Access 2016

Comprehensive

Shelley Gaskin
and Nancy Graviett

PEARSON

Boston Columbus Indianapolis New York San Francisco
Amsterdam Cape Town Dubai London Madrid Milan Munich Paris Montréal Toronto
Delhi Mexico City São Paulo Sydney Hong Kong Seoul Singapore Taipei Tokyo

Vice President, Career Skills: Andrew Gilfillan
Executive Editor: Jenifer Niles
Project Manager: Holly Haydash
Program Manager: Emily Biberger
Team Lead, Project Management: Laura Burgess
Development Editor: Toni Ackley
Editorial Assistant: Michael Campbell
Director of Product Marketing: Maggie Waples
Director of Field Marketing: Leigh Ann Sims
Product Marketing Manager: Kaylee Carlson
Field Marketing Managers: Molly Schmidt and Joanna Conley
Marketing Coordinator: Susan Osterlitz
Operations Specialist: Maura Zaldivar-Garcia
Senior Art Director: Maura Zaldivar-Garcia
Interior and Cover Design: Carie Keller/Cenveo
Project Manager, Permissions: Karen Sanatar
Cover Credits: GaudiLab, Rawpixel.com, Pressmaster, Eugenio Marongiu, Boggy, Gajus, Rocketclips, Inc
Senior Art Director: Diane Ernsberger
Associate Director of Design: Blair Brown
Vice President, Product Strategy: Jason Fournier
Director of Media Development: Blaine Christine
Senior Product Strategy Manager: Eric Hakanson
Product Team Lead, IT: Zachary Alexander
Course Producer, IT: Amanda Losonsky
Digital Project Manager, MyITLab: Becca Lowe
Media Project Manager, Production: John Cassar
Full-Service Project Management: Lumina Datamatics, Inc.
Composition: Lumina Datamatics, Inc.
Printer/Binder: RR Donnelley/Menasha
Cover Printer: Phoenix Color
Efficacy Curriculum Manager: Jessica Sieminski
Text Font: Times LT Pro

Library of Congress Cataloging-in-Publication Data

Library of Congress Control Number: 2016932297

2 16

ISBN 10: 0-13-444393-4
ISBN 13: 978-0-13-444393-5

Brief Contents

Table of Contents

About the Authors

Shelley Gaskin, Series Editor, is a professor in the Business and Computer Technology Division at Pasadena City College in Pasadena, California. She holds a bachelor's degree in Business Administration from Robert Morris College (Pennsylvania), a master's degree in Business from Northern Illinois University, and a doctorate in Adult and Community Education from Ball State University (Indiana). Before joining Pasadena City College, she spent 12 years in the computer industry, where she was a systems analyst, sales representative, and director of Customer Education with Unisys Corporation. She also worked for Ernst & Young on the development of large systems applications for their clients. She has written and developed training materials for custom systems applications in both the public and private sector, and has also written and edited numerous computer application textbooks.

This book is dedicated to my students, who inspire me every day.

Nancy Graviett is a professor and department chair in Business Technology at St. Charles Community College in Cottleville, Missouri. She holds a bachelor's degree in marketing and a master's degree in business education from the University of Missouri and has completed a certificate in online education. Nancy has authored textbooks on WordPerfect, Google, Microsoft Outlook, and Microsoft Access.

This book is dedicated to my husband, Dave, and my children, Matthew and Andrea. I cannot thank my family enough for the love and support they share every day.

GO! with Office 2016

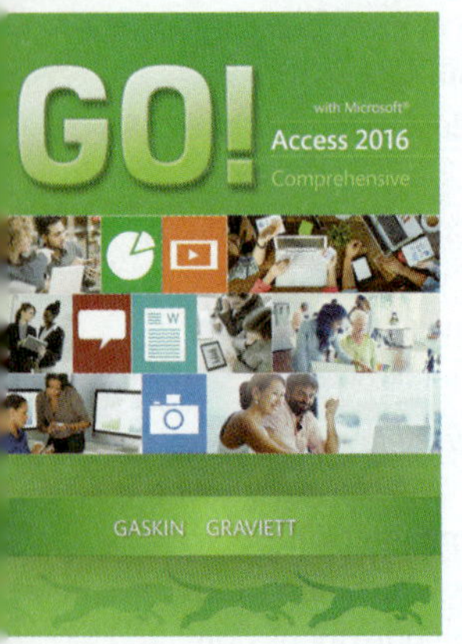

GO! with Office 2016 is the right approach to learning for today's fast-moving, mobile environment. The GO! Series focuses on the job and *success* skills students need to succeed in the workforce. Using job-related projects that put Microsoft Office into context, students learn the *how* and *why* at the moment they need to know, and because the GO! Series uses Microsoft procedural syntax, students never get lost in the instruction. For Office 2016, the hallmark GO! *guided practice-to-skill mastery pathway* is better than ever. Not only do students have multiple opportunities to work live in Microsoft Office to practice and apply the skills they have learned, but also, the *instructional* projects are now Grader projects, so students can work live in Office and receive auto-graded feedback as they learn!

By combining these new instructional Grader projects with the variety of existing Grader projects and the high-fidelity simulations that match the text, students have an effective pathway for learning, practicing, and assessing their abilities. After completing the instructional projects, students are ready to apply the skills with a wide variety of progressively challenging projects that require them to solve problems, think critically, and create projects on their own. The new *GO! with Google* projects also enable students to apply what they have learned in a different environment, and the integrated MOS objectives make this the one resource needed to learn Office, gain critical productivity skills, and prepare to get MOS certified!

What's New

Coverage of new features of Office 2016 ensures that students are learning the skills they need to work in today's job market.

NEW MyITLab 2016 Grader Projects In addition to the homework and assessment Graders already available, the A and B *instructional* projects are now Graders, enabling students to *learn by doing* live in the application *and* receive the instant feedback they need to ensure understanding.

MyITLab HTML 5 Training & Assessment Simulations for Office 2016 These simulations are rewritten by the authors to match the pedagogical approach of the textbook projects and to provide a direct one-to-one learning experience.

NEW Google Projects For each A and B instructional project in Chapters 1–3, students construct a parallel project using Google productivity tools. This gives students the opportunity to think critically and apply what they are learning about Microsoft Office to *other* productivity tools, which is an essential job skill.

NEW MOS Preparation MOS objectives are integrated into the text for easy review and reference for students who are preparing for a MOS certification exam. A MOS appendix is also included to provide a comprehensive list of the exam objectives.

NEW Lessons on the GO! How do you teach software that is constantly updated and getting new features all the time? This new project type will cover newer Microsoft apps such as Sway and MIX and things yet to come! These lessons are found in MyITLab and the Instructor Resource Center, and come with instructional content, student data files, solutions files, and rubrics for grading.

GO! To Work Page Here, students can review a summary of the chapter items focused on employability, including a MOS Objective summary, Build Your ePortfolio guidelines, and the GO! For Job Success soft skills videos or discussions.

Application Capstone Projects MyITLab grader Capstone projects for each application provide a variety of opportunities for students to ensure they have reached proficiency.

FOUR Types of Videos Students enjoy video learning, and these videos help students learn and gain skills and insight needed to succeed in the workforce.

- *(NEW)* ***GO! Walk Thru:*** Give students a quick 30-second preview of what they will do and create—from beginning to end—by completing each of the A and B Instructional Projects. These videos increase the student's confidence by letting the student see the entire project built quickly.
- ***GO! Learn How (formerly Student Training)*****:** Students learn visually by viewing these instructor-led videos that are broken down by Objective for direct guidance. This is the personal instruction students need—especially outside of the classroom—to answer the *How do I?* questions.
- ***GO! to Work*****:** These videos provide short interviews with real business information workers showing how they use Office in the workplace.
- ***GO! for Job Success:*** These videos or discussions relate to the projects in the chapter and cover important career topics such as *Dressing for Success*, *Time Management*, and *Making Ethical Choices*.

Expanded Project Summary chart This easy-to-use guide outlines all the instructional and end-of-chapter projects by category, including Instruction, Review, Mastery and Transfer of Learning, and Critical Thinking.

In-text boxed content for easy navigation *Another Way*, *Notes*, *More Knowledge*, *Alerts*, and *By Touch* instructions are included in line with the instruction—not in the margins—so students won't miss this important information and will learn it in context with what is on their screen.

MyITLab 2016 for GO! Let MyITLab do the work by giving students instantaneous feedback and saving hours of grading with GO!'s extensive Grader Project options. And the HTML5 Training and Assessment simulations provide a high-fidelity environment that provide step-by-step summary of student actions and include just-in-time learning aids to assist students: Read, Watch, Practice.

All other end-of-chapter projects, C, D, H, I, J, K, L, M, N, and O, have grading rubrics and solution files for easy hand grading. These are all Content-based, Outcomes-based, Problem-Solving, and Critical Thinking projects that enable you to add a variety of assessments—including authentic assessments—to evaluate a student's proficiency with the application.

IT Innovation Station Stay current with Office and Windows updates and important Microsoft and office productivity news and trends with help from your Pearson authors! Now that Microsoft Office is in the cloud, automatic updates occur regularly. These can affect how you to teach your course and the resources you are using. To keep you and your students completely up to date on the changes occurring in Office 2016 and Windows 10, we are launching the *IT Innovation Station*. This website will contain monthly updates from our product team and our author-instructors with tips for understanding updates, utilizing new capabilities, implementing new instructional techniques, and optimizing your Office use.

Why the GO! Approach Helps Students Succeed

GO! Provides Personalized Learning

MyITLab from Pearson is an online homework, training, and assessment system that will improve student results by helping students master skills and concepts through immediate feedback and a robust set of tools that allows instructors to easily gauge and address the performance of individuals and classrooms.

MyITLab learning experiences engage students using both realistic, high-fidelity simulations of Microsoft Office as well as auto-graded, live-in-the-application assignments, so they can understand concepts more thoroughly. With the ability to approach projects and problems as they would in real life—coupled with tutorials that adapt based on performance—students quickly complete skills they know and get help when and where they need it.

For educators, MyITLab establishes a reliable learning environment backed by the Pearson Education 24/7, 99.97 percent uptime service level agreement, and that includes the tools educators need to track and support both individual and class-wide student progress.

GO! Engages Students by Combining a Project-Based Approach with the Teachable Moment

GO!'s project-based approach clusters the learning objectives around the projects rather than around the software features. This tested pedagogical approach teaches students to solve real problems as they practice and learn the features.

GO! instruction is organized around student learning outcomes with numbered objectives and two instructional projects per chapter. Students can engage in a wide variety of end-of-chapter projects where they apply what they have learned in outcomes-based, problem-solving, and critical thinking projects—many of which require students to create the project from scratch.

GO! instruction is based on the teachable moment where students learn important concepts at the exact moment they are practicing the skill. The explanations and concepts are woven into the steps—not presented as paragraphs of text at the beginning of the project before students have even seen the software in action.

Each Project Opening Page clearly outlines Project Activities (what the student will do in this project), Project Files (what starting files are needed and how the student will save the files), and Project Results (what the student's finished project will look like). Additionally, to support this page, the GO! Walk Thru video gives students a 30-second overview of how the project will progress and what they will create.

GO! Demonstrates Excellence in Instructional Design

Student Learning Outcomes and Objectives are clearly defined so students understand what they will learn and what they will be able to do when they finish the chapter.

Clear Instruction provided through project steps written following Microsoft® Procedural Syntax to guide students where to go *and then* what to do, so they never get lost!

Teachable moment approach has students learn important concepts when they need to as they work through the instructional projects. No long paragraphs of text.

Clean Design presents textbook pages that are clean and uncluttered, with screenshots that validate the student's actions and that engage visual learners.

Sequential Pagination displays the pages sequentially numbered, like every other textbook a student uses, instead of using letters or abbreviations. Student don't spend time learning a new numbering approach.

Important information is boxed within the text so that students won't miss or skip the Another Way, By Touch, Note, Alert, or More Knowledge details so there are no distracting and "busy-looking" marginal notes.

Color-Coded Steps guide students through the projects with colors coded by project.

End-of-Project Icon helps students know when they have completed the project, which is especially useful in self-paced or online environments. These icons give students a clearly identifiable end point for each project.

GO! Learn How Videos provide step-by-step visual instruction for the A and B instructional projects—delivered by a real instructor! These videos provide the assistance and personal learning students may need when working on their own.

GO! Delivers Easy Course Implementation

Instructor Page

Teach the Course You Want in Less Time

The *GO!* series' one-of-a-kind instructional system provides you with everything you need to prepare for class, teach the material, and assess your students.

Prepare

- **Office 2013 to 2016 Transition Guide** provides an easy-to-use reference for updating your course for Office 2016 using GO!
- **Annotated Instructor Tabs** provide clear guidance on how to implement your course.
- **MyITLab Implementation Guide** is provided for course planning and learning outcome alignment.
- **Syllabus templates** outline various plans for covering the content in an 8-, 12-, or 16-week course.
- **List of Chapter Outcomes and Objectives** is provided for course planning and learning outcome alignment.
- **Student Assignment Tracker** for students to track their own work.
- **Assignment Planning Guide** Description of the *GO!* assignments with recommendations based on class size, delivery method, and student needs.
- **Solution Files** Examples of homework submissions to serve as examples for students.
- **Online Study Guide for Students** Interactive objective-style questions based on chapter content.

Teach

- **The Annotated Instructors Edition** includes the entire student text, spiral-bound and wrapped with teaching notes and suggestions for how to implement your course.
- **Scripted Lectures** present a detailed guide for delivering live in-class demonstrations of the A and B Instructional Projects.
- **PowerPoint Presentations** provide a visual walk-through of the chapter with suggested lecture notes included.
- **Audio PowerPoint Presentations** provide a visual walk-through of the chapter with the lecture notes read out loud.
- **Walk Thru Videos** provide a quick 30-second preview of what the student will do and create—from beginning to end—by completing each of the A and B Instructional projects. These videos increase the student's confidence by letting the student see the entire project built quickly.

Assess

- **A scoring checklist, task-specific rubric, or analytic rubric** accompanies every assignment.
- **Prepared Exams** provide cumulative exams for each project, chapter, and application that are easy to score using the provided scoring checklist and point suggestions for each task.
- **Solution Files** are provided in three formats: native file, PDF, and annotated PDF.
- **Rubrics** provide guidelines for grading open-ended projects.
- **Testbank questions** are available for you to create your own objective-based quizzes for review.

Grader Projects

- **Projects A & B** (Guided Instruction)
- **Project E Homework** (Formative) and Assesment (Summative) (Cover Objectives in Project A)
- **Project F Homework** (Formative) and Assesment (Summative) (Cover Objectives in Project B)
- **Project G Homework** (Formative) and Assesment (Summative) (Cover Objectives in Projects A and B)
- **Application Capstone Homework** (Formative review of core objectives covered in application)
- **Application Capstone Exam** (Summative review of core objectives covered in application—generates badge with 90 percent or higher)

GO! Series Hallmarks

Teach the Course You Want in Less Time

A Microsoft® Office textbook designed for student success!

- **Project-Based –** Students learn by creating projects that they will use in the real world.
- **Microsoft Procedural Syntax –** Steps are written to put students in the right place at the right time.
- **Teachable Moment –** Expository text is woven into the steps—at the moment students need to know it—not chunked together in a block of text that will go unread.
- **Sequential Pagination –** Students have actual page numbers instead of confusing letters and abbreviations.

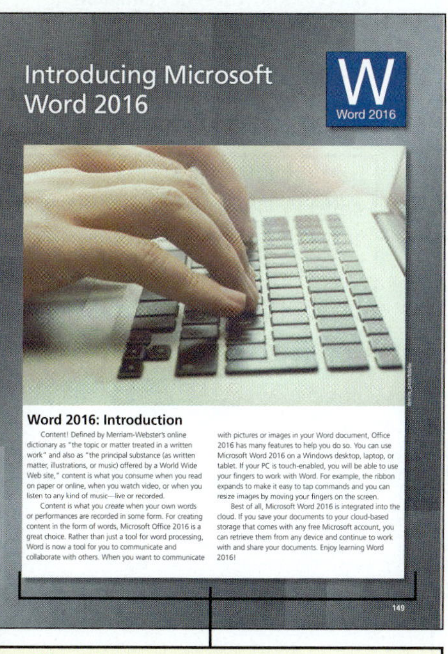

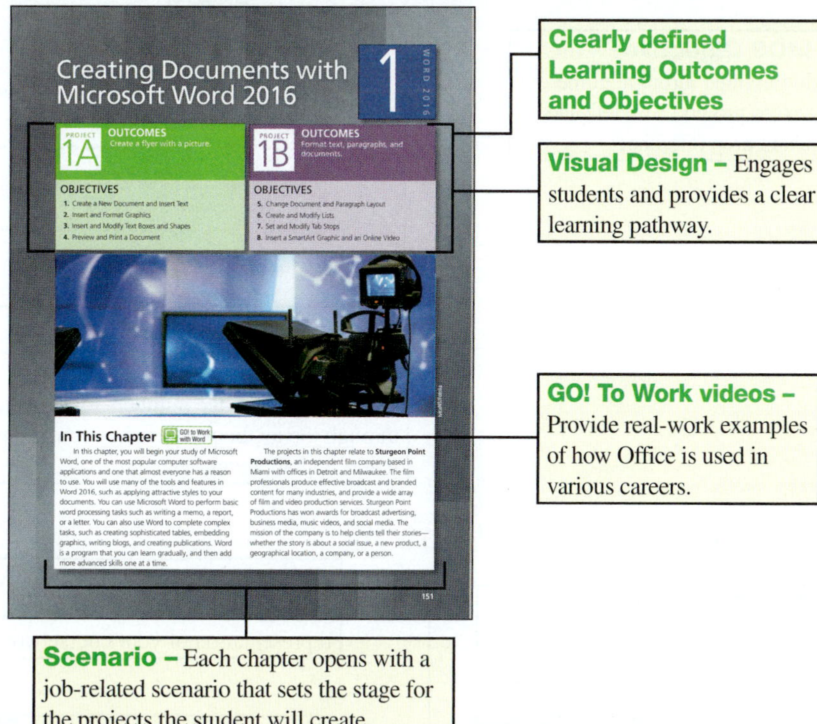

Clearly defined Learning Outcomes and Objectives

Visual Design – Engages students and provides a clear learning pathway.

GO! To Work videos – Provide real-work examples of how Office is used in various careers.

Application Introductions – Provide an overview of the application to prepare students for the upcoming chapters.

Scenario – Each chapter opens with a job-related scenario that sets the stage for the projects the student will create.

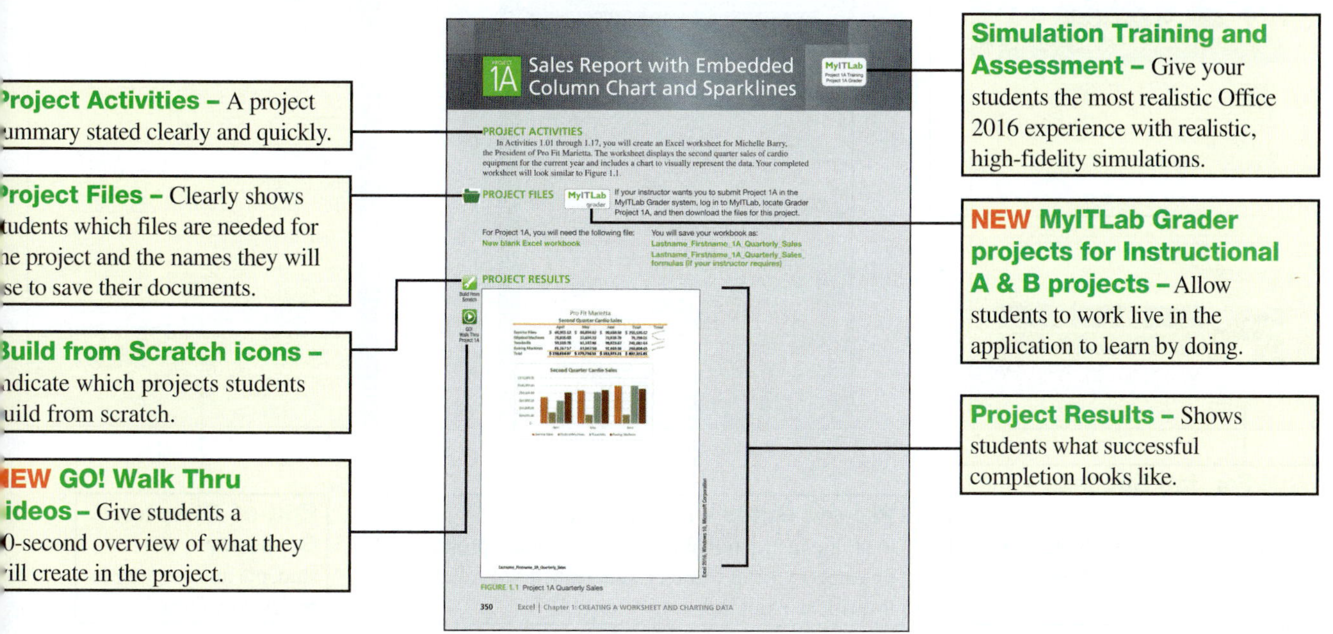

'roject Activities – A project ummary stated clearly and quickly.

'roject Files – Clearly shows tudents which files are needed for ne project and the names they will se to save their documents.

3uild from Scratch icons – ndicate which projects students uild from scratch.

IEW GO! Walk Thru ideos – Give students a 0-second overview of what they vill create in the project.

Simulation Training and Assessment – Give your students the most realistic Office 2016 experience with realistic, high-fidelity simulations.

NEW MyITLab Grader projects for Instructional A & B projects – Allow students to work live in the application to learn by doing.

Project Results – Shows students what successful completion looks like.

In-text Features

Another Way, Notes, More Knowledge, Alerts, and By Touch Instructions

Color Coding – Each chapter has two instructional projects, which is less overwhelming for students than one large chapter project. The projects are differentiated by different colored numbering and headings.

MOS Objectives – Are highlighted throughout the text to provide a review and exam prep reference.

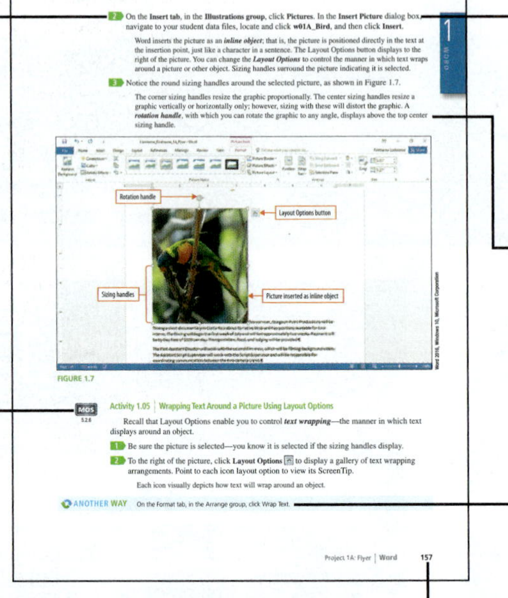

Microsoft Procedural Syntax – Steps are written to put the student at the right place at the right time.

Teachable Moment – Expository text is woven into the steps—at the moment students need to know it—not chunked together in a block of text that will go unread.

In-text Callouts – Ensure that students will read this important material—Another Way, Notes, More Knowledge, Alerts, and By Touch instructions.

Sequential Pagination – Students are given actual page numbers to navigate through the textbook instead of confusing letters and abbreviations.

End-of-Chapter

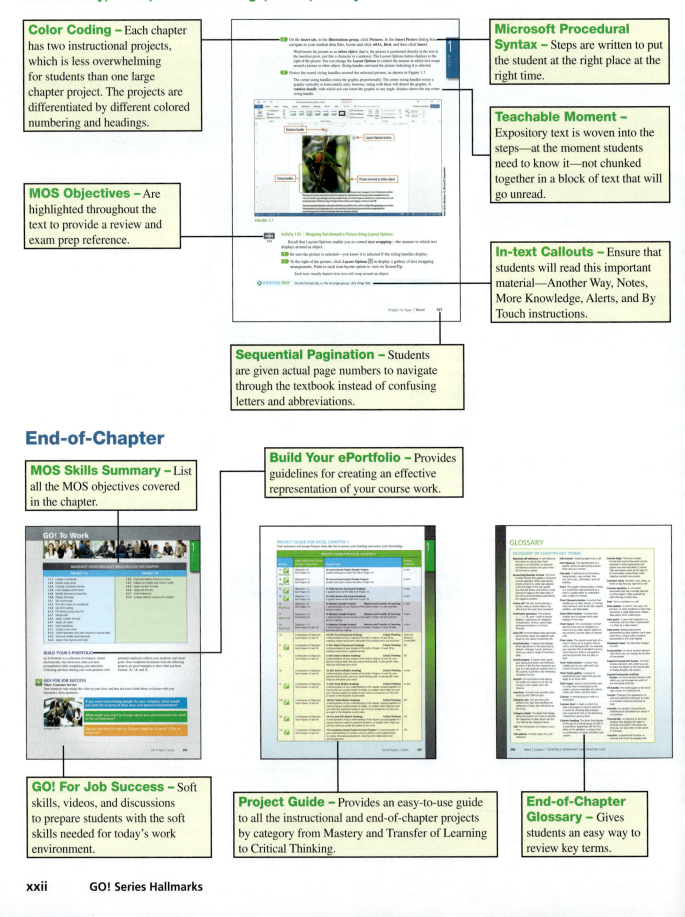

MOS Skills Summary – List all the MOS objectives covered in the chapter.

Build Your ePortfolio – Provides guidelines for creating an effective representation of your course work.

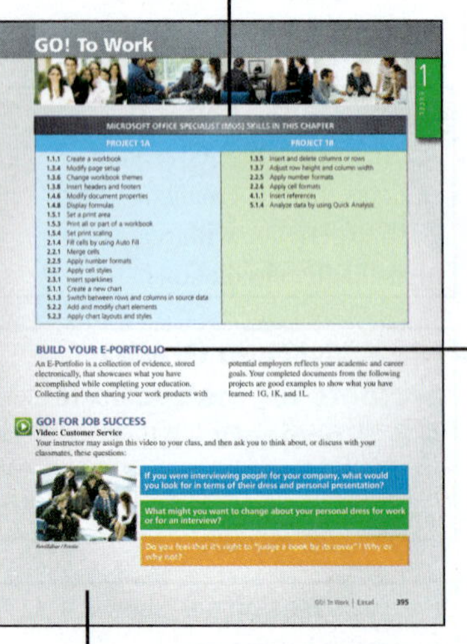

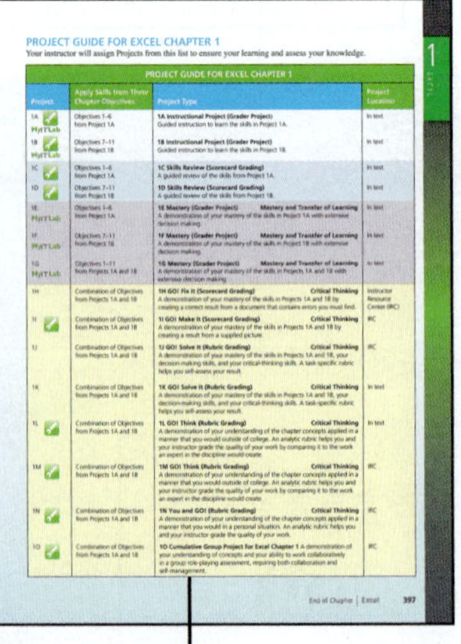

GO! For Job Success – Soft skills, videos, and discussions to prepare students with the soft skills needed for today's work environment.

Project Guide – Provides an easy-to-use guide to all the instructional and end-of-chapter projects by category from Mastery and Transfer of Learning to Critical Thinking.

End-of-Chapter Glossary – Gives students an easy way to review key terms.

End-of-Chapter

Objective List – Every end-of-chapter project includes a listing of covered Objectives from Projects A and B.

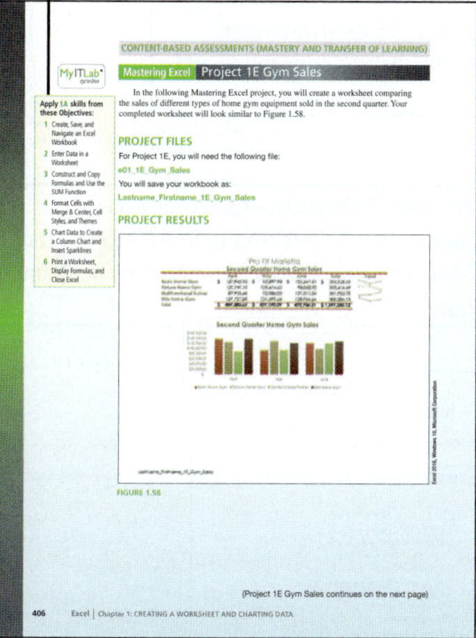

CONTENT-BASED ASSESSMENTS (MASTERY AND TRANSFER OF LEARNING)

MyITLab grader

Mastering Excel Project 1E Gym Sales

Apply 1A skills from these Objectives:

1 Create, Save, and Navigate an Excel Workbook
2 Enter Data in a Worksheet
3 Construct and Copy Formulas and Use the SUM Function
4 Format Cells with Merge & Center, Cell Styles, and Themes
5 Chart Data to Create a Column Chart and Insert Sparklines
6 Print a Worksheet, Display Formulas, and Close Excel

In the following Mastering Excel project, you will create a worksheet comparing the sales of different types of home gym equipment sold in the second quarter. Your completed worksheet will look similar to Figure 1.58.

PROJECT FILES

For Project 1E, you will need the following file:

e01_1E_Gym_Sales

You will save your workbook as:

Lastname_Firstname_1E_Gym_Sales

PROJECT RESULTS

FIGURE 1.58

(Project 1E Gym Sales continues on the next page)

Grader Projects – In addition to the two Grader Projects for the instructional portion of the chapter (Projects A and B), Chapters 1–3 have six MyITLab Grader projects within the end-of-chapter material—three homework and three assessment—and Chapters 4–10 have two MyITLab Grader projects, clearly indicated by the MyITLab logo.

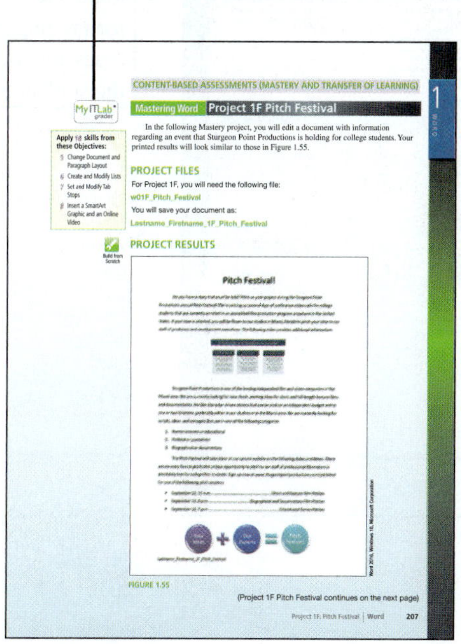

CONTENT-BASED ASSESSMENTS (MASTERY AND TRANSFER OF LEARNING)

MyITLab grader

Mastering Word Project 1F Pitch Festival

Apply 1B skills from these Objectives:

5 Change Document and Paragraph Layout
6 Create and Modify Lists
7 Set and Modify Tab Stops
8 Insert a SmartArt Graphic and an Online Video

In the following Mastery project, you will edit a document with information regarding an event that Sturgeon Point Productions is holding for college students. Your printed results will look similar to those in Figure 1.55.

PROJECT FILES

For Project 1F, you will need the following file:

w01F_Pitch_Festival

You will save your document as:

Lastname_Firstname_1F_Pitch_Festival

Build from Scratch

PROJECT RESULTS

Pitch Festival!

FIGURE 1.55

(Project 1F Pitch Festival continues on the next page)

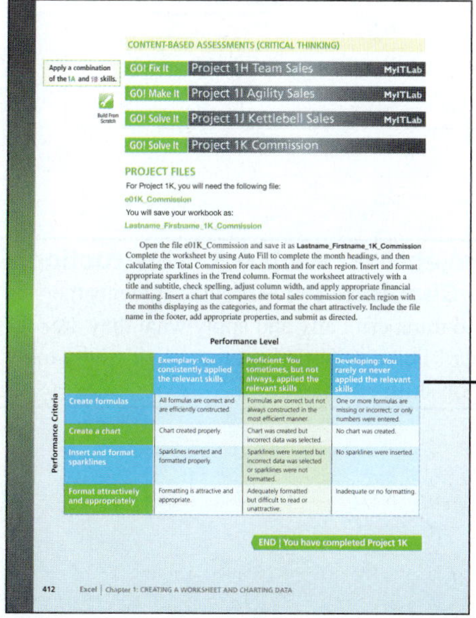

CONTENT-BASED ASSESSMENTS (CRITICAL THINKING)

Apply a combination of the 1A and 1B skills.

GO! Fix It Project 1H Team Sales MyITLab

GO! Make It Project 1I Agility Sales MyITLab

Build From Scratch

GO! Solve It Project 1J Kettlebell Sales MyITLab

GO! Solve It Project 1K Commission

PROJECT FILES

For Project 1K, you will need the following file:

e01K_Commission

You will save your workbook as:

Lastname_Firstname_1K_Commission

Open the file e01K_Commission and save it as **Lastname_Firstname_1K_Commission** Complete the worksheet by using Auto Fill to complete the month headings, and then calculating the Total Commission for each month and for each region. Insert and format appropriate sparklines in the Trend column. Format the worksheet attractively with a title and subtitle, check spelling, adjust column width, and apply appropriate financial formatting. Insert a chart that compares the total sales commission for each region with the months displaying as the categories, and format the chart attractively. Include the file name in the footer, add appropriate properties, and submit as directed.

Performance Level

Performance Criteria	Exemplary: You consistently applied the relevant skills	Proficient: You sometimes, but not always, applied the relevant skills	Developing: You rarely or never applied the relevant skills
Create formulas	All formulas are correct and are efficiently constructed.	Formulas are correct but not always constructed in the most efficient manner.	One or more formulas are missing or incorrect; or only numbers were entered.
Create a chart	Chart created properly.	Chart was created but incorrect data was selected.	No chart was created.
Insert and format sparklines	Sparklines inserted and formatted properly.	Sparklines were inserted but incorrect data was selected or sparklines were not formatted.	No sparklines were inserted.
Format attractively and appropriately	Formatting is attractive and appropriate.	Adequately formatted but difficult to read or unattractive.	Inadequate or no formatting.

END | You have completed Project 1K

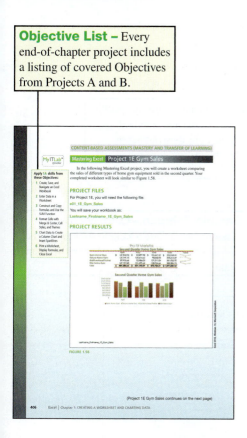

Task-Specific Rubric – A matrix specific to the GO! Solve It projects that states the criteria and standards for grading these defined-solution projects.

End-of-Chapter

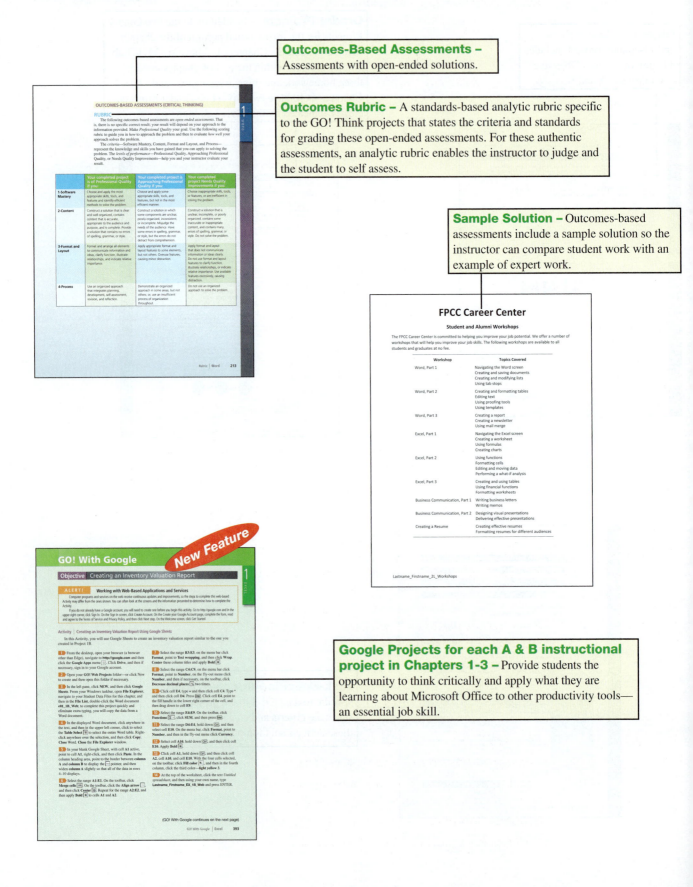

Outcomes-Based Assessments – Assessments with open-ended solutions.

Outcomes Rubric – A standards-based analytic rubric specific to the GO! Think projects that states the criteria and standards for grading these open-ended assessments. For these authentic assessments, an analytic rubric enables the instructor to judge and the student to self assess.

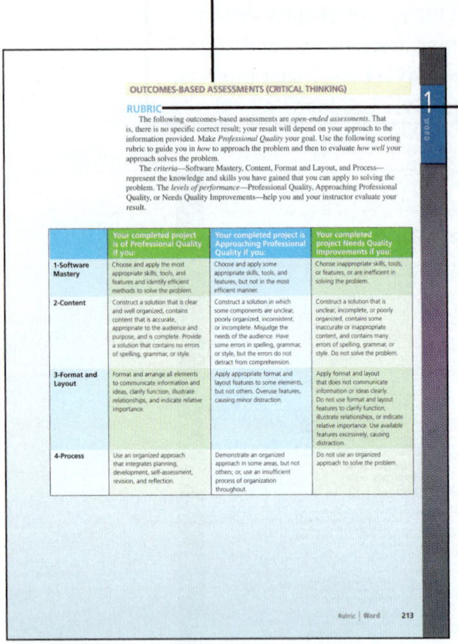

OUTCOMES-BASED ASSESSMENTS (CRITICAL THINKING)

RUBRIC

The following outcomes-based assessments are *open-ended assessments*. That is, there is no specific correct result; your result will depend on your approach to the information provided. Make *Professional Quality* your goal. Use the following scoring rubric to guide you in *how* to approach the problem and then to evaluate *how well* your approach solves the problem.

The *criteria*—Software Mastery, Content, Format and Layout, and Process—represent the knowledge and skills you have gained that you can apply to solving the problem. The *levels of performance*—Professional Quality, Approaching Professional Quality, or Needs Quality Improvements—help you and your instructor evaluate your result.

	Your completed project is of Professional Quality if you:	Your completed project is Approaching Professional Quality if you:	Your completed project Needs Quality Improvements if you:
1-Software Mastery	Choose and apply the most appropriate skills, tools, and features and identify efficient methods to solve the problem.	Choose and apply some appropriate skills, tools, and features, but not in the most efficient manner.	Choose inappropriate skills, tools, or features, or are inefficient in solving the problem.
2-Content	Construct a solution that is clear and well organized, contains content that is accurate, appropriate to the audience and purpose, and is complete. Provide a solution that contains no errors of spelling, grammar, or style.	Construct a solution in which some components are unclear, poorly organized, inconsistent, or incomplete. Misjudge the needs of the audience. Have some errors in spelling, grammar, or style, but the errors do not detract from comprehension.	Construct a solution that is unclear, incomplete, or poorly organized, contains some inaccurate or inappropriate content, and contains many errors of spelling, grammar, or style. Do not solve the problem.
3-Format and Layout	Format and arrange all elements to communicate information and ideas, clarify function, illustrate relationships, and indicate relative importance.	Apply appropriate format and layout features to some elements, but not others. Overuse features, causing minor distraction.	Apply format and layout that does not communicate information or ideas clearly. Do not use format and layout features to clarify function, illustrate relationships, or indicate relative importance. Use available features excessively, causing distraction.
4-Process	Use an organized approach that integrates planning, development, self-assessment, revision, and reflection.	Demonstrate an organized approach in some areas, but not others; or, use an insufficient process of organization throughout.	Do not use an organized approach to solve the problem.

Rubric | Word 213

Sample Solution – Outcomes-based assessments include a sample solution so the instructor can compare student work with an example of expert work.

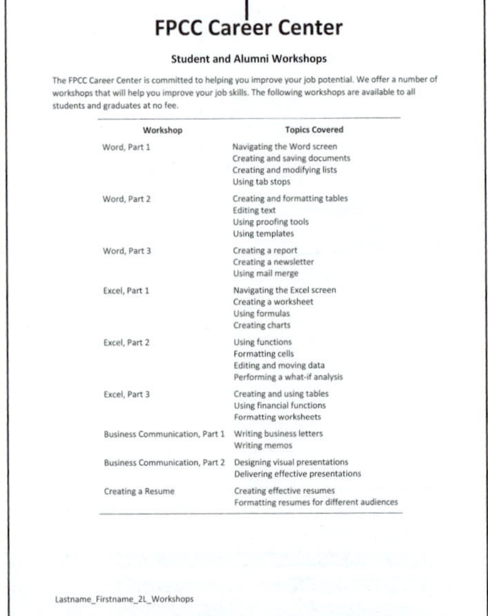

FPCC Career Center

Student and Alumni Workshops

The FPCC Career Center is committed to helping you improve your job potential. We offer a number of workshops that will help you improve your job skills. The following workshops are available to all students and graduates at no fee.

Workshop	Topics Covered
Word, Part 1	Navigating the Word screen Creating and saving documents Creating and modifying lists Using tab stops
Word, Part 2	Creating and formatting tables Editing text Using proofing tools Using templates
Word, Part 3	Creating a report Creating a newsletter Using mail merge
Excel, Part 1	Navigating the Excel screen Creating a worksheet Using formulas Creating charts
Excel, Part 2	Using functions Formatting cells Editing and moving data Performing a what-if analysis
Excel, Part 3	Creating and using tables Using financial functions Formatting worksheets
Business Communication, Part 1	Writing business letters Writing memos
Business Communication, Part 2	Designing visual presentations Delivering effective presentations
Creating a Resume	Creating effective resumes Formatting resumes for different audiences

Lastname_Firstname_2L_Workshops

GO! With Google

New Feature

Objective Creating an Inventory Valuation Report

ALERT! **Working with Web-Based Applications and Services**

Computer programs and services on the web receive continuous updates and improvements, so the steps to complete this web-based Activity may differ from the ones shown. You can often look at the screens and the information presented to determine how to complete the Activity.

If you do not already have a Google account, you will need to create one before you begin this activity. Go to http://google.com and in the upper right corner, click Sign In. On the Sign In screen, click Create Account. On the Create your Google Account page, complete the form, read and agree to the Terms of Service and Privacy Policy, and then click Next step. On the Welcome screen, click Get Started.

Activity | Creating an Inventory Valuation Report Using Google Sheets

In this Activity, you will use Google Sheets to create an inventory valuation report similar to the one you created in Project 1B.

1 From the desktop, open your browser (a browser other than Edge), navigate to **http://google.com** and then click the **Google Apps** menu. Click **Drive**, and then if necessary, sign in to your Google account.

2 Open your **GO! Web Projects** folder—or click New to create and then open this folder if necessary.

3 In the left pane, click **NEW**, and then click **Google Sheets**. From your Windows taskbar, open **File Explorer**, navigate to your Student Data Files for this chapter, and then in the **File List**, double-click the Word document **e01_1B_Web**; to complete this project quickly and eliminate extra typing, you will copy the data from a Word document.

4 In the displayed Word document, click anywhere in the text, and then in the upper left corner, click to select the **Table Select** to select the entire Word table. Right-click anywhere over the selection, and then click **Copy**. **Close** Word. **Close** the **File Explorer** window.

5 In your blank Google Sheet, with cell **A1** active, point to cell **A1**, right-click, and then click **Paste**. In the column heading area, point to the border between **column A** and **column B** to display the pointer, and then widen **column A** slightly so that all of the data in rows 4–10 displays.

6 Select the range **A1:E1**. On the toolbar, click **Merge cells**. On the toolbar, click the **Align arrow**, and then click **Center**. Repeat for the range **A2:E2**, and then apply **Bold** to cells **A1** and **A2**.

7 Select the range **B3:E3**, on the menu bar click **Format**, point to **Text wrapping**, and then click **Wrap**. **Center** these column titles and apply **Bold**.

8 Select the range **C4:C9**, on the menu bar click **Format**, point to **Number**, on the fly-out menu click **Number**, and then if necessary, on the toolbar, click **Decrease decimal places** two times.

9 Click cell **E4**, type = and then click cell **C4**. Type * and then click cell **D4**. Press Enter. Click cell **E4**, point to the fill handle in the lower right corner of the cell, and then drag down to cell **E9**.

10 Select the range **E4:E9**. On the toolbar, click **Functions**, click **SUM**, and then press Enter.

11 Select the range **D4:E4**, hold down Ctrl, and then select cell **E10**. On the menu bar, click **Format**, point to **Number**, and then in the fly-out menu click **Currency**.

12 Select cell **A10**, hold down Ctrl, and then click cell **E10**. Apply **Bold**.

13 Click cell **A1**, hold down Ctrl, and then click cell **A2**, cell **A10**, and cell **E10**. With the four cells selected, on the toolbar, click **Fill color**, and then in the fourth column, click the third color—**light yellow 3**.

14 At the top of the worksheet, click the text *Untitled spreadsheet*, and then using your own name, type **Lastname_Firstname_EX_1B_Web** and press ENTER.

(GO! With Google continues on the next page)

GO! With Google | Excel 393

Google Projects for each A & B instructional project in Chapters 1-3 – Provide students the opportunity to think critically and apply what they are learning about Microsoft Office to other productivity tools—an essential job skill.

Student Materials

Student Data Files – All student data files are available in MyITLab for Office 2016 or at www.pearsonhighered.com/go

FOUR Types of Videos help students learn and gain skills and insight needed to succeed in the workforce.

- ***(NEW) GO! Walk Thru*** is a brief overview of the A & B instructional projects to give students the context of what they will be doing in the projects
- ***GO! Learn How** (formerly Student Training)* instructor-led videos are broken down by Objective for direct guidance; this personal instruction answers the "how-do-I" questions students ask.
- ***GO! to Work*** videos provide short interviews with workers showing how they use Office in the workplace.
- ***GO! for Job Success*** videos or discussions relate to the projects in the chapter and cover important career topics such as *Dressing for Success*, *Time Management*, and *Making Ethical Choices*.

Matching and multiple choice questions provide a variety of review options for content in each chapter.

MOS Objective quiz provides a quick assessment of student understanding of the MOS objectives covered in the chapter. Helpful for courses focused on the pathway to MOS certification.

Available in MyITLab for Office 2016.

GO! with MyITLab

Gives you a completely integrated solution

Instruction ▪ Training ▪ Assessment

All of the content in the book and MyITLab is written by the authors, who are instructors, so the instruction works seamlessly with the simulation trainings and grader projects—true 1:1. eText, Training & Assessment Simulations, and Grader Projects.

Instructor Resources

All Instructor Resources found in MyITLab or at pearsonhighered.com/go

Annotated Instructor Edition – This instructor tool includes a full copy of the student textbook and a guide to implementing your course depending on the emphasis you want to place on digital engagement. Also included are teaching tips, discussion topics, and other useful pieces for teaching each chapter.

Assignment Sheets – Lists all the assignments for the chapter. Just add the course information, due dates, and points. Providing these to students ensures they will know what is due and when.

Scripted Lectures – A script to guide your classroom lecture of each instructional project.

Annotated Solution Files – Coupled with the scorecards, these create a grading and scoring system that makes grading easy and efficient.

PowerPoint Lectures – PowerPoint presentations for each chapter.

Audio PowerPoints – Audio versions of the PowerPoint presentations for each chapter.

Scoring Rubrics – Can be used either by students to check their work or by you as a quick check-off for the items that need to be corrected.

Syllabus Templates – For 8-week, 12-week, and 16-week courses.

Test Bank – Includes a variety of test questions for each chapter.

Instruction

Instruction: General

Syllabi templates demonstrate different approaches for covering the content in an 8-, 12-, or 16-week course.

Application Intro Videos provide a quick overview of what the application is and its primary function.

GO! to Work Videos put each chapter into context as related to how people use productivity software in their daily lives and work.

GO! For Success videos and discussions provide real-life scenarios exploring the essential soft skills needed to succeed in the workplace and professional settings.

Instruction: Hands-On *using one or more of the following:*

- **Interactive eText** allows students to read the narrative and instruction and also link directly to the various types of videos included.
- **(NEW) Walk Thru Videos** provide a quick 30-second overview of what students will do in the A & B instructional projects.
- **Scripted Lectures** are a detailed guide through the A & B projects from the book for you to use for in-class demonstration.
- **GO! Learn How** (previously Student Training) videos are instructor-led videos that provide guided instruction through each Objective and the related Activities.
- **PowerPoint Presentations** provide a visual walk-through of the chapter with suggested lecture notes included.
- **Audio PowerPoint Presentations** provide the visual walk-through of chapters with the lecture notes read aloud.
- **(NEW) A & B Instruction Projects** assigned to students. Students can complete the Instructional Projects 1A and 1B and submit for instructor review or manual grading. They can also submit as a MyITLab Grader project, which allows the students to work live in the application starting with files downloaded from MyITLab and then submitted for automatic grading and feedback.
- **(NEW) MOS Objectives** are covered throughout the chapter and are indicated with the MOS icon. Instructors use these to point students to content they would encounter on a MOS exam. If a course is focused on MOS preparation, this content would be emphasized in the instruction.

Practice

MyITLab Skill-based Training Simulation provides students with hands-on practice applying the skills they have learned in a simulated environment where they have access to Learning Aids to assist if needed (READ, WATCH, PRACTICE). All of the student's keystrokes are recorded so that instructors can review and provide support to the students. Instructor can set the number of times the students can complete the simulation.

MyITLab Homework Grader Projects (E, F, or G in Chapters 1–3, G in Chapters 4–10) provide students with live-in-the-application practice with the skills they learned in Projects A and B. These projects provide students with detailed reports showing them where they made errors and also provide "live comments" explaining the details.

Student Assignment Tracker for students to track their work.

Review

GO! Online activities (multiple choice and matching activities) provide objective-based quizzing to allow students to review how they are doing.

Testbank questions are available for instructors to create their own quizzes for review or assessment.

End-of-chapter online projects H–O provide Content-based, Outcome-based, and Critical Thinking projects that you can assign for additional review, practice, or assessments. These are graded manually by the instructor using the provided Solution Files and Grading Scorecards or Rubrics.

MOS Quizzes provide an objective-based quiz to review the MOS objective-related content covered in the chapter. Provides students with review to help if they plan to take a MOS Certification exam.

Assessment

MyITLab Skill-based Exam Simulation provides students with an assessment of their knowledge and ability to apply the skills they have learned. In the Simulated Exams, students do not have access to the Learning Aids. All of the student's keystrokes are recorded so that instructors can review and provide support to the students. Instructors can set the number of times the students can complete the simulation exam.

MyITLab Assessment Grader Projects (E, F, or G in Chapters 1–3 and G in Chapters 4–10) provide students with live-in-the-application testing of the skills they learned in Projects A and B. These projects provide students with detailed reports showing the student where they made errors and also provides "live comments" explaining the details.

Prepared Exams – these are additional projects created specifically for use as exams that the instructor will grade manually. They are available by Project, Chapter, and Unit.

Pre-built Chapter quizzes provide objective-based quizzing to allow students to review how they are doing.

Testbank questions are available for instructors to create their own quizzes for review or assessment.

Reviewers Of The GO! Series

Abul Sheikh	Abraham Baldwin Agricultural College
John Percy	Atlantic Cape Community College
Janette Hicks	Binghamton University
Shannon Ogden	Black River Technical College
Karen May	Blinn College
Susan Fry	Boise State University
Chigurupati Rani	Borough of Manhattan Community College / CUNY
Ellen Glazer	Broward College
Kate LeGrand	Broward College
Mike Puopolo	Bunker Hill Community College
Nicole Lytle-Kosola	California State University, San Bernardino
Nisheeth Agrawal	Calhoun Community College
Pedro Diaz-Gomez	Cameron
Linda Friedel	Central Arizona College
Gregg Smith	Central Community College
Norm Cregger	Central Michigan University
Lisa LaCaria	Central Piedmont Community College
Steve Siedschlag	Chaffey College
Terri Helfand	Chaffey College
Susan Mills	Chambersburg
Mandy Reininger	Chemeketa Community College
Connie Crossley	Cincinnati State Technical and Community College
Marjorie Deutsch	City University of New York - Queensborough Community College
Mary Ann Zlotow	College of Dupage
Christine Bohnsak	College of Lake County
Gertrude Brier	College of Staten Island
Sharon Brown	College of The Albemarle
Terry Rigsby	Columbia College
Vicki Brooks	Columbia College
Donald Hames	Delgado Community College
Kristen King	Eastern Kentucky University
Kathie Richer	Edmonds Community College
Gary Smith	Elmhurst College
Wendi Kappersw	Embry-Riddle Aeronautical University
Nancy Woolridge	Fullerton College
Abigail Miller	Gateway Community & Technical College
Deep Ramanayake	Gateway Community & Technical College
Gwen White	Gateway Community & Technical College
Debbie Glinert	Gloria K School
Dana Smith	Golf Academy of America
Mary Locke	Greenville Technical College
Diane Marie Roselli	Harrisburg Area Community College
Linda Arnold	Harrisburg Area Community College - Lebanon
Daniel Schoedel	Harrisburg Area Community College - York Campus
Ken Mayer	Heald College
Xiaodong Qiao	Heald College
Donna Lamprecht	Hopkinsville Community College
Kristen Lancaster	Hopkinsville Community College
Johnny Hurley	Iowa Lakes Community College
Linda Halverson	Iowa Lakes Community College
Sarah Kilgo	Isothermal Community College
Chris DeGeare	Jefferson College
David McNair	Jefferson College
Diane Santurri	Johnson & Wales
Roland Sparks	Johnson & Wales University
Ram Raghuraman	Joliet Junior College
Eduardo Suniga	Lansing Community College
Kenneth A. Hyatt	Lonestar College - Kingwood
Glenn Gray	Lonestar College North Harris
Gene Carbonaro	Long Beach City College
Betty Pearman	Los Medanos College
Diane Kosharek	Madison College
Peter Meggison	Massasoit Community College
George Gabb	Miami Dade College
Lennie Alice Cooper	Miami Dade College
Richard Mabjish	Miami Dade College
Victor Giol	Miami Dade College
John Meir	Midlands Technical College
Greg Pauley	Moberly Area Community College
Catherine Glod	Mohawk Valley Community College
Robert Huyck	Mohawk Valley Community College
Kevin Engellant	Montana Western
Philip Lee	Nashville State Community College
Ruth Neal	Navarro College
Sharron Jordan	Navarro College
Richard Dale	New Mexico State University
Lori Townsend	Niagara County Community College
Judson Curry	North Park University
Mary Zegarski	Northampton Community College
Neal Stenlund	Northern Virginia Community Colege
Michael Goeken	Northwest Vista College
Mary Beth Tarver	Northwestern State University
Amy Rutledge	Oakland University
Marcia Braddock	Okefenokee Technical College
Richard Stocke	Oklahoma State University - OKC
Jane Stam	Onondaga Community College
Mike Michaelson	Palomar College
Kungwen (Dave) Chu	Purdue University Calumet
Wendy Ford	CUNY - Queensborough CC
Lewis Hall	Riverside City College
Karen Acree	San Juan College
Tim Ellis	Schoolcraft College
Dan Combellick	Scottsdale Community College
Pat Serrano	Scottsdale Community College
Rose Hendrickson	Sheridan College
Kit Carson	South Georgia College
Rebecca Futch	South Georgia State College
Brad Hagy	Southern Illinois University Carbondale
Mimi Spain	Southern Maine Community College
David Parker	Southern Oregon University
Madeline Baugher	Southwestern Oklahoma State University
Brian Holbert	St. Johns River State College
Bunny Howard	St. Johns River State College
Stephanie Cook	State College of Florida
Sharon Wavle	Tompkins Cortland Community College
George Fiori	Tri-County Technical College
Steve St. John	Tulsa Community College
Karen Thessing	University of Central Arkansas
Richard McMahon	University of Houston-Downtown
Shohreh Hashemi	University of Houston-Downtown
Donna Petty	Wallace Community College
Julia Bell	Walters State Community College
Ruby Kowaney	West Los Angeles College
Casey Thompson	Wiregrass Georgia Technical College
DeAnnia Clements	Wiregrass Georgia Technical College

Introduction to Microsoft Office 2016 Features

PROJECT 1A

OUTCOMES

Create, save, and print a Microsoft Office 2016 document.

OBJECTIVES

1. Explore Microsoft Office 2016
2. Enter, Edit, and Check the Spelling of Text in an Office 2016 Program
3. Perform Commands from a Dialog Box
4. Create a Folder and Name and Save a File
5. Insert a Footer, Add Document Properties, Print a File, and Close a Desktop App

PROJECT 1B

OUTCOMES

Perform commands, apply formatting, and install apps for Office in Microsoft Office 2016

OBJECTIVES

6. Open an Existing File and Save it with a New Name
7. Sign in to Office and Explore Options for a Microsoft Office Desktop App
8. Perform Commands from the Ribbon and Quick Access Toolbar
9. Apply Formatting in Office Programs and Inspect Documents
10. Compress Files and Get Help with Office
11. Install Apps for Office and Create a Microsoft Account

Imagewell10/Fotolia

In This Chapter

GO! to Work with Office Features

In this chapter, you will practice using features in Microsoft Office 2016 that work similarly across Word, Excel, Access, and PowerPoint. These features include managing files, performing commands, adding document properties, signing in to Office, applying formatting to text, and searching for Office commands quickly. You will also practice installing apps from the Office Store and setting up a free Microsoft account so that you can use OneDrive.

The projects in this chapter relate to **Skyline Metro Grill**, which is a chain of 25 casual, full-service restaurants based in Boston. The Skyline Metro Grill owners are planning an aggressive expansion program. To expand by 15 additional restaurants in Chicago, San Francisco, and Los Angeles by 2020, the company must attract new investors, develop new menus, develop new marketing strategies, and recruit new employees, all while adhering to the company's quality guidelines and maintaining its reputation for excellent service. To succeed, the company plans to build on its past success and maintain its quality elements.

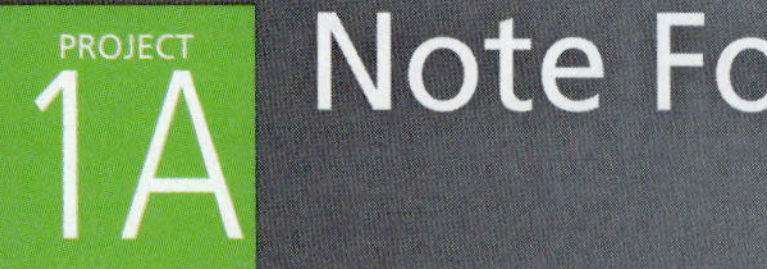

Note Form

PROJECT ACTIVITIES

In Activities 1.01 through 1.08, you will create a note form using Microsoft Word 2016, save it in a folder that you create by using File Explorer, and then print the note form or submit it electronically as directed by your instructor. Your completed note form will look similar to Figure 1.1.

PROJECT FILES

If your instructor wants you to submit Project 1A in the MyITLab Grader system, log in to MyITLab, locate Grader Project1A, and then download the files for this project.

For Project 1A, you will need the following file:
New blank Word document

You will save your file as:
Lastname_Firstname_1A_Note_Form

PROJECT RESULTS

Build From Scratch

GO! Walk Thru Project 1A

Skyline Metro Grill, Chef's Notes
Executive Chef, Sarah Jackson

Lastname_Firstname_1A_Note_Form

Word 2016, Windows 10, Microsoft Corporation

FIGURE 1.1 Project 1A Note Form

NOTE	If You Are Using a Touchscreen
	Tap an item to click it.
	Press and hold for a few seconds to right-click; release when the information or commands display.
	Touch the screen with two or more fingers and then pinch together to zoom out or stretch your fingers apart to zoom in.
	Slide your finger on the screen to scroll—slide left to scroll right and slide right to scroll left.
	Slide to rearrange—similar to dragging with a mouse.
	Swipe to select—slide an item a short distance with a quick movement—to select an item and bring up commands, if any.

Objective 1 Explore Microsoft Office 2016

NOTE Creating a Microsoft Account

Use a free Microsoft account to sign in to Office 2016 so that you can work on different PCs and use your OneDrive. If you already sign in to a Windows PC, tablet, or phone, or you sign in to Xbox Live, Outlook.com, or OneDrive, use that account to sign in to Office. To create a Microsoft account, you can use *any* email address as the user name for your new Microsoft account—including addresses from Outlook.com, Yahoo! or Gmail.

GO! Learn How Video OF1-1

The term ***desktop application*** or ***desktop app*** refers to a computer program that is installed on your PC and that requires a computer operating system such as Microsoft Windows. The programs in Microsoft Office 2016 are considered to be desktop apps. A desktop app typically has hundreds of features and takes time to learn.

An ***app*** refers to a self-contained program usually designed for a single purpose and that runs on smartphones and other mobile devices—for example, looking at sports scores or booking a flight on a particular airline. Microsoft's Windows 10 operating system supports both desktop apps that run only on PCs and ***Windows apps*** that run on all Windows device families—including PCs, Windows phones, Windows tablets, and the Xbox gaming system.

ALERT! **Is Your Screen More Colorful and a Different Size Than the Figures in This Textbook?**

Your installation of Microsoft Office 2016 may use the default Colorful theme, where the ribbon in each application is a vibrant color and the ribbon tabs display with white text. In this textbook, figures shown use the White theme, but you can be assured that all the commands are the same. You can keep your Colorful theme, or if you prefer, you can change your theme to White to match the figures here. To do so, open any application and display a new document. On the ribbon, click the File tab, and then on the left, click Options. With General selected on the left, under Personalize your copy of Microsoft Office, click the Office Theme arrow, and then click White.

Additionally, the figures in this book were captured using a screen resolution of 1280 x 768. If that is not your screen resolution, your screen will closely resemble, but not match, the figures shown. To view or change your screen's resolution on a Windows 10 PC, on the desktop, right-click in a blank area, click Display settings, and then on the right, click Advanced display settings. On a Windows 7 PC, right-click on the desktop, and then click Screen resolution.

MOS 1.1.1

Activity 1.01 | Exploring Microsoft Office 2016 and Creating a Blank Word Document

ALERT! **To submit as an autograded project, log into MyITLab, download the files for this project, and then begin with those files instead of a new blank document.**

1 On the computer you are using, start Microsoft Word 2016, and then compare your screen with Figure 1.2.

Depending on which operating system you are using and how your computer is set up, you might start Word from the taskbar in Windows 7, Windows 8, or Windows 10, or from the Start screen in Windows 8, or from the Start menu in Windows 10. On an Apple Mac computer, the program will display in the dock.

Documents that you have recently opened, if any, display on the left. On the right, you can select either a blank document or a ***template***—a preformatted document that you can use as a starting point and then change to suit your needs.

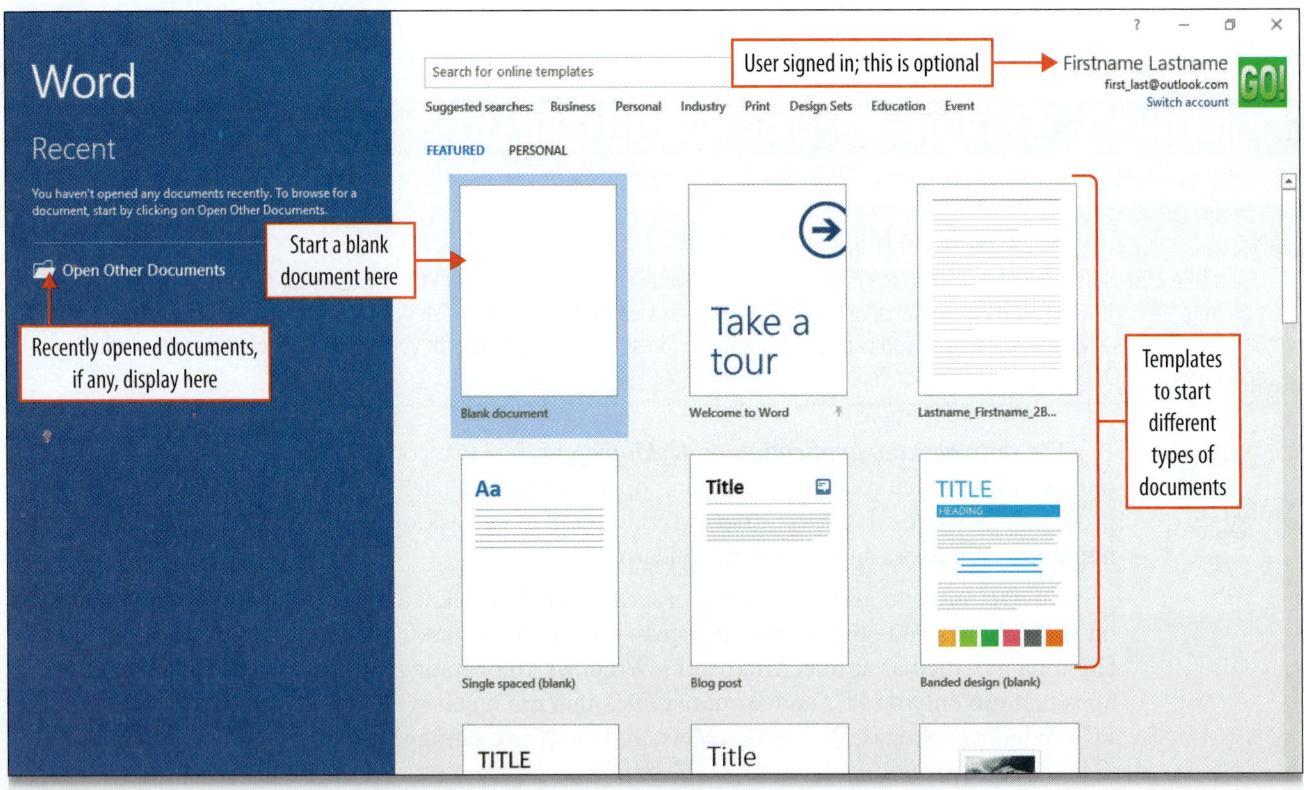

FIGURE 1.2

2 Click **Blank document**. Compare your screen with Figure 1.3, and then take a moment to study the description of these screen elements in the table in Figure 1.4.

NOTE Displaying the Full Ribbon

If your full ribbon does not display, click any tab, and then at the right end of the ribbon, click [pin icon] to pin the ribbon to keep it open while you work.

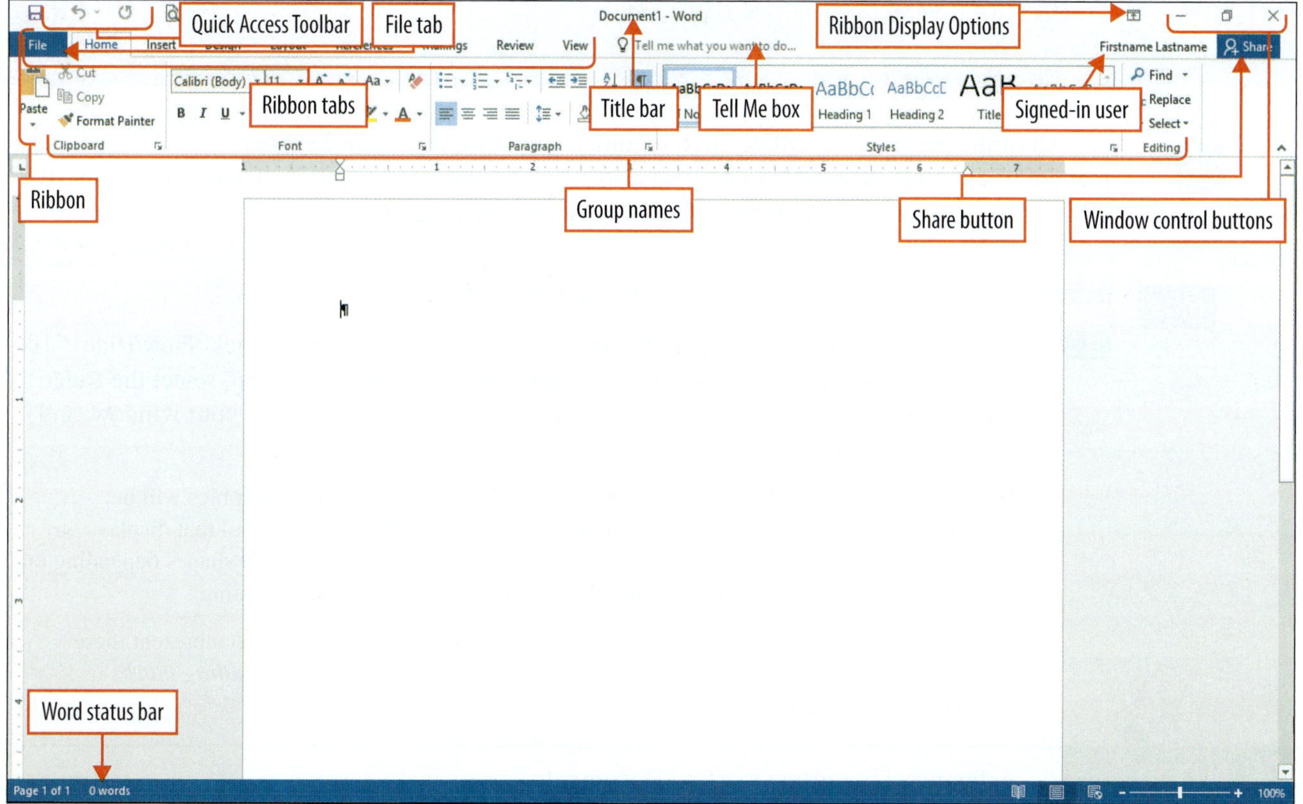

FIGURE 1.3

Word 2016, Windows 10, Microsoft Corporation

SCREEN ELEMENT	DESCRIPTION
File tab	Displays Microsoft Office Backstage view, which is a centralized space for all of your file management tasks such as opening, saving, printing, publishing, or sharing a file—all the things you can do *with* a file.
Group names	Indicate the name of the groups of related commands on the displayed tab.
Quick Access Toolbar	Displays buttons to perform frequently used commands and resources with a single click. The default commands include Save, Undo, and Redo. You can add and delete buttons to customize the Quick Access Toolbar for your convenience.
Ribbon	Displays a group of task-oriented tabs that contain the commands, styles, and resources you need to work in an Office 2016 desktop app. The look of your ribbon depends on your screen resolution. A high resolution will display more individual items and button names on the ribbon.
Ribbon Display Options	Displays three ways you can display the ribbon: Auto-hide Ribbon, Show Tabs, or Show Tabs and Commands.
Ribbon tabs	Display the names of the task-oriented tabs relevant to the open program.
Share button	Opens the Share pane from which you can save your file to the cloud—your OneDrive—and then share it with others so you can collaborate.
Signed-in user	Identifies the signed-in user.
Status bar	Displays file information on the left; on the right displays buttons for Read Mode, Print Layout, and Web Layout views; on the far right displays Zoom controls.
Tell Me box	Provides a search feature for Microsoft Office commands that you activate by typing what you are looking for in the Tell Me box; as you type, every keystroke refines the results so that you can click the command as soon as it displays.
Title bar	Displays the name of the file and the name of the program; the window control buttons are grouped on the right side of the title bar.
Window control buttons	Displays buttons for commands to change the Ribbon Display Options, Minimize, Restore Down, or Close the window.

Word 2016, Windows 10, Microsoft Corporation

FIGURE 1.4

Objective 2 Enter, Edit, and Check the Spelling of Text in an Office 2016 Program

GO! Learn How
Video OF1-2

All of the programs in Office 2016 require some typed text. Your keyboard is still the primary method of entering information into your computer. Techniques to enter text and to ***edit***—make changes to—text are similar across all of the Office 2016 programs.

1.4.6

Activity 1.02 | Entering and Editing Text in an Office 2016 Program

1 On the ribbon, on the **Home tab**, in the **Paragraph group**, if necessary, click **Show/Hide** ¶ so that it is active—shaded. If necessary, on the **View tab**, in the **Show group**, select the **Ruler** check box so that rulers display below the ribbon and on the left side of your window, and then redisplay the **Home tab**.

The ***insertion point***—a blinking vertical line that indicates where text or graphics will be inserted—displays. In Office 2016 programs, the mouse ***pointer***—any symbol that displays on your screen in response to moving your mouse device—displays in different shapes depending on the task you are performing and the area of the screen to which you are pointing.

When you press Enter, Spacebar, or Tab on your keyboard, characters display to represent these keystrokes. These screen characters do not print, and are referred to as ***formatting marks*** or ***nonprinting characters***.

NOTE Activating Show/Hide in Word Documents

When Show/Hide is active—the button is shaded—formatting marks display. Because formatting marks guide your eye in a document—like a map and road signs guide you along a highway—these marks will display throughout this instruction. Many expert Word users keep these marks displayed while creating documents.

2 Type **Skyline Grille Info** and notice how the insertion point moves to the right as you type. Point slightly to the right of the letter *e* in *Grille* and click one time to place the insertion point there. Compare your screen with Figure 1.5.

A ***paragraph symbol*** (¶) indicates the end of a paragraph and displays each time you press Enter. This is a type of formatting mark and does not print.

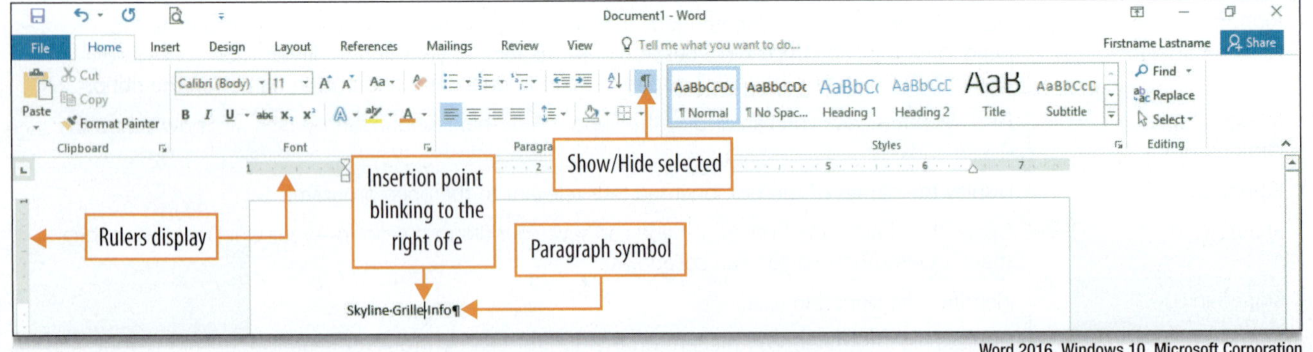

Word 2016, Windows 10, Microsoft Corporation

FIGURE 1.5

3 On your keyboard, locate and then press the Backspace key to delete the letter *e*.

Pressing Backspace removes a character to the left of the insertion point.

4 Press → one time to place the insertion point to the left of the *I* in *Info*. Type **Chef's** and then press Spacebar one time.

By ***default***, when you type text in an Office program, existing text moves to the right to make space for new typing. Default refers to the current selection or setting that is automatically used by a program unless you specify otherwise.

5 Press [Del] four times to delete *Info* and then type **Notes**

Pressing [Del] removes a character to the right of the insertion point.

6 With your insertion point blinking after the word *Notes*, on your keyboard, hold down the [Ctrl] key. While holding down [Ctrl], press [←] three times to move the insertion point to the beginning of the word *Grill*. Release [Ctrl].

This is a ***keyboard shortcut***—a key or combination of keys that performs a task that would otherwise require a mouse. This keyboard shortcut moves the insertion point to the beginning of the previous word.

A keyboard shortcut is indicated as [Ctrl] + [←] (or some other combination of keys) to indicate that you hold down the first key while pressing the second key. A keyboard shortcut can also include three keys, in which case you hold down the first two and then press the third. For example, [Ctrl] + [Shift] + [←] selects one word to the left.

7 With the insertion point blinking at the beginning of the word *Grill*, type **Metro** and press [Spacebar].

8 Press [Ctrl] + [End] to place the insertion point after the letter *s* in *Notes*, and then press [Enter] one time. With the insertion point blinking, type the following and include the spelling error: **Exective Chef, Madison Dunham**

9 With your mouse, point slightly to the left of the *M* in *Madison*, hold down the left mouse button, and then ***drag***—hold down the left mouse button while moving your mouse—to the right to select the text *Madison Dunham* but not the paragraph mark following it, and then release the mouse button. Compare your screen with Figure 1.6.

The ***mini toolbar*** displays commands that are commonly used with the selected object, which places common commands close to your pointer. When you move the pointer away from the mini toolbar, it fades from view.

Selecting refers to highlighting—by dragging or clicking with your mouse—areas of text or data or graphics so that the selection can be edited, formatted, copied, or moved. The action of dragging includes releasing the left mouse button at the end of the area you want to select.

The Office programs recognize a selected area as one unit to which you can make changes. Selecting text may require some practice. If you are not satisfied with your result, click anywhere outside of the selection, and then begin again.

BY TOUCH

Double-tap on *Madison* to display the gripper—a small circle that acts as a handle—directly below the word. This establishes the start gripper. If necessary, with your finger, drag the gripper to the beginning of the word. Then drag the gripper to the end of *Dunham* to select the text and display the end gripper.

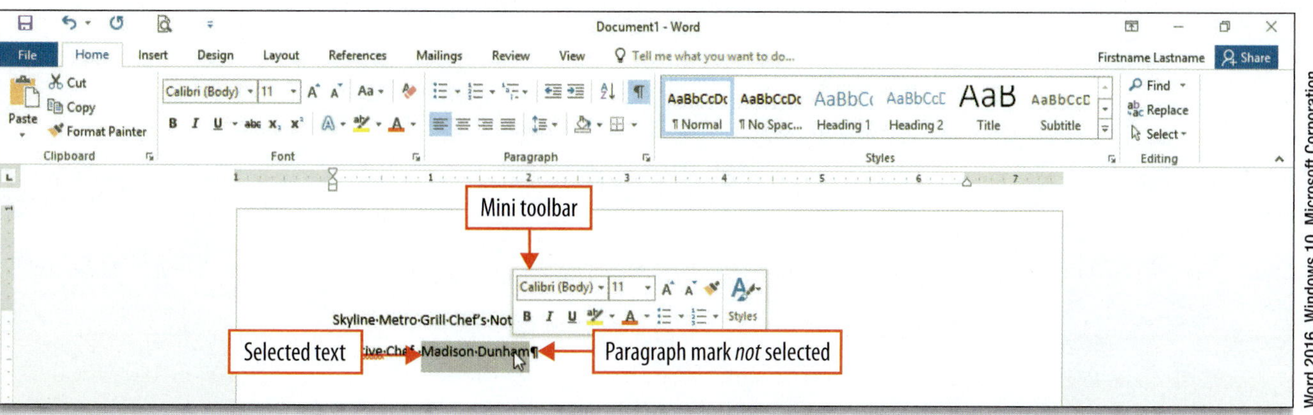

FIGURE 1.6

Word 2016, Windows 10, Microsoft Corporation

10 With the text *Madison Dunham* selected, type **Sarah Jackson**

In any Windows-based program, such as the Microsoft Office 2016 programs, selected text is deleted and then replaced when you begin to type new text. You will save time by developing good techniques for selecting and then editing or replacing selected text, which is easier than pressing the Del key numerous times to delete text.

Activity 1.03 | Checking Spelling

Office 2016 has a dictionary of words against which all entered text is checked. In Word and PowerPoint, words that are not in the dictionary display a wavy red line, indicating a possible misspelled word, a proper name, or an unusual word—none of which are in the Office 2016 dictionary.

In Excel and Access, you can initiate a check of the spelling, but red underlines do not display.

1 Notice that the misspelled word *Exective* displays with a wavy red underline.

2 Point to *Exective* and then ***right-click***—click your right mouse button one time.

A ***shortcut menu*** displays, which displays commands and options relevant to the selected text or object. These are ***context-sensitive commands*** because they relate to the item you right-clicked. These shortcut menus are also referred to as ***context menus***. Here, the shortcut menu displays commands related to the misspelled word.

Tap and hold a moment—when a square displays around the misspelled word, release your finger to display the shortcut menu.

3 Press Esc to cancel the shortcut menu, and then in the lower left corner of your screen, on the status bar, click the ***Proofing*** icon, which displays an *X* because some errors are detected. Compare your screen with Figure 1.7.

The Spelling pane displays on the right. Here you have many more options for checking spelling than you have on the shortcut menu. The suggested correct word, *Executive*, is highlighted.

You can click the speaker icon to hear the pronunciation of the selected word. If you have not already installed a dictionary, you can click *Get a Dictionary*—if you are signed in to Office with a Microsoft account—to find and install one from the online Office store; or if you have a dictionary app installed, it will display here and you can search it for more information.

In the Spelling pane, you can ignore the word one time or in all occurrences, change the word to the suggested word, select a different suggestion, or add a word to the dictionary against which Word checks.

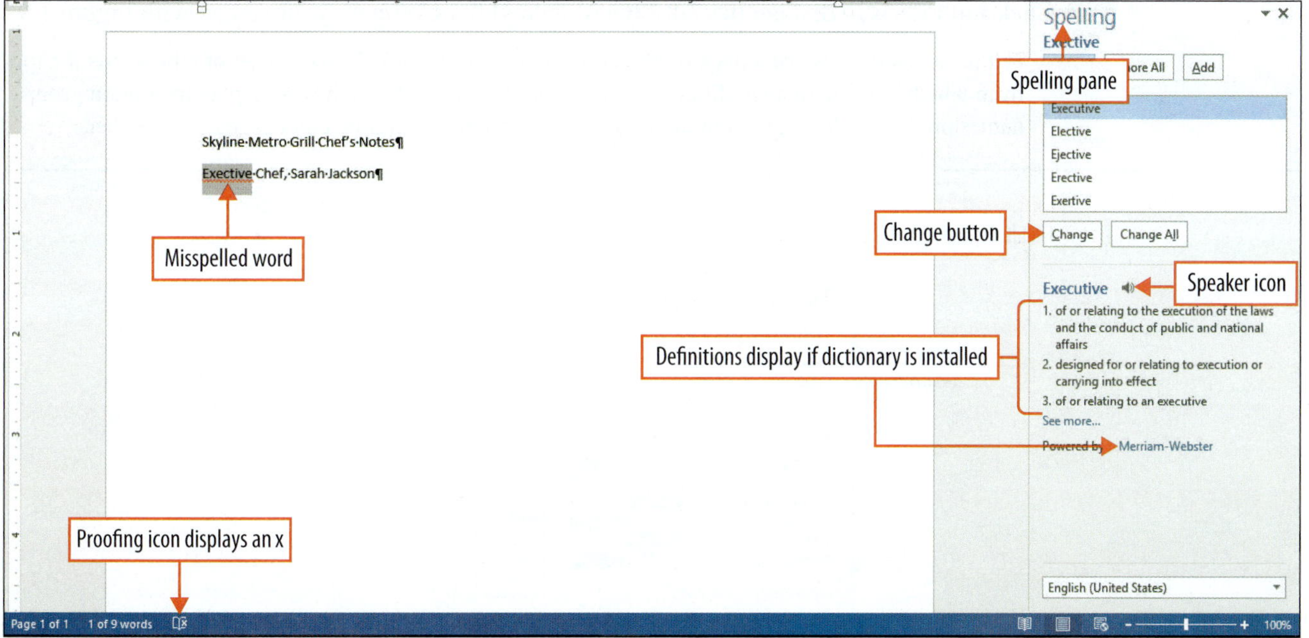

FIGURE 1.7

Word 2016, Windows 10, Microsoft Corporation

ANOTHER WAY Press F7 to display the Spelling pane; or, on the Review tab, in the Proofing group, click Spelling & Grammar.

4 In the ***Spelling*** pane, click **Change** to change the spelling to *Executive*. In the message box that displays, click **OK**.

Objective 3 Perform Commands from a Dialog Box

GO! Learn How
Video OF1-3

In a dialog box, you make decisions about an individual object or topic. In some dialog boxes, you can make multiple decisions in one place.

Activity 1.04 | Performing Commands from a Dialog Box

1.3.6

1 On the ribbon, click the **Design tab**, and then in the **Page Background group**, click **Page Color**.

2 At the bottom of the menu, notice the command ***Fill Effects*** followed by an **ellipsis** (...). Compare your screen with Figure 1.8.

An ***ellipsis*** is a set of three dots indicating incompleteness. An ellipsis following a command name indicates that a dialog box will display when you click the command.

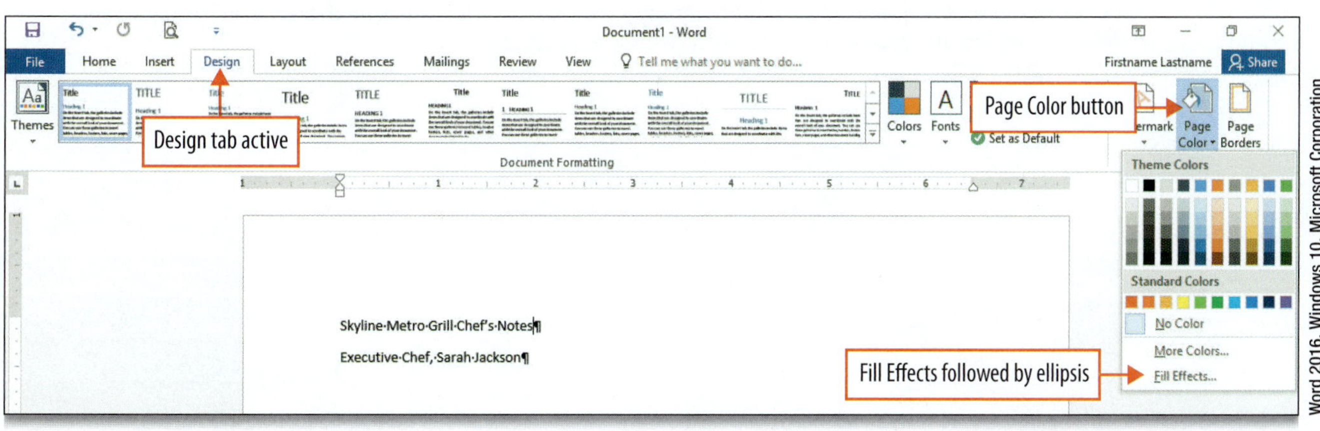

Word 2016, Windows 10, Microsoft Corporation

FIGURE 1.08

3 Click **Fill Effects** to display the **Fill Effects** dialog box. Compare your screen with Figure 1.9.

Fill is the inside color of a page or object. Here, the dialog box displays a set of tabs across the top from which you can display different sets of options. Some dialog boxes display the option group names on the left. The Gradient tab is active. In a ***gradient fill***, one color fades into another.

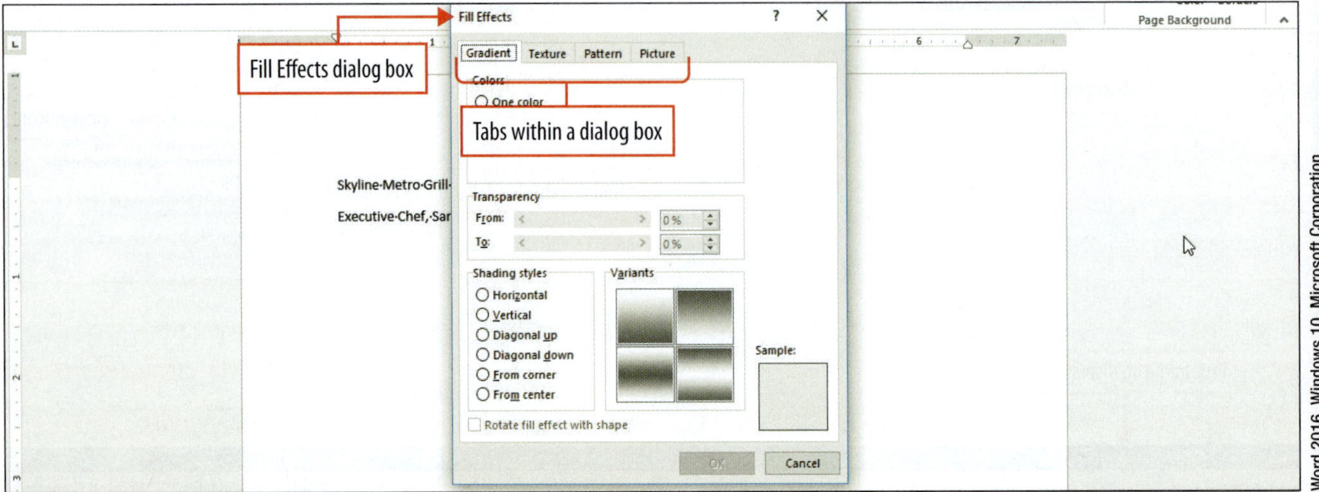

FIGURE 1.9

4 Under **Colors**, click the **One color** option button.

The dialog box displays settings related to the One color option. An ***option button*** is a round button that enables you to make one choice among two or more options.

5 Click the **Color 1 arrow**—the arrow under the text *Color 1*—and then in the third column, point to the second color to display the ScreenTip *Gray-25%, Background 2, Darker 10%*.

When you click an arrow in a dialog box, additional options display. A ***ScreenTip*** displays useful information about mouse actions, such as pointing to screen elements or dragging.

6 Click **Gray-25%, Background 2, Darker 10%**, and then notice that the fill color displays in the **Color 1** box. In the **Dark Light** bar, click the **Light arrow** as many times as necessary until the scroll box is all the way to the right. Under **Shading styles**, click the **Diagonal down** option button. Under **Variants**, click the **upper right variant**. Compare your screen with Figure 1.10.

This dialog box is a good example of the many different elements you may encounter in a dialog box. Here you have option buttons, an arrow that displays a menu, a slider bar, and graphic options that you can select.

BY TOUCH

In a dialog box, you can tap option buttons and other commands just as you would click them with a mouse. When you tap an arrow to display a color palette, a larger palette displays than if you used your mouse. This makes it easier to select colors in a dialog box.

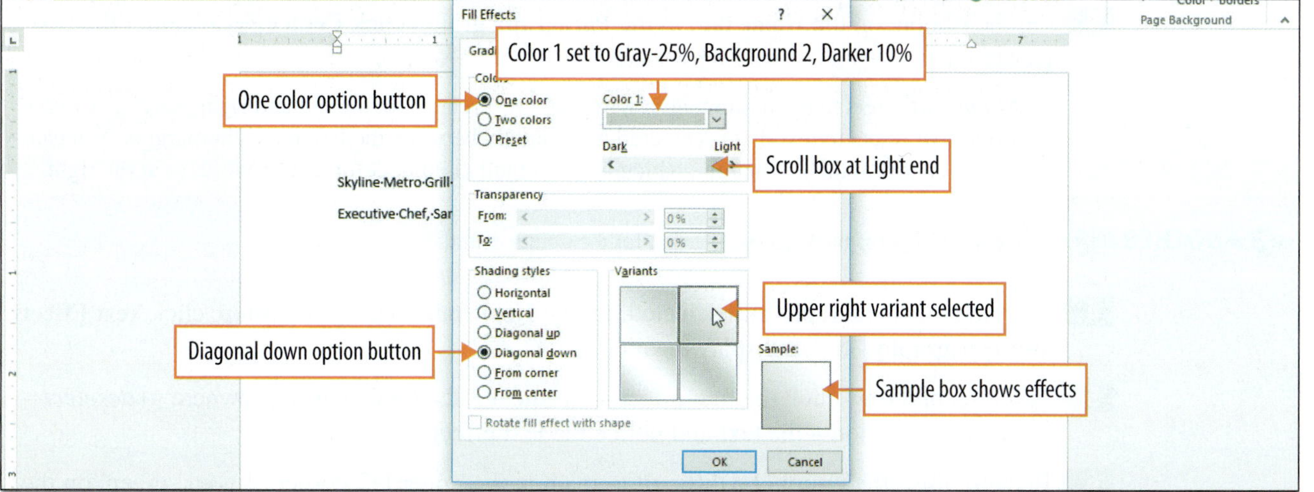

FIGURE 1.10

Word 2016, Windows 10, Microsoft Corporation

7 At the bottom of the dialog box, click **OK**, and notice the subtle page color.

In Word, the gray shading page color will not print—even on a color printer—unless you set specific options to do so. However, a subtle background page color is effective if people will be reading the document on a screen. Microsoft's research indicates that two-thirds of people who open Word documents on a screen never print them; they only read them.

MOS 2.2.6

Activity 1.05 | Using Undo and Applying a Built-In Style to Text

1 Point to the *S* in *Skyline*, and then drag down and to the right to select both paragraphs of text and include the paragraph marks. On the mini toolbar, click **Styles**, and then *point to* but do not click **Title**. Compare your screen with Figure 1.11.

A ***style*** is a group of ***formatting*** commands, such as font, font size, font color, paragraph alignment, and line spacing that can be applied to a paragraph with one command. Formatting is the process of establishing the overall appearance of text, graphics, and pages in an Office file—for example, in a Word document.

Live Preview is a technology that shows the result of applying an editing or formatting change as you point to possible results—before you actually apply it.

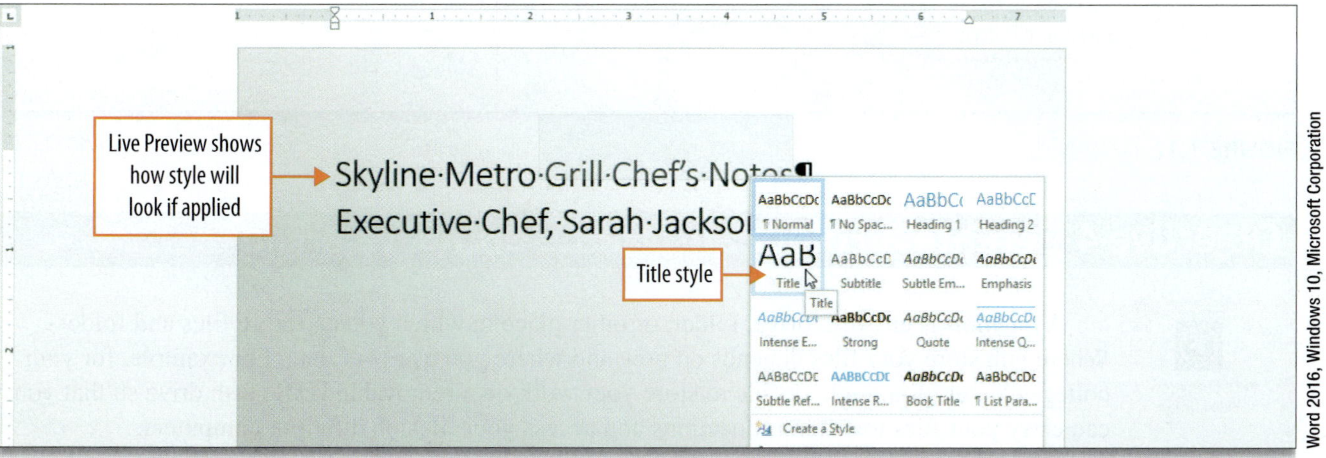

FIGURE 1.11

Word 2016, Windows 10, Microsoft Corporation

2 In the **Styles** gallery, click **Title**.

A ***gallery*** is an Office feature that displays a list of potential results.

3 On the ribbon, on the **Home tab**, in the **Paragraph group**, click **Center** [≡] to center the two paragraphs.

Alignment refers to the placement of paragraph text relative to the left and right margins. ***Center alignment*** refers to text that is centered horizontally between the left and right margins. You can also align text at the left margin, which is the default alignment for text in Word, or at the right.

ANOTHER WAY Press Ctrl + E as the keyboard shortcut for the Center command.

4 With the two paragraphs still selected, on the **Home tab**, in the **Font group**, click **Text Effects and Typography** [A] to display a gallery.

5 In the second row, click the first effect—**Gradient Fill – Gray**. Click anywhere to ***deselect***—cancel the selection—the text and notice the text effect.

6 Because this effect might be difficult to read, in the upper left corner of your screen, on the ***Quick Access Toolbar***, click **Undo** [↶].

The *Undo* command reverses your last action.

ANOTHER WAY Press Ctrl + Z as the keyboard shortcut for the Undo command.

7 With all of the text still selected, display the **Text Effects and Typography** [A] gallery again, and then in the second row, click the second effect—**Gradient Fill – Blue, Accent 1, Reflection**. Click anywhere to deselect the text and notice the text effect. Compare your screen with Figure 1.12.

As you progress in your study of Microsoft Office, you will practice using many dialog boxes and commands to apply interesting effects such as this to your Word documents, Excel worksheets, Access database objects, and PowerPoint slides.

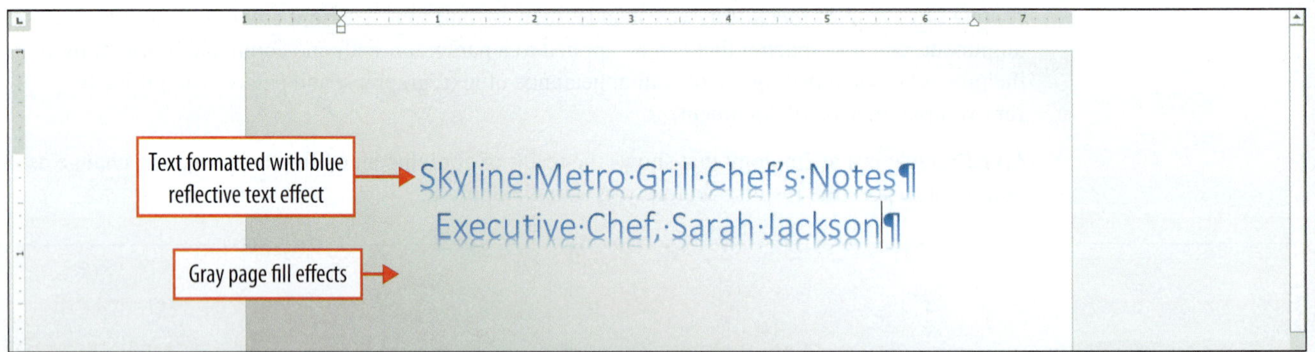

FIGURE 1.12

Objective 4 Create a Folder and Name and Save a File

GO! Learn How Video OF1-5

A ***location*** is any disk drive, folder, or other place in which you can store files and folders. Where you store your files depends on how and where you use your data. For example, for your college classes, you might decide to store your work on a removable USB flash drive so that you can carry your files to different locations and access your files on different computers.

If you do most of your work on a single computer, for example, your home desktop system or your laptop computer that you take with you to school or work, then you can store your files in one of the folders—Documents, Music, Pictures, or Videos—on your hard drive provided by your Windows operating system.

The best place to store files if you want them to be available anytime, anywhere, from almost any device is on your ***OneDrive***, which is Microsoft's free ***cloud storage*** for anyone with a free Microsoft account. Cloud storage refers to online storage of data so that you can access your data from different places and devices. ***Cloud computing*** refers to applications and services that are accessed over the Internet, rather than accessing applications installed on your local computer.

If you have an ***Office 365*** account—one of the versions of Microsoft Office to which you subscribe for an annual fee—your storage capacity on OneDrive is a terabyte or more, which is more than most individuals would ever require.

Because many people now have multiple computing devices—desktop, laptop, tablet, smartphone—it is common to store data *in the cloud* so that it is always available. ***Synchronization***, also called ***syncing***—pronounced SINK-ing—is the process of updating computer files that are in two or more locations according to specific rules. So if you create and save a Word document on your OneDrive using your laptop, you can open and edit that document on your tablet in OneDrive. When you close the document again, the file is properly updated to reflect your changes. Your OneDrive account will guide you in setting options for syncing files to your specifications.

You need not be connected to the Internet to access documents stored on OneDrive because an up-to-date version of your content is synched to your local system and available on OneDrive. You must, however, be connected to the Internet for the syncing to occur. Saving to OneDrive will keep the local copy on your computer and the copy in the cloud synchronized for as long as you need it. You can open and edit Office files by using Office apps available on a variety of device platforms, including iOS, Android, and Windows.

The Windows operating system helps you to create and maintain a logical folder structure, so always take the time to name your files and folders consistently.

Activity 1.06 | Creating a Folder and Naming and Saving a File

A Word document is an example of a file. In this Activity, you will create a folder in the storage location you have chosen to use for your files and then save your file. This example will use the Documents folder on the PC at which you are working. If you prefer to store on your OneDrive or on a USB flash drive, you can use similar steps.

1 Decide where you are going to store your files for this Project.

As the first step in saving a file, determine where you want to save the file, and if necessary, insert a storage device.

2 At the top of your screen, in the title bar, notice that *Document1 – Word* displays.

The Blank option on the opening screen of an Office 2016 program displays a new unsaved file with a default name— *Document1*, *Presentation1*, and so on. As you create your file, your work is temporarily stored in the computer's memory until you initiate a Save command, at which time you must choose a file name and a location in which to save your file.

3 In the upper left corner of your screen, click the **File tab** to display **Backstage** view. Compare your screen with Figure 1.13.

Backstage view is a centralized space that groups commands related to *file* management; that is why the tab is labeled *File*. File management commands include opening, saving, printing, publishing, or sharing a file. The ***Backstage tabs***—*Info*, *New*, *Open*, *Save*, *Save As*, *Print*, *Share*, *Export*, and *Close*—display along the left side. The tabs group file-related tasks together.

Here, the ***Info tab*** displays information—*info*—about the current file, and file management commands display under Info. For example, if you click the Protect Document button, a list of options that you can set for this file that relate to who can open or edit the document displays.

On the right, you can also examine the ***document properties***. Document properties, also known as ***metadata***, are details about a file that describe or identify it, such as the title, author name, subject, and keywords that identify the document's topic or contents. To close Backstage view and return to the document, you can click [back] in the upper left corner or press Esc.

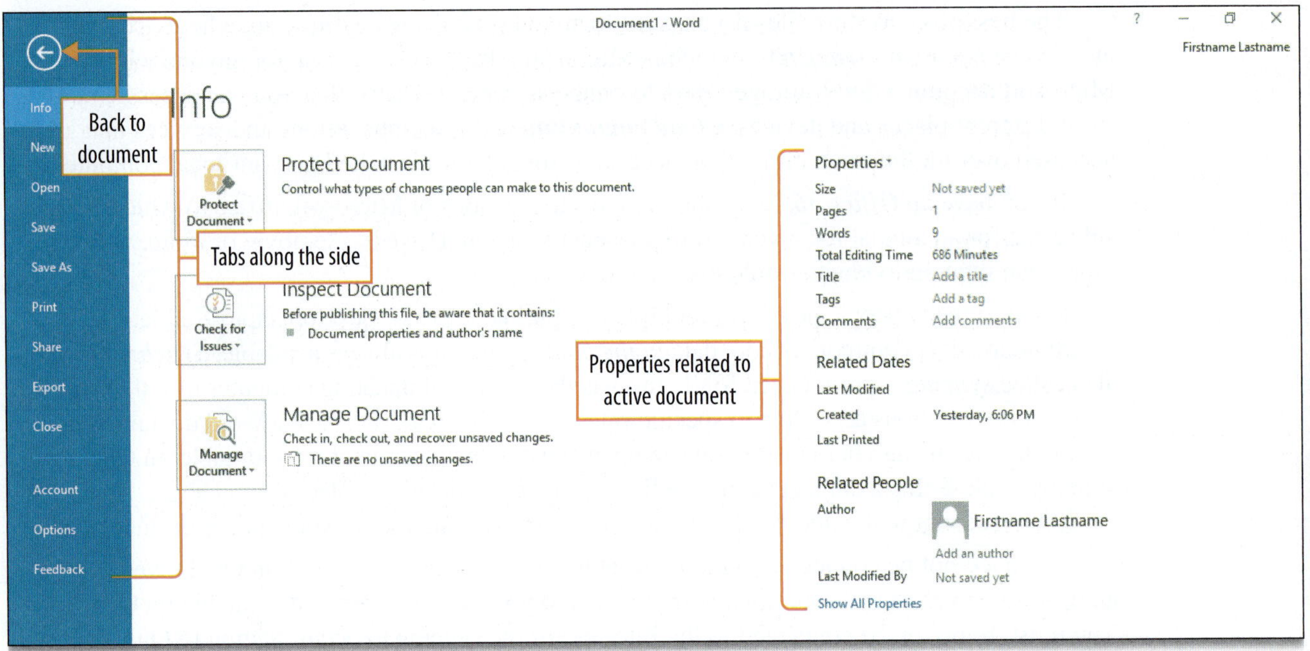

FIGURE 1.13

4 On the left, click **Save As**, and notice that the default location for storing Office files is your **OneDrive**—if you are signed in. Compare your screen with Figure 1.14.

When you are saving something for the first time, for example, a new Word document, the Save and Save As commands are identical. That is, the Save As commands will display if you click Save or if you click Save As.

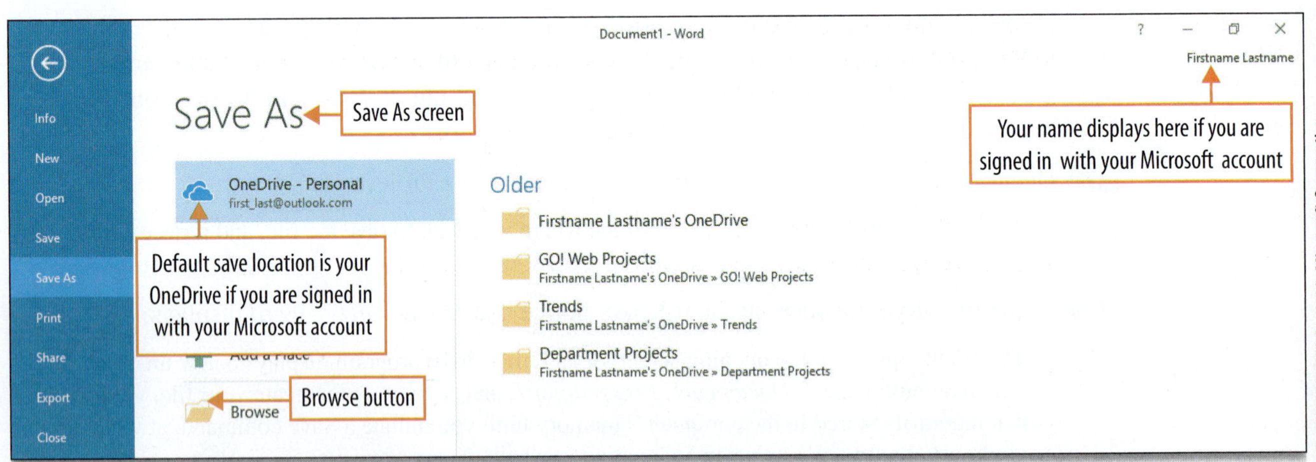

FIGURE 1.14

NOTE Saving After Your File Is Named

After you name and save a file, the Save command on the Quick Access Toolbar saves any changes you make to the file without displaying Backstage view. The Save As command enables you to name and save a *new* file based on the current one—in a location that you choose. After you name and save the new document, the original document closes, and the new document—based on the original one—displays.

5 To store your Word file in the **Documents** folder on your PC, click **Browse** to display the **Save As** dialog box. On the left, in the **navigation pane**, scroll down; if necessary click > to expand This PC, and then click **Documents**, or navigate to your USB flash drive or other location. In a college lab, your work may be lost if you store in the Documents folder. Compare your screen with Figure 1.15.

In the Save As dialog box, you must indicate the name you want for the file and the location where you want to save the file. When working with your own data, it is good practice to pause at this point and determine the logical name and location for your file.

In the Save As dialog box, a ***toolbar*** displays, which is a row, column, or block of buttons or icons, that displays across the top of a window and that contains commands for tasks you perform with a single click.

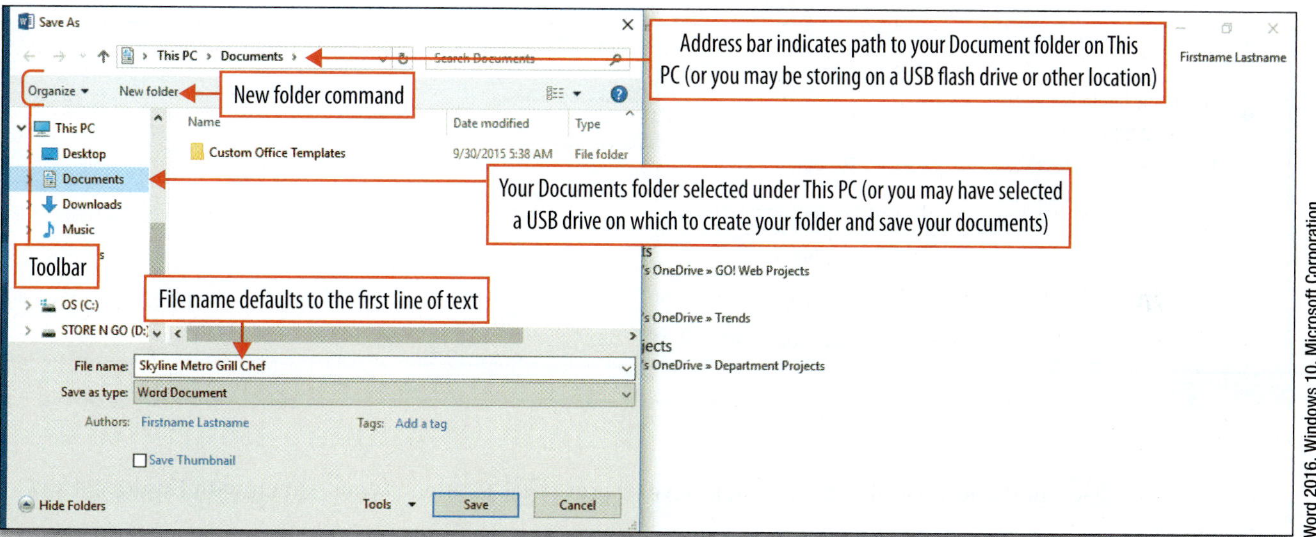

FIGURE 1.15

6 On the toolbar, click **New folder**.

In the file list, Windows creates a new folder, and the text *New folder* is selected.

7 Type **Office Features Chapter 1** and press Enter. Compare your screen with Figure 1.16.

In Windows-based programs, the Enter key confirms an action.

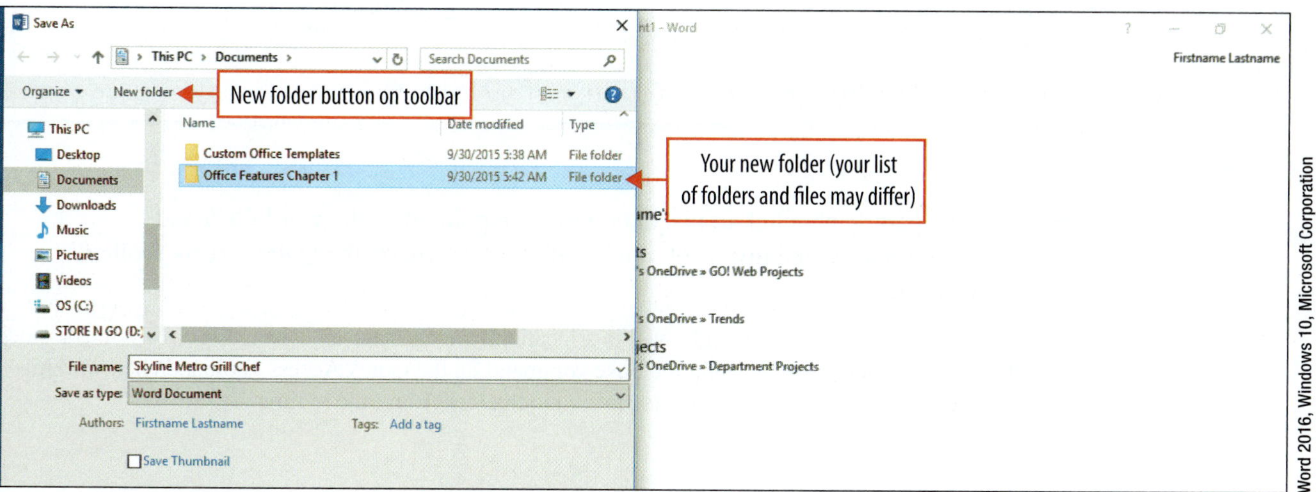

FIGURE 1.16

8 In the **file list**, double-click the name of your new folder to open it and display its name in the **address bar**.

9 In the lower portion of the dialog box, click in the **File name** box to select the existing text. Notice that as the suggested file name, Office inserts the text at the beginning of the document.

10 On your keyboard, locate the - key, to the right of zero on the number row. Notice that the Shift of this key produces the underscore character. With the text still selected and using your own name, type **Lastname_Firstname_1A_Note_Form** Compare your screen with Figure 1.17.

You can use spaces in file names, however, some people prefer not to use spaces. Some programs, especially when transferring files over the Internet, may insert the extra characters *%20* in place of a space. In general, however, unless you encounter a problem, it is OK to use spaces. In this instruction, underscores are used instead of spaces in file names.

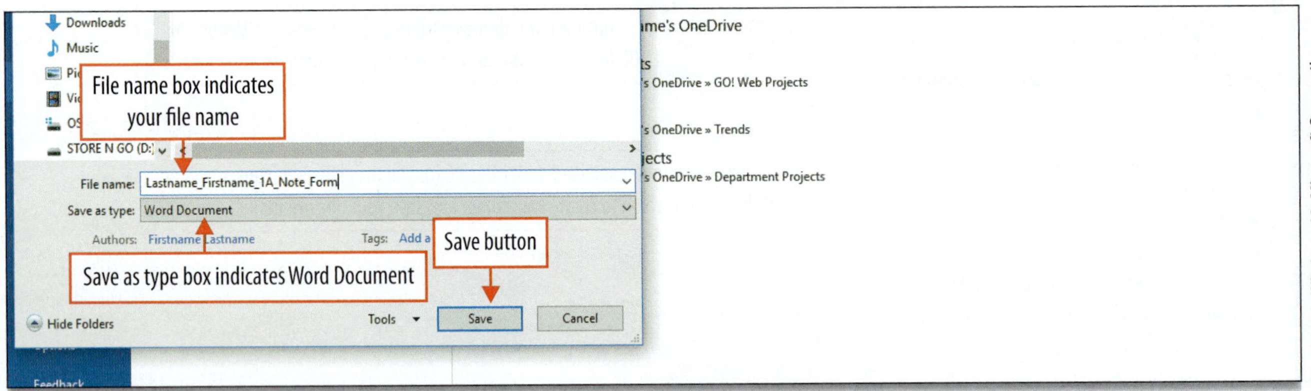

FIGURE 1.17

11 In the lower right corner, click **Save** or press Enter. Compare your screen with Figure 1.18.

The Word window redisplays and your new file name displays in the title bar, indicating that the file has been saved to the location that you have specified.

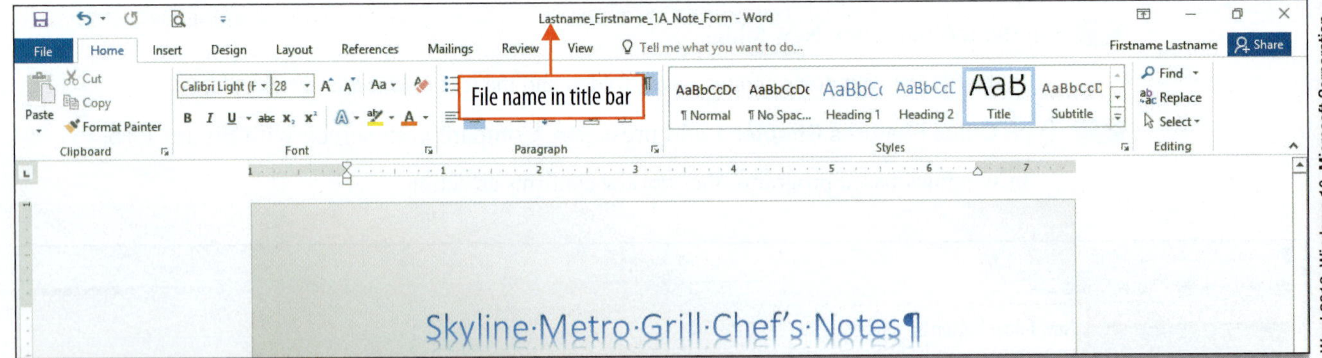

FIGURE 1.18

12 In the first paragraph, click to place the insertion point after the word *Grill* and type , (a comma). In the upper left corner of your screen, on the **Quick Access Toolbar**, click **Save**.

After a document is named and saved in a location, you can save any changes you have made since the last Save operation by using the Save command on the Quick Access Toolbar. When working on a document, it is good practice to save your changes from time to time.

Objective 5 Insert a Footer, Add Document Properties, Print a File, and Close a Desktop App

GO! Learn How Video OF1-5

MOS 1.3.4, 1.4.5

For most of your files, especially in a workplace setting, it is useful to add identifying information to help in finding files later. You might also want to print your file on paper or create an electronic printout. The process of printing a file is similar in all of the Office applications.

Activity 1.07 | Inserting a Footer, Inserting Document Info, and Adding Document Properties

NOTE What Does Your Instructor Require for Submission? A Paper Printout, an Image That Looks Like a Printed Document, or Your Word File?

In this Activity, you can produce a paper printout or an electronic image of your document that looks like a printed document. Or, your instructor may want only your completed Word file.

1. On the ribbon, click the **Insert tab**, and then in the **Header & Footer group**, click **Footer**.
2. At the bottom of the list, click **Edit Footer**. On the ribbon, notice that the **Header & Footer Tools** display.

   The *Header & Footer Tools Design* tab displays on the ribbon. The ribbon adapts to your work and will display additional tabs like this one—referred to as ***contextual tabs***—when you need them.

   A ***footer*** is a reserved area for text or graphics that displays at the bottom of each page in a document. Likewise, a ***header*** is a reserved area for text or graphics that displays at the top of each page in a document. When the footer (or header) area is active, the document area is dimmed, indicating it is unavailable.

3. On the ribbon, under **Header & Footer Tools**, on the **Design tab**, in the **Insert group**, click **Document Info**, and then click **File Name** to insert the name of your file in the footer, which is a common business practice. Compare your screen with Figure 1.19.

   Ribbon commands that display ▾ will, when clicked, display a list of options for the command.

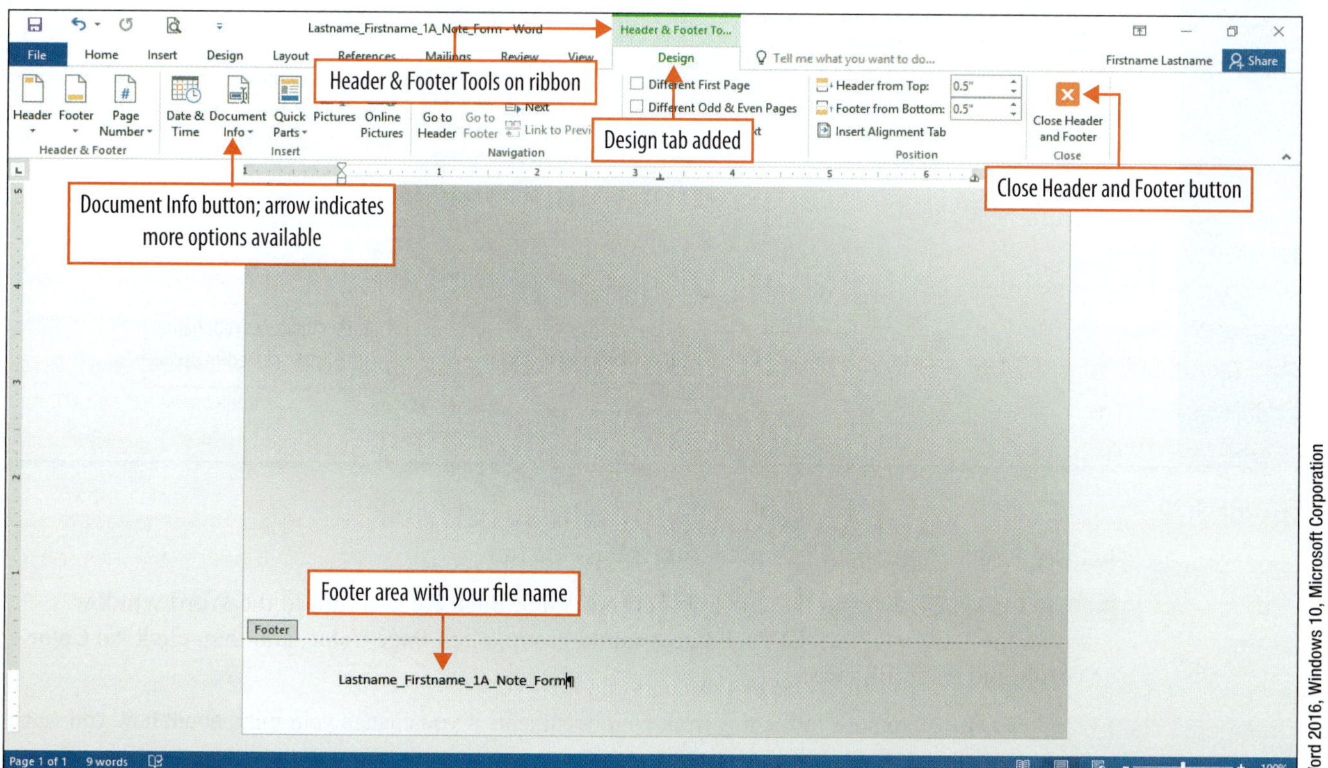

FIGURE 1.19

Word 2016, Windows 10, Microsoft Corporation

4 At the right end of the ribbon, click **Close Header and Footer**.

ANOTHER WAY Double-click anywhere in the dimmed document to close the footer.

5 Click the **File tab** to display **Backstage** view. On the right, at the bottom of the **Properties** list, click **Show All Properties**.

ANOTHER WAY Click the arrow to the right of Properties, and then click Advanced Properties to show and edit properties at the top of your document window.

6 On the list of **Properties**, click to the right of *Tags* to display an empty box, and then type **chef, notes, form**

Tags, also referred to as ***keywords***, are custom file properties in the form of words that you associate with a document to give an indication of the document's content. Adding tags to your documents makes it easier to search for and locate files in File Explorer, on your OneDrive, and in systems such as Microsoft ***SharePoint*** document libraries. SharePoint is collaboration software with which people in an organization can set up team sites to share information, manage documents, and publish reports for others to see.

BY TOUCH Tap to the right of Tags to display the Tags box and the onscreen keyboard.

7 Click to the right of *Subject* to display an empty box, and then type your course name and section #; for example, *CIS 10, #5543*.

8 Under **Related People**, be sure that your name displays as the author. If necessary, right-click the author name, click Edit Property, type your name, click outside of the Edit person dialog box, and then click OK. Compare your screen with Figure 1.20.

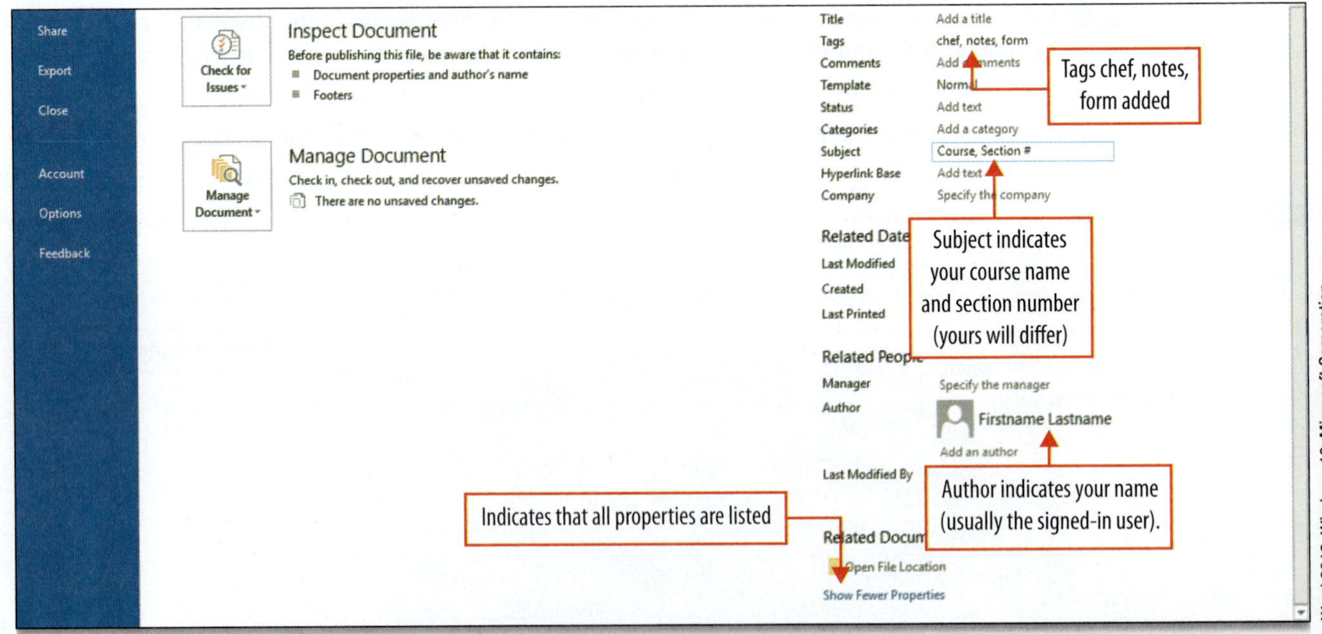

FIGURE 1.20

Activity 1.08 | Printing a File and Closing a Desktop App

1 In **Backstage** view, in the upper left corner, click **Back** to return to the Word window. On the **Design tab**, in the **Page Background group**, click **Page Color**, and then click **No Color** to remove the fill effects.

It's easy to remove formatting from your documents if you change your mind about how you want your document to look.

2 Click the **File tab** to return to **Backstage** view, on the left click **Print**, and then compare your screen with Figure 1.21.

Here you can select any printer connected to your system and adjust the settings related to how you want to print. On the right, the ***Print Preview*** displays, which is a view of a document as it will appear on paper when you print it.

At the bottom of the Print Preview area, in the center, the number of pages and page navigation arrows with which you can move among the pages in Print Preview display. On the right, the Zoom slider enables you to shrink or enlarge the Print Preview. ***Zoom*** is the action of increasing or decreasing the viewing area of the screen.

ANOTHER WAY From the document screen, press Ctrl + P or Ctrl + F2 to display Print in Backstage view.

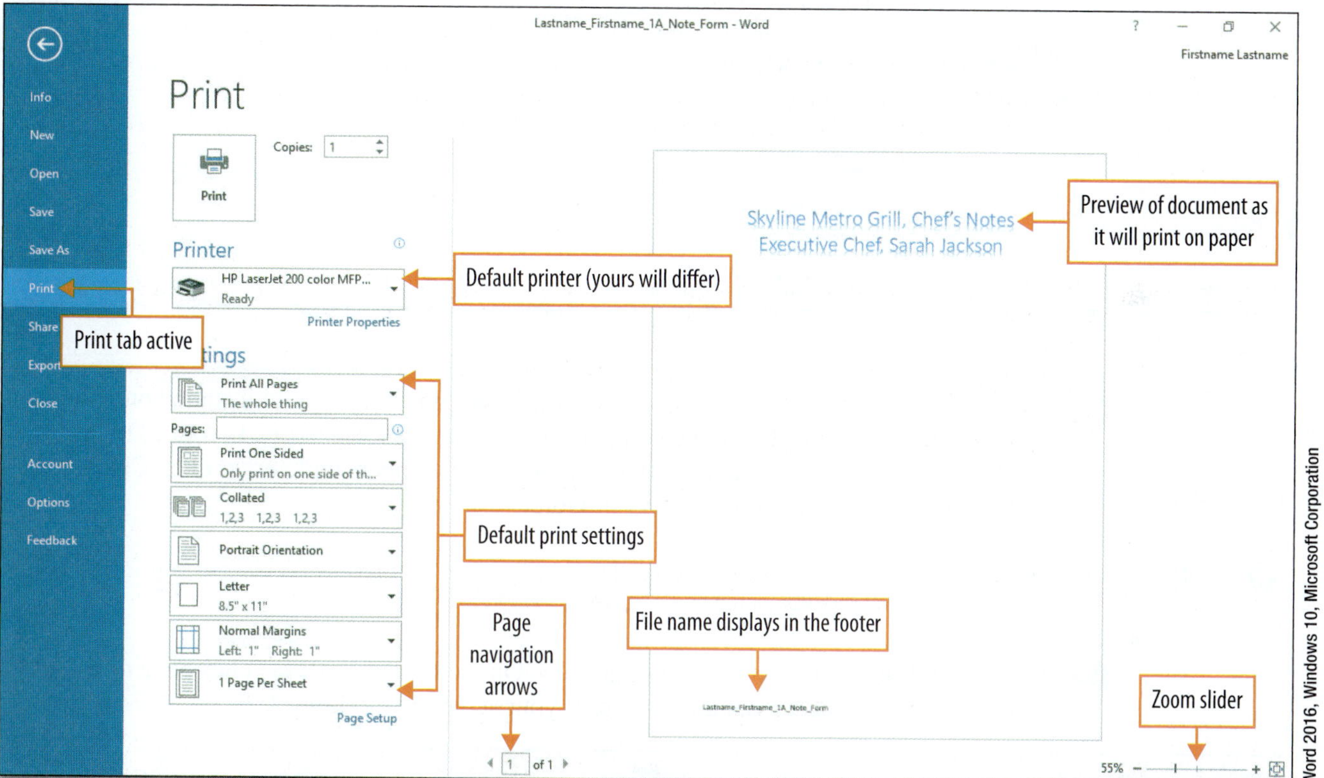

FIGURE 1.21

3 To create an electronic image of your document that looks like a printed document, skip this step and continue to Step 4. To print your document on paper using the default printer on your system, in the upper left portion of the screen, click **Print**.

The document will print on your default printer; if you do not have a color printer, the blue text will print in shades of gray. Backstage view closes and your file redisplays in the Word window.

4 To create an electronic image of your document that looks like a printed document, in **Backstage** view, on the left click **Export**. On the right, click the **Create PDF/XPS** button to display the **Publish as PDF or XPS** dialog box.

PDF stands for ***Portable Document Format***, which is a technology that creates an image that preserves the look of your file. This is a popular format for sending documents electronically, because the document will display on most computers.

XPS stands for ***XML Paper Specification***—a Microsoft file format that also creates an image of your document and that opens in the XPS viewer.

5 On the left in the **navigation pane**, if necessary expand > This PC, and then navigate to your **Office Features Chapter 1** folder in your **Documents** folder—or in whatever location you have created your Office Features Chapter 1 folder. Compare your screen with Figure 1.22.

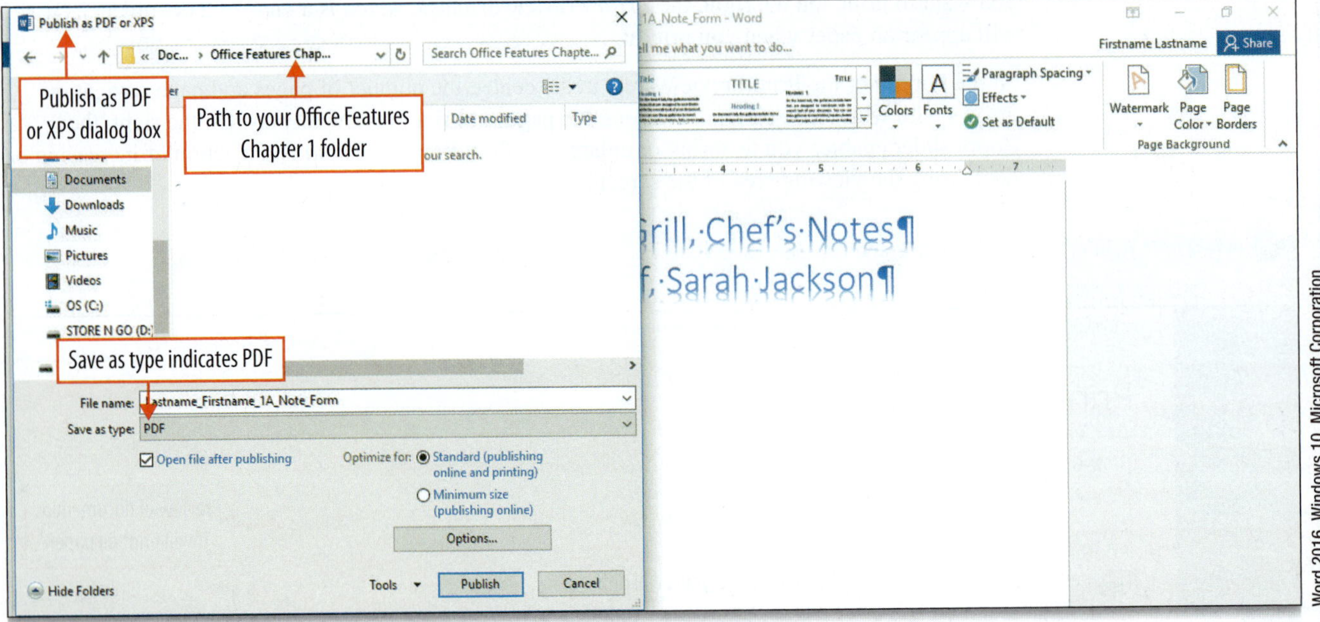

Word 2016, Windows 10, Microsoft Corporation

FIGURE 1.22

6 In the lower right corner of the dialog box, click **Publish**; if a program installed on your computer displays your PDF, in the upper right corner, click Close [×]. If your PDF displays in Microsoft Edge (on a Windows 10 computer), in the upper right corner click Close [×]. Notice that your document redisplays in Word.

ANOTHER WAY In Backstage view, click Save As, navigate to the location of your Chapter folder, click the Save as type arrow, on the list click PDF, and then click Save.

7 Click the **File tab** to redisplay **Backstage** view. On the left, click **Close**, click **Save** to save the changes you have made, and then compare your screen with Figure 1.23.

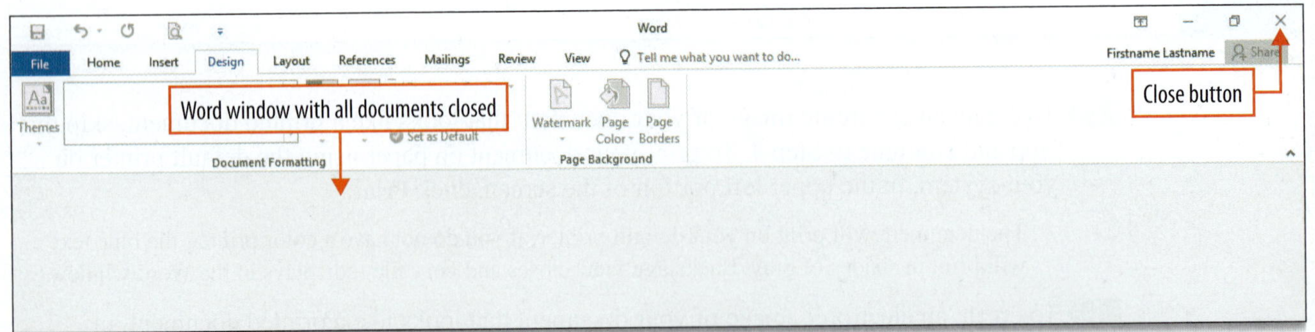

Word 2016, Windows 10, Microsoft Corporation

FIGURE 1.23

8 In the upper right corner of the Word window, click **Close** [×]. If directed by your instructor to do so, submit your paper printout, your electronic image of your document that looks like a printed document, or your original Word file.

END | You have completed Project 1A

PROJECT 1B

Memo

PROJECT ACTIVITIES

In Activities 1.09 through 1.24, you will open, edit, and then compress a Word file. You will also use the Tell Me help feature and install an app for Office. Your completed document will look similar to Figure 1.24.

PROJECT FILES

If your instructor wants you to submit Project 1B in the MyITLab Grader system, log in to MyITLab, locate Grader Project1B, and then download the files for this project.

For Project 1B, you will need the following file:
of01B_Rehearsal_Dinner

You will save your file as:
Lastname_Firstname_1B_Rehearsal_Dinner

PROJECT RESULTS

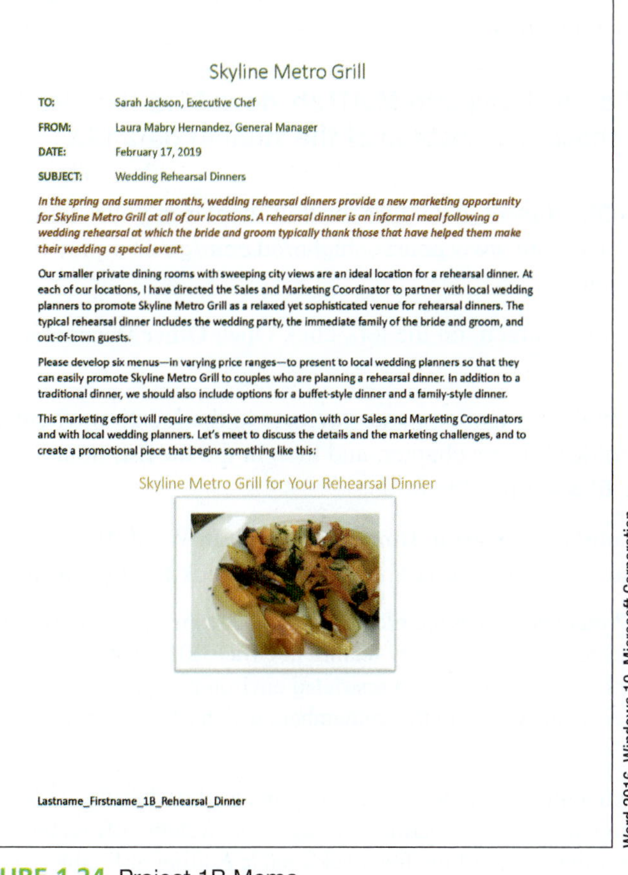

Skyline Metro Grill

TO: Sarah Jackson, Executive Chef

FROM: Laura Mabry Hernandez, General Manager

DATE: February 17, 2019

SUBJECT: Wedding Rehearsal Dinners

In the spring and summer months, wedding rehearsal dinners provide a new marketing opportunity for Skyline Metro Grill at all of our locations. A rehearsal dinner is an informal meal following a wedding rehearsal at which the bride and groom typically thank those that have helped them make their wedding a special event.

Our smaller private dining rooms with sweeping city views are an ideal location for a rehearsal dinner. At each of our locations, I have directed the Sales and Marketing Coordinator to partner with local wedding planners to promote Skyline Metro Grill as a relaxed yet sophisticated venue for rehearsal dinners. The typical rehearsal dinner includes the wedding party, the immediate family of the bride and groom, and out-of-town guests.

Please develop six menus—in varying price ranges—to present to local wedding planners so that they can easily promote Skyline Metro Grill to couples who are planning a rehearsal dinner. In addition to a traditional dinner, we should also include options for a buffet-style dinner and a family-style dinner.

This marketing effort will require extensive communication with our Sales and Marketing Coordinators and with local wedding planners. Let's meet to discuss the details and the marketing challenges, and to create a promotional piece that begins something like this:

Skyline Metro Grill for Your Rehearsal Dinner

Lastname_Firstname_1B_Rehearsal_Dinner

Word 2016, Windows 10, Microsoft Corporation

FIGURE 1.24 Project 1B Memo

Objective 6 Open an Existing File and Save It with a New Name

GO! Learn How Video OF1-6

In any Office program, you can display the ***Open dialog box***, from which you can navigate to and then open an existing file that was created in that same program.

The Open dialog box, along with the Save and Save As dialog boxes, is a common dialog box. These dialog boxes, which are provided by the Windows programming interface, display in all Office programs in the same manner. So the Open, Save, and Save As dialog boxes will all look and perform the same regardless of the Office program in which you are working.

ALERT! **To Complete This Project, You Will Need the Student Data Files That Accompany This Chapter**

To complete this project, you will need the Student Data Files that accompany this chapter. Possibly your instructor has provided these to you already; for example, in the learning management system used by your college. Alternatively, to download the files, go to **www.pearsonhighered.com/go** On the left, narrow your choice by selecting the appropriate topic, and then on the right, locate and click the image of this book. In the window that displays, click Download Data Files, and then click the chapter name. Using the commands for your browser, store the zipped file in your storage location, and then use the Extract tools in File Explorer to extract the zipped folder. Instructions for extracting can be found in the Getting Started with Windows 10 chapter.

Activity 1.09 | Opening an Existing File and Saving It with a New Name

In this Activity, you will display the Open dialog box, open an existing Word document, and then save it in your storage location with a new name.

ALERT! **To submit as an autograded project, log into MyITLab, download the files for this project, and begin with those files instead of the student data file.**

1. Be sure you have saved the folder **of01_student_data_files** for this chapter in your storage location; you can download this folder from **www.pearsonhighered.com/go** or it may have been provided to you by your instructor.

2. Start Word, and then on Word's opening screen, on the left, click **Open Other Documents**. Under **Open**, click **Browse**.

3. In the **Open** dialog box, on the left in the **navigation pane**, navigate to the location where you stored the **of01_student_data_files** folder for this chapter, and then in the **file list**, double-click the folder name **of01_student_data_files** to open the folder.

4. In the **file list**, double-click the file **of01B_Rehearsal_Dinner** to open it in Word. If **PROTECTED VIEW** displays at the top of your screen, in the center click **Enable Editing**.

   In Office 2016, a file will open in ***Protected View*** if the file appears to be from a potentially risky location, such as the Internet. Protected View is a security feature in Office 2016 that protects your computer from malicious files by opening them in a restricted environment until you enable them. ***Trusted Documents*** is another security feature that remembers which files you have already enabled.

   You might encounter these security features if you open a file from an email or download files from the Internet; for example, from your college's learning management system or from the Pearson website. So long as you trust the source of the file, click Enable Editing or Enable Content—depending on the type of file you receive—and then go ahead and work with the file.

5. With the document displayed in the Word window, be sure that **Show/Hide** is active; if necessary, on the Home tab, in the Paragraph group, click Show/Hide to activate it; on the View tab, be sure that Rulers are active. Compare your screen with Figure 1.25.

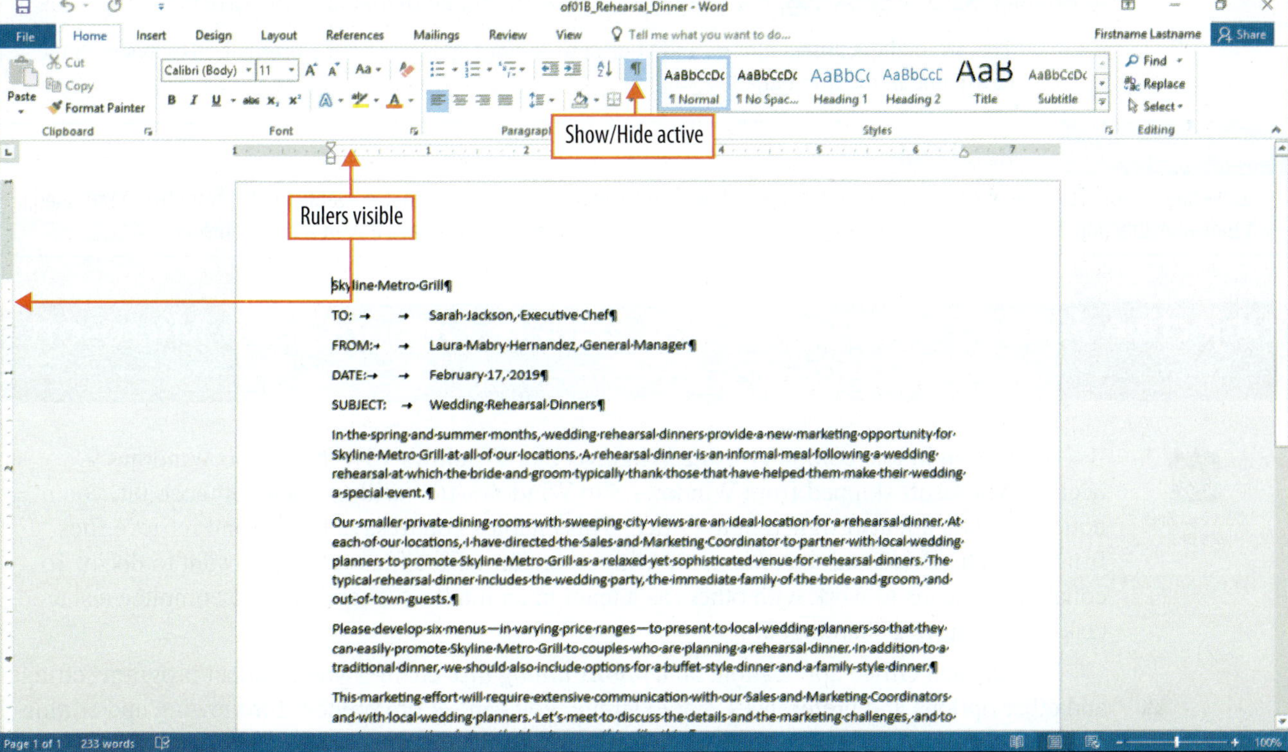

Word 2016, Windows 10, Microsoft Corporation

FIGURE 1.25

6 Click the **File tab** to display **Backstage** view, and then on the left, click **Save As**. Under **Save As**, click **Browse**.

7 In the **Save As** dialog box, use the **navigation pane** to navigate to and open the **Office Features Chapter 1** folder that you created to store your work from this chapter.

In Backstage view, on the right, you might also see your Office Features Chapter 1 folder listed, and if so, you can open it directly from there. The common dialog boxes Open, Save, and Save As remember your recently used locations and display them in Backstage view.

ANOTHER WAY From the Word window, press F12 to display the Save As dialog box.

8 Click in the **File name** box to select the existing text, and then, using your own name, type **Lastname_Firstname_1B_Rehearsal_Dinner** Compare your screen with Figure 1.26.

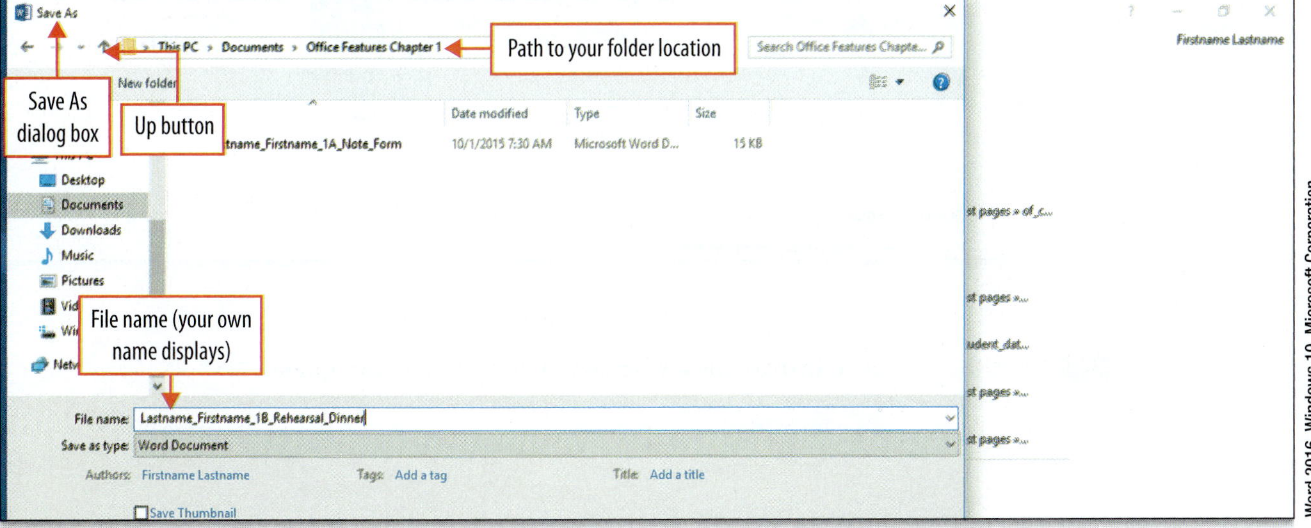

Word 2016, Windows 10, Microsoft Corporation

FIGURE 1.26

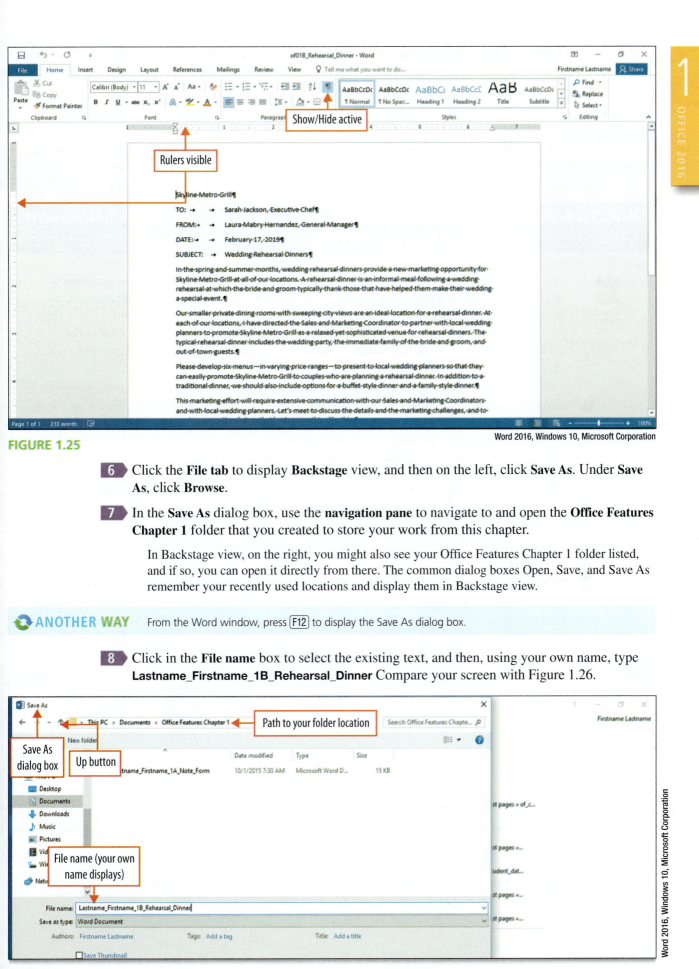

9 Click **Save** or press Enter; notice that your new file name displays in the title bar.

The original document closes, and your new document, based on the original, displays with the new name in the title bar.

> ***More* Knowledge** **Read-Only**
>
> Some files might display ***Read-Only*** in the title bar, which is a property assigned to a file that prevents the file from being modified; it indicates that you cannot save any changes to the displayed document unless you first save it with a new name.

Objective 7 Sign In to Office and Explore Options for a Microsoft Office Desktop App

GO! Learn How Video OF1-7

If you sign in to a computer using Windows 8 or Windows 10—there is no Windows 9, because Microsoft skipped from Windows 8 to Windows 10—with a Microsoft account, you may notice that you are also signed in to Office. This enables you to save files to and retrieve files from your OneDrive and to ***collaborate*** with others on Office files when you want to do so. To collaborate means to work with others as a team in an intellectual endeavor to complete a shared task or to achieve a shared goal.

Within each Office application, an ***Options dialog box*** enables you to select program settings and other options and preferences. For example, you can set preferences for viewing and editing files.

Activity 1.10 | Signing In to Office and Viewing Application Options

1 In the upper right corner of your screen, if you are signed in with a Microsoft account, click your name, and then compare your screen with Figure 1.27.

Here you can change your photo, go to About me to edit your profile, examine your Account settings, or switch accounts to sign in with a different Microsoft account.

> **ALERT!** **Not Signed In to Office or Have Not Yet Created a Microsoft Account?**
>
> In the upper right corner, click Sign in, and then enter your Microsoft account. If you have not created a free Microsoft account, click Sign in, type any email address that you currently use, click Next, and then click Sign up now. If you are working in a college lab, this process may vary.

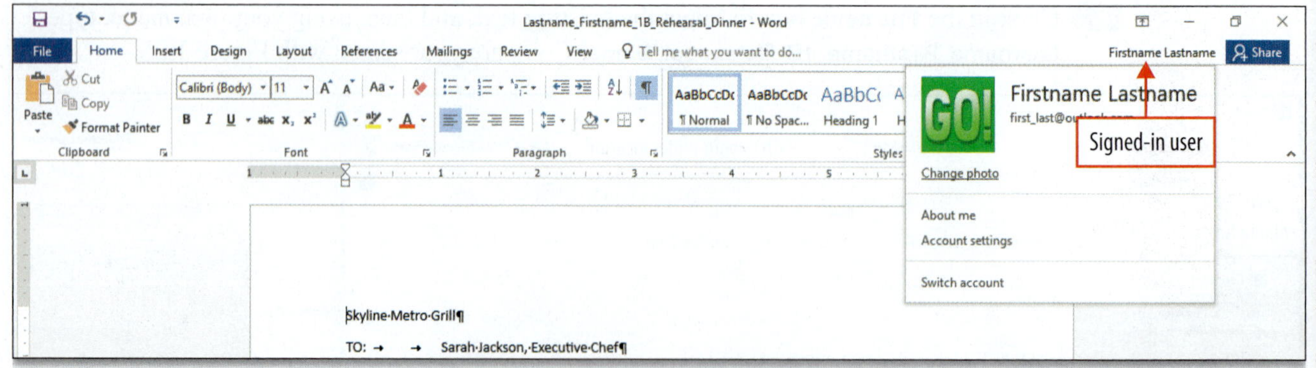

FIGURE 1.27

2 Click the **File tab** to display **Backstage** view. On the left, click **Options**.

3 In the **Word Options** dialog box, on the left, click **Display**, and then on the right, locate the information under **Always show these formatting marks on the screen**.

The Word Options dialog box—or the similar Options dialog box in any of the Office applications—controls nearly every aspect of the application. Next to many of the items, you will see small *i* icons, which when you point to them display a ScreenTip.

If you click each of the categories on the left side of the dialog box, you will see that the scope of each application is quite large and that you have a great deal of control over how the application behaves. For example, you can customize the tab names and group names in the ribbon.

If you are not sure what a setting or option does, in the upper right corner of the title bar, click the Help button—the question mark icon.

4 Under **Always show these formatting marks on the screen**, be sure the last check box, **Show all formatting marks**, is selected—select it if necessary. Compare your screen with Figure 1.28.

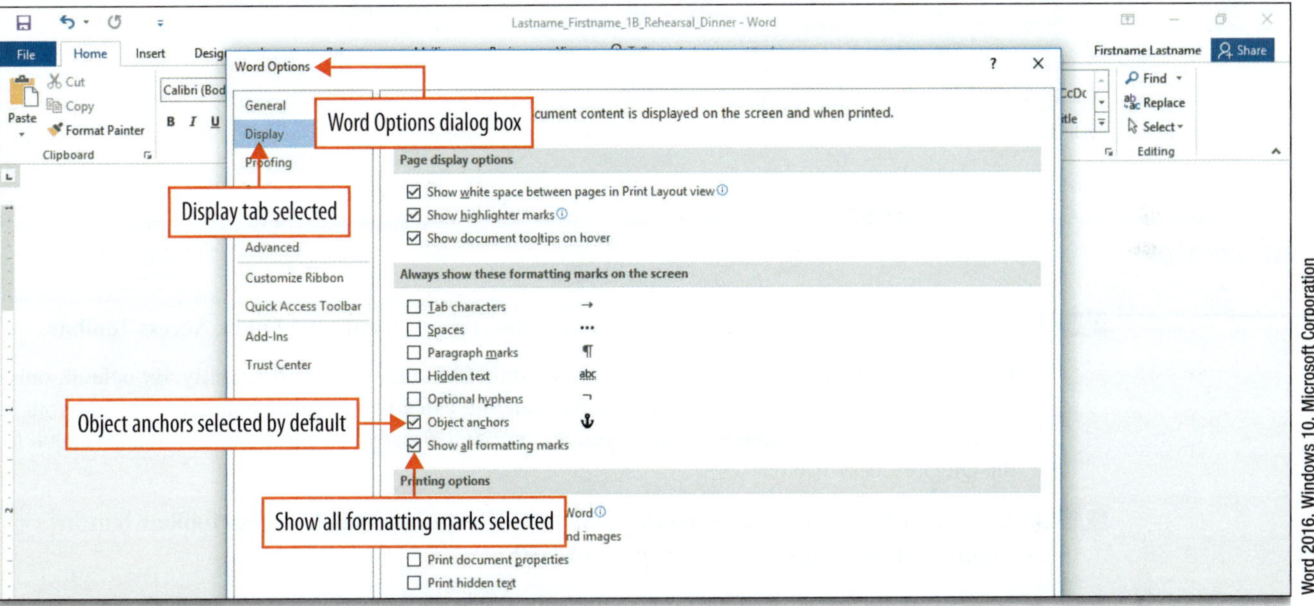

FIGURE 1.28

5 In the lower right corner of the dialog box, click **OK**.

Objective 8 Perform Commands from the Ribbon and Quick Access Toolbar

GO! Learn How
Video OF1-8

The ribbon that displays across the top of the program window groups commands in the way that you would most logically use them. The ribbon in each Office program is slightly different, but all contain the same three elements: ***tabs***, ***groups***, and ***commands***.

Tabs display across the top of the ribbon, and each tab relates to a type of activity; for example, laying out a page. Groups are sets of related commands for specific tasks. Commands—instructions to computer programs—are arranged in groups and might display as a button, a menu, or a box in which you type information.

You can also minimize the ribbon so only the tab names display, which is useful when working on a smaller screen such as a tablet computer where you want to maximize your screen viewing area.

1.4.3

Activity 1.11 | Performing Commands from and Customizing the Quick Access Toolbar

1 Take a moment to examine the document on your screen. If necessary, on the ribbon, click the View tab, and then in the Show group, click to place a check mark in the Ruler check box. Compare your screen with Figure 1.29.

This document is a memo from the General Manager to the Executive Chef regarding a new restaurant promotion for wedding rehearsal dinners.

When working in Word, display the rulers so that you can see how margin settings affect your document and how text and objects align. Additionally, if you set a tab stop or an indent, its location is visible on the ruler.

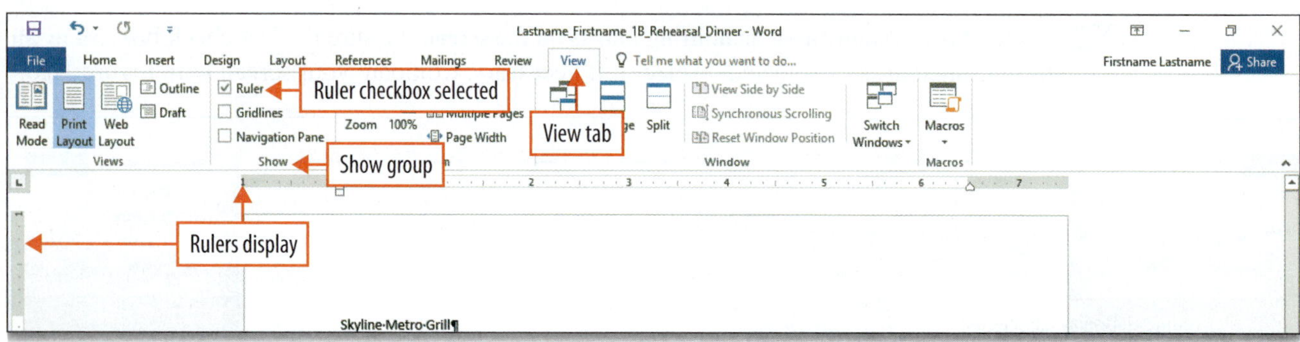

FIGURE 1.29

2 In the upper left corner of your screen, above the ribbon, locate the **Quick Access Toolbar**.

Recall that the Quick Access Toolbar contains commands that you use frequently. By default, only the commands Save, Undo, and Redo display, but you can add and delete commands to suit your needs. Possibly the computer at which you are working already has additional commands added to the Quick Access Toolbar.

3 At the end of the **Quick Access Toolbar**, click the **Customize Quick Access Toolbar** button, and then compare your screen with Figure 1.30.

A list of commands that Office users commonly add to their Quick Access Toolbar displays, including New, Open, Email, Quick Print, and Print Preview and Print. Commands already on the Quick Access Toolbar display a check mark. Commands that you add to the Quick Access Toolbar are always just one click away.

Here you can also display the More Commands dialog box, from which you can select any command from any tab to add to the Quick Access Toolbar.

BY TOUCH Tap once on Quick Access Toolbar commands.

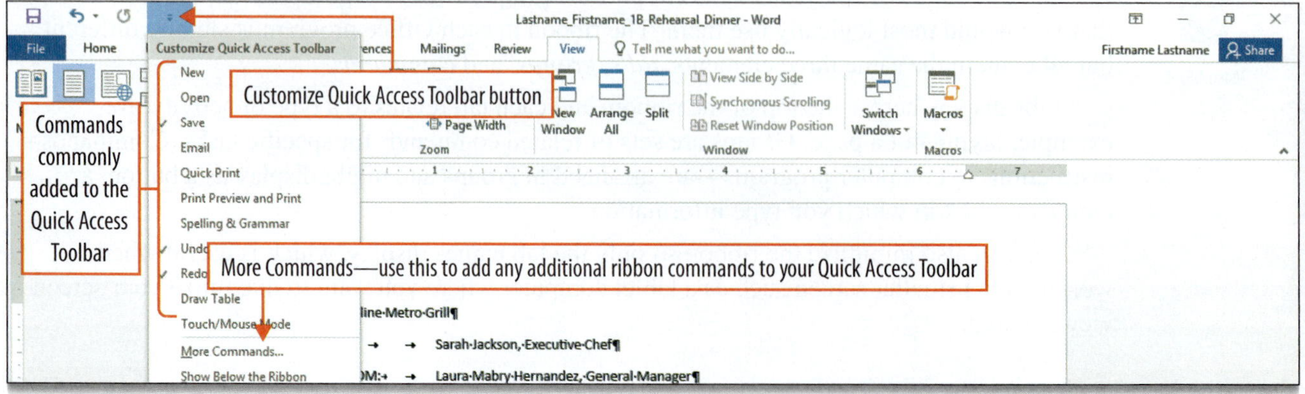

FIGURE 1.30

4 On the list, click **Print Preview and Print**, and then notice that the icon is added to the **Quick Access Toolbar**. Compare your screen with Figure 1.31.

The icon that represents the Print Preview command displays on the Quick Access Toolbar. Because this is a command that you will use frequently while building Office documents, you might decide to have this command remain on your Quick Access Toolbar.

ANOTHER WAY Right-click any command on the ribbon, and then on the shortcut menu, click Add to Quick Access Toolbar.

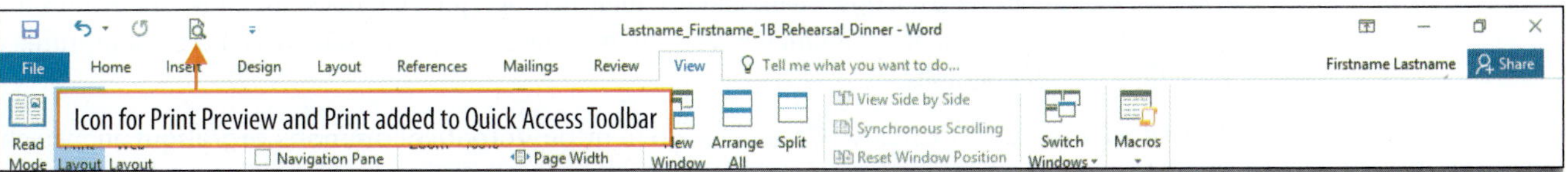

Word 2016, Windows 10, Microsoft Corporation

FIGURE 1.31

5.2.5

Activity 1.12 | Performing Commands from the Ribbon

1 In the first line of the document, if necessary, click to the left of the *S* in *Skyline* to position the insertion point there, and then press Enter one time to insert a blank paragraph. Press ↑ one time to position the insertion point in the new blank paragraph. Compare your screen with Figure 1.32.

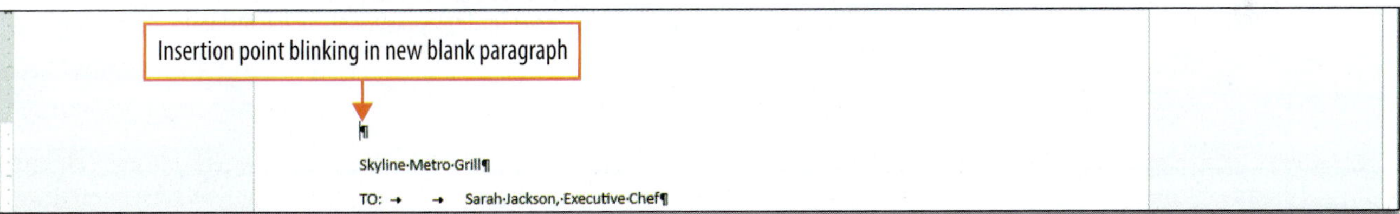

Word 2016, Windows 10, Microsoft Corporation

FIGURE 1.32

2 On the ribbon, click the **Insert tab**. In the **Illustrations group**, *point* to **Online Pictures** to display its ScreenTip.

Many buttons on the ribbon have this type of ***enhanced ScreenTip***, which displays useful descriptive information about the command.

3 Click **Online Pictures**, and then compare your screen with Figure 1.33.

In the Insert Pictures dialog box, you can search for online pictures using Bing Image Search, and, if you are signed in with your Microsoft account, you can also find images on your OneDrive by clicking Browse. At the bottom, you can click a logo to download pictures from your Facebook and other types of accounts if you have them.

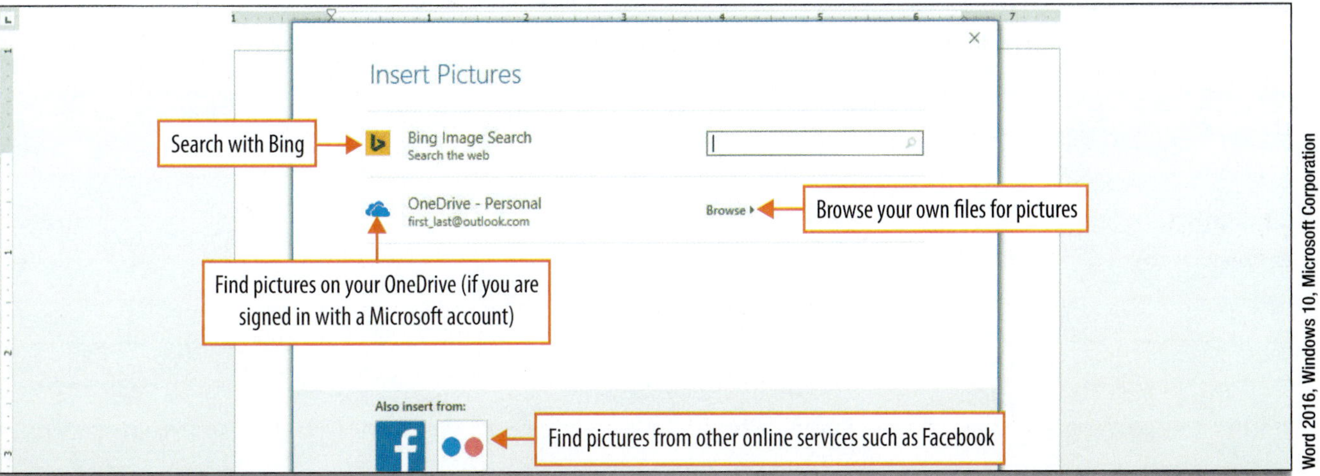

Word 2016, Windows 10, Microsoft Corporation

FIGURE 1.33

4 With the insertion point positioned in the **Bing Image Search** box, type **salad** and press Enter. Point to any of the results, and notice that keywords display. Compare your screen with Figure 1.34.

You can use various keywords to find images that are appropriate for your documents. The results shown indicate the images are licensed under ***Creative Commons***, which, according to **www.creativecommons.org** is "a nonprofit organization that enables the sharing and use of creativity and knowledge through free legal tools."

Creative Commons helps people share and use their photographs, but does not allow companies to sell them. For your college assignments, you can use these images so long as you are not profiting by selling the photographs.

To find out more about Creative Commons, go to **https://creativecommons.org/about** and watch the video.

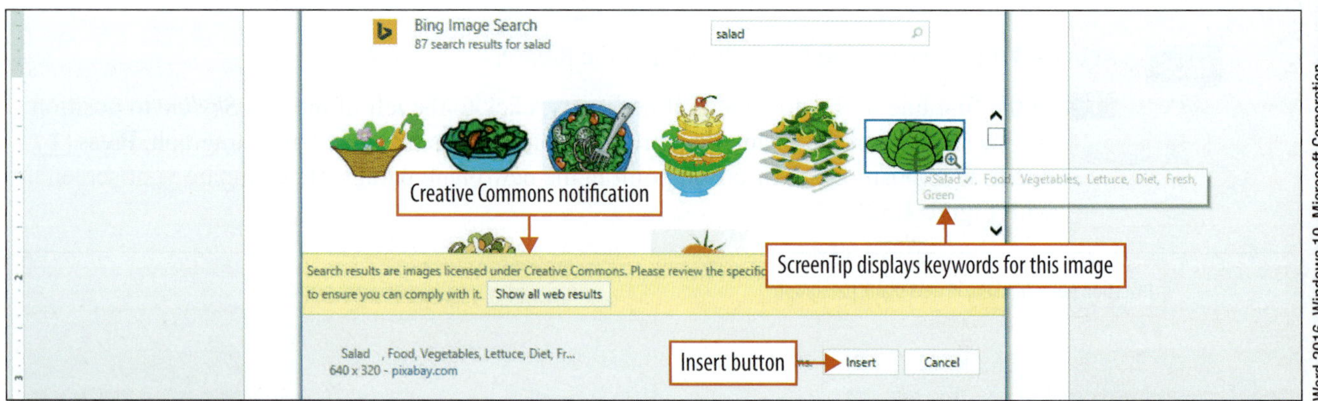

FIGURE 1.34

5 Locate an attractive picture of a salad on a plate or in a bowl that has a horizontal orientation—the picture is wider than it is tall—and then click that picture to select it. In the lower right corner, click **Insert**. In the upper right corner of the picture, point to the **Layout Options** button to display its ScreenTip, and then compare your screen with Figure 1.35.

Layout Options enable you to choose how the ***object***—in this instance an inserted picture—interacts with the surrounding text. An object is a picture or other graphic such as a chart or table that you can select and then move and resize.

When a picture is selected, the Picture Tools become available on the ribbon. Additionally, ***sizing handles***—small circles or squares that indicate an object is selected—surround the selected picture.

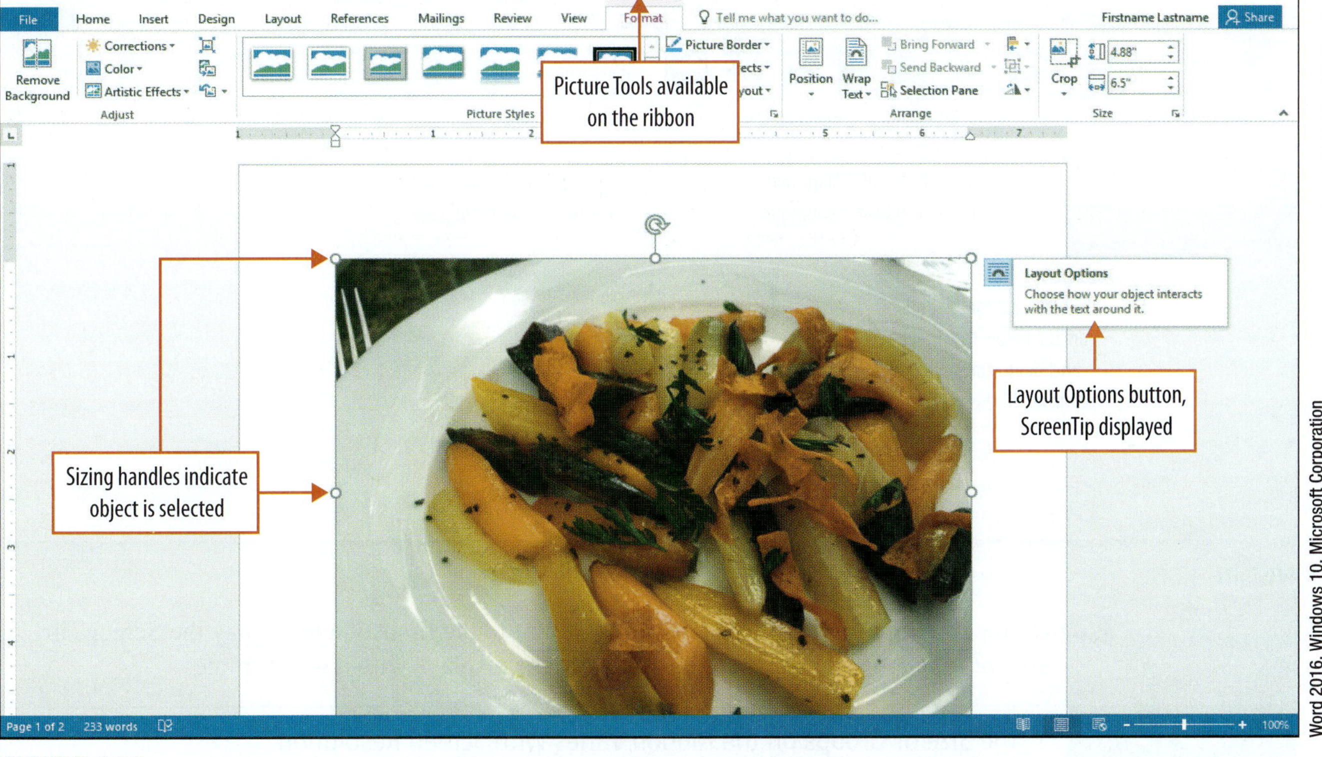

Word 2016, Windows 10, Microsoft Corporation

FIGURE 1.35

6 With the image selected, click **Layout Options** [icon], and then under **With Text Wrapping**, in the second row, click the first layout—**Top and Bottom**.

7 On the ribbon, with the **Picture Tools Format tab** active, at the right, in the **Size group**, click in the **Shape Height** box [icon] to select the existing text. Type **2** and press Enter.

8 Point to the image to display the [icon] pointer, hold down the left mouse button to display a green line at the left margin, and then drag the image to the right and slightly upward until a green line displays in the center of the image and at the top of the image, as shown in Figure 1.36, and then release the left mouse button. If you are not satisfied with your result, on the Quick Access Toolbar, click Undo [icon] and begin again.

Alignment guides are green lines that display to help you align objects with margins or at the center of a page.

Inserted pictures anchor—attach to—the paragraph at the insertion point location—as indicated by an anchor symbol.

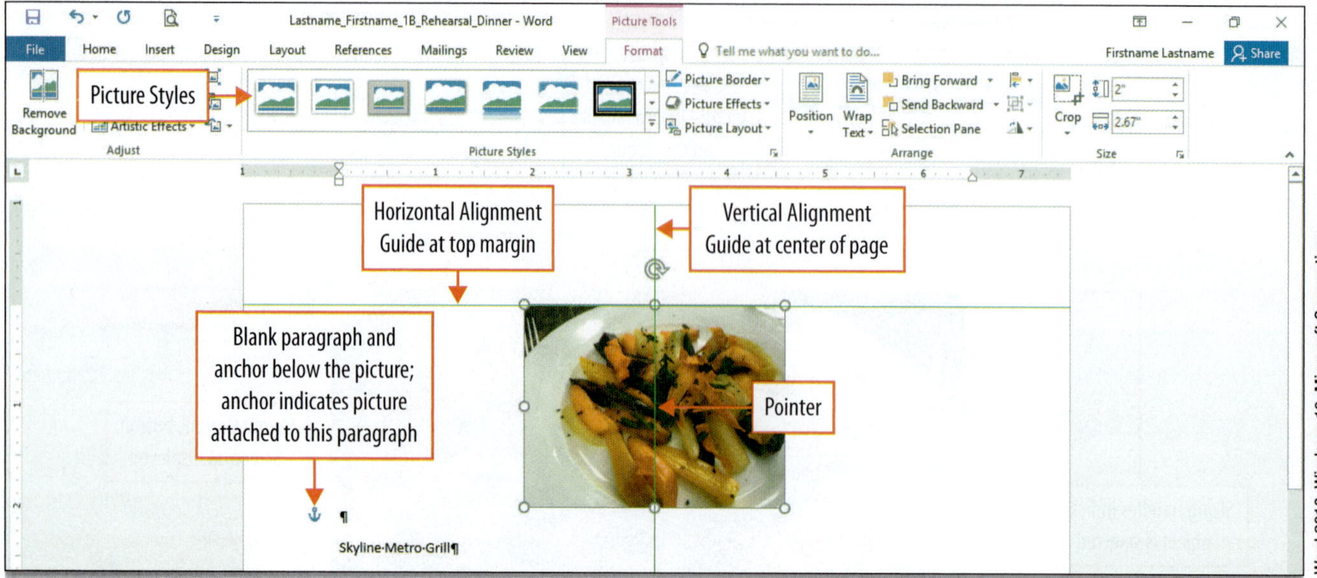

FIGURE 1.36

9 On the ribbon, in the **Picture Styles group**, point to the first style to display the ScreenTip *Simple Frame, White*, and notice that the image displays with a white frame.

> **NOTE** The Size of Groups on the Ribbon Varies with Screen Resolution
>
> Your monitor's screen resolution might be set higher than the resolution used to capture the figures shown here. At a higher resolution, the ribbon expands some groups to show more commands than are available with a single click, such as those in the Picture Styles group. Or, the group expands to add descriptive text to some buttons, such as those in the Arrange group. Regardless of your screen resolution, all Office commands are available to you. In higher resolutions, you will have a more robust view of the ribbon commands.

10 Watch the image as you point to the second picture style, and then to the third, and then to the fourth.

Recall that Live Preview shows the result of applying an editing or formatting change as you point to possible results—*before* you actually apply it.

11 In the **Picture Styles group**, click the second style—**Beveled Matte, White**—and then click anywhere outside of the image to deselect it. Notice that the Picture Tools no longer display on the ribbon. Compare your screen with Figure 1.37.

Contextual tabs on the ribbon display only when you need them.

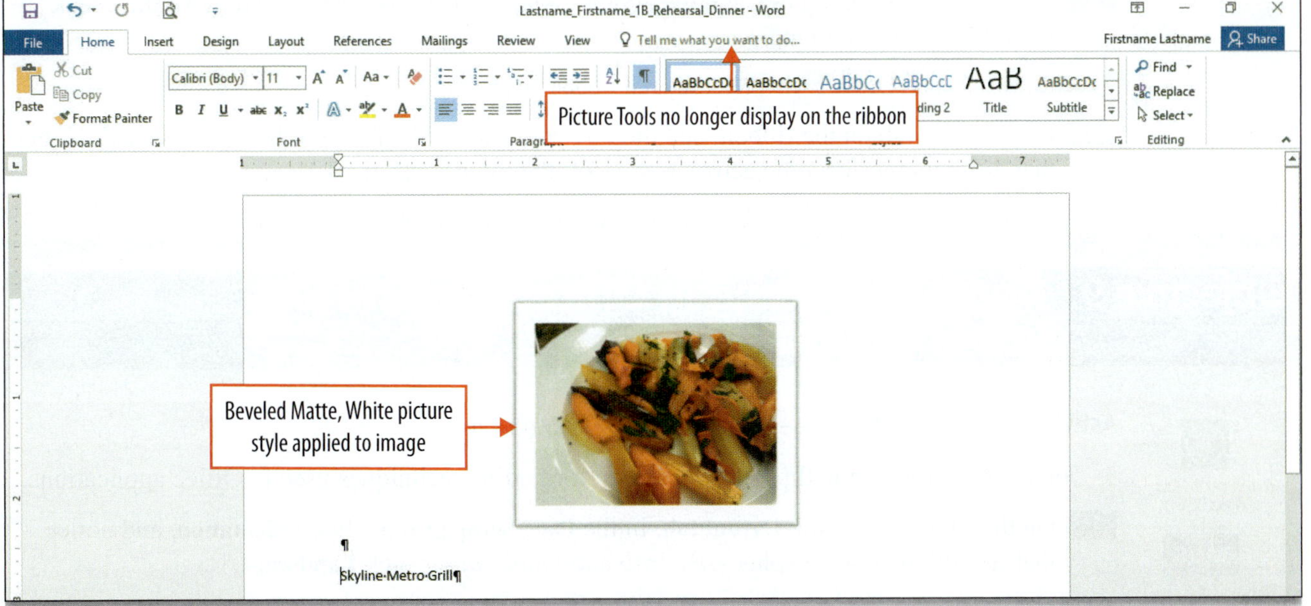

FIGURE 1.37

Word 2016, Windows 10, Microsoft Corporation

12 On the **Quick Access Toolbar**, click **Save** to save the changes you have made.

Activity 1.13 | Minimizing the Ribbon and Using the Keyboard to Control the Ribbon

Instead of a mouse, some individuals prefer to navigate the ribbon by using keys on the keyboard.

1 On your keyboard, press Alt, and then on the ribbon, notice that small labels display on the tabs. Press N to activate the commands on the **Insert tab**, and then compare your screen with Figure 1.38.

Each label represents a ***KeyTip***—an indication of the key that you can press to activate the command. For example, on the Insert tab, you can press F to open the Online Pictures dialog box.

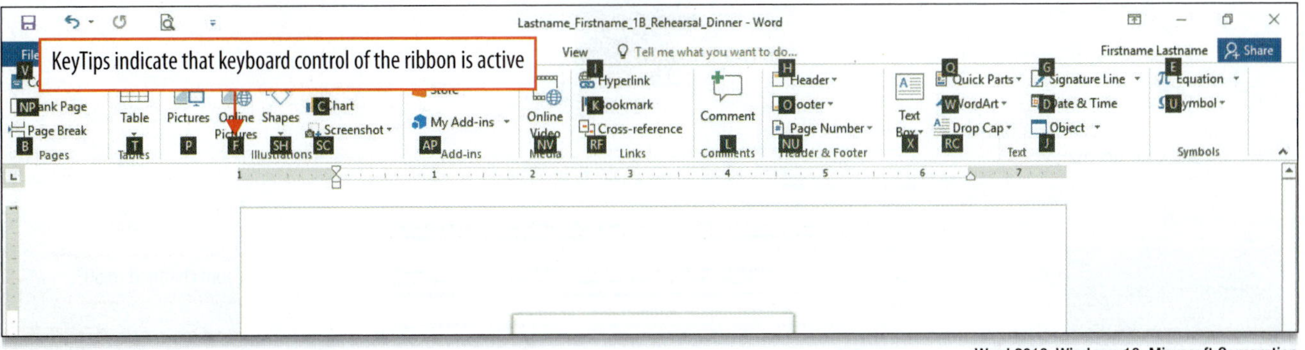

FIGURE 1.38

Word 2016, Windows 10, Microsoft Corporation

2 Press Esc to redisplay the KeyTips for the tabs. Then, press Alt or Esc again to turn off keyboard control of the ribbon.

3 Point to any tab on the ribbon and right-click to display a shortcut menu.

Here you can choose to display the Quick Access Toolbar below the ribbon or collapse the ribbon to maximize screen space. You can also customize the ribbon by adding, removing, renaming, or reordering tabs, groups, and commands, although this is not recommended until you become an expert Word user.

4 Click **Collapse the Ribbon**. Notice that only the ribbon tabs display. Click the **Home tab** to display the commands. Click anywhere in the document, and notice that the ribbon goes back to the collapsed display.

5 Right-click any ribbon tab, and then click **Collapse the Ribbon** again to remove the check mark from this command.

Most expert Office users prefer the full ribbon display.

6 Point to any tab on the ribbon, and then on your mouse device, roll the mouse wheel. Notice that different tabs become active as you roll the mouse wheel.

You can make a tab active by using this technique, instead of clicking the tab.

Objective 9 Apply Formatting in Office Programs and Inspect Documents

Activity 1.14 | Changing Page Orientation and Zoom Level

GO! Learn How
Video OF1-9

1.4.2

In this Activity, you will practice common formatting techniques used in Office applications.

1 On the ribbon, click the **Layout tab**. In the **Page Setup group**, click **Orientation**, and notice that two orientations display—*Portrait* and *Landscape*. Click **Landscape**.

In ***portrait orientation***, the paper is taller than it is wide. In ***landscape orientation***, the paper is wider than it is tall.

2 In the lower right corner of the screen, locate the **Zoom slider**.

Recall that to zoom means to increase or decrease the viewing area. You can zoom in to look closely at a section of a document, and then zoom out to see an entire page on the screen. You can also zoom to view multiple pages on the screen.

3 Drag the **Zoom slider** to the left until you have zoomed to approximately *60%*. Compare your screen with Figure 1.39.

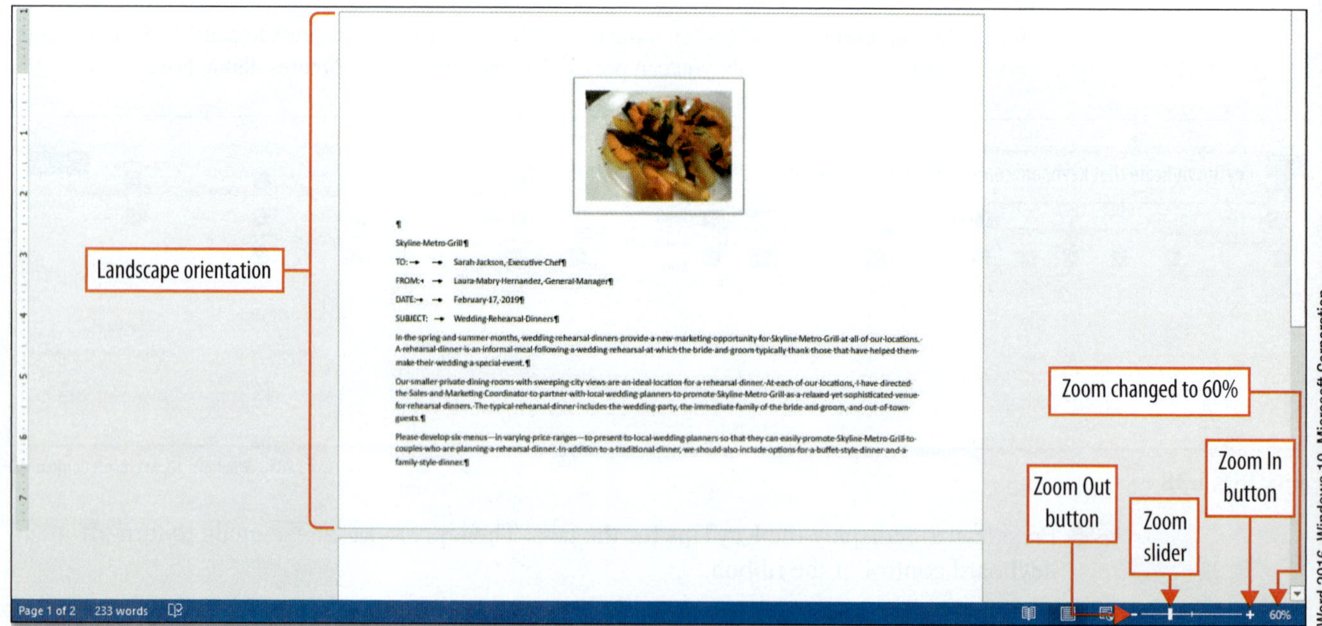

FIGURE 1.39

BY TOUCH Drag the Zoom slider with your finger.

4 Use the technique you just practiced to change the **Orientation** back to **Portrait**.

The default orientation in Word is Portrait, which is commonly used for business documents such as letters and memos.

5 In the lower right corner, click the **Zoom In** button as many times as necessary to return to the **100%** zoom setting.

Use the zoom feature to adjust the view of your document for editing and for your viewing comfort.

ANOTHER WAY You can also control Zoom from the ribbon. On the View tab, in the Zoom group, you can control the Zoom level and also zoom to view multiple pages.

6 On the **Quick Access Toolbar**, click **Save**.

More Knowledge **Zooming to Page Width**

Some Office users prefer ***Page Width***, which zooms the document so that the width of the page matches the width of the window. Find this command on the View tab, in the Zoom group.

Activity 1.15 | Formatting Text by Using Fonts, Alignment, Font Colors, and Font Styles

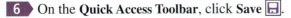

1 If necessary, on the right edge of your screen, drag the vertical scroll box to the top of the scroll bar. To the left of *Skyline Metro Grill*, point in the margin area to display the pointer and click one time to select the entire paragraph. Compare your screen with Figure 1.40.

Use this technique to select complete paragraphs from the margin area—drag downward to select multiple-line paragraphs—which is faster and more efficient than dragging through text.

FIGURE 1.40

2 On the ribbon, click the **Home tab**, and then in the **Paragraph group**, click **Center** to center the paragraph.

3 On the **Home tab**, in the **Font group**, click the **Font button arrow** Calibri (Body). On the alphabetical list of font names, scroll down and then locate and *point to* **Cambria**.

A ***font*** is a set of characters with the same design and shape. The default font in a Word document is Calibri, which is a ***sans serif font***—a font design with no lines or extensions on the ends of characters.

The Cambria font is a ***serif font***—a font design that includes small line extensions on the ends of the letters to guide the eye in reading from left to right.

The list of fonts displays as a gallery showing potential results. For example, in the Font gallery, you can point to see the actual design and format of each font as it would look if applied to text.

4 Point to several other fonts and observe the effect on the selected text. Then, scroll back to the top of the **Font** gallery. Under **Theme Fonts**, click **Calibri Light**.

A ***theme*** is a predesigned combination of colors, fonts, line, and fill effects that look good together and is applied to an entire document by a single selection. A theme combines two sets of fonts—one for text and one for headings. In the default Office theme, Calibri Light is the suggested font for headings.

5 With the paragraph *Skyline Metro Grill* still selected, on the **Home tab**, in the **Font group**, click the **Font Size button arrow** [11 ▾], point to **36**, and then notice how Live Preview displays the text in the font size to which you are pointing. Compare your screen with Figure 1.41.

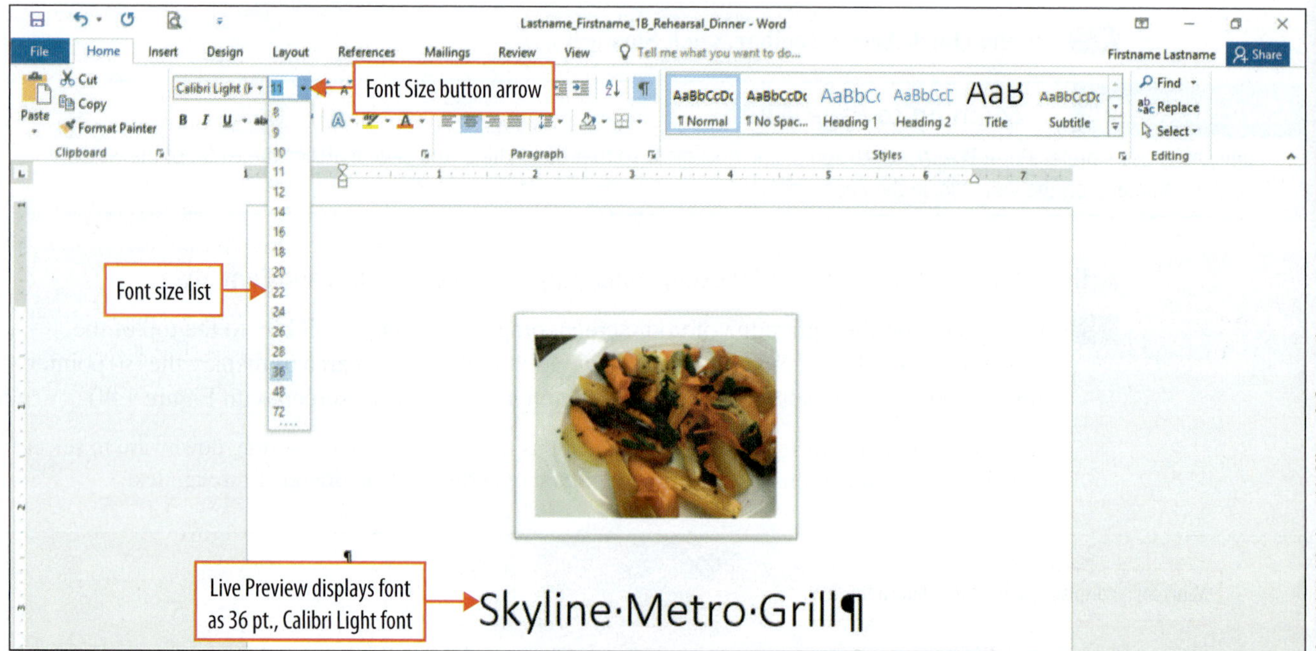

FIGURE 1.41

6 On the list of font sizes, click **20**.

Fonts are measured in ***points***, with one point equal to 1/72 of an inch. A higher point size indicates a larger font size. Headings and titles are often formatted by using a larger font size. The word *point* is abbreviated as ***pt***.

7 With *Skyline Metro Grill* still selected, on the **Home tab**, in the **Font group**, click the **Font Color button arrow** [A ▾]. Under **Theme Colors**, in the last column, click the last color—**Green, Accent 6, Darker 50%**. Click anywhere to deselect the text.

8 To the left of *TO:*, point in the left margin area to display the [pointer] pointer, hold down the left mouse button, drag down to select the four memo headings, and then release your mouse button. Compare your screen with Figure 1.42.

Use this technique to select complete paragraphs from the margin area—drag downward to select multiple paragraphs—which is faster and more efficient than dragging through text.

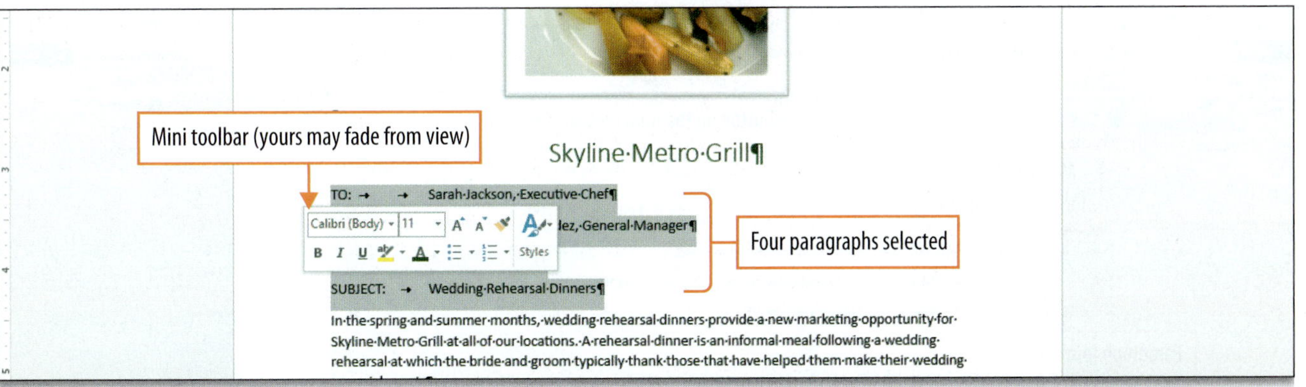

FIGURE 1.42

Word 2016, Windows 10, Microsoft Corporation

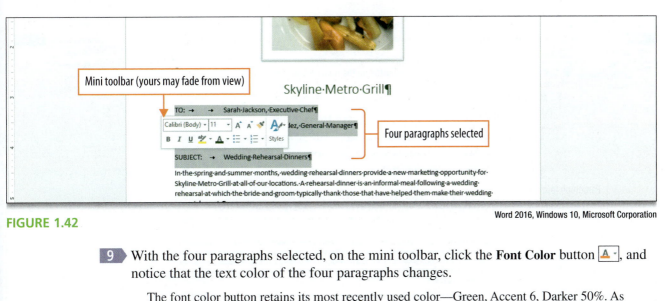

9 With the four paragraphs selected, on the mini toolbar, click the **Font Color** button [A], and notice that the text color of the four paragraphs changes.

The font color button retains its most recently used color—Green, Accent 6, Darker 50%. As you progress in your study of Microsoft Office, you will use other commands that behave in this manner; that is, they retain their most recently used format. This is commonly referred to as ***MRU***—most recently used.

Recall that the mini toolbar places commands that are commonly used for the selected text or object close by so that you reduce the distance that you must move your mouse to access a command. If you are using a touch screen device, most commands that you need are close and easy to touch.

10 On the right edge of your screen, if necessary drag the vertical scroll box down slightly to position more of the text on the screen. Click anywhere in the paragraph that begins *In the spring*, and then ***triple-click***—click the left mouse button three times—to select the entire paragraph. If the entire paragraph is not selected, click in the paragraph and begin again.

11 With the entire paragraph selected, on the mini toolbar, locate and then click the **Font Color button arrow** [A], and then under **Theme Colors**, in the sixth column, click the last color—**Orange, Accent 2, Darker 50%**.

12 In the memo headings, select the guide word **TO:** and then on the mini toolbar, click **Bold** [B] and **Italic** [I].

Font styles include bold, italic, and underline. Font styles emphasize text and are a visual cue to draw the reader's eye to important text.

13 On the mini toolbar, click **Italic** [I] again to turn off the Italic formatting.

A ***toggle button*** is a button that can be turned on by clicking it once, and then turned off by clicking it again.

MOS 2.2.2

Activity 1.16 | Using Format Painter

Use the Format Painter to copy the formatting of specific text or of a paragraph and then apply it in other locations in your document.

1 With TO: still selected, on the mini toolbar, click **Format Painter** [brush]. Then, move your mouse under the word *Sarah*, and notice the [brush pointer] mouse pointer. Compare your screen with Figure 1.43.

The pointer takes the shape of a paintbrush, and contains the formatting information from the paragraph where the insertion point is positioned. Information about the Format Painter and how to turn it off displays in the status bar.

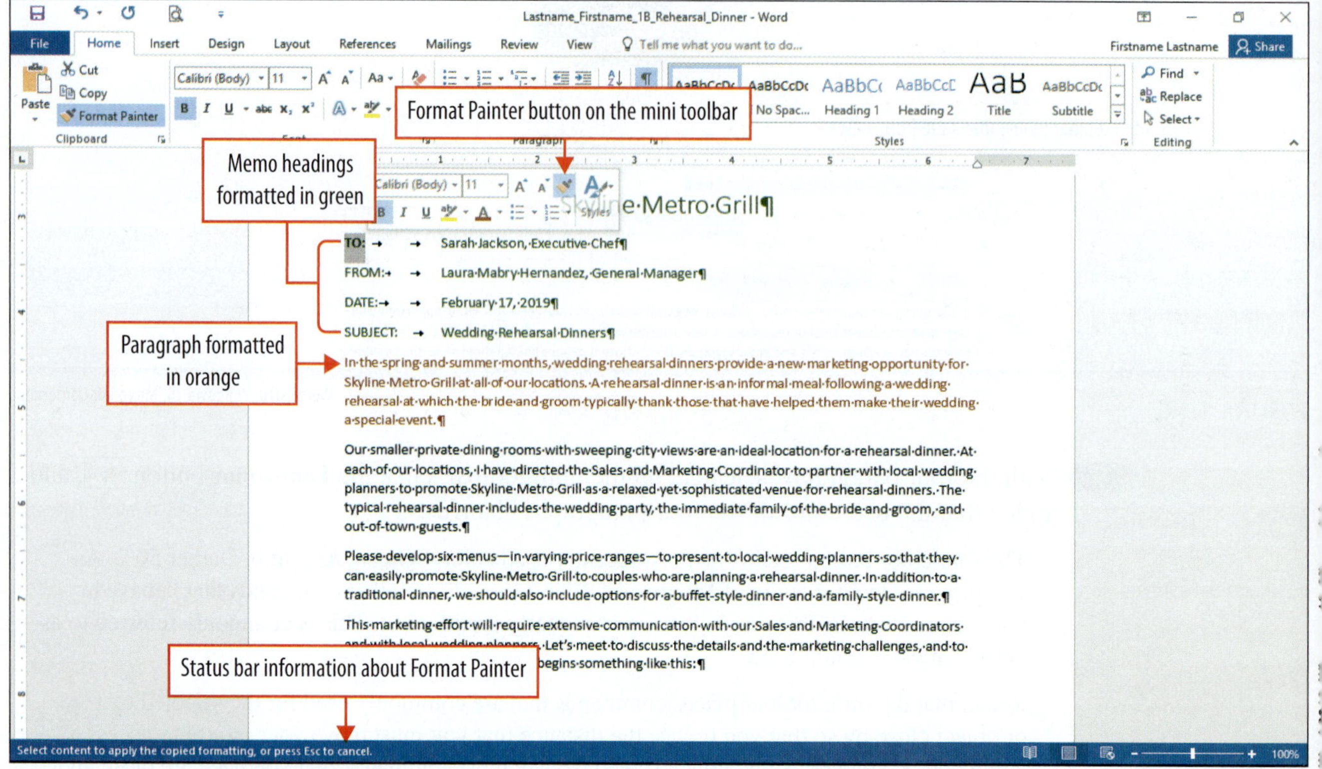

FIGURE 1.43

2 With the pointer, drag to select the guide word **FROM:** and notice that Bold formatting is applied. Then, point to the selected text *FROM:* and on the mini toolbar, *double-click* **Format Painter**.

3 Select the guide word **DATE:** to copy the Bold formatting, and notice that the pointer retains the shape.

When you *double-click* the Format Painter button, the Format Painter feature remains active until you either click the Format Painter button again, or press Esc to cancel it—as indicated on the status bar.

4 With **Format Painter** still active, select the guide word **SUBJECT:**, and then on the ribbon, on the **Home tab**, in the **Clipboard group**, notice that **Format Painter** is selected, indicating that it is active. Compare your screen with Figure 1.44.

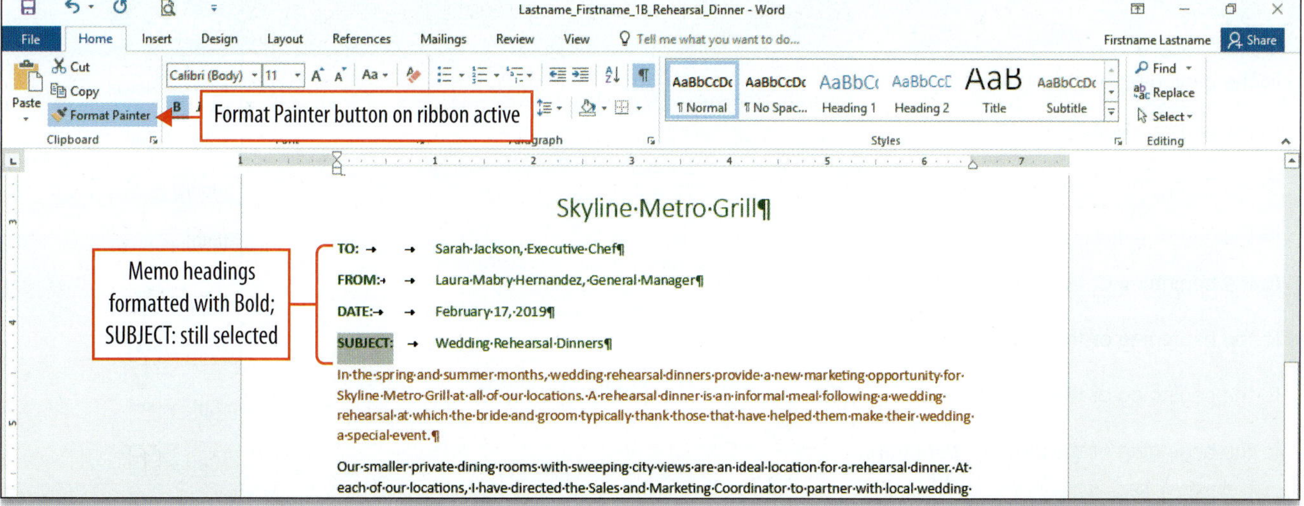

FIGURE 1.44

Word 2016, Windows 10, Microsoft Corporation

5 On the ribbon, click **Format Painter** to turn the command off.

ANOTHER WAY Press Esc to turn off Format Painter.

6 In the paragraph that begins *In the spring*, triple-click again to select the entire paragraph. On the mini toolbar, click **Bold** B and **Italic** I. Click anywhere to deselect.

7 On the **Quick Access Toolbar**, click **Save** to save the changes you have made to your document.

2.1.2

Activity 1.17 | Using Keyboard Shortcuts and Using the Clipboard to Copy, Cut, and Paste

The ***Clipboard*** is a temporary storage area that holds text or graphics that you select and then cut or copy. When you ***copy*** text or graphics, a copy is placed on the Clipboard and the original text or graphic remains in place. When you ***cut*** text or graphics, a copy is placed on the Clipboard, and the original text or graphic is removed—cut—from the document.

After copying or cutting, the contents of the Clipboard are available for you to ***paste***—insert—in a new location in the current document, or into another Office file.

1 On your keyboard, hold down Ctrl and press Home to move to the beginning of your document, and then take a moment to study the table in Figure 1.45, which describes similar keyboard shortcuts with which you can navigate quickly in a document.

TO MOVE	PRESS
To the beginning of a document	Ctrl + Home
To the end of a document	Ctrl + End
To the beginning of a line	Home
To the end of a line	End
To the beginning of the previous word	Ctrl + ←
To the beginning of the next word	Ctrl + →
To the beginning of the current word (if insertion point is in the middle of a word)	Ctrl + ←
To the beginning of the previous paragraph	Ctrl + ↑
To the beginning of the next paragraph	Ctrl + ↓
To the beginning of the current paragraph (if insertion point is in the middle of a paragraph)	Ctrl + ↑
Up one screen	PgUp
Down one screen	PgDn

FIGURE 1.45

2 To the left of *Skyline Metro Grill*, point in the left margin area to display the pointer, and then click one time to select the entire paragraph. On the **Home tab**, in the **Clipboard group**, click **Copy**.

Because anything that you select and then copy—or cut—is placed on the Clipboard, the Copy command and the Cut command display in the Clipboard group of commands on the ribbon. There is no visible indication that your copied selection has been placed on the Clipboard.

ANOTHER WAY Right-click the selection, and then click Copy on the shortcut menu; or, use the keyboard shortcut Ctrl + C.

3 On the **Home tab**, in the **Clipboard group**, to the right of the group name *Clipboard*, click the **Dialog Box Launcher** button, and then compare your screen with Figure 1.46.

The Clipboard pane displays with your copied text. In any ribbon group, the ***Dialog Box Launcher*** displays either a dialog box or a pane related to the group of commands. It is not necessary to display the Clipboard in this manner, although sometimes it is useful to do so.

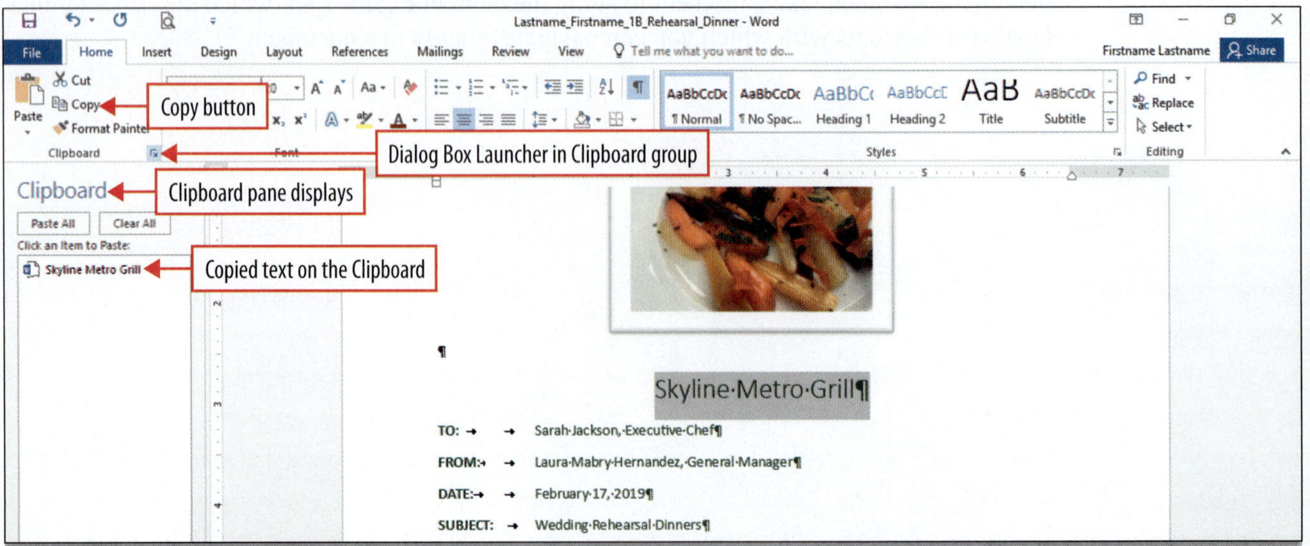

FIGURE 1.46

4 In the upper right corner of the **Clipboard** pane, click **Close** [X].

5 Press Ctrl + End to move to the end of your document. Press Enter one time to create a new blank paragraph. On the **Home tab**, in the **Clipboard group**, point to **Paste**, and then click the *upper* portion of this split button.

The Paste command pastes the most recently copied item on the Clipboard at the insertion point location. If you click the lower portion of the Paste button, a gallery of Paste Options displays. A ***split button*** is divided into two parts; clicking the main part of the button performs a command, and clicking the arrow displays a list or gallery with choices.

ANOTHER WAY Right-click, on the shortcut menu under Paste Options, click the desired option button; or, press Ctrl + V.

6 Below the pasted text, click **Paste Options** as shown in Figure 1.47.

Here you can view and apply various formatting options for pasting your copied or cut text. Typically you will click Paste on the ribbon and paste the item in its original format. If you want some other format for the pasted item, you can choose another format from the ***Paste Options gallery***.

The Paste Options gallery provides a Live Preview of the various options for changing the format of the pasted item with a single click. The Paste Options gallery is available in three places: on the ribbon by clicking the lower portion of the Paste button—the Paste button arrow; from the Paste Options button that displays below the pasted item following the paste operation; or on the shortcut menu if you right-click the pasted item.

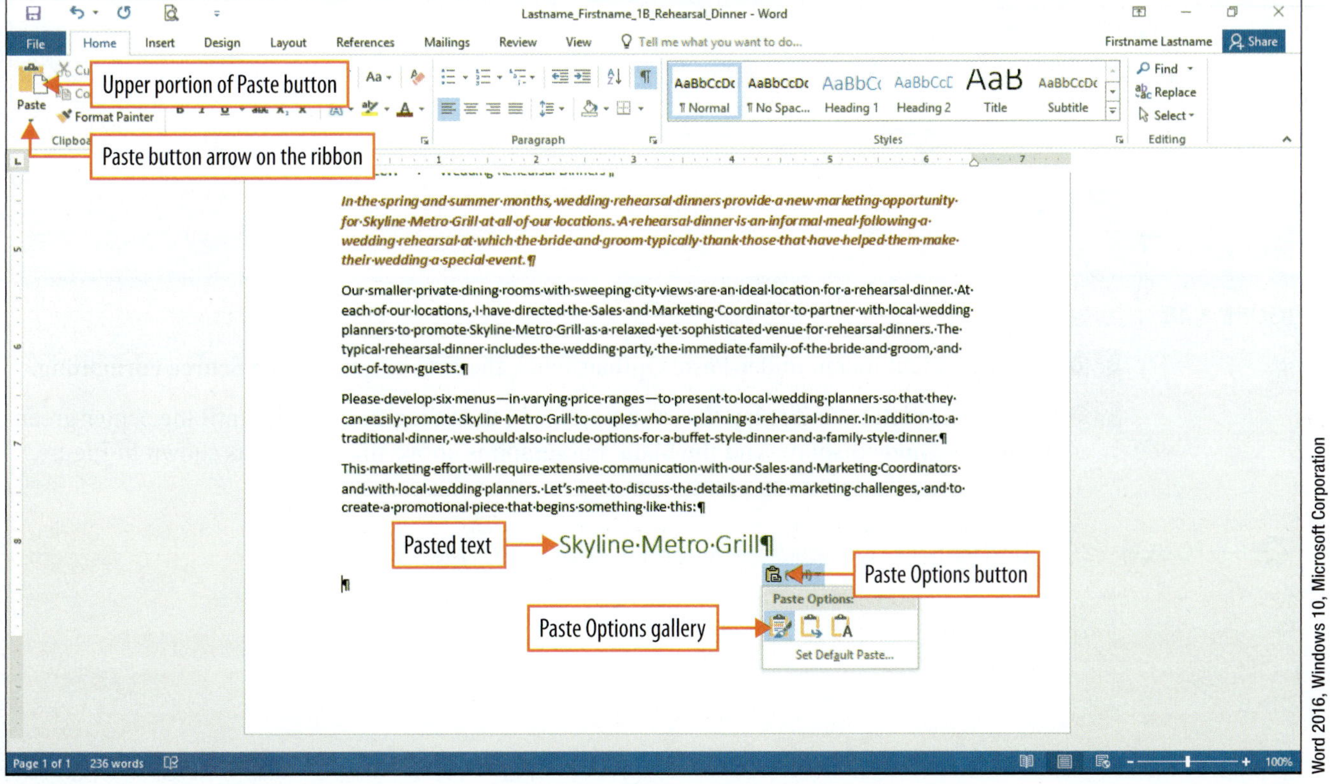

FIGURE 1.47

Word 2016, Windows 10, Microsoft Corporation

7 In the **Paste Options** gallery, *point* to each option to see the Live Preview of the format that would be applied if you clicked the button.

The contents of the Paste Options gallery are contextual; that is, they change based on what you copied and where you are pasting.

8 Press [Esc] to close the gallery; the button will remain displayed until you take some other screen action.

9 On your keyboard, press [Ctrl] + [Home] to move to the top of the document, and then click the **salad image** one time to select it. While pointing to the selected image, right-click, and then on the shortcut menu, click **Cut**.

Recall that the Cut command cuts—removes—the selection from the document and places it on the Clipboard.

ANOTHER WAY On the Home tab, in the Clipboard group, click the Cut button; or use the keyboard shortcut [Ctrl] + [X].

10 Press [Del] one time to remove the blank paragraph from the top of the document, and then press [Ctrl] + [End] to move to the end of the document.

11 With the insertion point blinking in the blank paragraph at the end of the document, right-click, and notice that the **Paste Options** gallery displays on the shortcut menu. Compare your screen with Figure 1.48.

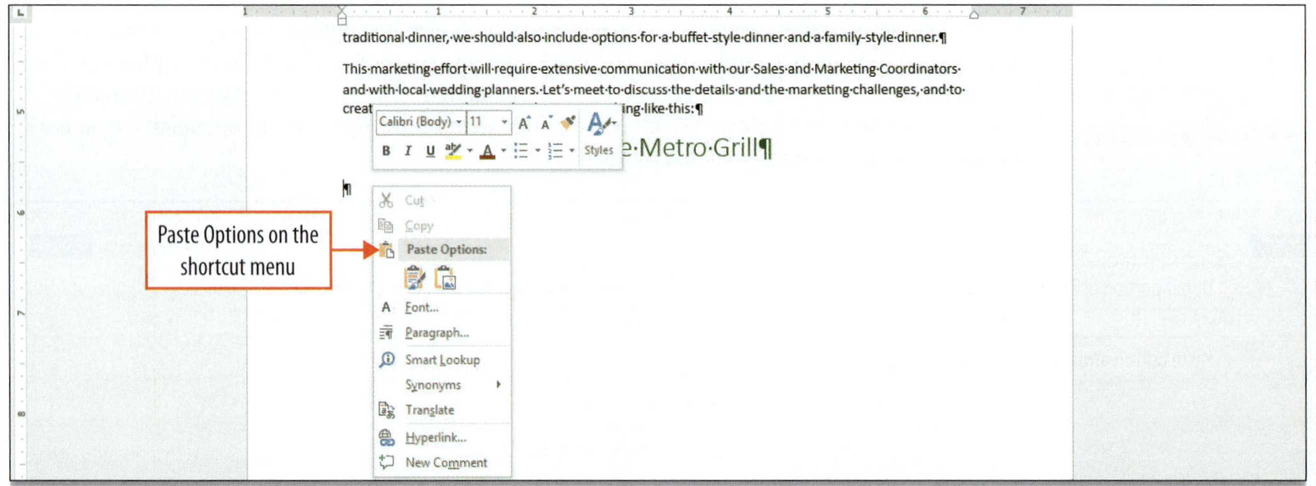

Word 2016, Windows 10, Microsoft Corporation

FIGURE 1.48

12 On the shortcut menu, under **Paste Options**, click the first button—**Keep Source Formatting**.

13 Point to the picture to display the [pointer] pointer, and then drag to the right until the center green **Alignment Guide** displays and the blank paragraph is above the picture, as shown in Figure 1.49. Release the left mouse button.

BY TOUCH Drag the picture with your finger to display the Alignment Guide.

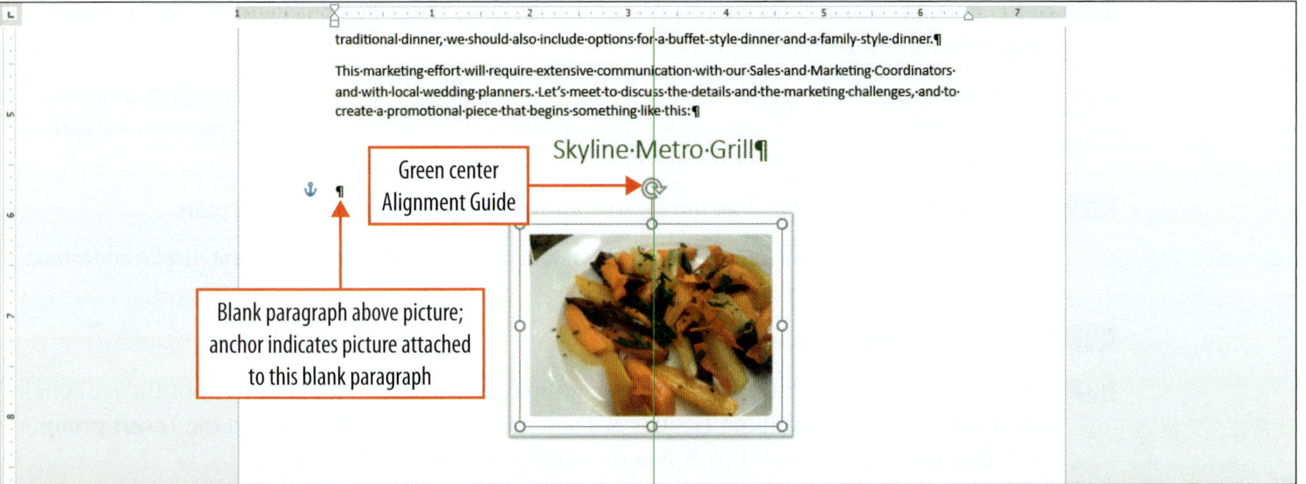

FIGURE 1.49

Word 2016, Windows 10, Microsoft Corporation

Activity 1.18 | Changing Text to WordArt and Adding Alternative Text for Accessibility

2.2.7, 5.2.8

1 Above the picture, click to position the insertion point at the end of the word *Grill*, press Spacebar one time, and then type **for Your Rehearsal Dinner**

2 Select the text *Skyline Metro Grill for Your Rehearsal Dinner*, and then on the **Insert tab**, in the **Text group**, click **Insert WordArt**.

WordArt is an Office feature available in Word, Excel, and PowerPoint that enables you to change normal text into decorative stylized text.

3 In the displayed gallery, use the ScreenTips to locate and then click **Fill - Gold, Accent 4, Soft Bevel**.

4 With the WordArt surrounded with a solid line, on the **Home tab**, in the **Font group**, change the font size to **16**.

5 Point to the solid line surrounding the WordArt to display the pointer, and then drag the WordArt slightly to the right until the green center alignment guides display, as shown in Figure 1.50, and then release the mouse button to center the WordArt above your picture. Click outside of the WordArt to deselect.

Word 2016, Windows 10, Microsoft Corporation

FIGURE 1.50

6 Point to the picture of the salad and right-click. On the shortcut menu, click **Format Picture**.

7 In the **Format Picture** pane that displays on the right, under **Format Picture**, click **Layout & Properties** [icon], and then click **Alt Text**.

Alternative text helps people using a ***screen reader***, which is software that enables visually impaired users to read text on a computer screen to understand the content of pictures. ***Alt text*** is the term commonly used for this feature.

8 As the Title, type **Salad** and as the Description, type **Picture of salad on a plate**

Anyone viewing the document with a screen reader will see the alternative text displayed instead of the picture.

9 **Close** [X] the **Format Picture** pane.

10 On the **Insert tab**, in the **Header & Footer group**, click **Footer**. At the bottom of the list, click **Edit Footer**, and then with the **Header & Footer Tools Design tab** active, in the **Insert group**, click **Document Info**. Click **File Name** to add the file name to the footer.

11 On the right end of the ribbon, click **Close Header and Footer**.

12 On the **Quick Access Toolbar**, point to the **Print Preview and Print icon** [icon] you placed there, right-click, and then click **Remove from Quick Access Toolbar**.

If you are working on your own computer and you want to do so, you can leave the icon on the toolbar; in a college lab, you should return the software to its original settings.

13 Click **Save** [icon] and then click the **File tab** to display **Backstage** view. With the **Info tab** active, in the lower right corner, click **Show All Properties**. As **Tags**, type **weddings, rehearsal dinners, marketing**

14 As the **Subject**, type your course name and number—for example, *CIS 10, #5543*. Under **Related People**, be sure your name displays as the author (edit it if necessary), and then on the left, click **Print** to display the Print Preview. Compare your screen with Figure 1.51.

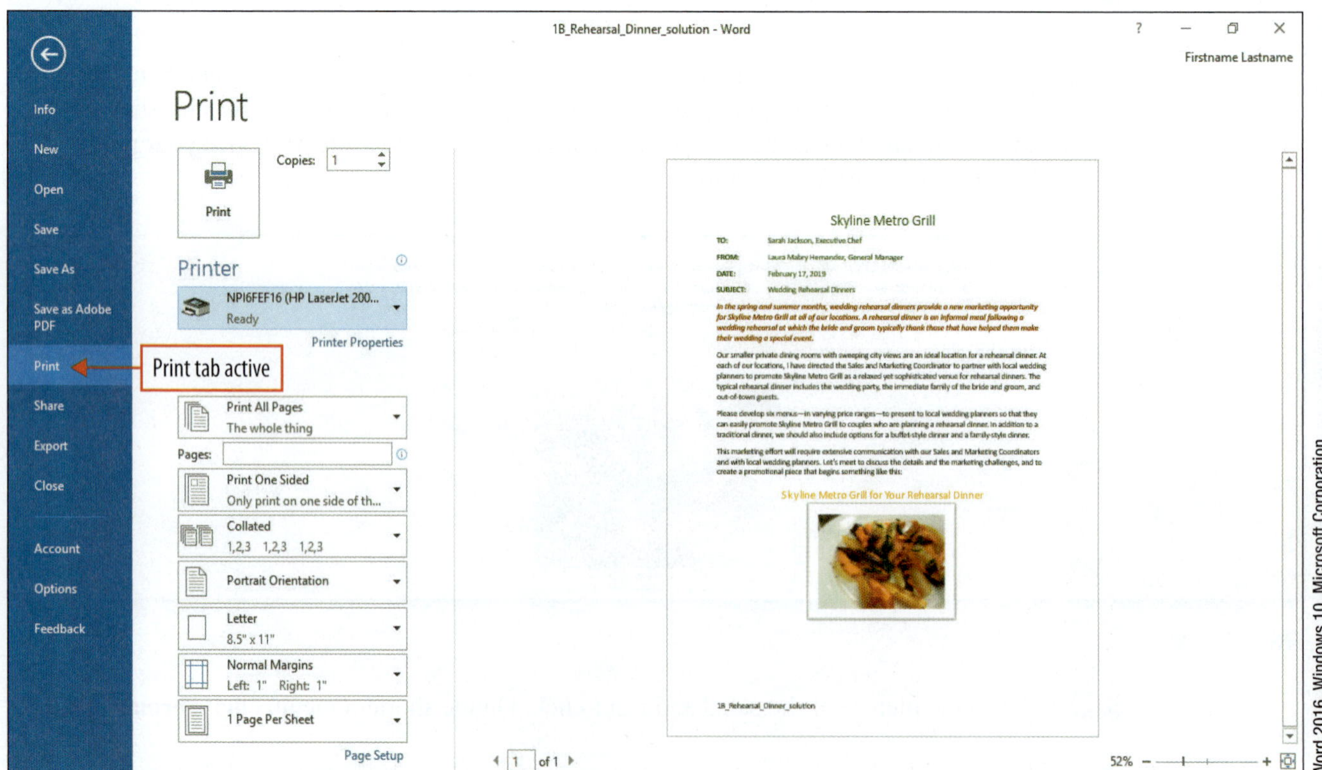

FIGURE 1.51

15 On the left side of **Backstage** view, click **Save**. In the upper right corner of the Word window, click **Close** [×]. If a message indicates *Do you want to keep the last item you copied?* click **No**.

This message displays if you have copied some type of image to the Clipboard. If you click Yes, the items on the Clipboard will remain for you to use in another program or document.

16 As directed by your instructor, create and submit a paper printout or an electronic image of your document that looks like a printed document; or, submit your completed Word file. If necessary, refer to Activity 1.08 in Project 1A.

1 OFFICE 2016

1.5.4, 1.5.5, 1.5.6

Activity 1.19 | Inspecting a Document

Word, Excel, and PowerPoint all have the same commands to inspect a file before sharing it.

1 If necessary, open your **Lastname_Firstname_1B_Rehearsal_Dinner** document.

2 Click the **File tab**, on the left, if necessary, click **Info**, and then on the right, click **Check for Issues**.

3 On the list, click **Inspect Document**.

The ***Inspect Document*** command searches your document for hidden data or personal information that you might not want to share publicly. This information could reveal company details that should not be shared.

4 In the lower right corner of the **Document Inspector** dialog box, click **Inspect**.

The Document Inspector runs and lists information that was found and that you could choose to remove.

5 Click **Close**, click **Check for Issues** again, and then click **Check Accessibility**.

The ***Check Accessibility*** command checks the document for content that people with disabilities might find difficult to read. The Accessibility Checker pane displays on the right and lists two objects that might require attention: a text box (your WordArt) and your picture.

6 **Close** [×] the **Accessibility Checker** pane, and then click the **File tab**.

7 Click **Check for Issues**, and then click **Check Compatibility**.

The ***Check Compatibility*** command checks for features in your document that may not be supported by earlier versions of the Office program. This is only a concern if you are sharing documents with individuals with older software.

8 Click **OK**. Leave your Word document displayed for the next Activity.

1.2.3

Activity 1.20 | Inserting a Bookmark

A ***bookmark*** identifies a word, section, or place in your document so that you can find it quickly without scrolling. This is especially useful in a long document.

1 In the paragraph that begins *Please develop*, select the text *six menus*.

2 On the **Insert tab**, in the **Links group**, click **Bookmark**.

3 In the Bookmark name box, type **menus** and then click **Add**.

4 Press [Ctrl] + [Home] to move to the top of your document.

5 Press [Ctrl] + [G], which is the keyboard shortcut for the Go To command.

6 Under **Go to what**, click **Bookmark**, and then with menus selected, click **Go To**. **Close** the **Find and Replace** dialog box, and notice that your bookmarked text is selected for you.

7 **Close** [×] Word, and then click **Save**. Close any open windows.

Objective 10 Compress Files and Get Help with Office

A ***compressed file*** is a file that has been reduced in size. Compressed files take up less storage space and can be transferred to other computers faster than uncompressed files. You can also combine a group of files into one compressed folder, which makes it easier to share a group of files.

Within each Office program, you will see the ***Tell Me*** feature at the right end of the ribbon tabs, which is a search feature for Microsoft Office commands that you activate by typing what you are looking for in the Tell Me box.

Another method to get help with an Office command is to point to the command on the ribbon, and then at the bottom of the displayed ScreenTip, click Tell me more, which will display step-by-step assistance.

Activity 1.21 | Compressing Files

In this Activity, you will combine the two files you created in this chapter into one compressed file.

1 On the Windows taskbar, click **File Explorer**. On the left, in the **navigation pane**, navigate to your storage location, and then open your **Office Features Chapter 1** folder. If you have been using this folder, in might appear under Quick access. Compare your screen with Figure 1.52.

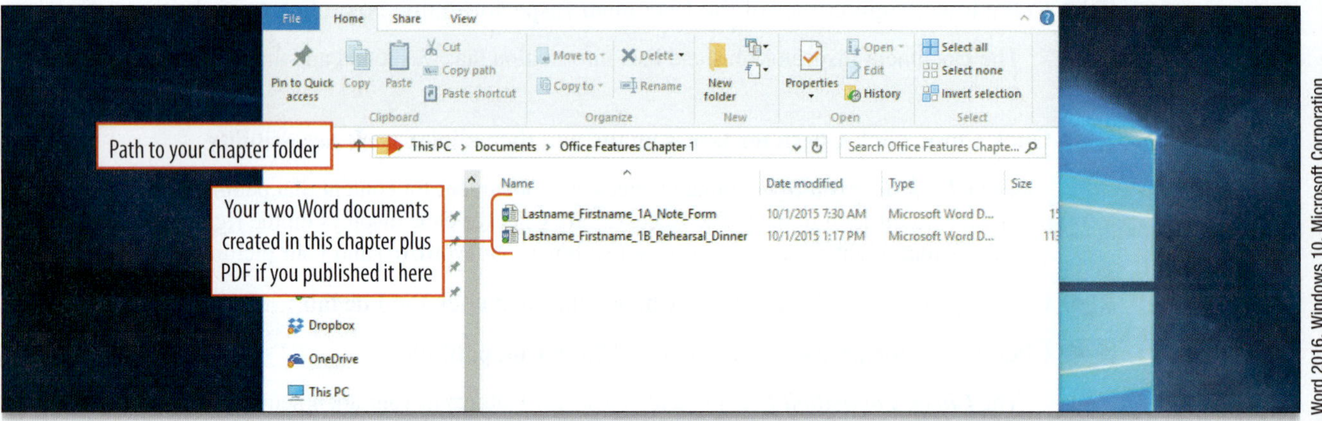

FIGURE 1.52

2 In the **file list**, click your **Lastname_Firstname_1A_Note_Form** Word file one time to select it. Then, hold down Ctrl, and click your **Lastname_Firstname_1B_Rehearsal_Dinner** file to select both files in the list.

In any Windows-based program, holding down Ctrl while selecting enables you to select multiple items.

3 On the **File Explorer** ribbon, click **Share**, and then in the **Send group**, click **Zip**. Compare your screen with Figure 1.53.

Windows creates a compressed folder containing a *copy* of each of the selected files. The folder name is selected—highlighted in blue—so that you can rename it. The default folder name is usually the name of the first file in the group that you select.

BY TOUCH Tap the ribbon commands.

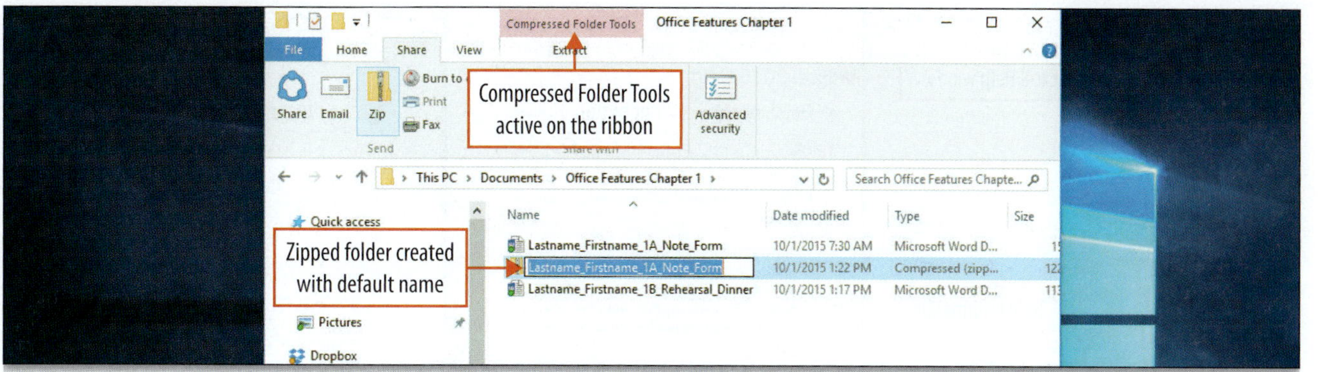

FIGURE 1.53

Word 2016, Windows 10, Microsoft Corporation

ANOTHER WAY Point to the selected files in the File List, right-click, point to Send to, and then click Compressed (zipped) folder.

4 With the folder name selected—highlighted in blue—using your own name, type **Lastname_Firstname_Office_Features_Chapter_1** and press Enter.

The compressed folder is ready to attach to an email or share in some other format.

5 In the upper right corner of the folder window, click **Close** ×.

Activity 1.22 | Using Microsoft Office Tell Me and Tell Me More to Get Help

In this Activity, you will use Tell Me to find information about formatting currency in Excel.

1 Start Excel and open a **Blank workbook**. With cell **A1** active, type **456789** and press Enter. Click cell **A1** again to make it the active cell.

2 At the top of the screen, click in the **Tell me what you want to do** box, and then type **format as currency** In the displayed list, point to **Accounting Number Formats**, and then click **$ English (United States)**.

As you type, every keystroke refines the results so that you can click the command as soon as it displays. This feature helps you apply the command immediately; it does not explain how to locate the command.

3 On the **Home tab**, in the **Alignment group**, *point to* **Merge & Center**, and then at the bottom of the displayed ScreenTip, click **Tell me more**. At the right edge of the displayed **Excel 2016 Help** window, use the scroll bar to scroll about halfway down the window, and then compare your screen with Figure 1.54.

The ***Tell me more*** feature opens the Office online Help system with explanations about how to perform the task.

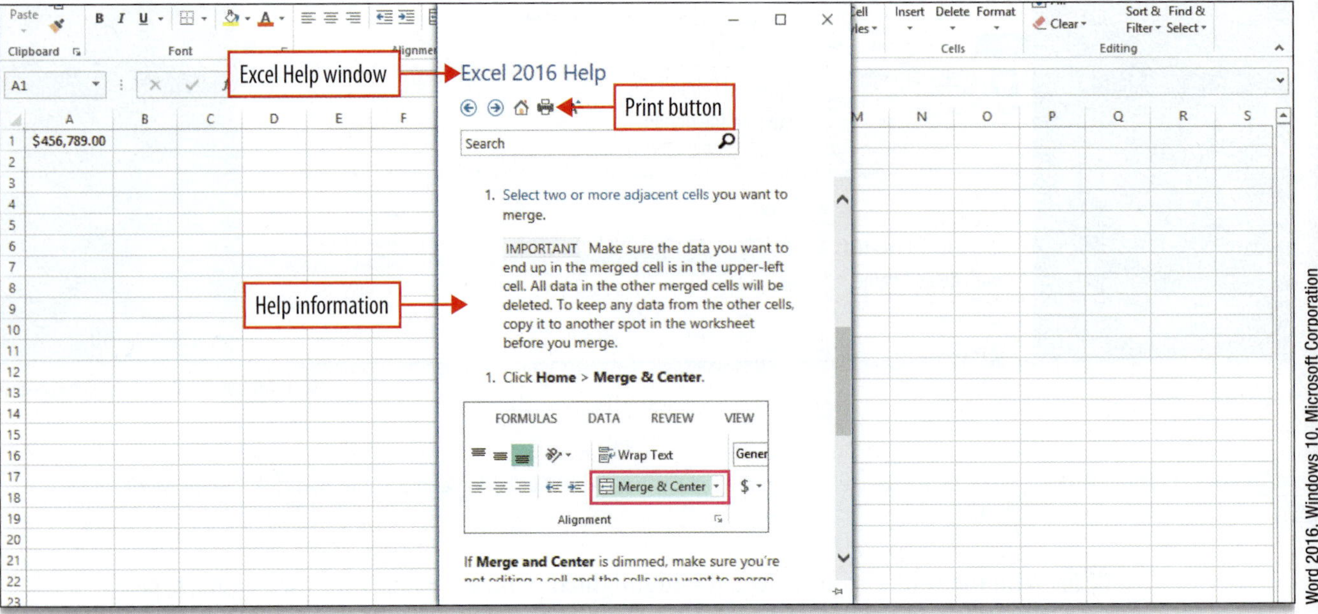
Excel Help window
Print button
Help information
Excel 2016 Help
Search
1. Select two or more adjacent cells you want to merge.
IMPORTANT Make sure the data you want to end up in the merged cell is in the upper-left cell. All data in the other merged cells will be deleted. To keep any data from the other cells, copy it to another spot in the worksheet before you merge.
1. Click Home > Merge & Center.
If Merge and Center is dimmed, make sure you're
$456,789.00
Word 2016, Windows 10, Microsoft Corporation

FIGURE 1.54

4 If you want to do so, at the top of the **Excel Help** window, click Print to print a copy of this information for your reference.

5 In the upper right corner of the Help window, click **Close** ×.

6 Leave Excel open for the next Activity.

Objective 11 Install Apps for Office and Create a Microsoft Account

ALERT! **Working with Web-Based Applications and Services**

Computer programs and services on the web receive continuous updates and improvements. Thus, the steps to complete the following web-based activities may differ from the ones shown. You can often look at the screens and the information presented to determine how to complete the activity.

GO! Learn How Video OF1-11

Apps for Office are a collection of downloadable apps that enable you to create and view information within your familiar Office programs. Apps for Office combine cloud services and web technologies within the user interface of Office. Some of these apps are developed by Microsoft, but many more are developed by specialists in different fields. As new apps are developed, they will be available from the online ***Office Store***—a public marketplace that Microsoft hosts and regulates on Office.com.

A ***task pane app*** works side-by-side with an Office document by displaying a separate pane on the right side of the window. For example, a task pane app can look up and retrieve product information from a web service based on the product name or part number selected in the document.

A ***content app*** integrates web-based features as content within the body of a document. For example, in Excel, you can use an app to look up and gather search results for a new apartment by placing the information in an Excel worksheet, and then use maps to determine the distance of each apartment to work and to family members. ***Mail apps*** display next to an Outlook item. For example, a mail app could detect a purchase order number in an email message and then display information about the order or the customer.

Activity 1.23 | Installing Apps for Office

1 With cell **A1** active, on your keyboard, press Delete to clear the cell. On the Excel ribbon, click the **Insert tab**. In the **Add-ins group**, click **Store**.

2 In the **Office Add-ins** dialog box, in the upper right, click in the **Search the Office Store** box, type **bing maps** and then press Enter.

3 Click the **Bing logo**, and then in the lower right corner, click **Trust It**.

4 If necessary, click Update. On the Welcome message, click **Insert Sample Data**.

Here, the Bing map displays information related to the sample data—this is a *content app*. Each city in the sample data displays a small pie chart that represents the two sets of data—revenue and expenses. Compare your screen with Figure 1.55.

This is just one example of many apps downloadable from the Office Store.

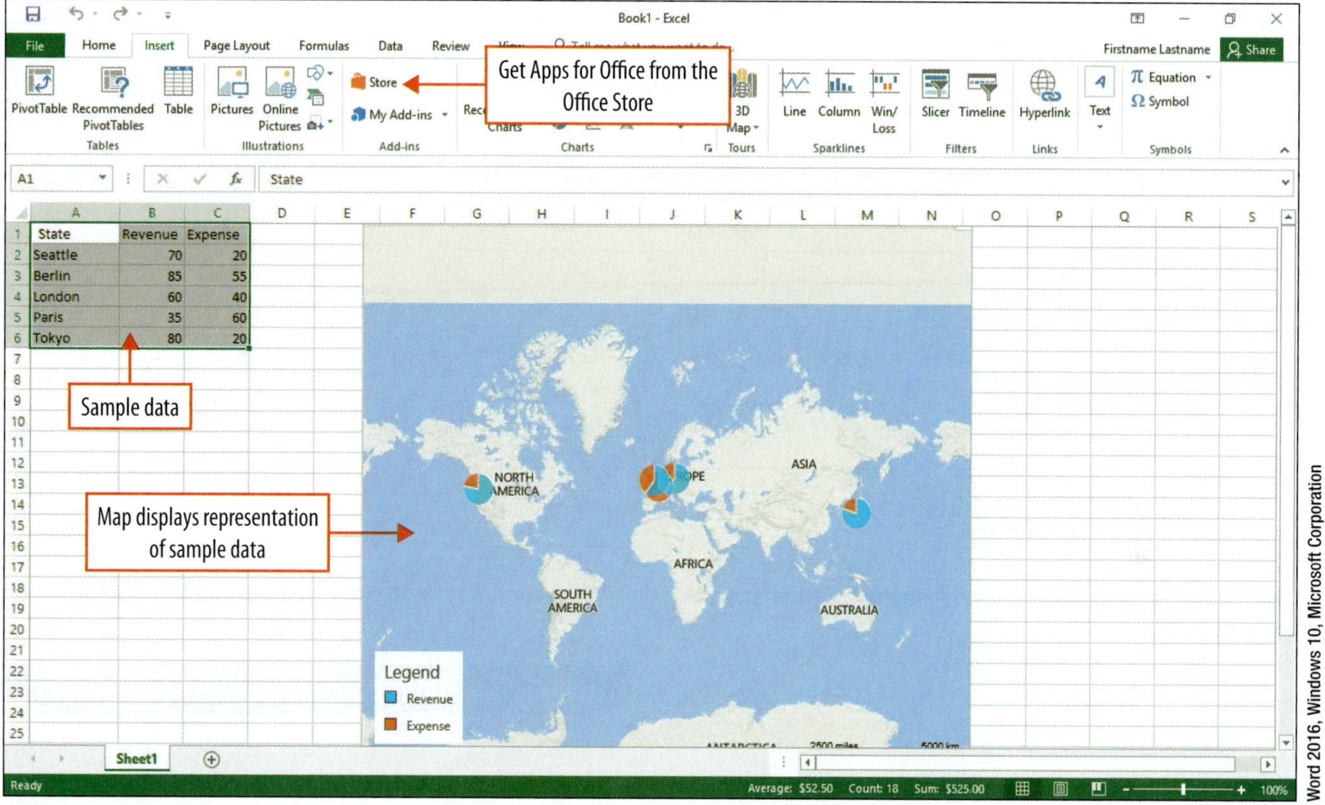

Word 2016, Windows 10, Microsoft Corporation

FIGURE 1.55

5 In the upper right corner of your screen, **Close** Excel without saving.

Activity 1.24 | Creating a Microsoft Account

> **ALERT!** **This is an optional activity.**
>
> You will find both Windows and Office to be much more useful if you sign in with a Microsoft account. If you already have an email account from **msn.com**, **hotmail.com**, **live.com**, or **outlook.com**, then you already have a Microsoft account. If you do not, you can create a free Microsoft account by following the steps in this activity.

In Windows 8 and Windows 10, you can use a Microsoft account to sign in to *any* Windows PC. Signing in with a Microsoft account is recommended because you can:

- Download Windows apps from the Windows Store.
- Get your online content—email, social network updates, updated news—automatically displayed in an app when you sign in.
- Synch settings online to make every Windows computer you use look and feel the same.
- Sign in to Office so that you can store documents on your OneDrive.

1 Use an Internet search engine to search for **create a microsoft account** or go to **signup.live.com** and at the bottom click **Sign up now**. You will see a screen similar to Figure 1.56. Complete the form to create your account.

You can use any email address that you currently have for your Microsoft account. Or, on this screen, you can create a new outlook.com account.

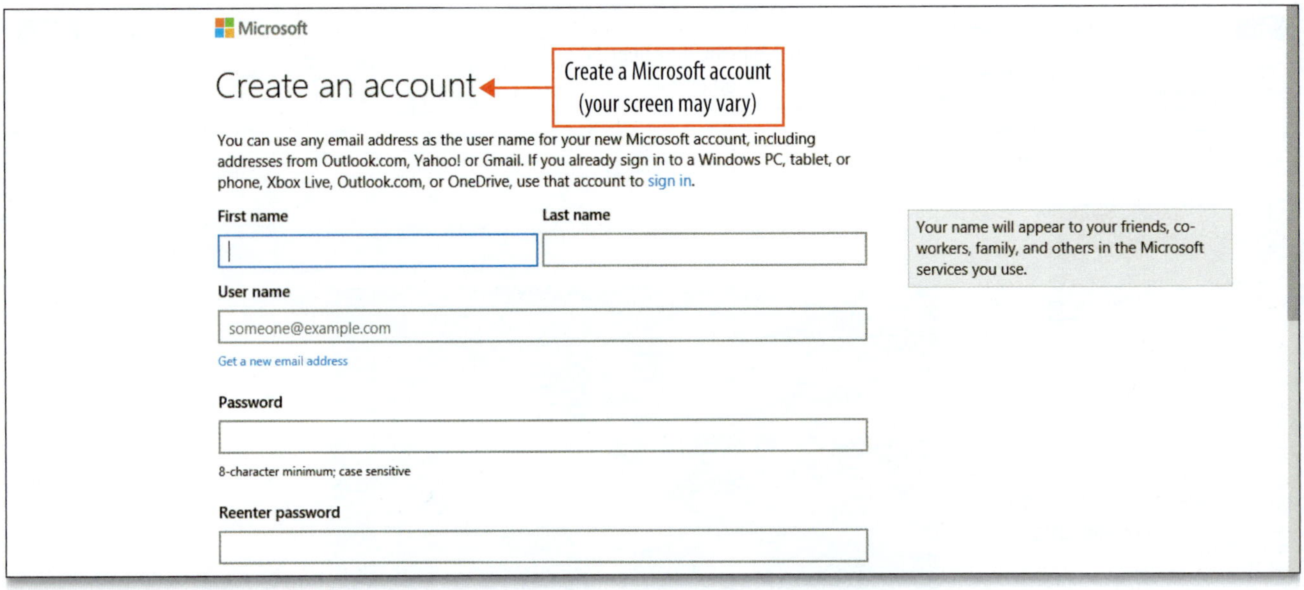

FIGURE 1.56

END | You have completed Project 1B

GO! To Work

Andres Rodriguez/Fotolia; FotolEdhar/Fotolia; Andrey Popov/Fotolia; Shutterstock

1 OFFICE

MICROSOFT OFFICE SPECIALIST (MOS) SKILLS IN THIS CHAPTER	
PROJECT 1A	**PROJECT 1B**
1.1.1 Create a blank document **1.3.4** Insert headers and footers **1.3.6** Format page background elements **1.4.5** Add document properties **1.4.6** Show or hide formatting symbols **2.2.6** Apply built-in styles to text	**1.2.3** Create bookmarks **1.4.2** Customize views by using zoom settings **1.4.3** Customize the Quick Access toolbar **1.5.4** Inspect a document for hidden properties or personal information **1.5.5** Inspect a document for accessibility issues **1.5.6** Inspect a document for compatibility issues **2.1.2** Cut, copy, and paste text **2.2.2** Apply formatting by using Format Painter **2.2.7** Change text to WordArt **5.2.5** Apply a picture style **5.2.8** Add alternative text to objects for accessibility

BUILD YOUR E-PORTFOLIO

An E-Portfolio is a collection of evidence, stored electronically, that showcases what you have accomplished while completing your education. Collecting and then sharing your work products with potential employers reflects your academic and career goals. Your completed documents from the following projects are good examples to show what you have learned: 1A and 1B.

END OF CHAPTER

SUMMARY

Many Office features and commands, such as accessing the Open and Save As dialog boxes, performing commands from the ribbon and from dialog boxes, and using the Clipboard are the same in all Office desktop apps.

A desktop app is installed on your computer and requires a computer operating system such as Microsoft Windows or Apple's Mac OS-X to run. The programs in Microsoft Office 2016 are considered to be desktop apps.

An app refers to a self-contained program usually designed for a single purpose and that runs on smartphones and other mobile devices—for example, looking at sports scores or booking a flight on a particular airline.

Within an Office app, you can add Apps for Office from the Office Store, which combine cloud services and web technologies within the Office user interface. Apps can be task pane apps, content apps, or mail apps.

GO! LEARN IT ONLINE

Review the concepts, key terms, and MOS skills in this chapter by completing these online challenges, which you can find at **MyITLab**.

Matching and Multiple Choice: Answer matching and multiple-choice questions to test what you learned in this chapter.

Lessons on the GO!: Learn how to use all the new apps and features as they are introduced by Microsoft.

MOS Prep Quiz: Answer questions to review the MOS skills that you practiced in this chapter.

GLOSSARY

GLOSSARY OF CHAPTER KEY TERMS

Alignment The placement of text or objects relative to the left and right margins.

Alignment guides Green lines that display when you move an object to assist in alignment.

Alt text Another name for alternative text.

Alternative text Text added to a picture or object that helps people using a screen reader understand what the object is.

App A self-contained program usually designed for a single purpose and that runs on smartphones and other mobile devices.

Apps for Office A collection of downloadable apps that enable you to create and view information within Office programs, and that combine cloud services and web technologies within the user interface of Office.

Backstage tabs The area along the left side of Backstage view with tabs to display screens with related groups of commands.

Backstage view A centralized space for file management tasks; for example, opening, saving, printing, publishing, or sharing a file. A navigation pane displays along the left side with tabs that group file-related tasks together.

Bookmark A command that identifies a word, section, or place in a document so that you can find it quickly without scrolling.

Center alignment The alignment of text or objects that is centered horizontally between the left and right margin.

Clipboard A temporary storage area that holds text or graphics that you select and then cut or copy.

Check Accessibility A command that checks the document for content that people with disabilities might find difficult to read.

Check Compatibility A command that searches your document for features that may not be supported by older versions of Office.

Cloud computing Applications and services that are accessed over the Internet, rather than accessing applications that are installed on your local computer.

Cloud storage Online storage of data so that you can access your data from different places and devices.

Collaborate To work with others as a team in an intellectual endeavor to complete a shared task or to achieve a shared goal.

Commands Instructions to a computer program that cause an action to be carried out.

Compressed file A file that has been reduced in size and thus takes up less storage space and can be transferred to other computers quickly.

Content app An app for Office that integrates web-based features as content within the body of a document.

Context menus Menus that display commands and options relevant to the selected text or object; also called *shortcut menus*.

Context-sensitive commands Commands that display on a shortcut menu that relate to the object or text that you right-clicked.

Contextual tabs Tabs that are added to the ribbon automatically when a specific object, such as a picture, is selected, and that contain commands relevant to the selected object.

Copy A command that duplicates a selection and places it on the Clipboard.

Creative Commons A nonprofit organization that enables sharing and use of images and knowledge through free legal tools.

Cut A command that removes a selection and places it on the Clipboard.

Default The term that refers to the current selection or setting that is automatically used by a computer program unless you specify otherwise.

Deselect The action of canceling the selection of an object or block of text by clicking outside of the selection.

Desktop app A computer program that is installed on your PC and requires a computer operating system such as Microsoft Windows; also known as a *desktop application*.

Desktop application A computer program that is installed on your PC and requires a computer operating system such as Microsoft Windows; also known as a *desktop app*.

Dialog Box Launcher A small icon that displays to the right of some group names on the ribbon and that opens a related dialog box or pane providing additional options and commands related to that group.

Document properties Details about a file that describe or identify it, including the title, author name, subject, and keywords that identify the document's topic or contents; also known as *metadata*.

Drag The action of holding down the left mouse button while moving your mouse.

Edit The process of making changes to text or graphics in an Office file.

Ellipsis A set of three dots indicating incompleteness; an ellipsis following a command name indicates that a dialog box will display if you click the command.

Enhanced ScreenTip A ScreenTip that displays more descriptive text than a normal ScreenTip.

Fill The inside color of an object.

Font A set of characters with the same design and shape.

Font styles Formatting emphasis such as bold, italic, and underline.

Footer A reserved area for text or graphics that displays at the bottom of each page in a document.

Formatting The process of establishing the overall appearance of text, graphics, and pages in an Office file—for example, in a Word document.

Formatting marks Characters that display on the screen, but do not print, indicating where the Enter key, the Spacebar, and the Tab key were pressed; also called *nonprinting characters*.

Gallery An Office feature that displays a list of potential results instead of just the command name.

Gradient fill A fill effect in which one color fades into another.

Groups On the Office ribbon, the sets of related commands that you might need for a specific type of task.

Header A reserved area for text or graphics that displays at the top of each page in a document.

Info tab The tab in Backstage view that displays information about the current file.

Inspect Document A command that searches your document for hidden data or personal information that you might not want to share publicly.

Insertion point A blinking vertical line that indicates where text or graphics will be inserted.

Keyboard shortcut A combination of two or more keyboard keys, used to perform a task that would otherwise require a mouse.

KeyTip The letter that displays on a command in the ribbon and that indicates the key you can press to activate the command when keyboard control of the Ribbon is activated.

Keywords Custom file properties in the form of words that you associate with a document to give an indication of the document's content; used to help find and organize files. Also called *tags*.

Landscape orientation A page orientation in which the paper is wider than it is tall.

Layout Options A button that displays when an object is selected and that has commands to choose how the object interacts with surrounding text.

Live Preview A technology that shows the result of applying an editing or formatting change as you point to possible results—*before* you actually apply it.

Location Any disk drive, folder, or other place in which you can store files and folders.

Mail app An app for Office that displays next to an Outlook item.

Metadata Details about a file that describe or identify it, including the title, author name, subject, and keywords that identify the document's topic or contents; also known as *document properties*.

Mini toolbar A small toolbar containing frequently used formatting commands that displays as a result of selecting text or objects.

MRU Acronym for *most recently used*, which refers to the state of some commands that retain the characteristic most recently applied; for example, the Font Color button retains the most recently used color until a new color is chosen.

Nonprinting characters Characters that display on the screen, but do not print, indicating where the Enter key, the Spacebar, and the Tab key were pressed; also called *formatting marks*.

Object A text box, picture, table, or shape that you can select and then move and resize.

Office 365 A version of Microsoft Office to which you subscribe for an annual fee.

Office Store A public marketplace that Microsoft hosts and regulates on Office.com.

OneDrive Microsoft's free cloud storage for anyone with a free Microsoft account.

Open dialog box A dialog box from which you can navigate to, and then open on your screen, an existing file that was created in that same program.

Option button In a dialog box, a round button that enables you to make one choice among two or more options.

Options dialog box A dialog box within each Office application where you can select program settings and other options and preferences.

Page Width A view that zooms the document so that the width of the page matches the width of the window. Find this command on the View tab, in the Zoom group.

Paragraph symbol The symbol ¶ that represents the end of a paragraph.

Paste The action of placing text or objects that have been copied or cut from one location to another location.

Paste Options gallery A gallery of buttons that provides a Live Preview of all the Paste options available in the current context.

PDF The acronym for *Portable Document Format*, which is a file format that creates an image that preserves the look of your file, but that cannot be easily changed; a popular format for sending documents electronically, because the document will display on most computers.

Pointer Any symbol that displays on your screen in response to moving your mouse.

Points A measurement of the size of a font; there are 72 points in an inch.

Portable Document Format A file format that creates an image that preserves the look of your file, but that cannot be easily changed; a popular format for sending documents electronically, because the document will display on most computers; also called a *PDF*.

Portrait orientation A page orientation in which the paper is taller than it is wide.

Print Preview A view of a document as it will appear when you print it.

Protected View A security feature in Office 2016 that protects your computer from malicious files by opening them in a restricted environment until you enable them; you might encounter this feature if you open a file from an e-mail or download files from the Internet.

pt The abbreviation for *point*; for example, when referring to a font size.

Quick Access Toolbar In an Office program window, the small row of buttons in the upper left corner of the screen from which you can perform frequently used commands.

Read-only A property assigned to a file that prevents the file from being modified or deleted; it indicates that you cannot save any changes to the displayed document unless you first save it with a new name.

Right-click The action of clicking the right mouse button one time.

Sans serif font A font design with no lines or extensions on the ends of characters.

Screen reader Software that enables visually impaired users to read text on a computer screen to understand the content of pictures.

ScreenTip A small box that that displays useful information when you perform various mouse actions such as pointing to screen elements or dragging.

Selecting Highlighting, by dragging with your mouse, areas of text or data or graphics, so that the selection can be edited, formatted, copied, or moved.

Serif font A font design that includes small line extensions on the ends of the letters to guide the eye in reading from left to right.

Share button Opens the Share pane from which you can save your file to the cloud—your OneDrive—and then share it with others so you can collaborate.

SharePoint Collaboration software with which people in an organization can set up team sites to share information, manage documents, and publish reports for others to see.

Shortcut menu A menu that displays commands and options relevant to the selected text or object; also called a *context menu*.

Sizing handles Small squares or circles that indicate a picture or object is selected.

Split button A button divided into two parts and in which clicking the main part of the button performs a command and clicking the arrow opens a menu with choices.

Status bar The area along the lower edge of an Office program window that displays file information on the left and buttons to control how the window looks on the right.

Style A group of formatting commands, such as font, font size, font color, paragraph alignment, and line spacing that can be applied to a paragraph with one command.

Synchronization The process of updating computer files that are in two or more locations according to specific rules—also called *syncing*.

Syncing The process of updating computer files that are in two or more locations according to specific rules—also called *synchronization*.

Tabs (ribbon) On the Office ribbon, the name of each task-oriented activity area.

Tags Custom file properties in the form of words that you associate with a document to give an indication of the document's content; used to help find and organize files. Also called *keywords*.

Task pane app An app for Office that works side-by-side with an Office document by displaying a separate pane on the right side of the window.

Tell Me A search feature for Microsoft Office commands that you activate by typing what you are looking for in the Tell Me box.

Tell me more A prompt within a ScreenTip that opens the Office online Help system with explanations about how to perform the command referenced in the ScreenTip.

Template A preformatted document that you can use as a starting point and then change to suit your needs.

Theme A predesigned combination of colors, fonts, and effects that looks good together and is applied to an entire document by a single selection.

Title bar The bar at the top edge of the program window that indicates the name of the current file and the program name.

Toggle button A button that can be turned on by clicking it once, and then turned off by clicking it again.

Toolbar In a folder window, a row of buttons with which you can perform common tasks, such as changing the view of your files and folders.

Triple-click The action of clicking the left mouse button three times in rapid succession.

Trusted Documents A security feature in Office that remembers which files you have already enabled; you might encounter this feature if you open a file from an e-mail or download files from the Internet.

Windows apps An app that runs on all Windows device families—including PCs, Windows phones, Windows tablets, and the Xbox gaming system.

WordArt An Office feature in Word, Excel, and PowerPoint that enables you to change normal text into decorative stylized text.

XML Paper Specification A Microsoft file format that creates an image of your document and that opens in the XPS viewer.

XPS The acronym for XML Paper Specification—a Microsoft file format that creates an image of your document and that opens in the XPS viewer.

Zoom The action of increasing or decreasing the size of the viewing area on the screen.

Getting Started with Microsoft Access 2016

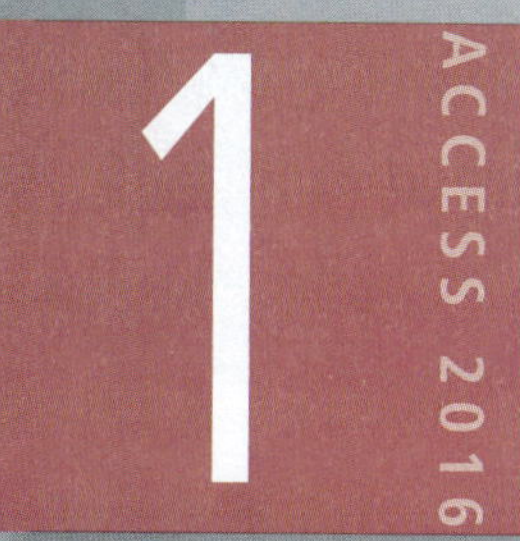

PROJECT 1A

OUTCOMES
Create a new database.

OBJECTIVES

1. Identify Good Database Design
2. Create a Table and Define Fields in a Blank Desktop Database
3. Change the Structure of Tables and Add a Second Table
4. Create a Query, Form, and Report
5. Close a Database and Close Access

PROJECT 1B

OUTCOMES
Create a database from a template.

OBJECTIVES

6. Use a Template to Create a Database
7. Organize Objects in the Navigation Pane
8. Create a New Table in a Database Created with a Template
9. Print a Report and a Table

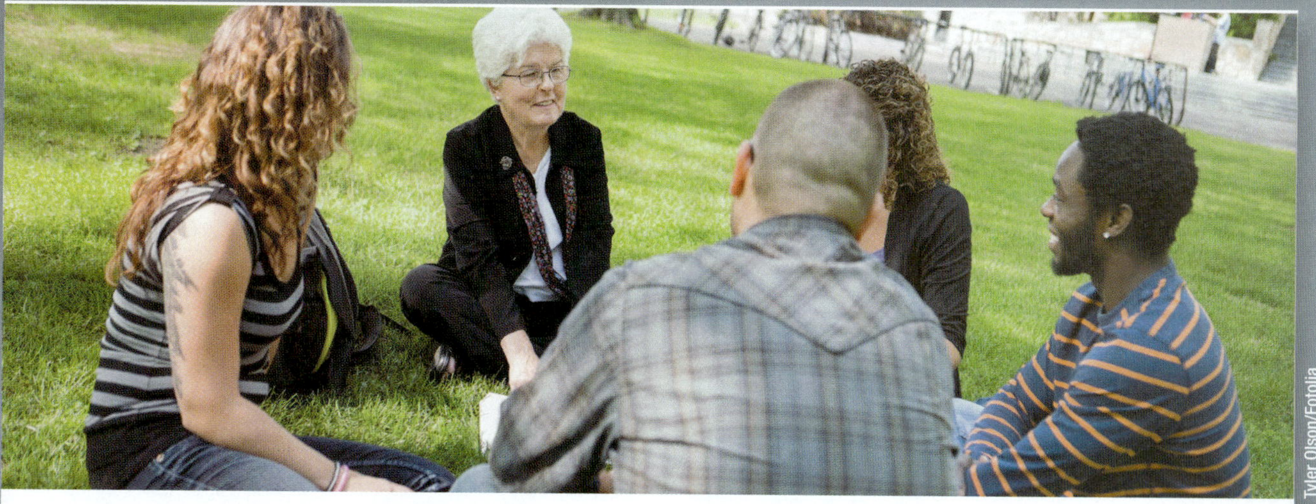

Tyler Olson/Fotolia

In This Chapter

GO! to Work with Access

In this chapter, you will use Microsoft Access 2016 to organize a collection of related information. You will create new databases, create tables, and enter data into the tables. You will create a query, a form, and a report—all of which are Access objects that make a database useful for locating and analyzing information. You will also create a complete database from a template that you can use as provided, or that you can modify to meet your needs. In this chapter, you will also learn how to apply good database design principles to your Access database and to define the structure of a database.

The projects in this chapter relate to **Texas Lakes Community College**, which is located in the Austin, Texas, area. Its four campuses serve over 30,000 students and offer more than 140 certificate programs and degrees. The college has a highly acclaimed Distance Education program and an extensive Workforce Development program. The college makes positive contributions to the community through cultural and athletic programs and has significant partnerships with businesses and nonprofit organizations. Popular fields of study include nursing and health care, solar technology, computer technology, and graphic design.

PROJECT 1A Student Advising Database with Two Tables

PROJECT ACTIVITIES

In Activities 1.01 through 1.17, you will assist Dr. Daniel Martinez, Vice President of Student Services at Texas Lakes Community College, in creating a new database for tracking students and their faculty advisors. Your completed database objects will look similar to Figure 1.1.

PROJECT FILES

If your instructor wants you to submit Project 1A in the MyITLab grader system, log in to MyITLab, locate grader Project1A, and then download the files for this project.

For Project 1A, you will need the following files:

Blank desktop database
a01A_Students (Excel workbook)
a01A_Faculty_Advisors (Excel workbook)

You will save your database as:

Lastname_Firstname_1A_Advising

PROJECT RESULTS

Build From Scratch

GO! Walk Thru Project 1A

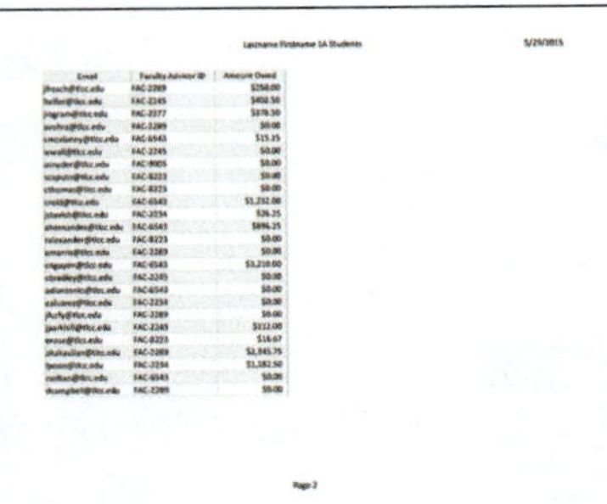

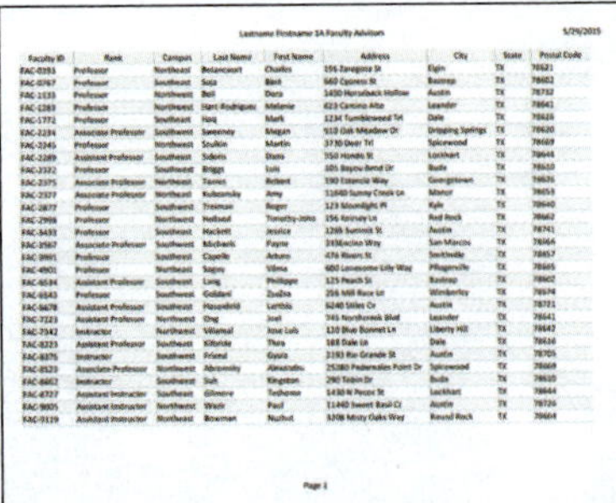

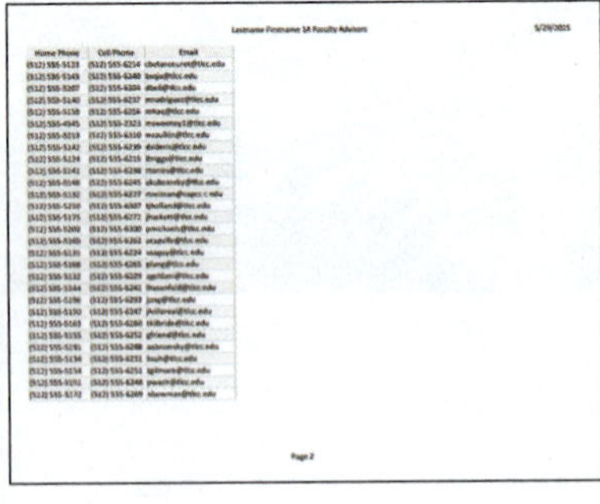

FIGURE 1.1 Project 1A Advising

NOTE	If You Are Using a Touchscreen
	Tap an item to click it.
	Press and hold for a few seconds to right-click; release when the information or command displays.
	Touch the screen with two or more fingers and then pinch together to zoom out or stretch your fingers apart to zoom in.
	Slide your finger on the screen to scroll—slide left to scroll right and slide right to scroll left.
	Slide to rearrange—similar to dragging with a mouse.
	Swipe to select—slide an item a short distance with a quick movement—to select an item and bring up commands, if any.

PROJECT RESULTS

In this project, using your own name, you will create the following database and objects. Your instructor may ask for printouts or PDF electronic images:

Lastname_Firstname_1A_Advising	Database file
Lastname Firstname 1A Students	Table
Lastname Firstname 1A Faculty Advisors	Table
Lastname Firstname 1A All Students Query	Query
Lastname Firstname 1A Student Form	Form
Lastname Firstname 1A Faculty Advisors Report	Report

Objective 1 Identify Good Database Design

GO! Learn How Video A1-1

A ***database*** is an organized collection of ***data***—facts about people, events, things, or ideas—related to a specific topic or purpose. ***Information*** is data that is accurate, timely, and organized in a useful manner. Your contact list is a type of database, because it is a collection of data about one topic—the people with whom you communicate. A simple database of this type is called a ***flat database*** because it is not related or linked to any other collection of data. Another example of a simple database is your music collection. You do not keep information about your music collection in your contact list because the data is not related to the people in your contact list.

A more sophisticated type of database is a ***relational database***, because multiple collections of data in the database are related to one another—for example, data about the students, the courses, and the faculty members at a college. Microsoft Access 2016 is a relational ***database management system***—also referred to as a ***DBMS***—which is software that controls how related collections of data are stored, organized, retrieved, and secured.

Activity 1.01 | Using Good Design Techniques to Plan a Database

ALERT!

To submit as an autograded project, log into MyITLab and download the files for this project, and begin with those files instead of a new, blank database. For Project 1A using Grader, read Activities 1.01 and 1.02 carefully. Begin working with the database in Activity 1.03. For Grader to award points accurately, when saving an object, do not include your Lastname Firstname at the beginning of the object name.

Before creating a new database, the first step is to determine the information you want to keep track of by asking yourself, *What questions should this database be able to answer?* The purpose of a database is to store the data in a manner that makes it easy to find the information you need by asking questions. For example, in a student database for Texas Lakes Community College, the questions to be answered might include:

- How many students are enrolled at the college?
- How many students have not yet been assigned a faculty advisor?
- Which students live in Austin, Texas?
- Which students owe money for tuition?
- Which students are majoring in Information Systems Technology?

Tables are the foundation of an Access database because all of the data is stored in one or more tables. A table is similar in structure to an Excel worksheet because data is organized into rows and columns. Each table row is a ***record***—all of the categories of data pertaining to one person, place, event, thing, or idea. Each table column is a ***field***—a single piece of information for every record. For example, in a table storing student contact information, each row forms a record for only one student. Each column forms a field for every record—for example, the student ID number or the student last name.

When organizing the fields of information in your table, break each piece of information into its smallest, most useful part. For example, create three fields for the name of a student—one field for the last name, one field for the first name, and one field for the middle name or initial.

The ***first principle of good database design*** is to organize data in the tables so that ***redundant***—duplicate—data does not occur. For example, record the student contact information in only *one* table, so that if a student's address changes, you can change the information in just one place. This conserves space, reduces the likelihood of errors when inputting new data, and does not require remembering all of the places where a student's address is stored.

The ***second principle of good database design*** is to use techniques that ensure the accuracy and consistency of data as it is entered into the table. Proofreading data is critical to maintaining accuracy in a database. Typically, many different people enter data into a database—think of all the people who enter data about students at your college. When entering a state in a student contacts table, one person might enter the state as *Texas*, while another might enter the state as *TX*. Use design techniques to help those who enter data into a database to enter the data more accurately and consistently.

Normalization is the process of applying design rules and principles to ensure that your database performs as expected. Taking the time to plan and create a database that is well designed will ensure that you can retrieve meaningful information from the database.

The tables of information in a relational database are linked or joined to one another by a ***common field***—a field in two or more tables that stores the same data. For example, a Students table includes the Student ID, name, and full address of every student. The Student Activities table includes the club name and the Student ID of members, but not the name or address, of each student in the club. Because the two tables share a common field—Student ID—you can use the data together to create a list of names and addresses of all of the students in a particular club. The names and addresses are stored in the Students table, and the Student IDs of the club members are stored in the Student Activities table.

Objective 2 Create a Table and Define Fields in a Blank Desktop Database

GO! Learn How Video A1-2

Three methods are used to create a new Access database. One method is to create a new database using a ***database template***—a preformatted database designed for a specific purpose. A second method is to create a new database from a ***blank desktop database***. A blank desktop database is stored on your computer or other storage device. Initially, it has no data and has no database tools; you create the data and the tools as you need them. A third method is to create a ***custom web app*** database from scratch or by using a template that you can publish and share with others over the Internet.

Regardless of the method you use, you must name and save the database before you can create any ***objects*** in it. Objects are the basic parts of a database; you create objects to store your data, to work with your data, and to display your data. The most common database objects are tables, queries, forms, and reports. Think of an Access database as a container for the objects that you create.

MOS 1.1.1

Activity 1.02 | Starting with a Blank Desktop Database

1 Start Microsoft Access 2016. Take a moment to compare your screen with Figure 1.2 and study the parts of the Microsoft Access opening screen described in the table in Figure 1.3.

From this Access opening screen, you can open an existing database, create a custom web app, create a blank desktop database, or create a new database from a template.

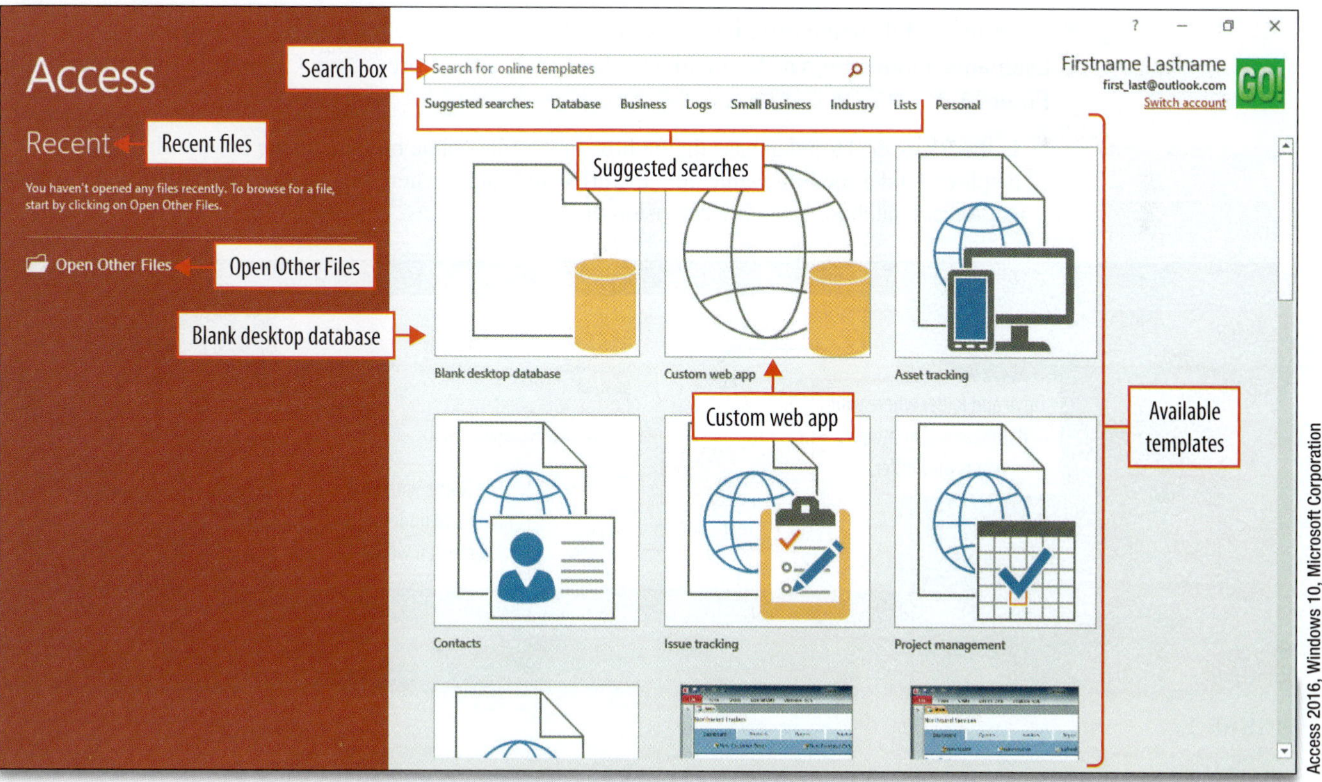

Access 2016, Windows 10, Microsoft Corporation

FIGURE 1.2

MICROSOFT ACCESS OPENING SCREEN ELEMENTS	
SCREEN ELEMENT	**DESCRIPTION**
Available templates	Starts a database for a specific purpose that includes built-in objects and tools ready for use.
Blank desktop database	Starts a blank database that is stored on your computer or on a portable storage device.
Custom web app	Starts a web app database that can be published and shared on the Internet.
Open Other Files	Enables you to open a database file from your computer, a shared location, or other location that you have designated.
Recent files	Displays a list of database files that have been recently opened.
Search box	Enables you to search the Microsoft Office website for templates.
Suggested searches	Enables you to click a category to start an online search for a template.

FIGURE 1.3

2 In the Access opening screen, click **Blank desktop database**. In the **Blank desktop database** dialog box, to the right of the **File Name** box, click **Browse** . In the **File New Database** dialog box, navigate to the location where you are saving your databases for this chapter, create a **New folder** named **Access Chapter 1** and then press Enter.

3 In the **File name** box, notice that *Database1* displays as the default file name—the number at the end of your file name might differ if you have saved a database previously with the default name. In the **Save as type** box, notice that the default database type is *Microsoft Access 2007 – 2016 Databases*, which means that you can open a database created in Access 2016 by using Access 2007, Access 2010, or Access 2013.

4 Click in the **File name** box. Using your own name, replace the existing text with **Lastname_Firstname_1A_Advising** and then click **OK** or press Enter. Compare your screen with Figure 1.4.

In the Blank desktop database dialog box, in the File Name box, the name of your database displays. Under the File Name box, the drive and folder where the database will be stored displays. An Access database has a file extension of *.accdb*.

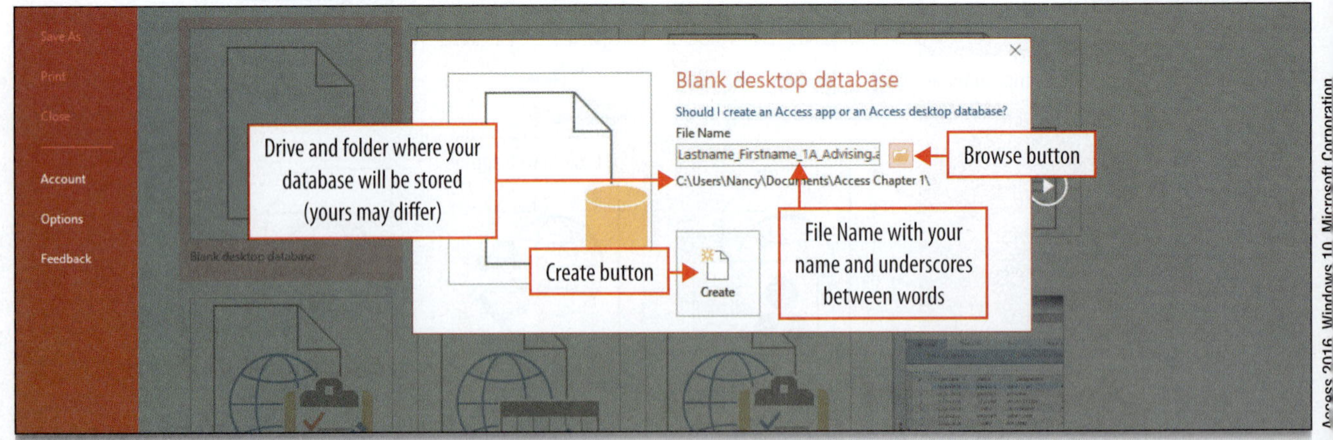

FIGURE 1.4

5 In the **Blank desktop database** dialog box, click **Create**. Compare your screen with Figure 1.5, and then take a moment to study the screen elements described in the table in Figure 1.6.

Access creates the new database and opens *Table1*. Recall that a table is an Access object that stores data in columns and rows, similar to the format of an Excel worksheet. Table objects are the foundation of a database because tables store data that is used by other database objects.

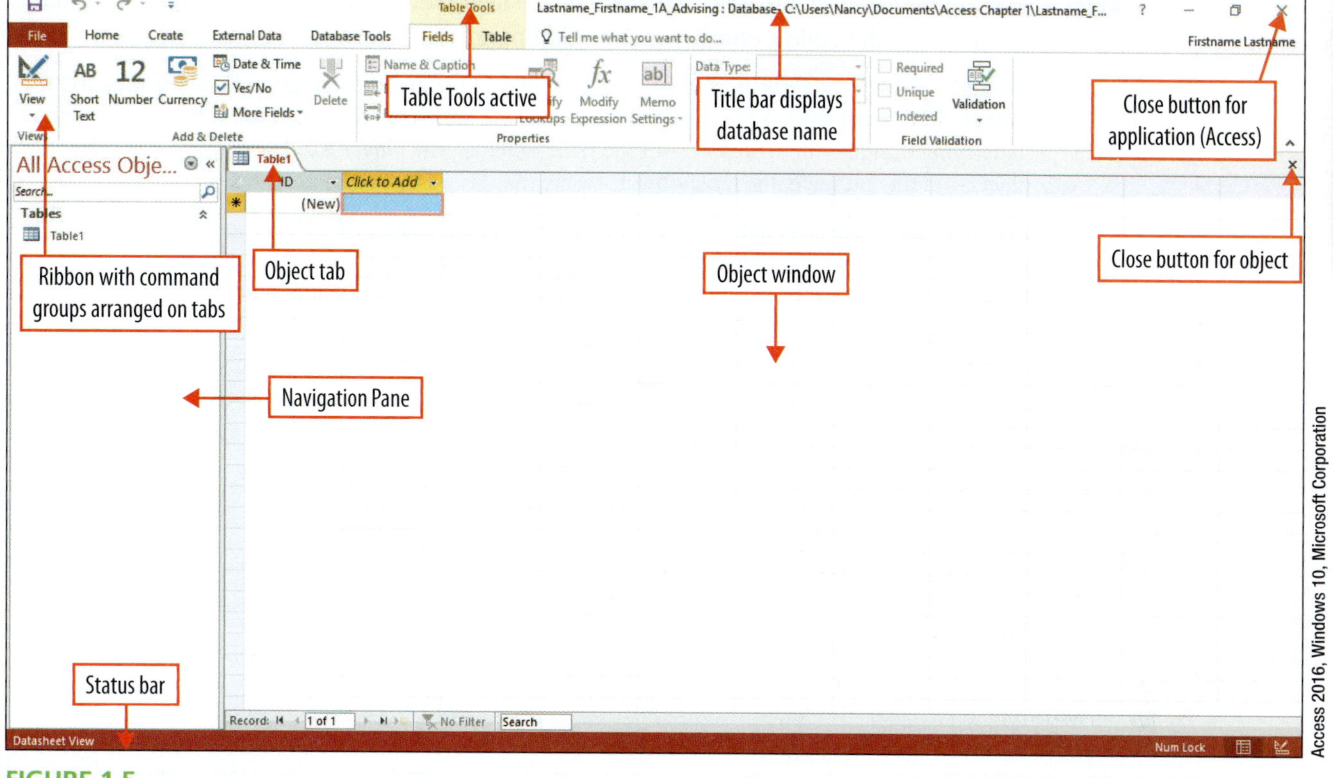

Access 2016, Windows 10, Microsoft Corporation

FIGURE 1.5

1 ACCESS

MICROSOFT ACCESS DATABASE WINDOW ELEMENTS	
ACCESS WINDOW ELEMENT	**DESCRIPTION**
Navigation Pane	Displays the database objects that can be opened in the object window.
Object tab	Identifies the open object.
Object window	Displays the active or open object(s), including tables, queries, or other objects.
Close button for object	Closes the active object.
Ribbon	Displays commands grouped by related tasks and stored on different tabs.
Status bar	Indicates the active view and the status of action occurring within the database on the left; provides buttons on the right to switch between Datasheet view and Design view.
Table Tools	Provides tools on two tabs for working with the active table object, these are contextual tabs—only available when a table object is active.
Close button for application (Access)	Closes the active database and Access.

Access 2016, Windows 10, Microsoft Corporation

FIGURE 1.6

2.1.1, 2.4.1

Activity 1.03 | Assigning the Data Type and Name to Fields

After you have named and saved your database, the next step is to consult your database design plan and then create the tables for your data. Limit the data in each table to *one* subject. For example, in this project, your database will have two tables—one for student information and one for faculty advisor information.

Recall that each column in a table is a field; field names display at the top of each column of the table. Recall also that each row in a table is a record—all of the data pertaining to one person, place, thing, event, or idea. Each record is broken up into its smallest usable parts—the fields. Use meaningful names for fields; for example, *Last Name*.

1 Notice the new blank table that displays in Datasheet view, and then take a moment to study the elements of the table's object window. Compare your screen with Figure 1.7.

The table displays in ***Datasheet view***, which displays the data in columns and rows similar to the format of an Excel worksheet. Another way to view a table is in ***Design view***, which displays the underlying design—the ***structure***—of the table's fields. The ***object window*** displays the open object—in this instance, the table object.

In a new blank database, there is only one object—a new blank table. Because you have not yet named this table, the object tab displays a default name of *Table1*. Access creates the first field and names it *ID*. In the ID field, Access assigns a unique sequential number—each number incremented by one—to each record as it is entered into the table.

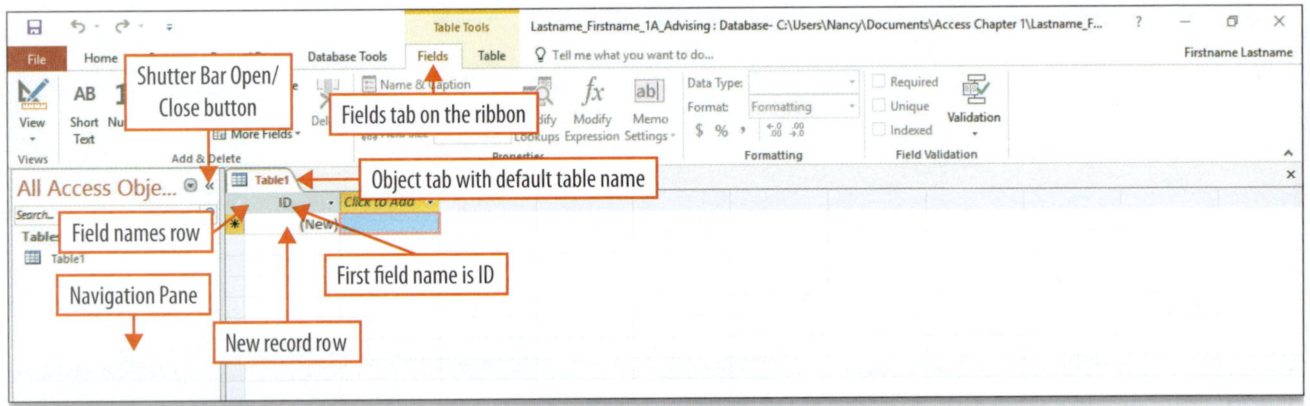

FIGURE 1.7

2 In the **Navigation Pane**, click **Shutter Bar Open/Close** [«] to collapse the **Navigation Pane** to a narrow bar on the left.

The ***Navigation Pane*** displays and organizes the names of the objects in a database. From the Navigation Pane, you can open objects. Collapse or close the Navigation Pane to display more of the object—in this case, the table.

ANOTHER WAY Press [F11] to close or open the Navigation Pane.

3 In the field names row, click anywhere in the text *Click to Add* to display a list of data types. Compare your screen with Figure 1.8.

A ***data type*** classifies the kind of data that you can store in a field, such as numbers, text, or dates. A field in a table can have only one data type. The data type of each field should be included in your database design. After selecting the data type, you can name the field.

ANOTHER WAY To the right of *Click to Add*, click the arrow.

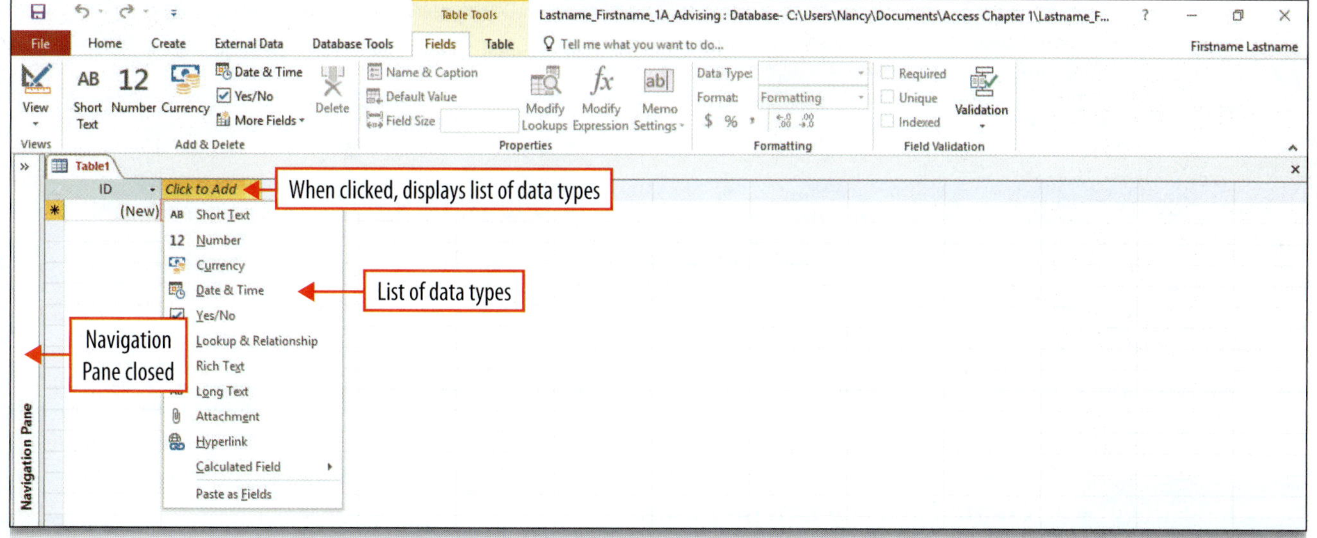

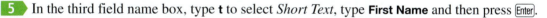

FIGURE 1.8

Access 2016, Windows 10, Microsoft Corporation

4 In the list of data types, click **Short Text**, and notice that in the second column, *Click to Add* changes to *Field1*, which is selected. Type **Last Name** and then press Enter.

The second column displays *Last Name* as the field name, and, in the third column, the data types list displays. The ***Short Text data type*** describes text, a combination of text and numbers, or numbers that do not represent a quantity or are not used in calculations, such as the Postal Code. This data type enables you to enter up to 255 characters in the field.

ANOTHER WAY With the list of data types displayed, type the character that is underscored to select the data type. For example, type *t* to select Short Text or type *u* to select Currency.

5 In the third field name box, type **t** to select *Short Text*, type **First Name** and then press Enter.

6 In the fourth field name box, click **Short Text**, type **Middle Initial** and then press Enter.

7 Create the remaining fields from the table below by first selecting the data type, typing the field name, and then pressing Enter. The field names in the table will display on one line—do not be concerned if the field names do not completely display in the column; you will adjust the column widths later.

Data Type		Short Text	Short Text	Short Text	**Short Text**	**Short Text**	**Short Text**	**Short Text**	**Short Text**	**Short Text**	**Short Text**	**Currency**
Field Name	ID	Last Name	First Name	Middle Initial	**Address**	**City**	**State**	**Postal Code**	**Phone**	**Email**	**Faculty Advisor ID**	**Amount Owed**

The Postal Code and Phone fields are assigned a data type of Short Text because the numbers are never used in calculations. The Amount Owed field is assigned the ***Currency data type***, which describes monetary values and numeric data that can be used in calculations and that have one to four decimal places. A U.S. dollar sign ($) and two decimal places are automatically included for all of the numbers in a field with the Currency data type.

8 If necessary, scroll to bring the first column—ID—into view, and then compare your screen with Figure 1.9.

Access automatically created the ID field, and you created 11 additional fields in the table.

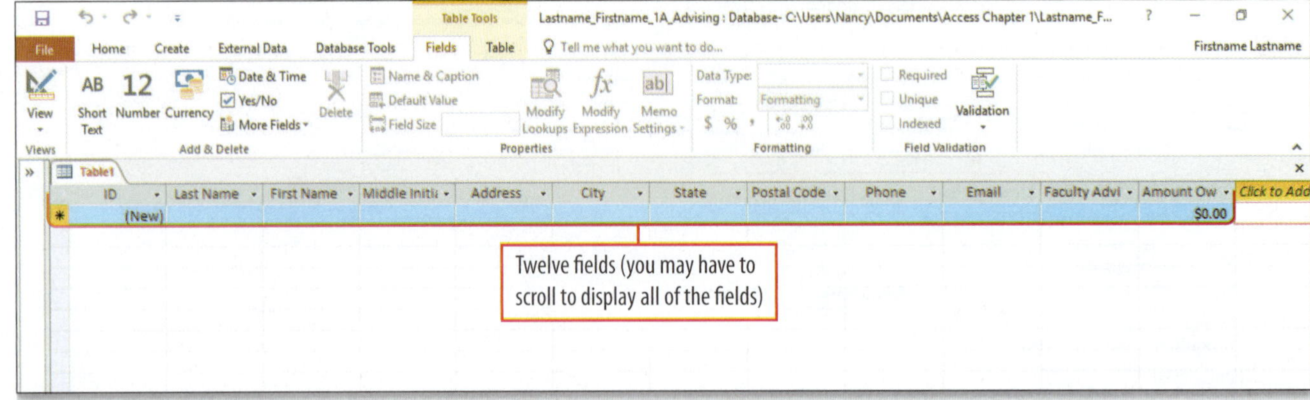

Access 2016, Windows 10, Microsoft Corporation

FIGURE 1.9

More Knowledge — Create Fields by Entering Data

You can create a new field in Datasheet view by typing the data in a new column. Access automatically assigns a data type based on the data you enter. For example, if you enter a date, Access assigns the Date & Time data type. If you enter a monetary amount, Access assigns the Currency data type. If Access cannot determine the data type based on the data entered, the Short Text data type is assigned. You can always change the data type if an incorrect data type is assigned. If you use this method to create fields, you must check the assigned data types to be sure they are correct. You must also rename the fields because Access assigns the names as *Field1*, *Field2*, and so on.

2.4.3, 2.4.6

Activity 1.04 | Renaming Fields and Changing Data Types in a Table

1 In the first column, click anywhere in the text *ID*. On the ribbon, under **Table Tools**, on the **Fields tab**, in the **Properties group**, click **Name & Caption**. In the **Enter Field Properties** dialog box, in the **Name** box, change *ID* to **Student ID**

The field name *Student ID* is a more precise description of the data contained in this field. In the Enter Field Properties dialog box, you have the option to use the ***Caption*** property to display a name for a field different from the one that displays in the Name box. Many database designers do not use spaces in field names; instead, they might name a field *LastName* or *LName* and then create a caption for the field so it displays as *Last Name* in tables, forms, or reports. In the Enter Field Properties dialog box, you can also provide a description for the field.

ANOTHER WAY Right-click the field name to display the shortcut menu, and then click Rename Field; or, double-click the field name to select the existing text, and then type the new field name.

2 Click **OK** to close the **Enter Field Properties** dialog box. On the ribbon, in the **Formatting group**, notice that the **Data Type** for the **Student ID** field is *AutoNumber*. Click the **Data Type arrow**, click **Short Text**, and then compare your screen with Figure 1.10.

In the new record row, the Student ID field is selected. By default, Access creates an ID field for all new tables and sets the data type for the field to AutoNumber. The ***AutoNumber data type*** describes a unique sequential or random number assigned by Access as each record is entered. Changing the data type of this field to Short Text enables you to enter a custom student ID number.

When records in a database have *no* unique value, such as a book ISBN or a license plate number, the AutoNumber data type is a useful way to automatically create a unique number. In this manner, you are sure that every record is different from the others.

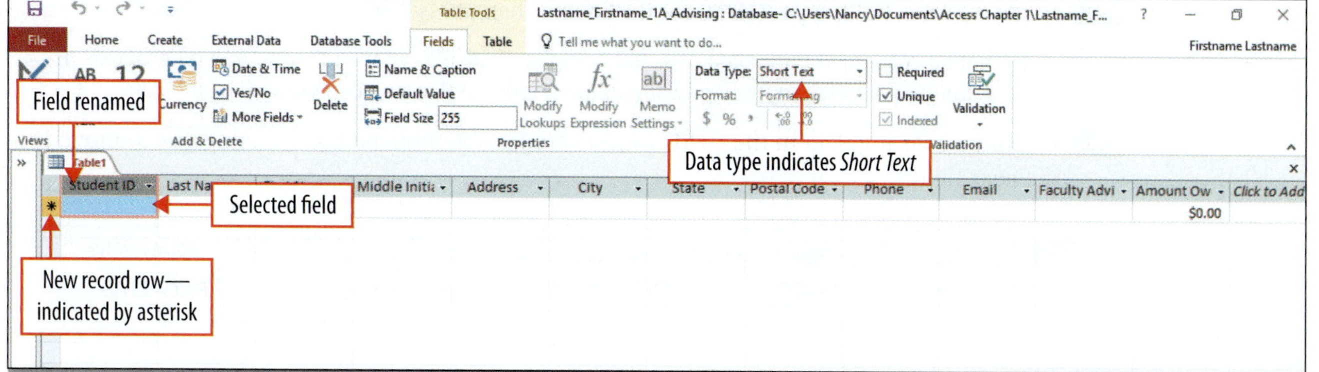

FIGURE 1.10

Access 2016, Windows 10, Microsoft Corporation

2.3.2, 2.2.4

Activity 1.05 | Adding a Record to a Table

A new contact list is not useful until you fill it with names and phone numbers. Likewise, a new database is not useful until you ***populate*** it by filling one or more tables with data. You can populate a table with records by typing data directly into the table.

1 In the new record row, click in the **Student ID** field to display the insertion point, type **1023045** and then press Enter. Compare your screen with Figure 1.11.

The pencil icon in the ***record selector box*** indicates that a record is being entered or edited. The record selector box is the small box at the left of a record in Datasheet view. When clicked, the entire record is selected.

ANOTHER WAY Press Tab to move the insertion point to the next field.

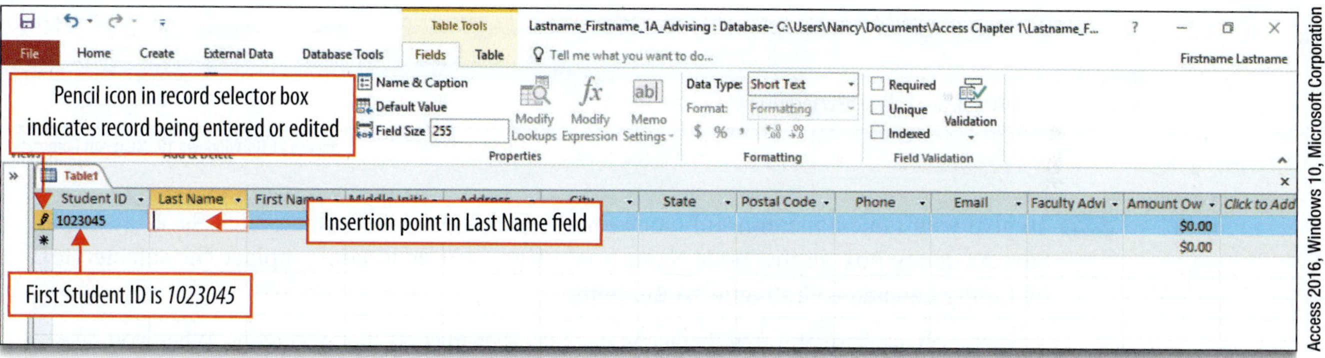

FIGURE 1.11

Access 2016, Windows 10, Microsoft Corporation

2 With the insertion point positioned in the **Last Name** field, type **Fresch** and then press Enter.

NOTE Correcting Typing Errors

Correct any typing errors you make by using the techniques you have practiced in other Office applications. For example, use Backspace to remove characters to the left of the insertion point. Use Del to remove characters to the right of the insertion point. Or select the text you want to replace and type the correct information. Press Esc to exit out of a record that has not been completely entered.

3 In the **First Name** field, type **Jenna** and then press Enter.

4 In the **Middle Initial** field, type **A** and then press Enter.

5 In the **Address** field, type **7550 Douglas Ln** and then press Enter.

Do not be concerned if the data does not completely display in the column. As you progress in your study of Access, you will adjust column widths so that you can view all of the data.

6 Continue entering data in the fields as indicated in the table below, pressing Enter to move to the next field.

City	State	Postal Code	Phone	Email	Faculty Advisor ID
Austin	**TX**	**78749**	**(512) 555-7550**	**jfresch@tlcc.edu**	**FAC-2289**

NOTE **Format for Typing Telephone Numbers in Access**

Access does not require a specific format for typing telephone numbers in a record. The examples in this textbook use the format of Microsoft Outlook. Using such a format facilitates easy transfer of Outlook information to and from Access.

7 In the **Amount Owed** field, type **250** and then press Enter. Compare your screen with Figure 1.12.

Pressing Enter or Tab in the last field moves the insertion point to the next row to begin a new record. Access automatically saves the record as soon as you move to the next row; you do not have to take any specific action to save a record.

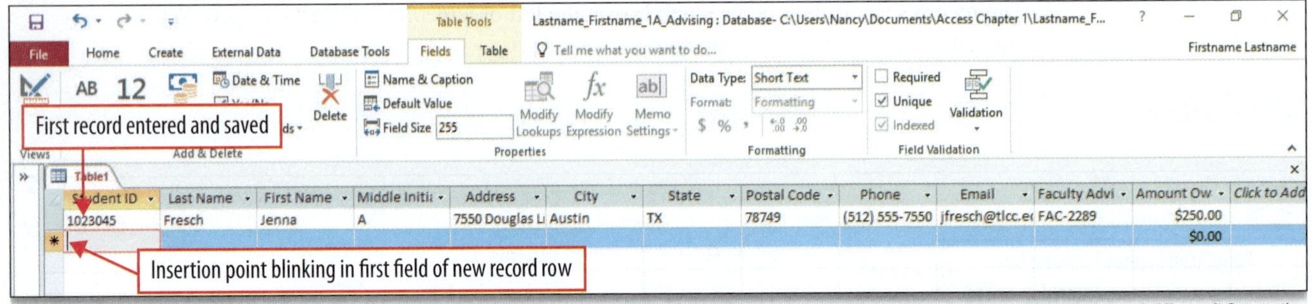

FIGURE 1.12

8 To give your table a meaningful name, on the Quick Access Toolbar, click **Save**. In the **Save As** dialog box, in the **Table Name** box, using your own name, replace the selected text by typing **Lastname Firstname 1A Students**

Save each database object with a name that identifies the data that it contains. When you save objects within a database, it is not necessary to use underscores in place of the spaces between words. Your name is included as part of the object name so that you and your instructor can identify your printouts or electronic files easily.

9 In the **Save As** dialog box, click **OK**. Notice that the object tab—located directly above the *Student ID* field name—displays the new table name that you just entered.

***More* Knowledge** **Renaming or Deleting a Table**

To change the name of a table, close the table, display the Navigation Pane, right-click the table name, and then click Rename. Type the new name or edit as you would any selected text. To delete a table, close the table, display the Navigation Pane, right-click the table name, and then click Delete.

2.3.2

Activity 1.06 | Adding Additional Records to a Table

1 In the new record row, click in the **Student ID** field, and then enter the data for two additional students as shown in the table below. Press Enter or Tab to move from field to field. The data in each field will display on one line in the table.

Student ID	Last Name	First Name	Middle Initial	Address	City	State	Postal Code	Phone	Email	Faculty Advisor ID	Amount Owed
2345677	**Ingram**	**Joseph**	**S**	**621 Hilltop Dr**	**Leander**	**TX**	**78646**	**(512) 555-0717**	**jingram@tlcc.edu**	**FAC-2377**	**378.5**
3456689	**Snyder**	**Amanda**	**J**	**4786 Bluff St**	**Buda**	**TX**	**78610**	**(512) 555-9120**	**asnyder@tlcc.edu**	**FAC-9005**	**0**

2 Press Enter, and compare your screen with Figure 1.13

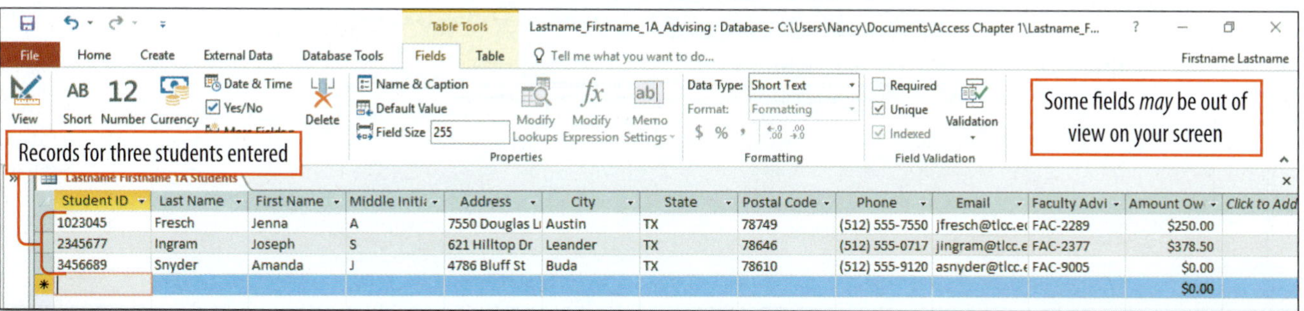

Access 2016, Windows 10, Microsoft Corporation

FIGURE 1.13

2.3.4

Activity 1.07 | Importing Data from an Excel Workbook into an Existing Access Table

You can type records directly into a table. You can also ***import*** data from a variety of sources. Importing is the process of copying data from one source or application to another application. For example, you can import data from a Word table or an Excel spreadsheet into an Access database because the data is arranged in columns and rows, similar to a table in Datasheet view.

In this Activity, you will ***append***—add on—data from an Excel spreadsheet to your *1A Students* table. To append data, the table must already be created, and it must be closed.

1 In the upper right corner of the table, below the ribbon, click **Object Close** [X] to close your **1A Students** table. Notice that no objects are open.

2 On the ribbon, click the **External Data tab**. In the **Import & Link group**, click **Excel**. In the **Get External Data – Excel Spreadsheet** dialog box, click **Browse**.

3 In the **File Open** dialog box, navigate to the student data files that accompany this chapter, double-click the Excel file **a01A_Students**, and then compare your screen with Figure 1.14.

The path to the ***source file***—the file being imported—displays in the File name box. There are three options for importing data from an Excel spreadsheet: import the data into a *new* table in the current database, append a copy of the records to an existing table, or link the data from the spreadsheet to a linked table in the database. A ***link*** is a connection to data in another file. When linking, Access creates a table that maintains a link to the source data, so that changes to the data in one file are automatically made in the other—linked—file.

ANOTHER WAY Click the file name, and then in the File Open dialog box, click Open.

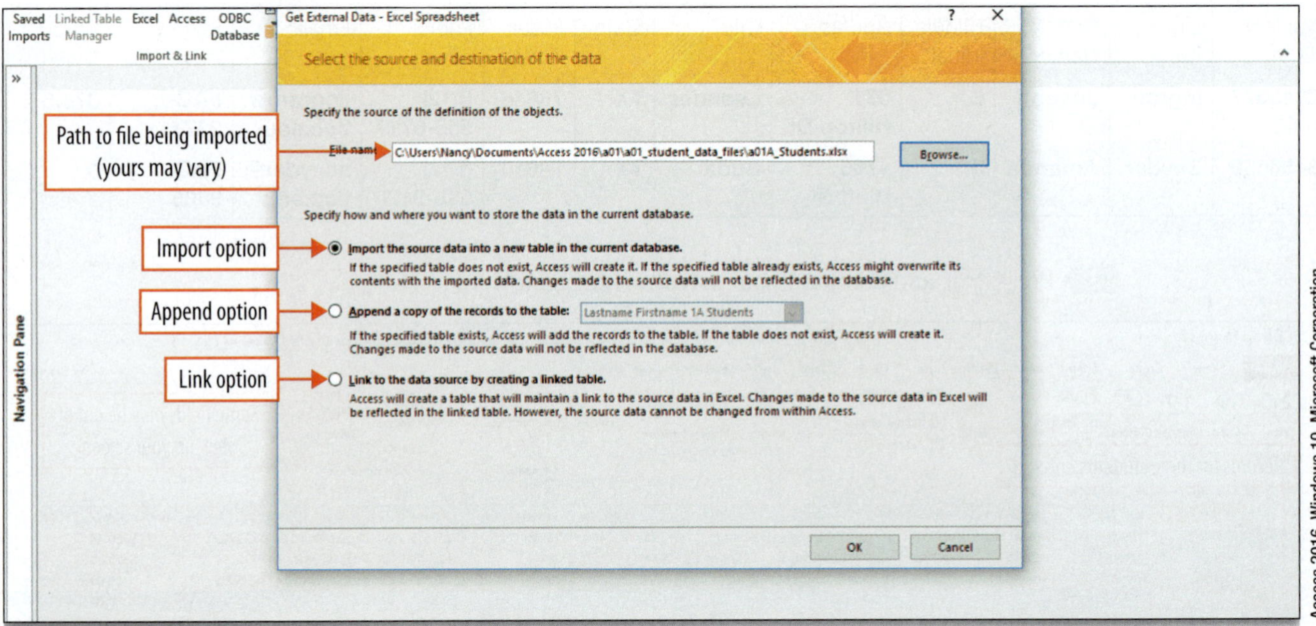

FIGURE 1.14

4 Click the **Append a copy of the records to the table** option button, and then, in the box to the right, click the **arrow**.

Currently, your database has only one table, so no other tables display on the list. However, when a database has multiple tables, click the arrow to select the table to which you want to append records. The table into which you import or append data is referred to as the ***destination table***.

5 Press Esc to cancel the list, and in the dialog box, click **OK**. If a security message displays, click Open. Compare your screen with Figure 1.15.

The first screen of the Import Spreadsheet Wizard displays. A ***wizard*** is a feature in a Microsoft Office program that walks you step by step through a process. The presence of scroll bars in the window indicates that records and fields are out of view. To append records from an Excel workbook to an existing database table, the column headings in the Excel worksheet or spreadsheet must be identical to the field names in the table. The wizard identified the first row of the spreadsheet as column headings, which are equivalent to field names.

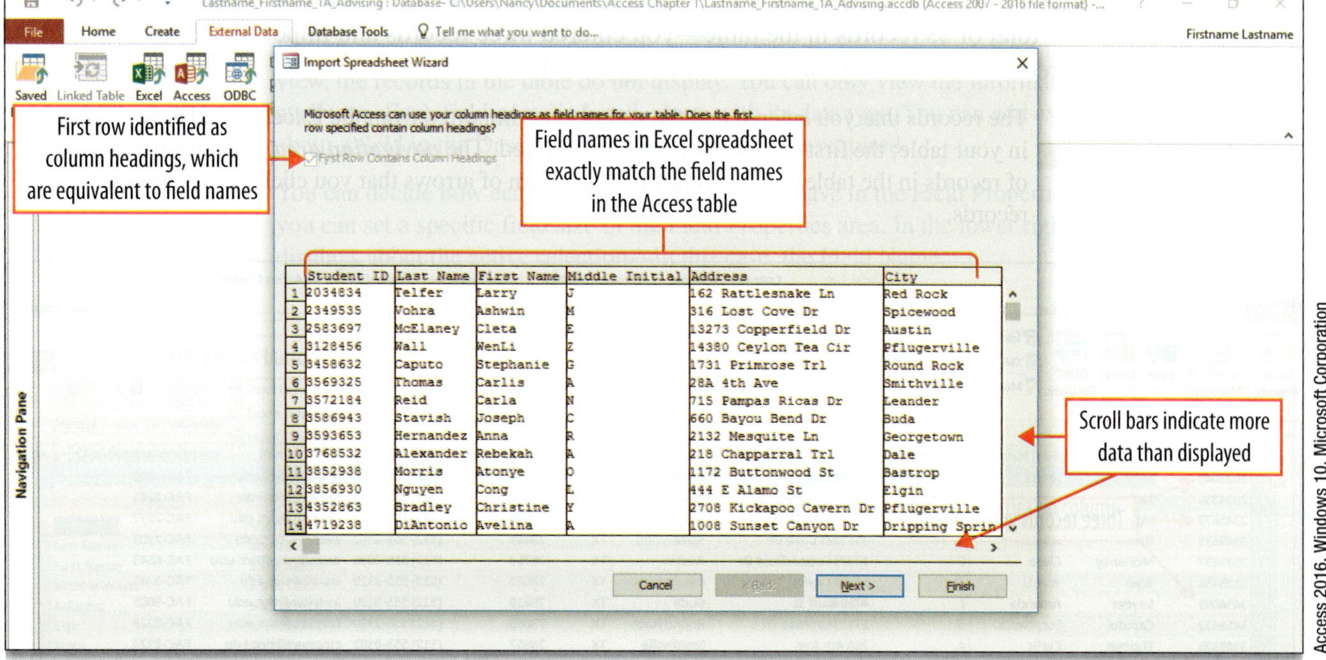

Access 2016, Windows 10, Microsoft Corporation

FIGURE 1.15

6 In the lower right corner of the wizard, click **Next**. Notice that the name of your table displays under **Import to Table**. In the lower right corner of the wizard, click **Finish**.

7 In the **Get External Data – Excel Spreadsheet** dialog box, click **Close**. **Open** » the **Navigation Pane**.

8 Point to the right edge of the **Navigation Pane** to display the ⟺ pointer. Drag to the right to increase the width of the **Navigation Pane** so that the entire table name displays, and then compare your screen with Figure 1.16.

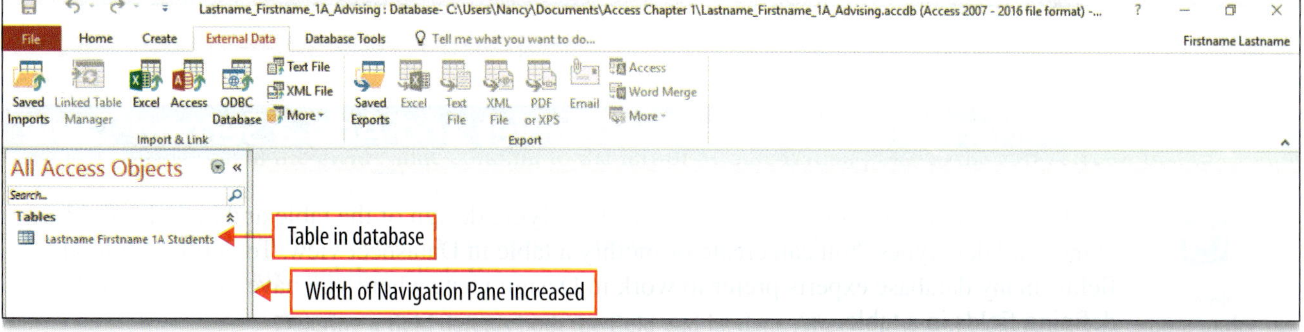

Access 2016, Windows 10, Microsoft Corporation

FIGURE 1.16

9 In the **Navigation Pane**, double-click your **1A Students** table to open the table in Datasheet view, and then **Close** « the **Navigation Pane**.

ANOTHER WAY To open an object from the Navigation Pane, right-click the object name, and then click Open.

2.4.4, 2.2.3

Activity 1.09 | Changing a Field Size and Adding a Description

Typically, many different individuals have the ability to enter data into a table. For example, at your college, many Registration Assistants enter and modify student and course information daily. Two ways to help reduce errors are to restrict what can be typed in a field and to add descriptive information to help the individuals when entering the data.

1 With your table still displayed in **Design** view, in the **Field Name** column, click anywhere in the **Student ID** field name.

2 In the lower area of the screen, under **Field Properties**, click **Field Size** to select the text **255**, and then type **7**

This action limits the size of the Student ID field to no more than seven characters. ***Field properties*** control how the field displays and how data can be entered into the field. You can define properties for each field in the Field Properties area by first clicking the field name to display the properties for that specific data type.

The default field size for a Short Text field is 255. Limiting the Field Size property to seven ensures that no more than 7 characters can be entered for each Student ID. However, this does not prevent someone from entering seven characters that are incorrect or entering fewer than seven characters. Setting the proper data type for the field and limiting the field size are two ways to help reduce errors during data entry.

ANOTHER WAY In Datasheet view, click in the field. Under Table Tools, on the Fields tab, in the Properties group, click in the Field Size box, and then type the number that represents the maximum number of characters for that field.

3 In the **Student ID** row, click in the **Description** box, type **Seven-digit Student ID number** and then press Enter. Compare your screen with Figure 1.19.

Descriptions for fields in a table are optional. Include a description if the field name does not provide an obvious explanation of the type of data to be entered. If a description is provided for a field, when data is being entered in that field in Datasheet view, the text in the Description displays on the left side of the status bar to provide additional information for the individuals who are entering the data.

When you enter a description for a field, a Property Update Options button displays below the text you typed, which enables you to copy the description for the field to all other database objects that use this table as an underlying source.

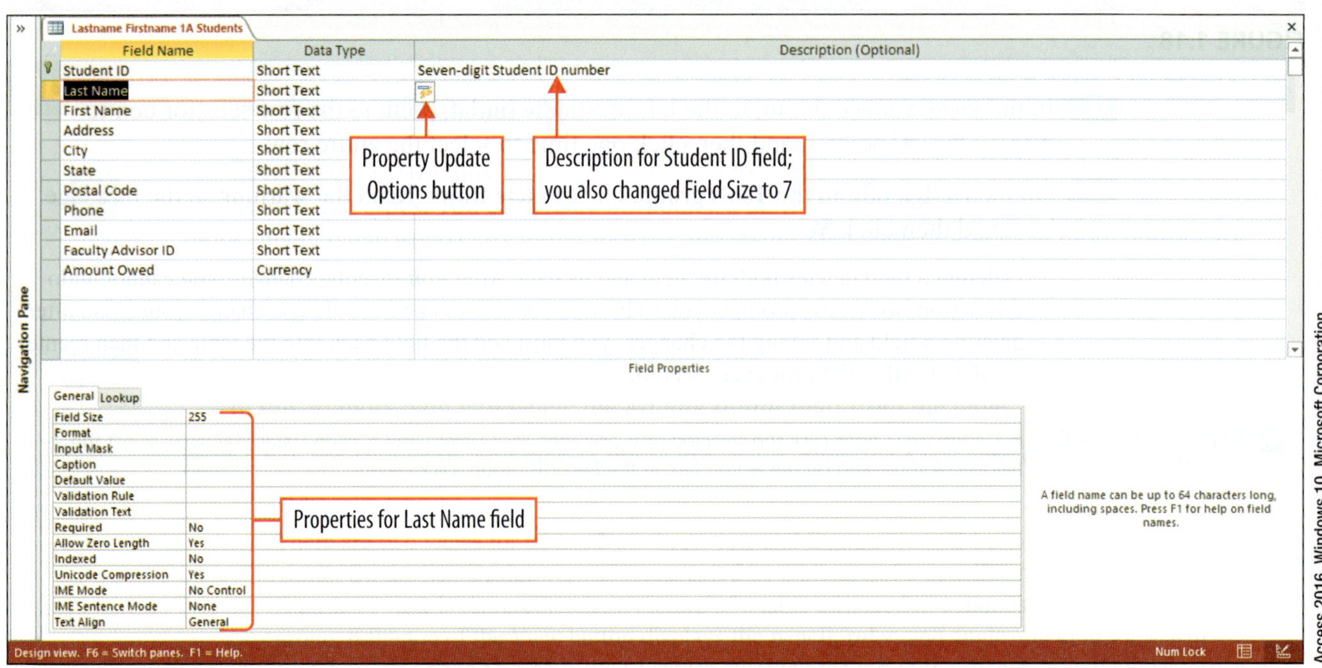

FIGURE 1.19

4 Click in the **State** field name box. In the **Field Properties** area, change the **Field Size** to **2** and in the **Description** box for this field, type **Two-character state abbreviation** and then press Enter.

5 Click in the **Faculty Advisor ID** field name box. In the **Field Properties** area, change the **Field Size** to **8** and in the **Description** box for this field, type **Eight-character ID of the instructor assigned as advisor** and then press Enter.

6 On the Quick Access Toolbar, click **Save** to save the design changes to your table, and then notice the message.

The message indicates that the field size property of one or more fields has changed to a shorter size. If more characters are currently present in the Student ID, State, or Faculty Advisor ID fields than you have allowed, the data will be ***truncated***—cut off or shortened—because the fields were not previously restricted to these specific number of characters.

7 In the message box, click **Yes**.

More Knowledge Add a Table Description

You can create a description to provide more information to users regarding the entire table. With the table displayed in Design view, click the Design tab. In the Show/Hide group, click Property Sheet. Click in the Description box, type the table description, and then press Enter. Close the Property Sheet.

1.3.5

Activity 1.10 | Viewing the Primary Key in Design View

Primary key refers to the required field in the table that uniquely identifies a record. For example, in a college registration database, your Student ID number identifies you as a unique individual—every student has a student number and no other student at the college has your exact student number. In the 1A Students table, the Student ID uniquely identifies each student.

When you create a table using the blank desktop database template, Access designates the first field as the primary key field and names the field ID. It is good database design practice to establish a primary key for every table, because doing so ensures that you do not enter the same record more than once. You can imagine the confusion if another student at your college had the same Student ID number as you do.

1 With your table still displayed in **Design** view, in the **Field Name** column, click in the **Student ID** box. To the left of the box, notice the small icon of a key, as shown in Figure 1.20.

Access automatically designates the first field as the primary key field, but you can set any field as the primary key by clicking the field name, and then in the Tools group, clicking Primary Key.

Access 2016, Windows 10, Microsoft Corporation

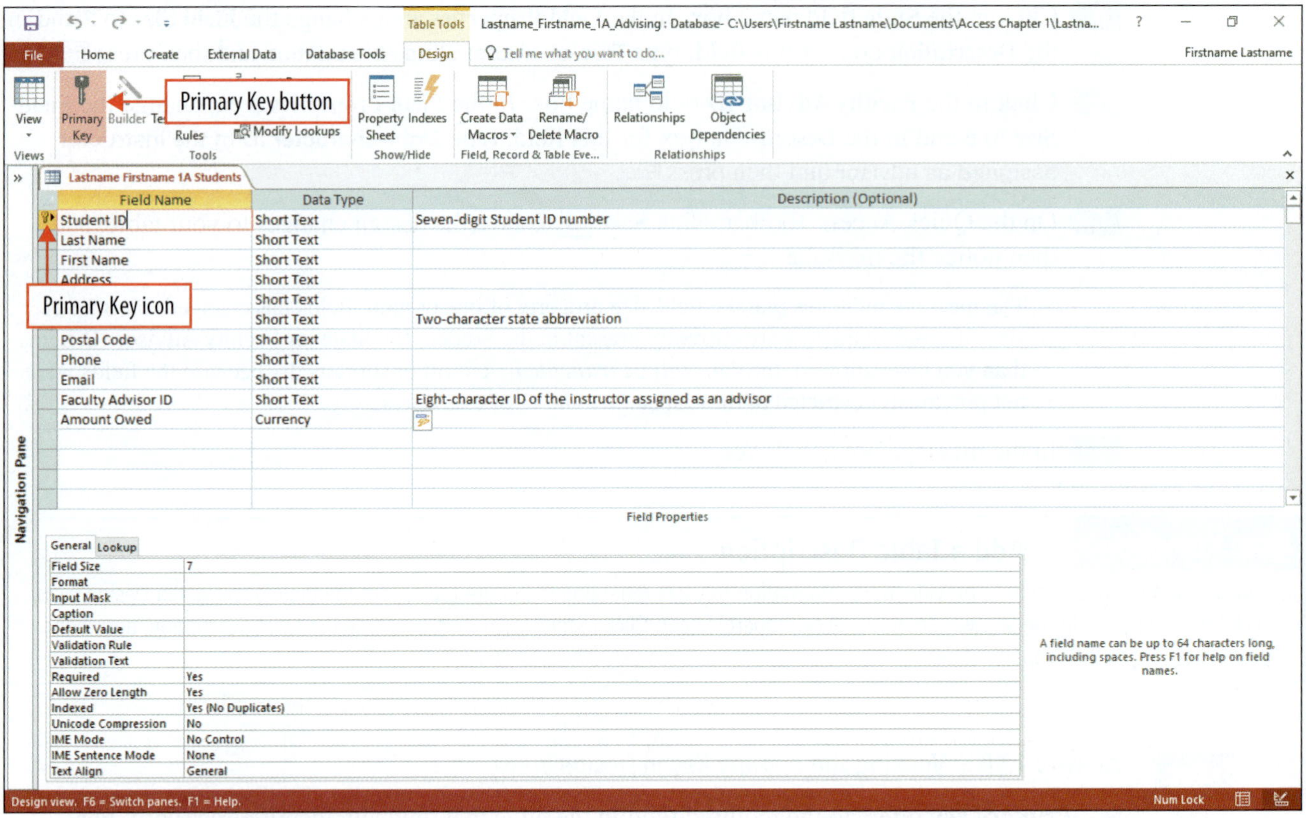

FIGURE 1.20

2 On the **Design tab**, in the **Views group**, notice that the View button displays a picture of a datasheet, indicating that clicking View will switch the view to Datasheet view. Click the top of the **View** button.

If you make design changes to a table and switch views without first saving the table, Access will prompt you to save the table before changing views.

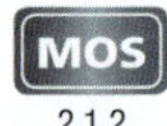

MOS 2.1.2

Activity 1.11 | Adding a Second Table to a Database by Importing an Excel Spreadsheet

Many Microsoft Office users track data in an Excel spreadsheet. The sorting and filtering capabilities of Excel are useful for a simple database where all of the information resides in one large Excel spreadsheet. However, Excel is limited as a database management tool because it cannot *relate* the information in multiple spreadsheets in a way that you can ask a question and get a meaningful result. Because data in an Excel spreadsheet is arranged in columns and rows, the spreadsheet can easily convert to an Access table by importing the spreadsheet.

1 On the ribbon, click the **External Data tab**, and then in the **Import & Link group**, click **Excel**. In the **Get External Data – Excel Spreadsheet** dialog box, to the right of the **File name** box, click **Browse**.

2 In the **File Open** dialog box, navigate to the location where your student data files are stored, and then double-click **a01A_Faculty_Advisors**. Compare your screen with Figure 1.21.

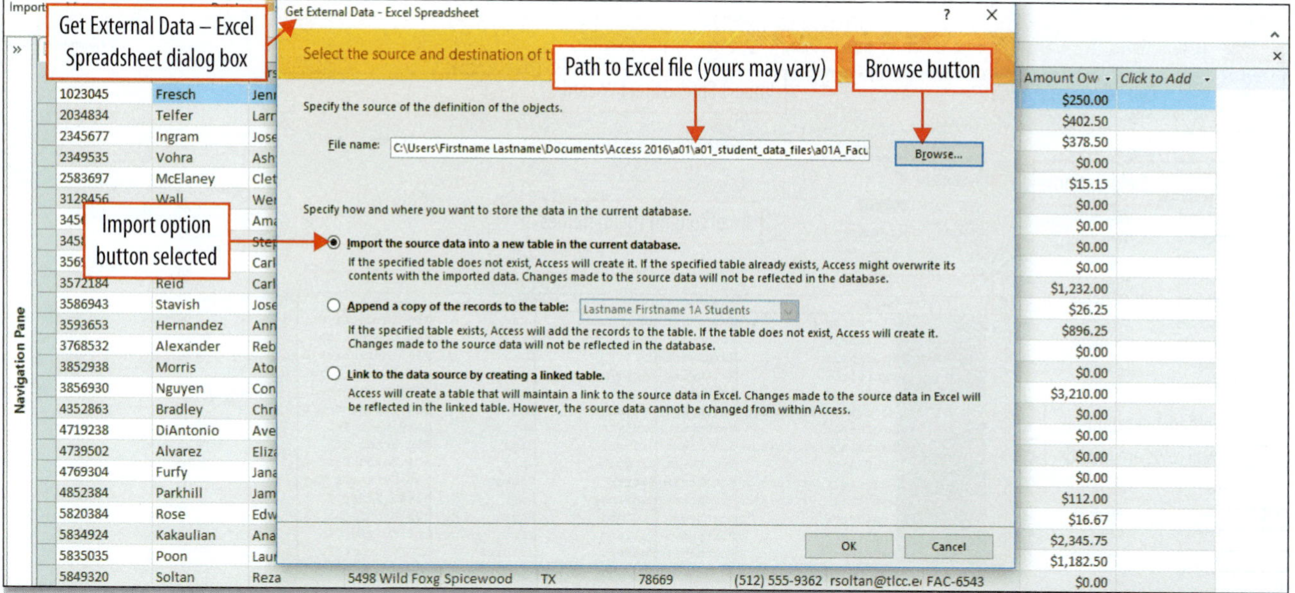

FIGURE 1.21

Access 2016, Windows 10, Microsoft Corporation

3 Be sure that the **Import the source data into a new table in the current database** option button is selected, click **OK**. If a security message displays, click Open.

The Import Spreadsheet Wizard displays the spreadsheet data.

4 In the upper left corner of the wizard, select the **First Row Contains Column Headings** check box.

The Excel data is framed, indicating that the first row of Excel column titles will become the Access table field names, and the remaining rows will become the individual records in the new Access table.

5 Click **Next**. Notice that the first column—*Faculty ID*—is selected, and in the upper area of the wizard, the **Field Name** and the **Data Type** display. Compare your screen with Figure 1.22.

In this step, under Field Options, you can review and change the name or the data type of each selected field. You can also identify fields in the spreadsheet that you do not want to import into the Access table by selecting the Do not import field (Skip) check box.

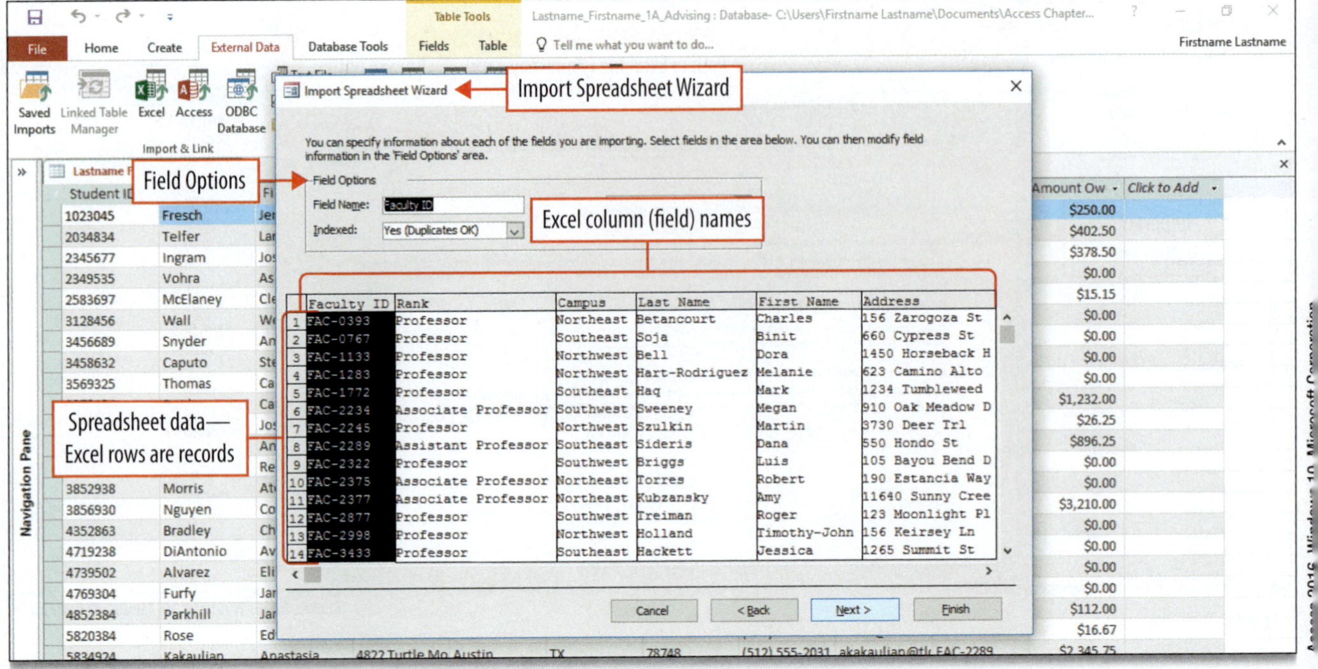

FIGURE 1.22

6 Click **Next**. In the upper area of the wizard, click the **Choose my own primary key** option button, and then be sure that **Faculty ID** displays.

In the new table, Faculty ID will be the primary key. Every faculty member has a Faculty ID and no two faculty members have the same Faculty ID. By default, Access selects the first field as the primary key, but you can click the arrow and select a different field.

7 Click **Next**. In the **Import to Table** box, using your own name, type **Lastname Firstname 1A Faculty Advisors** and then click **Finish**.

8 In the **Get External Data – Excel Spreadsheet** dialog box, click **Close**. **Open** » the **Navigation Pane**.

9 In the **Navigation Pane**, double-click your **1A Faculty Advisors** table to open it in Datasheet view, and then **Close** « the **Navigation Pane**.

Two tables that are identified by their object tabs are open in the object window. Your 1A Faculty Advisors table is the active table and displays the 29 records that you imported from the Excel spreadsheet.

10 In your **1A Faculty Advisors** table, click in the **Postal Code** field in the first record. On the ribbon, under **Table Tools**, click the **Fields tab**. In the **Formatting group**, click the **Data Type arrow**, and then click **Short Text**. Compare your screen with Figure 1.23.

When you import data from an Excel spreadsheet, check the data types of all fields to ensure they are correct. Recall that if a field, such as the Postal Code, contains numbers that do not represent a quantity or are not used in calculations, the data type should be set to Short Text. To change the data type of a field, click in the field in any record.

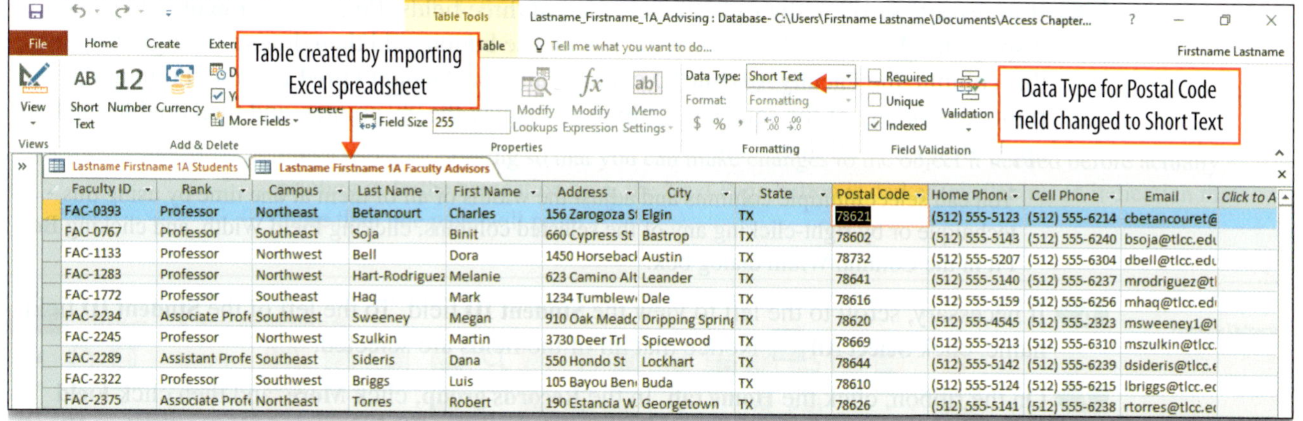

FIGURE 1.23

Access 2016, Windows 10, Microsoft Corporation

Activity 1.12 | Adjusting Column Widths

You can adjust the column widths in a table displayed in Datasheet view by using techniques similar to those you use for Excel spreadsheets.

1 In the object window, click the ***object tab*** for your **1A Students** table to make it the active object and to display it in the object window.

Clicking an object tab along the top of the object window enables you to display the open object and make it active so that you can work with it. All of the columns in the datasheet are the same width, regardless of the length of the data in the field, the length of the field name, or the field size that was set. If you print the table as currently displayed, some of the data or field names will not print completely, so you will want to adjust the column widths.

2 In the column headings row, point to the right edge of the **Address** field to display the [+] pointer, and then compare your screen with Figure 1.24.

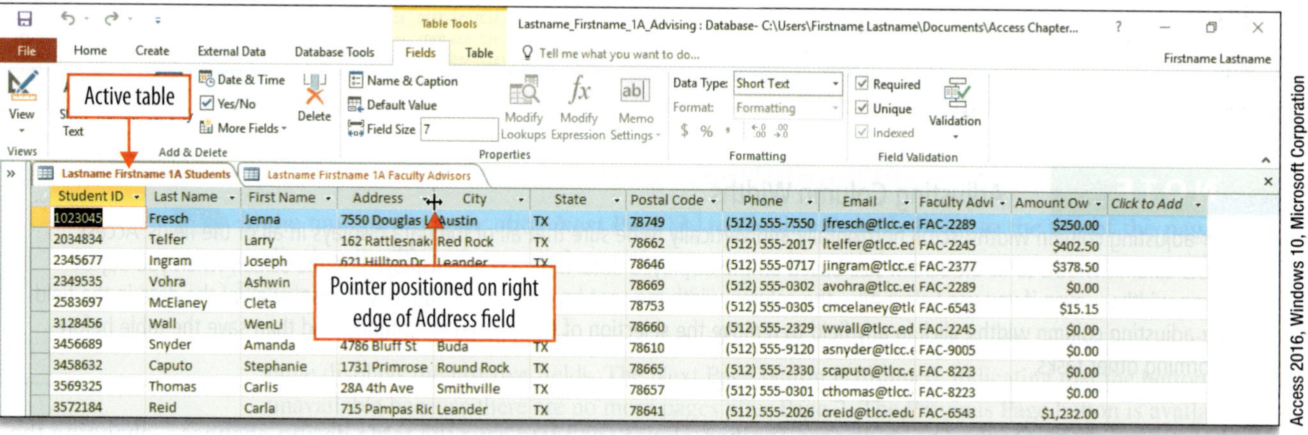

FIGURE 1.24

Access 2016, Windows 10, Microsoft Corporation

3 With the [+] pointer positioned as shown in Figure 1.24, double-click the right edge of the **Address** field.

The column width of the Address field widens to display the longest entry in the field fully. In this manner, the width of a column can be increased or decreased to fit its contents in the same manner as a column in an Excel spreadsheet. In Access, adjusting the column width to fit the contents is referred to as ***Best Fit***.

4 Point to the **City** field name to display the [↓] pointer, right-click to select the entire column and display the shortcut menu. Click **Field Width**, and then in the **Column Width** dialog box, click **Best Fit**.

This is a second way to adjust column widths.

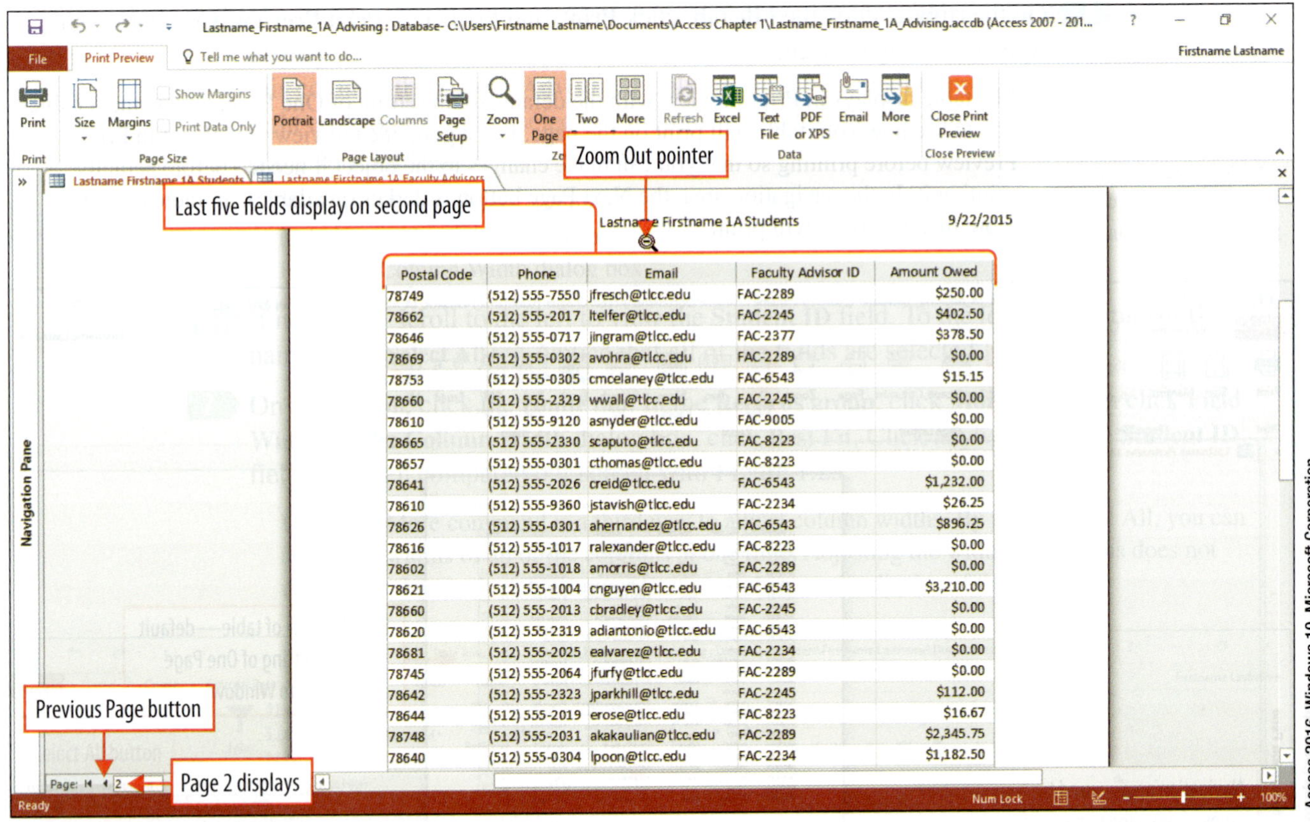

FIGURE 1.27

3 On the ribbon, on the **Print Preview tab**, in the **Zoom group**, click **Zoom** to change the zoom setting back to the default setting of One Page.

ANOTHER WAY With the [Zoom Out] pointer displayed on the page, click to zoom back to the One Page setting.

4 In the **Page Layout group**, click **Landscape**, and notice that there are only three fields on Page 2. In the navigation area, click **Previous Page** [◂] to display Page 1, and then compare your screen with Figure 1.28.

The orientation of the page to be printed changes. The header on the page includes the table name and current date, and the footer displays the page number. The change in orientation from portrait to landscape is not saved with the table. Each time you print, you must check the page orientation, the margins, and any other print parameters so that the object prints as you intend.

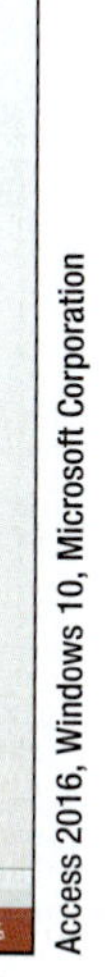

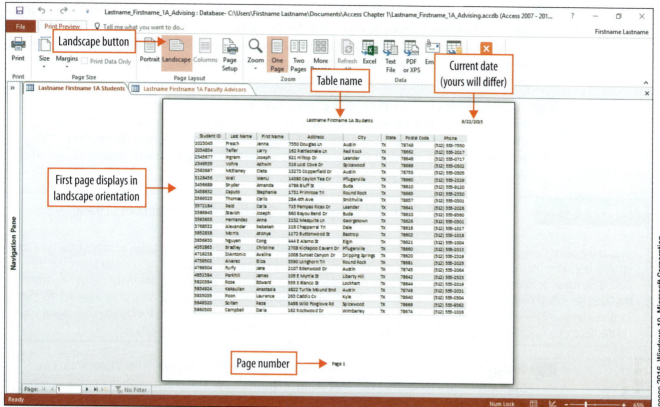

FIGURE 1.28

NOTE Headers and Footers in Access Objects

The headers and footers in Access tables and queries are controlled by default settings; you cannot enter additional information or edit the information. The object name displays in the center of the header area, and the current date displays on the right. Adding your name to the object name is helpful in identifying your paper printouts or electronic results. The page number displays in the center of the footer area. The headers and footers in Access forms and reports are more flexible; you can add to and edit the information.

5 On the **Print Preview tab**, in the **Print group**, click **Print**. In the **Print** dialog box, under **Print Range**, verify that **All** is selected. Under **Copies**, verify that the **Number of Copies** is **1**. Compare your screen with Figure 1.29.

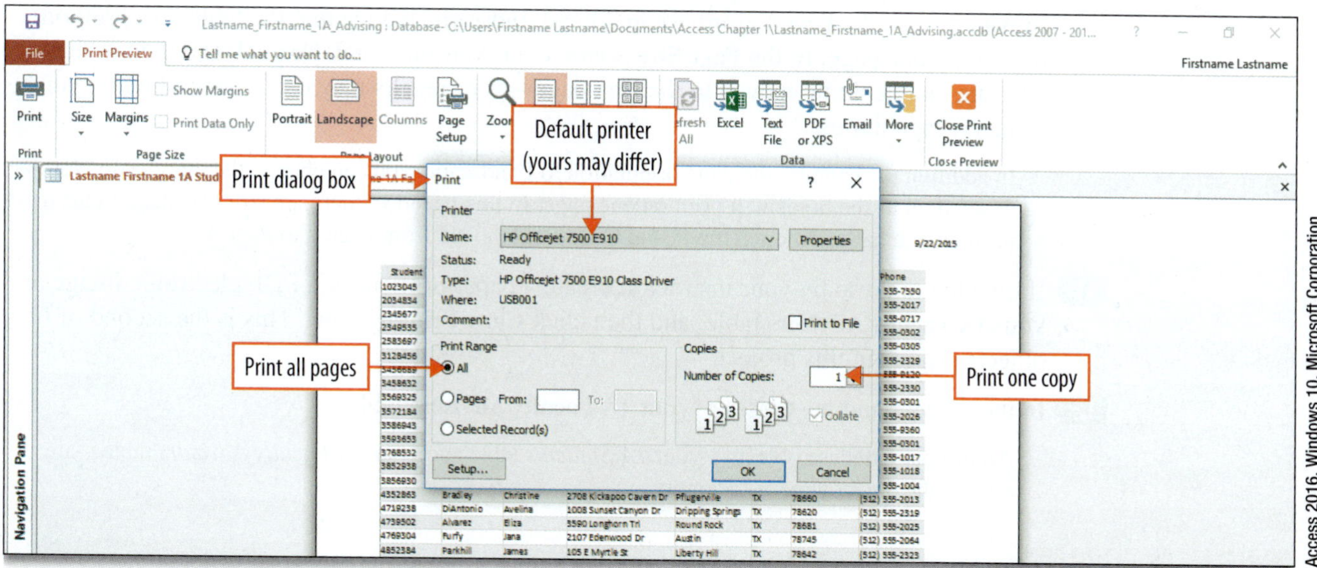

FIGURE 1.29

6 Determine if your instructor wants you to submit the individual database objects that you create within this Project, or if you will submit only your completed database file. Then, if you are creating and submitting the individual database objects—this is the first of five in this Project—determine if you are submitting the objects as a paper printout or as an electronic image that looks like a printed document.

7 To print on paper, in the **Print** dialog box, click **OK**, and then on the ribbon, in the **Close Preview group**, click **Close Print Preview**. If you are required to create and submit an electronic image of your document that looks like a printed document, in the Print dialog box, click Cancel, and then follow the steps in the following Note—or follow the specific directions provided by your instructor.

NOTE Creating a PDF Electronic Image of Your Database Object That Looks Like a Printed Document

Display the object (table, query, form, report, and so on) in Print Preview and adjust margins and orientation as needed. On the Print Preview tab, in the Data group, click PDF or XPS. In the Publish as PDF or XPS dialog box, navigate to your chapter folder. Use the default file name, or follow your instructor's directions to name the object. If you wish to view the PDF file, in the dialog box, select the Open file after publishing check box. In the Publish as PDF or XPS dialog box, click Publish. If necessary, close any windows that try to display your PDF—Adobe Reader, Adobe Acrobat, or the Microsoft Edge browser, and then close the Export – PDF dialog box. On the ribbon, click Close Print Preview; your electronic image is saved. Close the Save Export Steps dialog box.

8 In the upper right corner of the object window, click **Close Object** [X] to close your **1A Students** table. Notice that the **1A Faculty Advisors** table is the active object in the object window.

ANOTHER WAY In the object window, right-click the 1A Students object tab, and then click Close.

9 In your **1A Faculty Advisors** table, to the left of the **Faculty ID** field name, click **Select All** to select all of the columns. On the **Home tab**, in the **Records group**, click **More**, and then click **Field Width**. In the **Column Width** dialog box, click **Best Fit** to adjust the widths of all of the columns so that all of the data displays. Click in any field in the table to cancel the selection. Scroll horizontally and vertically to be sure that all of the data displays in each field; if necessary, use the techniques you practiced to apply Best Fit to individual columns. **Save** the changes you made to the table's column widths, and then click in any record to cancel the selection, if necessary

10 On the ribbon, click the **File tab**, click **Print**, and then click **Print Preview**. On the **Print Preview tab**, in the **Page Layout group**, click **Landscape**. Notice that the table will print on more than one page. In the **Page Size group**, click **Margins**, click **Normal**, and then notice that one more column moved to the first page—your results may differ depending on your printer's capabilities.

In addition to changing the page orientation to Landscape, you can change the margins to Normal to see if all of the fields will print on one page. In this instance, there are still too many fields to print on one page, although the Postal Code field moved from Page 2 to Page 1.

11 If directed to do so by your instructor, create a paper printout or a PDF electronic image of your **1A Faculty Advisors** table, and then click **Close Print Preview**. This is the second of five objects printed in this project.

12 In the object window, **Close** [X] your **1A Faculty Advisors** table.

All of your database objects—your *1A Students* table and your *1A Faculty Advisors* table—are closed; the object window is empty.

Objective 4 Create a Query, Form, and Report

GO! Learn How Video A1-4

Recall that tables are the foundation of an Access database because all of the data is stored in one or more tables. You can use the data stored in tables in other database objects such as queries, forms, and reports.

3.1.1

Activity 1.14 | Creating a Query by Using the Simple Query Wizard

A ***query*** is a database object that retrieves specific data from one or more database objects—either tables or other queries—and then, in a single datasheet, displays only the data that you specify when you design the query. Because the word *query* means *to ask a question*, think of a query as a question formed in a manner that Access can answer.

A ***select query*** is one type of Access query. A select query, also called a ***simple select query***, retrieves (selects) data from one or more tables or queries and then displays the selected data in a datasheet. A select query creates a subset of the data to answer specific questions; for example, *Which students live in Austin, TX?*

The objects from which a query selects the data are referred to as the query's ***data source***. In this Activity, you will create a simple query using a wizard that walks you step by step through the process. The process involves selecting the data source and indicating the fields that you want to include in the query results. The query—the question you want to ask—is *What is the name, email address, phone number, and Student ID of every student?*

1 On the ribbon, click the **Create tab**, and then in the **Queries group**, click **Query Wizard**. In the **New Query** dialog box, be sure **Simple Query Wizard** is selected, and then click **OK**. If a security message displays, click Open. Compare your screen with Figure 1.30.

In the wizard, the displayed table or query name is the object that was last selected on the Navigation Pane. The last object you worked with was your 1A Faculty Advisors table, so that object name displayed in the wizard.

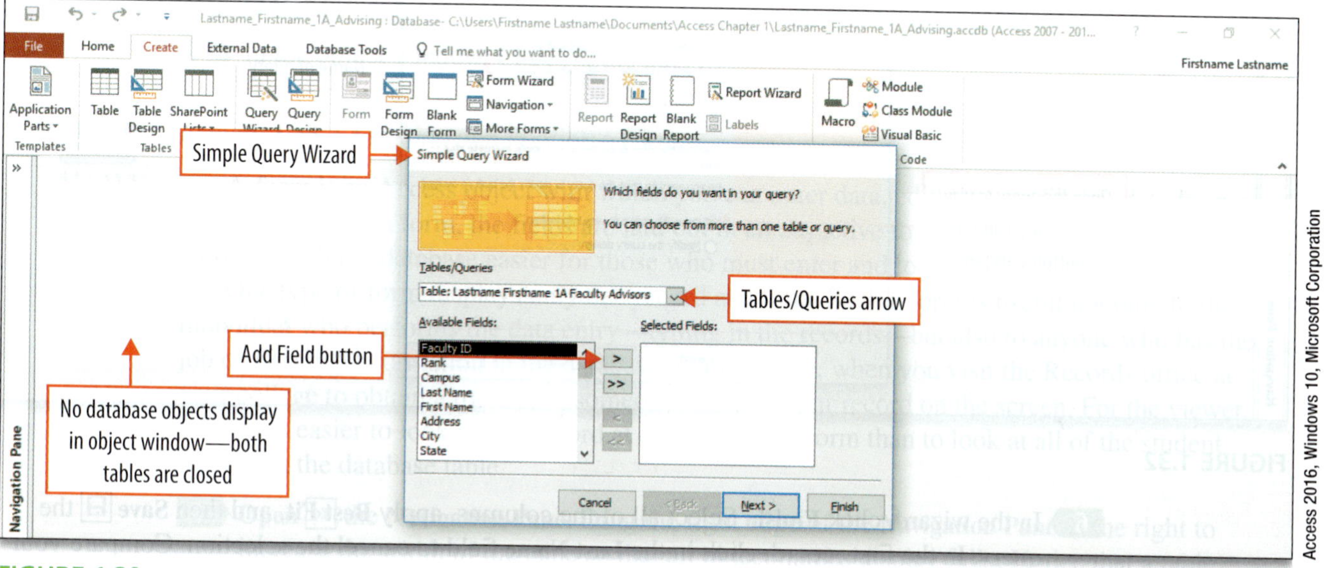

FIGURE 1.30

2 In the wizard, click the **Tables/Queries arrow**, and then click your **Table: Lastname Firstname 1A Students**.

To create a query, first select the data source—the object from which the query is to select the data. The information you need to answer the question is stored in your 1A Students table, so this table is your data source.

11 On the **File tab**, click **Print**, and then click **Print Preview**. On the **Print Preview tab**, in the **Zoom group**, click **Two Pages**, and then compare your screen with Figure 1.37.

As currently formatted, the report will print on two pages, because the page number at the bottom of the report is positioned beyond the right margin of the report.

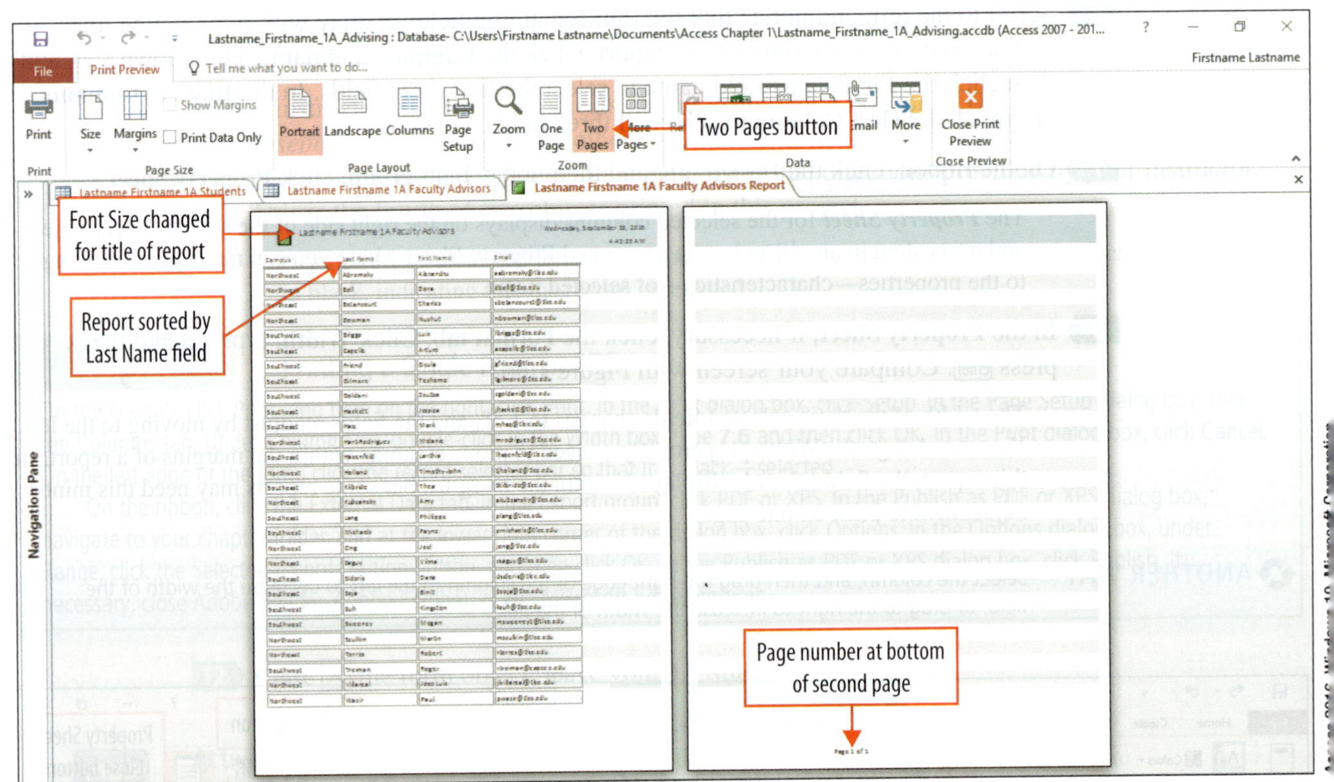

FIGURE 1.37

12 In the **Close Preview group**, click **Close Print Preview**. Scroll down to display the bottom of the report, and then, if necessary, scroll right to display the page number. Click the page number—**Page 1 of 1**—and then press Del.

Because all of the data will print on one page, the page number is not necessary for this report. If you want the page number to display, you can drag it within the margins of the report.

13 Display the report in **Print Preview**, and notice that the report will now print on one page. In the **Zoom group**, click **One Page**. Click **Save** to save the changes to the design of the report, and then create a paper printout or PDF electronic image as directed. Click **Close Print Preview**. This is the fifth or last object printed in this project.

When you create a report by using the Report tool, the default margins are 0.25 inch. Some printers require a greater margin, so your printed report may result in two pages. As you progress in your study of Access, you will practice making these adjustments. Also, if a printer is not installed on your system, the electronic PDF printout might result in a two-page report.

14 In the object window, right-click any **object tab**, and then click **Close All** to close all of the open objects. Notice that the object window is empty.

Objective 5 Close a Database and Close Access

GO! Learn How
Video A1-5

When you close a table, any changes made to the records are saved automatically. If you made changes to the structure or adjusted column widths, you will be prompted to save the table when you close the table or when you switch views. Likewise, you will be prompted to save queries, forms, and reports if you make changes to the layout or design. If the Navigation Pane is open when you close Access, it will display when you reopen the database. When you are finished using your database, close the database, and then close Access.

Activity 1.17 | Closing a Database and Closing Access

1 **Open** [»] the **Navigation Pane**. If necessary, increase the width of the Navigation Pane so that all object names display fully. Notice that your report object displays with a green report icon. Compare your screen with Figure 1.38.

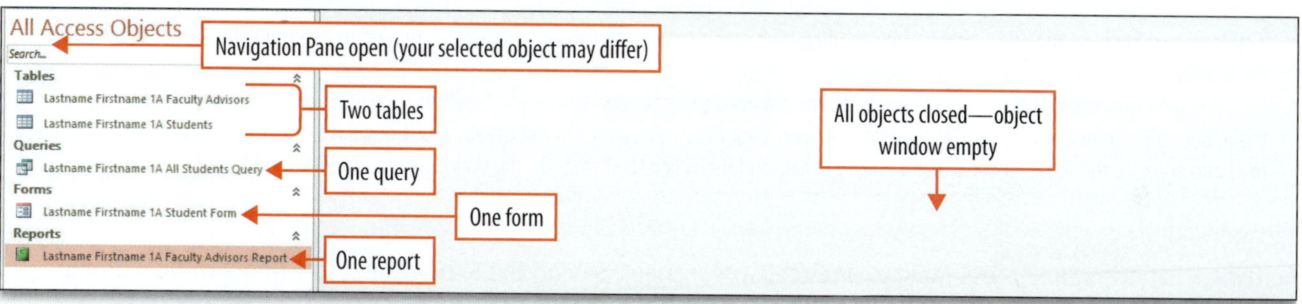

FIGURE 1.38

Access 2016, Windows 10, Microsoft Corporation

2 On the **File tab**, click **Close** to close the database but leave Access open. This action enables you to continue working in Access with another database if you want to do so. In the Access application window, in the upper right corner, click **Close** [X] to close Access. As directed by your instructor, submit your database and the paper printouts or PDF electronic images of the five objects—two tables, one query, one form, and one report—that are the results of this project.

END | You have completed Project 1A

GO! With Google

Objective Export an Access Table to an Excel Spreadsheet, Open as a Google Sheet, Edit a Record, and Save to Your Computer

Access web apps are designed to work with Microsoft's ***SharePoint***, a service for setting up websites to share and manage documents. Your college may not have SharePoint installed, so you will use other tools to share objects from your database so that you can work collaboratively with others. Recall that Google Drive is Google's free, web-based word processor, spreadsheet, slide show, form, and data storage and sharing service. For Access, you can ***export*** a database object to an Excel worksheet, a PDF file, or a text file, and then save the file to Google Drive.

ALERT! **Working with Web-Based Applications and Services**

Computer programs and services on the web receive continuous updates and improvements. Therefore, the steps to complete this web-based Activity may differ from the ones shown. You can often look at the screens and the information presented to determine how to complete the activity.

If you do not already have a Google account, you will need to create one before you begin this activity. Go to http://google.com and, in the upper right corner, click Sign In. On the Sign In screen, click Create Account. On the Create your Google Account page, complete the form, read and agree to the Terms of Service and Privacy Policy, and then click Next step. On the Welcome screen, click Get Started.

Activity | Exporting an Access Table to an Excel Spreadsheet, Saving the Spreadsheet to Google Drive, Editing a Record in Google Drive, and Saving to Your Computer

In this Activity, you will export your 1A Faculty Advisors table to an Excel spreadsheet, upload your Excel file to Google Drive as a Google Sheet, edit a record in the Google Sheet, and then download a copy of the edited spreadsheet to your computer.

1 Start Access, navigate to your **Access Chapter 1** folder, and then **Open** your **1A_Advising** database file. If necessary, on the Message Bar, click **Enable Content**. In the **Navigation Pane**, click your **1A Faculty Advisors** table to select it—do not open it.

2 On the ribbon, click the **External Data tab**, and then in the **Export group**, click **Excel**. In the **Export – Excel Spreadsheet** dialog box, click **Browse**, and then navigate to your **Access Chapter 1** folder. In the **File Save** dialog box, click in the **File name** box, type **Lastname_ Firstname_a1A_Web** and then click **Save**.

3 In the **Export – Excel Spreadsheet** dialog box, under **Specify export options**, select the first two check boxes—**Export data with formatting and layout** and **Open the destination file after the export operation is complete**—and then click **OK**. Take a moment to examine the data in the file, and then **Close** Excel. In the **Export – Excel Spreadsheet** dialog box, click **Close**, and then **Close** Access. **Close** Excel.

4 Open your browser software, navigate to **http:// drive.google.com**, and sign in to your Google account. On the right side of the screen, click **Settings**, and then click **Settings**. In the **Settings** dialog box, to the right of *Convert uploads*, if necessary, select the **Convert uploaded files to Google Docs editor format** check box. In the upper right, click **Done**.

It is necessary to select this setting; otherwise, your document will upload as a pdf file and cannot be edited without further action.

5 Open your **GO! Web Projects** folder—or create and then open this folder by clicking **NEW** and then **Folder**. On the left, click **NEW**, and then click **File upload**. In the **Open** dialog box, navigate to your **Access Chapter 1** folder, and then double-click your **a1A_Web** Excel file to upload it to Google Drive. When the message *Uploads completed* displays, **Close** the message box.

6 Double-click your **Lastname_Firstname_a1A_Web** file to display the file, and then compare your screen with Figure A.

The worksheet displays column letters, row numbers, and data.

(GO! With Google continues on the next page)

GO! With Google

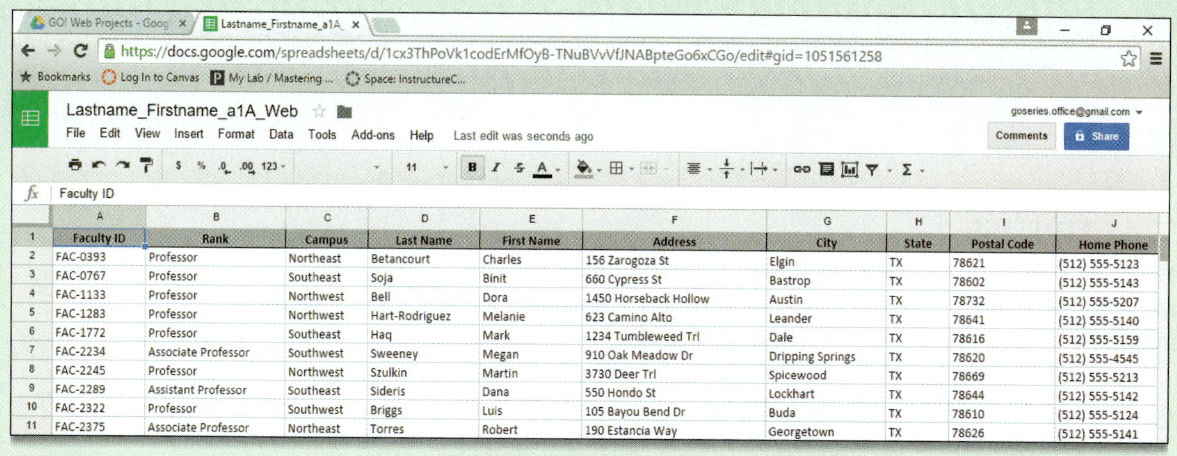

	A	B	C	D	E	F	G	H	I	J
1	Faculty ID	Rank	Campus	Last Name	First Name	Address	City	State	Postal Code	Home Phone
2	FAC-0393	Professor	Northeast	Betancourt	Charles	156 Zarogoza St	Elgin	TX	78621	(512) 555-5123
3	FAC-0767	Professor	Southeast	Soja	Binit	660 Cypress St	Bastrop	TX	78602	(512) 555-5143
4	FAC-1133	Professor	Northwest	Bell	Dora	1450 Horseback Hollow	Austin	TX	78732	(512) 555-5207
5	FAC-1283	Professor	Northwest	Hart-Rodriguez	Melanie	623 Camino Alto	Leander	TX	78641	(512) 555-5140
6	FAC-1772	Professor	Southeast	Haq	Mark	1234 Tumbleweed Trl	Dale	TX	78616	(512) 555-5159
7	FAC-2234	Associate Professor	Southwest	Sweeney	Megan	910 Oak Meadow Dr	Dripping Springs	TX	78620	(512) 555-4545
8	FAC-2245	Professor	Northwest	Szulkin	Martin	3730 Deer Trl	Spicewood	TX	78669	(512) 555-5213
9	FAC-2289	Assistant Professor	Southeast	Sideris	Dana	550 Hondo St	Lockhart	TX	78644	(512) 555-5142
10	FAC-2322	Professor	Southwest	Briggs	Luis	105 Bayou Bend Dr	Buda	TX	78610	(512) 555-5124
11	FAC-2375	Associate Professor	Northeast	Torres	Robert	190 Estancia Way	Georgetown	TX	78626	(512) 555-5141

FIGURE A

7 Click in cell **C2**, and replace the current Campus with **Southwest** Click in cell **D2** and replace Betancourt with your last name. Press Tab and then replace Charles with your first name.

8 Above row **1** and to the left of column **A**, click **Select All** [button]. On the menu bar, click **Format**, and then click **Clear formatting** so that the font is the same for all data; the cell borders are removed, and the formatting of the field names is removed.

9 In the column headings row, click **I** to select the entire column. On the menu bar, click **Format**, point to **Number**, and then click **Plain text** to format every number in the columns as text. Click in cell **A1** to deselect the column.

Recall that in Access, numbers that are not used in calculations should be formatted as Short Text. Because the formatting is cleared, you can enter new records into the spreadsheet in the same format as the existing records.

10 Click **File** to display the menu, point to **Download as**, and then click **Microsoft Excel (.xlsx)**. In the message box—usually displayed at the bottom of your screen—click the **Save arrow**, and then click **Save as**. In the **Save As** dialog box, navigate to your **Access Chapter 1** folder, click in the **File name** box, and type **Lastname_Firstname_a1A_Web_Download** and then click **Save**. **Close** the message box.

NOTE Saving the Downloaded File to the Access Chapter 1 Folder

Depending on the browser you are using, you may need to open the file in Excel and then save the a1A_Web_Download worksheet to your Access Chapter 1 folder.

11 In Google Drive, at the upper right corner of your screen, click your user name, and then click **Sign out**. **Close** your browser window.

12 Start Excel. In the Excel opening screen, click **Open Other Workbooks**, and then click **Browse**. Navigate to your **Access Chapter 1** folder, and then double-click your **a1A_Web** Excel file. Notice that this file is the original file—the new record is not entered. If you are required to print your documents, use one of the methods in the following Note. **Close** your Excel file; and, if prompted, save the changes to your worksheet. Then **Open** and print your a **1A_Web_Download** Excel file using one of the methods in the following Note. **Close** Excel; and, if prompted, save the changes to your worksheet. As directed by your instructor, submit your two workbooks and the two paper printouts or PDF electronic images that are the results of this project.

NOTE Adding the File Name to the Footer and Printing or Creating a PDF Electronic Image of an Excel Spreadsheet on One Page

Click the File tab, click Print, and then click Page Setup. In the Page Setup dialog box, on the Page tab, under Orientation, click Landscape. Under Scaling, click the Fit to option button. In the Page Setup dialog box, click the Header/Footer tab, and then click Custom Footer. With the insertion point blinking in the Left section box, click the Insert File Name button, and then click OK. In the Page Setup dialog box, click OK.

To print on paper, click Print. To create a PDF electronic image, on the left side of your screen, click Export. Under Export, be sure Create PDF/XPS Document is selected, and then click Create PDF/XPS. Navigate to your Access Chapter 1 folder, and then click Publish to save the file with the default name and an extension of pdf.

PROJECT 1B

Student Workshops Database

PROJECT ACTIVITIES

In Activities 1.18 through 1.25, you will assist Dr. Miriam Yong, Director of Student Activities, in creating a database to store information about student workshops held at Texas Lakes Community College campuses. You will use a database template that tracks event information, add workshop information to the database, and then print the results. Your completed report and table will look similar to Figure 1.39.

PROJECT FILES

If your instructor wants you to submit Project 1B in the MyITLab Grader system, log in to MyITLab, locate Grader Project1B, and then download the files for this project.

For Project 1B, you will need the following files:
Desktop event management template
a01B_Workshops (Excel workbook)

You will save your database as:
Lastname_Firstname_1B_Student_Workshops

PROJECT RESULTS

Build From Scratch

GO! Walk Thru Project 1B

Lastname Firstname 1B All Events — Tuesday, July 28, 2015 11:41:10 AM

Title	Start Time	End Time	Location
Your Online Reputation	3/9/2021 7:00:00 PM	3/9/2021 9:00:00 PM	Northeast Campus
Internet Safety			
Writing a Research Paper	3/10/2021 4:00:00 PM	3/10/2021 6:00:00 PM	Southwest Campus
Computer Skills			
Resume Writing	3/18/2021 2:00:00 PM	3/18/2021 4:00:00 PM	Northwest Campus
Job Skills			
Careers in the Legal Profession	3/19/2021 2:00:00 PM	3/19/2021 4:00:00 PM	Southeast Campus
Careers			
Transferring to a 4-Year University	4/8/2021 11:00:00 AM	4/8/2021 12:30:00 PM	Northeast Campus
Transfer			
Financial Aid	4/14/2021 7:00:00 PM	4/14/2021 8:30:00 PM	Southeast Campus
CC Info			
Sensitivity Training	4/15/2021 8:00:00 AM	4/15/2021 9:00:00 AM	Northwest Campus
Human Behavior			
Preparing for the Job Interview	4/15/2021 12:30:00 PM	4/15/2021 2:00:00 PM	Northwest Campus
Job Skills			
Class Note Taking	4/18/2021 12:30:00 PM	4/18/2021 1:30:00 PM	Southeast Campus
Study Skills			
Managing Time and Stress	4/18/2021 6:00:00 PM	4/18/2021 7:30:00 PM	Southwest Campus
Study Skills			
Work Smart at Your Computer	4/20/2021 10:00:00 AM	4/20/2021 11:00:00 AM	Northeast Campus
Computer Skills			
Preparing for Tests	4/20/2021 4:00:00 PM	4/20/2021 5:00:00 PM	Southeast Campus
Study Skills			

Page 1 of 1

Lastname Firstname 1B Workshop Locations — 5/30/2015

Room ID	Campus/Location	Room	Seats	Room Arrangement	Equipment
NE-01	Northeast Campus	H265	150	Theater	Computer Projector, Surround Sound, Microphone
NE-02	Northeast Campus	B105	25	U-shaped	25 Computers, Projector
NW-01	Northwest Campus	C202	50	Lecture Classroom	Smart Board
SE-01	Southeast Campus	D148	20	U-shaped	White Board
SW-01	Southwest Campus	A15	35	Lecture Classroom	Computer Projector

Page 1

FIGURE 1.39 Project 1B Student Workshops

PROJECT RESULTS

In this project, using your own name, you will create the following database and objects. Your instructor may ask for printouts or PDF electronic images:

Lastname_Firstname_1B_Student Workshops	Database file
Lastname Firstname 1B All Events	Report
Lastname Firstname 1B Workshop Locations	Table

Objective 6 Use a Template to Create a Database

GO! Learn How Video A1-6

A *database template* contains prebuilt tables, queries, forms, and reports that perform a specific task, such as tracking events. For example, your college may hold events such as athletic contests, plays, lectures, concerts, and club meetings. Using a predefined template, your college's Activities Director can quickly create a database to manage these events. The advantage of using a template to start a new database is that you do not have to create the objects—all you need to do is enter the data and modify the prebuilt objects to suit your needs.

The purpose of the database in this project is to track the student workshops that are held by Texas Lakes Community College. The questions to be answered might include:

- What workshops will be offered, and when will they be offered?
- In what rooms and on what campuses will the workshops be held?
- Which workshop locations have a computer projector for PowerPoint presentations?

1.1.2

Activity 1.18 | Using a Template to Create a Database

ALERT!

To submit as an autograded project, log into MyITLab and download the files for this project, and begin with those files instead of the Desktop event managment template database. For Project 1B using Grader, read Activity 1.18 carefully. Begin working with the database in Activity 1.19. For Grader to award points accurately, when saving an object, do not include your Lastname Firstname at the beginning of the object name.

There are two types of database templates—those that will be stored on your desktop and those that are designed to share with others over the Internet. In this Activity, you will use a desktop template to create your database.

1 Start Access. In the Access opening screen, scroll down to display a **Desktop vehicle maintenance** template and an **Asset tracking** template. Compare your screen with Figure 1.40.

These templates are included with the Access program. To store a database to manage vehicle maintenance on your desktop, select the *Desktop Vehicle maintenance* template. To publish a database to track assets and share it with others, select the *Asset tracking* template—the one that displays a globe image. The names of templates designed to create databases stored on your computer start with the word *Desktop*.

You can search the Microsoft Office website for more templates. You can also click a category under the search box, where templates will be suggested.

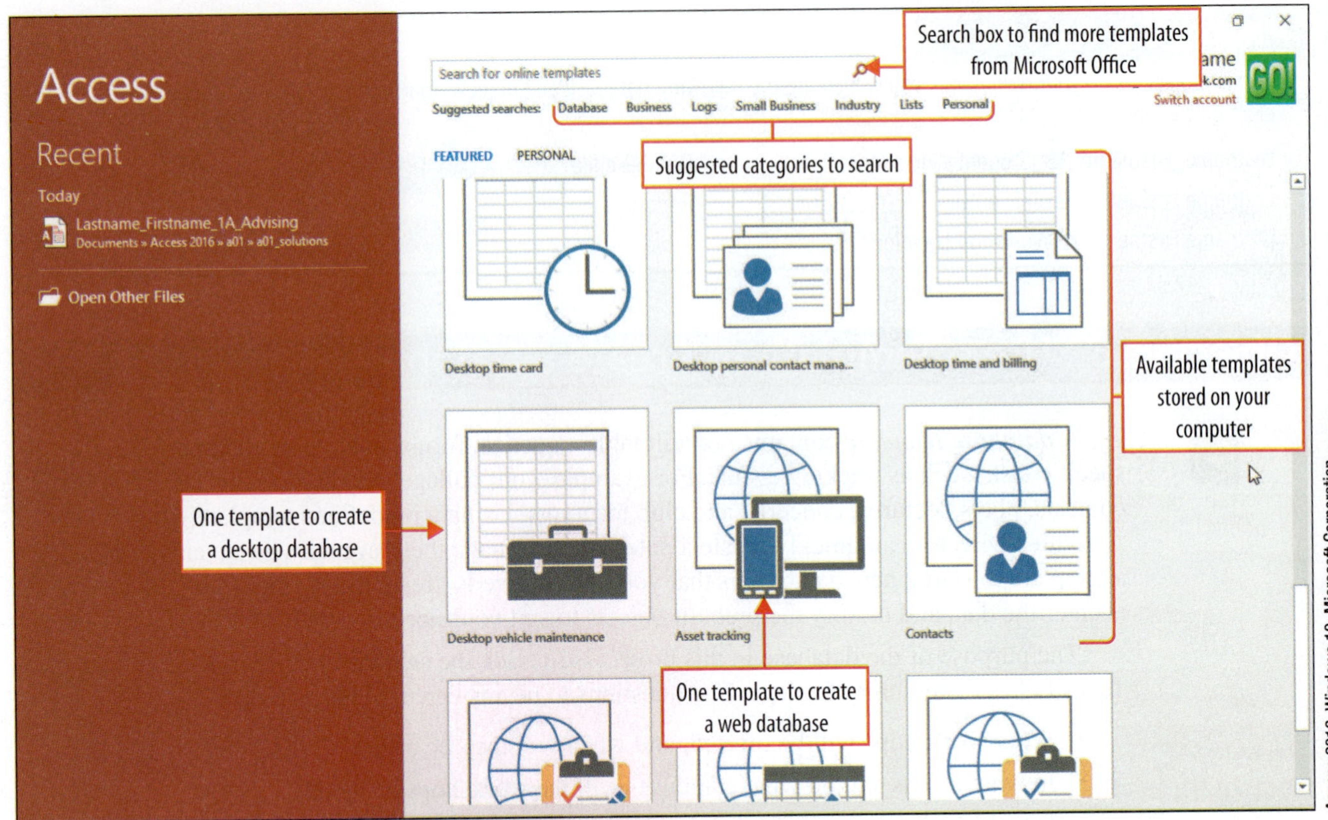

FIGURE 1.40

2 At the top of the window, click in the **Search for online templates** box, type **event** and then press Enter. Compare your screen with Figure 1.41.

You must have an Internet connection to search for online templates. Access displays several templates, including the event management template.

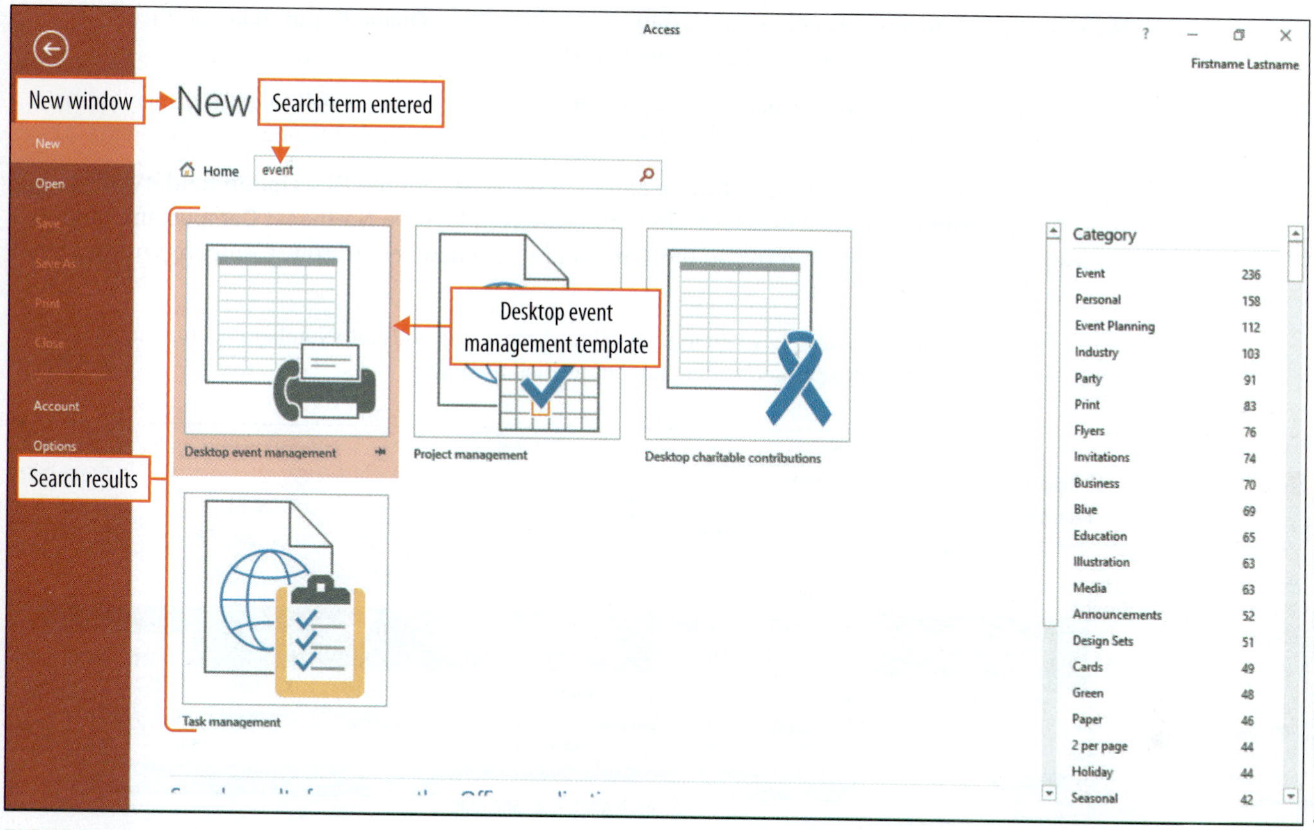

FIGURE 1.41

Access 2016, Windows 10, Microsoft Corporation

3 Click the **Desktop event management** template, and notice the description of the template. In the dialog box, to the right of the **File Name** box, click **Browse**, and then navigate to your **Access Chapter 1** folder.

4 In the **File New Database** dialog box, click in the **File name** box to select the existing text. Using your own name, type **Lastname_Firstname_1B_Student_Workshops** and then press Enter.

5 In the **Desktop event management** dialog box, click **Create** to download the template and to save the database. If a welcome message box displays, click Get Started.

Access creates the *1B_Student_Workshops* database, and the database name displays in the title bar. A predesigned *form*—Event List—displays in the object window. Although you can enter events for any date, when you open the database in the future, the Event List form will display only those events for the current date and future dates.

6 Under the ribbon, on the **Message Bar**, a *SECURITY WARNING* may display. If it is, on the **Message Bar**, click **Enable Content**.

Databases provided by Microsoft are safe to use on your computer.

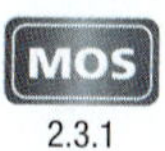

MOS
2.3.1

Activity 1.19 | Building a Table by Entering Records in a Multiple-Items Form and a Single-Record Form

One purpose of a form is to simplify the entry of data into a table—either for you or for others who enter data. In Project 1A, you created a simple form that enabled you to display or enter records in a table one record at a time. The Desktop Event management template creates a ***multiple-items form*** that enables you to display or enter *multiple* records in a table, but with an easier and simplified layout rather than typing directly into the table itself.

1 In the new record row, click in the **Title** field. Type **Your Online Reputation** and then press Tab. In the **Start Time** field, type **3/9/21 7p** and then press Tab.

Access formats the date and time. As you enter dates and times, a small calendar displays to the right of the field. You can use the calendar to select a date instead of typing it.

2 In the **End Time** field, type **3/9/21 9p** and then press Tab. In the **Description** field, type **Internet Safety** and then press Tab. In the **Location** field, type **Northeast Campus** and then press Tab three times to move to the **Title** field in the new record row. Compare your screen with Figure 1.42.

Because the workshops have no unique value, Access uses the AutoNumber data type in the ID field to assign a unique, sequential number to each record.

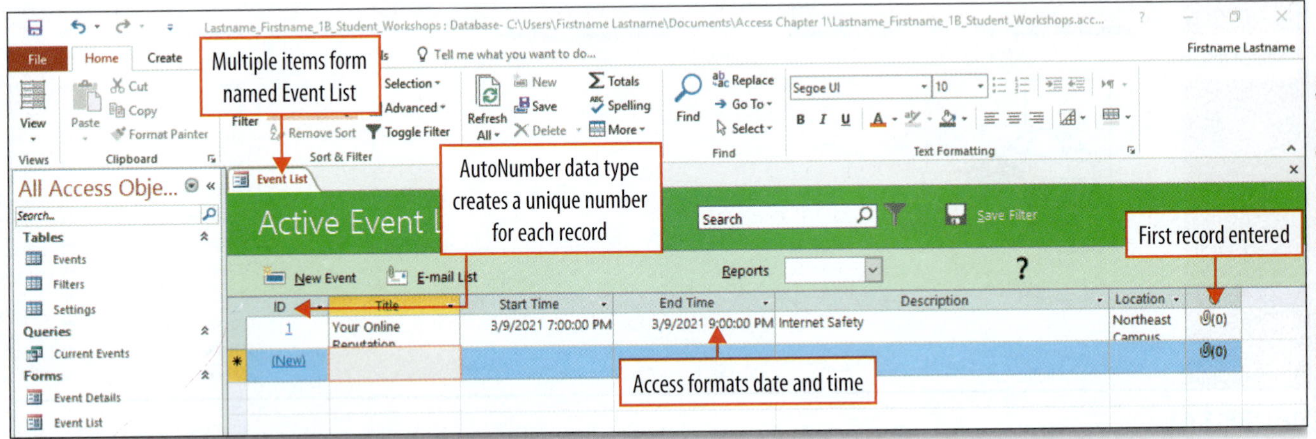

FIGURE 1.42

3 In the form, directly above the field names row, click **New Event**.

A ***single-record form*** with the name *Event Details* displays, similar to the simple form you created in Project 1A. A single-record form enables you to display or enter one record at a time into a table.

4 Using Tab to move from field to field, enter the following record in the **Event Details** form—after entering the **End Time**, click in the **Description** field. Then compare your screen with Figure 1.43.

Title	Location	Start Time	End Time	Description
Writing a Research Paper	**Southwest Campus**	**3/10/21 4p**	**3/10/21 6p**	**Computer Skills**

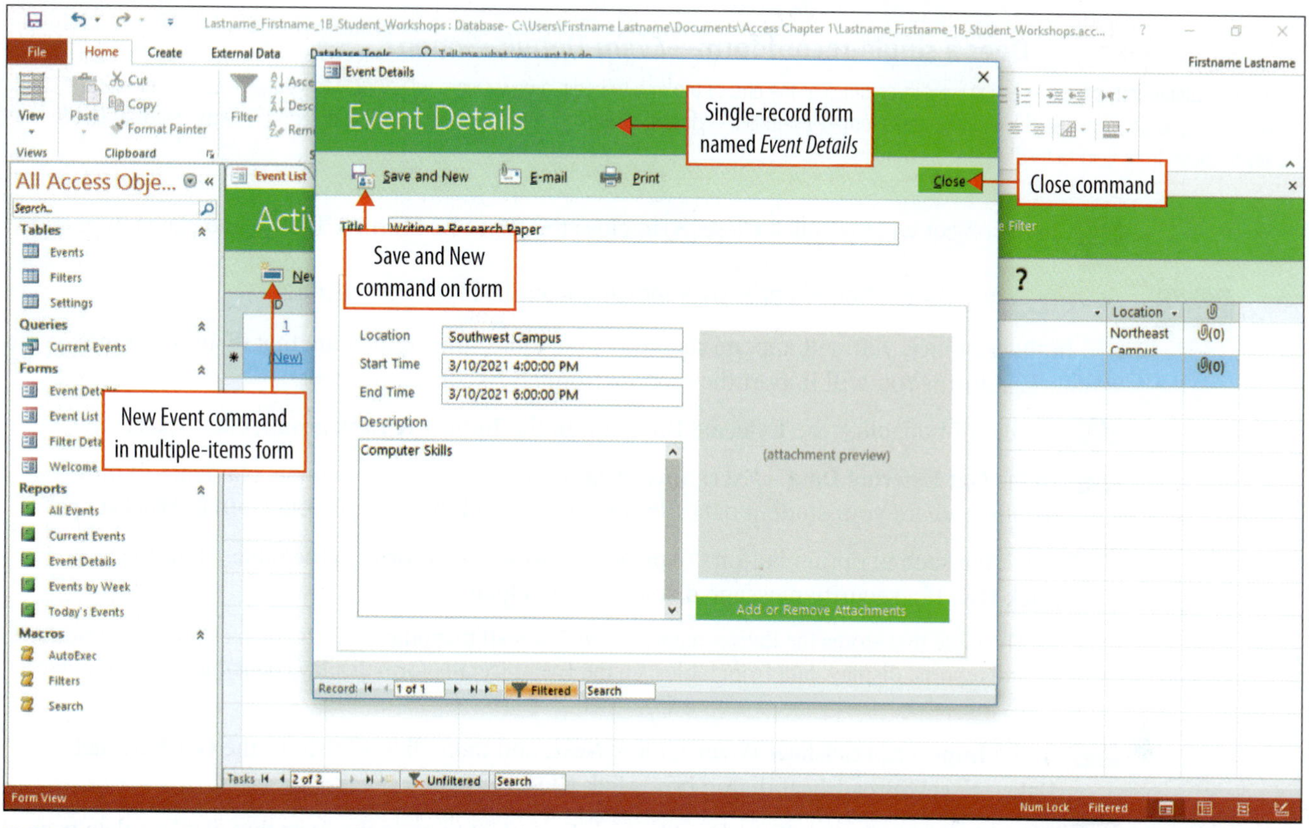

FIGURE 1.43

Access 2016, Windows 10, Microsoft Corporation

5 In the **Event Details** single-record form, in the upper right corner, click **Close**, and notice that the new record displays in the multiple-items form—*Event List*.

6 Enter the following records by using either the **Event List** form—the multiple-items form—or the **Event Details** form—the single-record form that is accessed by clicking the *New Event* command on the Event List form. Be sure the multiple-items form displays, and then compare your screen with Figure 1.44.

ID	Title	Start Time	End Time	Description	Location
3	**Resume Writing**	**3/18/21 2p**	**3/18/21 4p**	**Job Skills**	**Northwest Campus**
4	**Careers in the Legal Profession**	**3/19/21 2p**	**3/19/21 4p**	**Careers**	**Southeast Campus**

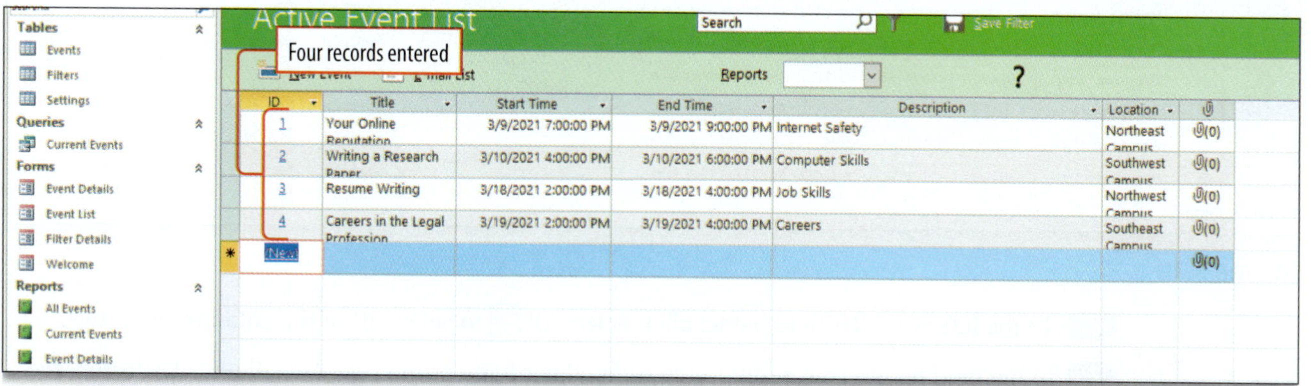

FIGURE 1.44

Access 2016, Windows 10, Microsoft Corporation

ALERT! **Does a single-record form—*Event Details*—open?**

In the multiple-items form, pressing Enter three times at the end of the row to begin a new record will display the single-record form—*Event Details*. If you prefer to use the multiple-items form—Event List—close the single-record form and continue entering records, using the Tab key to move from field to field.

7 In the object window, click **Close** [X] to close the **Event List** form. Close [«] the Navigation Pane.

2.3.4

Activity 1.20 | Appending Records by Importing from an Excel Spreadsheet

In this Activity, you will append records to the table storing the data that displays in the Events List form. You will import the records from an Excel spreadsheet.

1 On the ribbon, click the **External Data tab**. In the **Import & Link group**, click **Excel**.

2 In the **Get External Data – Excel Spreadsheet** dialog box, click **Browse**. Navigate to the location where your student data files are stored, and then double-click **a01B_Workshops**.

3 Click the second option button—**Append a copy of the records to the table**—and then click **OK**. If a security message displays, click Open.

The table that stores the data is named *Events*. Recall that other objects, such as forms, queries, and reports, display data from tables; so the Event Details form displays data that is stored in the Events table.

4 In the **Import Spreadsheet Wizard**, click **Next**, and then click **Finish**. In the **Get External Data – Excel Spreadsheet** dialog box, click **Close**.

5 **Open** [»] the **Navigation Pane**. Double-click **Event List** to open the form that displays data from the Events table, and then **Close** [«] the **Navigation Pane**. Compare your screen with Figure 1.45.

A total of 12 records display; you entered four records, and you appended eight records from the a01B_Workshops Excel workbook. The data displays truncated in several fields because the columns are not wide enough to display all of the data.

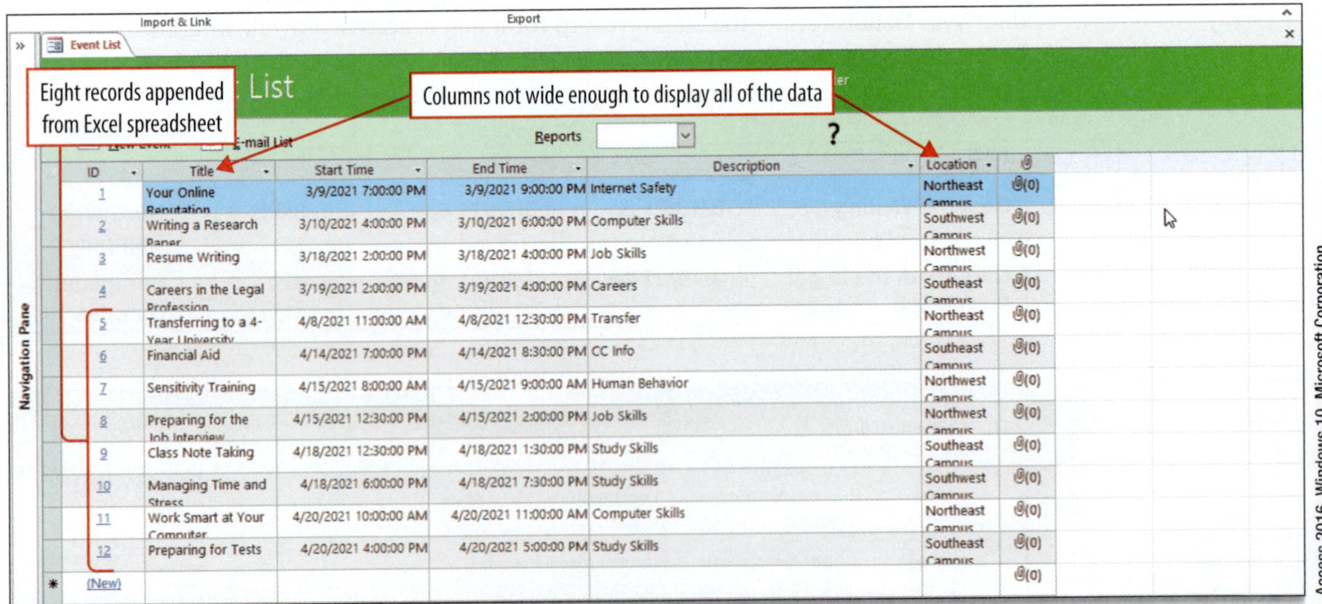

FIGURE 1.45

6 To the left of the **ID** field name, click **Select All** [ ] to select all of the columns and rows.

7 In the field names row, point to the right edge of any of the selected columns to display the [+] pointer, and then double-click to apply Best Fit to all of the columns. Click in any field to cancel the selection, and then **Save** [ ] the form.

Objective 7 Organize Objects in the Navigation Pane

GO! Learn How
Video A1-7

Use the Navigation Pane to open objects, organize database objects, and perform common tasks, such as renaming an object or deleting an object.

1.3.4

Activity 1.21 | Grouping Database Objects in the Navigation Pane

The Navigation Pane groups and displays your database objects and can do so in predefined arrangements. In this Activity, you will group your database objects using the ***Tables and Related Views*** category, which groups objects by the table to which the objects are related. This grouping is useful because you can determine easily the table that is the data source of queries, forms, and reports.

1 **Open** [»] the **Navigation Pane**. At the top of the **Navigation Pane**, click **All Access Objects** arrow [▾]. On the list, under **Navigate To Category**, click **Tables and Related Views**. Compare your screen with Figure 1.46.

In the Navigation Pane, you can see the number of objects that are included in the Desktop Events Management template, including the table named *Events*. Other objects in the database that display data from the Events table include one query, two forms, and five reports. In the Navigation Pane, the Event List form is selected because it is open in the object window and is the active object.

Other objects might display on the Navigation Pane; for example, Filters and Unrelated Objects. These filters are objects created for use by the Desktop Event management template.

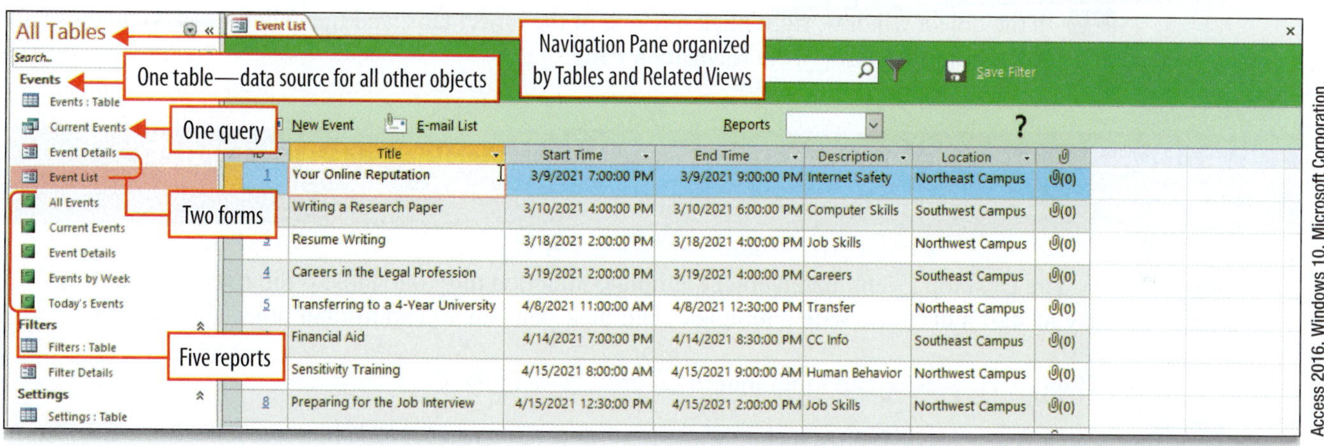

FIGURE 1.46

2 In the **Navigation Pane**, point to **Events: Table**, right-click, and then click **Open** to display the records in the underlying table.

The Events table is the active object in the object window. Use the Navigation Pane to open objects for use. The 12 records that display in the Event List multiple-items form are stored in this table. Recall that tables are the foundation of your database because your data must be stored in a table. You can enter records directly into a table or you can use a form to enter records.

ANOTHER WAY Double-click the table name to open it in the object window.

3 In the object window, click the **Event List tab** to display the form as the active object in the object window.

Recall that a form presents a more user-friendly screen for entering records into a table.

4 In the **Navigation Pane**, double-click the **Current Events** *report* (green icon) to open the report. Compare your screen with Figure 1.47.

An advantage of using a template to create a database is that many objects, such as reports, are already designed for you.

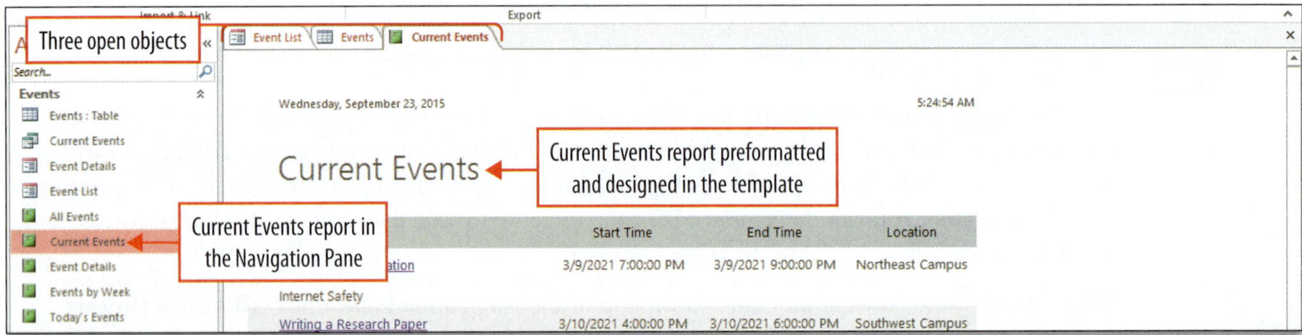

Access 2016, Windows 10, Microsoft Corporation

FIGURE 1.47

5 In the object window, **Close** [X] the **Current Events** report.

6 By double-clicking or right-clicking, from the **Navigation Pane**, open the **Events by Week** report.

In this predesigned report, the events are displayed by week. After entering records in the form or table, the preformatted reports are updated with the records from the table.

7 In the object window, right-click any one of the **object tabs**, and then click **Close All** to close all of the objects. **Close** [«] the **Navigation Pane**.

Objective 8 Create a New Table in a Database Created with a Template

GO! Learn How Video A1-8

The Desktop Event management template included only one table—the *Events* table. It is easy to start a database with a template, and then you can add additional objects as needed.

Activity 1.22 | Using the Table Tool to Create a New Table

2.1.1, 2.1.5

Dr. Yong has information about the various locations where workshops are held. For example, on the Northeast Campus, she has information about the room, seating arrangements, number of seats, and multimedia equipment. In the Events table, workshops are scheduled in rooms at each of the four campuses. It would not make sense to store information about the campus rooms multiple times in the same table. It is *not* considered good database design to have duplicate information in a table.

When data becomes redundant, it is usually an indication that you need a new table to contain that information. In this Activity, you will create a table to track the workshop locations, the equipment, and the seating arrangements in each location.

1 On the ribbon, click the **Create tab**, and then in the **Tables group**, click **Table**.

2 In the field names row, click **Click to Add**, click **Short Text**, type **Campus/Location** and then press [Enter].

3 In the third column, click **Short Text**, type **Room** and then press [Enter]. In the fourth column, click **Number**, type **Seats** and then press [Enter].

The ***Number data type*** describes numbers that represent a quantity and may be used in calculations. For the Seats field, you may need to determine how many seats remain after reservations are booked for a room. In the new record row, a *0* displays in the field.

4 In the fifth column, type **t** to select *Short Text*, type **Room Arrangement** and then press Enter. In the sixth column, type **t** and then type **Equipment** On your keyboard, press ↓.

With the data type list displayed, you can select the data type by either clicking it or typing the letter that is underscored for the data type.

This table has six fields. Access automatically creates the first field in the table—the ID field—to ensure that every record has a unique value. Before naming each field, you must define the data type for the field.

5 Right-click the **ID** field name, and then click **Rename Field**. Type **Room ID** and then press Enter. On the **Fields tab**, in the **Formatting group**, click the **Data Type arrow**, and then click **Short Text**. On the ribbon, in the **Field Validation group**, notice that **Unique** is selected.

Recall that, by default, Access creates the ID field with the AutoNumber data type so that the field can be used as the primary key. Here, this field will store a unique room ID that is a combination of letters, symbols, and numbers; therefore, it is appropriate to change the data type to Short Text. In Datasheet view, the primary key field is identified by the selection of the Unique check box.

More Knowledge **Create a Table from a Template with Application Parts**

To create a table using the Application Parts gallery, click the Create tab, and in the Templates group click Application Parts. Under Quick Start, click Comments. In the Create Relationship dialog box, specify a relationship between the Comments table and an associated table, and click Next to choose the lookup column, and then click Create to create the table. If you choose No relationship, click Create to create the table. The Comments table displays in the Navigation Pane.

2.3.2

Activity 1.23 | Entering Records Into a New Table

1 In the new record row, click in the **Room ID** field. Enter the following record, pressing Enter or Tab to move from one field to the next. Do not be concerned that all of your text does not display; you will adjust the column widths later. After entering the record, compare your screen with Figure 1.48.

Recall that Access saves a record when you move to another row within the table. You can press either Enter or Tab to move between fields in a table.

Room ID	Campus/Location	Room	Seats	Room Arrangement	Equipment
NE-01	**Northeast Campus**	**H265**	**150**	**Theater**	**Computer Projector, Surround Sound, Microphone**

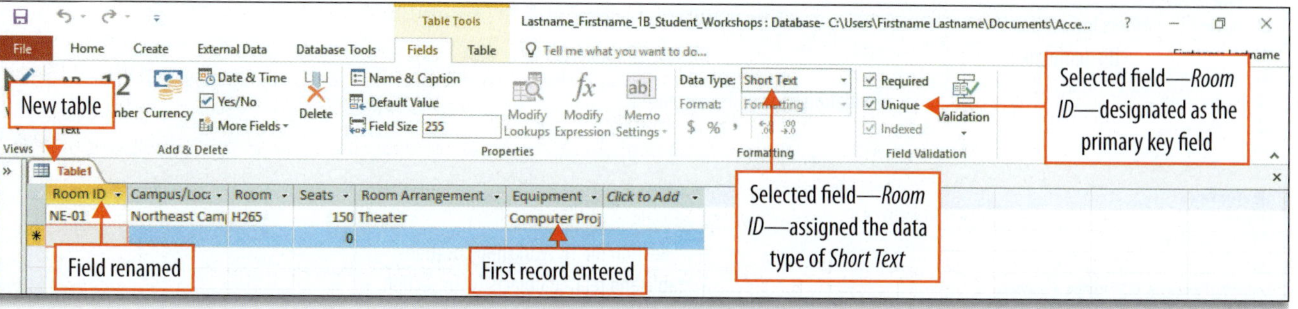

FIGURE 1.48

Access 2016, Windows 10, Microsoft Corporation

2 In the **Views group**, click the top of the **View** button to switch to **Design** view. In the **Save As** dialog box, in the **Table Name** box, using your own name, type **Lastname Firstname 1B Workshop Locations** and then click **OK**.

Recall that when you switch views or when you close a table, Access prompts you to save the table if you have not previously saved it.

ANOTHER WAY On the right side of the status bar, click Design View to switch to Design view.

3 In the **Field Name** column, to the left of **Room ID**, notice the key icon.

In Design view, the key icon indicates that the field—Room ID—is the primary key field.

4 In the **Views group**, click the top of the **View** button to switch back to **Datasheet** view.

ANOTHER WAY On the right side of the status bar, click Datasheet View to switch to Datasheet view.

5 In the new record row, click in the **Room ID** field. Enter the following records, pressing Enter or Tab to move from one field to the next.

Room ID	Campus/Location	Room	Seats	Room Arrangement	Equipment
SW-01	**Southwest Campus**	**A15**	**35**	**Lecture Classroom**	**Computer Projector**
NW-01	**Northwest Campus**	**C202**	**50**	**Lecture Classroom**	**Smart Board**
SE-01	**Southeast Campus**	**D148**	**20**	**U-shaped**	**White Board**
NE-02	**Northeast Campus**	**B105**	**25**	**U-shaped**	**25 Computers, Projector**

6 To the left of the **Room ID** field name, click **Select All** to select all of the columns and rows in the table. On the **Home tab**, in the **Records group,** click **More**, and then click **Field Width**. In the **Column Width** dialog box, click **Best Fit** to display all of the data in each column. Click in any field to cancel the selection, and then **Save** the changes to the table. In the object window, **Close** your **1B Workshop Locations** table.

7 **Open** the **Navigation Pane**, and notice that your new table displays in its own group. Point to the right edge of the **Navigation Pane** to display the pointer. Drag to the right to increase the width of the **Navigation Pane** so that your entire table name displays. Compare your screen with Figure 1.49.

Recall that organizing the Navigation Pane by Tables and Related Views groups the objects by each table and displays the related objects under each table name.

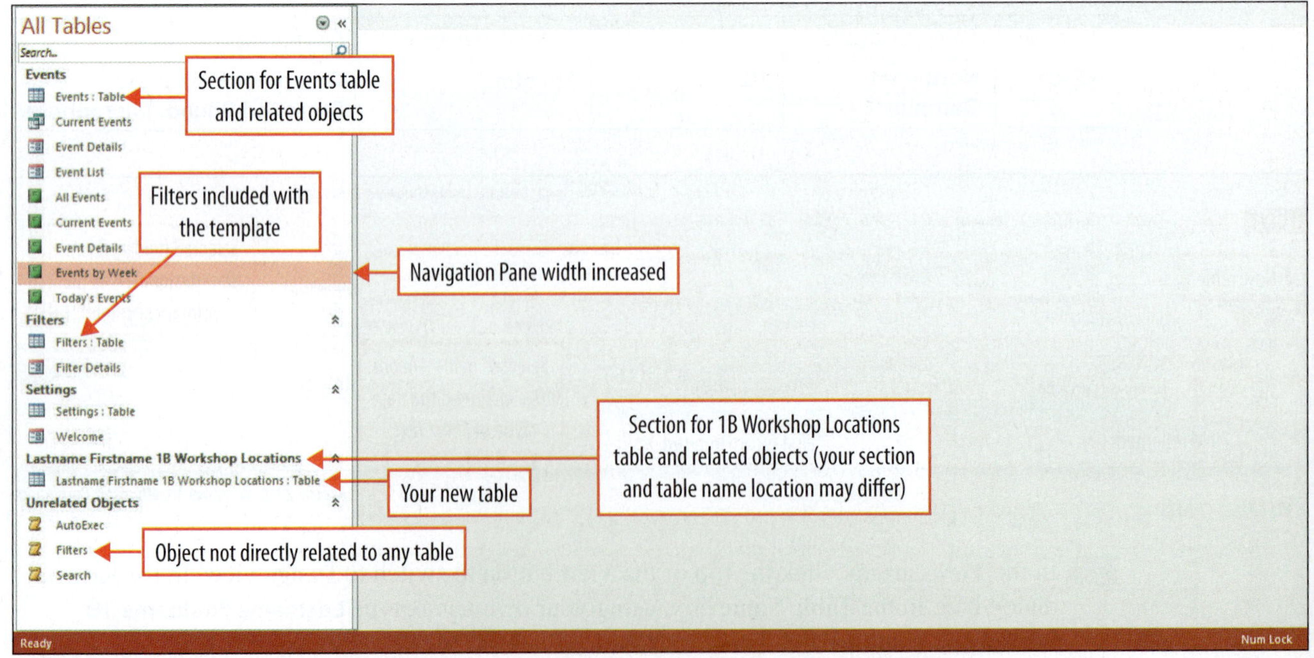

FIGURE 1.49

Objective 9 Print a Report and a Table

GO! Learn How Video A1-9

Recall that one advantage to starting a new database with a template, instead of from a blank database, is that many report objects are already created for you.

1.5.1

Activity 1.24 | Viewing Reports and Printing a Report

1. In the **Navigation Pane**, double-click the report (not the form) name **Event Details** to open it in the object window.

   This prebuilt Event Details report displays in an attractively arranged format.

2. **Close** the **Event Details** report. Open the **All Events** report, and then **Close** the **Navigation Pane**. On the **Home** tab, in the **Views group**, click the top of the **View** button to switch to **Layout** view.

   Recall that Layout view enables you to make changes to an object while viewing the data in the fields. Each prebuilt report displays the records in the table in different useful formats.

ANOTHER WAY On the right side of the status bar, click Layout View to switch to Layout view.

3. At the top of the report, click the title—*All Events*—to display a colored border around the title. Click to the left of the letter *A* to place the insertion point there. Using your own name, type **Lastname Firstname 1B** and then press Spacebar. Press Enter, and then **Save** the report.

   Including your name in the title will help you and your instructor identify any submitted work.

4. On right side of the status bar, click **Print Preview**. In the navigation area, notice that the navigation arrows are unavailable, an indication that this report will print on one page.

ANOTHER WAY On the Home tab, in the Views group, click the View arrow, and then click Print Preview. Or, on the File tab, click Print, and then click Print Preview. Or, right-click the object tab, and then click Print Preview.

5. Create a paper printout or PDF electronic image as instructed. Click **Close Print Preview**, and then **Close** the report, saving any changes. This is the first of two objects printed in this project.

1.5.2

Activity 1.25 | Printing a Table

When printing a table, use the Print Preview command to determine if the table will print on one page or if you need to adjust column widths, margins, or page orientation. Recall that there will be occasions when you print a table for a quick reference or for proofreading. For a more professional-looking format, create and print a report.

1. **Open** the **Navigation Pane**, double-click your **1B Workshop Locations** table to open it in the object window, and then **Close** the **Navigation Pane**.

2. On the ribbon, click the **File tab**, click **Print**, and then click **Print Preview**.

   The table displays how it will look when printed. Generally, tables are not printed, so there is no Print Preview option on the View button or on the status bar.

   The navigation area displays *1* in the Pages box, and the navigation arrows to the right of the box are active, an indication that the table will print on more than one page.

3. In the navigation area, click **Next Page**.

   The second page of the table displays the last field. Whenever possible, try to print all of the fields horizontally on one page. Of course, if there are many records, more than one page may be needed to print all of the records and all of the fields.

4 On the **Print Preview tab**, in the **Page Layout group**, click **Landscape**, and then compare your screen with Figure 1.50. In landscape orientation, notice that the entire table will print on one page—all of the navigation buttons are unavailable.

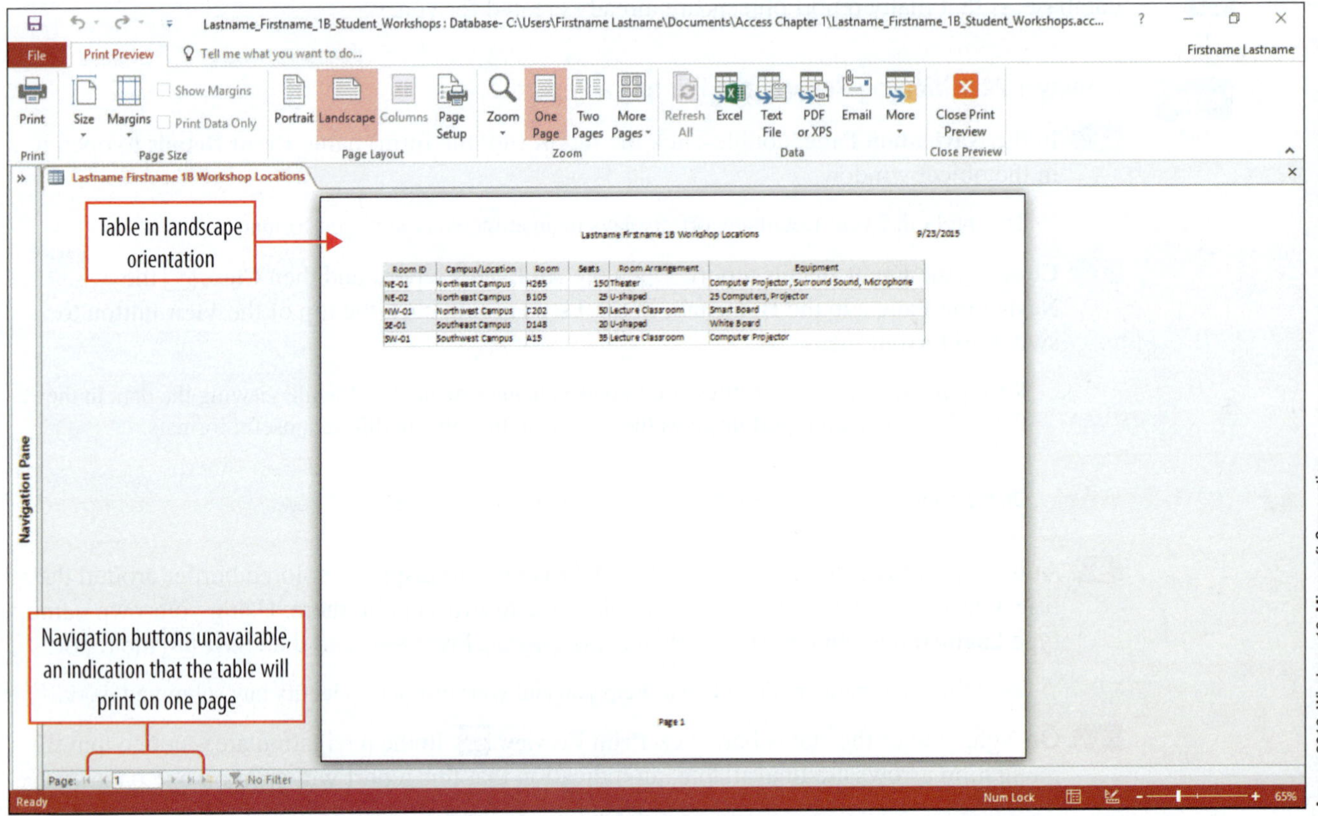

FIGURE 1.50

5 Create a paper printout or PDF electronic image as instructed, and then click **Close Print Preview**. This is the second or last object printed in this project.

6 **Close** [X] your **1B Workshop Locations** table. For the convenience of the next individual opening the database, **Open** [»] the **Navigation Pane**.

7 On the right side of the title bar, click **Close** [X] to close the database and to close Access. As directed by your instructor, submit your database and the paper printout or PDF electronic images of the two objects—one report and one table—that are the results of this project.

END | You have completed Project 1B

GO! With Google

Objective Export an Access Table to a Word Document, Save to Google Drive, Add a Record, and Save to Your Computer

Access web apps are designed to work with Microsoft's SharePoint, a service for setting up websites to share and manage documents. Your college may not have SharePoint installed, so you will use other tools to share objects from your database so that you can work collaboratively with others. Recall that Google Drive is Google's free, web-based word processor, spreadsheet, slide show, form, and data storage and sharing service. For Access, you can export a database object to an Excel worksheet, a PDF file, or a text file, and then save the file to Google Drive.

ALERT! **Working with Web-Based Applications and Services**

Computer programs and services on the web receive continuous updates and improvements. Therefore, the steps to complete this web-based activity may differ from the ones shown. You can often look at the screens and the information presented to determine how to complete the activity.

If you do not already have a Google account, you will need to create one before you begin this activity. Go to http://google.com and, in the upper right corner, click Sign In. On the Sign In screen, click Create Account. On the Create your Google Account page, complete the form, read and agree to the Terms of Service and Privacy Policy, and then click Next step. On the Welcome screen, click Get Started.

Activity | Exporting an Access Table to a Word Document, Saving the Document to Google Drive, Adding a Record in Google Drive, and Saving to Your Computer

In this Activity, you will export your 1B Workshop Locations table to a Word document, upload your Word file to Google Drive as a Google Doc, add a record in Google Drive, and then download a copy of the edited document to your computer.

1 Start Access, navigate to your **Access Chapter 1** folder, and then **Open** your **1B_Student_Workshops** database file. If necessary, on the Message Bar, click **Enable Content**, and then **Close** the **Event List** form. In the **Navigation Pane**, click your **1B Workshop Locations** table to select it—do not open it.

2 On the ribbon, click the **External Data tab**. In the **Export group**, click **More**, and then click **Word**. In the **Export – RTF File** dialog box, click **Browse**, and then navigate to your **Access Chapter 1** folder. In the **File Save** dialog box, click in the **File name** box, using your own name, type **Lastname_Firstname_a1B_Web** and then click **Save**.

3 In the **Export – RTF File** dialog box, under **Specify export options**, select the second check box—**Open the destination file after the export operation is complete**—and then click **OK**. Take a moment to examine the data in the file, and then **Close** Word. In the **Export – RTF File** dialog box, click **Close**, and then **Close** Access.

Notice that the table is too wide to display fully with Portrait orientation

4 Open your browser software, navigate to **http://drive.google.com**, and sign in to your Google account. On the right side of the screen, click **Settings** [⚙▾], and then click **Settings**. In the **Settings** dialog box, to the right of *Convert uploads*, if necessary, select the **Convert uploaded files to Google Docs editor format** check box. In the upper right, click **Done**.

It is necessary to select this setting; otherwise, your document will upload as a pdf file and cannot be edited without further action.

5 Open your **GO! Web Projects** folder—or create and then open this folder by clicking **NEW** and then clicking **New folder**. On the left, click **NEW**, and then click **File upload**. In the **Choose File to Upload** dialog box, navigate to your **Access Chapter 1** folder, and then double-click your **a1B_Web** Word file to upload it to Google Drive. When the title bar of the message box indicates *Upload complete*, **Close** the message box.

6 Double-click your **a1B_Web** file to open the file in Google Docs. Notice that the table is not fully displayed on the page.

(GO! With Google continues on the next page)

GO! With Google

7 Click **File** to display a menu, and then click **Page setup**. In the **Page setup** dialog box, under **Orientation**, click **Landscape**. Click **OK**.

The table displays fully with Landscape orientation.

8 Click in the last cell in the table, and press Tab. Add the following record, and compare with Figure A

Field	Room ID	Campus/Location	Room	Seats	Room Arrangement	Equipment
	SE-02	**Southeast Campus**	**D120**	**20**	**Testing Lab**	**20 Computers**

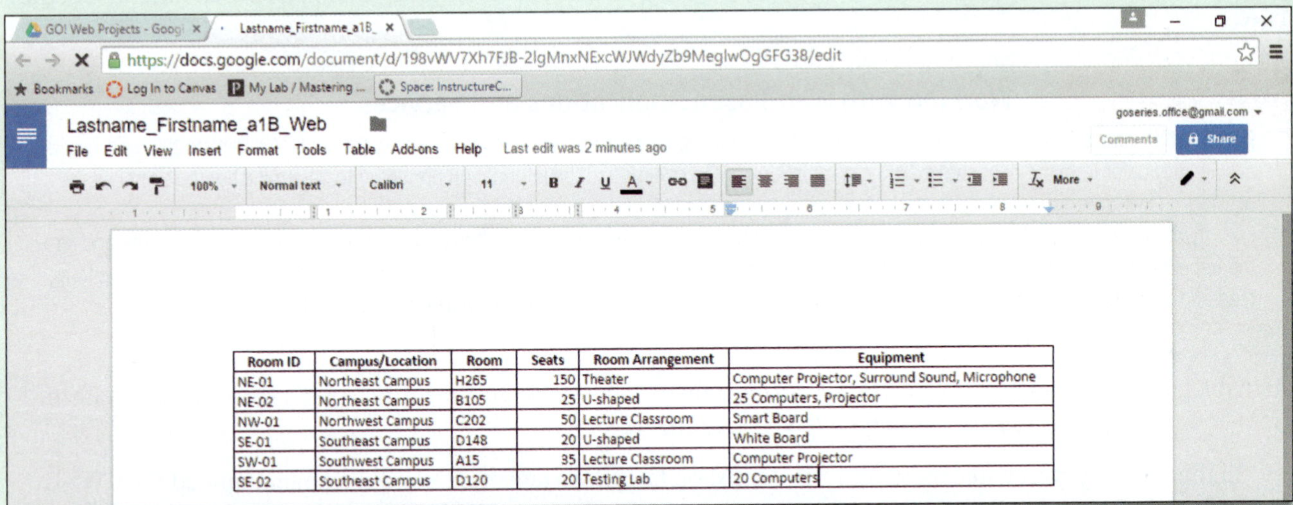

Room ID	Campus/Location	Room	Seats	Room Arrangement	Equipment
NE-01	Northeast Campus	H265	150	Theater	Computer Projector, Surround Sound, Microphone
NE-02	Northeast Campus	B105	25	U-shaped	25 Computers, Projector
NW-01	Northwest Campus	C202	50	Lecture Classroom	Smart Board
SE-01	Southeast Campus	D148	20	U-shaped	White Board
SW-01	Southwest Campus	A15	35	Lecture Classroom	Computer Projector
SE-02	Southeast Campus	D120	20	Testing Lab	20 Computers

FIGURE A

9 On the menu, click **File**, point to **Download as**, and then click **Microsoft Word (.docx)**. In the message box—usually displays at the bottom of your screen—click the **Save arrow**, and then click **Save as**. In the **Save As** dialog box, navigate to your **Access Chapter 1** folder, click in the **File name** box, and type **Lastname_Firstname_a1B_Web_Download** and then click **Save**. **Close** the message box.

10 In Google Drive, at the upper right corner of your screen, click your user name, and then click **Sign out**. **Close** your browser window.

11 Start Word. In the Word opening screen, click **Open**. Under **Open**, click **Browse**. Navigate to your **Access Chapter 1** folder, and then double-click your **a1B_Web** Word file. Notice that this file is the original file—the new record is not entered. If you are required to print your documents, use one of the methods in the following Note. **Close** your Word file; and, if prompted, save the changes to your document. Then **Open** and print your **a1B_Web_Download** Word file using one of the methods in the following Note. **Close** Word; and, if prompted, save the changes to your document. As directed by your instructor, submit your two documents and the two paper printouts or PDF electronic images that are the results of this project.

NOTE Adding the File Name to the Footer and Printing or Creating a PDF Electronic Image

Click the Insert tab. In the Header & Footer group, click Footer, and then click Blank. With Type here selected, in the Insert group, click Document Info, and then click File Name. Close the Footer window. Click the Layout tab. In the Page Setup group, click Orientation, and then click Landscape.

To print on paper, click File, and then click Print. To create a pdf electronic image of your printout, click File, and then click Export. Under Export, be sure Create PDF/XPS Document is selected, and then click Create PDF/XPS. Navigate to your Access Chapter 1 folder, and then click Publish to save the file with the default name and an extension of pdf.

GO! To Work

Andres Rodriguez/Fotolia; FotolEdhar/Fotolia; Andrey Popov/Fotolia; Shutterstock

MICROSOFT OFFICE SPECIALIST (MOS) SKILLS IN THIS CHAPTER	
PROJECT 1A	**PROJECT 1B**
1.1.1 Create a blank desktop database	**1.1.2** Create a database from a template
1.3.5 Change views of objects	**1.3.4** Display objects in the Navigation Pane
1.5.1 Print reports	**1.5.1** Print reports
1.5.2 Print records	**1.5.2** Print records
2.1.1 Create a table	**2.1.1** Create a table
2.1.2 Import data into tables	**2.1.5** Create a table from a template with application parts
2.2.3 Add table descriptions	**2.3.1** Update records
2.3.2 Add records	**2.3.4** Append records from external data
2.3.4 Append records from external data	
2.4.1 Add fields to tables	
2.4.3 Change field captions	
2.4.4 Change field sizes	
2.4.5 Change field data types	
2.4.6 Configure fields to auto-increment	
2.4.9 Delete fields	
3.1.1 Run a query	
4.1.1 Create a form	
4.1.3 Save a form	
5.1.1 Create a report based on a query or table	

BUILD YOUR E-PORTFOLIO

An E-Portfolio is a collection of evidence, stored electronically, that showcases what you have accomplished while completing your education. Collecting and then sharing your work products with potential employers reflects your academic and career goals. Your completed documents from the following projects are good examples to show what you have learned: 1G, 1K, and 1L.

GO! FOR JOB SUCCESS

Video: Goal Setting

Your instructor may assign this video to your class, and then ask you to think about, or discuss with your classmates, these questions:

FotolEdhar/Fotolia

Is there anything you would change about Theo's behavior at his performance evaluation? Why or why not?

SMART goals are goals that are specific, measurable, achievable, realistic, and time-frame specific. Is Theo's first goal of beating his sales numbers by 10 percent next year a SMART goal?

How important do you think it is to set career development goals for yourself? Why?

END OF CHAPTER

SUMMARY

Principles of good database design, also known as normalization, help ensure that the data in your database is accurate and organized in a way that you can retrieve information that is useful.

You can create a database from scratch by using the blank desktop database template or a custom web app or by using a template that contains prebuilt tables, queries, forms, reports, and other objects.

Tables are the foundation of a database, but before entering records in a table, you must define the data type and name the field. Common data types are Short Text, Number, Currency, and Date/Time.

Use forms to enter data into a table or view the data in a table. Use queries to retrieve information from tables. Reports display information from tables in a professional-looking format.

GO! LEARN IT ONLINE

Review the concepts, key terms, and MOS Skills in this chapter by completing these online challenges, which you can find at **MyITLab**.

Matching and Multiple Choice: Answer matching and multiple-choice questions to test what you learned in this chapter.

Lessons on the GO!: Learn how to use all the new apps and features as they are introduced by Microsoft.

MOS Prep Quiz: Answer questions to review the MOS skills that you have practiced in this chapter.

GO! COLLABORATIVE TEAM PROJECT (Available in MyITLab and Instructor Resource Center)

If your instructor assigns this project to your class, you can expect to work with one or more of your classmates—either in person or by using Internet tools—to create work products similar to those that you created in this chapter. A team is a group of workers who work together to solve a problem, make a decision, or create a work product. Collaboration is when you work together with others as a team in an intellectual endeavor to complete a shared task or achieve a shared goal.

PROJECT GUIDE FOR ACCESS CHAPTER 1

Your instructor will assign Projects from this list to ensure your learning and assess your knowledge.

PROJECT GUIDE FOR ACCESS CHAPTER 1			
Project	**Apply Skills from These Chapter Objectives**	**Project Type**	**Project Location**
1A MyITLab	Objectives 1–5 from Project 1A	**1A Instructional Project (Grader Project)** Guided instruction to learn the skills in Project A.	In MyITLab and in text
1B MyITLab	Objectives 6–9 from Project 1B	**1B Instructional Project (Grader Project)** Guided instruction to learn the skills in Project A.	In MyITLab and in text
1C	Objectives 1–5 from Project 1A	**1C Chapter Review (Scorecard Grading)** A guided review of the skills from Project 1A.	In text
1D	Objectives 6–9 from Project 1B	**1D Chapter Review (Scorecard Grading** A guided review of the skills from Project 1B.	In text
1E MyITLab	Objectives 1–5 from Project 1A	**1E Mastery (Grader Project)** **Mastery and Transfer of Learning** A demonstration of your mastery of the skills in Project 1A with extensive decision making.	In MyITLab and in text
1F MyITLab	Objectives 6–9 from Project 1B	**1F Mastery (Grader Project)** **Mastery and Transfer of Learning** A demonstration of your mastery of the skills in Project 1B with extensive decision making.	In MyITLab and in text
1G MyITLab	Combination of Objectives from Projects 1A and 1B	**1G Mastery (Grader Project)** **Mastery and Transfer of Learning** A demonstration of your mastery of the skills in Projects 1A and 1B with extensive decision making.	In MyITLab and in text
1H	Combination of Objectives from Projects 1A and 1B	**1H GO! Fix It (Scorecard Grading)** **Critical Thinking** A demonstration of your mastery of the skills in Projects 1A and 1B by creating a correct result from a document that contains errors you must find.	Instructor Resource Center (IRC) and MyITLab
1I	Combination of Objectives from Projects 1A and 1B	**1I GO! Make It (Scorecard Grading)** **Critical Thinking** A demonstration of your mastery of the skills in Projects 1A and 1B by creating a result from a supplied picture.	IRC and MyITLab
1J	Combination of Objectives from Projects 1A and 1B	**1J GO! Solve It (Rubric Grading)** **Critical Thinking** A demonstration of your mastery of the skills in Projects 1A and 1B, your decision-making skills, and your critical-thinking skills. A task-specific rubric helps you self-assess your result.	IRC and MyITLab
1K	Combination of Objectives from Projects 1A and 1B	**1K GO! Solve It (Rubric Grading)** **Critical Thinking** A demonstration of your mastery of the skills in Projects 1A and 1B, your decision-making skills, and your critical thinking skills. A task-specific rubric helps you self-assess your result.	In text
1L	Combination of Objectives from Projects 1A and 1B	**1L GO! Think (Rubric Grading)** **Critical Thinking** A demonstration of your understanding of the Chapter concepts applied in a manner that you would outside of college. An analytic rubric helps you and your instructor grade the quality of your work by comparing it to the work an expert in the discipline would create.	In text
1M	Combination of Objectives from Projects 1A and 1B	**1M GO! Think (Rubric Grading)** **Critical Thinking** A demonstration of your understanding of the Chapter concepts applied in a manner that you would outside of college. An analytic rubric helps you and your instructor grade the quality of your work by comparing it to the work an expert in the discipline would create.	IRC and MyITLab
1N	Combination of Objectives from Projects 1A and 1B	**1N You and GO! (Rubric Grading)** **Critical Thinking** A demonstration of your understanding of the Chapter concepts applied in a manner that you would in a personal situation. An analytic rubric helps you and your instructor grade the quality of your work.	IRC and MyITLab
1O	Combination of Objectives from Project 1A and 1B	**1O Collaborative Team Project for ACCESS Chapter 1** **Critical Thinking** A demonstration of your understanding of concepts and your ability to work collaboratively in a group role-playing assessment, requiring both collaboration and self-management.	IRC and MyITLab

GLOSSARY

GLOSSARY OF CHAPTER KEY TERMS

Append To add on to the end of an object; for example, to add records to the end of an existing table.

AutoNumber data type A data type that describes a unique sequential or random number assigned by Access as each record is entered and that is useful for data that has no distinct field that can be considered unique.

Best Fit An Access command that adjusts the width of a column to accommodate the column's longest entry.

Blank desktop database A database that has no data and has no database tools—you must create the data and tools as you need them; the database is stored on your computer or other storage device.

Caption A property setting that displays a name for a field in a table, query, form, or report different from the one listed as the field name.

Common field A field included in two or more tables that stores the same data.

Currency data type An Access data type that describes monetary values and numeric data that can be used in mathematical calculations involving values with one to four decimal places.

Custom web app A database that you can publish and share with others over the Internet.

Data Facts about people, events, things, or ideas.

Data source The table or tables from which a query, form, or report gathers its data.

Data type Classification identifying the kind of data that can be stored in a field, such as numbers, text, or dates.

Database An organized collection of facts about people, events, things, or ideas related to a specific topic or purpose.

Database management system (DBMS) Database software that controls how related collections of data are stored, organized, retrieved, and secured; also known as a DBMS.

Database template A preformatted database that contains prebuilt tables, queries, forms, and reports that perform a specific task, such as tracking events.

Datasheet view The Access view that displays data organized in columns and rows similar to an Excel worksheet.

DBMS An acronym for database management system.

Design view An Access view that displays the detailed structure of a table, query, form, or report. For forms and reports, may be the view in which some tasks must be performed, and only the controls, and not the data, display in this view.

Destination table The table to which you import or append data.

Export The process of copying data from one file into another file, such as an Access table into an Excel spreadsheet.

Field A single piece of information that is stored in every record; represented by a column in a database table.

Field properties Characteristics of a field that control how the field displays and how data can be entered in the field; vary for different data types.

First principle of good database design A principle of good database design stating that data is organized in tables so that there is no redundant data.

Flat database A simple database file that is not related or linked to any other collection of data.

Form An Access object you can use to enter new records into a table, edit or delete existing records in a table, or display existing records.

Form view The Access view in which you can view records, but you cannot change the layout or design of the form.

Import The process of copying data from another file, such as a Word table or an Excel workbook, into a separate file, such as an Access database.

Information Data that is accurate, timely, and organized in a useful manner.

Layout view The Access view in which you can make changes to a form or report while the data from the underlying data source displays.

Link A connection to data in another file.

Multiple-items form A form that enables you to display or enter multiple records in a table.

Navigation area An area at the bottom of the Access window that indicates the number of records in the table and contains controls in the form of arrows that you click to move among the records.

Navigation Pane An area of the Access window that displays and organizes the names of the objects in a database; from here, you open objects for use.

Normalization The process of applying design rules and principles to ensure that your database performs as expected.

Number data type An Access data type that represents a quantity, how much or how many, and may be used in calculations.

Object tab In the object window, a tab that identifies the object and which enables you to make an open object active.

Object window An area of the Access window that displays open objects, such as tables, queries, forms, or reports; by default, each object displays on its own tab.

Objects The basic parts of a database that you create to store your data and to work with your data; for example, tables, queries, forms, and reports.

Populate The action of filling a database table with records.

Primary key A required field that uniquely identifies a record in a table; for example, a Student ID number at a college.

Property Sheet A list of characteristics—properties—for fields or controls on a form or report in which you can make precise changes to each property associated with the field or control.

Query A database object that retrieves specific data from one or more database objects—either tables or other queries—and then, in a single datasheet, displays only the data you specify.

Record All of the categories of data pertaining to one person, place, event, thing, or idea; represented by a row in a database table.

Record selector bar The bar at the left edge of a record when it is displayed in a form, and which is used to select an entire record.

Record selector box The small box at the left of a record in Datasheet view that, when clicked, selects the entire record.

Redundant In a database, information that is duplicated in a manner that indicates poor database design.

Relational database A sophisticated type of database that has multiple collections of data within the file that are related to one another.

Report A database object that summarizes the fields and records from a table or query in an easy-to-read format suitable for printing.

Run The process in which Access searches the records in the table(s) included in the query design, finds the records that match the specified criteria, and then displays the records in a datasheet; only the fields that have been included in the query design display.

Second principle of good database design A principle stating that appropriate database techniques are used to ensure the accuracy and consistency of data as it is entered into the table.

Select query A type of Access query that retrieves (selects) data from one or more tables or queries, displaying the selected data in a datasheet; also known as a simple select query.

SharePoint A Microsoft application used for setting up websites to share and manage documents.

Short Text data type An Access data type that describes text, a combination of text and numbers, or numbers that are not used in calculations, such as the Postal Code.

Simple select query Another name for a select query.

Single-record form A form that enables you to display or enter one record at a time from a table.

Source file When importing a file, refers to the file being imported.

Structure In Access, the underlying design of a table, including field names, data types, descriptions, and field properties.

Table A format for information that organizes and presents text and data in columns and rows; the foundation of a database.

Tables and Related Views An arrangement in the Navigation Pane that groups objects by the table to which they are related.

Truncated Data that is cut off or shortened because the field or column is not wide enough to display all of the data or the field size is too small to contain all of the data.

Wizard A feature in Microsoft Office that walks you step by step through a process.

CHAPTER REVIEW

Apply 1A skills from these Objectives:

1. Identify Good Database Design
2. Create a Table and Define Fields in a Blank Desktop Database
3. Change the Structure of Tables and Add a Second Table
4. Create a Query, Form, and Report
5. Close a Database and Exit Access

Skills Review Project 1C College Administrators

In the following Skills Review, you will create a database to store information about the administrators of Texas Lakes Community College and their departments. Your completed database objects will look similar to Figure 1.51.

PROJECT FILES

For Project 1C, you will need the following files:

Blank desktop database

a01C_Administrators (Excel workbook)

a01C_Departments (Excel workbook)

You will save your database as:

Lastname_Firstname_1C_College_Administrators

Build From Scratch

PROJECT RESULTS

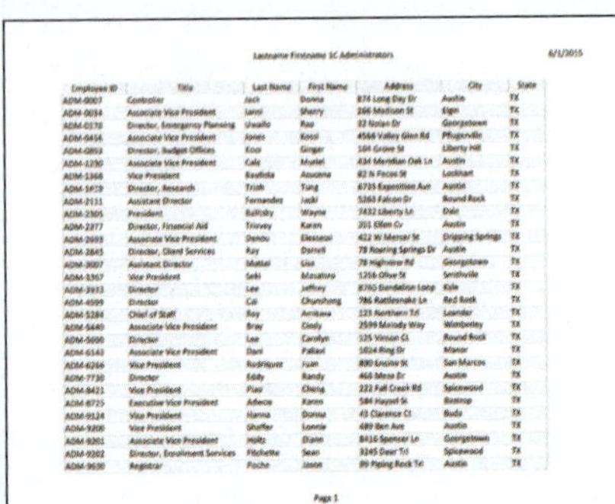

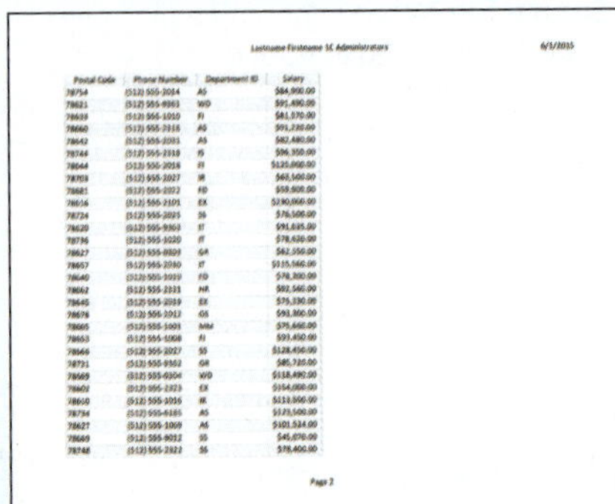

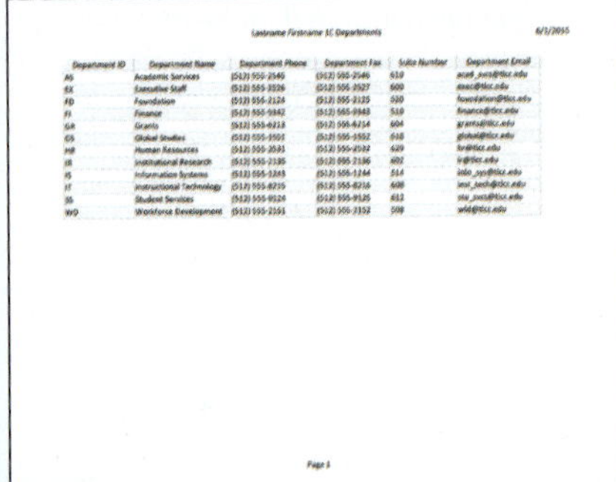

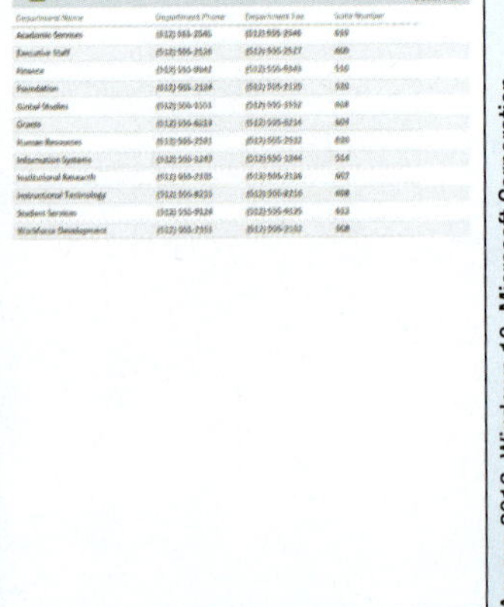

Access 2016, Windows 10, Microsoft Corporation

FIGURE 1.51

(Project 1C College Administrators continues on the next page)

Skills Review Project 1C College Administrators (continued)

1 Start Access. In the Access opening screen, click **Blank desktop database**. In the **Blank desktop database** dialog box, to the right of the **File Name** box, click **Browse**. In the **File New Database** dialog box, navigate to your **Access Chapter 1** folder. In the **File New Database** dialog box, click in the **File name** box, type **Lastname_Firstname_1C_College_Administrators** and then press Enter. In the **Blank desktop database** dialog box, click **Create**.

a. **Close** the **Navigation Pane**. In the field names row, click in the text *Click to Add*, and then click **Short Text**. Type **Title** and then press Enter.

b. In the third field name box, click **Short Text**, type **Last Name** and then press Enter. In the fourth field name box, click **Short Text**, type **First Name** and then press Enter. Create the remaining fields shown in **Table 1**, pressing Enter after the last field name. All of the data is typed on one line.

c. If necessary, scroll to bring the first column into view, and then click the **ID** field name. On the **Fields tab**, in the **Properties group**, click **Name & Caption**. In the **Name** box, change *ID* to **Employee ID** and then click **OK**. On the ribbon, in the **Formatting group**, click the **Data Type arrow**, and then click **Short Text**.

d. In the new record row, click in the **Employee ID** field, type **ADM-9200** and press Enter. In the **Title** field, type **Vice President** and press Enter. Continue entering data in the fields shown in **Table 2**, pressing Enter or Tab to move to the next field and to the next row.

e. On the Quick Access Toolbar, click **Save**. In the **Save As** dialog box, in the **Table Name** box, using your own name, replace the selected text by typing **Lastname Firstname 1C Administrators** and then click **OK**.

f. In the new record row, enter the data for two college administrators shown in Table 3, pressing Enter or Tab to move from field to field and to the next row.

TABLE 1

Data Type		Short Text	Short Text	Short Text	**Short Text**	**Short Text**	**Short Text**	**Short Text**	**Short Text**	**Short Text**	**Short Text**	**Currency**
Field Name	ID	Title	Last Name	First Name	**Middle Initial**	**Address**	**City**	**State**	**Postal Code**	**Phone Number**	**Department ID**	**Salary**

(Return to Step 1c)

TABLE 2

Last Name	First Name	Middle Initial	Address	City	State	Postal Code	Phone Number	Department ID	Salary
Shaffer	**Lonnie**	**J**	**489 Ben Ave**	**Austin**	**TX**	**78734**	**(512) 555-6185**	**AS**	**123500**

(Return to Step 1e)

TABLE 3

Employee ID	Title	Last Name	First Name	Middle Initial	Address	City	State	Postal Code	Phone Number	Department ID	Salary
ADM-9201	**Associate Vice President**	**Holtz**	**Diann**	**S**	**8416 Spencer Ln**	**Georgetown**	**TX**	**78627**	**(512) 555-1069**	**AS**	**101524**
ADM-9202	**Director, Enrollment Services**	**Fitchette**	**Sean**	**H**	**3245 Deer Trl**	**Spicewood**	**TX**	**78669**	**(512) 555-9012**	**SS**	**45070**

(Return to Step 1g)

(Project 1C College Administrators continues on the next page)

Skills Review Project 1C College Administrators (continued)

g. **Close** your **1C Administrators** table. On the **External Data tab**, in the **Import & Link group**, click **Excel**. In the **Get External Data – Excel Spreadsheet** dialog box, click **Browse**. In the **File Open** dialog box, navigate to your student data files, and then double-click the **a01C_Administrators** Excel file.

h. Click the **Append a copy of the records to the table** option button, and then click **OK**. In the **Import Spreadsheet Wizard**, click **Next**, and then click **Finish**. In the **Get External Data – Excel Spreadsheet** dialog box, click **Close**.

i. **Open** the **Navigation Pane**. Resize the Navigation Pane so that the entire table name displays. In the **Navigation Pane**, double-click your **1C Administrators** table to open it, and then **Close** the **Navigation Pane**—there are 30 records in this table.

2 Click the **Home tab**, and then in the **Views group**, click the top of the **View** button to switch to **Design** view. In the **Field Name** column, to the left of **Middle Initial**, click the row selector box to select the entire row. On the **Design tab**, in the **Tools group**, click **Delete Rows**. In the message box, click **Yes**.

a. Click in the **Employee ID** field name box. Under **Field Properties**, click **Field Size** to select the existing text. Type **8** and then in the **Employee ID** field row, click in the **Description** box. Type **Eight-character Employee ID** and then press Enter.

b. Click in the **State** field name box. In the **Field Properties** area, click **Field Size**, and then type **2** In the **State Description** box, type **Two-character state abbreviation** and then press Enter.

c. **Save** the design changes to your table, and in the message box, click **Yes**. On the **Design tab**, in the **Views group**, click the top of the **View** button to switch to **Datasheet** view.

d. On the ribbon, click the **External Data tab**, and then in the **Import & Link group**, click **Excel**. In the **Get External Data – Excel Spreadsheet** dialog box, to the right of the **File name** box, click **Browse**. In the **File Open** dialog box, navigate to your student data files, and then double-click **a01C_Departments**. Be sure that the **Import the source data into a new table in the current database** option button is selected, and then click **OK**.

e. In the upper left corner of the wizard, select the **First Row Contains Column Headings** check box, and then click **Next**. Click **Next** again. Click the **Choose my own primary key** option button, be sure that **Department ID** displays, and then click **Next**. In the **Import to Table** box, type **Lastname Firstname 1C Departments** and then click **Finish**. In the **Get External Data – Excel Spreadsheet** dialog box, click **Close**.

f. **Open** the **Navigation Pane**, double-click your **1C Departments** table, and then **Close** the **Navigation Pane**. There are 12 records in your **1C Departments** table.

g. To the left of the **Department** field name, click **Select All**. On the ribbon, click the **Home tab**, and in the **Records group**, click **More**, and then click **Field Width**. In the **Column Width** dialog box, click **Best Fit**. Click in any field to cancel the selection, and then **Save** your table. In the object window, click the **object tab** for your **1C Administrators** table. Using the techniques you just practiced, apply **Best Fit** to the columns, cancel the selection, and then **Save** the table.

h. With your **1C Administrators** table displayed, on the ribbon, click the **File tab**, click **Print**, and then click **Print Preview**. On the **Print Preview tab**, in the **Page Layout group**, click **Landscape**. Create a paper printout or PDF electronic image as directed by your instructor—two pages result. On the ribbon, click **Close Print Preview**, and then **Close** your **1C Administrators** table.

i. With your **1C Departments** table displayed, view the table in **Print Preview**. Change the orientation to **Landscape**, and then create a paper printout or PDF electronic image as directed by your instructor—one page results. Click **Close Print Preview**, and then **Close** your **1C Departments** table.

3 On the ribbon, click the **Create tab**, and then in the **Queries group**, click **Query Wizard**. In the **New Query** dialog box, be sure **Simple Query Wizard** is selected, and then click **OK**. In the wizard, click the **Tables/Queries arrow**, and then click your **Table: 1C Administrators**.

a. Under **Available Fields**, click **Last Name**, and then click **Add Field** to move the field to the **Selected Fields** list on the right. Double-click the **First Name** field to move it to the **Selected Fields** list. By using **Add Field** or by double-clicking the field name, add

(Project 1C College Administrators continues on the next page)

Skills Review Project 1C College Administrators (continued)

the following fields to the **Selected Fields** list in the order specified: **Title**, **Department ID**, and **Phone Number**. This query will answer the question, *What is the last name, first name, title, Department ID, and phone number of every administrator?*

b. In the wizard, click **Next**. Click in the **What title do you want for your query?** box. Using your own name, edit as necessary so that the query name is **Lastname Firstname 1C All Administrators Query** and then click **Finish**. If necessary, apply Best Fit to the columns, and then Save the query. Display the query in **Print Preview**, and then create a paper printout or PDF electronic image as directed—one page results. Click **Close Print Preview**, and then **Close** the query.

c. **Open** the **Navigation Pane**, right-click your **1C Administrators** table, and then click **Open** to display the table in the object window. **Close** the **Navigation Pane**. Notice that the table has 11 fields. On the ribbon, click the **Create tab**, and in the **Forms group**, click **Form**. On the Quick Access Toolbar, click **Save**. In the **Save As** dialog box, click in the **Form Name** box, edit to name the form **Lastname Firstname 1C Administrator Form** and then click **OK**.

d. In the navigation area, click **Last Record**, and then click **Previous Record** two times to display the record for *Diann Holtz*. By using the instructions in Activity 1.15, print or create a PDF electronic image of only this record on one page. **Close** the form object, saving it if prompted. Your **1C Administrators** table object remains open.

e. **Open** the **Navigation Pane**, open your **1C Departments** table by double-clicking the table name or by right-clicking the table name and clicking Open. **Close** the **Navigation Pane**. On the **Create tab**, in the **Reports group**, click **Report**.

f. Click the **Department ID** field name, and then on the ribbon, under **Report Layout Tools**, click the **Arrange tab**. In the **Rows & Columns group**, click **Select Column**, and then press Del. Using the same technique, delete the **Department Email** field.

g. Click the **Department Phone** field name. Hold down Shift, and then click the **Suite Number** field name to select the last three field names. In the **Rows & Columns group**, click **Select Column**. On the ribbon, click the **Design tab**, and then in the **Tools group**, click **Property Sheet**. In the **Property Sheet**, on the **Format tab**, click **Width**, type **1.5** and then press Enter. **Close** the **Property Sheet**.

h. Click the **Department Name** field name. On the ribbon, click the **Home tab.** In the **Sort & Filter group**, click **Ascending** to sort the report in alphabetic order by *Department Name*. At the bottom of the report, on the right side, click **Page 1 of 1**, and then press Del.

i. **Save** the report as **Lastname Firstname 1C Departments Report** and then click **OK**. Display the report in **Print Preview**, and then create a paper printout or PDF electronic image of the report as directed. Click **Close Print Preview**. In the object window, right-click any **object tab**, and then click **Close All** to close all open objects, leaving the object window empty.

4 **Open** the **Navigation Pane**. If necessary, increase the width of the Navigation Pane so that all object names display fully. On the right side of the title bar, click **Close** to close the database and to close Access. As directed by your instructor, submit your database and the paper printouts or PDF electronic images of the five objects—two tables, one query, one form, and one report—that are the results of this project. Specifically, in this project, using your own name, you created the following database and printouts or PDF electronic images:

1. Lastname_Firstname_1C_College_Administrators	Database file
2. Lastname Firstname 1C Administrators	Table
3. Lastname Firstname 1C Departments	Table
4. Lastname Firstname 1C All Administrators Query	Query
5. Lastname Firstname 1C Administrator Form	Form
6. Lastname Firstname 1C Departments Report	Report

END | You have completed Project 1C

CHAPTER REVIEW

Apply 1B skills from these Objectives:

6 Use a Template to Create a Database
7 Organize Objects in the Navigation Pane
8 Create a New Table in a Database Created with a Template
9 Print a Report and a Table

Skills Review Project 1D Certification Events

In the following Skills Review, you will create a database to store information about certification test preparation events at Texas Lakes Community College. Your completed report and table will look similar to Figure 1.52.

PROJECT FILES

For Project 1D, you will need the following file:

Desktop event management template
a01D_Certification_Events (Excel workbook)

You will save your database as:

Lastname_Firstname_1D_Certification_Events

PROJECT RESULTS

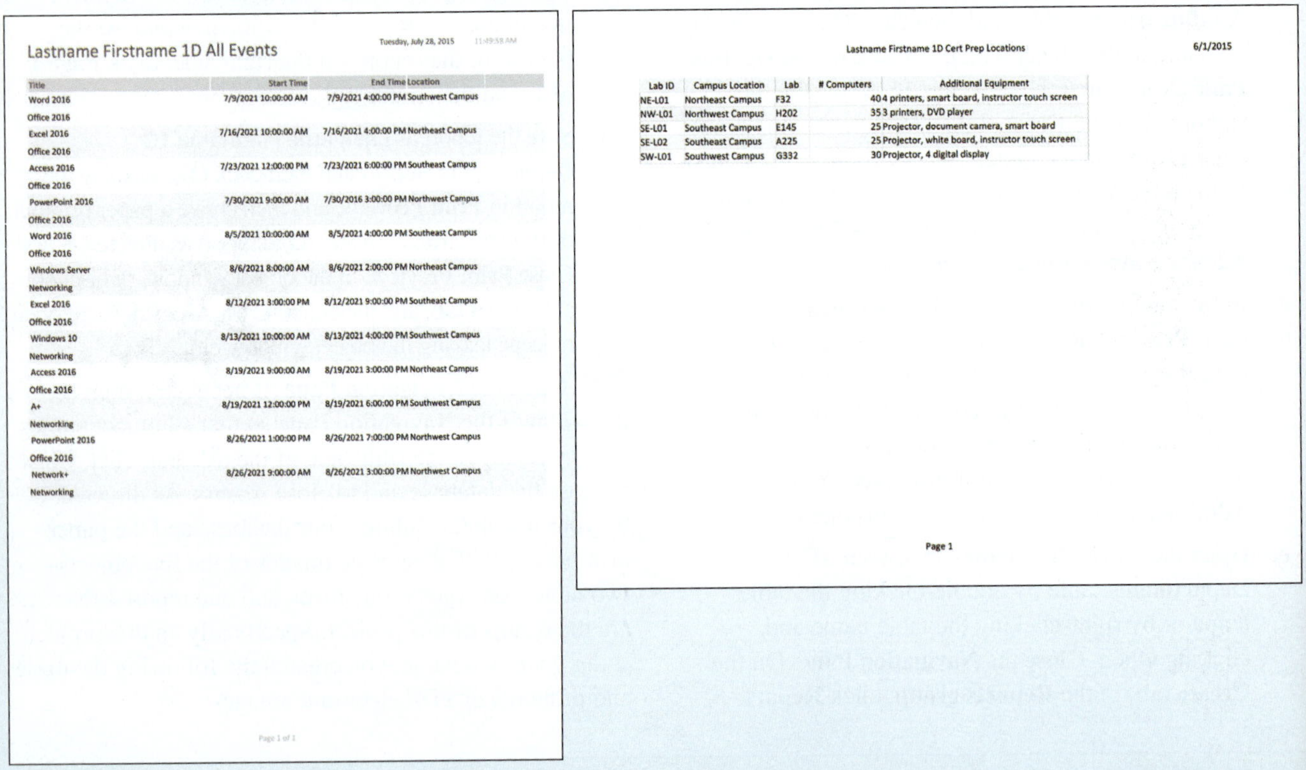

Lastname Firstname 1D All Events

Tuesday, July 28, 2015 11:49:58 AM

Title	Start Time	End Time	Location
Word 2016 Office 2016	7/9/2021 10:00:00 AM	7/9/2021 4:00:00 PM	Southwest Campus
Excel 2016 Office 2016	7/16/2021 10:00:00 AM	7/16/2021 4:00:00 PM	Northeast Campus
Access 2016 Office 2016	7/23/2021 12:00:00 PM	7/23/2021 6:00:00 PM	Southeast Campus
PowerPoint 2016 Office 2016	7/30/2021 9:00:00 AM	7/30/2016 3:00:00 PM	Northwest Campus
Word 2016 Office 2016	8/5/2021 10:00:00 AM	8/5/2021 4:00:00 PM	Southeast Campus
Windows Server Networking	8/6/2021 8:00:00 AM	8/6/2021 2:00:00 PM	Northeast Campus
Excel 2016 Office 2016	8/12/2021 3:00:00 PM	8/12/2021 9:00:00 PM	Southeast Campus
Windows 10 Networking	8/13/2021 10:00:00 AM	8/13/2021 4:00:00 PM	Southwest Campus
Access 2016 Office 2016	8/19/2021 9:00:00 AM	8/19/2021 3:00:00 PM	Northeast Campus
A+ Networking	8/19/2021 12:00:00 PM	8/19/2021 6:00:00 PM	Southwest Campus
PowerPoint 2016 Office 2016	8/26/2021 1:00:00 PM	8/26/2021 7:00:00 PM	Northwest Campus
Network+ Networking	8/26/2021 9:00:00 AM	8/26/2021 3:00:00 PM	Northwest Campus

Page 1 of 1

Lastname Firstname 1D Cert Prep Locations

6/1/2015

Lab ID	Campus Location	Lab	# Computers	Additional Equipment
NE-L01	Northeast Campus	F32	40	4 printers, smart board, instructor touch screen
NW-L01	Northwest Campus	H202	35	3 printers, DVD player
SE-L01	Southeast Campus	E145	25	Projector, document camera, smart board
SE-L02	Southeast Campus	A225	25	Projector, white board, instructor touch screen
SW-L01	Southwest Campus	G332	30	Projector, 4 digital display

Page 1

FIGURE 1.52

(Project 1D Certification Events continues on the next page)

Skills Review Project 1D Certification Events (continued)

1 Start Access. In the Access opening screen, click in the **Search** box, type **event** and then press Enter to search for a template to manage events. Click the **Desktop event management** template. In the **Desktop event management** dialog box, to the right of the **File Name** box, click **Browse**, and then navigate to your **Access Chapter 1** folder. In the **File New Database** dialog box, click in the **File name** box to select the existing text. Using your own name, type **Lastname_Firstname_1D_Certification_Events** and then press Enter. In the **Desktop event management** dialog box, click **Create** to download the template and to save the database. Under the ribbon, on the **Message Bar**, click **Enable Content**.

a. In the first row, click in the **Title** field, type **Word 2016** and then press Tab. In the **Start Time** field, type **7/9/21 10a** and then press Tab. In the **End Time** field, type **7/9/21 4p** and then press Tab. In the **Description** field, type **Office 2016** and then press Tab. In the **Location** field, type **Southwest Campus** and then press Tab three times to move to the **Title** field in the new record row.

b. In the form, directly above the field names row, click **New Event** to open the **Event Details** single-record form. Using Tab to move from field to field, enter the record shown in Table 1. Press Tab three times to move from the **End Time** field to the **Description** field.

c. In the **Events Detail** form, click **Close**. Using either the **Event List** multiple-items form or the **Event Details** single-record form, enter the records shown in Table 2. If you use the Events Detail form, be sure to Close it after entering records to display the records in the Event List form.

d. **Close** the **Event List** form. On the ribbon, click the **External Data tab**, and in the **Import & Link group**, click **Excel**. In the **Get External Data – Excel Spreadsheet** dialog box, click **Browse**. Navigate to your student data files, and then double-click **a01D_Certification_Events**. Click the second option button—**Append a copy of the records to the table**—and then click **OK**.

e. In the **Import Spreadsheet Wizard**, click **Next**, and then click **Finish**. In the **Get External Data – Excel Spreadsheet** dialog box, click **Close**. **Open** the **Navigation Pane**, and then double-click **Event List** to open the form that displays data stored in the Events table—12 total records display. **Close** the **Navigation Pane**.

f. To the left of the **ID** field name, click **Select All**. In the field names row, point to the right edge of any of the selected columns to display the ✛ pointer, and then double-click to apply Best Fit to all of the columns. Click in any field to cancel the selection, and then **Save** the form.

2 **Open** the **Navigation Pane**. At the top of the **Navigation Pane**, click **More**. On the list, under **Navigate To Category**, click **Tables and Related Views**.

a. In the **Navigation Pane**, point to **Events: Table**, right-click, and then click **Open** to display the records in the underlying table. In the **Navigation Pane**, double-click the **Current Events** *report* (green icon) to view this predesigned report. From the **Navigation Pane**, open the **Events by Week** report to view this predesigned report.

TABLE 1

Title	Location	Start Time	End Time	Description
Excel 2016	Northeast Campus	7/16/21 10a	7/16/21 4p	Office 2016

(Return to Step 1c)

TABLE 2

ID	Title	Start Time	End Time	Description	Location
3	Access 2016	7/23/21 12p	7/23/21 6p	Office 2016	Southeast Campus
4	PowerPoint 2016	7/30/21 9a	7/30/21 3p	Office 2016	Northwest Campus

(Return to Step 1d)

(Project 1D Certification Events continues on the next page)

Skills Review Project 1D Certification Events (continued)

b. In the object window, right-click any of the **object tabs**, and then click **Close All**. **Close** the **Navigation Pane**.

3 On the ribbon, click the **Create tab**, and in the **Tables group**, click **Table**.

a. In the field names row, click **Click to Add**, click **Short Text**, type **Campus Location** and then press Enter. In the third column, click **Short Text**, type **Lab** and then press Enter. In the fourth column, click **Number**, type **# Computers** and then press Enter. In the fifth column, click **Short Text**, type **Additional Equipment** and then press ↓.

b. Right-click the **ID** field name, and then click **Rename Field**. Type **Lab ID** and then press Enter. On the **Fields tab**, in the **Formatting group**, click the **Data Type arrow**, and then click **Short Text**.

c. In the new record row, click in the **Lab ID** field, and then enter the records shown in Table 3, pressing Enter or Tab to move from one field to the next.

d. In the **Views group**, click the upper portion of the **View** button to switch to **Design** view. In the **Save As** dialog box, in the **Table Name** box, using your own name, type **Lastname Firstname 1D Cert Prep Locations** and then click **OK**. Notice that the **Lab ID** field is the **Primary Key**. On the **Design tab**, in the **Views group**, click the upper portion of the **View** button to switch to **Datasheet** view.

e. To the left of the **Lab ID** field name, click **Select All** to select all of the columns and rows in the table. On the **Home tab**, in the **Records group**, click **More**, and then click **Field Width**. In the **Column Width** dialog box, click **Best Fit**. Click in any field to cancel the selection, and then **Save** the changes to the table. **Close** the table, and then **Open** the **Navigation Pane**. Increase the width of the **Navigation Pane** so that your entire table name displays.

4 In the **Navigation Pane**, double-click the **All Events** report to open it in the object window. **Close** the **Navigation Pane**. On the **Home tab**, in the **Views group**, click the top of the **View** button to switch to **Layout** view. At the top of the report, click the title—*All Events*—to display a colored border around the title. Click to the left of the letter *A* to place the insertion point there. Using your own name, type **Lastname Firstname 1D** and then press Spacebar. Press Enter, and then **Save** the report.

a. On the right side of the status bar, click **Print Preview**, and notice that the report will print on one page. Create a paper printout or PDF electronic image as instructed. Click **Close Print Preview**, and then **Close** the report.

b. **Open** the **Navigation Pane**, double-click your **1D Cert Prep Locations** table, and then **Close** the **Navigation Pane**. On the ribbon, click the **File tab**, click **Print**, and then click **Print Preview**. On the **Print Preview tab**, in the **Page Layout group**, click **Landscape**. Create a paper printout or PDF electronic image as directed, and then click **Close Print Preview**. Close your **1D Cert Prep Locations** table.

c. **Open** the **Navigation Pane**. On the right side of the title bar, click **Close** to close the database and to close Access. As directed by your instructor,

TABLE 3

Lab ID	Campus Location	Lab	# Computers	Additional Equipment
NW-L01	**Northwest Campus**	**H202**	**35**	**3 printers, DVD player**
SE-L01	**Southeast Campus**	**E145**	**25**	**Projector, document camera, smart board**
NE-L01	**Northeast Campus**	**F32**	**40**	**4 printers, smart board, instructor touch screen**
SW-L01	**Southwest Campus**	**G332**	**30**	**Projector, 4 digital display**
SE-L02	**Southeast Campus**	**A225**	**25**	**Projector, white board, instructor touch screen**

(Return to Step 3d)

(Project 1D Certification Events continues on the next page)

Skills Review Project 1D Certification Events (continued)

submit your database and the paper printouts or PDF electronic images of the two objects—one report and one table—that are the results of this project.

Specifically, in this project, using your own name, you created the following database and printouts or PDF electronic images:

1. Lastname_Firstname_1D_Certification_Events	Database file
2. Lastname Firstname 1D Cert Prep Locations	Table
3. Lastname Firstname 1D All Events	Report

END | You have completed Project 1D

CONTENT-BASED ASSESSMENTS (MASTERY AND TRANSFER OF LEARNING)

Mastering Access Project 1E Kiosk Inventory (continued)

Inventory Report and then display the report in **Print Preview**. Create a paper printout or PDF electronic image as directed. Click **Close Print Preview.**

9 **Close All** open objects. **Open** the **Navigation Pane** and be sure that all object names display fully. **Close** the database, and then **Close** Access. As directed by your instructor, submit your database and the paper printouts or PDF electronic images of the five objects—two tables, one query, one form, and one report—that are the results of this project. Specifically, in this project, using your own name, you created the following database and printouts or PDF electronic images:

1. Lastname_Firstname_1E_Kiosk_Inventory	Database file
2. Lastname Firstname 1E Inventory	Table
3. Lastname Firstname 1E Inventory Storage	Table
4. Lastname Firstname 1E Inventory Query	Query
5. Lastname Firstname 1E Inventory Form	Form
6. Lastname Firstname 1E Inventory Report	Report

END | You have completed Project 1E

Apply 1B skills from these Objectives:

6 Use a Template to Create a Database

7 Organize Objects in the Navigation Pane

8 Create a New Table in a Database Created with a Template

9 Print a Report and a Table

Mastering Access Project 1F Recruiting Events

In the following Mastering Access project, you will create a database to store information about the recruiting events that are scheduled to attract new students to Texas Lakes Community College. Your completed report and tables will look similar to Figure 1.54.

PROJECT FILES

For Project 1F, you will need the following file:

Desktop event management template

a01F_Recruiting_Events (Excel workbook)

You will save your database as:

Lastname_Firstname_1F_Recruiting_Events

PROJECT RESULTS

Build From Scratch

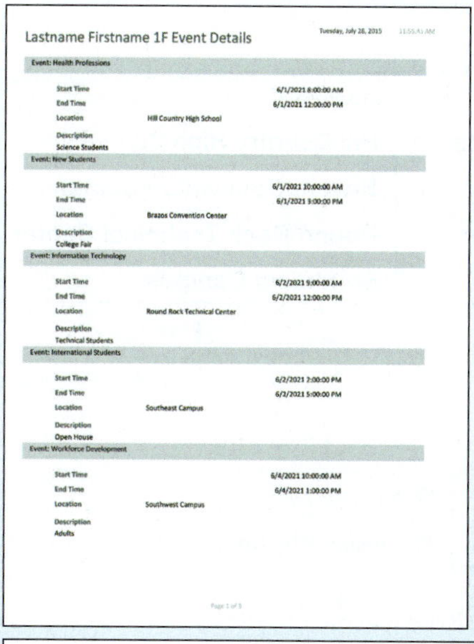

Lastname Firstname 1F Event Details — Tuesday, July 28, 2015 11:55:41 AM

Event: Health Professions

Start Time 6/1/2021 8:00:00 AM
End Time 6/1/2021 12:00:00 PM
Location Hill Country High School
Description
Science Students

Event: New Students

Start Time 6/1/2021 10:00:00 AM
End Time 6/1/2021 3:00:00 PM
Location Brazos Convention Center
Description
College Fair

Event: Information Technology

Start Time 6/2/2021 9:00:00 AM
End Time 6/2/2021 12:00:00 PM
Location Round Rock Technical Center
Description
Technical Students

Event: International Students

Start Time 6/2/2021 2:00:00 PM
End Time 6/2/2021 5:00:00 PM
Location Southeast Campus
Description
Open House

Event: Workforce Development

Start Time 6/4/2021 10:00:00 AM
End Time 6/4/2021 1:00:00 PM
Location Southwest Campus
Description
Adults

Page 1 of 3

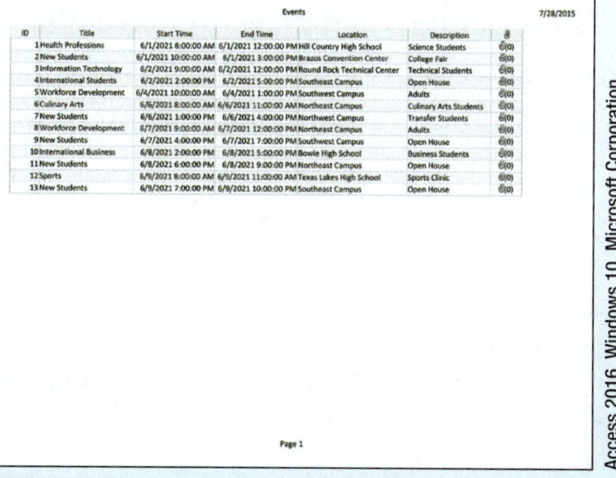

Events — 7/28/2015

ID	Title	Start Time	End Time	Location	Description	📎
1	Health Professions	6/1/2021 8:00:00 AM	6/1/2021 12:00:00 PM	Hill Country High School	Science Students	(0)
2	New Students	6/1/2021 10:00:00 AM	6/1/2021 3:00:00 PM	Brazos Convention Center	College Fair	(0)
3	Information Technology	6/2/2021 9:00:00 AM	6/2/2021 12:00:00 PM	Round Rock Technical Center	Technical Students	(0)
4	International Students	6/2/2021 2:00:00 PM	6/2/2021 5:00:00 PM	Southeast Campus	Open House	(0)
5	Workforce Development	6/4/2021 10:00:00 AM	6/4/2021 1:00:00 PM	Southwest Campus	Adults	(0)
6	Culinary Arts	6/6/2021 8:00:00 AM	6/6/2021 11:00:00 AM	Northeast Campus	Culinary Arts Students	(0)
7	New Students	6/6/2021 1:00:00 PM	6/6/2021 4:00:00 PM	Northwest Campus	Transfer Students	(0)
8	Workforce Development	6/7/2021 9:00:00 AM	6/7/2021 12:00:00 PM	Northeast Campus	Adults	(0)
9	New Students	6/7/2021 4:00:00 PM	6/7/2021 7:00:00 PM	Southwest Campus	Open House	(0)
10	International Business	6/8/2021 2:00:00 PM	6/8/2021 5:00:00 PM	Bowie High School	Business Students	(0)
11	New Students	6/8/2021 6:00:00 PM	6/8/2021 9:00:00 PM	Northeast Campus	Open House	(0)
12	Sports	6/9/2021 8:00:00 AM	6/9/2021 11:00:00 AM	Texas Lakes High School	Sports Clinic	(0)
13	New Students	6/9/2021 7:00:00 PM	6/9/2021 10:00:00 PM	Southeast Campus	Open House	(0)

Page 1

Access 2016, Windows 10, Microsoft Corporation

Lastname Firstname 1F Recruiters — 6/1/2015

Recruiter ID	Location	Last Name	First Name	Email Address	Business Phone
R-01	Hill Country High School	Rostamo	Robyn	rrostamo@hillcohs.sch	(512) 555-3410
R-02	Brazos Convention Center	Hart	Roberto	rlhart@brazosconv.ctr	(512) 555-1938
R-03	Round Rock Technical Center	Sedlacek	Belinda	bsedlacek@rrocktech.sch	(512) 555-0471
R-04	Southeast Campus	Nguyen	Thao	tnguyen@tlcc.edu	(512) 555-2387

Page 1

FIGURE 1.54

(Project 1F Recruiting Events continues on the next page)

Mastering Access Project 1F Recruiting Events (continued)

1 Start Access. In the Access opening screen, search for **event** and then click the **Desktop event management** template. Save the database in your **Access Chapter 1** folder as **Lastname_Firstname_1F_Recruiting_Events** and on the **Message Bar**, click **Enable Content**.

2 In the **Event List** multiple-items form or the **Event Details** single-record form—open by clicking New Event on the Event List form—enter the records shown in Table 1.

3 **Close** the **Event List** form. From your student data files, import and **Append** the data from the **Excel** file **a01F_Recruiting_Events** to the **Events** table. **Open** the **Navigation Pane**, organize the objects by **Tables and Related Views**, and then open the **Events** table to display 13 records. **Close** the table, and then **Close** the **Navigation Pane**.

4 **Create** a new **Table** defining the new fields shown in Table 2.

5 For the **ID** field, change the **Data Type** to **Short Text**, rename the field to **Recruiter ID** and then enter the records shown in Table 3.

6 Apply **Best Fit** to all of the columns. **Save** the table as **Lastname Firstname 1F Recruiters** and then **Close** the table.

7 From the **Navigation Pane**, open the **Event Details** *report* (green icon). Switch to **Layout** view. In the report, click in the title—*Event Details*—and then click to position the insertion point to the left of the word *Event*. Using your own type, type **Lastname Firstname 1F** and then press Spacebar and Enter. If necessary, decrease the font size of the title so that the title does not overlap the date on the right side or does not extend to two lines.

TABLE 1

ID	Title	Start Time	End Time	Description	Location
1	**Health Professions**	**6/1/21 8a**	**6/1/21 12p**	**Science Students**	**Hill Country High School**
2	**New Students**	**6/1/21 10a**	**6/1/21 3p**	**College Fair**	**Brazos Convention Center**
3	**Information Technology**	**6/2/21 9a**	**6/2/21 12p**	**Technical Students**	**Round Rock Technical Center**
4	**International Students**	**6/2/21 2p**	**6/2/21 5p**	**Open House**	**Southeast Campus**

(Return to Step 3)

TABLE 2

Data Type		Short Text	Short Text	Short Text	Short Text	Short Text
Field Name	ID	**Location**	**Last Name**	**First Name**	**Email Address**	**Business Phone**

(Return to Step 5)

TABLE 3

Recruiter ID	Location	Last Name	First Name	Email Address	Business Phone
R-01	**Hill Country High School**	**Rostamo**	**Robyn**	**rrostamo@hillcohs.sch**	**(512) 555-3410**
R-02	**Brazos Convention Center**	**Hart**	**Roberto**	**rlhart@brazosconv.ctr**	**(512) 555-1938**
R-03	**Round Rock Technical Center**	**Sedlacek**	**Belinda**	**bsedlacek@rrocktech.sch**	**(512) 555-0471**
R-04	**Southeast Campus**	**Nguyen**	**Thao**	**tnguyen@tlcc.edu**	**(512) 555-2387**

(Return to Step 6)

(Project 1F Recruiting Events continues on the next page)

Mastering Access Project 1F Recruiting Events (continued)

Save the report, and then display it in **Print Preview**. If directed to create a paper printout, in the **Print group**, click **Print**. In the **Print** dialog box, under **Print Range**, to the right of **Pages**, click in the **From** box, type **1** and then click in the **To** box and type **1** and then click **OK** to print only the first page. If directed to create a PDF electronic image, in the **Publish as PDF or XPS** dialog box, click **Options**, and then under **Range**, click the **Page(s)** option button, and then click **OK**. **Close Print Preview**, and then **Close** the report.

8 From the **Navigation Pane**, open the **Events** table, select all of the columns, and then apply **Best Fit** to all of the columns by double-clicking the right edge of any of the selected columns. Cancel the selection, and then **Save** the table. Display the table in **Print Preview**, change the orientation to **Landscape**, change the **Margins** to **Normal**, and then create a paper printout or PDF electronic image as directed. **Close Print Preview**, and then **Close** the table.

9 From the **Navigation Pane**, open your **1F Recruiters** table. Display the table in **Print Preview**, change the orientation to **Landscape**, and then create a paper printout or PDF electronic image as directed. **Close Print Preview**, and then **Close** the table.

10 Open the **Navigation Pane**, and be sure that all object names display fully. **Close** Access. As directed by your instructor, submit your database and the paper printouts or PDF electronic images of the three objects—one report and two tables—that are the results of this project. Specifically, in this project, using your own name, you created the following database and printouts or PDF electronic images:

1. Lastname_Firstname_1F_Recruiting_Events	Database file
2. Lastname Firstname 1F Event Details	Report
3. Lastname Firstname 1F Events	Table
4. Lastname Firstname 1F Recruiters	Table

END | You have completed Project 1F

Mastering Access Project 1G College Construction (continued)

number—**Page 1 of 1**. **Save** the report as **Lastname Firstname 1G Projects Report** and then display the report in **Print Preview**. Create a printout or PDF electronic image as directed. **Close Print Preview**.

9 **Close All** open objects. **Open** the **Navigation Pane**, arrange the objects by **Tables and Related Views**, and be sure that all object names display fully. **Close** the database, but do *not* close Access.

10 In the Access opening screen, search for **event** and then click the **Desktop Event management** template. Save the database in your **Access Chapter 1** folder as **Lastname_Firstname_1G_Public_Events** and on the **Message Bar**, click **Enable Content**.

11 In the **Event List** multiple-items form or the **Event Details** single-record form—open by clicking New Event on the Event List form—enter the three records shown in **Table 3**.

12 **Close** the **Event List** form. **Open** the **Navigation Pane**, organize the objects by **Tables and Related Views**, and then open the **Current Events** *report* (green icon). Switch to **Layout** view. In the report, click in the title—*Current Events*—and then click to position the insertion point to the left of the letter *C*. Using your own name, type **Lastname Firstname 1G** and then press Spacebar and Enter. If necessary, decrease the font size of the title so that the title does not overlap the date on the right side or does not extend to two lines. **Save** the report, display it in **Print Preview**, and then create a paper printout or PDF electronic image as directed. **Close Print Preview**, and then **Close** the report.

13 Open the **Navigation Pane**, and be sure that all object names display fully. **Close** Access. As directed by your instructor, submit your database and the paper printouts or PDF electronic images of the six objects—two tables, one query, one form and two reports—that are the results of this project. Specifically, in this project, using your own name, you created the following database and printouts or PDF electronic images:

1. Lastname_Firstname_1G_College_Construction	Database file
2. Lastname_Firstname_1G_Public_Events	Database file
3. Lastname Firstname 1G Projects	Table
4. Lastname Firstname 1G Contractors	Table
5. Lastname Firstname 1G Projects Query	Query
6. Lastname Firstname 1G Project Form	Form
7. Lastname Firstname 1G Projects Report	Report
8. Lastname Firstname 1G Current Events	Report

TABLE 3

ID	Title	Start Time	End Time	Description	Location
1	**Groundbreaking**	**6/13/21 10a**	**6/13/21 11a**	**Student Center groundbreaking**	**Northeast Campus**
2	**Dedication**	**8/26/21 12:30 p**	**8/26/21 2p**	**Gymnasium building dedication**	**Southwest Campus**
3	**Community Arts Expo**	**10/5/21 6p**	**10/5/21 9p**	**Book and Art Expo at Library**	**Southeast Campus**

(Return to Step 12)

END | You have completed Project 1G

CONTENT-BASED ASSESSMENTS (CRITICAL THINKING)

Apply a combination of the 1A and 1B skills.

GO! Fix It Project 1H Scholarships **MyITLab**

GO! Make It Project 1I Theater Events **MyITLab**

GO! Solve It Project 1J Athletic Scholarships **MyITLab**

GO! Solve It Project 1K Student Activities

Build From Scratch

PROJECT FILES

For Project 1K, you will need the following files:

Desktop event management template
a01K_Student_Activities (Word document)

You will save your database as:

Lastname_Firstname_1K_Student_Activities

Use the Desktop event management template to create a database, and save it in your Access Chapter 1 folder as **Lastname_Firstname_1K_Student_Activities** From your student data files, use the information in the Word document a01K_Student_Activities to enter data into the Event List multiple-items form. Each event begins at 7 p.m. and ends at 10 p.m.

After entering the records, close the form, and arrange the Navigation Pane by Tables and Related Views. Open the Event Details *report*, and then add **Lastname Firstname 1K** to the beginning of the report title. If necessary, decrease the font size of the title so that it does not overlap the date and displays on one line. Create a paper printout or PDF electronic image as directed. As directed, submit your database and the paper printout or PDF electronic image that results.

Performance Level

Performance Criteria	Exemplary: You consistently applied the relevant skills	Proficient: You sometimes, but not always, applied the relevant skills	Developing: You rarely or never applied the relevant skills
Create database using Desktop event management template and enter data	Database created using the correct template, named correctly, and all data entered correctly.	Database created using the correct template, named correctly, but not all data entered correctly.	Database created using the correct template, but numerous errors in database name and data.
Modify report	Event Details report title includes name and project on one line.	Event Details report title includes name and project, but not on one line.	Event Details report title does not include name and project and does not display on one line.
Create report printout	Event Details report printout is correct.	Event Details printout is incorrect.	Event Details report printout not created.

END | You have completed Project 1K

OUTCOMES-BASED ASSESSMENTS (CRITICAL THINKING)

RUBRIC

The following outcomes-based assessments are open-ended assessments. That is, there is no specific correct result; your result will depend on your approach to the information provided. Make Professional Quality your goal. Use the following scoring rubric to guide you in how to approach the problem and then to evaluate how well your approach solves the problem.

The *criteria*—Software Mastery, Content, Format & Layout, and Process—represent the knowledge and skills you have gained that you can apply to solving the problem. The *levels of performance*—Professional Quality, Approaching Professional Quality, or Needs Quality Improvements—help you and your instructor evaluate your result.

	Your completed project is of Professional Quality if you:	Your completed project is Approaching Professional Quality if you:	Your completed project Needs Quality Improvements if you:
1-Software Mastery	Choose and apply the most appropriate skills, tools, and features and identify efficient methods to solve the problem.	Choose and apply some appropriate skills, tools, and features, but not in the most efficient manner.	Choose inappropriate skills, tools, or features, or are inefficient in solving the problem.
2-Content	Construct a solution that is clear and well organized, contains content that is accurate, appropriate to the audience and purpose, and is complete. Provide a solution that contains no errors of spelling, grammar, or style.	Construct a solution in which some components are unclear, poorly organized, inconsistent, or incomplete. Misjudge the needs of the audience. Have some errors in spelling, grammar, or style, but the errors do not detract from comprehension.	Construct a solution that is unclear, incomplete, or poorly organized, contains some inaccurate or inappropriate content, and contains many errors of spelling, grammar, or style. Do not solve the problem.
3-Format and Layout	Format and arrange all elements to communicate information and ideas, clarify function, illustrate relationships, and indicate relative importance.	Apply appropriate format and layout features to some elements, but not others. Overuse features, causing minor distraction.	Apply format and layout that does not communicate information or ideas clearly. Do not use format and layout features to clarify function, illustrate relationships, or indicate relative importance. Use available features excessively, causing distraction.
4-Process	Use an organized approach that integrates planning, development, self-assessment, revision, and reflection.	Demonstrate an organized approach in some areas, but not others; or, use an insufficient process of organization throughout.	Do not use an organized approach to solve the problem.

Apply a combination of the 1A and 1B skills.

OUTCOMES-BASED ASSESSMENTS (CRITICAL THINKING)

GO! Think Project 1L Student Clubs

Build From Scratch

PROJECT FILES

For Project 1L, you will need the following files:

Blank desktop database
a01L_Clubs (Word document)
a01L_Student_Clubs (Excel workbook)
a01L_Club_Presidents (Excel workbook)

You will save your database as

Lastname_Firstname_1L_Student_Clubs

Dr. Daniel Martinez, Vice President of Student Services, needs a database that tracks information about student clubs. The database should contain two tables—one for club information and one for contact information for the club presidents.

Create a desktop database, and save the database in your Access Chapter 1 folder as **Lastname_Firstname_1L_Student_Clubs** From your student data files, use the information in the Word document a01L_Clubs to create the first table and to enter two records. Name the table appropriately to include your name and 1L, and then append the 23 records from the Excel workbook a01L_Student_Clubs to your table. For the Club ID and President ID fields, add a description and change the field size.

Create a second table in the database by importing 25 records from the Excel workbook a01L_Club_Presidents, and name the table appropriately to include your name and 1L. For the State and Postal Code fields, add a description and change the field size. Be sure that the field data types are correct—recall that numbers that are not used in calculations should have a data type of Short Text. Be sure all of the data and field names display in each table.

Create a simple query based on the Clubs table that answers the question, *What is the club name, meeting day, meeting time, campus, and Room ID for all of the clubs?* Create a form based on the Clubs table, saving it with an appropriate name that includes your name and 1L. Create a report based on the Presidents table, saving it with an appropriate name that includes your name and 1L, that displays the president's last name (in ascending order), the president's first name, and the phone number of every president. Change the width of the three fields so that there is less space between them, but being sure that each record prints on a single line.

Create paper printout or PDF electronic images of the two tables, the query, only Record 21 of the form, and the report as directed being sure that each object prints on one page. Organize the objects on the Navigation Pane by Tables and Related Views, and be sure that all object names display fully. As directed, submit your database and the paper printouts or PDF electronic images of the five objects—two tables, one query, one form, and one report—that are the results of this project.

END | You have completed Project 1L

Build From Scratch

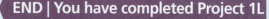

GO! Think Project 1M Faculty Training MyItLab

Build From Scratch

You and GO! Project 1N Personal Contacts MyItLab

GO! Collaborative Team Project Project 1O Bell Orchid Hotels MyItLab

Sort and Query a Database

2

ACCESS 2016

PROJECT 2A

OUTCOMES
Sort and query a database

OBJECTIVES
1. Open and Save an Existing Database
2. Create Table Relationships
3. Sort Records in a Table
4. Create a Query in Design View
5. Create a New Query from an Existing Query
6. Sort Query Results
7. Specify Criteria in a Query

PROJECT 2B

OUTCOMES
Create complex queries

OBJECTIVES
8. Specify Numeric Criteria in a Query
9. Use Compound Criteria in a Query
10. Create a Query Based on More Than One Table
11. Use Wildcards in a Query
12. Create Calculated Fields in a Query
13. Calculate Statistics and Group Data in a Query
14. Create a Crosstab Query
15. Create a Parameter Query

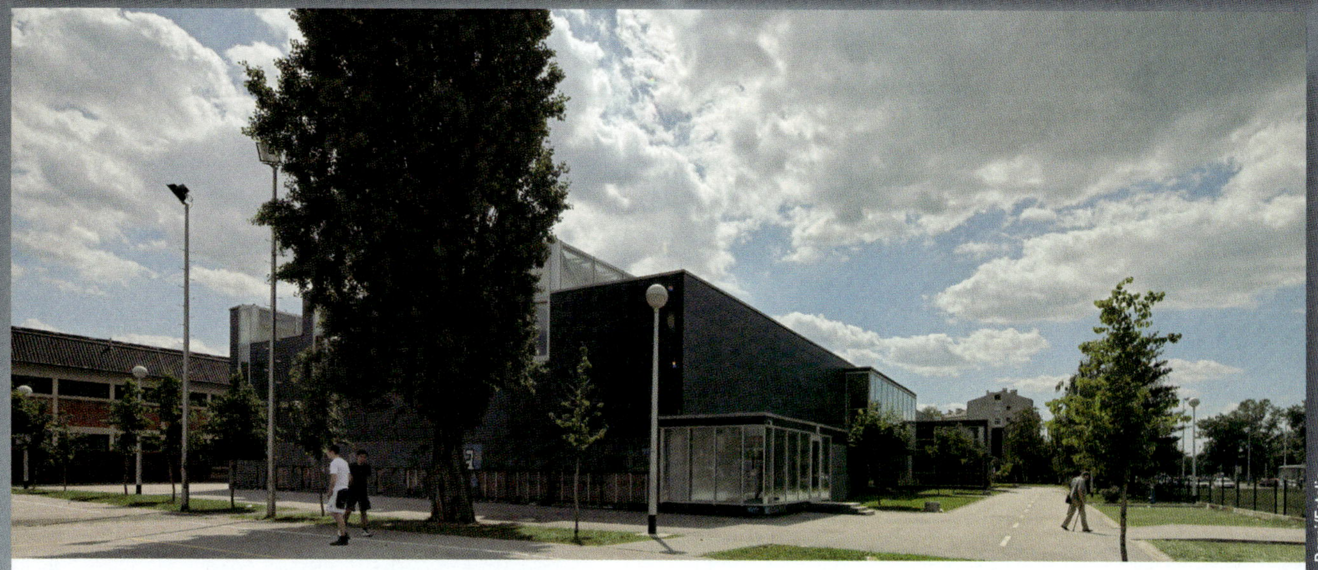

Berni/Fotolia

In This Chapter

GO! to Work with Access

In this chapter, you will sort Access database tables and create and modify queries. To convert data into meaningful information, you must manipulate your data in a way that you can answer questions. One question might be: *Which students have a grade point average of 3.0 or higher?* With this information, you could send information about scholarships or internships to students who meet the grade point average criteria.

The projects in this chapter relate to **Texas Lakes Community College**, which is located in the Austin, Texas, area. Its four campuses serve over 30,000 students and offer more than 140 certificate programs and degrees. The college has a highly acclaimed Distance Education program and an extensive Workforce Development program. The college makes positive contributions to the community through cultural and athletic programs and has maintained partnerships with businesses and nonprofit organizations.

PROJECT 2A Instructors and Courses Database

PROJECT ACTIVITIES

In Activities 2.01 through 2.17, you will assist Dr. Carolyn Judkins, Dean of the Business Division at the Northeast Campus of Texas Lakes Community College, in locating information about instructors and courses in the Division. Your completed database objects will look similar to Figure 2.1.

PROJECT FILES

If your instructor wants you to submit Project 2A in the MyITLab Grader system, log in to MyITLab, locate Grader Project 2A, and then download the files for this project.

For Project 2A, you will need the following file:
a02A_Instructors_Courses

You will save your database as:
Lastname_Firstname_2A_Instructors_Courses

PROJECT RESULTS

GO! Walk Thru Project 2A

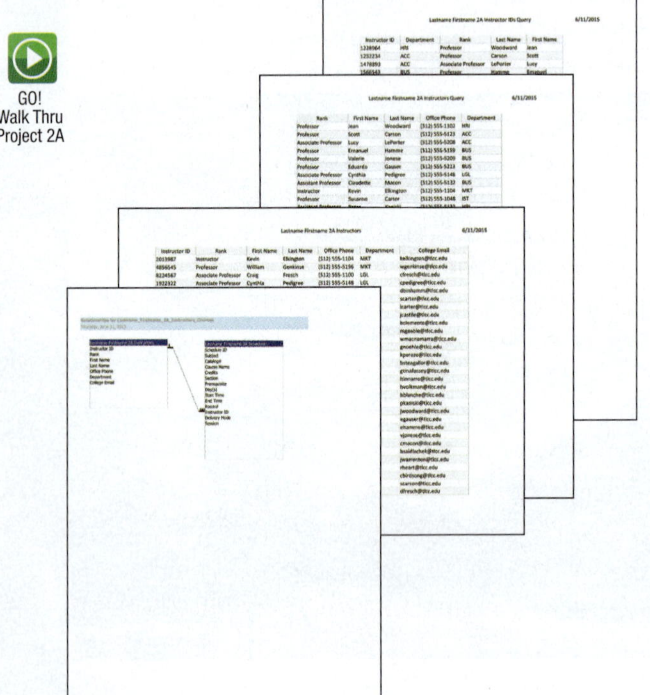

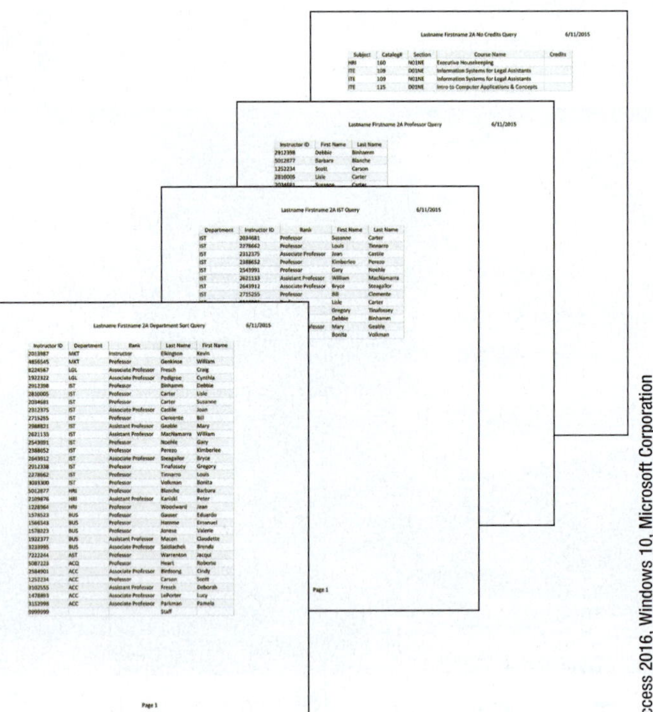

Access 2016, Windows 10, Microsoft Corporation

FIGURE 2.1 Project 2A Instructors and Courses

PROJECT RESULTS

In this project, using your own name, you will create the following database and objects. Your instructor may ask you to submit printouts or PDF electronic images:

Lastname_Firstname_2A_Instructors_Courses	Database file
Relationships for Lastname_Firstname_2A_Instructors_Courses	Relationships Report
Lastname Firstname 2A Instructors table sorted (not saved)	Table sorted (Page 1)
Lastname Firstname 2A Instructors Query	Query
Lastname Firstname 2A Instructor IDs Query	Query
Lastname Firstname 2A Department Sort Query	Query
Lastname Firstname 2A IST Query	Query
Lastname Firstname 2A Professor Query	Query
Lastname Firstname 2A No Credits Query	Query

Objective 1 Open and Save an Existing Database

GO! Learn How Video A2-1

There will be instances where you need to work with a database and still keep the original, unaltered version of the database. Like the other Microsoft Office 2016 applications, you can open a database file and save it with another name.

Activity 2.01 | Opening and Saving an Existing Database

ALERT!

To submit as an autograded project, log into MyITLab and download the files for this project, and begin with those files instead of the 02A_Instructors_Courses file from your student data files. For Project 2A using Grader, read Activity 2.01 carefully. Begin working with the database in Activity 2.02. For Grader to award points accurately, when saving an object, do not include your Lastname Firstname at the beginning of the object name.

1. Start Access. In the Access opening screen, click **Open Other Files**. Under **Open**, click **Browse**. In the **Open** dialog box, navigate to the location where your student data files for this chapter are stored, and then double-click **a02A_Instructors_Courses** to open the database.

2. On the ribbon, click the **File tab**, and then click **Save As**. Under **File Types**, be sure **Save Database As** is selected. On the right, under **Database File Types**, be sure **Access Database** is selected, and then at the bottom of the screen, click **Save As**.

   The Access Database file type saves your database in a format that enables the database to be opened with Access 2007, Access 2010, Access 2013, or Access 2016. If you are sharing your database with individuals who have an earlier version of Access, you can save the database in a version that will be compatible with that application, although some functionality might be lost since earlier versions of Access do not have the same features as later versions of Access. None of the features added to Access since that earlier version will be available in a database saved with backward compatibility.

3. In the **Save As** dialog box, navigate to the location where you are saving your databases. Create a **New folder** named **Access Chapter 2**, and then **Open** the folder. Click in the **File name** box to select the existing text, and using your own name, type **Lastname_Firstname_2A_Instructors_Courses** and then click **Save** or press Enter.

   Use this technique when you need to keep a copy of the original database file.

The Show Table dialog box displays in the Relationships window. In the Show Table dialog box, the Tables tab displays the two tables that are in this database.

4 Point to the title bar of the **Show Table** dialog box, and then, holding down the left mouse button, drag downward and slightly to the right to move the dialog box away from the top of the **Relationships** window. Release the mouse button.

Moving the Show Table dialog box enables you to see the tables as they are added to the Relationships window.

5 In the **Show Table** dialog box, if necessary, click your **2A Instructors** table, and then click **Add**. In the **Show Table** dialog box, double-click your **2A Schedule** table to add it to the **Relationships** window. In the **Show Table** dialog box, click **Close**, and then compare your screen with Figure 2.5.

You can use either technique to add a table to the Relationships window; tables are displayed in the order in which they are added. A ***field list***—a list of the field names in a table—for each of the two table objects displays, and each table's primary key is identified by a key icon. Although this database has only two tables, it is not uncommon for larger databases to have many tables. Scroll bars in a field list indicate that there are fields in the table that are not currently in view.

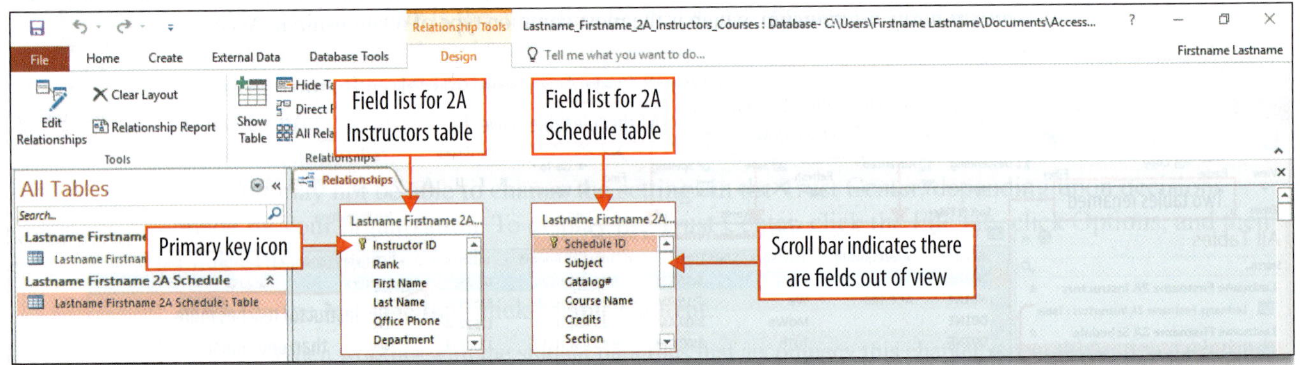

FIGURE 2.5

ALERT!

Are there more than two field lists in the Relationships window?

In the Show Table dialog box, if you double-click a table name more than one time, a duplicate field list displays in the Relationships window. To remove a field list from the Relationships window, right-click the title bar of the field list, and then click Hide table. Alternatively, click anywhere in the field list, and then on the Design tab, in the Relationships group, click Hide Table.

6 In the **2A Schedule** field list—the field list on the right—point to the title bar to display the [pointer icon] pointer. Drag the field list to the right until there are about two inches of space between the field lists.

7 In the **2A Instructors** field list—the field list on the left—point to the lower right corner of the field list to display the [resize pointer icon] pointer, and then, holding down the left mouse button, drag downward and to the right to increase the height and width of the field list until the entire name of the table in the title bar displays and all of the field names display. Release the mouse button.

This action enables you to see all of the available fields and removes the vertical scroll bar.

8 Use the same technique to resize the **2A Schedule** field list so that the table name and all of the field names display as shown in Figure 2.6.

Recall that *one* instructor can teach *many* scheduled courses. The arrangement of field lists in the Relationships window displays the *one table* on the left side and the *many table* on the right side. Recall also that the primary key in each table is the required field that contains the data that uniquely identifies each record in the table. In the 2A Instructors table, each instructor is uniquely identified by the Instructor ID. In the 2A Schedule table, each scheduled course section is uniquely identified by the Schedule ID.

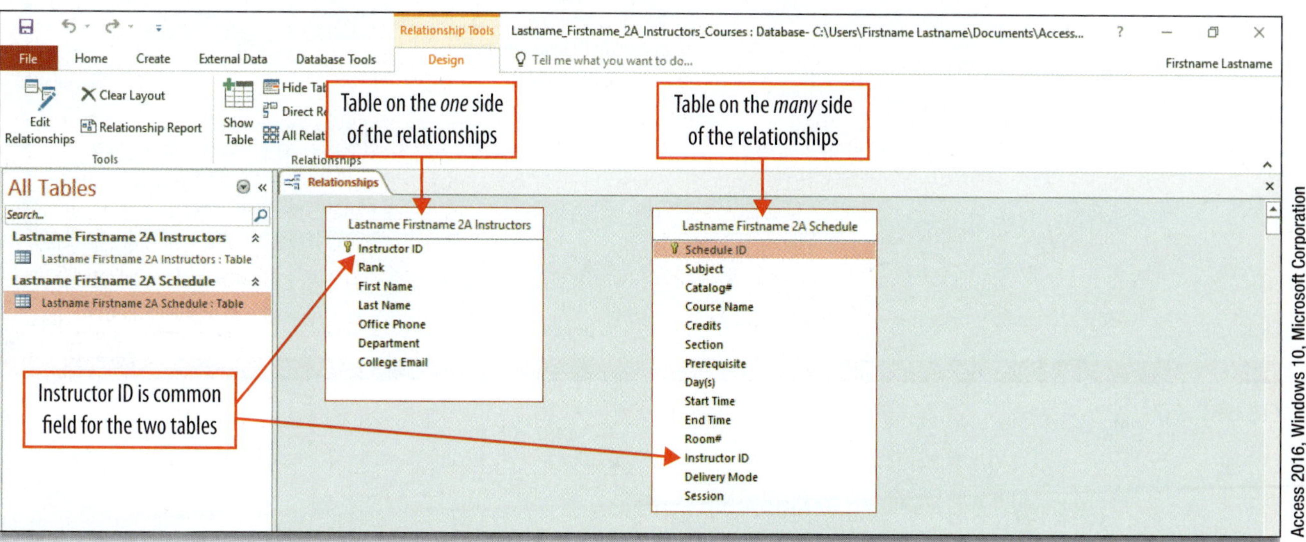

Access 2016, Windows 10, Microsoft Corporation

FIGURE 2.6

NOTE The Field That Is Highlighted Does Not Matter

After you rearrange the field lists in the Relationships window, the highlighted field name indicates the active field list, which is the list that you moved last. This is of no consequence for this activity.

9 In the **2A Instructors** field list, point to **Instructor ID**, and then, holding down the left mouse button, drag the field name downward and to the right into the **2A Schedule** field list until the pointer's arrow is on top of **Instructor ID**. Release the mouse button to display the **Edit Relationships** dialog box.

As you drag, a small graphic displays to indicate that you are dragging a field name from one field list to another. A table relationship works by matching data in two fields—the common field. In these two tables, the common field has the same name—*Instructor ID*. Common fields are not required to have the same name; however, they must have the same data type and field size.

ANOTHER WAY On the Design tab, in the Tools group, click Edit Relationships. In the Edit Relationships dialog box, click Create New. In the Create New dialog box, designate the tables and fields that will create the relationship.

10 Point to the title bar of the **Edit Relationships** dialog box, and then, holding down the left mouse button, drag the dialog box downward and to the right below the two field lists as shown in Figure 2.7. Release the mouse button.

By dragging the common field, you create the *one-to-many* relationship. In the 2A Instructors table, Instructor ID is the primary key. In the 2A Schedule table, Instructor ID is the ***foreign key*** field. The foreign key is the field in the related table used to connect to the primary key in another table. The field on the *one* side of the relationship is typically the primary key.

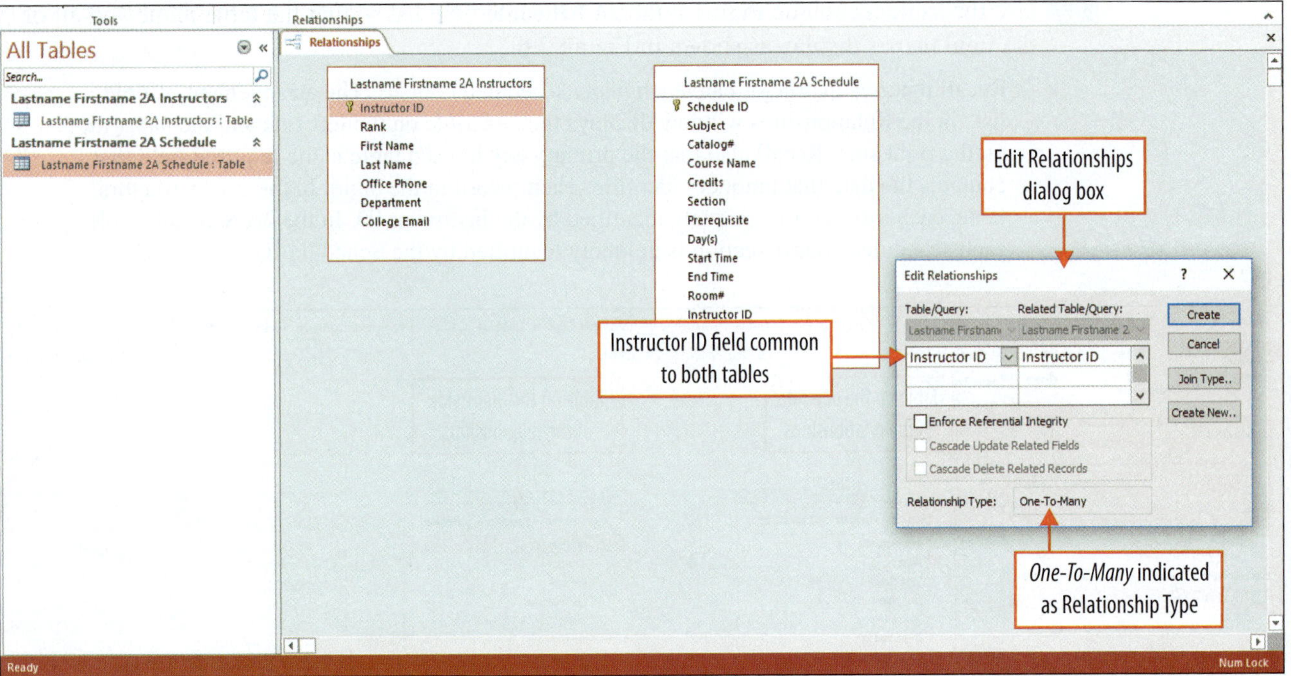

FIGURE 2.7

Activity 2.04 | Setting Relationship Options

In this Activity you will set relationship options that will enable you to work with records in the related tables.

1.2.3

1 In the **Edit Relationships** dialog box, click to select the **Enforce Referential Integrity** check box. Notice that the two options under **Enforce Referential Integrity** are now available.

Referential integrity is a set of rules that Access uses to ensure that the data between related tables is valid. Enforcing referential integrity ensures that an Instructor ID cannot be added to a course in the 2A Schedule table if the Instructor ID is *not* included in the 2A Instructors table first. Similarly, enforcing referential integrity ensures that you cannot delete an instructor from the 2A Instructors table if there is a course that has been assigned to that instructor in the 2A Schedule table.

After selecting Enforce Referential Integrity, ***cascade options***—relationship options that enable you to update records in related tables when referential integrity is enforced—become available for use.

2 In the **Edit Relationships** dialog box, click to select the **Cascade Update Related Fields** check box.

The ***Cascade Update Related Fields*** option enables you to change the data in the primary key field for the table on the *one* side of the relationship, and updates automatically change any fields in the related table that store the same data. For example, in the 2A Instructors table, if you change the data in the Instructor ID field for one instructor, Access automatically finds every scheduled course assigned to that instructor in the 2A Schedule table and changes the data in the common field, in this case, the Instructor ID field. Without this option, if you try to change the ID number for an instructor, an error message displays if there is a related record in the related table on the *many* side of the relationship.

3 In the **Edit Relationships** dialog box, click to select the **Cascade Delete Related Records** check box, and then compare your screen with Figure 2.8

The ***Cascade Delete Related Records*** option enables you to delete a record in the table on the *one* side of the relationship and also delete all of the related records in related tables. For example, if an instructor retires or leaves the college and the courses that the instructor teaches must be canceled because no other instructor can be found, you can delete the instructor's record from the 2A Instructors table, and then all of the courses that are assigned to that instructor in the 2A Schedule table are also deleted. Without this option, an error message displays if you try to delete the instructor's record from the 2A Instructors table. Use caution when applying this option; in many instances, another instructor would be found so you would not want the course to be deleted. In this instance, you would need to change the Instructor ID in the related records before deleting the original instructor from the 2A Instructors table.

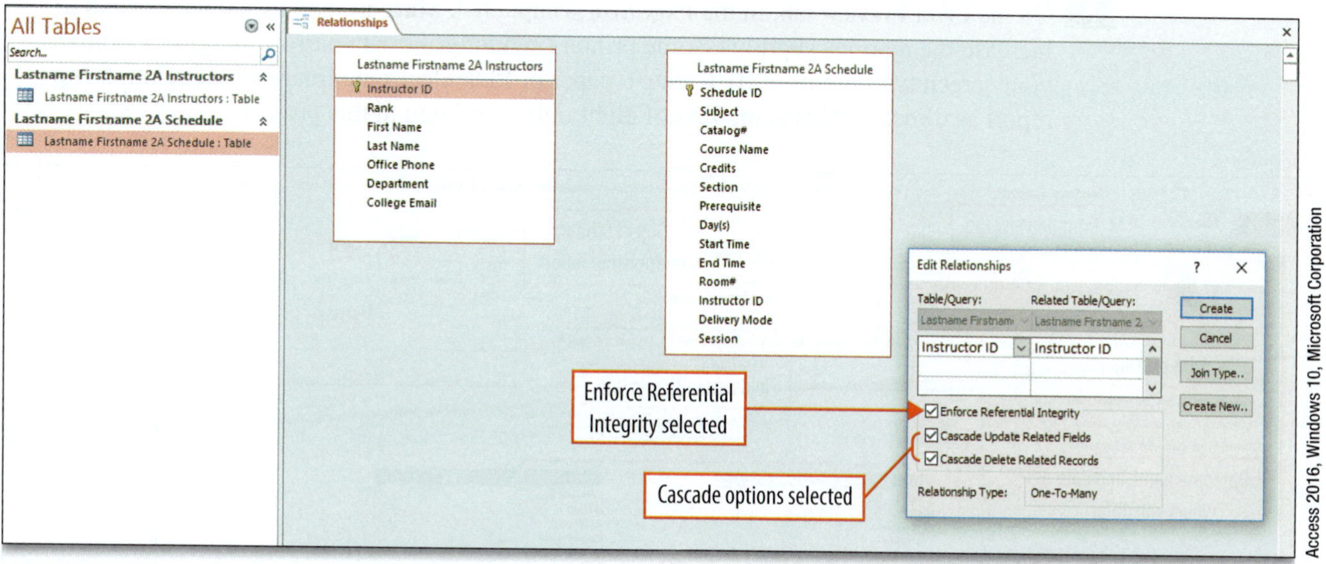

FIGURE 2.8

4 In the **Edit Relationships** dialog box, click **Create**, and then compare your screen with Figure 2.9

A ***join line***—the line connecting or joining the two tables—displays between the two tables. The join line connects the primary key field—Instructor ID—in the 2A Instructors field list to the common field—Instructor ID—in the 2A Schedule field list. On the join line, *1* indicates the *one* side of the relationship, and the infinity symbol (∞) indicates the *many* side of the relationship. These symbols display when referential integrity is enforced.

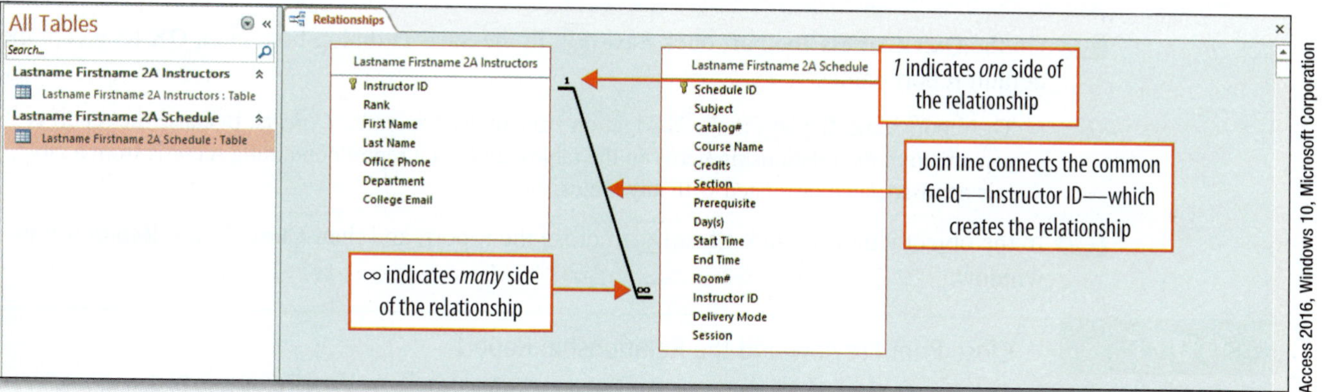

FIGURE 2.9

More Knowledge **Edit or Delete a Relationship**

To modify or delete an existing relationship, right-click the join line. From the shortcut menu, click Delete to remove the join line and the relationship. If you want to edit the relationship options, click Edit Relationship to display the Edit Relationships dialog box.

Activity 2.05 | Printing and Saving a Relationship Report

1.5.1

The Relationships window provides a map of how your database tables are related, and you can print and save this information as a report.

1. On the **Design tab**, in the **Tools group**, click **Relationship Report**.

   The report is created and displays in the object window in Print Preview.

2. On the **Print Preview tab**, in the **Page Size group**, click **Margins**, and then click **Normal** to increase the margins slightly—some printers cannot print with narrow margins. Compare your screen with Figure 2.10. Create a paper or PDF electronic image of the relationship report as directed. This is the first of eight objects printed in this project.

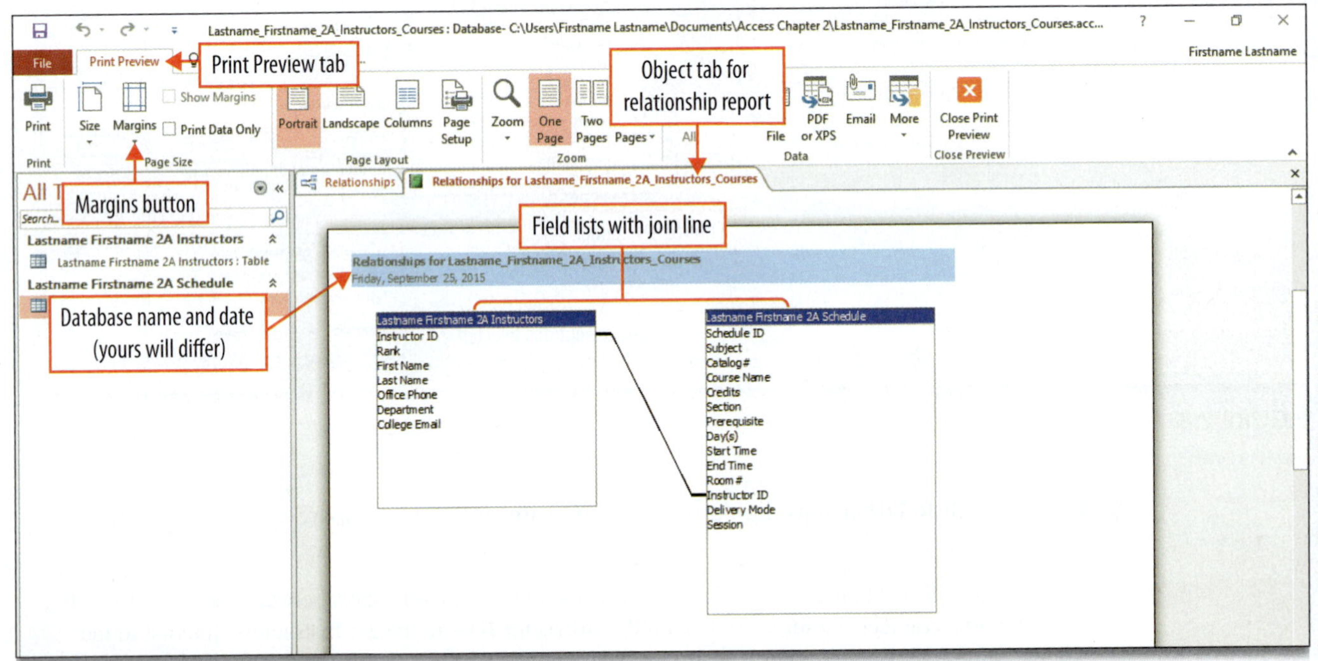

FIGURE 2.10

3. On the **Quick Access Toolbar**, click **Save**. In the **Save As** dialog box, click **OK** to accept the default report name.

   The report name displays in the Navigation Pane under *Unrelated Objects*. Because the report is just a map of the relationship between the tables, and not a report containing records from a table, it is not associated or related with any tables.

4. In the object window, click **Close** to close the report, and then **Close** the **Relationships** window.

NOTE **Close Print Preview and the Relationship Report**

If you click Close Print Preview when the report is displayed in Print Preview, the Relationship report will display in Design view in the object window. If this happens, you can Close the object while it is displayed in this view.

Activity 2.06 | Displaying Subdatasheet Records

When you open the table on the *one* side of the relationship, the related records from the table on the *many* side are available for you to view and to modify.

1 In the **Navigation Pane**, double-click your **2A Instructors** table to open it in the object window, and then **Close** « the **Navigation Pane**.

2 On the left side of the first record—*Instructor ID* of *1224567*—click **+**, and then compare your screen with Figure 2.11.

A plus sign (+) to the left of a record in a table indicates that *related* records may exist in another table. Click the plus sign to display the related records in a ***subdatasheet***. In the first record for *Craig Fresch*, you can see that related records exist in the 2A Schedule table—he is scheduled to teach five LGL (Legal) courses. The plus signs display because you created a relationship between the two tables using the Instructor ID field—the common field.

When you click + to display the subdatasheet, the symbol changes to a minus sign (–), an indication that the subdatasheet is expanded. Click - to collapse the subdatasheet.

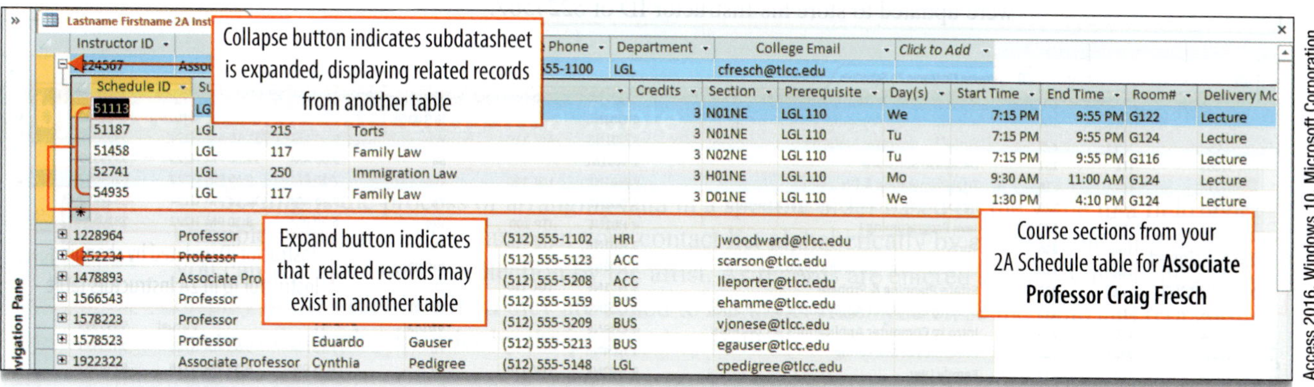

FIGURE 2.11

> ***More Knowledge*** **Other Types of Relationships: One-to-One and Many-to-Many**
>
> The type of relationship is determined by the placement of the primary key field. A one-to-one relationship exists between two tables when a record in one table is related to only one record in a second table. In this case, both tables use the same field as the primary key. This is most often used when data is placed in a separate table because access to that information is restricted; for example, using an Employee ID field as the primary key field, there is one table for contact information, and a second table with payroll information.
>
> A many-to-many relationship between tables exists where many records in one table can be related to many records in another table. For example, many students can enroll in many courses. To create a many-to-many relationship, you must create a third table that contains the primary key fields from both tables. In the Relationships window, you create a join line from this table to the other two tables. In effect, you create multiple one-to-many relationships.

Activity 2.07 | Testing Cascade Options

2.3.3

Recall that cascade options enable you to make changes to records on the *one* side table of the relationship and update or delete records in the table on the *many* side of the relationship. In this Activity you will change the data in the Instructor ID field—the primary key field—for one instructor, and then delete all of the records associated with another instructor from both tables.

1 In the subdatasheet for the first record—*Instructor ID* of *1224567*—notice that the first course that the instructor is scheduled to teach has a *Schedule ID* of *51113—LGL 216*. In the **2A Instructors** table, to the left of the first record, click **–** (minus sign) to collapse the subdatasheet.

Objective 4 Create a Query in Design View

GO! Learn How
Video A2-4

Recall that a select query is a database object that retrieves (selects) specific data from one or more tables and then displays the specified data in a table in Datasheet view. A query answers a question such as *Which instructors teach courses in the IST department?* Unless a query has already been designed to ask this question, you must create a new query.

Database users rarely need to see all of the records in all of the tables. That is why a query is so useful; it creates a ***subset*** of records—a portion of the total records—according to your specifications, and then displays only those records.

Activity 2.10 | Creating a New Select Query in Design View

3.2.2

Previously, you created a query using the Query Wizard. To create queries with more control over the results that are displayed, use Query Design view. The table or tables from which a query selects its data is referred to as the ***data source***.

1 On the ribbon, click the **Create tab**, and then in the **Queries group**, click **Query Design**. Compare your screen with Figure 2.15.

A new query opens in Design view, and the Show Table dialog box displays, which lists both tables in the database.

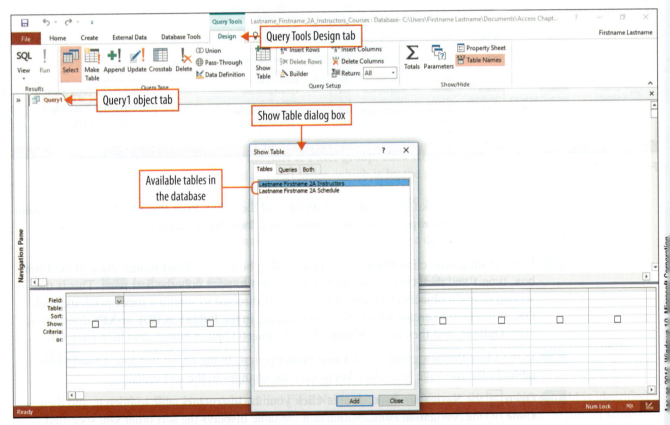

FIGURE 2.15

2 In the **Show Table** dialog box, double-click your **2A Instructors** table, and then, in the dialog box, click **Close**.

A field list for your 2A Instructors table displays in the upper area of the Query window. Instructor ID is the primary key field in this table. The Query window has two parts: the ***table area*** (upper area), which displays the field lists for tables that are used in the query, and the ***query design grid*** (lower area), which displays the design of the query.

ALERT!

Is there more than one field list in the table area?

If you double-click a table more than one time, a duplicate field list displays in the table area of the Query window. To remove a field list from the Query window, right-click the title bar of the field list, and then click Remove Table.

2 ACCESS

3 Point to the lower right corner of the field list to display the pointer, and then, holding down the left mouse button, drag downward and to the right to resize the field list, displaying all of the field names and the entire table name. Release the mouse button. In the **2A Instructors** field list, double-click **Rank**, and then look at the design grid.

The Rank field name displays in the design grid in the Field row. You limit the fields that display in the query results by placing only the desired field names in the design grid.

4 In the **2A Instructors** field list, point to **First Name**, holding down the left mouse button, drag the field name down into the design grid until the pointer displays in the **Field** row in the second column, and then release the mouse button. Compare your screen with Figure 2.16.

This is a second way to add field names to the design grid. When you release the mouse button, the field name displays in the Field row.

FIGURE 2.16

5 In the design grid, in the **Field** row, click in the third column, and then click the **arrow** that displays. From the list, click **Last Name** to add the field to the design grid.

This is a third way to add field names to the design grid.

6 Using one of the three techniques you just practiced, add the **Office Phone** field to the fourth column and the **Department** field to the fifth column in the design grid.

ALERT!

Is there a duplicate field name or an incorrect field name in the design grid?

If you double-click a field name more than one time, a duplicate field name displays in the design grid. To remove a duplicate field name, in the design grid, in the Field row, right-click the duplicate field name, and then click Cut. Use this same method to delete a field name that you placed in the design grid by mistake. As you progress in your study of query design, you will learn alternate ways to delete field names from the design grid.

Activity 2.11 | Running, Saving, Printing, and Closing a Query

3.1.1, 3.1.6

Once a query is designed, you ***run*** it to display the results. When you run a query, Access looks at the records in the table (or tables) you have included in the query, finds the records that match the specified conditions (if any), and displays only those records in a datasheet. Only the fields that you have added to the design grid display in the query results. The query always runs using the current table or tables, presenting the most up-to-date information.

1 On the **Design tab**, in the **Results group**, click **Run**, and then compare your screen with Figure 2.17.

This query answers the question, *What is the rank, first name, last name, office phone number, and department of all of the instructors in the 2A Instructors table?* A query is a subgroup of the records in the table, arranged in Datasheet view, using the fields and conditions that you specify in the design grid. The five fields you specified in the design grid display in columns, and the records from the 2A Instructors table display in rows.

ANOTHER WAY On the Design tab, in the Results group, click the upper portion of the View button, which runs the query by switching to Datasheet view.

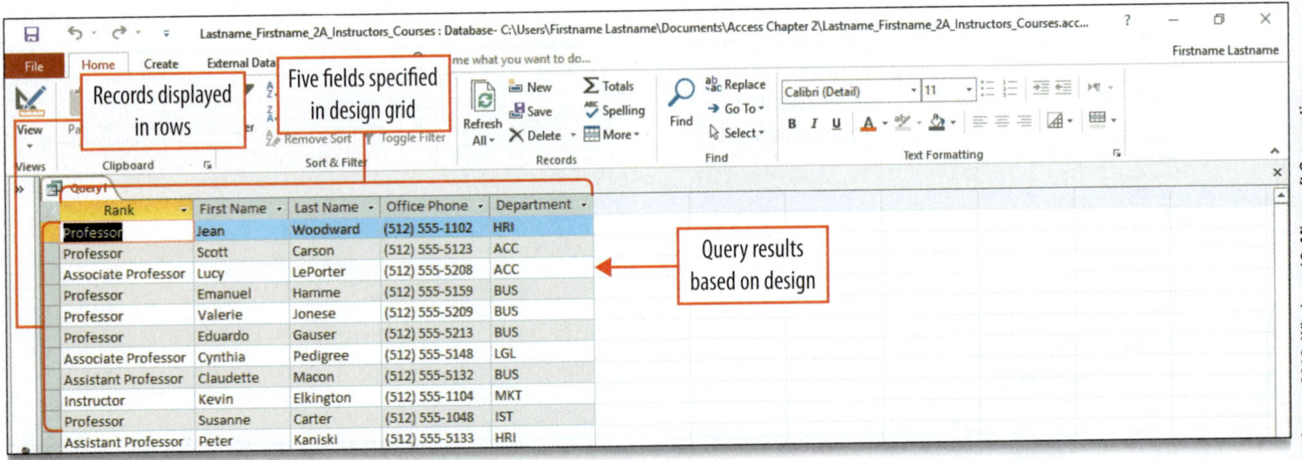

Rank	First Name	Last Name	Office Phone	Department
Professor	Jean	Woodward	(512) 555-1102	HRI
Professor	Scott	Carson	(512) 555-5123	ACC
Associate Professor	Lucy	LePorter	(512) 555-5208	ACC
Professor	Emanuel	Hamme	(512) 555-5159	BUS
Professor	Valerie	Jonese	(512) 555-5209	BUS
Professor	Eduardo	Gauser	(512) 555-5213	BUS
Associate Professor	Cynthia	Pedigree	(512) 555-5148	LGL
Assistant Professor	Claudette	Macon	(512) 555-5132	BUS
Instructor	Kevin	Elkington	(512) 555-1104	MKT
Professor	Susanne	Carter	(512) 555-1048	IST
Assistant Professor	Peter	Kaniski	(512) 555-5133	HRI

FIGURE 2.17

2 On the **Quick Access Toolbar**, click **Save**. In the **Save As** dialog box, type **Lastname Firstname 2A Instructors Query** and then click **OK**.

The query name displays on the object tab in the object window. Save your queries if you are likely to ask the same question again; doing so will save you the effort of creating the query again to answer the same question—just run the query again.

ALERT! Does a message display after entering a query name?

Query names are limited to 64 characters. For all projects, if you have a long last name or first name that results in your query name exceeding the 64-character limit, ask your instructor how you should abbreviate your name.

3 Click the **File tab**, click **Print**, and then click **Print Preview**. Create a paper or PDF electronic image as directed, and then click **Close Print Preview**. This is the third of eight objects printed in this project.

Queries answer questions and gather information from the data in tables. Typically, queries are created as a basis for a report, but query results can be printed like any table of data.

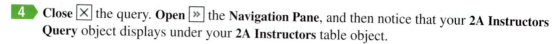

4 **Close** [X] the query. **Open** [»] the **Navigation Pane**, and then notice that your **2A Instructors Query** object displays under your **2A Instructors** table object.

The new query name displays in the Navigation Pane under the table with which it is related—the 2A Instructors table, which is the data source. Only the design of the query is saved; the records reside in the table object. Each time you open a query, Access runs it and displays the results based on the data stored in the data source. Thus, the results of the query always reflect the most up-to-date information.

2 ACCESS

Objective 5 Create a New Query from an Existing Query

GO! Learn How Video A2-5

You can create a new query from scratch or you can open an existing query, save it with a new name, and modify the design to answer another question. Using an existing query saves you time if your new query uses all or some of the same fields and conditions in an existing query.

Activity 2.12 | Copying an Existing Query

3.1.6, 3.2.1

1 In the **Navigation Pane**, right-click your **2A Instructors Query**, and then click **Copy**.

2 In the **Navigation Pane**, point to a blank area, right-click, and then click Paste.

The Paste As dialog box displays, which enables you to name the copied query.

ANOTHER WAY To create a copy of the query, in the Navigation Pane, click the query name to select it. On the Home tab, in the Clipboard group, click Copy. On the Home tab, in the Clipboard group, click the upper portion of the Paste button.

3 In the **Paste As** dialog box, type **Lastname Firstname 2A Instructor IDs Query** and then click **OK**.

A new query, based on a copy of your 2A Instructors Query, is created and displays in the object window and in the Navigation Pane under its data source—your 2A Instructors table.

ANOTHER WAY To create a copy of an open query using a new name, click the File tab, and then click Save As. Under Save As, double-click Save Object As. In the Save As dialog box, click in the Name box and type the name of the new query.

4 In the **Navigation Pane**, double-click your **2A Instructor IDs Query** to run the query and display the query results in **Datasheet** view. **Close** [«] the **Navigation Pane**.

More Knowledge **Rename a Query**

If the query name is not correct, you can rename it as long as the query is closed. In the Navigation Pane, right-click the query name, and then click Rename. Edit the current name or type a new name, and then press Enter to accept the change.

Activity 2.13 | Modifying the Design of a Query

3.2.2, 1.3.5, 3.2.3, 3.1.1, 3.1.6

1 On the **Home tab**, in the **Views group**, click **View** to switch to **Design** view.

ANOTHER WAY On the Home tab, in the Views group, click the View arrow, and then click Design View; or on the right side of the status bar, click the Design View button.

8 **Run** the query, and then notice that the *Rank* field does not display even though it was used to specify criteria in the query.

The same 18 records display, but the *Rank* field is hidden from the query results. Although the Rank field is included in the query design so that you could specify the criteria of *professor*, it is not necessary to display the field in the results. When appropriate, clear the Show check box to avoid cluttering the query results with data that is not useful.

9 **Save** the query as **Lastname Firstname 2A Professor Query** and then display the query results in **Print Preview**. Create a paper or PDF electronic image as directed, and then click **Close Print Preview**. This is the seventh of eight objects printed in this project. **Close** the query.

Activity 2.17 | Using *Is Null* Criteria to Find Empty Fields

3.1.1, 3.2.2, 3.3.2, 3.2.5, 3.1.6

Sometimes you must locate records where data is missing. You can locate such records by using ***Is Null*** as the criteria in a field. *Is Null* is used to find empty fields. Additionally, you can display only the records where data has been entered in the field by using the criteria of ***Is Not Null***, which excludes record3s where the specified field is empty. In this Activity you will design a query to answer the question, *Which scheduled courses have no credits listed?*

1 On the **Create tab**, in the **Queries group**, click **Query Design**. In the **Show Table** dialog box, double-click your **2A Schedule** table to add it to the table area, and then **Close** the **Show Table** dialog box.

2 Resize the field list, and then add the following fields to the design grid in the order given: **Subject**, **Catalog#**, **Section**, **Course Name**, and **Credits**.

3 Click in the **Criteria** row under **Credits**, type **is null** and then press Enter.

Access capitalizes *is null*. The criteria *Is Null* examines the Credits field and locates records that do *not* have any data entered in the field.

4 Click in the **Sort** row under **Subject**, click the **arrow**, and then click **Ascending**. **Sort** the **Catalog#** field in **Ascending** order, and then **Sort** the **Section** field in **Ascending** order. Compare your screen with Figure 2.25.

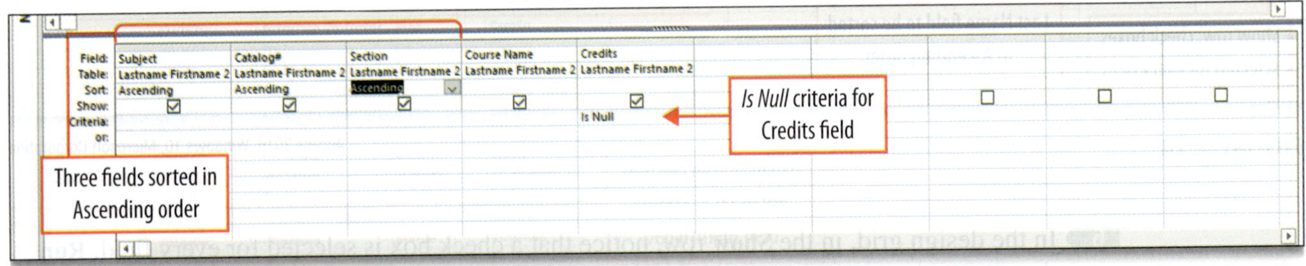

Access 2016, Windows 10, Microsoft Corporation

FIGURE 2.25

5 **Run** the query, and then compare your screen with Figure 2.26.

Four scheduled courses do not have credits listed—the Credits field is empty. The records are sorted in ascending order first by the Subject field, then by the Catalog# field, and then by the Section field. Using the information displayed in the query results, a course scheduler can more easily locate the records in the table and enter the credits for these courses.

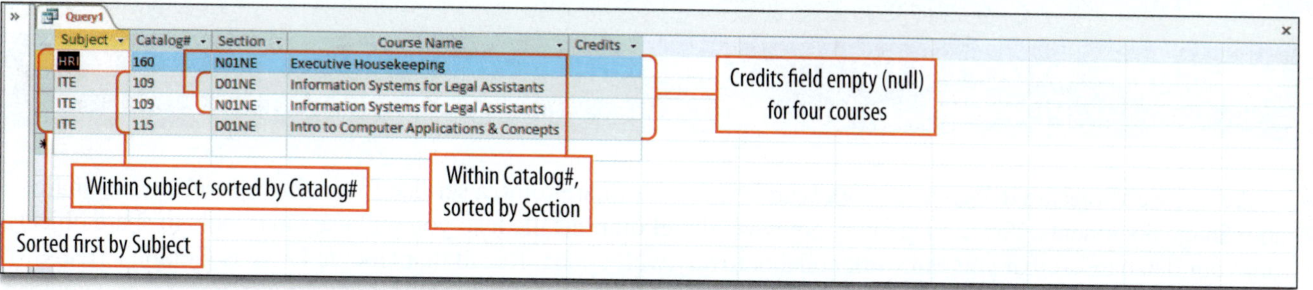

FIGURE 2.26

6 **Save** the query as **Lastname Firstname 2A No Credits Query**, and then display the query results in **Print Preview**. Create a paper or PDF electronic image as instructed, and then click **Close Print Preview**. This is the eighth of eight objects printed in this project.

7 **Close** the query. **Open** the **Navigation Pane**, and then notice that your **2A No Credits Query** object displays under your **2A Schedule** table object, its data source.

8 On the right side of the title bar, click **Close** to close the database and **Close** Access. As directed by your instructor, submit your database and the paper or PDF electronic images of the eight objects—relationship report, sorted table, and six queries—that are the results of this project.

END | You have completed Project 2A

GO! With Google

Objective Export a Relationship Report to a PDF File, Save the PDF File to Google Drive, and then Share the File

Access web apps are designed to work with Microsoft's SharePoint, a service for setting up websites to share and manage documents. Your college may not have SharePoint installed, so you will use other tools to share objects from your database so that you can work collaboratively with others. Recall that Google Drive is Google's free, web-based word processor, spreadsheet, slide show, form, and data storage and sharing service. For Access, you can export a database object to an Excel worksheet, a PDF file, or a text file, and then save the file to Google Drive.

ALERT! Working with Web-Based Applications and Services

Computer programs and services on the web receive continuous updates and improvements, so the steps to complete this web-based activity may differ from the ones shown. You can often look at the screens and the information presented to determine how to complete the activity.

If you do not already have a Google account, you will need to create one before doing this activity. Go to http://google.com and in the upper right corner, click Sign In. On the Sign In screen, click Create Account. On the Create your Google Account page, complete the form, read and agree to the Terms of Service and Privacy Policy, and then click Next step. On the Welcome screen, click Get Started.

Activity | Exporting a Relationship Report to a PDF File, Saving the PDF file to Google Drive, and Sharing the File

In this Activity you will export your Relationships Report object to a PDF file, upload your PDF file to Google Drive, and then share the file.

1 Start Access, navigate to your **Access Chapter 2** folder, and then open your **2A_Instructors_Courses** database file. On the **Message Bar**, click **Enable Content**. In the **Navigation Pane**, click your **Relationships for 2A Instructors Courses** object to select it.

2 On the ribbon, click the **External Data tab**, and then in the **Export group**, click **PDF or XPS**. In the **Publish as PDF or XPS** dialog box, navigate to your **Access Chapter 2** folder. In the **File Save** dialog box, click in the **File name** box, and then using your own name, type **Lastname_Firstname_AC_2A_Web** and be sure that the **Open file after publishing** check box is selected and the **Minimum size (publishing online)** option button is selected. Click **Publish**. If necessary, choose the application with which you want to display the file.

The PDF file is created and opens in Microsoft Edge, Adobe Reader, or Adobe Acrobat, depending on the software that is installed on your computer.

3 If necessary, close the view of the PDF file. In the **Export – PDF** dialog box, click **Close**, and then **Close** [×] Access.

4 From the desktop, open your browser, navigate to **http://google.com**, and then sign in to your Google account. Click the **Google Apps** menu, and then click **Drive**. Open your **GO! Web Projects** folder—or click New to create and then open this folder if necessary.

5 On the left, click **NEW**, click **File upload**. In the **Open** dialog box, navigate to your **Access Chapter 2** folder, and then double-click your **Lastname_Firstname_AC_2A_Web** file to upload it to Google Drive. When the title bar of the message box indicates *Uploads completed*, **Close** the message box. A second message box may display temporarily.

6 In the file list, click your **Lastname_Firstname_AC_2A_Web** PDF file one time to select it.

7 At the top of the window, click **Share**.

8 In the **Share with others** dialog box, with your insertion point blinking in the **Enter names or email addresses** box, type the email address that you use at your college. Click **Can edit**, and click **Can comment**. Click in the **Add a note** box, and then type **This relationship report identifies tables that can be used together to create other objects in the database.** Compare your screen with Figure A.

If you upload a table that you exported as an Excel spreadsheet or Word document and to which you want to enable others to add records, be sure that you change the Sharing permission to *Can edit*.

(GO! With Google continues on the next page)

GO! With Google

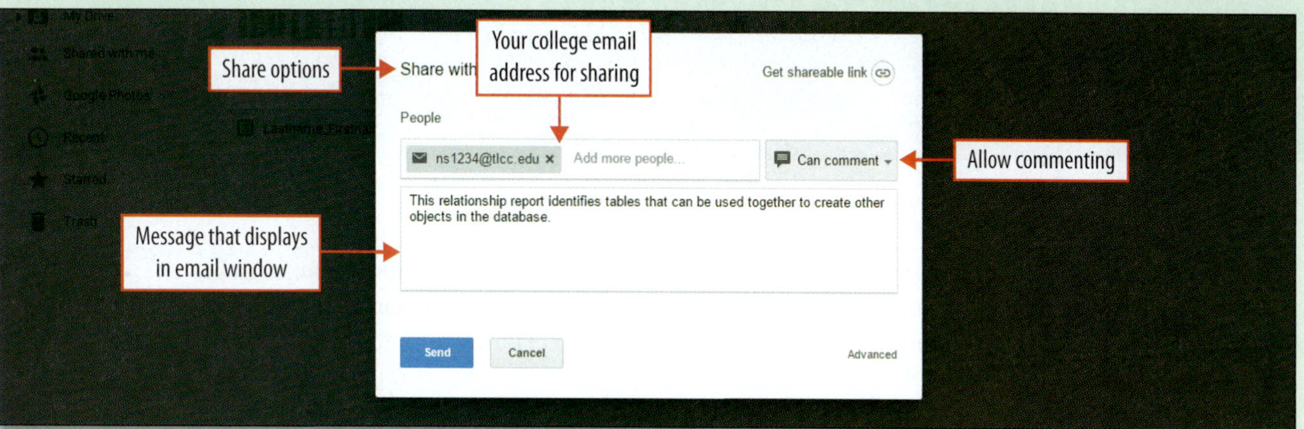

FIGURE A

9 In the **Share with others** dialog box, click **Send**.

If your college is not using Google accounts, you may have to confirm sending the message with a link.

10 At the top of the window, click **Share**. In the **Share with others** dialog box, notice that the file has been shared with your college email account. Start the **Snipping Tool**. In the **Snipping Tool** dialog box, click the **New arrow**, and then click **Full-screen Snip**.

11 On the **Snipping Tool** toolbar, click **Save Snip**. In the **Save As** dialog box, navigate to your **Access Chapter 2** folder. Click in the **File name** box, type **Lastname_Firstname_AC_2A_Web_Snip** and then be sure that the **Save as type** box displays **JPEG file**, and then click **Save**. **Close** the **Snipping Tool** window.

12 In the **Share with Others** dialog box, click **Done** in Google Drive, click your Google Drive name, and then click **Sign out**. **Close** your browser window.

13 If directed to submit a paper printout of your PDF and snip file, follow the directions given in the Note below. As directed by your instructor, submit your file and your snip file that are the results of this project. Your instructor may also request that you submit a copy of the email that was sent to you notifying you of the shared file.

NOTE Printing your PDF and Snip .JPG File

Using File Explorer, navigate to your Access Chapter 2 folder. Locate and double-click your a2A_Google file. On the toolbar, click the Print file button. Then Close your default PDF reader. In your Access Chapter 2 folder, locate and double-click your AC_2A_Web_Snip file. If this is the first time you have tried to open a .jpg file, you will be asked to identify a program. If you are not sure which program to use, select Paint or Windows Photo Viewer. From the ribbon, menu bar, or toolbar, click the Print command, and then Close the program window.

PROJECT

2B Athletic Scholarships Database

PROJECT ACTIVITIES

In Activities 2.18 through 2.33, you will assist Roberto Garza, Athletic Director for Texas Lakes Community College, in creating queries to locate information about athletic scholarships that have been awarded to students. Your completed database objects will look similar to Figure 2.27.

PROJECT FILES

If your instructor wants you to submit Project 2B in the MyITLab Grader system, log in to MyITLab, locate Grader Project 2B, and then download the files for this project.

For Project 2B, you will need the following files:
a02B_Athletes_Scholarships
a02B_Athletes (Excel workbook)

You will save your document as:
Lastname_Firstname_2B_Athletes_Scholarships

PROJECT RESULTS

GO! Walk Thru Project 2B

Access 2016, Windows 10, Microsoft Corporation

FIGURE 2.27 Project 2B Athletic Scholarships

PROJECT RESULTS

In this project, using your own name, you will create the following database and objects. Your instructor may ask you to submit printouts or PDF electronic images:

Lastname_Firstname_2B_Athletes_Scholarships	Database file
Lastname Firstname 2B Relationships	Relationships Report
Lastname Firstname 2B $300 or More Query	Query
Lastname Firstname 2B Awards May-June Query	Query
Lastname Firstname 2B Football AND Over $500	Query
Lastname Firstname 2B Volleyball OR Golf AND Over $200 Query	Query
Lastname Firstname 2B Tennis OR Swimming Query	Query
Lastname Firstname 2B Wildcard Query	Query
Lastname Firstname 2B Alumni Donations Query	Query
Lastname Firstname 2B Total by Sport Query	Query
Lastname Firstname 2B Sport and Team Crosstab Query	Query
Lastname Firstname 2B City Parameter Query	Query (Round Rock)

Objective 8 Specify Numeric Criteria in a Query

GO! Learn How
Video A2-8

Criteria can be set for fields containing numeric data. When you design your table, set the appropriate data type for fields that will contain numbers, currency, or dates so that mathematical calculations can be performed.

2.2.4, 1.1.3, 1.2.2, 2.4.5, 1.3.5

Activity 2.18 | Opening, Renaming, and Saving an Existing Database and Importing a Spreadsheet as a New Table

ALERT!

To submit as an autograded project, log into MyITLab and download the files for this project, and begin with those files instead of the a02B_Athletes_Scholarships file from your student data files. For Project 2B using Grader, begin working with the database in Step 3. For Grader to award points accurately, when saving an object, do not include your Lastname Firstname at the beginning of the object name.

In this Activity you will open, rename, and save an existing database, and then import an Excel spreadsheet as a new table in the database.

1. Start Access. In the Access opening screen, click **Open Other Files**. Under **Open**, click **Browse** and then navigate to the location where your student data files are stored. Double-click **a02B_Athletes_Scholarships** to open the database.

2. On the **File tab**, click **Save As**. Under **File Types**, be sure **Save Database As** is selected, and on the right, under **Database File Types**, be sure **Access Database** is selected, and then click **Save As**. In the **Save As** dialog box, navigate to your **Access Chapter 2** folder, click in the **File name** box, type **Lastname_Firstname_2B_Athletes_Scholarships** and then press Enter.

3. On the **Message Bar**, click **Enable Content**. In the **Navigation Pane**, right-click **2B Scholarships Awarded**, and then click **Rename**. Type **Lastname Firstname 2B Scholarships Awarded** and then press Enter. Double-click the table name to open it in **Datasheet** view. **Close** « the **Navigation Pane**, and then examine the data in the table. Compare your screen with Figure 2.28.

   In this table, Mr. Garza tracks the names and amounts of scholarships awarded to student athletes. Students are identified only by their Student ID numbers, and the primary key is the Scholarship ID field.

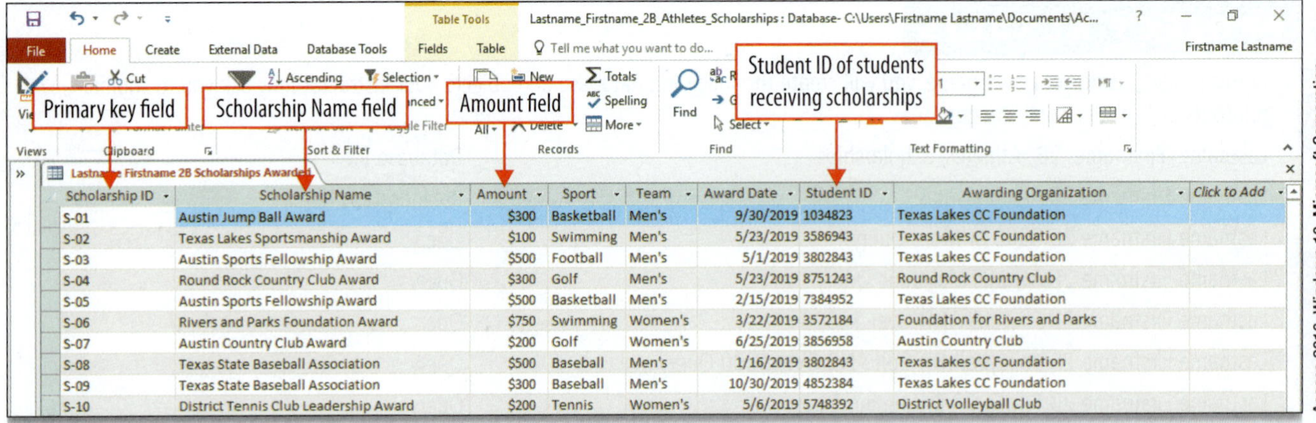

FIGURE 2.28

4 **Close** [X] the table. On the ribbon, click the **External Data tab**, and then in the **Import & Link group**, click **Excel**. In the **Get External Data – Excel Spreadsheet** dialog box, to the right of the **File name** box, click **Browse**.

5 In the **File Open** dialog box, navigate to your student data files, and then double-click **a02B_Athletes**. Be sure that the **Import the source data into a new table in the current database** option button is selected, and then click **OK**.

The Import Spreadsheet Wizard opens and displays the spreadsheet data.

6 In the upper left area of the wizard, select the **First Row Contains Column Headings** check box. In the wizard, click **Next**, and then click **Next** again.

7 In the wizard, click the **Choose my own primary key** option button, and then be sure that **Student ID** displays in the box.

In the new table, Student ID will be designated as the primary key. No two students have the same Student ID.

8 Click **Next**. With the text selected in the **Import to Table** box, type **Lastname Firstname 2B Athletes** and then click **Finish**. In the **Get External Data – Excel Spreadsheet** dialog box, click **Close**.

9 **Open** [»] the **Navigation Pane**, and increase the width of the pane so that the two table names display fully. In the **Navigation Pane**, right-click your **2B Athletes** table, and then click **Design View**. **Close** [«] the **Navigation Pane**.

10 To the right of **Student ID**, click in the **Data Type** box, click the **arrow**, and then click **Short Text**. For the **Postal Code** field, change the **Data Type** to **Short Text**, and in the **Field Properties** area, click **Field Size**, type **5** and then press [Enter]. In the **Field Name** column, click **State**, set the **Field Size** to **2** and then press [Enter]. Compare your screen with Figure 2.29.

Recall that numeric data that does not represent a quantity and is not used in a calculation, such as the Student ID and Postal Code, should be assigned a data type of Short Text.

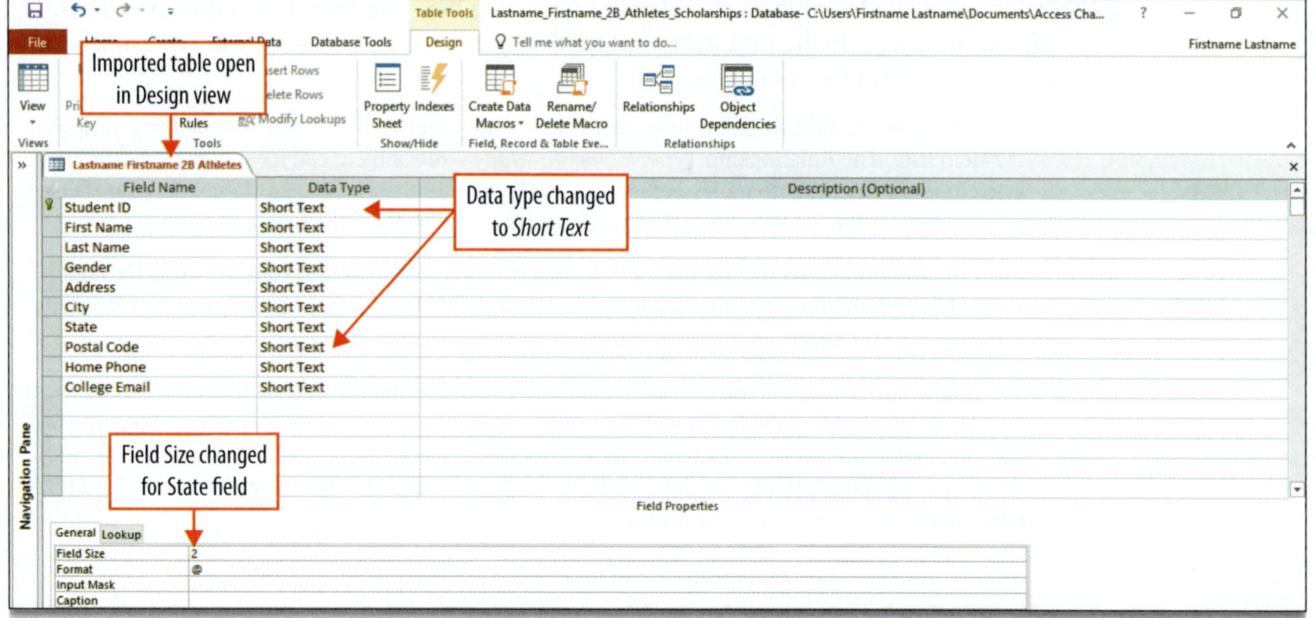

FIGURE 2.29

Access 2016, Windows 10, Microsoft Corporation

11 On the **Design tab**, in the **Views group**, click the top half of the **View button** to switch to **Datasheet** view. In the message box, click **Yes** to save the table. In the second message box, click **Yes**—no data will be lost. Take a moment to examine the data in the imported table.

12 In the datasheet, to the left of the **Student ID** field name, click the **Select All** button. On the **Home tab**, in the **Records group**, click **More**, and then click **Field Width**. In the **Column Width** dialog box, click **Best Fit**. Click in any record to cancel the selection, **Save** the table, and then **Close** the table.

1.2.1, 1.2.3, 1.2.4

Activity 2.19 | Creating a One-to-Many Table Relationship

In this Activity you will create a one-to-many relationship between your 2B Athletes table and your 2B Scholarships Awarded table by using the common field—*Student ID*.

1 Click the **Database Tools tab**, and then in the **Relationships group**, click **Relationships**.

2 In the **Show Table** dialog box, double-click your **2B Athletes** table, and then double-click your **2B Scholarships Awarded** table to add both tables to the **Relationships** window. **Close** the **Show Table** dialog box.

3 Point to the title bar of the field list on the right, and drag the field list to the right until there are approximately three inches of space between the field lists. By dragging the lower right corner of the field list, resize each field list to display all of the field names and the entire table name.

Repositioning and resizing the field lists are not required, but doing so makes it easier for you to view the field names and the join line when creating relationships.

4 In the **2B Athletes** field list, point to **Student ID**, and then, holding down the left mouse button, drag the field name into the **2B Scholarships Awarded** field list on top of **Student ID**. Release the mouse button to display the **Edit Relationships** dialog box.

5 Point to the title bar of the **Edit Relationships** dialog box, and then drag it downward below the two field lists. In the **Edit Relationships** dialog box, be sure that **Student ID** displays as the common field for both tables.

Repositioning the Edit Relationships dialog box is not required, but doing so enables you to see the field lists. The Relationship Type is *One-To-Many—one* athlete can have *many* scholarships. The common field in both tables is the *Student ID* field. In the 2B Athletes table, Student ID is the primary key. In the 2B Scholarships Awarded table, Student ID is the foreign key.

6 In the **Edit Relationships** dialog box, click to select the **Enforce Referential Integrity** check box, the **Cascade Update Related Fields** check box, and the **Cascade Delete Related Records** check box. Click **Create**, and then compare your screen with Figure 2.30.

The one-to-many relationship is established. The *1* and ∞ symbols indicate that referential integrity is enforced, which ensures that a scholarship cannot be awarded to a student whose Student ID is not included in the 2B Athletes table. Recall that the Cascade options enable you to update and delete records automatically on the *many* side of the relationship when changes are made in the table on the *one* side of the relationship.

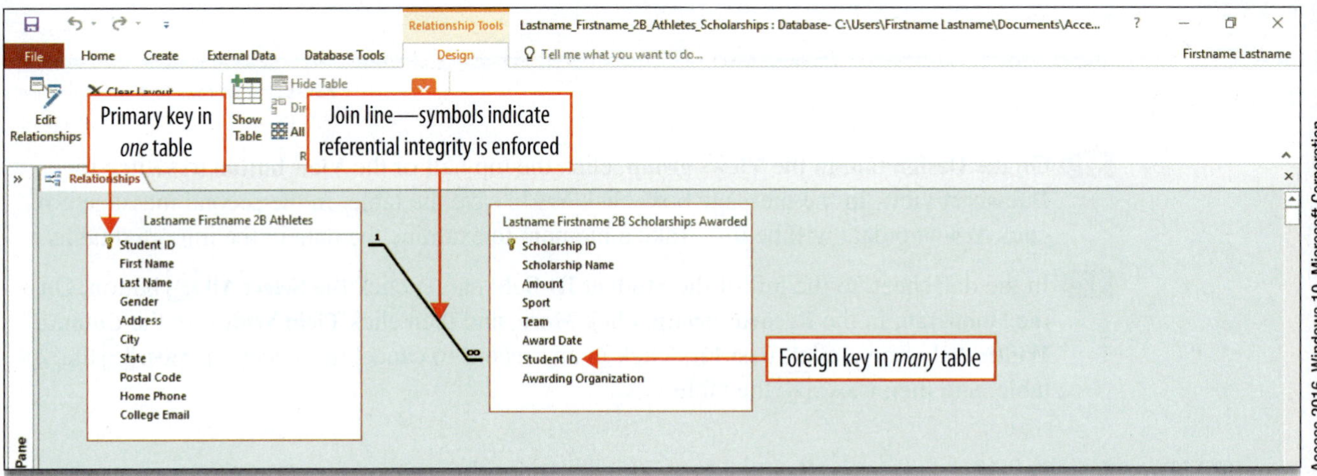

FIGURE 2.30

7 On the **Design tab**, in the **Tools group**, click **Relationship Report**. On the **Print Preview tab**, in the **Page Size group**, click **Margins**, and then click **Normal**. **Save** the report as **Lastname Firstname 2B Relationships** and then create a paper or PDF electronic image as directed. This is the first of eleven objects printed in this project.

8 In the object window, right-click either **object tab**, and then click **Close All** to close the Relationships Report and the Relationships window.

9 **Open** » the **Navigation Pane**, double-click your **2B Athletes** table to open it, and then **Close** « the **Navigation Pane**. On the left side of the first record, click + (plus sign) to display the subdatasheet for the record.

In the first record, for *Joel Barthmaier*, one related record exists in the 2B Scholarships Awarded table. Joel has been awarded the *Austin Jump Ball Award* in the amount of *$300*. The subdatasheet displays because you created a relationship between the two tables using Student ID as the common field.

10 **Close** the **2B Athletes** table.

When you close the table, the subdatasheet will collapse—you do not need to click – (minus sign) before closing a table.

3.1.1 3.2.2, 3.2.4, 3.3.2

Activity 2.20 | Specifying Numeric Criteria in a Query

In this Activity you will create a query to answer the question, *Which scholarships are in the amount of $300, and for which sports?*

1. Click the **Create tab**. In the **Queries group**, click **Query Design**.
2. In the **Show Table** dialog box, double-click your **2B Scholarships Awarded** table to add it to the table area, and then **Close** the **Show Table** dialog box. Resize the field list to display all of the fields and the entire table name.
3. Add the following fields to the design grid in the order given: **Scholarship Name**, **Sport**, and **Amount**.
4. Click in the **Sort** row under **Sport**, click the **arrow**, and then click **Ascending**.
5. Click in the **Criteria** row under **Amount**, type **300** and then press Enter. Compare your screen with Figure 2.31.

   When you enter currency values as criteria, do not type the dollar sign. Include a decimal point only if you are looking for a specific amount that includes cents; for example, 300.49. Access does not insert quotation marks around the criteria because the data type of the field is Currency, which is a numeric format.

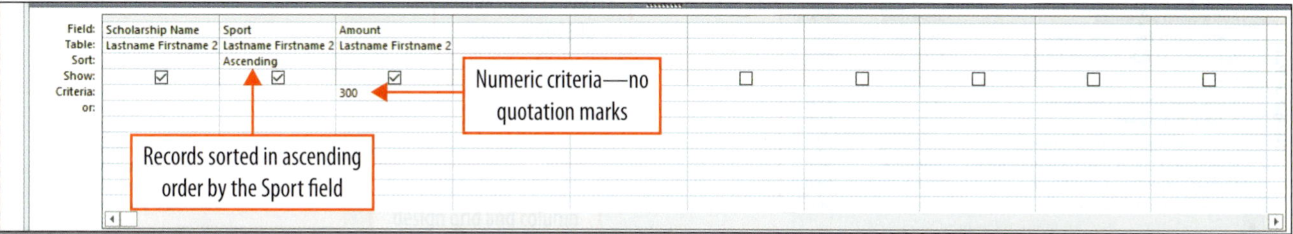

Access 2016, Windows 10, Microsoft Corporation

FIGURE 2.31

6. On the **Design tab**, in the **Results group**, click **Run** to display the query results.

   Five scholarships in the exact amount of $300 were awarded to student athletes. In the navigation area, *1 of 5* displays—1 represents the first record that is selected, and 5 represents the total number of records that meet the criteria.

7. On the **Home tab**, in the **Views group**, click **View** to switch to **Design** view.

Activity 2.21 | Using Comparison Operators in Criteria

3.3.4, 1.3.5, 3.1.6

Comparison operators are symbols that are used to evaluate data in the field to determine if it is the same (=), greater than (>), less than (<), or in between a range of values as specified by the criteria. If no comparison operator is specified, equal (=) is assumed. For example, in the previous Activity you created a query to display only those records where the *Amount* is *300*. The comparison operator of = was assumed, and the query results displayed only those records that had values in the Amount field equal to 300.

1. In the design grid, in the **Criteria** row under **Amount**, select the existing criteria—*300*—and then type **>300** and press Enter. **Run** the query.

   Fourteen records display, and each has a value *greater than* $300 in the Amount field; there are no records for which the Amount is *equal to* $300.

Objective 9 Use Compound Criteria in a Query

GO! Learn How
Video A2-9

You can specify more than one condition—criteria—in a query; this is called ***compound criteria***. Compound criteria use AND and OR ***logical operators***. Logical operators enable you to enter multiple criteria for the same field or for different fields.

Activity 2.23 | Using AND Criteria in a Query

3.1.1, 3.2.2, 3.3.4, 3.3.5, 1.3.5, 3.1.6

The ***AND condition*** is an example of a compound criteria used to display records that match all parts of the specified criteria. In this Activity you will help Mr. Garza answer the question, *Which scholarships over $500 were awarded for football?*

1. Click the **Create tab**, and in the **Queries group**, click **Query Design**. In the **Show Table** dialog box, double-click your **2B Scholarships Awarded** table to add it to the table area, and then **Close** the **Show Table** dialog box. Resize the field list to display all of the fields and the table name.

2. Add the following fields to the design grid in the order given: **Scholarship Name**, **Sport**, and **Amount**.

3. Click in the **Criteria** row under **Sport**, type **football** and then press Enter.

4. In the **Criteria** row under **Amount**, type **>500** and then press Enter. Compare your screen with Figure 2.34.

   You create the AND condition by placing the criteria for both fields on the same line in the Criteria row. The criteria indicates that records should be located that contain *Football* in the Sport field AND a value greater than *500* in the Amount field. Both conditions must exist or be true for the records to display in the query results.

Access 2016, Windows 10, Microsoft Corporation

FIGURE 2.34

5. **Run** the query, and notice that two records display that match both conditions—*Football* in the Sport field AND a value greater than *$500* in the Amount field.

6. **Save** the query as **Lastname Firstname 2B Football AND Over $500 Query** and then **Close** the query.

7. **Open** » the **Navigation Pane**, and then click to select your **2B Football AND Over $500 Query** object. Click the **File tab**, click **Print**, and then click **Print Preview**.

   You can view an object in Print Preview or print any selected object in the Navigation Pane—the object does not need to be open in the object window to print it.

8. Create a paper or PDF electronic image as directed, and then click **Close Print Preview**. This is the fourth of eleven objects printed in this project. **Close** « the **Navigation Pane**.

Activity 2.24 | Using OR Criteria in a Query

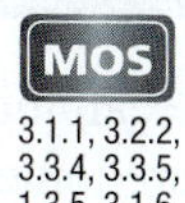

3.1.1, 3.2.2, 3.3.4, 3.3.5, 1.3.5, 3.1.6

The ***OR condition*** is an example of a compound criteria used to display records that meet one or more parts of the specified criteria. The OR condition can specify criteria in a single field or in different fields. In this Activity you will help Mr. Garza answer the question, *Which scholarships over $200 were awarded for volleyball or golf, and what is the award date of each?*

1 On the **Create tab**, in the **Queries group**, click **Query Design**.

2 In the **Show Table** dialog box, double-click your **2B Scholarships Awarded** table to add it to the table area, and then **Close** the **Show Table** dialog box. Resize the field list, and then add the following fields to the design grid in the order given: **Scholarship Name**, **Sport**, **Amount**, and **Award Date**.

3 In the design grid, click in the **Criteria** row under **Sport**, type **volleyball** and then press ↓.

The insertion point is blinking in the *or* row under Sport.

4 In the **or** row under **Sport**, type **golf** and then press Enter. **Run** the query.

Six records were located in the 2B Scholarships Awarded table that have either *volleyball* OR *golf* stored in the Sport field. This is an example of using the OR condition to locate records that meet one or more parts of the specified criteria in a single field—*Sport*.

5 Switch to **Design** view. In the **or** row under **Sport**, select "**golf**" and then press Del. In the **Criteria** row under **Sport**, select and delete "**volleyball**". Type **volleyball or golf** and then press Enter.

6 In the **Criteria** row under **Amount**, type **>200** and then press Enter. Compare your screen with Figure 2.35.

This is an alternative way to enter the OR condition in the Sport field and is a good method to use when you add an AND condition to the criteria. Access will locate records where the Sport field contains *volleyball* OR *golf* AND where the Amount field contains a value greater than *200*.

If you enter *volleyball* in the Criteria row, and *golf* in the or row for the Sport field, then you must enter >*200* in both the Criteria row and the or row for the Amount field so that the correct records are located when the query is run.

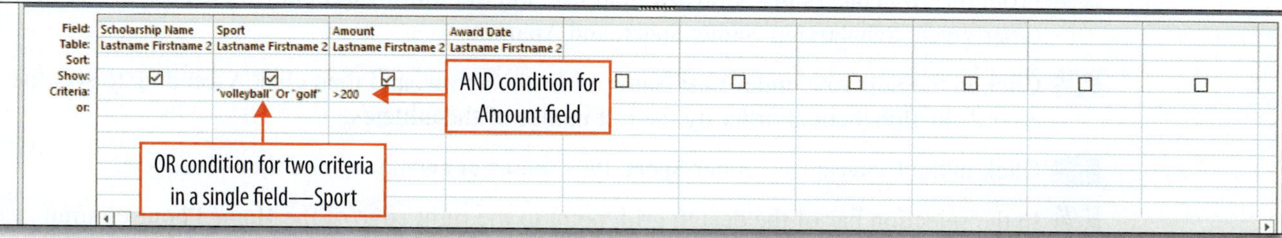

FIGURE 2.35 Access 2016, Windows 10, Microsoft Corporation

7 **Run** the query.

Two records were located in the 2B Scholarships Awarded table that have either *Volleyball* OR *Golf* stored in the Sport field AND a value greater than $200 in the Amount field. This is an example of using the OR condition in combination with an AND condition.

8 **Save** the query as **Lastname Firstname 2B Volleyball OR Golf AND Over $200 Query** and then display the query results in **Print Preview**. Create a paper or PDF electronic image as directed, click **Close Print Preview**, and then **Close** the query. This is the fifth of eleven objects printed in this project.

Objective 10 Create a Query Based on More Than One Table

GO! Learn How Video A2-10

In a relational database, you can retrieve information from more than one table. Recall that a table in a relational database contains all of the records about a single topic. Tables are joined to one another by relating the primary key in one table to the foreign key in another table. This common field is used to create the relationship and is used to find records from multiple tables when the query is created and run.

For example, the Athletes table stores all of the data about the student athletes—name, address, and so on. The Scholarships Awarded table stores data about the scholarship name, the amount, and so on. When an athlete receives a scholarship, only the Student ID of the athlete is used to identify the athlete in the Scholarships Awarded table. It is not necessary to include any other data about the athlete in the Scholarships Awarded table; doing so would result in redundant data.

Activity 2.25 | Creating a Query Based on More Than One Table

3.1.1, 3.2.2, 3.1.5, 3.2.5, 3.3.5, 3.1.6

In this Activity you will create a query that selects records from two tables. This is possible because you created a relationship between the two tables in the database. The query will answer the questions, *What is the name, email address, and phone number of athletes who have received a scholarship for tennis or swimming, and what is the name and amount of the scholarship?*

1. On the **Create tab**, in the **Queries group**, click **Query Design**. In the **Show Table** dialog box, double-click your **2B Athletes** table, and then double-click your **2B Scholarships Awarded** table to add both tables to the table area. In the **Show Table** dialog box, click **Close**. Drag the **2B Scholarships Awarded** field list to the right so that there are approximately three inches of space between the two field lists, and then resize each field list to display all of the field names and the entire table name.

   The join line displays because you created a one-to-many relationship between the two tables using the common field of Student ID; *one* athlete can have *many* scholarships.

2. From the **2B Athletes** field list, add the following fields to the design grid in the order given: **First Name**, **Last Name**, **College Email**, and **Home Phone**.

3. From the **2B Scholarships Awarded** field list, add the following fields to the design grid in the order given: **Scholarship Name**, **Sport**, and **Amount**.

4. Click in the **Sort** row under **Last Name**, click the **arrow**, and then click **Ascending** to sort the records in alphabetical order by the last names of the athletes.

5. Click in the **Criteria** row under **Sport**, type **tennis or swimming** and then press Enter.

6. In the selection bar of the design grid, point to the right edge of the **Home Phone** column to display the + pointer, and then double-click to increase the width of the column and to display the entire table name on the **Table** row. Using the same technique, increase the width of the **Scholarship Name** column. If necessary, scroll to the right to display both of these columns in the design grid, and then compare your screen with Figure 2.36.

   When locating data from multiple tables, the information in the Table row is helpful, especially when different tables include the same field name, such as Address. Although the field name is the same, the data may be different—for example, an athlete's address or a coach's address from two different related tables.

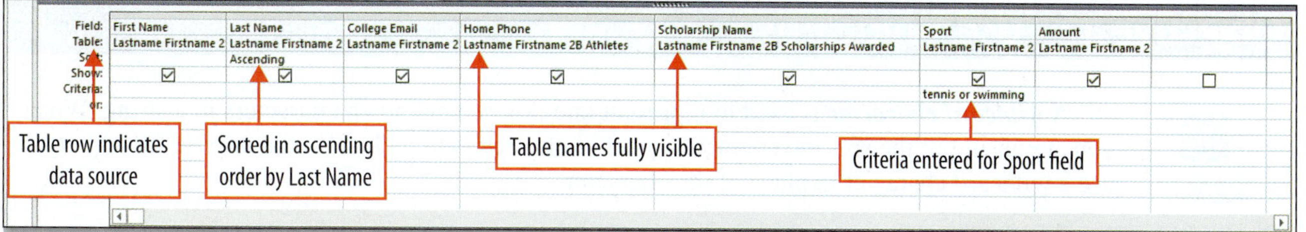

FIGURE 2.36

Access 2016, Windows 10, Microsoft Corporation

7 **Run** the query, and then compare your screen with Figure 2.37.

Eight records display for athletes who received either a Swimming *or* Tennis scholarship, and the records are sorted in ascending order by the Last Name field. Because the common field of Student ID is included in both tables, Access can locate the specified fields in both tables by using one query. Two students—*Carla Reid* and *Florence Zimmerman*—received two scholarships, one for swimming and one for tennis. Recall that *one* student athlete can receive *many* scholarships.

FIGURE 2.37

Access 2016, Windows 10, Microsoft Corporation

8 **Save** the query as **Lastname Firstname 2B Tennis OR Swimming Query** and then display the query results in **Print Preview**. Change the orientation to **Landscape**, and the **Margins** to **Normal**. Create a paper or PDF electronic image as directed, and then click **Close Print Preview**. This is the sixth of eleven objects printed in this project.

9 **Close** the query, **Open** the **Navigation Pane**, increase the width of the **Navigation Pane** to display all object names fully, and then compare your screen with Figure 2.38.

Your *2B Tennis OR Swimming Query* object name displays under both tables from which it selected records.

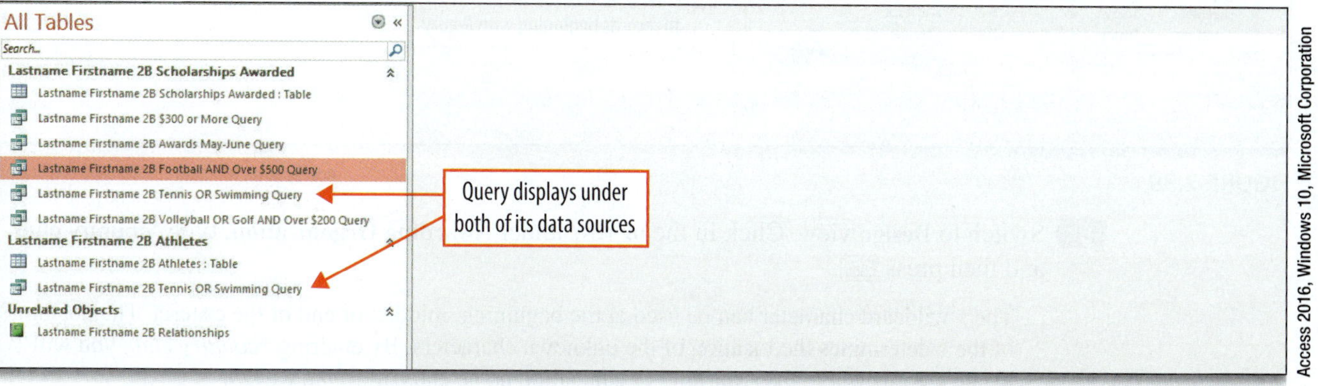

FIGURE 2.38

Access 2016, Windows 10, Microsoft Corporation

10 **Close** the **Navigation Pane**.

Objective 11 Use Wildcards in a Query

GO! Learn How Video A2-11

A ***wildcard character*** is used to represent one or more unknown characters in a string. When you are unsure of the specific character or set of characters to include in the criteria for a query, use a wildcard character in place of the character.

Activity 2.26 | Using a Wildcard in a Query

3.1.1, 3.2.2, 3.3.5, 3.2.4, 1.3.5, 3.1.6

Use the asterisk (*) wildcard character to represent one or more unknown characters. For example, entering Fo* as the criteria in a last name field will result in displaying records containing last names of Foster, Forrester, Fossil, or any other last name that begins with *Fo*. In this Activity you will use the asterisk (*) wildcard character in criteria to answer the question, *Which athletes received scholarships from local Rotary Clubs, country clubs, or foundations?*

1. On the **Create tab**, in the **Queries group**, click **Query Design**. In the **Show Table** dialog box, double-click your **2B Athletes** table, and then double-click your **2B Scholarships Awarded** table to add both tables to the table area. In the **Show Table** dialog box, click **Close**. Drag the **2B Scholarships Awarded** field list to the right so that there are approximately three inches of space between the two field lists, and then resize each field list to display all of the field names and the entire table name.

2. From the **2B Athletes** field list, add the following fields to the design grid in the order given: **First Name** and **Last Name**. From the **2B Scholarships Awarded** field list, add the **Awarding Organization** field to the design grid.

3. Click in the **Sort** row under **Last Name**, click the **arrow**, and then click **Ascending** to sort the records in alphabetical order by the last names of the athletes.

4. Click in the **Criteria** row under **Awarding Organization**, type **rotary*** and then press Enter.

   The * wildcard character is a placeholder used to match one or more unknown characters. After pressing Enter, Access adds *Like* to the beginning of the criteria.

5. **Run** the query, and then compare your screen with Figure 2.39.

   Three athletes received scholarships from a Rotary Club from different cities. The results are sorted alphabetically by the Last Name field.

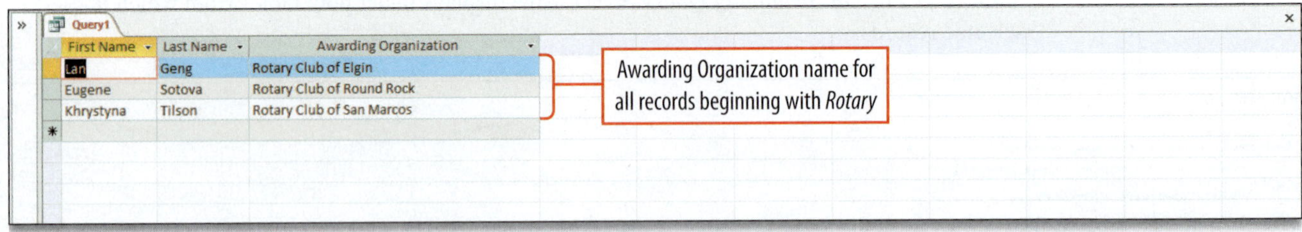

FIGURE 2.39

Access 2016, Windows 10, Microsoft Corporation

6. Switch to **Design** view. Click in the **or** row under **Awarding Organization**, type ***country club** and then press Enter.

   The * wildcard character can be used at the beginning, middle, or end of the criteria. The position of the * determines the location of the unknown characters. By entering **country club*, you will locate records where the Awarding Organization name ends in *Country Club*.

7. **Run** the query.

   Six records display for students receiving scholarships; three from organizations with a name that begins with *Rotary*, and three from organizations with a name that ends with *Country Club*.

8 Switch to **Design** view. In the design grid under **Awarding Organization** and under **Like "*country club"**, type ***foundation*** and then press Enter. Compare your screen with Figure 2.40.

This query will also display records where the Awarding Organization has *Foundation* anywhere in the organization name—at the beginning, middle, or end. Three *OR* criteria have been entered for the Awarding Organization field. When run, this query will locate records where the Awarding Organization has a name that begins with *Rotary*, OR ends with *Country Club*, OR that has *Foundation* anywhere in its name.

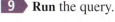

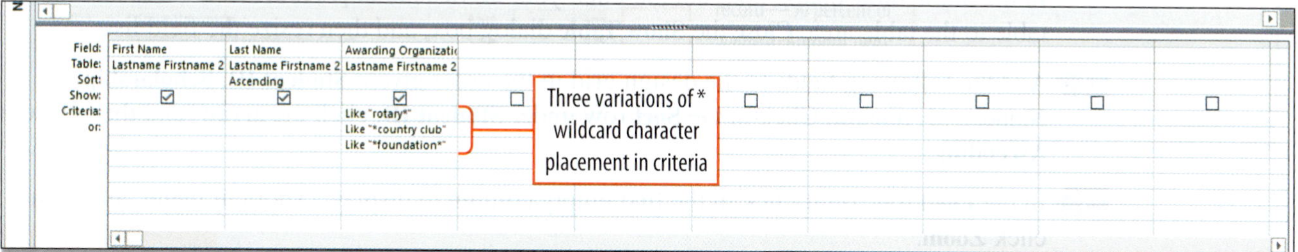

FIGURE 2.40 Access 2016, Windows 10, Microsoft Corporation

9 **Run** the query.

Twenty-eight scholarships were awarded from organizations where the name of the organization begins with Rotary, ends with Country Club, or has Foundation anywhere in its name. The records are sorted alphabetically by the Last Name field.

10 **Save** the query as **Lastname Firstname 2B Wildcard Query** and then display the query results in **Print Preview**. Create a paper or PDF electronic image as directed, and then click **Close Print Preview**. This is the seventh of eleven objects printed in this project.

11 **Close** the query, and then **Open** the **Navigation Pane**. Notice that your **2B Wildcard Query** displays under both tables because the query selected data from both tables—the data sources.

More Knowledge **Using the ? Wildcard Character to Search for a Single Unknown Character**

The question mark (?) wildcard character is used to search for a single unknown character. For each question mark included in the criteria, any character can be located. For example, entering *b?d* as the criteria will result in the display of words such as *bed*, *bid*, or *bud*, or any three-character word that begins with *b* and ends with *d*. Entering *b??d* as the criteria will results in the display of words such as *bard*, *bend*, or *bind*, or any four-character word that begins with *b* and ends with *d*.

Objective 12 Create Calculated Fields in a Query

GO! Learn How Video A2-12

Queries can create calculated values that are stored in a ***calculated field***. A calculated field stores the value of a mathematical operation. For example, you can multiply the value stored in a field named Total Hours Worked by the value stored in a field named Hourly Pay to display the Gross Pay value for each work study student.

There are two steps to create a calculated field in a query. First, name the field that will store the results of the calculation. Second, enter the ***expression***—the formula—that will perform the calculation. When entering the information for the calculated field in the query, the new field name must be followed by a colon (:), and each field name from the table used in the expression must be enclosed within its own pair of brackets.

3 In the **Zoom** dialog box, click **OK**, and then **Run** the query.

The value in the *Total Scholarship* field is calculated by adding together the values in the Amount field and the Matching Donation field. The values in the Total Scholarship field are formatted with dollar signs, commas, and decimal points, which is carried over from the Currency format in the Amount field.

Activity 2.29 | Formatting Calculated Fields

1.3.5, 3.2.6, 3.1.1, 3.1.6

In this Activity you will format the calculated fields so that the values display in a consistent manner.

1 Switch to **Design** view. In the **Field** row, click in the **Alumni Donation** field name box.

2 On the **Design tab**, in the **Show/Hide group**, click **Property Sheet**.

The Property Sheet displays on the right side of your screen. Recall that a Property Sheet enables you to make precise changes to the properties—characteristics—of selected items, in this case, a field.

ANOTHER WAY In the design grid, on the Field row, right-click in the Alumni Donation field name box, and then click Properties.

3 In the **Property Sheet**, with the **General tab** active, click **Format**. In the property setting box, click the **arrow**, and then compare your screen with Figure 2.44.

A list of available formats for the Alumni Donation field displays.

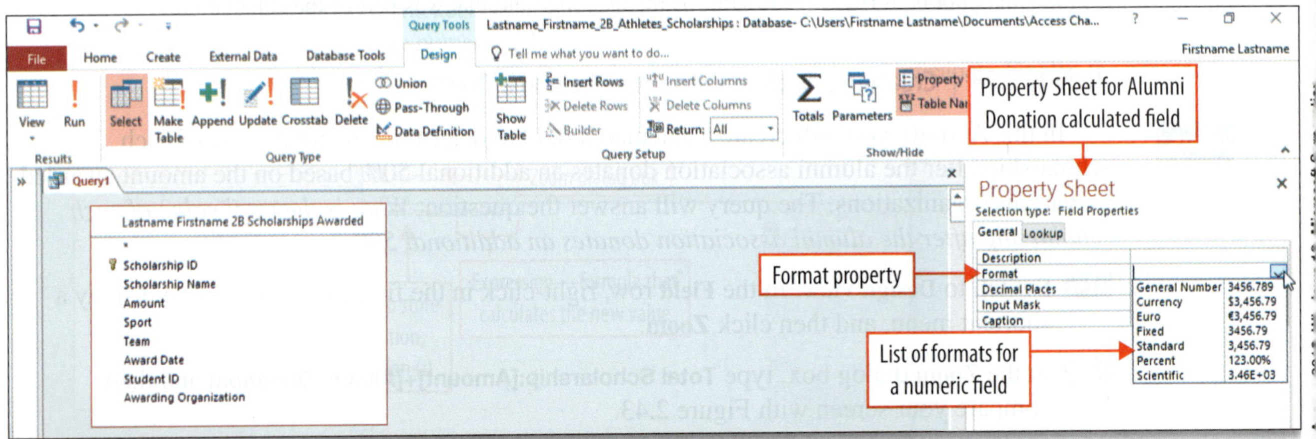

FIGURE 2.44

4 In the list, click **Currency**. In the **Property Sheet**, click **Decimal Places**. In the property setting box, click the **arrow**, and then click **0**.

5 In the design grid, in the **Field** row, click in the **Total Scholarship** field name. In the **Property Sheet**, set the **Format** property setting to **Currency** and the **Decimal Places** property setting to **0**.

6 **Close** ☒ the **Property Sheet**, and then **Run** the query.

The Alumni Donation and Total Scholarship fields are formatted as Currency with 0 decimal places.

7 To the left of the **Student ID** field name, click the **Select All** button. On the **Home tab**, in the **Records group**, click **More**, and then click **Field Width**. In the **Column Width** dialog box, click **Best Fit**. Click in any field, and then **Save** the query as **Lastname Firstname 2B Alumni Donations Query**

The field widths are adjusted to display fully the calculated field names.

8 Display the query results in **Print Preview**. Change the **Margins** to **Normal**. Create a paper or PDF electronic image as directed, and then click **Close Print Preview**. This is the eighth of eleven objects printed in this project. **Close** the query.

Objective 13 Calculate Statistics and Group Data in a Query

GO! Learn How Video A2-13

Queries can be used to perform statistical calculations known as ***aggregate functions*** on a group of records. For example, you can find the total or average amount for a group of records, or you can find the lowest or highest number in a group of records.

Activity 2.30 | Using the Min, Max, Avg, and Sum Functions in a Query

3.1.1, 3.2.2, 3.3.3, 1.3.5

In this Activity you will use aggregate functions to find the lowest and highest scholarships amounts and the average and total scholarship amounts. The last query in this Activity will answer the question, *What is the total dollar amount of all scholarships awarded?*

1 On the **Create tab**, in the **Queries group**, click **Query Design**. In the **Show Table** dialog box, double-click your **2B Scholarships Awarded** table to add the table to the table area, **Close** the **Show Table** dialog box, and then resize the field list.

2 Add the **Amount** field to the design grid.

Include only the field to summarize in the design grid, so that the aggregate function is applied only to that field.

3 On the **Design tab**, in the **Show/Hide group**, click **Totals** to add a **Total** row as the third row in the design grid. Notice that in the design grid, on the **Total** row under **Amount**, *Group By* displays.

Use the Total row to select an aggregate function for the selected field.

4 In the **Total** row under **Amount**, click in the box that displays *Group By*, and then click the **arrow** to display a list of aggregate functions. Compare your screen with Figure 2.45, and then take a moment to review the available aggregate functions and the purpose of each function as shown in Figure 2.46.

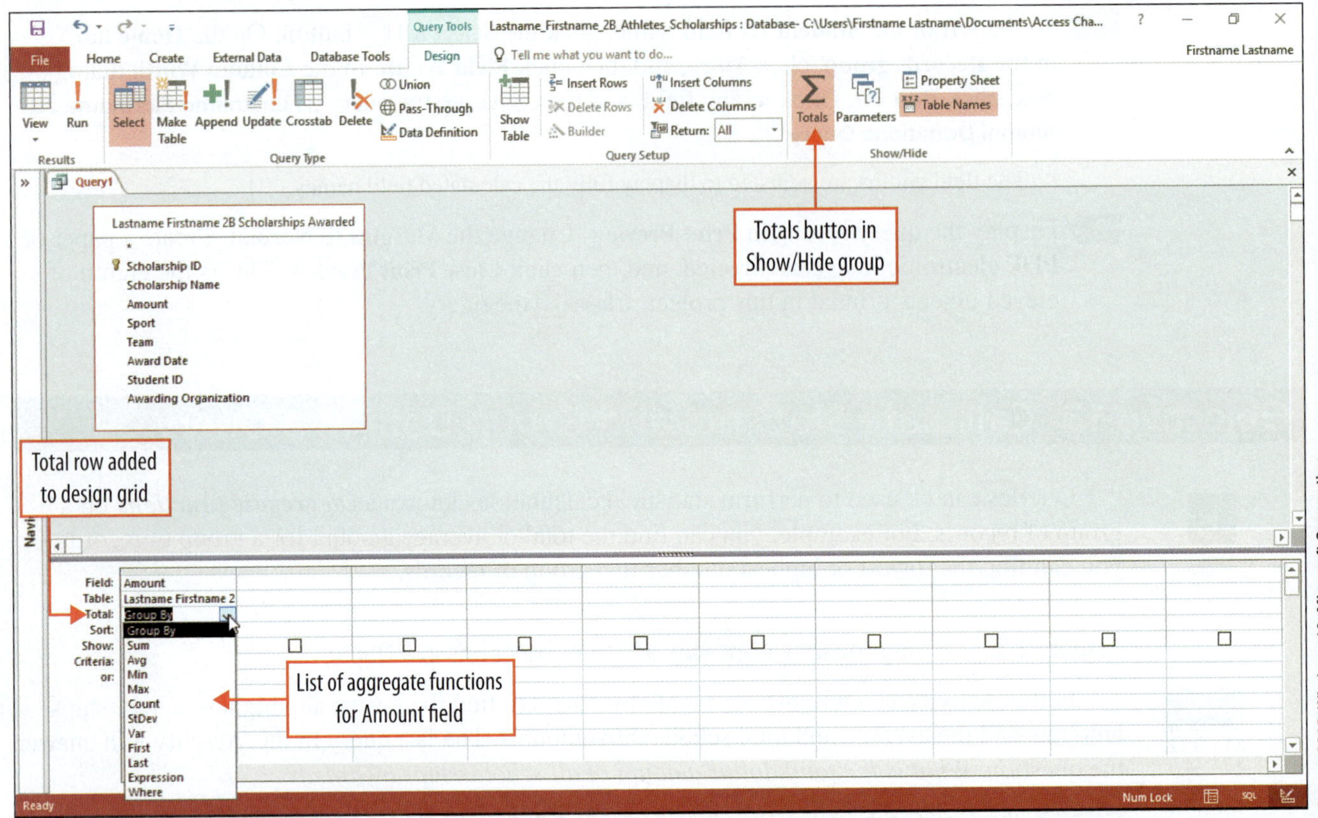

FIGURE 2.45

AGGREGATE FUNCTIONS	
FUNCTION NAME	**PURPOSE**
Group By	Combines data based on matching data in the selected field
Sum	Totals the values in a field
Avg	Averages the values in a field
Min	Locates the smallest value in a field
Max	Locates the largest value in a field
Count	Displays the number of records based on a field
StDev	Calculates the standard deviation for the values in a field
Var	Calculates the variance for the values in a field
First	Displays the first value in a field for the first record
Last	Displays the last value in a field for the last record
Expression	Creates a calculated field that includes an aggregate function
Where	Limits the records to those that match a condition specified in the Criteria row of a field

FIGURE 2.46

5 In the list of functions, click **Min**, and then **Run** the query. Point to the right edge of the first column to display the [+] mouse pointer, and then double-click to apply **Best Fit** to the field.

Access locates the minimum (smallest) value—*$100*—in the Amount field for all of the records in the 2B Scholarships Awarded table. The field name *MinOfAmount* is automatically created. This query answers the question, *What is the minimum (smallest) scholarship amount awarded to athletes?*

6 Switch to **Design** view. In the **Total** row under **Amount**, click the **arrow**, and then click **Max**. **Run** the query.

The maximum (largest) value for a scholarship award amount is *$750.00*.

7 Switch to **Design** view. In the **Total** row, select the **Avg** function, and then **Run** the query.

The average scholarship award amount is *$358.33*.

8 Switch to **Design** view. In the **Total** row, select the **Sum** function, and then **Run** the query.

The values in the Amount field for all records are summed and display a result of *$10,750.00*. The field name *SumOfAmount* is automatically created. The query answers the question, *What is the total dollar amount of all scholarships awarded?*

Activity 2.31 | Grouping Records in a Query

1.3.5, 3.3.3, 3.1.6, 3.2.6

You can use aggregate functions and group the records by the data in a field. For example, to group (summarize) the amount of scholarships awarded to each student, you include the Student ID field in addition to the Amount field. Using the Sum aggregate function, the records will be grouped by the Student ID so you can see the total amount of scholarships awarded to each student. Similarly, you can group the records by the Sport field so you can see the total amount of scholarships awarded for each sport.

1 Switch to **Design** view. From the field list, drag the **Student ID** field to the first column of the design grid—the **Amount** field moves to the second column. In the **Total** row under **Student ID**, notice that *Group By* displays.

This query will group—combine—the records by Student ID and will calculate a total amount for each student.

2 **Run** the query, and then compare your screen with Figure 2.47.

The query calculates the total amount of all scholarships for each student.

Student ID	SumOfAmount
1034823	$300.00
1298345	$250.00
1846834	$200.00
2845209	$200.00
2849523	$600.00
2934853	$200.00
3572184	$1,150.00
3586943	$100.00
3802843	$1,000.00

FIGURE 2.47

3 Switch to **Design** view. In the design grid, above **Student ID**, point to the selection bar to display the [↓] pointer. Click to select the column, and then press [Del] to remove the **Student ID** field from the design grid.

4 From the field list, drag the **Sport** field to the first column in the design grid—the **Amount** field moves to the second column. Click in the **Sort** row under **Amount**, click the **arrow**, and then click **Descending**.

5 On the **Design tab**, in the **Show/Hide group**, click **Property Sheet**. In the **Property Sheet**, set the **Format** property to **Currency**, and then set the **Decimal Places** property to **0**. **Close** [X] the **Property Sheet**.

6 **Run** the query, and then compare your screen with Figure 2.48.

Access groups—summarizes—the records by each sport and displays the groupings in descending order by the total amount of scholarships awarded for each sport. Basketball scholarships were awarded the largest total amount—*$3,500*—and Volleyball scholarships were awarded the smallest total amount—*$650*.

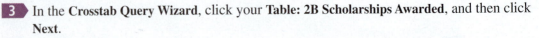

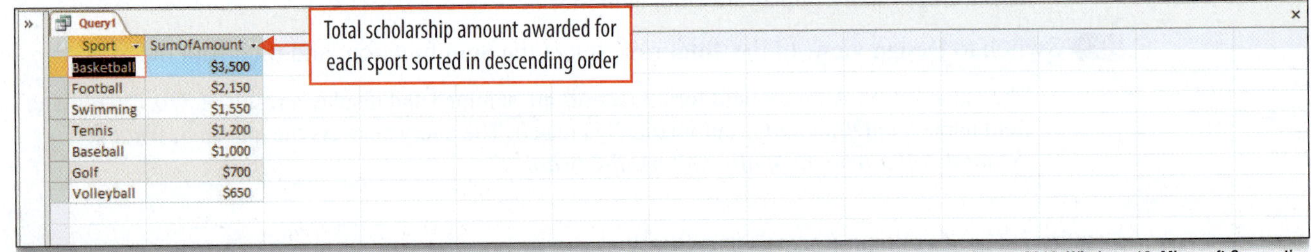

FIGURE 2.48

7 **Save** the query as **Lastname Firstname 2B Total by Sport Query** and then display the query results in **Print Preview**. Create a paper or PDF electronic image as directed, click **Close Print Preview**, and then **Close** the query. This is the ninth of eleven objects printed in this project.

Objective 14 Create a Crosstab Query

GO! Learn How Video A2-14

A ***crosstab query*** uses an aggregate function for data that can be grouped by two types of information, and displays the data in a compact, spreadsheet-like format with column headings and row headings. A crosstab query always has at least one row heading, one column heading, and one summary field. Use a crosstab query to summarize a large amount of data in a compact space that is easy to read.

Activity 2.32 | Creating a Crosstab Query Using the Query Wizard

3.1.2, 3.2.6

In this Activity you will create a crosstab query that displays the total amount of scholarships awarded for each sport and for each type of team—men's or women's.

1 On the **Create tab**, in the **Queries group**, click **Query Wizard**.

2 In the **New Query** dialog box, click **Crosstab Query Wizard**, and then click **OK**.

3 In the **Crosstab Query Wizard**, click your **Table: 2B Scholarships Awarded**, and then click **Next**.

4 In the wizard under **Available Fields**, double-click **Sport** to group the scholarship amounts by the sports—the sports will display as row headings. Click **Next**, and then compare your screen with Figure 2.49.

The sport names will be grouped and displayed as row headings, and you are prompted to select column headings.

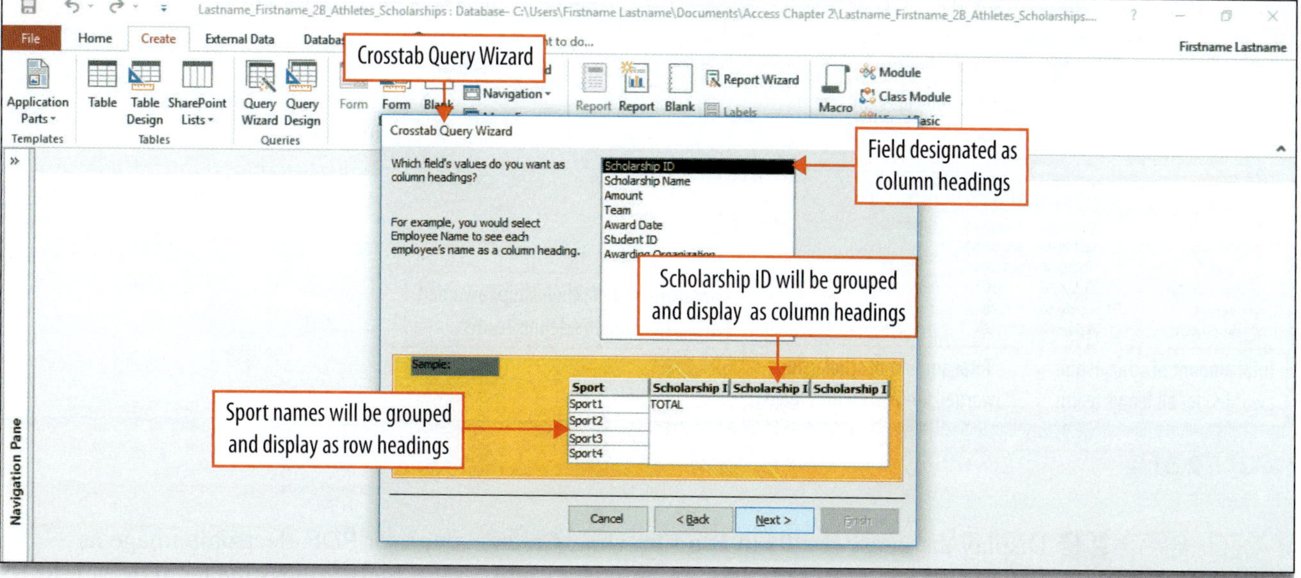

Access 2016, Windows 10, Microsoft Corporation

FIGURE 2.49

5 In the wizard, in the field list, click **Team** to select the column headings. Click **Next**, and then compare your screen with Figure 2.50.

The Team types—*Men's* and *Women's*—will display as column headings, and you are prompted to select a field to summarize.

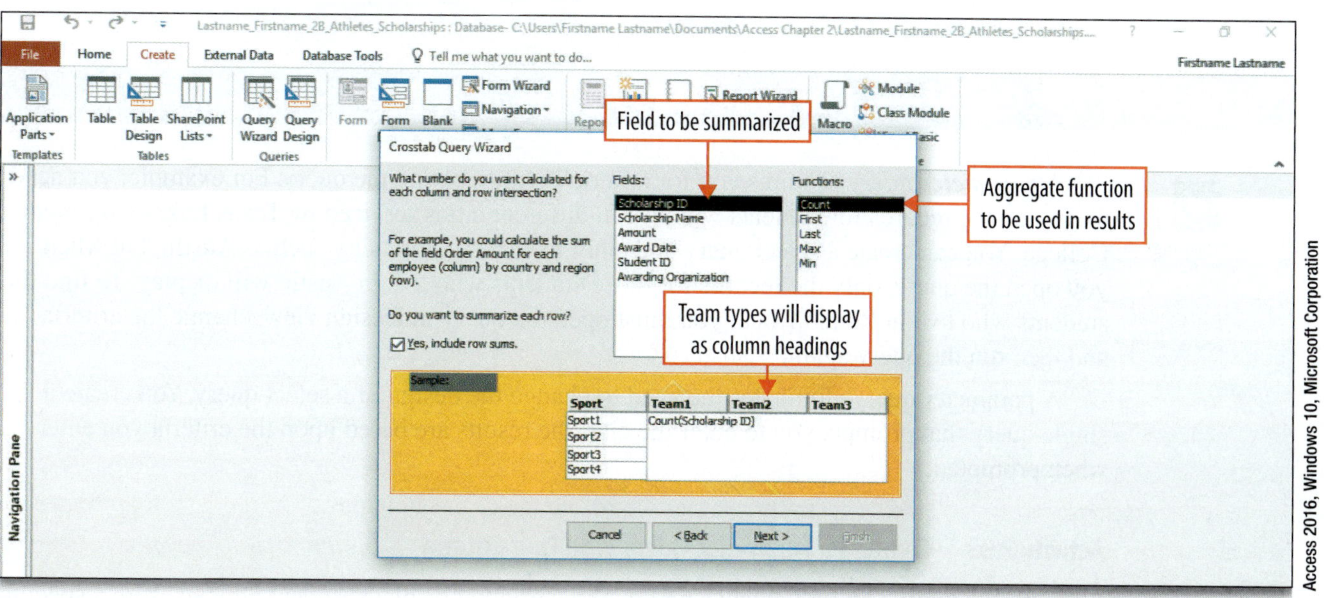

Access 2016, Windows 10, Microsoft Corporation

FIGURE 2.50

6 In the wizard under **Fields**, click **Amount**. Under **Functions**, click **Sum**.

The crosstab query will calculate the total scholarship amount for each sport and for each type of team.

7 Click **Next**. In the **What do you want to name your query?** box, select the existing text, type **Lastname Firstname 2B Sport and Team Crosstab Query** and then click **Finish**. Apply **Best Fit** to the datasheet, click in any field to cancel the selection, **Save** the query, and then compare your screen with Figure 2.51.

The field widths are adjusted to display fully the calculated field names.

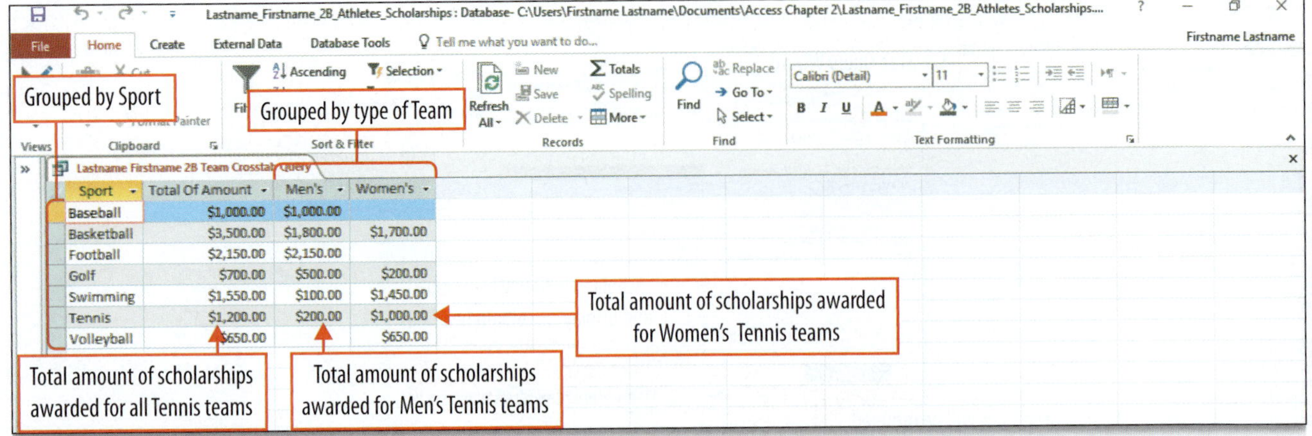

FIGURE 2.51

8 Display the query results in **Print Preview**. Create a paper or PDF electronic image as directed, click **Close Print Preview**, and then **Close** [X] the query. This is the tenth of eleven objects printed in this project.

> ***More* Knowledge** **Creating a Crosstab Query Using Data from Two Related Tables**
>
> To create a crosstab query using fields from more than one table, you must first create a select query with the fields from both tables, and then use the query as the data source for the crosstab query.

Objective 15 Create a Parameter Query

GO! Learn How Video A2-15

A ***parameter query*** prompts you for criteria before running the query. For example, you need to display the records for students who live in different cities serviced by Texas Lakes Community College. You can create a select query and enter the criteria for a city such as Austin, but when you open the query, only the records for those students who live in Austin will display. To find the students who live in Round Rock, you must open the query in Design view, change the criteria, and then run the query again.

A parameter query eliminates the need to change the design of a select query. You create a single query that prompts you to enter the city; the results are based upon the criteria you enter when prompted.

Activity 2.33 | Creating a Parameter Query with One Criteria

3.1.1, 3.2.2, 3.1.3, 3.2.5, 3.1.6

In this Activity you will create a parameter query that displays student athletes from a specific city in the areas serviced by Texas Lakes Community College.

1 On the **Create tab**, in the **Queries group**, click **Query Design**.

2 In the **Show Table** dialog box, double-click your **2B Athletes** table to add it to the table area, **Close** the **Show Table** dialog box, and then resize the field list.

3 Add the following fields to the design grid in the order given: **First Name**, **Last Name Address**, **City**, **State**, and **Postal Code**.

4 In the **Sort** row under **Last Name**, click the **arrow**, and then click **Ascending**.

5 In the **Criteria** row under **City**, type **[Enter a City]** and then press Enter. Compare your screen with Figure 2.52.

The bracketed text indicates a ***parameter***—a value that can be changed—rather than specific criteria.

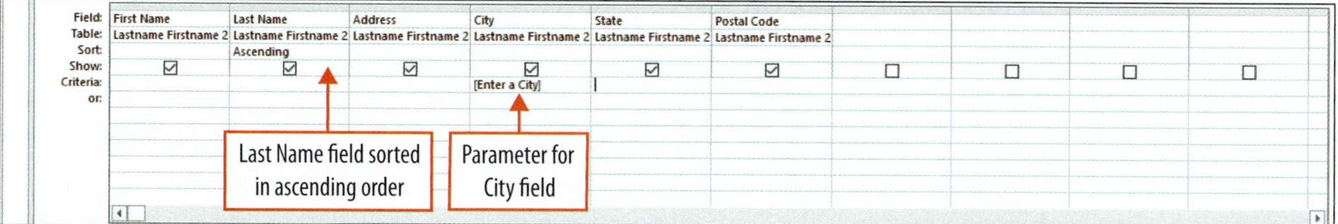

FIGURE 2.52

6 **Run** the query. In the **Enter Parameter Value** dialog box, type **austin** and then compare your screen with Figure 2.53.

The Enter Parameter Value dialog box prompts you to *Enter a City*, which is the text enclosed in brackets that you entered in the criteria row under City. The city you enter will be set as the criteria for the query. Because you are prompted for the criteria, you can reuse this query without having to edit the criteria row in Design view. The value you enter is not case sensitive—you can enter *austin*, *Austin*, or *AUSTIN*.

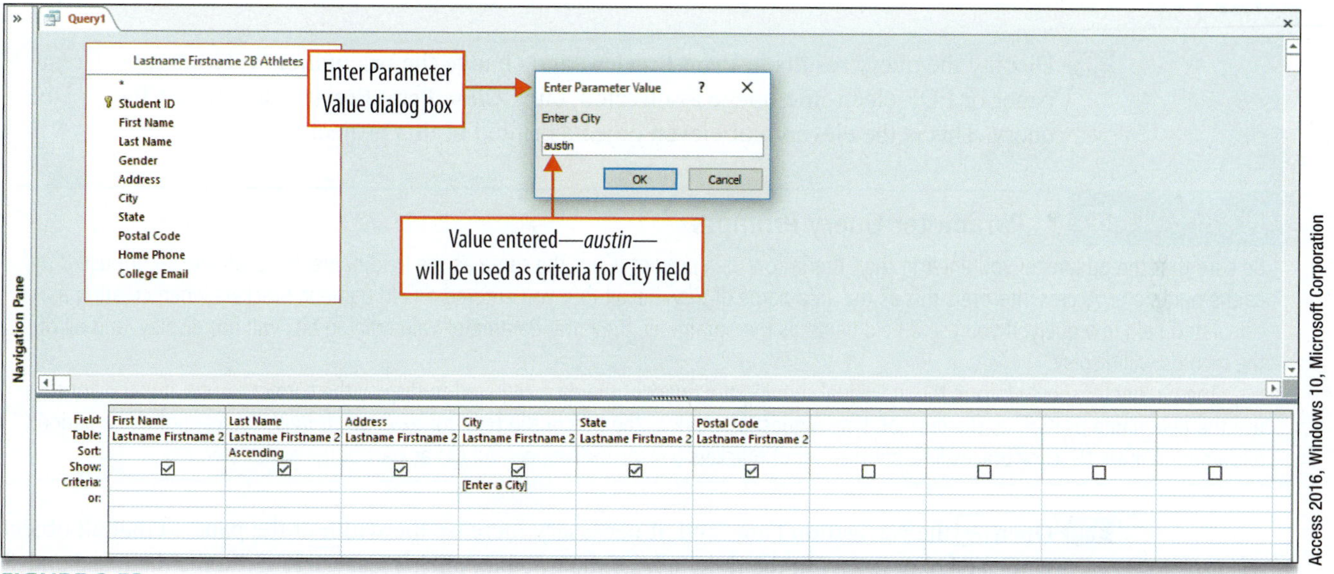

FIGURE 2.53

ALERT! **Did the Enter Parameter Value dialog box not display?**

If the Enter Parameter Value dialog box does not display, you may have typed the parameter incorrectly in the design grid. Common errors include using parentheses or curly braces instead of brackets around the parameter text, which Access interprets as specific criteria, resulting in no records matching the criteria. If you typed curly braces instead of brackets, the query will not run. To correct, display the query in Design view and change the parameter entered in the Criteria row.

7 In the **Enter Parameter Value** dialog box, click **OK**.

Twenty-three students live in the city of Austin, and the records are sorted in alphabetical order by the Last Name field.

8 **Save** [icon] the query as **Lastname Firstname 2B City Parameter Query**, and then **Close** [X] the query.

9 **Open** [»] the **Navigation Pane**. In the **Navigation Pane**, under your **2B Athletes** table, double-click your **2B City Parameter Query**. In the **Enter Parameter Value** dialog box, type **round rock** and then click **OK**. **Close** [«] the **Navigation Pane**. Compare your screen with Figure 2.54.

Nine students live in the city of Round Rock. Every time you open a parameter query, you are prompted to enter criteria. You may have to apply Best Fit to the columns if all of the data in the fields does not display and you wish to print the query results—the length of the data in the fields changes as new records display depending upon the criteria entered. Recall that only the query design is saved; each time you open a query, it is run using the most up-to-date information in the data source.

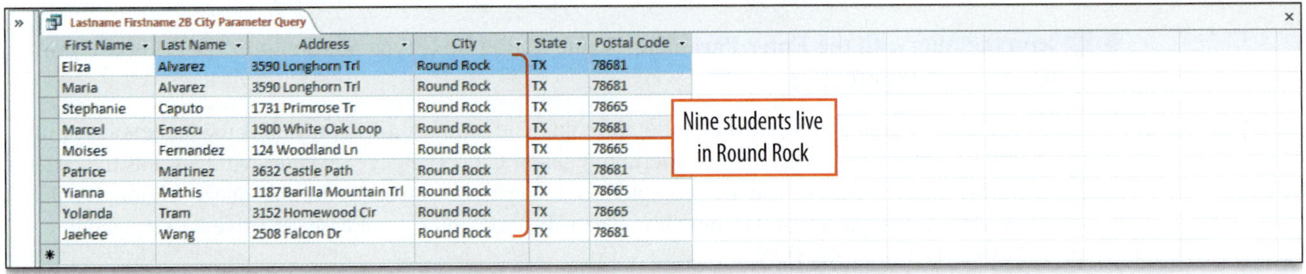

First Name	Last Name	Address	City	State	Postal Code
Eliza	Alvarez	3590 Longhorn Trl	Round Rock	TX	78681
Maria	Alvarez	3590 Longhorn Trl	Round Rock	TX	78681
Stephanie	Caputo	1731 Primrose Tr	Round Rock	TX	78665
Marcel	Enescu	1900 White Oak Loop	Round Rock	TX	78681
Moises	Fernandez	124 Woodland Ln	Round Rock	TX	78665
Patrice	Martinez	3632 Castle Path	Round Rock	TX	78681
Yianna	Mathis	1187 Barilla Mountain Trl	Round Rock	TX	78665
Yolanda	Tram	3152 Homewood Cir	Round Rock	TX	78665
Jaehee	Wang	2508 Falcon Dr	Round Rock	TX	78681

Access 2016, Windows 10, Microsoft Corporation

FIGURE 2.54

10 Display the query results in **Print Preview**, and change the orientation to **Landscape**. Create a paper or PDF electronic image as directed, click **Close Print Preview**, and then **Close** [X] the query. This is the eleventh of eleven objects printed in this project.

More Knowledge **Parameter Query Prompts**

Be sure that the parameter you enter in the Criteria row as a prompt is not the same as the field name. For example, do not use *[City]* as the parameter. Access interprets this as the field name of *City*. Recall that you entered a field name in brackets when creating a calculated field in a query. If you use a field name as the parameter, the Enter Parameter Value dialog box will not display, and all of the records will display.

The parameter should inform the individual running the query of the data required to display the correct results. If you want to use the field name by itself as the prompt, type a question mark at the end of the text; for example, *[City?]*. You cannot use a period, exclamation mark (!), curly braces ({ }), another set of brackets ([ ]), or the ampersand (&) as part of the parameter.

11 **Open** [»] the **Navigation Pane**, and, if necessary increase the width of the pane so that all object names display fully. On the right side of the title bar, click **Close** [X] to close the database and **Close** Access. As directed by your instructor, submit your database and the paper or PDF electronic images of the 11 objects—relationship report and 10 queries—that are the results of this project.

END | You have completed Project 2B

GO! With Google

2 ACCESS

Objective Export an Access Query to an Excel Spreadsheet, Save It in Google Drive, and Create a Chart

Access web apps are designed to work with Microsoft's SharePoint, a service for setting up websites to share and manage documents. Your college may not have SharePoint installed, so you will use other tools to share objects from your database so that you can work collaboratively with others. Recall that Google Drive is Google's free, web-based word processor, spreadsheet, slide show, form, and data storage and sharing service. For Access, you can export a database object to an Excel worksheet, a PDF file, or a text file, and then save the file to Google Drive.

ALERT! Working with Web-Based Applications and Services

Computer programs and services on the web receive continuous updates and improvements, so the steps to complete this web-based activity may differ from the ones shown. You can often look at the screens and the information presented to determine how to complete the activity.

If you do not already have a Google account, you will need to create one before doing this activity. Go to http://google.com and in the upper right corner, click Sign In. On the Sign In screen, click Create Account. On the Create your Google Account page, complete the form, read and agree to the Terms of Service and Privacy Policy, and then click Next step. On the Welcome screen, click Get Started.

Activity | Exporting an Access Query to an Excel Spreadsheet, Saving the Spreadsheet to Google Drive, Editing a Record in Google Drive, and Saving to Your Computer

In this Activity you will export your 2B Sport and Team Crosstab Query table to an Excel spreadsheet, upload the Excel file to your Google Drive as a Google Sheet, edit a record in Google Drive, and then download a copy of the edited spreadsheet to your computer.

1 Start Access, navigate to your **Access Chapter 2** folder, and then open your **2B_Athletes_Scholarships** database file. If necessary, on the Message Bar, click **Enable Content**. In the **Navigation Pane**, click your **2B Sport and Team Crosstab** Query one time to select it—do not open it.

2 Click the **External Data tab**, and then in the **Export group**, click **Excel**. In the **Export – Excel Spreadsheet** dialog box, click **Browse**, and then navigate to your **Access Chapter 2** folder. In the **File Save** dialog box, click in the **File name** box, type **Lastname_Firstname_AC_2B_Web** and then click **Save**.

3 In the **Export – Excel Spreadsheet** dialog box, under **Specify export options**, select the first two check boxes—**Export data with formatting and layout** and **Open the destination file after the export operation is complete**—and then click **OK**. Take a moment to examine the data in the file, and then **Close** Excel. In the **Export – Excel Spreadsheet** dialog box, click **Close**, and then **Close Access**.

4 From the desktop, open your browser, navigate to **http://google.com**, and then sign in to your Google account. Click the **Google Apps** menu, and then click **Drive**. Open your **GO! Web Projects** folder—or click New to create and then open this folder if necessary.

5 In the upper right corner, click **Settings**, and then on the menu click **Settings**. In the **Settings** dialog box, next to *Convert uploads*, be sure that **Convert uploaded files to Google Docs editor format** is selected. In the upper right, click **Done**.

If this setting is not selected, your document will upload as a PDF file and cannot be edited without further action.

6 On the left, click **NEW**, and then click **File upload**. In the **Open** dialog box, navigate to your **Access Chapter 2** folder, and then double-click your **Lastname_Firstname_AC_2B_Web** Excel file to upload it to Google Drive. In the lower right corner, when the title bar of the message box indicates *Uploads completed*, **Close** the message box. A second message box may display temporarily.

7 In the file list, double-click your **Lastname_Firstname_AC_2B_Web** file to open it in Google Sheets. Compare your screen with Figure A.

The worksheet displays column letters, row numbers, and data.

(GO! With Google continues on the next page)

GO! With Google

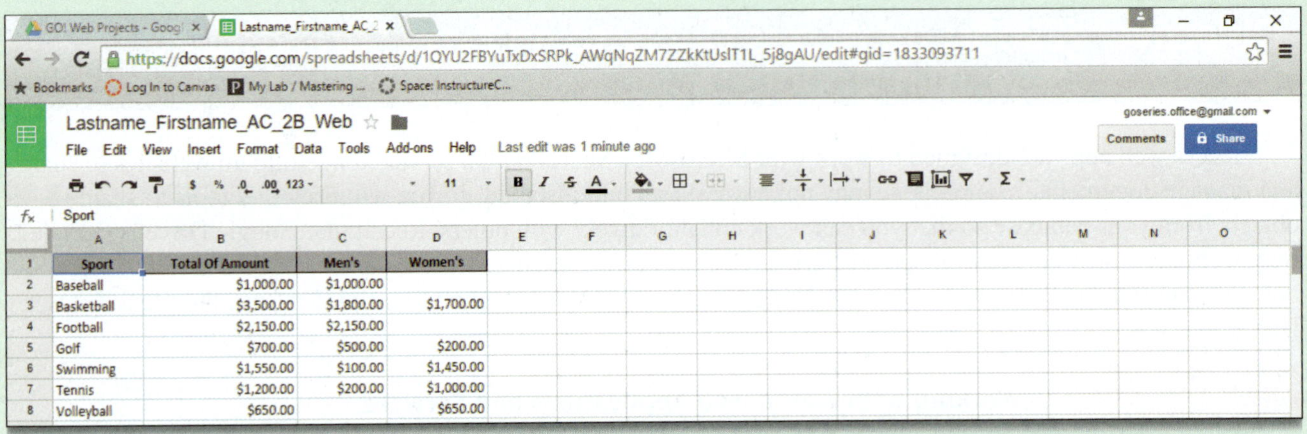

Sport	Total Of Amount	Men's	Women's
Baseball	$1,000.00	$1,000.00	
Basketball	$3,500.00	$1,800.00	$1,700.00
Football	$2,150.00	$2,150.00	
Golf	$700.00	$500.00	$200.00
Swimming	$1,550.00	$100.00	$1,450.00
Tennis	$1,200.00	$200.00	$1,000.00
Volleyball	$650.00		$650.00

FIGURE A

8 Select the range **A1:B8**. On the menu bar, click **Insert**, and then click **Chart**. At the bottom of the **Chart Editor** dialog box, click **Insert** to insert the column chart in the spreadsheet.

The chart is placed in the spreadsheet, covering some of the data.

9 Click the **Chart title**, type **Lastname Firstname Total Scholarships by Sport** Above the title, click the **font size arrow**, click **12**, and then press Enter to apply the title. On the right side of the chart, point to the legend, right-click, and click **Clear legend**.

10 Click to select the chart, if necessary. Point to the top of the chart window until the pointer displays. Hold down the left mouse button, and then drag the chart below the data in the spreadsheet.

11 On the menu, click **File**, point to **Download as**, and then click **Microsoft Excel (.xlsx)**. Use your browser commands to save the file in your **Access Chapter 2** folder as **Lastname_Firstname_AC_2B_Web_Download**

NOTE Saving The Downloaded File to the Access Chapter 2 Folder

Depending on the browser you are using, you may need to open the file in Excel and then save the AC_2B_Web_Download worksheet to your Access Chapter 2 folder.

12 In Google Drive, in the upper right corner, click your name, and then click Sign out. Close your browser window.

13 Start Excel. In the Excel opening screen, in the lower left corner, click **Open Other Workbooks**. Navigate to your **Lastname_Firstname_AC_2B_Web_Download** file and then open the file.

14 If directed to submit a paper printout of your AC_2B_Web_Download file, follow the directions given in the Note below. As directed by your instructor, submit your Excel file created in this project. Your instructor may also request that you submit a copy of the email that was sent to you notifying you of the shared file.

NOTE Printing or Creating a PDF Electronic Image of an Excel Spreadsheet

To print on paper, click Print. To create a PDF electronic image of your printout, on the left side of your screen, click Export. Under Export, be sure Create PDF/XPS Document is selected, and then click Create PDF/XPS. Navigate to your Access Chapter 2 folder, and then click Publish to save the file with the default name and an extension of pdf.

GO! To Work

Andres Rodriguez/Fotolia; FotolEdhar/Fotolia; Andrey Popov/Fotolia; Shutterstock

MICROSOFT OFFICE SPECIALIST (MOS) SKILLS IN THIS CHAPTER	
PROJECT 2A	**PROJECT 2B**
1.2.1 Create and modify relationships **1.2.3** Enforce referential integrity **1.2.4** Set foreign keys **1.3.5** Change views of objects **1.5.1** Print reports **1.5.2** Print records **2.2.4** Rename tables **2.3.3** Delete records **2.3.6** Sort records **3.1.1** Run a query **3.1.6** Save a query **3.2.1** Rename a query **3.2.2** Add fields **3.2.3** Remove fields **3.2.4** Hide fields **3.2.5** Sort data within queries **3.3.2** Set filtering criteria	**1.2.1** Create and modify relationships **1.2.2** Set the primary key **1.2.3** Enforce referential integrity **1.2.4** Set foreign keys **1.3.5** Change views of object **2.2.4** Rename tables **3.1.1** Run a query **3.1.2** Create a crosstab query **3.1.3** Create a parameter query **3.1.5** Create a multi-table query **3.1.6** Save a query **3.2.2** Add fields **3.2.5** Sort data within queries **3.2.6** Format fields within queries **3.3.1** Add calculated fields **3.3.2** Set filtering criteria **3.3.3** Group and summarize data **3.3.4** Group data by using comparison operators **3.3.5** Group data by using arithmetic and logical operators

BUILD YOUR E-PORTFOLIO

An E-Portfolio is a collection of evidence, stored electronically, that showcases what you have accomplished while completing your education. Collecting and then sharing your work products with potential employees reflects your academic and career goals. Your completed documents from the following projects are good examples to show what you have learned: 2G, 2K, and 2L.

GO! FOR JOB SUCCESS

Video: Making Ethical Choices

Your instructor may assign this video to your class, and then ask you to think about, or discuss with your classmates, these questions:

FotolEdhar/Fotolia

Which behaviors in this video do you think were unethical?

Is it unethical to "borrow" things from your employer? Why? What would you do if you saw this behavior going on?

What do you think an employer could do to prevent unethical behavior?

END OF CHAPTER

SUMMARY

Table relationships are created by joining the common fields in tables providing a means for you to modify data simultaneously and use data from multiple tables to create queries, forms, and reports.

Queries are created to answer questions and to extract information from your database tables; saving a query with your database saves you time when you need to answer the question many times.

Queries range from simple queries where you ask a single question to complex queries where you use compound criteria, wildcard characters, logical operators, and create calculated fields.

A crosstab query displays information grouped by two fields, an easy way to display complex data, and a parameter query prompts you to enter the criteria each time you open or run the query.

GO! LEARN IT ONLINE

Review the concepts, key terms, and MOS Skills in this chapter by completing these online challenges, which you can find at **MyITLab**.

Matching and Multiple Choice: Answer matching and multiple-choice questions to test what you learned in this chapter.

Lessons on the GO!: Learn how to use all the new apps and features as they are introduced by Microsoft.

MOS Prep Quiz: Answer questions to review the MOS skills that you have practiced in this chapter.

GO! COLLABORATIVE TEAM PROJECT (available in MyITLab and Instructor Resource Center)

If your instructor assigns the project to your class, you can expect to work with one or more of your classmates—either in class or by using Internet tools—to create work products similar to those you created in this chapter. A team is a group of workers who work together to solve a problem, make a decision, or create a work product. Collaboration is when you work together with others as a team in an intellectual endeavor to complete a shared task or achieve a shared goal.

PROJECT GUIDE FOR ACCESS CHAPTER 2

Your instructor will assign Projects from this list to ensure your learning and assess your knowledge.

PROJECT GUIDE FOR ACCESS CHAPTER 2			
Project	**Apply Skills from These Chapter Objectives**	**Project Type**	**Project Location**
2A **MyITLab**	Objectives 1–7 from Project 2A	**2A Instructional Project (Grader Project)** Guided instruction to learn the skills in Project 2A.	MyITLab and in text
2B **MyITLab**	Objectives 8–15 from Project 2B	**2A Instructional Project (Grader Project)** Guided instruction to learn the skills in Project 2B.	MyITLab and in text
2C	Objectives 1–7 from Project 2A	**2C Chapter Review (Scorecard Grading)** A guided review of the skills from Project 2A.	In text
2D	Objectives 8–15 from Project 2B	**2D Chapter Review (Scorecard Grading)** A guided review of the skills from Project 2B.	In text
2E **MyITLab**	Objectives 1–7 from Project 2A	**2E Mastery (Grader Project)** **Mastery and Transfer of Learning** A demonstration of your mastery of the skills in Project 2A with extensive decision making.	MyITLab and in text
2F **MyITLab**	Objectives 8–15 from Project 2B	**2F Mastery (Grader Project)** **Mastery and Transfer of Learning** A demonstration of your mastery of the skills in Project 2B with extensive decision making.	MyITLab and in text
2G **MyITLab**	Combination of Objectives from Projects 2A and 2B	**2G Mastery (Grader Project)** **Mastery and Transfer of Learning** A demonstration of your mastery of the skills in Projects 2A and 2B with extensive decision making.	MyITLab and in text
2H	Combination of Objectives from Projects 2A and 2B	**2H GO! Fix It (Scorecard Grading)** **Critical Thinking** A demonstration of your mastery of the skills in Projects 2A and 2B Resource by creating a correct result from a document that contains errors Center (IRC) you must find.	Instructor Resource Center (IRC) and MyITLab
2I	Combination of Objectives from Projects 2A and 2B	**2I GO! Make It (Scorecard Grading)** **Critical Thinking** A demonstration of your mastery of the skills in Projects 2A and 2B by creating a result from a supplied picture.	IRC and MyITLab
2J	Combination of Objectives from Projects 2A and 2B	**2J GO! Solve It (Rubric Grading)** **Critical Thinking** A demonstration of your mastery of the skills in Projects 2A and 2B, your decision-making skills, and your critical-thinking skills. A task-specific rubric helps you self-assess your result.	IRC and MyITLab
I2K	Combination of Objectives from Projects 2A and 2B	**2K GO! Solve It (Rubric Grading)** **Critical Thinking** A demonstration of your mastery of the skills in Projects 2A and 2B, your decision-making skills, and your critical-thinking skills. A task-specific rubric helps you self-assess your result.	In text
2L	Combination of Objectives from Projects 2A and 2B	**2L GO! Think (Rubric Grading)** **Critical Thinking** A demonstration of your understanding of the chapter concepts applied in a manner that you would outside of college. An analytic rubric helps you and your instructor grade the quality of your work by comparing it to the work an expert in the discipline would create.	In text
2M	Combination of Objectives from Projects 2A and 2B	**2M GO! Think (Rubric Grading)** **Critical Thinking** A demonstration of your understanding of the chapter concepts applied in a manner that you would outside of college. An analytic rubric helps you and your instructor grade the quality of your work by comparing it to the work an expert in the discipline would create.	IRC and MyITLab
2N	Combination of Objectives from Projects 2A and 2B	**2N You and GO! (Rubric Grading)** **Critical Thinking** A demonstration of your understanding of the chapter concepts applied in a manner that you would in a personal situation. An analytic rubric helps you and your instructor grade the quality of your work.	IRC and MyITLab
2O	Combination of Objectives from Projects 2A and 2B	**2O Collaborative Team Project for ACCESS Chapter 2** **Critical Thinking** A demonstration of your understanding of concepts and your ability to work collaboratively in a group role-playing assessment, requiring both collaboration and self-management.	IRC and MyITLab

GLOSSARY

GLOSSARY OF CHAPTER KEY TERMS

Aggregate functions Calculations such as Min, Max, Avg, and Sum that are performed on a group of records.

AND condition A compound criteria used to display records that match all parts of the specified criteria.

Ascending order A sorting order that arranges text alphabetically (A to Z) and numbers from the lowest number to the highest number.

Between … And operator A comparison operator that looks for values within a range.

Calculated field A field that stores the value of a mathematical operation.

Cascade Delete Related Records A cascade option that enables you to delete a record in a table and also delete all of the related records in related tables.

Cascade options Relationship options that enable you to update records in related tables when referential integrity is enforced.

Cascade Update Related Fields A cascade option that enables you to change the data in the primary key field in the table on the *one* side of the relationship and update that change to any fields storing that same data in related tables.

Comparison operators Symbols that are used to evaluate data in the field to determine if it is the same (=), greater than (>), less than (<), or in between a range of values as specified by the criteria.

Compound criteria Multiple conditions in a query or filter.

Criteria Conditions in a query that identify the specific records you are looking for.

Crosstab query A query that uses an aggregate function for data that can be grouped by two types of information and displays the data in a compact, spreadsheet-like format with column headings and row headings.

Data source The table or tables from which a form, query, or report retrieves its data.

Descending order A sorting order that arranges text in reverse alphabetical order (Z to A) and numbers from the highest number to the lowest number.

Expression A formula that will perform the calculation.

Field list A list of field names in a table.

Foreign key The field that is included in the related table so the field can be joined with the primary key in another table for the purpose of creating a relationship.

Innermost sort field When sorting on multiple fields in Datasheet view, the field that will be used for the second level of sorting.

Is Not Null A criteria that searches for fields that are not empty.

Is Null A criteria that searches for fields that are empty.

Join line In the Relationships window, the line joining two tables that visually indicates the common fields and the type of relationship.

Logical operators Operators that combine criteria using AND and OR. With two criteria, AND requires that both conditions be met and OR requires that either condition be met for the record to display in the query results.

Message Bar The area directly below the ribbon that displays information such as security alerts when there is potentially unsafe, active content in an Office document that you open.

One-to-many relationship A relationship between two tables where one record in the first table corresponds to many records in the second table—the most common type of relationship in Access.

OR condition A compound criteria used to display records that match at least one of the specified criteria.

Outermost sort field When sorting on multiple fields in Datasheet view, the field that will be used for the first level of sorting.

Parameter A value that can be changed.

Parameter query A query that prompts you for criteria before running the query.

Query design grid The lower area of the query window that displays the design of the query.

Referential integrity A set of rules that Access uses to ensure that the data between related tables is valid.

Relationship An association that you establish between two tables based on common fields.

Run The process in which Access looks at the records in the table(s) included in the query design, finds the records that match the specified criteria, and then displays the records in a datasheet; only the fields included in the query design display.

Sorting The process of arranging data in a specific order based on the value in a field.

Subdatasheet A format for displaying related records when you click the plus sign (+) next to a record in a table on the *one* side of the relationship.

Subset A portion of the total records available.

Table area The upper area of the query window that displays field lists for the tables that are used in a query.

Text string A sequence of characters.

Trust Center An area of Access where you can view the security and privacy settings for your Access installation.

Wildcard character In a query, a character that represents one or more unknown characters in criteria; an asterisk (*) represents one or more unknown characters, and a question mark (?) represents a single unknown character.

Apply 2A skills from these Objectives:

1. Open and Save an Existing Database
2. Create Table Relationships
3. Sort Records in a Table
4. Create a Query in Design View
5. Create a New Query from an Existing Query
6. Sort Query Results
7. Specify Criteria in a Query

Skills Review Project 2C Freshman Orientation

In the following Skills Review, you will assist Dr. Wendy Bowie, the Director of Counseling at the Southwest Campus, in using her database to answer several questions about the freshman orientation sessions that will be held prior to class registration. Your completed database objects will look similar to Figure 2.55.

PROJECT FILES

For Project 2C, you will need the following file:

a02C_Freshman_Orientation

You will save your database as:

Lastname_Firstname_2C_Freshman_Orientation

PROJECT RESULTS

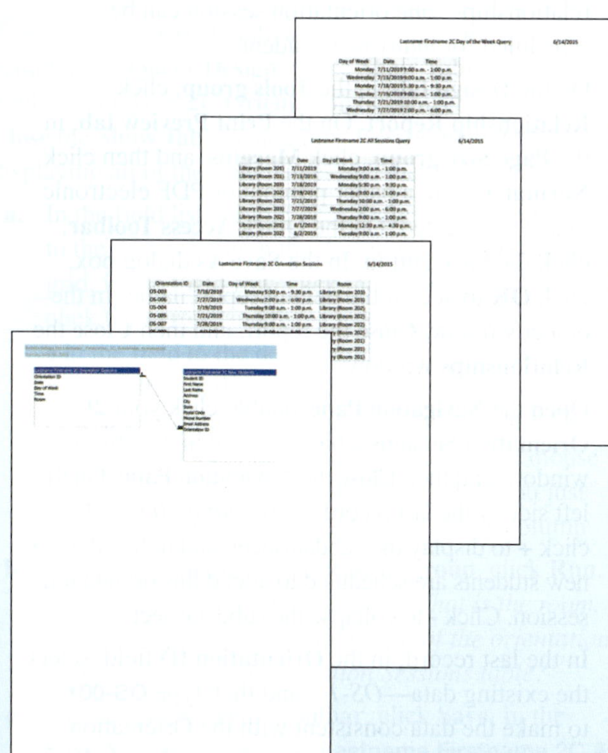

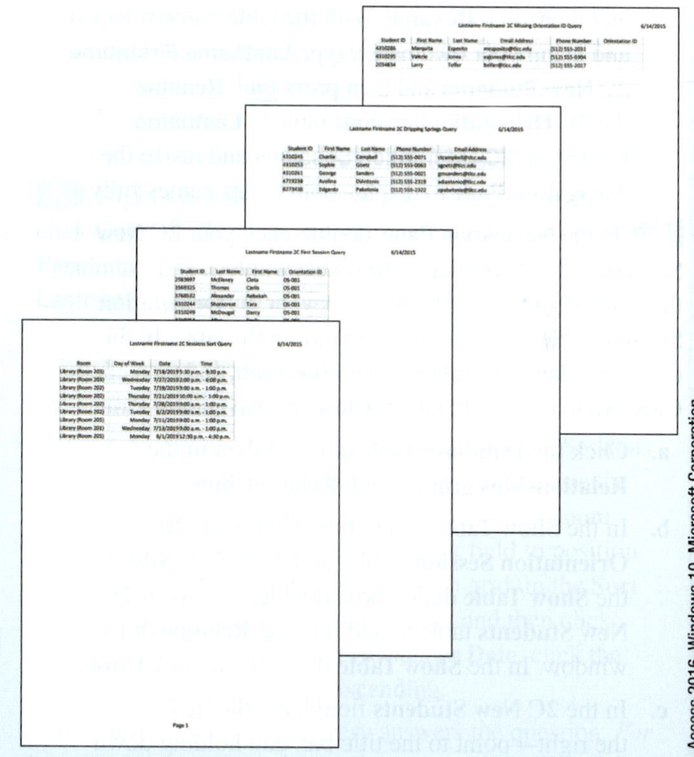

FIGURE 2.55

(Project 2C Freshman Orientation continues on the next page)

Mastering Access Project 2E Biology Supplies (continued)

1 **Start** Access. From your student data files, open **a02E_Biology_Supplies**. Save the database in your **Access Chapter 2** folder as **Lastname_Firstname_2E_Biology_Supplies** and then enable the content. In the **Navigation Pane**, **Rename** each table by adding **Lastname Firstname** to the beginning of the table name. Increase the width of the **Navigation Pane** so that all object names display fully.

2 Open both tables to examine the fields and data, and then **Close** both tables. Create a *one-to-many* relationship between your **2E Vendors** table and your **2E Biology Lab Supplies** table using the common field **Vendor ID**. **Enforce Referential Integrity**, and enable both cascade options. *One* vendor can supply *many* supplies. Create a **Relationship Report** with **Normal Margins**, saving it with the default name. Create a paper or PDF electronic image as directed, and then **Close All** open objects. Open your **2E Vendors** table. In the last record, in the **Vendor ID** field, select **V-100**, type **V-001** and then press [↓] to save the record. **Close** the table.

3 Open your **2E Biology Lab Supplies** table. Sort the records first in **Descending** order by **Price Per Item** and then in **Ascending** order by **Category**. Using **Landscape** orientation, create a paper printout or PDF electronic image as directed. **Close** the table, and do *not* save changes to the table.

4 **Create** a query in **Query Design** view using your **2E Biology Lab Supplies** table to answer the question, *What is the item ID, item name, room, location, and quantity in stock for all of the items, sorted in ascending order by the Room field and the Location field?* Display the fields in the order listed in the question. **Save** the query as **Lastname Firstname 2E Items by Room Query** and then create a paper printout or PDF electronic image as directed. **Close** the query.

5 In the **Navigation Pane**, use your **2E Items by Room Query** to create a new query object named **Lastname Firstname 2E Item Categories Query** and then redesign the query to answer the question, *What is the item ID, item name, category, vendor ID, and quantity in stock for all items, sorted in ascending order by the Category field and the Vendor ID field?* Display only the fields necessary to answer the question and in the order listed in the question. Create a paper printout or PDF electronic image as directed. **Close** the query, saving the design changes.

6 In the **Navigation Pane**, use your **2E Items by Room Query** to create a new query object named **Lastname Firstname 2E Supplies Sort Query** and then open the new query in **Design** view. Redesign the query to answer the question, *What is the item name, category, price per item, and quantity in stock for all supplies, sorted in ascending order by the Category field and then in descending order by the Price Per Item field?* Display only the fields necessary to answer the question and in the order listed in the question. Create a paper printout or PDF electronic image as directed. **Close** the query, saving the design changes.

7 Using your **2E Supplies Sort Query**, create a new query object named **Lastname Firstname 2E Kits Query** and then redesign the query to answer the question, *What is item name, category, price per item, quantity in stock, and vendor ID for all items that have a category of kits, sorted in ascending order by the Item Name field?* Do not display the **Category** field in the query results, and display the rest of the fields in the order listed in the question. Six records match the criteria. Create a paper printout or PDF electronic image as directed. **Close** the query, saving the design changes.

8 **Create** a query in **Query Design** view using your **2E Vendors** table to answer the question, *What is the vendor ID, vendor name, and phone number where the phone number is blank, sorted in ascending order by the Vendor Name field?* Display the fields in the order listed in the question. Two records match the criteria. **Save** the query as **Lastname Firstname 2E Missing Phone Query** and then create a paper printout or PDF electronic image as directed. **Close** the query.

(Project 2E Biology Supplies continues on the next page)

Mastering Access Project 2E Biology Supplies (continued)

9 Be sure all objects are closed. **Open** the **Navigation Pane**, be sure that all object names display fully, and then **Close Access**. As directed by your instructor, submit your database and the paper printout or PDF electronic images of the seven objects—relationship report, sorted table, and five queries—that are the results of this project.

1. Lastname_Firstname_2E_Biology_Supplies	Database file
2. Relationships for Lastname_Firstname_2E_Biology_Supplies Relationships	Report
3. Lastname Firstname 2E Biology Lab Supplies table sorted (not saved)	Table sorted
4. Lastname Firstname 2E Items by Room Query	Query
5. Lastname Firstname 2E Item Categories Query	Query
6. Lastname Firstname 2E Supplies Sort Query	Query
7. Lastname Firstname 2E Kits Query	Query
8. Lastname Firstname 2E Missing Phone Query	Query

END | You have completed Project 2E

Apply a combination of the 2A and 2B skills.

CONTENT-BASED ASSESSMENTS (CRITICAL THINKING)

GO! Fix It Project 2H Social Sciences **MyITLab**

GO! Make It Project 2I Faculty Awards **MyITLab**

GO! Solve It Project 2J Student Refunds **MyITLab**

GO! Solve It Project 2K Leave

PROJECT FILES

For Project 2K, you will need the following file:

a02K_Leave

You will save your database as:

Lastname_Firstname_2K-Leave

Start Access, navigate to your student data files, open a02K_Leave, and then save the database in your Access Chapter 2 folder as **Lastname_Firstname_2K_Leave** Add **Lastname Firstname** to the beginning of both table names, create a one-to-many relationship with cascade options between the two tables—*one* employee can receive *many* leave transactions—and then create a relationship report saving it as **Lastname Firstname 2K Relationships**

Create and save four queries to answer the following questions; be sure that all data displays fully:

- What is the last name and first name of employees who have used personal leave, sorted in ascending order by the Last Name and First Name fields? Do not display the Leave field in the query results.
- What is the last name, first name, and email address of employees who have no phone number listed, sorted in ascending order by the Last Name and First Name fields?
- Grouped by the Leave Classification field, what is the total of each type of leave used? (Hint: Use the aggregate function Count.)
- What is the total number of leave transactions grouped in rows by the Employee# field and grouped in columns by the Leave Classification field?

As directed, create paper or PDF electronic images of the relationship report and the four queries. Be sure that each object prints on one page, and that the object names display fully in the Navigation Pane. As directed, submit your database and the paper printouts or PDF electronic images of the five objects that are the results of this project.

(Project 2K Leave continues on the next page)

GO! Solve It Project 2K Leave (continued)

Performance Level

Performance Criteria	Exemplary: You consistently applied the relevant skills	Proficient: You sometimes, but not always, applied the relevant skills	Developing: You rarely or never applied the relevant skills
Create relationship and relationship report	Relationship and relationship report created correctly.	Relationship and relationship report created with one error.	Relationship and relationship report created with two or more errors, or missing entirely.
Create 2K Personal Leave query	Query created with correct name, fields, sorting, and criteria.	Query created with one element incorrect.	Query created with two or more elements incorrect, or missing entirely.
Create 2K Missing Phone query	Query created with correct name, fields, sorting, and criteria.	Query created with one element incorrect.	Query created with two or more elements incorrect, or missing entirely.
Create 2K Type of Leave query	Query created with correct name, fields, and aggregate function.	Query created with one element incorrect.	Query created with two or more elements incorrect, or missing entirely.
Create 2K Crosstab query	Query created with correct name, row headings, column headings, and aggregate function.	Query created with one element incorrect.	Query created with two or more two elements incorrect, or missing entirely.

END | You have completed Project 2K

OUTCOMES-BASED ASSESSMENTS (CRITICAL THINKING)

RUBRIC

The following outcomes-based assessments are open-ended assessments. That is, there is no specific correct result; your result will depend on your approach to the information provided. Make Professional Quality your goal. Use the following scoring rubric to guide you in how to approach the problem and then to evaluate how well your approach solves the problem.

The *criteria*—Software Mastery, Content, Format and Layout, and Process—represent the knowledge and skills you have gained that you can apply to solving the problem. The *levels of performance*—Professional Quality, Approaching Professional Quality, or Needs Quality Improvements—help you and your instructor evaluate your result.

	Your completed project is of Professional Quality if you:	Your completed project is Approaching Professional Quality if you:	Your completed project Needs Quality Improvements if you:
1-Software Mastery	Choose and apply the most appropriate skills, tools, and features and identify efficient methods to solve the problem.	Choose and apply some appropriate skills, tools, and features, but not in the most efficient manner.	Choose inappropriate skills, tools, or features, or are inefficient in solving the problem.
2-Content	Construct a solution that is clear and well organized, contains content that is accurate, appropriate to the audience and purpose, and is complete. Provide a solution that contains no errors of spelling, grammar, or style.	Construct a solution in which some components are unclear, poorly organized, inconsistent, or incomplete. Misjudge the needs of the audience. Have some errors in spelling, grammar, or style, but the errors do not detract from comprehension.	Construct a solution that is unclear, incomplete, or poorly organized, contains some inaccurate or inappropriate content, and contains many errors of spelling, grammar, or style. Do not solve the problem.
3-Format and Layout	Format and arrange all elements to communicate information and ideas, clarify function, illustrate relationships, and indicate relative importance.	Apply appropriate format and layout features to some elements, but not others. Overuse features, causing minor distraction.	Apply format and layout that does not communicate information or ideas clearly. Do not use format and layout features to clarify function, illustrate relationships, or indicate relative importance. Use available features excessively, causing distraction.
4-Process	Use an organized approach that integrates planning, development, self-assessment, revision, and reflection.	Demonstrate an organized approach in some areas, but not others; or, use an insufficient process of organization throughout.	Do not use an organized approach to solve the problem.

2 ACCESS

Apply a combination of the 2A and 2B skills.

OUTCOMES-BASED ASSESSMENTS (CRITICAL THINKING)

GO! Think Project 2L Coaches

PROJECT FILES

For Project 2L, you will need the following file:

a02L_Coaches

You will save your database as

Lastname_Firstname_2L_Coaches

Start Access, navigate to your student data files, open a02L_Coaches, and then save the database in your Access Chapter 2 folder as **Lastname_Firstname_2L_Coaches** Add **Lastname Firstname** to the beginning of both table names, create a one-to-many relationship with cascade options between the two tables—*one* coach can participate in *many* activities—and then create a relationship report saving it as **Lastname Firstname 2L Relationships**

Create queries to assist Randy Garza, the Athletic Director, answer the following questions about the coaches at Texas Lakes Community College:

- What is the last name and first name of every coach involved in *Dive* activities, sorted in ascending order by the Last Name field? Do not display the activity name.
- What is the last name and first name of every coach involved in basketball or football activities, sorted in ascending first by the Activity Name field and then by the Last Name field?
- Grouped by division, what is the total number of activity names, sorted in descending order by the total number? (Hint: Use the Count aggregate function.)
- What is the skill specialty, first name, last name, and phone number for coaches in a specified position that is entered when prompted for the Position, sorted in ascending order first by the Skill Specialty field and then by the Last Name field? (When prompted, enter the position of *director* for your paper or PDF electronic image.)

As directed, create paper or PDF electronic images of the relationship report and the four queries. Be sure that each object prints on one page, and that the object names display fully in the Navigation Pane. As directed, submit your database and the paper printout or PDF electronic images of the five objects that are the results of this project.

End | You have completed Project 2L

GO! Think Project 2M Club Donations MyITLab

Build From Scratch

You and GO! Project 2N Personal Inventory MyITLab

GO! Collaborative Team Project Project 2O Bell Orchid Hotels MyITLab

4 On the **Message Bar**, click **Enable Content**. In the **Navigation Pane**, right-click the **3A Majors** table, and then click **Rename**. With the table name selected and using your own name, type **Lastname Firstname 3A Majors** and then press Enter to rename the table. Use the same technique to **Rename** the **3A New Students** table to **Lastname Firstname 3A New Students**

5 Point to the right edge of the **Navigation Pane** to display the ⇔ pointer. Drag to the right to increase the width of the pane until both table names display fully.

6 On the ribbon, click the **Database Tools tab**. In the **Relationships group**, click **Relationships**. Under Relationship Tools, on the **Design tab**, in the **Relationships group**, click **All Relationships**. If necessary, resize and move the field lists so that the entire table name and fields display for each field list.

Because you renamed the tables, the field lists do not automatically display in the Relationships window.

7 In the **Relationships** window, click the **join line** between the two field lists. In the **Tools group**, click **Edit Relationships**. Point to the title bar of the **Edit Relationships** dialog box, and drag the dialog box to the right of the two field lists. Compare your screen with Figure 3.2.

One major is associated with *many* students. A one-to-many relationship is established between your 3A Majors table and your 3A New Students table using the Major ID field as the common field. Recall that Cascade Update Related Fields enables you to change the primary key in the 3A Majors table, and then the data in the foreign key field in the 3A New Students field is automatically updated. Recall that Cascade Delete Related Records enables you to delete a record in the 3A Majors table, and then all related records in the 3A New Students table are automatically deleted.

ANOTHER WAY In the Relationships window, double-click the join line to display the Edit Relationships dialog box.

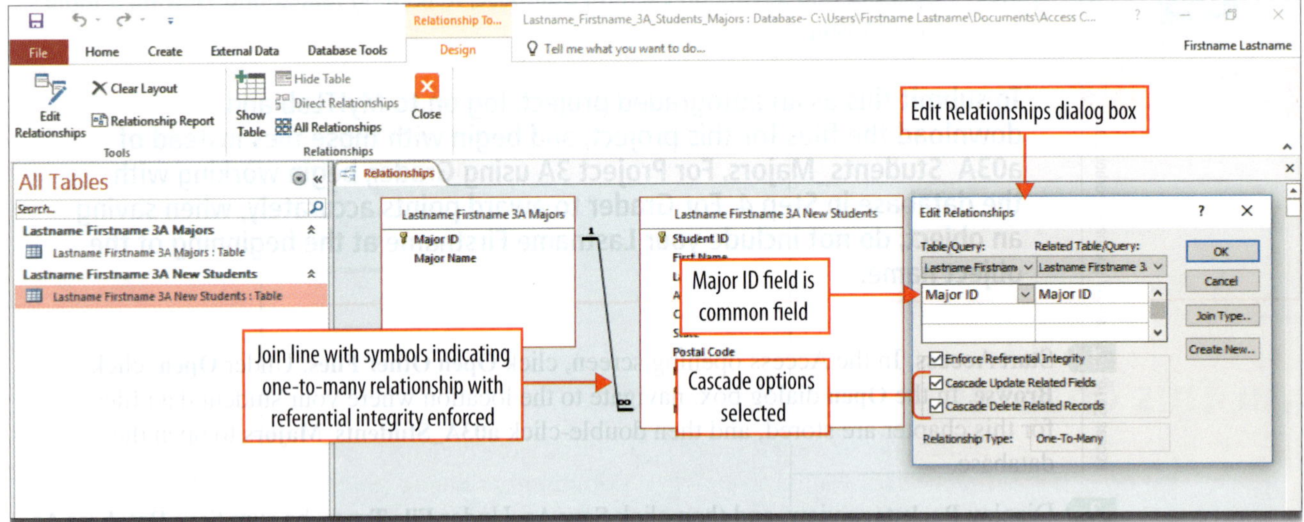

FIGURE 3.2

ALERT! **Is your Edit Relationships dialog box empty?**

The Edit Relationships dialog box does not display any information if you do not first click the join line. If this happens, close the Edit Relationships dialog box, and then be sure that you click the join line—when selected, the join line is darker.

8 Close the **Edit Relationships** dialog box, and then **Close** the **Relationships** window. In the message box, click **Yes** to save changes to the layout of the relationships.

Activity 3.02 | Creating a Form and Viewing Records

4.1.1, 4.1.3

There are several ways to create a form in Access, but the fastest and easiest way is to use the ***Form tool***. With a single mouse click, all fields from the data source are placed on the form. You can modify the form in Layout view or in Design view, or you can switch to Form view and use the new form immediately.

The Form tool uses all of the field names and all of the records from an existing table or query. Records that you create or edit using a form are automatically updated in the underlying table or tables. In this Activity, you will create a form and then view records from the underlying table—the data source.

1 In the **Navigation Pane**, double-click your **3A New Students** table to open it. Scroll as needed to view all 10 fields—*Student ID*, *First Name*, *Last Name*, *Address*, *City*, *State*, *Postal Code*, *Home Phone*, *College Email*, and *Major ID*. **Close** the table.

2 In the **Navigation Pane**, be sure your **3A New Students** table is selected. On the ribbon, click the **Create tab**, and then in the **Forms group**, click **Form**. **Close** the **Navigation Pane**, and then compare your screen with Figure 3.3.

The form is created based on the currently selected object—your 3A New Students table—and displays in ***Layout view***. In Layout view, you can modify the form with the data displayed in the fields. For example, you can adjust the size of the text boxes to fit the data.

The form is created in a simple top-to-bottom layout, with all 10 fields from your 3A New Students table lined up in a single column. The data for the first record in the data source displays.

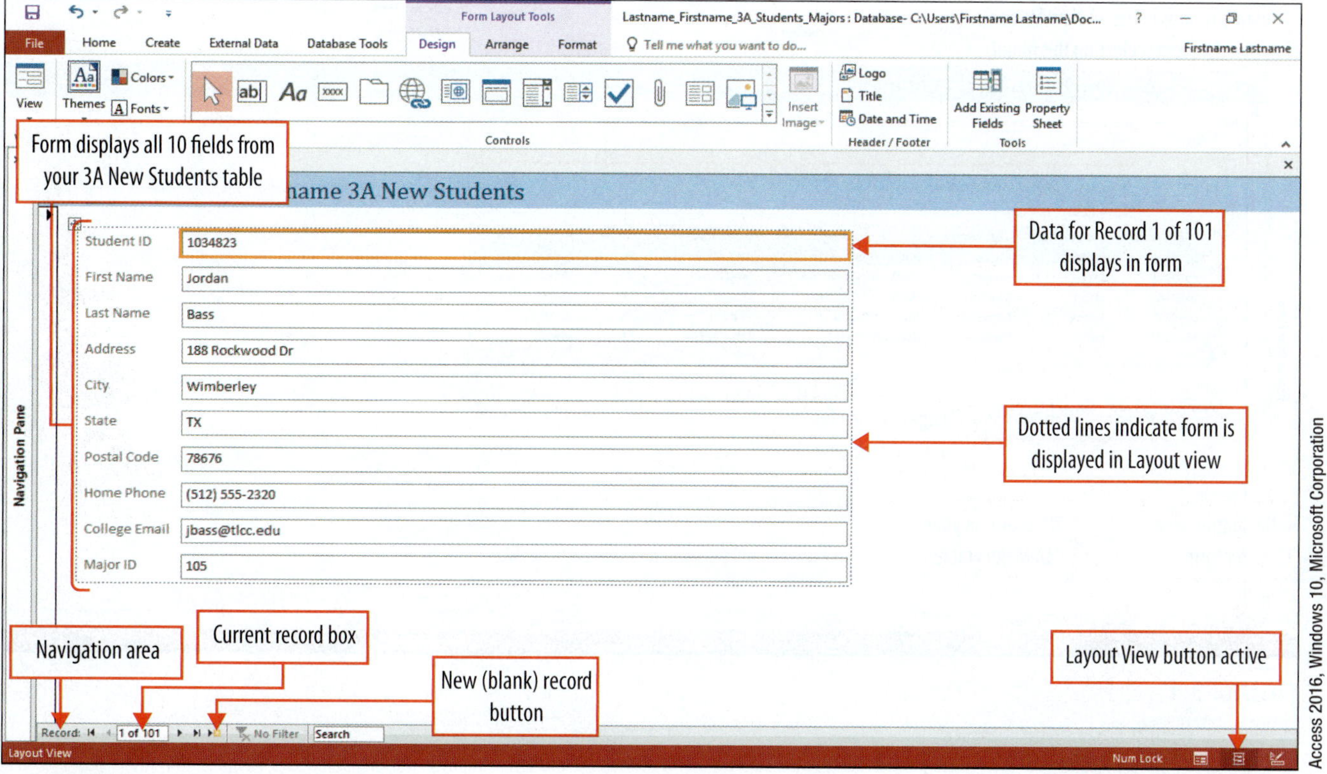

FIGURE 3.3

3 In the navigation area, click **Next record** ▶ four times to display the fifth record—*Student ID 1298345*. In the navigation area, select the text in the Current record box, type **62** and then press Enter to display the record for *Student ID 5720358*. In the navigation area, click **Last record** ▶| to display the record for *Student ID 9583924*, and then click **First record** |◀ to display the record for *Student ID 1034823*.

Use the navigation buttons to scroll among the records or the Current record box to display any single record.

4 **Save** the form as **Lastname Firstname 3A New Student Form** and then **Close** ✕ the form object.

5 **Open** » the **Navigation Pane**. Notice that your new form displays under the table with which it is related—your **3A New Students** table.

Activity 3.03 | Creating a Second Form

MOS 4.1.1, 4.1.3

In this Activity, you will use the Form tool to create a form for your 3A Majors table.

1 In the **Navigation Pane**, click your **3A Majors** table to select it. On the ribbon, click the **Create tab**, and then in the **Forms group**, click **Form**. **Close** « the **Navigation Pane**, and then compare your screen with Figure 3.4.

Because a one-to-many relationship is established, the form displays related records in the 3A New Students table for each record in the 3A Majors table. Five new students have selected a major of *Diagnostic Medical Sonography—Major ID 105*.

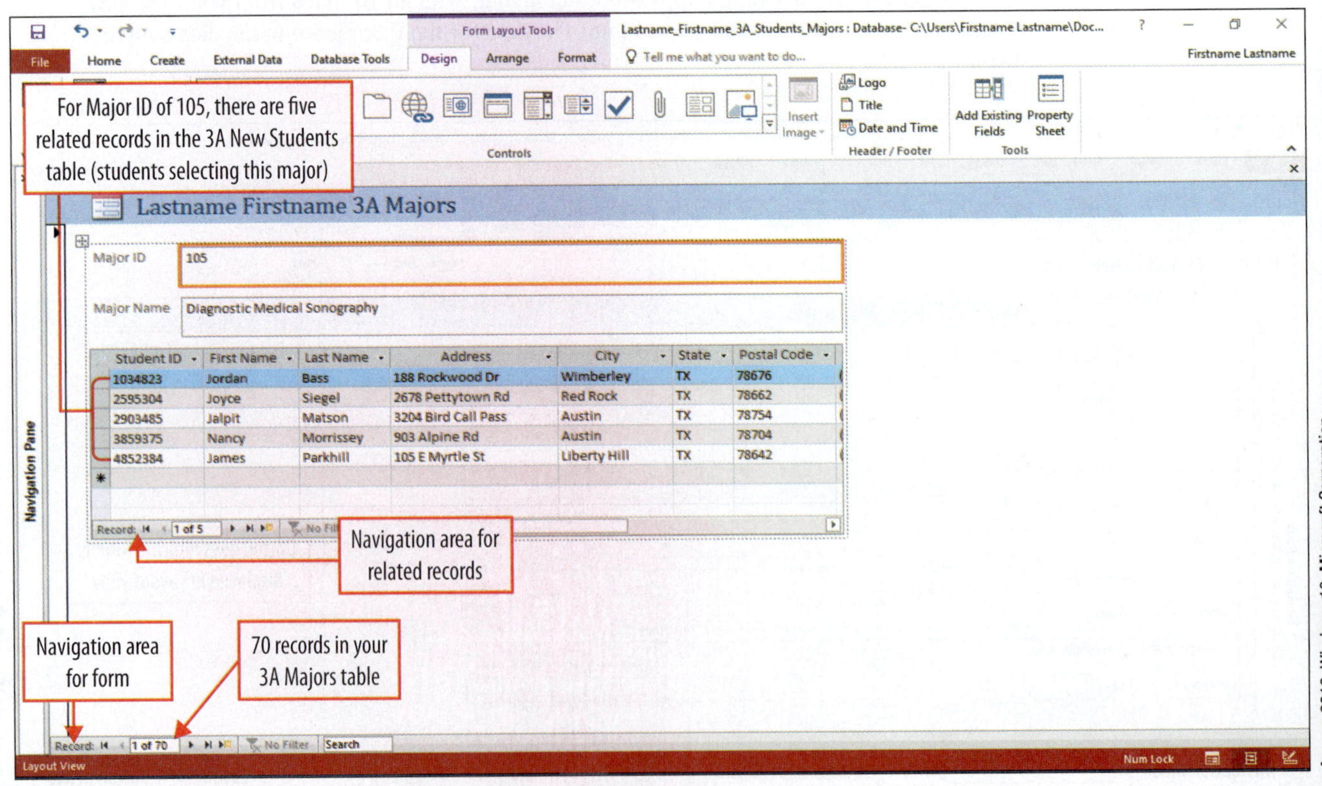

FIGURE 3.4

2 **Close** [X] your **3A Majors** form. In the message box, click **Yes**. In the **Save As** dialog box, in the **Form Name** box, type **Lastname Firstname 3A Major Form** and then click **OK**.

Recall that if you do not save an object, you are prompted to do so when you close the object.

3 **Open** [»] the **Navigation Pane**. Notice that your new form displays under the table with which it is related—your **3A Majors** table.

Activity 3.04 | Adding Records to a Table by Using a Form

2.3.2

By using a single-record form to add, modify, and delete records, you can reduce the number of data entry errors, because the individual performing the data entry is looking at only one record at a time. Recall that your database is useful only if the information is accurate—just like your contact list is useful only if it contains accurate phone numbers and email addresses.

Forms are based on—also referred to as ***bound*** to—the table where the records are stored. When a record is entered in a form, the new record is added to the underlying table. The reverse is also true—when a record is added to the table, the new record can be viewed in the related form.

In this Activity, you will add a new record to both tables by using the forms that you just created.

1 In the **Navigation Pane**, double-click your **3A New Student Form** object to open it, and then **Close** [«] the **Navigation Pane**. In the navigation area, click **New (blank) record** to display a new blank form.

When you open a form, the first record in the underlying table displays in ***Form view***, which is used to view, add, modify, and delete records stored in the table.

2 In the **Student ID** field, type **9712345** and then press [Tab].

Use the [Tab] key to move from field to field in a form. ***Tab order*** is the order in which the insertion point moves from one field to the next when you press the [Tab] key. As you start typing, the pencil icon displays in the ***record selector bar*** at the left—the bar used to select an entire record. The pencil icon displays when a record is being created or edited.

ANOTHER WAY Press the [Enter] key, provided there are no special links on the form, such as a link to create a new form or a link to print the form.

3 Using your own first name and last name and using the first initial of your first name and your last name for the *College Email* field, continue entering the data shown in the following table, and then compare your screen with Figure 3.5.

Student ID	First Name	Last Name	Address	City	State	Postal Code	Home Phone	College Email	Major ID
9712345	**First Name**	**Last Name**	**5820 Sweet Basil Ct**	**Austin**	**TX**	**78726**	**(512) 555-5712**	**flastname@tlcc.edu**	**339**

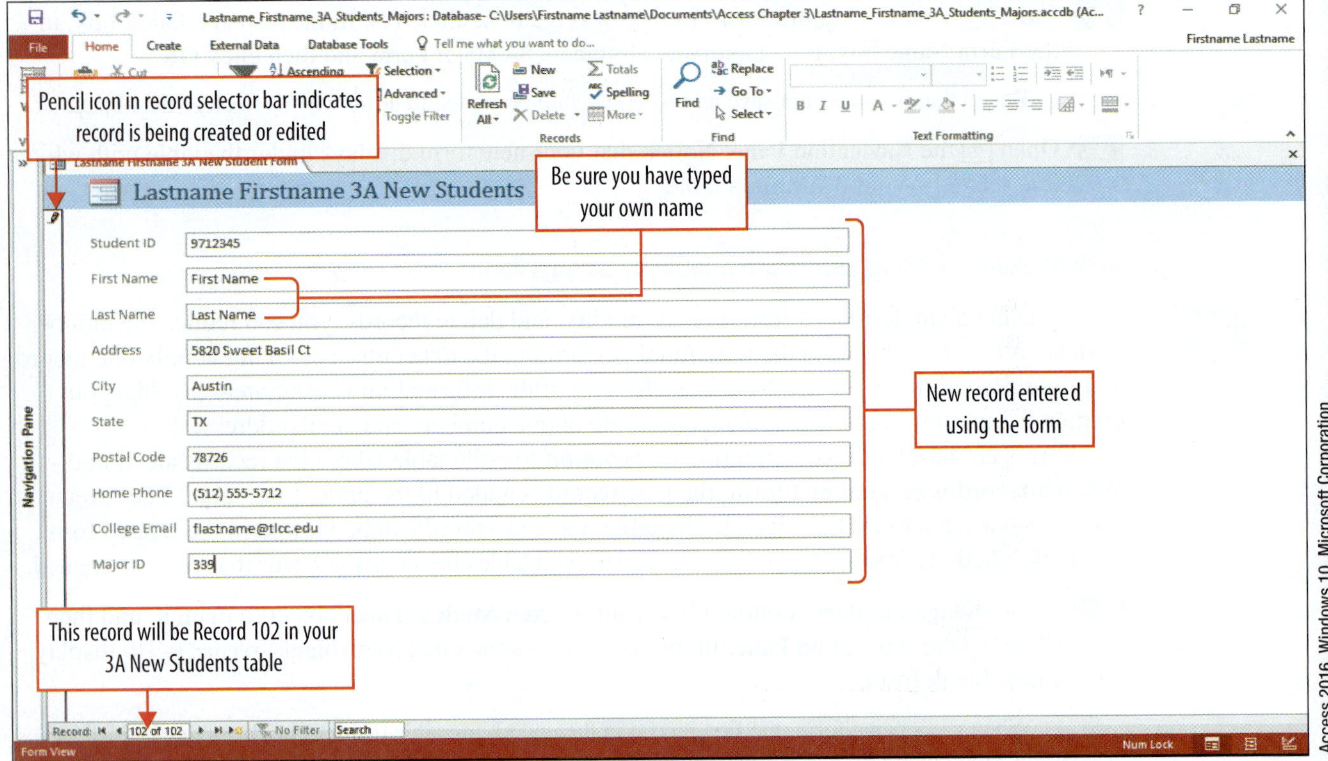

FIGURE 3.5

4 With the insertion point positioned in the last field, press Enter to save the record and display a new blank record. **Close** your **3A New Student Form** object.

5 **Open** the **Navigation Pane**, and then double-click your **3A New Students** table to open it. In the navigation area, click **Last record** to verify that the record you entered in the form is stored in the underlying table. **Close** your **3A New Students** table.

6 In the **Navigation Pane**, double-click your **3A Major Form** object to open it. At the bottom of the screen, in the navigation area for the form—*not* the navigation area for the subdatasheet—click **New (blank) record**. In the blank form, enter the data shown in the following table:

Major ID	Major Name
339.555.22	**Network Security**

7 **Close** your **3A Major Form** object. In the **Navigation Pane**, double-click your **3A Majors** table, and then scroll to verify that the record for *Major ID 339.555.22 Network Security* displays in the table—records are sorted by the *Major ID* field. **Close** the table.

Activity 3.05 | Deleting Records from a Table by Using a Form

2.3.3, 2.3.5

You can delete records from a database table by using a form. In this Activity, you will delete the record for *Major ID 800.03* because the program has been discontinued.

1 In the **Navigation Pane**, double-click your **3A Major Form** object to open it, and then **Close** the **Navigation Pane**. On the **Home tab**, in the **Find group**, click **Find** to open the **Find and Replace** dialog box.

ANOTHER WAY Press Ctrl + F to open the Find and Replace dialog box.

2 In the **Look In** box, notice that *Current field* displays. In the **Find What** box, type **800.03** and then click **Find Next**. Compare your screen with Figure 3.6, and verify that the record for *Major ID 800.03* displays.

Because the insertion point was positioned in the *Major ID* field before opening the dialog box, Access will search for data in this field—the *Current field*.

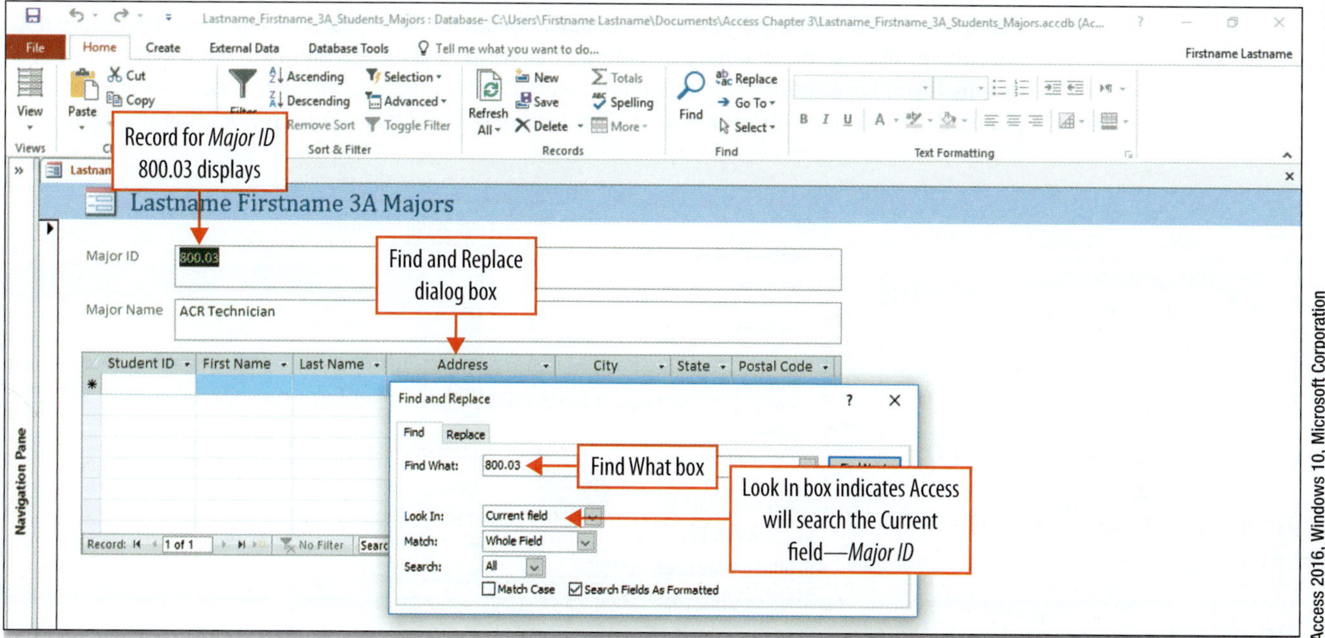

FIGURE 3.6

3 **Close** [X] the **Find and Replace** dialog box. On the **Home tab**, in the **Records group**, click the **Delete arrow**, and then click **Delete Record**.

The record is removed from the screen, and a message displays alerting you that you are about to delete *1 record(s)*. Once you click *Yes*, you cannot click Undo to reverse this action. If you delete a record by mistake, you must re-create the record by reentering the data. Because no students are associated with this major and the program is being discontinued, you can delete it from the table.

4 In the message box, click **Yes** to delete the record. In the navigation area for the form, notice that the total number of records in the table is *70*. **Close** [X] your **3A Major Form** object.

5 **Open** [»] the **Navigation Pane**, and then double-click your **3A Majors** table to open it. Examine the table to verify that the *Major ID 800.03* record has been deleted from the table, and then **Close** [X] the table.

Adding and deleting records in a form updates the records stored in the underlying table.

Activity 3.06 | Printing a Form

1.5.2, 4.3.2

When a form is displayed, clicking Print causes *all* of the records to print in the form layout. In this Activity, you will print only *one* record.

1 In the **Navigation Pane**, double-click your **3A New Student Form** object to open it, and then **Close** [«] the **Navigation Pane**. Press [Ctrl] + [F] to open the **Find and Replace** dialog box. In the **Find What** box, type **9712345** and then click **Find Next** to display the record with your name. **Close** [X] the **Find and Replace** dialog box.

2 On the **File tab**, click **Print**, and then on the right, click **Print**. In the **Print** dialog box, under **Print Range**, click the **Selected Record(s)** option button. In the lower left corner of the dialog box, click **Setup**.

3 In the **Page Setup** dialog box, click the **Columns tab**. Under **Column Size**, double-click in the **Width** box to select the existing value, type **7.5** and then compare your screen with Figure 3.7.

Change the width of the column in this manner so that the form prints on one page. Forms are not typically printed, so the width of the column in a form might be greater than the width of the paper on which you are printing. The maximum column width that you can enter is dependent upon the printer that is installed on your system. This setting is saved when you save or close the form.

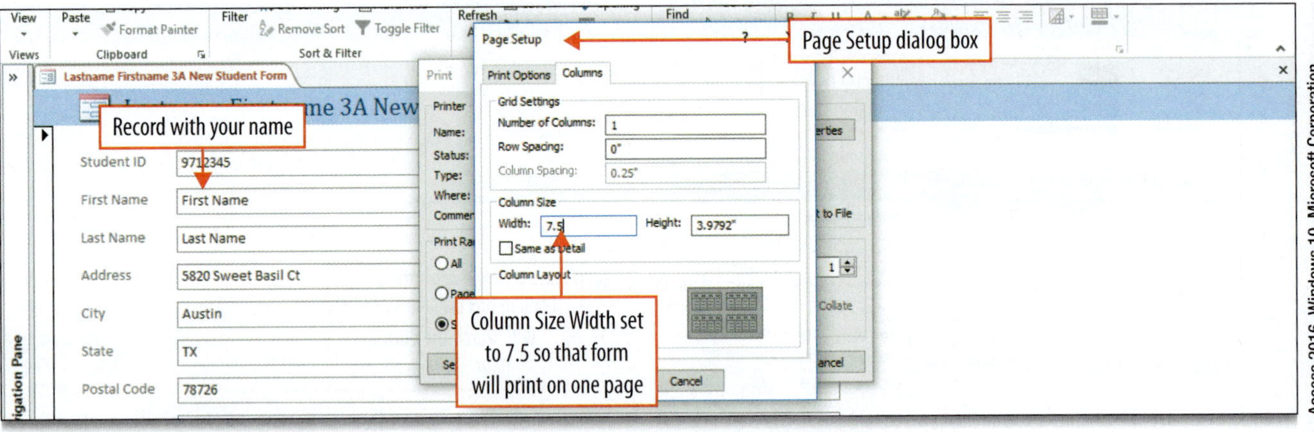

FIGURE 3.7

4 In the **Page Setup** dialog box, click **OK**. To create a paper printout, in the **Print** dialog box click **OK**. To create a PDF electronic image of this single form, click **Cancel** and then follow the instructions in the Note below.

NOTE Printing a Single Form as a PDF Electronic Image

To create a PDF electronic image of a single form as a PDF electronic image, change the column width to 7.5 as described in Step 3 above, and then in the Print dialog box, click Cancel. On the left side of the form, click the Record Selector bar so that it is black—selected. Click the External Data tab. In the Export group, click PDF or XPS.

In the Publish as PDF or XPS dialog box, navigate to your chapter folder. In the File name box, the file has the same name as the form. Be sure that the Open file after publishing check box is selected, and that the Minimum size (publishing online) option button is selected. In the Publish as PDF or XPS dialog box, click Options. In the Options dialog box, under Range, click the Selected records option button, click OK, and then click Publish. Close the Windows Edge Reader, Adobe Reader or Adobe Acrobat window, and then submit the file as directed by your instructor.

5 **Close** your **3A New Student Form** object, **Open** the **Navigation Pane**, and then double-click your **3A Major Form** object to open it. **Close** the **Navigation Pane**.

6 Use the techniques you just practiced to **Find** the record for the **Major ID** of **339.555.22**, and then create a paper printout or PDF electronic image as directed by your instructor of that record only on one page. After printing, **Close** your **3A Major Form** object.

If there are no related records in the subdatasheet, the empty subdatasheet does not display in the printed form.

Objective 2 Filter Records

GO! Learn How Video A3-2

Filtering records in a form displays only a portion of the total records—a ***subset***—based on matching specific values. Filters are commonly used to provide a quick answer to a question, and the result is not generally saved for future use. For example, by filtering records in a form, you can quickly display a subset of records for students majoring in Information Systems Technology, which is identified by the Major ID of 339.

A form provides an interface for the database. For example, because of security reasons, the registration assistants at your college may not have access to the entire student database. Rather, by using a form, they can access and edit only some information—the information necessary for them to do their jobs. Filtering records within a form provides individuals who do not have access to the entire database a way to ask questions of the database without constructing a query. You can save the filter with the form if you are going to use the filter frequently.

Activity 3.07 | Filtering Data by Selection of One Field

2.3.7

In this Activity, you will assist a counselor at the college who wants to see records for students majoring in Information Systems Technology. In a form, you can use the ***Filter By Selection*** command to display only the records that contain the value in the selected field and to hide the records that do *not* contain the value in the selected field.

1 **Open** [»] the **Navigation Pane**, double-click your **3A New Student Form** object to open it in **Form** view, and then **Close** [«] the **Navigation Pane**.

2 In the first record, click the **Major ID** field name—or you can click in the field box. Press [Ctrl] + [F] to display the **Find and Replace** dialog box. In the **Find What** box, type **339** If necessary, in the Match box, click the arrow, and then click Whole Field. Click **Find Next**, and then compare your screen with Figure 3.8.

This action finds and displays a record with a *Major ID* of *339*—the major of *Information Systems Technology*. You will use this action to filter the records using the value of *339*.

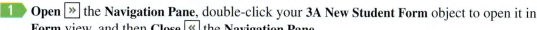

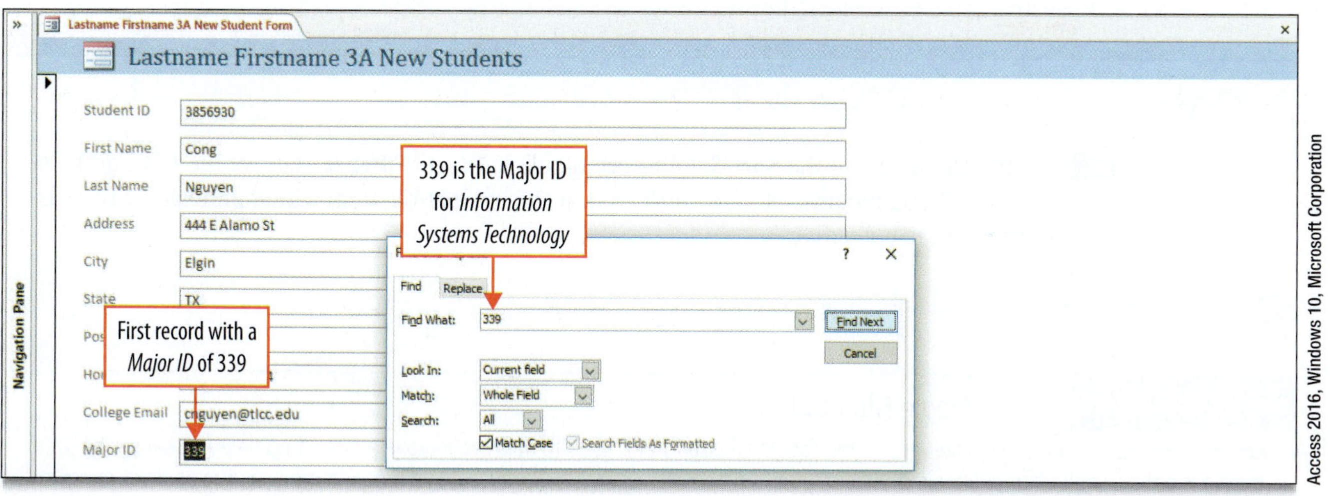

FIGURE 3.8

3 **Close** ☒ the **Find and Replace** dialog box. On the **Home tab**, in the **Sort & Filter group**, click **Selection**, and then click **Equals "339"**. Compare your screen with Figure 3.9.

Seven records match the contents of the selected Major ID field—*339*—the Major ID for the Information Systems Technology major. In the navigation area, *Filtered* with a funnel icon displays next to the number of records. *Filtered* also displays on the right side of the status bar to indicate that a filter is applied. On the Home tab, in the Sort & Filter group, Toggle Filter is active.

ANOTHER WAY With the data selected in the field, right-click the selection, and then click Equals "339".

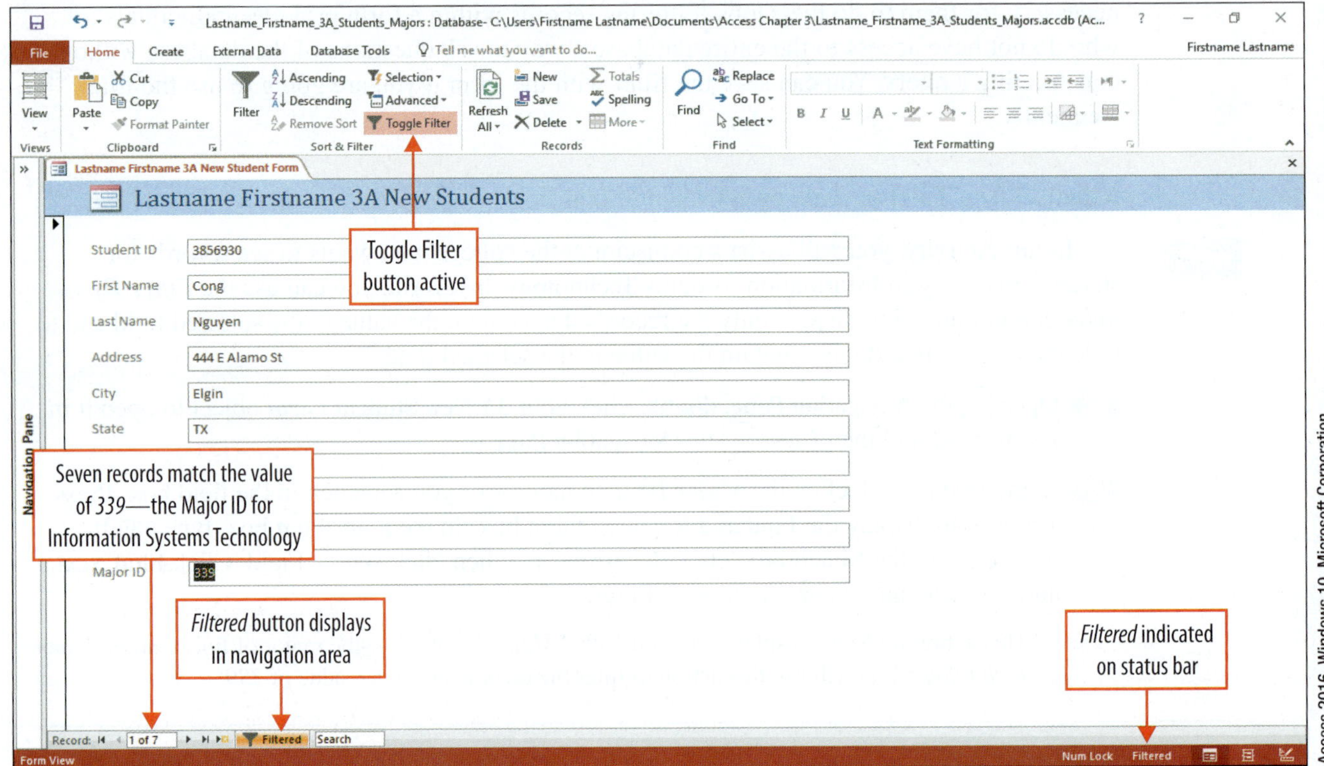

FIGURE 3.9

4 On the **Home tab**, in the **Sort & Filter group**, click **Toggle Filter** to remove the filter and display all 102 records. Notice *Unfiltered* in the navigation area, which indicates a filter is created but is not active.

ANOTHER WAY Click Filtered in the navigation area to remove the filter.

NOTE The Toggle Filter Button

On the Home tab, in the Sort & Filter group, the Toggle Filter button is used to apply or remove a filter. If no filter is created, the button is not available. After a filter is created, the button becomes available. Because it is a toggle button used to apply or remove a filter, the ScreenTip that displays for this button alternates between Apply Filter—when a filter is created but is not currently applied—and Remove Filter—when a filter is applied.

5 Be sure that the first record—for *Jordan Bass*—displays. On the **Home tab**, in the **Sort & Filter group**, click **Toggle Filter** to reapply the filter. In the navigation area, click **Last record** ▸| to display the last of the seven records that match a Major ID of *339*.

The record for *Student ID 9712345* displays—the record with your name. Use Toggle Filter to apply or remove filters as needed.

6 In the navigation area, click **Filtered** to remove the filter and display all of the records.

In the navigation area, *Filtered* changes to *Unfiltered*.

7 In the first record for *Jordan Bass*, in the **Last Name** field, select the first letter—**B**—in *Bass*. In the **Sort & Filter group**, click **Selection**, and then click **Begins with "B"**.

A new filter is applied that displays eight records in which the *Last Name* begins with the letter *B*.

ANOTHER WAY With the letter *B* selected, right-click the selection, and then click Begins with "B".

8 Use either **Toggle Filter** in the **Sort & Filter group** or **Filtered** in the navigation area to remove the filter and display all of the records.

9 In the **Sort & Filter group**, click **Advanced**, and then click **Clear All Filters**. Notice, that in the navigation area, *Unfiltered* changed to *No Filter*.

The filter is removed from the form and must be re-created to apply it. If you toggle the filter off and save the form, the filter is saved with the form even though the filter is not currently applied.

Activity 3.08 | Using Filter By Form

2.3.7

Use the ***Filter By Form*** command to filter the records based on one or more fields, or based on more than one value in the same field. The Filter By Form command offers greater flexibility than the Filter By Selection command and can be used to answer a question that requires matching multiple values. In this Activity, you will filter records to help Mr. Fitchette determine how many students live in Dripping Springs or Austin.

1 On the **Home tab**, in the **Sort & Filter group**, click **Advanced**, and then click **Filter By Form**. Compare your screen with Figure 3.10.

The Filter by Form window displays all of the field names, but without any data. In the empty text box for each field, you can type a value or select a value from a list. The *Look for* and *Or* tabs display at the bottom.

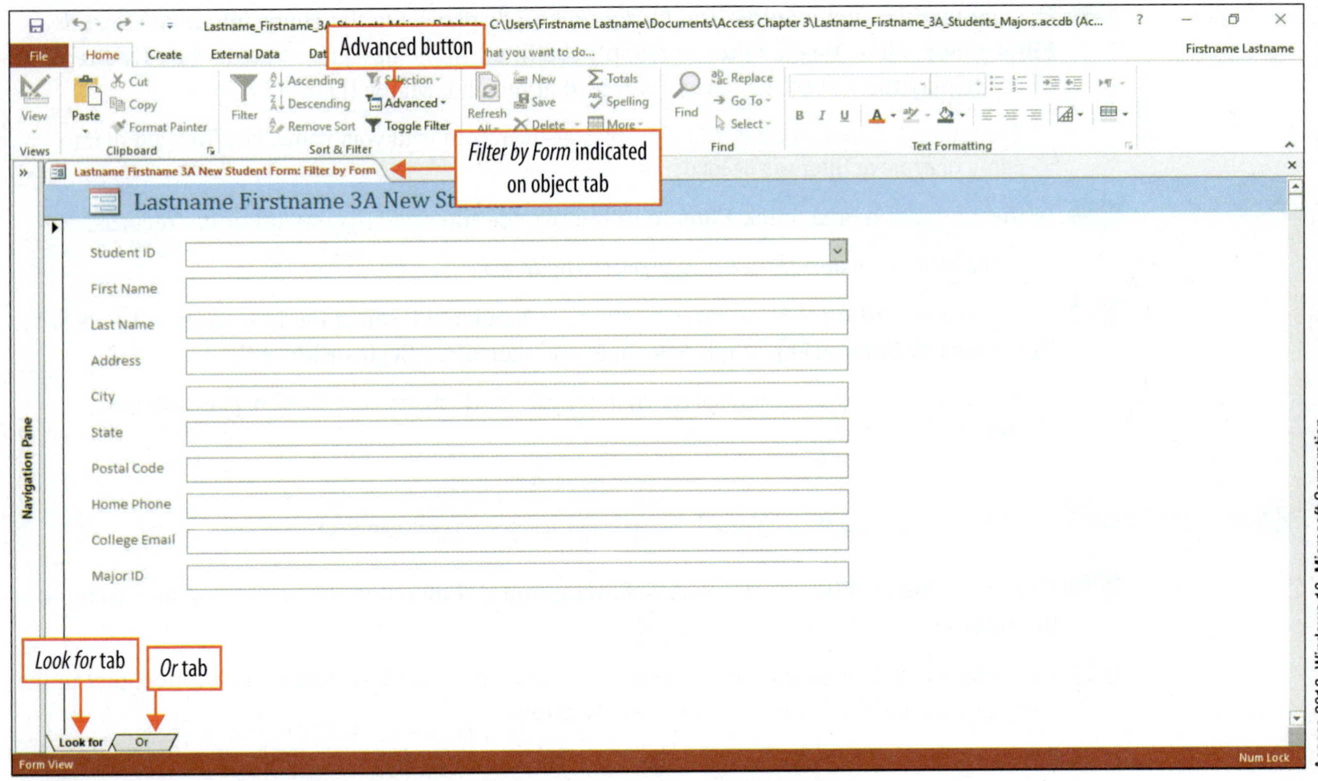

FIGURE 3.10

2 In the form, click the **City** field name to position the insertion point in the **City** field box. At the right edge of the **City** field box, click the **arrow**, and then click **Dripping Springs**. In the **Sort & Filter group**, click **Toggle Filter**.

As displayed in the navigation area, four student records have *Dripping Springs* stored in the City field.

3 In the **Sort & Filter group**, click **Advanced**, and then click **Filter By Form**. In the lower left corner of the form, click the **Or tab**. Click the **City** field box **arrow**, and then click **Austin**. In the **Sort & Filter group**, click **Toggle Filter**, and then compare your screen with Figure 3.11.

As displayed in the navigation area, 28 student records have either *Dripping Springs* OR *Austin* stored in the City field. You have created an ***OR condition***; that is, records display where, in this instance, either of two values—Dripping Springs *or* Austin—is present in the selected field.

ANOTHER WAY Click in the field box, and type the criteria separated by the word *or*. For example, in the City field box, type *Dripping Springs or Austin*.

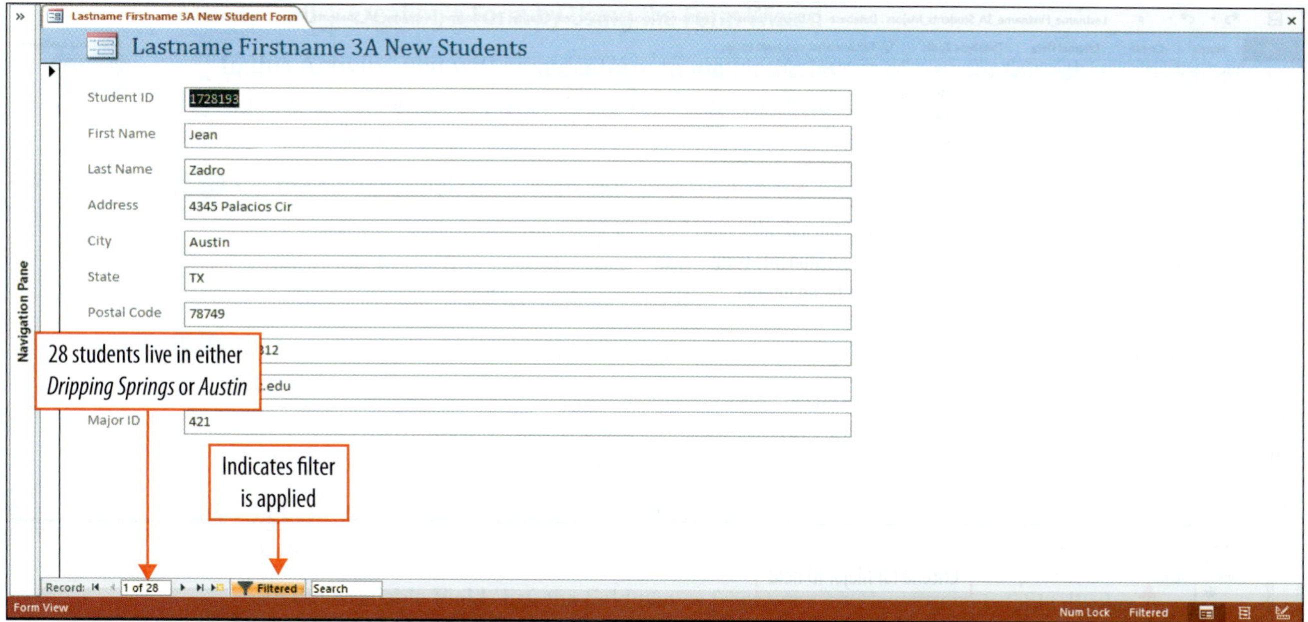

Access 2016, Windows 10, Microsoft Corporation

FIGURE 3.11

4 In the **Sort & Filter group**, click **Advanced**, and then click **Clear All Filters** to display all 102 records.

Activity 3.09 | Using Advanced Filter/Sort

2.3.7

In this Activity, you will use the Advanced Filter/Sort command to filter records to locate students who live in Austin with a Major ID of *339*—Information Systems Technology.

1 In the **Sort & Filter group**, click **Advanced**, and then click **Advanced Filter/Sort**.

The Advanced Filter design grid displays, which is similar to the query design grid, although not all rows display in the bottom half of the window. A field list for the underlying table of the form displays.

2 In the table area, resize the field list so that the entire table name and all of the field names display.

3 In the **3A New Students** field list, double-click **City**, and then double-click **Major ID** to add both fields to the design grid. In the **Criteria** row, under **City**, type **Austin** and then press Enter. In the **Criteria** row, under **Major ID**, type **339** and then press Enter. Compare your screen with Figure 3.12.

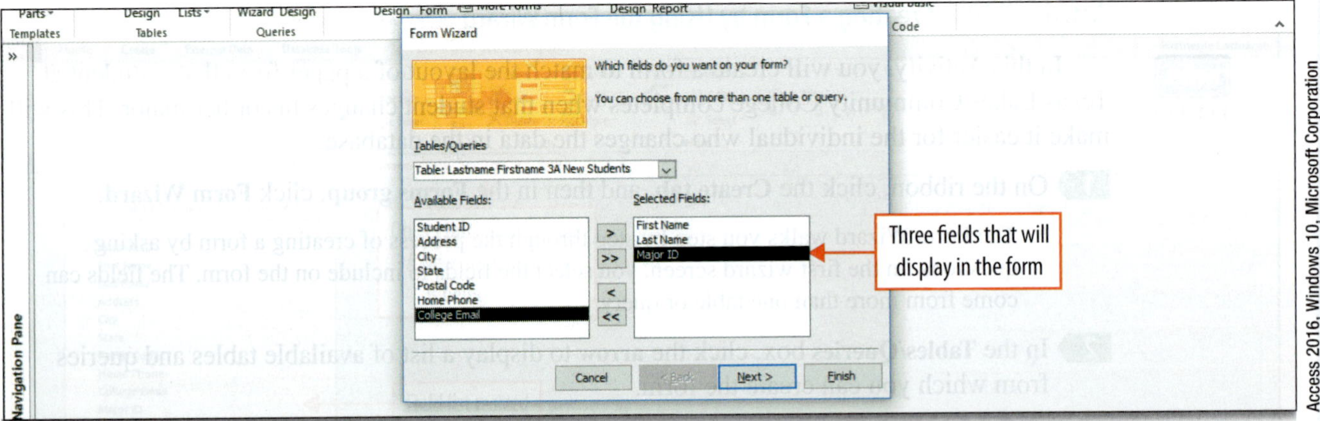

Access 2016, Windows 10, Microsoft Corporation

FIGURE 3.14

5 Click **Next**. In the wizard, verify that **Columnar** is selected as the layout, and then click **Next**. In the **What title do you want for your form?** box, select the existing text, type **Lastname Firstname 3A Student Major Change Form** and then click **Finish** to close the wizard and create the form.

The three fields and the data from the first record in your 3A New Students table display in Form view.

6 **Open** [»] the **Navigation Pane**. If necessary, increase the width of the Navigation Pane so that all object names display fully. Compare your screen with Figure 3.15.

In the Navigation Pane, the form displays under its data source—your 3A New Students table.

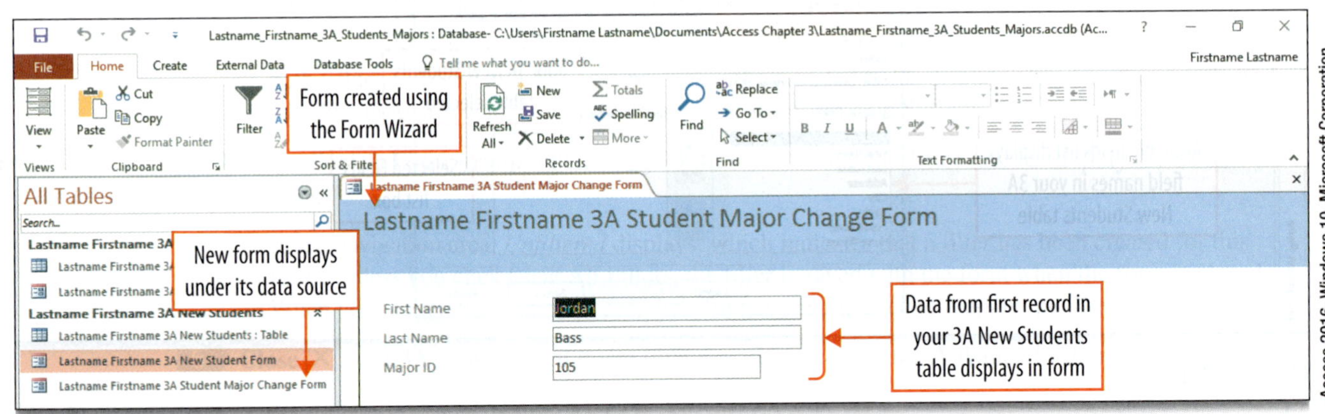

Access 2016, Windows 10, Microsoft Corporation

FIGURE 3.15

Objective 4 Modify a Form in Layout View and in Design View

GO! Learn How Video A3-4

After you create a form, you can make changes to it. For example, you can group the fields, resize the fields, add more fields to the form, and change the style of the form. Layout view enables you to see the data in the form as you modify the form. Most changes to a form can be made in Layout view.

Activity 3.11 | Grouping Controls in Layout View

4.2.5

In this Activity, you will group ***controls*** in the form so that you can work with them as one unit. Controls are objects on a form that display data or text, perform actions, and let you view and work with information.

1 **Close** [«] the **Navigation Pane**, and be sure that your **3A Student Major Change Form** object displays in the object window. On the **Home tab**, in the **Views group**, click the top portion of the **View** button to switch to **Layout** view. If the Field List pane displays on the right side of your screen, click Close [X] to close the pane. Compare your screen with Figure 3.16.

The field names and data for the first record in your 3A New Students record display in controls. The data for the first record displays in ***text box controls***. The most commonly used control is the text box control, which typically displays data from a field in the underlying table. A text box control is a ***bound control***—its data comes from a field in a table or query.

The field names—*First Name*, *Last Name*, and *Major ID*—display in ***label controls***. A label control displays to the left of a text box control and contains descriptive information that displays on the form, usually the field name. A control that does not have a data source is an ***unbound control***. Another example of an unbound control is a label control that displays the title of a form.

ANOTHER WAY On the right side of the status bar, click Layout View [icon] to switch from Form view to Layout view.

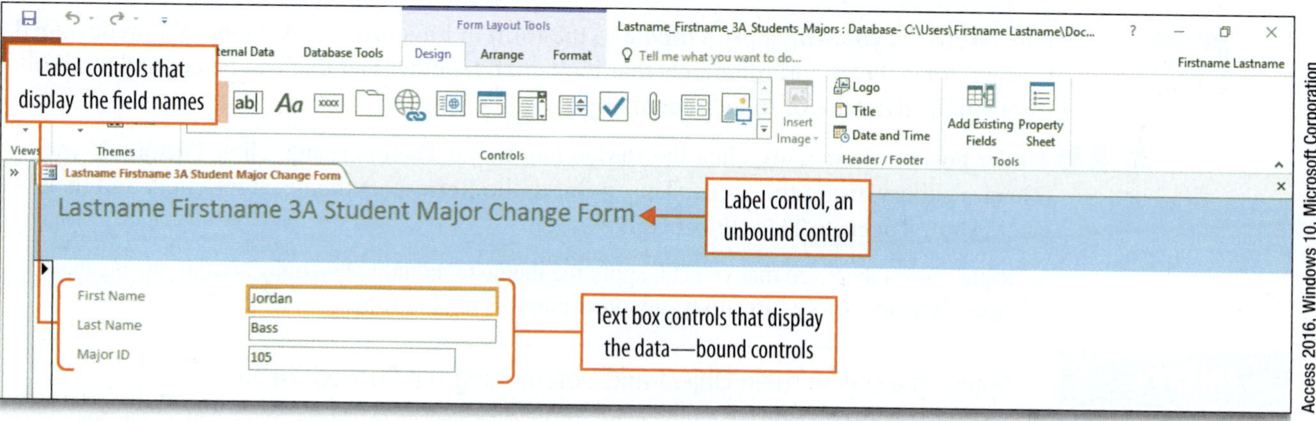

Access 2016, Windows 10, Microsoft Corporation

FIGURE 3.16

2 Click the **First Name label control**. Hold down [Shift], and then click the **Last Name label control**, the **Major ID label control**, and the three **text box controls** to select all of the label and text box controls on the form.

ALERT! **Do your controls change order when selecting?**

If, when selecting multiple controls, the controls change order, click Undo, and then select the controls again. Be careful not to drag the mouse when you are selecting multiple controls.

3 With all six controls selected—surrounded by a colored border—on the ribbon, under **Form Layout Tools**, click the **Arrange tab**. In the **Table group**, click **Stacked**. Click the **First Name label control** to cancel the selection of all of the controls and to surround the **First Name label control** with a dotted border. Compare your screen with Figure 3.17.

This action groups the controls together in the ***Stacked layout*** format—a layout similar to a paper form, with labels to the left of each field. Because the controls are grouped, you can move and edit the controls more easily as you redesign your form.

A dotted line forms a border around the controls, which indicates that the controls are grouped together. Above and to the left of the first label control that displays *First Name*, the ***layout selector*** [icon] displays. The layout selector is used to select and move or format the entire group of controls.

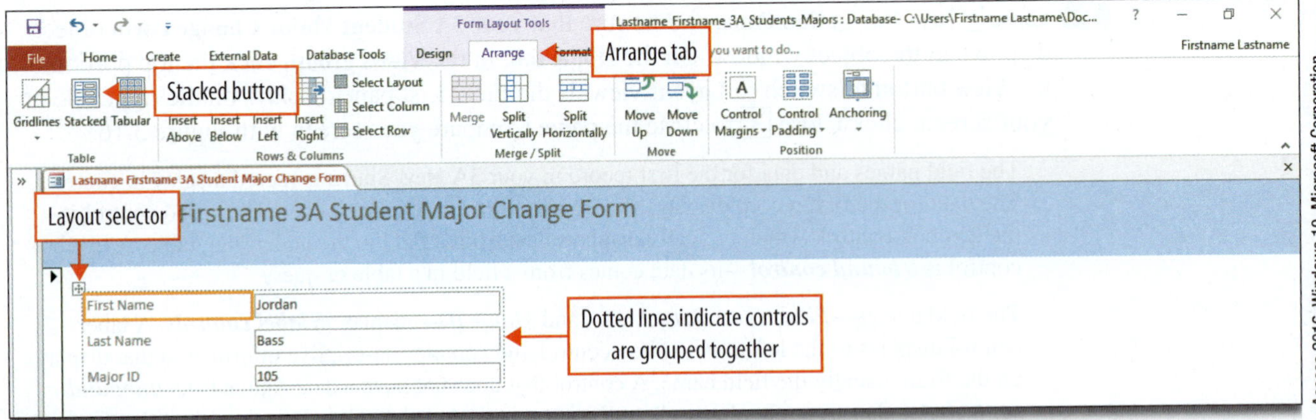

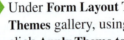

FIGURE 3.17

Activity 3.12 | Applying a Theme and Formatting a Form in Layout View

4.2.6, 4.3.4

In this Activity, you will apply a ***theme*** to the form in Layout view. A theme is a predesigned set of colors, fonts, lines, and fill effects that look good together and that can be applied to all of the objects in the database or to individual objects in the database.

1 Under **Form Layout Tools**, click the **Design tab**. In the **Themes group**, click **Themes**. In the **Themes** gallery, using the ScreenTips, point to the **Retrospect** theme, right-click, and then click **Apply Theme to This Object Only**.

Right-click a theme so that you can apply the theme to an individual object within the database. Apply a theme before formatting any other controls in your form.

NOTE Applying a Theme to an Object and Determining the Applied Theme

If you click a theme rather than right-clicking it and selecting an option, the theme is applied to all objects in the database. You cannot click Undo to cancel the application of the theme to all objects. To determine the applied theme, in the Themes group, point to Themes. The ScreenTip displays the name of the current theme.

2 Click anywhere in the title of the form—*Lastname Firstname 3A Student Major Change Form*—to select the title. Under **Form Layout Tools**, click the **Format tab**. In the **Font group**, click the **Font Size arrow** [11], and then click **14**. In the **Font group**, click **Bold** [B]. Click the **Font Color arrow** [A], and then under **Theme Colors**, in the fourth column, click the last color—**Olive Green, Text 2, Darker 50%**.

Activity 3.13 | Adding, Resizing, and Moving Controls in Layout View

4.2.1, 4.2.2, 4.2.3, 4.2.5, 4.2.6

In Layout view, you can change the form's ***control layout***—the grouped arrangement of controls.

1 Be sure that your **3A Student Major Change Form** object displays in **Layout** view. On the **Design tab**, and in the **Tools group**, click **Add Existing Fields**. Compare your screen with Figure 3.18.

The Field List pane displays, which lists the fields in the underlying table—your 3A New Students table.

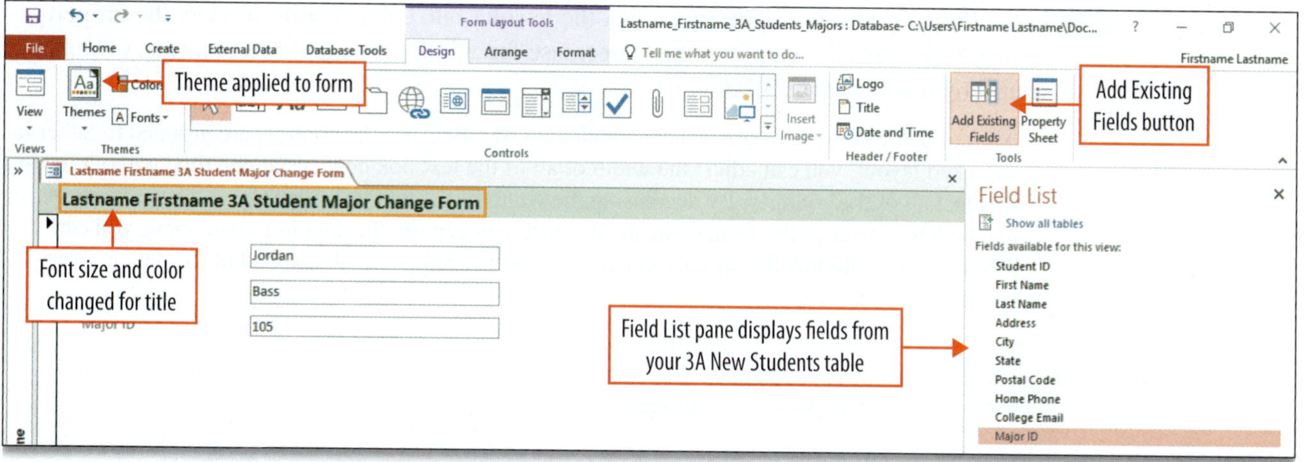

FIGURE 3.18 Access 2016, Windows 10, Microsoft Corporation

2 In the **Field List** pane, click **Student ID**, and then drag the field name to the left until the pointer displays above the **First Name label control** and a colored line displays above the control. Release the mouse button, and then compare your screen with Figure 3.19. If you are not satisfied with the result, click Undo, and begin again.

This action adds the Student ID label control and text box control to the form above the First Name controls.

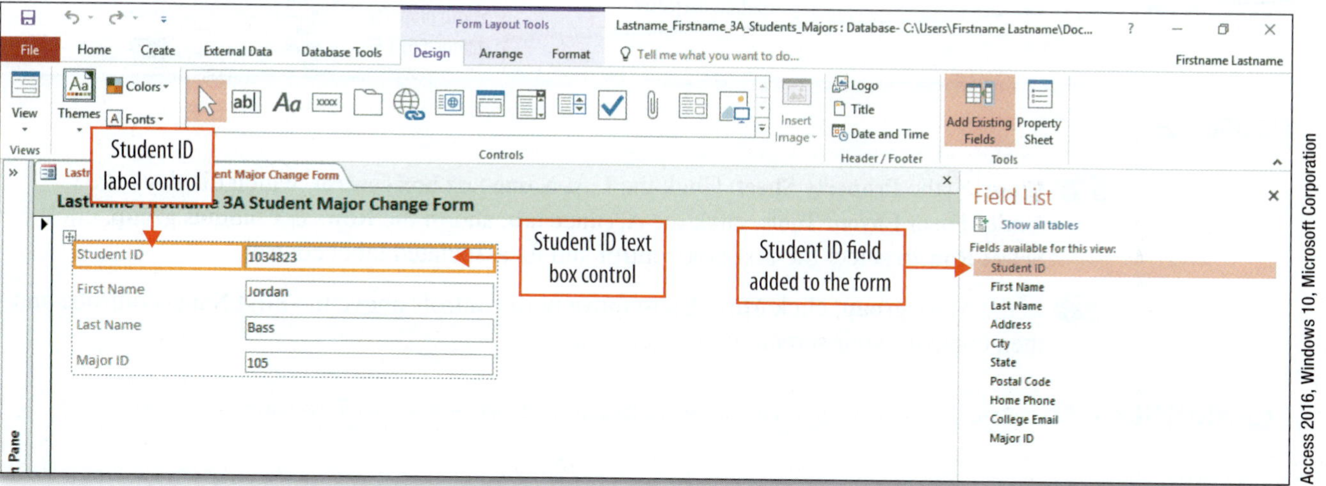

FIGURE 3.19 Access 2016, Windows 10, Microsoft Corporation

3 **Close** the **Field List** pane. Click the **Student ID text box control**, which displays *1034823*, to surround it with a border and to remove the border from the label control.

4 On the **Design tab**, in the **Tools group**, click **Property Sheet**.

The Property Sheet for the Student ID text box control displays. Recall that each control has an associated Property Sheet where precise changes to the properties—characteristics—of selected controls can be made. At the top of the Property Sheet, to the right of *Selection type: Text Box* displays because you selected the Student ID text box control.

5 In the **Property Sheet**, if necessary, click the **Format tab**. Click **Width** to select the property setting, type **1.5** and then press Enter to decrease the width of the text box controls. Compare your screen with Figure 3.20.

All four text box controls are resized simultaneously. Because the controls are grouped together in a stacked layout, you can adjust the width of all of the text box controls at one time without having to select all of the controls. By decreasing the width of the text box controls, you have more space in which to rearrange the form controls. Because you can see the data in Layout view, you can determine visually that the space you have allotted is adequate to display all of the data in every field for every record.

ANOTHER WAY With the text box control selected, point to the right edge of the text box control until the ⟺ pointer displays, and then drag left to the desired location.

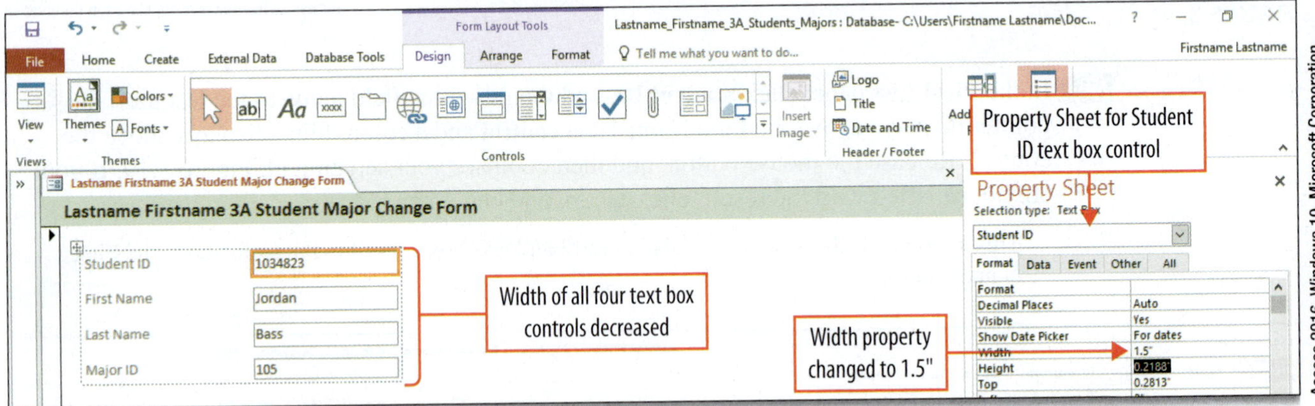

FIGURE 3.20

6 Close the **Property Sheet**. Click the **Last Name text box control**, which displays *Bass*. Under **Form Layout Tools**, click the **Arrange tab**, and in the **Rows & Columns group**, click **Select Row** to select the text box control and its associated label control.

7 In the **Move group**, click **Move Up** to move both controls above the **First Name** controls, and then compare your screen with Figure 3.21.

ANOTHER WAY
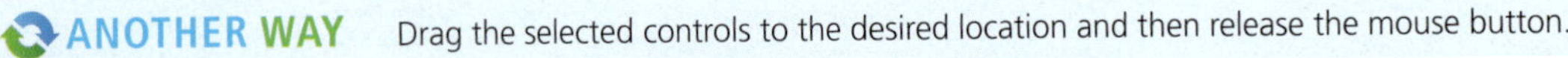
Drag the selected controls to the desired location and then release the mouse button.

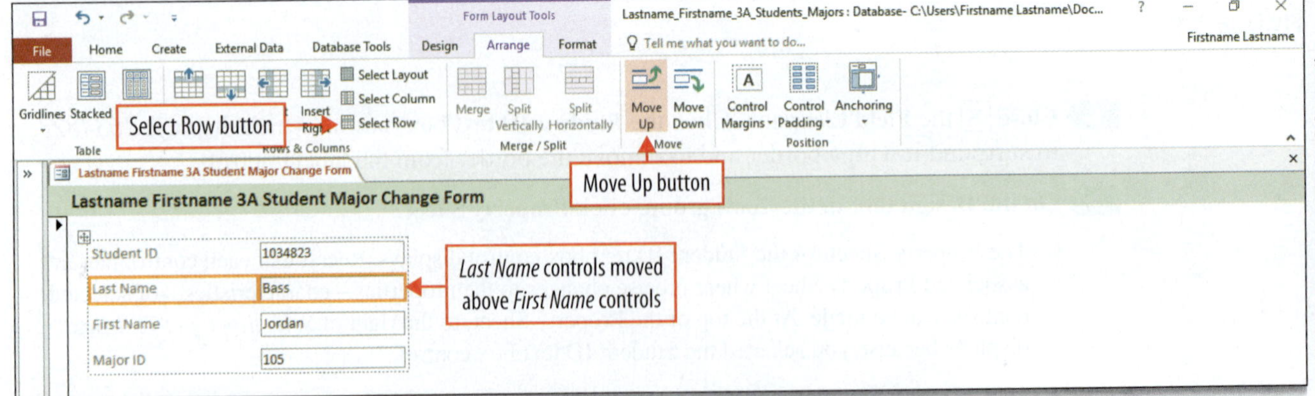

FIGURE 3.21

ALERT! **Did the Last Name label control not move with the Last Name text box control?**

Be sure to select both the text box control and the label control before moving the controls; otherwise, only one of the controls will move. If this happens, click Undo, select both controls, and try again. Controls are stacked from top to bottom, not right to left.

8 **Save** the changes you have made to the design of your form.

Activity 3.14 | Formatting Controls in Layout View

4.2.5, 4.2.6

In this Activity, you will format and change the property settings for multiple controls.

1 With the form displayed in **Layout** view, click the **Student ID text box control**, which displays *1034823*. On the **Arrange tab**, in the **Rows & Columns group**, click **Select Column** to select all four text box controls.

ANOTHER WAY Click the first text box control, hold down Shift, and then click the last text box control to select all four text box controls.

2 With all four text box controls selected, on the **Format tab**, in the **Font group**, click the **Background Color arrow**. Under **Theme Colors**, in the last column, click the second color—**Green, Accent 6, Lighter 80%**.

All of the text box controls display a background color of light green. This formatting is not applied to the label controls on the left.

3 Click the **Student ID label control**. On the ribbon, click the **Arrange tab**, and then in the **Rows & Columns group**, click **Select Column**. On the **Format tab**, click the **Font Color arrow**—*not* the Background Color arrow. Under **Theme Colors**, in the fourth column, click the first color—**Olive Green, Text 2**. Click **Bold** B. Click in a blank area of the form to cancel the selection, and then compare your screen with Figure 3.22.

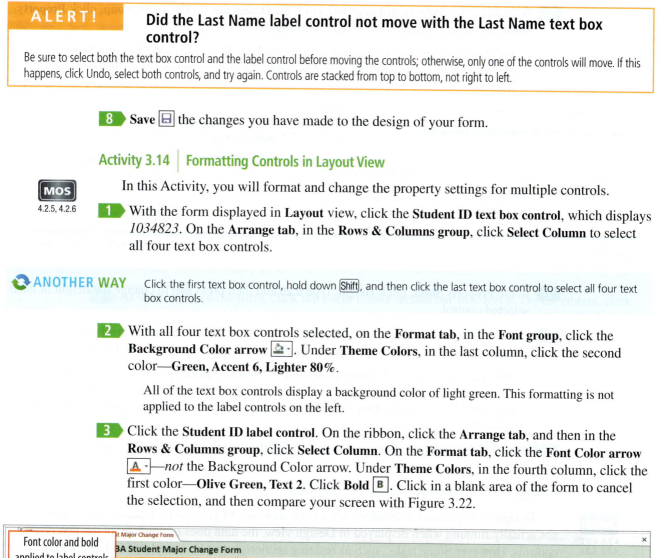

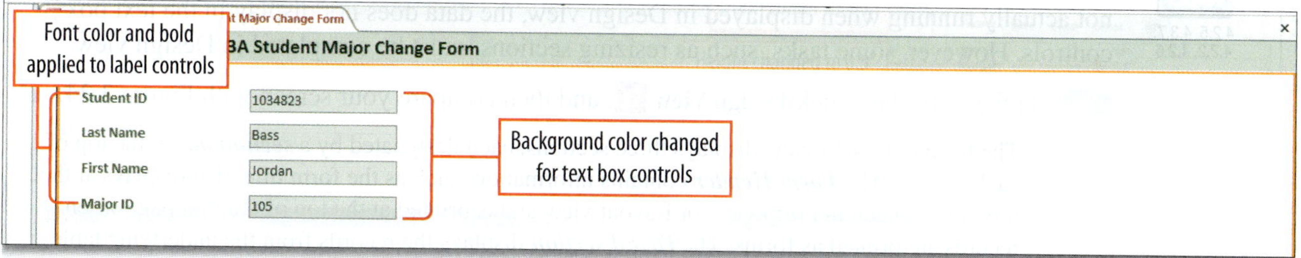

FIGURE 3.22

4 Click any **label control** to display the **layout selector**, and then click the **layout selector** to select all of the grouped controls.

Recall that the layout selector, which displays to the left and above the Student ID label control, enables you to select and move the entire group of controls in Layout view.

ANOTHER WAY Click any control, and then on the Arrange tab, in the Rows & Columns group, click Select Layout.

5 On the **Format tab**, in the **Font group**, click the **Font Size arrow** 11, and then click **12** to change the font size of all of the text in all of the controls.

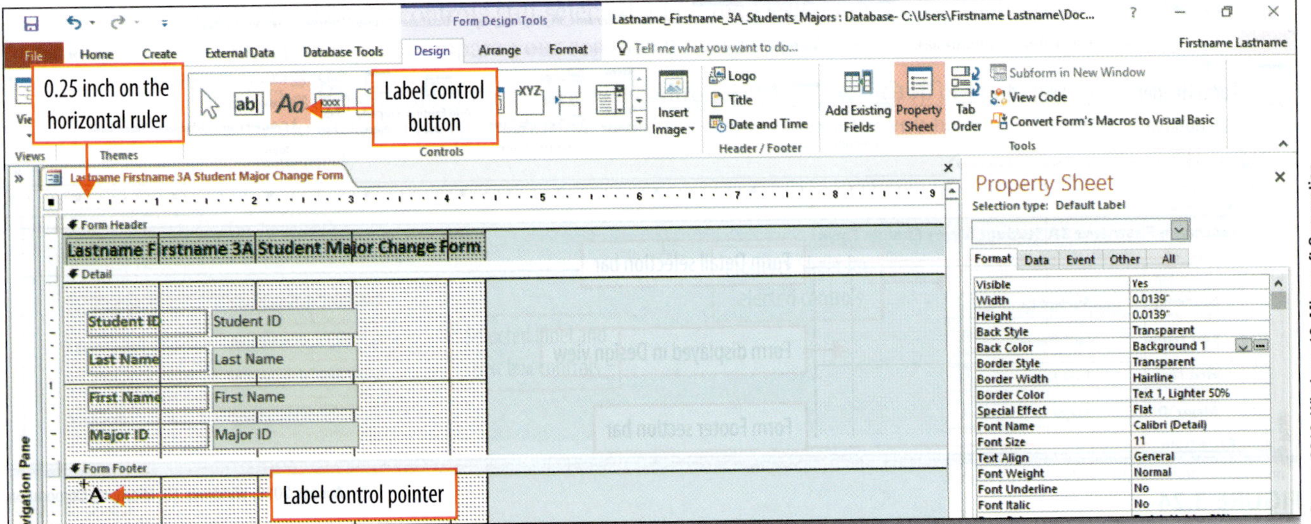

FIGURE 3.26

4 Click one time. Type **Texas Lakes Community College** and then press Enter. With the **label control** selected, click the **Format tab**. In the **Font group**, click **Bold** [B]. Click the **Font Color arrow**, and then under **Theme Colors**, in the fourth column, click the first color—**Olive Green, Text 2**.

5 With the **label control** still selected, in the **Property Sheet**, click **Top**, type **0.1** and then press Enter. In the **Property Sheet**, in the **Left** property setting, type **0.6** and then press Enter. **Close** the **Property Sheet**, and then **Save** the design changes to your form.

The top edge of the label control in the Form Footer section displays 0.1 inch from the lower edge of the Form Footer section bar. The left edge of the label control aligns at 0.6 inch from the left margin of the form. In this manner, you can place a control in a specific location on the form.

6 On the right side of the status bar, click **Form View**, and then compare your screen with Figure 3.27.

Form Footer text displays on the screen at the bottom of the form and prints only on the last page if all of the forms are printed. Recall, that in Form view, you can add, modify, or delete records stored in the underlying table.

ANOTHER WAY On the Home tab, in the Views group, click the View arrow, and then click Form View; or right-click the object tab, and then click Form View.

Access 2016, Windows 10, Microsoft Corporation

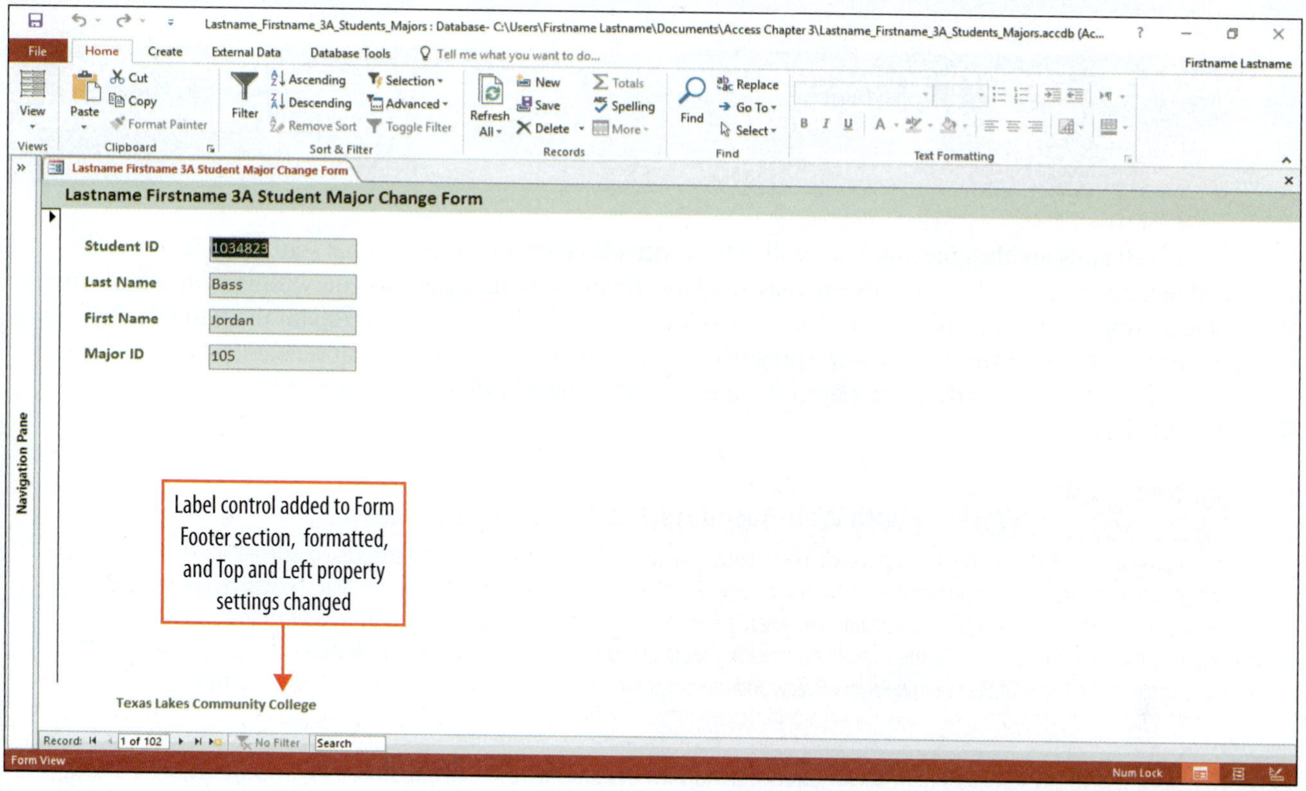

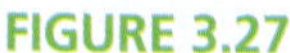

FIGURE 3.27

7 In the navigation area, click **Last record** [▶|] to display the record containing your name.

8 On the **File tab**, click **Print**, and then on the right, click **Print**. In the **Print** dialog box, under **Print Range**, click the **Selected Records(s)** option button. Create a paper printout or electronic printout as directed by your instructor. To create a PDF electronic image, follow the directions given in the Note in Activity 3.06.

Because you decreased the width of the text box controls, you do *not* have to adjust the column size width in the Page Setup dialog box as you did with the form you created by using the Form tool.

9 **Close** [X] all open objects, and then **Open** [»] the **Navigation Pane**. On the right side of the title bar, click **Close** [X] to close the database and to close Access. As directed by your instructor, submit your database and the paper printouts or PDF electronic images of the three forms that are the results of this project.

END | You have completed Project 3A

GO! With Google

Objective Export an Access Form to an Excel Spreadsheet, Save to Google Drive as a Google Sheet, Edit a Record, and Save to Your Computer

Access web apps are designed to work with Microsoft's SharePoint, a service for setting up websites to share and manage documents. Your college may not have SharePoint installed, so you will use other tools to share objects from your database so that you can work collaboratively with others. Recall that Google Drive is Google's free, web-based word processor, spreadsheet, slide show, form, and data storage and sharing service. For Access, you can export a database object to an Excel worksheet, a PDF file, or a text file, and then save the file to Google Drive.

ALERT! Working with Web-Based Applications and Services

Computer programs and services on the web receive continuous updates and improvements, so the steps to complete this web-based activity may differ from the ones shown. You can often look at the screens and the information presented to determine how to complete the activity.

If you do not already have a Google account, you will need to create one before you begin this activity. Go to http://google.com and in the upper right corner, click Sign In. On the Sign In screen, click Create account. On the Create your Google Account page, complete the form, read and agree to the Terms of Service and Privacy Policy, and then click Next step. On the Welcome screen, click Get Started.

Activity | Exporting an Access Form to an Excel Spreadsheet, Saving the Spreadsheet to Google Drive, Editing a Record in Google Sheets, and Saving to Your Computer

In this Activity, you will export your 3A Student Major Change Form object to an Excel spreadsheet, upload your Excel file to Google Drive, edit a record in Google Sheets, and then download a copy of the edited spreadsheet to your computer.

1 Start Access, on the left click **Open Other Files**, navigate to your **Access Chapter 3** folder, and then **Open** your **Lastname_Firstname_3A_Students_Majors** database file. If necessary, on the Message Bar, click Enable Content. In the **Navigation Pane**, click your **3A Student Major Change Form** object to select it.

2 On the **External Data tab**, in the **Export group**, click **Excel**. In the **Export – Excel Spreadsheet** dialog box, click **Browse**, and then navigate to your **Access Chapter 3** folder. In the **File Save** dialog box, click in the **File name** box, type **Lastname_Firstname_AC_3A_Web** and then click **Save**.

3 In the **Export – Excel Spreadsheet** dialog box, under **Specify export options**, select the second check box—**Open the destination file after the export operation is complete**—and then click **OK**.

The records from the underlying table of the form display in Excel. When you export a form to Excel, the formatting and layout are automatically saved. For example, notice the olive green background color of the cells, which was the color that was applied to the text box controls in the form.

4 In the **Microsoft Excel** window, in the column headings row, to the left of column **A**, click **Select All**. On the **Home tab**, in the **Cells group**, click **Format**, and then click **AutoFit Column Width**. Click in cell **A1** to cancel the selection, and then compare your screen with Figure A.

5 **Save** the spreadsheet, and then **Close** Excel. In the **Export – Excel Spreadsheet** dialog box, click **Close**, and then **Close** Access.

6 From the desktop, open your browser, navigate to **http://google.com**, and then sign in to your Google account. Click the **Google Apps menu**, and then click **Drive**. Open your **GO! Web Projects** folder—or click New to create and then open this folder if necessary.

7 In the upper right corner, click **Settings**, and then on the menu click **Settings**. In the **Settings** dialog box, next to **Convert uploads**, be sure that **Convert uploaded files to Google Docs editor format** is selected. In the upper right, click **Done**.

If this setting is not selected, your document will upload as a PDF file and cannot be edited without further action.

(GO! With Google continues on the next page)

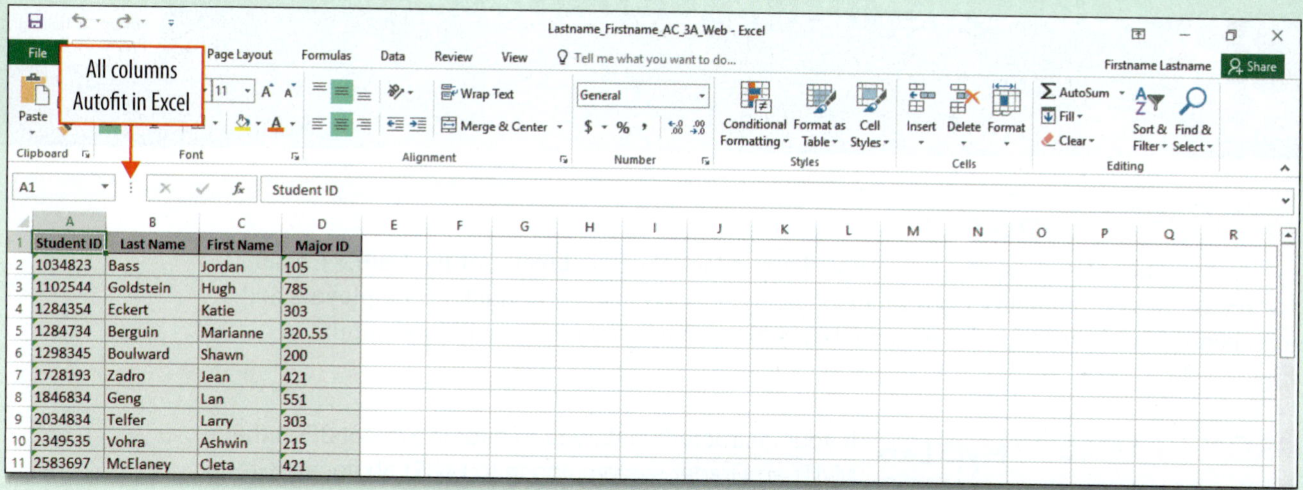

FIGURE A

8 On the left, click **NEW**, and then click **File upload**. In the **Open** dialog box, navigate to your **Access Chapter 3** folder, and then double-click your **Lastname_Firstname_AC_3A_Web** file to upload it to Google Drive. When the title bar of the message box indicates *Uploads completed*, **Close** the message box. A second box may display temporarily.

9 In your **GO! Web Projects** folder, double-click your **Lastname_Firstname_AC_3A_Web** file to open it in Google Sheets.

10 In the second record (row 3), click in the **Last Name** field, using your own last name, type **Lastname** and then press Enter. In the **First Name** field, using your own first name, type **Firstname** and then press Enter to save the record. Compare your screen with Figure B.

11 On the menu bar, click **File**, point to **Download as**, and then click **Microsoft Excel (.xlsx)**. As necessary, open the downloaded file in Excel, enable editing, and then **Save** the file in your **Access Chapter 3** folder as **Lastname_Firstname_AC_3A_Web_Download**

12 **Close** Excel. In Google Drive, in the upper right corner, click your user name, and then click **Sign out**. **Close** your browser window.

13 As directed by your instructor, submit your two workbooks.

> **NOTE** Printing or Creating a PDF Electronic Image of an Excel Spreadsheet
>
> To print on paper, click Print. To create a PDF electronic image of your printout, on the left side of your screen, click Export. Under Export, be sure Create PDF/XPS Document is selected, and then click Create PDF/XPS. Navigate to your Access Chapter 3 folder, and then click Publish to save the file with the default name and an extension of PDF.

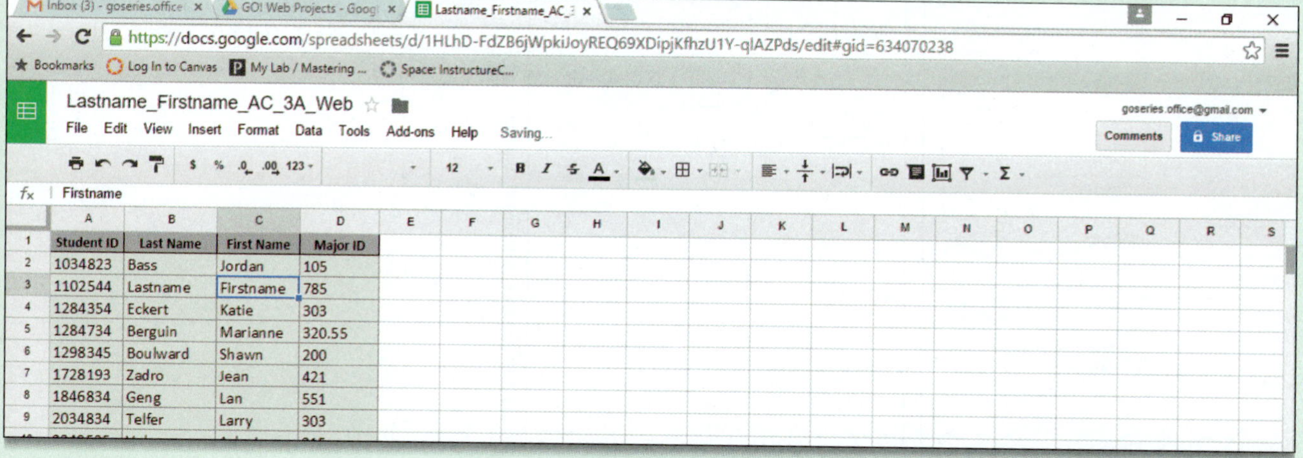

FIGURE B

PROJECT 3B

Job Openings Database

PROJECT ACTIVITIES

In Activities 3.16 through 3.24, you will assist Jack Woods, director of the Career Center for Texas Lakes Community College, in using his Access database to track the employees and job openings advertised for the annual job fair. Your completed reports will look similar to Figure 3.28.

PROJECT FILES

If your instructor wants you to submit Project 3B in the MyITLab Grader system, log in to MyITLab, locate Grader Project 3B, and then download the files for this project.

For Project 3B, you will need the following file:
a03B_Job_Openings

You will save your database as:
Lastname_Firstname_3B_Job_Openings

PROJECT RESULTS

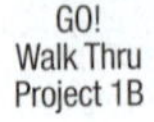

FIGURE 3.28 Project 3B Job Openings

PROJECT RESULTS

In this project, using your own name, you will create the following database and objects. Your instructor may ask you to submit printouts or PDF electronic images:

Lastname_Firstname_3B_Job_Openings	Database file
Lastname Firstname 3B Salary $40,000 or More Report	Report (two pages)
Lastname Firstname 3B Booth Fees by Industry Report	Report (two pages)

Objective 5 Create a Report by Using the Report Tool and Modify the Report in Layout View

GO! Learn How
Video A3-5

A ***report*** is a database object that summarizes the fields and records from a query or from a table in an easy-to-read format suitable for printing. A report consists of information extracted from queries or tables and report design controls, such as labels, headings, and graphics. The queries or tables that provide the underlying data for a report are referred to as the report's ***record source***.

Activity 3.16 | Opening and Saving an Existing Database, Renaming Objects, and Viewing a Table Relationship

ALERT!

To submit this as an autograded project, log on to MyITLab and download the files for this project, and begin with those files instead of a03B_Job_Openings. For Project 3B using Grader, begin working with the database in Step 3. For Grader to award points accurately, when saving an object, do not include your Lastname Firstname at the beginning of the object name.

1.2.5, 2.2.4

1. Start Access. In the Access opening screen, click **Open Other Files**. Under **Open**, click **Browse**, and then navigate to the location where your student data files are stored. Double-click **a03B_Job_Openings** to open the database.

2. On the **File tab**, click **Save As**. Under **File Types**, be sure **Save Database As** is selected. On the right, under **Database File Types**, be sure **Access Database** is selected, and then click **Save As**. In the **Save As** dialog box, navigate to your **Access Chapter 3** folder. In the **File name** box, replace the existing text with **Lastname_Firstname_3B_Job_Openings** and then press Enter.

3. On the **Message Bar**, click **Enable Content**. In the **Navigation Pane**, right-click the **3B Employers** table, and then click **Rename**. With the table name selected and using your own name, type **Lastname Firstname 3B Employers** and then press Enter to rename the table. Use the same technique to **Rename** the **3B Job Openings** table to **Lastname Firstname 3B Job Openings** and then **Rename** the first **3B Salary $40,000 or More Query** object to **Lastname Firstname 3B Salary $40,000 or More Query**

   Recall that a query that selects data from more than one table displays under both table names in the Navigation Pane. When you rename one of the query objects, the name of the second occurrence automatically changes.

4. Point to the right edge of the **Navigation Pane** to display the ⟺ pointer. Drag to the right to increase the width of the pane until all object names display fully.

3 On the **Report Layout Tools**, click the **Design tab**, in the **Tools group**, click **Property Sheet**. In the **Property Sheet**, on the **Format tab**, click **Width**, type **2.5** and then press Enter. Compare your screen with Figure 3.31.

Recall that you can use the Property Sheet to make precise changes to control properties.

ANOTHER WAY Point to the right edge of the text box control to display the ⟺ pointer. Drag to the right slightly until the data in the text box control displays on correctly.

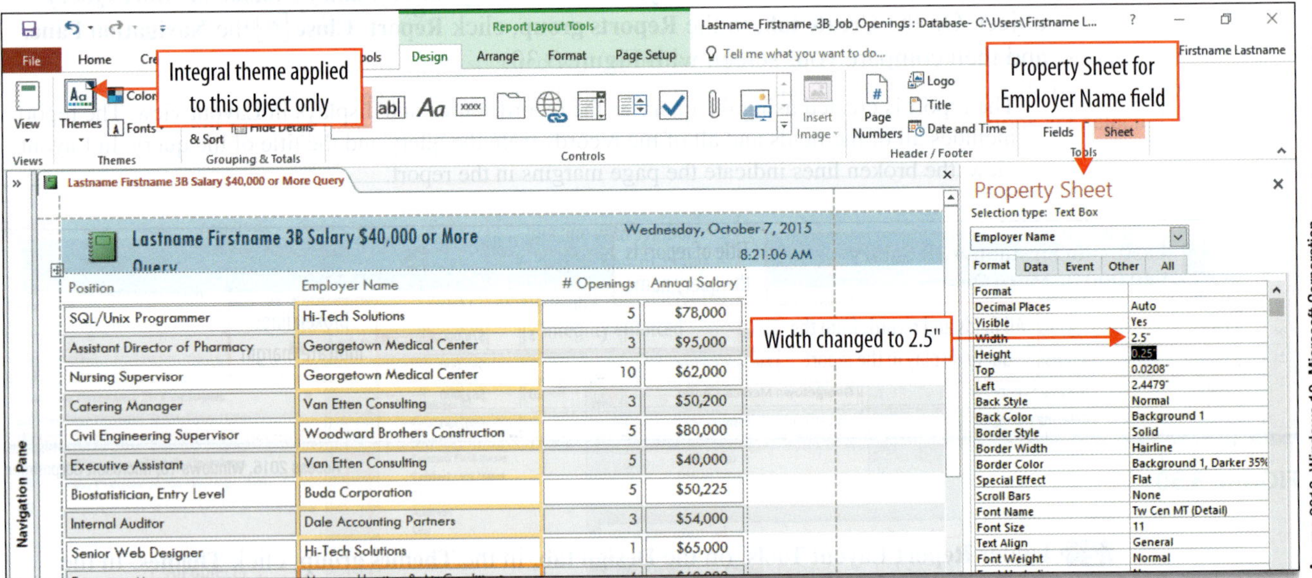

FIGURE 3.31

4 **Close** ☒ the **Property Sheet**. Click the **Position** field name, and then on the **Home tab**, in the **Sort & Filter group**, click **Ascending** to sort the records in ascending order by the Position field.

ANOTHER WAY Right-click the selected field name and then click Sort A to Z.

5 Scroll to the bottom of the report, and then click the **calculated control** that displays *$2,157,625*, which is shortened at the bottom cutting off part of the data. Press Del to remove this control.

In a report created by using the Report tool, a ***calculated control*** is automatically created to sum any field that is formatted as currency. A calculated control contains an expression, often a formula or a function. Here, the total is not a useful number and thus can be deleted.

6 Scroll to the bottom of the report again, and then under the last column, click the horizontal line that is the border between the last record and the calculated control that you deleted. Press Del to remove this line, and then scroll to the bottom of the report to verify that the line has been deleted.

7 Scroll to the top of the report, and then click the **# Openings** field name. On the **Design tab**, in the **Grouping & Totals group**, click **Totals**, and then click **Sum**.

8 Scroll to the bottom of the report, and then click the **calculated control** that displays *100*. On the **Design tab**, in the **Tools group**, click **Property Sheet**. In the **Property Sheet**, on the **Format tab**, click **Height**, type **0.25** and then press Enter. Compare your screen with Figure 3.32.

The total number of job openings for positions with a salary of $40,000 or more is 100.

ANOTHER WAY Point to the lower edge of the text box control to display the [↕] pointer, and then double-click to resize the control, or drag downward to increase the height of the control.

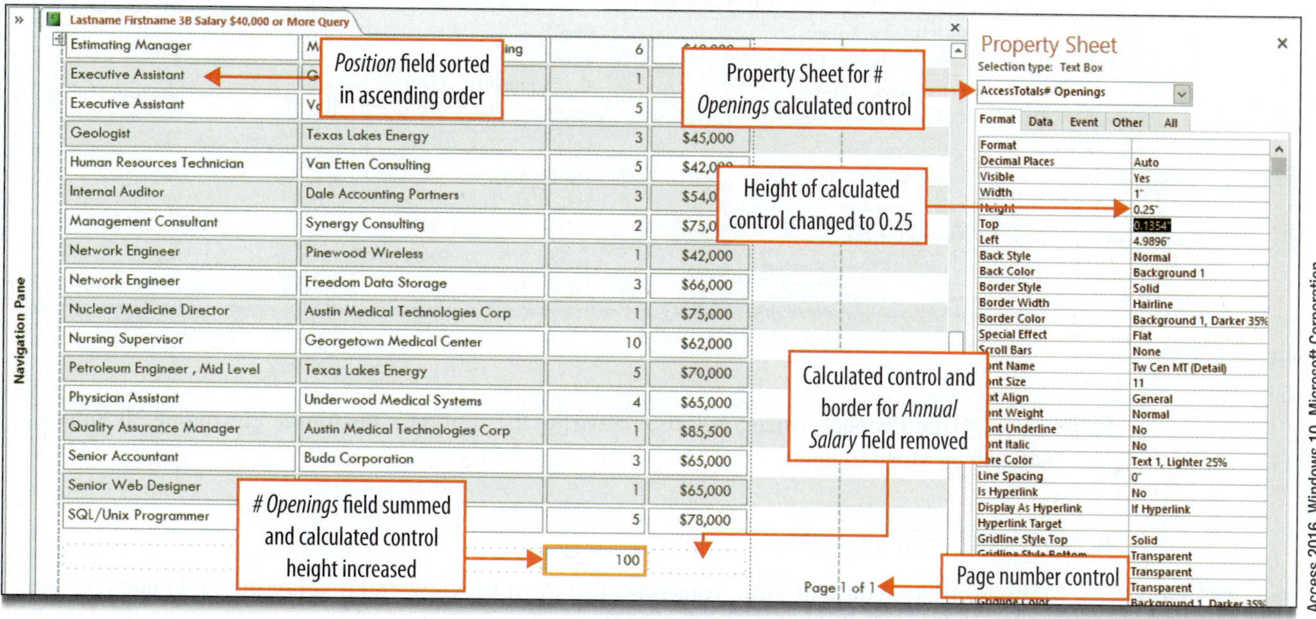

FIGURE 3.32

9 At the bottom of the report to the right of the calculated control, notice that the control that displays the page number does not fit entirely within the margins of the report. Click the **control** that displays *Page 1 of 1*. In the **Property Sheet**, click **Left**, type **2.5** and then press Enter.

The control moves within the margins of the report with the left edge of the control 2.5 inches in from the left margin of the report. When you click different controls in a report or form, the Property Sheet changes to match the selected control. Before printing, always scroll through the report to be sure that all of the controls display on one page and not outside of the margins.

ANOTHER WAY Click the control, point to the selected control to display the [move] pointer, and then drag the control to the left within the margins of the report.

10 Scroll to the top of the report, and then click the **label control** that displays the title of the report—*Lastname Firstname 3B Salary $40,000 or More Query*. On the **Report Layout Tools**, click the **Format tab**. In the **Font group**, click the **Font Size arrow** [11], and then click **14**.

11 With the **label control** for the title still selected, double-click **Query** to select the word, type **Report** and then press Enter to change the name of the report to *Lastname Firstname 3B Salary $40,000 or More Report*.

12 Click the **Position** field name. In the **Property Sheet**, click **Left**, type **0.5** and then press Enter to move this field 0.5 inch in from the left margin of the report. Compare your screen with Figure 3.33.

The other fields adjust by moving to the right. The fields are centered approximately within the margins of the report.

ANOTHER WAY Click the layout selector [⊞] to select all of the controls, and then drag it slightly downward and to the right until the columns are visually centered between the margins of the report. If your columns rearrange, click Undo and begin again.

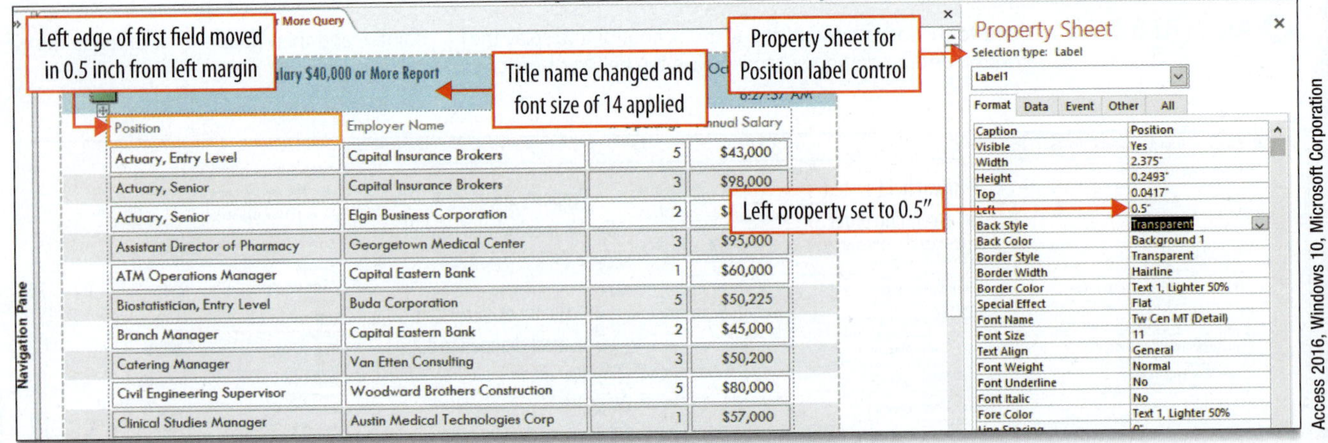

FIGURE 3.33

13 **Close** the **Property Sheet**, and then **Save** the report as **Lastname Firstname 3B Salary $40,000 or More Report**.

Activity 3.19 | Printing a Report

1.5.1

In this Activity, you will view your report in Print Preview and display the two pages of the report.

1 On the right side of the status bar, click **Print Preview**.

> **ANOTHER WAY** On the Design tab or the Home tab, in the Views group, click the View arrow, and then click Print Preview; or, in the object window, right-click the object tab, and then click Print Preview.

2 On the **Print Preview tab**, in the **Zoom group**, click **Two Pages** to view the two pages of your report. Notice that the page number displays at the bottom of each page.

3 Create a paper printout or PDF electronic image as directed—two pages result, and then click **Close Print Preview**. **Close** the report, and then **Open** the **Navigation Pane**.

The report displays under both tables from which the query was created. The report object name displays with a small green notebook icon.

4 **Close** the **Navigation Pane**.

Objective 6 Create a Report by Using the Report Wizard

Use the ***Report Wizard*** when you need more flexibility in the design of your report. You can group and sort data by using the wizard and use fields from more than one table or query if you have created the relationships between tables. The Report Wizard is similar to the Form Wizard; the wizard walks you step by step through the process of creating the report by asking you questions and then designs the report based on your answers.

GO! Learn How
Video A3-6

Activity 3.20 | Creating a Report by Using the Report Wizard

5.1.3, 5.2.1, 5.3.1

In this activity, you will prepare a report for Mr. Woods that displays the employers, grouped by industry, and the total fees paid by employers for renting a booth at the Job Fair.

1 On the **Create tab**, in the **Reports group**, click **Report Wizard**.

In the first wizard screen, you select the fields to include on the report. The fields can come from more than one table or query.

2 In the **Tables/Queries** box, click the **arrow**, and then click **Table: Lastname Firstname 3B Employers**. In the **Available Fields** list, double-click the following field names in the order given to move them to the **Selected Fields** list: **Industry**, **Employer Name**, and **Fee Paid** (scroll as necessary to locate the *Fee Paid* field). Compare your screen with Figure 3.34.

Three field names from your 3B Employers table display in the Selected Fields list.

ANOTHER WAY Click the field name, and then click One Field [>] to move a field from the Available Fields list to the Selected Fields list.

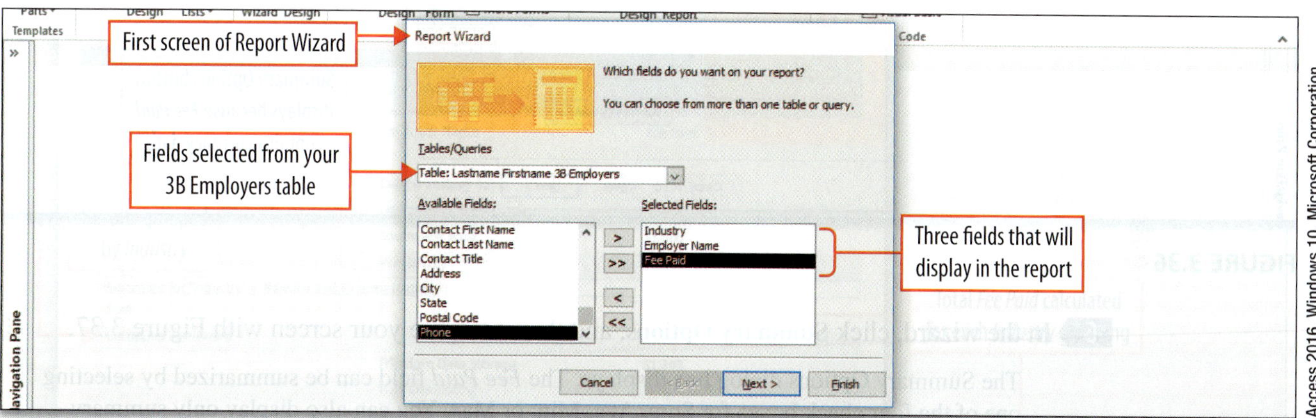

FIGURE 3.34

3 Click **Next**. In the wizard, notice that you can add grouping levels and that a preview of the grouping level displays on the right.

Grouping data helps to organize and summarize the data in your report.

4 On the left, double-click **Industry**, and then compare your screen with Figure 3.35.

The preview displays how the data will be grouped in the report. Grouping data in a report places all of the records that have the same data in a field together as a group—in this instance, the records will be grouped by *Industry*. Within each Industry name, the Employer Name and Fee Paid will display.

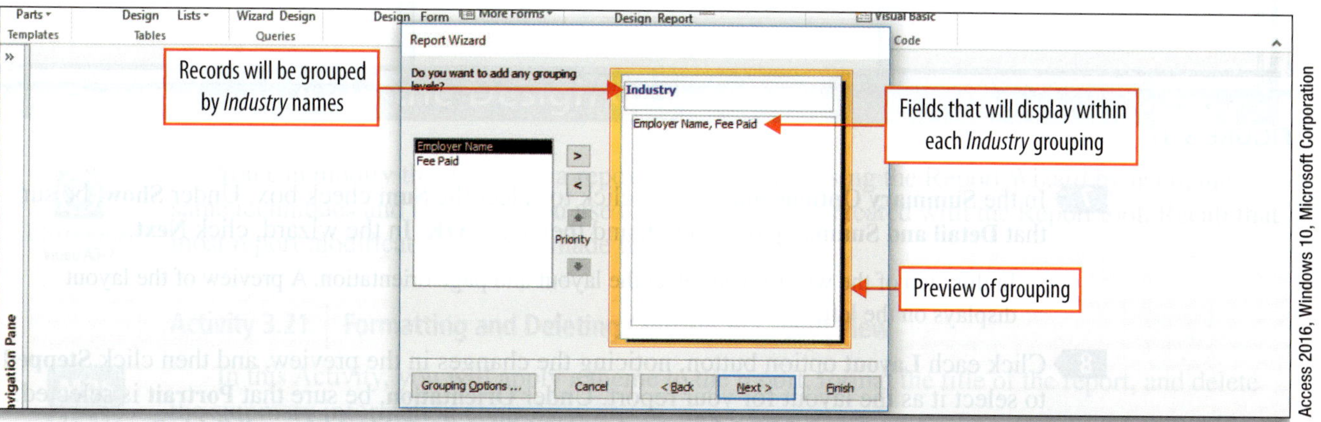

FIGURE 3.35

2 In the **Page Footer** section of the report, examine the two controls in this section. Recall that information in the Page Footer section displays at the bottom of every page in the report.

On the left side, the ***date control*** displays *=Now( )*, which inserts the current date each time the report is opened. On the right side, the ***page number control*** displays *="Page " & [Page] & " of " & [Pages]*, which inserts the page number, for example, *Page 1 of 2*, when the report is displayed in Print Preview or when printed. Both of these controls contain examples of functions that are used by Access to create controls in a report.

3 In the **Industry Footer** section, click the **Total Booth Fees by Industry label control**. Hold down Shift, and in the **Report Footer** section, click the **Grand Total label control** to select both label controls.

4 Under **Report Design Tools**, click the **Arrange tab**. In the **Sizing & Ordering group**, click **Align**, and then click **Left**.

The left edge of the *Grand Total label control* is aligned with the left edge of the *Total Booth Fees by Industry label control*. When using the Align Left command, the left edges of the selected controls are aligned with the control that is the farthest to the left in the report.

5 In the **Page Header** section, click the **Fee Paid label control**. Hold down Shift while you click the following: in the **Detail** section, click the **Fee Paid text box control**; in the **Industry Footer** section, click the **calculated control** that begins with *=Sum*; and in the **Report Footer** section, click the **calculated control** that begins with *=Sum*.

Four controls are selected.

6 On the **Arrange tab**, in the **Sizing & Ordering group**, click **Align**, and then click **Right**. **Save** the design changes to your report, and then compare your screen with Figure 3.45.

The right edges of the four selected controls are aligned with the right edge of the *Fee Paid text box control*. When using the Align Right command, the right edges of the selected controls are aligned with the control that is the farthest to the right in the report.

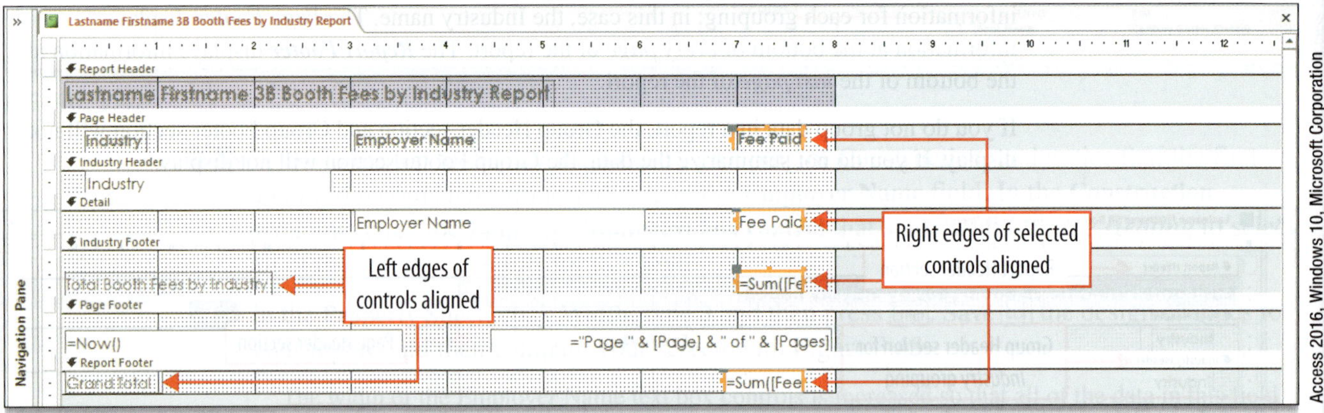

FIGURE 3.45

7 On the status bar, click **Layout View** to display the underlying data in the controls. Scroll to view the bottom of the report. On the left side, notice that the **Total Booth Fees by Industry label control** and the **Grand Total label control** are left aligned. Also, notice the right alignment of the controls in the **Fee Paid** column.

Objective 8 Keep Grouped Data Together in a Printed Report

GO! Learn How
Video A3-8

Before you print a report, examine the report in Print Preview to be sure that all of the labels and data display fully and to be sure that all of the data is properly grouped. Sometimes a page break occurs in the middle of a group of data, leaving the labels on one page and the data or summary information on another page.

Activity 3.24 | Keeping Grouped Data Together in a Printed Report

1.5.1, 5.3.4

In this Activity, you will preview the document and then will keep the data in each group together so a grouping is not split between two pages of the report. This is possible if the data in a grouping does not exceed the length of a page.

1 On the status bar, click **Print Preview**. On the **Print Preview tab**, in the **Zoom group**, click **Two Pages**, and then compare your screen with Figure 3.46.

The report will print on two pages. For the Industry grouping of *Hotel and Food Service*, one record and the summary data display at the top of Page 2 and are separated from the rest of the grouping that displays at the bottom of page 1. Your display may differ depending upon your printer configuration.

In Print Preview, the One Page or Two Pages Zoom view causes the records to be compressed slightly and might display with the bottoms of records truncated. The records, however, will print correctly.

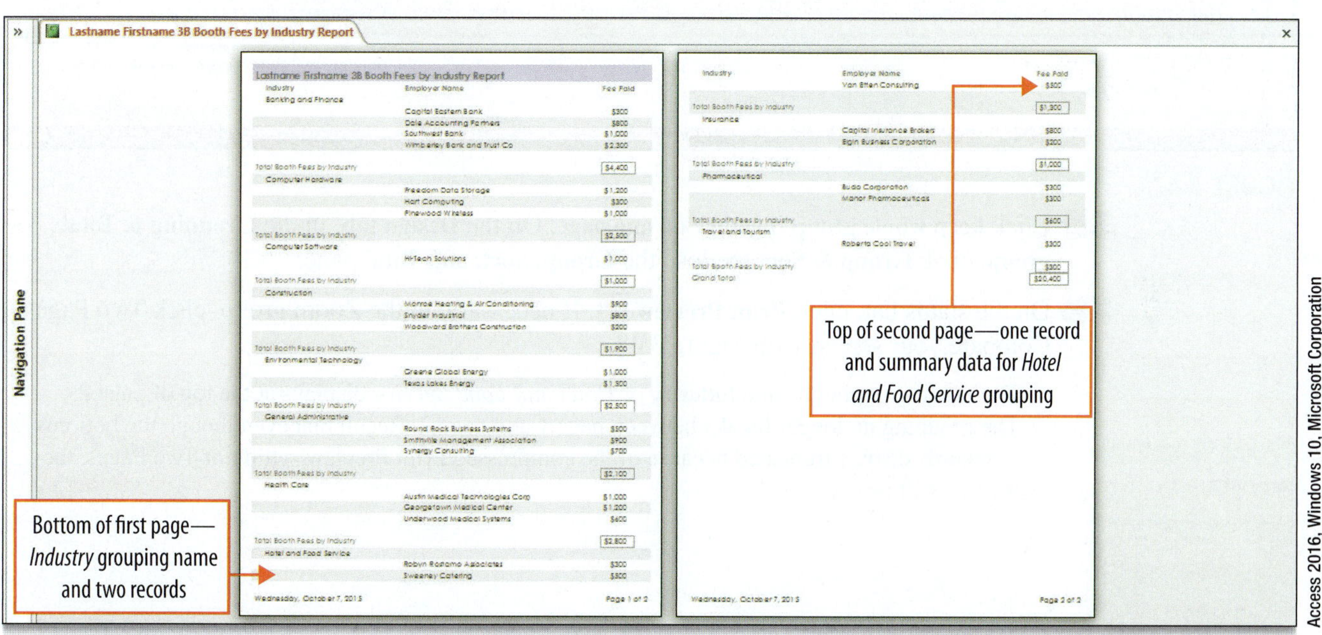

FIGURE 3.46

2 Click **Close Print Preview** to return to **Layout** view. On the **Design tab**, in the **Grouping & Totals group**, click **Group & Sort**.

At the bottom of the screen, the ***Group, Sort, and Total pane*** displays. This pane is used to control how information is grouped, sorted, or totaled. Layout view is the preferred view in which to accomplish these tasks because you can see how the changes affect the display of the data in the report.

3 In the **Group, Sort, and Total** pane, on the **Group on Industry** bar, click **More**. To the right of **do not keep group together on one page**, click the **arrow**, and then compare your screen with Figure 3.47.

The *keep whole group together on one page* command keeps each industry group together, from the name in the Group Header section through the summary information in the Group Footer section. The default setting is *do not keep group together on one page*. Next to *Group on Industry, with A on top* indicates that the industry names are sorted in ascending order.

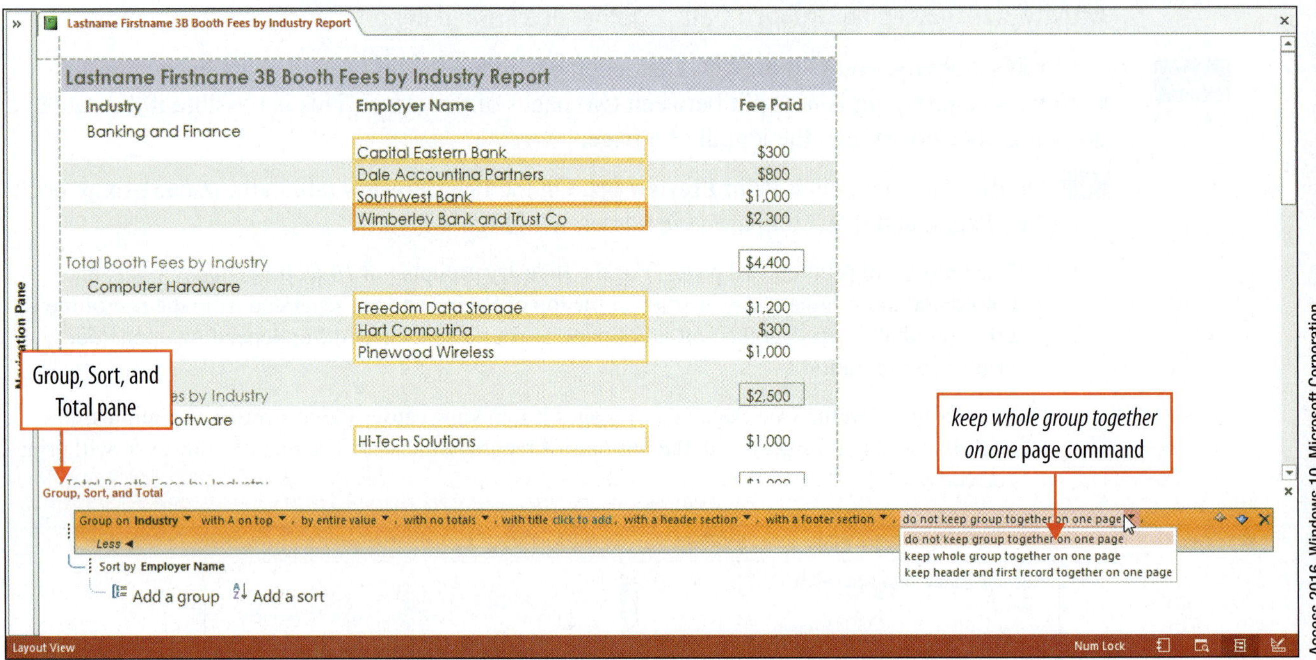

FIGURE 3.47

4 Click **keep whole group together on one page**. On the **Design tab**, in the **Grouping & Totals group**, click **Group & Sort** to close the **Group, Sort, and Total** pane.

5 On the status bar, click **Print Preview**. If necessary, in the Zoom group, click Two Pages. Compare your screen with Figure 3.48.

The entire grouping for the Industry of *Hotel and Food Service* displays at the top of page 2. The grouping no longer breaks between page 1 and page 2. Recall that even though the bottoms of records display truncated because of the compressed Print Preview setting of Two Pages, the records will print correctly.

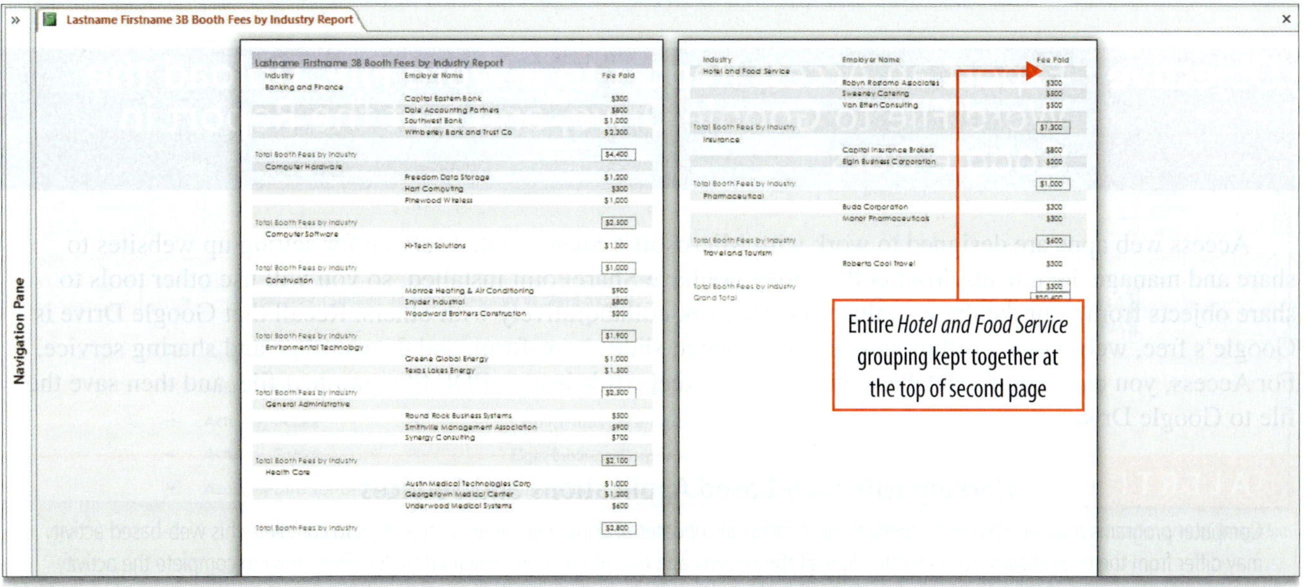

Access 2016, Windows 10, Microsoft Corporation

FIGURE 3.48

6. **Save** the design changes to your report, and then create a paper printout or electronic printout of the report as directed—two pages result.

7. **Close** the report, and then **Open** the **Navigation Pane**. If necessary, increase the width of the Navigation Pane so that all object names display fully.

8. On the right side of the title bar, click **Close** to close the database and to close Access. As directed by your instructor, submit your database and the paper printouts or PDF electronic images of the two reports—each report is two pages—that are the results of this project.

END | You have completed Project 3B

Access web apps are designed to work with Microsoft's SharePoint, a service for setting up websites to share and manage documents. Your college may not have SharePoint installed, so you will use other tools to share objects from your database so that you can work collaboratively with others. Recall that Google Drive is Google's free, web-based word processor, spreadsheet, slide show, form, and data storage service. For Access, you can [illegible] file to Google Drive.

Working with Web Based [illegible]

[illegible] may differ from the ones shown. You can often look at the screens and the information presented to determine how to complete the activity. If you do not already have a Google account, you will need to create one before you begin [illegible]

[illegible]

In this Activity, you will export your 3B Salary $40,000 or [illegible] upload the file to Google Drive, and then edit the report in Google Docs.

1. Start Access. On the left, click Open Other [illegible] Database [illegible] If necessary, on the Message Bar, click Enable Content. In the Navigation Pane, click one time to select the report Lastname Firstname 3B Salary $40,000 or More Report object to select it.

2. On the External Data tab, in the Export group, click More, and then click Word.

   The report will be exported as a Rich Text Format (RTF)—a standard file format that contains text and some formatting such as underline, bold, italic, font sizes, and colors. RTF documents can be opened in many word processing programs and text editors.

3. In the Export – RTF File dialog box, click [illegible] and [illegible] your Access Chapter 3 folder. In the File Save dialog box, click in the File name box to select the existing text. Type Lastname_Firstname_AC_3B_Web and then click Save. In the Export – RTF File dialog box, select the Open the destination file after the export [illegible]

4. In Word, click the File tab, click Save As, and then click Browse. In the Save As dialog box, navigate to your Access Chapter 3 folder. In the File name box, [illegible] In the Save as type box, click the arrow and select Word [illegible] preserve the formatting of the document as created in Access.

5. From the desktop, open your browser, navigate to http://google.com, and then sign in to your Google account. Click the Google Apps menu, and then click Drive. Open your GO! Web Projects folder—or click [illegible] this folder if necessary.

6. In the upper right, click Settings, and then [illegible] click Settings. In the Settings dialog box, next to Convert uploads, be sure that Convert uploaded files to Google Docs editor format is selected. In the [illegible]

   If this setting is not selected, your document will upload as a PDF file and cannot be edited without further action.

(GO! With Google continues on the next page)

GO! To Work

Andres Rodriguez/Fotolia; FotolEdhar/Fotolia; Andrey Popov/Fotolia; Shutterstock

3 ACCESS

MICROSOFT OFFICE SPECIALIST (MOS) SKILLS IN THIS CHAPTER			
3A MOS SKILLS		**3B MOS SKILLS**	
1.2.5	View relationships	**1.2.5**	View relationships
1.5.2	Print records	**1.5.1**	Print reports
2.2.4	Rename tables	**2.2.4**	Rename tables
2.3.2	Add records	**5.1.1**	Create a report based on the query or table
2.3.3	Delete records	**5.1.3**	Create a report by using a wizard
2.3.5	Find and replace data	**5.2.1**	Group and sort fields
2.3.7	Filter records	**5.2.4**	Add and modify labels
4.1.1	Create a form	**5.3.1**	Format reports into multiple columns
4.1.3	Save a form	**5.3.2**	Add calculated fields
4.2.1	Move form controls	**5.3.4**	Format report elements
4.2.2	Add form controls	**5.3.6**	Insert header and footer information
4.2.3	Modify data sources	**5.3.8**	Apply a theme
4.2.5	Set form control properties		
4.2.6	Manage labels		
4.3.2	Configure print settings		
4.3.4	Apply a theme		
4.3.7	Insert headers and footers		

BUILD YOUR E-PORTFOLIO

An E-Portfolio is a collection of evidence, stored electronically, that showcases what you have accomplished while completing your education. Collecting and then sharing your work products with potential employers reflects your academic and career goals. Your completed documents from the following projects are good examples to show what you have learned: 3G, 3K, and 3L.

GO! FOR JOB SUCCESS

Video: Performance Evaluations

Your instructor may assign this video to your class, and then ask you to think about, or discuss with your classmates, these questions:

FotolEdhar/Fotolia

What kind of message is Sara sending by forgetting to do the self-assessment review she was assigned for her evaluation? Why is it important to do a self-assessment for a review?

How should Sara react to her supervisor's criticisms in her review?

How important is it to follow a company's dress code policy? Do you think Sara's response to not following the dress code is appropriate? Why or why not?

GLOSSARY

GLOSSARY OF CHAPTER KEY TERMS

AND condition A condition in which records display only when all of the specified values are present in the selected fields.

Bound A term used to describe objects and controls that are based on data that is stored in tables.

Bound control A control that retrieves its data from an underlying table or query; a text box control is an example of a bound control.

Calculated control A control that contains an expression, often a formula or function, that most often summarizes a field that contains numerical data.

Control An object on a form or report that displays data or text, performs actions, and lets you view and work with information.

Control layout The grouped arrangement of controls on a form or report; for example, the Stacked layout.

Data entry The action of entering the data into a record in a database table or form.

Date control A control on a form or report that inserts the current date each time the form or report is opened.

Design view The Access view that displays the detailed structure of a query, form, or report; for forms and reports, may be the view in which some tasks must be performed, and displays only the controls, not the data.

Detail section The section of a form or report that displays the records from the underlying table or query.

Filter by Form An Access command that filters the records in a form based on one or more fields, or based on more than one value in the field.

Filter by Selection An Access command that displays only the records that contain the value in the selected field and hides the records that do not contain the value.

Filtering The process of displaying only a portion of the total records (a subset) based on matching specific values to provide a quick answer to a question.

Form A database object that you can use to enter new records into a table, or to edit, delete, and display existing records in a table.

Form Footer Information displayed at the bottom of the screen in Form view or Layout view that is printed after the last detail section on the last page of a printout.

Form Header Information such as a form's title that displays at the top of the screen in Form view or Layout view and is printed at the top of the first page when records are printed as forms.

Form tool An Access tool that creates a form with a single mouse click, which includes all of the fields from the underlying data source (table or query).

Form view The Access view in which you can view, modify, delete, or add records in a table but you cannot change the layout or design of the form.

Form Wizard An Access tool that walks you step by step through the creation of a form and that gives you more flexibility in the design, layout, and number of fields in a form.

Group Footer Information printed at the end of each group of records to display summary information for the group.

Group Header Information printed at the beginning of each new group of records; for example, the group name.

Group, Sort, and Total pane A pane that displays at the bottom of the window in Design view in which you can control how information is sorted and grouped in a report; provides the most flexibility for adding or modifying groups, sort orders, or totals options on a report.

Label control A control on a form or report that contains descriptive information, usually a field name or title.

Layout selector A small symbol that displays in the upper left corner of a selected control layout in a form or report that is displayed in Layout view or Design view and is used to move or format an entire group of controls.

Layout view The Access view in which you can make changes to a form or report while the data from the underlying data source displays.

OR condition A condition in which records display that match at least one of the specified values.

Page Footer Information printed at the bottom of every page in a report and most often includes the page number.

Page Header Information printed at the top of every page in a report.

Page number control A control on a form or report that inserts the page number when displayed in Print Preview or when printed.

Record selector bar The vertical bar at the left edge of a record used to select an entire record in Form view.

Record source The tables or queries that provide the underlying data for a form or report.

Report A database object that summarizes the fields and records from a query or table in an easy-to-read format suitable for printing.

Report Footer Information printed at the bottom of the last page of a report.

Report Header Information printed on the first page of a report that is used for logos, titles, and dates.

Report tool An Access tool that creates a report with one mouse click and displays all of the fields and records from the record source that you select.

Report Wizard An Access tool that walks you step by step through the creation of a report and that gives you more flexibility in the design, layout, and number of fields in a report.

Rich Text Format (RTF) A standard file format that contains some formatting such as underline, bold, font sizes, and colors. RTF documents can be opened in many applications.

Section bar In Design view, a gray bar in a form or report that identifies and separates one section from another; used to select the section and to change the size of the section.

Stacked layout A control layout format that is similar to a paper form, with label controls placed to the left of each text box control; the controls are grouped together for easy editing.

Subset A portion of the total records available.

Tab order The order in which the insertion point moves from one field to another in a form when you press the Tab key.

Text box control A bound control on a form or report that displays the data from the underlying table or query.

Theme A predesigned set of colors, fonts, lines, and fill effects that look good together and that can be applied to all of the objects in the database or to individual objects in the database.

Unbound control A control that does not have a source of data, such as the title in a form or report.

Apply 3A skills from these Objectives:

1. Create and Use a Form to Add and Delete Records
2. Filter Records
3. Create a Form by Using the Form Wizard
4. Modify a Form in Layout View and in Design View

Skills Review Project 3C Student Internships

In the following Skills Review, you will assist Erinique Jerlin, the Dean of Business at the Northwest Campus, in using her database to track business students and their internship placements for the current semester. Your completed forms will look similar to Figure 3.49.

PROJECT FILES

For Project 3C, you will need the following file:

a03C_Student_Internships

You will save your database as:

Lastname_Firstname_3C_Student_Internships

PROJECT RESULTS

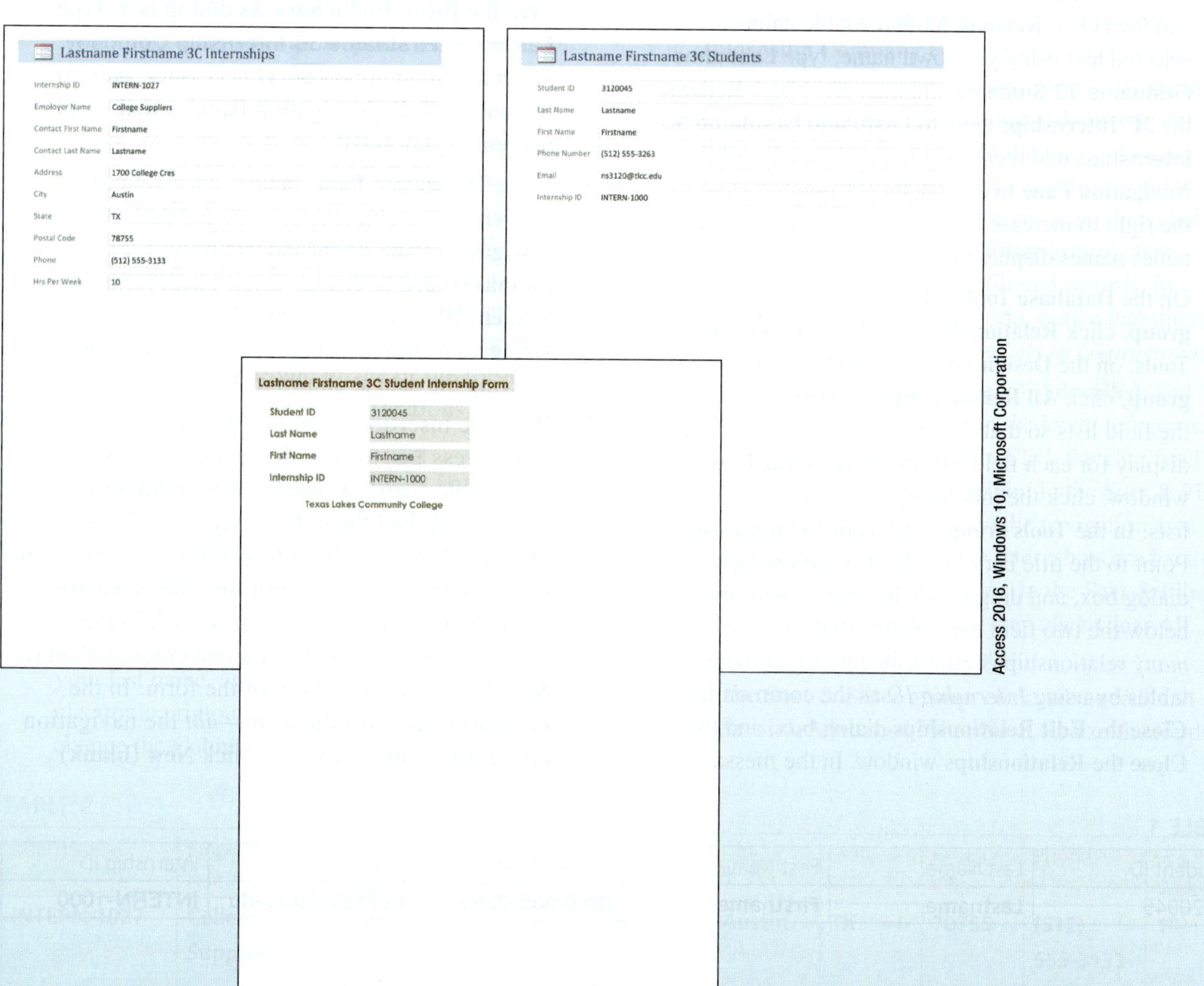

Lastname Firstname 3C Internships

Internship ID	INTERN-1027
Employer Name	College Suppliers
Contact First Name	Firstname
Contact Last Name	Lastname
Address	1700 College Cres
City	Austin
State	TX
Postal Code	78755
Phone	(512) 555-3133
Hrs Per Week	10

Lastname Firstname 3C Students

Student ID	3120045
Last Name	Lastname
First Name	Firstname
Phone Number	(512) 555-3263
Email	ns3120@tlcc.edu
Internship ID	INTERN-1000

Lastname Firstname 3C Student Internship Form

Student ID	3120045
Last Name	Lastname
First Name	Firstname
Internship ID	INTERN-1000

Texas Lakes Community College

FIGURE 3.49

(Project 3C Student Internships continues on the next page)

CHAPTER REVIEW

Apply 3B skills from these Objectives:

5 Create a Report by Using the Report Tool and Modify the Report in Layout View
6 Create a Report by Using the Report Wizard
7 Modify the Design of a Report
8 Keep Grouped Data Together in a Printed Report

Skills Review Project 3D Student Parking

In the following Skills Review, you will assist Carlos Medina, the Chief of Security, in using his Access database to track the details about students who have paid for parking in designated lots at the Southeast Campus of Texas Lakes Community College. Your completed reports will look similar to Figure 3.50.

PROJECT FILES

For Project 3D, you will need the following file:

a03D_Student_Parking

You will save your database as:

Lastname_Firstname_3D_Student_Parking

PROJECT RESULTS

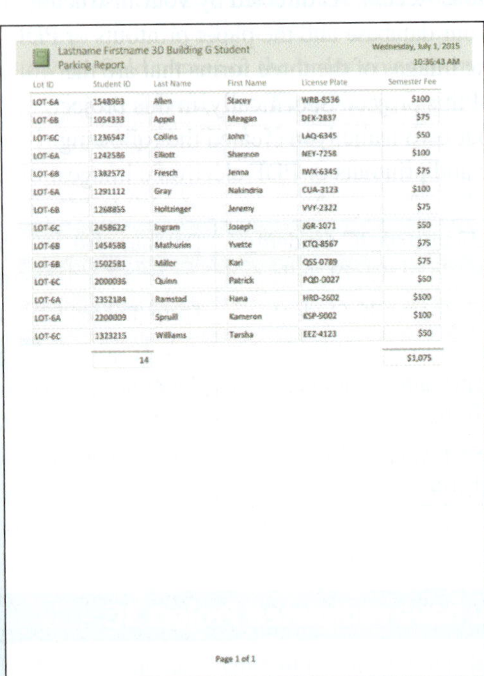

Lastname Firstname 3D Building G Student Parking Report — Wednesday, July 1, 2015 — 10:36:43 AM

Lot ID	Student ID	Last Name	First Name	License Plate	Semester Fee
LOT-6A	1548963	Allen	Stacey	WRB-8536	$100
LOT-6B	1054333	Appel	Meagan	DEX-2837	$75
LOT-6C	1236547	Collins	John	LAQ-6345	$50
LOT-6A	1242586	Elliott	Shannon	MEY-7258	$100
LOT-6B	1382572	Fresch	Jenna	IWX-6345	$75
LOT-6A	1291112	Gray	Nakindria	CUA-3123	$100
LOT-6B	1268855	Holtzinger	Jeremy	VVY-2322	$75
LOT-6C	2458622	Ingram	Joseph	JGR-1071	$50
LOT-6B	1454588	Mathurim	Yvette	KTQ-8567	$75
LOT-6B	1502581	Miller	Kari	QSS-0789	$75
LOT-6C	2000036	Quinn	Patrick	PQD-0027	$50
LOT-6A	2352184	Ramstad	Hana	HRD-2602	$100
LOT-6A	2200009	Spruill	Kameron	KSP-9002	$100
LOT-6C	1323215	Williams	Tarsha	EEZ-4123	$50
	14				$1,075

Page 1 of 1

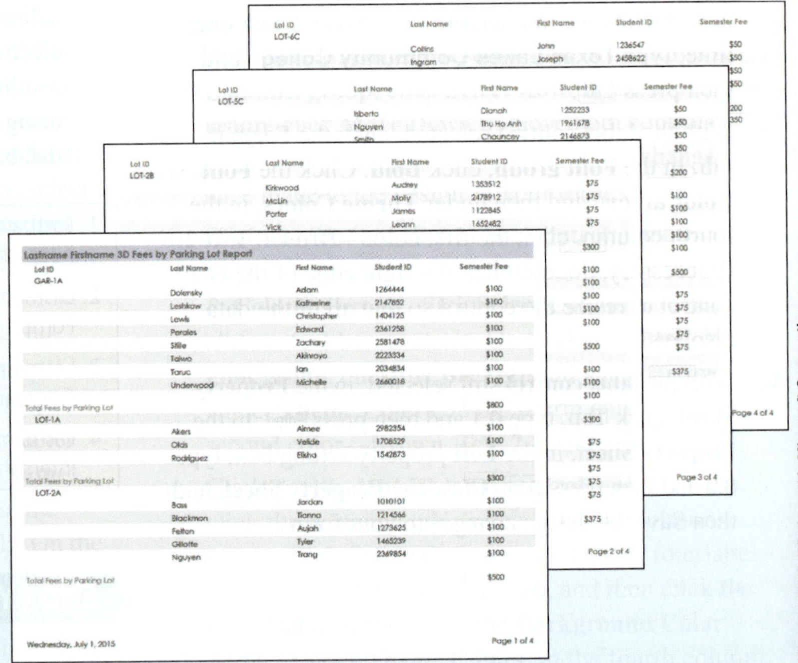

Lastname Firstname 3D Fees by Parking Lot Report

Lot ID	Last Name	First Name	Student ID	Semester Fee
GAR-1A				
	Dolensky	Adam	1264444	$100
	Leshkow	Katherine	2147852	$100
	Lewis	Christopher	1404125	$100
	Perales	Edward	2361258	$100
	Sifile	Zachary	2581478	$100
	Taiwo	Akinroyo	2223334	$100
	Taruc	Ian	2034834	$100
	Underwood	Michelle	2660018	$100
Total Fees by Parking Lot				$800
LOT-1A				
	Akers	Aimee	2982354	$100
	Olds	Velide	1708529	$100
	Rodriguez	Elisha	1542873	$100
Total Fees by Parking Lot				$300
LOT-2A				
	Bass	Jordan	1010101	$100
	Blackmon	Tianna	1214566	$100
	Felton	Aujah	1273625	$100
	Gillotte	Tyler	1465239	$100
	Nguyen	Trang	2369854	$100
Total Fees by Parking Lot				$500

Wednesday, July 1, 2015 — Page 1 of 4

FIGURE 3.50

(Project 3D Student Parking continues on the next page)

Skills Review Project 3D Student Parking (continued)

1 Start Access. In the Access opening screen, click **Open Other Files**. Under **Open**, click **Browse** and then navigate to the location where your student data files are stored. Double-click **a03D_Student_Parking** to open the database.

a. On the **File tab**, click **Save As**. Under **File Types**, be sure **Save Database As** is selected. On the right, under **Database File Types**, be sure **Access Database** is selected, and then at the bottom of the screen, click **Save As**. In the **Save As** dialog box, navigate to your **Access Chapter 3** folder. In the **File name** box, replace the existing text with **Lastname_Firstname_3D_Student_Parking** and then press Enter. On the **Message Bar**, click **Enable Content**.

b. In the **Navigation Pane**, right-click the **3D Parking Lots** table, and then click **Rename**. Using your own name, type **Lastname Firstname 3D Parking Lots** and then press Enter. Use this same technique to add your last name and first name to the beginning of the names of the two queries and the **3D Students** table. Increase the width of the **Navigation Pane** so that all object names display fully.

c. On the **Database Tools tab**, in the **Relationships group**, click **Relationships**. On the **Design tab**, in the **Relationships group**, click **All Relationships**. Resize and move the field lists so that the entire table name and fields display for each field list. In the **Relationships** window, click the **join line** between the two field lists. In the **Tools group**, click **Edit Relationships**. Point to the title bar of the **Edit Relationships** dialog box, and drag the dialog box downward below the two field lists. Notice that a *one-to-many* relationship is established between the two tables by using *Lot ID* as the common field. **Close** the **Edit Relationships** dialog box, and then **Close** the **Relationships** window. In the message box, click **Yes** to save changes to the layout of the relationships.

d. In the **Navigation Pane**, double-click each table to open them, and then examine the fields and data in each table. In the **Navigation Pane**, double-click your **3D Building G Student Parking Query** object to run the query and view the results. Apply **Best Fit** to the query results, and then **Save** the query. Switch to **Design** view to examine the design grid. This query answers the question, *What is the lot ID, lot location, student ID, student last name, student first name, license plate, state, and semester fee for students who have paid for parking in front of Building G, in ascending order by the Last Name field?* In the **Navigation Pane**, double-click your **3D Student Parking by Lots Query** object, apply **Best Fit** to the query results, **Save** the query, and then switch to **Design** view to examine the design grid. This query answers the question, *What is the lot ID, student ID, student last name, student first name, license plate, state, and semester fee for all students?* In the object window, right-click any **object tab**, and then click **Close All**.

e. In the **Navigation Pane**, click to select your **3D Building G Student Parking Query** object. On the **Create tab**, in the **Reports group**, click **Report**. **Close** the **Navigation Pane**. Under **Report Layout Tools**, on the **Design tab**, in the **Themes group**, click **Themes**. In the **Themes** gallery, use the ScreenTips to locate the **Retrospect** theme, right-click the **Retrospect** theme, and then click **Apply Theme to This Object Only**.

f. Click the **Lot Location** field name. On the **Report Layout Tools**, click the **Arrange tab**. In the **Rows & Columns group**, click **Select Column** to select the field name and all of the data for each record in the field. Press Del to remove the field from the report.

g. Click the **Last Name** field name, hold down Shift, and then click the **First Name** field name. On the **Design tab**, in the **Tools group**, click **Property Sheet**. In the **Property Sheet**, on the **Format tab**, click **Width**, type **1.25** and then press Enter to decrease the width of the two fields. **Close** the **Property Sheet**.

h. Click the **Last Name** field name to cancel the selection of both fields and to select only this field. On the **Home tab**, in the **Sort & Filter group**, click **Ascending** to sort the records in ascending order by the Last Name field.

i. If necessary, scroll to the bottom of the report, and notice that the *Semester Fee* column is automatically totaled. At the top of the report, click the **Student ID** field name. On the **Design tab**, in the **Grouping & Totals group**, click **Totals**, and then click **Count Records**. If necessary, scroll to the bottom of the report, and notice that *14* students have paid for parking in front of Building G.

(Project 3D Student Parking continues on the next page)

Mastering Access Project 3F Degrees and Students (continued)

1 Start Access. From your student data files, open **a03F_Degrees_Students**. **Save** the database in your **Access Chapter 3** folder as **Lastname_Firstname_3F_Degrees_Students** and then enable the content. In the **Navigation Pane**, **Rename** the two tables and two queries by adding **Lastname Firstname** to the beginning of each object name, and then increase the width of the **Navigation Pane** so that all object names display fully. View the relationship that is established between the *3F Degrees* tables and the *3F Students* table—*one* type of degree can be awarded to *many* students. Save the changes to the layout of the relationships. **Run** each query to display the query results, apply **Best Fit**, and then **Save** each query.

Open each query in **Design** view to examine the design grid. The *3F Summa Cum Laude Graduates Query* answers the question, *What is the GPA, student ID, last name, first name, degree, and program for students graduating with a grade point average of 3.8 or higher, in descending order by GPA and ascending order by Last Name?* The *3F GPAs by Degree Program Query* answers the question, *What is the program, last name, first name, and GPA for all students, in ascending order by the Last Name field within the Program field?* **Close All** objects.

2 Based on your **3F Summa Cum Laude Graduates Query** object, use the **Report** tool to create a report. Apply the **Facet** theme to only this report. Delete the **Student ID** field from the report. For the **Last Name**, **First Name**, and **Degree text box controls**, set the **Width** property to **1.25** and then **Sort** the **Last Name** field in **Ascending** order. For the **Program text box controls**, set the **Width** property to **2.5**.

At the bottom of the report, for the **calculated control**, which displays *8*, set the **Height** to **0.25** and then for the **page number control**, set the **Left** property to **5**. For the title of the report, set the **Font Size** to **14** and change the word *Query* to **Report** For the **GPA** field, set the **Left** property to **0.25** to approximately center the fields within the margins of the report. **Save** the report as **Lastname Firstname 3F Summa Cum Laude Graduates Report** and then create a paper printout or PDF electronic image as directed. **Close Print Preview**, **Close** the **Property Sheet**, and then **Close** the report.

3 Use the **Report Wizard** to create a report based on your **3F GPAs by Degree Program Query** object that includes the following fields in the order given: **Program**, **GPA**, **Last Name**, and **First Name**. View your data by **3F Degrees** and do not add any other grouping to the report. Sort first in **Descending** order by **GPA**, and second in **Ascending** order by **Last Name**. Summarize the report by averaging the **GPA** field for each degree. Be sure the layout is **Stepped** and the orientation is **Portrait**. For the report title, type **Lastname Firstname 3F GPAs by Program Report** and then switch to **Layout** view.

4 Apply the **Wisp** theme to only this report. For the report title, change the **Font Size** to **16**, and then apply **Bold**. Delete the controls that begin with **Summary for 'Program'**. Under **Program**, for the **text box controls**, set the **Width** property to **2.75**. Change the text in the **Avg label control** to **Average GPA by Program**. At the top of the report, select the four **label controls** that display the field names, and then apply **Bold**. Select the **GPA label control**, the **GPA text box controls**, and the **calculated controls** for the average GPA, and then set the **Width** property to **1** and the **Left** property to **3**. **Close** the **Property Sheet**. Display the report in **Design** view. Under **Program Header**, click the **Program text box control**, hold down Shift, and under **Program Footer**, click the **Average GPA by Program label control**. **Align** the controls on the **Right**, and then **Save** the design changes to your report.

5 Switch to **Print Preview**, **Zoom** to display **Two Pages** of the report, and examine how the groupings break across the pages. Switch to **Layout** view, display the **Group, Sort, and Total** pane, select **keep whole group together on one page**, and then close the **Group, Sort, and Total** pane. Switch to **Print Preview**, and notice that the groupings are not split between pages. **Save** the report, and then create a paper printout or PDF electronic image as directed—two pages result.

6 **Close Print Preview**, and then **Close** the report. **Open** the **Navigation Pane**, and, if necessary, increase the width of the pane so that all object names display

(Project 3F Degrees and Students continues on the next page)

Mastering Access Project 3F Degrees and Students (continued)

fully. On the right side of the title bar, click **Close** to close the database and to close Access. As directed by your instructor, submit your database and the paper printouts or PDF electronic images of the two reports—one report is two pages—that are the results of this project. Specifically, in this project, using your own name, you created the following database and printouts or PDF electronic images:

1. Lastname_Firstname_3F_Degrees_Students	Database file
2. Lastname Firstname 3F Summa Cum Laude Graduates Report	Report
3. Lastname Firstname 3F GPAs by Program Report	Report

END | You have completed Project 3F

Apply 3A and 3B skills from these Objectives:

1. Create and Use a Form to Add and Delete Records
2. Filter Records
3. Create a Form by Using the Form Wizard
4. Modify a Form in Layout View and in Design View
5. Create a Report by Using the Report Tool and Modify the Report in Layout View
6. Create a Report by Using the Report Wizard
7. Modify the Design of a Report
8. Keep Grouped Data Together in a Printed Report

Mastering Access Project 3G Career Books

In the following Mastering Access project, you will assist Rebecca Hennelly, Head Librarian at the Southwest Campus of Texas Lakes Community College, in using her database to track publishers and book titles that assist students in finding employment. Your completed forms and report will look similar to Figure 3.53.

PROJECT FILES

For Project 3G, you will need the following file:

a03G_Career_Books

You will save your database as:

Lastname_Firstname_3G_Career_Books

PROJECT RESULTS

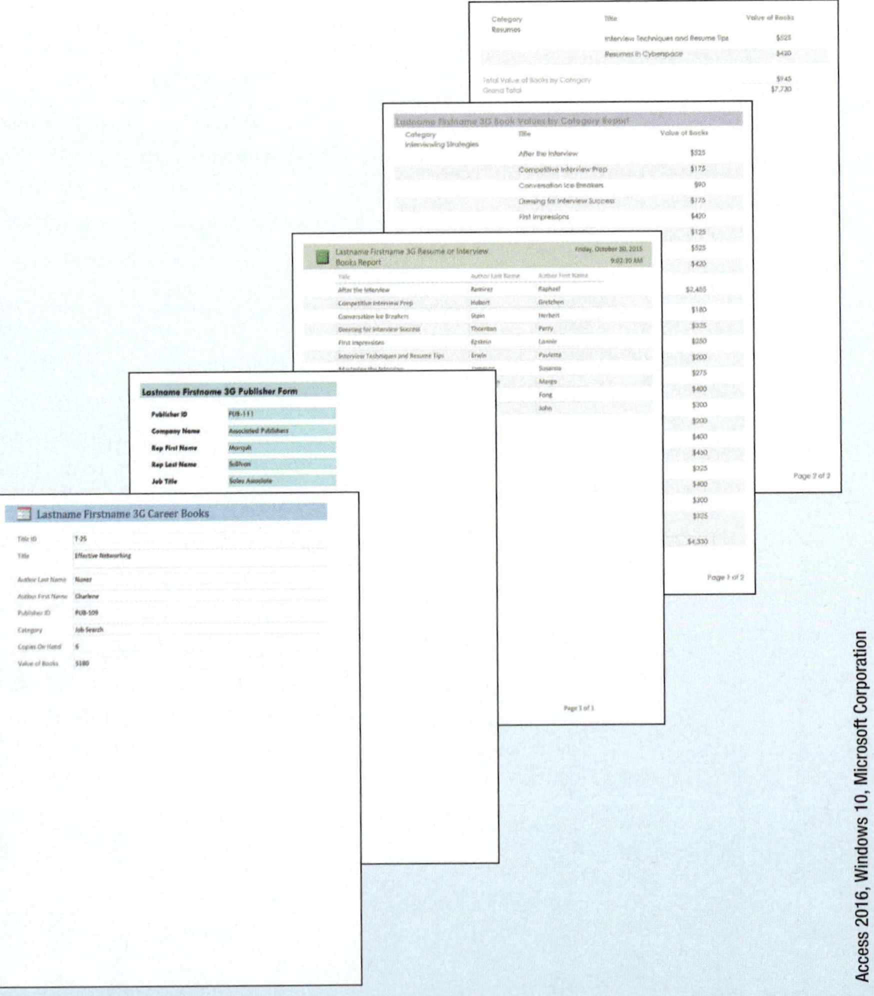

Access 2016, Windows 10, Microsoft Corporation

FIGURE 3.53

(Project 3G Career Books continues on the next page)

Mastering Access Project 3G Career Books (continued)

1 Start Access. From your student data files, open **a03G_Career_Books**. Save the database in your **Access Chapter 3** folder as **Lastname_Firstname_3G_Career_Books** and then enable the content. In the **Navigation Pane**, **Rename** the two tables and one query by adding **Lastname Firstname** to the beginning of each object name. Increase the width of the **Navigation Pane** so that all object names display fully. View the relationship that is established between the *3G Publishers* table and the *3G Career Books* table—*one* publisher can publish *many* career books. Save the changes to the layout of the relationships.

Open the **3G Resume or Interview Books Query**, apply **Best Fit**, and then **Save** the query. Switch the query to **Design** view, examine the design of the query, and then **Close** the query object.

2 Based on your **3G Career Books** table, use the **Form** tool to create a form. **Save** the form as **Lastname Firstname 3G Career Book Form** and then switch to **Form** view. Using the form, add a new record to the underlying table as shown in **Table 1**.

3 Display the first record, and click in the **Title ID** field. **Find** the record for the **Title ID** of **T-19**, and then **Delete** the record. Display the record you entered for **T-25**, and then, as directed, create a paper printout or electronic printout of only that record, changing the **Column Size Width** in the **Print** dialog box to **7.5**. **Save** the design changes to your form.

4 Use the **Filter By Form** tool in your **3G Career Book Form** object to create a filter that displays records with a **Category** of **Interviewing Strategies** or **Resumes**. After verifying that 10 records match this criteria, click **Toggle Filter** to display all 24 records. **Save** the form, and then **Close** the form.

5 Use the **Form Wizard** to create a form based on your **3G Publishers** table that includes the following fields in the order given: **Company Name, Rep Last Name, Rep First Name, Job Title**, and **Phone Number**. Apply a **Columnar** layout, and name the form **Lastname Firstname 3G Publisher Form**.

6 In **Layout** view, apply the **Stacked** layout to all of the controls, and then apply the **Integral** theme to this form only. For the title of the form, change the **Font Size** to **16**, apply **Bold**, and then change the **Font Color** to **Dark Teal, Text 2, Darker 50%**—under **Theme Colors**, in the fourth column, the last color. **Save** the design changes to the form.

7 From the **Field List** pane, add the **Publisher ID** field to the form directly above the **Company Name** field. **Close** the **Field List** pane. Move the **Rep First Name** controls directly above the **Rep Last Name** controls. Click the **Job Title text box control**, set the **Width** property to **2.5** and then **Save** the design changes to your form.

8 Select all six **text box controls**, and change the **Background Color** to **Turquoise, Accent 1, Lighter 80%**—under **Theme Colors**, in the fifth column, the second color. Select all six **label controls**, and change the **Font Color** to **Dark Teal, Text 2, Darker 50%**—under **Theme Colors**, in the fourth column, the last color. Apply **Bold** to the **label controls**. With the **label controls** still selected, set the **Width** property to **1.75** and then select all of the **label controls** and all of the **text box controls**. Change the **Font Size** to **12**, set the **Height** property to **0.25** and then **Save** the design changes to your form.

9 In **Design** view, set the **Form Footer** section **Height** property to **0.5**. Add a **Label** control to the **Form Footer** section that displays **Texas Lakes Southwest Campus**. For this **label control**, change the **Font Color** to **Dark Teal, Text 2, Darker 50%**—under **Theme Colors**, in the fourth column, the last color —and then apply **Bold**. For this **label control**, set the **Width** property to **2.2**, set the **Top** property to **0.1** and then set the **Left** property to **1.25**. **Close** the **Property Sheet**, **Save** your form, and then

TABLE 1

Title ID	Title	Author Last Name	Author First Name	Publisher ID	Category	Copies On Hand	Value of Books
T-25	**Effective Networking**	**Nunez**	**Charlene**	**PUB-109**	**Job Search**	**6**	**180**

(Project 3G Career Books continues on the next page)

Mastering Access Project 3G Career Books (continued)

switch to **Form** view. Using the form, add a new record to the underlying table as shown in **Table 2**.

10 Display the record that you just created, and then, as directed, create a paper printout or PDF electronic image of only this record. Because you changed the field widths, you do not need to change the Column Size Width in the **Print** dialog box. **Close** the form.

11 Based on your **3G Resume or Interview Books Query** object, use the **Report** tool to create a report. Apply the **Retrospect** theme to only this report. Delete the following fields from the report: **Publisher ID**, **Category**, and **Company Name**. For the **Title text box controls**, set the **Width** property to **3** and then **Sort** the **Title** field in **Ascending** order. For the **Author Last Name text box controls** and the **Author First Name text box controls**, set the **Width** property to **1.5**.

12 Click the **Title** field name, and then add a calculated control that counts the number of records. At the bottom of the report, for the **calculated control**, which displays *10*, set the **Height** to **0.25** and then for the **page number control**, set the **Left** property to **5**. For the title of the report, set the **Font Size** to **14** and change the word *Query* to **Report**. Click the **Title** field name, and then set the **Left** property to **0.75** to move all of the controls to the right. **Save** the report as **Lastname Firstname 3G Resume or Interview Books Report** and then create a paper printout or PDF electronic image as directed. **Close Print Preview**, **Close** the **Property Sheet**, and then **Close** the report.

13 Use the **Report Wizard** to create a report based on your **3G Career Books** table that includes the following fields in the order given: **Category, Title**, and **Value of Books**. Group your data by **Category**, sort in **Ascending** order by **Title**, and then summarize the report by summing the **Value of Books** field. Be sure the layout is **Stepped** and the orientation is **Portrait**. For the report title, type **Lastname Firstname 3G Book Values by Category Report** and then switch to **Layout** view.

14 Apply the **Ion Boardroom** theme to only this report. For the report title, change the **Font Size** to **14**, and then apply **Bold**. Delete the controls that begin with **Summary for 'Category'**. Select the **Category**, **Title**, and **Value of Books label controls**, and then apply **Bold**. Under **Title**, for the **text box controls**, set the **Width** property to **3.5**. For the **Value of Books label control**, set the **Left** property to **6** and then **Save** the design changes to your report.

15 At the bottom of the report in the last column, select the following three controls: **text box control** that displays *$420*, **calculated control** that displays *$945*, and the **calculated control** that displays *7,730 (Grand Total control, may be too small to view number)*. Set the **Width** property to **1.25** and the **Left** property to **6**. For the **Grand Total label control**, set the **Width** property to **1** and then change the text in the **Sum label control** to **Total Value of Books by Category**. Click any **Title text box control**, set the **Height** property to **0.35** and then **Save** your report.

16 **Close** the **Property Sheet**, and then display your report in **Design** view. Under **Category Footer**, click the **label control** that displays *Total Value of Books by Category*, hold down Shift, and then under **Report Footer**, click the **Grand Total label control**. **Align** the controls on the **Left**, and then **Save** the design changes to your report.

17 Switch to **Print Preview**, **Zoom** to display **Two Pages** of the report, and examine how the groupings break across the pages. Switch to **Layout** view, display the **Group, Sort, and Total** pane, select **keep whole group together on one page**, and then close the **Group, Sort, and Total** pane. Switch to **Print Preview**, and notice that the groupings are no longer split between pages. **Save** the report, and then create a paper printout or PDF electronic image as directed—two pages result.

TABLE 2

Publisher ID	Company Name	Rep First Name	Rep Last Name	Job Title	Phone Number
PUB-111	**Associated Publishers**	**Marquis**	**Sullivan**	**Sales Associate**	**(512) 555-7373**

(Project 3G Career Books continues on the next page)

Mastering Access Project 3G Career Books (continued)

18 **Close Print Preview**, and then **Close** the report. **Open** the **Navigation Pane**, and, if necessary, increase the width of the pane so that all object names display fully. On the right side of the title bar, click **Close** to close the database and to close Access. As directed by your instructor, submit your database and the paper printout or PDF electronic images of the two forms and two reports—one report is two pages—that are the results of this project. Specifically, in this project, using your own name, you created the following database and printouts or PDF electronic images:

1. Lastname_Firstname_3G_Career_Books	Database file
2. Lastname Firstname 3G Career Book Form	Form (Record 24)
3. Lastname Firstname 3G Publisher Form	Form (Record 12)
4. Lastname Firstname 3G Resume or Interview Books Report	Report
5. Lastname Firstname 3G Book Values by Category Report	Report

END | You have completed Project 3G

Apply a combination of the 3A and 3B skills.

CONTENT-BASED ASSESSMENTS (CRITICAL THINKING)

GO! Fix It Project 3H Resume Workshops MyITLab

GO! Make It Project 3I Study Abroad MyITLab

GO! Solve It Project 3J Job Offers MyITLab

GO! Solve It Project 3K Financial Aid

PROJECT FILES

For Project 3K, you will need the following file:

a03K_Financial_Aid

You will save your database as:

Lastname_Firstname_3K_Financial_Aid

Start Access, navigate to your student data files, open **a03K_Financial_Aid**, and then save the database in your **Access Chapter 3** folder as **Lastname_Firstname_3K_Financial_Aid**. Using your own name, add **Lastname Firstname** to the beginning of all objects. Sivia Long, the Financial Aid Director, would like you to create an form and a report, using the following guidelines:

- In the form, move the Last Name field above the First Name field. Enter a new record using your own information with a Student ID of **9091246** and Financial Aid ID of **FA-07** and a Home Phone of **(512) 555-9876** and a College Email of **ns246@tlcc.edu** Create a filter to display the only those students whose last name begin with the letter *S*. Add a footer that displays **Texas Lakes Community College Financial Aid**. Save the form as **Lastname Firstname 3K FA Student Update Form** and then create a paper printout or PDF electronic image of your record only.
- The report will use the query and list the Award Name, Student ID, and Award Amount, viewed by students, grouped by the Award Name field, and sorted in ascending order by the Student ID field. Include a total for the Award Amount field, save the report as **Lastname Firstname 3K FA Amount by Award Report** and be sure the groupings do not break across pages. Create a paper printout or PDF electronic image as directed—multiple pages result.

Open the Navigation Pane, be sure that all object names display fully, and then close Access. As directed, submit your database and the paper printout or PDF electronic images of the form and report that are the results of this project.

Performance Level

Performance Criteria	Exemplary: You consistently applied the relevant skills	Proficient: You sometimes, but not always, applied the relevant skills	Developing: You rarely or never applied the relevant skills
Create 3K FA Student Update Form	Form created with correct fields, new record, footer, and filter in an attractive format.	Form created with no more than two missing elements.	Form created with more than two missing elements.
Create 3K FA Amount by Award Report	Report created with correct fields, grouped, sorted, and summarized correctly, with groupings kept together in an attractive format.	Report created with no more than two missing elements.	Report created with more than two missing elements.

END | You have completed Project 3K

OUTCOMES-BASED ASSESSMENTS (CRITICAL THINKING)

RUBRIC

The following outcomes-based assessments are *open-ended assessments*. That is, there is no specific correct result; your result will depend on your approach to the information provided. Make *Professional Quality* your goal. Use the following scoring rubric to guide you in *how* to approach the problem and then to evaluate *how well* your approach solves the problem.

The *criteria*—Software Mastery, Content, Format & Layout, and Process—represent the knowledge and skills you have gained that you can apply to solving the problem. The *levels of performance*—Professional Quality, Approaching Professional Quality, or Needs Quality Improvements—help you and your instructor evaluate your result.

	Your completed project is of Professional Quality if you:	Your completed project is Approaching Professional Quality if you:	Your completed project Needs Quality Improvements if you:
1-Software Mastery	Choose and apply the most appropriate skills, tools, and features and identify efficient methods to solve the problem.	Choose and apply some appropriate skills, tools, and features, but not in the most efficient manner.	Choose inappropriate skills, tools, or features, or are inefficient in solving the problem.
2-Content	Construct a solution that is clear and well organized, contains content that is accurate, appropriate to the audience and purpose, and is complete. Provide a solution that contains no errors in spelling, grammar, or style.	Construct a solution in which some components are unclear, poorly organized, inconsistent, or incomplete. Misjudge the needs of the audience. Have some errors in spelling, grammar, or style, but the errors do not detract from comprehension.	Construct a solution that is unclear, incomplete, or poorly organized; contains some inaccurate or inappropriate content; and contains many errors in spelling, grammar, or style. Do not solve the problem.
3-Format & Layout	Format and arrange all elements to communicate information and ideas, clarify function, illustrate relationships, and indicate relative importance.	Apply appropriate format and layout features to some elements, but not others. Overuse features, causing minor distraction.	Apply format and layout that does not communicate information or ideas clearly. Do not use format and layout features to clarify function, illustrate relationships, or indicate relative importance. Use available features excessively, causing distraction.
4-Process	Use an organized approach that integrates planning, development, self-assessment, revision, and reflection.	Demonstrate an organized approach in some areas, but not others; or, use an insufficient process of organization throughout.	Do not use an organized approach to solve the problem.

Apply a combination of the 3A and 3B skills.

OUTCOMES-BASED ASSESSMENTS (CRITICAL THINKING)

GO! Think Project 3L Food Services

PROJECT FILES

For Project 3L, you will need the following file:

a03L_Food_Services

You will save your database as:

Lastname_Firstname_3L_Food_Services

Start Access, navigate to your student data files, open **a03L_Food_Services**, save the database in your **Access Chapter 3** folder as **Lastname_Firstname_3L_Food_Services** and then enable the content. Using your own name, add **Lastname Firstname** to the beginning of both table names. Luciano Gonzalez, the Hospitality Director, would like you to create an attractive form and a report to assist him with the staff scheduling of food services for a two-day student orientation workshop using the following guidelines:

- The form will be used to update records in the 3L Staff table. Be sure that the Last Name field displays above the First Name field. After the form is created, enter a new record using your own last name and first name with a Staff ID of **STAFF-1119** and a Phone Number of **(512) 555-0845** and a Title of **Server**. Create a filter that when toggled on displays the records for staff with a Title of *Server*. Add a footer to the form that displays **Texas Lakes Community College Hospitality Services**. Save the form as **Lastname Firstname 3L Staff Update Form** and then create a paper printout or PDF electronic image of your record only.
- The report will be used by Mr. Gonzalez to call staff members when the schedule changes, so it should be grouped by title. Add a report footer that displays **Texas Lakes Community College Hospitality Services** and then save the report as **Lastname Firstname 3L Staff Phone List**. Create a paper printout or PDF electronic image as directed.

Open the Navigation Pane, be sure that all object names display fully, and then close Access. As directed, submit your database and the paper or electronic printout of the form and report that are the results of this project. Specifically, in this project, using your own name, you created the following database and printouts or PDF electronic images.

END | You have completed Project 3L

GO! Think Project 3M Donor Gifts MyITLab

Build From Scratch

You and GO! Project 3N Personal Inventory MyITLab

GO! Collaborative Team Project Project 3O Bell Orchid Hotels MyITLab

Enhancing Tables

OUTCOMES
Maneuver and manage data.

OBJECTIVES

1. Manage Existing Tables
2. Modify Existing Tables
3. Change Data Types
4. Attach Files to Records

PROJECT 4B

OUTCOMES
Format tables and validate data entry.

OBJECTIVES

5. Create a Table in Design View
6. Create a Lookup Field
7. Set Field Properties
8. Create Data Validation Rules and Validation Text

Fuyu liu/Shutterstock

In This Chapter

GO! to Work with Access

In this chapter, you will enhance tables and improve data accuracy and data entry. You will begin by identifying secure locations where databases will be stored and by backing up existing databases to protect the data. You will edit existing tables for more effective design and copy data and a table design across tables. You will create a new table in Design view and determine the best data type for each field based on its characteristics. You will use the field properties to enhance the table and to improve data accuracy and data entry, including looking up data in another table and attaching an existing document to a record.

Golden Grove, California, is a growing city located between Los Angeles and San Diego. Just 10 years ago the population was under 100,000; today it has grown to almost 300,000. Its growth in population is based on its growth as a community. Community leaders have always focused on quality of life and economic development in decisions on housing, open space, education, and infrastructure, making the city a model for other communities its size around the United States. The city provides many recreational and cultural opportunities with a large park system and library system, thriving arts, and a friendly business atmosphere.

City Directory

PROJECT ACTIVITIES

Dario Soto, the new city manager of Golden Grove, has a database of city directory information. This database has three tables that have duplicate information in them. In Activities 4.01 through 4.12, you will redesign the tables, edit and proofread data, change data types, and attach files to records. Your completed tables will look similar to those in Figure 4.1.

PROJECT FILES

If your instructor wants you to submit Project 4A in the MyITLab Grader system, log in to MyITLab, locate Grader Project 4A, and then download the files for this project.

For Project 4A, you will need the following files:

a04A_GG_Directory
a04A_GG_Employees
a04A_PZ_Schedule
a04A_Bldg_Permit_App

You will save your databases as:

Lastname_Firstname_4A_GG_Directory
Lastname_Firstname_a04A_GG_Directory_2019-07-07 (date will vary)
Lastname_Firstname_4A_GG_Employees

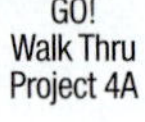

PROJECT RESULTS

GO!
Walk Thru
Project 4A

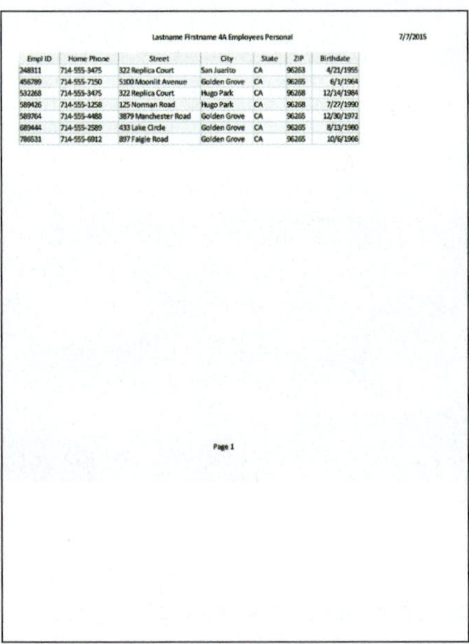

Lastname Firstname 4A Employees Personal 7/7/2015

Empl ID	Home Phone	Street	City	State	ZIP	Birthdate
248311	714-555-3475	322 Replica Court	San Juarito	CA	96263	4/21/1955
456789	714-555-7150	5100 Moonlit Avenue	Golden Grove	CA	96265	6/1/1964
532268	714-555-3475	322 Replica Court	Hugo Park	CA	96268	12/14/1984
589426	714-555-1258	125 Norman Road	Hugo Park	CA	96268	7/27/1990
589764	714-555-4488	3879 Manchester Road	Golden Grove	CA	96265	12/30/1972
689444	714-555-2589	433 Lake Circle	Golden Grove	CA	96265	8/13/1980
786531	714-555-6912	897 Faigle Road	Golden Grove	CA	96265	10/6/1966

Page 1

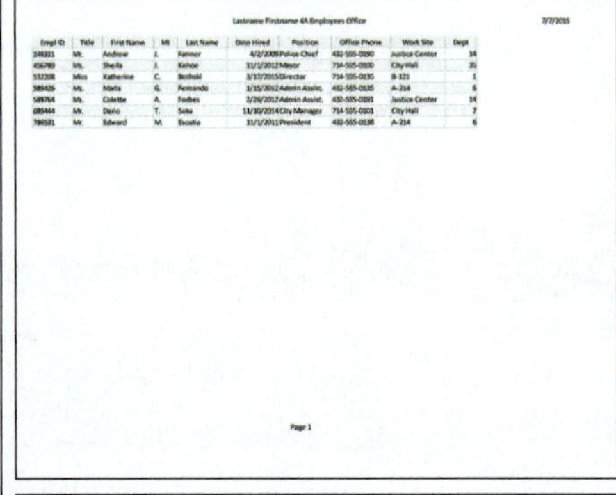

Lastname Firstname 4A Employees Office 7/7/2015

Empl ID	Title	First Name	MI	Last Name	Date Hired	Position	Office Phone	Work Site	Dept
248311	Mr.	Andrew	J.	Farmer	4/2/2009	Police Chief	432-555-0190	Justice Center	14
456789	Ms.	Sheila	J.	Kehoe	11/1/2012	Mayor	714-555-0100	City Hall	35
532268	Miss	Katherine	C.	Bothski	3/17/2015	Director	714-555-0135	B-121	1
589426	Ms.	Maria	G.	Fernando	1/15/2012	Admin Assist.	432-555-0135	A-214	6
589764	Ms.	Colette	A.	Forbes	2/26/2012	Admin Assist.	432-555-0193	Justice Center	14
689444	Mr.	Dario	T.	Soto	11/10/2014	City Manager	714-555-0101	City Hall	7
786531	Mr.	Edward	M.	Escalia	11/1/2011	President	432-555-0138	A-214	6

Page 1

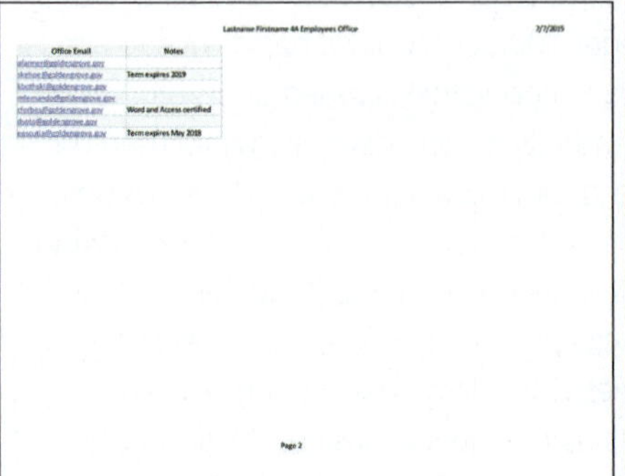

Lastname Firstname 4A Employees Office 7/7/2015

Office Email	Notes
[illegible]	
[illegible]	Term expires 2019
[illegible]	
[illegible]	
[illegible]	Word and Access certified
[illegible]	
[illegible]	Term expires May 2018

Page 2

Lastname Firstname 4A Departments Revised 7/7/2015

Dept ID	Department	Dept Phone	📎
1	Animal Control	714-555-0109	(0)
2	Building Permits & Inspections	714-555-0199	(1)
3	Constituent Relations	714-555-0132	(0)
4	City Attorney	714-555-0145	(0)
6	City Council	714-555-0135	(0)
7	City Manager	714-555-0100	(0)
8	City Treasurer	714-555-0155	(0)
9	Fire Administration	714-555-0168	(0)
10	Public Administrator	714-555-0111	(0)
11	Housing & Rental Inspections	714-555-0139	(0)
12	Human Resources	714-555-0194	(0)
13	Planning & Zoning	714-555-0128	(1)
14	City Police	714-555-0190	(0)
15	Social Services	714-555-0152	(0)
16	Trash Pickup	714-555-0144	(0)
17	City Jail	714-555-0191	(0)
18	Community Relations	714-555-0164	(0)
19	Finance	714-555-0122	(0)
20	Municipal Court	714-555-0141	(0)
21	General Services	714-555-0116	(0)
22	Golf Courses	714-555-0162	(0)
23	Information Technology	714-555-0115	(0)
24	Library	714-555-0171	(0)
25	Community Center	714-555-0178	(0)
26	Permits & Licenses	714-555-0133	(0)
27	Parks & Recreation	714-555-0149	(0)
28	City Utilities	714-555-0112	(0)
29	School Administration	714-555-0182	(0)
30	Street Repairs	714-555-0118	(0)
31	Traffic	714-555-0120	(0)
32	Visitor Information	714-555-0143	(0)
33	Waste Management	714-555-0175	(0)
34	Health & Wellness	714-555-0136	(0)
35	City Mayor	714-555-0162	(0)
36	City Engineer	714-555-0198	(0)
37	City Planner	714-555-0151	(0)

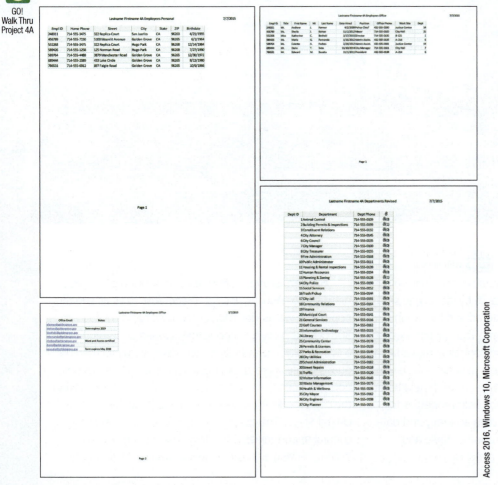

FIGURE 4.1 Project 4A City Directory

NOTE	If You Are Using a Touchscreen
	Tap an item to click it.
	Press and hold for a few seconds to right-click; release when the information or command displays.
	Touch the screen with two or more fingers and then pinch together to zoom out or stretch your fingers apart to zoom in.
	Slide your finger on the screen to scroll—slide left to scroll right and slide right to scroll left.
	Slide to rearrange—similar to dragging with a mouse.
	Swipe to select—slide an item a short distance with a quick movement—to select an item and bring up commands, if any.

PROJECT RESULTS

In this project, using your own name, you will create the following database and objects. Your instructor may ask you to submit printouts or PDF electronic images:

Lastname_Firstname_4A_GG_Directory	Database file
Lastname_Firstname_a04A_GG_Directory_2019-07-07 (date will vary)	Backup database file
Lastname Firstname 4A Employees Personal	Table
Lastname Firstname 4A Employees Office	Table
Lastname Firstname 4A Departments Revised	Table

Objective 1 Manage Existing Tables

GO! Learn How Video A4-1

A database is most effective when the data is maintained accurately and efficiently. It is important to back up your database often to be sure you can always obtain a clean copy if the data is corrupted or lost. Maintaining the accuracy of the field design and data is also critical for a useful database; regular reviews and updates of design and data are necessary. It is also helpful to avoid retyping data that already exists in a database; using copy/paste or appending records reduces the chances for additional errors as long as the source data is accurate.

Activity 4.01 | Backing Up a Database

ALERT!

To submit as an autograded project, log into MyITLab and download the files for this project, and begin with those files instead of a04A_GG_Directory. For Project 4A using Grader, read Activities 4.01 and 4.02 carefully. Begin working with the database in Activity 4.03. For Grader to award points accurately, when saving an object, do not include your Lastname Firstname at the beginning of the object name.

1.4.3, 1.4.6

Before modifying the structure of an existing database, it is important to ***back up*** the database so that a copy of the original database will be available if you need it. It is also important to back up databases regularly to avoid losing data.

1 **Start** Access. Navigate to the location where the student data files for this chapter are saved. Locate and open the **a04A_GG_Directory** file and enable the content.

4 In the **Microsoft Office Trusted Location** dialog box, under **Description**, using your own first and last name, type **Databases created by Firstname Lastname** and then click **OK**.

The Trusted Locations pane displays the path of the *Access Chapter 4* folder. You will no longer receive a security warning when you open databases from this location.

5 Using the technique you just practiced, add the location of your student data files to the Trust Center. For the description, type **Student data files created for GO! Series**

Only locations that you know are secure should be added to the Trust Center. If other people have access to the databases and can change the information in the database, the location is not secure.

6 At the lower-right corner of the **Trust Center** dialog box, click **OK**. In the displayed **Microsoft Office Security Options** dialog box, click **OK**.

The message bar no longer displays—you opened the database from a trusted location.

7 Display **Backstage** view, and then click **Close**. Open **Lastname_Firstname_4A_GG_Directory**.

The database opens, and the message bar with the Security Alert does not display. Using the Trust Center button is an efficient way to open databases that are saved in a safe location.

> ***More* Knowledge** **Remove a Trusted Location**
>
> Display Backstage view, and then click Options. In the Access Options dialog box, in the left pane, click Trust Center. In the right pane, click the Trust Center Settings button, and then click Trusted Locations. Under Path, click the trusted location that you want to remove, and then click the Remove button. Click OK to close the dialog box.

Activity 4.03 | Duplicating a Table and Modifying the Structure

1.2.2, 1.3.5, 2.3.6, 2.4.6, 2.4.9

In this Activity, you will duplicate the *4A Departments* table, modify the structure by deleting fields and data that are duplicated in other tables, and then designate a primary key field.

1 In the **Navigation Pane**, double-click **4A Departments** to open the table. **Close** « the **Navigation Pane**. Click the **File tab**, and then click **Save As**. Under **File Types**, double-click **Save Object As**. Compare your screen to Figure 4.5.

The Save As command displays the Save As dialog box, where you can name and save a new object based on the currently displayed object. After you name and save the new table, the original table closes, and the new table—based on the original one—displays.

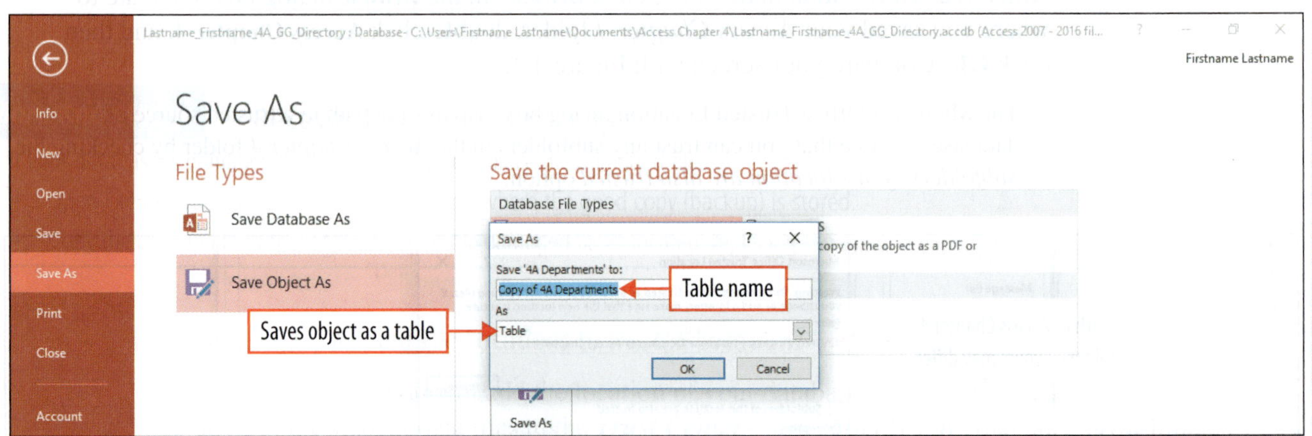

Access 2016, Windows 10, Microsoft Corporation

FIGURE 4.5

2 In the displayed **Save As** dialog box, under **Save '4A Departments' to:**, type **Lastname Firstname 4A Departments Revised** and then click **OK**.

The *4A Departments Revised* table is open; it is an exact duplicate of the *4A Departments* table. Working with a duplicate table ensures that the original table will be available if needed.

3 Point to the **Dept Head** field name until the [⬇] pointer displays. Hold down the left mouse button, and drag to the right to the **Admin Asst** field name to select both fields. On the **Home tab**, in the **Records group**, click **Delete**. In the displayed message box, click **Yes** to permanently delete the fields and the data.

The names of the employees are deleted from this table to avoid having employee data in more than one table. Recall that a table should store data about one subject—this table now stores only departmental data. In addition to needing duplicate data removed, the fields that you deleted were also poorly designed. They combined both the first and last names in the same field, limiting the use of the data to entire names only.

4 Switch to **Design** view. To the left of **Department**, click the **row selector** box. Under **Table Tools**, on the **Design tab**, in the **Tools group**, click **Insert Rows** to insert a blank row (field) above the *Department* field.

5 Under **Field Name**, click in the blank field name box, type **Dept ID** and then press Tab. In the **Data Type** box, type **a** and then press Tab. Alternatively, click the Data Type arrow, and then select the AutoNumber data type. Under **Table Tools**, on the **Design tab**, in the **Tools group**, click **Primary Key**, and then compare your screen with Figure 4.6.

Recall that a primary key field is used to ensure that each record is unique. Because each department has a unique name, you might question why the *Department* field is not designated as the primary key field. Primary key fields should be data that does not change often. When organizations or companies are reorganized, department names are often changed.

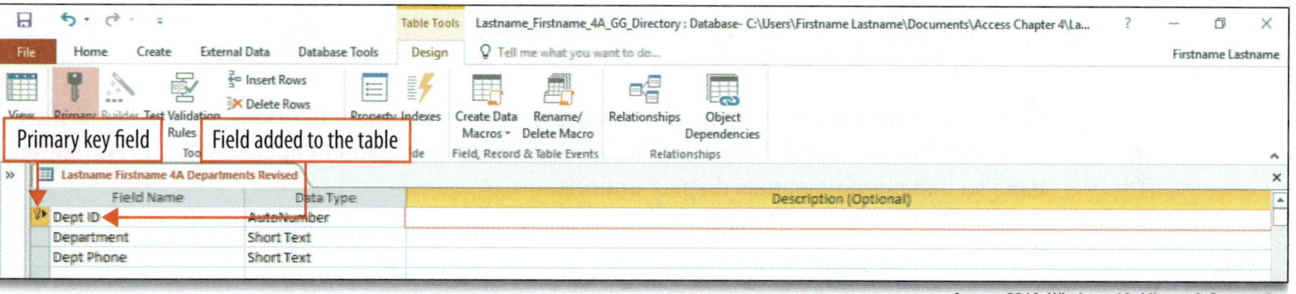

FIGURE 4.6

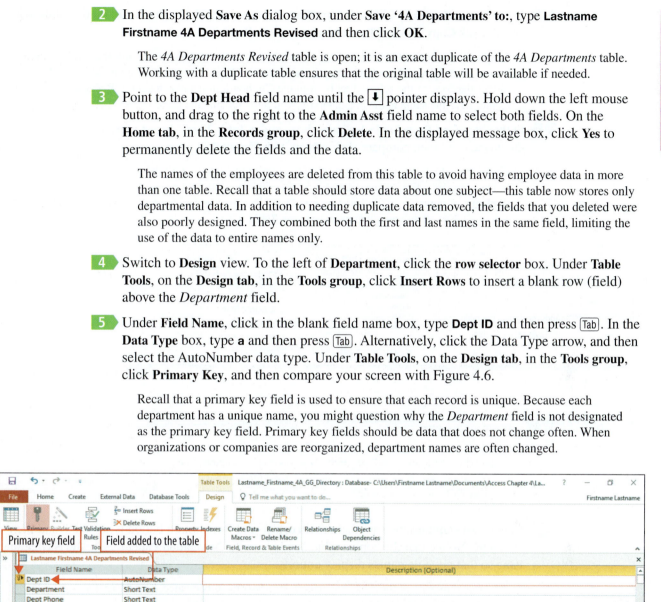

Access 2016, Windows 10, Microsoft Corporation

6 Switch to **Datasheet** view, and in the displayed message box, click **Yes** to save the table.

Because the *Dept ID* field has a data type of AutoNumber, each record is sequentially numbered. The data in this field cannot be changed because it is generated by Access.

7 In the datasheet, next to **Department**, click the **Sort and Filter arrow** [▾], and then click **Sort A to Z**.

Sorting the records by the department name makes it easier to locate a department.

8 **Save** [💾] the table. **Close** the table. **Open** [»] the **Navigation Pane**.

Activity 4.04 | Copying and Appending Records to a Table

2.3.4, 2.2.3

In this Activity, you will copy the *4A City Council Members* table to use as the basis for a single employees table. You will then copy the data in the *4A Police Dept Employees* table and ***append***—add on—the data to the new employees table.

1 In the **Navigation Pane**, click **4A City Council Members**. On the **Home tab**, in the **Clipboard group**, click **Copy**. In the **Clipboard group**, click **Paste**.

Copy sends a duplicate version of the selected table to the Clipboard, leaving the original table intact. The ***Clipboard*** is a temporary storage area in Office that can store up to 24 items. ***Paste*** moves the copy of the selected table from the Clipboard into a new location. Because two tables cannot have the same name in a database, you must rename the pasted version.

2 In the displayed **Paste Table As** dialog box, under **Table Name**, type **Lastname Firstname 4A Employees** and then compare your screen with Figure 4.7.

Under Paste Options, you can copy the structure only, including all the items that are displayed in Design view—field names, data types, descriptions, and field properties. To make an exact duplicate of the table, click Structure and Data. To copy the data from the table into another existing table, click Append Data to Existing Table.

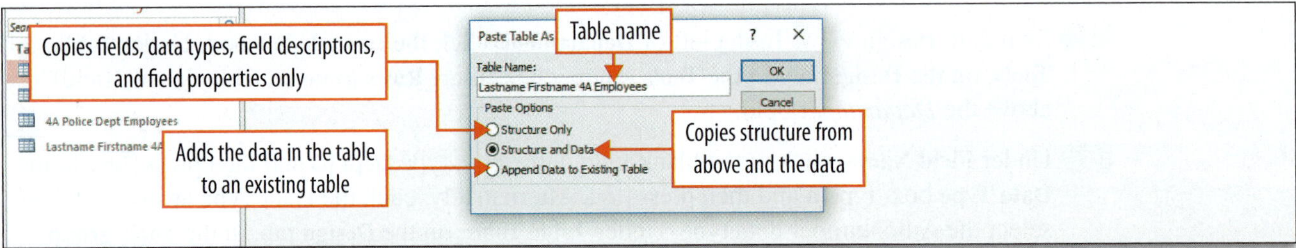

FIGURE 4.7

ANOTHER WAY There are two other methods to copy and paste selected tables:

- In the Navigation Pane, right-click the table, and from the displayed list, click Copy. To paste the table, right-click the Navigation Pane, and click Paste from the options listed.
- In the Navigation Pane, click the table, hold down Ctrl, and then press C. To paste the table, hold down Ctrl, and then press V.

3 Under **Paste Options**, be sure that the **Structure and Data** option button is selected, and then click **OK**. Notice that the copied table displays in the **Navigation Pane**. Resize the **Navigation Pane** so that all table names display entirely.

An exact duplicate of the *4A City Council Members* table is created. The *4A Employees* table will be used to build a table of all employees.

***More* Knowledge** **Add a Table Description**

A table description can also be added to the table properties to provide more information about the table. With the table displayed in Design view, under Table Tools, click the Design tab. In the Show/Hide group, click Property Sheet. Alternatively, in the Navigation Pane, right-click the table name, and then click Table Properties. On the Property sheet, click in the Description box, and type a description of the table. Close the Property Sheet.

4 Open the **4A Employees** table, and notice the duplicate records that were copied from the *4A City Council Members* table.

5 **Copy** the **4A Police Dept Employees** table, and then click **Paste**. In the **Paste Table As** dialog box, under **Table Name**, type **Lastname Firstname 4A Employees** Under **Paste Options**, click the **Append Data to Existing Table** option button, and then click **OK**. With the **4A Employees table** active, on the **Home tab**, in the **Records group**, click **Refresh All**, and then compare your screen with Figure 4.8.

The table to which you are appending the records must exist before using the Append option. Clicking the Refresh All button causes Access to refresh or update the view of the table, displaying the newly appended records. The *4A Employees* table then displays the two records for the police department employees—last names of *Farmer* and *Forbes*—and the records are arranged in ascending order by the first field. The records still exist in the *4A Police Dept Employees* table. If separate tables existed for the employees for each department, you would repeat these steps until every employee's record was appended to the *4A Employees* table.

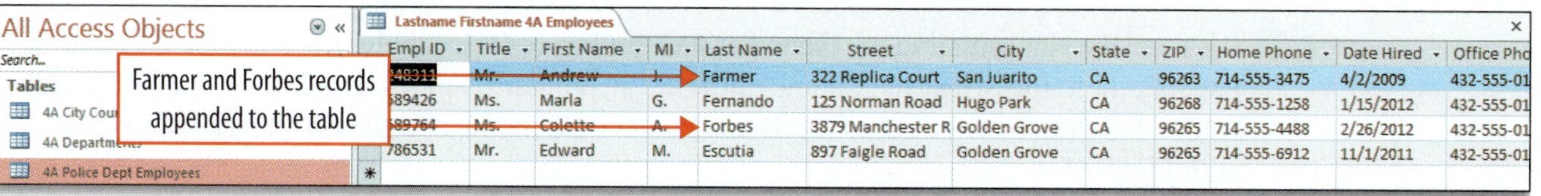

Access 2016, Windows 10, Microsoft Corporation

FIGURE 4.8

ALERT! **Does a message box display?**

If a message box displays stating that the Microsoft Office Access database engine could not find the object, you probably mistyped the name of the table in the Paste Table As dialog box. In the Navigation Pane, note the spelling of the table name to which you are copying the records. In the message box, click OK, and then in the Paste Table As dialog box, under Table Name, correctly type the table name.

6 **Close** [X] the table.

***More* Knowledge** **Append Records**

Access appends all records from the ***source table***—the table from which you are copying records—into the ***destination table***—the table to which the records are appended—as long as the field names and data types are the same in both tables. Exceptions include:

- If the source table does not have all of the fields that the destination table has, Access will still append the records, leaving the data in the missing fields blank in the destination table.
- If the source table has a field name that does not exist in the destination table or the data type is incompatible, the append procedure will fail.

Before performing an append procedure, carefully analyze the structure of both the source table and the destination table.

Activity 4.05 | Splitting a Table into Two Tables

2.3.4, 2.4.9

The *4A Employees* table stores personal data and office data about the employees. Although the table contains data about one subject—employees—you will split the table into two separate tables to keep the personal information separate from the office information.

1 Double-click the **4A Employees** table to open it in **Datasheet** view. **Close** [«] the **Navigation Pane**. Click the **File tab**, and then in **Backstage** view, click **Save As**. Under File Types, double-click **Save Object As**.

2 In the **Save As** dialog box, in the **Save to** box, type **Lastname Firstname 4A Employees Office** Notice the *As* box displays Table, and then click **OK**. Using the technique you just practiced, create a copy of the open table named **Lastname Firstname 4A Employees Personal**

These two new tables will be used to split the *4A Employees* table into two separate tables, one storing personal data and the other storing office data.

3 In the **4A Employees Personal** table, scroll to the right, if necessary, to display the **Date Hired**, **Office Phone**, **Position**, **Office Email**, and **Notes** fields. Select all five fields. On the **Home tab**, in the **Records group**, click **Delete**. In the displayed message box, click **Yes** to permanently delete the fields and data.

Because these fields contain office data, they are deleted from the *4A Employees Personal* table. These fields will be stored in the *4A Employees Office* table.

4 Select the **Title**, **First Name**, **MI**, and **Last Name** fields, and then delete the fields. **Close** [X] the table.

The fields you deleted are stored in the *4A Employees Office* table. You have deleted redundant data from the *4A Employees Personal* table.

5 **Open** [»] the **Navigation Pane**. Open the **4A Employees Office** table. **Close** [«] the **Navigation Pane**. Point to the **Street** field name until the [⬇] pointer displays. Hold down the left mouse button and drag to the right to the **Home Phone** field name, and then compare your screen with Figure 4.9.

Five fields are selected and will be deleted from this table. This is duplicate data that exists in the *4A Employees Personal* table. The *Empl ID* field will be the common field between the two tables.

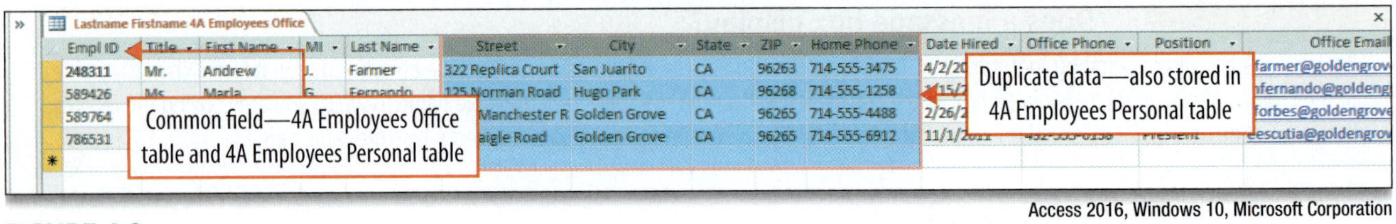

Common field—4A Employees Office table and 4A Employees Personal table
Duplicate data—also stored in 4A Employees Personal table
Access 2016, Windows 10, Microsoft Corporation

FIGURE 4.9

6 Delete the selected fields and data from the table.

The *4A Employees Office* table now stores only office data about the employees and can be linked to the *4A Employees Personal* table through the common field, *Empl ID*.

7 Click the **Position** field name. Under **Table Tools**, on the **Fields tab**, in the **Add & Delete group**, click **Number**.

A blank field is inserted between the *Position* field and the *Office Email* field, and it holds numeric data. Because this field will be used to link to the *4A Departments Revised* Dept ID field, which has a data type of AutoNumber, this field must use a data type of Number, even though it will not be used in a calculation.

8 The default name *Field1* is currently selected; type **Dept** to replace it and name the new field. Press [Enter].

9 **Open** [»] the **Navigation Pane**. Open the **4A Departments Revised** table.

The *4A Departments Revised* table opens in Datasheet view, and the records are sorted in ascending order by the *Department* field.

10 Locate the **Dept ID** for the **City Police** department. On the **tab row**, click the **4A Employees Office tab** to make the table active. In the record for *Andrew Farmer*, enter the City Police Dept ID **14** in the **Dept** field. Press [↓] two times. In the third record, for **Colette Forbes**, type **14**

11 Using the techniques you just practiced, find the **Dept ID** for the **City Council** department, and then enter that number in the **Dept** field for the second and fourth records in the **4A Employees Office** table. Compare your screen with Figure 4.10.

The *Dept* field is a common field with the *Dept ID* field in the *4A Departments Revised* table and will be used to link or join the two tables.

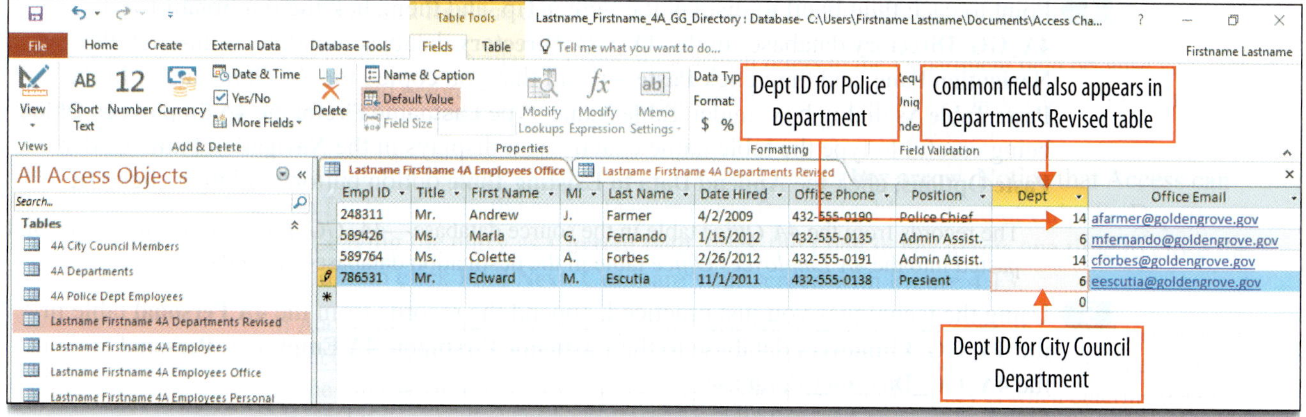

Access 2016, Windows 10, Microsoft Corporation

FIGURE 4.10

12 On the **tab row**, right-click any table tab, and then click **Close All**.

Activity 4.06 | Appending Records from Another Database

2.3.4

Additional employee records are stored in another database. In this Activity, you will open a second database to copy and paste records from tables in the second database to tables in the *4A_GG_Directory* database.

1 Point to the **Start** button in the lower-left corner of your screen, and then click one time to display the menu. Click **All Apps** to display your program list, and then click **Access 2016** to open a second instance of Access.

2 On the left side of the Access startup window, at the bottom, click **Open Other Files**. Under **Open**, click **Browse**. In the **Open** dialog box, navigate to the location where the student data files for this chapter are saved. Locate and open the **a04A_GG_Employees** file. Display **Backstage** view, click **Save As**, and save the database as **Lastname_Firstname_4A_GG_Employees** in your **Access Chapter 4** folder.

3 In the **4A_GG_Employees** database window, in the **Navigation Pane**, right-click **4A Office**, and then click **Copy**. Click the **Access** in the taskbar to see two instances of Access open. Compare your screen with Figure 4.11.

Each time you start Access, you open an ***instance*** of it. Two instances of Access are open, and each instance displays in the taskbar.

You cannot open multiple databases in one instance of Access. If you open a second database in the same instance, Access closes the first database. You can, however, open multiple instances of Access that display different databases. The number of times you can start Access at the same time is limited by the amount of your computer's available RAM.

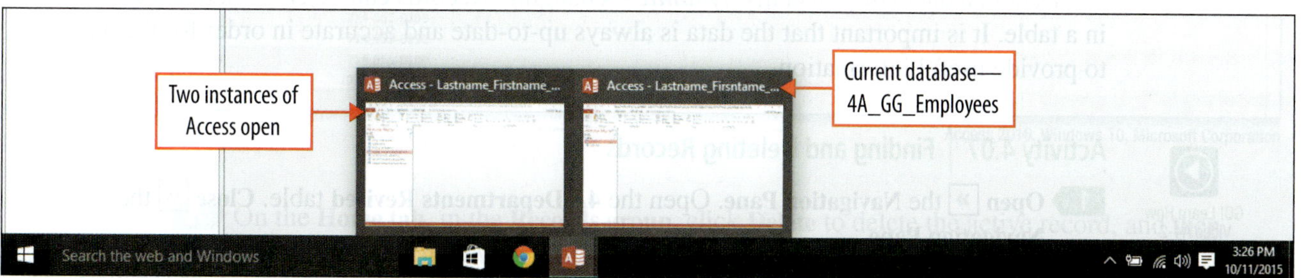

Access 2016, Windows 10, Microsoft Corporation

FIGURE 4.11

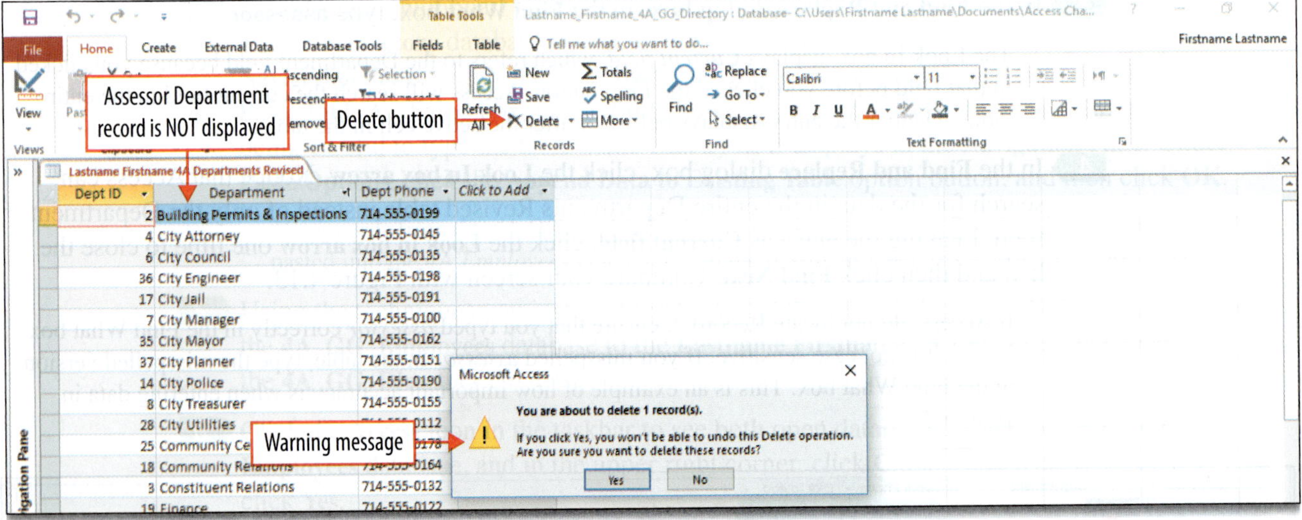

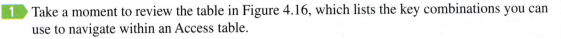

FIGURE 4.15

ANOTHER WAY There are two other methods to delete selected records in a table:

- On the selected record, right-click and then click Delete Record.
- From the keyboard, press Delete.

8 In the message box, click **Yes** to confirm the deletion.

The record holding information for *Assessor* no longer displays in the table; it has been permanently deleted from the table, and will no longer display in any other objects that were created using the Departments Revised table. The record number of Dept ID 2—Building Permits & Inspections—is now record 2 and is the current record.

More Knowledge **Why the Dept ID Field Data Did Not Renumber Sequentially**

You added the Dept ID field with an AutoNumber data type. Because of this, when data is entered into the table, Dept ID is automatically numbered sequentially, and those numbers are not changed as records are added, deleted, or modified.

Activity 4.08 | Finding and Modifying Records

1.3.1, 2.3.1, 2.3.6

When data needs to be changed or updated, you must locate and modify the record with the data. Recall that you can move among records in a table using the navigation buttons at the bottom of the window and that you can use Find to locate specific data. Other navigation methods include using keys on the keyboard and using the Search box in the navigation area.

1 Take a moment to review the table in Figure 4.16, which lists the key combinations you can use to navigate within an Access table.

4 ACCESS

KEY COMBINATIONS FOR NAVIGATING A TABLE	
KEYSTROKE	MOVEMENT
↑	Moves the selection up one record at a time.
↓	Moves the selection down one record at a time.
PageUp	Moves the selection up one screen at a time.
PageDown	Moves the selection down one screen at a time.
Ctrl + Home	Moves the selection to the first field in the table or the beginning of the selected field.
Ctrl + End	Moves the selection to the last field in the table or the end of the selected field.
Tab	Moves the selection to the next field in the table.
Shift + Tab	Moves the selection to the previous field in the table.
Enter	Moves the selection to the next field in the table.

FIGURE 4.16

2 On the keyboard, press ↓ to move the selection down one record. Record 3—*City Attorney*—is now the current record.

3 On the keyboard, hold down Ctrl, and then press Home to move to the first field of the first record in the table—Dept ID *1*.

4 In the navigation area, click **Next record** ▶ six times to navigate to Record 7—Dept ID 7.

5 On the keyboard, hold down Ctrl, and then press End to move to the last field in the last record in the table—Dept Phone *714-555-0175*.

6 On the keyboard, hold down Shift, and then press Tab to move to the previous field in the same record in the table—*Waste Management* in the Department field.

7 In the navigation area, click in the **Search** box. In the **Search** box, type **b**

Record 2 is selected, and the letter *B* in *Building Permits & Inspections* is highlighted. Search found the first occurrence of the letter *b*. It is not necessary to type capital letters in the Search box; Access will locate the words regardless of capitalization.

8 Click in the **Search** box again, select the existing text, and type **sani**

Record 30 is selected, and the letters *Sani* in *Sanitation* are highlighted. Search found the first occurrence of the letters *sani*. This is the record that needs to be modified. It is not necessary to type an entire word into the Search box to locate a record containing that word.

9 In the Department field box, double-click the word *Sanitation* to select it. Type **Trash Pickup** to replace the current entry. The Small Pencil icon in the Record Selector box means that the record is being edited and has not yet been saved. Press ↓ to move to the next record and save the change.

If you must edit part of a name, drag through letters or words to select them. You can then type the new letters or words over the selection to replace the text without having to press Delete or Backspace.

10 In the field name row, next to **Department**, click the **Sort and Filter arrow** [▾], and then click **Sort A to Z**.

Sorting the records by the department name again is necessary because a department changed its name.

11 **Save** [🖫] and **Close** [×] the table. **Open** [»] the **Navigation Pane**.

Activity 4.09 | Adding and Moving Fields in Design View and Datasheet View

1.3.5, 2.4.1, 2.2.1, 1.5.2

In this Activity, you will add and move fields in Design view and in Datasheet view.

1 Right-click the **4A Employees Personal** table to display a shortcut menu, and click **Design View** to open the table in Design view. **Close** [«] the **Navigation Pane**.

2 In the **Field Name** column, click the **Home Phone** Field Name box. Under **Table Tools**, on the **Design tab**, in the **Tools** group, click **Insert Rows**.

A new row is inserted above the *Home Phone* field. Recall that a row in Design view is a field.

3 In the empty **Field Name** box, type **Birthdate** and then press [Tab] to move to the **Data Type** column. Click the **Data Type arrow** to display the list of data types, and then click **Date/Time** to set the data type for this field. Compare your screen with Figure 4.17.

A new field to display the employee's date of birth has been created in the *Lastname Firstname 4A Employees Personal* table. An advantage of adding a field in Design view is that you name the field and set the data type when you insert the field.

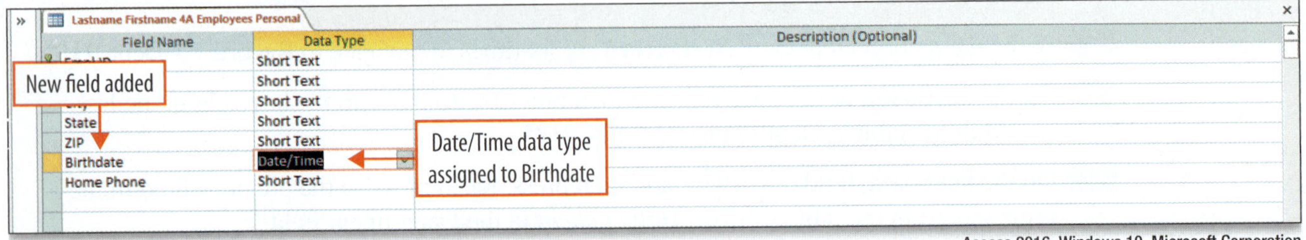

Access 2016, Windows 10, Microsoft Corporation

FIGURE 4.17

4 In the **Field Name** column, locate **Home Phone**, and then click the **Row Selector** box to select the field. Point to the **Row Selector** box to display the [➡] pointer. Hold down the left mouse button and drag the field up until you see a dark horizontal line following *Empl ID*, and then release the mouse button. Compare your screen with Figure 4.18.

Access 2016, Windows 10, Microsoft Corporation

FIGURE 4.18

5 Switch the **Lastname Firstname 4A Employees Personal** table to **Datasheet** view. In the displayed message box, click **Yes** to save the design changes.

The *Home Phone* field displays to the left of the *Street* field.

6 In the first record—248311—click in the **Birthdate** field. Using the techniques you have practiced, enter the birthdate for each record shown in the following list, pressing ↓ after each entry to move to the next record.

EMPL ID	BIRTHDATE
248311	**4/21/1955**
456789	**6/1/1964**
532268	**12/14/1984**
589426	**7/27/1990**
589764	**12/30/1972**
689444	**8/13/1980**
786531	**10/6/1966**

7 Apply **Best Fit** to all columns, ensuring that all of the field names and all of the field data display. View the table in **Print Preview**. On the **Print Preview tab**, in the **Page Size group**, click **Margins** and then click **Normal**. If you are instructed to submit this result, create a paper printout or PDF electronic image. On the **Print Preview tab**, in the **Close Preview group,** click **Close Print Preview**.

8 Close the **4A Employees Personal** table, saving changes. Open » the **Navigation Pane**. Open the **4A Employees Office** table in **Datasheet** view. Close « the **Navigation Pane**.

9 Select the **Office Phone** column. Under **Table Tools**, on the **Fields tab**, in the **Add & Delete group**, click **Short Text**. Alternatively, right-click the selected field and, from the shortcut menu, click Insert Field. A new column is inserted to the right of *Office Phone*.

10 If necessary, double-click **Field1**—the name of your field may differ if you have been experimenting with adding fields—to select the field name. Type **Work Site** and press Enter to save the field name.

11 In the first record—248311—click in the **Work Site** field. Using the techniques you have practiced, enter the work site for each record shown in the following list, pressing ↓ after each entry to move to the next record.

EMPL ID	WORK SITE
248311	**Justice Center**
456789	**City Hall**
532268	**B-121**
589426	**A-214**
589764	**Justice Center**
689444	**City Hall**
786531	**A-214**

12 Point to **Position** until the ↓ pointer displays, and then click one time to select the column. Hold down the left mouse button and drag the field left until you see a dark vertical line between *Date Hired* and *Office Phone*, and then release the mouse button. Compare your screen with Figure 4.19.

The *Position* field is moved after the *Date Hired* field and before the *Office Phone* field. If you move a field to the wrong position, select the field again, and then drag it to the correct position. Alternatively, on the Quick Access Toolbar, click Undo to place the field back in its previous position.

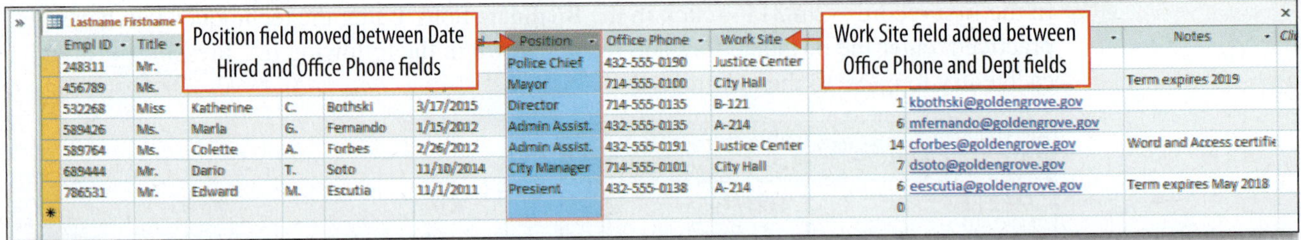

Access 2016, Windows 10, Microsoft Corporation

FIGURE 4.19

> **More Knowledge** **Hide/Unhide Fields in a Table**
>
> If you do not want a field to display in Datasheet view or on a printed copy of the table, you can hide the field.
>
> - Right-click the field name at the top of the column.
> - On the shortcut menu, click Hide Fields.
> - To display the field again, right-click any field name. On the shortcut menu, click Unhide Fields. In the dialog box, click the fields to unhide, and then click OK.

Activity 4.10 | Checking Spelling

In this Activity you will use the Spell Check feature to find spelling errors in your data. It is important to realize that Spell Check will not find all data entry mistakes, so you will need to use additional proofreading methods to ensure the accuracy of the data.

1 In the first record—248311—click in the **Empl ID** field. On the **Home tab**, in the **Records group**, click **Spelling** or press F7. Compare your screen with Figure 4.20.

The Spelling dialog box displays, and *Bothski* is highlighted because it is not in the Office dictionary. Many proper names will be ***flagged***—highlighted—by the spelling checker. Take a moment to review the options in the Spelling dialog box; these are described in Figure 4.21.

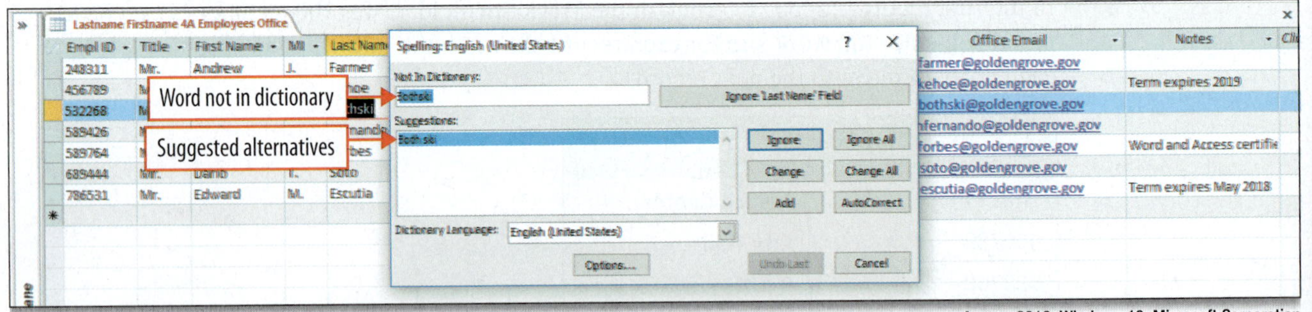

Access 2016, Windows 10, Microsoft Corporation

FIGURE 4.20

SPELLING DIALOG BOX BUTTONS	
BUTTON	**ACTION**
Ignore 'Last Name' Field	Ignores any words in the selected field.
Ignore	Ignores this one occurrence of the word but continues to flag other instances of the word.
Ignore All	Discontinues flagging any instance of the word anywhere in the table.
Change	Changes the identified word to the word highlighted under Suggestions.
Change All	Changes every instance of the word in the table to the word highlighted under Suggestions.
Add	Adds the highlighted word to a custom dictionary, which can be edited. This option does not change the built-in Office dictionary.
AutoCorrect	Adds the flagged word to the AutoCorrect list, which will subsequently correct the word automatically if misspelled in the future.
Options	Displays the Access Options dialog box.
Undo Last	Undoes the last change.

FIGURE 4.21

2 In the **Spelling** dialog box, click **Ignore 'Last Name' Field**.

Presient, which displays in the Position field, is flagged by the spelling checker. In the Spelling dialog box under Suggestions, *President* is highlighted.

3 In the **Spelling** dialog box, click **Change** to change the word from *Presient* to *President*.

When the spelling checker has completed checking the table and has found no other words missing from its dictionary, a message displays stating *The spelling check is complete*.

4 In the message box, click **OK**.

Objective 3 Change Data Types

GO! Learn How Video A4-3

Before creating a table, it is important to decide on the data types for the fields in the table. Setting a specific data type helps to ensure that the proper data will be entered into a field; for example, it is not possible to enter text into a field with a Currency data type. It is also important to choose a number data type when it is appropriate to avoid problems with calculations and sorting.

Activity 4.11 | Changing Data Types

1.3.5, 2.4.5, 1.5.2

Once data is entered into a field, caution must be exercised when changing the data type—existing data may not be completely visible or may be deleted. You can change the data type in either Datasheet view or Design view.

1 With the **4A Employees Office** table open, switch to **Design** view. Change the **Data Type** for the **Date Hired** field to **Date/Time**. Press F6 to move to the **Field Properties** pane at the bottom of the screen. Click in the **Format** property and select **Short Date**.

The data type of Date/Time is more appropriate for this field because it will display dates and restrict other entries. This will also allow the field to be accurately used in calculations, comparisons, and sorts.

PROJECT 4B

IT Tasks

PROJECT ACTIVITIES

Matthew Shoaf, director of the Information Technology department, has created a table to keep track of tasks that he has assigned to the employees in his department. In Activities 4.13 through 4.23, you will create a table in Design view that stores records about assigned tasks, modify its properties, and customize its fields. You will add features to the database table that will help to reduce data entry errors and that will make data entry easier. Your completed tables will look similar to the tables shown in Figure 4.24.

PROJECT FILES

If your instructor wants you to submit Project 4B in the MyITLab Grader system, log in to MyITLab, locate Grader Project 4B, and then download the files for this project.

For Project 4B, you will need the following file:
a04B_IT_Workload

You will save your database as:
Lastname_Firstname_4B_IT_Workload

PROJECT RESULTS

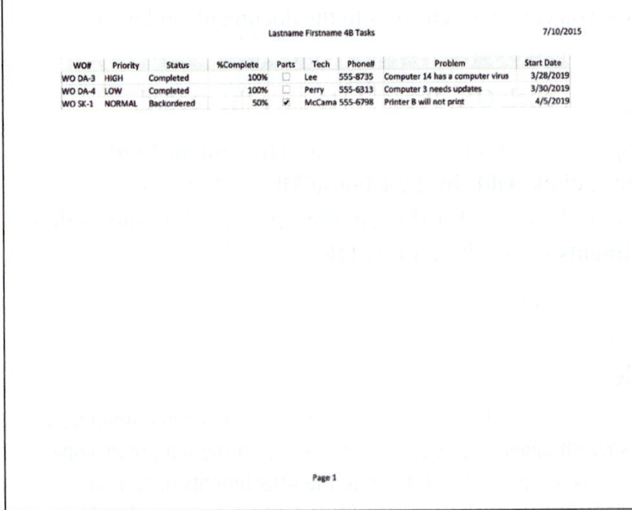

Lastname Firstname 4B Tasks 7/10/2015

WO#	Priority	Status	%Complete	Parts	Tech	Phone#	Problem	Start Date
WO DA-3	HIGH	Completed	100%	☐	Lee	555-8735	Computer 14 has a computer virus	3/28/2019
WO DA-4	LOW	Completed	100%	☐	Perry	555-6313	Computer 3 needs updates	3/30/2019
WO SK-1	NORMAL	Backordered	50%	☑	McCama	555-6798	Printer B will not print	4/5/2019

Page 1

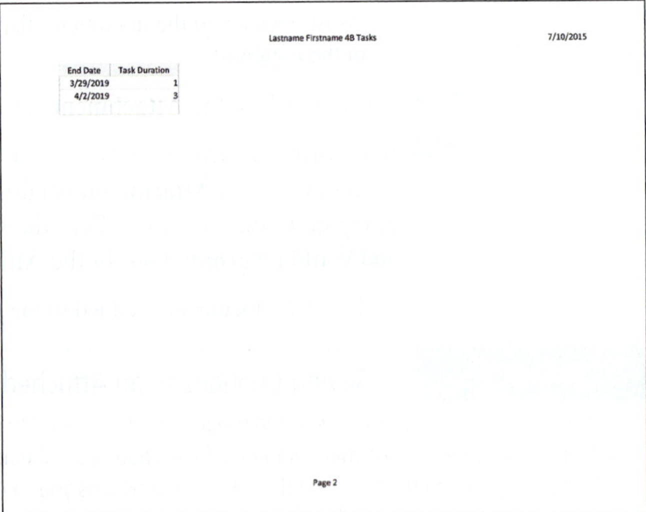

Lastname Firstname 4B Tasks 7/10/2015

End Date	Task Duration
3/29/2019	1
4/2/2019	3

Page 2

FIGURE 4.24 Project 4B IT Tasks

PROJECT RESULTS

In this project, using your own name, you will create the following database and object. Your instructor may ask you to submit printouts or PDF electronic images:

Lastname_Firstname_4B_IT_Workload	Database file
Lastname Firstname 4B Tasks	Table (2 pages)

4 ACCESS

Objective 5 Create a Table in Design View

Creating a table in Design view gives you the most control over the characteristics of the table and the fields. Most database designers use Design view to create tables, setting the data types and formats before entering any records. Design view is a good way to create a table when you know exactly how you want to set up your fields.

GO! Learn How
Video A4-5

Activity 4.13 | Creating a Table in Design View

ALERT!

To submit this as an autograded project, log into MyITLab and download the files for this project, and begin with those files instead of a04B_IT_Workload. For Project 4B using Grader, begin working with the database in Step 2. For Grader to award points accurately, when saving an object, do not include your Lastname Firstname at the beginning of the object name.

2.1.1, 2.4.1, 2.4.4, 2.4.3, 2.2.4

In this Activity, you will create a table to keep track of the tasks that the IT department will be completing.

1 **Start** Access. On the left side of the Access startup window, click **Open Other Files**. Under **Open**, click **Browse**. In the **Open** dialog box, navigate to the student data files for this chapter. Locate and open **a04B_IT_Workload** file. **Save** the database in your **Access Chapter 4** folder as **Lastname_Firstname_4B_IT_Workload**

2 If you did not add the **Access Chapter 4** folder to the Trust Center, enable the content. In the **Navigation Pane**, under **Tables**, rename **4B Employees** by adding **Lastname Firstname** to the beginning of the table name. **Close** « the **Navigation Pane**.

3 On the ribbon, click the **Create tab**. In the **Tables group**, click **Table Design** to open an empty table in Design view, and then compare your screen with Figure 4.25.

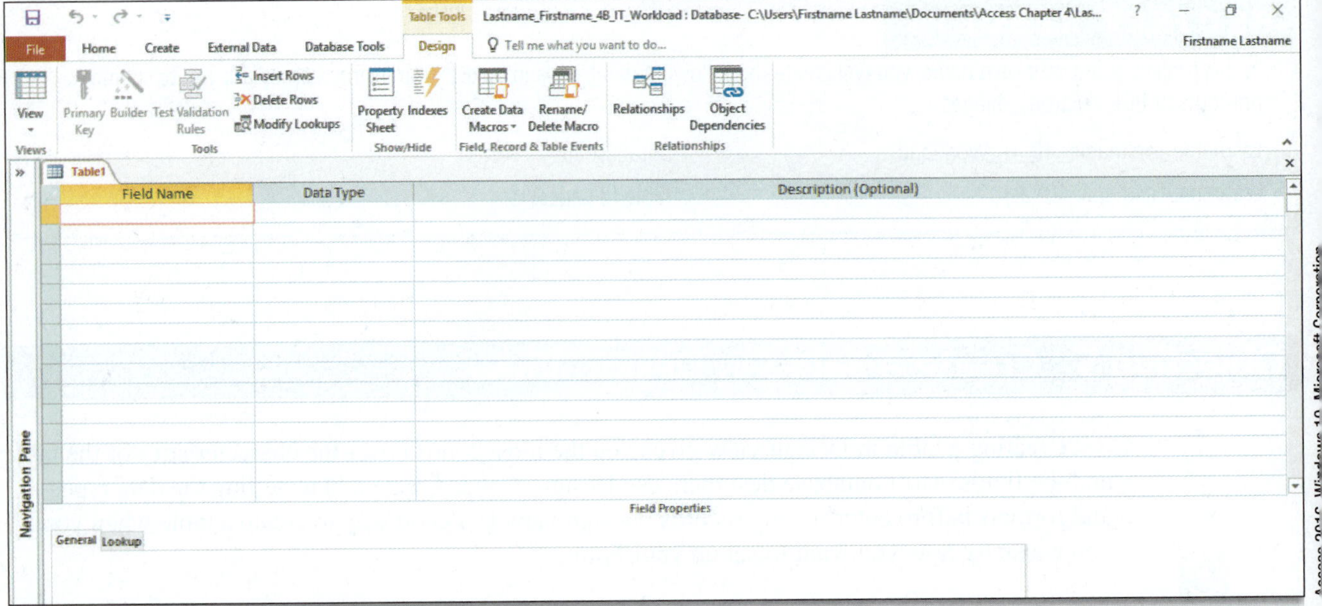

FIGURE 4.25

4 In the first **Field Name** box, type **WO#** press Tab, and then, under **Table Tools**, on the **Design tab**, in the **Tools group**, click **Primary Key**.

5 Click the **Data Type arrow** to display a list of data types, as shown in Figure 4.26. Take a moment to study the table in Figure 4.27 that describes all 12 possible choices.

In Design view, all the data types are displayed. In Datasheet view, the list depends on the data entered in the field and does not display several data types including AutoNumber, Calculated, and Lookup Wizard.

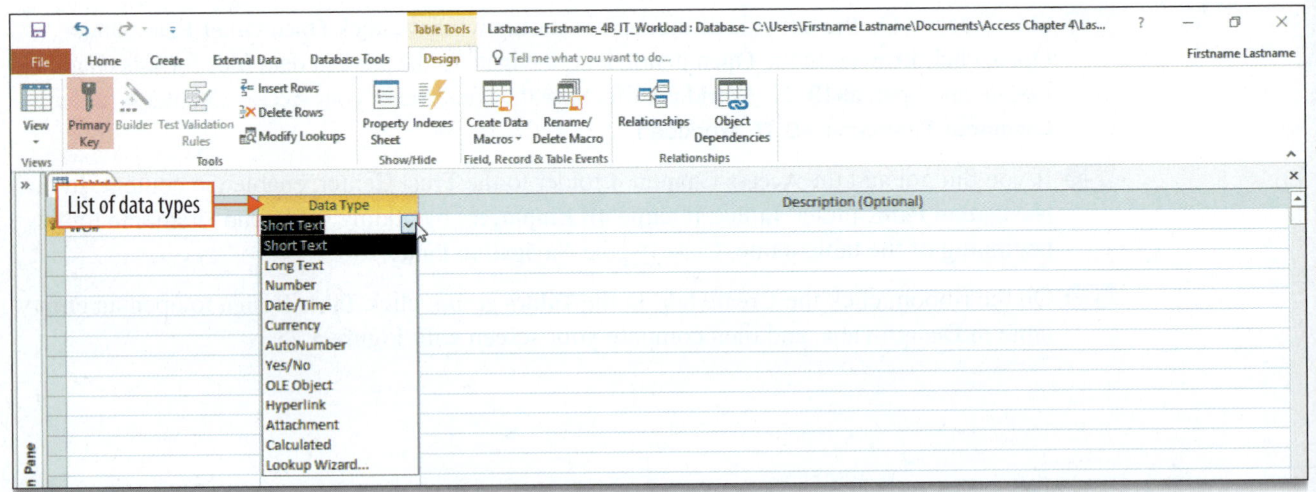

FIGURE 4.26

DATA TYPES		
DATA TYPE	**DESCRIPTION**	**EXAMPLE**
Short Text	Text or combinations of text and numbers; also, numbers that are not used in calculations. Limited to 255 characters or length set on field, whichever is less. Access does not reserve space for unused portions of the text field. This is the default data type.	An inventory item, such as towels, or a phone number or postal code that is not used in calculations and that may contain characters other than numbers
Long Text	Lengthy text or combinations of text and numbers that can hold up to 65,535 characters depending on the size of the database.	A description of a product
Number	Numeric data used in mathematical calculations with varying field sizes.	A quantity, such as 500
Date/Time	Date and time values for the years 100 through 9999.	An order date, such as 11/10/2018 3:30 p.m.
Currency	Monetary values and numeric data that can be used in mathematical calculations involving data with one to four decimal places. Accurate to 15 digits on the left side of the decimal separator and to 4 digits on the right side. Use this data type to store financial data and when you do not want Access to round values.	An item price, such as $8.50
AutoNumber	Available in Design view. A unique sequential or random number assigned by Access as each record is entered that cannot be updated.	An inventory item number, such as 1, 2, 3, or a randomly assigned employee number, such as 38527
Yes/No	Contains only one of two values—Yes/No, True/False, or On/Off. Access assigns 1 for all Yes values and 0 for all No values.	Whether an item was ordered—Yes or No
OLE Object	An object created by a program other than Access that is linked to or embedded in the table. *OLE* is an abbreviation for *object linking and embedding*, a technology for transferring and sharing information among programs. Stores up to two gigabytes of data (the size limit for all Access databases). Must have an OLE server registered on the server that runs the database. Should usually use Attachment data type instead.	A graphics file, such as a picture of a product, a sound file, a Word document, or an Excel spreadsheet stored as a bitmap image
Hyperlink	Web or email address.	An email address, such as dwalker@ityourway.com, or a Web page, such as http://www.ityourway.com
Attachment	Any supported type of file—images, spreadsheet files, documents, or charts. Similar to email attachments.	Same as OLE Object
Calculated	Available in Design view. Opens the Expression Builder to create an expression based on existing fields or numbers. Field must be designated as a Calculated field when it is inserted into the table; the expression can be edited in the Field Properties.	Adding two existing fields such as [field1]+[field2], or performing a calculation with a field and a number such as [field3]*.5
Lookup Wizard	Available in Design view. Not really a data type, but will display in the list of data types. Links to fields in other tables to display a list of data instead of having to manually type the data.	Link to another field in the same or another table

FIGURE 4.27

6 From the displayed list, click **Short Text**, and then press Tab to move to the **Description** box. In the **Description** box, type **Identification number assigned to task reported on work order form**

Field names should be short; use the description box to display more information about the contents of the field.

7 Press F6 to move to the **Field Properties** pane at the bottom of the screen. In the **Field Size** box, type **8** to replace the 255. Compare your screen with Figure 4.28.

Pressing F6 while in the Data Type column moves the insertion point to the first field property box in the Field Properties pane. Alternatively, click in the Field Size property box.

Recall that a field with a data type of Short Text can store up to 255 characters. You can change the field size to limit the number of characters that can be entered into the field to ensure accuracy. For example, if you use the two-letter state abbreviations for a state field, limit the size of the field to two characters. When entering a state in the field, you will be unable to type more than two characters.

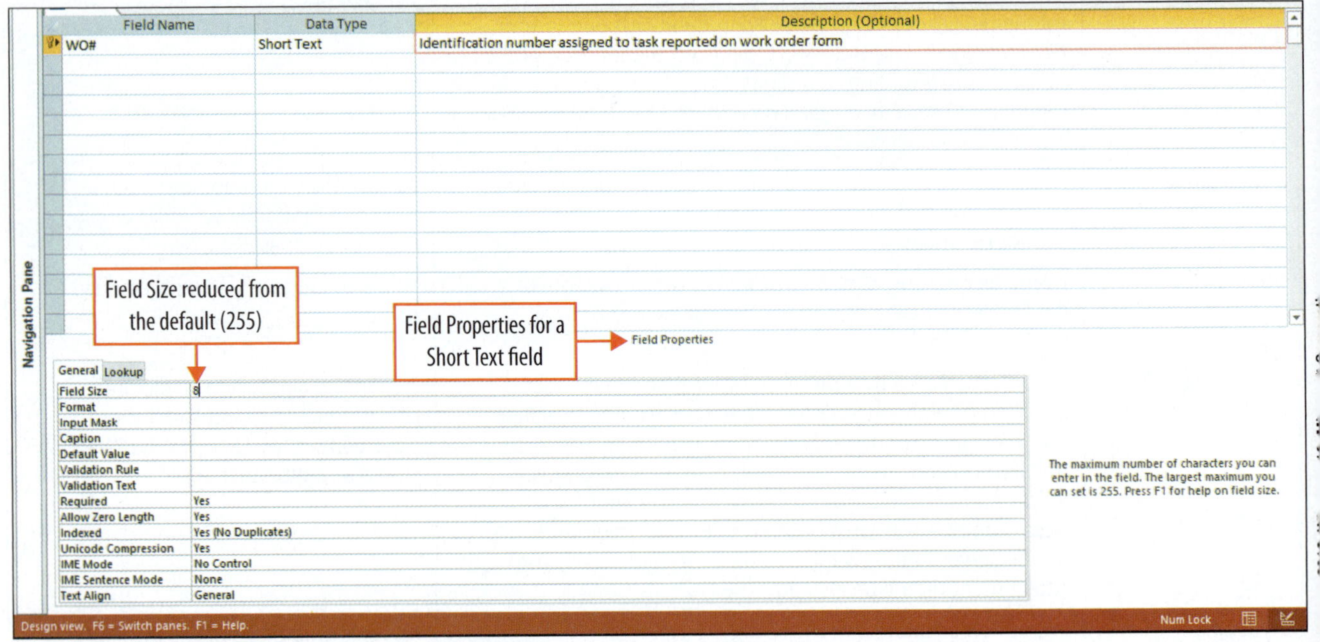

FIGURE 4.28

8 Click in the second **Field Name** box, type **Priority** and then press Tab twice to move to the **Description** box. Type **Indicate the priority level of this task** Press F6 to move to the **Field Properties** pane at the bottom of the screen. Click in the **Format** box and type **>**

Because Short Text is the default data type, you do not have to select it if it is the correct data type for the field. Additionally, if the field name is descriptive enough, the Description box is optional.

A greater than symbol (>) in the Format property box in a Text field converts all entries in the field to uppercase. Using a less than symbol (<) would force all entries to be lowercase.

More Knowledge **The Caption Property**

The Caption property is used to give a name to fields used on forms and reports. Many database administrators create short and abbreviated field names in tables. In a form or report based on the table, a more descriptive name is desired. The value in the Caption property is used in label controls on forms and reports instead of the field name. If the Caption property is blank, the field name is used in the label control. A caption can contain up to 2,048 characters.

9 In the third **Field Name** box, type **Status** and then press Tab three times to move to the next **Field Name** box.

10 In the fourth **Field Name** box, type **%Complete** Press Tab and then click the **Data Type arrow**. From the displayed list, click **Number**. Press Tab to move to the **Description** box, and then type **Percentage of the task that has been completed** Press F6 to move to the **Field Properties** pane. Click the **Field Size** property arrow and select **Single**. Click the **Format** property arrow and select **Percent**. Click the **Decimal Places** property arrow and select 0.

The data type of Number is appropriate for this field because it will display only the amount of a task that has been completed. Defining the number as a percent with zero decimal places further restricts the entries. This allows the field to be used accurately in calculations, comparisons, and sorts.

11 In the fifth **Field Name** box, type **Parts** Press Tab and then click the **Data Type arrow**. From the displayed list, click **Yes/No**. Press Tab to move to the **Description** box. Type **Click the field to indicate parts have been ordered to complete the task**

The data type of Yes/No is appropriate for this field because there are only two choices: parts are on order (yes) or parts are not on order (no). In Datasheet view, click the check box to indicate yes with a checkmark.

Activity 4.14 | Adding Fields to a Table in Design View

2.4.1, 2.4.4, 2.4.5

1 In the sixth **Field Name** box, type **Tech** and then press Tab three times to move to the next Field Name box.

2 In the seventh **Field Name** box, type **Phone#** Press Tab two times to move to the **Description** box, type **Enter as ###-####** and then change the **Field Size** property to **8**

3 Click in the eighth **Field Name** box, and then type **Problem** Press Tab and then click the **Data Type arrow**. From the displayed list, click **Long Text**. Press Tab to move to the **Description** box, and then type **Description of the IT problem**

The data type of Long Text is appropriate for this field because it may require more than 255 characters and spaces to effectively describe the IT problem that needs attention.

4 Click in the ninth **Field Name** box, and then type **Start Date** Press Tab and then click the **Data Type arrow**. From the displayed list, click **Date/Time**.

The data type of Date/Time is appropriate for this field because it will only display date information. Because Date/Time is a type of number, this field can be used in calculations.

5 Click in the tenth **Field Name** box and then type **End Date** Press Tab and then click the **Data Type arrow**. From the displayed list, click **Date/Time**.

6 Click in the eleventh **Field Name** box and then type **Task Duration** Press Tab and then click the **Data Type arrow**. From the displayed list, click **Calculated**, and the **Expression Builder** dialog box displays. In the **Expression Builder** dialog box, type **[End Date]-[Start Date]** and then compare your screen to Figure 4.29.

The data type of Calculated is appropriate for this field because the entry is calculated with an expression—subtracting *Start Date* from *End Date*. The *Task Duration* field will remain blank if the task has not yet been completed; nothing can be entered in the field.

The ***Expression Builder*** is a feature used to create formulas (expressions) in calculated fields, query criteria, form and report controls and table validation rules. An expression can be entered using field names or numbers, and the only spaces included are those that separate words in field names. Any time a field name is used in the expression, it should be enclosed in square brackets. An existing field cannot be changed to a Calculated data type; it must be assigned when the field is added to the table. It cannot be changed to a Calculated data type later without deleting the field and reinserting it. The expression can be edited in the Field Properties.

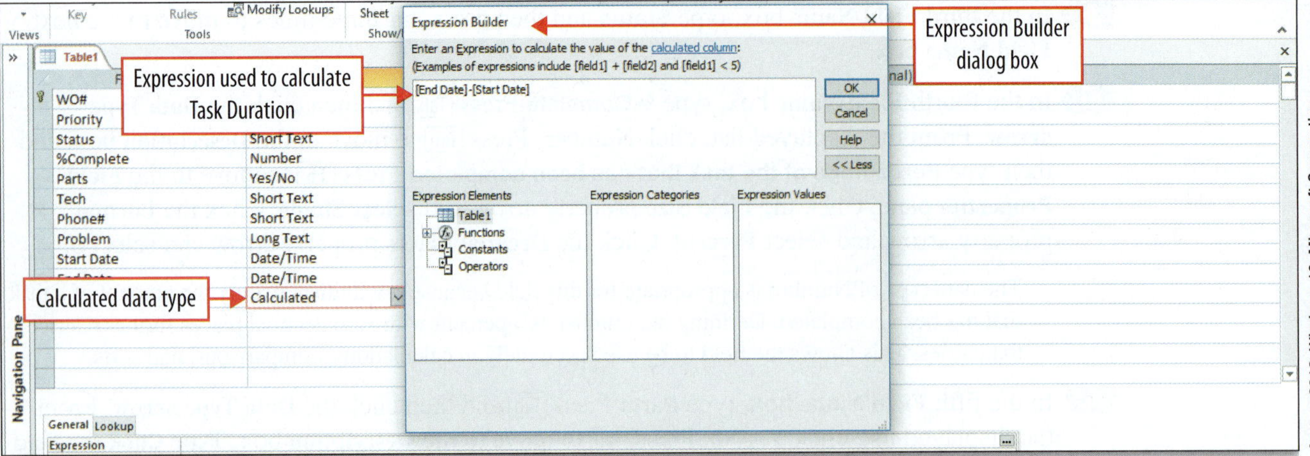

FIGURE 4.29

7 Click **OK**. Click in the **Description** box, and type **Number of days necessary to complete the task** Press F6 to move to the **Field Properties** pane at the bottom of the screen. Click in the **Result Type** property arrow, and then select **Single**.

8 On the **Quick Access** toolbar, click **Save**. In the **Save As** dialog box, type **Lastname Firstname 4B Tasks** and then click **OK**. Switch to **Datasheet** view to view the table you have just created; there are no records in the table yet.

Objective 6 Create a Lookup Field

GO! Learn How Video A4-6

Creating a ***lookup field*** can restrict the data entered in a field because the person entering data selects that data from a list retrieved from another table, query, or list of entered values. The choices can be displayed in a ***list box***—a box containing a list of choices—or a ***combo box***—a box that is a combination of a list box and a text box. You can create a lookup field by using the Lookup Wizard or manually by setting the field's lookup field properties. Whenever possible, use the Lookup Wizard because it simplifies the process, ensures consistent data entry, automatically populates the associated field properties, and creates the needed table relationships.

Activity 4.15 | Creating a Lookup Field Based on a List of Values

2.4.5

In this Activity, you will create a lookup field for the Status field.

1 With the **4B Tasks** table open, switch to **Design** view. In the **Status** field, click in the **Data Type** box, and then click the **arrow**. From the displayed list of data types, click **Lookup Wizard**.

2 In the first **Lookup Wizard** dialog box, click the **I will type in the values that I want** option button, and then click **Next**. Compare your screen with Figure 4.30.

The first step of the Lookup Wizard enables you to choose whether you want Access to locate the information from another table or query or whether you would like to type the information to create a list.

The second step enables you to select the number of columns you want to include in the lookup field. The values are typed in the grid, and you can adjust the column width of the displayed list.

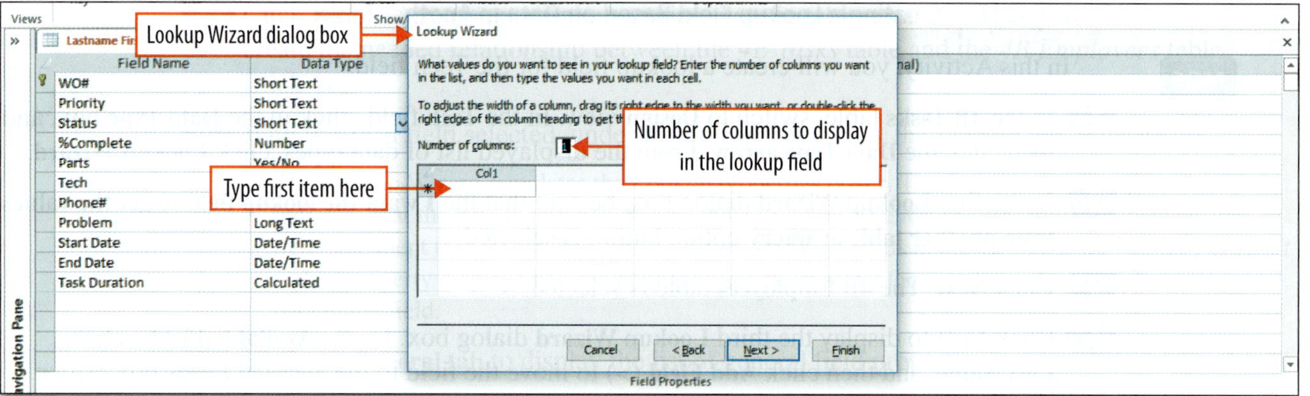

FIGURE 4.30

Access 2016, Windows 10, Microsoft Corporation

3 Be sure the number of columns is **1**. Under **Col1**, click in the first row, type **Not Started** and then press Tab or ↓ to save the first item.

If you mistakenly press Enter, the next dialog box of the wizard displays. If that happens, click the Back button.

4 Type the following data, and then compare your screen with Figure 4.31.

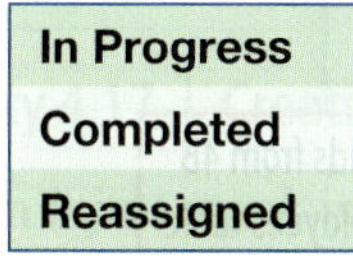

In Progress
Completed
Reassigned

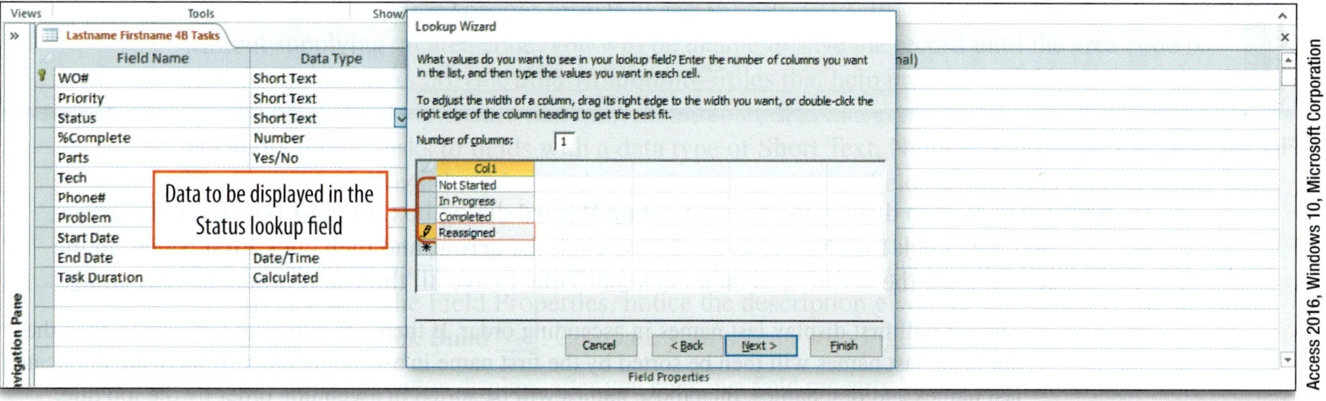

FIGURE 4.31

Access 2016, Windows 10, Microsoft Corporation

5 Double-click the right edge of Col1 to apply Best Fit, adjusting the column width so all entries display, if necessary, and then click **Next**. In the final dialog box, click **Finish**. With the **Status** field selected, under **Field Properties**, click the **Lookup tab**.

The Lookup Wizard populates the Lookup property boxes. The *Row Source Type* property indicates that the data is retrieved from a Value List, a list that you created. The *Row Source* property displays the data you entered in the list. The *Limit to List* property displays No, so you can type alternative data in the field if necessary.

6 **Save** the changes, and switch to **Datasheet** view. Click the **Status** field in the first record, and then click the **arrow** to view the lookup list. Press Esc to return to a blank field.

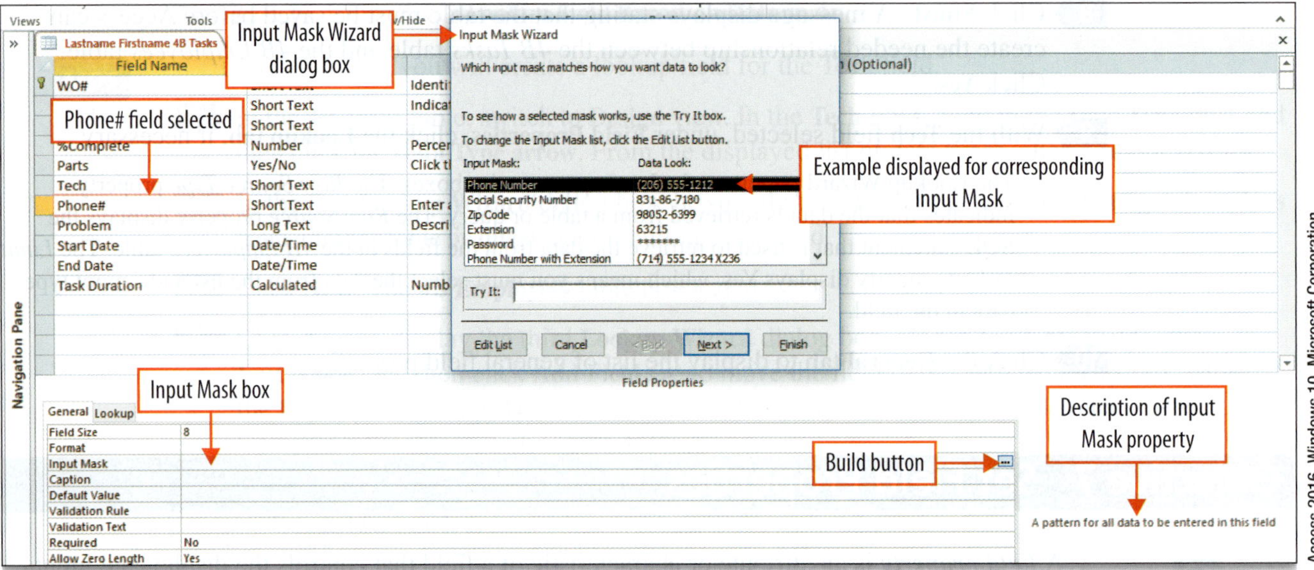

FIGURE 4.33

2 In the displayed **Input Mask Wizard** dialog box, with **Phone Number** selected, click **Next**, and then compare your screen with Figure 4.34. In the **Input Mask Wizard** dialog box, notice the entry in the **Input Mask** box.

A *0* indicates a required digit; a *9* indicates an optional digit or space. The area code is enclosed in parentheses, and a hyphen (-) separates the three-digit prefix from the four-digit number. The exclamation point (!) causes the input mask to fill in from left to right. The Placeholder character indicates that the field will display an underscore character (_) for each digit before data is entered in Datasheet view.

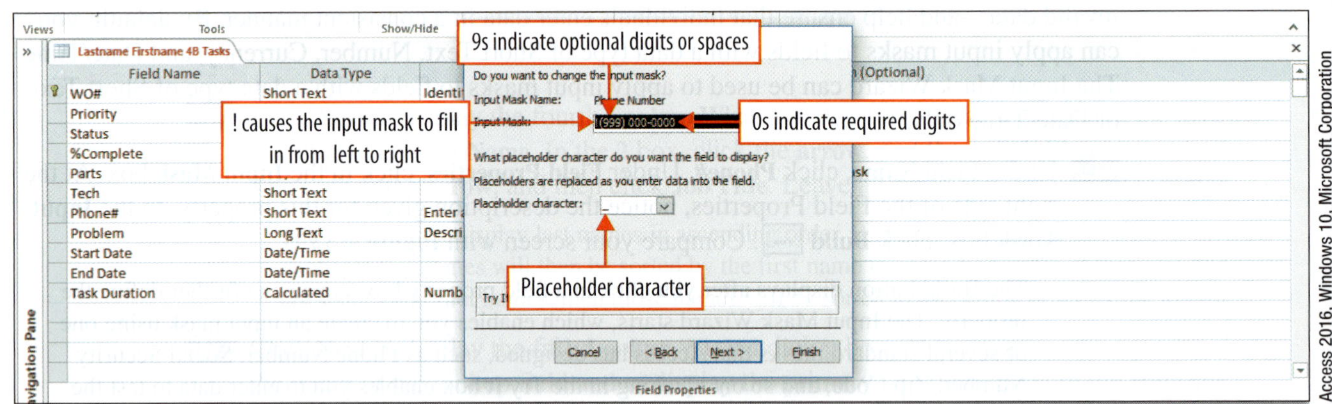

FIGURE 4.34

3 In the **Input Mask Wizard** dialog box, click **Back**, and then click **Edit List**.

The Customize Input Mask Wizard dialog box displays, which enables you to edit the default input mask or add an input mask.

4 In the **Customize Input Mask Wizard** dialog box, in the navigation area, click **New (blank) record** [icon]. In the **Description** box, type **Local Phone Number** Press Tab to move to the **Input Mask** box, and type **!000-0000** Press Tab to move to the **Placeholder** box, and type **#** Press Tab to move to the **Sample Data** box, and type **555-2090** Compare your screen with Figure 4.35.

Because tasks are assigned to local personnel, the area code is unnecessary. Instead of displaying an underscore as the placeholder in the field, the number sign (#) displays.

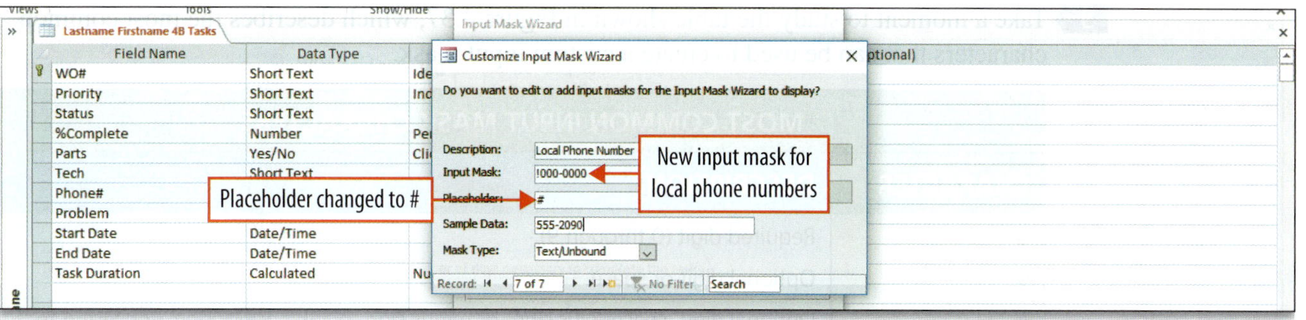

Access 2016, Windows 10, Microsoft Corporation

FIGURE 4.35

5 In the **Customize Input Mask Wizard** dialog box, click **Close**.

The newly created input mask for Local Phone Number displays below the input mask for Password.

6 Under **Input Mask**, click **Local Phone Number**, and then click **Next**. Click the **Placeholder character arrow** to display other symbols that can be used as placeholders. Be sure that # is displayed as the placeholder character, and then click **Next**.

After creating an input mask to be used with the Input Mask Wizard, you can change the placeholder character for individual fields.

7 The next wizard screen enables you to decide how you want to store the data. Be sure that the **Without the symbols in the mask, like this** option button is selected, as shown in Figure 4.36.

Saving the data without the symbols makes the database size smaller.

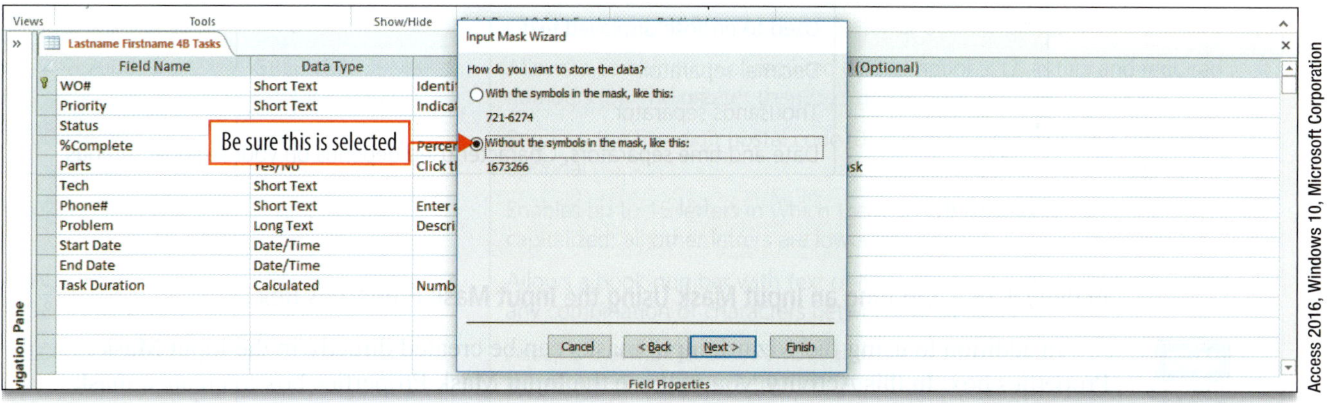

Access 2016, Windows 10, Microsoft Corporation

FIGURE 4.36

8 Click **Next**. In the final wizard screen, click **Finish**. Notice that the entry in the *Input Mask* box displays as *!000\-0000;;#*. **Save** the table.

Recall that the exclamation point (!) fills the input mask from left to right, and the 0s indicate required digits. The two semicolons (;) are used by Access to separate the input mask into three sections. This input mask has data in the first section—the 0s—and in the third section—the placeholder of #.

The second and third sections of an input mask are optional. The second section, which is not used in this input mask, determines whether the literal characters—in this case, the hyphen (-)—are stored with the data. A *0* in the second section will store the literal characters; a *1* or leaving it blank stores only the characters entered in the field. The third section of the input mask indicates the placeholder character—in this case, the # sign. If you want to leave the fill-in spaces blank instead of using a placeholder, type " "—there is a space between the quotation marks—in the third section.

3 Switch to **Datasheet** view, and click **Yes** to save the table. In the **WO#** field in the first record, type **da3** and then press Tab or Enter to go to the next field.

The input mask adds the WO and a space. The *da* is automatically capitalized, and the hyphen is inserted before the 3.

4 In the **Priority** field, type **High** and then press Tab or Enter to go to the next field.

5 In the **Status** field, type **C** to display the **Completed** item in the lookup list, and then press Tab or Enter to move to the next field.

6 In the **%Complete** field, type **100** and then press Tab or Enter three times to bypass the **Parts** and **Tech** fields.

Leaving the Yes/No field blank assigns a No value in the Parts field, so parts are not on order for this task.

7 In the **Phone#** field, type **5558735** and then press Tab or Enter to move to the next field.

8 In the **Problem** field, type **Computer 14 has a computer virus** and then press Tab or Enter to move to the next field.

9 In the **Start Date** field, type **3/28/2019** and then press Tab or Enter to move to the next field.

10 In the **End Date** field, type **3/29/19** and then press Tab or Enter to move to the **Task Duration** field. Notice the calculated field now displays a *1*. Apply **Best Fit** to adjust the width of all columns, and then compare your screen with Figure 4.40.

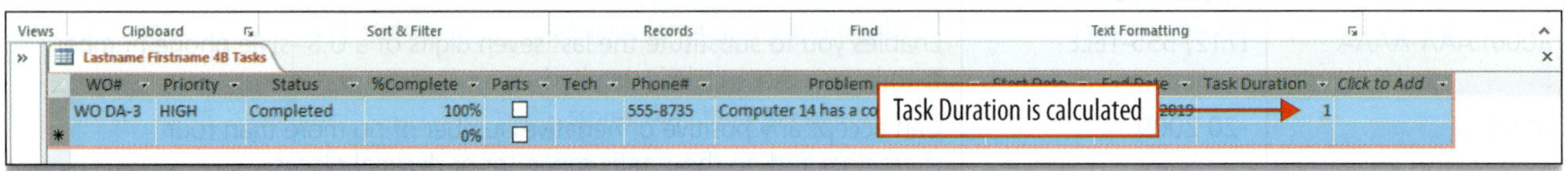

Access 2016, Windows 10, Microsoft Corporation

FIGURE 4.40

11 Switch to **Design** view. The data entry is automatically saved when the record is complete.

Activity 4.19 | Specifying a Required Field

Recall that if a table has a field designated as the primary key field, an entry for the field is ***required***; it cannot be left empty. You can set this requirement on other fields in either Design view or Datasheet view. In this Activity, you will require an entry in the Status field. Use the Required field property to ensure that a field contains data and is not left blank.

1 Under **Field Name**, click in the **Status** field, and then under **Field Properties**, click in the **Required** box. Click the **Required arrow**, and then compare your screen with Figure 4.41.

Only Yes and No options display in the list.

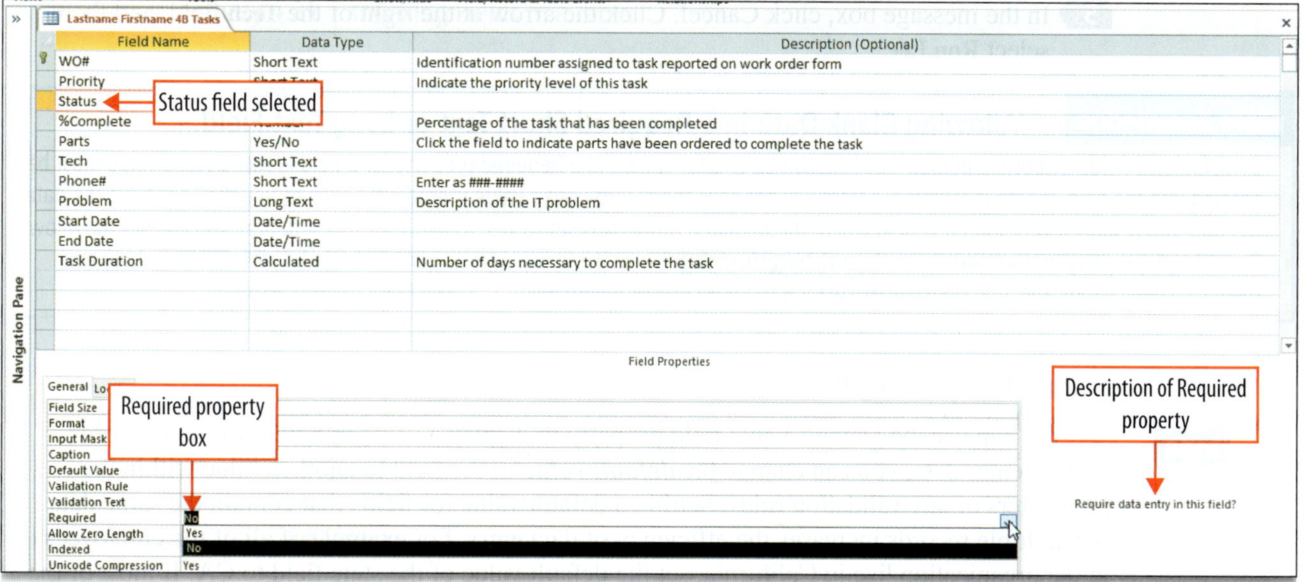

FIGURE 4.41 Access 2016, Windows 10, Microsoft Corporation

2 Click **Yes** to require an individual to enter the status for each record. **Save** the changes to the table.

A message displays stating that data integrity rules have been changed and that existing data may not be valid for the new rules. This message displays when you change field properties where data exists in the field. Clicking Yes requires Access to examine the field in every record to see if the existing data meets the new data validation rule. For each record Access finds in which data does not meet the new validation rule, a new message displays that prompts you to keep testing with the new setting. You also can revert to the prior validation setting and continue testing or cancel testing of the data.

3 If the message displays, click **No**. Switch to **Datasheet** view. Click in the **Status** field. Under **Table Tools**, on the **Fields tab**, in the **Field Validation group**, notice that the **Required** check box is selected.

4 In the table, click in the **Tech** field. On the **Fields tab**, in the **Field Validation group**, click the **Required** check box. Compare your screen with Figure 4.42.

A message displays stating that the existing data violates the Required property for the Tech field because the field is currently blank.

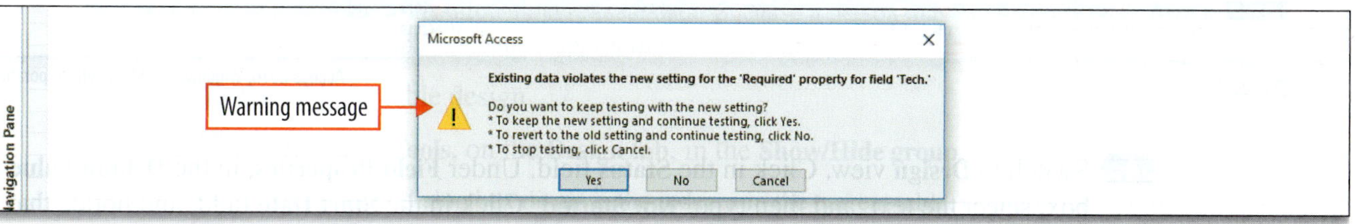

FIGURE 4.42 Access 2016, Windows 10, Microsoft Corporation

Objective 8 Create Data Validation Rules and Validation Text

GO! Learn How Video A4-8

You have practiced different techniques to help ensure that data entered into a field is valid. Data types restrict the type of data that can be entered into a field. Field sizes control the number of characters that can be entered into a field. Field properties further control how data is entered into a field, including the use of input masks to require individuals to enter data in a specific way.

Another way to ensure the accuracy of data is by using the Validation Rule property. A ***validation rule*** is an expression that precisely defines the range of data that will be accepted in a field. An ***expression*** is a combination of functions, field values, constants, and operators that brings about a result. ***Validation text*** is the error message that displays when an individual enters a value prohibited by the validation rule.

Activity 4.22 | Creating Data Validation Rules and Validation Text

2.4.2

In this Activity, you will create data validation rules and validation text for the %Complete field, the Start Date field, and the Priority field.

1 Under **Field Name**, click **%Complete**. Under **Field Properties**, click in the **Validation Rule** box, and then click **Build** [...].

The Expression Builder dialog box displays. Recall that the Expression Builder is a feature used to create formulas (expressions) in query criteria, form and report controls, and table validation rules. Take a moment to study the table shown in Figure 4.45, which describes the operators that can be used in building expressions.

OPERATORS USED IN EXPRESSIONS		
OPERATOR	**FUNCTION**	**EXAMPLE**
Not	Tests for values NOT meeting a condition.	**Not** > 10 (the same as <=10)
In	Tests for values equal to existing members in a list.	**In** ("High","Normal","Low")
Between...And	Tests for a range of values, including the values on each end.	**Between** 0 **And** 100 (the same as >=0 **And** <=100)
Like	Matches pattern strings in Text and Memo fields.	**Like** "Car*"
Is Not Null	Requires individuals to enter values in the field. If used in place of the Required field, you can create Validation Text that better describes what should be entered in the field.	**Is Not Null** (the same as setting Required property to Yes)
And	Specifies that all of the entered data must fall within the specified limits.	>=#01/01/2016# **And** <=#03/01/2016# (date must be between 01/01/2016 and 03/01/2016). Can use And to combine validation rules; for example, **Not** "USA" **And Like** "U*"
Or	Specifies that one of many entries can be accepted.	"High" **Or** "Normal" **Or** "Low"
<	Less than.	<100
<=	Less than or equal to.	<=100
>	Greater than.	>0
>=	Greater than or equal to.	>=0
=	Equal to.	=Date()
<>	Not equal to.	<>#12/24/53#

FIGURE 4.45

4 ACCESS

2 In the upper box of the **Expression Builder** dialog box, type **>=0 and <=1** In the **Expression Builder** dialog box, click **OK**.

The %Complete field has a data type of Number and is formatted as a percent. Recall that the Format property changes the way the stored data displays. To convert the display of a number to a percent, Access multiplies the value by 100 and appends the percent sign (%). Therefore, 100% is stored as 1—Access multiplies 1 by 100, resulting in 100. A job that is halfway completed—50%—has the value stored as .5 because .5 times 100 equals 50.

ANOTHER WAY When using the expression builder to create an expression, you can either type the entire expression or, on the small toolbar in the dialog box, click an existing button, such as the > button, to insert operators into the expression.

3 Click in the **Validation Text** box, and then type **Enter a value between 0 and 100** so that the percentages are reflected accurately. Compare your screen with Figure 4.46.

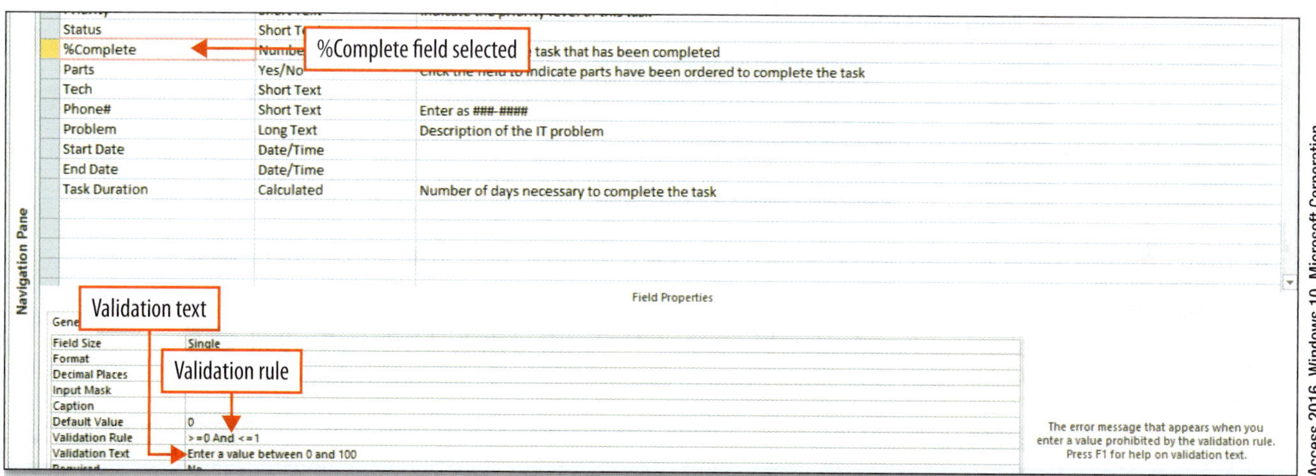

FIGURE 4.46

4 Under **Field Name**, click **Start Date** to make the field active. Under **Field Properties**, click in the **Validation Rule** box, and then type **>=3/15/2019** Click in the **Validation Text** box, and then type **You cannot enter a date prior to 3/15/2019** Compare your screen with Figure 4.47.

In expressions, Access inserts a number or pound sign (#) before and after a date. This validation rule ensures that the person entering data cannot enter a date prior to 3/15/2019.

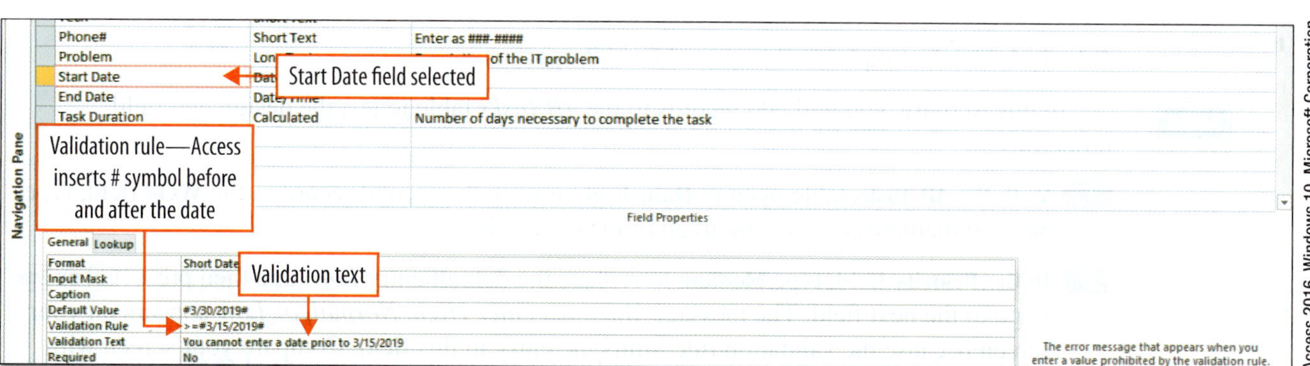

FIGURE 4.47

END OF CHAPTER

SUMMARY

Backup files are copies of a database created to protect the data. Adding trustworthy storage locations to the Trust Center as secure locations allows the user full use of the content in the database.

Using existing tables as the basis to create new ones eliminates the chances of mistakes in table design, and they can be continually modified and updated to keep the data useful over time.

Creating a table in Design view allows control over the fields in the table, the choice of the data type based on the content, and the ability to set field properties to minimize errors in data entry.

Reducing errors starts with using a lookup or calculated data type to minimize manual entry, formatting properties and input masks to ensure accurate presentation, and validation rules to restrict data entry.

GO! LEARN IT ONLINE

Review the concepts, key terms, and MOS Skills in this chapter by completing these online challenges, which you can find at **MyITLab**.

Matching and Multiple Choice: Answer matching and multiple choice questions to test what you learned in this chapter.

Lessons on the GO!: Learn how to use all the new apps and features as they are introduced by Microsoft.

MOS Prep Quiz: Answer questions to review the MOS skills that you have practiced in this chapter.

PROJECT GUIDE FOR ACCESS CHAPTER 4

Your instructor will assign Projects from this list to ensure your learning and assess your knowledge.

PROJECT GUIDE FOR ACCESS CHAPTER 4			
Project	**Apply Skills from These Chapter Objectives**	**Project Type**	**Project Location**
4A **MyITLab**	Objectives 1-4 from Project 4A	**4A Instructional Project (Grader Project)** Guided instruction to learn the skills in Project 4A.	In MyITLab and in text
4B **MyITLab**	Objectives 5-8 from Project 4B	**4B Instructional Project (Grader Project)** Guided instruction to learn the skills in Project 4B.	In MyITLab and in text
4C	Objectives 1–4 from Project 4A	**4C Chapter Review (Scorecard Grading)** A guided review of the skills from Project 4A.	In text
4D	Objectives 5–8 from Project 4B	**4D Chapter Review (Scorecard Grading)** A guided review of the skills from Project 4B.	In text
4E	Objectives 1–4 from Project 4A	**4E Mastery (Scorecard Grading) Mastery and Transfer of Learning** A demonstration of your mastery of the skills in Project 4A with extensive decision making.	In text
4F	Objectives 5–8 from Project 4B	**4F Mastery (Scorecard Grading) Mastery and Transfer of Learning** A demonstration of your mastery of the skills in Project 4B with extensive decision making.	In text
4G **MyITLab**	Objectives 1–8 from Projects 4A and 4B	**4G Mastery (Grader Project) Mastery and Transfer of Learning** A demonstration of your mastery of the skills in Projects 4A and 4B with extensive decision making.	In MyITLab and in text
4H	Combination of Objectives from Projects 4A and 4B	**4H GO! Fix It (Scorecard Grading) Critical Thinking** A demonstration of your mastery of the skills in Projects 4A and 4B by creating a correct result from a document that contains errors you must find.	Instructor Resource Center (IRC) and MyITLab
4I	Combination of Objectives from Projects 4A and 4B	**4I GO! Make It (Scorecard Grading) Critical Thinking** A demonstration of your mastery of the skills in Projects 4A and 4B by creating a result from a supplied picture.	IRC and MyITLab
4J	Combination of Objectives from Projects 4A and 4B	**4J GO! Solve It (Rubric Grading) Critical Thinking** A demonstration of your mastery of the skills in Projects 4A and 4B, your decision-making skills, and your critical thinking skills. A task-specific rubric helps you self-assess your result.	IRC and MyITLab
4K	Combination of Objectives from Projects 4A and 4B	**4K GO! Solve It (Rubric Grading) Critical Thinking** A demonstration of your mastery of the skills in Projects 4A and 4B, your decision-making skills, and your critical thinking skills. A task-specific rubric helps you self-assess your result.	In text
4L	Combination of Objectives from Projects 4A and 4B	**4L GO! Think (Rubric Grading) Critical Thinking** A demonstration of your understanding of the chapter concepts applied in a manner that you would use outside of college. An analytic rubric helps you and your instructor grade the quality of your work by comparing it to the work an expert in the discipline would create.	In text
4M	Combination of Objectives from Projects 4A and 4B	**4M GO! Think (Rubric Grading) Critical Thinking** A demonstration of your understanding of the chapter concepts applied in a manner that you would use outside of college. An analytic rubric helps you and your instructor grade the quality of your work by comparing it to the work an expert in the discipline would create.	IRC and MyITLab
4N	Combination of Objectives from Projects 4A and 4B	**4N You and GO (Rubric Grading) Critical Thinking** A demonstration of your understanding of the chapter concepts applied in a manner that you would use in a personal situation. An analytic rubric helps you and your instructor grade the quality of your work.	IRC and MyITLab

GLOSSARY

GLOSSARY OF CHAPTER KEY TERMS

Append An action that allows you to add data to an existing table.

Backup A feature that creates a copy of the original database to protect against lost data.

Clipboard A temporary storage area in Windows that can hold up to 24 items.

Combo box A box that is a combination of a list box and a text box in a lookup field.

Copy A command that duplicates a selection and places it on the Clipboard.

Data validation Rules that help prevent invalid data entries and ensure data is entered consistently.

Default value A specified value to be automatically entered in a field in new records.

Destination table The table to which records are appended.

Dynamic An attribute applied to data in a database that changes.

Expression A combination of functions, field values, constants, and operators that produces a result.

Expression Builder A feature used to create formulas (expressions) in calculated fields, query criteria, form and report controls, and table validation rules.

Field property An attribute or a characteristic of a field that controls the display and input of data.

Flagged Action of highlighting a word that Spell Check does not recognize from the Office dictionary.

Index A special list created in Access to speed up searches and sorting.

Multivalued field A field that holds multiple values.

Paste An action of placing text or other objects that have been copied or cut from one location to a new location.

Path The location of a folder or file on your computer or storage device.

Required A field property that ensures a field cannot be left empty.

Source table The table from which records are being extracted or copied.

System tables Tables used to keep track of multiple entries in an attachment field that you cannot work with or view.

Trust Center A security feature that checks documents for macros and digital signatures.

Trusted source A person or organization that you know will not send you databases with malicious content.

Validation rule An expression that precisely defines the range of data that will be accepted in a field.

Validation text The error message that displays when an individual enters a value prohibited by the validation rule.

Zero-length string An entry created by typing two quotation marks with no spaces between them ("") to indicate that no value exists for a required text or memo field.

Apply 4A skills from these Objectives:

1 Manage Existing Tables
2 Modify Existing Tables
3 Change Data Types
4 Attach Files to Records

Skills Review Project 4C Commerce

Dario Soto, the city manager of Golden Grove, has a database of the city's industry information. This database has five tables. The Industries table contains summary information from the other four tables. Each update to an individual industry table would require updates to the summary table. In the following Skills Review, you will redesign the tables, taking advantage of table relationships to avoid entering and storing redundant data. Your completed tables and relationships will look similar to those in Figure 4.51.

PROJECT FILES

For Project 4C, you will need the following files:

a04C_Commerce
a04C_GCH_Contacts

You will save your databases as:

Lastname_Firstname_4C_Commerce
Lastname_Firstname_4C_Commerce_2019-10-30 (date will vary)

PROJECT RESULTS

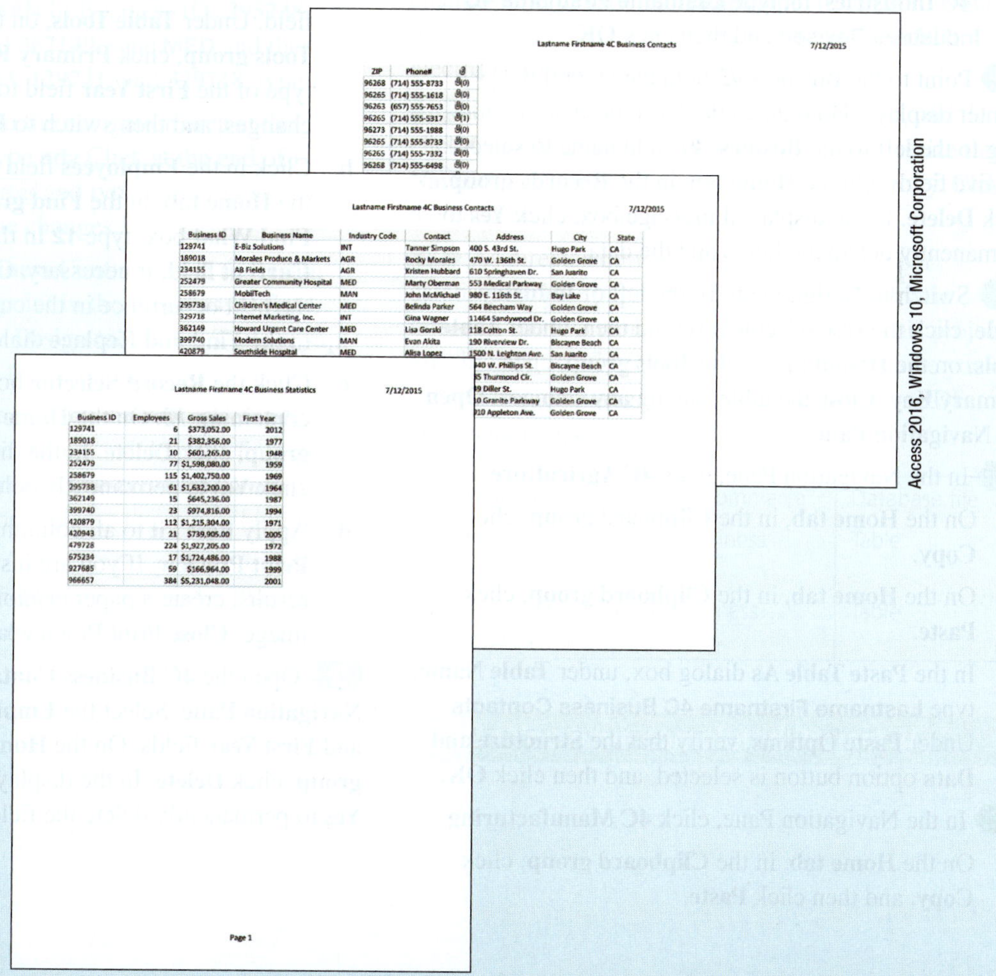

Lastname Firstname 4C Business Contacts 7/12/2015

ZIP	Phone#	
96268	(714) 555-8733	(0)
96265	(714) 555-1618	(0)
96263	(657) 555-7653	(0)
96265	(714) 555-5317	(1)
96273	(714) 555-1988	(0)
96265	(714) 555-8733	(0)
96265	(714) 555-7332	(0)
96268	(714) 555-6498	(0)

Lastname Firstname 4C Business Contacts 7/12/2015

Business ID	Business Name	Industry Code	Contact	Address	City	State
129741	E-Biz Solutions	INT	Tanner Simpson	400 S. 43rd St.	Hugo Park	CA
189018	Morales Produce & Markets	AGR	Rocky Morales	470 W. 136th St.	Golden Grove	CA
234155	AB Fields	AGR	Kristen Hubbard	610 Springhaven Dr.	San Juarito	CA
252479	Greater Community Hospital	MED	Marty Oberman	553 Medical Parkway	Golden Grove	CA
258679	MobilTech	MAN	John McMichael	980 E. 116th St.	Bay Lake	CA
295738	Children's Medical Center	MED	Belinda Parker	564 Beecham Way	Golden Grove	CA
329718	Internet Marketing, Inc.	INT	Gina Wagner	11464 Sandywood Dr.	Golden Grove	CA
362149	Howard Urgent Care Center	MED	Lisa Gorski	118 Cotton St.	Hugo Park	CA
399740	Modern Solutions	MAN	Evan Akita	190 Riverview Dr.	Biscayne Beach	CA
420879	Southside Hospital	MED	Alisa Lopez	1500 N. Leighton Ave.	San Juarito	CA
				40 W. Phillips St.	Biscayne Beach	CA
				5 Thurmond Cir.	Golden Grove	CA
				9 Diller St.	Hugo Park	CA
				0 Granite Parkway	Golden Grove	CA
				10 Appleton Ave.	Golden Grove	CA

Lastname Firstname 4C Business Statistics 7/12/2015

Business ID	Employees	Gross Sales	First Year
129741	6	$373,052.00	2012
189018	21	$382,356.00	1977
234155	10	$601,265.00	1948
252479	77	$1,598,080.00	1959
258679	115	$1,402,750.00	1969
295738	61	$1,632,200.00	1964
362149	15	$645,236.00	1987
399740	23	$974,816.00	1994
420879	112	$1,215,304.00	1971
420943	21	$739,905.00	2005
479728	224	$1,927,205.00	1972
675234	17	$1,724,486.00	1988
927685	59	$166,964.00	1999
966657	384	$5,231,048.00	2001

Page 1

Access 2016, Windows 10, Microsoft Corporation

FIGURE 4.51

(Project 4C Commerce continues on the next page)

Skills Review Project 4D City Airport (continued)

If you are instructed to submit this result, create a paper printout or PDF electronic image of the **4D Employee Benefits** table. If you are to submit your work electronically, follow your instructor's directions. **Close** the table.

3 In the **Navigation Pane**, under **Tables**, rename the **4D Employees** table by adding your **Lastname Firstname** to the beginning of the table name. Double-click **4D Employees** to open the table. **Close** the **Navigation Pane**.

a. Switch to **Design** view. Make **Empl ID** the **Primary Key** field. Change the data type for the **Date Hired** field to **Date/Time**. Change the data type for the **Annual Salary** field to **Currency**. Change the data type for the **Office E-mail** field to **Hyperlink**. **Save** your work. You will see two message boxes warning about data. Click **Yes** to continue in both.

b. In the **Dept** field, click in the **Data Type** box, click the **arrow**, and then click **Lookup Wizard**. In the first **Lookup Wizard** dialog box, verify that **I want the lookup field to get the values from another table or query** option button is selected. Click **Next**. Select the **4D Departments** table. Click **Next** to display the third **Lookup Wizard** dialog box. Under **Available Fields**, with **Department** selected, click **Add Field** to move the field to the **Selected Fields** box.

c. Click **Next** to display the fourth **Lookup Wizard** dialog box. In the **1** box, click the **arrow**, and then click **Department**. Leave the sort order as **Ascending**. Click **Next** twice to display the sixth and final **Lookup Wizard** dialog box. Under **What label would you like for your lookup field?**, leave the default of **Dept** and be sure that **Allow Multiple Values** is *not* selected. Click **Finish**. Click **Yes** to save the table. Click **Yes** to close the message box.

d. Under **Field Name**, click **Office Phone**. Under **Field Properties**, click in the **Input Mask** box and then click **Build**.

e. In the displayed **Input Mask Wizard** dialog box, with **Phone Number** selected, click **Edit List**. In the **Customize Input Mask Wizard** dialog box, click **New (blank) record**. In the **Description** box, type **Phone Number with Extension** In the **Input Mask** box, type **!(999) 000-0000 \X999** Click in the **Placeholder** box, and then change _ to # Click in the **Sample Data** box, and type **714 5551234236** In the **Customize Input Mask Wizard** dialog box, click **Close**.

f. Under **Input Mask**, scroll down, click **Phone Number with Extension**, and then click **Next**. Verify that # is displayed as the placeholder character, and then click **Next**. The next wizard screen enables you to decide how you want to store the data. Verify that the **Without the symbols in the mask, like this** option button is selected, and then click **Next**. In the final wizard screen, click **Finish**.

g. Click in the **Date Hired** field. Under **Field Properties**, click in the **Format** box, and then click the **Format arrow**. From the displayed list, click **Medium Date**. Click in the **Required** box. Click the **Required arrow**, and then click **Yes**. Click in the **Monthly Earn** field. Under **Field Properties**, click in the **Expression** box, and edit the expression to read **[Annual Salary]/12** Click the **Result Type arrow**, and then select **Currency** from the displayed list.

h. Under **Field Name**, click **State**. Under **Field Properties**, click in the **Format** box, and then type > Click in the **Default Value** box, and then type **CA** Using the same technique, set the **Default Value** of the **City** field to **Golden Grove**

i. Under **Field Name**, click **Last Name**. Under **Field Properties**, click in the **Indexed** property box, and then click the displayed **arrow**. Click **Yes (Duplicates OK)**. **Save** your work. In the message box, click **Yes** to test the existing data with the new rules. Under **Table Tools**, on the **Design tab**, in the **Show/Hide group**, click the **Indexes** button. Hold down Alt, and then press PrintScrn.

j. Start **Microsoft Word**. In a new blank document, type your first and last names, press Enter, and then type **4D Indexes** Press Enter, and then press Ctrl + V. **Save** the document in your **Access Chapter 4** folder as **Lastname_Firstname_4D_Indexes** If you are instructed to submit this result, create a paper printout or PDF electronic image. **Close** Word. **Close** the Indexes dialog box.

(Project 4D City Airport continues on the next page)

Skills Review Project 4D City Airport (continued)

4 Switch to **Datasheet** view, saving changes to the table if necessary.

a. Click **New (blank) record**. Type the following data:

Empl ID	**543655**
Title	**Mr.**
First Name	**Mark**
Last Name	**Roberts**
Street	**1320 Woodbriar Court**
City	**Golden Grove**
State	**CA**
Postal Code	**96265**
Dept	**Operations**
Date Hired	**3/9/2017**
Salary	**92000**
Office Phone	**714 555 0167 101**
Office E-Mail	**mroberts@goldengrove.gov**

b. Apply **Best Fit** to all columns so all data displays fully.

c. If you are instructed to submit this result, create a paper printout or PDF electronic image of the **4D Employees** table in **Landscape** orientation with **Normal** margins. This table will print on two pages. **Close 4D Employees**, saving changes. If you are to submit your work electronically, follow your instructor's directions.

5 **Open** the **Navigation Pane**. Resize the Navigation Pane so all object names display fully. **Close** the database, saving changes if necessary, and **Close** Access.

6 As directed by your instructor, submit your database and the paper printouts or PDF electronic image of the two Word documents and two tables that are the result of this project. Specifically, in this project, using your own name you created the following database and printouts or PDF electronic images:

1. Lastname_Firstname_4D_City_Airport	Database file
2. Lastname_Firstname_4D_Validation	Word document
3. Lastname Firstname 4D Employee Benefits	Table
4. Lastname_Firstname_4D_Indexes	Word document
5. Lastname Firstname 4D Employees	Table

END | You have completed Project 4D

Mastering Access Project 4E Cultural Events

Apply 4A skills from these Objectives:

1. Manage Existing Tables
2. Modify Existing Tables
3. Change Data Types
4. Attach Files to Records

In the following Mastering Access project, you will manage and modify tables in a database that contains cultural information about the city of Golden Grove. The database will be used by the arts council. Your completed tables and report will look similar to those in Figure 4.53.

PROJECT FILES

For Project 4E, you will need the following files:

a04E_Cultural_Events

a04E_Concert_Flyer

a04E_Quilts_Flyer

You will save your database as:

Lastname_Firstname_4E_Cultural_Events

PROJECT RESULTS

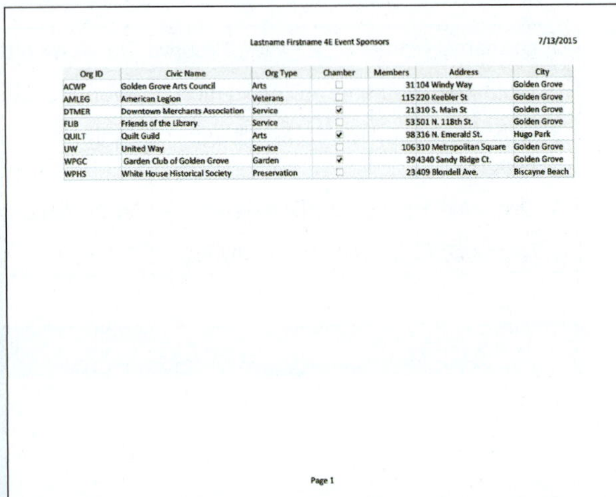

Lastname Firstname 4E Event Sponsors — 7/13/2015

Org ID	Civic Name	Org Type	Chamber	Members	Address	City
ACWP	Golden Grove Arts Council	Arts	☐	31	104 Windy Way	Golden Grove
AMLEG	American Legion	Veterans	☐	115	220 Keebler St	Golden Grove
DTMER	Downtown Merchants Association	Service	☑	21	310 S. Main St	Golden Grove
FLIB	Friends of the Library	Service	☐	53	501 N. 118th St.	Golden Grove
QUILT	Quilt Guild	Arts	☑	98	316 N. Emerald St.	Hugo Park
UW	United Way	Service	☐	106	310 Metropolitan Square	Golden Grove
WPGC	Garden Club of Golden Grove	Garden	☑	39	4340 Sandy Ridge Ct.	Golden Grove
WPHS	White House Historical Society	Preservation	☐	23	409 Blondell Ave.	Biscayne Beach

Page 1

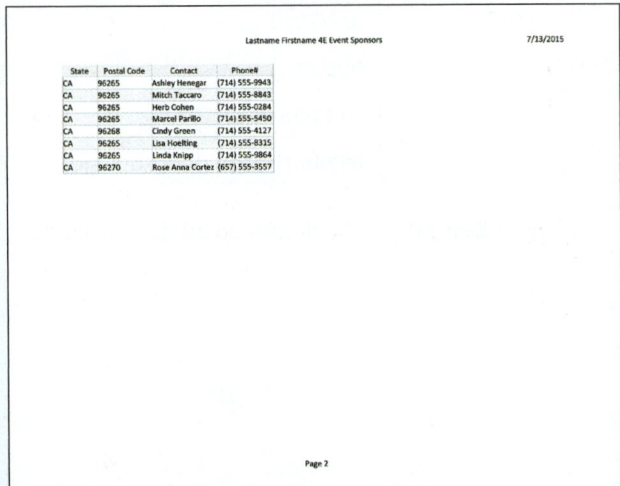

Lastname Firstname 4E Event Sponsors — 7/13/2015

State	Postal Code	Contact	Phone#
CA	96265	Ashley Henegar	(714) 555-9943
CA	96265	Mitch Taccaro	(714) 555-8843
CA	96265	Herb Cohen	(714) 555-0284
CA	96265	Marcel Parillo	(714) 555-5450
CA	96268	Cindy Green	(714) 555-4127
CA	96265	Lisa Hoelting	(714) 555-8315
CA	96265	Linda Knipp	(714) 555-9864
CA	96270	Rose Anna Cortez	(657) 555-3557

Page 2

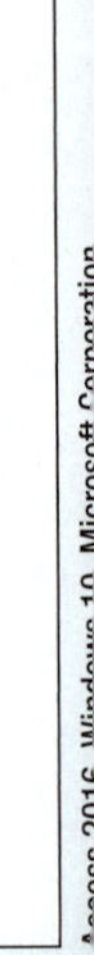

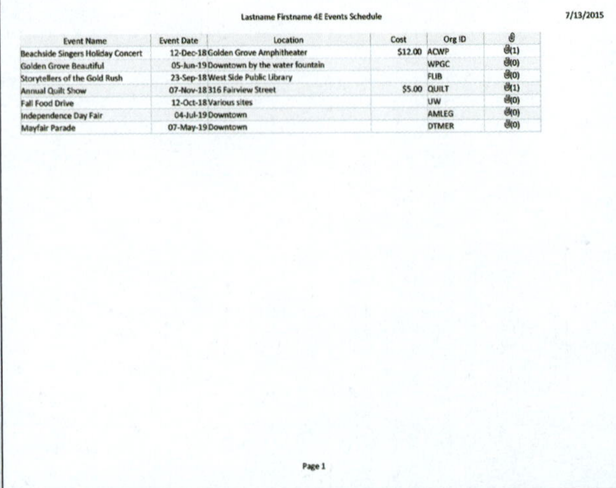

Lastname Firstname 4E Events Schedule — 7/13/2015

Event Name	Event Date	Location	Cost	Org ID	📎
Beachside Singers Holiday Concert	12-Dec-18	Golden Grove Amphitheater	$12.00	ACWP	(1)
Golden Grove Beautiful	05-Jun-19	Downtown by the water fountain		WPGC	(0)
Storytellers of the Gold Rush	23-Sep-18	West Side Public Library		FLIB	(0)
Annual Quilt Show	07-Nov-18	316 Fairview Street	$5.00	QUILT	(1)
Fall Food Drive	12-Oct-18	Various sites		UW	(0)
Independence Day Fair	04-Jul-19	Downtown		AMLEG	(0)
Mayfair Parade	07-May-19	Downtown		DTMER	(0)

Page 1

FIGURE 4.53

(Project 4E Cultural Events continues on the next page)

Mastering Access Project 4E Cultural Events (continued)

1 **Start** Access. Locate and open the **a04E_Cultural_Events** file. **Save** the database in the **Microsoft Access Database** format in your **Access Chapter 4** folder as **Lastname_Firstname_4E_Cultural_Events**

2 Open the **4E Cultural Events** table. In **Backstage** view, click **Save As**. Under **File Types**, double-click **Save Object As**. In the **Save As** dialog box, type **Lastname Firstname 4E Events Schedule** Click **OK**.

3 Make a second copy of the table. Name the table **Lastname Firstname 4E Event Sponsors**

4 With the **4E Event Sponsors** table open in **Datasheet** view, select the first four columns, the **Event Name** field through the **Cost** field. Press Delete, and then click **Yes** to delete the fields and data. Switch to **Design** view, and then make the **Org ID** field the **Primary Key** field.

5 Insert a row above the **Members** field, and add a field named **Chamber** with a data type of **Yes/No**. Switch to **Datasheet** view, saving the changes.

6 In **Datasheet** view, click the **Chamber** field to place a checkmark for the **Downtown Merchants Association**, **Quilt Guild**, and **Garden Club of Golden Grove**. If you are instructed to submit this result, create a paper printout or PDF electronic image of the **4E Event Sponsors** table in **Landscape** orientation. It will print on two pages. **Close Print Preview** and the table.

7 Open the **4E Events Schedule** table in **Datasheet** view. **Close** the **Navigation Pane**. Select and delete the following fields: **Civic Name**, **Org Type**, **Members**, **Address**, **City**, **State**, **Postal Code**, **Contact**, and **Phone#**.

8 Using **Find**, find **1876** in the **Event Name** field; in the **Match** field, select **Any Part of Field**, if necessary. Select and delete the record. On the **Home tab**, in the **Records group**, click **Spelling**. Make any spelling corrections necessary in the table.

9 In the navigation area at the bottom of the window, search for *k* in the records. When it stops at *Make Golden Grove Beautiful*, delete the word **Make** and the space following the word from the Event Name.

10 Switch to **Design** view. Select the **Event Date** field, and, holding down the left mouse button, drag it up until it is between **Event Name** and **Location**. Add a **Flyer** field at the bottom of the field list using an **Attachment** data type.

11 Switch to **Datasheet** view, saving the changes to the table design. Attach the **a04E_Concert_Flyer** to the *Beachside Singers Holiday Concert* record, and add the **a04E_Quilts_Flyer** to the *Annual Quilt Show* record. Apply **Best Fit** to all columns to display all of the data and field names.

12 If you are instructed to submit this result, create a paper printout or PDF electronic image of the **4E Events Schedule** table in **Landscape** orientation with **Normal** margins. **Close** the table.

13 **Open** the **Navigation Pane** and resize it so all object names display fully. **Close** the database, and **Close** Access.

14 As directed by your instructor, submit your database and the paper printouts or PDF electronic image of the two tables that are the result of this project. Specifically, in this project, using your own name you created the following database and printouts or PDF electronic images:

1. Lastname_Firstname_4E_Cultural_Events	Database file
2. Lastname Firstname 4E Event Sponsors	Table
3. Lastname Firstname 4E Events Schedule	Table

END | You have completed Project 4E

Mastering Access Project 4G Parks and Recreation (continued)

1 **Start** Access. Locate and open the **a04G_Parks_and_Recreation** file. **Save** the database in the **Microsoft Access Database** format in your **Access Chapter 4** folder as **Lastname_Firstname_4G_Parks_and_Recreation** Rename all tables by adding your **Lastname Firstname** to the beginning of each table name. Resize the **Navigation Pane** to display all object names fully.

2 Select the **4G Community Centers** table. **Copy** and **Paste** the table. Name the table **Lastname Firstname 4G Facilities** In the **Paste Table As** dialog box, verify the **Structure and Data** option is selected. Click **OK**.

3 Select the **4G Parks** table. **Copy** and **Paste** the table. In the **Table Name** box, type **Lastname Firstname 4G Facilities** Under **Paste Options**, select **Append Data to Existing Table**, and then click **OK** to create one table that contains all of the facility information for the Parks and Recreation Department.

4 Open the **4G Facilities** table in **Design** view. **Close** the **Navigation Pane**. Change the **Data Type** for the **Entry Fee** field to **Currency**. In the **Contact** field, change the field size to **20**

5 Add a new **Monthly Pass** field between the **Entry Fee** and **Contact** fields, and use a data type of **Calculated**. In the **Expression Builder** dialog box, type **[Entry Fee]*15** Change the **Result Type** to **Currency**.

6 Below the **Phone#** field add a new **Directions** field to the table and assign a data type of **Attachment**. In the description box, type **Directions to facility**

7 Select the **Phone#** field. In the **Input Mask** box, type **!000-0000** Change the field size to **8** Set the **Field Property** of **Required** to **Yes**. Using the Clipboard and Word, submit a printed copy of the **Phone#** Field Properties if you are requested to do so. **Save** the document as **Lastname_Firstname_4G_Phone_Properties** **Close** the document, and **Close** Word.

8 Display the **4G Facilities** table and switch to **Datasheet** view. Save your changes. You will see a message box warning that some data may be lost. Click **Yes** to continue. You will also see a message explaining that data integrity rules have changed. Click **No** to testing the data with the new rules.

9 In the **Biscayne Park** record, double-click in the **Attachment** field, and then from the student data files, attach **a04G_Biscayne_Park**. Click **OK**.

10 Using the same technique, for the **Hugo West Center**, add the directions that are in the **a04G_Hugo_West** file.

11 Create a table in **Design** view. In the first **Field Name** box, type **Sport ID** Select an **AutoNumber** data type. Set this as the primary key.

12 In the second **Field Name** box, type **Sport** In the third **Field Name** box, type **Season** and select the **Lookup Wizard** data type. Type the following four items into the lookup list: **Winter Spring Summer** and **Fall** Save the table as **Lastname Firstname 4G Youth Sports**

13 Switch to **Datasheet** view, and populate the table with the following data:

Sport ID	Sport	Season
1	**t-ball**	**Spring**
2	**baseball**	**Summer**
3	**fast pitch softball**	**Fall**
4	**basketball**	**Winter**
5	**volleyball**	**Fall**

14 Apply **Best Fit** to all columns to display all of the data and field names.

15 If you are instructed to submit this result, create a paper printout or PDF electronic image of the **4G Facilities** table and **4G Youth Sports** table. Be sure that all field names and data display.

16 **Close** the tables, saving changes if necessary. **Close** the database, and **Close** Access.

17 As directed by your instructor, submit your database and the paper printouts or PDF electronic image of the Word document and two tables that are the result of this project. Specifically, in this project, using your own name you created the following database and printouts or PDF electronic images:

1. Lastname_Firstname_4G_Parks_and_Recreation	Database file
2. Lastname_Firstname_4G_Phone_Properties	Word document
3. Lastname Firstname 4G Facilities	Table
4. Lastname Firstname 4G Youth Sports	Table

END | You have completed Project 4G

Apply a combination of the 4A and 4B skills.

CONTENT-BASED ASSESSMENTS (CRITICAL THINKING)

GO! Fix It — Project 4H Permit Applications — MyITLab

GO! Make It — Project 4I Medical Centers — MyITLab

GO! Solve It — Project 4J Fire Department — MyITLab

GO! Solve It — Project 4K City Zoo

PROJECT FILES

For Project 4K, you will need the following files:

a04K_City_Zoo
a04K_Dragonfly

You will save your database as:

Lastname_Firstname_4K_City_Zoo

Mandi Cartwright, public relations director of Golden Grove, California, and city manager Dario Soto are meeting with Mayor Sheila Kehoe to discuss the funding for the city zoo. Mandi has outlined a database to organize the sponsorships.

From the student files that accompany this chapter, open the a04K_City_Zoo database file, and then save the database in your Access Chapter 4 folder as **Lastname_Firstname_4K_City_Zoo**

In this project, you will open the **a04K_City_Zoo** database and examine the tables. Rename the tables by adding your **Lastname Firstname** to each table name. Resize the Navigation Pane so all object names are fully visible. Modify the *4K Sponsored Events* table to eliminate redundancy between it and the *4K Sponsors* table. Also, change data types to match the data, including a lookup field for the Sponsor field, and apply an input mask to the Event Date. In the *4K Sponsors* table, create data validation for sponsor type; it must be Individual, Family, or Corporate. In the *4K Sponsors* table, use the *4K Sponsor Levels* table as a lookup field. To the *4K Sponsor Levels* table, add an attachment field named Logo. Add the **a04K_Dragonfly** file to the appropriate record. If you are instructed to submit this result, create a paper or electronic printout of the tables.

(Project 4K City Zoo continues on the next page)

CONTENT-BASED ASSESSMENTS (CRITICAL THINKING)

GO! Solve It Project 4K City Zoo (continued)

Performance Level

Performance Element	Exemplary: You consistently applied the relevant skills	Proficient: You sometimes, but not always, applied the relevant skills	Developing: You rarely or never applied the relevant skills
Modify the 4K Sponsored Events table to eliminate redundancy	Table was modified with correct fields in easy-to-follow format.	Table was modified with no more than two missing elements.	Table was modified with more than two missing elements.
Change data types and field properties in the 4K Sponsored Events and 4K Sponsors tables	Data types and field properties were assigned effectively for the data that each field will hold.	Data types and field properties were assigned with no more than two missing or incorrect elements.	Data types and field properties were assigned with more than two missing or incorrect elements.
Add field to 4K Sponsor Levels table and populate field	Field was added with correct data type and correct data was added to the table.	Field was added with no more than two missing or incorrect elements.	Field was added with more than two missing or incorrect elements.

END | You have completed Project 4K

OUTCOME-BASED ASSESSMENTS (CRITICAL THINKING)

RUBRIC

The following outcomes-based assessments are open-ended assessments. That is, there is no specific correct result; your result will depend on your approach to the information provided. Make Professional Quality your goal. Use the following scoring rubric to guide you in how to approach the problem, and then to evaluate how well your approach solves the problem.

The *criteria*—Software Mastery, Content, Format and Layout, and Process—represent the knowledge and skills you have gained that you can apply to solving the problem. The *levels of performance*—Professional Quality, Approaching Professional Quality, or Needs Quality Improvements—help you and your instructor evaluate your result.

	Your completed project is of Professional Quality if you:	Your completed project is Approaching Professional Quality if you:	Your completed project Needs Quality Improvements if you:
1-Software Mastery	Choose and apply the most appropriate skills, tools, and features and identify efficient methods to solve the problem.	Choose and apply some appropriate skills, tools, and features, but not in the most efficient manner.	Choose inappropriate skills, tools, or features, or are inefficient in solving the problem.
2-Content	Construct a solution that is clear and well organized, contains content that is accurate, appropriate to the audience and purpose, and is complete. Provide a solution that contains no errors of spelling, grammar, or style.	Construct a solution in which some components are unclear, poorly organized, inconsistent, or incomplete. Misjudge the needs of the audience. Have some errors in spelling, grammar, or style, but the errors do not detract from comprehension.	Construct a solution that is unclear, incomplete, or poorly organized, contains some inaccurate or inappropriate content, and contains many errors of spelling, grammar, or style. Do not solve the problem.
3-Format and Layout	Format and arrange all elements to communicate information and ideas, clarify function, illustrate relationships, and indicate relative importance.	Apply appropriate format and layout features to some elements, but not others. Overuse features, causing minor distraction.	Apply format and layout that does not communicate information or ideas clearly. Do not use format and layout features to clarify function, illustrate relationships, or indicate relative importance. Use available features excessively, causing distraction.
4-Process	Use an organized approach that integrates planning, development, self-assessment, revision, and reflection.	Demonstrate an organized approach in some areas, but not others; or, use an insufficient process of organization throughout.	Do not use an organized approach to solve the problem.

Apply a combination of the 4A and 4B skills.

OUTCOMES-BASED ASSESSMENTS (CRITICAL THINKING)

GO! Think Project 4L Streets Department

PROJECT FILES

For Project 4L, you will need the following files:

a04L_Streets_Department
a04L_Work_Order

You will save your database as:

Lastname_Firstname_4L_Streets_Department

In this project, you will examine the database that has been created to help the deputy city manager of infrastructure services organize and track the constituent work requests for the city street repairs. Save the database as **Lastname_Firstname_4L_Streets_Department** Rename all of the tables by adding your **Lastname_Firstname** to the beginning of each table name. Resize the Navigation Pane so all object names display fully. Modify the design of the *4L Work Requests* table. Set the Work Order # field as the primary key field, and then create an input mask to match the data for that field in the first record. For the Type field, create a lookup table using the *4L Repair Types* table. In the Repair Team field, create a Lookup Wizard data type using the *4L Repair Teams* table. In the Priority field, create a validation rule requiring an entry of A, B, or C. Explain this rule with appropriate validation text. Add a long text field called Description between Type and Repair Team. Open **a04L_Work_Order**, and then use the data to add information to the first record in the table. Use today's date as the start date, and leave the completion date blank. Add an attachment field to the table, and then add **a04L_Work_Order** as the attachment. If you are instructed to submit this result, create a paper printout or PDF electronic image of the *4L Work Requests* table.

END | You have completed Project 4L

GO! Think Project 4M Police Department MyITLab

Build From Scratch

You and GO! Project 4N Club Directory MyITLab

Enhancing Queries

OUTCOMES

Create special-purpose queries.

OBJECTIVES

1. Create Calculated Fields in a Query
2. Use Aggregate Functions in a Query
3. Create a Crosstab Query
4. Find Duplicate and Unmatched Records
5. Create a Parameter Query

PROJECT 5B

OUTCOMES

Create action queries and modify join types.

OBJECTIVES

6. Create a Make Table Query
7. Create an Append Query
8. Create a Delete Query
9. Create an Update Query
10. Modify the Join Type

Mayok21/Shutterstock

In This Chapter

Queries can do more than extract data from tables and other queries. You can create queries to perform special functions, such as calculate and summarize numeric data. Queries can also be used to find duplicate and unmatched records in tables, which is useful for maintaining data integrity. You can create a parameter query, where an individual is prompted for the criteria each time the query is run, for more flexibility in the data extracted. Queries can create additional tables in the database, append records to an existing table, delete records from a table, and modify data in the tables based on specific criteria.

S-Boards, Inc., a surf and snowboard shop, combines the expertise and favorite sports of two friends after they graduated from college. Gina Pollard and Steven Michaels grew up in the sun of Southern California, but they also spent time in the mountain snow. The store carries top brands of men's and women's apparel, goggles and sunglasses, boards, and gear. The surfboard selection includes both classic boards and the latest high-tech boards. Snowboarding gear can be purchased in packages or customized for the most experienced boarders. Pollard and Michaels are proud to serve Southern California's board enthusiasts.

2. If necessary, enable the content or add the Access Chapter 5 folder to the Trust Center. In the **Navigation Pane**, rename each table by adding your **Lastname Firstname** to the beginning of each table name. Resize the **Navigation Pane** so all table names are fully displayed.

3. In the **Navigation Pane**, double-click **5A Inventory**. If the Field List pane opens, close it. Take a moment to study the fields in the table.

   Snowboarding items have a catalog number beginning with 8; surfing items have a catalog number beginning with 9. The Category field is a Lookup column. If you click in the Category field, and then click the arrow, a list of category numbers and their descriptions display. The Supplier field identifies the supplier numbers. Cost is the price the company pays to a supplier for each item. Selling Price is what the company will charge its customers for each item. On Hand refers to the current inventory for each item.

4. Switch to **Design** view, and then take a moment to study the data structure. Notice the Category field has a data type of Number; this reflects the AutoNumber field (ID field) in the Category table used in the Lookup field. When you are finished, **Close** the table, and then **Close** « the **Navigation Pane**.

5. On the ribbon, click the **Create tab**, and then, in the **Queries group**, click **Query Design**. In the **Show Table** dialog box, double-click **5A Inventory** to add the table to the query design workspace, and then click **Close**. Resize the list so the table name and all fields are fully displayed.

   If you add the wrong table to the workspace or have two copies of the same table, right-click the extra table, and click Remove Table.

6. From the **5A Inventory** field list, add the following fields, in the order specified, to the design grid: **Catalog#**, **Item**, **Cost**, and **Selling Price**.

   Recall that you can double-click a field name to add it to the design grid, or you can drag the field name to the field box on the design grid. You can also click in the field box, click the arrow, and click the field name from the displayed list.

7. Under **Query Tools**, on the **Design tab**, in the **Results group**, click **Run** to display the four fields used in the query, and then compare your screen with Figure 5.2.

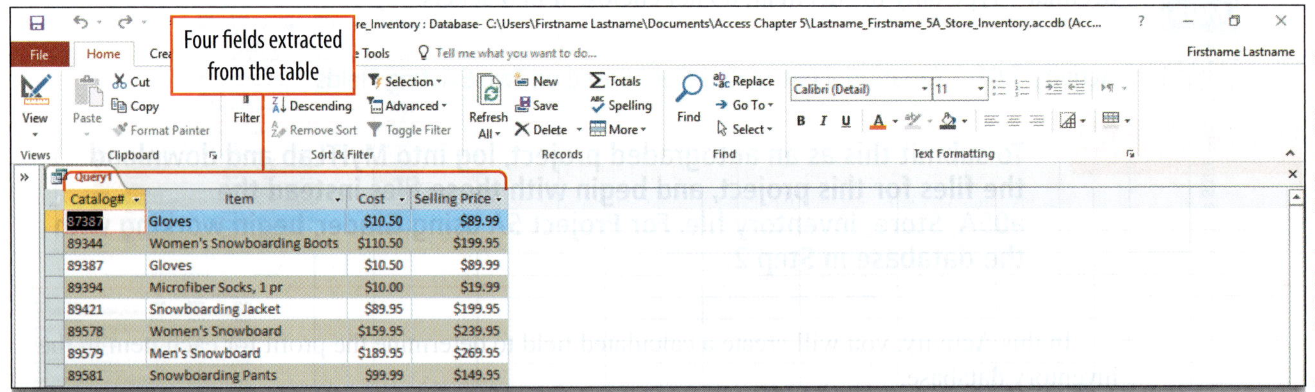

FIGURE 5.2

5 ACCESS

8 Switch to **Design** view. In the **Field row**, right-click in the first empty column—the fifth column—to display a shortcut menu, and then click **Zoom** to display the **Zoom** dialog box. ***Arithmetic operators*** are mathematical symbols used to build expressions in calculated fields. Take a moment to study the arithmetic operators as described in Figure 5.3.

ARITHMETIC OPERATORS			
OPERATOR	**DESCRIPTION**	**EXAMPLE**	**RESULT**
+	Addition	Cost:[Price]+[Tax]	Adds the value in the Price field to the value in the Tax field and displays the result in the Cost field.
–	Subtraction	Cost:[Price]–[Markdown]	Subtracts the value in the Markdown field from the value in the Price field and displays the result in the Cost field.
*	Multiplication	Tax:[Price]*.05	Multiplies the value in the Price field by .05 (5%) and displays the result in the Tax field. (Note: This is an asterisk, not an x.)
/	Division	Average:[Total]/3	Divides the value in the Total field by 3 and displays the result in the Average field.
^	Exponentiation	Required:2^[Bits]	Raises 2 to the power of the value in the Bits field and stores the result in the Required field.
\	Integer division	Average:[Children]\[Families]	Divides the value in the Children field by the value in the Families field and displays the integer portion—the digits to the left of the decimal point—in the Average field.

FIGURE 5.3

9 In the **Zoom** dialog box, type **Per Item Profit:[Selling Price]-[Cost]** and then compare your screen with Figure 5.4.

The first element of the calculated field—*Per Item Profit*—is the new field name that will display the calculated value. The field name must be unique for the table being used in the query. Following the new field name is a colon (:). A colon in a calculated field separates the new field name from the expression. *Selling Price* is enclosed in square brackets because it is an existing field name in the *5A Inventory* table and contains data that will be used in the calculation. Following *[Selling Price]* is a hyphen (-), which, in math calculations, signifies subtraction. Finally, *Cost*, an existing field in the *5A Inventory* table, is enclosed in square brackets. This field also contains data that will be used in the calculation.

5 Switch to **Design** view. Under **Query Tools**, on the **Design tab**, in the **Show/Hide group**, click **Table Names**.

In the design grid, the Table row no longer displays. If all of the fields in the design grid are from one table, you can hide the Table row. The Table Names button is a toggle button; if you click it again, the Table row displays in the design grid.

6 In the **Field row**, click in the **Discount** field box. Under **Query Tools**, on the **Design tab**, in the **Show/Hide group**, click **Property Sheet**. Alternatively, right-click in the field box and click Properties, or hold down Alt and press Enter.

The Property Sheet for the selected field—Discount—displays on the right side of the screen. In the Property Sheet, under the title of Property Sheet, is the subtitle—Selection type: Field Properties.

ALERT! **Does the Property Sheet display a subtitle of Selection Type: Query Properties?**

To display the Property Sheet for a field, you must first click in the field; otherwise, the Property Sheet for the query might display. If this occurs, in the Field row, click the Discount field box to change the Property Sheet to this field.

7 In the **Property Sheet**, on the **General tab**, click in the **Format** box, and then click the displayed **arrow**. Compare your screen with Figure 5.7.

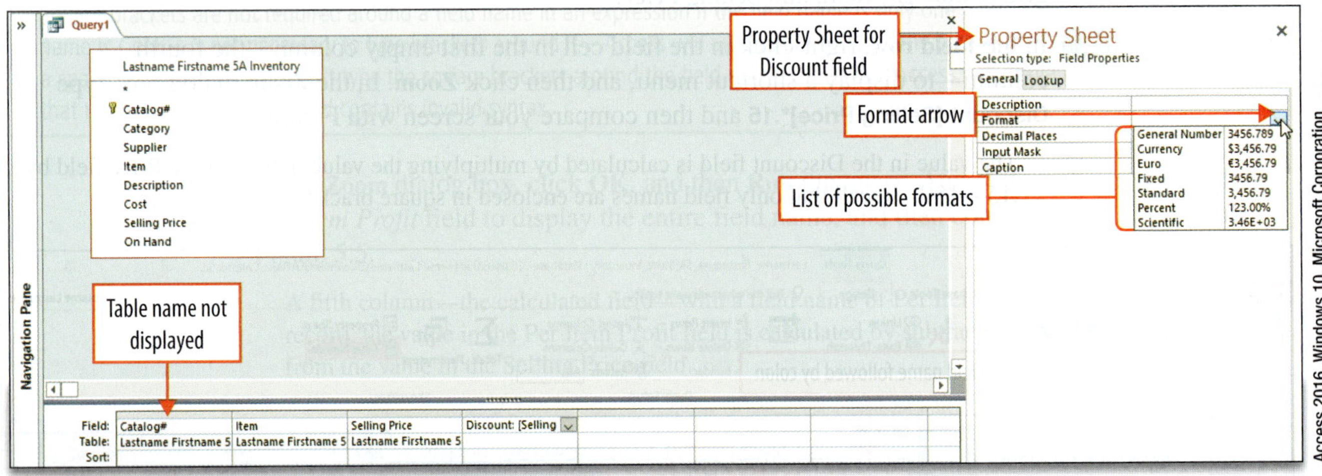

FIGURE 5.7

8 From the list of formats, click **Currency**. On the **Property Sheet** title bar, click **Close**. **Run** the query to display the results.

The values in the Discount field now display with a dollar sign, and the first record's discount—$13.50—displays with two decimal places.

9 Switch to **Design** view. In the **Field row**, right-click in the first empty column, and then click **Zoom**. In the **Zoom** dialog box, type **Sale Price:[Selling Price]-[Discount]** and then click **OK**. **Run** the query to display the results.

The Sale Price for Catalog #87387, Gloves, is $76.49. The value in the Sale Price field is calculated by subtracting the value in the Discount field from the value in the Selling Price field. The field names are not case sensitive—you can type a field name in lower case, such as [selling price]. Because you used only existing fields in the expression that were formatted as currency, the values in the Sale Price field are formatted as currency.

10 Switch to **Design** view. In the design grid, click in the **Criteria row** under **Catalog#**, type **9*** and then press Enter.

Recall that the asterisk (*) is a wildcard. With the criteria, Access will extract those records where the catalog number begins with 9 followed by one or more characters. Also, recall that Access formats the criteria. For example, you typed 9*, and Access formatted the criteria as Like "9*".

11 **Run** the query. Notice that only the records with a **Catalog#** beginning with a **9** display—surfboarding items.

12 **Save** the query as **Lastname Firstname 5A Surfboarding Sale Query** View the query in **Print Preview**, ensuring that the query prints on one page. If you are instructed to submit this result, create a paper printout or PDF electronic image. **Close** the query.

Objective 2 Use Aggregate Functions in a Query

GO! Learn How Video A5-2

In Access queries, you can use ***aggregate functions*** to perform a calculation on a column of data and return a single value. Examples are the Sum function, which adds a column of numbers, and the Average function, which adds a column of numbers and divides by the number of records with values, ignoring null values. Access provides two ways to use aggregate functions in a query—you can add a total row in Datasheet view or create a totals query in Design view.

Activity 5.03 | Adding a Total Row to a Query

3.3.1, 3.2.2, 2.2.2, 1.3.5, 3.1.1, 3.1.6

In this Activity, you will create and run a query. In Datasheet view, you will add a Total row to insert an aggregate function in one or more columns without having to change the design of the query.

1 Create a new query in **Query Design**. Add the **5A Inventory** table to the query design workspace, and then **Close** the **Show Table** dialog box. Resize the field list. From the **5A Inventory** field list, add the following fields, in the order specified, to the design grid: **Catalog#**, **Item**, **Cost**, and **On Hand**.

2 In the **Field row**, right-click in the first empty column, and then click **Zoom**. In the **Zoom** dialog box, type **Inventory Cost:[Cost]*[On Hand]**

The value in the Inventory Cost field is calculated by multiplying the value in the Cost field by the value in the On Hand field. This field will display the cost of all of the inventory items, not just the cost per item.

3 In the **Zoom** dialog box, click **OK**, and then **Run** the query to display the results in Datasheet view. Adjust the column width of the **Inventory Cost** field to display the entire field name, and then compare your screen with Figure 5.8.

If the *Inventory Cost* for Catalog #87387, Gloves, is not $525.00, switch to Design view and edit the expression you entered for the calculated field.

6 **Save** the query as **Lastname Firstname 5A Total Inventory Cost Query** View the query in **Print Preview**, ensuring that the query prints on one page; if you are instructed to submit this result, create a paper printout or PDF electronic image. **Close** the query.

> ***More* Knowledge** **Removing the Aggregate Function and Removing the Total Row**
>
> To remove an aggregate function from a column in a query or table, on the Total row under the field, click the arrow and then click None. To remove the Total row, on the Home tab, in the Records group, click Totals. You cannot cut or delete a Total row; you can only turn it on or off. You can copy a Total row and paste it into another file—for example, an Excel worksheet or a Word document.

Activity 5.04 | Creating a Totals Query

3.2.2, 3.1.5, 1.3.5, 3.3.3, 2.4.3, 3.1.6

In this Activity, you will create a ***totals query***—a query that calculates subtotals across groups of records. For example, to subtotal the number of inventory items by suppliers, use a totals query to group the records by the supplier and then apply an aggregate function to the On Hand field. In the previous Activity, you created a Total row, which applied an aggregate function to one column—field—of data. A totals query is used when you need to apply an aggregate function to some or all of the records in a query. A totals query can then be used as a source for another database object, such as a report.

1 Create a new query in **Query Design**. Add the **5A Suppliers** table and the **5A Inventory** table to the query design workspace, and then **Close** the **Show Table** dialog box. Resize both field lists. Notice that there is a one-to-many relationship between the tables—*one* supplier can supply *many* items. From the **5A Inventory** field list, add **On Hand** to the first field box in the design grid.

2 Under **Query Tools**, on the **Design tab**, in the **Show/Hide group**, click **Totals**.

Like the Totals button on the Home tab, this button is a toggle button. In the design grid, a Total row displays under the Table row, and Group By displays in the box.

3 In the design grid, click in the **Total row** under **On Hand** to display the arrow. Click the **arrow**, and then compare your screen with Figure 5.12.

A list of aggregate functions displays. This list displays more functions than the list in Datasheet view, and the function names are abbreviated.

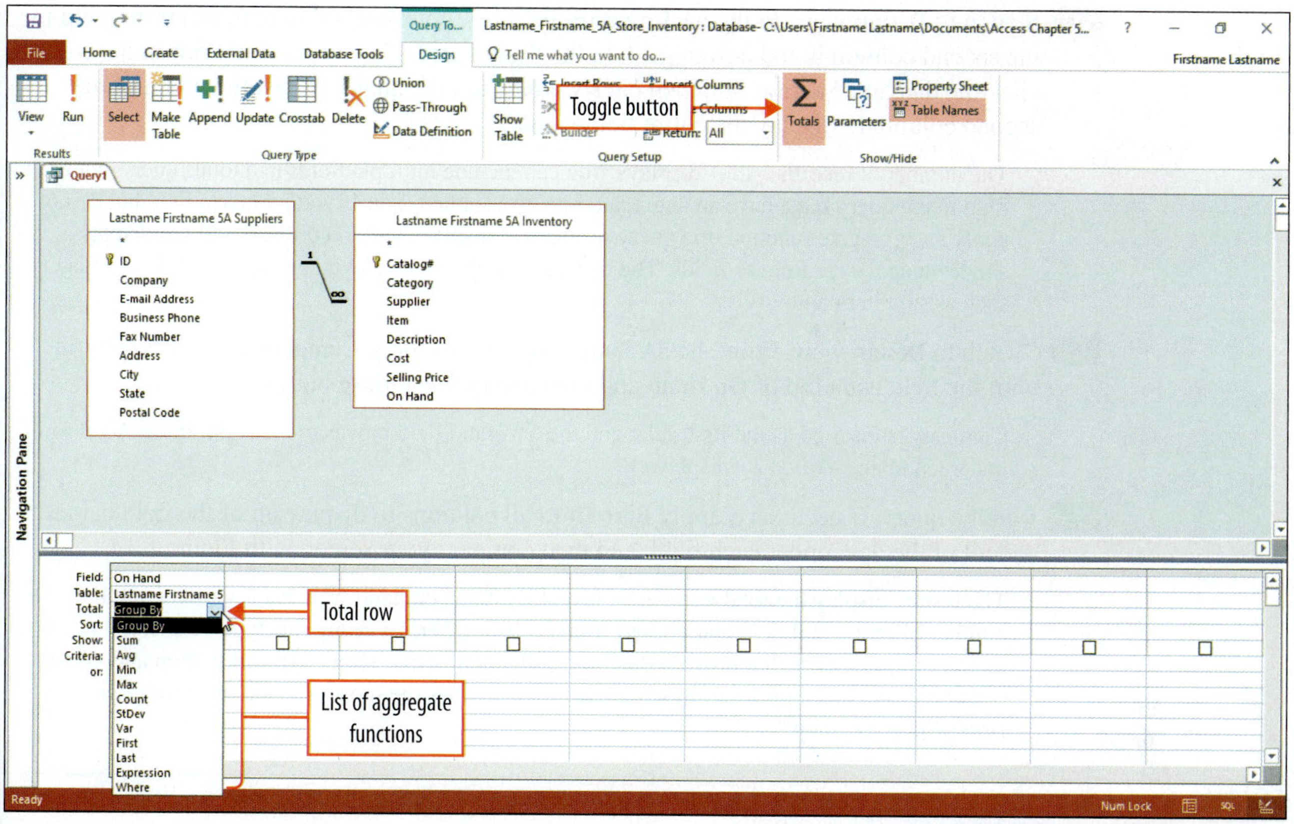

Access 2016, Windows 10, Microsoft Corporation

FIGURE 5.12

4 From the displayed list, click **Sum**. **Run** the query, and then adjust the width of the column to display the entire field name. Compare your screen with Figure 5.13.

When you run a totals query, the result of the aggregate function—*1244*—is displayed; the records are not displayed. The name of the function and the field used are displayed in the column heading.

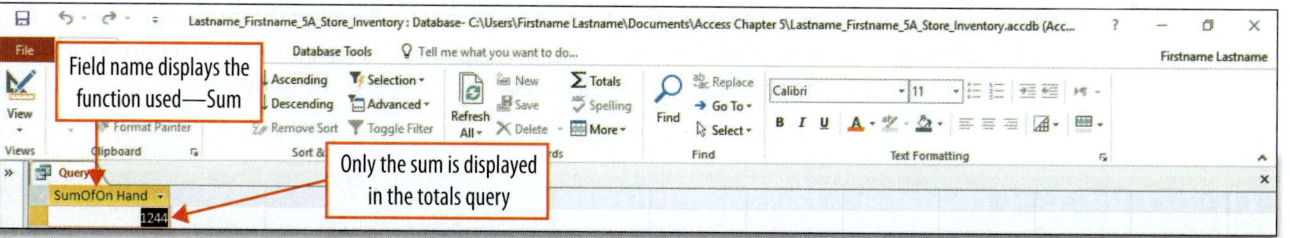

FIGURE 5.13

Access 2016, Windows 10, Microsoft Corporation

More Knowledge Changing the Name of the Totals Query Result

To change the name from the combination aggregate function and field name to something more concise and descriptive, in Design view, in the Field row, click in the On Hand field box. Under Query Tools, on the Design tab, in the Show/Hide group, click Property Sheet. In the Property Sheet, on the General tab, click in the Caption box, and type the new name for the result.

5 Switch to **Design** view. In the **5A Inventory** field list, double-click **Item** to insert the field in the second column in the design grid. In the design grid, click in the **Total row** under **Item**, click the displayed **arrow**, and then click **Count**. **Run** the query. Adjust the width of the second column to display the entire field name.

The number of records—25—displays. You can include multiple fields in a totals query, but each field in the query must have an aggregate function applied to it. If you include a field but do not apply an aggregate function, the query results will display every record and will not display a single value for the field or fields. The exception to this is when you group records by a category, such as supplier name.

6 Switch to **Design** view. From the **5A Suppliers** field list, drag **Company** to the design grid until the field is on top of **On Hand** and then release the mouse button.

Company is inserted as the first field, and the On Hand field moves to the right. In the Total row under Company, *Group By* displays.

7 **Run** the query. If necessary, apply **Best Fit** to all columns to display all of the field names and all of the data under each field, and then compare your screen with Figure 5.14.

The results display the total number of inventory items on hand from each supplier and the number of individual items purchased from each supplier. By using this type of query, you can identify the suppliers that provide the most individual items—Bob's Sporting Shop and Wetsuit Country—and the supplier from whom the company has the most on-hand inventory items—Bob's Sporting Shop.

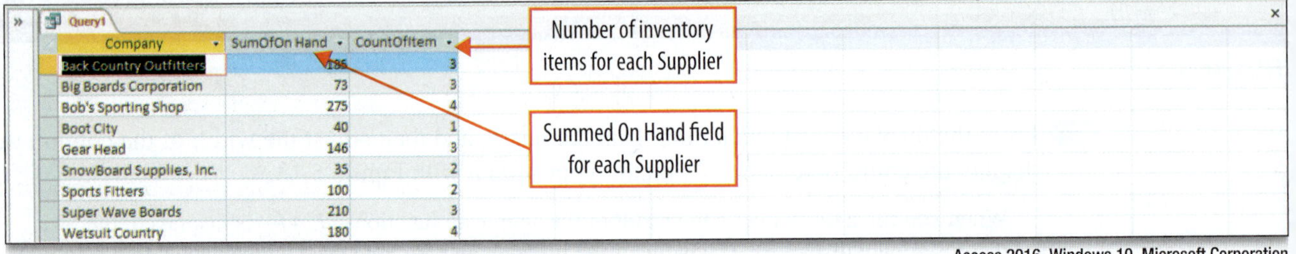

Company	SumOfOn Hand	CountOfItem
Back Country Outfitters	185	3
Big Boards Corporation	73	3
Bob's Sporting Shop	275	4
Boot City	40	1
Gear Head	146	3
SnowBoard Supplies, Inc.	35	2
Sports Fitters	100	2
Super Wave Boards	210	3
Wetsuit Country	180	4

Access 2016, Windows 10, Microsoft Corporation

FIGURE 5.14

8 **Save** the query as **Lastname Firstname 5A Inventory By Supplier Query** View the query in **Print Preview**, ensuring that the query prints on one page. If you are instructed to submit this result, create a paper printout or PDF electronic image. **Close** the query.

Objective 3 Create a Crosstab Query

GO! Learn How
Video A5-3

A ***crosstab query*** uses an aggregate function for data that is grouped by two types of information and displays the data in a compact, spreadsheet-like format. A crosstab query always has at least one row heading, one column heading, and one summary field. Use a crosstab query to summarize a large amount of data in a small space that is easy to read.

Activity 5.05 | Creating a Select Query as the Source for a Crosstab Query

3.1.5, 3.2.2, 3.2.5, 3.3.3, 3.1.1, 3.1.6

In this Activity, you will create a select query displaying suppliers, the category of the inventory item, the inventory item, and the number on hand. Recall that a select query is the most common type of query, and it extracts data from one or more tables or queries, displaying the results in a datasheet. After creating the select query, you will use it to create a crosstab query to display the data in a format that is easier to analyze. Because most crosstab queries extract data from more than one table or query, it is helpful to create a select query containing all of the fields necessary for the crosstab query.

1 Create a new query in **Query Design**. Add the following tables to the query design workspace: **5A Category**, **5A Inventory**, and **5A Suppliers**. In the **Show Table** dialog box, click **Close**. Resize the field lists.

2 In the **5A Suppliers** field list, double-click **Company** to add it to the first field box in the design grid. In the **5A Category** field list, double-click **CatName** to add it to the second field box in the design grid. In the **5A Inventory** field list, double-click **On Hand** to add it to the third field box in the design grid. In the design grid, click in the **Sort** box under **Company**. Click the **arrow**, and then click **Ascending**. Sort the **CatName** field in **Ascending** order.

3 Under **Query Tools**, on the **Design tab**, in the **Show/Hide group**, click **Totals**. Click in the **Total row** under **On Hand**, click the **arrow**, and then click **Sum**. Compare your screen with Figure 5.15.

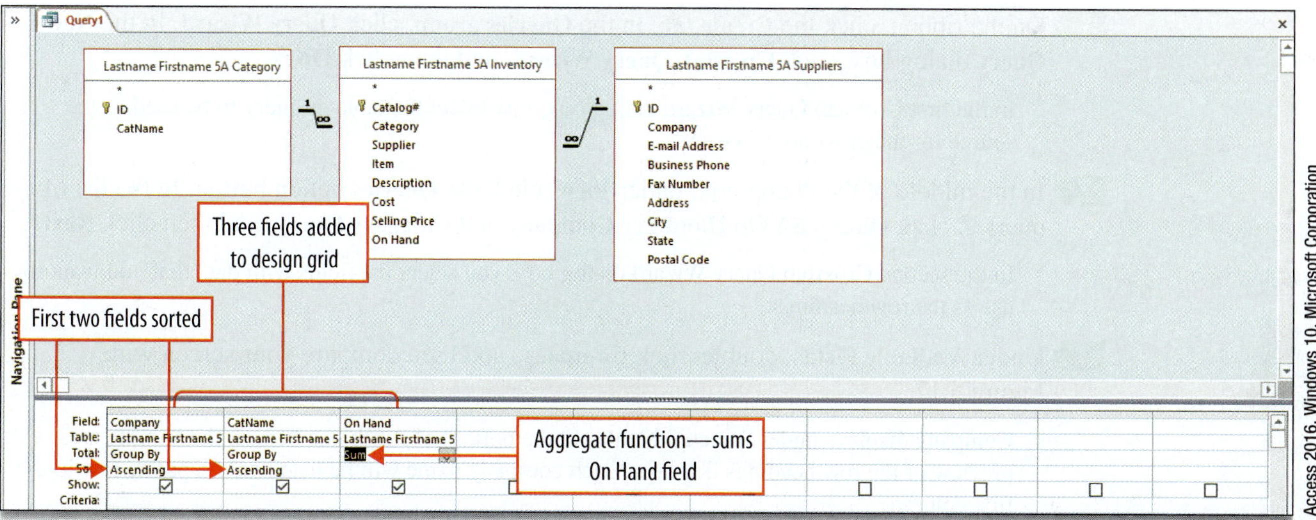

Access 2016, Windows 10, Microsoft Corporation

FIGURE 5.15

NOTE Selecting Multiple Fields for Row Headings

You can select up to three fields for row headings in a crosstab query. An example would be sorting first by state, then by city, and then by postal code. State would be the first row heading, city would be the second row heading, and postal code would be the third row heading. Regardless of the number of fields used for row headings, at least two fields must remain available to complete the crosstab query.

4 **Run** the query. In the datasheet, apply **Best Fit** to all columns to display the entire field name and the data for each record. Click in the first record, and then compare your screen with Figure 5.16.

The select query groups the totals vertically by company and then by category.

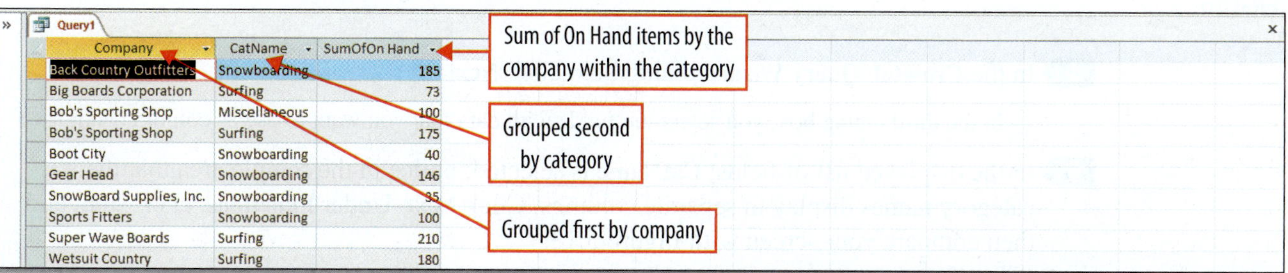

Company	CatName	SumOfOn Hand
Back Country Outfitters	Snowboarding	185
Big Boards Corporation	Surfing	73
Bob's Sporting Shop	Miscellaneous	100
Bob's Sporting Shop	Surfing	175
Boot City	Snowboarding	40
Gear Head	Snowboarding	146
SnowBoard Supplies, Inc.	Snowboarding	35
Sports Fitters	Snowboarding	100
Super Wave Boards	Surfing	210
Wetsuit Country	Surfing	180

FIGURE 5.16

Access 2016, Windows 10, Microsoft Corporation

5 Switch to **Design** view. Under **Query Tools**, on the **Design tab**, in the **Show/Hide group**, click **Totals** to remove the **Total row** from the design grid.

This select query will be used to create the crosstab query. When you create a crosstab query, you will be prompted to use an aggregate function on a field, so it should not be summed prior to creating the query.

6 **Save** the query as **Lastname Firstname 5A On Hand Per Company and Category Query** and then **Close** the query.

Activity 5.06 | Creating a Crosstab Query

3.1.2

In this Activity, you will create a crosstab query using the 5A On Hand Per Company and Category query as the source.

1 On the ribbon, click the **Create tab**, in the **Queries group**, click **Query Wizard**. In the **New Query** dialog box, click **Crosstab Query Wizard**, and then click **OK**.

In the first Crosstab Query Wizard dialog box, you select the table or query to be used as the source for the crosstab query.

2 In the middle of the dialog box, under **View**, click the **Queries** option button. In the list of queries, click **Query: 5A On Hand Per Company and Category Query**, and then click **Next**.

In the second Crosstab Query Wizard dialog box, you select the fields with data that you want to use as the row headings.

3 Under **Available Fields**, double-click **Company**, and then compare your screen with Figure 5.17.

Company displays under Selected Fields. At the bottom of the dialog box, in the Sample area, a preview of the row headings displays. Each company name will be listed on a separate row in the first column.

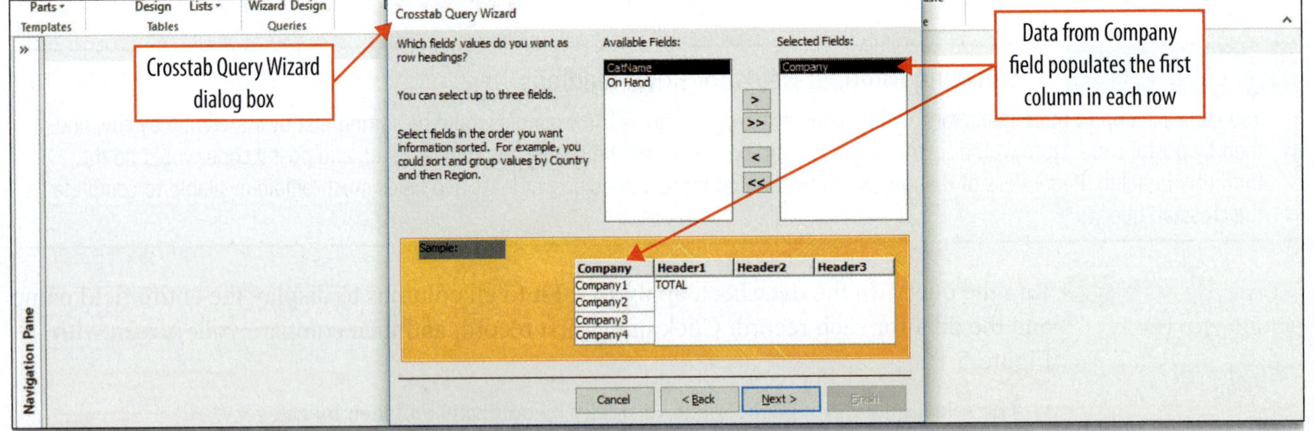

Access 2016, Windows 10, Microsoft Corporation

FIGURE 5.17

4 In the **Crosstab Query Wizard** dialog box, click **Next**.

In the third dialog box, you select the fields with data that you want to use as column headings.

5 In the displayed list of fields, **CatName** is selected; notice in the sample area that the category names display in separate columns. Click **Next**. Under **Functions**, click **Sum**, and then compare your screen with Figure 5.18.

This dialog box enables you to apply an aggregate function to one or more fields. The function will add the number on hand for every item sold by each company for each category. Every row can also be summed.

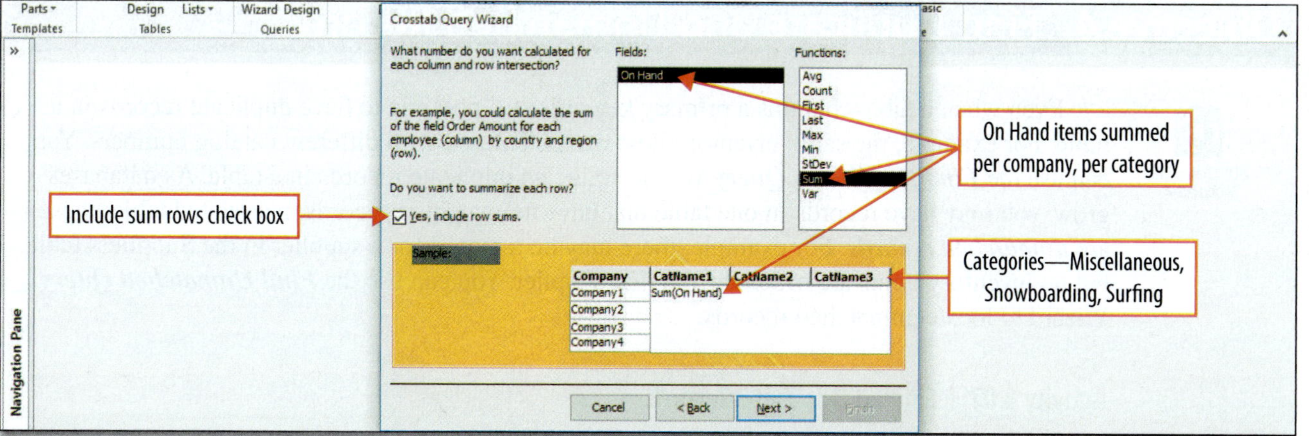

FIGURE 5.18

Access 2016, Windows 10, Microsoft Corporation

6 On the left side of the **Crosstab Query Wizard** dialog box, above the **Sample** area, clear the **Yes, include row sums** check box, and then click **Next**.

If the check box is selected, a column will be inserted between the first and second column that sums all of the numeric data per row.

7 Under **What do you want to name your query?**, select the existing text, type **Lastname Firstname 5A Crosstab Query** and then click **Finish**. Apply **Best Fit** to all columns to display the entire field name and the data in each field, and then compare your screen with Figure 5.19. Then take a moment to compare this screen with Figure 5.16, the select query you created with the same extracted data.

The same data is extracted using the select query as shown in Figure 5.16; however, the crosstab query displays the data differently. A crosstab query reduces the number of records displayed, as shown by the entry for Bob's Sporting Shop. In the select query, there are two records displayed, one for the Miscellaneous category and one for the Surfing category. The crosstab query combines the data into one record.

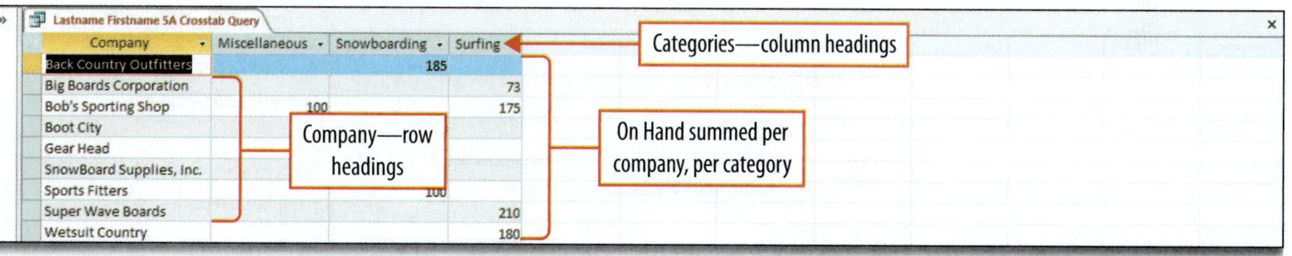

FIGURE 5.19

Access 2016, Windows 10, Microsoft Corporation

> **NOTE** Including Row Sums
>
> If you include row sums in a crosstab query, the sum will display in a column following the column for the row headings. In this Activity, the row sums column would display following the Company column. For Bob's Sporting Shop, the row sum would be 275—100 plus 175.

8 View the query in **Print Preview**, ensuring that the query prints on one page. If you are instructed to submit this result, create a paper printout or PDF electronic image. **Close** the query, saving changes—you adjusted the column widths.

Objective 4 Find Duplicate and Unmatched Records

GO! Learn How
Video A5-4

Even when a table contains a primary key, it is still possible to have duplicate records in a table. For example, the same inventory item can be entered with different catalog numbers. You can use the ***Find Duplicates Query*** Wizard to locate duplicate records in a table. As databases grow, you may have records in one table that have no matching records in a related table; these are ***unmatched records***. For example, there may be a record for a supplier in the Suppliers table, but no inventory items are ordered from that supplier. You can use the ***Find Unmatched Query*** Wizard to locate unmatched records.

Activity 5.07 | Finding Duplicate Records

3.2.2, 3.1.1, 3.1.6

In this Activity, you will find duplicate records in the *5A Inventory* table by using the Find Duplicates Query Wizard.

1. On the **Create tab**, in the **Queries group**, click **Query Wizard**. In the **New Query** dialog box, click **Find Duplicates Query Wizard**, and then click **OK**.

2. In the first **Find Duplicates Query Wizard** dialog box, in the list of tables, click **Table: 5A Inventory**, and then click **Next**.

   The second dialog box displays, enabling you to select the field or fields that may contain duplicate data. If you select all of the fields, then every field must contain the same data, which cannot be the case for a primary key field.

3. Under **Available fields**, double-click **Item** to move it under **Duplicate-value fields**, and then click **Next**.

   The third dialog box displays, enabling you to select one or more fields that will help you distinguish duplicate from nonduplicate records.

4. Under **Available fields**, add the following fields, in the order specified, to the **Additional query fields** box: **Catalog#**, **Category**, **Supplier**, **Cost**, and **Selling Price**. Compare your screen with Figure 5.20.

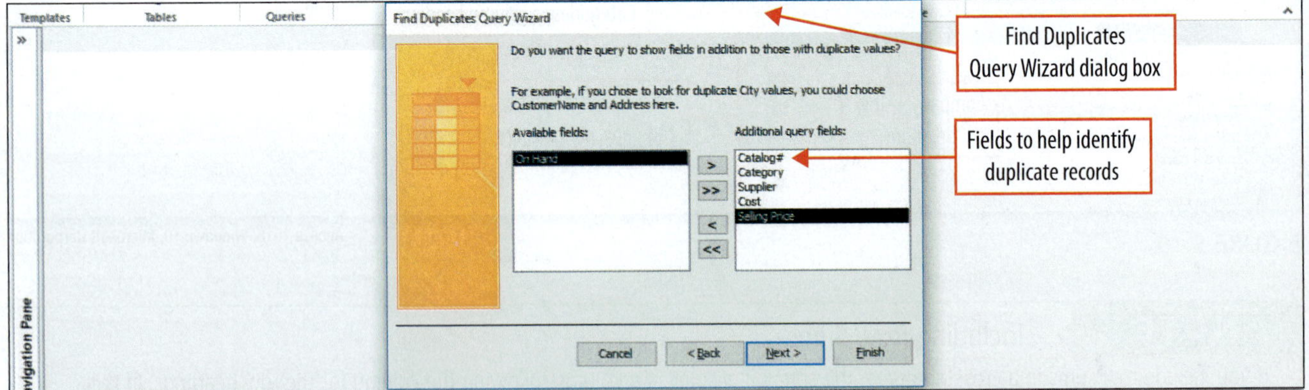

FIGURE 5.20

5. Click **Next**. Click **Finish** to accept the suggested query name—*Find duplicates for Lastname Firstname 5A Inventory*—and then compare your screen with Figure 5.21.

   Three records display with a duplicate value in the *Item* field. Using the displayed fields, you can determine that the second and third records are duplicates; the *Catalog#* was entered incorrectly for one of the records. By examining the *5A Inventory* table, you can determine that Category 1 is Snowboarding and Category 2 is Surfing. Be careful when using the Find Duplicates Query Wizard. If you do not include additional fields to help determine whether the records are duplicates or not, you might mistakenly identify them as duplicates.

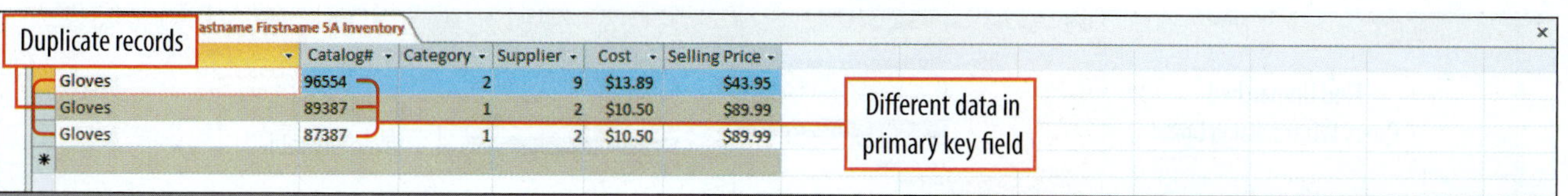

FIGURE 5.21

Access 2016, Windows 10, Microsoft Corporation

5 ACCESS

6 Apply **Best Fit** to all columns, as needed. View the query in **Print Preview**, ensuring that the query prints on one page. If you are instructed to submit this result, create a paper printout or PDF electronic image. **Close** the query, saving changes.

Normally, you would delete the duplicate record, but your instructor needs to verify that you have found the duplicate record by using a query.

More Knowledge **Removing Duplicate Records**

If you choose to delete duplicate records, you must first deal with existing table relationships. If the record you want to delete exists in the table on the *many* side of the relationship, you can delete the record without taking additional steps. If the record exists in the table on the *one* side of the relationship, you must first delete the relationship, and then delete the record. You should then re-create the relationship between the tables. You can either manually delete the duplicate records or create a delete query to remove the duplicate records.

Activity 5.08 | Finding Unmatched Records

3.2.2, 3.1.1, 3.1.6

In this Activity, you will find unmatched records in related tables—*5A Suppliers* and *5A Inventory*—by using the Find Unmatched Query Wizard.

1 On the **Create tab**, in the **Queries group**, click **Query Wizard**. In the **New Query** dialog box, click **Find Unmatched Query Wizard**, and then click **OK**.

2 In the first **Find Unmatched Query Wizard** dialog box, in the list of tables, click **Table: 5A Suppliers**, and then click **Next**.

The second dialog box displays, enabling you to select the related table or query that you would like Access to compare to the first table to find unmatched records.

3 In the list of tables, click **Table: 5A Inventory**, and then click **Next**.

The third dialog box displays, enabling you to select the matching fields in each table.

4 Under **Fields in '5A Suppliers'**, if necessary, click **ID**. Under **Fields in '5A Inventory'**, if necessary, click **Supplier**. Between the two fields columns, click the button that displays <=>. Click **Next**.

Your table names may require two lines, depending on the length of your name. At the bottom of the dialog box, Access displays the matching fields of ID and Supplier.

5 Under **Available fields**, double-click **ID**, and then double-click **Company** to move the field names under **Selected fields**. Notice that these fields will display in the query results, and then compare your screen with Figure 5.22.

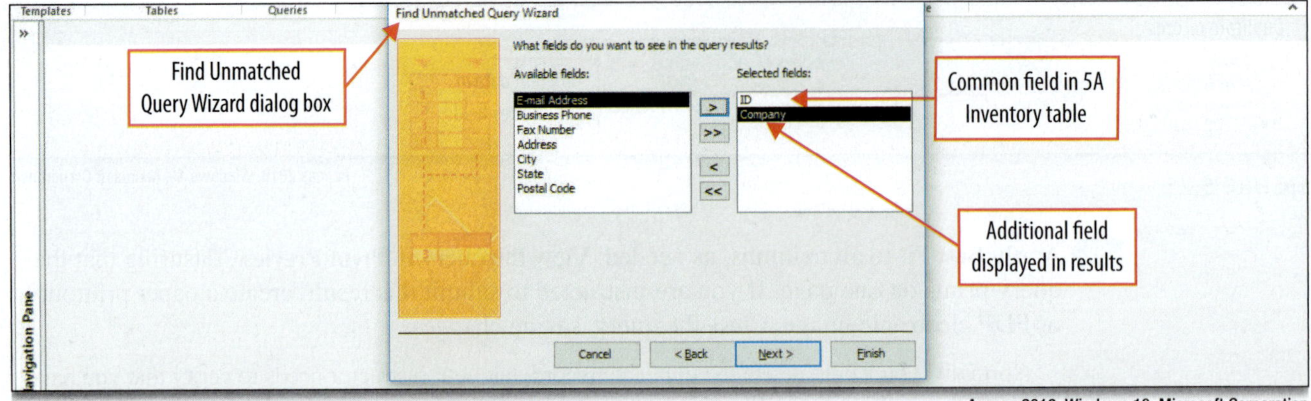

Access 2016, Windows 10, Microsoft Corporation

FIGURE 5.22

6 Click **Next**. In the last dialog box, under **What would you like to name your query?**, type **Lastname Firstname 5A Find Unmatched Query** and then click **Finish**. Compare your screen with Figure 5.23.

The query results display one company—*Cold Sports Club*—that has no inventory items in the *5A Inventory* table. Normally, you would either delete the Cold Sports Club record from the *5A Suppliers* table or add inventory items in the related *5A Inventory* table for the Cold Sports Club, but your instructor needs to verify that you have located an unmatched record by using a query.

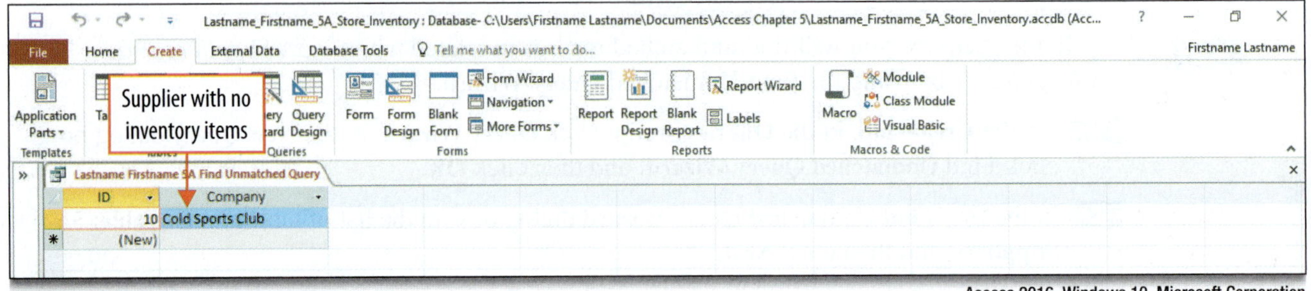

Access 2016, Windows 10, Microsoft Corporation

FIGURE 5.23

7 Apply **Best Fit** to all columns, if necessary, so all field names and data display fully. View the query in **Print Preview**, ensuring that the query prints on one page. If you are instructed to submit this result, create a paper printout or PDF electronic image. **Close** the query, saving changes.

***More* Knowledge** **Finding Unmatched Records in a Table with Multivalued Fields**

You cannot use the Find Unmatched Query Wizard with a table that has ***multivalued fields***—fields that appear to hold multiple values. If your table contains multivalued fields, you must first create a query to extract all of the fields except the multivalued fields, and then create the query to find unmatched records.

Objective 5 Create a Parameter Query

GO! Learn How Video A5-5

A ***parameter query*** prompts you for criteria before running the query. For example, if you had a database of snowboarding events, you might need to find all of the snowboarding events in a particular state. You can create a select query for a state, but when you need to find information about snowboarding events in another state, you must open the original select query in Design view, change the criteria, and then run the query again. With a parameter query, you can create one query—Access will prompt you to enter the state and then display the results based upon the criteria you enter in the dialog box.

Activity 5.09 | Creating a Parameter Query Using One Criterion

3.1.5, 3.2.2, 3.1.3, 3.3.2, 3.1.1, 3.1.6

In this Activity, you will create a parameter query to display a specific category of inventory items. You can enter a parameter anywhere you use text, number, or date criteria.

1. **Open** [»] the **Navigation Pane**. Under **Tables**, double-click **5A Inventory** to open the table in **Datasheet** view. In any record, click in the **Category** field, and then click the **arrow** to display the list of categories. Take a moment to study the four categories used in this table. Be sure you do not change the category for the selected record. **Close** the table, and **Close** [«] the **Navigation Pane**.

2. Create a new query in **Query Design**. Add the **5A Category** table, the **5A Inventory** table, and the **5A Suppliers** table to the query design workspace, and then **Close** the **Show Table** dialog box. Resize the field lists. From the **5A Category** field list, add **CatName** to the first column in the design grid. From the **5A Inventory** field list, add **Catalog#** and **Item** to the second and third columns in the design grid. From the **5A Suppliers** field list, add **Company** to the fourth column in the design grid.

3. In the **Criteria row** under **CatName**, type **[Enter a Category]** and then compare your screen with Figure 5.24.

   The brackets indicate a ***parameter***—a value that can be changed—rather than specific criteria. When you run the query, a dialog box will display, prompting you to *Enter a Category*. The category you type will be set as the criteria for the query. Because you are prompted for the criteria, you can reuse this query without resetting the criteria in Design view.

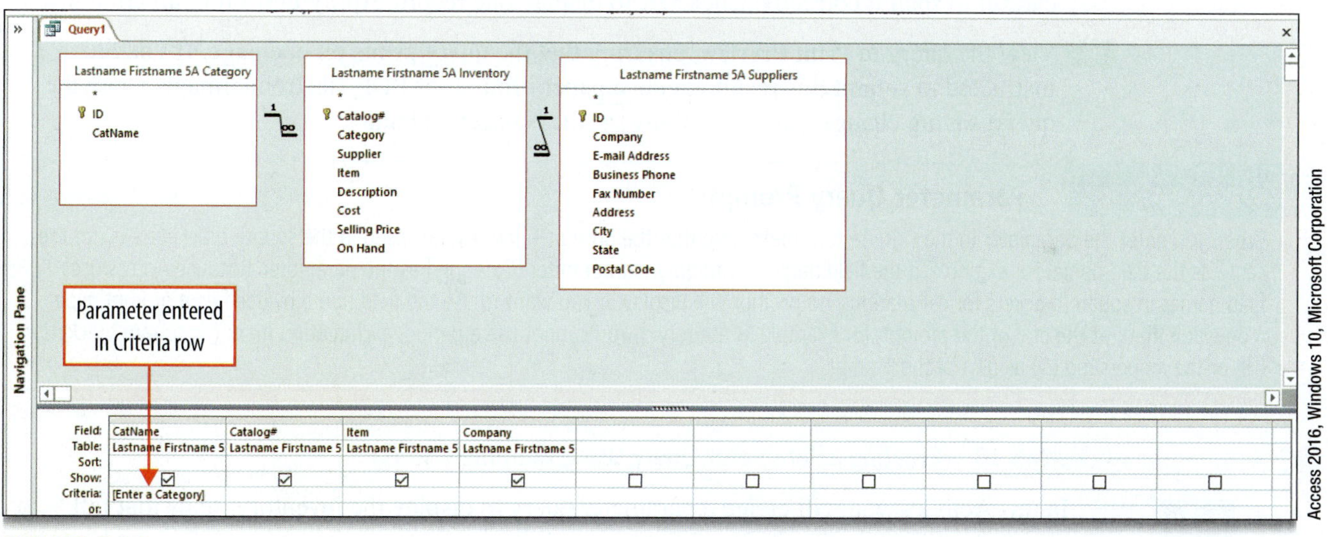

Access 2016, Windows 10, Microsoft Corporation

FIGURE 5.24

4. **Run** the query. In the **Enter Parameter Value** dialog box, type **Surfing** and then compare your screen with Figure 5.25.

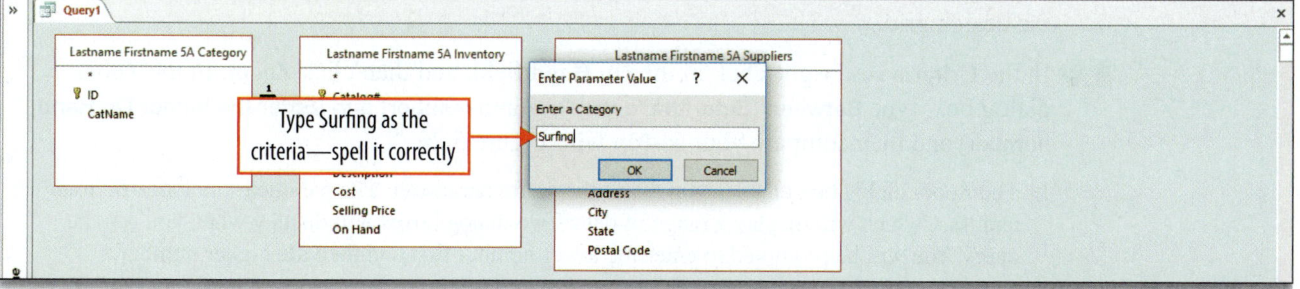

FIGURE 5.25

Access 2016, Windows 10, Microsoft Corporation

ALERT! **Does your screen differ?**

If the Enter Parameter Value dialog box does not display, you may have typed the parameter incorrectly in the design grid. Common errors include using parentheses or curly braces instead of square brackets around the parameter text, causing Access to interpret the text as specific criteria. If you use parentheses, when you run the query no records will display. If you use curly braces, the query will not run. To correct this, display the query in Design view, and then correct the parameter entered in the Criteria row.

5 In the **Enter Parameter Value** dialog box, click **OK**.

Thirteen records display where the CatName field is Surfing.

6 Apply **Best Fit** to all columns, if necessary, and **Save** the query as **Lastname Firstname 5A Category Parameter Query Close** the query, and then **Open** » the **Navigation Pane**.

7 In the **Navigation Pane**, under **Queries**, double-click **5A Category Parameter Query**. In the **Enter Parameter Value** dialog box, type **Snowboarding** and then click **OK**.

Eleven items categorized as Snowboarding display. Recall that when you open a query, Access runs the query so that the most up-to-date data is extracted from the underlying table or query. When you have entered a parameter as the criteria, you will be prompted to enter the criteria every time you open the query.

8 Switch to **Design** view. Notice that the parameter—[Enter a Category]—is stored with the query. Access does not store the criteria entered in the Enter Parameter Value dialog box.

9 **Run** the query, and in the **Enter Parameter Value** dialog box, type **Miscellaneous** being careful to spell it correctly. Click **OK** to display one record. Apply **Best Fit** to all columns.

10 View the query in **Print Preview**, ensuring that the query prints on one page. If you are instructed to submit this result, create a paper printout or PDF electronic image. **Close** the query, saving changes, and then **Close** « the **Navigation Pane**.

***More* Knowledge** **Parameter Query Prompts**

When you enter the parameter in the Criteria row, make sure that the prompt—the text enclosed in the square brackets—is not the same as the field name. For example, if the field name is Category, do not enter [Category] as the parameter. Because Access uses field names in square brackets for calculations, no prompt will display. If you want to use the field name by itself as a prompt, type a question mark at the end of the prompt; for example, [Category?]. You cannot use a period, exclamation mark (!), square brackets ([]), or the ampersand (&) as part of the prompt.

Activity 5.10 | Creating a Parameter Query Using Multiple Criteria

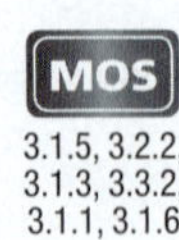

3.1.5, 3.2.2, 3.1.3, 3.3.2, 3.1.1, 3.1.6

In this Activity, you will create a parameter query to display the inventory items that fall within a certain range in the On Hand field.

1 Create a new query in **Query Design**. Add the **5A Suppliers** table and the **5A Inventory** table to the query design workspace, and then **Close** the **Show Table** dialog box. Resize the field lists. From the **5A Inventory** field list, add **Item** and **On Hand** to the first and second columns in the design grid. From the **5A Suppliers** field list box, add **Company** to the third column in the design grid.

2 In the **Criteria row**, right-click in the **On Hand** field, and then click **Zoom**. In the **Zoom** dialog box, type **Between [Enter the lower On Hand number] and [Enter the higher On Hand number]** and then compare your screen with Figure 5.26.

The Zoom dialog box enables you to see the entire parameter. The parameter includes *Between* and *And*, which will display a range of data. Two dialog boxes will display when you run the query. You will be prompted to enter the lower number first and then the higher number.

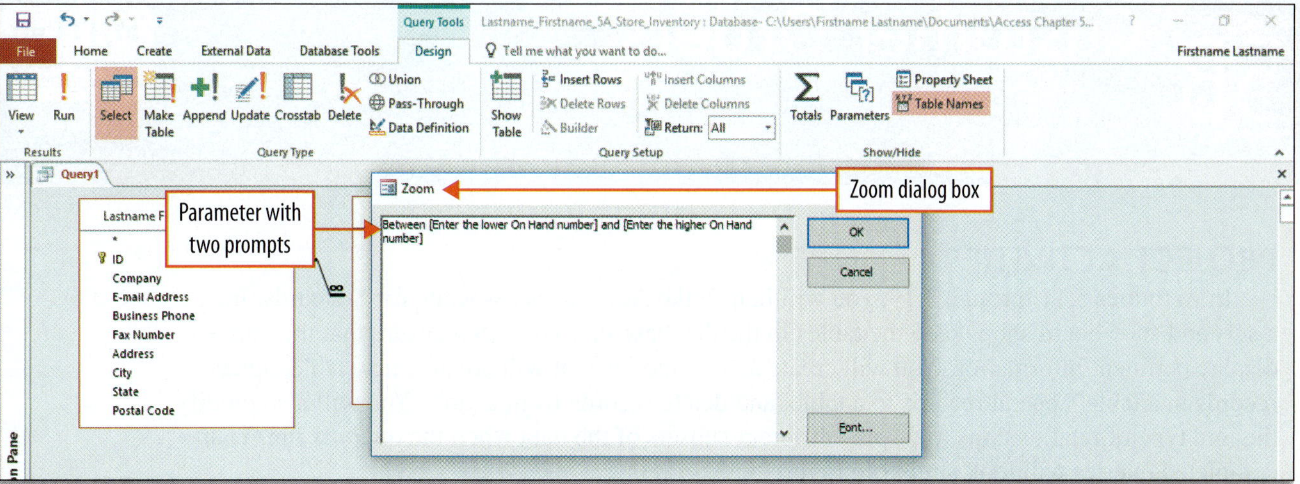

FIGURE 5.26

Access 2016, Windows 10, Microsoft Corporation

3. After verifying that you have entered the correct parameter, in the **Zoom** dialog box, click **OK**, and then **Run** the query. In the first **Enter Parameter Value** dialog box, type **10** and then click **OK**. In the second **Enter Parameter Value** dialog box, type **25** and then click **OK**. Compare your screen with Figure 5.27.

   Six records have On Hand items in the range of 10 to 25. These might be inventory items that need to be ordered soon.

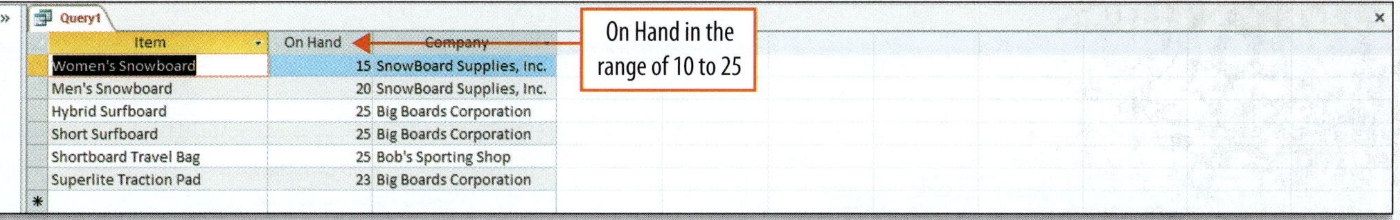

FIGURE 5.27

Access 2016, Windows 10, Microsoft Corporation

More Knowledge **Creating a Parameter Query Using Multiple Criteria**

When you create a query using more than one field with parameters, the individual sees the prompts in the order that the fields are arranged from left to right in the design grid. When you create a query using more than one parameter in a single field, the individual sees the prompts in the order displayed, from left to right, in the Criteria box.

If you want the prompts to display in a different order, under Query Tools, on the Design tab, in the Show/Hide group, click Parameters. In the Parameter column, type the prompt for each parameter exactly as it was typed in the design grid. Enter the parameters in the order you want the dialog boxes to display when the query is run. In the Data Type column, next to each entered parameter, specify the data type by clicking the arrow and displaying the list of data types. Click OK, and then run the query.

4. Apply **Best Fit** to all columns, and **Save** the query as **Lastname Firstname 5A On Hand Parameter Query**

5. View the query in **Print Preview**, ensuring that the query prints on one page. If you are instructed to submit this result, create a paper printout or PDF electronic image. **Close** the query.

6. **Open** » the **Navigation Pane**. Resize the **Navigation Pane** so all object names are fully visible. **Close** the database, and **Close** Access.

7. As directed by your instructor, submit your database and the paper printouts or PDF electronic image of the nine queries that are the result of this project.

END | You have completed Project 5A

PROJECT 5B Customer Orders

PROJECT ACTIVITIES

In Activities 5.11 through 5.19, you will help Miko Adai, sales associate for S-Boards, Inc., a surf and snowboard shop, keep the tables in the database up to date and ensure that the queries display pertinent information. You will create action queries that will create a new table, update records in a table, append records to a table, and delete records from a table. You will also modify the join type of relationships to display different subsets of the data when the query is run. Your completed queries will look similar to Figure 5.28.

PROJECT FILES

If your instructor wants you to submit Project 5B in the MyITLab grader system, log in to MyITLab, locate Grader Project 5B, and then download the files for this project.

For Project 5B, you will need the following files:
a05B_Customer_Orders
a05B_Potential_Customers

You will save your databases as:
Lastname_Firstname_5B_Customers_ Orders
Lastname_Firstname_5B_Potential_Customers

PROJECT RESULTS

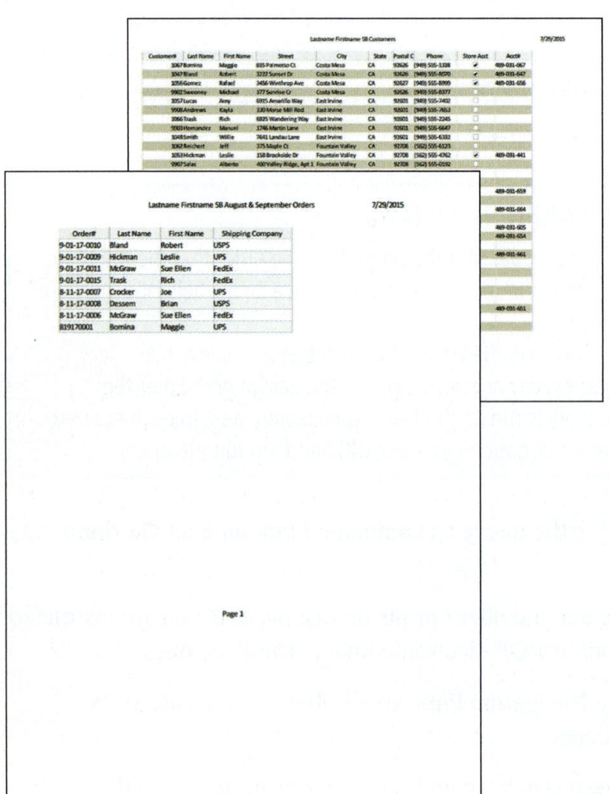

Lastname Firstname 5B Customers 7/29/2015

Customer#	Last Name	First Name	Street	City	State	Postal C	Phone	Store Acct	Acct#
1067	Bomina	Maggie	835 Palmetto Ct	Costa Mesa	CA	92626	(949) 555-1338	✓	489-031-667
1047	Bland	Robert	3232 Sunset Dr	Costa Mesa	CA	92626	(949) 555-8070	✓	489-031-647
1056	Gomez	Rafael	3456 Winthrop Ave	Costa Mesa	CA	92627	(949) 555-8999	✓	489-031-656
9902	Sweeney	Michael	377 Sunrise Cr	Costa Mesa	CA	92626	(949) 555-8377		
1057	Lucas	Amy	6915 Amarillo Way	East Irvine	CA	92601	(949) 555-7402		
9908	Andrews	Kayla	330 Morse Mill Rod	East Irvine	CA	92601	(949) 555-7653		
1066	Trask	Rich	6825 Wandering Way	East Irvine	CA	92601	(949) 555-2245		
9303	Hernandez	Manuel	1746 Martin Lane	East Irvine	CA	92601	(949) 555-6647		
1048	Smith	Willie	7641 Landau Lane	East Irvine	CA	92601	(949) 555-6332		
1062	Reichert	Jeff	375 Maple Ct	Fountain Valley	CA	92708	(562) 555-6123		
1053	Hickman	Leslie	158 Brockside Dr	Fountain Valley	CA	92708	(562) 555-4762	✓	489-031-441
9907	Salas	Alberto	400 Valley Ridge, Apt 1	Fountain Valley	CA	92708	(562) 555-0192		

Lastname Firstname 5B August & September Orders 7/29/2015

Order#	Last Name	First Name	Shipping Company
9-01-17-0010	Bland	Robert	USPS
9-01-17-0009	Hickman	Leslie	UPS
9-01-17-0011	McGraw	Sue Ellen	FedEx
9-01-17-0015	Trask	Rich	FedEx
8-11-17-0007	Crocker	Joe	UPS
8-11-17-0008	Dessem	Brian	USPS
8-11-17-0006	McGraw	Sue Ellen	FedEx
819170001	Bomina	Maggie	UPS

Page 1

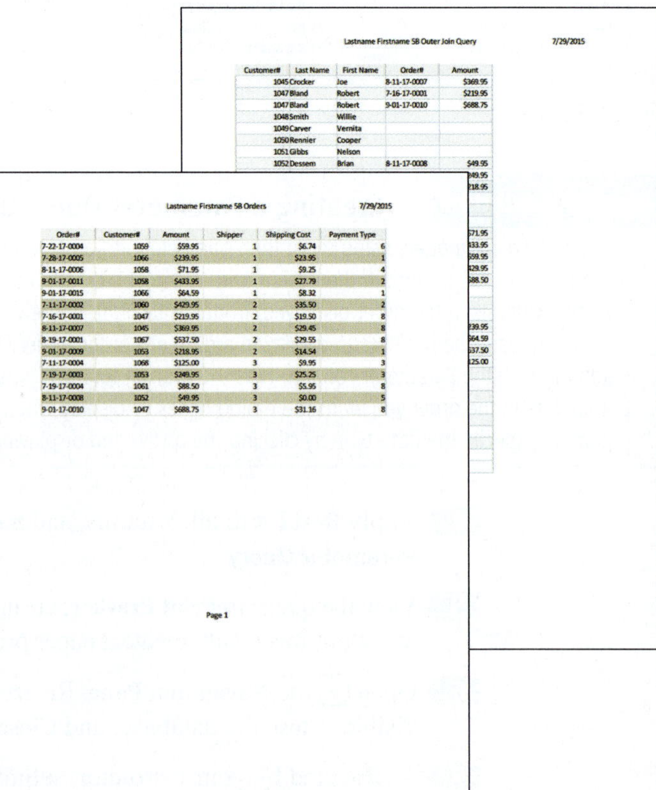

Lastname Firstname 5B Outer Join Query 7/29/2015

Customer#	Last Name	First Name	Order#	Amount
1045	Crocker	Joe	8-11-17-0007	$369.95
1047	Bland	Robert	7-16-17-0001	$219.95
1047	Bland	Robert	9-01-17-0010	$688.75
1048	Smith	Willie		
1049	Carver	Vernita		
1050	Rennier	Cooper		
1051	Gibbs	Nelson		
1052	Dessem	Brian	8-11-17-0008	$49.95

Lastname Firstname 5B Orders 7/29/2015

Order#	Customer#	Amount	Shipper	Shipping Cost	Payment Type
7-22-17-0004	1059	$59.95	1	$6.74	6
7-28-17-0005	1066	$239.95	1	$23.95	1
8-11-17-0006	1058	$71.95	1	$9.25	4
9-01-17-0011	1058	$433.95	1	$27.79	2
9-01-17-0015	1066	$64.59	1	$8.32	1
7-11-17-0002	1060	$429.95	2	$35.50	2
7-16-17-0001	1047	$219.95	2	$19.50	8
8-11-17-0007	1045	$369.95	2	$29.45	8
8-19-17-0001	1067	$537.50	2	$29.55	8
9-01-17-0009	1053	$218.95	2	$14.54	1
7-11-17-0004	1068	$125.00	3	$9.95	3
7-19-17-0003	1053	$249.95	3	$25.25	3
7-19-17-0004	1061	$88.50	3	$5.95	8
8-11-17-0008	1052	$49.95	3	$0.00	5
9-01-17-0010	1047	$688.75	3	$31.16	8

Page 1

FIGURE 5.28 Project 5B Customer Orders

PROJECT RESULTS

In this project, using your own name, you will create the following databases and objects. Your instructor may ask you to submit printouts or PDF electronic images:

Lastname_Firstname_5B_Customer_Orders	Database file
Lastname Firstname 5B August & September Orders	Table
Lastname_Firstname_5B_Potential_Customers	Database file
Lastname Firstname 5B Customers	Table
Lastname Firstname 5B Orders	Table
Lastname Firstname 5B Outer Join Query	Query

Objective 6 Create a Make Table Query

GO! Learn How Video A5-6

An ***action query*** enables you to create a new table or change data in an existing table. A ***make table query*** is an action query that creates a new table by extracting data from one or more tables. Creating a new table from existing tables is useful when you need to copy or back up data. For example, you may wish to create a table that displays the orders for the past month. You can extract that data and store it in another table, using the new table as a source for reports or queries. Extracting data and storing it in a new table reduces the time to retrieve ***static data***—data that does not change—and creates a convenient backup of the data.

Activity 5.11 | Creating a Select Query

ALERT!

To submit as an autograded project, log into MyITLab and download the files for this project, and begin with those files instead of the a05B_Customer_Orders file. For Project 5B using Grader, begin working with the database in Step 2.

2.2.4, 3.1.5, 3.2.2, 3.1.1

In this Activity, you will create a select query to extract the fields you wish to store in the new table.

1. **Start** Access. Navigate to the location where the student data files for this chapter are saved. Locate and open the **a05B_Customer_Orders** file. **Save** the database in your **Access Chapter 5** folder as **Lastname_Firstname_5B_Customer_Orders**

2. If you did not add the **Access Chapter 5** folder to the Trust Center, enable the content. In the **Navigation Pane**, under **Tables**, rename the four tables by adding **Lastname Firstname** to the beginning of each table name. Resize the **Navigation Pane** so all table names are fully displayed. Take a moment to open each table and observe the data in each. In the **5B Orders** table, make a note of the data type for the **Order#** field and the pattern of data entered in the field. When you are finished, close all of the tables, and **Close** « the **Navigation Pane**.

   In the *5B Orders* table, the first record contains an Order# of 7-11-17-0002. The first section of the order number is the month of the order and the second section is the day of the month. The last section is a sequential number. Records with orders for July, August, and September are contained in this table.

ALERT! **Action Queries and Trusted Databases**

To run an action query, the database must reside in a trusted location, or you must enable the content. If you try running an action query and nothing happens, check the status bar for the following message: *This action or event has been blocked by Disabled Mode*. Either add the storage location to Trusted Locations or enable the content. Then, run the query again.

3 Create a new query in **Query Design**. From the **Show Table** dialog box, add the following tables to the query design workspace: **5B Customers**, **5B Orders**, and **5B Shippers**. **Close** the **Show Table** dialog box, and then resize the field lists. Notice the relationships between the tables.

The *5B Customers* table has a one-to-many relationship with the *5B Orders* table—*one* customer can have *many* orders. The *5B Shippers* table has a one-to-many relationship with the *5B Orders* table—*one* shipper can ship *more* than one order.

4 From the **5B Orders** field list, add **Order#** to the first column of the design grid. From the **5B Customers** field list, add **Last Name** and **First Name** to the second and third columns of the design grid. From the **5B Shippers** field list, add **Shipping Company** to the fourth column of the design grid.

5 In the design grid, click in the **Criteria row** under **Order#**, type **9*** and then compare your screen with Figure 5.29.

Recall that the asterisk is a wildcard that stands for one or more characters—Access will extract the records where the Order# starts with a 9, and it does not matter what the following characters are. The first section of the Order# contains the month the order was placed without any regard for the year; all September orders will display whether they were placed in 2017, 2018, or any other year. You do not need criteria in a select query to convert it to a make table query.

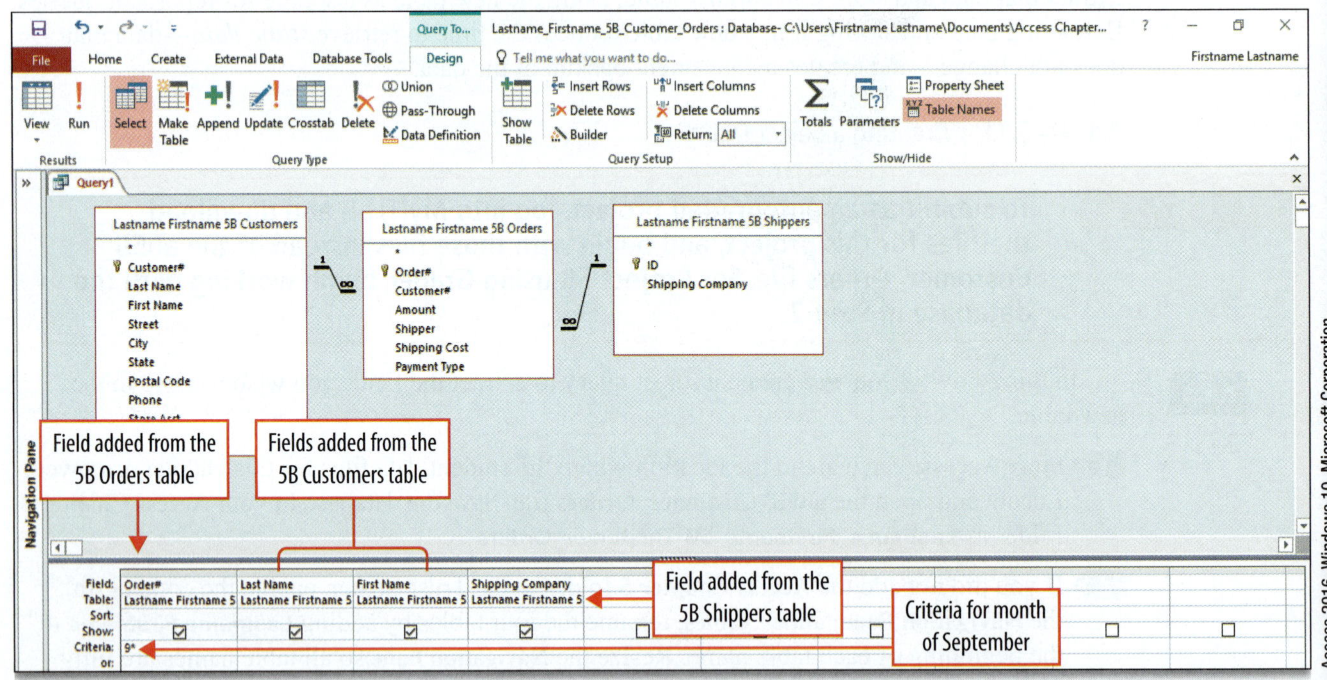

FIGURE 5.29

NOTE Using Expressions and Aggregate Functions in a Make Table Query

In addition to using criteria in a select query upon which a make table query is based, you can use expressions to create a calculated field; for example, *Gross Pay:[Hourly Wage]*[Hours Worked]*. You can also use aggregate functions; for example, you may want to sum the *Hours Worked* field.

6 **Run** the query, and notice that four orders were placed in September.

The select query displays the records that will be stored in the new table.

Activity 5.12 | Converting a Select Query to a Make Table Query

3.1.4, 3.1.6, 1.3.5

In this Activity, you will convert the select query you just created to a make table query.

1 Switch to **Design** view. Under **Query Tools**, on the **Design tab**, in the **Query Type group**, click **Make Table**. Notice the exclamation point (!) in several of the buttons in the Query Type group—these are action queries. In the **Make Table** dialog box, in the **Table Name** box, type **Lastname Firstname 5B September Orders** and then compare your screen with Figure 5.30.

The table name should be a unique table name for the database in which the table will be saved. If it is not, you will be prompted to delete the first table before the new table can be created. You can save a make table query in the current database or in another existing database.

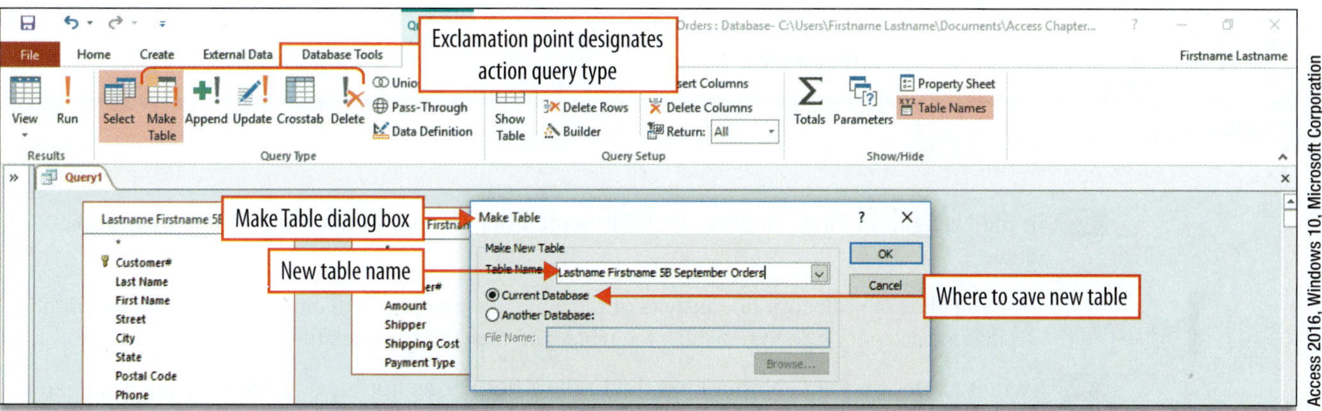

FIGURE 5.30

2 In the **Make Table** dialog box, verify that **Current Database** is selected, and then click **OK**. **Run** the query.

A message displays indicating that *You are about to paste 4 row(s) into a new table* and that you cannot use the Undo command.

3 In the displayed message box, click **Yes**. **Close** the query, click **Yes** in the message box prompting you to save changes, and then name the query **Lastname Firstname 5B Make Table Query**

4 **Open** » the **Navigation Pane**. Notice that under Tables, the new table you created—*5B September Orders*—is displayed. Under Queries, the *5B Make Table Query* is displayed.

5 In the **Navigation Pane**, click the title—**All Access Objects**. Under **Navigate To Category**, click **Tables and Related Views**, widen the **Navigation Pane**, and then compare your screen with Figure 5.31.

The Navigation Pane is grouped by tables and related objects. Because the 5B Make Table Query extracted records from three tables—*5B Customers*, *5B Orders*, and *5B Shippers*—it is displayed under all three tables. Changing the grouping in the Navigation Pane to Tables and Related Views enables you to easily determine which objects are dependent upon other objects in the database.

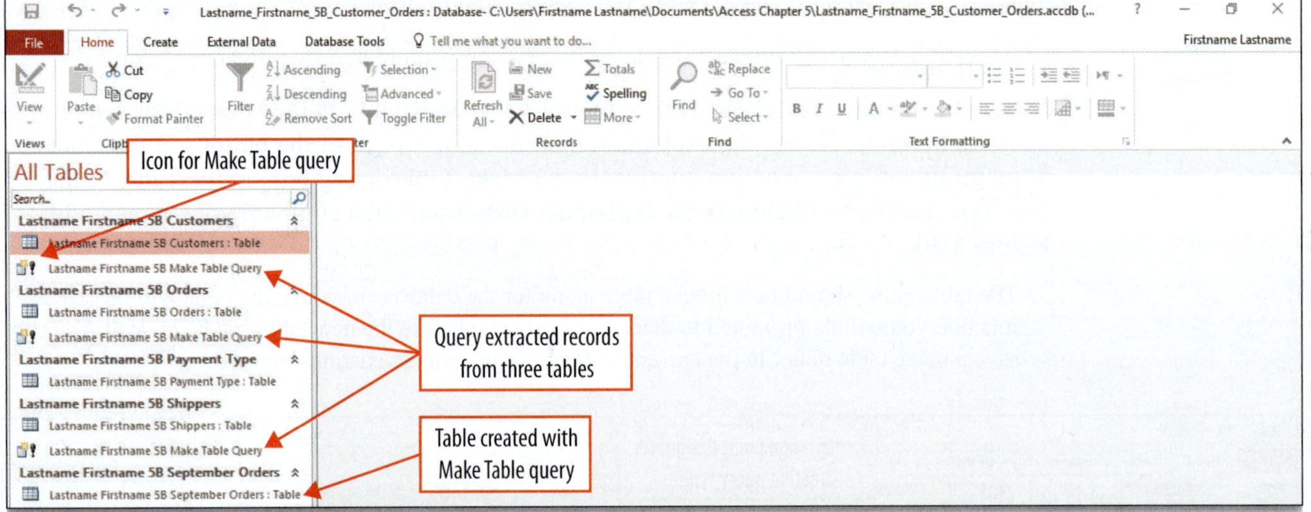

Access 2016, Windows 10, Microsoft Corporation

FIGURE 5.31

6 In the **Navigation Pane**, double-click **5B September Orders** to open the table in **Datasheet** view.

If you click the category title instead of the table, the category will close—if that happens, double-click the category title to redisplay the table, and then double-click the table.

7 Switch to **Design** view. Notice that the Order# field does not have an input mask associated with it and that there is no Primary Key field for this table.

When using a make table query to create a new table, the data in the new table does not inherit the field properties or the Primary Key field setting from the original table.

8 Switch to **Datasheet** view, and then adjust all column widths. **Close** the table, saving changes.

NOTE Updating a Table Created with a Make Table Query

The data stored in a table created with a make table query is not automatically updated when records in the original tables are modified. To keep the new table up to date, you must run the make table query periodically to be sure the information is current.

Objective 7 Create an Append Query

GO! Learn How Video A5-7

An ***append query*** is an action query that adds new records to an existing table by adding data from another Access database or from a table in the same database. An append query can be limited by criteria. Use an append query when the data already exists and you do not want to manually enter it into an existing table. Like the make table query, you first create a select query and then convert it to an append query.

Activity 5.13 | Creating an Append Query for a Table in the Current Database

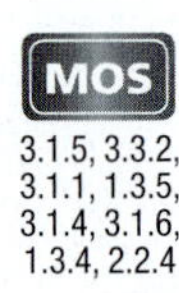

3.1.5, 3.3.2, 3.1.1, 1.3.5, 3.1.4, 3.1.6, 1.3.4, 2.2.4

In this Activity, you will create a select query to extract the records for customers who have placed orders in August and then append the records to the *5B September Orders* table.

1 **Close** « the **Navigation Pane**. Create a new query in **Query Design**. From the **Show Table** dialog box, add the following tables to the Query design workspace: **5B Customers**, **5B Orders**, and **5B Shippers**. **Close** the **Show Table** dialog box, and then resize the field lists.

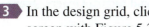

2 From the **5B Customers** field list, add **First Name** and **Last Name**, in the order specified, to the first and second columns of the design grid. From the **5B Orders** field list, add **Order#** and **Shipping Cost**, in the order specified, to the third and fourth columns of the design grid. From the **5B Shippers** field list, add **Shipping Company** to the fifth column of the design grid.

3 In the design grid, click in the **Criteria row** under **Order#**, type **8*** and then compare your screen with Figure 5.32.

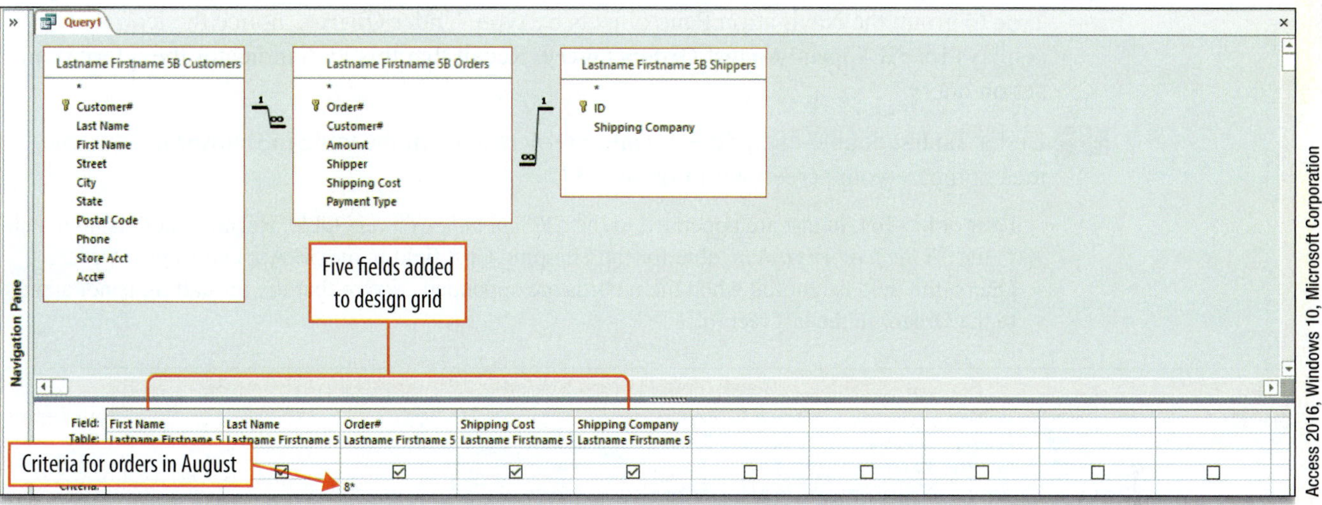

FIGURE 5.32

4 **Run** the query, and notice that four customers placed orders in August.

5 Switch to **Design** view. Under **Query Tools**, on the **Design tab**, in the **Query Type group**, click **Append**. In the **Append** dialog box, click the **Table Name arrow**, and then from the displayed list, click **5B September Orders**. Click **OK**. Compare your screen with Figure 5.33.

In the design grid, Access inserts an *Append To* row above the Criteria row. Access compares the fields in the query with the fields in the ***destination table***—the table to which you are appending the fields—and attempts to match fields. If a match is found, Access adds the name of the destination field to the Append To row in the query. If no match is found, Access leaves the destination field blank. You can click the box in the Append To row and select a destination field.

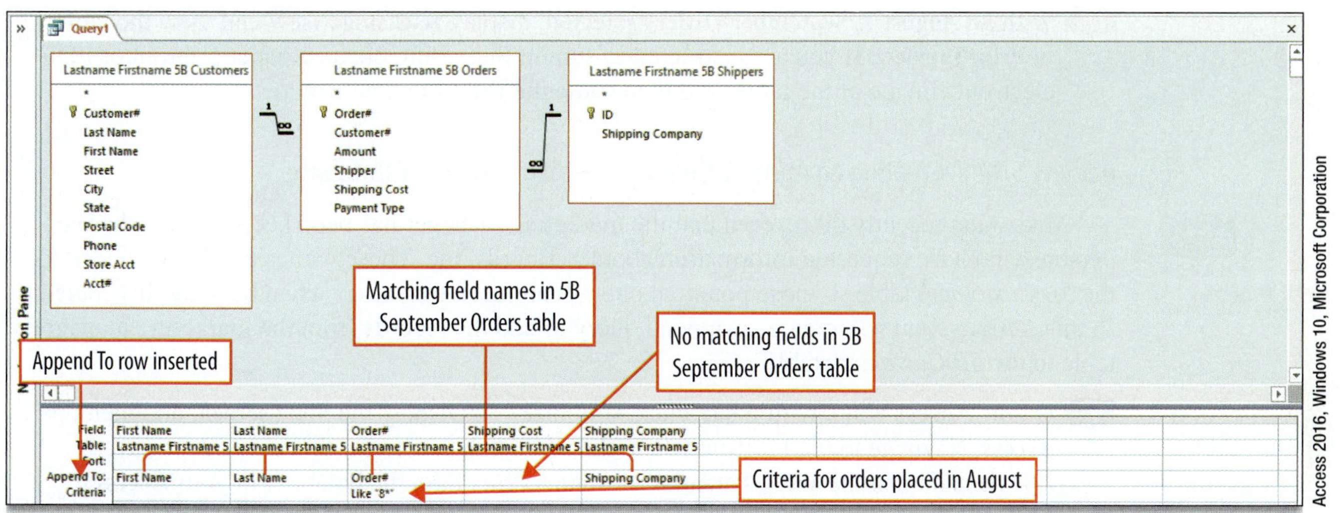

FIGURE 5.33

6 **Run** the query. In the displayed message box, click **Yes** to append the four rows to the *5B September Orders* table.

7 **Close** the query, and then save it as **Lastname Firstname 5B Append August Orders Query**

8 **Open** [»] the **Navigation Pane**. Notice that **5B Append August Orders Query** displays under the three tables from which data was extracted.

9 In the **Navigation Pane**, click the title—**All Tables**. Under **Navigate To Category**, click **Object Type** to group the Navigation Pane objects by type. Under **Queries**, notice the icon that displays for **5B Append August Orders Query**. Recall that this icon indicates the query is an action query.

10 Under **Tables**, double-click **5B September Orders** to open the table in **Datasheet** view, and then compare your screen with Figure 5.34.

Four orders for August are appended to the *5B September Orders* table. Because there is no match in the *5B September Orders* table for the Shipping Cost field in the 5B Append August Orders Query, the field is ignored when the records are appended. Notice that the formatting is not applied to the Order# in the last record.

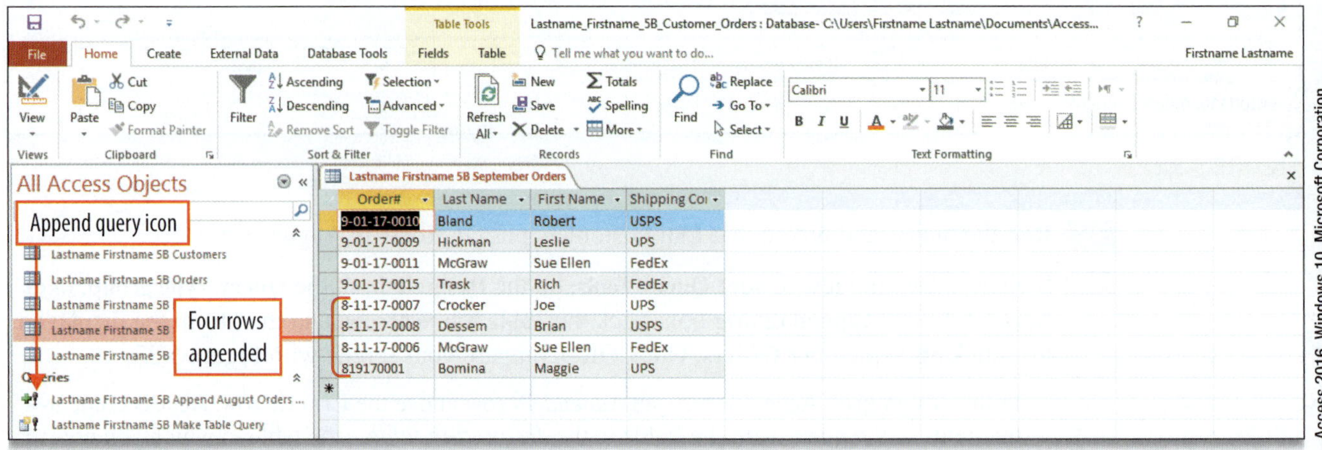

FIGURE 5.34

11 **Close** the table. In the **Navigation Pane**, under **Tables**, right-click **5B September Orders**, and then click **Rename**. **Rename** the table as **Lastname Firstname 5B August & September Orders**

12 With **5B August & September Orders** selected, display **Backstage** view and view the table in **Print Preview**. If you are instructed to submit this result, create a paper printout or PDF electronic image of the table, and then **Close** the Print Preview window.

Activity 5.14 | Creating an Append Query for a Table in Another Database

3.1.4, 2.2.4, 2.1.2, 3.1.1, 3.2.2, 3.1.6

Miko Adai recently discovered that the marketing manager has been keeping a database of persons who have requested information about S-Boards, Inc. These names need to be added to the *5B Customers* table so those potential clients can receive catalogs when they are distributed. In this Activity, you will create an append query to add the records from the marketing manager's table to the *5B Customers* table.

1 On the Access window title bar, click **Minimize** [–]. Display the **Start screen**, and then open **Access**. Navigate to the location where the student data files for this chapter are saved. Locate and open the **a05B_Potential_Customers** file. **Save** the database in your **Access Chapter 5** folder as **Lastname_Firstname_5B_Potential_Customers**

2 If you did not add the **Access Chapter 5** folder to the Trust Center, enable the content. In the **Navigation Pane**, under **Tables**, rename the table by adding **Lastname Firstname** to the beginning of **5B Potential Customers**. Resize the **Navigation Pane** so the entire table name is visible. Take a moment to open the table, noticing the fields and field names. When you are finished, **Close** the table, and **Close** « the **Navigation Pane**.

The *5B Potential Customers* table in this database contains fields similar to those in the *5B Customers* table in the *5B_Customer_Orders* database.

3 Create a new query in **Query Design**. From the **Show Table** dialog box, add the **5B Potential Customers** table to the query design workspace, and then **Close** the **Show Table** dialog box. Resize the field list.

4 In the **5B Potential Customers** field list, click **Customer#**, hold down Shift, and then click **Phone** to select all of the fields. Drag the selection down into the first column of the design grid.

Although you could click the asterisk (*) in the field list to add all of the fields to the design grid, it is easier to detect which fields have no match in the destination table when the field names are listed individually in the design grid.

5 Under **Query Tools**, on the **Design tab**, in the **Query Type group**, click **Append**. In the **Append** dialog box, click the **Another Database** option button, and then click **Browse**. Navigate to your **Access Chapter 5** folder, and then double-click **5B Customer Orders**. (Be sure to use the version of the file that you worked on and saved earlier.)

The *5B Customer Orders* database contains the destination table.

6 In the **Append** dialog box, click the **Table Name arrow**, click **5B Customers**, and then compare your screen with Figure 5.35.

Once you select the name of another database, the tables contained in that database display.

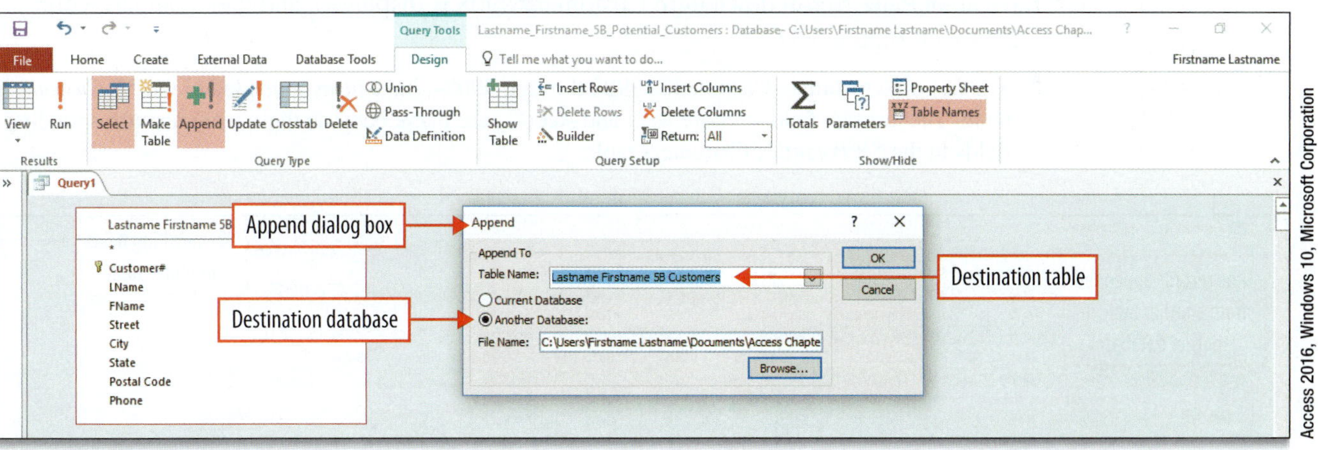

FIGURE 5.35

7 Click **OK**. In the design grid, notice that in the **Append To row**, Access found field name matches for all fields except **LName** and **FName**.

8 In the design grid, click in the **Append To row** under **LName**, click the **arrow**, and then compare your screen with Figure 5.36.

A list displays the field names contained in the *5B Customers* table. If the field names are not exactly the same in the source and destination tables, Access will not designate them as matched fields. A ***source table*** is the table from which records are being extracted.

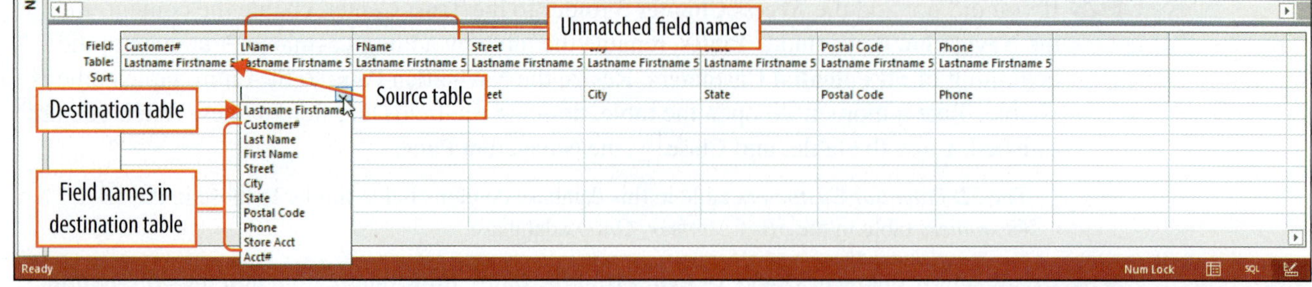

FIGURE 5.36

Access 2016, Windows 10, Microsoft Corporation

9 From the displayed list, click **Last Name**. Click in the **Append To** row under **FName**, and then click the **arrow**. In the displayed list, click **First Name**.

10 **Save** the query as **Lastname Firstname 5B Append to 5B Customers Query** and then **Run** the query, clicking **Yes** to append 9 rows. **Close** the query, and then **Open** » the **Navigation Pane**, resizing it if necessary. **Close** the database, and then **Close** this instance of Access.

ALERT! **To trust or not to trust? That is the question!**

When you allow someone else to run an action query that will modify a table in your database, be sure that you can trust that individual. One mistake in the action query could destroy your table. A better way of running an action query that is dependent upon someone else's table is to obtain a copy of the table, place it in a database that you have created, and examine the table for malicious code. Once you are satisfied that the table is safe, you can create the action query to modify the data in your tables. Be sure to make a backup copy of the destination database before running action queries.

11 If necessary, on the taskbar, click the button for your **5B_Customer_Orders** database. If you mistakenly closed the *5B_Customer_Orders* database, reopen it. In the **Navigation Pane**, under **Tables**, double-click **5B Customers** to open the table in **Datasheet** view. **Close** « the **Navigation Pane**. Scroll down until Customer# 9908 is displayed, and then compare your screen with Figure 5.37.

The last nine records—Customer#s 9900 through 9908—have been appended to the *5B Customers* table. The last two fields—Store Acct and Acct#—are blank because there were no corresponding fields in the *5B Potential Customers* table.

Lastname Firstname 5B Customers

Customer#	Last Name	First Name	Street	City	State	Post	Phone	Store Acct	Acct#	Click to
		Cindy	5119 Patricia St	Irvine	CA	92603	(949) 555-0477	☐		
		Blake	4724 Candle Ct	Irvine	CA	92604	(949) 555-7355	☑	489-031-664	
		Zack	15 Avalon Lane	Santa Ana	CA	97204	(714) 555-5593	☐		
		Rich	6825 Wandering Way	East Irvine	CA	92650	(949) 555-2245	☐		
		Maggie	835 Palmetto Ct	Costa Mesa	CA	92626	(949) 555-1338	☑	489-031-667	
1068	Zoltek	Cindy	6440 Waterstone Dr	Newport Beach	CA	92660	(949) 555-2866	☐		
1069	Polenski	Elizabeth	9915 Split Rock Way	Laguna Hills	CA	92653	(949) 555-4664	☐		
9900	Diego	Jake	112 S. Washington St	Irvine	CA	92603	(714) 555-8112	☐		
9901	Sanders	Rachel	2843 Frisco Dr	Santa Ana	CA	97201	(714) 555-6843	☐		
9902	Sweeney	Michael	377 Sunrise Cr	Costa Mesa	CA	92626	(949) 555-8377	☐		
9903	Hernandez	Manuel	1746 Martin Lane	East Irvine	CA	92650	(949) 555-6647	☐		
9904	Roberts	Megan	1002 Sandy Ave	Newport Beach	CA	92658	(949) 555-7002	☐		
9905	Snyder	Amanda	238 Pebblestone Rd	Huntington Beach	CA	92605	(714) 555-8238	☐		
9906	Landsbaum	Jean	8544 N. Richland Dr	Tustin	CA	92780	(714) 555-0544	☐		
9907	Salas	Alberto	400 Valley Ridge, Apt :	Fountain Valley	CA	92708	(562) 555-0192	☐		
9908	Andrews	Kayla	330 Morse Mill Rod	East Irvine	CA	92650	(949) 555-7653	☐		
*					CA			☐		

Nine records appended from another table in another database

No matching fields in source table

Navigation Pane

FIGURE 5.37

Access 2016, Windows 10, Microsoft Corporation

> ***More* Knowledge** **Running the Same Append Query a Second Time**
>
> If you run the same append query a second time with the same records in the source table and no primary key field is involved in the appending of records, you will have duplicate records in the destination table. If a primary key field is part of the records being duplicated, a message will display stating that Access cannot append all of the records due to one of several rule violations. If new records were added to the source table that were not originally appended to the destination table, clicking Yes in the message dialog box will enable those records to be added without adding duplicate records.

Objective 8 Create a Delete Query

GO! Learn How
Video A5-8

A ***delete query*** is an action query that removes records from an existing table in the same database. When information becomes outdated or is no longer needed, the records should be deleted from your database. Recall that one method you can use to find unnecessary records is to create a find unmatched query. Assuming outdated records have common criteria, you can create a select query, convert it to a delete query, and then delete all of the records at one time rather than deleting the records one by one. Use delete queries only when you need to remove many records quickly. Before running a delete query, you should back up the database because you cannot undo the deletion.

Activity 5.15 | Creating a Delete Query

2.3.6, 1.2.5, 3.1.1, 3.2.2, 3.3.2, 1.3.5, 3.1.4, 3.1.6

A competing store has opened in Santa Ana, and the former customers living in that city have decided to do business with that store. In this Activity, you will create a select query and then convert it to a delete query to remove records for clients living in Santa Ana.

1. With the **5B Customers** table open in **Datasheet** view, under **City**, click in any row. On the **Home tab**, in the **Sort & Filter group**, click **Descending** to arrange the cities in descending alphabetical order.

2. At the top of the datasheet, in the record for **Customer# 1060**, click the **plus (+) sign** to display the subdatasheet. Notice that this customer has placed one order that has been shipped.

3. Display the subdatasheets for the four customers residing in **Santa Ana**, and then compare your screen with Figure 5.38.

   The four customers residing in Santa Ana have not placed orders.

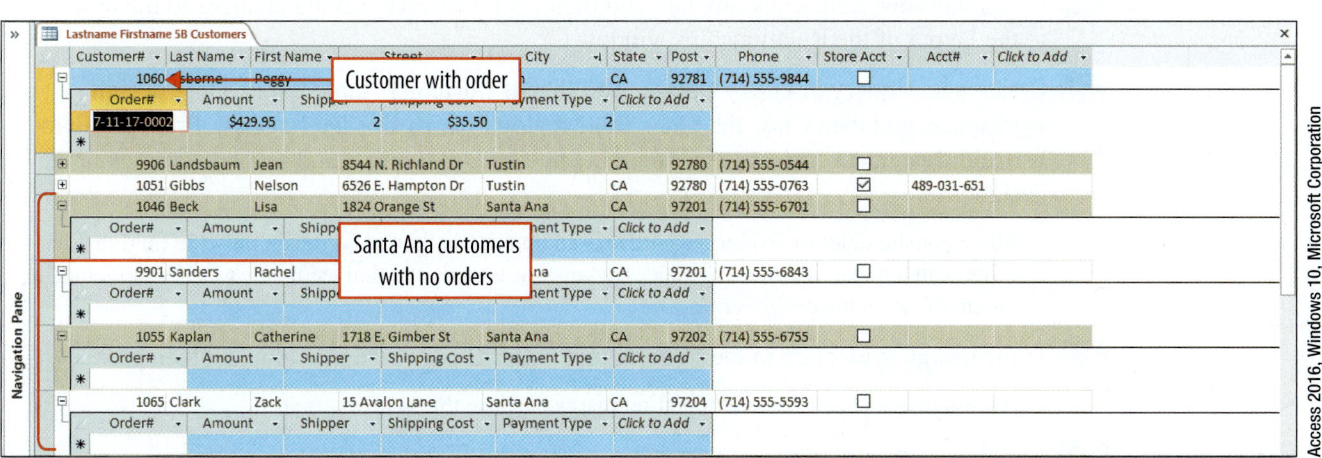

Access 2016, Windows 10, Microsoft Corporation

FIGURE 5.38

4 Collapse all of the subdatasheets by clicking each **minus (–) sign**.

5 On the ribbon, click the **Database Tools tab**. In the **Relationships group**, click **Relationships**. Under **Relationship Tools**, on the **Design tab**, in the **Relationships group**, click **All Relationships**. Resize the field lists and rearrange the field lists to match the layout displayed in Figure 5.39.

The *5B Customers* table has a one-to-many relationship with the *5B Orders* table, and referential integrity has been enforced. By default, Access will prevent the deletion of records from the table on the *one* side of the relationship if related records are contained in the table on the *many* side of the relationship. Because the records for the Santa Ana customers do not have related records in the related table, you will be able to delete the records from the *5B Customers* table, which is on the *one* side of the relationship.

To delete records from the table on the *one* side of the relationship that have related records in the table on the *many* side of the relationship, you must either delete the relationship or enable Cascade Delete Related Records. If you need to delete records on the *many* side of the relationship, you can do so without changing or deleting the relationship.

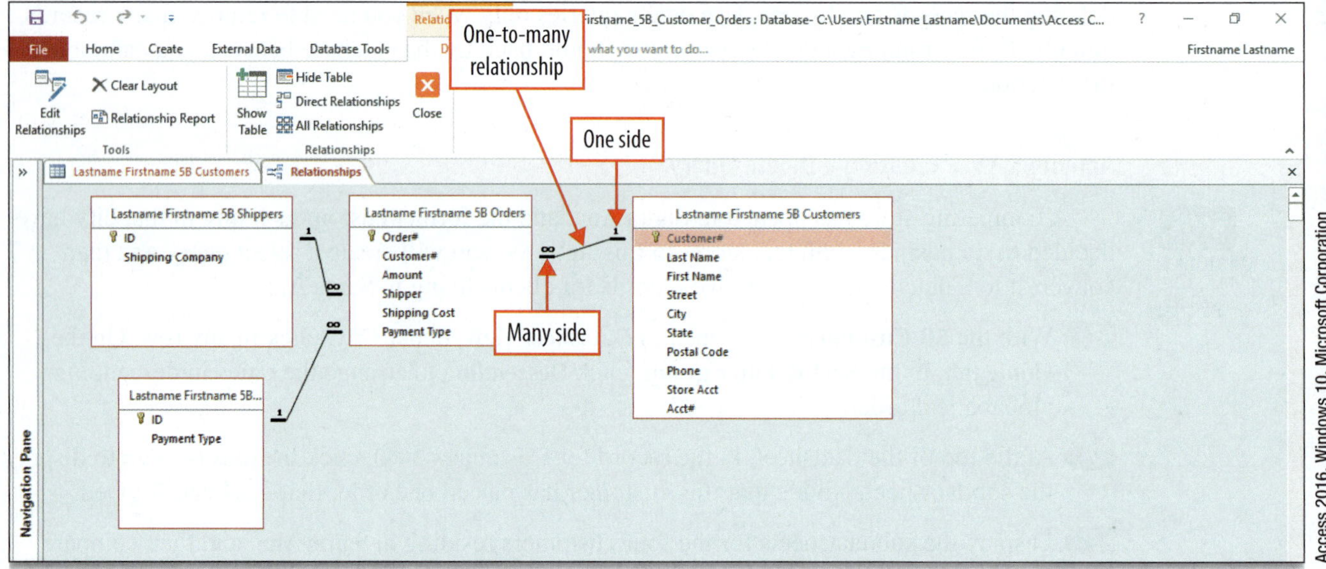

FIGURE 5.39

6 On the **tab row**, right-click any tab, and then click **Close All**, saving changes to the table and to the layout of the Relationships window.

7 Create a new query in **Query Design**. Add the **5B Customers** table to the query design workspace, and then **Close** the **Show Table** dialog box. Resize the field list. From the field list, add **Customer#** and **City**, in the order specified, to the first and second columns in the design grid.

Since you are deleting existing records based on criteria, you need to add only the field that has criteria attached to it—the City field. However, it is easier to analyze the results if you include another field in the design grid.

8 In the design grid, click in the **Criteria** row under **City**, type **Santa Ana** and then press ↓.

Access inserts the criteria in quotation marks because this is a Text field.

9 **Run** the query, and then compare your screen with Figure 5.40.

Four records for customers in Santa Ana are displayed. If your query results display an empty record, switch to Design view and be sure that you typed the criteria correctly.

Customer#	City
1046	Santa Ana
1055	Santa Ana
1065	Santa Ana
9901	Santa Ana

Customers living in Santa Ana

FIGURE 5.40

Access 2016, Windows 10, Microsoft Corporation

10 Switch to **Design** view. In the query design workspace, to the right of the field list, right-click in the empty space. From the displayed shortcut menu, point to **Query Type**, and click **Delete Query** or, under **Query Tools**, on the **Design tab**, in the **Query Type** group, click **Delete**. Compare your screen with Figure 5.41.

In the design grid, a Delete row is inserted above the Criteria row with the word *Where* in both columns. Access will delete all records *Where* the City is Santa Ana. If you include all of the fields in the query using the asterisk (*), Access inserts the word *From* in the Delete row, and all of the records will be deleted.

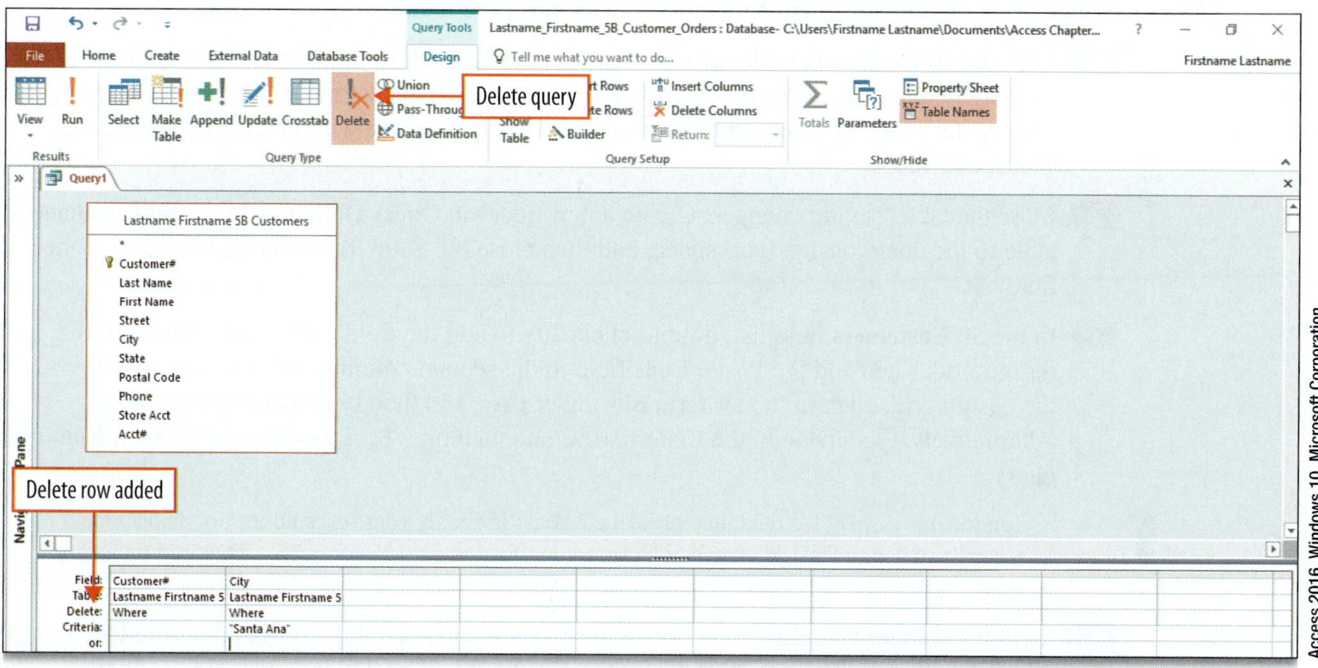

FIGURE 5.41

Access 2016, Windows 10, Microsoft Corporation

11 **Save** the query as **Lastname Firstname 5B Delete Santa Ana Customers Query** and then **Run** the query. In the message box stating that *You are about to delete 4 row(s) from the specified table*, click **Yes**.

12 **Close** the query, and then **Open** [»] the **Navigation Pane**. Under **Queries**, notice the icon that is associated with a delete query—**5B Delete Santa Ana Customers Query**. Under **Tables**, open the **5B Customers** table in **Datasheet** view. Notice that the records are still in descending order by the **City** field, and notice that the four records for customers living in **Santa Ana** have been deleted from the table.

13 **Close** [«] the **Navigation Pane**, leaving the table open for the next Activity. On the **Home tab**, in the **Sort & Filter group**, click **Remove Sort** to clear all sorts from the **City** field.

Objective 9 Create an Update Query

GO! Learn How
Video A5-9

An ***update query*** is an action query that is used to add, change, or delete data in fields of one or more existing records. Combined with criteria, an update query is an efficient way to change data for a large number of records at one time, and you can change records in more than one table at a time. If you need to change data in a few records, you can use the Find and Replace dialog box. You are unable to use update queries to add or delete records in a table; use an append query or delete query as needed. Because you are changing data with an update query, you should back up your database before running one.

Activity 5.16 | Creating an Update Query

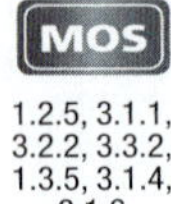

1.2.5, 3.1.1, 3.2.2, 3.3.2, 1.3.5, 3.1.4, 3.1.6

The postal codes for all of the customers living in Irvine or East Irvine are changing to a consolidated postal code. In this Activity, you will create a select query to extract the records from the *5B Customers* table for customers living in these cities, and then convert the query to an update query so that you change the postal codes for all of the records at one time.

1. With the **5B Customers** table open in **Datasheet** view, click in the **City** field in any row. Sort the **City** field in **Ascending** order. Notice that there are five customers living in **East Irvine** with postal codes of **92650** and five customers living in **Irvine** with postal codes of **92602**, **92603**, and **92604**.

2. **Close** the table, saving changes. Create a new query in **Query Design**. Add the **5B Customers** table to the query design workspace, and then close the **Show Table** dialog box. Resize the field list.

3. In the **5B Customers** field list, double-click **City** to add the field to the first column of the design grid. Then add the **Postal Code** field to the second column of the design grid. In the design grid, click in the **Criteria row** under **City**, and then type **Irvine or East Irvine** Alternatively, type **Irvine** in the Criteria row, and then type **East Irvine** in the Or row. **Run** the query.

   Ten records display for the cities of Irvine or East Irvine. If your screen does not display ten records, switch to Design view and be sure you typed the criteria correctly. Then run the query again.

4. Switch to **Design** view, and then notice how Access changed the criteria under the **City** field, placing quotation marks around the text and capitalizing *or*. Under **Query Tools**, on the **Design tab**, in the **Query Type group**, click **Update**.

   In the design grid, an Update To row is inserted above the Criteria row.

5. In the design grid, click in the **Update To** row under **Postal Code**, type **92601** and then compare your screen with Figure 5.42.

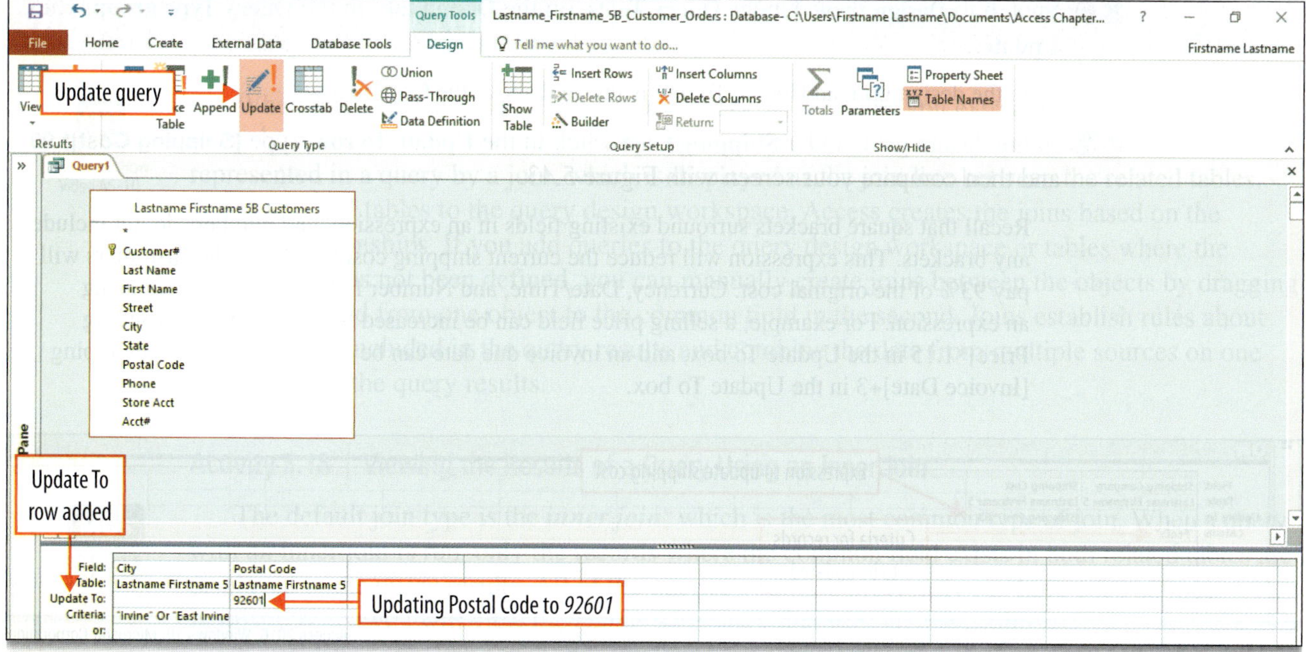

FIGURE 5.42 Access 2016, Windows 10, Microsoft Corporation

6 **Save** the query as **Lastname Firstname 5B Update Postal Codes Query** and then **Run** the query. In the message box stating that *You are about to update 10 row(s)*, click **Yes**.

7 **Close** the query, and then **Open** the **Navigation Pane**. Under **Queries**, notice the icon that is associated with an update query—**5B Update Postal Codes Query**. Under **Tables**, open the **5B Customers** table in **Datasheet** view. Notice that the 10 records for customers living in **East Irvine** and **Irvine** have a **Postal Code** of **92601**.

8 View the table in **Print Preview**. Change the orientation to **Landscape** and the margins to **Normal** so the table prints on one page. If you are instructed to submit this result, create a paper printout or PDF electronic image, and then **Close** the Print Preview window. **Close** the table.

Activity 5.17 | Creating an Update Query with an Expression

2.3.6, 3.1.5, 3.2.2, 3.3.2, 1.3.5, 3.3.1

There was a computer problem, and customers were overcharged for items shipped by FedEx. In this Activity, you will create an update query to correct the field to reflect an accurate shipping cost. Any item shipped by FedEx will be discounted 7 percent.

1 Open the **5B Orders** table in **Datasheet** view, and **Close** the **Navigation Pane**. Click the right side of the **Shipper** field to see the lookup list. Notice an entry of **1** means the order was shipped using FedEx. Press Esc to return to the field box. Sort the **Shipper** field from **Smallest to Largest**. Notice that there are five orders that were shipped using FedEx. Make note of the shipping cost for each of those items.

2 **Close** the table, saving changes. Create a new query in **Query Design**. From the **Show Table** dialog box, add the **5B Shippers** table and the **5B Orders** table to the query design workspace, and then **Close** the **Show Table** dialog box. Resize the field lists.

3 From the **5B Shippers** field list, add **Shipping Company** to the design grid. From the **5B Orders** field list, add **Shipping Cost** to the design grid. In the **Criteria row** under **Shipping Company**, type **FedEx Run** the query.

Five records display for FedEx. If your screen does not display five records, switch to Design view and be sure you typed the criteria correctly. Then run the query again.

3 In the **Edit Relationships** dialog box, click **Join Type**, and then compare your screen with Figure 5.45. In the displayed **Join Properties** dialog box, notice that option **1** is selected—*Only include rows where the joined fields from both tables are equal.*

Option 1 is the default join type, which is an inner join. Options 2 and 3 are outer join types.

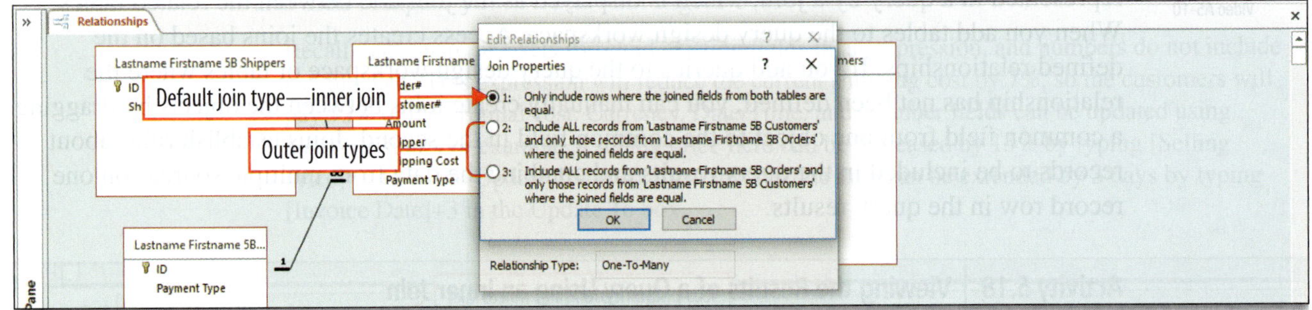

Access 2016, Windows 10, Microsoft Corporation

FIGURE 5.45

4 In the **Join Properties** dialog box, click **Cancel**. In the **Edit Relationships** dialog box, click **Cancel**. **Close** the **Relationships** window.

Because the relationships have been established and saved in the database, you should not change the join properties in the Relationships window. You should only change join properties in the query design workspace.

5 **Open** » the **Navigation Pane**. In the **Navigation Pane**, open the **5B Orders** table and the **5B Customers** table, in the order specified, and then **Close** « the **Navigation Pane**.

6 With the **5B Customers** table active, on the **Home tab**, in the **Sort & Filter group**, click **Remove Sort** to remove the ascending sort from the **City** field. Notice that the records are now sorted by the **Customer#** field—the primary key field.

7 In the third record, click the **plus (+) sign** to expand the subdatasheet—the related record in the *5B Orders* table—and then notice that **Willie Smith** has no related records—he has not placed any orders. Click the **minus (–) sign** to collapse the subdatasheet.

8 Expand the subdatasheet for **Customer# 1045**, and then notice that **Joe Crocker** has one related record in the *5B Orders* table—he has placed one order. Collapse the subdatasheet.

9 Expand the subdatasheet for **Customer# 1047**, and then notice that **Robert Bland** has two related records in the *5B Orders* table—he has placed *many* orders. Collapse the subdatasheet.

10 On the **tab row**, click the **5B Orders tab** to make the datasheet active, and then notice that 15 orders have been placed. On the **tab row**, right-click any tab, and then click **Close All**, saving changes, if prompted.

11 Create a new query in **Query Design**. From the **Show Table** dialog box, add the **5B Customers** table and the **5B Orders** table to the query design workspace, and then close the **Show Table** dialog box. Resize both field lists.

12 From the **5B Customers** field list, add **Customer#**, **Last Name**, and **First Name**, in the order specified, to the design grid. In the design grid, under **Customer#**, click in the **Sort row**, click the **arrow**, and then click **Ascending**. **Run** the query, and then compare your screen with Figure 5.46. There is no record for Willie Smith, there is one record for Customer# 1045—Joe Crocker—and there are two records for Customer# 1047—Robert Bland.

Because the default join type is an inner join, the query results display records only where there is a matching Customer#—the common field—in both related tables, even though you did not add any fields from the *5B Orders* table to the design grid. All of the records display for the table on the *many* side of the relationship—*5B Orders*. For the table on the *one* side of the relationship—*5B Customers*—only those records that have matching records in the related table display. Recall that there were 30 records in the *5B Customers* table and 15 records in the *5B Orders* table.

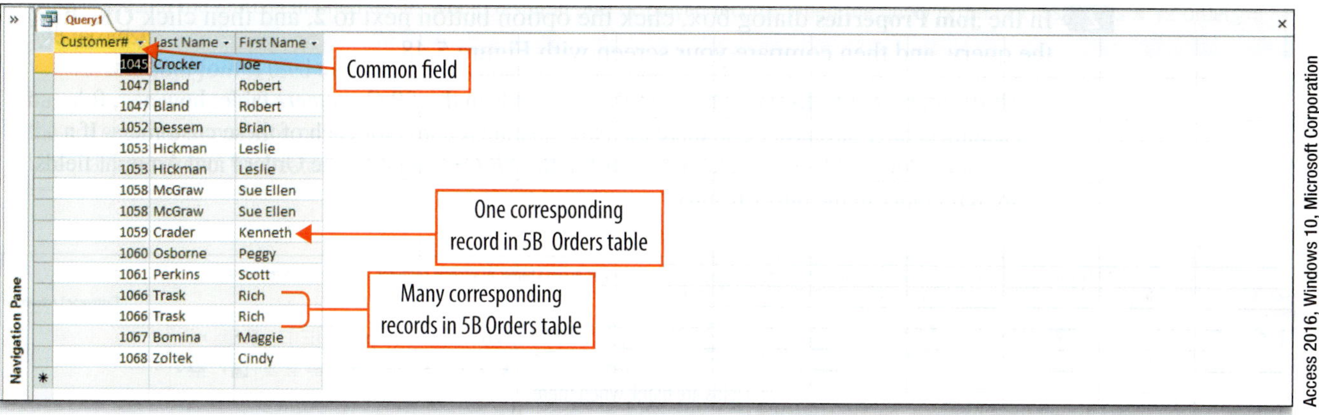

FIGURE 5.46

13 Switch to **Design** view. From the **5B Orders** field list, add **Order#** to the fourth column of the design grid, and then add **Amount** to the fifth column of the design grid. **Run** the query to display the results.

The same 15 records display but with two additional fields.

Activity 5.19 | Changing the Join Type to an Outer Join

1.3.5, 3.1.6

An ***outer join*** is typically used to display records from both tables, regardless of whether there are matching records. In this Activity, you will modify the join type to display all of the records from the *5B Customers* table, regardless of whether the customer has placed an order.

1 Switch to **Design** view. In the query design workspace, right-click the join line, and then click **Join Properties** or double-click the **join line** to display the **Join Properties** dialog box. Compare your screen with Figure 5.47.

The Join Properties dialog box displays the tables used in the join and the common field from both tables. Option 1—inner join type—is selected by default. Options 2 and 3 are two different types of outer joins.

Option 2 is a ***left outer join***. Select a left outer join when you want to display all of the records on the *one* side of the relationship, whether or not there are matching records in the table on the *many* side of the relationship. Option 3 is a ***right outer join***. Selecting a right outer join will display all of the records on the *many* side of the relationship, whether or not there are matching records in the table on the *one* side of the relationship. This should not occur if referential integrity has been enforced because all orders should have a related customer.

FIGURE 5.48

Save [illegible] the query as **Lastname Firstname 5B Outer Join Query**. View the query in Print Preview, ensuring that the table prints on one page. If you are instructed to submit this result, create a paper or PDF electronic image. Close the Print Preview [illegible]

GO! To Work

Andres Rodriguez/Fotolia; FotolEdhar/Fotolia; Andrey Popov/Fotolia; Shutterstock

5 ACCESS

MICROSOFT OFFICE SPECIALIST (MOS) SKILLS IN THIS CHAPTER

PROJECT 5A		PROJECT 5B	
1.3.5	Change views of objects	**1.2.5**	View relationships
2.2.2	Add total rows	**1.3.4**	Display objects in the Navigation Pane
2.2 4	Rename tables	**1.3.5**	Change views of objects
2.4.3	Change field captions	**2.1.2**	Import data into tables
3.1.1	Run a query	**2.2.4**	Rename tables
3.1.2	Create a crosstab query	**2.3.6**	Sort records
3.1.3	Create a parameter query	**3.1.1**	Run a query
3.1.5	Create a multi-table query	**3.1.4**	Create an action query
3.1.6	Save a query	**3.1.5**	Create a multi-table query
3.2.2	Add fields	**3.1.6**	Save a query
3.2.5	Sort data within queries	**3.2.2**	Add fields
3.2.6	Format fields within queries	**3.2.5**	Sort data within a query
3.3.1	Add calculated fields	**3.3.2**	Set filtering criteria
3.3.2	Set filtering criteria		
3.3.3	Group and summarize data		
3.3.5	Group data by using arithmetic and logical operators		

BUILD YOUR E-PORTFOLIO

An E-Portfolio is a collection of evidence, stored electronically, that showcases what you have accomplished while completing your education. Collecting and then sharing your work products with potential employers reflects your academic and career goals. Your completed documents from the following projects are good examples to show what you have learned: 5G, 5K, and 5L.

GO! FOR JOB SUCCESS

Discussion: Business Culture

Your instructor may assign these questions to your class, and then ask you to think about them or discuss them with your classmates:

Markets and technologies move fast in today's high-tech environment. Companies that need to adapt quickly are adopting an agile business culture. Agile businesses focus on customer needs and welcome the changes to products or services that customers request. Constant innovation toward more effective strategies is seen as the norm.

FotolEdhar/Fotolia

What are some businesses that you interact with that might benefit from the quicker innovation and response to customer input provided by an agile culture?

Do you see areas at your college that you think would benefit from a more agile culture?

Are there areas of your life where an agile approach to change and innovation might be beneficial?

END OF CHAPTER

SUMMARY

Queries are powerful database objects created to do more than extract data from tables and other queries; results can provide tools for analyzing, updating, and maintaining the integrity of the data.

Special-purpose queries are created to calculate fields, use aggregate functions, display data for easier analysis, find duplicate and unmatched records to avoid problems, and create prompts to use.

Action queries are used to create new tables, append records from source data in the same and other databases, delete records, and update data in tables. The results must be viewed in the original table.

Query results can be modified to display additional records by changing from the default inner join to an outer join between tables.

GO! LEARN IT ONLINE

Review the concepts, key terms, and MOS Skills in this chapter by completing these online challenges, which you can find at **MyITLab**.

Matching and Multiple Choice: Answer matching and multiple choice questions to test what you learned in this chapter.

Lessons on the GO!: Learn how to use all the new apps and features as they are introduced by Microsoft.

MOS Prep Quiz: Answer questions to review the MOS skills that you have practiced in this chapter.

PROJECT GUIDE FOR ACCESS CHAPTER 5

Your instructor will assign Projects from this list to ensure your learning and assess your knowledge.

PROJECT GUIDE FOR ACCESS CHAPTER 5			
Project	**Apply Skills from These Chapter Objectives**	**Project Type**	**Project Location**
5A **MyITLab**	Objectives 1–5 from Project 5A	**5A Instructional Project (Grader Project)** Guided instruction to learn the skills in Project 5A.	In MyITLab and in text
5B **MyITLab**	Objectives 6–10 from Project 5B	**5B Instructional Project (Grader Project)** Guided instruction to learn the skills in Project 5B.	In MyITLab and in text
5C	Objectives 1–5 from Project 5A	**5C Chapter Review (Scorecard Grading)** A guided review of the skills from Project 5A.	In text
5D	Objectives 6–10 from Project 5B	**5D Chapter Review (Scorecard Grading** A guided review of the skills from Project 5B.	In text
5E	Objectives 1–5 from Project 5A	**5E Mastery (Scorecard Grading)** **Mastery and Transfer of Learning** A demonstration of your mastery of the skills in Project 5A with extensive decision making.	In text
5F	Objectives 6–10 from Project 5B	**5F Mastery (Scorecard Grading)** **Mastery and Transfer of Learning** A demonstration of your mastery of the skills in Project 5B with extensive decision making.	In text
5G **MyITLab**	Objectives 1–3, 9 from Projects 5A and 5B	**5G Mastery (Grader Project)** **Mastery and Transfer of Learning** A demonstration of your mastery of the skills in Projects 5A and 5B with extensive decision making.	In MyITLab and in text
5H	Combination of Objectives from Projects 5A and 5B	**5H GO! Fix It (Scorecard Grading)** **Critical Thinking** A demonstration of your mastery of the skills in Projects 5A and 5B by creating a correct result from a document that contains errors you must find.	Instructor Resource Center (IRC) and MyITLab
5I	Combination of Objectives from Projects 5A and 5B	**5I GO! Make It (Scorecard Grading)** **Critical Thinking** A demonstration of your mastery of the skills in Projects 5A and 5B by creating a result from a supplied picture.	IRC and MyITLab
5J	Combination of Objectives from Projects 5A and 5B	**5J GO! Solve It (Rubric Grading)** **Critical Thinking** A demonstration of your mastery of the skills in Projects 5A and 5B, your decision-making skills, and your critical thinking skills. A task-specific rubric helps you self-assess your result.	IRC and MyITLab
5K	Combination of Objectives from Projects 5A and 5B	**5K GO! Solve It (Rubric Grading)** **Critical Thinking** A demonstration of your mastery of the skills in Projects 5A and 5B, your decision-making skills, and your critical thinking skills. A task-specific rubric helps you self-assess your result.	In text
5L	Combination of Objectives from Projects 5A and 5B	**5L GO! Think (Rubric Grading)** **Critical Thinking** A demonstration of your understanding of the chapter concepts applied in a manner that you would use outside of college. An analytic rubric helps you and your instructor grade the quality of your work by comparing it to the work an expert in the discipline would create.	In text
5M	Combination of Objectives from Projects 5A and 5B	**5M GO! Think (Rubric Grading)** **Critical Thinking** A demonstration of your understanding of the chapter concepts applied in a manner that you would use outside of college. An analytic rubric helps you and your instructor grade the quality of your work by comparing it to the work an expert in the discipline would create.	IRC and MyITLab
5N	Combination of Objectives from Projects 5A and 5B	**5N You and GO! (Rubric Grading)** **Critical Thinking** A demonstration of your understanding of the chapter concepts applied in a manner that you would use in a personal situation. An analytic rubric helps you and your instructor grade the quality of your work.	IRC and MyITLab

GLOSSARY

GLOSSARY OF CHAPTER KEY TERMS

Action query A query that creates a new table or changes data in an existing table.

Aggregate function A function that performs a calculation on a column of data and returns a single value.

Append query An action query that adds new records to an existing table by adding data from another Access database or from a table in the same database.

Arithmetic operators Mathematical symbols used in building expressions.

Calculated field A field that obtains its data by using a formula to perform a calculation or computation.

Cross join A join that displays when each row from one table is combined with each row in a related table, usually created unintentionally when you do not create a join line between related tables.

Crosstab query A query that uses an aggregate function for data that is grouped by two types of information and displays the data in a compact, spreadsheet-like format. A crosstab query always has at least one row heading, one column heading, and one summary field.

Delete query An action query that removes records from an existing table in the same database.

Destination table In an append query, the table to which you are appending records, attempting to match the fields.

Expression The formula that will perform a calculation.

Find Duplicates Query A query used to locate duplicate records in a table.

Find Unmatched Query A query used to locate unmatched records so they can be deleted from the table.

Inner join A join that allows only the records where the common field exists in both related tables to be displayed in query results.

Join A relationship that helps a query return only the records from each table you want to see, based on how those tables are related to other tables in the query.

Left outer join A join used when you want to display all of the records on the *one* side of a one-to-many relationship, whether or not there are matching records in the table on the *many* side of the relationship.

Make table query An action query that creates a new table by extracting data from one or more tables.

Multivalued fields Fields that hold multiple values.

Outer join A join that is typically used to display records from both tables, regardless of whether there are matching records.

Parameter A value that can be changed.

Parameter query A query that prompts you for one or more criteria before running.

Right outer join A join used when you want to display all of the records on the *many* side of a one-to-many relationship, whether or not there are matching records in the table on the *one* side of the relationship.

Source table In a make table or append query, the table from which records are being extracted.

Static data Data that does not change.

Totals query A query that calculates subtotals across groups of records.

Unequal join A join used to combine rows from two data sources based on field values that are not equal; can be created only in SQL view.

Unmatched records Records in one table that have no matching records in a related table.

Update query An action query used to add, change, or delete data in fields of one or more existing records.

CHAPTER REVIEW

Apply 5A skills from these Objectives:

1. Create Calculated Fields in a Query
2. Use Aggregate Functions in a Query
3. Create a Crosstab Query
4. Find Duplicate and Unmatched Records
5. Create a Parameter Query

Skills Review Project 5C Employee Payroll

Derek Finkel, human resource specialist at S-Boards, Inc., a surf and snowboard shop, has a database containing employee data and payroll data. In the following Skills Review, you will create special-purpose queries to perform calculations on data, summarize and group data, display data in a spreadsheet-like format, and find duplicate and unmatched records. You will also create a query that prompts an individual to enter the criteria. Your completed queries will look similar to Figure 5.49.

PROJECT FILES

For Project 5C, you will need the following file:

a05C_Employee_Payroll

You will save your database as:

Lastname_Firstname_5C_Employee_Payroll

PROJECT RESULTS

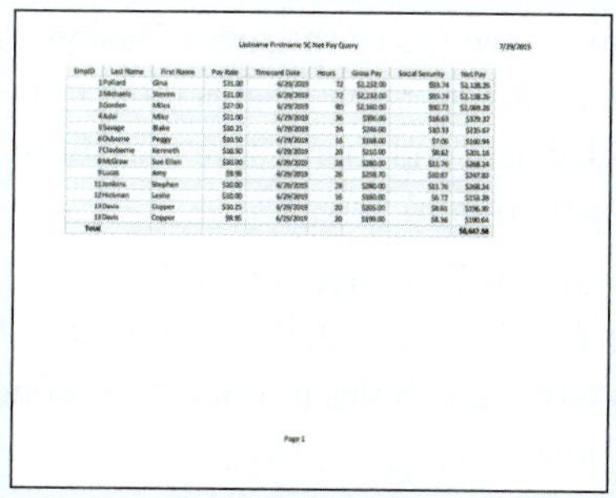

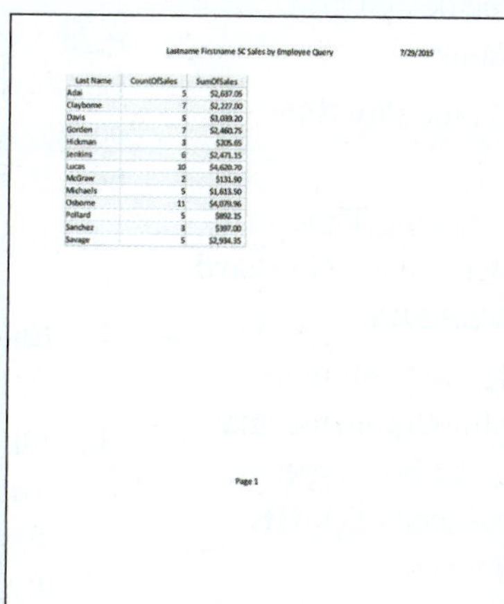

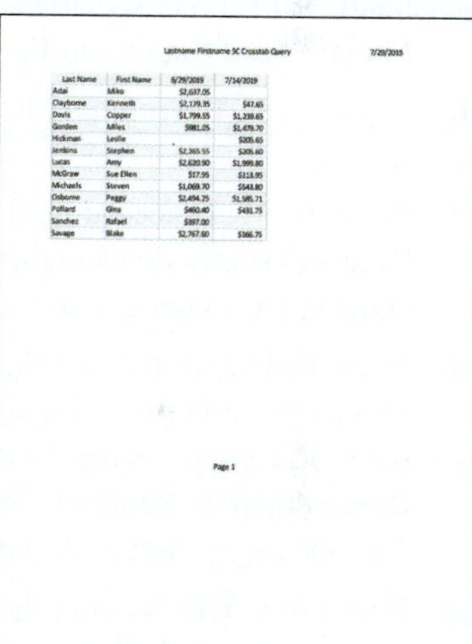

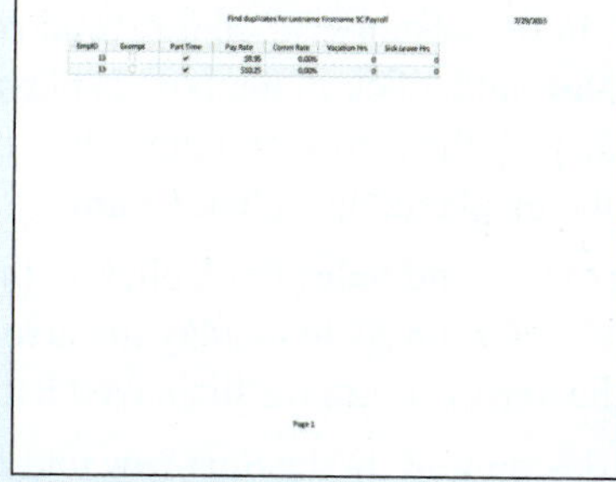

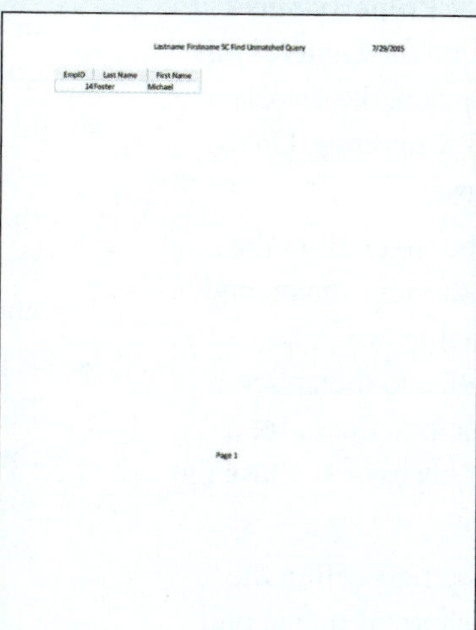

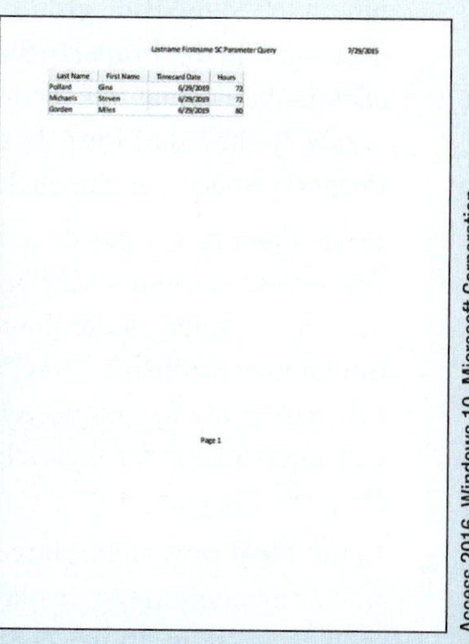

Access 2016, Windows 10, Microsoft Corporation

FIGURE 5.49

(Project 5C Employee Payroll continues on the next page)

Skills Review Project 5C Employee Payroll (continued)

1 Start Access. Locate and open the **a05C_Employee_Payroll** file. **Save** the database in your **Access Chapter 5** folder as **Lastname_Firstname_5C_Employee_Payroll**

a. If necessary, enable the content or add the Access Chapter 5 folder to the Trust Center.

b. Rename the tables by adding your **Lastname Firstname** to the beginning of each table name. **Close** the **Navigation Pane**.

2 On the ribbon, click the **Create tab**. In the **Queries group**, click **Query Design**. In the **Show Table** dialog box, add the following three tables to the query design workspace—**5C Employees**, **5C Payroll**, and **5C Timecard**—and then click **Close**. Resize the field lists.

a. From the **5C Employees** field list, add the following fields, in the order specified, to the design grid: **EmpID**, **Last Name**, and **First Name**.

b. From the **5C Payroll** field list, add the **Pay Rate** field.

c. From the **5C Timecard** field list, add the **Timecard Date** and **Hours** fields in this order. Under **Timecard Date**, in the **Criteria row**, type **6/29/2019**

d. In the **Field row**, right-click in the first cell in the first empty column to display a shortcut menu, and then click **Zoom**. In the **Zoom** dialog box, type **Gross Pay:[Pay Rate]*[Hours]** and then click **OK**. **Run** the query. Return to **Design** view.

e. If the **Gross Pay** does not show as **Currency**, click in the **Gross Pay** field that you just added. On the **Design tab**, in the **Show/Hide group**, click **Property Sheet**, if necessary. In the **Property Sheet**, on the **General tab**, click in the **Format** box, and then click the displayed **arrow**. In the list of formats, click **Currency**. On the **Property Sheet** title bar, click **Close**.

f. In the **Field row**, right-click in the first cell in the first empty column to display a shortcut menu, and then click **Zoom**. In the **Zoom** dialog box, type **Social Security:[Gross Pay]*0.042** and then click **OK**. Using the technique you just practiced, set a Currency format for this field, if necessary. **Close** the Property Sheet.

g. In the **Field row**, right-click in the first cell in the first empty column to display a shortcut menu, and then click **Zoom**. In the **Zoom** dialog box, type **Net Pay:[Gross Pay]-[Social Security]** and then click **OK**. **Run** the query to display the payroll calculations. Adjust column widths to display all field names and all data under each field.

h. On the **Home tab**, in the **Records group**, click **Totals**. In the **Total row**, under **Net Pay**, click in the empty box, and then click the **arrow** at the left edge. From the displayed list, click **Sum**.

i. On the **tab row**, right-click the **Query1 tab**, and then click **Save**. In the **Save As** dialog box, under **Query Name**, type **Lastname Firstname 5C Net Pay Query** and then click **OK**. View the query in **Print Preview**. Change the orientation to **Landscape** to ensure the table prints on one page. If you are instructed to submit this result, create a paper printout or PDF electronic image. **Close** the query.

3 Create a new query in **Query Design**. Add the **5C Employees** table and the **5C Sales** table to the query design workspace, and then **Close** the **Show Table** dialog box. Resize both field lists.

a. From the **5C Employees** field list, add **Last Name** to the first field box in the design grid. From the **5C Sales** table, add **Sales** to both the second and third field boxes.

b. On the **Design tab**, in the **Show/Hide group**, click **Totals**. In the design grid, in the **Total row** under the first **Sales** field, click in the box displaying *Group By* to display the arrow, and then click the **arrow**. From the displayed list, click **Count**.

c. Under the second **Sales** field, click in the box displaying *Group By* to display the arrow, and then click the **arrow**. From the displayed list, click **Sum**.

d. In the design grid, in the **Sort row** under **Last Name**, click in the box to display the arrow, and then click the **arrow**. From the displayed list, click **Ascending**. **Run** the query to display the total number of sales and the total amount of the sales for each associate.

e. If necessary, adjust column widths to display all field names and all data under each field. **Save** the query as **Lastname Firstname 5C Sales by Employee Query** View the query in **Print Preview**, ensuring that the query prints on one page. If you are instructed to submit this result, create a paper printout or PDF electronic image. **Close** the query.

(Project 5C Employee Payroll continues on the next page)

Skills Review Project 5C Employee Payroll (continued)

4 **Create** a new query in **Query Design**. Add the following tables to the query design workspace: **5C Employees** and **5C Sales**. In the **Show Table** dialog box, click **Close**. Resize the field lists.

a. From the **5C Employees** table, add the **Last Name** and **First Name** fields. From the **5C Sales** table, add the **Timecard Date** and **Sales** fields. **Run** the query to display the sales by date. **Save** the query as **Lastname Firstname 5C Sales by Date Query** and then **Close** the query.

b. On the ribbon, click the **Create tab**. In the **Queries group**, click **Query Wizard**. In the **New Query** dialog box, click **Crosstab Query Wizard**, and then click **OK**. In the middle of the dialog box, under **View**, click the **Queries** option button. In the list of queries, click **Query: 5C Sales by Date Query**, and then click **Next**.

c. Under **Available Fields**, double-click **Last Name** and **First Name**, and then click **Next**. In the displayed list of fields, double-click **Timecard Date**. Select an interval of **Date**, and then click **Next**. Under **Functions**, click **Sum**. On the left side of the **Crosstab Query Wizard** dialog box, above the **Sample** area, clear the **Yes, include row sums** check box, and then click **Next**.

d. Under **What do you want to name your query?**, select the existing text, type **Lastname Firstname 5C Crosstab Query** and then click **Finish**. Adjust all of the column widths to display the entire field name and the data in each field. The result is a spreadsheet view of total sales by employee by payroll date. View the query in **Print Preview**, ensuring that the query prints on one page. If you are instructed to submit this result, create a paper printout or PDF electronic image. **Close** the query, saving changes.

5 On the **Create tab**, in the **Queries group**, click **Query Wizard**. In the **New Query** dialog box, click **Find Duplicates Query Wizard**, and then click **OK**.

a. In the first **Find Duplicates Query Wizard** dialog box, in the list of tables, click **Table: 5C Payroll**, and then click **Next**. Under **Available fields**, double-click **EmpID** to move it under **Duplicate-value fields**, and then click **Next**.

b. Under **Available fields**, add all of the fields to the **Additional query fields** box. Click **Next**. Click **Finish** to accept the suggested query name—*Find duplicates for Lastname Firstname 5C Payroll*. Adjust all column widths. View the query in **Print Preview**, ensuring that the query prints on one **Landscape** page. If you are instructed to submit this result, create a paper printout or PDF electronic image. **Close** the query, saving your changes.

6 On the **Create tab**, in the **Queries group**, click **Query Wizard**. In the **New Query** dialog box, click **Find Unmatched Query Wizard**, and then click **OK**.

a. In the first **Find Unmatched Query Wizard** dialog box, in the list of tables, click **Table: 5C Employees**, if necessary, and then click **Next**. In the list of tables, click **Table: 5C Payroll**, and then click **Next**. Under **Fields in '5C Employees'**, if necessary, click **EmpID**. Under **Fields in 5C Payroll**, if necessary, click **EmpID**. Click the <=> button. Click **Next**.

b. Under **Available fields**, double-click **EmpID**, **Last Name**, and **First Name** to move the field names under **Selected fields**. Click **Next**. In the last dialog box, under **What would you like to name your query?**, type **Lastname Firstname 5C Find Unmatched Query** and then click **Finish**.

c. Adjust all column widths. View the query in **Print Preview**, ensuring that the query prints on one page. If you are instructed to submit this result, create a paper printout or PDF electronic image. **Close** the query, saving changes if necessary.

7 **Create** a new query in **Query Design**. Add the **5C Employees** table and the **5C Timecard** table to the query design workspace, and then **Close** the **Show Table** dialog box. Resize the field lists.

a. From the **5C Employees** field list, add **Last Name** and **First Name** to the first and second columns in the design grid. From the **5C Timecard** field list, add **Timecard Date** and **Hours** to the third and fourth columns in the design grid.

b. In the **Criteria row** under **Timecard Date** field, type **[Enter date]**

c. In the **Criteria row**, right-click in the **Hours** field, and then click **Zoom**. In the **Zoom** dialog box, type **Between [Enter the minimum Hours] And [Enter the maximum Hours]** and then click **OK**.

(Project 5C Employee Payroll continues on the next page)

Skills Review Project 5C Employee Payroll (continued)

d. **Run** the query. In the **Enter Parameter Value** dialog box, type **6/29/19** and then click **OK**. Type **60** and then click **OK**. Type **80** and then click **OK**. Three employees have worked between 60 and 80 hours during the pay period for 6/29/19.

e. Adjust all column widths, and **Save** the query as **Lastname Firstname 5C Parameter Query** View the query in **Print Preview**, ensuring that the query prints on one page. If you are instructed to submit this result, create a paper or PDF electronic image. **Close** the query.

8 Open the **Navigation Pane**, resize it so all object names are fully visible. **Close** the database, and then **Close** Access.

9 As directed by your instructor, submit your database and the paper printouts or PDF electronic image of the six queries that are the result of this project. Specifically, in this project, using your own name you created the following database and printouts or PDF electronic images:

1. Lastname_Firstname_5C_Employee_Payroll	Database file
2. Lastname Firstname 5C Net Pay Query	Query
3. Lastname Firstname 5C Sales by Employee Query	Query
4. Lastname Firstname 5C Crosstab Query	Query
5. Find duplicates for Lastname Firstname 5C Payrol	Query
6. Lastname Firstname 5C Find Unmatched Query	Query
7. Lastname Firstname 5C Parameter Query	Query

END | You have completed Project 5C

CHAPTER REVIEW

Apply 5B skills from these Objectives:

6 Create a Make Table Query
7 Create an Append Query
8 Create a Delete Query
9 Create an Update Query
10 Modify the Join Type

Skills Review Project 5D Clearance Sale

Miles Gorden, purchasing manager for S-Boards, Inc., a surf and snowboard shop, must keep the tables in the database up to date and ensure that the queries display pertinent information. Two of the suppliers, Super Wave Boards and Boot City, will no longer provide merchandise for S-Boards, Inc. This merchandise must be moved to a new discontinued items table. In the following Skills Review, you will create action queries that will create a new table, update records in a table, append records to a table, and delete records from a table. You will also modify the join type of relationships to display different subsets of the data when the query is run. Your completed queries will look similar to Figure 5.50.

PROJECT FILES

For Project 5D, you will need the following files:

a05D_Store_Items
a05D_Warehouse_Items

You will save your databases as:

Lastname_Firstname_5D_Store_Items
Lastname_Firstname_5D_Warehouse_Items

PROJECT RESULTS

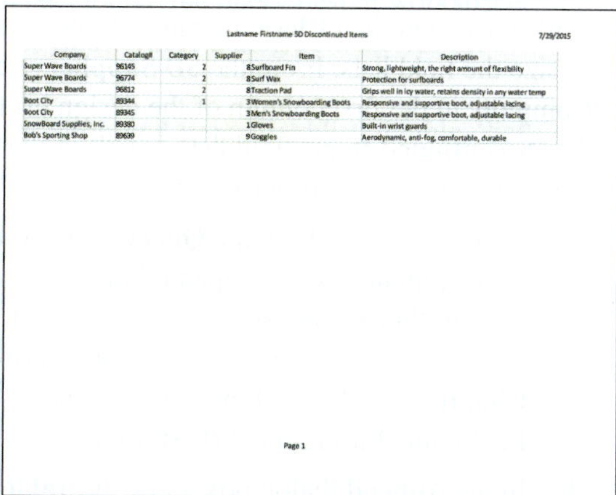

Lastname Firstname 5D Discontinued Items 7/29/2015

Company	Catalog#	Category	Supplier	Item	Description
Super Wave Boards	96145	2	8	Surfboard Fin	Strong, lightweight, the right amount of flexibility
Super Wave Boards	96774	2	8	Surf Wax	Protection for surfboards
Super Wave Boards	96812	2	8	Traction Pad	Grips well in icy water, retains density in any water temp
Boot City	89344	1	3	Women's Snowboarding Boots	Responsive and supportive boot, adjustable lacing
Boot City	89345		3	Men's Snowboarding Boots	Responsive and supportive boot, adjustable lacing
SnowBoard Supplies, Inc.	89380		1	Gloves	Built-in wrist guards
Bob's Sporting Shop	89639		9	Goggles	Aerodynamic, anti-fog, comfortable, durable

Page 1

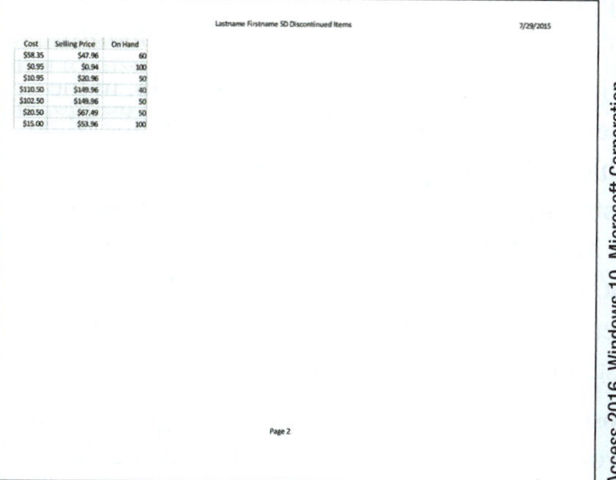

Lastname Firstname 5D Discontinued Items 7/29/2015

Cost	Selling Price	On Hand
$58.35	$47.96	60
$0.95	$0.94	100
$10.95	$20.96	50
$110.50	$149.96	40
$102.50	$149.96	50
$20.50	$67.49	50
$15.00	$53.96	100

Page 2

Access 2016, Windows 10, Microsoft Corporation

Lastname Firstname 5D Outer Join Query 7/29/2015

Company	Business Phone	Catalog#	Item	On Hand
Back Country Outfitters	(800) 555-3694			
Big Boards Corporation	(800) 555-3788			
Bob's Sporting Shop	(757) 555-7139	89639	Goggles	100
Boot City	(541) 555-1170	89344	Women's Snowboarding Boots	40
Boot City	(541) 555-1170	89345	Men's Snowboarding Boots	50
Cold Sports Club	(800) 555-6781			
Gear Head	(206) 555-8499			
SnowBoard Supplies, Inc.	(248) 555-1000	89380	Gloves	50
Sports Fitters	(800) 555-4084			
Super Wave Boards	(800) 555-5874	96145	Surfboard Fin	60
Super Wave Boards	(800) 555-5874	96774	Surf Wax	100
Super Wave Boards	(800) 555-5874	96812	Traction Pad	50
Wetsuit Country	(866) 555-2877			

Page 1

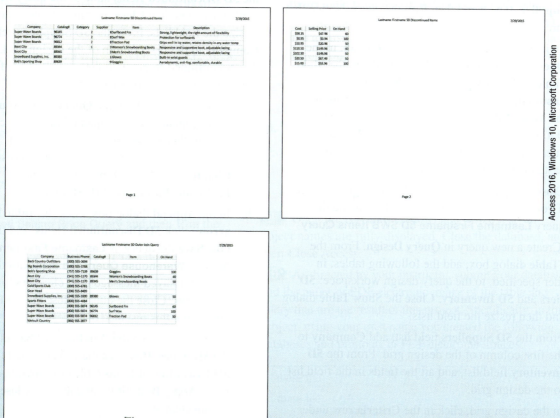

FIGURE 5.50

(Project 5D Clearance Sale continues on the next page)

Apply 5A skills from these Objectives:

1. Create Calculated Fields in a Query
2. Use Aggregate Functions in a Query
3. Create a Crosstab Query
4. Find Duplicate and Unmatched Records
5. Create a Parameter Query

Mastering Access Project 5E Surfing Lessons

Gina Pollard, one of the owners of S-Boards, Inc., a surf and snowboard shop, has a database containing student, instructor, and surfing lesson data. In the following Mastering Access project, you will create special-purpose queries to calculate data, summarize and group data, display data in a spreadsheet-like format, and find duplicate and unmatched records. You will also create a query that prompts an individual to enter the criteria. Your completed queries will look similar to Figure 5.51.

PROJECT FILES

For Project 5E, you will need the following file:

a05E_Surfing_Lessons

You will save your database as:

Lastname_Firstname_5E_Surfing_Lessons

PROJECT RESULTS

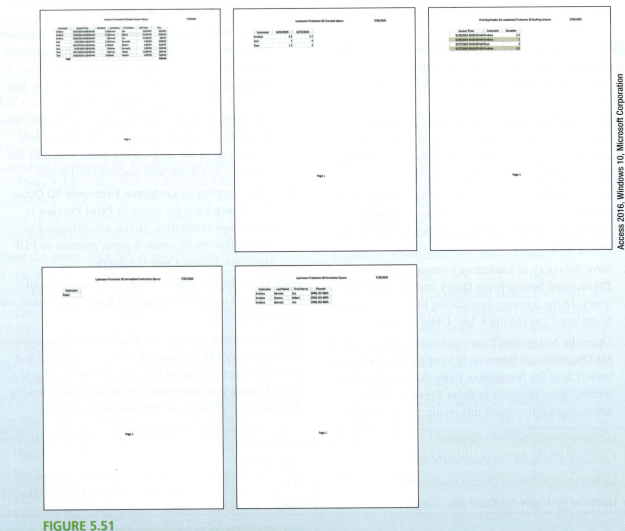

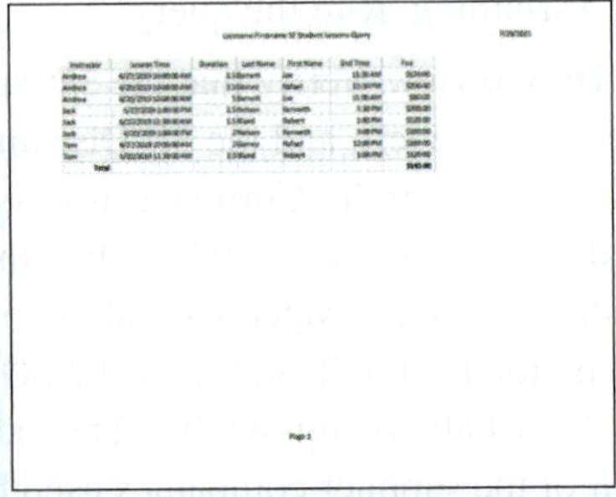

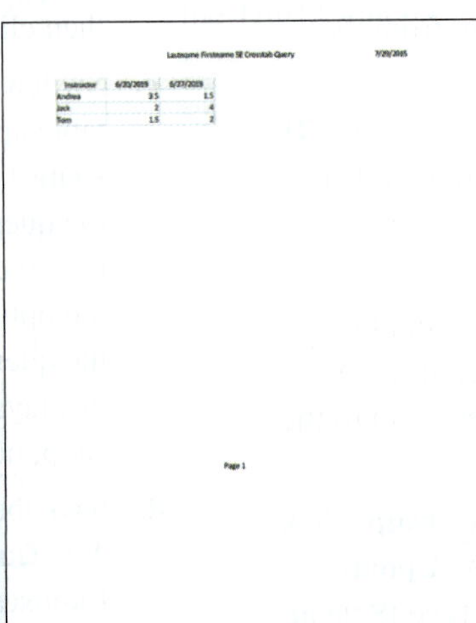

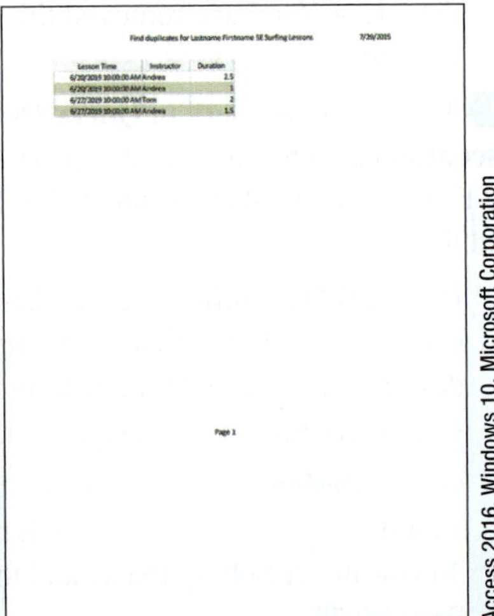

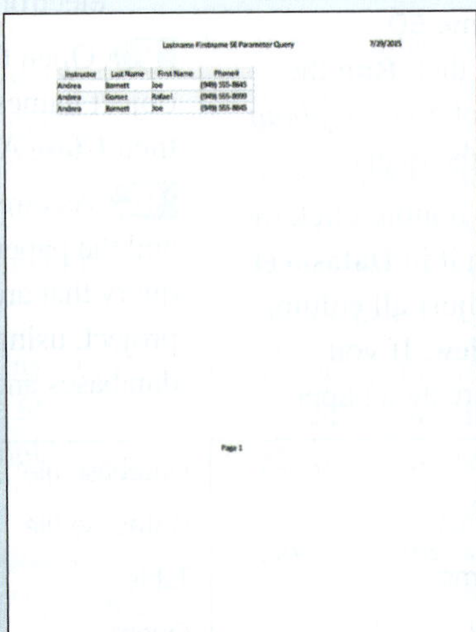

Access 2016, Windows 10, Microsoft Corporation

FIGURE 5.51

(Project 5E Surfing Lessons continues on the next page)

Mastering Access Project 5E Surfing Lessons (continued)

1 Start Access. Locate and open the **a05E_Surfing_Lessons** file. Save the database in your **Access Chapter 5** folder as **Lastname_Firstname_5E_Surfing_Lessons** If necessary, enable the content or add the Access Chapter 5 folder to the Trust Center. Rename the tables by adding your **Lastname Firstname** to the beginning of each table name.

2 **Create** a query in **Query Design** using the **5E Surfing Lessons** table and the **5E Students** table. From the **5E Surfing Lessons** table, add the **Instructor** field, the **Lesson Time** field, and the **Duration** field to the first, second, and third columns of the design grid. From the **5E Students** table, add the **Last Name** and **First Name** fields to the fourth and fifth columns.

3 In the sixth column of the design grid, add a calculated field. In the **field name row**, type **End Time:[Duration]/24+[Lesson Time]** Display the **Field Properties** property sheet, and then format this field as **Medium Time**. This field will display the time the lesson ends.

4 In the first blank column, in the field name row, add the calculated field **Fee:[Duration]*80** Display the **Field Properties** property sheet, and then format this field as **Currency**. Surfing lessons cost $80.00 an hour.

5 In the **Instructor** field, in the **Sort row**, click **Ascending**. In the **Lesson Time** field, in the **Sort row**, click **Ascending**. **Run** the query.

6 On the **Home tab**, in the **Records group**, click **Totals**. In the **Fee** column, in the **Total row**, click the **arrow**, and then click **Average**. Adjust field widths as necessary.

7 **Save** the query as **Lastname Firstname 5E Student Lessons Query** View the query in **Print Preview**, ensuring that the query prints on one page in **Landscape** orientation. If you are instructed to submit this result, create a paper printout or PDF electronic image. **Close** the query.

8 **Create** a new query using the **Crosstab Query Wizard**. Select the **Query: 5E Student Lessons Query**. Click **Next**. From the **Available Fields**, add **Instructor** to the **Selected Fields** column. Click **Next**. Double-click **Lesson Time**, and then click **Date**. Click **Next**. From the **Fields column**, select **Duration**, and then from **Functions**, select **Sum**. Clear the **Yes, include row sums** check box.

9 Click **Next**. Name the query **Lastname Firstname 5E Crosstab Query** Select **View the query**, and then click **Finish**. This query displays each instructor and the number of hours he or she taught by date. Adjust field widths as necessary.

10 View the query in **Print Preview**, ensuring that the query prints on one page. If you are instructed to submit this result, create a paper printout or PDF electronic image. **Close** the query, saving changes.

11 Create a new query using the **Find Duplicates Query Wizard**. Select **Table: 5E Surfing Lessons**, click **Next**, and then select the **Lesson Time** field for duplicate information. Click **Next**. From **Available fields**, add the **Instructor** and **Duration** fields to the **Additional query fields** column. Click **Next**, and then accept the default name for the query. Click **Finish**. The query results show that there are duplicate lesson times. Adjust field widths as necessary.

12 View the query in **Print Preview**, ensuring that the query prints on one page. If you are instructed to submit this result, create a paper printout or PDF electronic image. **Close** and **Save** the query.

13 Create a new query in the **Find Unmatched Query Wizard**. Select **Table: 5E Surfing Instructors**. From the **Which table or query contains the related records?** dialog box, click **Table: 5E Surfing Lessons**. Click **Instructor** as the **Matching** field. Display the one field **Instructor** in the query results. Name the query **Lastname Firstname 5E Unmatched Instructors Query** and then click **Finish**. Ralph is the only instructor who has no students.

14 View the query in **Print Preview**. If you are instructed to submit this result, create a paper printout or PDF electronic image. **Close** the query.

15 **Create** a query in **Design** view using the **5E Surfing Lessons** table and the **5E Students** table. From the **5E Surfing Lessons** table, add the **Instructor** field. From the **5E Students** table, add the **Last Name**, **First Name**, and **Phone#** fields in that order to the design grid. In the **Criteria row** under **Instructor**, type **[Enter Instructor's First Name]**

16 **Run** the query. In the **Enter Parameter Value** dialog box, type **Andrea** and then press Enter. The query displays Andrea's students and their phone numbers.

17 **Save** the query as **Lastname Firstname 5E Parameter Query** Adjust field widths as necessary.

(Project 5E Surfing Lessons continues on the next page)

Apply 5A and 5B skills from these Objectives:

1 Create Calculated Fields in a Query
2 Use Aggregate Functions in a Query
3 Create a Crosstab Query
4 Find Duplicate and Unmatched Record
5 Create a Parameter Query
6 Create a Make Table Query
7 Create an Append Query
8 Create a Delete Query
9 Create an Update Query
10 Modify the Join Type

Mastering Access Project 5G Advertising Options

Steven Michaels, one of the owners of S-Boards, Inc., a surf and snowboard shop, is responsible for all of the advertising for the business. In the following Mastering Access project, you will create special-purpose queries to perform calculations on data, and then summarize and group data for advertising cost analysis. You will also create a query that prompts an individual to enter the criteria for a specific type of advertisement media. Your completed queries will look similar to Figure 5.53.

PROJECT FILES

For Project 5G, you will need the following file:

a05G_Advertising_Options

You will save your database as:

Lastname_Firstname_5G_Advertising_Options

PROJECT RESULTS

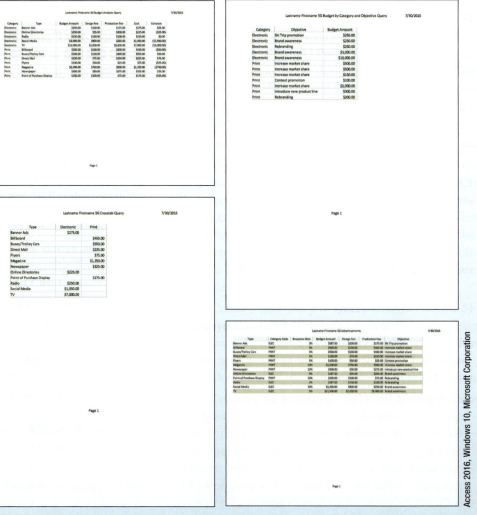

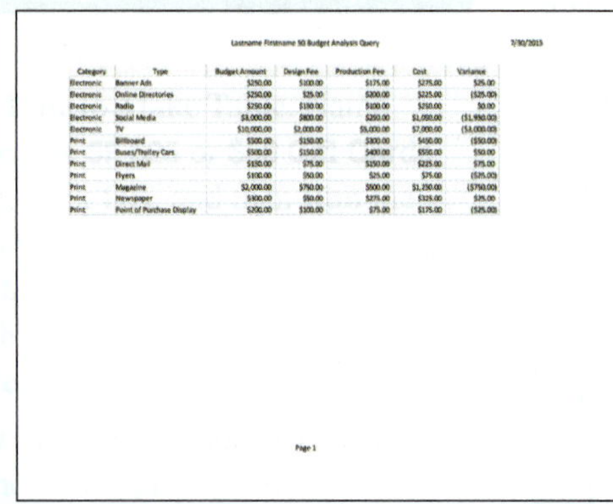

Lastname Firstname 5G Budget Analysis Query 7/30/2015

Category	Type	Budget Amount	Design Fee	Production Fee	Cost	Variance
Electronic	Banner Ads	$250.00	$100.00	$175.00	$275.00	$25.00
Electronic	Online Directories	$250.00	$25.00	$200.00	$225.00	($25.00)
Electronic	Radio	$250.00	$150.00	$100.00	$250.00	$0.00
Electronic	Social Media	$3,000.00	$800.00	$250.00	$1,050.00	($1,950.00)
Electronic	TV	$10,000.00	$2,000.00	$5,000.00	$7,000.00	($3,000.00)
Print	Billboard	$500.00	$150.00	$300.00	$450.00	($50.00)
Print	Buses/Trolley Cars	$500.00	$150.00	$400.00	$550.00	$50.00
Print	Direct Mail	$150.00	$75.00	$150.00	$225.00	$75.00
Print	Flyers	$100.00	$50.00	$25.00	$75.00	($25.00)
Print	Magazine	$2,000.00	$750.00	$500.00	$1,250.00	($750.00)
Print	Newspaper	$300.00	$50.00	$275.00	$325.00	$25.00
Print	Point of Purchase Display	$200.00	$100.00	$75.00	$175.00	($25.00)

Page 1

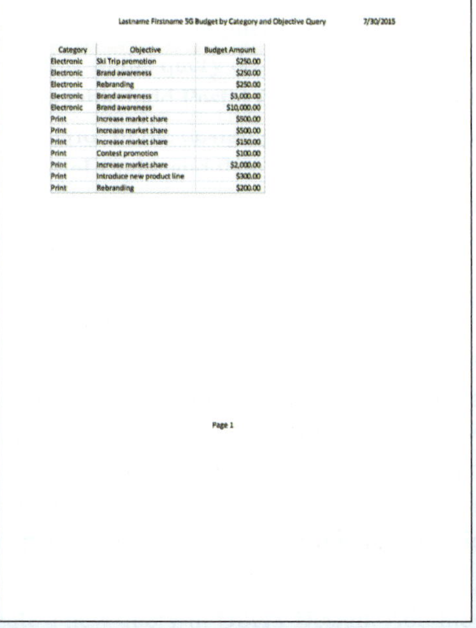

Lastname Firstname 5G Budget by Category and Objective Query 7/30/2015

Category	Objective	Budget Amount
Electronic	Ski Trip promotion	$250.00
Electronic	Brand awareness	$250.00
Electronic	Rebranding	$250.00
Electronic	Brand awareness	$3,000.00
Electronic	Brand awareness	$10,000.00
Print	Increase market share	$500.00
Print	Increase market share	$500.00
Print	Increase market share	$150.00
Print	Contest promotion	$100.00
Print	Increase market share	$2,000.00
Print	Introduce new product line	$300.00
Print	Rebranding	$200.00

Page 1

Lastname Firstname 5G Crosstab Query 7/30/2015

Type	Electronic	Print
Banner Ads	$275.00	
Billboard		$450.00
Buses/Trolley Cars		$550.00
Direct Mail		$225.00
Flyers		$75.00
Magazine		$1,250.00
Newspaper		$325.00
Online Directories	$225.00	
Point of Purchase Display		$175.00
Radio	$250.00	
Social Media	$1,050.00	
TV	$7,000.00	

Page 1

Lastname Firstname 5G Advertisements 7/30/2015

Type	Category Code	Response Rate	Budget Amount	Design Fee	Production Fee	Objective
Banner Ads	ELEC	2%	$287.50	$100.00	$175.00	Ski Trip promotion
Billboard	PRNT	5%	$500.00	$150.00	$300.00	Increase market share
Buses/Trolley Cars	PRNT	5%	$500.00	$150.00	$400.00	Increase market share
Direct Mail	PRNT	2%	$150.00	$75.00	$150.00	Increase market share
Flyers	PRNT	5%	$100.00	$50.00	$25.00	Contest promotion
Magazine	PRNT	10%	$2,000.00	$750.00	$500.00	Increase market share
Newspaper	PRNT	10%	$300.00	$50.00	$275.00	Introduce new product line
Online Directories	ELEC	5%	$287.50	$25.00	$200.00	Brand awareness
Point of Purchase Display	PRNT	10%	$200.00	$100.00	$75.00	Rebranding
Radio	ELEC	2%	$287.50	$150.00	$100.00	Rebranding
Social Media	ELEC	10%	$3,450.00	$800.00	$250.00	Brand awareness
TV	ELEC	5%	$11,500.00	$2,000.00	$5,000.00	Brand awareness

Page 1

FIGURE 5.53

(Project 5G Advertising Options continues on the next page)

Mastering Access Project 5G Advertising Options (continued)

1 Start Access. Locate and open the **a05G_Advertising_Options** file. Save the database in your **Access Chapter 5** folder as **Lastname_Firstname_5G_Advertising_Options** If necessary, enable the content or add the Access Chapter 5 folder to the Trust Center. Rename the tables by adding your **Lastname Firstname** to the beginning of the table names. **Close** the **Navigation Pane**.

2 Create a new query in **Query Design**. From the **5G Categories** table, add the **Category** field to the design grid. From the **5G Advertisements** table, add the **Type**, **Budget Amount**, **Design Fee**, and **Production Fee** fields to the design grid in this order.

3 In the first blank field column, add a calculated field. Type **Cost:[Design Fee]+[Production Fee]** In the next blank field column, add a second calculated field: **Variance:[Cost]-[Budget Amount]**

4 **Run** the query. Save it as **Lastname Firstname 5G Budget Analysis Query** View the results in **Print Preview**, ensuring that it fits on one page in **Landscape** orientation. If you are instructed to submit this result, create a paper printout or PDF electronic image. **Close** the query.

5 Create a new query in **Query Design**. From the **5G Categories** table, add the **Category** field to the design grid. From the **5G Advertisements** table, add the **Objective** and **Budget Amount** fields to the design grid. On the **Design tab**, in the **Show/Hide group**, click **Totals**. In the design grid, in the **Total row** under **Budget Amount**, click **Sum**.

6 **Run** the query. Save it as **Lastname Firstname 5G Budget by Category and Objective Query** View the results in **Print Preview**, ensuring that it fits on one page. If you are instructed to submit this result, create a paper or PDF electronic image. **Close** the query.

7 Create a new crosstab query using the **Query Wizard**. Select **Query: 5G Budget Analysis Query**. For row headings, use **Type**, and for column headings, use **Category**. Select **Cost** for the calculated field, using the **Sum** function. Do not summarize each row. Save it as **Lastname Firstname 5G Crosstab Query** and then click **Finish**

8 View the query in **Print Preview**, ensuring that the query prints on one page. If you are instructed to submit this result, create a paper printout or PDF electronic image. **Close** the query.

9 Create a new query in **Query Design**. From the **5G Advertisements** table, add the **Budget Amount** field to the design grid. From the **5G Categories** table, add the **Category** field to the design grid. In the design grid, click in the **Criteria row** under **Category**, and type **Electronic**

10 Change the **Query Type** to **Update**. In the design grid, click in the **Update To row** under **Budget Amount**, and type **[Budget Amount]*1.15**

11 **Run** the query. Click **Yes** to update five rows. **Close** the query, saving it as **Lastname Firstname 5G Update Electronics Budget Query** **Open** the **Navigation Pane**. **Open** the **5G Advertisements** table. View the table in **Print Preview**, ensuring that the table prints on one page. If you are instructed to submit this result, create a paper printout or PDF electronic image. **Close** the table.

12 **Open** the **Navigation Pane**, and resize it so all object names are displayed fully. **Close** the database, and then **Close** Access.

13 As directed by your instructor, submit your database and the paper or PDF electronic image of the four queries and one table that are the result of this project. Specifically, in this project, using your own name you created the following database and printouts or PDF electronic images:

1. Lastname_Firstname_5G_Advertising_Options	Database file
2. Lastname Firstname 5G Budget Analysis Query	Query
3. Lastname Firstname 5G Budget by Category and Objective Query	Query
4. Lastname Firstname 5G Crosstab Query	Query
5. Lastname Firstname 5G Advertisements	Table
6. Lastname Firstname 5G Update Electronics Budget Query	Query

END | You have completed Project 5G

Apply a combination of the 5A and 5B skills.

CONTENT-BASED ASSESSMENTS (CRITICAL THINKING)

GO! Fix It Project 5H Contests **MyITLab**

GO! Make It Project 5I Ski Trips **MyITLab**

GO! Solve It Project 5J Applications **MyITLab**

GO! Solve It Project 5K Ski Apparel

PROJECT FILES

For Project 5K, you will need the following file:

a05K_Ski_Apparel

You will save your database as:

Lastname_Firstname_5K_Ski_Apparel

Miles Gorden is the purchasing manager for S-Boards, Inc., a surf and snowboard shop. It is his responsibility to keep the clothing inventory current and fashionable. You have been asked to help him with this task. From the student files that accompany this chapter, open the **a05K_Ski_Apparel** database file, and then save the database in your Access Chapter 5 folder as **Lastname_Firstname_5K_Ski_Apparel**

The database consists of a table of ski apparel for youth, women, and men. Create a query to identify the inventory by status of the items (promotional, in stock, and discontinued clothing), and the number of items that are in each category. Update the selling price of the discontinued items to 80 percent of the current selling price. Use a make table query to place the promotional items into their own table and a delete query to remove those items from the *5K Ski Apparel* table. Save your queries using your last and first names followed by the query type. View the queries in Print Preview, ensuring that each query prints on one page. If you are instructed to submit this result, create a paper printout or PDF electronic image.

Performance Level

Performance Criteria	Exemplary: You consistently applied the relevant skills	Proficient: You sometimes, but not always, applied the relevant skills	Developing: You rarely or never applied the relevant skills
Create 5K Totals Query	Query created to display inventory by status.	Query created with no more than two missing elements.	Query created with more than two missing elements.
Create 5K Update Query	Query created to update clearance sale prices.	Query created with no more than two missing elements.	Query created with more than two missing elements.
Create 5K Make Table Query	Query created to make a table for promotional items.	Query created with no more than two missing elements.	Query created with more than two missing elements.
Create 5K Delete Query	Query created to delete promotional items from the Ski Apparel table.	Query created with no more than two missing elements.	Query created with more than two missing elements.

END | You have completed Project 5K

OUTCOMES-BASED ASSESSMENTS (CRITICAL THINKING)

RUBRIC

The following outcomes-based assessments are open-ended assessments. That is, there is no specific correct result; your result will depend on your approach to the information provided. Make Professional Quality your goal. Use the following scoring rubric to guide you in how to approach the problem and then to evaluate how well your approach solves the problem.

The *criteria*—Software Mastery, Content, Format and Layout, and Process—represent the knowledge and skills you have gained that you can apply to solving the problem. The *levels of performance*—Professional Quality, Approaching Professional Quality, or Needs Quality Improvements—help you and your instructor evaluate your result.

	Your completed project is of Professional Quality if you:	Your completed project is Approaching Professional Quality if you:	Your completed project Needs Quality Improvements if you:
1-Software Mastery	Choose and apply the most appropriate skills, tools, and features and identify efficient methods to solve the problem.	Choose and apply some appropriate skills, tools, and features, but not in the most efficient manner.	Choose inappropriate skills, tools, or features, or are inefficient in solving the problem.
2-Content	Construct a solution that is clear and well organized, contains content that is accurate, appropriate to the audience and purpose, and is complete. Provide a solution that contains no errors of spelling, grammar, or style.	Construct a solution in which some components are unclear, poorly organized, inconsistent, or incomplete. Misjudge the needs of the audience. Have some errors in spelling, grammar, or style, but the errors do not detract from comprehension.	Construct a solution that is unclear, incomplete, or poorly organized, contains some inaccurate or inappropriate content, and contains many errors of spelling, grammar, or style. Do not solve the problem.
3-Format and Layout	Format and arrange all elements to communicate information and ideas, clarify function, illustrate relationships, and indicate relative importance.	Apply appropriate format and layout features to some elements, but not others. Overuse features, causing minor distraction.	Apply format and layout that does not communicate information or ideas clearly. Do not use format and layout features to clarify function, illustrate relationships, or indicate relative importance. Use available features excessively, causing distraction.
4-Process	Use an organized approach that integrates planning, development, self-assessment, revision, and reflection.	Demonstrate an organized approach in some areas, but not others; or, use an insufficient process of organization throughout.	Do not use an organized approach to solve the problem.

Apply a combination of the 5A and 5B skills.

OUTCOMES-BASED ASSESSMENTS (CRITICAL THINKING)

GO! Think Project 5L Surfboards

PROJECT FILES

For Project 5L, you will need the following file:

a05L_Surfboards

You will save your database as

Lastname_Firstname_5L_Surfboards

Miles Gorden, purchasing manager for S-Boards, Inc., a surf and snowboard shop, is stocking the shop with a variety of surfboards and accessories for the upcoming season. In this project, you will open the **a05L_Surfboards** database and create queries to perform special functions. Save the database as **Lastname_Firstname_5L_Surfboards** Create a query to display the item, cost, selling price, on hand, and two calculated fields: Item Profit by subtracting the cost from the selling price, and Inventory Profit by multiplying Item Profit by the number on hand for each item. Be sure both fields display as Currency. Include a sum for the Inventory Profit column at the bottom of the query results. Check the supplier against the inventory using a find unmatched records query; display all fields in the supplier table. Create a query to show the company that supplies each item, its email address, and then the Item and On Hand fields for each item in the inventory. Before running the query, create an outer join query using the *5L Suppliers* table and the *5L Inventory* table. Save your queries using your last and first names followed by the query type. View the queries in Print Preview, ensuring that the queries print on one page. If you are instructed to submit this result, create a paper printout or PDF electronic image.

END | You have completed Project 5L

GO! Think Project 5M Shop Promotions MyITLab

Build From Scratch

You and GO! Project 5N Club Directory MyITLab

Customizing Forms and Reports

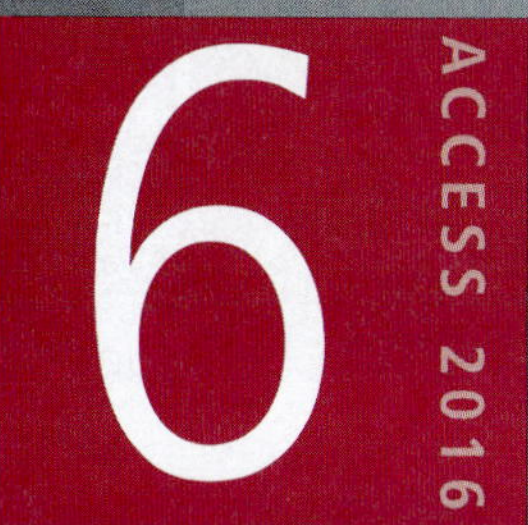

OUTCOMES
Customize forms.

OBJECTIVES

1. Create a Form in Design View
2. Change and Add Controls
3. Format a Form
4. Make a Form User Friendly

PROJECT 6B

OUTCOMES
Customize reports.

OBJECTIVES

5. Create a Report Based on a Query Using a Wizard
6. Create a Report in Design View
7. Add Controls to a Report
8. Group, Sort, and Total Records in Design View

Timof/Shutterstock

In This Chapter

Forms provide a way to enter, edit, and display data from underlying tables. You have created forms using the Form tool and Wizard. Forms can also be created in Design view. Access provides tools to enhance the appearance of forms, like adding color, backgrounds, borders, or guidelines to assist the person using the form. Forms can also be created from multiple tables if a relationship exists between the tables.

Reports display data in a professional-looking format suitable for printing. Like forms, reports can be created using the Report tool or a wizard, or in Design view, and they can all be enhanced using Access tools. Reports can be based on tables or queries in the database.

Rosebud Cafe is a "fast casual" franchise restaurant chain with headquarters in Florida and locations throughout the United States. The founders wanted to create a restaurant where fresh flavors would be available at reasonable prices in a comfortable atmosphere. The menu features quality ingredients in offerings that include grilled meat and vegetable skewers, wraps, salads, frozen yogurt, smoothies, coffee drinks, and seasonal favorites. All 81 outlets offer wireless Internet connections and meeting space, making Rosebud Cafe the perfect place for groups and people who want some quiet time or to work with others.

PROJECT 6A Locations

PROJECT ACTIVITIES

In Activities 6.01 through 6.10, you will help Linda Kay, president, and James Cecil, vice president of franchising, create robust forms to match the needs of Rosebud Cafe. For example, forms can include color and different types of controls and can manipulate data from several tables. You will customize your form to make it easier to use and more attractive. Your completed form will look similar to Figure 6.1.

PROJECT FILES

If your instructor wants you to submit Project 6A in the MyITLab Grader system, log in to MyITLab, locate Grader Project 6A, and then download the files for this project.

For Project 6A, you will need the following files:

a06A_Locations
a06A_Logo
a06A_Background

You will save your database as:

Lastname_Firstname_6A_Locations

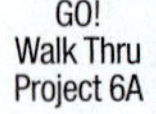

PROJECT RESULTS

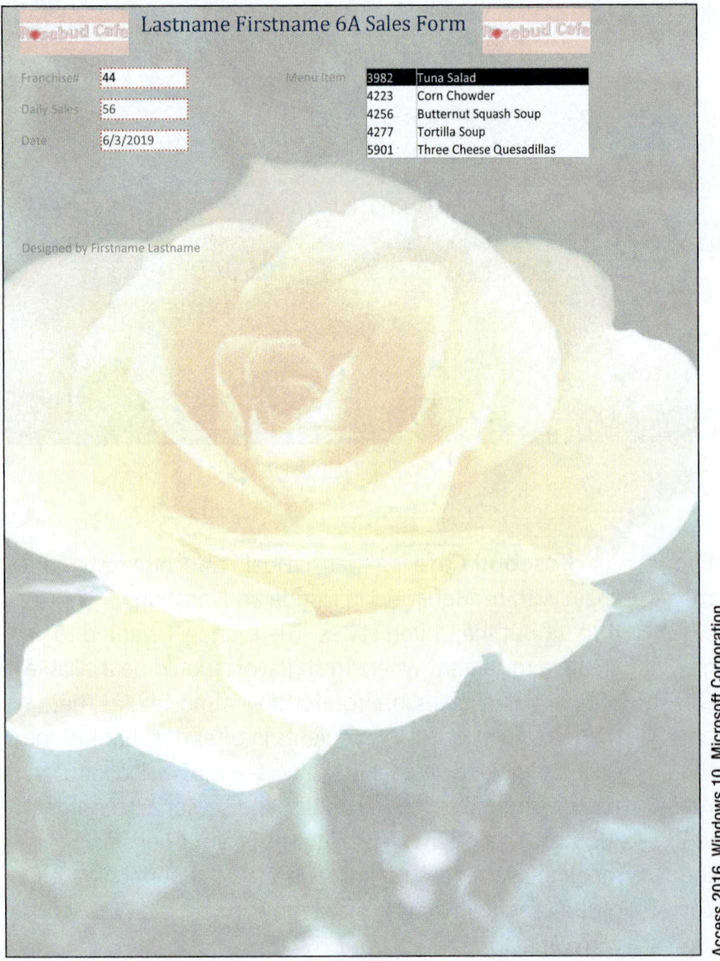

Access 2016, Windows 10, Microsoft Corporation

FIGURE 6.1 Project 6A Locations

PROJECT RESULTS

In this project, using your own name, you will create the following database and object. Your instructor may ask you to submit printouts or PDF electronic images:

Lastname_Firstname_6A_Locations	Database file
Lastname_Firstname_6A_Sales_Form	Form

Objective 1 Create a Form in Design View

Forms are usually created using the Form tool or the Form Wizard and then modified in Design view to suit your needs. Use Design view to create a form when these tools do not meet your needs or if you want more control in the creation of a form. Creating or modifying a form in Design view is a common technique when additional controls, such as combo boxes or images, need to be added to the form.

GO! Learn How Video A6-1

Activity 6.01 | Creating a Form in Design View

ALERT!

To submit as an autograded project, log into MyITLab and download the files for this project, and begin with those files instead of the a06A_ Locations file. Begin working with the database in Step 2. For Grader to award points accurately, when saving an object, do not include your Lastname Firstname at the beginning of the object name.

4.1.1, 4.2.3, 4.2.2, 4.1.3

In this Activity, you will create a form in Design view that will enable employees to enter the daily sales data for each franchise of Rosebud Cafe.

1. Start Access. Navigate to the location where the student data files for this textbook are saved. Locate and open the **a06A_Locations** file. Display **Backstage** view. Click **Save As**, and then, under *File Types*, double-click **Save Database As**. In the **Save As** dialog box, navigate to the drive on which you will be saving your folders and projects for this chapter. Create a new folder named **Access Chapter 6** and then save the database as **Lastname_Firstname_6A_Locations** in the folder.

2. Enable the content or add the Access Chapter 6 folder to the Trust Center.

3. In the **Navigation Pane**, double-click **6A Sales** to open the table in **Datasheet** view. Take a moment to examine the fields in the table. In any record, click in the **Franchise#** field, and then click the **arrow**. This field is a Lookup field—the values are looked up in the *6A Franchises* table. The Menu Item field is also a Lookup field—the values are looked up in the *6A Menu Items* table.

4. **Close** [X] the table, and then **Close** [«] the **Navigation Pane**. On the **Create tab**, in the **Forms group**, click **Form Design**.

   The design grid for the Detail section displays.

5. Under **Form Design Tools**, on the **Design tab**, in the **Tools group**, click **Property Sheet**. Compare your screen with Figure 6.2. Notice that the *Selection type* box displays *Form*—this is the Property Sheet for the entire form.

   Every object on a form, including the form itself, has an associated ***Property Sheet*** that can be used to further enhance the object. ***Properties*** are characteristics that determine the appearance, structure, and behavior of an object. This Property Sheet displays the properties that affect the appearance and behavior of the form. The left column displays the property name, and the right column displays the property setting. Some of the text in the property setting boxes may be truncated.

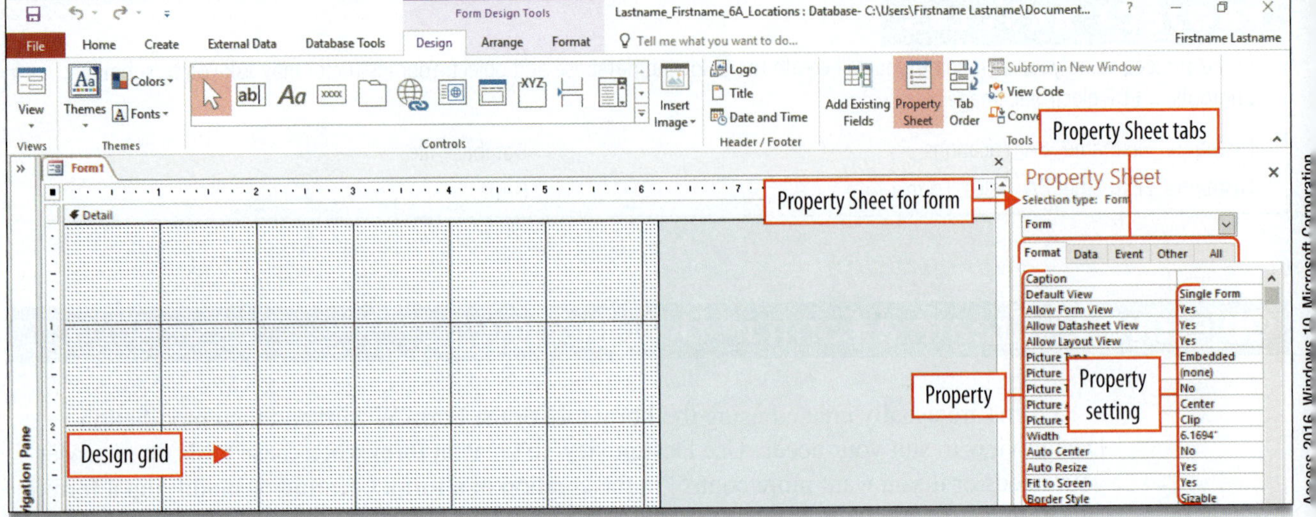

FIGURE 6.2

6 On the **Property Sheet**, with the **Format tab** displayed, scroll down, if necessary, to display the **Split Form Orientation** property box. Point to the left edge of the **Property Sheet** until the ⟺ pointer displays, and then drag to the left until the setting in the **Split Form Orientation** property box—**Datasheet on Top**—displays entirely.

7 On the **Property Sheet**, click the **Data tab**. Click the **Record Source property setting box arrow**, and then click **6A Sales**.

The ***Record Source property*** enables you to specify the source of the data for a form or a report. The property setting can be a table name, a query name, or an SQL statement.

8 **Close** [X] the **Property Sheet**. Under **Form Design Tools**, on the **Design tab**, in the **Tools group**, click **Add Existing Fields**, and then compare your screen with Figure 6.3.

The Field List for the record source—6A Sales—displays.

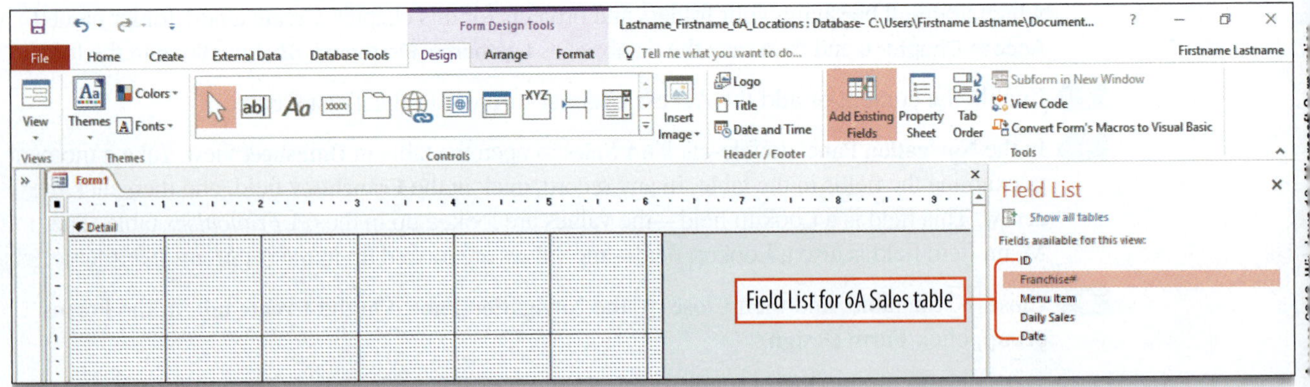

FIGURE 6.3

9 In the **Field List**, click **Franchise#**, if necessary. To select multiple fields, hold down Shift, and then click **Date**. Drag the selected fields onto the design grid until the top of the arrow of the pointer is **three dots** below the bottom edge of the **Detail section bar** and aligned with the **1.5-inch mark on the horizontal ruler**, as shown in Figure 6.4, and then release the mouse button.

Drag the fields to where the text box controls should display. If you drag to where the label controls should display, the label controls and text box controls will overlap. If you move the controls to an incorrect position, click Undo, and move them again.

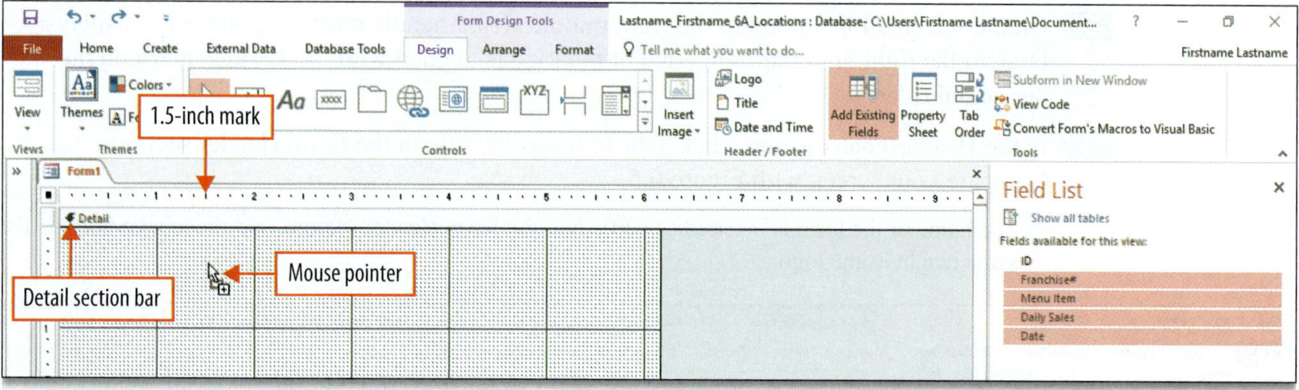

FIGURE 6.4

Access 2016, Windows 10, Microsoft Corporation

In the Field List, double-click each field name to add the fields to the form. It is not possible to select all the fields and then double-click. Alternatively, in the Field List, right-click a field name, and then click Add Field to View.

10 Close [X] the **Field List**.

> **More Knowledge** **Remove Unnecessary Form Controls**
>
> If controls that you no longer need are displayed, click to select one of the controls. Holding down Shift, select all extra controls at one time. Press Delete.

11 With all controls selected, under **Form Design Tools**, click the **Arrange tab**. In the **Table group**, click **Stacked**.

When you create a form in Design view, the controls are not automatically grouped in a stacked or tabular layout. Grouping the controls makes it easier to format the controls and keeps the controls aligned.

12 **Save** the form as **Lastname Firstname 6A Sales Form**

> **More Knowledge** **Horizontal and Vertical Spacing Between Controls**
>
> If the controls on a form are not grouped in a tabular or stacked layout, you can change the spacing between the controls. With the controls selected, click the Arrange tab. In the Sizing & Ordering group, click Size/Space, and then click the appropriate button to control spacing. Spacing options include Equal Horizontal, Increase Horizontal, Decrease Horizontal, Equal Vertical, Increase Vertical, and Decrease Vertical.

Activity 6.02 | Adding Sections to a Form

1.3.5, 4.3.7, 4.3.8,

The only section that is automatically added to a form when it is created in Design view is the Detail section. In this Activity, you will add a Form Header section and a Form Footer section.

1 Switch to **Form** view, and notice that the form displays only the data. There is no header section with a logo or name of the form.

2 Switch to **Design** view. Under **Form Design Tools**, on the **Design tab**, in the **Header/Footer group**, click **Logo**. Navigate to the location where the student data files for this textbook are saved. Locate and double-click **a06A_Logo** to insert the logo in the Form Header section.

Two sections—the Form Header and the Form Footer—are added to the form along with the logo. Sections can be added only in Design view.

3 On the selected logo, point to the right middle sizing handle until the pointer [↔] displays. Drag to the right until the right edge of the logo is aligned with the **1.5-inch mark on the horizontal ruler**.

4 In the **Header/Footer group**, click **Title** to insert the title in the Form Header section. Compare your screen with Figure 6.5.

The name of the form is inserted as a title into the Form Header section, and the label control is the same height as the logo.

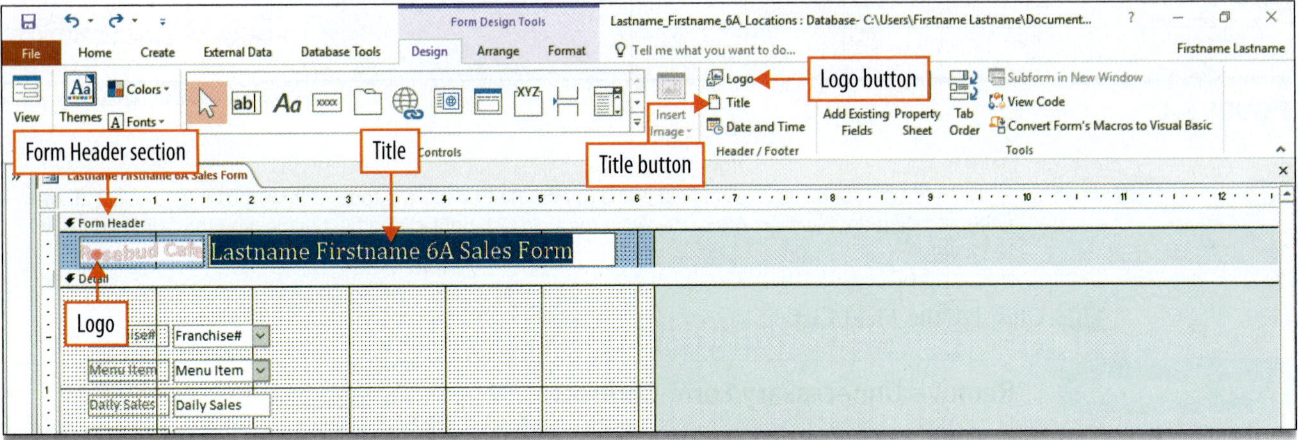

FIGURE 6.5

5 Scroll down until the **Form Footer** section bar displays. Point to the top of the **Form Footer** section bar until the pointer [+] displays. Drag upward until the top of the Form Footer section bar aligns with the **2-inch mark on the vertical ruler**.

The height of the Detail section is decreased. Extra space at the bottom of the Detail section will cause blank space to display between records if the form is printed.

6 Under **Form Design Tools**, on the **Design tab**, in the **Controls group**, click **Label** [Aa]. Point to the **Form Footer** section until the plus sign (+) of the pointer aligns with the bottom of the **Form Footer** section bar and with the left edge of the **Date label control** in the Detail section. Click and drag downward to the bottom of the **Form Footer** section and to the right to **3 inches on the horizontal ruler**. Using your own first name and last name, type **Designed by Firstname Lastname** Press Enter, and then compare your screen with Figure 6.6.

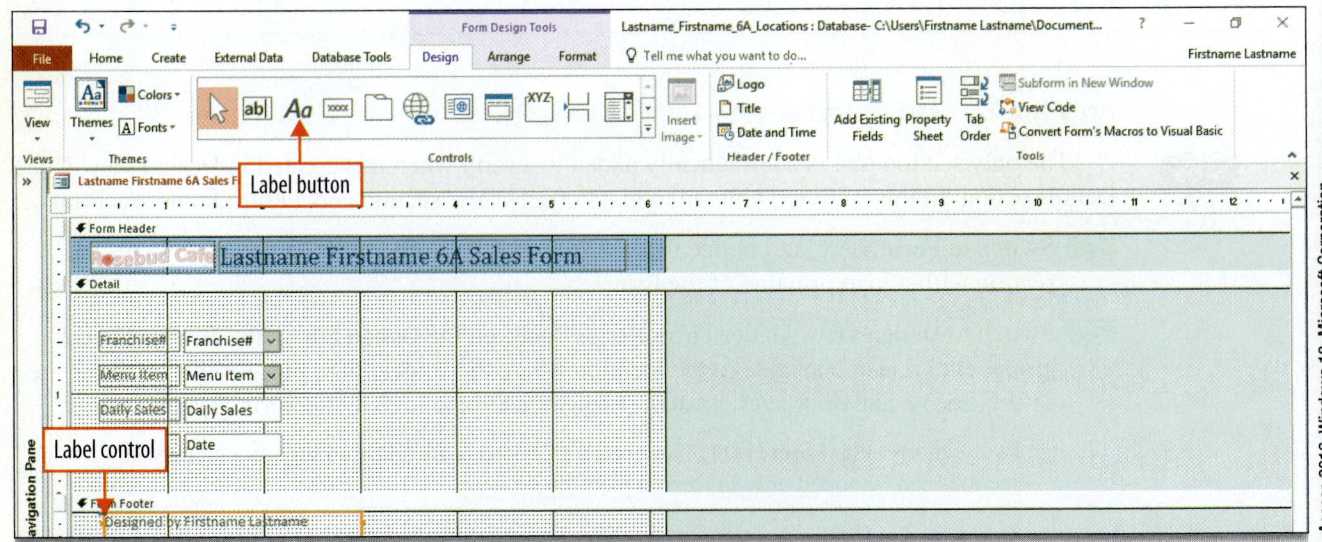

FIGURE 6.6

7 With the label control in the Form Footer section selected, hold down Shift, and then click each of the label controls in the Detail section. Under **Form Design Tools,** click the **Arrange tab**. In the **Sizing & Ordering group**, click **Align**, and then select **Left**. **Save** the form, and then switch to **Form** view.

The Form Header section displays the logo and the title of the form. The Form Footer section displays the label control that is aligned with the label controls in the Detail section. Both the Form Header and Form Footer sections display on every form page.

Objective 2 Change and Add Controls

GO! Learn How Video A6-2

A ***control*** is an object, such as a label or text box, in a form or report that enables you to view or manipulate information stored in tables or queries. You have worked with label controls, text box controls, and, earlier in the chapter, logo controls, but there are more controls that can be added to a form. More controls are available in Design view than in Layout view. By default, when you create a form, Access uses the same field definitions as those in the underlying table or query.

Activity 6.03 | Changing Controls on a Form

4.2.1, 1.3.5

In this Activity, you will change a combo box control to a list box control.

1 Click the **Menu Item field arrow**.

Because the underlying table—*6A Sales*—designated this field as a lookup field, Access inserted a combo box control for this field instead of a text box control. The Franchise# field is also a combo box control. A ***combo box*** enables individuals to select from a list or to type a value.

2 Switch to **Design** view. In the **Detail** section, click the **Menu Item label control**, hold down Shift, and then click the **Menu Item combo box control**. Under **Form Design Tools,** click the **Arrange tab**. In the **Table group**, click **Remove Layout**.

Remove Layout is used to remove a field from a stacked or tabular layout—it does not delete the field or remove it from the form. If fields are in the middle of a stacked layout column and are removed from the layout, the remaining fields in the column will display over the removed field. To avoid the clutter, first move the fields that you want to remove from the layout to the bottom of the column.

3 Click **Undo**. Point to the **Menu Item label control** until the pointer displays. Click and drag downward until a thin orange line displays on the bottom edges of the **Date** controls. Release the mouse button.

ALERT! **Did the control stay in the same location?**

In Design view, the orange line that indicates the location where controls will be moved is much thinner than—and not as noticeable as—the line in Layout view. If you drag downward too far, Access will not move the selected fields.

4 In the **Table group**, click **Remove Layout** to remove the Menu Item field from the stacked layout. Point to the selected controls, and then drag to the right and upward until the **Menu Item label control** is aligned with the **Franchise#** controls and with the **3.25-inch mark on the horizontal ruler**. Compare your screen with Figure 6.7.

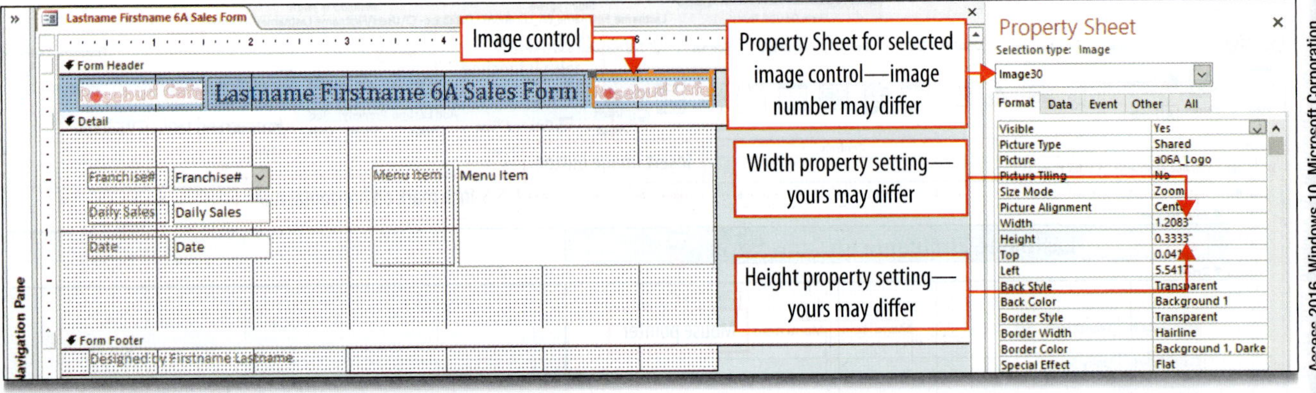

FIGURE 6.10

5 If necessary, change the **Width** property setting to **1.25** and then change the **Height** property setting to **0.5** In the **Form Header** section, on the left side, click the **logo control**, and then notice that the Property Sheet for the logo control displays. On the **Property Sheet**, change the **Width** property setting to **1.25** and then change the **Height** property setting to **0.5** **Close** [X] the **Property Sheet**.

The width and height of the two controls are now the same.

6 With the logo control selected, hold down Shift, and then click the **image control**. Under **Form Design Tools**, click the **Arrange tab**. In the **Sizing & Ordering group**, click **Align**, and then click **Bottom**. Click the **title's label control**. In the **Table group**, click **Remove Layout**, and then point to the left middle sizing handle until the pointer ↔ displays. Drag to the right until there is **one dot** displayed between the right edge of the logo control and the left edge of the title's label control.

The logo control and the image control are aligned at the bottom, and the title's label control is resized.

7 Under **Form Design Tools**, click the **Design tab**. At the right edge of the **Controls gallery**, click **More** [▾], and verify that the **Use Control Wizards** option is active. Click **Button** [xxxx]. Move the mouse pointer down into the **Detail** section. Align the plus sign (+) of the pointer at **1.5 inches on the vertical ruler** and **1.5 inches on the horizontal ruler**, and then click. If a security message displays, click Open. Compare your screen with Figure 6.11.

The Command Button Wizard dialog box displays. The first dialog box enables you to select an action for the button based on the selected category.

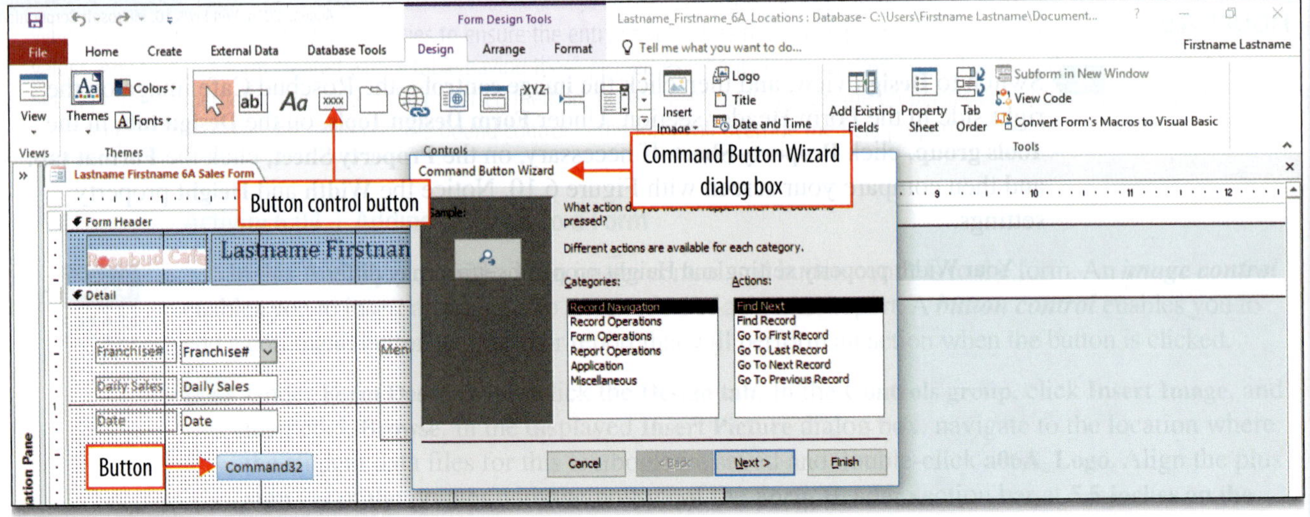

FIGURE 6.11

8 Take a moment to click the different categories to display the actions associated with each category. When you are finished, under **Categories**, if necessary, click **Record Navigation**. Under **Actions**, click **Go To Previous Record**, and then click **Next**.

The second Command Button Wizard dialog box displays, which enables you to select what will display on the button—either text or a picture. If you select Picture, you can then click Browse to navigate to a location on your computer where pictures are saved, and then select any picture. If you select Text, you can accept the default text or type new text. A preview of the button displays on the left side of the dialog box.

9 Next to **Picture**, verify **Go To Previous** is selected, and then click **Next**.

The third Command Button Wizard dialog box displays, which enables you to name the button. If you need to refer to the button later—usually in creating macros—a meaningful name is helpful. The buttons created with the Command Button Wizard are linked to macros or programs.

10 In the text box, type **btnPrevRecord** and then click **Finish**.

When you are creating controls that can later be used in programming, it is a good idea to start the name of the control with an abbreviation of the type of control—btn—and then a descriptive abbreviation of the purpose of the control.

11 Using the techniques you have just practiced, add a **button control** about **1 inch** to the right of the **Previous Record button control**. Under **Categories**, click **Record Navigation**, if necessary. Under **Actions**, click **Go To Next Record**. For **Picture**, click **Go To Next**, name the button **btnNxtRecord** and then click **Finish**. Do not be concerned if the button controls are not exactly aligned.

12 With the **Next Record button control** selected, hold down Shift, and then click the **Previous Record button control**. Under **Form Design Tools,** click the **Arrange tab**. In the **Sizing & Ordering group**, click **Align**, and then click **Top**. Click **Size/Space**, and then, under **Spacing**, click either **Increase Horizontal** or **Decrease Horizontal** until there is approximately **1 inch** of space between the two controls. Compare your screen with Figure 6.12.

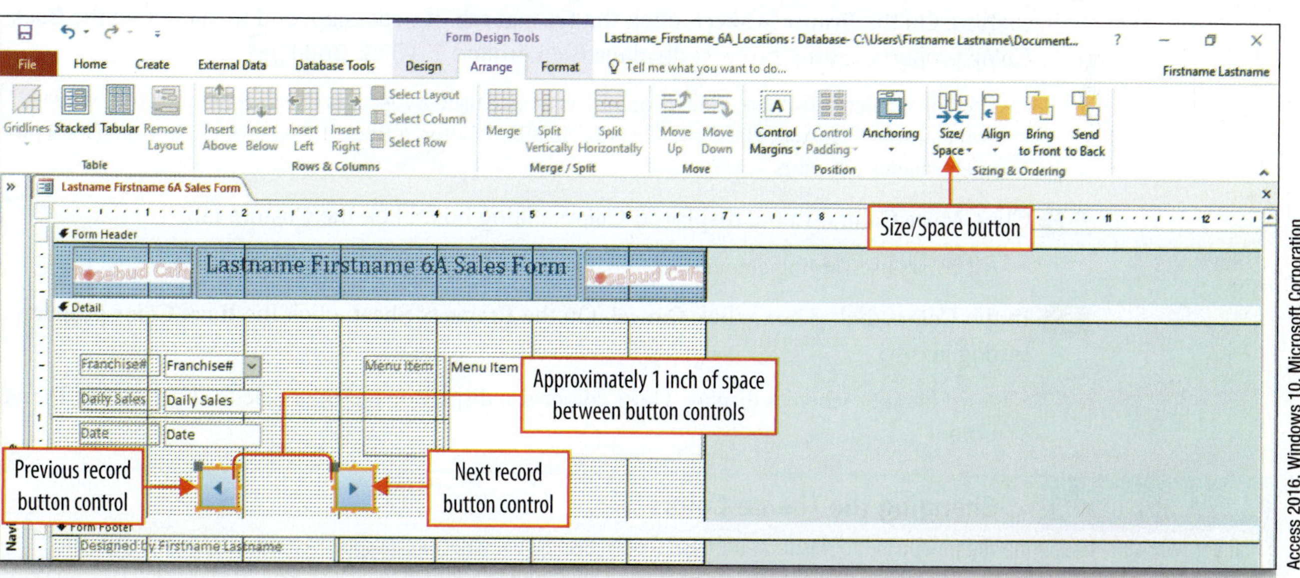

FIGURE 6.12

13 **Save** the form, and then switch to **Form** view. Experiment by clicking the **Next Record** button and the **Previous Record** button, and notice in the record navigator that you are displaying different records.

14 Switch to **Design** view. Under **Form Design Tools**, on the **Design tab**, in the **Controls group**, click **Button** [xxxx] Align the plus sign (+) of the pointer at **1.5 inches on the vertical ruler** and at **5.5 inches on the horizontal ruler**, and then click.

15 In the **Command Button Wizard** dialog box, under **Categories**, click **Form Operations**. Under **Actions**, click **Print Current Form**, and then click **Next**. Click the **Text** option button to accept *Print Form*, and then click **Next**. Name the button **btnPrtForm** and then click **Finish**.

You will use this button to print one record when you are finished formatting the form.

16 **Save** the form.

Objective 3 Format a Form

GO! Learn How
Video A6-3

There are several methods you can use to modify the appearance of a form. Each section and control on a form has properties. Some properties can be modified by using buttons in the groups on a tab or by changing the property setting on the Property Sheet.

Activity 6.05 | Adding a Background Color

4.3.6, 4.3.4, 1.3.5

1 With **6A Sales Form** open in **Design** view, click the **Form Header** section bar.

The darkened bar indicates that the entire Form Header section of the form is selected.

2 Under **Form Design Tools**, click the **Format tab**. In the **Font group**, click **Background Color arrow**. Under **Theme Colors**, in the second row, click the sixth color—**Red, Accent 2, Lighter 80%**.

The background color for the Form Header section changes to a light shade of red.

3 Double-click the **Form Footer** section bar to display the Property Sheet for the Form Footer section. On the **Property Sheet**, click the **Format tab**, if necessary, and then click in the **Back Color** property setting box—it displays Background 1. Click **Build** [...].

The color palette displays. Background 1 is a code used by Access to represent the color white. You can select an Access Theme Color, a Standard Color, a Recent Color, or click More Colors to select shades of colors.

4 Click **More Colors**. In the displayed **Colors** dialog box, click the **Custom tab**.

All colors use varying amounts of Red, Green, and Blue.

5 In the **Colors** dialog box, click **Cancel**. On the **Property Sheet**, click the **Back Color property setting arrow**.

A list of color schemes display. These colors also display on the color palette under Access Theme Colors.

More Knowledge **Changing the Theme Colors**

If you want to change the theme applied to this form (or object) only, display the object in Design or Layout view. On the Design tab, in the Themes group, click Themes to display a list of available themes. Right-click the theme you want to apply, and click Apply Theme to This Object Only.

6 ACCESS

6 From the displayed list, experiment by clicking on different color schemes and viewing the effects of the background color change. You will have to click the property setting arrow each time to select another color scheme. When you are finished, click **Build** [...]. Under **Theme Colors**, in the second row, click the sixth color—**Red, Accent 2, Lighter 80%**. **Close** [X] the **Property Sheet**.

You can change the background color either by using the Background Color button in the Font group or by changing the Back Color property setting on the Property Sheet.

ANOTHER WAY Open the form in Layout view. To select a section, click in an empty area of the section. On the Home tab, in the Text Formatting group, click the Background Color button.

7 Using one of the techniques you have just practiced, change the background color of the **Detail** section to **Red, Accent 2, Lighter 80%**. Switch to **Form** view, and then compare your screen with Figure 6.13.

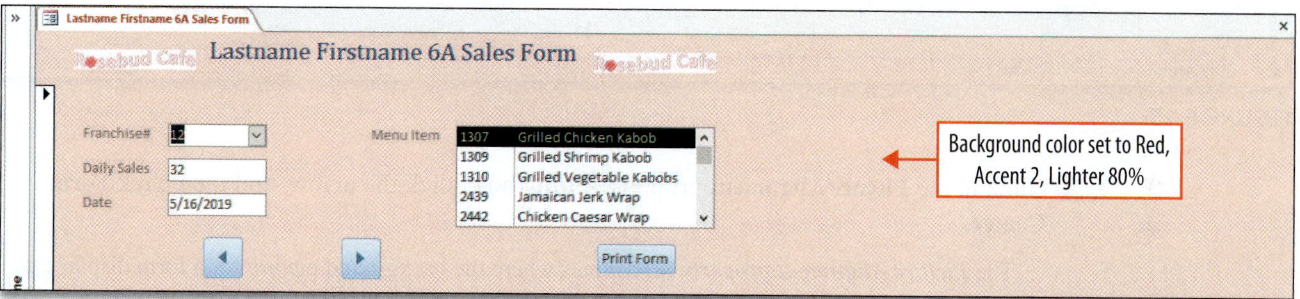

FIGURE 6.13

Access 2016, Windows 10, Microsoft Corporation

8 **Save** [save] the form, and then switch to **Design** view.

More Knowledge **Adding a Shape Fill to Controls**

You can also add fill color to controls. First, click the control or controls to which you want to add a fill color. If you want to use color schemes, open the Property Sheet, and then click the Back Color property setting arrow. If you want to use the color palette, in Design view, under Form Design Tools, on the Format tab, in the Font group, click Background Color.

Activity 6.06 | Adding a Background Picture to a Form

4.3.6, 4.3.8, 4.2.5, 1.3.5

In this Activity, you will add a picture to the background of *6A Sales Form*.

1 With **6A Sales Form** open in **Design** view, locate the **Form selector**, as shown in Figure 6.14.

The ***Form selector*** is the box where the rulers meet, in the upper left corner of a form in Design view. Use the Form selector to select the entire form.

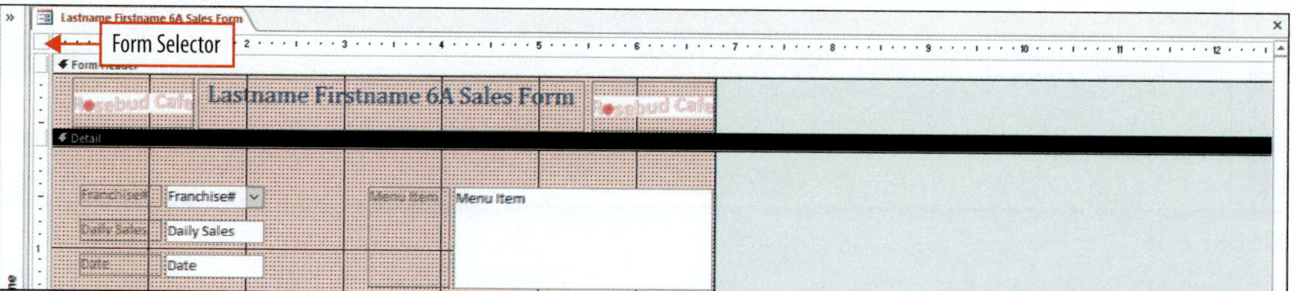

FIGURE 6.14

Access 2016, Windows 10, Microsoft Corporation

2 Double-click the **Form selector** to open the **Property Sheet** for the form.

3 On the **Property Sheet**, on the **Format tab**, click in the **Picture** property setting box. Click **Build** [...]. Navigate to the location where the student data files for this textbook are saved. Locate and double-click **a06A_Background** to insert the picture in the form, and then compare your screen with Figure 6.15.

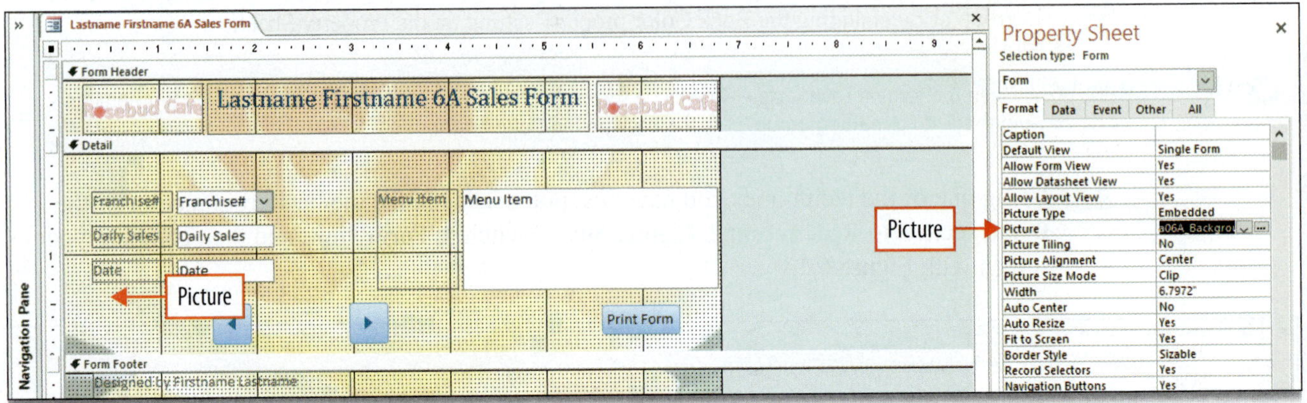

FIGURE 6.15

4 Click in the **Picture Alignment** property setting box, click the **arrow**, and then click **Form Center**.

The ***Picture Alignment property*** determines where the background picture for a form displays on the form. Center places the picture in the center of the page when the form is printed. Form Center places the picture in the center of the form data when the form is printed.

5 Click in the **Picture Size Mode** property setting box, and then click the **arrow** to display the options. From the displayed list, click **Stretch**.

The ***Picture Size Mode property*** determines the size of the picture in the form. The Clip setting retains the original size of the image. The Stretch setting stretches the image both vertically and horizontally to match the size of the form—the image may be distorted. The Zoom setting adjusts the image to be as large as possible without distorting the image. Both Stretch Horizontal and Stretch Vertical can distort the image. If you have a background color and set the Picture Type property setting to Stretch, the background color will not display.

6 **Close** [X] the **Property Sheet**, **Save** [save] the form, and then switch to **Layout** view. Compare your screen with Figure 6.16.

FIGURE 6.16

Activity 6.07 | Modifying the Borders of Controls

4.2.6, 1.3.5

In this Activity, you will modify the borders of some of the controls on *6A Sales Form*. There are related property settings on the Property Sheet.

1 With **6A Sales Form** open in **Layout** view, click the **Franchise#** combo box control. Holding down Shift, click the **Daily Sales** text box control, and then click the **Date** text box control. Under **Form Layout Tools**, on the **Format tab**, in the **Control Formatting group**, click **Shape Outline**. Notice the options that are used to modify borders—Colors, Line Thickness, and Line Type. Compare your screen with Figure 6.17.

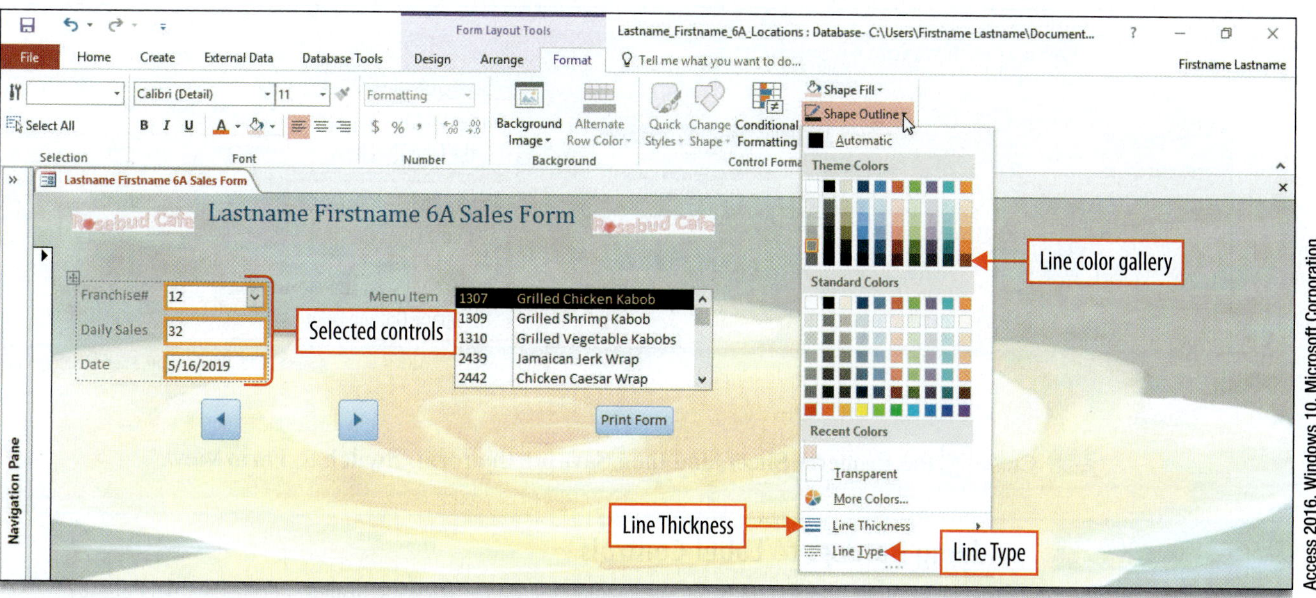

FIGURE 6.17

2 Point to **Line Type** and point to each line type to display the **ScreenTip**. The second line type—Solid—is the default line type. Click the fifth line type—**Dots**—and then switch to **Form** view to display the results. Notice that the borders of the three controls display a dotted line. Switch to **Layout** view.

You can review the results in Layout view, but you would have to deselect the three controls.

3 With the three controls still selected, under **Form Layout Tools**, on the **Format tab**, in the **Control Formatting group**, click **Shape Outline**. Point to **Line Thickness** and point to each line thickness to display the **ScreenTip**. The first line thickness—Hairline—is the default line thickness. Click the second line type—**1 pt**.

4 In the **Control Formatting group**, click **Shape Outline**. Under **Theme Colors**, point to a few colors to display the **ScreenTip**, and then in the first row, click the sixth color—**Red, Accent 2**. Switch to **Form** view to display the results.

The borders of the three controls display a line thickness of 1 point, and the color of the borders is a dark red shade. A ***point*** is 1/72 of an inch.

5 Switch to **Layout** view. With the three controls still selected, under **Form Layout Tools**, on the **Design tab**, in the **Tools group**, click **Property Sheet**, and then compare your screen with Figure 6.18. Notice the properties that are associated with the buttons on the ribbon with which you changed the borders of the selected controls.

Because multiple items on the form are selected, the Property Sheet displays *Selection type: Multiple selection*. You changed the property settings of the controls by using buttons, and the Property Sheet displays the results of those changes. You can also select multiple controls, open the Property Sheet, and make the changes to the properties. The Property Sheet displays more settings than those available through the use of buttons.

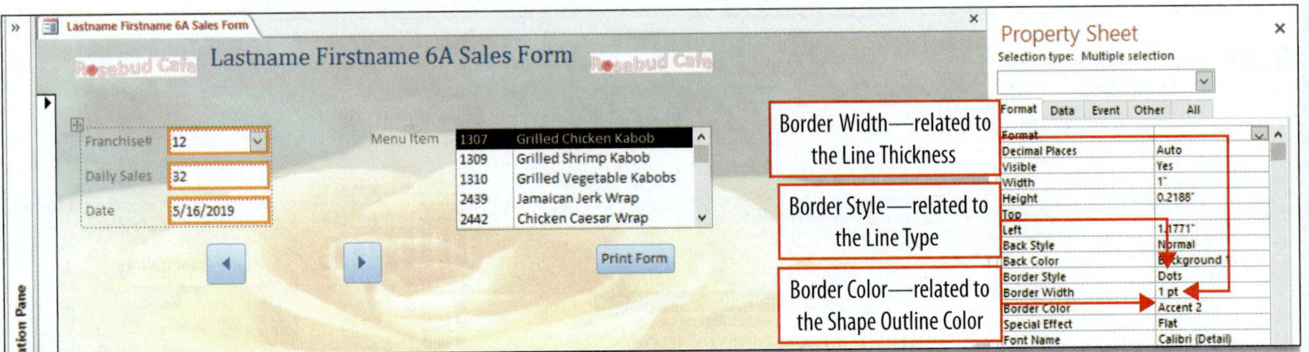

Access 2016, Windows 10, Microsoft Corporation

FIGURE 6.18

6 **Close** the **Property Sheet**, and then **Save** the form. Switch to **Form** view.

***More* Knowledge** **Adding Borders to Label Controls**

By default, the line type of a label control is transparent, effectively hiding the border from the display. Because borders display around bound controls that contain data, it is recommended that you do not add borders to label controls so that individuals can easily distinguish the control that holds data.

Objective 4 Make a Form User Friendly

GO! Learn How Video A6-4

To make forms easy to use, you can add instructions to the status bar while data is being entered and custom ***ControlTips*** that display when an individual points to a control on a form. Additionally, you can change the tab order of the fields on a form. ***Tab order*** refers to the order in which the fields are selected when the Tab key is pressed. By default, the tab order is created based on the order in which the fields are added to the form.

Activity 6.08 | Adding a Message to the Status Bar

4.2.5, 1.3.5

When you created tables, you may have added a description to the field, and the description displayed in the status bar of the Access window. If a description is included for a field in the underlying table of a form, the text of the description will also display in the status bar when an individual clicks in the field on the form. In this Activity, you will add a description to the Daily Sales field in the *6A Sales* table, and then ***propagate***—disseminate or apply—the changes to *6A Sales Form*. You will also add status bar text to a field on a form using the Property Sheet of the control.

1 With **6A Sales Form** open in **Form** view, click in the **Daily Sales** field. On the left side of the status bar, *Form View* displays—there is no text to assist an individual entering data.

2 **Close** [X] the form, and then **Open** [»] the **Navigation Pane**. Under **Tables**, right-click **6A Sales**, and then from the shortcut menu, click **Design View**. In the **Daily Sales** field, click in the **Description** box. Type **How many items were sold?** and then press Enter. Compare your screen with Figure 6.19.

A ***Property Update Options button*** displays in the Description box for the Date field. When you make changes to the design of a table, Access displays this button, which enables individuals to update the Property Sheet for this field in all objects that use this table as the record source.

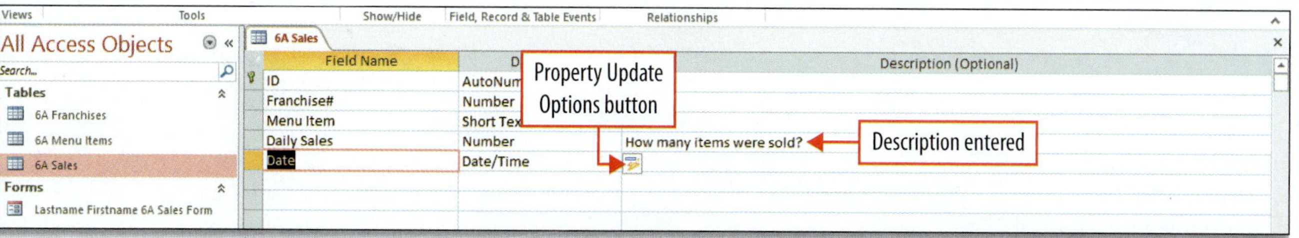

FIGURE 6.19

Access 2016, Windows 10, Microsoft Corporation

3 Click **Property Update Options** [icon], and then click **Update Status Bar Text everywhere Daily Sales is used**. In the displayed **Update Properties** dialog box, under **Update the following objects?**, notice that only one object—*Form: 6A Sales Form*—displays, and it is selected. In the **Update Properties** dialog box, click **Yes**. **Close** [X] the table, saving changes.

The changes in the Description field in the table will be propagated to *6A Sales Form*. If multiple objects use the *6A Sales* table as the underlying object, you can propagate the change to all of the objects.

4 In the **Navigation Pane**, under **Forms**, double-click **6A Sales Form** to open it in **Form** view. **Close** [«] the **Navigation Pane**. Click in the **Daily Sales** field, and then notice that on the left side of the status bar, *How many items were sold?* displays.

Access propagated the change made in the underlying table to the form.

5 Switch to **Design** view. Click the **Daily Sales text box control**. Under **Form Design Tools**, on the **Design tab**, in the **Tools group**, click **Property Sheet**.

6 On the **Property Sheet**, click the **Other tab**. Locate the **Status Bar Text** property, and notice the setting *How many items were sold?*

When Access propagated the change to the form, it populated the Status Bar Text property setting. The ***Status Bar Text property*** enables individuals to add descriptive text that will display in the status bar for a selected control.

7 In the **Detail** section, click the **Date text box control**, and then notice that the **Property Sheet** changes to display the properties for the Date text box control. Click in the **Status Bar Text** property setting box, type **Enter the date of sales report** and then press Enter.

Entering a Status Bar Text on the Text Box Property Sheet does not display Property Update Options to propagate changes to the underlying table or add the information to the Description box for the field in the table.

8 **Save** [icon] the form, and then switch to **Form** view. Click in the **Date** field, and then compare your screen with Figure 6.20.

The status bar displays the text you entered in the Status Bar Text property setting box.

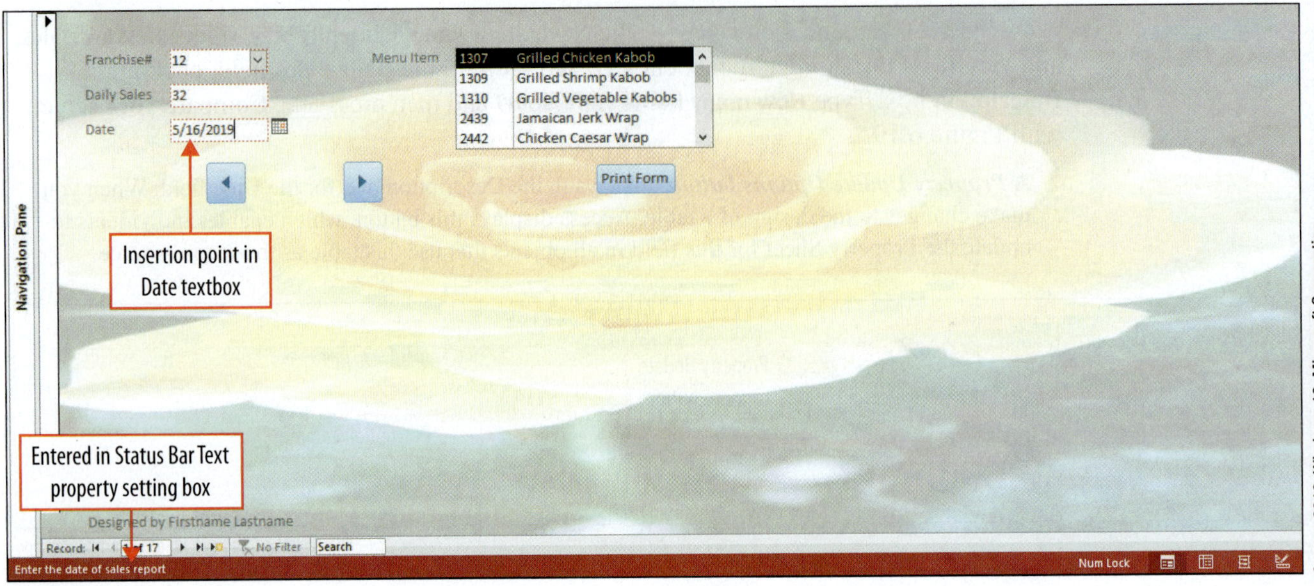

FIGURE 6.20

9 Switch to **Design** view.

***More* Knowledge** **Conflicting Field Description and Status Bar Text Property Setting**

When you create a form, the fields inherit the property settings from the underlying table. You can change the Status Bar Text property setting for the form, and it will override the setting that is inherited from the table. If you later change field properties in Table Design view, Property Update Options displays—you must manually propagate those changes to the table's related objects; propagation is not automatic. An exception to this is entering Validation Rules—changes are automatically propagated.

Activity 6.09 | Creating Custom ControlTips

4.2.5, 1.3.5

Another way to make a form easier to use is to add custom ControlTips to objects on the form. A ControlTip is similar to a ScreenTip, and temporarily displays descriptive text while the mouse pointer is paused over the control. This method is somewhat limited because most individuals press Tab or Enter to move from field to field and thus do not see the ControlTip. However, a ControlTip is a useful tool in a training situation when an individual is learning how to use the data entry form. In this Activity, you will add a ControlTip to the Print Form button control.

1 With **6A Sales Form** open in **Design** view and the **Property Sheet** displayed, click the **Print Form** button. If necessary, click the **Other tab** to make it active. Notice the **Property Sheet** displays *Selection type: Command Button* and the Selection type box displays *btnPrtForm*, the name you gave to the button when you added it to the form.

2 Click in the **ControlTip Text** property setting box, type **Prints the selected record** and then press Enter. Compare your screen with Figure 6.21.

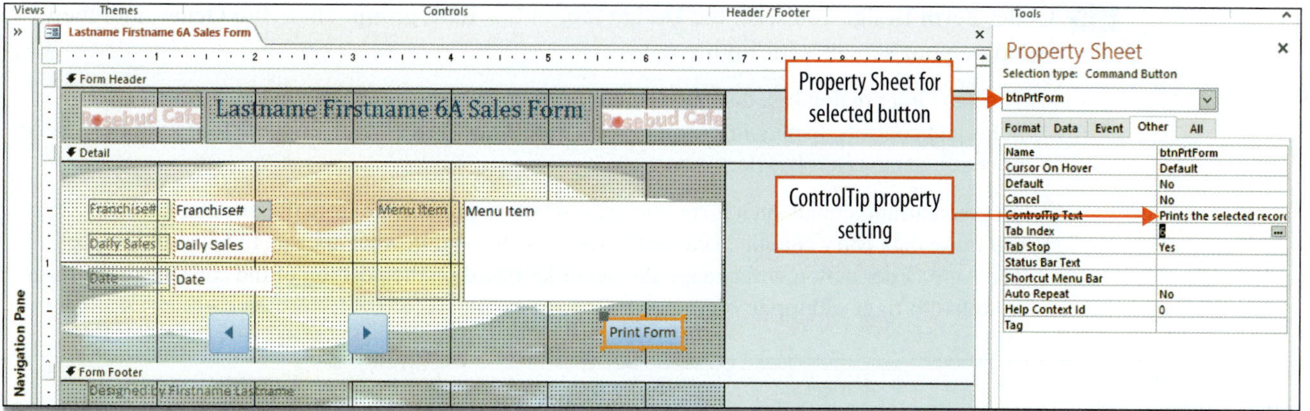

FIGURE 6.21

Access 2016, Windows 10, Microsoft Corporation

3 **Close** the **Property Sheet**, **Save** the form, and then switch to **Form** view. Point to the **Print Form** button, and then compare your screen with Figure 6.22.

A ControlTip displays the message you typed for the ControlTip Text property setting.

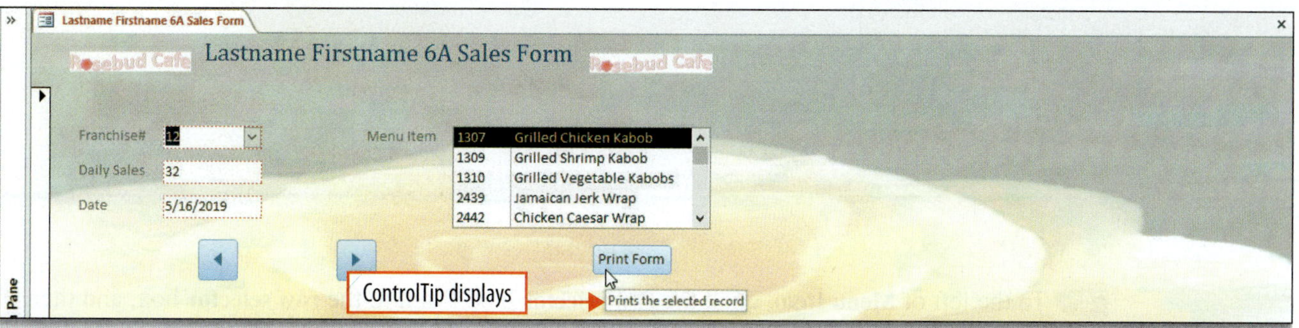

FIGURE 6.22

Access 2016, Windows 10, Microsoft Corporation

Activity 6.10 | Changing the Tab Order

4.3.1, 1.3.5, 4.2.5, 4.3.2, 4.3.3, 1.5.2, 4.3.5

You can customize the order in which you enter data on a form by changing the tab order. Recall that tab order refers to the order in which the fields are selected each time Tab is pressed. As you press Tab, the focus of the form changes from one control to another control. ***Focus*** refers to the control that is selected and currently being acted upon.

1 With **6A Sales Form** open in **Form** view, in the record navigator, click **New (blank) record**. If necessary, click in the **Franchise#** combo box. Press Tab three times, and then notice that the insertion point moves from field to field, ending with the **Date** text box. Press Tab three more times, and then notice the **Print Form** button is the focus. The button displays with a darker border. Press Enter.

Because the focus is on the Print Form button, the Print dialog box displays.

2 In the **Print** dialog box, click **Cancel**. Switch to **Design** view.

3 Under **Form Design Tools**, on the **Design tab**, in the **Tools group**, click **Tab Order**, and then compare your screen with Figure 6.23.

The Tab Order dialog box displays. Under Section, Detail is selected. Under Custom Order, the fields and controls display in the order they were added to the form. To the left of each field name or button name is a row selector box.

As you rearrange fields on a form, the tab order does not change from the original tab order. This can make data entry chaotic because the focus is changed in what appears to be an illogical order. The Auto Order button will change the tab order based on the position of the controls in the form from left to right and top to bottom.

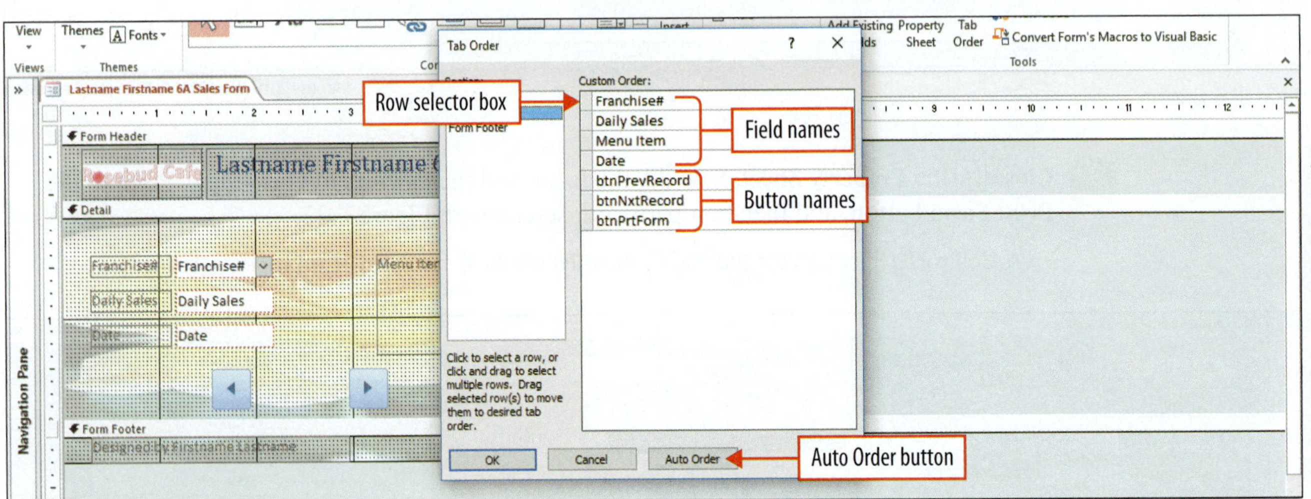

FIGURE 6.23

4 To the left of **Menu Item**, click the **row selector** box. Point to the **row selector** box, and then drag downward until a dark horizontal line displays between **Date** and **btnPrevRecord**.

The Menu Item field will now receive the focus after the Date field.

ALERT! **Did the field stay in the same location?**

You must point to the row selector box before dragging the field. If you point to the field name, the field will not move.

5 In the **Tab Order** dialog box, click **OK**. **Save** the form, and then switch to **Form** view. In the record navigator, click **Last record**. When the Menu Item field has the focus, it is easier to see it on a blank record. In the record navigator, click **New (blank) record**.

The insertion point displays in the Franchise# field.

6 Press Tab three times. Even though it is difficult to see, the focus changes to the **Menu Item** list box. Press Tab again, and then notice that the focus changes to the **btnPrevRecord** button.

Before allowing individuals to enter data into a form, you should always test the tab order to ensure that the data will be easy to enter.

7 Switch to **Design** view. In the **Detail** section, right-click the **Date text box control**, and click **Properties**. If necessary, click the **Other** tab, and then compare your screen with Figure 6.24.

Text box controls have three properties relating to tab order: Tab Index, Tab Stop, and Auto Tab. Combo box controls and list box controls do not have an Auto Tab property.

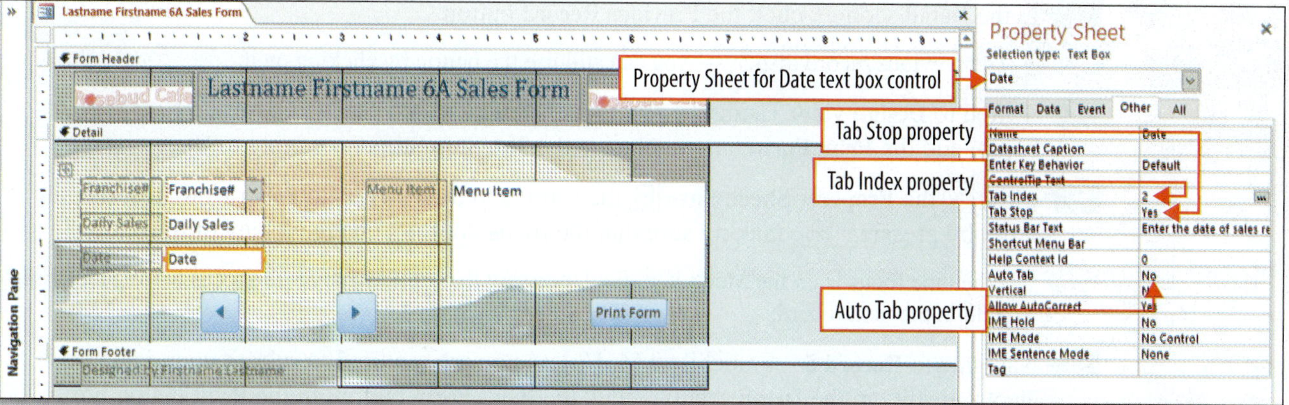

FIGURE 6.24

Access 2016, Windows 10, Microsoft Corporation

8 On the **Property Sheet**, click in the **Tab Index** property setting box, which displays *2*. Click **Build** [...].

Tab Index settings begin with 0. Franchise# has a Tab Index setting of 0, which indicates that this field has the focus when the form is opened. Daily Sales has a Tab Index setting of 1—it will receive the focus when Tab is pressed one time. Date has a Tab Index setting of 2—it will receive the focus when Tab is pressed a second time. Menu Item has a Tab Index setting of 3—it will receive the focus when Tab is pressed a third time.

9 In the **Tab Order** dialog box, click **Cancel**. On the **Property Sheet**, notice that the **Tab Stop** property setting is **Yes**, which means individuals can press Tab to move to this field.

The Auto Tab property setting is No. It should be changed to Yes only when a text field has an input mask. Recall that an input mask controls how the data is entered into a field; for example, the formatting of a phone number.

10 In the **Detail** section, click the **Franchise# combo box control**, and then on the **Property Sheet**, notice the settings for the **Tab Index** and **Tab Stop** properties.

The Tab Index setting is 0, which means this field has the focus when the form page is displayed—it is first on the tab order list. The Tab Stop setting is Yes. Because an input mask cannot be applied to a combo box, there is no Auto Tab property. The Auto Tab property applies only to a text box control.

11 In the **Detail** section, click the **Previous Record** button control. On the **Property Sheet**, click in the **Tab Stop** property setting box, click the **arrow**, and then click **No**.

Changing the Tab Stop property setting to No means that the focus will not be changed to the button by pressing Tab.

12 **Save** the form, and then switch to **Form** view. In the record navigator, click **Last record**. Press Tab two times, watching the focus change from the **Franchise#** field to the **Date** field. Press Tab two more times, and then compare your screen with Figure 6.25.

Because the Tab Stop property setting for the Previous Record button control was changed to No, the button does not receive the focus by pressing the Tab key.

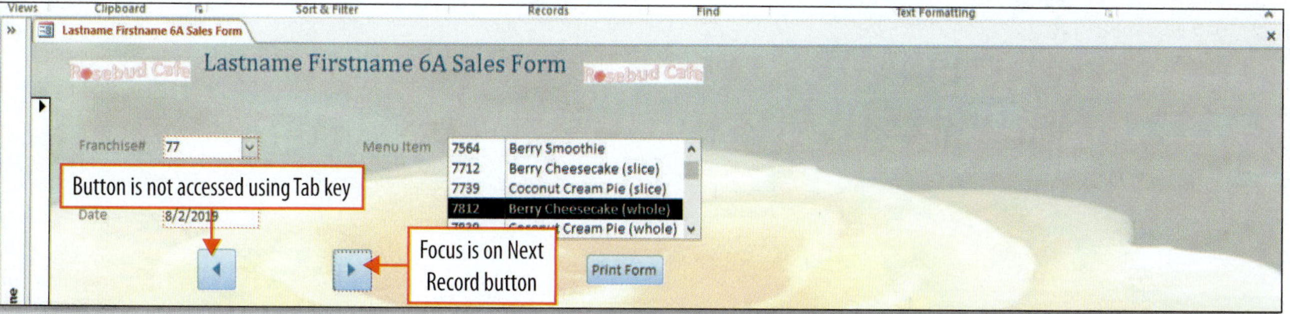

FIGURE 6.25

Access 2016, Windows 10, Microsoft Corporation

13 In the **Detail** section, click the **Previous Record** button.

The previous record displays—you can still use the button by clicking on it.

14 Switch to **Design** view. Using the techniques you have just practiced, for the **Next Record** button and the **Print Form** button, change the **Tab Stop** property setting to **No**.

15 **Close** the **Property Sheet**. **Save** the form, and then switch to **Form** view. Test the tab order by pressing Tab, making sure that the focus does not change to any of the buttons.

When the focus is on the Menu Item field, pressing the Tab key moves the focus to the Franchise# field in the next record.

16 Navigate to **Record 5**—Franchise# 44. Unless you are required to submit your database electronically, in the **Detail** section, click the **Print Form** button. In the **Print** dialog box, under **Print Range**, click **Selected Record(s)**, and then click **OK**. If you are instructed to submit this result as an electronic printout, select the record using the selector bar, and then from **Backstage** view, click **Save As**. Click **Save Object As**, and double-click **PDF or XPS**. Navigate to the folder where you store your electronic printouts. Click the **Options** button, click **Selected records**, and then click **OK**. Click **Publish**.

17 **Close** the form, and then **Open** » the **Navigation Pane**. **Close** the database, and then **Close** Access.

18 As directed by your instructor, submit your database and the paper printout or PDF electronic image of the form that is the result of this project.

***More* Knowledge** **Changing the Margins in the Print Dialog Box**

In the Print dialog box, at the bottom left, click Setup. In the Page Setup dialog box, on the Print Options tab, adjust the left and right margins to balance the form on the page, and then click OK.

END | You have completed Project 6A

PROJECT 6B

Rosebud Cafe

MyITLab
Project 6B Training
Project 6B Grader

PROJECT ACTIVITIES

In Activities 6.11 through 6.18, you will create customized reports for Jane Chin. The corporate office of Rosebud Cafe (RBC) maintains a database about the franchises, including daily sales of menu items per franchise, the franchise owners, and franchise fees and payments. Reports are often run to summarize data in the tables or queries. Creating customized reports will help the owners and officers of the company view the information in the database in a meaningful way. Your completed reports will look similar to Figure 6.26.

PROJECT FILES

If your instructor wants you to submit Project 6B in the MyITLab grader system, log in to MyITLab, locate Grader Project 6B, and then download the files for this project.

For Project 6B, you will need the following files:
a06B_RBC
a06B_Logo

You will save your database as:
Lastname_Firstname_6B_RBC

PROJECT RESULTS

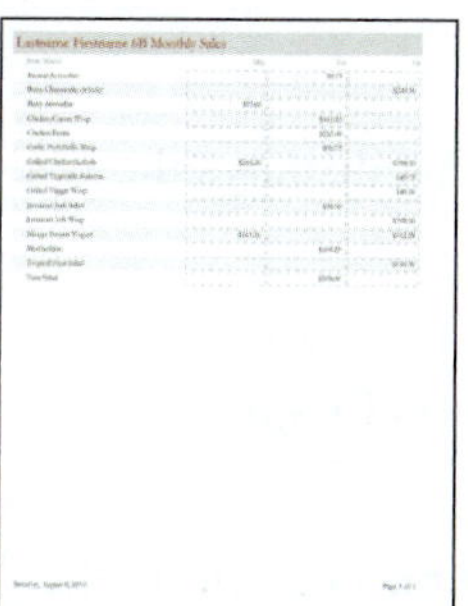

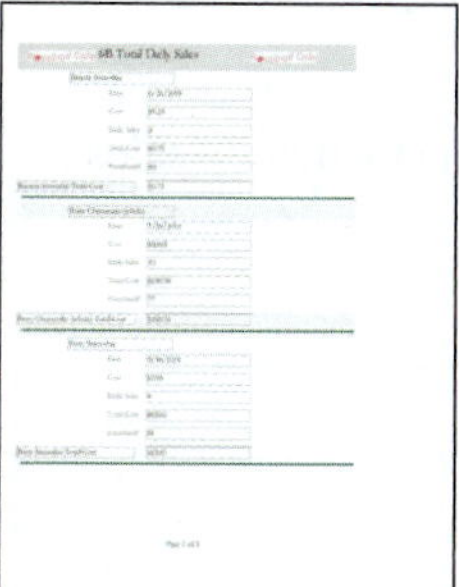

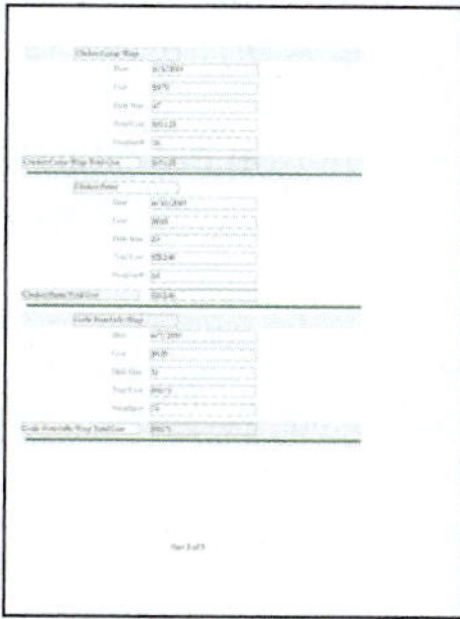

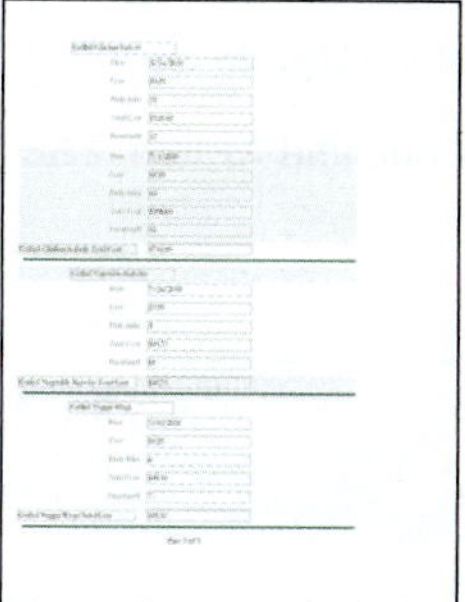

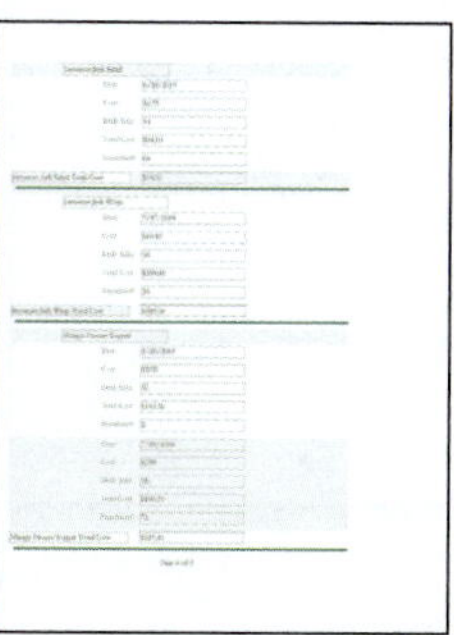

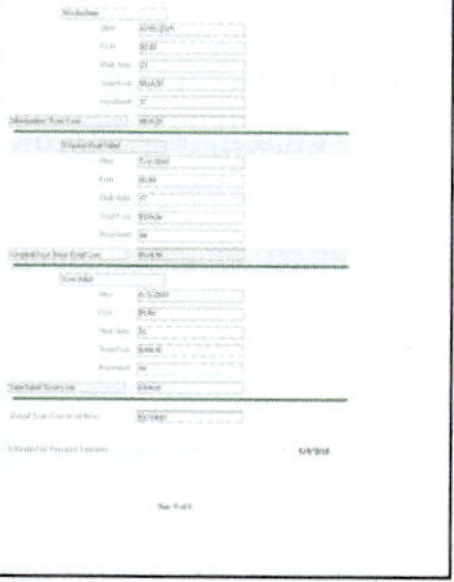

FIGURE 6.26 Project 6B Rosebud Cafe

PROJECT RESULTS

In this project, using your own name, you will create the following database and objects. Your instructor may ask you to submit printouts or PDF electronic images:

Lastname_Firstname_6B_RBC	Database file
Lastname Firstname 6B Monthly Sales	Report
Lastname Firstname 6B Total Daily Sales	Report

Objective 5 Create a Report Based on a Query Using a Wizard

GO! Learn How Video A6-5

A report wizard is a more efficient way to start a report, although Design view does offer more control as you create your report. Once the report has been created, its appearance can be modified in Design or Layout view.

Activity 6.11 | Creating a Report Using a Wizard

ALERT!

To submit as an autograded project, log into MyITLab and download the files for this project, and begin with those files instead of the a06B_RBC file. Begin working with the database in Step 2. For Grader to award points accurately, when saving an object, do not include your Lastname Firstname at the beginning of the object name.

5.1.1, 5.1.3, 5.2.1, 5.3.1, 5.3.5

In this Activity, you will use a wizard to create a report for Rosebud Cafe that displays the data from the 6B Total Daily Sales Crosstab Query.

1. Start Access. Navigate to the location where the student data files for this textbook are saved. Locate and open the **a06B_RBC** file. Save the database in your **Access Chapter 6** folder as **Lastname_Firstname_6B_RBC**

2. If you did not add the Access Chapter 6 folder to the Trust Center, enable the content. In the **Navigation Pane**, under **Queries**, double-click **6B Total Daily Sales Crosstab Query**. Take a moment to study the data in the query, as shown in Figure 6.27.

   The data is grouped by Item Name and Month. The Sum function calculates the total daily sales for each item per month.

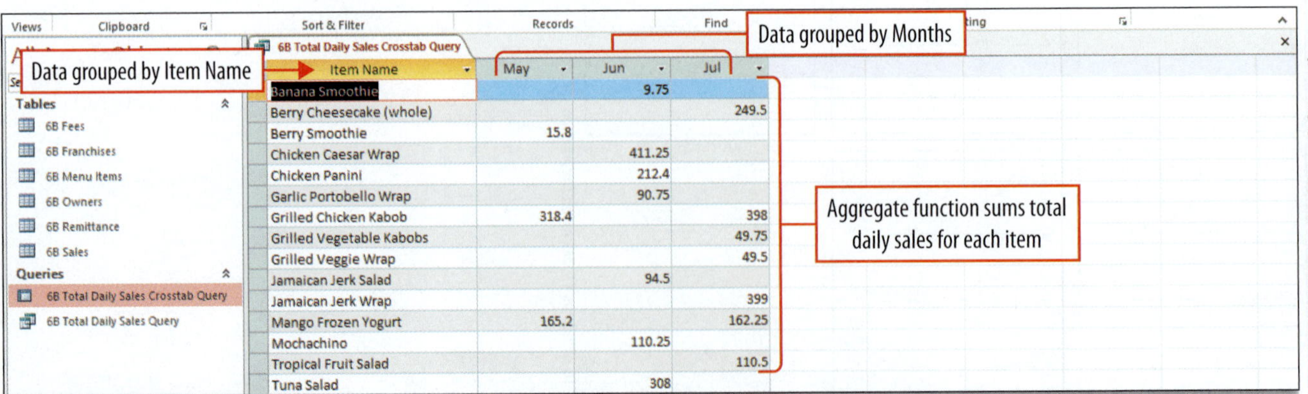

Item Name	May	Jun	Jul
Banana Smoothie		9.75	
Berry Cheesecake (whole)			249.5
Berry Smoothie	15.8		
Chicken Caesar Wrap		411.25	
Chicken Panini		212.4	
Garlic Portobello Wrap		90.75	
Grilled Chicken Kabob	318.4		398
Grilled Vegetable Kabobs			49.75
Grilled Veggie Wrap			49.5
Jamaican Jerk Salad		94.5	
Jamaican Jerk Wrap			399
Mango Frozen Yogurt	165.2		162.25
Mochachino		110.25	
Tropical Fruit Salad			110.5
Tuna Salad		308	

FIGURE 6.27

ALERT! **Are blank columns displayed for months besides May, June, and July?**

If blank columns are displayed for months besides May, June, and July, select the blank columns for Jan, Feb, Mar, and Apr and right-click. From the shortcut menu, click Hide Fields. Using the same technique, hide the columns for Aug, Sep, Oct, Nov, and Dec.

3 **Close** [X] the query, saving if necessary. With **6B Total Daily Sales Crosstab Query** still selected, **Close** [«] the **Navigation Pane**.

4 On the **Create tab**, in the **Reports group**, click **Report Wizard**.

5 Because the crosstab query was selected in the Navigation Pane, in the **Report Wizard** dialog box, in the **Tables/Queries** box, **Query: 6B Total Daily Sales Crosstab Query** displays. If it does not display, click the **Tables/Queries** arrow, and then click **Query: 6B Total Daily Sales Crosstab Query**.

6 Under **Available Fields**, notice there are more months than those that were displayed in 6B Total Daily Sales Crosstab Query.

Because there was data for the months of May, June, and July only, the other months may have been hidden from the display in the query.

7 Under **Available Fields**, double-click each field name, in the order specified, to add the field names to the Selected Fields box: **Item Name**, **May**, **Jun**, and **Jul**.

8 In the **Report Wizard** dialog box, click **Next**. Because no grouping levels will be used, click **Next**.

9 To sort the records within the report by Item Name, click the **arrow** next to the **1** box. From the displayed list, click **Item Name**. Leave the sort order as **Ascending**, and then click **Next**.

10 Under **Layout**, verify the **Tabular** option button is selected. Under **Orientation**, verify the **Portrait** option button is selected, and then click **Next**.

Choose Landscape orientation to display more data across the page.

11 In the **What title do you want for your report?** box, type **Lastname Firstname 6B Monthly Sales** and then click **Finish**. Compare your screen with Figure 6.28.

The report displays in Print Preview. Because this report uses a crosstab query as the record source, it displays calculated data grouped by two different types of information.

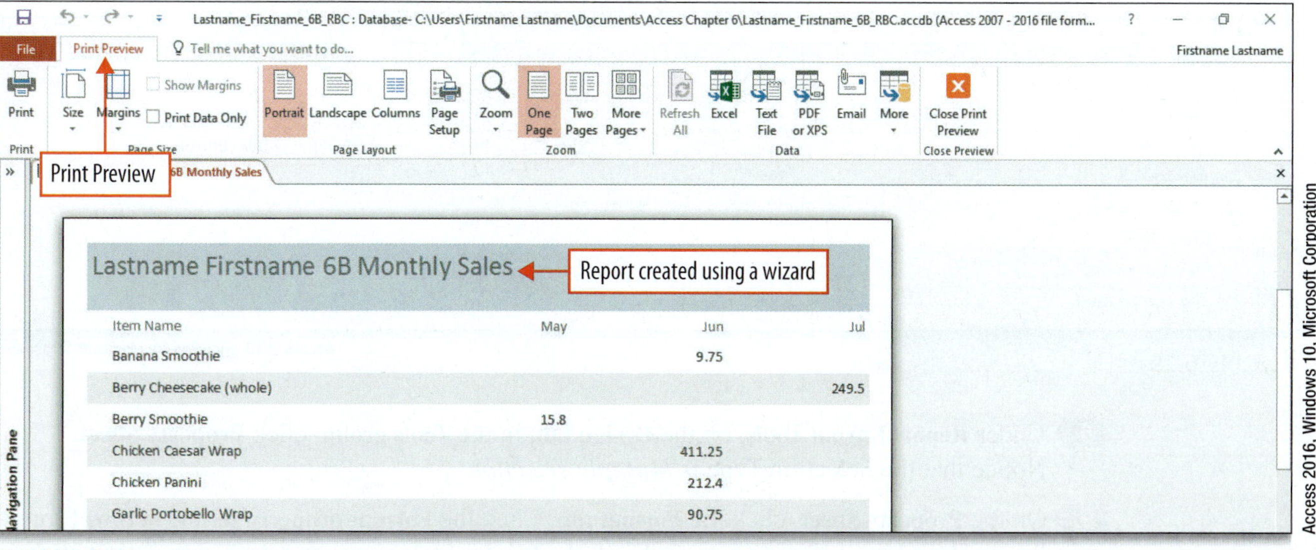

Access 2016, Windows 10, Microsoft Corporation

FIGURE 6.28

Activity 6.12 | Modifying a Report Created Using a Wizard

5.3.8, 5.3.4, 1.3.5, 1.5.1

In this Activity, you will modify controls in the report to change its appearance. Although the report was created using a wizard, its appearance can be modified in Design view and Layout view.

1 On the **Print Preview tab**, in the **Close Preview group**, click **Close Print Preview**. If the **Field List** or **Property Sheet** displays, **Close** it.

2 Under **Report Design Tools**, on the **Design tab**, in the **Themes group**, click **Themes** to display a list of available themes. Under **Office**, on the second row, click the second theme—**Organic**.

   Themes simplify the process of creating professional-looking objects within one program or across multiple programs. A theme includes theme colors and theme fonts that will be applied consistently throughout the objects in the database. It is a simple way to provide professional, consistent formatting in a database.

3 Click the **Report title text box control** to select it. Under **Report Design Tools**, click the **Format tab**, and in the **Font group**, click the **Font Color arrow** [A ▾]. Under **Theme Colors**, in the first row, click the eighth color—**Red, Accent 4**. If necessary, resize the title text box so the entire title is visible.

4 Select all of the controls in the **Page Header** section by pointing to the top left of the **Page Header** section, holding down your mouse button, dragging the mouse across the Page Header controls and to the bottom of the Page Header section, and then releasing the mouse button. Use the techniques you have practiced to change the font color to **Red, Accent 4**. Click anywhere in the **Detail** section to deselect the **Page Header** controls.

   Any group of controls can be selected using this lasso method. It can be more efficient than holding down Shift while clicking each control.

5 In the **Detail** section, click the **Item Name** control. Hold down Shift and, in the Page **Header** section, click the **Item Name label control**. Point to the right edge of any control until the pointer [↔] displays. Drag to the left until the box is approximately **2.5 inches** wide.

6 **Save** [💾] the report, and then switch to **Layout** view. Be sure none of the data in the **Item Name** column is truncated or cut off.

7 To select all of the text box controls, in the **May** column, click **15.8**. Holding down Shift, in the **Jun** and **Jul** columns, click a **text box control**. Compare your screen with Figure 6.29.

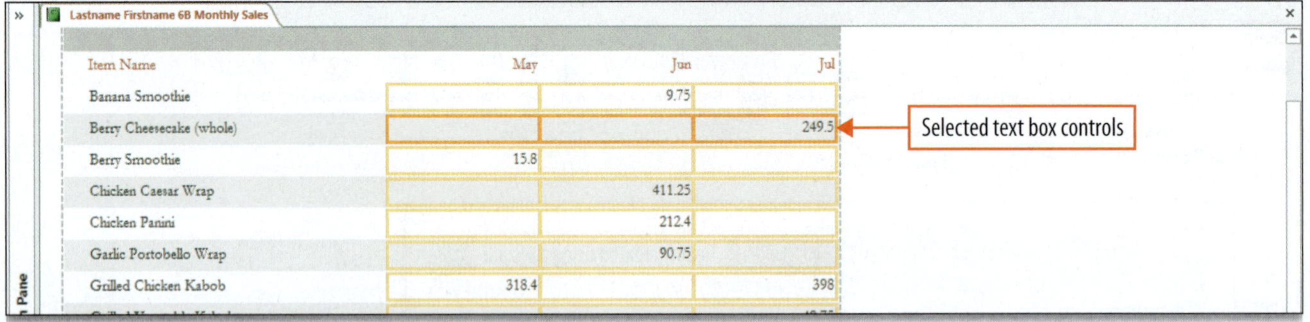

Access 2016, Windows 10, Microsoft Corporation

FIGURE 6.29

8 Under **Report Layout Tools**, on the **Design tab**, in the **Tools group**, click **Property Sheet**. Notice that the Selection Type is *Multiple selection*.

9 On the **Property Sheet**, click the **Format tab**. Click the **Format property setting arrow**. From the displayed list, select **Currency**. Click the **Border Style property setting arrow**, and click **Short Dashes**. **Close** [X] the **Property Sheet**.

10 **Save** the report, and then switch to **Print Preview** view. If you are instructed to submit this result, create a paper printout or PDF electronic image. On the **Print Preview tab**, in the **Close Preview group**, click **Close Print Preview**.

11 **Close** the report, and then **Open** the **Navigation Pane**.

6 ACCESS

Objective 6 Create a Report in Design View

GO! Learn How Video A6-6

You usually create a report using the Report tool or the Report Wizard, and then modify the report in Design view to suit your needs. Use Design view to create a report when these tools do not meet your needs or if you want more control in the creation of a report. Creating or modifying a report in Design view is a common technique when additional controls, such as calculated controls, need to be added to the report or properties need to be changed.

Activity 6.13 | Creating a Report in Design View

5.1.1, 5.1.2, 5.2.2, 5.2.3, 5.3.1, 5.3.8

Creating a report with the Report tool or the Report Wizard is the easiest way to start the creation of a customized report, but you can also create a report from scratch in Design view. Once you understand the sections of a report and how to manipulate the controls within the sections, it is easier to modify a report that has been created using the report tools.

1 In the **Navigation Pane**, open **6B Total Daily Sales Query** in **Design** view, and then notice the underlying tables that were used in the creation of the query. Notice the calculated field—*Total Cost*.

Recall that a calculated field contains the field name, followed by a colon, and then an expression. In the expression, the existing field names must be enclosed in square brackets. The Total Cost was calculated by multiplying the value in the Cost field by the value in the Daily Sales field.

2 When you are finished, **Close** the query, and **Close** the **Navigation Pane**. Click the **Create tab**, and then, in the **Reports group**, click **Report Design**. When the design grid displays, scroll down to display all of the report sections.

Three sections are included in the blank design grid: the Page Header section, the Detail section, and the Page Footer section. A page header displays at the top of every printed page, and a page footer displays at the bottom of every printed page.

3 Double-click the report selector to display the **Property Sheet**. On the **Property Sheet**, click the **Data tab**. Click the **Record Source property setting box arrow**, and then compare your screen with Figure 6.30. If necessary, increase the width of the Property Sheet.

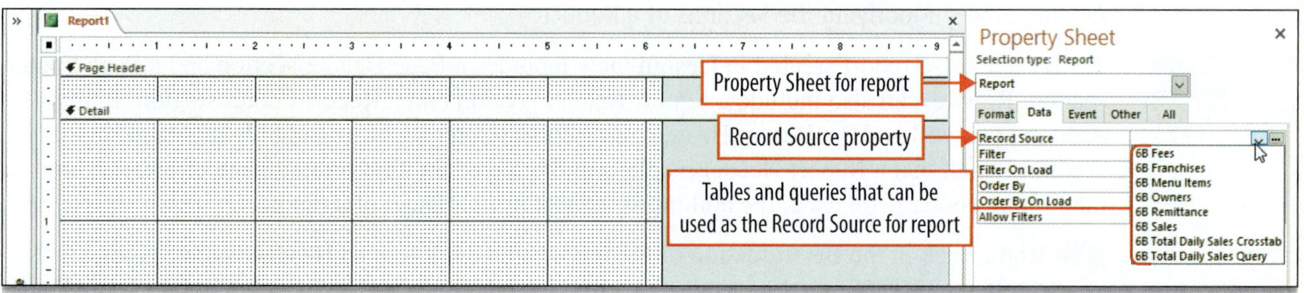

Access 2016, Windows 10, Microsoft Corporation

FIGURE 6.30

4 From the displayed list of tables and queries, click **6B Total Daily Sales Query**, and then **Close** the **Property Sheet**.

6B Total Daily Sales Query is the record source—underlying query—for this report.

5 Under **Report Design Tools**, on the **Design tab**, in the **Tools group**, click **Add Existing Fields** to display the fields in 6B Total Daily Sales Query.

6 In the **Field List**, click **Date**. Hold down Shift, and then click **Franchise#** to select all of the fields.

> **ALERT!** **Are multiple tables displayed in the field list?**
>
> If all tables display in the field list, click Show only fields in the current record source at the bottom of the Field List box.

7 Drag the selected fields into the **Detail** section of the design grid until the top of the arrow of the pointer is **one dot** below the bottom edge of the **Detail** section bar and aligned with the **3-inch mark on the horizontal ruler**. **Close** the **Field List**, and then compare your screen with Figure 6.31.

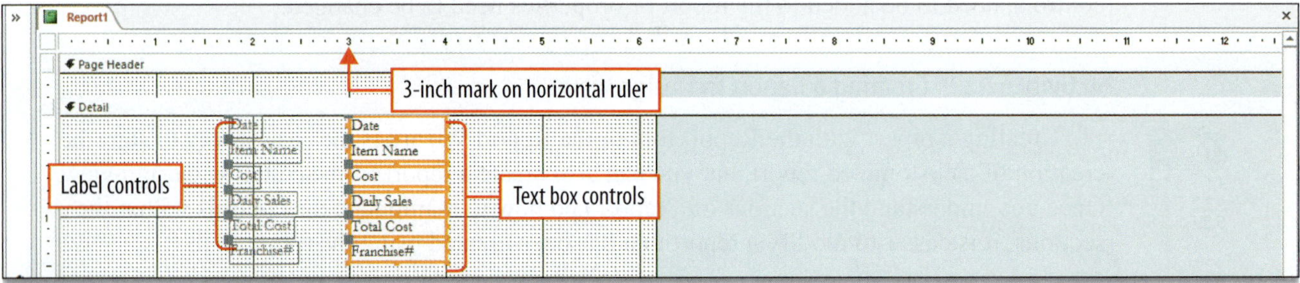

FIGURE 6.31

Access 2016, Windows 10, Microsoft Corporation

8 With the label controls and text box controls for the fields selected, under **Report Design Tools** click the **Arrange tab**. In the **Table group**, click **Stacked** to group the fields together for easier formatting.

> ***More* Knowledge** **Using the Tabular Arrangement**
>
> When you want your data to display professionally in a report, on the Arrange tab, in the Table group, click the Tabular button. This will place the labels in the Page Header and the data in the Detail section for a table-like appearance.

9 Under **Report Design Tools**, on the **Design tab**, in the **Themes group**, click **Themes**. Under **In This Database**, notice the theme used in this database—**Organic**. Press Esc to close the gallery.

10 **Save** the report as **Lastname Firstname 6B Total Daily Sales**

Activity 6.14 | Modifying the Sections of a Report

5.3.7, 5.2.4, 5.3.6

By default, a report created in Design view includes a Page Header section and a Page Footer section. Reports can also include a Report Header section and a Report Footer section. In this Activity, you will add the Report Header and Report Footer sections and hide the Page Header section. Recall that a Report Header displays at the top of the first printed page of a report, and the Report Footer displays at the bottom of the last printed page of a report.

1 Right-click in the **Detail** section of the report, and click **Report Header/Footer**. Notice that the **Report Header** section displays at the top of the design grid. Scroll down to display the **Report Footer** section.

2 Scroll up to display the **Report Header** section. Under **Report Design Tools**, click the **Design tab**, and then, in the **Header/Footer group**, click **Logo**. Locate and double-click **a06B_Logo** to insert the logo in the Report Header section. On the selected logo, point to the right middle sizing handle until the pointer ↔ displays. Drag to the right until the right edge of the logo is aligned with the **1.5-inch mark on the horizontal ruler**.

3 Under **Report Design Tools**, on the **Design tab**, in the **Header/Footer group**, click **Title**. In the **title's label control**, click to the left of your **Lastname**, delete your **Lastname Firstname** and the space, and then press Enter. On the **title's label control**, point to the right middle sizing handle until the pointer displays ↔, and then double-click to adjust the size of the label control to fit the text. Alternatively, drag the right middle sizing handle to the left.

4 Scroll down until the **Page Footer** section bar displays. Point to the top edge of the **Page Footer** section bar until the pointer ↕ displays. Drag upward until the top of the **Page Footer** section bar aligns with the **2.25-inch mark on the vertical ruler**.

This prevents extra blank space from printing between the records.

5 Scroll up until the **Report Header** section displays. Point to the top edge of the **Detail** section bar until the pointer ↕ displays. Drag upward until the top edge of the **Detail** section bar aligns with the bottom edge of the **Page Header** section bar, and then compare your screen with Figure 6.32.

The Page Header and Page Footer sections are paired together. Likewise, the Report Header and Report Footer sections are paired together. You cannot remove only one section of the pair. If you wish to remove one section of a paired header/footer, decrease the height of the section. Alternatively, set the Height property for the section to 0. Because there is no space in the Page Header section, nothing will print at the top of every page. To remove both of the paired header/footer sections, right click in the Detail section, and click Page Header/Footer to deselect it.

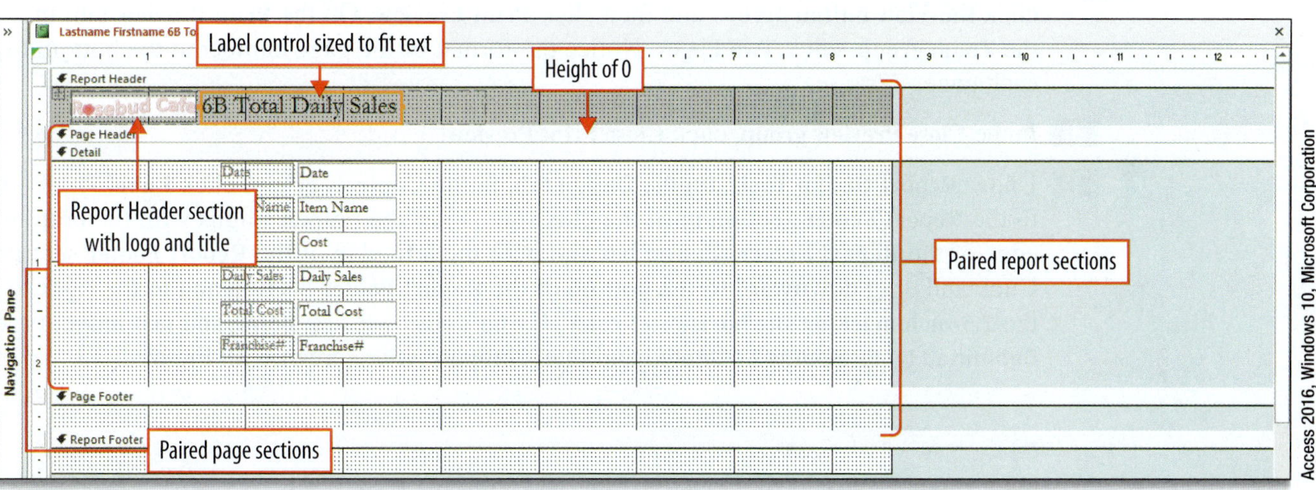

Access 2016, Windows 10, Microsoft Corporation

FIGURE 6.32

6 Drag the right edge of the design grid to the left until it aligns with the **6.5-inch mark on the horizontal ruler**. **Save** the report.

The width of the report page is decreased, which will enable the report to fit within the margins of paper in portrait orientation.

***More* Knowledge** **Formatting a Report**

You can add a background picture to a report or change the background color of a report using the same techniques you used for forms.

Objective 7 Add Controls to a Report

GO! Learn How Video A6-7

Reports are not used to manipulate data in the underlying table or query, so they contain fewer types of controls. You can add label controls, text box controls, images, hyperlinks, or calculated controls to a report.

Activity 6.15 | Adding Label and Text Box Controls to a Report

5.2.3, 1.3.5, 5.2.4, 5.3.6

In this Activity, you will add controls to the report that will contain the page number, the date, and your first name and last name.

1. Under **Report Design Tools**, on the **Design tab**, in the **Header/Footer group**, click **Page Numbers**. In the displayed **Page Numbers** dialog box, under **Format**, click **Page N of M**. Under **Position**, click **Bottom of Page [Footer]**. Alignment should remain **Center**; click **OK**.

   A text box control displays in the center of the Page Footer section. The control displays an expression that will display the page number. Every expression begins with an equal sign (=). "Page " is enclosed in quotation marks. Access interprets anything enclosed in quotation marks as text and will display it exactly as it is typed within the quotation marks, including the space. The & symbol is used for ***concatenation***—linking or joining—of strings. A ***string*** is a series of characters. The word *Page* followed by a space will be concatenated—joined—to the string that follows the & symbol. [Page] is a reserved name that retrieves the current page number. This is followed by another & symbol that concatenates the page number to the next string—" of ". The & symbol continues concatenation of [Pages], a reserved name that retrieves the total number of pages in the report.

2. **Save** the report. Under **Report Design Tools**, on the **Design tab**, in the **Views group**, click the **View button arrow**, and then click **Print Preview**. On the **Print Preview tab**, in the **Zoom group**, click **Two Pages**. Notice the format of the page number at the bottom of each page.

3. In the **Close Preview group**, click **Close Print Preview**.

4. Under **Report Design Tools**, on the **Design tab**, in the **Controls group**, click **Label** Aa. Point to the **Report Footer** section until the plus sign (+) of the pointer aligns with the bottom edge of the **Report Footer** section bar and with the left edge of the **Report Footer** section. Click and drag downward to the bottom of the **Report Footer** section and to the right to the **2.5-inch mark on the horizontal ruler**. Using your own first name and last name, type **Submitted by Firstname Lastname** and then compare your screen with Figure 6.33.

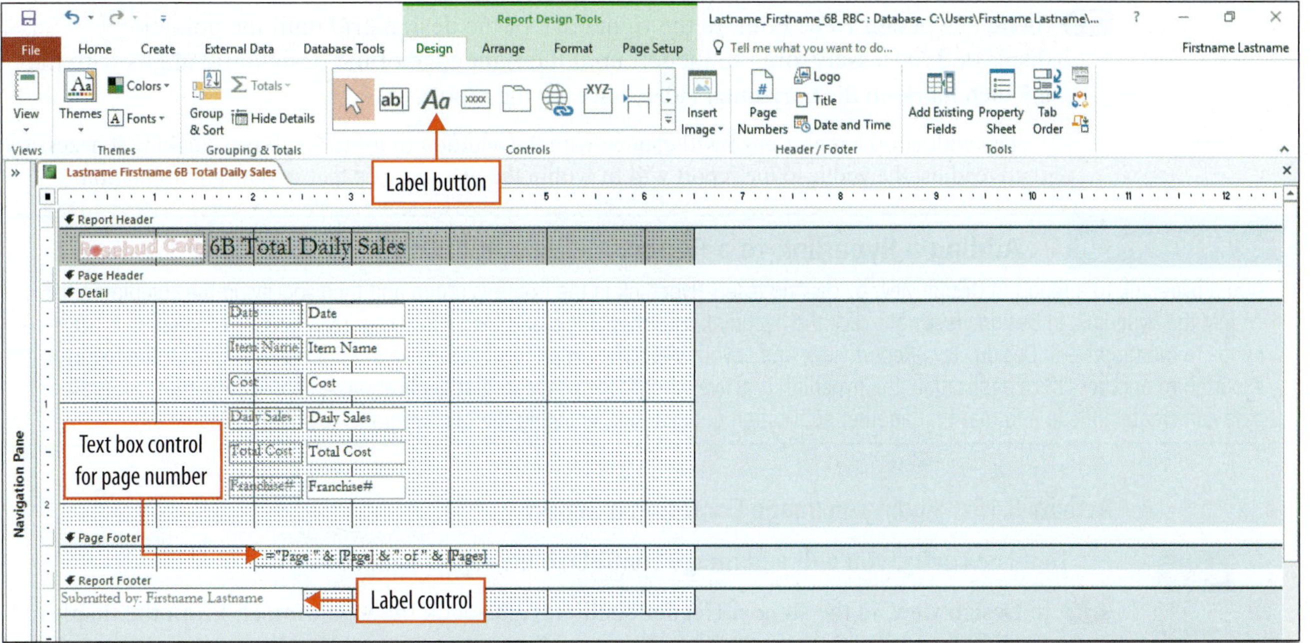

Access 2016, Windows 10, Microsoft Corporation

FIGURE 6.33

5 Click away from the label box, and then **Save** the report. Under **Report Design Tools**, on the **Design tab**, in the **Header/Footer group**, click **Date and Time**. In the **Date and Time** dialog box, under **Include Date**, click the third option button, which displays the date as mm/dd/yyyy. Click to clear the **Include Time** check box, and then click **OK**.

A text box control with an expression for the current date displays in the Report Header section. It may display over the Report title.

6 In the **Report Header**, click the **Date text box control** to select it. Under **Report Design Tools**, click the **Arrange tab**, and, in the **Table group**, click **Remove Layout** so the Date text box control can be moved. Right-click the selected control, and click **Cut**. Point to the **Report Footer** section bar, right-click, and then click **Paste**. Drag the text box control until the right edge of the text box control aligns with the **6.25-inch mark on the horizontal ruler**. Click the **Title label control** which has been resized to a bar next to the logo, to select it, point to the right middle sizing handle until the pointer ↔ displays, and then drag to the right until the right edge of the text box control aligns with the **4.5-inch mark on the horizontal ruler**.

When the Date control was removed from the layout, the Title label control was resized.

7 **Save** the report, and then switch to **Layout** view. Notice that, for the first record, the data for the **Item Name** field does not fully display. Click the **Item Name text box control**, which partially displays *Banana Smoothie*. Point to the right edge of the **Item Name text box control** until the pointer ↔ displays. Drag to the right approximately **1.5 inches**. Because no ruler displays in Layout view, you will have to estimate the distance to drag.

Because the controls are in a stacked layout, the widths of all of the text box controls are increased.

8 Scroll down, observing the data in the **Item Name** field. Ensure that all of the data displays. If the data is not all visible in a record, use the technique you just practiced to increase the width of the text box control until all of the data displays.

9 Switch to **Design** view. Point to the right edge of the design grid until the pointer [+] displays. If necessary, drag to the left until the right edge of the design grid aligns with the **6.5-inch mark on the horizontal ruler**. **Save** [Save] the report.

The width of the report page will change with the addition of more text boxes, making it necessary to readjust the width so the report will fit within the margins of paper in portrait orientation.

More Knowledge | **Adding a Hyperlink to a Report**

Add a hyperlink to a report in Design view by clicking Insert Hyperlink in the Controls group and then specifying the complete URL. To test the hyperlink, in Design view, right-click the hyperlink, click Hyperlink, and then click Open Hyperlink. The hyperlink is active—jumps to the target—in Design view, Report view, and Layout view. The hyperlink is not active in Print Preview view. If the report is exported to another Office application, the hyperlink is active when it is opened in that application. An application that can export data can create a file in a format that another application understands, enabling the two programs to share the same data.

Activity 6.16 | Adding an Image Control to a Report

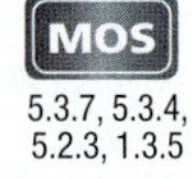

5.3.7, 5.3.4, 5.2.3, 1.3.5

In this Activity, you will add image controls to the report header.

1 In **Design view**, in the **Report Header** section, right-click the **logo control**. From the displayed shortcut menu, click **Copy**. Right-click anywhere in the **Report Header** section, and then from the shortcut menu, click **Paste**.

A copy of the image displays on top and slightly to the left of the original logo control.

2 Point to the selected logo until the pointer [move pointer] displays. Drag to the right until the left edge of the outlined control is the same distance from the title as the logo control on the left. Point to the top edge of the **Page Header** section bar until the pointer [↕] displays. Drag upward until the top of the **Page Header** section bar aligns with the **0.5-inch mark on the vertical ruler**.

Recall that when you created a form in Design view, you clicked Insert Image and selected the location in the header section. You then had to change the properties of the image to match the size of the image in the logo control. Because you copied the original image from the logo, the images are the same size.

3 With the image control on the right selected, hold down Ctrl, and then click the **logo control**. Under **Report Design Tools**, click the **Arrange tab**, and, in the **Sizing & Ordering group**, click **Align**, and select **Bottom**. Compare your screen with Figure 6.34.

Both the logo control and the image control are aligned along the bottom edges.

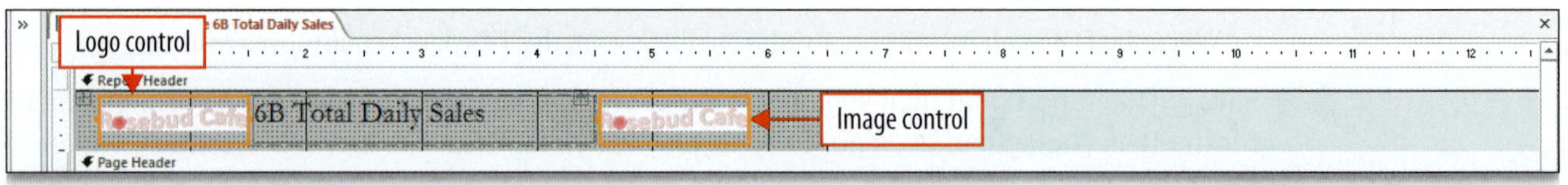

FIGURE 6.34

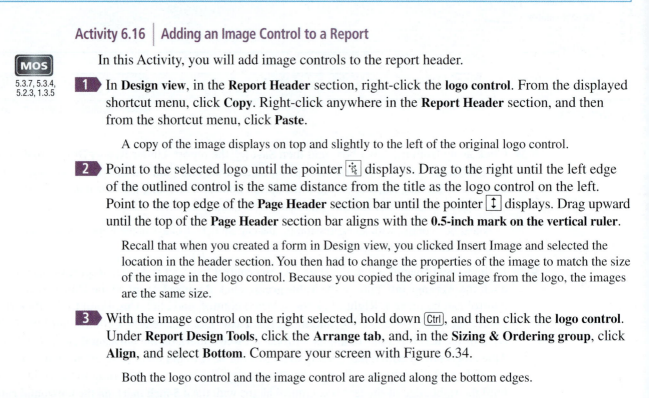

Access 2016, Windows 10, Microsoft Corporation

4 Under **Report Design Tools**, click the **Design tab**, and, in the **Controls group**, click the **More** button [More], and then click **Line** [Line]. Point to the **Detail** section until the middle of the plus sign (+) of the pointer aligns at **2 inches on the vertical ruler** and **0 inches on the horizontal ruler**, as shown in Figure 6.35.

A ***line control*** enables an individual to insert a line in a form or report.

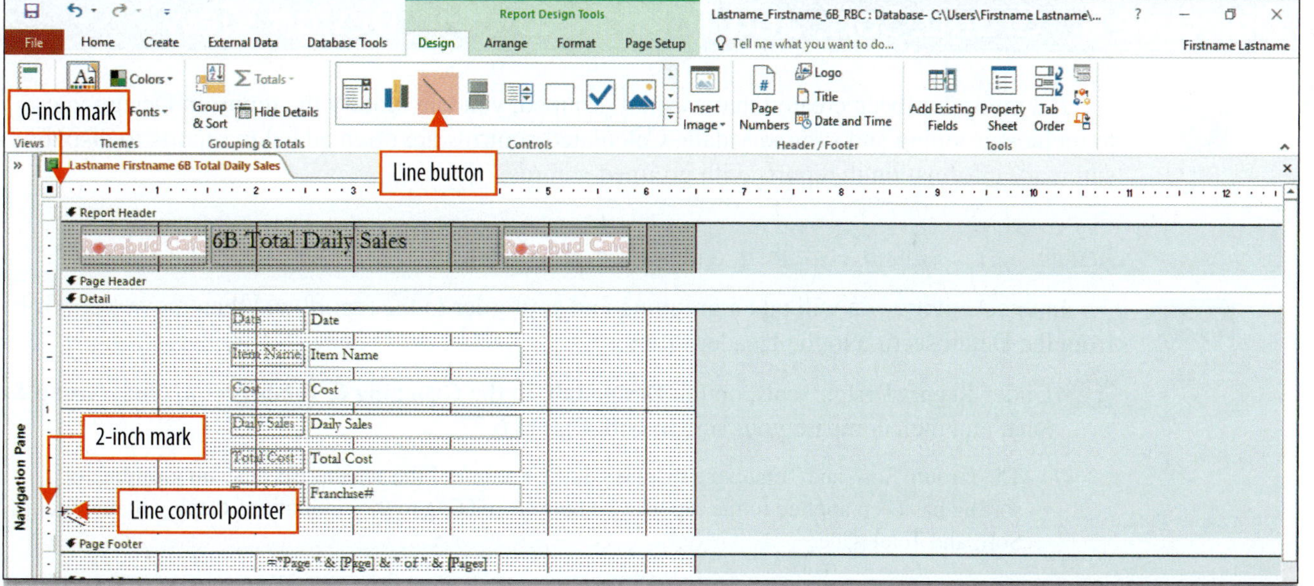

FIGURE 6.35

Access 2016, Windows 10, Microsoft Corporation

5 Hold down Shift, drag to the right to **6.5 inches on the horizontal ruler**, and then release the mouse button.

An orange line control displays. Holding down the Shift key ensures that the line will be straight.

6 Under **Report Design Tools**, click the **Format tab**, and, in the **Control Formatting group**, click **Shape Outline**. Point to **Line Thickness** and then click the third line—**2 pt**. In the **Control Formatting group**, click **Shape Outline**. Under **Theme Colors**, on the fifth row, click the sixth color—**Teal, Accent 2, Darker 25%**.

7 **Save** the report, and then switch to **Report** view. Compare your screen with Figure 6.36. Notice the horizontal line that displays between the records.

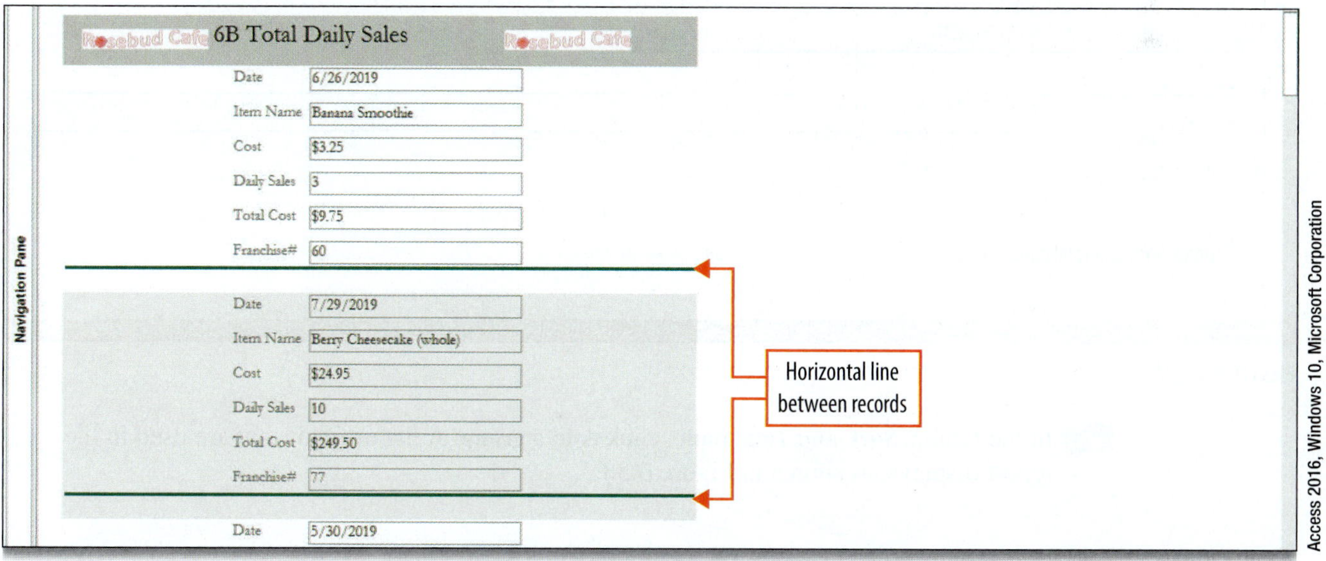

FIGURE 6.36

Access 2016, Windows 10, Microsoft Corporation

8 Switch to **Design** view. Click anywhere in the **Detail** area to deselect the line.

Objective 8 Group, Sort, and Total Records in Design View

GO! Learn How
Video A6-8

If a report has been created that was not grouped, you can modify the report in Design view to include grouping and summary data. Calculated controls are often added to reports to display summary information in reports with grouped records.

Activity 6.17 | Adding a Grouping and Sort Level to a Report

5.2.1, 5.3.3, 1.3.5

In this Activity, you will add a grouping and sort order to the report, and then move a control from the Detail section to the Header section.

1 Under **Report Design Tools**, on the **Design tab**, in the **Grouping & Totals group**, click **Group & Sort**, and then compare your screen with Figure 6.37.

The Group, Sort, and Total pane displays at the bottom of the screen. Because no grouping or sorting has been applied to the report, two buttons relating to these functions display in the Group, Sort, and Total pane.

Group & Sort button

Group, Sort, and Total pane

FIGURE 6.37

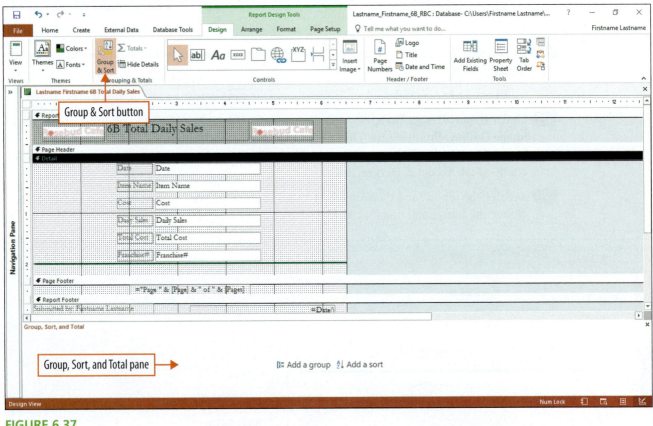

2 In the **Group, Sort, and Total pane**, click **Add a group**. A list of fields that are used in the report displays, as shown in Figure 6.38.

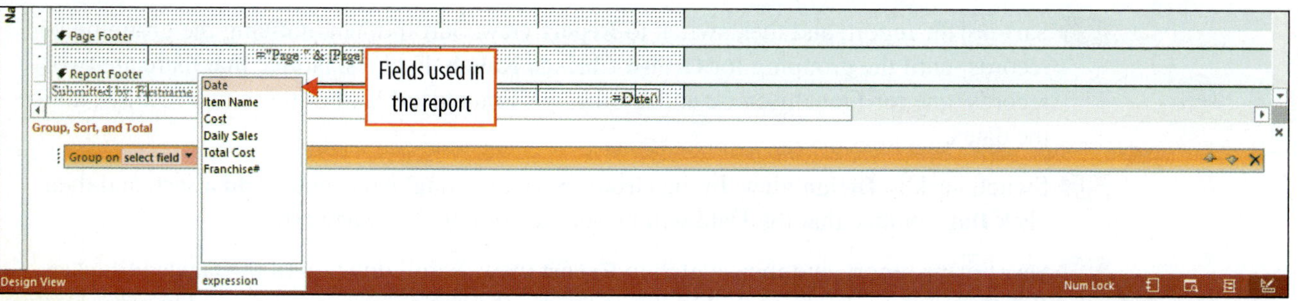

Access 2016, Windows 10, Microsoft Corporation

FIGURE 6.38

3 From the displayed list, click **Item Name**.

An empty Item Name Header section is inserted above the Detail section. The report will be grouped by the Item Name, and the Item Names will be sorted in ascending order.

4 In the **Detail** section, click the **Item Name text box control**. Point to the selected text box control until the pointer displays. Drag downward until a thin orange line displays below the **Franchise#** controls.

The text box control for this field will be moved to the Item Name Header section in the report. Recall that moving the controls to the bottom of the stacked layout makes it easier to remove the controls from the stacked layout.

5 Under **Report Design Tools**, click the **Arrange tab**, and, in the **Table group**, click **Remove Layout**.

The label control and the text box control for the Item Name field are removed from the stacked layout.

6 Right-click the selected **Item Name text box control** to display the shortcut menu, and click **Cut**. Click the **Item Name Header** section bar to select it, right-click to display the shortcut menu, and click **Paste**.

The controls for the Item Name are moved from the Detail section to the Item Name Header section. Because the report is being grouped by this field, the controls should be moved out of the Detail section.

7 In the **Item Name Header** section, click the **Item Name label control**, and then press Delete. Click the **Item Name text box control** to select it, and then drag it to the right until the left edge of the control aligns with the **1-inch mark on the horizontal ruler**. Compare your screen with Figure 6.39.

Because the records are grouped by the data in the Item Name field, the name of the field is unnecessary.

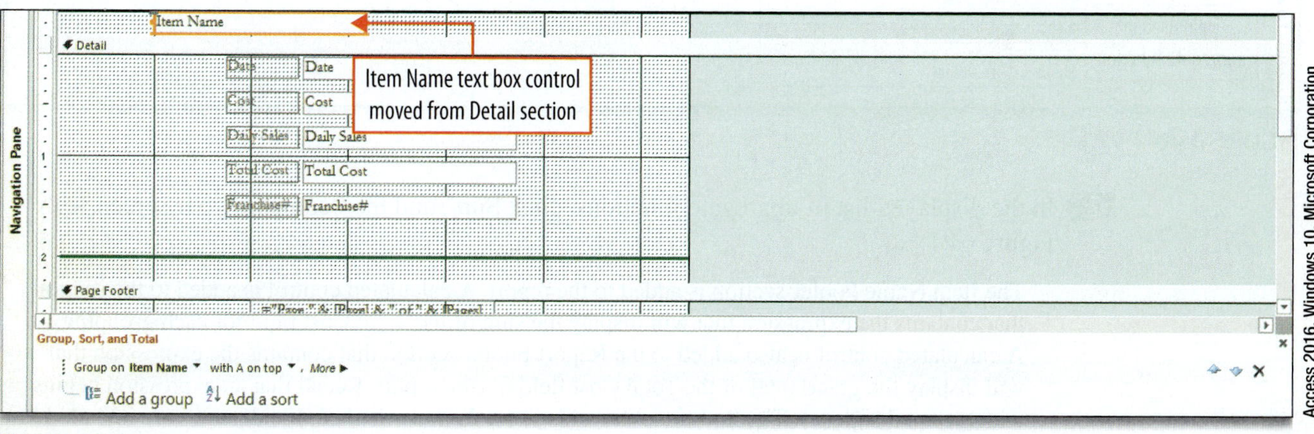

Access 2016, Windows 10, Microsoft Corporation

FIGURE 6.39

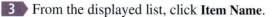

8 **Save** the report, and then switch to **Report** view. Scroll down, noticing the grouping of records, until the grouping for **Grilled Chicken Kabob** displays. Notice that there are two records, one for Franchise# 62 and another for Franchise# 12. For these two records, notice the dates.

9 Switch back to **Design** view. In the **Group, Sort, and Total pane**, click **Add a sort**, and then click **Date**. Notice that the Date will be sorted from oldest to newest.

10 **Save** the report, and then switch to **Report** view. Scroll down until the **Grilled Chicken Kabob** grouping displays. Within the grouping, the two records are arranged in order by the date with the oldest date listed first.

11 Switch to **Design** view, and then **Close** the **Group, Sort, and Total pane**. Be sure to click the Close button located in the title bar and not the Delete button that is inside the pane. Alternatively, to close the Group & Sort pane, on the Design tab, in the Grouping & Totals group, click Group & Sort.

Activity 6.18 | Adding Calculated Controls to a Report

MOS
5.3.2, 1.3.5, 5.2.4, 5.3.3, 1.5.1

In this Activity, you will add an aggregate function and appropriate section to the report.

1 In the **Detail** section, click the **Total Cost text box control**. Under **Report Design Tools**, on the **Design tab**, in the **Grouping & Totals group**, click **Totals**, and then compare your screen with Figure 6.40.

A list of ***aggregate functions***—functions that group and perform calculations on multiple fields—displays. Before selecting Totals, the field that will be used in the aggregate function must be selected. If you wish to perform aggregate functions on multiple fields, you must select each field individually, and then select the aggregate function to apply to the field.

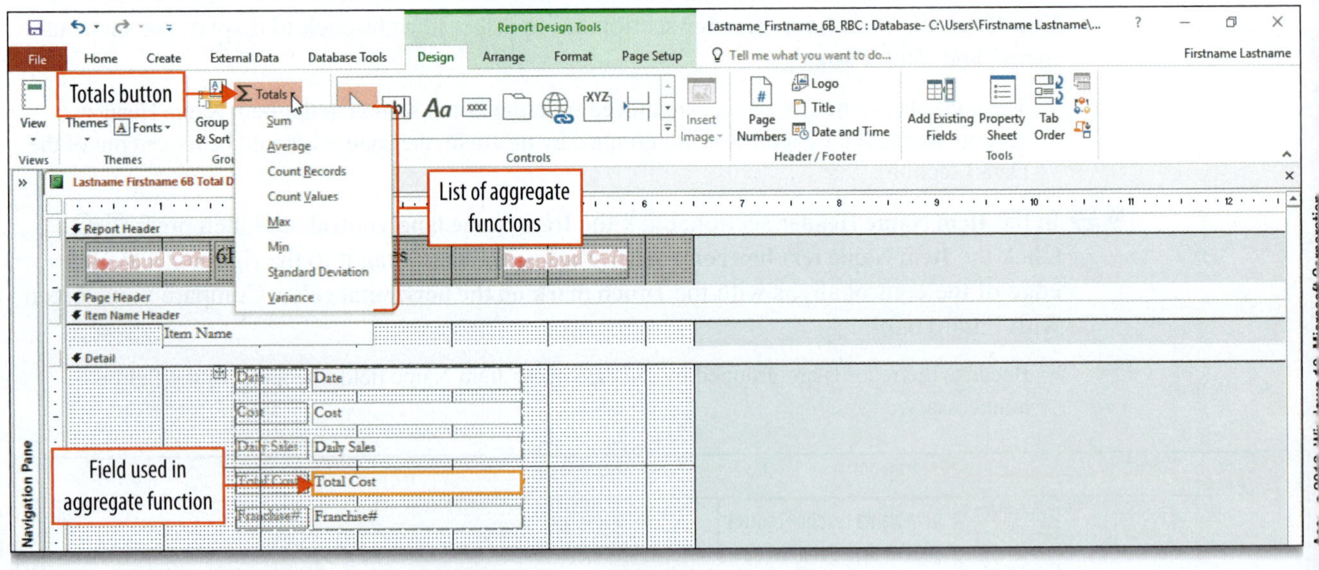

FIGURE 6.40

2 In the displayed list of aggregate functions, click **Sum**, and then compare your screen with Figure 6.41.

The Item Name Footer section is added to the report. A calculated control is added to the section that contains the expression that will display the sum of the Total Cost field for each grouping. A calculated control is also added to the Report Footer section that contains the expression that will display the grand total of the Total Cost field for the report. Recall that an expression begins with an equal sign (=). The Sum function adds or totals numeric data. Field names are included in square brackets.

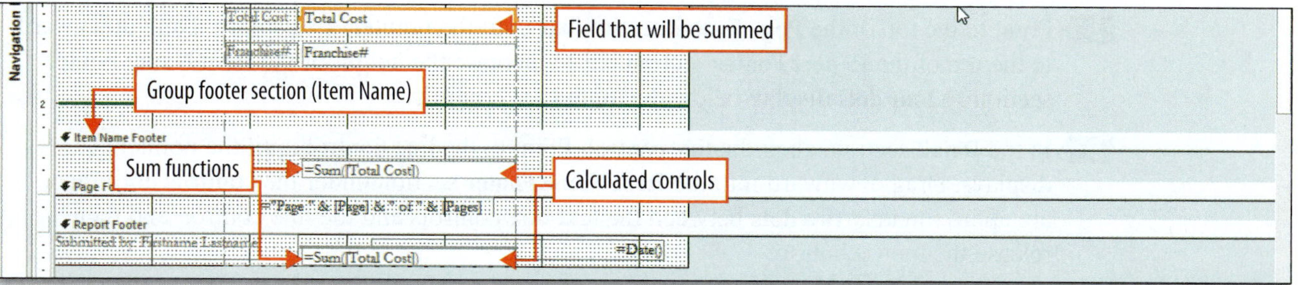

FIGURE 6.41

Access 2016, Windows 10, Microsoft Corporation

3 **Save** the report, and then switch to **Report** view. Notice that for the first grouping—Banana Smoothie—which only contains one record, the sum of the grouping displays below the horizontal line. Scroll down to the **Grilled Chicken Kabob** grouping, and then notice that the total for the grouping—**$716.40**—displays below the horizontal line for the second record in the grouping.

The placement of the horizontal line is distracting in the report, and there is no label attached to the grouping total.

4 Switch to **Design** view. Under **Report Design Tools**, on the **Design tab**, in the **Controls group**, click **Text Box** [ab|]. Point to the **Item Name Footer** section until the plus sign (+) of the pointer aligns with the bottom edge of the **Item Name Footer** section bar and with the **0.25-inch mark on the horizontal ruler**. Drag downward to the bottom of the **Item Name Footer** section and to the right to the **2.5-inch mark on the horizontal ruler**.

5 Click inside the text box, and type **=[Item Name] & " Total Cost:"** ensuring that you include a space between the quotation mark and *Total* and that *Item Name* is enclosed in square brackets. Compare your screen with Figure 6.42.

Because a field name is included in the description of the total, a text box control must be used. This binds the control to the Item Name field in the underlying query, which makes this control a bound control. If you wish to insert only string characters as a description—for example, Total Cost—add a label control, which is an unbound control.

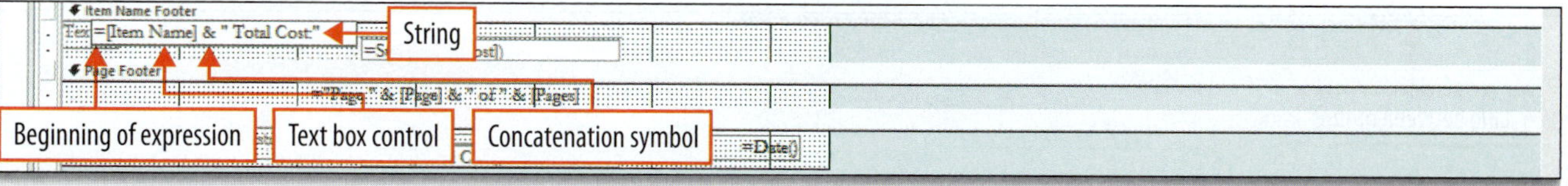

FIGURE 6.42

Access 2016, Windows 10, Microsoft Corporation

6 In the **Item Name Footer** section, click the **label control** that displays to the left of the text box control where you typed the expression. Press Delete to delete the text box control's associated label control.

The data in the text box control is descriptive and does not require an additional label control.

7 In the **Item Name Footer** section, click the **text box control** that contains the expression you typed. Point to the left middle sizing handle until the pointer displays. Drag to the left until the left edge of the text box control aligns with the left edge of the design grid. With the text box control selected, hold down Shift. In the **Item Name Footer** section, click the **calculated control** for the sum. Under **Report Design Tools**, click the **Arrange tab**. In the **Sizing & Ordering group**, click **Size/Space**, and then click **To Tallest**. In the **Sizing & Ordering group**, click **Align**, and then click **Bottom** to align both controls at the bottom.

The two controls are now the same height and aligned at the top edges of the controls.

8 Point to the top of the **Page Footer** section bar until the pointer [↕] displays. Drag downward to the top of the **Report Footer** section bar to increase the height of the Item Name Footer section so **four dots** display below the **Total Cost** controls.

9 In the **Detail** section, click the **line control**. Point to the line control until the pointer [✥] displays. Drag downward into the **Item Name Footer** section under the controls until there are approximately **two dots** between the text box controls and the line control, and then release the mouse button.

The line control is moved from the Detail section to the Item Name Footer section.

10 Point to the top of the **Item Name Footer** section bar until the pointer [↕] displays. Drag upward until approximately **two dots** display between the **Franchise#** controls and the top edge of the **Item Name Footer** section bar. Compare your screen with Figure 6.43.

The height of the Detail section is changed.

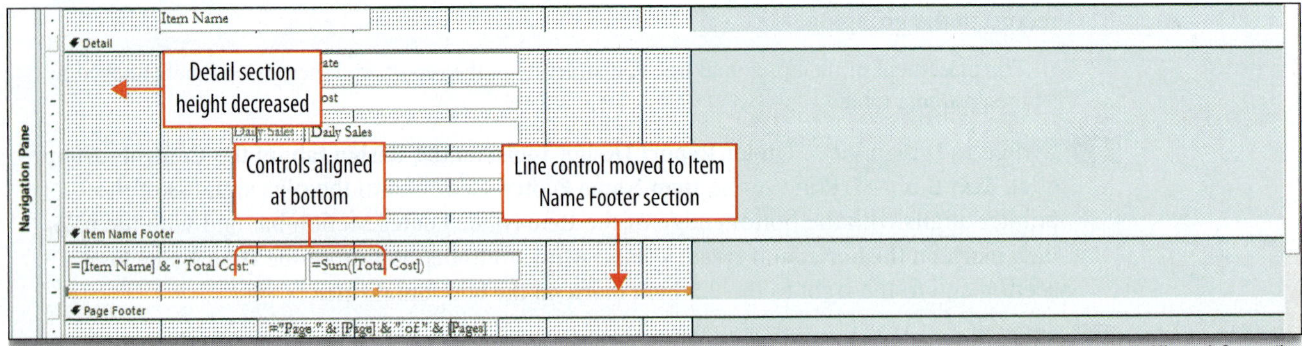

FIGURE 6.43

11 **Save** [💾] the report, and then switch to **Report** view. Scroll down until the **Grilled Chicken Kabob** grouping displays, and then compare your screen with Figure 6.44.

The report is easier to read with the horizontal line moved to the grouping footer section and with an explanation of the total for the grouping.

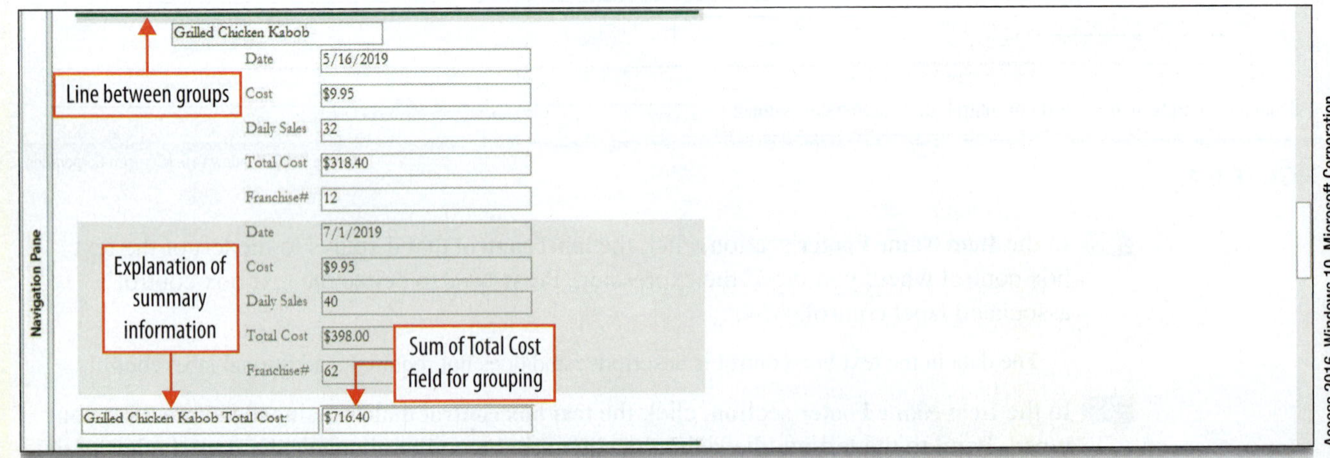

FIGURE 6.44

12 Hold down Ctrl, and then press End to move to the end of the report. Notice the sum of **$3,154.80**.

By default, when you insert an aggregate function into a report, a calculated control for the grand total is inserted in the Report Footer section. The control is aligned with the text box control that is being used in the aggregate function. If the Report Footer section is not tall enough and multiple aggregate functions are used, the controls will display on top of one another.

13 Switch to **Design** view. In the **Report Footer** section, the calculated control displays *=Sum([Total Cost])*. Point to the bottom of the **Report Footer** section—not the section bar—until the pointer displays. Drag downward until the height of the **Report Footer** section is approximately **1 inch**.

14 Click the label control that displays **Submitted by Firstname Lastname**. Hold down Shift, and then click the text box control that displays the **Date** expression. Under **Report Design Tools**, click the **Arrange tab**. In the **Sizing & Ordering group**, click **Size/Space**, and then click **To Tallest**. In the **Sizing & Ordering group**, click **Align**, and then click **Bottom**.

The two controls are the same height and aligned at the bottom edges of the controls.

15 Point to either of the selected controls until the pointer displays. Drag downward until the bottom edges of the controls align with the bottom edge of the Report Footer section, and then compare your screen with Figure 6.45.

The controls are moved to the bottom of the Report Footer section to increase readability and to make space to insert a label control for the grand total.

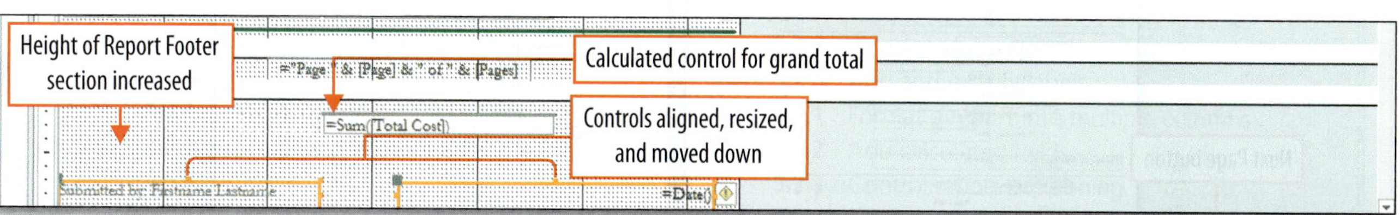

FIGURE 6.45 Access 2016, Windows 10, Microsoft Corporation

16 Under **Report Design Tools**, click the **Design tab**. Use the techniques you have practiced previously to add a **label control** in the **Report Footer** section to the left of the calculated control—the left edge of the control should be aligned with the **0-inch mark on the horizontal ruler** and the right edge should be **one dot** to the left of the calculated control. In the label control, type **Grand Total Cost of All Items:** Align the label control with the calculated control and be sure that the controls are the same height. Compare your screen with Figure 6.46.

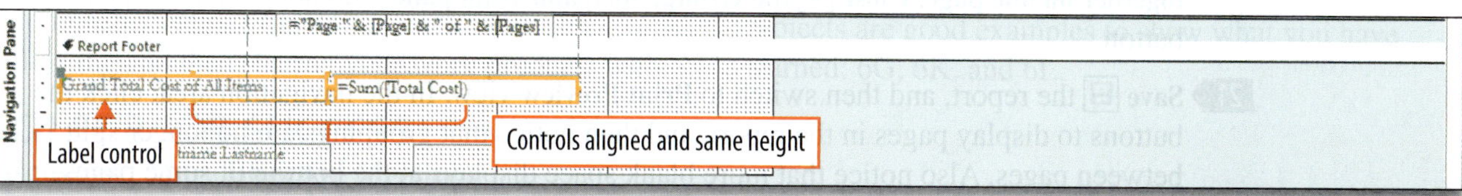

FIGURE 6.46 Access 2016, Windows 10, Microsoft Corporation

ALERT! **Does your control display with two boxes?**

If your control displays with two boxes—one that displays text and a number, for example Text35, and one that displays Unbound—you selected the Text Box button instead of the Label button. If that happens, click Undo, and then begin again

17 **Save** the report, and then switch to **Report** view. Hold down Ctrl, and then press End to move to the end of the report. Notice that the grand total is now easier to distinguish because a description of the control has been added and the other controls are moved down.

18 Display the report in **Print Preview** view. If necessary, on the **Print Preview tab**, in the **Zoom group**, click **Two Pages**. Look at the bottom of Page 1 and the top of Page 2, and notice that the grouping breaks across two pages. In the navigation area, click **Next Page** to display Pages 3 and 4. Groupings are split between these pages. Compare your screen with Figure 6.47.

For a more professional-looking report, avoid splitting groupings between pages.

END OF CHAPTER

SUMMARY

Forms are database objects used to interact with the data in tables; however, specific records can be printed. Sections and controls can be added, formatted, and modified to make the form user friendly.

Reports are database objects used to present data from tables or queries in a professional format. Grouping and sorting levels are added for organization, and then aggregate functions can be used to summarize the data.

Forms and reports can be created in Design view or by using a wizard. Some editing can be done in Layout view, but specific modifications can be done only in Design view.

Controls added to forms and reports include label controls, image controls, command button controls, and line controls. Text box controls with expressions and concatenated strings are used to clarify data.

GO! LEARN IT ONLINE

Review the concepts, key terms, and MOS Skills in this chapter by completing these online challenges, which you can find at MyITLab.

Matching and Multiple Choice: Answer matching and multiple choice questions to test what you learned in this chapter.

Lessons on the GO!: Learn how to use all the new apps and features as they are introduced by Microsoft.

MOS Prep Quiz: Answer questions to review the MOS skills that you have practiced in this chapter.

PROJECT GUIDE FOR ACCESS CHAPTER 6

Your instructor will assign Projects from this list to ensure your learning and assess your knowledge.

PROJECT GUIDE FOR ACCESS CHAPTER 6			
Project	**Apply Skills from These Chapter Objectives**	**Project Type**	**Project Location**
6A MyITLab	Objectives 1–4 from Project 6A	**6A Instructional Project (Grader Project)** Guided instruction to learn the skills in Project 6A.	In MyITLab and in text
6B MyITLab	Objectives 5–8 from Project 6B	**6B Instructional Project (Grader Project)** Guided instruction to learn the skills in Project 6B.	In MyITLab and in text
6C	Objectives 1–4 from Project 6A	**6C Chapter Review (Scorecard Grading)** A guided review of the skills from Project 6A.	In text
6D	Objectives 5–8 from Project 6B	**6D Chapter Review (Scorecard Grading)** A guided review of the skills from Project 6B.	In text
6E	Objectives 1–4 from Project 6A	**6E Mastery (Scorecard Grading)** **Mastery and Transfer of Learning** A demonstration of your mastery of the skills in Project 6A with extensive decision making.	In text
6F	Objectives 5–8 from Project 6B	**6F Mastery (Scorecard Grading)** **Mastery and Transfer of Learning** A demonstration of your mastery of the skills in Project 6B with extensive decision making.	In text
6G MyITLab	Objectives 1–8 from Projects 6A and 6B	**6G Mastery (Grader Project)** **Mastery and Transfer of Learning** A demonstration of your mastery of the skills in Projects 6A and 6B with extensive decision making.	In MyITLab and in text
6H	Combination of Objectives from Projects 6A and 6B	**6H GO! Fix It (Scorecard Grading)** **Critical Thinking** A demonstration of your mastery of the skills in Projects 6A and 6B by creating a correct result from a document that contains errors you must find.	Instructor Resource Center (IRC) and MyITLab
6I	Combination of Objectives from Projects 6A and 6B	**6I GO! Make It (Scorecard Grading)** **Critical Thinking** A demonstration of your mastery of the skills in Projects 6A and 6B by creating a result from a supplied picture.	IRC and MyITLab
6J	Combination of Objectives from Projects 6A and 6B	**6J GO! Solve It (Rubric Grading)** **Critical Thinking** A demonstration of your mastery of the skills in Projects 6A and 6B, your decision-making skills, and your critical thinking skills. A task-specific rubric helps you self-assess your result.	IRC and MyITLab
6K	Combination of Objectives from Projects 6A and 6B	**6K GO! Solve It (Rubric Grading)** **Critical Thinking** A demonstration of your mastery of the skills in Projects 6A and 6B, your decision-making skills, and your critical thinking skills. A task-specific rubric helps you self-assess your result.	In text
6L	Combination of Objectives from Projects 6A and 6B	**6L GO! Think (Rubric Grading)** **Critical Thinking** A demonstration of your understanding of the chapter concepts applied in a manner that you would use outside of college. An analytic rubric helps you and your instructor grade the quality of your work by comparing it to the work an expert in the discipline would create.	In text
6M	Combination of Objectives from Projects 6A and 6B	**6M GO! Think (Rubric Grading)** **Critical Thinking** A demonstration of your understanding of the chapter concepts applied in a manner that you would use outside of college. An analytic rubric helps you and your instructor grade the quality of your work by comparing it to the work an expert in the discipline would create.	IRC and MyITLab
6N	Combination of Objectives from Projects 6A and 6B	**6N You and GO! (Rubric Grading)** **Critical Thinking** A demonstration of your understanding of the chapter concepts applied in a manner that you would use in a personal situation. An analytic rubric helps you and your instructor grade the quality of your work.	IRC and MyITLab
Capstone Project for Access Chapters 4–6	Combination of Objectives from Projects 4A, 4B, 5A, 5B, 6A, and 6B	A demonstration of your mastery of the skills in Chapters 4–6 with extensive decision making. **(Grader Project)**	IRC and MyITLab

GLOSSARY

GLOSSARY OF CHAPTER KEY TERMS

Aggregate function A function that groups and performs calculations on multiple values.

Button control A control that enables individuals to add a command button to a form or report that will perform an action when the button is clicked.

Combo box A control that enables individuals to select from a list or to type a value.

Concatenation Linking or joining strings.

Control An object, such as a label or text box, in a form or report that enables individuals to view or manipulate information stored in tables or queries.

ControlTip A message that displays descriptive text when the mouse pointer is paused over the control.

Focus A control that is selected and currently being acted upon.

Form selector The box in the upper-left corner of a form in Design view where the rulers meet; used to select the entire form.

Image control A control that enables individuals to insert an image into any section of a form or report.

Line control A control that enables an individual to insert a line into a form or report.

List box A control that enables individuals to select from a list but does not enable individuals to type anything that is not in the list.

Picture Alignment property A property that determines where the background picture for a form displays on the form.

Picture Size Mode property A property that determines the proportions of a picture in a form.

Point A unit of measure that is 1/72 of an inch.

Propagate To disseminate or apply changes to an object.

Properties The characteristics that determine the appearance, structure, and behavior of an object.

Property Sheet A pane that is available for every object on a form, including the form itself, to further enhance the object.

Property Update Options button An option button that displays when you make changes to the design of a table; it enables individuals to update the Property Sheet for a field in all objects that use a table as the record source.

Record Source property A property that enables you to specify the source of the data for a form or a report; the property setting can be a table name, a query name, or an SQL statement.

Status Bar Text property A form property that enables individuals to enter text that will display in the status bar for a selected control.

String A series of characters.

Tab order A setting that refers to the order in which the fields are selected when the Tab key is pressed.

Theme A design tool that simplifies the process of creating professional-looking objects within one program or across multiple programs; includes theme colors and theme fonts that will be applied consistently throughout the objects in a database.

Apply 6A skills from these Objectives:

1 Create a Form in Design View
2 Change and Add Controls
3 Format a Form
4 Make a Form User Friendly

Skills Review Project 6C Party Orders

Marty Kress, vice president of marketing for the Rosebud Cafe franchise restaurant chain, wants to expand the chain's offerings to include party trays for advance order and delivery. In the following project, you will create a form to use for the data entry of these party order items. Your completed form, if printed, will look similar to Figure 6.48. An electronic version of the form will look slightly different.

PROJECT FILES

For Project 6C, you will need the following files:

a06C_Party_Orders
a06C_Logo
a06C_Rose

You will save your database as:

Lastname_Firstname_6C_Party_Orders

PROJECT RESULTS

FIGURE 6.48

(Project 6C Party Orders continues on the next page)

Skills Review Project 6C Party Orders (continued)

1 Start Access. Locate and open the **a06C_Party_Orders** file. Save the database in your **Access Chapter 6** folder as **Lastname_Firstname_6C_Party_Orders** If necessary, click **Enable Content**.

2 Double-click **6C Party Orders** to open the table in **Datasheet** view. Take a moment to examine the fields in the table.

a. In any record, click in the **Party Tray** field, and then click the **arrow**. This field is a Lookup field in the *6C Trays* table. In any record, click in the **Extras** field, and then click the **arrow**. This field is a Lookup field in the *6C Menu Items* table.

b. **Close** the table, and then **Close** the **Navigation Pane**.

3 On the **Create tab**, in the **Forms group**, click **Form Design**.

a. If necessary, under **Form Design Tools**, on the **Design tab**, in the **Tools group**, click **Property Sheet**. On the **Property Sheet**, click the **Data tab**. Click the **Record Source arrow**, and then click **6C Party Orders**. Close the **Property Sheet**.

4 Under **Form Design Tools**, on the **Design tab**, in the **Tools group**, click **Add Existing Fields**.

a. In the **Field List**, click **Order ID**, hold down Shift, and then click **Extras**. Drag the selected fields onto the design grid until the top of the pointer arrow is aligned at **0.25 inch on the vertical ruler** and **2 inches on the horizontal ruler**, and then release the mouse button. **Close** the **Field List**.

b. With all of the controls still selected, under **Form Design Tools**, on the **Arrange tab**, in the **Table group**, click **Stacked**.

c. Drag the left edge of the label controls to the **0.5-inch mark on the horizontal ruler**. Increase the width of the text boxes by approximately **0.5 inches**. **Save** the form as **Lastname Firstname 6C Party Orders Form**

5 Under **Form Design Tools**, on the **Design tab**, in the **Header/Footer group**, click **Logo**.

a. Navigate to the location where the student data files for this textbook are saved. Locate and double-click **a06C_Logo** to insert the logo in the **Form Header**.

b. On the selected logo, point to the right-middle sizing handle until the pointer displays. Drag to the right until the right edge of the logo is aligned with the **1.5-inch mark on the horizontal ruler**.

6 In the **Header/Footer group**, click **Title**.

a. In the **label control** for the title, replace the text with **6C Party Orders** and then press Enter.

b. Drag the right edge of the title to align it with the **4-inch mark on the horizontal ruler**.

c. With the title selected, under **Form Design Tools**, on the **Format tab**, in the **Font group**, click **Center**.

7 Scroll down until the **Form Footer** section bar displays. Point to the top of the **Form Footer** section bar until the pointer displays. Drag upward until the top of the **Form Footer** section bar aligns with the **2.5-inch mark on the vertical ruler**.

a. Under **Form Design Tools**, on the **Design tab**, in the **Controls group**, click **Label**. Point to the **Form Footer** section until the plus sign (+) of the pointer aligns with the bottom of the **Form Footer** section bar and the **0.25-inch mark on the horizontal ruler**. Drag downward to the bottom of the **Form Footer** section and to the right to the **3.25-inch mark on the horizontal ruler**.

b. Type **Order online at www.rosebudcafe.net** and then press Enter.

c. With the **label control** in the **Form Footer** section selected, hold down Shift, and then click the **Logo control** and the **Extras label control**. Under **Form Design Tools**, on the **Arrange tab**, in the **Sizing & Ordering group**, click **Align**, and then click **Left**. **Save** the form.

8 Click and hold the **Party Tray text box control** until the pointer displays. Drag downward until a thin orange line displays on the bottom edges of the **Extras** controls and then release the mouse button.

a. With the **Party Tray text box control** selected, hold down Shift, and then click the **Party Tray label control, Extras text box control**, and **Extras label control**.

b. Under **Form Design Tools**, on the **Arrange tab**, in the **Table group**, click **Remove Layout** to remove the *Extras* field and the *Party Tray* field from the stacked layout.

c. Click in a blank area in the **Detail** section to deselect the controls. Right-click the **Party Tray combo box control**. From the shortcut menu, point to **Change To**, and then click **List Box**.

(Project 6C Party Orders continues on the next page)

Skills Review Project 6C Party Orders (continued)

d. **Save** the form, and then switch to **Form** view. Notice that the **Party Tray list box control** is not wide enough to display all columns and that there are horizontal and vertical scroll bars to indicate there is more data. Click the **Extras combo box arrow** to see if any menu item names or prices are cut off. Press Esc.

e. Switch to **Design** view, and click the **Party Tray list box control**, if necessary. Point to the right edge of the control until the pointer displays. Drag to the right until the right edge of the control aligns with the **4.25-inch mark on the horizontal ruler**.

f. Switch to **Layout** view. Resize the **Extras combo box control** to be the same size as the **Party Tray list box control**. **Save** the form and switch to **Design** view.

9 Click the **Form Header section bar**. Under **Form Design Tools**, on the **Design tab**, in the **Controls group**, click **Insert Image**, and then click **Browse**. In the displayed **Insert Picture** dialog box, navigate to the location where the student data files for this textbook are saved.

a. Locate and double-click **a06C_Logo**.

b. Align the plus sign (+) with the bottom of the **Form Header** section bar and with the **4-inch mark on the horizontal ruler**. Drag downward to the top of the **Detail** section bar and to the right to the **5.25-inch mark on the horizontal ruler**.

c. Click the **image control**—the Rosebud Cafe image on the right side in the **Form Header** section—if necessary. On the **Design tab**, in the **Tools group**, click **Property Sheet**. If necessary, on the **Format tab**, change the **Width** property setting to **1.25** and then change the **Height** property setting to **0.5**.

d. In the **Form Header** section, click the **logo control**. On the **Property Sheet**, change the **Width** property setting to **1.25** and change the **Height** property setting to **0.5**. **Close** the **Property Sheet**.

e. With the logo control selected, hold down Shift, and then click the **image control**. On the **Arrange tab**, in the **Sizing & Ordering group**, click **Align**, and then click **Top**.

10 Under **Form Design Tools**, on the **Design tab**, in the **Controls group**, click **Button**.

a. Move the mouse pointer down into the **Detail** section. Align the plus sign (+) of the pointer at **0.25 inches on the vertical ruler** and **3.25 inches on the horizontal ruler**, and then click.

b. Under **Categories**, verify **Record Navigation** is selected. Under **Actions**, click **Find Record**, and then click **Next** two times. In the text box, type **btnFindRcrd** and then click **Finish**.

c. Using the technique you just practiced, add a **button control** right next to the **Find Record button**. Under **Categories**, click **Record Operations**. Under **Actions**, click **Print Record**, and then click **Next** two times. Name the button **btnPrtForm** Click **Finish**.

d. With the **Print Current Form button control** selected, hold down Shift, and then click the **Find Record button control**. Under **Form Design Tools**, on the **Arrange tab**, in the **Sizing & Ordering group**, click **Align**, and then click **Top**.

11 Switch to **Layout** view. Click in the **Form Footer** section to the right of the label control to select the entire section.

a. Under **Form Layout Tools**, on the **Format tab**, in the **Control Formatting group**, click **Shape Fill**. Under **Theme Colors**, in the third row, click the seventh color—**Olive Green, Accent 3, Lighter 60%**.

b. Using the technique you just practiced, change the color of the **Form Header** section to match the **Form Footer** section.

12 Switch to **Design** view, and then double-click the **Form selector** to open the Property Sheet for the form.

a. On the **Property Sheet**, on the **Format tab**, click in the **Picture** property setting box, and then click **Build**. Navigate to where the student data files for this textbook are saved. Locate and double-click **a06C_Rose** to insert the picture in the form.

b. Click in the **Picture Alignment** property setting box, click the **arrow**, and then click **Form Center**. **Close** the **Property Sheet**, and then **Save** the form.

13 Switch to **Layout** view, click the **Order ID text box control**, hold down Shift, and then click the **Cust Name text box control** and the **Cust Phone# text box control**.

a. Under **Form Layout Tools**, on the **Format tab**, in the **Control Formatting group**, click **Shape Outline**. Point to **Line Type**, and click the fifth line type—**Dots**.

(Project 6C Party Orders continues on the next page)

Skills Review Project 6D Catering (continued)

20 In the **Detail** section, click the **Tray Desc text box control**. On the **Design tab**, in the **Grouping & Totals group**, click **Totals**. In the displayed list of aggregate functions, click **Count Records**.

21 In the **Pickup Time Footer** section, select the **Count text box control**, and then holding down Shift, in the **Report Footer** select the **Count text box control**.

a. Under **Report Design Tools**, on the **Arrange tab**, in the **Table group**, click **Remove Layout**.

b. Align and resize each control so the left edge of each control is even with the **5.5-inch marker on the horizontal ruler** and the right edge of each control is even with the **6-inch marker on the horizontal ruler**.

c. Under **Report Design Tools**, on the **Design tab**, in the **Controls group**, click **Text Box**. Drag the plus sign (+) from the bottom edge of the **Pickup Time Footer** section bar at the **2.75-inch mark on the horizontal ruler** to the bottom of the **Pickup Time Footer** section and to the right to the **5.5-inch mark on the horizontal ruler**.

d. In the unbound text box, type **=[Pickup Time] & " # of Orders:"** In the **Pickup Time Footer** section, click the **label control** that displays to the left of the text box control, and then press Delete.

e. In the **Pickup Time Footer** section, click the **text box control** that contains the expression you typed. Hold down Shift and click the **Count calculated control** in the **Pickup Time Footer**. On the **Arrange tab**, in the **Sizing & Ordering group**, click **Size/Space**, and then click **To Tallest**. In the **Sizing & Ordering group**, click **Align**, and then click **Top**.

22 Drag the right edge of the design grid to the left until it aligns with the **6.5-inch mark on the horizontal ruler**. Switch to **Report** view. Hold down Ctrl, and then press End to move to the end of the report.

23 Switch to **Design** view. Point to the bottom of the **Report Footer** section, and then drag downward until it reaches the **0.5-inch mark on the vertical ruler**.

a. In the **Report Footer** section, click the **Count text box control**, and then drag downward until the bottom edge of the control aligns with the bottom edge of the **Report Footer** section.

b. Use the techniques you have practiced to add a label control in the **Report Footer** section to the left of the calculated control—the left edge of the control should be aligned with the **4-inch mark on the horizontal ruler**. In the **label control**, type **Total # of Orders:**

c. Align the label control with the calculated control at the bottom and then be sure that the controls are the same height.

24 Under **Report Design Tools**, on the **Design tab**, in the **Controls group**, click **Line**. Point to the bottom of the **Pickup Time Footer** section until the middle of the plus sign (+) of the pointer aligns with the top of the **Page Footer** section bar and the **0-inch mark on the horizontal ruler**. Click, hold down Shift, drag to the right to the **6.5-inch mark on the horizontal ruler**, and then release the mouse button and Shift.

25 Under **Report Design Tools**, on the **Format tab**, in the **Control Formatting group**, click **Shape Outline**. Click **Line Thickness**, and then click the third line—**2 pt**. In the **Control Formatting group**, click **Shape Outline**. Under **Theme Colors**, in the first row, click the eighth color—**Green, Accent 4**. **Save** the report.

26 Switch to **Print Preview**. Adjust the margins or report width as needed. If you are instructed to submit this result, create a paper printout or PDF electronic image. **Close Print Preview**.

27 **Close** the report. **Open** the **Navigation Pane** and resize so all object names display fully. **Close** the database, and then **Close** Access.

28 As directed by your instructor, submit your database and the paper printout or PDF electronic image of both reports that are the result of this project. Specifically, in this project, using your own name you created the following database and printouts or electronic printouts:

1. Lastname_Firstname_6D_Catering	Database file
2. Lastname Firstname 6D Catering by Date	Report
3. Lastname Firstname 6D Catering Report	Report

END | You have completed Project 6D

Apply 6A skills from these Objectives:

1 Create a Form in Design View
2 Change and Add Controls
3 Format a Form
4 Make a Form User Friendly

Mastering Access Project 6E Monthly Promotions

In the following project, you will create a form that will be used to enter the data for the monthly promotions that are offered to guests at the Rosebud Cafe restaurant franchise. Your task includes designing a form that will be attractive and provide easy data entry for the staff. Your completed form will look similar to Figure 6.50.

PROJECT FILES

For Project 6E, you will need the following files:

a06E_Monthly_Promotions
a06E_Logo
a06E_Dollar

You will save your database as:

Lastname_Firstname_6E_Monthly_Promotions

PROJECT RESULTS

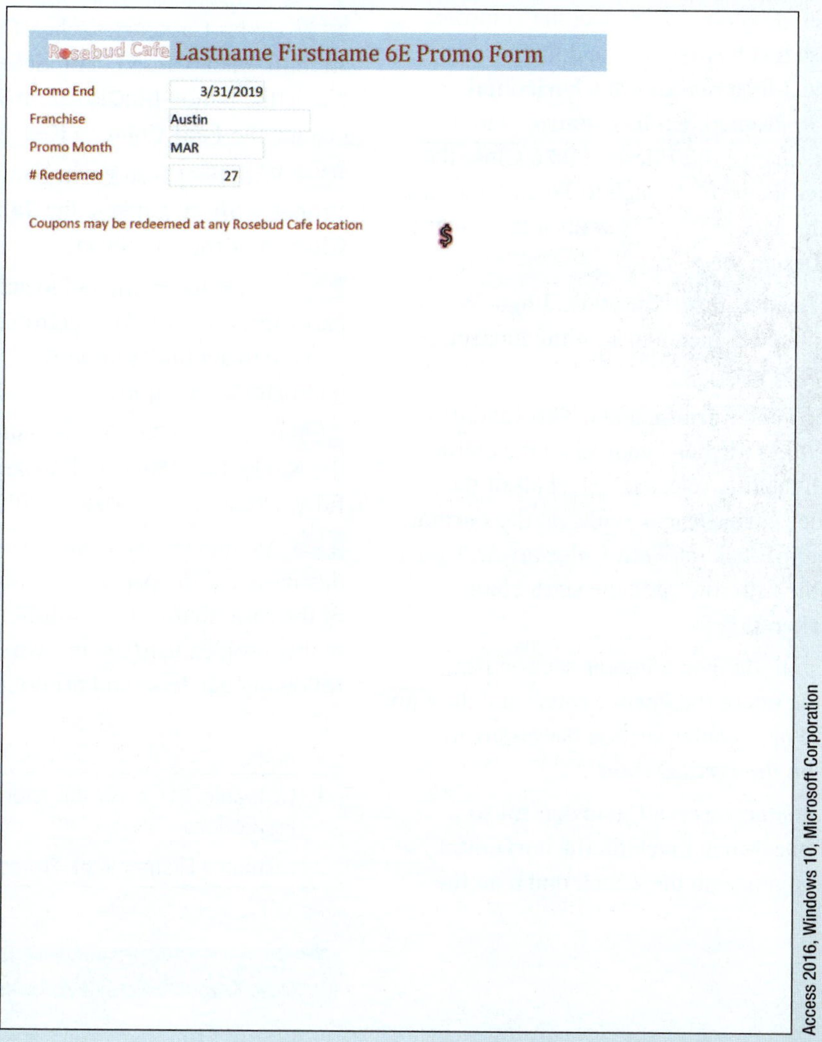

FIGURE 6.50

(Project 6E Monthly Promotions continues on the next page)

Mastering Access Project 6E Monthly Promotions (continued)

1 Start Access. Locate and open the **a06E_Monthly_Promotions** file. Save the database in your **Access Chapter 6** folder as **Lastname_Firstname_6E_Monthly_Promotions** If necessary, click **Enable Content**.

2 Create a form in **Form Design**. For the **Record Source**, use the **6E Monthly Results** table. Select all of the fields, and then drag them onto the design grid until the top of the arrow is aligned with the **1-inch mark on the horizontal ruler** and the **0.25-inch mark on the vertical ruler**. **Save** the form as **Lastname Firstname 6E Promo Form**

3 With all of the text box controls selected, display the **Property Sheet**, and then click the **Format tab**. In the **Left** property box, type **1.5** and press Enter. Click anywhere in the **Detail** section to deselect the controls. Select the **Franchise text box control**, and then drag the right edge to the **3-inch mark on the horizontal ruler**. Select the **# Redeemed text box control**, and in the **Property Sheet**, change the **Width** to **0.75 Close** the Property Sheet. **Save** the form. Switch to **Form** view, and then click the **Promo Month** text box control to view the entries. Switch to **Design** view.

4 In the **Form Header**, insert the **a06E_Logo**. Widen the selected logo to the **1.5-inch mark on the horizontal ruler**.

5 In the **Header/Footer group**, add a **Title**, and then, if necessary, resize the **Title label control** so the entire title is visible. With the title selected, select all of the label controls. Under **Form Design Tools**, on the **Format tab**, in the **Font group**, click the **Font Color** arrow, Under **Theme Colors**, in the fifth row click the sixth color—**Red, Accent 2, Darker 25%**.

6 Scroll down until the **Form Footer** section bar displays. Point to the top of the **Form Footer**, and drag up until the top of the **Form Footer** section bar aligns with the **1.5-inch mark on the vertical ruler**.

7 In the **Form Footer**, insert a **Label** control so the left aligns with the **0-inch mark on the horizontal ruler** and the right aligns with the **4-inch mark on the horizontal ruler**. Type **Coupons may be redeemed at any Rosebud Cafe location** Press Enter. Change the font color to **Red, Accent 2, Darker 25%**.

8 In the **Form Footer**, insert the **a06E_Dollar** image at the top of the **Form Footer** section and at the **4.25-inch mark on the horizontal ruler**.

9 Display the **Property Sheet**, and change the **Width** and **Height** to **0.35** Point to the bottom of the **Form Footer** and drag up until the bottom of the Form Footer section bar aligns with the **0.5-inch mark on the vertical ruler**. **Close** the Property Sheet.

10 In the **Detail** section, insert a **Button** control aligning the plus sign (+) of the pointer with the **0.5-inch mark on the vertical ruler** and the **3.5-inch mark on the horizontal ruler**.

11 Under **Categories**, click **Form Operations**. Under **Actions**, click **Close Form**. Select the **Text** option button. Name the button **btnCloseFrm** With the button selected, change the **Font Color** to **Red, Accent 2, Darker 25%**.

12 With the **Close Form** button selected, open the **Property Sheet**. Change the **Tab Stop** property to **No**. **Close** the **Property Sheet**.

13 If you are instructed to submit this result, create a paper printout or PDF electronic image of **record 8**. If you are to submit your work electronically, follow your instructor's directions.

14 Click the **Close Form** button, saving changes. **Open** the **Navigation Pane**, and resize to display all objects fully. **Close** the database, and then **Close** Access.

15 As directed by your instructor, submit your database and the paper printout or PDF electronic image of the form that is the result of this project. Specifically, in this project, using your own name you created the following database and printout or electronic printout:

1. Lastname_Firstname_6E_Monthly_Promotions	Database file
2. Lastname Firstname 6E Promo Form	Form

END | You have completed Project 6E

CONTENT-BASED ASSESSMENTS (MASTERY AND TRANSFER OF LEARNING)

6 ACCESS

Apply 6B skills from these Objectives:

5 Create a Report Based on a Query Using a Wizard
6 Create a Report in Design View
7 Add Controls to a Report
8 Group, Sort, and Total Records in Design View

Mastering Access Project 6F Promotional Results

In the following project, you will create a report that will display the promotions that are offered to guests of the Rosebud Cafe restaurant franchise. You will also create a crosstab report that will summarize the results of the promotions. Creating customized reports will help the managers of each location view the information in the database in a meaningful way. Your completed reports will look similar to Figure 6.51.

PROJECT FILES

For Project 6F, you will need the following files:

a06F_Promotional_Results
a06F_Logo

You will save your database as:

Lastname_Firstname_6F_Promotional_Results

PROJECT RESULTS

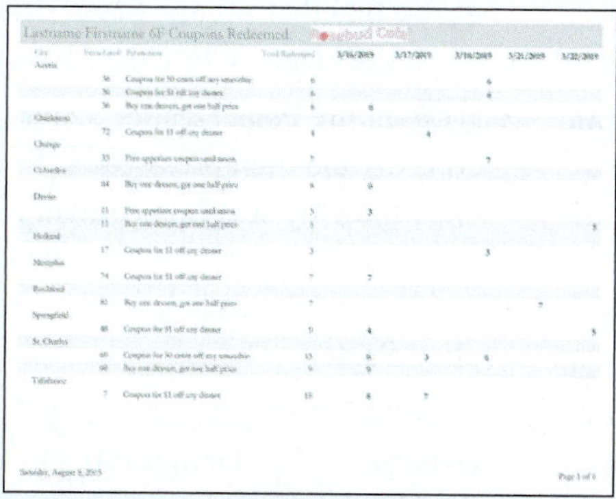

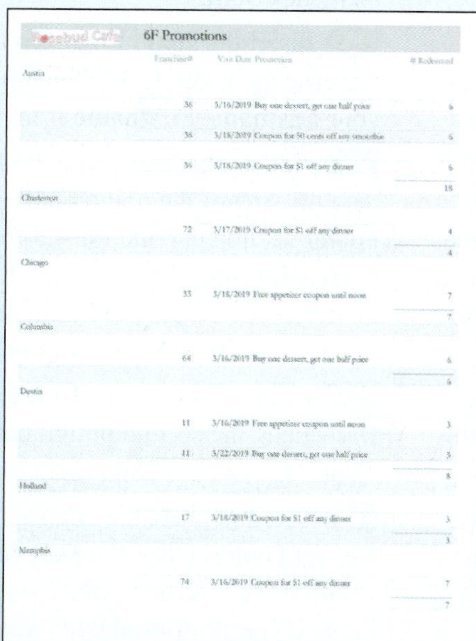

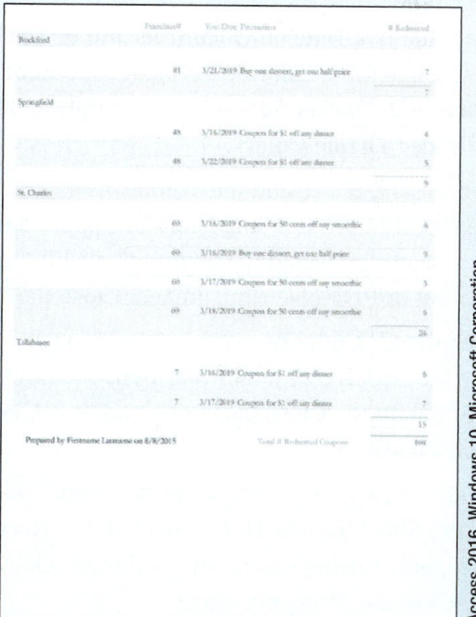

Access 2016, Windows 10, Microsoft Corporation

FIGURE 6.51

(Project 6F Promotional Results continues on the next page)

Mastering Access Project 6F Promotional Results (continued)

1 Start Access. Locate and open the **a06F_Promotional Results** file. Save the database in your **Access Chapter 6** folder as **Lastname_Firstname_6F_Promotional_Results** If necessary, click **Enable Content**.

2 Under **Queries**, open the **6F Coupons Crosstab Query**. Take a moment to study the data in the query. **Close** the query, and then **Close** the **Navigation Pane**.

3 **Create** a report using the **Report Wizard**. From the **Query: 6F Coupons Crosstab Query**, select all of the fields. Under **Do you want to add any grouping levels?**, select **City**. **Sort** the records within the report by **Franchise#** in **Ascending** order. Under **Layout**, be sure the **Stepped** option button is selected. Under **Orientation**, click the **Landscape** option button. Be sure the **Adjust the field width so all fields fit on a page** check box is selected. For the title of the report, type **Lastname Firstname 6F Coupons Redeemed** Select **Modify the report's design**, and then click **Finish**.

4 Switch to **Layout** view, and then apply the **Organic** theme. If any data is cut off, select the label control and drag to widen the column to display all data. Reduce the width of any columns that display a lot of blank space to allow for the widened columns.

5 Switch to **Design** view. Insert the **a06F_Logo** image so it appears from the **5.25-inch mark on the horizontal ruler** to the **7-inch mark**, and is the height of the Report Header section.

6 Select the five **Date label controls and textbox controls**. Change the width to **0.8**. Change the **Font Color** to **Teal, Accent 2, Darker 50%**—the sixth option in the sixth row under **Theme Colors**.

7 If necessary, resize and move controls so you can resize the report to print on one landscape page. **Save** the report. If you are instructed to submit this result, create a paper printout or PDF electronic image. **Close** the report.

8 Open the **6F Coupons** query in **Design** view, and notice the underlying tables that were used in the creation of the query. **Close** the query, and then **Close** the **Navigation Pane**.

9 Create a new report using **Report Design**. Display the **Property Sheet**. On the **Data tab**, click the **Record Source property setting box arrow**, and then select **6F Coupons**. **Close** the **Property Sheet**.

10 Display the **Field List**. From the **Field List**, select all fields included in the query. Drag the selected fields into the **Detail** section of the design grid until the top of the pointer is aligned with the **0.25-inch mark on the vertical ruler** and the **1-inch mark on the horizontal ruler**. With the controls selected, under **Report Design Tools**, on the **Arrange tab**, in the **Table group**, click **Tabular**. **Close** the **Field List**. Drag the **Page Footer section bar** up to the **0.5-inch mark on the vertical ruler**.

11 **Save** the report as **Lastname Firstname 6F Promotions** Switch to **Layout** view to be sure all data is visible in the report. If necessary, adjust the width of any columns where data is cut off. Switch to **Design** view.

12 Under **Report Design Tools**, on the **Design tab**, click the **Group & Sort** button. Click **Add a group**, and then from the displayed list, click **City**. Apply **Keep whole group together on one page**. Click **Add a sort**, and then click **Visit Date**. **Close** the **Group, Sort, and Total Pane**.

13 In the **Page Header** section, click the **City** label control, and then press Delete. In the **Detail** section, right-click the **City text box control** to display the shortcut menu, and click **Cut**. Click the **City Header** section bar to select it, right-click to display the shortcut menu, and click **Paste**.

14 In the **Detail** section, click the **# Redeemed text box control**. On the **Design tab**, click the **Totals** button, and then click **Sum**.

15 Insert the **a06F_Logo**. On the **Property Sheet**, increase the width to **1.75 inches**. Insert a **Title**. Delete your **Lastname Firstname** from the beginning of the title.

16 Add a **label control** to the **Report Footer**. Position the plus sign of the pointer at the bottom of the **Report Footer** section bar and the **4.5-inch mark on the horizontal ruler**. Drag upward to the top of the **Report Footer** section and to the right to the left edge of the Sum control box. Type **Total # Redeemed Coupons**

17 Click the **Date and Time** button. Under **Include Date**, click the second option button. Do not **Include Time**. Remove the **Date text box control** from the layout.

18 **Cut and paste** the control to the left edge of the **Report Footer**. Click the **Date text box control** two times. Position the insertion point between the equal sign and the *D*. Type **"Prepared by Firstname Lastname on "&** and

(Project 6F Promotional Results continues on the next page)

Mastering Access Project 6F Promotional Results (continued)

then press Enter. Click the **Title label control**, and resize it so the right edge aligns with the **4-inch mark on the horizontal ruler**. **Center** the text in the control. Resize the report to **7.75 inches wide**.

19 Select all of the controls in the **Report Footer**. Be sure they are all the same height and aligned at the bottom.

20 Switch to **Layout** view, and then adjust all controls to fit the data without extending beyond the right margin. **Save** the report. If you are instructed to submit this result, create a paper printout or PDF electronic image. **Close** the report.

21 **Open** the **Navigation Pane**, and resize to display all objects fully. **Close** the database, and then **Close** Access.

22 As directed by your instructor, submit your database and the paper printout or PDF electronic image of both reports that are the result of this project. Specifically, in this project, using your own name you created the following database and printouts or electronic printouts:

1. Lastname_Firstname_6F_Promotional_Results	Database file
2. Lastname Firstname 6F Coupons Redeemed	Report
3. Lastname Firstname 6F Promotions	Report

END | You have completed Project 6F

CONTENT-BASED ASSESSMENTS (MASTERY AND TRANSFER OF LEARNING)

Apply 6A and 6B skills from these Objectives:

1. Create a Form in Design View
2. Change and Add Controls
3. Format a Form
4. Make a Form User Friendly
5. Create a Report Based on a Query Using a Wizard
6. Create a Report in Design View
7. Add Controls to a Report
8. Group, Sort, and Total Records in Design View

Mastering Access Project 6G Wireless Usage

Marty Kress, vice president of marketing for Rosebud Cafe franchises, keeps a database on the wireless usage per franchise on a monthly basis. The individual restaurants report the number of customers using the wireless connections and the average length of usage per customer. In this project, you will design a form for the data entry of this data and design a report that can be used by Mr. Kress to plan next year's marketing strategies. Your completed work will look similar to Figure 6.52.

PROJECT FILES

For Project 6G, you will need the following files:

a06G_Wireless_Usage

a06G_Logo

You will save your database as:

Lastname_Firstname_6G_Wireless_Usage

PROJECT RESULTS

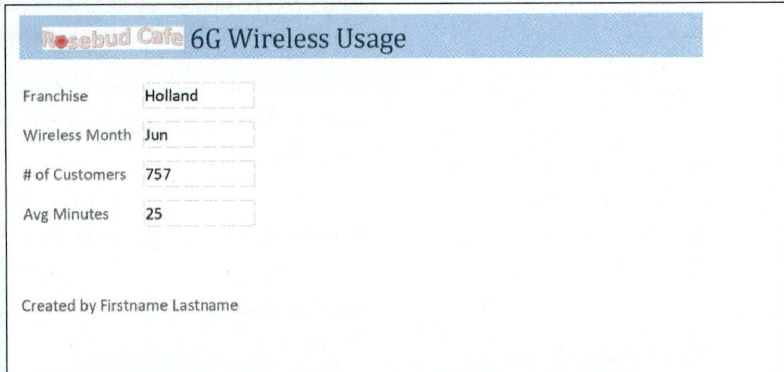

6G Wireless Usage by Month

City	Total Of # of Customers	Jul	Aug	Sep
Austin	1722	469	542	711
Charleston	983	223	209	551
Chicago	1256	712	294	250
Clearwater	1794	318	1265	211
Columbia	2128	670	1010	448
Destin	1698	398	630	670
Grand Haven	1815	634	603	578
Holland	1992	655		580
Macon	1353	641	244	468
Memphis	1492	379	662	451
Providence	2006	580	687	739
Santa Monica	1321	573		748
Springfield	2137	788	787	562
St. Charles	1946	644	754	548
Tallahasee	1103	245	619	239

Prepared by Firstname Lastname on 8/8/2015 5:33:36 PM   Page 1 of 1

FIGURE 6.52

(Project 6G Wireless Usage continues on the next page)

Mastering Access Project 6G Wireless Usage (continued)

1 Start Access. Locate and open the **a06G_Wireless_Usage** file. Save the database in your **Access Chapter 6** folder as **Lastname_Firstname_6G_Wireless_Usage** If necessary, click **Enable Content**.

2 Create a form in **Form Design**. For the **Record Source**, use the **6G Wireless Usage** table. Select all of the fields, and then drag them onto the design grid until the top of the arrow is aligned with the **1-inch mark on the horizontal ruler** and the **0.25-inch mark on the vertical ruler**. **Save** the form as **Lastname Firstname 6G Wireless Usage**

3 Apply a **Stacked** layout. Add a **Red, Accent 2** dashed outline to the text box controls in the **Detail** section.

4 Insert the **a06G_Logo**. Widen the selected logo to the **1.5-inch mark on the horizontal ruler**.

5 Insert a **Title**. Delete **Lastname Firstname** and the following space, and then press Enter. Adjust the right edge of the title label control to just fit the text.

6 Add a **Button** in the **Detail** section at the **0.5-inch mark on the vertical ruler** and the **2.5-inch mark on the horizontal ruler**. Click **Record Operations**, and then **Add New Record**. Apply the **Go To New Picture**, and then name the button **btnNewRcrd** Add a button to print the record below the **Add New Record** button. Place a picture on it, and name it **btnPrtRcrd**

7 With the **New Record** and **Print Record** buttons selected, change the **Tab Stop** property to **No**. If necessary, **Align** the buttons at the **Right**.

8 Drag the top of the **Form Footer** section bar until it aligns with the **2-inch mark on the vertical ruler**. In the **Form Footer** section, insert a label aligned with the bottom of the **Form Footer** section bar and the left edge of the form. Type **Created by Firstname Lastname** and then press Enter.

9 Switch to **Form** view. Click the **New Record** button. From the list of **Franchises**, select **Holland MI**. In the **Wireless Month text box control**, select **June 1, 2019**. In the **# of Customers text box control**, type **757** In the **Avg Minutes text box control**, type **25**

10 If you are instructed to submit this result, create a paper printout or PDF electronic image of the new, selected record only. **Close** the form and **Save** changes.

11 **Create** a report using the **Report Wizard**. From the **Query: 6G Wireless Crosstab Query**, select the **City, Total Of # of Customers, Jul**, **Aug**, and **Sep** fields. Do not add any grouping levels. **Sort** records within the report by **City**, in **Ascending** order. Use a **Tabular** layout and a **Landscape** orientation. Title your report as **6G Wireless Usage by Month**

12 Switch to **Design** view. Select the **Title** label control and all of the label controls in the **Page Header** section. Change the font color to **Orange, Accent 6, Darker 50%**. Reduce the width of the **Page # control** so the right edge aligns with the **8-inch mark on the horizontal ruler**.

13 Resize the **Jul**, **Aug**, and **Sep textbox controls** and **label controls** to **1 inch**. Move the controls so there is one dot between the monthly columns. Resize the report to **9.5 inches** wide.

14 Modify the **Page Footer** by adding **Prepared by Firstname Lastname on** before Now().Be sure to use correct syntax when adding the text. Widen the control to the **5-inch mark on the horizontal ruler**. Switch to **Print Preview**.

15 If you are instructed to submit this result, create a paper printout or PDF electronic image. **Close** the report and **Save** changes.

16 **Open** the **Navigation Pane**, and resize to display all objects fully. **Close** the database, and then **Close** Access.

17 As directed by your instructor, submit your database and the paper printout or PDF electronic image of the form and report that are the result of this project. Specifically, in this project, using your own name you created the following database and printouts or electronic printouts:

1. Lastname_Firstname_6G_Wireless_Usage	Database file
2. Lastname Firstname 6G Wireless Usage	Form
3. Lastname Firstname 6G Wireless Usage by Month	Report

END | You have completed Project 6G

Apply a combination of the 6A and 6B skills.

CONTENT-BASED ASSESSMENTS (CRITICAL THINKING)

GO! Fix It Project 6H Advertising Contracts MyITLab

GO! Make It Project 6I Supply Orders MyITLab

GO! Solve It Project 6J Menu Items MyITLab

GO! Solve It Project 6K Birthday Coupons

PROJECT FILES

For Project 6K, you will need the following files:

a06K_Birthday_Coupons
a06K_Rose
a06K_Birthday
a06K_Cupcake

You will save your database as:

Lastname_Firstname_6K_Birthday_Coupons

The vice president of marketing, Marty Kress, encourages each location of the Rosebud Cafe franchise to offer birthday coupons to its customers as a promotional venture. Open the a06K_Birthday_Coupons database, and then save it as **Lastname_Firstname_6K_Birthday_Coupons** Use the 6K Birthdates table to create a form to enter the names, birthday months, and email addresses of the customers visiting one of the restaurants. Save the form as **Lastname Firstname 6K Birthday Form** Add a button control to print the current record. Include the Rose image as the logo, and title the form **6K Happy Birthday** Remove the background from the Form Header. Resize the Detail area to 1.5 inches. Be sure all data is visible on the form. Add a new record using the form and your own information.

Create a report to display the customer name and email address grouped by birthday month using the months as a section header and sorted by customer name. Add the a06K_Birthday image as the logo, resized to 1 inch tall and wide. Add a title. Draw a line above the Birthday Month header control to separate the months; apply a Line Color and Line Type. Add a footer that includes your name. Save the report as **Lastname Firstname 6K Birthdate Report**

Create a report based on the 6K First Quarter Birthdays query. Include both of the fields arranged in a tabular format. Save the report as **Lastname Firstname 6K First Quarter Birthdays** Add a title to the report, **Lastname Firstname 6K First Quarter Birthdays** Add the current date and time to the Report Header section. Delete the Page Footer controls, and resize the Page Footer section to 0. Apply a dotted outline to the label controls in the Page Header section; choose a Line Color and Line Thickness. Add a count of how many first quarter birthdays there are to the Report Footer. Include a descriptive label to the right of the count. Be sure the controls are the same size and aligned. Adjust the width of the report to 7.5 inches, making necessary adjustments to textbox controls. Add the a06K_Cupcake image and place it in the bottom right of the Report Footer. Resize it to 1 inch tall and wide. Save the changes. If you are instructed to submit the results, create a paper printout or PDF electronic image of the objects created.

(Project 6K Birthday Coupons continues on the next page)

GO! Solve It Project 6K Birthday Coupons (continued)

Performance Level

Performance Criteria	Exemplary: You consistently applied the relevant skills	Proficient: You sometimes, but not always, applied the relevant skills	Developing: You rarely or never applied the relevant skills
Create 6K Birthday Form	Form created with the correct fields and formatted as directed.	Form created with no more than two missing elements.	Form created with more than two missing elements.
Create 6K Birthdate Report	Report created with the correct fields and formatted as directed.	Report created with no more than two missing elements.	Report created with more than two missing elements.
Create 6K First Quarter Birthdays Report	Report created with the correct fields and formatted as directed.	Report created with no more than two missing elements.	Report created with more than two missing elements.

END | You have completed Project 6K

OUTCOMES-BASED ASSESSMENTS (CRITICAL THINKING)

RUBRIC

The following outcomes-based assessments are open-ended assessments. That is, there is no specific correct result; your result will depend on your approach to the information provided. Make Professional Quality your goal. Use the following scoring rubric to guide you in how to approach the problem and then to evaluate how well your approach solves the problem.

The *criteria*—Software Mastery, Content, Format and Layout, and Process—represent the knowledge and skills you have gained that you can apply to solving the problem. The *levels of performance*—Professional Quality, Approaching Professional Quality, or Needs Quality Improvements—help you and your instructor evaluate your result.

	Your completed project is of Professional Quality if you:	Your completed project is Approaching Professional Quality if you:	Your completed project Needs Quality Improvements if you:
1-Software Mastery	Choose and apply the most appropriate skills, tools, and features and identify efficient methods to solve the problem.	Choose and apply some appropriate skills, tools, and features, but not in the most efficient manner.	Choose inappropriate skills, tools, or features, or are inefficient in solving the problem.
2-Content	Construct a solution that is clear and well organized, contains content that is accurate, appropriate to the audience and purpose, and is complete. Provide a solution that contains no errors of spelling, grammar, or style.	Construct a solution in which some components are unclear, poorly organized, inconsistent, or incomplete. Misjudge the needs of the audience. Have some errors in spelling, grammar, or style, but the errors do not detract from comprehension.	Construct a solution that is unclear, incomplete, or poorly organized, contains some inaccurate or inappropriate content, and contains many errors of spelling, grammar, or style. Do not solve the problem.
3-Format and Layout	Format and arrange all elements to communicate information and ideas, clarify function, illustrate relationships, and indicate relative importance.	Apply appropriate format and layout features to some elements, but not others. Overuse features, causing minor distraction.	Apply format and layout that does not communicate information or ideas clearly. Do not use format and layout features to clarify function, illustrate relationships, or indicate relative importance. Use available features excessively, causing distraction.
4-Process	Use an organized approach that integrates planning, development, self-assessment, revision, and reflection.	Demonstrate an organized approach in some areas, but not others; or, use an insufficient process of organization throughout.	Do not use an organized approach to solve the problem.

Apply a combination of the 6A and 6B skills.

OUTCOMES-BASED ASSESSMENTS (CRITICAL THINKING)

GO! Think Project 6L Vacation Days

PROJECT FILES

For Project 6L, you will need the following files:

a06L_Vacation_Days

a06L_Logo

You will save your database as:
Lastname_Firstname_6L_Vacation_Days

In this project, you will create a report to display the information for the Rosebud Cafe employees and their vacation days. Open the **a06L_Vacation_Days** database and save it as **Lastname_Firstname_6L_Vacation_Days** From the *6L Vacation Days* table, add the following fields to the report: Employee Name, Days Allotted, and Days Taken. Add a calculated text box control to display the number of vacation days each employee has remaining (Days Allotted-Days Taken) with a label control to describe the field, and format the result as a General Number. Change the Theme to Ion. In the Report Header section, add the Rosebud Cafe logo and a descriptive title. Add a label control to the Report Footer section that reads **Report Designed by Firstname Lastname** Align the left edge with the label controls in the Detail section. Change the background color and font color used in the Report Header and Report Footer sections so they are easy to read. Sort the report on Employee Name. Adjust all label and text controls to display all field names and data. Adjust the width of the report so it is 6 inches wide. Add a dotted line between employees to make it easier to read. Center page numbers in the page footer. Resize the Detail section to reduce the blank space. Close the space for the Page Header. Save the report as **Lastname Firstname 6L Vacation Information** If you are instructed to submit this result, create a paper printout or PDF electronic image.

END | You have completed Project 6L

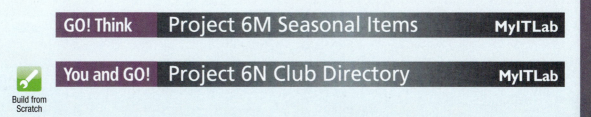

GO! Think Project 6M Seasonal Items MyITLab

Build from Scratch

You and GO! Project 6N Club Directory MyITLab

Creating Advanced Forms and Reports

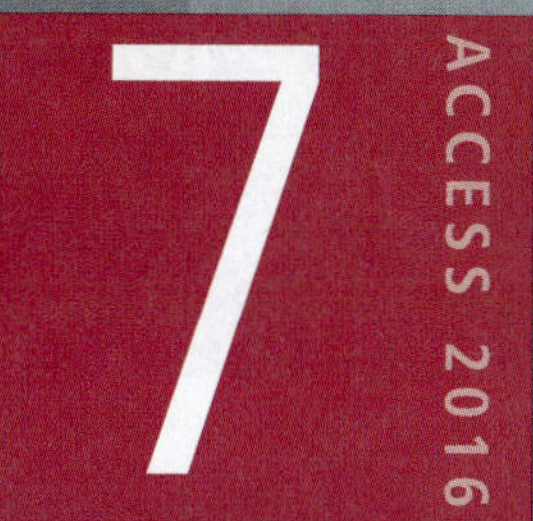

OUTCOMES
Create advanced forms.

OBJECTIVES

1. Create a Split Form
2. Create a Form and a Subform
3. Create a Multi-Page Form

PROJECT 7B

OUTCOMES
Create advanced reports.

OBJECTIVES

4. Create and Modify a Subreport
5. Create a Report Based on a Parameter Query
6. Create an Alphabetic Index

Elesi/Shutterstock

In This Chapter

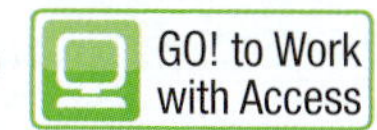

Forms provide a way to enter, edit, and display data; reports display the data in a professional manner. Access 2016 enables you to create a form that also displays the data in Datasheet view or to create multiple-page forms. If a one-to-many relationship exists between the underlying tables, forms can be used to manipulate data from multiple tables, and reports can display data from multiple tables. You have also practiced creating a parameter query, which, in turn, can be used to create a report based on the criteria entered when the report is opened. Specialty reports, like an alphabetic index, can also be created.

Gardening has increased in popularity in many areas of the country. The stylish simplicity and use of indigenous, hardy plants make for beautiful, environmentally friendly gardens in any region of the country. Gardeners also enjoy learning about plants and gardens in other parts of the country and the world. Produced by MWB Productions, ***Midwest Botanicals*** is a syndicated television show that is broadcast nationwide. The show and its website provide tips and tricks for beautiful plants and gardens, highlight new tools and techniques, and present tours of public and private gardens to inspire home gardeners.

PROJECT 7A

MWB Schedule

PROJECT ACTIVITIES

In Activities 7.01 through 7.08, you will help Gina Donaldson, office manager of MWB Productions, customize the company's forms. She wants the database forms to display related data. For example, she is interested in displaying the advertisers of the television shows on one form. You will display data in two ways on the same form, display data from multiple tables on one form, and display data on multiple pages on a form. Your completed forms will look similar to Figure 7.1.

PROJECT FILES

If your instructor wants you to submit Project 7A in the MyITLab Grader system, log in to MyITLab, locate Grader Project 7A, and then download the files for this project.

For Project 7A, you will need the following files:

a07A_MWB_Schedule
a07A_MWB_Logo
A blank Word document

You will save your documents as:

Lastname_Firstname_7A_MWB_Schedule
Lastname_Firstname_7A_Tab_Control_Form

PROJECT RESULTS

GO! Walk Thru Project 7A

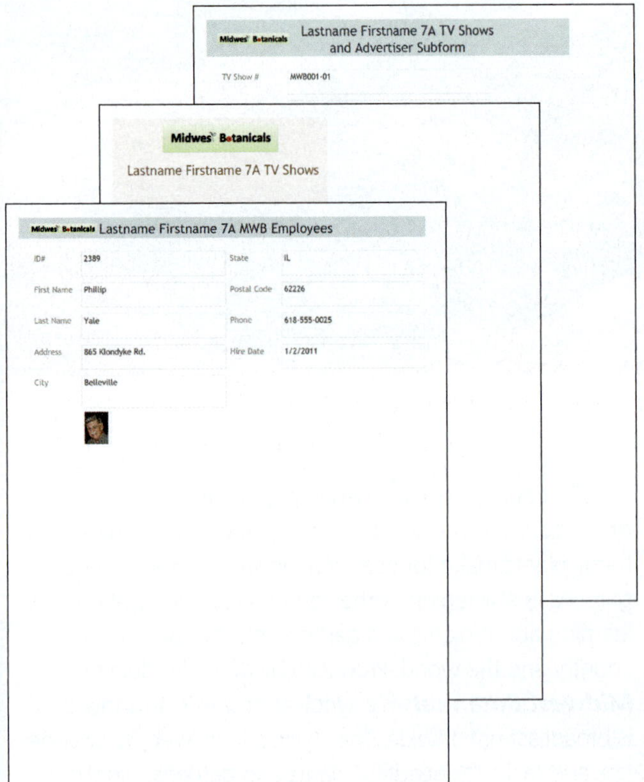

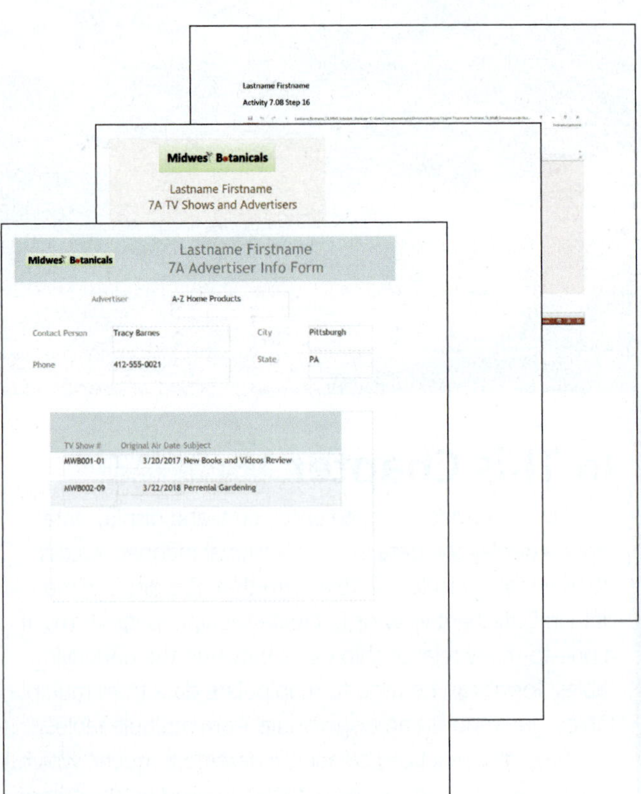

FIGURE 7.1 Project 7A MWB Schedule

NOTE If You Are Using a Touchscreen

- Tap an item to click it.
- Press and hold for a few seconds to right-click; release when the information or commands display.
- Touch the screen with two or more fingers and then pinch together to zoom out or stretch your fingers apart to zoom in.
- Slide your finger on the screen to scroll—slide left to scroll right and slide right to scroll left.
- Slide to rearrange—similar to dragging with a mouse.
- Swipe to select—slide an item a short distance with a quick movement—to select an item and bring up commands, if any.

PROJECT RESULTS

In this project, using your own name, you will create the following database and objects. Your instructor may ask for printouts or PDF electronic images:

Lastname_Firstname_7A_MWB_Schedule	Database file
Lastname Firstname 7A MWB Employees Split Form	Form
Lastname Firstname 7A Split Form	Form
Lastname Firstname 7A TV Shows Form	Form
Lastname Firstname 7A TV Shows Main Form	Form
Lastname Firstname 7A Advertiser Info Form	Form
Lastname Firstname 7A TV Shows and Advertisers	Form
Lastname_Firstname_7A_Tab_Control_Form	Word document

Objective 1 Create a Split Form

GO! Learn How Video A7-1

A ***split form*** displays data in two views—Form view and Datasheet view—on a single form. The two views display data from the same source and are synchronized with each other at all times. When you select a field in one of the views, the same field displays in the other view. You can add, delete, or edit data in either view. An advantage of displaying data in a split form is the flexibility of finding a record in Datasheet view and then editing the same record in Form view.

4.1.1, 4.1.3

Activity 7.01 | Creating a Split Form Using the Split Form Tool

In this Activity you will create a split form from scratch.

ALERT!

To submit this as an autograded project, log into MyITLab and download the files for this project and begin with those files instead of a07A_MWB_Schedule. For Project 7A using Grader, begin working with the database in Step 2. For Grader to award points accurately, when saving an object, do not include your Lastname Firstname at the beginning of the object name.

1 Start Access. Navigate to the location where the student data files for this chapter are saved. Locate and **Open** the **a07A_MWB_Schedule** file. Display **Backstage** view, click **Save As** and then, under File Types, double-click **Save Database As**. In the **Save As** dialog box, navigate to the drive on which you will be saving your folders and projects for this chapter. Create a new folder named **Access Chapter 7** and **Save** the database as **Lastname_Firstname_7A_MWB_Schedule** in the folder. Enable the content or add the Access Chapter 7 folder to the Trust Center.

2 In the **Navigation Pane**, double-click **7A TV Show Advertisers** to open the table in Datasheet view. In the first record, in the **TV Show #** field, click the **arrow** to the right of *MWB001-01* to display a list of television show codes. In the first record, click in the **Advertiser** field, and then click the **arrow** to the right of *A-Z Home Products* to display a list of advertisers.

Both of these fields are lookup fields. The TV Show # field looks up data in the 7A TV Shows table. The Advertiser field looks up data in the 7A Advertiser Info table. Because these fields look up data in specific tables, you will not change the names of the existing tables and forms in this database. If you did rename the tables, the lookup fields would not be able to locate the related tables.

3 Press Esc to close the list. If the small pencil displays in the record selector box, press Esc one more time. **Close** ☒ the table.

4 In the **Navigation Pane**, double-click **7A MWB Employees** to open the table in Datasheet view. Take a moment to review the fields in the table. Scroll to the right, if necessary, until the **Attachment** field displays. In the **Attachment** field, double-click any record. In the displayed **Attachments** dialog box, click **Open** to display a photograph of the employee. **Close** ☒ the window with the picture, and then **Close** ☒ the **Attachments** dialog box. **Close** ☒ the table.

5 With the **7A MWB Employees** table selected, **Close** « the **Navigation Pane**. On the **Create tab**, in the **Forms group**, click **More Forms**, and then click **Split Form**. Compare your screen with Figure 7.2.

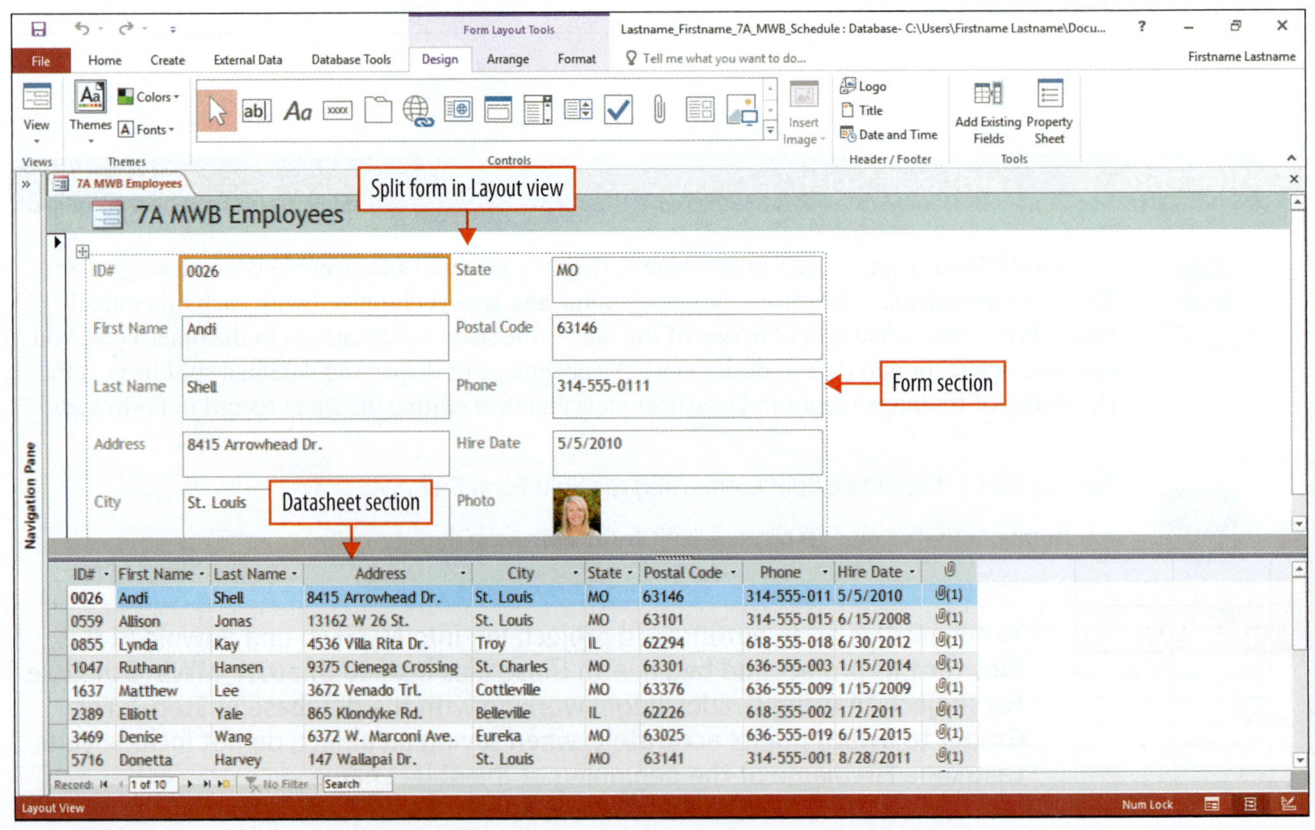

FIGURE 7.2

The underlying table or query does not need to be open to create a split form as long as it is selected before clicking the Create tab on the ribbon.

The split form displays in Layout view. The top section of the split form displays the data in Form view, and the bottom section of the split form displays the data in Datasheet view.

6 In the datasheet section of the split form, click anywhere in the first record, and then press ↓. Notice that the form section displays the data and photograph for the second record—the two sections are synchronized.

7 **Save** the split form as **Lastname Firstname 7A MWB Employees Split Form**

Activity 7.02 | Formatting a Split Form

MOS 4.2.5, 4.2.4, 4.2.2, 4.3.8, 4.3.2

In this Activity you will enhance the split form by modifying the fields and form properties.

1 In the datasheet section of the split form, click anywhere in the first record. In the form section of the split form, click the **Photo** for *Andi Shell*, and then compare your screen with Figure 7.3.

A mini toolbar displays above Andi's photograph. If the mini toolbar does not display, point to the picture. A ***mini toolbar*** is a miniature, semitransparent toolbar that is used to work with objects on the screen. In this case, the mini toolbar displays a Back button, a Forward button, and a Manage Attachments button. If there were multiple attachments for this record, clicking the Forward button would display the next attachment, and clicking the Back button would display the previous attachment. Clicking the Manage Attachments button would display the Attachments dialog box.

Recall that the Layout Selector is used to select all of the fields in the current layout. Clicking any field in a column displays the Layout Selector for the column.

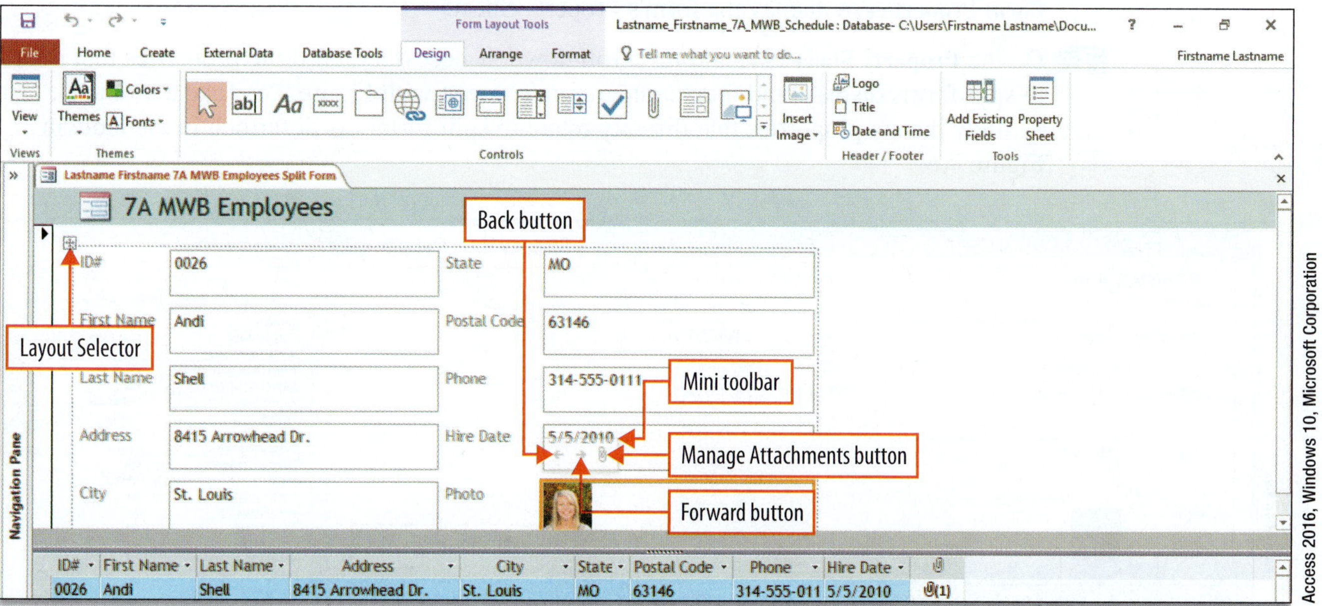

FIGURE 7.3

Access 2016, Windows 10, Microsoft Corporation

2 Select the **Photo attachment control**—the box displaying the photograph—and **Photo label control**, and then on the ribbon, under **Form Layout Tools**, click the **Arrange tab**. In the **Table group**, click **Stacked**. Notice that both controls have been removed from the stacked layout.

The Photo field is moved outside of the form arrangement, to the left margin, because it was removed from the stacked layout. A dotted placeholder displays the original position in the stacked layout.

3 Click in the **Photo attachment control**. Under **Form Layout Tools**, on the **Design tab**, in the **Tools group**, click **Property Sheet**. Verify that the Property Sheet displays *Selection type: Attachment*. On the **Property Sheet Format tab**, click in the **Picture Alignment** property setting box, and then click the **arrow** to review the options. Click **Bottom Left**, and then **Close** [X] the **Property Sheet**.

Aligning the photograph at the left edge of the attachment control makes it easier to adjust the width of the control. Recall that you must remove a field from the predefined layout to resize only that field.

4 Point to the right edge of the **Photo attachment control** until the [+|+] pointer displays. Drag to the left until the border aligns with the right edge of the photograph, and then compare your screen with Figure 7.4.

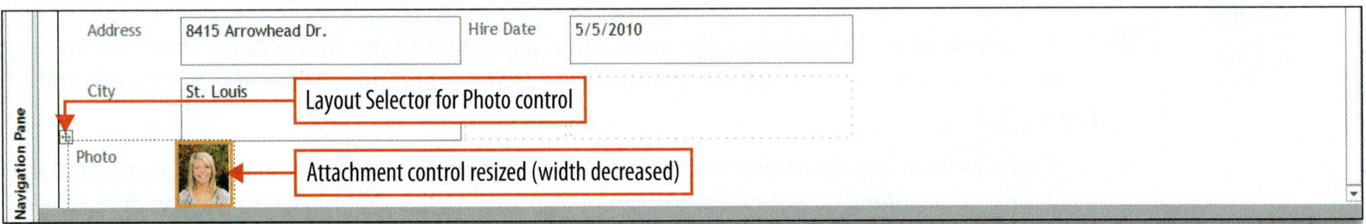

Access 2016, Windows 10, Microsoft Corporation

FIGURE 7.4

5 Press PageDown to display the second record. Scroll down, if necessary, and notice that the width of the attachment control is also decreased for this record.

6 **Save** [Save icon] the split form. With the **Photo attachment control** selected, right-click and then click **Form Properties** to display the form's Property Sheet.

7 On the **Property Sheet Format tab**, scroll down, if necessary, until the properties that relate to split forms display, and then compare your screen with Figure 7.5. Take a moment to study the six properties that directly relate to split forms, as described in the table in Figure 7.6.

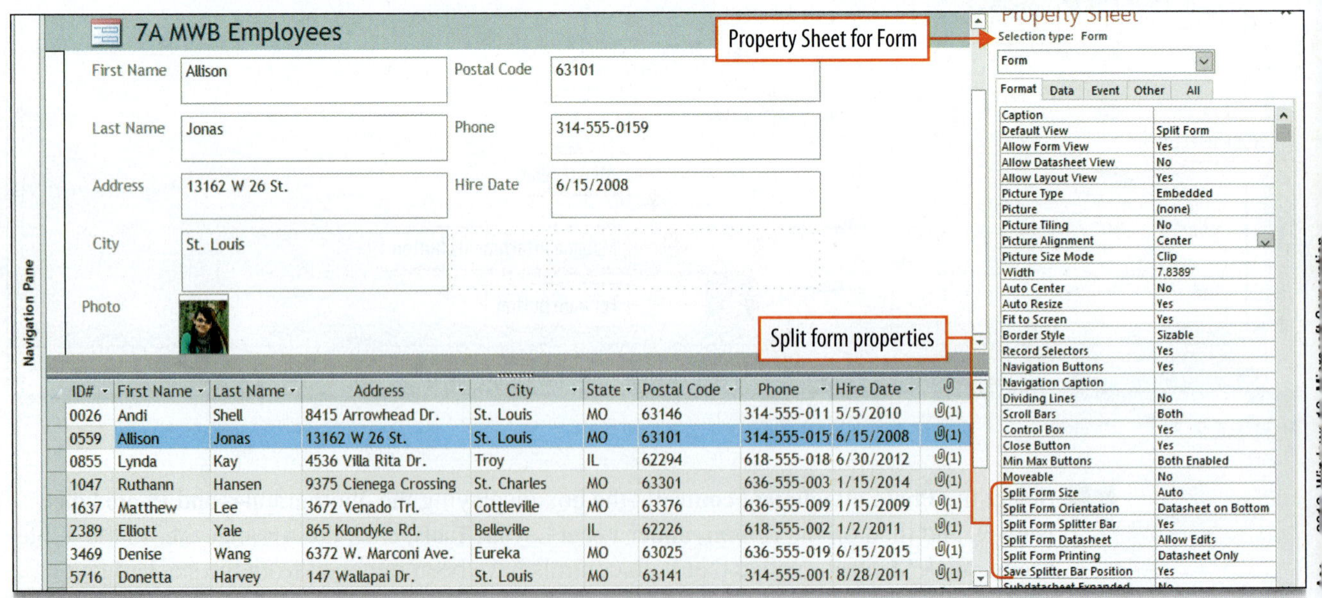

FIGURE 7.5

SPLIT FORM PROPERTIES		
PROPERTY	**DESCRIPTION**	**VIEW(S) IN WHICH THE PROPERTY CAN BE SET**
Split Form Size	Specify an exact height or width, depending on whether the form is split vertically or horizontally, for the form section of the split form. For example, type *1* to set the form height or width to 1 inch. Type *Auto* to set the size by other means, such as dragging the splitter bar in Layout view. The default is *Auto*.	Design or Layout
Split Form Orientation	Define whether the datasheet displays above, below, to the left, or to the right of the form. The default is *Datasheet on Bottom*.	Design
Split Form Splitter Bar	If set to *Yes*, the form and datasheet can be resized by moving the splitter bar that separates the two sections. If set to *No*, the splitter bar is hidden, and the form and datasheet cannot be resized. The default is *Yes*.	Design
Split Form Datasheet	If set to *Allow Edits* and the form's source can be updated, editing can be done in the datasheet section. If set to *Read Only*, editing cannot be done in the datasheet section. The default is *Allow Edits*.	Design or Layout
Split Form Printing	Define which section of the form is printed. If set to *Form Only*, only the form section is printed. If set to *Datasheet Only*, only the datasheet section is printed. The default is *Datasheet Only*.	Design or Layout
Save Splitter Bar Position	If set to *Yes*, the form opens with the splitter bar in the same position in which it was saved. If set to *No*, the form and datasheet cannot be resized, and the splitter bar is hidden. The default is *Yes*.	Design

FIGURE 7.6

8 On the **Property Sheet**, click in the property setting box for **Split Form Printing**, click the **arrow**, and then click **Form Only**. Notice that you can print either the Form or the Datasheet, but not both.

9 On the **tab row**, right-click **7A MWB Employees Split Form**, and then click **Design View**. On the **Property Sheet** for the form, click in the **Split Form Orientation** property setting box, and then click the **arrow**. Compare your screen with Figure 7.7. If necessary, increase the width of the Property Sheet to display all four of the property settings.

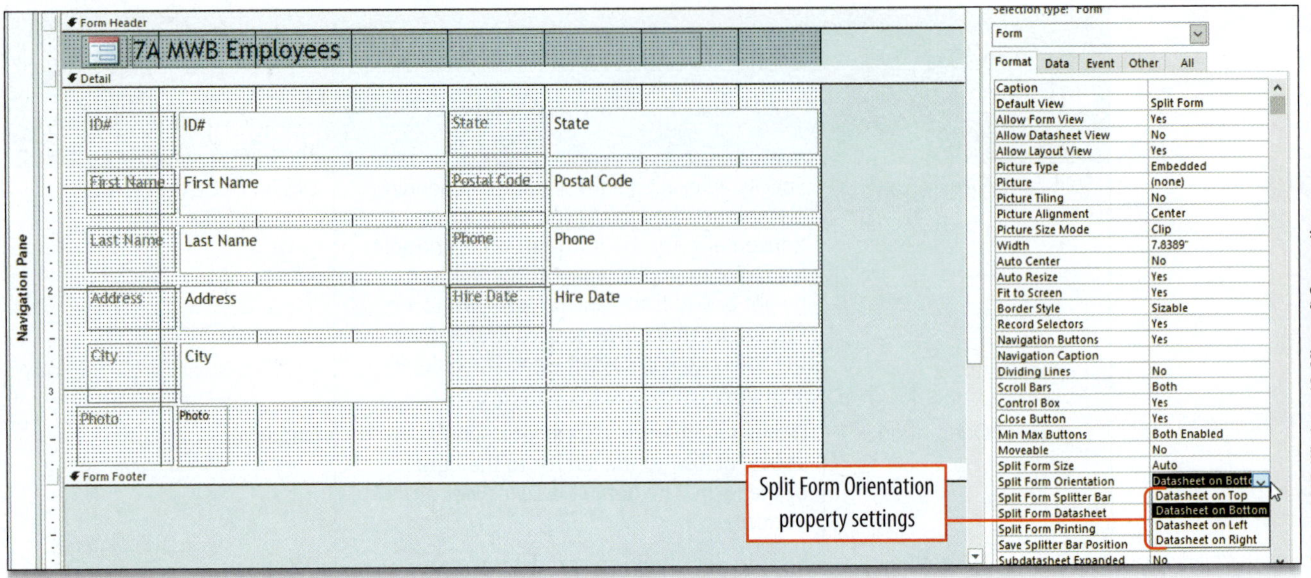

FIGURE 7.7

10 Click **Datasheet on Top**, and then **Close** ☒ the Property Sheet.

ALERT! **Does a message display, prompting you to change to Design View?**

If you try to change a property that can only be changed in Design view, Access displays a message prompting you to change to Design view. If you then try to change a property that can only be changed in Layout view, Access will display the same message. If this happens, switch to Design view and then switch back to Layout view, or change to Design view, and then change the property settings. All split form properties can be changed in Design view.

11 Switch to **Layout** view. Click the **Photo label control**, and press Delete. Click the **Photo attachment control**, and drag it to the right until the left edge aligns with the left edge of the City text box control.

Some editing in the form can be done in Layout view. The datasheet section displays above the form section of the split form. A splitter bar divides the two sections.

12 Point to the splitter bar until the ‡ pointer displays. Drag upward until the dark horizontal line displays between the records with an **ID#** of **0855** and **1047**.

In the datasheet section, Records 1 through 3 display, and the height of the form section is increased.

13 Switch to **Design** view. Under **Form Design Tools**, on the **Design tab**, in the **Header/Footer group**, click **Logo**. Navigate to the location where the student data files are saved, and then double-click **a07A_MWB_Logo**. In the **Tools group**, click **Property Sheet** to display the Property Sheet for the logo. Click in the **Size Mode** setting box—*Clip* is displayed. Click the arrow, and then click **Zoom**. **Close** ☒ the **Property Sheet**.

When the logo is inserted in a form or report that includes a logo placeholder, the Size Mode property is set to *Clip*, and the image may be too large to display in the control. By setting the property to *Zoom*, the image is resized to fit the control while maintaining the proportions of the object.

14 Increase the width of the **logo control** to the **1.5-inch mark on the horizontal ruler**. Click in the title's **label control**, and then click at the beginning of the line. Using your own first and last names, type **Lastname Firstname** and press Spacebar to add your name before the title of the form and press Enter to accept the changes. Switch to **Form** view, and then compare your screen with Figure 7.8.

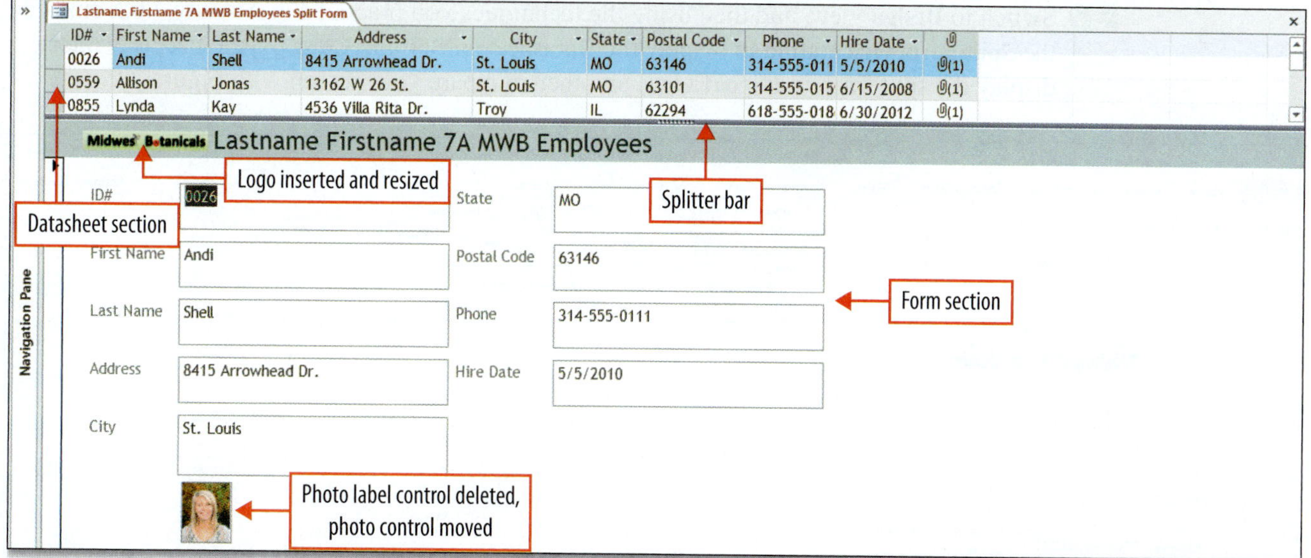

FIGURE 7.8

Access 2016, Windows 10, Microsoft Corporation

15 **Save** the form. Press PageDown to display **Record 6**. In the form section, change the **First Name** from *Elliott* to **Phillip** and then press Tab. Notice that in the datasheet section, the same record—*ID#* 2389—is selected and is in the editing mode. Also notice that the **First Name** field has been updated in the datasheet section.

Recall that you can only make changes to the data in the fields with the form displayed in Form view.

16 In the form section, on the left side, click the **Record Selector** bar. If you are instructed to submit this result, create a paper printout or PDF electronic image of the selected record. **Close** the form. **Open** the **Navigation Pane**.

The form section prints because you set the Split Form Printing property to Form Only.

More Knowledge **Adding or Deleting a Field**

To add a field to a split form in Layout view, display the Field List—on the Design tab, in the Tools group, click Add Existing Fields. Drag the field from the Field List to the datasheet section or the form section. The field will be added to both sections of the split form.

To delete a field from a split form, you must delete it from the form section. The field will then be removed automatically from the datasheet section.

Activity 7.03 | Converting an Existing Form into a Split Form

4.2.5, 4.2.6, 4.3.2, 1.5.2

In this Activity you will convert the 7A TV Shows Form into a split form.

1 In the **Navigation Pane**, under **Forms**, right-click **7A TV Shows Form**, and then click **Design View**. **Close** the **Navigation Pane**. Under **Form Design Tools**, on the **Design tab**, in the **Tools** group, click **Property Sheet** to display the Property Sheet for the form. If the Property Sheet does not display *Selection type: Form*, click the Selection type arrow, and then click Form.

To convert an existing form to a split form, the form must be open in Design view.

2 On the **Property Sheet Format tab**, click in the **Default View** property setting box—*Single Form* is displayed. Click the **arrow**, and then click **Split Form**. **Close** the **Property Sheet**, and then switch to **Layout** view.

The split form displays with the datasheet section on top; Access applied the same Split Form Orientation to this split form as the previous split form.

3 Switch to **Design** view, and then using the techniques you practiced in Activity 7.02, change the **Split Form Orientation** to display the **Datasheet on Bottom**. **Close** [X] the **Property Sheet**, display the split form in **Layout** view, and then compare your screen with Figure 7.9.

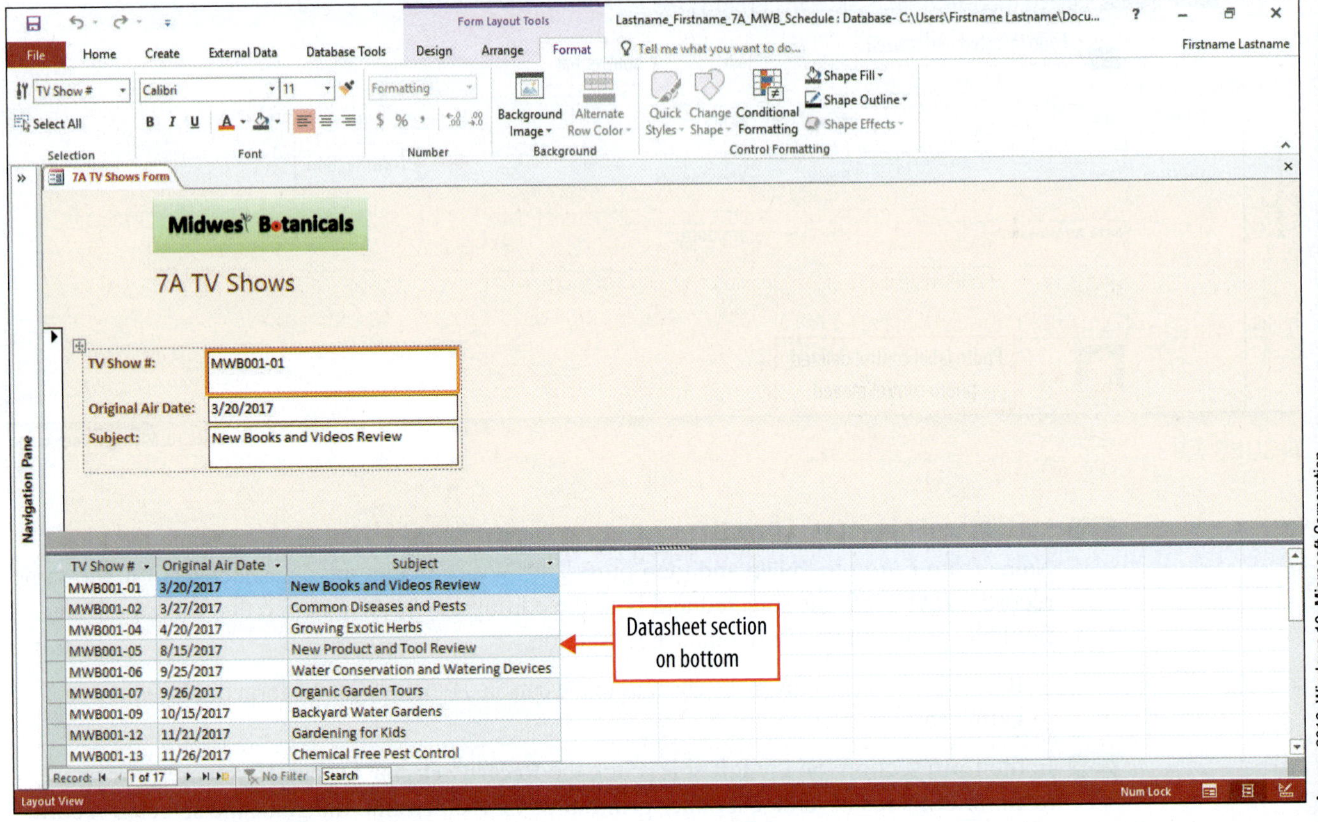

FIGURE 7.9

4 In the form section, click the **title's label control**, and then click at the beginning of the line. Using your own first and last names, type **Lastname Firstname** and then press Spacebar.

5 Switch to **Design** view. Hold down Shift, click the **title's label control**, and then click the **label control** for **TV Show #**. Under **Form Design Tools**, click the **Arrange tab**. In the **Sizing & Ordering group**, click **Align**, and then click **Left**.

The left edge of the title's label control is aligned with the left edge of the TV Show # label control.

6 Click in an empty area of the design grid to deselect the controls, and then click the **title's label control**. Point to the right edge of the **title's label control** until the [↔] pointer displays. Drag to the right until the right edge of the label control aligns with the right edges of the text box controls in the Detail section. If your entire name does not display within the title's label control, click the **Home tab**, and in the **Text Formatting group**, reduce the font size of the text.

Even though the entire title displays in Layout view and in Form view, if the title is truncated in Design view, it will be truncated when you print the form.

7 **Save** [save icon] and **Close** [X] the form. **Open** [»] the **Navigation Pane**. Under **Forms**, right-click **7A TV Shows Form**, and then click **Rename**. Type **Lastname Firstname 7A TV Shows Split Form** and then press Enter.

Recall that an object must be closed before you can rename it.

8 Double-click **7A TV Shows Split Form** to open it in Form view. Be sure that **Record 1** is displayed. In the form section, on the left side, click the **Record Selector** bar. If you are instructed to submit this result, create a paper printout or PDF electronic image of the selected record.

9 **Close** ☒ the form, and then **Close** « the **Navigation Pane**.

7 ACCESS

Objective 2 Create a Form and a Subform

GO! Learn How Video A7-2

In the previous Activities, you created a split form that displayed the datasheet of the underlying table—the data in the form section was the same data as that displayed in the datasheet section. A ***subform*** is a form that is embedded within another form—the ***main form***—and is used to view, enter, and edit data that is related to data in the main form. A subform is similar to a subdatasheet—the data in the related table is displayed without having to open another table or form.

Activity 7.04 | Creating a Form and a Subform Using the Form Tool

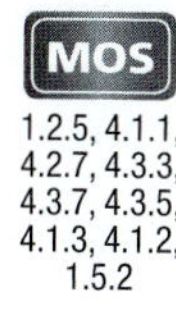
1.2.5, 4.1.1, 4.2.7, 4.3.3, 4.3.7, 4.3.5, 4.1.3, 4.1.2, 1.5.2

If Access finds a single table that has a one-to-many relationship with the table used to create a form, Access adds the datasheet as a subform to display the related records. In this Activity you will create the main form using the 7A TV Shows table. Because a one-to-many relationship has been created between this table and the 7A TV Show Advertisers table, the datasheet for the 7A TV Show Advertisers table will be inserted as a subform.

1 Click the **Database Tools tab**, and then in the **Relationships group**, click **Relationships**. If the tables do not display in the Relationships window, under **Relationship Tools**, on the **Design tab**, in the **Relationships group**, click **All Relationships**. If necessary, expand the table boxes and rearrange them so that it is easier to view the relationships as shown in Figure 7.10. Take a moment to study the established relationships.

This is an example of a ***many-to-many relationship*** between the *7A TV Shows* table and the *7A Advertiser Info* table. *Many* television shows can have *many* advertisers. Conversely, *many* advertisers can advertise on *many* television shows.

To create the *many-to-many relationship* between *7A TV Shows* and *7A Advertiser Info*, the *7A TV Show Advertisers* table was created. This table is known as a ***junction table***. It breaks down the many-to-many relationship into two *one-to-many relationships*. The data from the primary key fields—*TV Show #* and *Advertiser*—from the two tables are added to the junction table, which records each instance of the relationship. The primary key fields from the two tables are connected to the foreign key fields in the junction table.

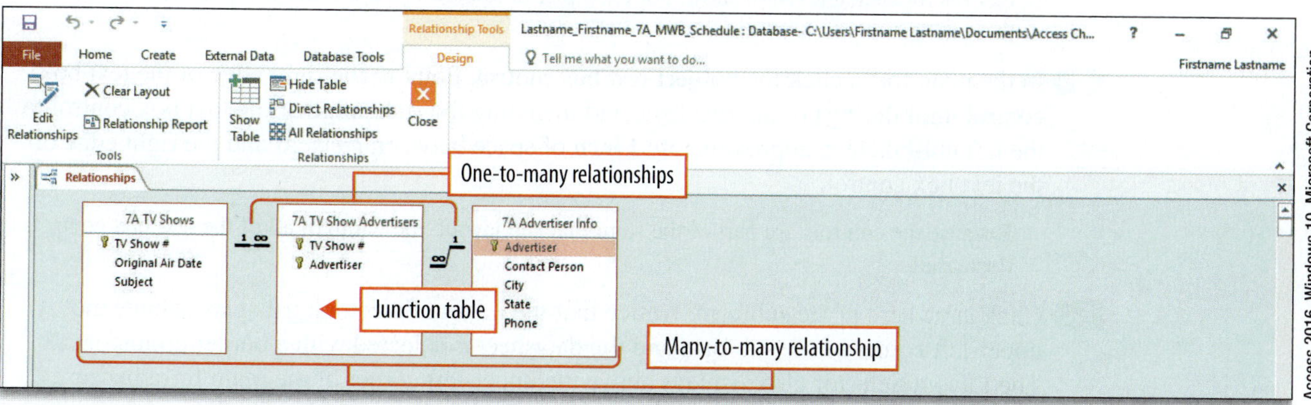

Access 2016, Windows 10, Microsoft Corporation

FIGURE 7.10

> **NOTE** Specifying Multiple Primary Key Fields
>
> A junction table contains data from the primary key fields in two tables. The fields in the junction table are designated as primary key fields. In Design view, to specify multiple fields as primary key fields, hold down the Ctrl key, and then click the row selector boxes for each primary key field. Under Table Tools, on the Design tab, in the Tools group, click Primary Key. A junction table can include fields other than the common fields from the two related tables.

2 **Close** the Relationships window, saving changes if prompted. **Open** the **Navigation Pane**. Under **Tables**, click **7A TV Shows**. On the **Create tab**, in the **Forms group**, click **Form**. **Close** the **Navigation Pane**, and then compare your screen with Figure 7.11.

The data in the *7A TV Shows* table displays in the main form and the subform displays the Advertiser information from the related table, *7A TV Show Advertisers*.

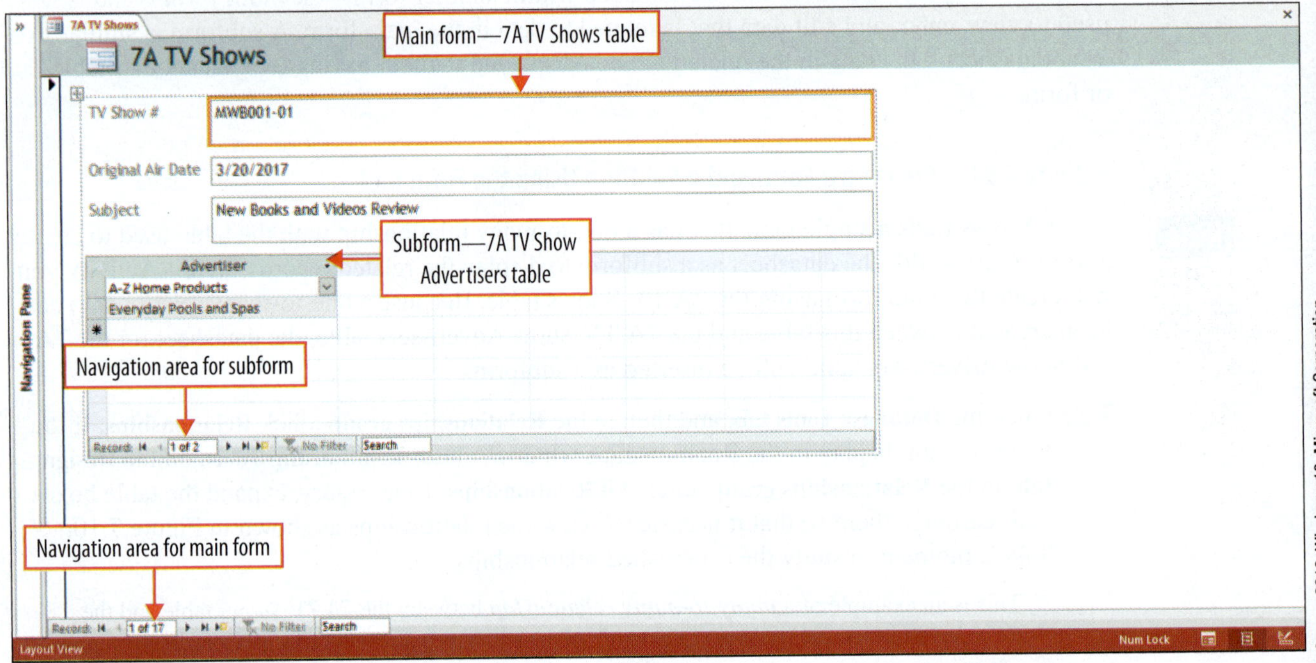

FIGURE 7.11

3 In the main form, click the **TV Show # text box control**, if necessary, and then press PageDown until Record **5** is displayed, observing changes in the subform and in the two record navigators.

As you scroll through the records in the *7A TV Shows* table, the subform displays the related records for each television show. For example, in Record 5, the TV Show # is *MWB001-06*, and three advertisers support this show.

4 In the main form, click the **Subject text box control**. Point to the right edge of the text box control until the ↔ pointer displays, and then drag the right edge of the text box control to the left until there is approximately **1 inch** of space between *Devices* and the right edge of the text box control.

Because the controls are part of the same stacked layout, the width of all of the text box controls is decreased.

5 Click anywhere in the subform. Notice that the Layout Selector displays above the upper-left corner of the subform and the datasheet is selected with a border around it. The Layout Selector also displays above the upper-left corner of the main form because the forms are stacked. Switch to **Design** view. Click in the Table.7A TV Show Advertisers subform placeholder. Under **Form Design Tools**, click the **Arrange tab**. In the **Table group**, click **Remove Layout** to remove the subform from the stacked layout.

6 Switch to **Layout** view. Click the subform, and then compare your screen with Figure 7.12.

Notice that the Layout Selector only displays above the upper-left corner of the form because the forms are no longer stacked.

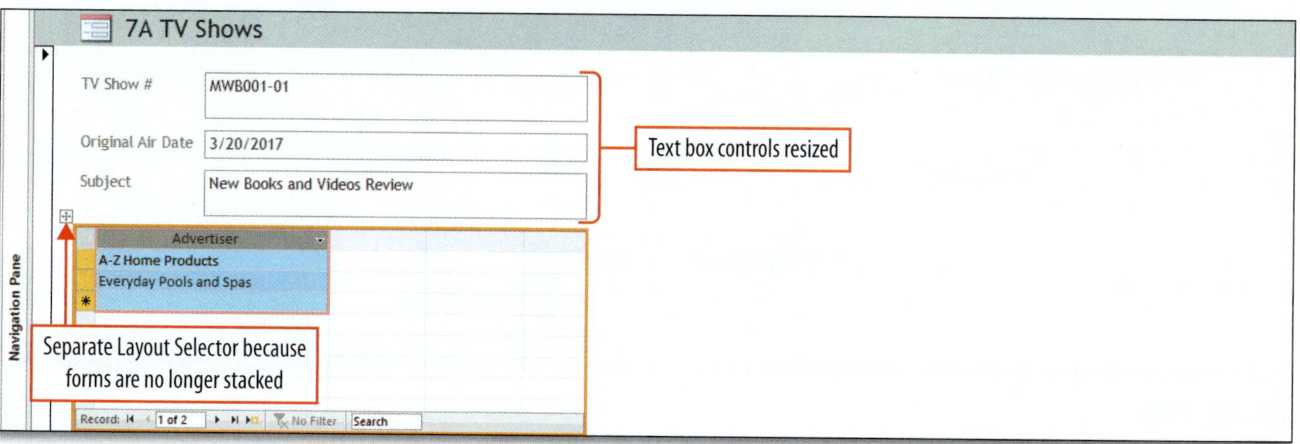

FIGURE 7.12 Access 2016, Windows 10, Microsoft Corporation

More Knowledge Sort Records in a Form

In a form or subform, records are sorted by the primary key field. To modify the sort order, click the text box control for the field to be sorted. On the Home tab, in the Sort & Filter group, click Ascending or Descending (depending on the sort you want to perform). To remove the sort, on the Home tab, in the Sort & Filter group, click Remove Sort.

7 With the subform selected, point to the right edge of the subform until the pointer displays, and then drag the right edge of the subform to the left until it aligns with the right edge of the **Advertiser** control box. Point to the subform **Layout Selector** until the pointer displays, and then drag to the right until the subform is centered under the controls in the main form. **Save** the form as **Lastname Firstname 7A TV Shows and Advertisers**

Be sure to leave some space between the main form and the subform so it is not returned to the Stacked Layout. If it returns to that layout, click Undo, and move the subform again.

8 Switch to **Design** view. Under **Form Design Tools**, on the **Design tab**, in the **Header/Footer group**, click **Logo**. Navigate to the location where the student data files for this chapter are saved. Locate and double-click **a07A_MWB_Logo** to insert the logo in the form header. In the **Tools group**, click **Property Sheet** to display the Property Sheet for the logo. Click in the **Size Mode** property box, click the arrow, and then click **Zoom**. **Close** the **Property Sheet**. Point to the center right edge of the control until the pointer displays; drag to the right until it is between the *S* and *h* in *Shows*, and then compare your screen to Figure 7.13.

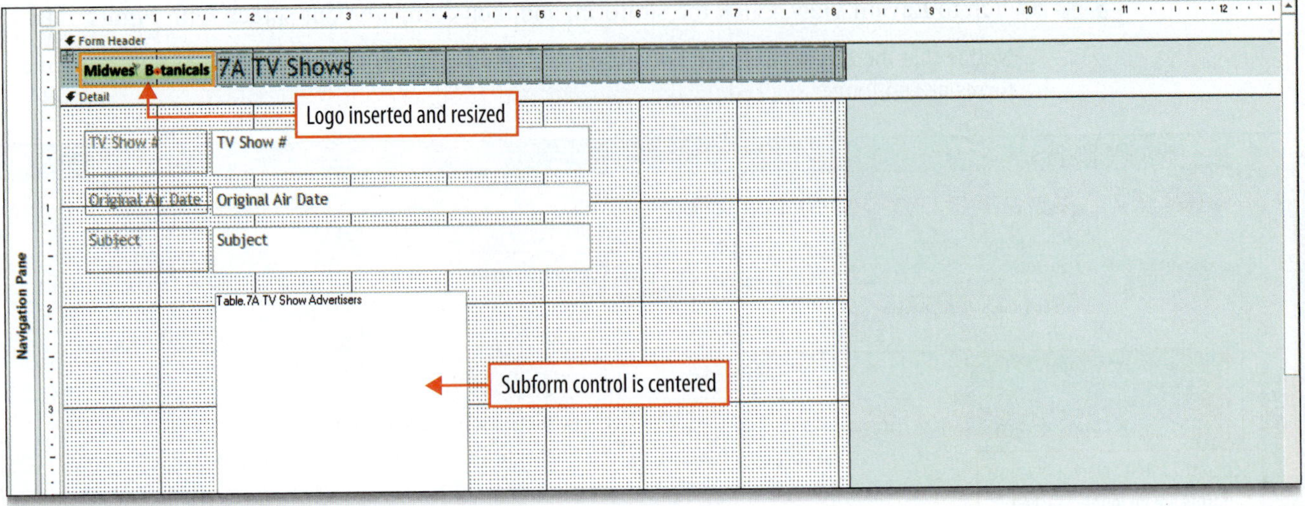

FIGURE 7.13

9 Click at the beginning of the title label control, and type **Lastname Firstname** and then press Spacebar once. To the right of *Shows*, press Spacebar one time, hold down Shift, and then press Enter. Type **and Advertiser Subform** Press Enter.

Pressing Shift + Enter creates a line break so the title displays on two lines in the label control.

10 Point to the right edge of the **title's label control** until the pointer displays—the right edge may display at the very right side of your screen. Drag to the left until the right edge aligns with the **5.75-inch mark on the horizontal ruler**. With the **title's label control** selected, under **Form Design Tools**, click the **Format tab**. In the **Font group**, click **Center**.

11 Resize the width of the form to **7 inches**. Compare your screen with Figure 7.14. Notice that the subform control displays the related table's name—*Table.7A TV Show Advertisers*. Also, notice that the title's label control may not display the entire title. Be sure it is visible before moving on.

Although you can make most adjustments to a form in Layout view, you should adjust the title's control in Design view to ensure the form's title will print as desired. With narrow margins for a form and with Portrait orientation, the right edge of the form should not exceed 7.5 inches on the horizontal ruler; otherwise, pages will print with only the background color in the form header.

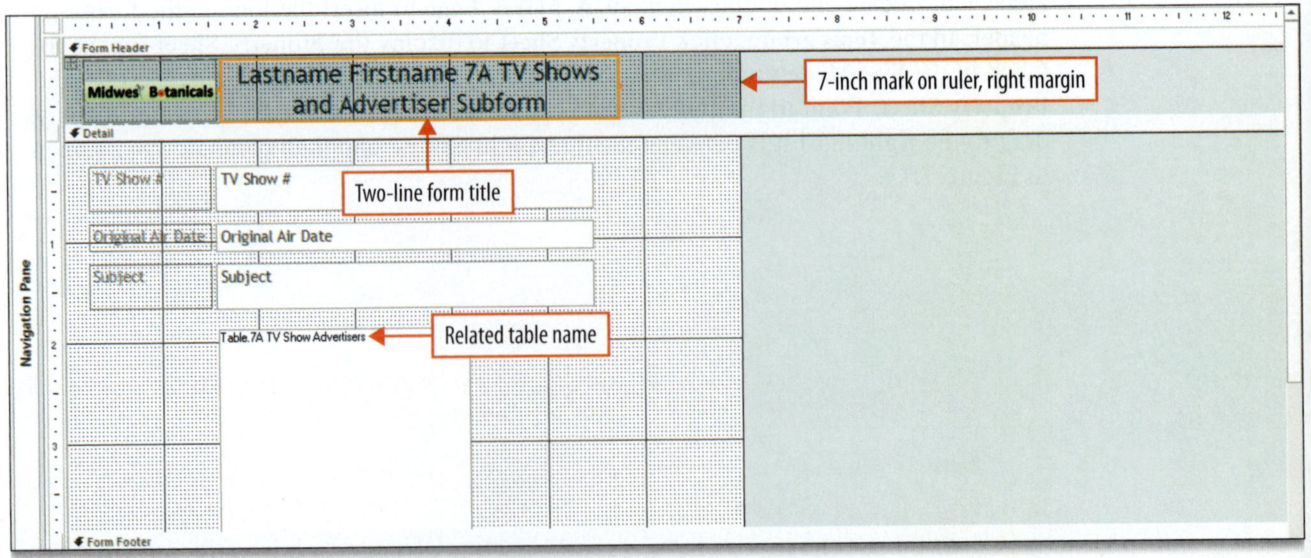

FIGURE 7.14

12 **Save** the form, and then switch to **Form** view. On the left side of the form, click the **Record Selector** bar, and then if you are instructed to submit this result, create a paper printout or PDF electronic image of only Record 1—the selected record. Notice that both the main form and the subform print. **Close** the form.

More Knowledge **Create a Form with Application Parts**

Create a form using application parts by clicking the Create tab. In the Templates group, click the Application Parts arrow, and then click the template you want to use for the form. Once you assign the Record Source to the form, you can add fields to the form.

Activity 7.05 | Creating a Form and a Subform Using the Form Wizard

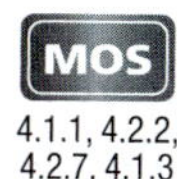

4.1.1, 4.2.2, 4.2.7, 4.1.3

Use the Form Wizard to create a form and a subform when you want to have more control over the design of the subform or if the underlying table or query has more than one relationship established. If the underlying table or query that is on the *one* side of the relationship is related to more than one table or query on the *many* side of the relationship, the subform will not automatically be created when the form is created. The same technique can be used to create a split form between two tables that have a many-to-many relationship.

1 On the **Create tab**, in the **Forms group**, click **Form Wizard**. In the **Form Wizard** dialog box, if necessary, click the **Tables/Queries arrow**, and then click **Table: 7A TV Shows**, which is on the *one* side of the relationship with **7A Advertiser Info** using the junction table.

It does not matter which table you select first; in a later dialog box, you can select the table that displays in the main form and the table that displays in the subform.

2 Under **Available Fields**, click **All Fields** >> to add all of the fields to the **Selected Fields** box. In the same dialog box, click the **Tables/Queries arrow**, and from the displayed list, click **Table: 7A Advertiser Info**, which is on the *many* side of the relationship with the **7A TV Shows** table. Again, add **All Fields** to the **Selected Fields** box. Click **Next**, and then compare your screen with Figure 7.15.

The second Form Wizard dialog box displays with a preview of how the data will be arranged. The order in which you select the tables or queries to be included in the main form and subform does not matter because you can change the way the data is displayed in this Form Wizard dialog box. If a relationship between the tables has not been established, this Form Wizard dialog box will not display.

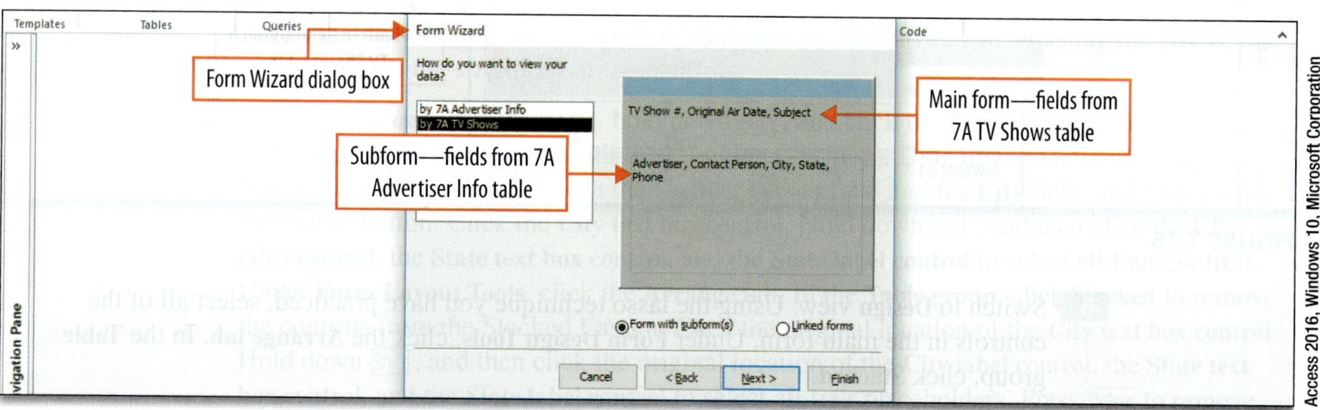

FIGURE 7.15

3 Under **How do you want to view your data?**, click **by 7A Advertiser Info**, and notice that the form will display with the *7A Advertiser Info* table as the main form and the *7A TV Shows* table as the subform. Under the preview of the form, click **Linked forms**, and notice the preview displays two separate forms with a button on the main form that represents the link between the two forms.

space between the **Contact Person text box control** and the **City label control**. Click in a blank area of the form to deselect the controls. Click the **City label control**, and then point to the right edge of the **City label control** until the [pointer] pointer displays. Drag the right edge of the **City label control** to the left until there is approximately **0.5 inches** of space between the word *City* and the right edge of the **City label control**. Using the same technique, resize the **City text box control**. **Save** [Save] the form. Compare your screen with Figure 7.18.

After removing the fields from the stacked layout, they are grouped as a separate layout for ease in making adjustments to the controls. The widths of the City and State label controls are decreased so that the text box controls will not exceed the allowable width when printed.

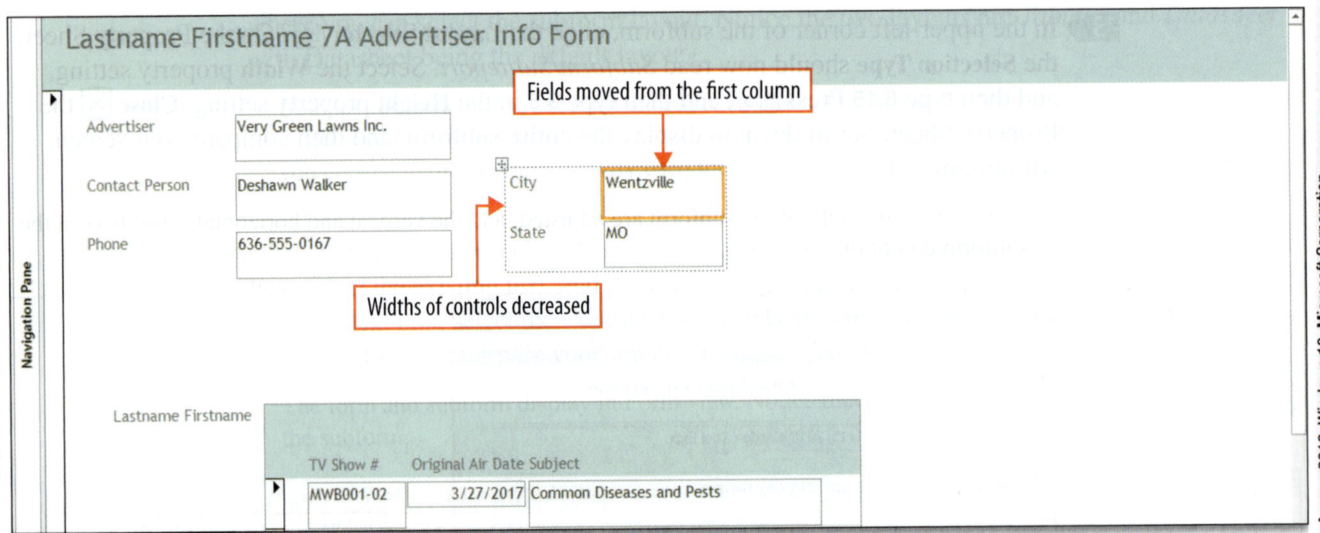

FIGURE 7.18

7 Using the techniques you have practiced, remove the **Advertiser text box control** and the **Advertiser label control** from the stacked layout, and then delete the placeholders from the stacked layout. Move the left column down so the **Contact Person** field aligns with the **City** field. Click the **Advertiser label control**. Hold down Shift, and then click the **Advertiser text box control** to select both controls. Point to one of the selected controls until the [pointer] pointer displays. Drag upward and to the right until the controls are approximately centered above the controls on the left and the controls on the right.

The Advertiser field is contained in its own stacked layout.

8 Click the **subform label control**—*Lastname Firstname 7A TV Shows*—and press Delete to remove the label from the subform control. Click the **subform** to display the **Layout Selector** for the subform. Point to the **Layout Selector** until the [pointer] pointer displays. Drag the subform upward until there is approximately **0.5 inches** of space between the **Phone** field and the subform, and the right edge of the subform aligns with the right edge of the **State text box control**. Compare your screen with Figure 7.19.

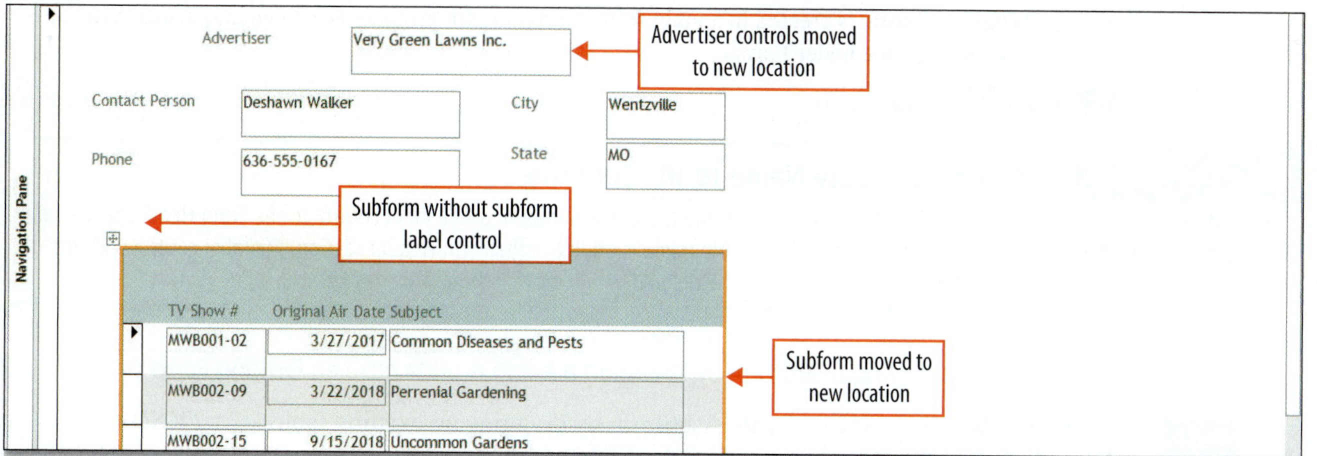

FIGURE 7.19

Access 2016, Windows 10, Microsoft Corporation

9 **Save** the form, and switch to **Design** view. Using the techniques you have practiced, in the main form, add a **Logo** to the **Form Header** section using **a07A_MWB_Logo**, and then **Delete** the accompanying label control. Move the **form title's label control** so the left edge aligns with the **2-inch mark on the horizontal ruler**, and place *7A Advertiser Info Form* on the second line of the title. Resize the **title label control** by aligning the right edge of the form title's label control with the right edge of the subform. **Center** the text in the form title's label control. Adjust the size of the logo so there is one dot between it and the title label control and it is the same height as the title. Resize the form width to **7.25 inches** so no extraneous pages print when the form is printed. Compare your screen with Figure 7.20.

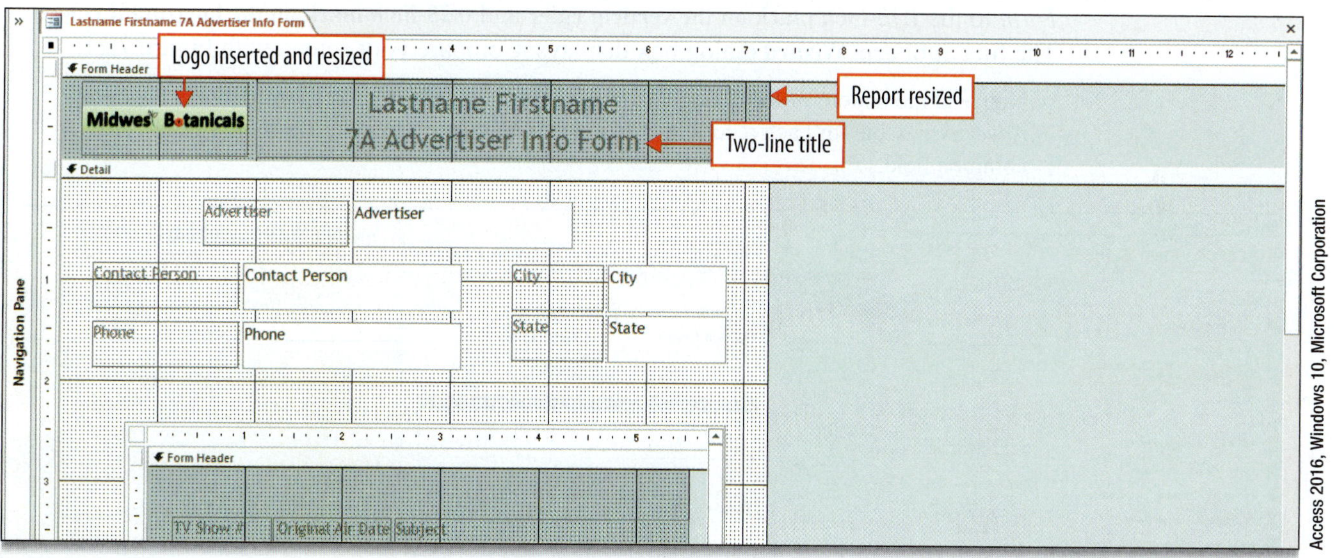

FIGURE 7.20

Access 2016, Windows 10, Microsoft Corporation

10 Switch to **Form** view. Press PageDown until the record for **A-Z Home Products**—*Record 4*— displays. If you are instructed to submit this result, create a paper printout or PDF electronic image of only this record.

11 **Close** the form, saving changes. **Open** the **Navigation Pane**. Under **Forms**, **7A Advertiser Info Form** and **7A TV Shows Subform** display. Double-click **7A Advertiser Info Form** to open it in Form view. The subform is embedded in the form. Double-click **7A TV Shows Subform** to open it in Form view. This form displays the fields from the *7A TV Shows* table that are used in the subform of *7A Advertiser Info Form*.

When a subform is created in a main form, a separate form object is created and displays in the Navigation Pane under Forms.

12 **Close** [X] all forms.

More Knowledge **Adding the Table Name to the Subform**

To add the name of the table used to create the subform at the top of the subform, add a label control to the Form Header section of the subform, and then type the name of the table. If the table name is added to the Form Header section, the label control with the table name that displays to the left of the subform should be deleted.

Activity 7.07 | Creating a Subform by Dragging a Related Table onto an Existing Form

4.2.7, 1.3.5, 4.2.4, 4.2.6, 1.5.2

In this Activity you will create a subform by dragging an existing table—*7A TV Show Advertisers*—on the *many* side of the relationship onto an existing form—*7A TV Shows Main Form*—on the *one* side of the relationship. When a table has more than one relationship with other tables, this method is helpful in adding a subform to a form.

1 In the **Navigation Pane**, under **Forms**, open **7A TV Shows Main Form** in **Design** view. Under **Form Design Tools**, on the **Design tab**, in the **Controls group**, click **More** and verify that the **Use Control Wizards** option is active.

The existing form must be open in Design view before you drag a related table onto it. If you try to drag a related table onto a form in Layout view, an error message displays.

2 In the form, point to the top of the **Form Footer section bar** until the [+] pointer displays. Drag downward until the Detail section is **3 inches** high.

3 In the **Navigation Pane**, under **Tables**, drag **7A TV Show Advertisers** onto *7A TV Shows Main Form* to the **1.75-inch mark on the vertical ruler** and **0.25-inch mark on the horizontal ruler**. The first **SubForm Wizard** dialog box displays. Compare your screen with Figure 7.21.

Notice at the bottom of the dialog box that Access will display records from the *7A TV Show Advertisers* table for each record in the *7A TV Shows* table using the *TV Show #* field—the common field.

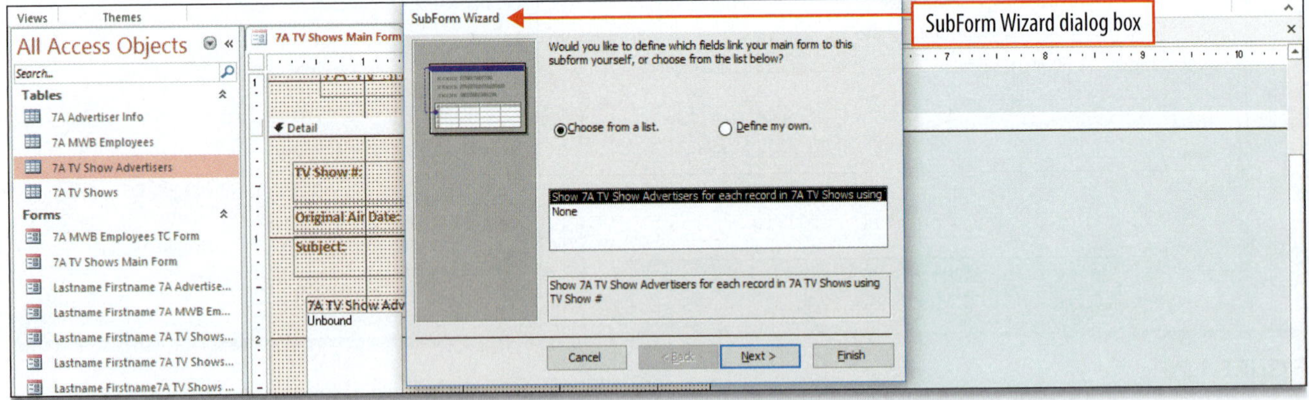

FIGURE 7.21

4 In the **SubForm Wizard** dialog box, click **Define my own**.

The SubForm Wizard dialog box changes to display list boxes in which you can select the fields that link the main form to the subform.

5 Under **Form/report fields**, in the **first list box**, click the **arrow**, and then click **TV Show #**. Under **Subform/subreport fields**, in the **first list box**, click the **arrow**, and then click **TV Show #**. Compare your screen with Figure 7.22.

The same field is used to link the form and the subform as when *Choose from a list* was selected. By default, Access uses the fields that are used to create the join line in the relationship between the tables. You should select *Define my own* when you want to use fields other than the common fields as defined in the relationship.

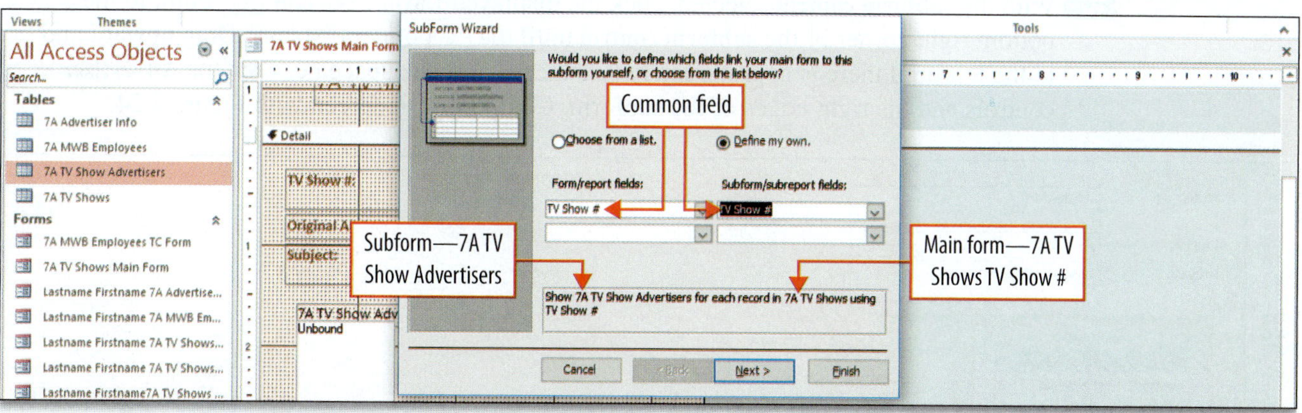

FIGURE 7.22

Access 2016, Windows 10, Microsoft Corporation

6 Click **Next**. Under **What name would you like for your subform or subreport?**, type **Lastname Firstname 7A TV Show Advertisers Subform** and then click **Finish**. Compare your screen with Figure 7.23.

The subform displays under the label and text box controls of the main form, and a subform label control displays above the subform.

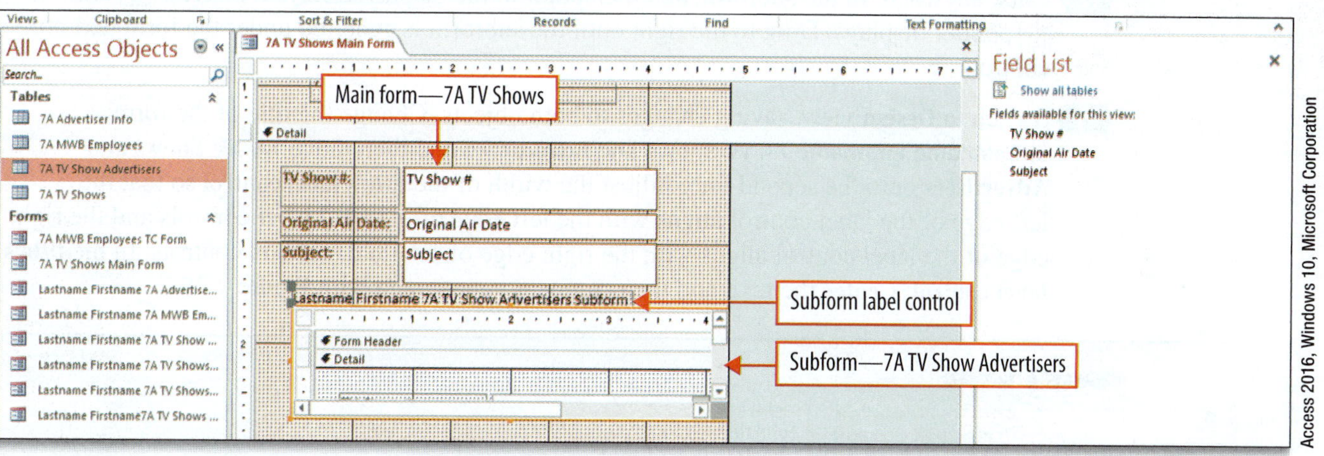

FIGURE 7.23

Access 2016, Windows 10, Microsoft Corporation

7 With the subform control selected, point to the **bottom-middle sizing handle** of the subform control until the [↕] pointer displays. If the subform is not selected, point to the bottom edge of the subform control, and then click to display the sizing handles. Drag downward about **0.5 inches**. If necessary, point to the top of the **Form Footer section bar** until the [+] pointer displays, and then drag upward to the bottom of the subform control. **Close** [X] the **Field List**, if necessary. **Save** [Save] the form, and then **Close** [«] the **Navigation Pane**.

8 Switch to **Layout** view. If necessary, resize controls so both fields are visible in the subform. Press PageDown to display the record for each television show and the related record(s) in the subform. Notice that the **TV Show #** field displays in both the main form and the subform.

9 In the record navigator for the main form, click **First Record** [|◄]. Switch to **Design** view. In the subform control, click the **TV Show # label control**, hold down Shift, and click the **TV Show # text box control**. Press Delete, and then switch to **Layout** view. Press PageDown until the record for **MWB001-09**—*Record 7*—displays. Double-click the right edge of the **Advertiser label control** to resize for the longest item in the list.

The *TV Show #* field is removed from the subform.

10 With the **subform control** selected, click the displayed **Layout Selector** ⊞. Point to the bottom right corner of the **subform control** until the ⤡ pointer displays. Drag upward and to the left until there is approximately **0.25 inches** of blank space between the **Advertiser** controls and the right edges of the subform. Compare your screen with Figure 7.24.

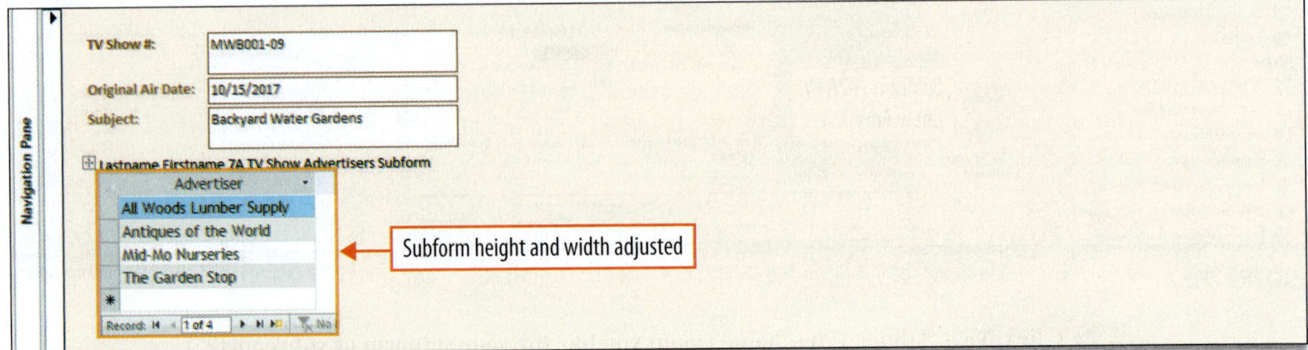

FIGURE 7.24

11 Click the **subform label control**, which displays *Lastname Firstname 7A Show Advertisers Subform*, and then press Delete to remove the label control from the subform.

12 Click anywhere in the subform, and then point to the displayed **Layout Selector** ⊞ until the ✥ pointer displays. Drag to the right until the subform is centered under the form text box controls.

13 Switch to **Design** view, saving changes to both objects. Change the title of the form to **Lastname Firstname 7A TV Shows and Advertisers** and then move **7A TV Shows and Advertisers** onto the second line. Adjust the width of the **title's label control** so that the left edge of the label control aligns with the left edge of the field label controls and the right edge of the label control aligns with the right edge of the field text box controls. In the **title's label control**, **Center** the text, and then compare your screen with Figure 7.25.

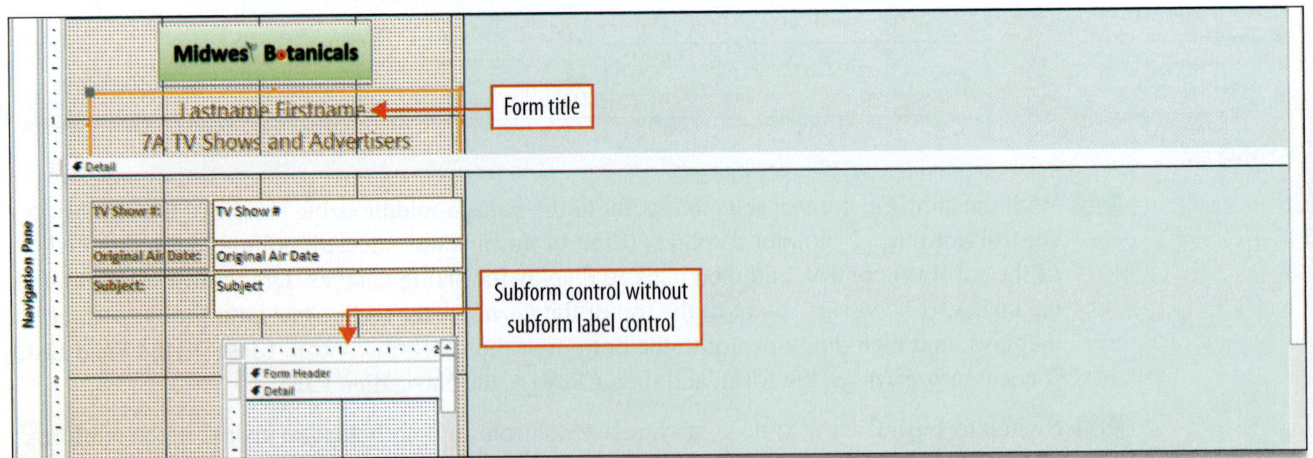

FIGURE 7.25

14 **Save** the form, and in the **Microsoft Access** dialog box, click **Yes**. Switch to **Form** view. If you are instructed to submit this result, create a paper printout or PDF electronic image of only the last record.

15 **Close** the form and **Open** the **Navigation Pane**. Under **Forms**, **Rename** *7A TV Shows Main Form* as **Lastname Firstname 7A TV Shows Main Form and Advertisers Subform**

> ***More Knowledge*** **Creating a Form with Two Subforms or Nested Subforms**
>
> A form can contain more than one subform. The main form should have a one-to-many relationship with the first subform. The first subform should have a one-to-many relationship with the second subform. The main form would contain both subform controls. To create a form with two subforms, use the Form Wizard, selecting each table from the Tables/Queries list and each table's fields.
>
> A form can also contain ***nested subforms***. The main form should have a one-to-many relationship with the first subform. The first subform should have a one-to-many relationship with the second subform. Instead of the main form containing both subform controls, the first subform would contain the second subform control. You can have a maximum of seven levels of subforms.

Objective 3 Create a Multi-Page Form

GO! Learn How
Video A7-3

A ***multi-page form*** displays the data from the underlying table or query on more than one page. Creating a multi-page form enables you to divide a long form into sections that display on separate pages or to display subforms on different tabs within the main form. A multi-page form enables the user to display only the data that needs to be accessed and displays the form in a more organized format.

Activity 7.08 | Creating a Multi-Page Form Using the Tab Control

4.1.1, 4.2.2, 4.2.5, 4.2.3, 1.3.5, 4.1.3

In this Activity you will modify a form to create a multi-page form using the tab control. A ***tab control*** is used to display data on the main form on different tabs, similar to the way database objects, such as forms and tables, display on different tabs.

1 In the **Navigation Pane**, under **Forms**, open **7A MWB Employees TC Form** in Design view, and then **Close** the **Navigation Pane**. Point to the top of the **Form Footer section bar** until the pointer displays. Drag downward to the **2.25-inch mark on the vertical ruler** to increase the height of the Detail section.

2 Under **Form Design Tools**, on the **Design tab**, in the **Controls group**, click **Tab Control**. Move the pointer into the **Detail** section until the plus (+) sign of the pointer is aligned approximately with the **0.25-inch mark on the horizontal ruler** and with the **0.25-inch mark on the vertical ruler**. Click one time, and then compare your screen with Figure 7.26.

A tab control is inserted into the Detail section of the form. There are two tabs on the tab control. Each tab represents a separate page on the form. Do not be concerned if the page numbers on your tabs differ from those displayed in Figure 7.26.

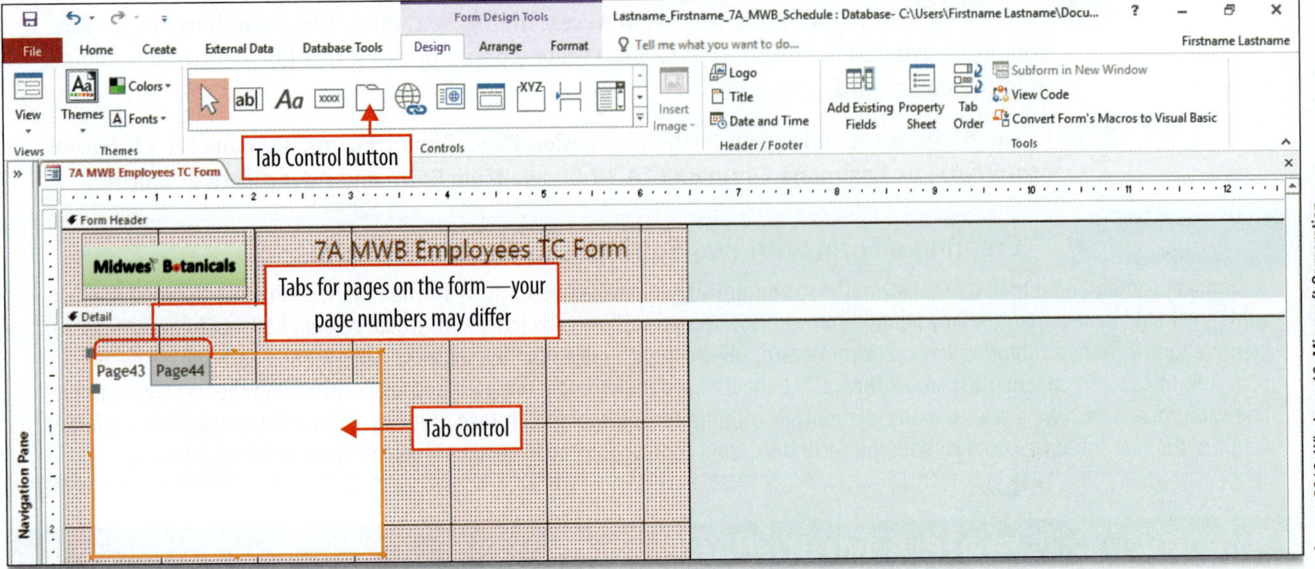

FIGURE 7.26

3 In the selected **tab control**, point to the **right-middle sizing handle** until the ↔ pointer displays. Drag to the right until the right edge of the tab control aligns with the **6-inch mark on the horizontal ruler**.

4 Under **Form Design Tools**, on the **Design tab**, in the **Tools group**, click **Add Existing Fields**.

The Field List for the *7A MWB Employees* table displays.

5 In the **Field List**, click **ID#**. Hold down Shift, and then click **Last Name** to select three fields. Hold down Ctrl, click **Hire Date**, and then click **Photo** to select two additional fields. Point to a selected field, and then drag downward and to the left onto the first tab until the top of the arrow of the pointer aligns with the **1.5-inch mark on the horizontal ruler** and with the **0.75-inch mark on the vertical ruler**. Release the mouse button. Compare your screen with Figure 7.27.

The controls for the fields are arranged in a column on the first tab in the tab control, and Access automatically adjusts the height of the tab control so that all of the controls display. The controls are not grouped together.

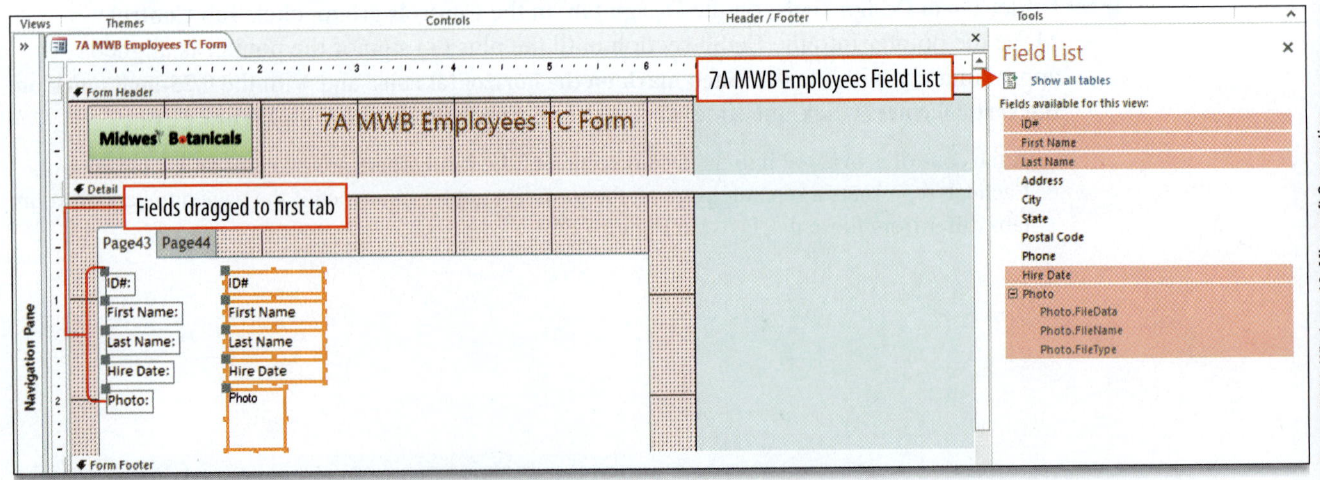

FIGURE 7.27

6 **Close** ☒ the **Field List**. Click in an empty area of the tab control to deselect the controls. Hold down Shift, and then click the **label controls** for the **Hire Date** and **Photo** fields, the **text box control** for **Hire Date**, and the **control** for the **Photo**. Point to the selected controls until the pointer displays. Drag to the right and upward until the *Hire Date* controls align with the *ID#* controls and there is approximately **0.5 inches** of space between the two columns. Do not be concerned if the controls do not exactly align.

7 With the controls selected, under **Form Design Tools**, click the **Arrange tab**. In the **Table group**, click **Stacked** to group the controls together. Click the **ID# label control** to deselect the controls in the second column. Using the techniques you have just practiced, select all of the controls in the first column, and then group them together in a **Stacked** layout.

8 Click the **Layout Selector** for the first column. Hold down Shift, click the **Hire Date label control**, and then click the **Layout Selector** above the second column to select both columns. Under **Form Design Tools**, on the **Arrange tab**, in the **Sizing & Ordering group**, click **Align**, and then click **Top**. Compare your screen with Figure 7.28.

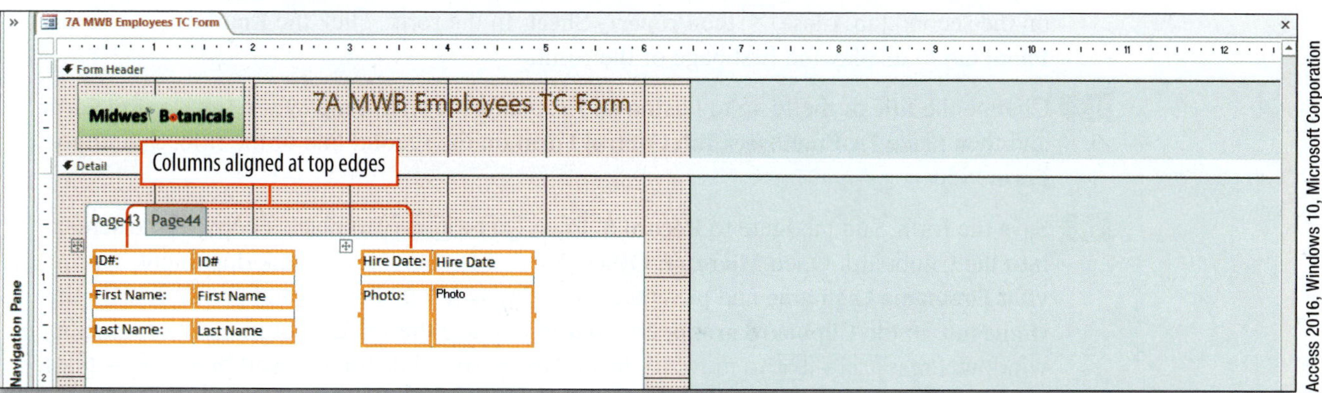

Access 2016, Windows 10, Microsoft Corporation

FIGURE 7.28

9 **Save** the form, and then switch to **Layout** view. Press PageDown several times to display the other records in the table, ensuring that all of the data displays in all of the fields.

10 Switch to **Design** view. In the **Detail** section, click the **tab control** to select it, and then click the **second tab**, which has no controls added to it. Under **Form Design Tools**, click the **Design tab**, and then, in the **Tools group**, click **Add Existing Fields**. In the **Field List**, click **Address**. Hold down Shift, and then click **Phone** to select five fields. Point to the selected fields, and then drag downward and to the left onto the second tab until the top of the arrow of the pointer aligns with the **1.5-inch mark on the horizontal ruler** and with the **0.75-inch mark on the vertical ruler**.

11 Using the techniques you have practiced, move the **Phone label control** and **Phone text box control** up and to the right until the controls are aligned with the **Address** controls. Arrange the **Phone controls** in a **Stacked** layout. Arrange the eight controls in the first column in a **Stacked** layout. Align the tops of both columns. **Close** the **Field List**, and then compare your screen with Figure 7.29.

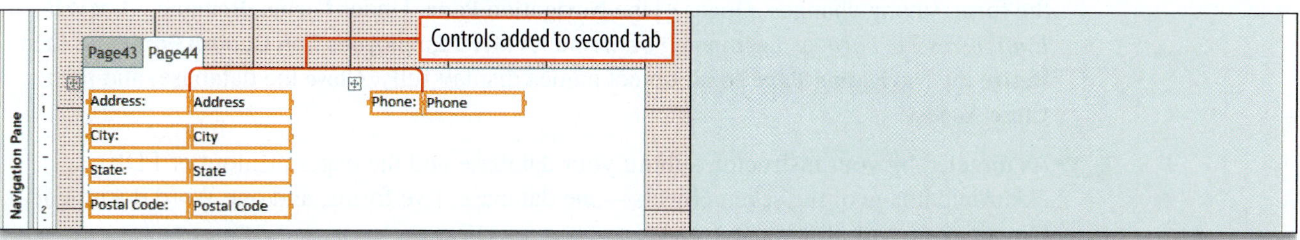

Access 2016, Windows 10, Microsoft Corporation

FIGURE 7.29

12 **Save** the form, and then switch to **Layout** view. Click the **second tab** and notice that the data in the **Address** field is truncated. Press PageDown three times to display **Record 4**. Point to the right edge of the **Address text box control** until the [pointer] pointer displays, and then drag to the right until the entire address displays in the text box control. Move the **Phone label control** to the right so the columns are about 0.5 inches apart, if necessary. Click the **first tab** of the form.

13 Right-click in the **first page** of the form, and then click **Properties**. The Property Sheet should display *Selection type: Page*, and the Selection type box should display the tab's page number. If necessary, change the Selection type. On the **Property Sheet Format tab**, click in the **Caption** property setting box, type **Employee Name and Photo** and then press Enter.

The first tab displays the text you entered in the Caption property setting box.

14 In the form, click the **second tab** to display the Property Sheet for the second tab. Click in the **Caption** property setting box, type **Address and Phone** and then press Enter to change the text on the second tab. **Close** [X] the **Property Sheet**. In the form, click the **Employee Name and Photo tab** to display the first page of the form.

15 Change the **title** of the form to **Lastname Firstname 7A MWB Employees Tab Control Form** and then place **7A Employees Tab Control Form** on the second line of the title. Switch to **Form** view.

16 **Save** the form, and navigate to **Record 5**. Press Alt + PrintScrn to place a copy of the screen into the Clipboard. Open **Microsoft Office Word 2016**. In a New, Blank document, type your **Firstname Lastname** and press Enter. Type **Activity 7.08 Step 16** and press Enter. On the **Home tab**, in the **Clipboard group**, click **Paste** to place the screenshot in the Word document window. Press Ctrl + End to move to the end of the Word document, and press Ctrl + Enter to move to the next page. **Minimize** the Word window.

Because it takes a long time for Access to format a form that contains a tab control for printing, you are copying the screens displaying the data on the tabs into Word, and then printing the Word document.

17 In the **Access** window, on the form, click the **Address and Phone tab**. Press Alt + PrintScrn to place a copy of the screen into the Clipboard. On the taskbar, click the **Microsoft Word** [W] button to display the Word document. In the **Word** window, on the **Home tab**, in the **Clipboard group**, click **Paste** to place the second page of the form in the Word document window.

18 In the **Word** window, on the **Quick Access Toolbar**, click **Save** [Save]. Under **Save As**, click **Browse**, navigate to the **Access Chapter 7** folder, and then save the file as **Lastname_Firstname_7A_Tab_Control_Form** If you are instructed to submit this result, create a paper printout or PDF electronic image of the document.

The screen copy of the first tab prints on the first page, and the screen copy of the second tab prints on the second page.

19 **Close** [X] **Word**. If necessary, on the taskbar, click the **Access** [A] button. In **Access**, **Close** [X] the form, saving changes. **Open** [»] the **Navigation Pane**. Under **Forms**, **Rename** *7A MWB Employees TC Form* as **Lastname Firstname 7A MWB Employees Tab Control Form** and then **Resize** the **Navigation Pane** so all object names display fully. **Close** the database, and then **Close** Access.

20 As directed by your instructor, submit your database and the paper printout or PDF electronic image of the seven objects—one database, five forms, and one Word document—that are the result of this project.

END | You have completed Project 7A

PROJECT 7B

Online Orders

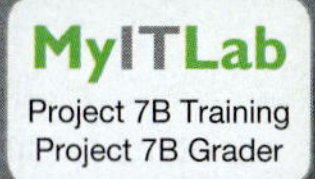

7 ACCESS

PROJECT ACTIVITIES

In Activities 7.09 through 7.15, you will create advanced reports that will help the president and officers of the production company view the information in a database in a different way. MWB Productions maintains a website where customers can order gardening supplies that are featured in the *Midwest Botanicals* television show. You will create advanced reports that display data from multiple tables and from a parameter query. You will also create an alphabetic index of garden suppliers. Your completed reports will look similar to Figure 7.30.

PROJECT FILES

If your instructor wants you to submit Project 7B in the MyITLab grader system, log in to MyITLab, locate Grader Project 7B, and then download the files for this project.

For Project 7B, you will need the following file:
a07B_Online_Orders

You will save your database as:
Lastname_Firstname_7B_Online_Orders

PROJECT RESULTS

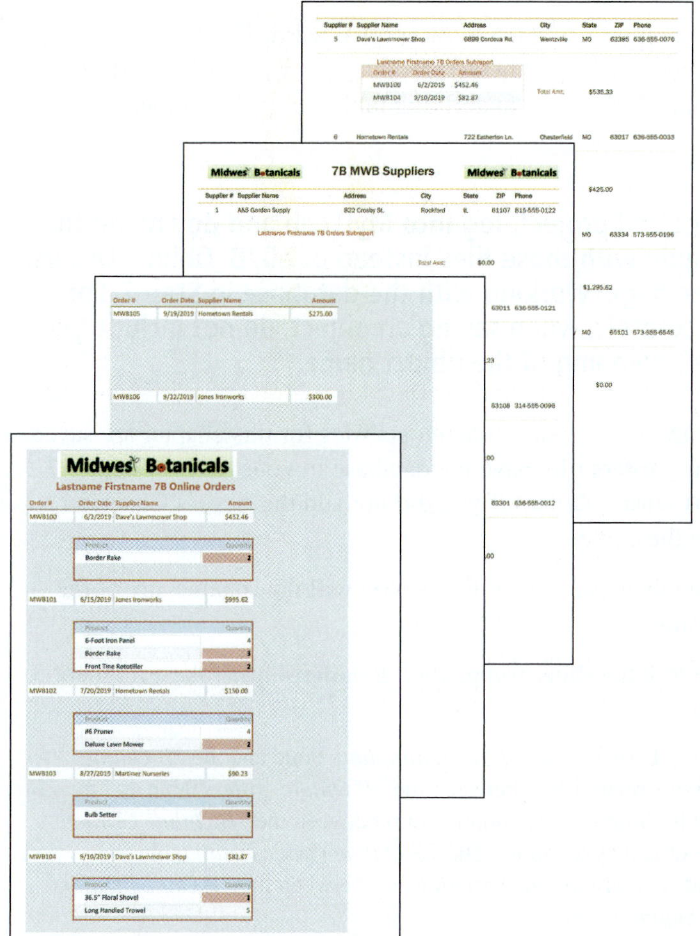

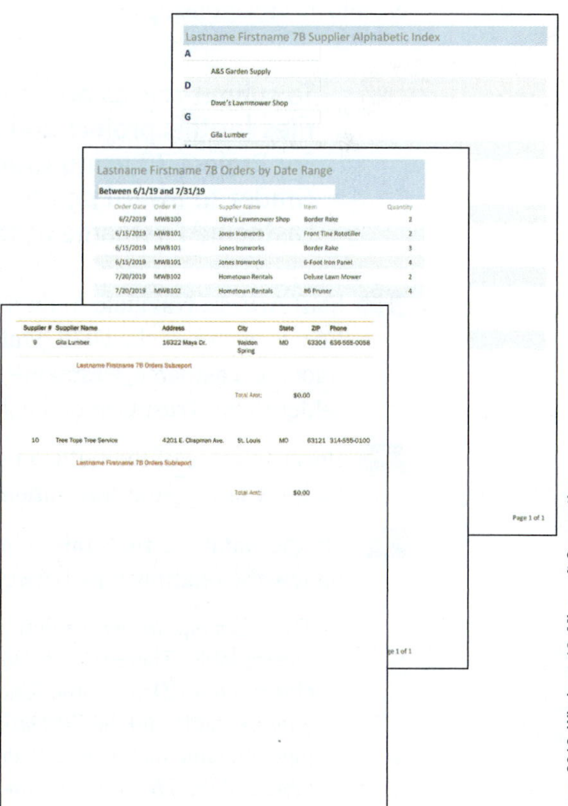

FIGURE 7.30 Project 7B Online Orders

PROJECT RESULTS

In this project, using your own name, you will create the following database and objects. Your instructor may ask for printouts or PDF electronic images:

Lastname_Firstname_7B_Online Orders	Database file
Lastname Firstname 7B Orders Main Report	Report
Lastname Firstname 7B MWB Suppliers Report	Report
Lastname Firstname 7B Orders by Date Range	Report
Lastname Firstname 7B Supplier Alphabetic Index	Report

Objective 4 Create and Modify a Subreport

GO! Learn How Video A7-4

A ***subreport*** is a report that is embedded within another report—the ***main report***. The main report is either bound or unbound. A ***bound report*** displays data from an underlying table, query, or SQL statement as specified in the report's Record Source property; an ***unbound report*** does not. An ***SQL statement*** is an instruction using Structured Query Language. An example of an unbound report being used as the main form would be a report that displays a title, logo, and date, similar to a report header. A main report can also contain a subform instead of a subreport. A main report can contain up to seven levels of subforms and subreports.

Activity 7.09 | Using the SubReport Wizard to Create a Subreport

1.2.5, 5.2.2, 5.2.4, 5.2.3

In this Activity you will create a subreport using the SubReport Wizard. The main report will display the online orders, and the subreport will display the products that were ordered. Before creating a subreport using the SubReport Wizard, the underlying tables or queries should have established relationships.

ALERT!

To submit this as an autograded project, log into MyITLab and download the files for this project and begin with those files instead of a07B_Online_Orders. For Project 7B using Grader, begin working with the database in Step 2. For Grader to award points accurately, when saving an object, do not include your Lastname Firstname at the beginning of the object name.

1. Start Access. Navigate to the location where the student data files for this chapter are saved. Locate and open the **a07B_Online_Orders** file. Save the database in your **Access Chapter 7** folder as **Lastname_Firstname_7B_Online_Orders** If you did not add the Access Chapter 7 folder to the Trust Center, enable the content.

2. Because some of the fields in the tables are lookup fields, you will not rename any of the tables. **Close** « the **Navigation Pane**.

3. On the **Database Tools tab**, in the **Relationships group**, click **Relationships**. Take a moment to review the relationships between the tables.

   There is a *one-to-many* relationship between the *7B MWB Suppliers* table and the *7B Online Orders* table. There is a *one-to-many* relationship between the *7B Online Orders* table and the *7B Online Order Detail* table. There is a *one-to-many* relationship between the *7B Online Garden Supplies* table and the *7B Online Order Detail* table. The *7B Online Order Detail* table is a junction table that is used to create a *many-to-many* relationship between the *7B Online Orders* table and the *7B Online Garden Supplies* table.

4 **Close** [X] the **Relationships tab**, and then **Open** [»] the **Navigation Pane**. Under **Reports**, right-click **7B Orders Report**, and then click **Copy**. On the **Home tab**, in the **Clipboard group**, click **Paste**. In the **Paste As** dialog box, under **Report Name**, and with the existing text selected, type **Lastname Firstname 7B Orders Main Report** and then click **OK**.

In the Navigation Pane under Reports, the newly named copy of the *7B Orders Report* displays.

5 Open **7B Orders Main Report** in **Design** view, and then **Close** [«] the **Navigation Pane**. Click the **small box** in the upper-left corner of the report, where the top and left margins intersect. Recall that clicking this box selects the report. Under **Report Design Tools**, on the **Design tab**, in the **Tools group**, click **Property Sheet**.

The Property Sheet should display *Selection type: Report*.

6 Click the **Property Sheet Data tab**. Notice that the **Record Source** property setting is *7B Online Orders*. **Close** [X] the **Property Sheet**.

7B Orders Main Report is bound to the *7B Online Orders* table.

7 In the **Report Header** section, click the **title's label control**, and change *Lastname Firstname* to your own last and first names, and then press Enter. In the report, point to the top of the **Page Footer section bar** until the [+] pointer displays. Drag downward to the **1-inch mark on the vertical ruler** to make room in the Detail section for the subreport.

8 Under **Report Design Tools**, on the **Design tab**, in the **Controls group**, click **More** [▾], and verify that the **Use Control Wizards** option is active. In the **Controls group**, click **Subform/ Subreport** [▤]. Move the mouse pointer down into the **Detail** section until the top of the plus (+) sign of the pointer aligns with the **1-inch mark on the horizontal ruler** and with the **0.5-inch mark on the vertical ruler**, and then click. Compare your screen with Figure 7.31.

A subreport control is inserted into the Detail section of the report, and the SubReport Wizard dialog box displays. The control displays *Unbound* because the control has not yet been linked to a record source.

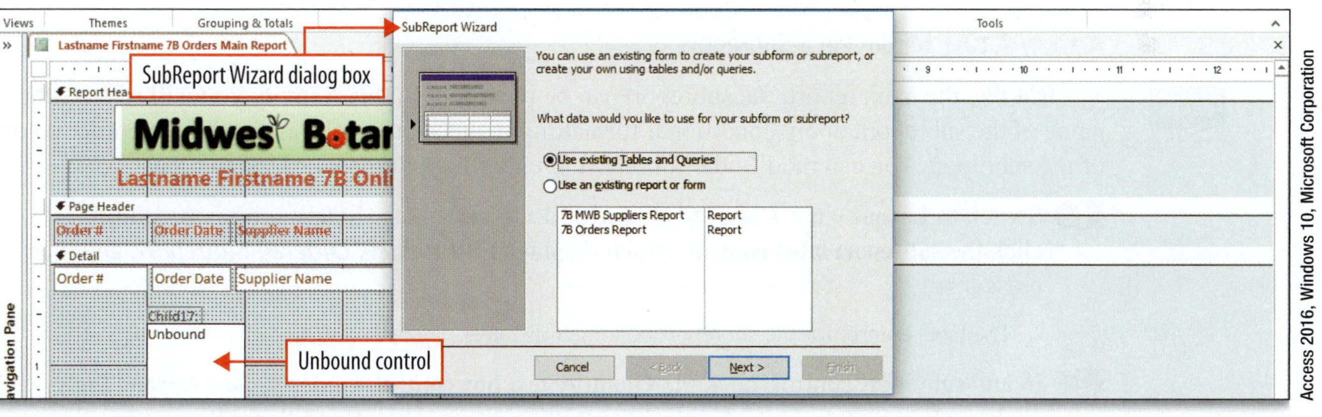

FIGURE 7.31

9 In the **SubReport Wizard** dialog box, verify that **Use existing Tables and Queries** is selected, and then click **Next**.

The second SubReport Wizard dialog box enables you to select the table or query and the fields to use in the subreport.

10 Click the **Tables/Queries box arrow**, and from the displayed list, click **Table: 7B Online Order Detail**. Under **Available Fields**, double-click **Product**, and then double-click **Quantity** to move the fields to the **Selected Fields** box. Click **Next**.

The third SubReport Wizard dialog box enables you to define the fields that link the main form to the subreport. Because there is a one-to-many relationship between the two tables, the default setting is to show the data in the *7B Online Order Detail* table for each record in the *7B Online Orders* table.

11 Click **Next**, name the report **Lastname Firstname 7B Products Ordered Subreport** and then click **Finish**. **Save** the Main report. Switch to **Report** view, and then compare your screen with Figure 7.32.

The subreport data displays under each record from the *7B Online Orders* table. For example, for *Order # MWB100*, two Border Rakes were ordered.

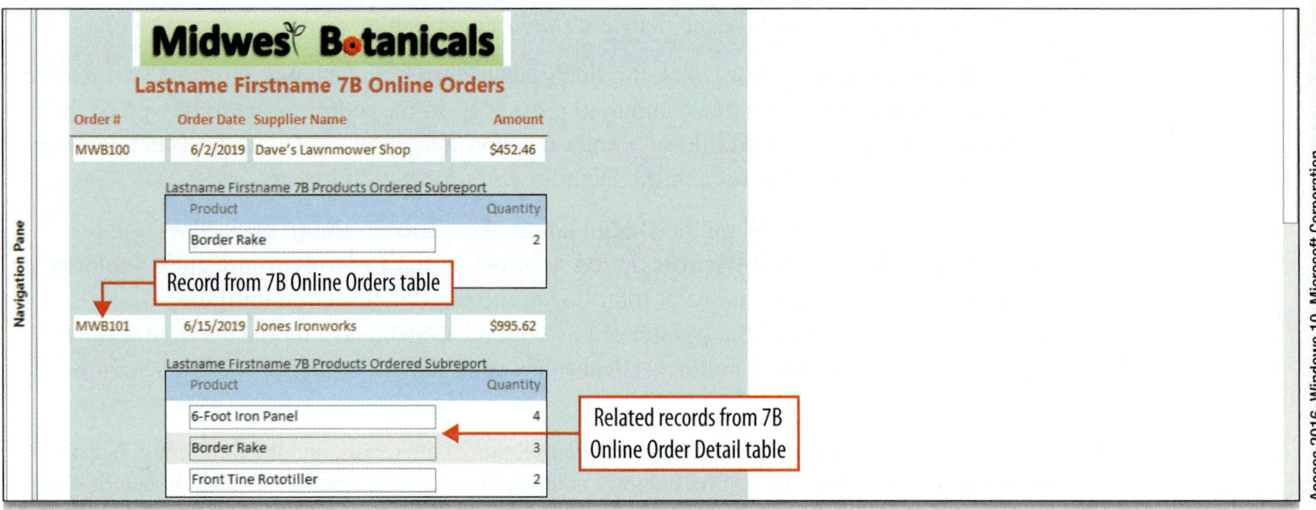

FIGURE 7.32

Activity 7.10 | Modifying a Subreport

1.3.5, 5.3.4, 5.2.3

Just like the main report, the subreport can be modified. In this Activity you will remove the name of the subreport, apply conditional formatting in the subreport, and change the border color of the subreport. You can modify the subreport in either Layout view or Design view.

1 Switch to **Layout** view. **Close** the **Field List**, if necessary. In any subreport control, click the **subreport label control**, which displays *7B Products Ordered Subreport*, and then press Delete.

The label control for the subreport no longer displays.

2 In any subreport control, click the **Quantity text box control**. Under **Report Layout Tools**, click the **Format tab**. In the **Control Formatting** group, click **Conditional Formatting**. The **Conditional Formatting Rules Manager** dialog box displays to show formatting rules for the *Quantity* field. Click **New Rule**, and compare your screen with Figure 7.33.

Conditional formatting is a way to apply formatting to specific controls based on a comparison to a rule set in the New Rule dialog box. It is one way to draw attention to an entry that might require additional action.

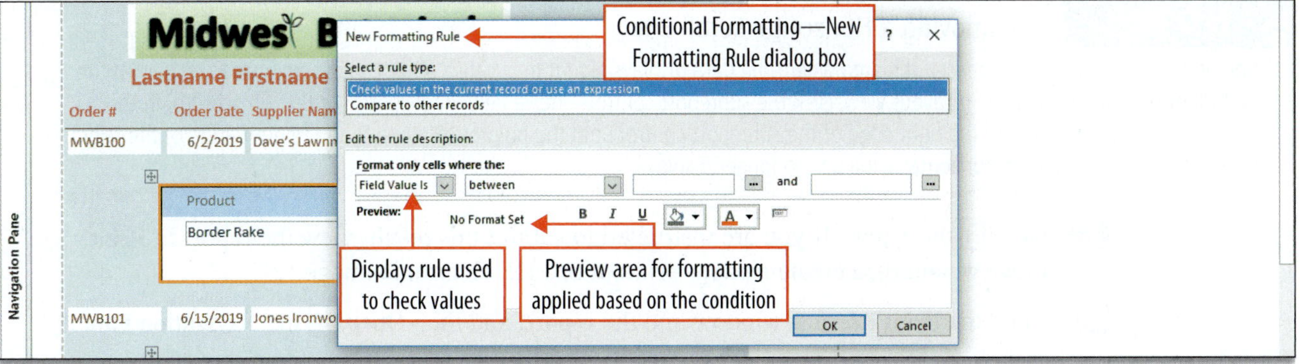

Access 2016, Windows 10, Microsoft Corporation

FIGURE 7.33

3 Click the arrow to the right of the box that displays *between*, and select **less than or equal to**. Click in the empty text box, and type **3** The rule will format only cells where the *Field Value is less than or equal to 3*.

The rule has now been set; however, no format options have been set. These settings are applied using the buttons below the rule.

4 Click **Bold** [B], and then click the **Background color arrow** [icon]. Under **Standard Colors**, on the fourth row, click the sixth color—**Maroon 3**. Click **OK** to close the **New Formatting Rule** dialog box. Click **OK** to close the **Conditional Formatting Rules Manager**.

For any items ordered, if the quantity is 3 or less, the quantity will display in bold with a light maroon background. This will alert the staff to determine if special marketing strategies might be helpful to increase sales.

5 Click anywhere in the subreport, if necessary, and then click the **Layout Selector**. Under **Report Layout Tools**, on the **Format tab**, in the **Control Formatting group**, click the **Shape Outline arrow**. Under **Theme Colors**, on the first row, click the sixth color—**Red, Accent 2**. Again, click the **Shape Outline arrow**, and then point to **Line Thickness**. In the displayed list, click the third line—**2 pt**—and then click anywhere in the main report to display the results of the formatting. Switch to **Report** view. Compare your screen with Figure 7.34.

The subreport displays with a thicker maroon border.

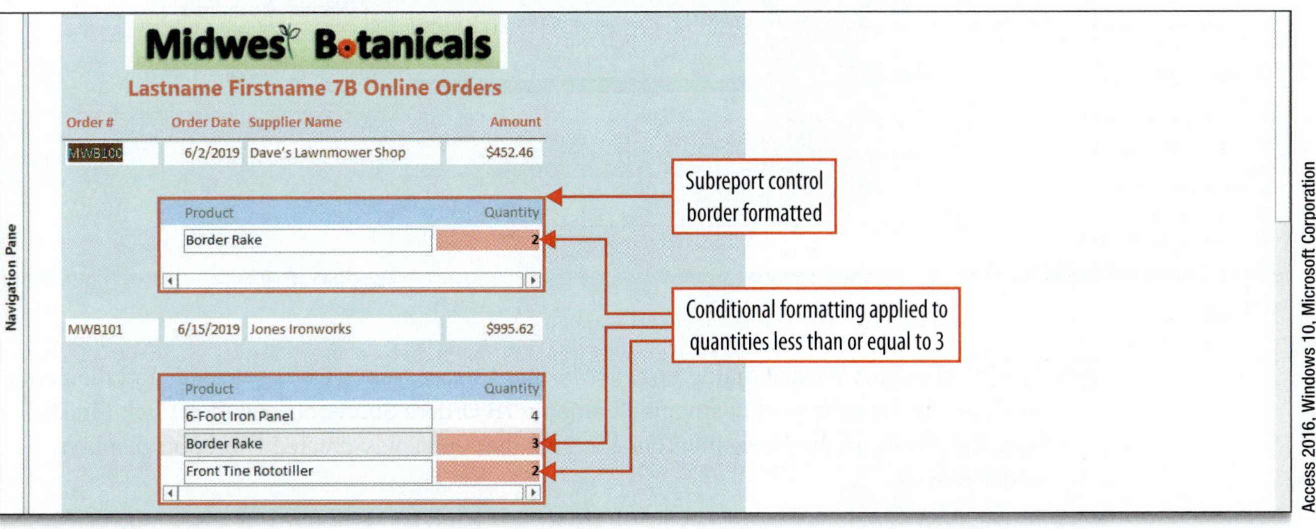

Access 2016, Windows 10, Microsoft Corporation

FIGURE 7.34

> **NOTE** Removing a Horizontal Scroll Bar
>
> Adding the thicker border decreased the area where the data displays, and it may cause a horizontal scroll bar to display at the bottom of the subreport. If so, in Layout view, click the subreport control—not a field label control or text box control in the subreport—and then point to the right edge of the subreport control until the pointer displays. Drag the right edge of the subreport control to the right until the horizontal scroll bar no longer displays.

6 **Save** the report. If you are instructed to submit this result, view the report in **Print Preview**, and then create a paper printout or PDF electronic image.

7 **Close** the **Print Preview** window and the **report**, and then **Open** the **Navigation Pane**.

Activity 7.11 | Creating a Subreport by Adding an Object to an Existing Report

5.2.2, 5.3.4, 1.3.5

In this Activity you will drag the *7B Online Orders* table onto the *7B MWB Suppliers Report* to create a subreport. For the subreport to be linked to the main report, the underlying tables should have an established relationship. You can also create a subreport by dragging an existing form, subform, query, report, or subreport onto a report.

1 In the **Navigation Pane**, under **Reports**, locate **7B MWB Suppliers Report**, and then open the report in **Design** view. In the report, point to the top of the **Page Footer section bar** until the pointer displays. Drag downward to the **1.25-inch mark on the vertical ruler** to make room in the Detail section for the subreport.

2 In the **Navigation Pane**, under **Tables**, click **7B Online Orders**, and then drag the table to the right onto the **Detail** section until the top of the pointer aligns with the **1-inch mark on the horizontal ruler** and the **0.5-inch mark on the vertical ruler**. The **SubReport Wizard** dialog box displays, as shown in Figure 7.35.

The SubReport Wizard suggests that the report shows the Online Orders for each record in the Suppliers using Supplier Name. If you were dragging an existing report onto this report that had an established relationship between the underlying tables, the SubReport Wizard dialog box would not display.

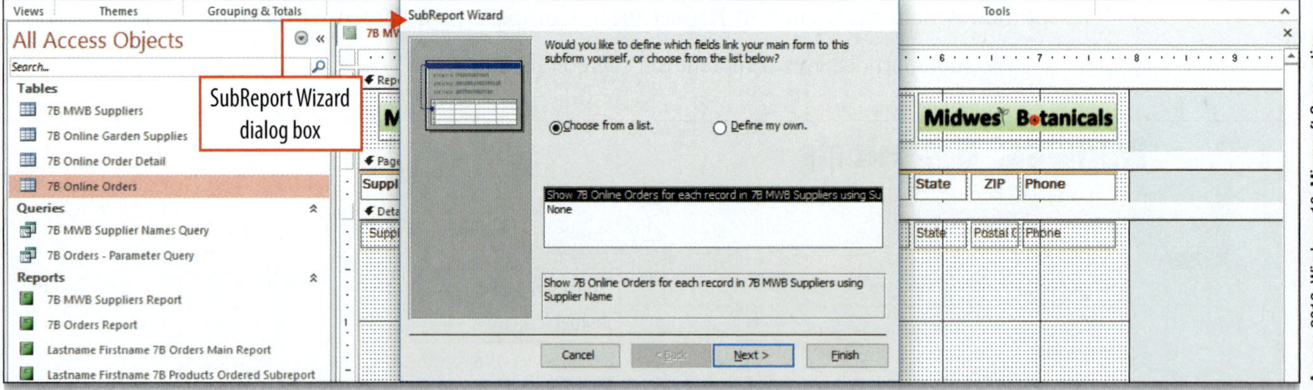

FIGURE 7.35

3 In the **SubReport Wizard** dialog box, verify that **Choose from a list** is selected, and then click **Next**. Name the subreport **Lastname Firstname 7B Orders Subreport** and then click **Finish**. **Save** the report. In the **Navigation Pane**, notice that the newly created subreport displays under **Reports**.

4 If necessary, **Close** the **Field List**, if necessary. Press F4 to display the Property Sheet for the subreport, and then **Close** the **Navigation Pane**. If necessary, click the **Property Sheet Data tab**, click in the **Link Master Fields** property setting box, and then click **Build**.

The Subreport Field Linker dialog box displays. The fields that are used to link the two underlying record sources are displayed; the Master Fields property setting box displays the linked field in the main report, and the Child Fields property setting box displays the linked field in the subreport. Use the Subreport Field Linker dialog box to change the linked fields if the subreport does not display the data in the manner you intended. If you are unsure of which fields to link, click Suggest.

5 In the **Subreport Field Linker** dialog box, click **OK**. **Close** the **Property Sheet**, and then switch to **Layout** view. Notice that **Record 1** displays no data in the subreport; no orders have been placed with A&S Garden Supply.

6 In the main report, locate Record 2—**Martinez Nurseries**. Notice that Record 2 displays one order in the subreport and displays the name of the supplier in the third field. In the **subreport control** for **Record 2**, click **Martinez Nurseries**, press Shift, and click the **Supplier Name label control**. Press Delete to remove the label and text box controls and the redundant data. Resize the other three controls so they are wide enough to just view the data. Move the controls to close large gaps between fields.

7 Click the **subreport's Layout Selector**, and then press F4 to display the Property Sheet for the subreport. Click the **Property Sheet Format tab**, select the text in the **Width** property setting box, type **3.5** and then press Enter to change the width of the subreport control. **Close** the **Property Sheet**.

The subreport has been modified, and the redundant field has been removed. A horizontal scroll bar displays in the subreport.

8 Click the **subreport label control**—*Lastname Firstname 7B Orders Subreport*. Change the **Font Color** of the text in the selected label control to **Red, Accent 2**, and then add **Bold** formatting to the text. Point to the selected label control until the pointer displays, and then drag the control to the right until it is approximately centered between the margins of the subreport control.

9 Switch to **Design** view, saving changes to the main report and subreport. Select the **Subreport Header**, and under **Report Design Tools**, click the **Format tab**. Click the **Background color arrow**. Under **Standard Colors**, on the third row, click the sixth color—**Maroon 2**. Click the **Order # label control**, hold down Shift, click the **Order Date label control**, and then click the **Amount label control** to select all three label controls, scrolling to the right as necessary. Change the **Font Color** to **Red, Accent 2**. Switch to **Layout** view, and then compare your screen with Figure 7.36.

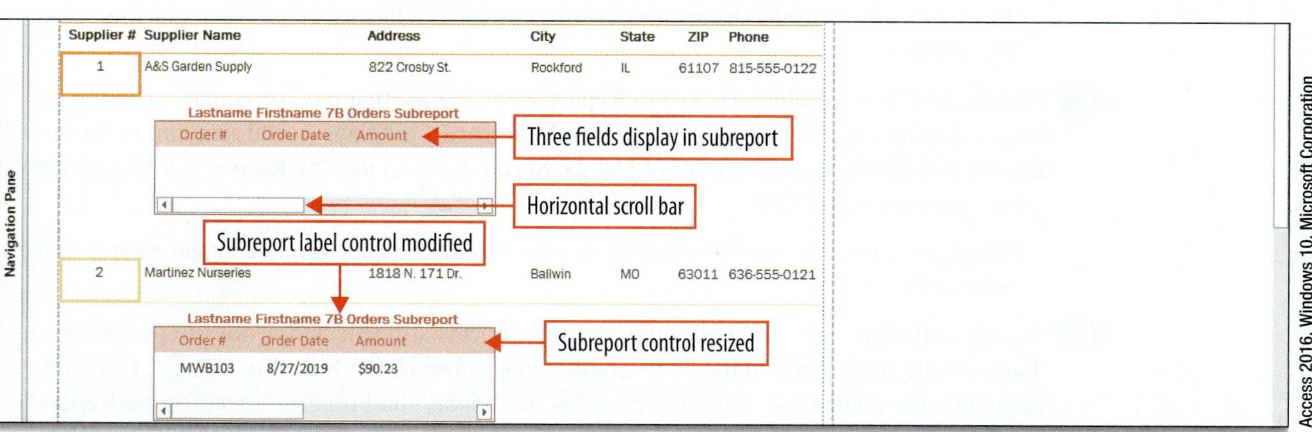

FIGURE 7.36

10 **Save** the report, and then switch to **Design** view.

Activity 7.12 | Displaying a Total from a Subreport on the Main Report

5.3.3, 5.3.2, 5.3.6, 1.3.5, 5.2.4, 5.3.4, 1.5.1

In this Activity you will display a total from the subreport on the main report.

1 Click the subreport to select it. Under **Report Design Tools**, on the **Design tab**, in the **Tools** group, click **Subreport in New Window**.

The subreport displays on its own tab, and all of the controls are displayed, which makes it easier to edit.

2 Under **Report Design Tools**, on the **Design tab**, in the **Tools group**, click **Property Sheet**. Verify that the Property Sheet displays *Selection type: Report*. On the **Property Sheet Format tab**, change the **Width** property setting to **3.45** and press Enter. Compare your screen with Figure 7.37.

Recall that the subreport control displayed a horizontal scroll bar—this is because the actual subreport's width was wider than the size of the control. By making the width of the report smaller than the width of the subreport control, the scroll bar will no longer display in the *7B MWB Suppliers Report* because it is not really necessary to view data.

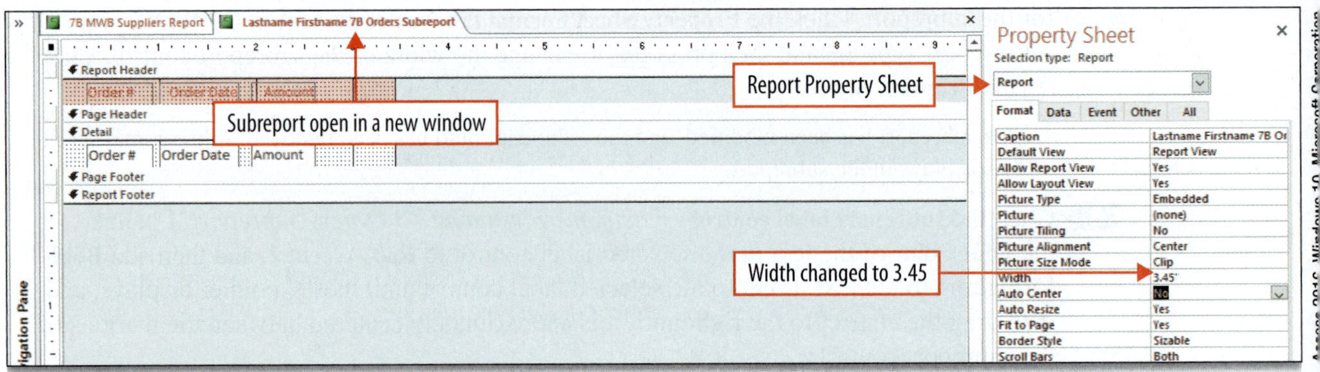

FIGURE 7.37

3 Close the **Property Sheet**. In the **Detail** section, click the **Amount text box control**. Under **Report Design Tools**, on the **Design tab**, in the **Grouping & Totals group**, click **Totals**, and then click **Sum** to insert a calculated control into the Report Footer section.

4 **Save** the subreport, and then **Close** *7B Orders Subreport*.

To view the results of the changes made to the subreport in the main report, you first must close the subreport.

5 Switch *7B MWB Suppliers Report* to **Report** view. Notice that the horizontal scroll bar no longer displays, and in the subreport controls, **Record 1** displays a total Amount of **$0.00** and **Record 2** displays a total Amount of **$90.23**. Scroll down to display **Record 5**, which displays a total Amount of **$535.33**.

Adding a sum to a field in the subreport causes the sum to display in the subreport control on the main form.

6 Switch to **Design** view, and verify that the subreport is still selected. Under **Report Design Tools**, on the **Design tab**, in the **Tools group**, click **Subreport in New Window**. Click the **Report Footer section bar**, and then press F4 to display the Property Sheet for the Report Footer section. On the **Property Sheet Format tab**, click in the **Visible** property setting box, which displays **Yes**. Click the **arrow**, and then click **No**.

The data in the Report Footer section will not display when the report is displayed in any view other than Design view. You will be displaying the calculated field in the main form, so it is being hidden from view.

7 In the **Report Footer** section, click the **calculated control**. The **Property Sheet** displays *Selection type: Text Box*, and the **Selection type** box displays *AccessTotalsAmount*. Click the **Property Sheet Other tab**, and then click in the **Name** property setting box. Select **AccessTotalsAmount**, type **Total Amount** and then press Enter. Compare your screen with Figure 7.38.

The Selection type box displays Total Amount, which is the new name of the text box control that displays the sum of the amount field. Rename controls to easily remember the name, especially if the control name is used somewhere else in the form. You will be using this control name to display the total of the amount field in the main form.

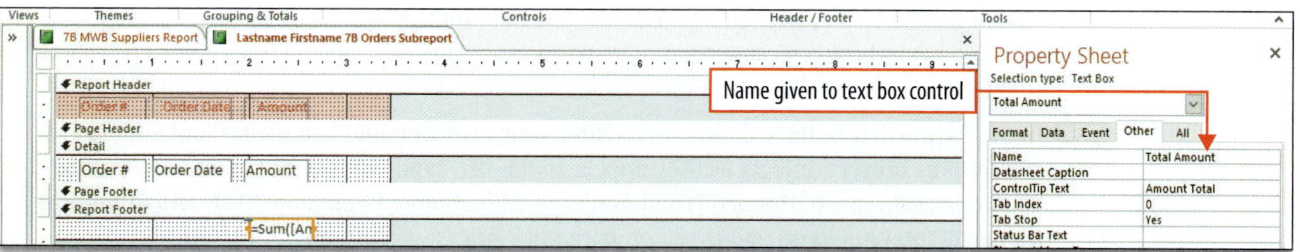

Access 2016, Windows 10, Microsoft Corporation

FIGURE 7.38

8 **Close** the **Property Sheet**, **Save** the report, and then **Close** *7B Orders Subreport*. Switch *7B MWB Suppliers Report* to **Report** view, and notice that the sum of the Amount field no longer displays in the subreport control.

9 Switch to **Design** view. Under **Report Design Tools**, on the **Design tab**, in the **Controls group**, click **Text Box** [ab|]. Move the mouse pointer down to the **Detail** section until the top of the plus (+) sign aligns with the **6-inch mark on the horizontal ruler** and with the **1-inch mark on the vertical ruler**, and then click. Compare your screen with Figure 7.39.

A text box control with an associated label control displays in the Detail section. The text box control displays Unbound because the control is not linked to a field.

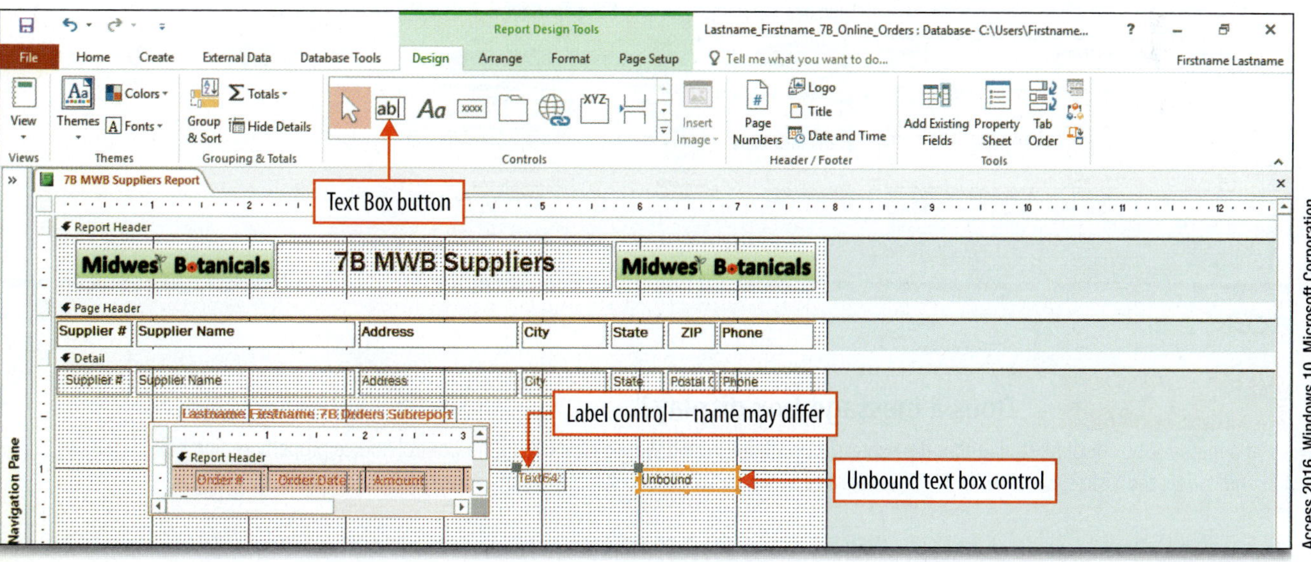

Access 2016, Windows 10, Microsoft Corporation

FIGURE 7.39

10 In the **Detail** section, click the **label control** that is associated with the unbound text box control, and then press F4 to display the Property Sheet for the label control. Click the **Property Sheet Format tab**, select the text in the **Caption** property setting box, and then type

Total Amt: Select the text in the **Width** property setting box, type **.75** and then press Enter to increase the width of the label control.

The Caption property setting controls the text that is displayed in the label control associated with the unbound text box control.

11 In the **Detail** section, click the **unbound text box control**. If the control is hidden behind the Property Sheet, decrease the width of the Property Sheet by dragging the left edge of the Property Sheet to the right. Click the **Property Sheet Data tab**, and then in the **Control Source** property setting box, click **Build** [...].

The Expression Builder dialog box displays. Although you can type the expression directly in the Control Source property setting box, the Expression Builder dialog box is similar to the Zoom dialog box, where you can see the entire typed expression. The Control Source property setting is used to link the text box control to a field.

12 In the **Expression Builder** dialog box, using your own first and last names and double-clicking the correct objects as they appear in the list, type **=IIf(IsError([Lastname Firstname 7B Orders Subreport].[Report]![Total Amount]),0,[Lastname Firstname 7B Orders Subreport].[Report]![Total Amount])** and then compare your screen with Figure 7.40.

The expression starts with an equal (=) sign and is followed by the IsError function within the IIf function. The IIf function checks for the #Error message in the Total Amount field of 7B Orders Subreport. If #Error is found, 0 is displayed in the field; otherwise, the data in the Total Amount field is displayed. A period separates the report name from the object name, which is also enclosed in brackets. The object name, in this case [Report], is only necessary if the name of the report is the same as the underlying record source. The exclamation (!) mark is called the ***bang operator***. The bang operator tells Access that what follows it is an object that belongs to the object that precedes it in the expression. In this expression, Total Amount is an object in the 7B Orders Subreport report.

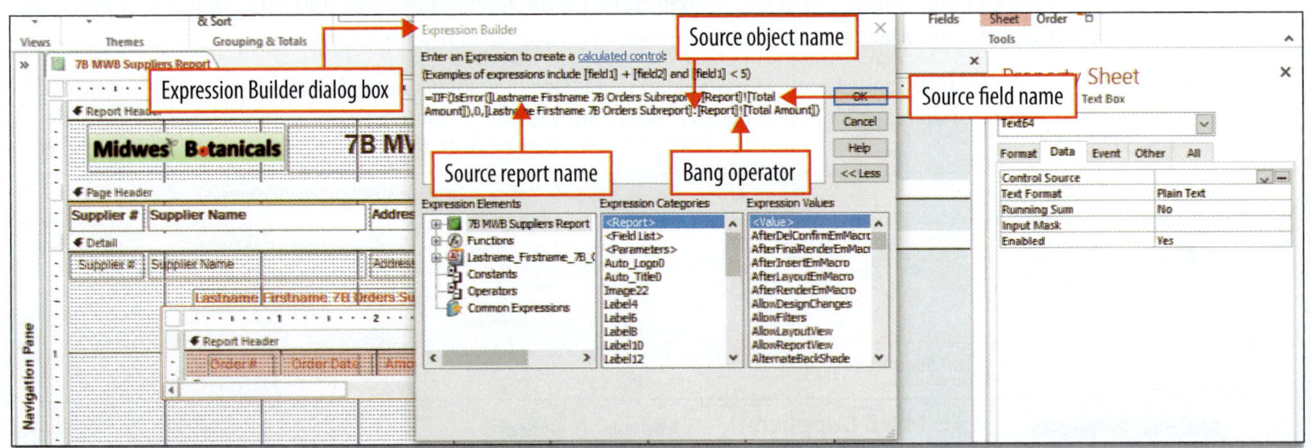

FIGURE 7.40

ALERT!

Does a message box display?

If a message box displays stating that the expression contains invalid syntax, click OK. In the Control Source property setting box, click Build, and correct the expression. ***Syntax*** is the set of rules by which words and symbols in an expression are combined.

ANOTHER WAY

If the subreport contained data for each control on the main report, you could have typed a simpler expression of =[Lastname Firstname 7B Online Orders Subreport].[Report]![Total Amount]. The expression starts with an equal (=) sign and is followed by the name of the report enclosed in brackets. A period separates the report name from the object name—Report—which is also enclosed in brackets. The bang operator is used to identify Total Amount as an object in the 7B Orders Subreport report. If the subreport does not contain any data for any control on the main report, the control on the main report displays #Error when printed using the simplified expression.

7 ACCESS

13 In the **Expression Builder** dialog box, click **OK**, and then press Enter.

The expression displays in the Control Source property setting box.

14 Click the **Property Sheet Format tab**. Click in the **Format** property setting box, click the displayed **arrow**, and then select **Currency**. **Close** the **Property Sheet**.

The data that was typed in the Control Source property setting box displays in the text box control.

15 With the **text box control selected**, point to the small gray box that displays in the upper-left corner of the text box control until the pointer displays. Drag to the left until the left edge of the text box control aligns with the right edge of the label control that displays *Total Amt:*.

Dragging the small box that displays in the upper-left corner of a control enables you to move only that control. If you point to any other part of the control before dragging, the control and its associated controls are moved.

16 **Save** the report, and click **Yes** in the dialog box if necessary. Switch to **Report** view. Scroll down to display **Records 6 and 7**, and then compare your screen with Figure 7.41.

The sum of the Amount field in the subreport is displayed in the main report and is formatted as Currency.

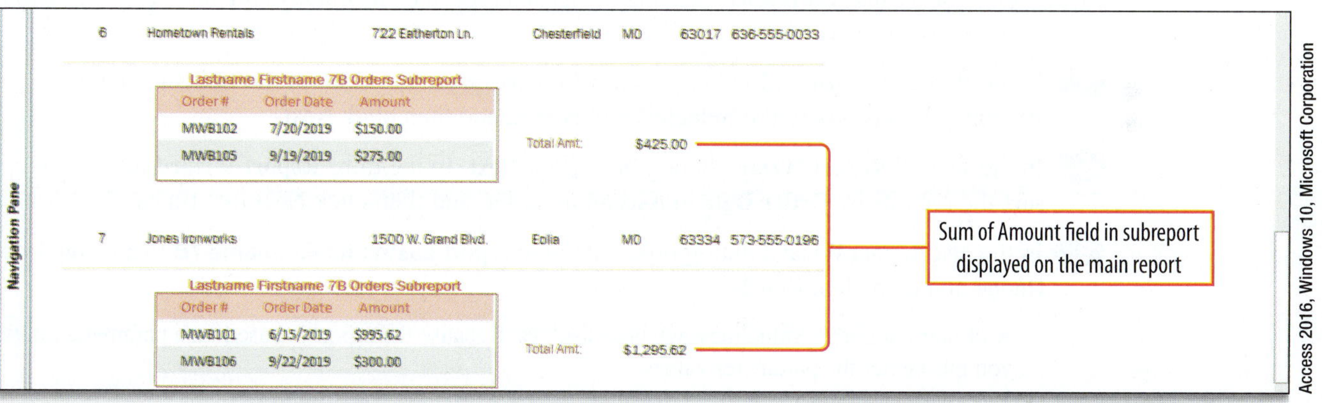

Access 2016, Windows 10, Microsoft Corporation

FIGURE 7.41

ALERT! **Does an Enter Parameter Value message box display?**

If an Enter Parameter Value message box displays, you probably typed the name of the subreport or the name of the field incorrectly. If this occurs, repeat Steps 11 and 12, ensuring that you type the expression correctly.

17 If you are instructed to submit this result, view the report in **Print Preview**, and then create a paper printout or PDF electronic image.

18 **Close** the **Print Preview** window and the **report**, and then **Open** the **Navigation Pane**. Rename the 7B MWB Suppliers Report to **Lastname Firstname 7B MWB Suppliers Report**

Objective 5 Create a Report Based on a Parameter Query

GO! Learn How Video A7-5

Recall that a ***parameter query*** prompts you for criteria before running the query. Using a parameter query as the record source for a report enables the user to set the criteria for the report when the report is opened. Recall that when a report is opened, the underlying table or query in the report is read to ensure that the report displays the most current data. MWB Productions maintains a table to keep track of the website orders. A parameter query was created to display the orders between a range of dates.

Activity 7.13 | Creating a Report Based on a Parameter Query

5.1.3, 5.2.4, 1.3.5, 5.3.3

In this Activity you will view the design of the *7B Orders Parameter Query*, and then create a report based on the parameter query.

1 In the **Navigation Pane**, under **Tables**, double-click **7B Online Orders** to open the table in **Datasheet** view. Notice that the **Order Date** data ranges from 6/2/2019 to 9/22/2019.

When you run the parameter query, if you enter a range for which there is no data or if you enter the data incorrectly, the resulting fields will be empty.

2 **Close** [X] the table. In the **Navigation Pane**, under **Queries**, double-click **7B Orders - Parameter Query**. In the **Enter Parameter Value** message box, under **Enter first date**, type **6/1/19** and then click **OK**. In the second message box, under **Enter second date**, type **July 31, 2019** and then click **OK**.

Because the Order Date field has a data type of Date, you can enter the date in several formats. The query is run and displays orders between June 1, 2019, and July 31, 2019.

3 **Close** [X] the query, and then **Close** [«] the **Navigation Pane**. On the **Create tab**, in the **Reports group**, click **Report Wizard**.

Because the query was selected in the Navigation Pane, the *7B Orders - Parameter Query* displays in the Tables/Queries box.

4 In the **Report Wizard** dialog box, click **All Fields** [>>] to move all of the fields from the Available Fields box to the Selected Fields box, and then click **Next**.

5 In the second **Report Wizard** dialog box, click **Next**. In the third **Report Wizard** dialog box, **sort** the records by **Order Date** in **Ascending** order, and then click **Next** two times.

6 In the last **Report Wizard** dialog box, name the report **Lastname Firstname 7B Orders by Date Range** and then click **Finish**.

An Enter Parameter Value message box displays. Because the report is based on a parameter query, you must enter the parameter values.

7 For the first date, type **6/1/19** and click **OK**. For the second date, type **7/31/19** Click **OK**, and then compare your screen with Figure 7.42.

Six records are extracted from the underlying tables based on the parameter values entered. Five fields are included in the report, but all data may not be visible on this page. In that case, adjustments will need to be made to controls so all data is visible and the report prints on one page.

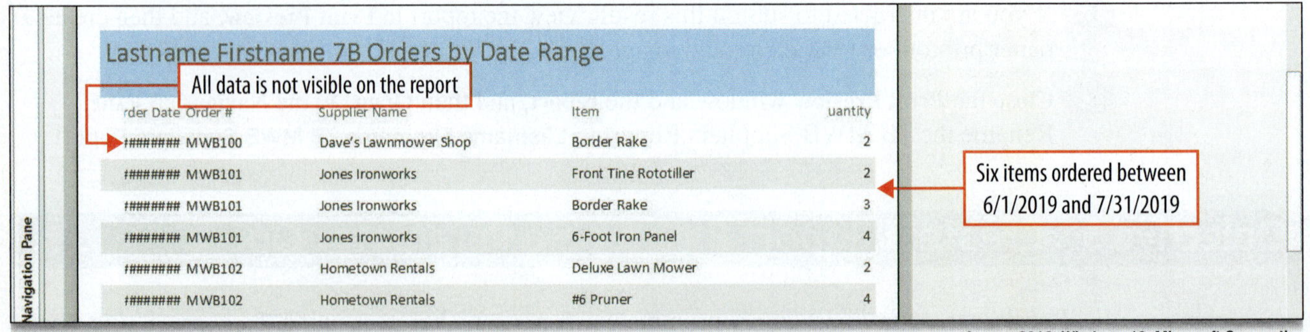

Access 2016, Windows 10, Microsoft Corporation

FIGURE 7.42

8 Right-click the object tab, and click **Layout View**. Close the Field List, if necessary. Resize the text box controls and label controls for the **Item** and **Supplier Name** so they are just wide enough to display the longest item in each column. Resize the **Order Date** field to fully display the data, and then resize the **Quantity** field to fit the label control.

9 Switch to **Design** view. Adjust the field placement so all fields display on the page and the right edge of the **Quantity** field aligns at the **7-inch mark on the horizontal ruler**.

10 In the **Page Footer** section, click to select the **Page Numbering** text box. Point to the right middle sizing handle until the ↔ pointer displays. Drag to the left until the right edge of the text box control aligns with the right edge of the **Quantity** controls. Resize the width of the report to **7.25 inches**. **Save** the report.

Activity 7.14 | Printing the Parameters in the Report

5.3.6, 5.2.4, 1.5.1

The parameters used in the creation of the report can be printed as a part of the report by adding a text box control to a section. In this Activity you will add a text box control to the Report Header section to display the parameter values as a subtitle.

1 Point to the top of the **Page Header section bar** until the + pointer displays. Drag downward to the top of the **Detail section bar** to increase the size of the **Report Header**.

2 Under **Report Design Tools**, on the **Design tab**, in the **Controls group**, click **Text Box** ab|. In the **Report Header** section, align the top of the plus (+) sign of the pointer **one dot** from the left margin and **three dots** below the label control for the report title, and then click.

Recall that adding a text box control to the design also adds an associated label control that can be used to describe the data in the text box control.

3 Click the **label control** that is associated with the newly added text box control, and then press Delete.

4 Click the unbound **text box control**, and then press F4 to display the Property Sheet for the control. Click the **Property Sheet Data tab**, click in the **Control Source** property setting box, and then click **Build** .... In the displayed **Expression Builder** dialog box, type **="Between** press Spacebar, and then continue typing **"&[Enter first date]&"** Press Spacebar, and then type **and** Press Spacebar again, and then continue typing **"&[Enter second date]** Compare your screen with Figure 7.43.

Recall that an expression must begin with an equal sign (=). The word *Between* and a space will print. The & symbol concatenates the string with the next part of the expression. *Enter first date* is enclosed in square brackets because it is part of the criteria that is retrieved from the parameter query. You must type the criteria exactly as it displays in the criteria of the parameter query. The criteria will be concatenated with the space, the word *and*, and another space. This is concatenated with the second criteria.

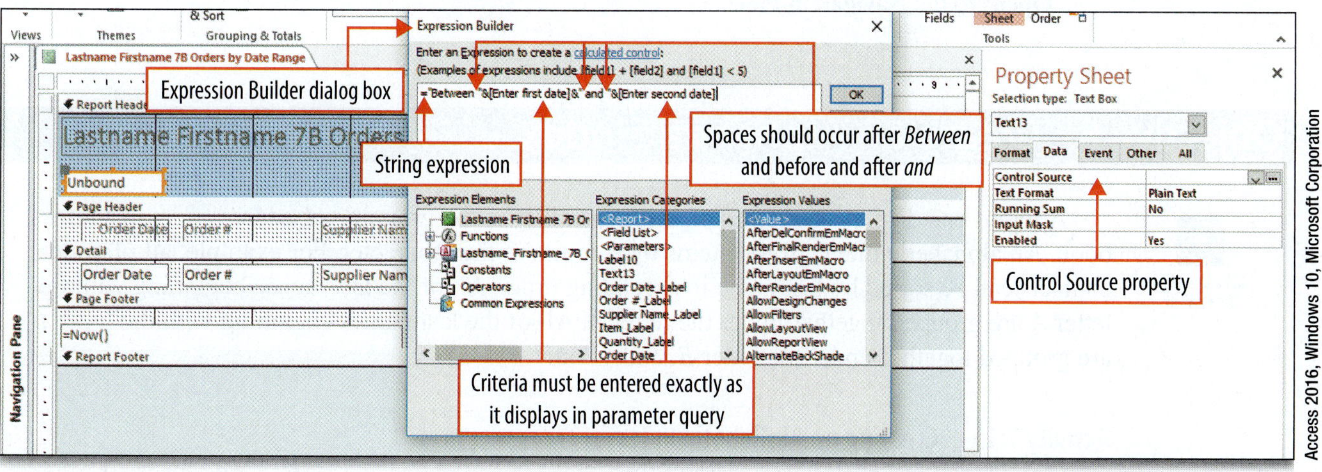

FIGURE 7.43

5 In the **Expression Builder** dialog box, click **OK**, and then press Enter to save the property setting.

ALERT! Did a message box display?

If a message box displays stating that the expression you entered contains invalid syntax, click OK. Click the Control Source Build button, and then view Figure 7.43 to be sure that you typed the expression correctly. Common errors include not typing the equal sign, using parentheses instead of square brackets, leaving out the beginning or ending quotation marks, or leaving out one of the & symbols.

6 **Close** the **Property Sheet**. Under **Report Design Tools**, on the **Format tab**, in the **Font group**, click the **Font Color arrow**. Under **Theme Colors**, on the sixth row, click the fourth color—**Dark Blue, Text 2, Darker 50%**.

7 With the text box control selected, in the **Font group**, click the **Font Size arrow**, and from the displayed list, click **14**. Increase the width of the text box until the entire expression displays.

8 Under **Report Design Tools**, click the **Arrange tab**, and then, in the **Sizing & Ordering group**, click **Size/Space**, and then click **To Fit**.

The height of the text box control is increased to fit the size of the text, and the width of the text box control will adjust to fit the title that displays in Layout view, Report view, and Print Preview view.

9 **Save** the report, and switch to **Report** view. For the first date, enter **6/1/19** and for the second date, enter **7/31/19**

The report displays with a subtitle of *Between 6/1/19 and 7/31/19*. When the criteria is displayed in the report, be sure to enter the criteria in a consistent manner. For example, do not enter 6/1/19 for the first date and July 31, 2019, for the second date. If you do, the subtitle will display as *Between 6/1/19 and July 31, 2019*.

ALERT! Did another message box display?

If an unexpected Enter Parameter Value message box displays when you try to print or preview a report, you may have misspelled one of the criteria or a field name in the expression. If this happens, click Cancel to return to Design view and correct the error. The parameter criteria in this report must match exactly to the parameter criteria used in the query.

10 Switch to **Print Preview** view. If you are instructed to submit this result, create a paper printout or PDF electronic image. **Close** the **Print Preview** window and the **report**, and then **Open** the **Navigation Pane**.

Objective 6 Create an Alphabetic Index

GO! Learn How Video A7-6

A report can display an ***alphabetic index***, similar to the grouping of addresses in an address book. An alphabetic index groups items by a common first character. For example, all of your contacts can be sorted by last name in ascending order. All of the last names beginning with the letter *A* are grouped together under the letter *A*. All of the last names beginning with the letter *B* are grouped together under the letter *B*, and so on.

Activity 7.15 | Creating an Alphabetic Index

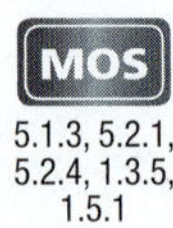

5.1.3, 5.2.1, 5.2.4, 1.3.5, 1.5.1

In this Activity you will create an alphabetic index of the suppliers' names from the *7B MWB Suppliers* table, using the *7B MWB Supplier Names Query*.

1 In the **Navigation Pane**, under **Queries**, double-click **7B MWB Supplier Names Query**. Take a moment to review the data in the query, and then switch to **Design** view.

The query displays the Supplier Name field in ascending order from the *7B MWB Suppliers* table.

2 **Close** [X] the query, and then **Close** [«] the **Navigation Pane**.

3 On the **Create tab**, in the **Reports group**, click **Report Wizard**.

4 Because the query was selected in the Navigation Pane, in the **Report Wizard** dialog box, in the **Tables/Queries** box, **Query: 7B MWB Supplier Names Query** displays. If it does not display, click the **Tables/Queries arrow**, and then click **Query: 7B MWB Supplier Names Query**.

5 Under **Available Fields**, double-click **Supplier Name** to add the field name to the **Selected Fields** box, and then click **Next**.

Because the query sorts the Supplier Name in ascending order, the field will automatically be sorted in the same manner in the report.

6 Click **Next**. Under **Layout**, verify that the **Tabular** option button is selected. Under **Orientation**, verify that the **Portrait** option button is selected, and then click **Next**.

7 For the title of the report, type **Lastname Firstname 7B Supplier Alphabetic Index** and then click **Finish**. Compare your screen with Figure 7.44.

The report displays in Print Preview.

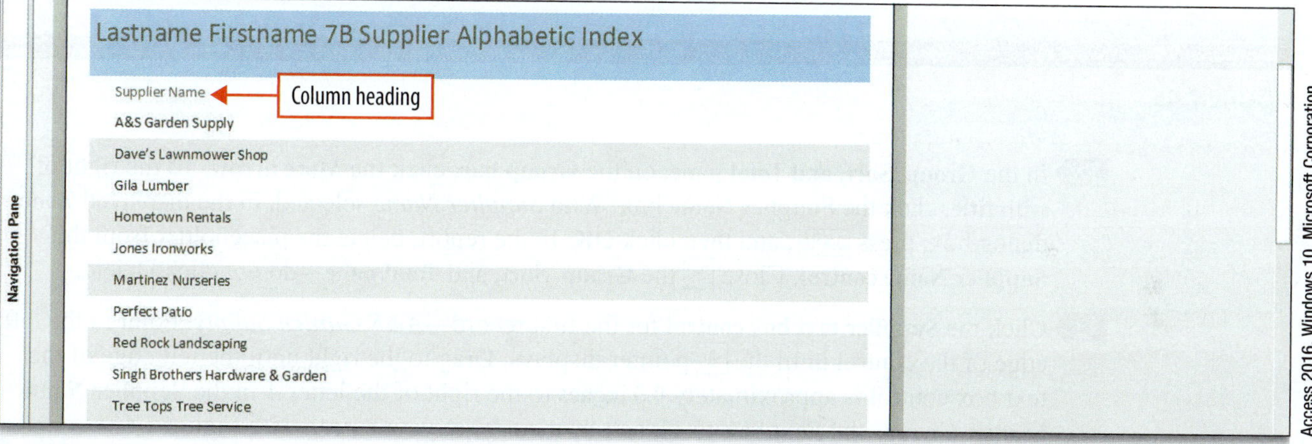

FIGURE 7.44

8 **Close** Print Preview. In **Design** view, click anywhere in an empty area of the design grid to deselect the controls, if necessary, and then click the **Supplier Name label control**. Be sure that the orange border only displays around the Supplier Name label control. Press [Delete] to remove the Supplier Name label control from the report.

9 **Save** [save icon] the report, and then switch to **Layout** view.

10 Under **Report Layout Tools**, on the **Design tab**, in the **Grouping & Totals group**, click **Group & Sort**. In the **Group, Sort, and Total pane**, click **Add a group**. From the displayed list, click **Supplier Name**.

The report must be grouped by Supplier Name to create an alphabetic index of the names.

11 In the **Group, Sort, and Total pane**, on the **Group bar**, click the **More arrow**. Click the **by entire value arrow**, and from the displayed list, click the **by first character** option button. Verify that the third option from the right displays **with a header section**. Click in an empty area of the report, and then compare your screen with Figure 7.45.

The first letter of the Supplier Name displays above the supplier names along with a label control that displays Supplier Name. You can select more than one character for the index.

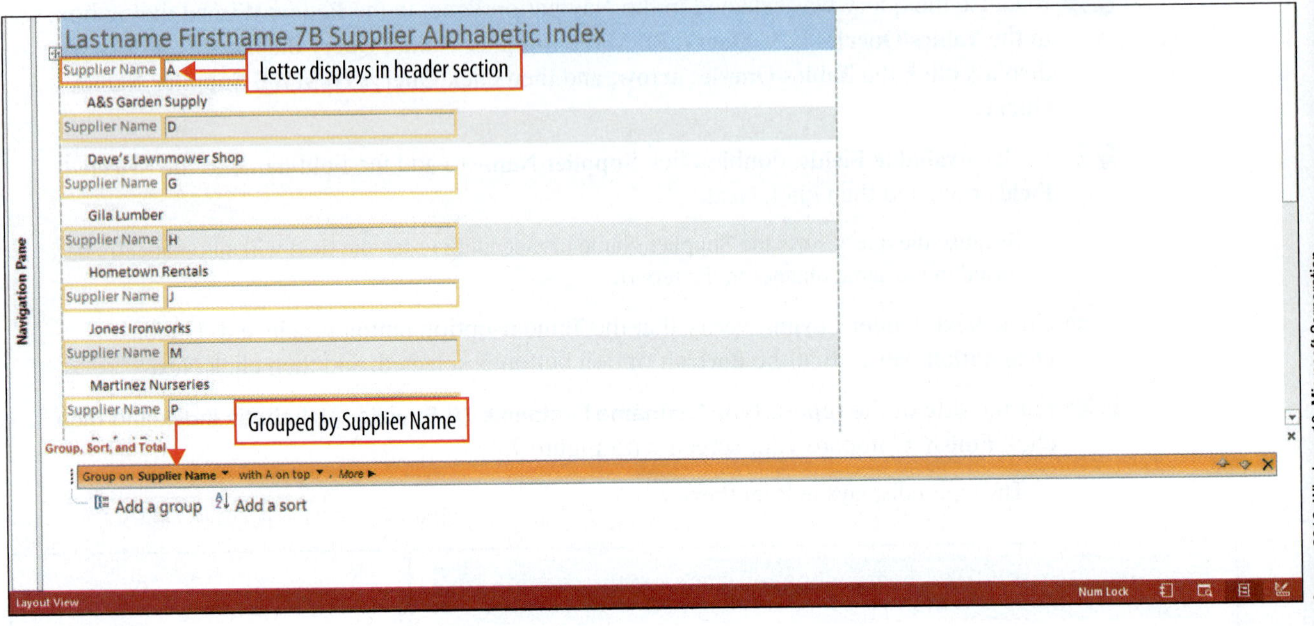

FIGURE 7.45

12 In the **Group, Sort, and Total pane**, on the **Group bar**, click the **More arrow**. To the right of **with title**, click the **Supplier Name** link. With *Supplier Name* selected, in the displayed **Zoom** dialog box, press Delete, and then click **OK**. In the report, delete the placeholder from the **Supplier Name control**. Close ☒ the **Group, Sort, and Total pane**—do *not* click Delete.

13 Click the **Supplier text box control** for the first record—*A&S Garden Supply*. Point to the left edge of the control until the ⟷ pointer displays. Drag to the right until the left edge of the text box control is approximately **0.5 inches** to the right of the letter *A* in the **Supplier Name header**. Change the **Font Size** to **12**, and then compare your screen with Figure 7.46.

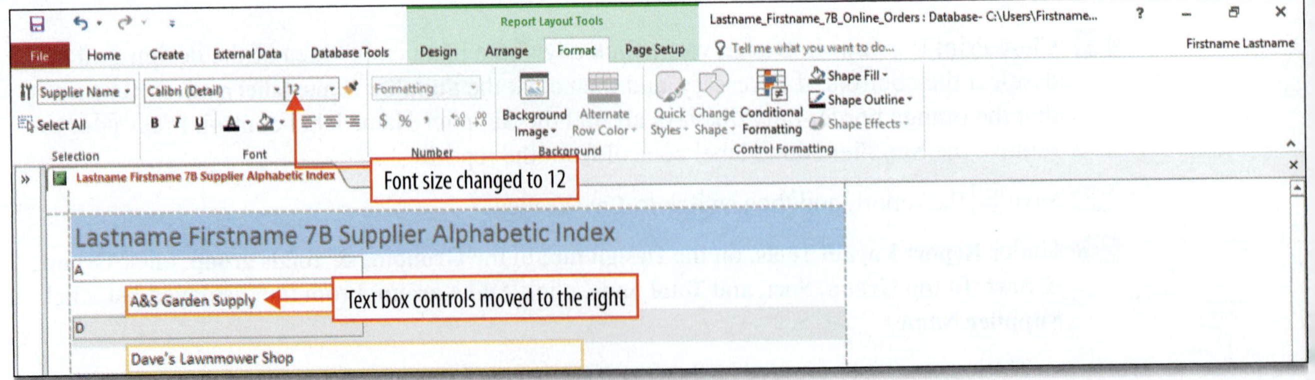

FIGURE 7.46

14 Click the **text box control** that displays the letter *A*, and change the **Font Size** to **16**. Change the **Font Color** to **Dark Blue, Text 2**, and then add **Bold** formatting to the text.

15 **Save** [icon] the report, and then switch to **Report** view. Compare your screen with Figure 7.47.

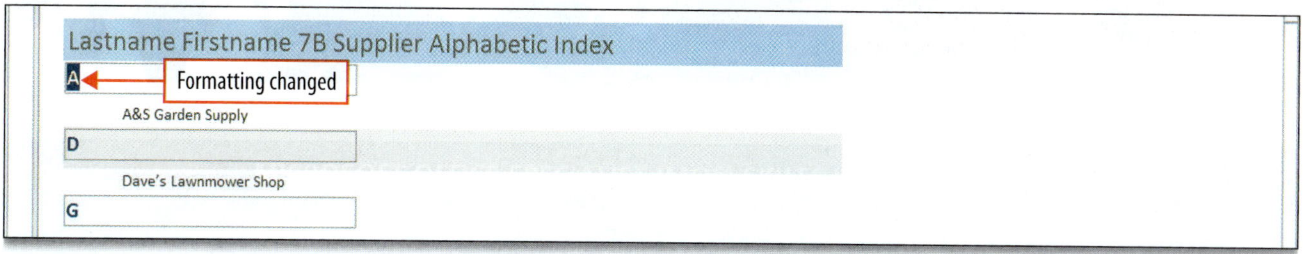

Lastname Firstname 7B Supplier Alphabetic Index
A ← Formatting changed
A&S Garden Supply
D
Dave's Lawnmower Shop
G

FIGURE 7.47

Access 2016, Windows 10, Microsoft Corporation

16 Switch to **Print Preview** view. If you are instructed to submit this result, create a paper printout or PDF electronic image. On the **Print Preview tab**, in the **Close Preview group**, click **Close Print Preview**.

17 **Close** [X] the report, and then **Open** [»] the **Navigation Pane**. Resize the **Navigation Pane** to be sure all object names display fully. **Close** the database, and **Close** Access.

18 As directed by your instructor, submit your database and the paper printout or PDF electronic image of the five objects—one database and four reports—that are the result of this project.

END | You have completed Project 7B

END OF CHAPTER

SUMMARY

Advanced forms can display data from one or more record sources. Split forms display data from one table in two different ways in the same form: Form view and Datasheet view.

Subforms display data from related tables on one form; they can be created using the Form Tool and the Form Wizard or by dragging a related table onto an existing form. Forms can be displayed on multiple pages by using the tab control.

Reports can be simple or complex; advanced reports use some of the same techniques as advanced forms. Subreports can be created using the SubReport Wizard and by dragging a related table onto a report.

A report can be created from a parameter query, and the criteria can be displayed in an unbound control in the report. A report can also use grouping and sorting features to display an alphabetic index.

GO! LEARN IT ONLINE

Review the concepts, key terms, and MOS skills in this chapter by completing these online challenges, which you can find at **MyITLab**.

Matching and Multiple Choice: Answer matching and multiple choice questions to test what you learned in this chapter.

Lessons on the GO!: Learn how to use all the new apps and features as they are introduced by Microsoft.

MOS Prep Quiz: Answer questions to review the MOS skills that you have practiced in this chapter.

PROJECT GUIDE FOR ACCESS CHAPTER 7

Your instructor will assign Projects from this list to ensure your learning and assess your knowledge.

PROJECT GUIDE FOR ACCESS CHAPTER 7			
Project	**Apply Skills from These Chapter Objectives**	**Project Type**	**Project Location**
7A **MyITLab**	Objectives 1–3 from Project 7A	**7A Instructional Project (Grader Project)** Guided instruction to learn the skills in Project 7A.	In MyITLab and in text
7B **MyITLab**	Objectives 4–6 from Project 7B	**7B Instructional Project (Grader Project)** Guided instruction to learn the skills in Project 7B.	In MyITLab and in text
7C	Objectives 1–3 from Project 7A	**7C Chapter Review (Scorecard Grading)** A guided review of the skills from Project 7A.	In text
7D	Objectives 4–6 from Project 7B	**7D Chapter Review (Scorecard Grading)** A guided review of the skills from Project 7B.	In text
7E	Objectives 1–3 from Project 7A	**7E Mastery (Scorecard Grading) Mastery and Transfer of Learning** A demonstration of your mastery of the skills in Project 7A with extensive decision making.	In text
7F	Objectives 4–6 from Project 7B	**7F Mastery (Scorecard Grading) Mastery and Transfer of Learning** A demonstration of your mastery of the skills in Project 7B with extensive decision making.	In text
7G **MyITLab**	Objectives 1–6 from Projects 7A and 7B	**7G Mastery (Grader Project) Mastery and Transfer of Learning** A demonstration of your mastery of the skills in Projects 7A and 7B with extensive decision making.	In MyITLab and in text
7H	Combination of Objectives from Projects 7A and 7B	**7H GO! Fix It (Scorecard Grading) Critical Thinking** A demonstration of your mastery of the skills in Projects 7A and 7B by creating a correct result from a document that contains errors you must find.	Instructor Resource Center (IRC) and MyITLab
7I	Combination of Objectives from Projects 7A and 7B	**7I GO! Make It (Scorecard Grading) Critical Thinking** A demonstration of your mastery of the skills in Projects 7A and 7B by creating a result from a supplied picture.	IRC and MyITLab
7J	Combination of Objectives from Projects 7A and 7B	**7J GO! Solve It (Rubric Grading) Critical Thinking** A demonstration of your mastery of the skills in Projects 7A and 7B, your decision-making skills, and your critical thinking skills. A task-specific rubric helps you self-assess your result.	IRC and MyITLab
7K	Combination of Objectives from Projects 7A and 7B	**7K GO! Solve It (Rubric Grading) Critical Thinking** A demonstration of your mastery of the skills in Projects 7A and 7B, your decision-making skills, and your critical thinking skills. A task-specific rubric helps you self-assess your result.	In text
7L	Combination of Objectives from Projects 7A and 7B	**7L GO! Think (Rubric Grading) Critical Thinking** A demonstration of your understanding of the chapter concepts applied in a manner that you would use outside of college. An analytic rubric helps you and your instructor grade the quality of your work by comparing it to the work an expert in the discipline would create.	In text
7M	Combination of Objectives from Projects 7A and 7B	**7M GO! Think (Rubric Grading) Critical Thinking** A demonstration of your understanding of the chapter concepts applied in a manner that you would use outside of college. An analytic rubric helps you and your instructor grade the quality of your work by comparing it to the work an expert in the discipline would create.	IRC and MyITLab
7N	Combination of Objectives from Projects 7A and 7B	**7N You and GO! (Rubric Grading) Critical Thinking** A demonstration of your understanding of the chapter concepts applied in a manner that you would use in a personal situation. An analytic rubric helps you and your instructor grade the quality of your work.	IRC and MyITLab

GLOSSARY

GLOSSARY OF CHAPTER KEY TERMS

Alphabetic index Grouping of items by a common first character.

Bang operator The exclamation (!) mark that tells Access that what follows is an object that belongs to the object that precedes it in the expression.

Bound report A report that displays data from an underlying table, query, or SQL statement as specified in the report's Record Source property.

Conditional formatting A way to apply formatting to specific controls based on a comparison to a rule set.

Junction table A table that breaks down the many-to-many relationship into two one-to-many relationships.

Linked form A form related to the main form that is not stored within the main form.

Main form A form that contains a subform.

Main report A report that contains a subreport.

Many-to-many relationship A relationship between tables where one record in one table has many matching records in a second table, and a single record in the related table has many matching records in the first table.

Mini toolbar A miniature, semitransparent toolbar that is used to work with objects on the screen.

Multi-page form A form that displays the data from the underlying table or query on more than one page.

Nested subform A subform that is embedded within another subform.

Parameter query A query that prompts an individual for criteria before running the query.

Split form An object that displays data in two views—Form view and Datasheet view—on a single form.

SQL statement An instruction using Structured Query Language.

Subform A form that is embedded within another form.

Subreport A report that is embedded within another report.

Syntax The set of rules by which words and symbols in an expression are combined.

Tab control A control that is used to display data on the main form on different tabs, similar to the way database objects, such as forms and tables, display on different tabs.

Unbound report A report that does not display data from an underlying table, query, or SQL statement and has an empty Record Source property setting.

Apply 7A skills from these Objectives:

1 Create a Split Form
2 Create a Form and a Subform
3 Create a Multi-Page Form

Skills Review Project 7C Historical Gardens

Matthew Lee, coordinator for cultural and historical events of MWB Productions, wants the database forms to display related data. For example, he is interested in displaying the contacts for the historical gardens on one form. In this project, you will customize the company's forms to display data in two ways on the same form, to display data from multiple tables on one form, and to display data on multiple pages on a form. Your completed work will look similar to Figure 7.48.

PROJECT FILES

For Project 7C, you will need the following files:

a07C_Historical_Gardens
a07C_MWB_Logo
A new blank Word document

You will save your files as:

Lastname_Firstname_7C_Historical_Gardens
Lastname_Firstname_7C_Tab_Control_Form

PROJECT RESULTS

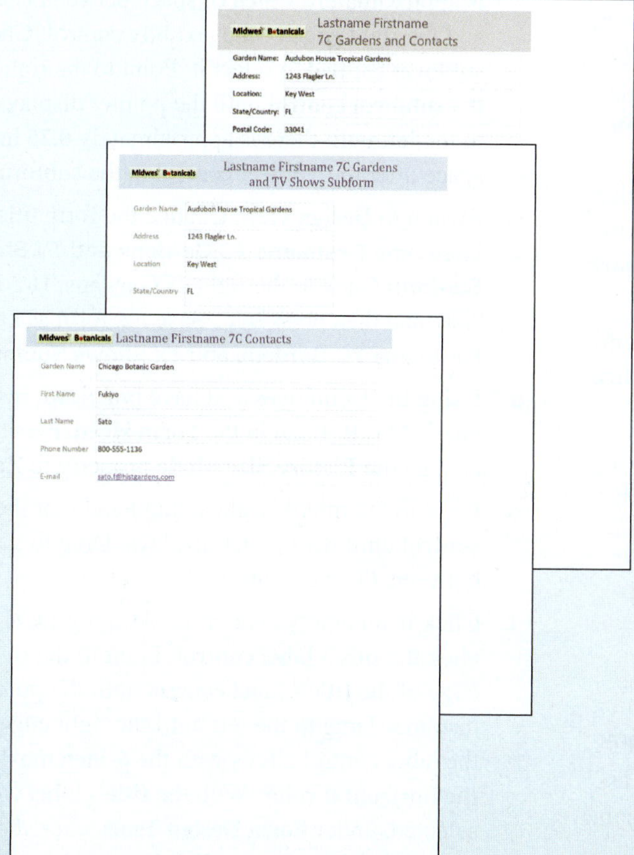

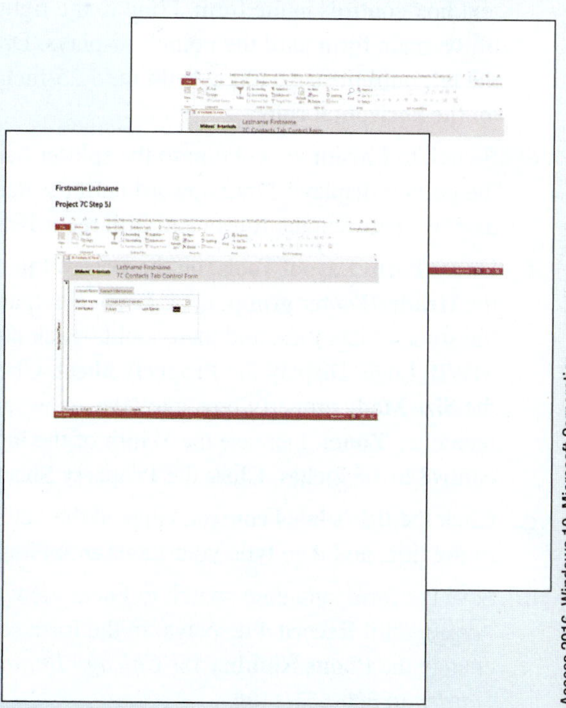

FIGURE 7.48

Access 2016, Windows 10, Microsoft Corporation

(Project 7C Historical Gardens continues on the next page)

Skills Review Project 7C Historical Gardens (continued)

1 Start Access. Open the **a07C_Historical_Gardens** file. Save the database in your **Access Chapter 7** folder as **Lastname_Firstname_7C_Historical_Gardens** If necessary, enable the content.

2 In the **Navigation Pane**, click **7C Contacts** to select the table. **Close** the **Navigation Pane**.

a. On the **Create tab**, in the **Forms group**, click **More Forms**, and then click **Split Form**. **Save** the split form as **Lastname Firstname 7C Contacts Split Form**

b. Under **Form Layout Tools**, on the **Design tab**, in the **Tools group**, click **Property Sheet**. Click the **Selection type arrow**, and then click **Form**.

c. Click the **Form Property Sheet Format tab**, if necessary. In the property setting box for **Split Form Printing**, click the **arrow**, and then click **Form Only**.

d. Switch to **Design** view. Click in the **Split Form Orientation** property setting box, and then click the **arrow**. Click **Datasheet on Top**, and then **Close** the **Property Sheet**. Select the **title's label control**. Point to the right edge of the **title's label control** until the pointer displays. Drag to the left until the right edge of the label control aligns with the **7-inch mark on the horizontal ruler**. Repeat the process with the text box controls in the form. Point to the right edge of the main form until the pointer displays. Drag to the left until the edge aligns with the **7.25-inch mark on the horizontal ruler**.

e. Switch to **Layout** view. Point to the splitter bar until the pointer displays. Drag upward until the dark line displays between the fourth and fifth records.

f. Under **Form Layout Tools**, on the **Design tab**, in the **Header/Footer group**, click **Logo**. Navigate to the student data files, and then double-click **a07C_MWB_Logo**. Display the **Property Sheet**. Click in the **Size Mode** property box, click the arrow, and then click **Zoom**. Increase the **Width** of the **logo control** to **1.5 inches**. **Close** the **Property Sheet**.

g. Click the **title's label control**. Click at the beginning of the title, and then type your **Lastname Firstname**

h. **Save** the form, and then switch to **Form** view. Press PageDown until **Record 4** displays. In the form section, change the **Phone Number** for *Chicago Botanic Garden* to **800-555-1136**

i. On the left side of the form, click the **Record Selector** bar, and then if you are instructed to submit this result, create a paper printout or PDF electronic image of only Record 4—the selected record. **Close** the form. **Open** the **Navigation Pane**.

3 Under **Tables**, click **7C Gardens**. On the **Create tab**, in the **Forms group**, click **Form**. **Close** the **Navigation Pane**.

a. Switch to **Design** view. In the **Detail** section, click on the **Layout Selector** to select the controls in the main form and subform. Under **Form Design Tools**, click the **Arrange tab**. In the **Table group**, click **Remove Layout**. Click an empty area of the design grid to deselect the controls.

b. Switch to **Layout** view. In the main form, click the **Garden Name text box control**. Press Shift and then click each of the text boxes in the main form. Point to the right edge of one of the text box controls until the pointer displays, and then drag to the left until there is approximately **1 inch** of space between *Gardens* and the right edge of the text box control. Click the **subform control** to select it. Point to the right edge of the **subform control** until the pointer displays. Drag to the left until there is approximately **0.25 inches** of space after the **Subject control** in the subform.

c. Switch to **Design** view. Change the form title to **Lastname Firstname 7C Gardens and TV Shows Subform** Click to the right of **Gardens**. Hold down Shift, and then press Enter. **Save** the form as **Lastname Firstname 7C Gardens and TV Shows Subform**

d. Using the techniques you have practiced, insert **a07C_MWB_Logo** in the **Form Header** section, and change the **Picture Size Mode** property to **Zoom**.

e. Point to the middle right sizing handle of the **logo control** until the pointer displays. Drag to the right between *TV* and *Shows*.

f. Click in an empty area of the design grid, and then click the **title's label control**. Point to the right edge of the **title's label control** until the pointer displays. Drag to the left until the right edge of the label control aligns with the **6-inch mark on the horizontal ruler**. With the **title's label control** selected, under **Form Design Tools**, click the **Format tab**. In the **Font group**, click **Center**.

(Project 7C Historical Gardens continues on the next page)

Skills Review Project 7C Historical Gardens (continued)

g. Point to the right edge of the main form until the pointer displays. Drag to the left until the edge aligns with the **6.5-inch mark on the horizontal ruler**.

h. **Save** the form, and then switch to **Form** view. If you are instructed to submit this result, create a paper printout or PDF electronic image of only Record 1—the selected record. **Close** the form.

4 **Open** the **Navigation Pane**. Under **Forms**, open **7C Gardens Main Form** in **Design** view.

a. Under **Form Design Tools**, on the **Design tab**, in the **Controls group**, verify that the **Use Control Wizards** option is active. In the form, point to the top of the **Form Footer section bar** until the pointer displays. Drag downward **1 inch**.

b. In the **Navigation Pane**, under **Tables**, drag **7C Contacts** onto **7C Gardens Main Form** at the **1.75-inch mark on the vertical ruler** and even with the left edge of the form.

c. In the **SubForm Wizard** dialog box, click **Define my own**. Under **Form/report fields**, in the **first list box**, click the **arrow**, and then click **Garden Name**. Under **Subform/subreport fields**, in the **first list box**, click the **arrow**, and then click **Garden Name**. Click **Next**. Under **What name would you like for your subform or subreport?**, type **Lastname Firstname 7C Garden Contact Subform** and then click **Finish**. **Close** the **Navigation Pane**. Close the **Field List**, if necessary.

d. **Save** the form. With the subform selected, under **Form Design Tools**, on the **Design tab**, in the **Tools group**, click **Property Sheet**. Verify that the Selection type is *Form*. Change the **Default View** property to **Single Form**. **Close** the **Property Sheet**.

e. In the subform, click the **Garden Name label control**, press Shift, click the **Garden Name combo box control**, and then press Delete. Move the other controls up to close the empty space. Switch to **Layout** view.

f. Reduce the size of the **First Name**, **Last Name**, and **Phone Number** controls so there is approximately **0.5 inches** of blank space to the right of the data. Point to the lower ight corner of the **subform control** until the pointer displays. Drag to the left and up until the **right edge of the subform control** aligns with the **right edge of the text box controls** and the **bottom edge of the subform control** aligns with the **bottom of the E-mail controls**.

g. Delete the **subform label control**, which displays *Lastname Firstname 7C Garden Contact Subform.*

h. Switch to **Design** view, saving changes if necessary. Change the title of the form to **Lastname Firstname 7C Gardens and Contacts** and then place *7C Gardens and Contacts* on the second line. Adjust the width of the **title's label control** so that the **right edge of the title's label control** aligns with the **right edge of the main form field's text box controls**.

i. **Save** the form. Switch to **Form** view. If you are instructed to submit this result, create a paper printout or PDF electronic image of only the first record. **Close** the form. **Open** the **Navigation Pane**. In the **Navigation Pane**, under **Forms**, **Rename** *7C Gardens Main Form* to **Lastname Firstname 7C Gardens and Contacts Form**

5 In the **Navigation Pane**, under **Forms**, open **7C Contacts TC Form** in **Design** view, and then **Close** the **Navigation Pane**.

a. Point to the top of the **Form Footer section bar**, and drag downward to the **3-inch mark on the vertical ruler**. Under **Form Design Tools**, on the **Design tab**, in the **Controls group**, click **Tab Control**. Move the pointer into the **Detail** section until the plus (+) sign of the pointer is aligned approximately with the **0.25-inch mark on the horizontal and vertical rulers**, and then click.

b. In the selected **tab control**, point to the **right middle sizing handle** until the pointer displays. Drag to the right until the right edge of the tab control aligns with the **6-inch mark on the horizontal ruler**.

c. Under **Form Design Tools**, on the **Design tab**, in the **Tools group**, click **Add Existing Fields**. In the **Field List**, click **Garden Name**. Hold down Shift, and then click **Last Name**. Point to a selected field, and then drag onto the first tab until the top of the arrow of the pointer aligns with the **1.5-inch mark on the horizontal ruler** and with the **0.75-inch mark on the vertical ruler**. **Close** the **Field List**.

d. Click anywhere in the form to deselect the controls. Click the **Garden Name combo box control**, and point to the **right edge** of the control until the pointer

(Project 7C Historical Gardens continues on the next page)

Skills Review Project 7D Featured Gardens (continued)

d. Under **Report Design Tools**, on the **Design tab**, in the **Controls group**, click **Text Box**. In the **Report Header** section, align the top of the plus (+) sign of the pointer with the **0.25-inch mark on the horizontal ruler** and the **0.5-inch mark on the vertical ruler**, and then click. Click the associated **label control**, and then press Delete.

e. Click the **unbound text box control**, and then press F4. Click the **Property Sheet Data tab**, click in the **Control Source** property setting box, and then click **Build**. In the displayed **Expression Builder** dialog box, type **="Original Air Date Between " & [Enter first date] &" and " & [Enter second date]** making sure that you press Spacebar after *Between* and before and after *and*. Click **OK**. **Close** the Property Sheet.

f. With the text box control selected, under **Report Design Tools**, click the **Format tab**. In the **Font group**, click **Center**. In the **Font group**, click the **Font Size arrow**, and click **14**. Increase the size of the text box control until it is the same size and aligns with the right edge of the report title or to the **5-inch mark on the horizontal ruler** (whichever is greater).

g. **Save** the report, and switch to **Report** view. For the first date, enter **1/1/18** and for the second date, enter **12/31/18** Switch to **Print Preview** view. If you are instructed to submit this result, create a paper printout or PDF electronic image. **Close** the **Print Preview** window and the **report**, and then **Open** the **Navigation Pane**.

5 In the **Navigation Pane**, under **Queries**, click **7D Garden Contacts Query**, and then **Close** the **Navigation Pane**. On the **Create tab**, in the **Reports group**, click **Report Wizard**.

a. In the **Report Wizard** dialog box, **Query: 7D Garden Contacts Query** should display. Move all of the fields to the **Selected Fields** box, and then click **Next**. Click **Remove Field** to remove the grouping. Click **Next** three times. For the title of the report, type **Lastname Firstname 7D Contacts Index** and then click **Finish**. **Close** Print Preview.

b. **Save** the report, and then switch to **Layout** view. Adjust the width of all controls so that all of the data displays for every record.

c. Under **Report Layout Tools**, on the **Design tab**, in the **Grouping & Totals group**, click **Group & Sort**. In the **Group, Sort, and Total pane**, click **Add a group**. From the displayed list, click **Last Name**. On the **Group bar**, click the **More arrow**. Click the **by entire value arrow**, and click the **by first character** option button. Click in an empty area of the report.

d. In the **Group, Sort, and Total pane**, on the **Group bar**, click **More**, and then to the right of **with title**, click the **Last Name** link. With *Last Name* selected in the displayed **Zoom** dialog box, press Delete, and then click **OK**. Delete the empty label control box placeholder. **Close** the **Group, Sort, and Total pane**.

e. Click the **text box control** that displays the letter *B*. Under **Report Layout Tools**, click the **Format tab**, in the **Font group**, change the **Font Size** to **16**. Resize the control to approximately **1 inch**.

f. **Save** the report, and then switch to **Report** view. If you are instructed to submit this result, switch to **Print Preview** view, and then create a paper printout or PDF electronic image of the report. **Close** Print Preview.

g. **Close** the report, and then **Open** the **Navigation Pane**. **Resize** the **Navigation Pane** so all object names display fully. **Close** the database, and **Close** Access.

6 As directed by your instructor, submit your database and the paper printout or PDF electronic image of the five objects—one database and four reports—that are the result of this project. Specifically, in this project, using your own name you created the following database and printouts or PDF electronic images:

1. Lastname_Firstname_7D_Featured_Gardens	Database file
2. Lastname Firstname 7D Gardens Main Report	Report
3. Lastname Firstname 7D Featured Gardens Report	Report
4. Lastname Firstname 7D 2018 TV Shows	Report
5. Lastname Firstname 7D Contacts Index	Report

END | You have completed Project 7D

Apply 7A skills from these Objectives:

1 Create a Split Form
2 Create a Form and a Subform
3 Create a Multi-Page Form

Mastering Access Project 7E Phone Orders

MWB Productions maintains a database where customers can place telephone orders for the gardening supplies that are featured in the *Midwest Botanicals* television show. Ruthann Hansen, president of MWB Productions, wants the database forms to display related data. For example, she is interested in displaying the orders on one form. She also wants to display the CSR (customer service representative) information in a tab control form. In the following project, you will customize the company's forms to display data in two ways on the same form, to display data from multiple tables on one form, and to display data on multiple pages on a form. Your completed forms will look similar to Figure 7.50.

PROJECT FILES

For Project 7E, you will need the following files:

a07E_Phone_Orders
a07E_MWB_Logo
A new blank Word document

You will save your files as:

Lastname_Firstname_7E_Phone_Orders
Lastname_Firstname_7E_Tab_Control_Form

PROJECT RESULTS

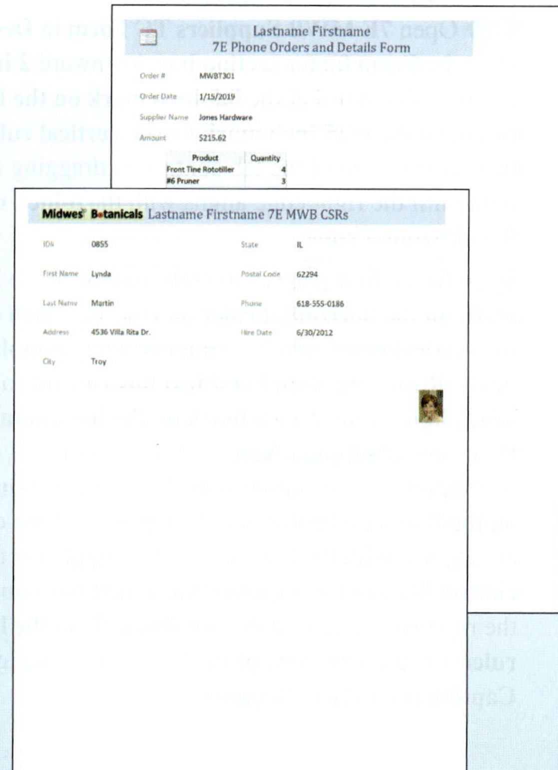

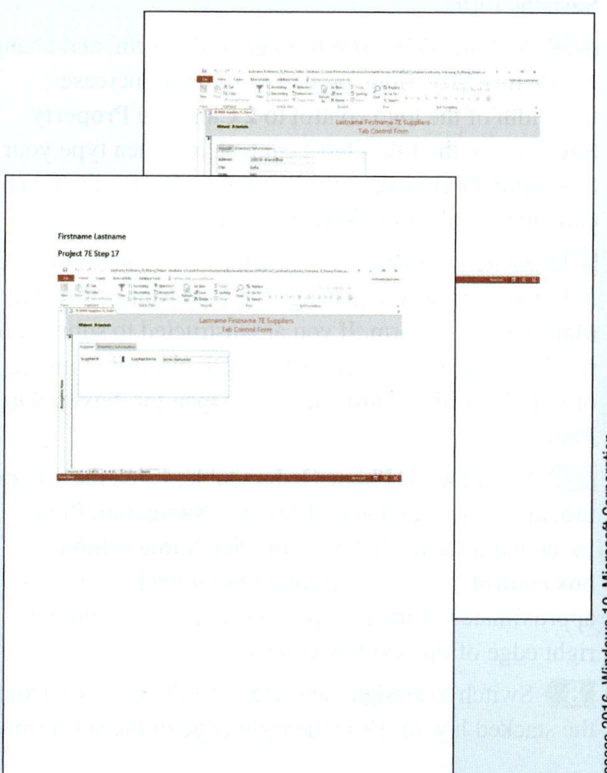

FIGURE 7.50

(Project 7E Phone Orders continues on the next page)

Mastering Access Project 7F Customer Service (continued)

15 If you are instructed to submit this result, create a paper printout or PDF electronic image. **Close** the report, saving changes. **Open** the **Navigation Pane**.

16 Click **7F CSR Last Names Query**. Create a report using the **Report Wizard**. From the **Available Fields** list, add **Last Name** to the **Selected Fields** list. No sorting is required. Use **Tabular** layout and **Portrait** orientation. Title the report **Lastname Firstname 7F CSR Index Close** Print Preview. **Close** the **Navigation Pane**.

17 Switch to **Layout** view. In the **Group, Sort, and Total** pane, click **Add a group**, and then click **Last Name**. On the **Group bar**, click the **More arrow**. Click the **by entire value arrow**, and click the **by first character** option button. Click in an empty area of the report. On the **Group bar**, click **do not keep group together on one page arrow**, and from the displayed list, click **keep whole group together on one page**. Remove the **Lastname Firstname** title and placeholder. **Save** the report.

18 Click the **text box control** that displays the letter *A*, and change the **Font Size** to **16**. Click the **Font Color arrow**. Under **Theme Colors**, on the first line, click the sixth color—**Red, Accent 2**—and then apply **Bold** and **Italic**.

19 **Save** the report, and then switch to **Print Preview**. If you are instructed to submit this result, create a paper printout or PDF electronic image of the first page of the report.

20 **Close** the report, and then **Open** the **Navigation Pane**. **Resize** the **Navigation Pane** so all object names display fully. **Close** the database, and then **Close** Access.

21 As directed by your instructor, submit your database and the paper printout or PDF electronic image of the four objects—one database and three reports—that are the result of this project. Specifically, in this project, using your own name you created the following database and printouts or PDF electronic images:

1. Lastname_Firstname_7F_Customer_Service	Database file
2. Lastname Firstname 7F CSR Orders	Report
3. Lastname Firstname 7F Orders by CSR	Report
4. Lastname Firstname 7F CSR Index	Report

END | You have completed Project 7F

Apply 7A and 7B skills from these Objectives:

3 Create a Multi-Page Form

5 Create a Report Based on a Parameter Query

Mastering Access Project 7G Garden Tours

MWB Productions produces the television show *Midwest Botanicals*. The show's hosts present tours of public and private gardens that showcase the various styles. Matthew Lee maintains an updated database about the tours of the featured historic gardens. In this project, you will design a multi-page form for the gardens and tour information that will be used to update this part of the production. You will also create a report based on a parameter query using the name of the garden. Your completed work will look similar to Figure 7.52.

PROJECT FILES

For Project 7G, you will need the following files:

a07G_Garden_Tours

A new blank Word document

You will save your files as:

Lastname_Firstname_7G_Garden_Tours

Lastname_Firstname_7G_Garden_Tours_Tabs

PROJECT RESULTS

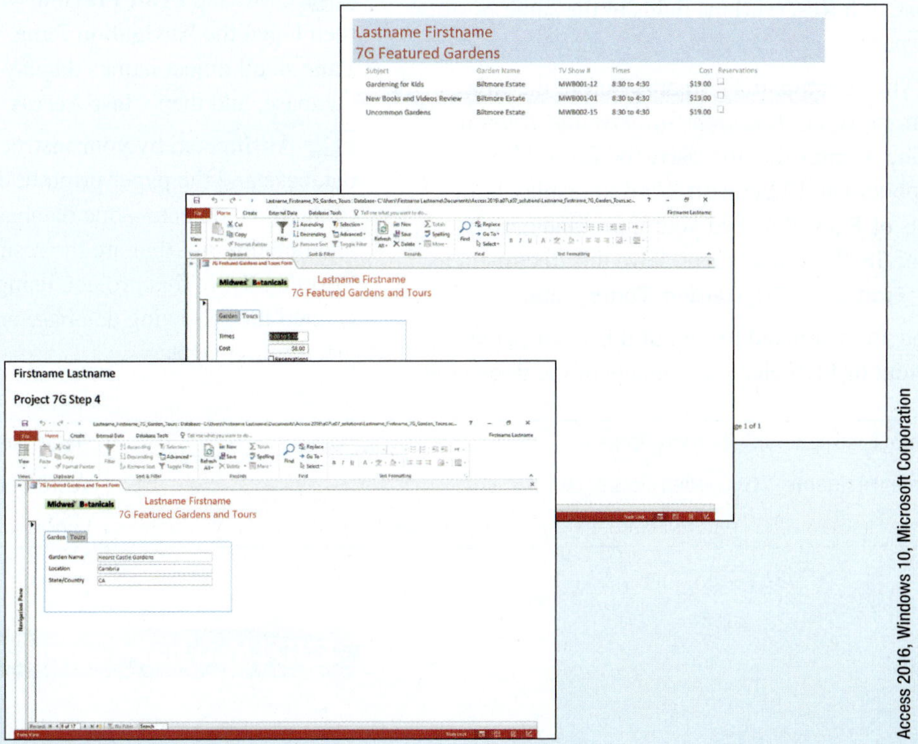

Access 2016, Windows 10, Microsoft Corporation

FIGURE 7.52

(Project 7G Garden Tours continues on the next page)

Mastering Access Project 7G Garden Tours (continued)

1 Start Access. Open the **a07G_Garden_Tours** file. Save the database in your **Access Chapter 7** folder as **Lastname_Firstname_7G_Garden_Tours** If necessary, enable the content.

2 Open **7G Featured Gardens and Tours Form** in **Design** view, and then **Close** the **Navigation Pane**. Drag the top of the **Form footer section bar** down to the **3-inch mark on the vertical ruler**. In the Detail section, add a **tab control** at the **0.25-inch mark on the vertical and horizontal rulers**.

3 Extend the right edge of the **tab control** to the **5-inch mark on the horizontal ruler**. To the first page of the **tab control**, on the **Property Sheet**, add a caption of **Garden** From the **Field List**, add the **Garden Name**, **Location**, and **State/Country** field at the **1.5-inch mark on the horizontal ruler** and the **0.75-inch mark on the vertical ruler**. Extend the **text box controls** to the **4.5-inch mark on the horizontal ruler**. To the second page of the **tab control**, add a caption of **Tours** Add the **Times**, **Cost**, and **Reservations** fields to the same position as the first page.

4 Add your **Lastname Firstname** before the **title** of the form, move *7G Featured Gardens and Tours* to a second line. **Center** the title. **Save** the form. Use the Office Clipboard and Microsoft Word to display both tab controls of **Record 6**. Add your name and activity at the top of the Word document. **Save** this document as **Lastname_Firstname_7G_Garden_Tours_Tabs**.

5 If you are instructed to submit this result, create a paper printout or PDF electronic image of the document. Close **Word**. Return to the **Access** window, **Close** the form, and then **Open** the **Navigation Pane**.

6 Click the **7G Garden and Tours Query**. **Close** the **Navigation Pane**. Create a report using the **Report Wizard**. Use all of the fields. Do not add any grouping levels. **Sort** by **Subject** in **Ascending** order. Use **Tabular** layout and **Landscape** orientation. Title the report **Lastname Firstname 7G Featured Gardens** Modify the report's design.

7 Select the **title control**. Move *7G Featured Gardens* to a second line. Change the **Font Color** to **Red, Accent 2** and the font size to **24**. Set the width of the **title control** to **4** Resize the controls so the report width can be adjusted to **9.5 inches** wide.

8 Switch to **Layout** view. In the **Enter Parameter Value** message box, type **Biltmore Estate Save** the report.

9 If you are instructed to submit this result, create a paper printout or PDF electronic image.

10 Close the **Print Preview** window and the report, and then **Open** the **Navigation Pane**. **Resize** the **Navigation Pane** so all object names display fully. **Close** the database, and then **Close Access**.

11 As directed by your instructor, submit your database and the paper printout or PDF electronic image of the three objects—one database, one Word document, and one report—that are the result of this project. Specifically, in this project, using your own name you created the following database and printouts or PDF electronic images:

1. Lastname_Firstname_7G_Garden_Tours	Database file
2. Lastname_Firstname_7G_Garden_Tours_Tabs	Word document
3. Lastname Firstname 7G Featured Gardens	Report

END | You have completed Project 7G

Apply a combination of the 7A and 7B skills.

CONTENT-BASED ASSESSMENTS (CRITICAL THINKING)

GO! Fix It Project 7H Contests MyITLab

GO! Make It Project 7I Advertising MyITLab

GO! Solve It Project 7J Host Travel MyITLab

GO! Solve It Project 7K Special Programming

PROJECT FILES

For Project 7K, you will need the following files:

a07K_Special_Programming
a07K_MWB_Logo
A new blank Word document

You will save your files as:

Lastname_Firstname_7K_Special_Programming
Lastname_Firstname_7K_TV_Shows_Form

Ruthann Hansen, president of MWB Productions, has scheduled special programming segments for the *Midwest Botanicals* television show. These segments will focus on holiday and seasonal topics.

Open the **a07K_Special_Programming** database and save it as **Lastname_Firstname_7K_Special_Programming** In this project, you will use the *7K TV Shows Form* to create a multi-page form. To the first tab, add the TV Show # and the Original Air Date fields with a caption of **Show** To the second tab, add the Subject, Featured Garden, and Program fields with a caption of **Programming** Adjust all controls to display all data. In the title, replace *Lastname Firstname* with your first and last names. Rename the form as **Lastname Firstname 7K TV Shows Form** Create a Microsoft Word document to display both tabs for Record 15. Save this document as **Lastname_Firstname_7K_TV_Shows_Form** If you are instructed to submit this result, create a paper printout or PDF electronic image of this document.

Open the *7K Special Programs* report in Design view. Add the *7K Show Sponsors* table as a subreport. Link the reports using the TV Show # field. Accept the default name for the subreport. Remove the TV Show # controls from the subreport and reduce the width of the subreport to 3 inches. Delete the subreport label control. Add a logo and two-line title including your Lastname Firstname. Apply color in backgrounds, outlines, and fonts to create a well-formatted report on a portrait page. If you are instructed to submit this result, create a paper printout or PDF electronic image of the first page of the report.

Create an alphabetic index on *7K Special Programs* using the Program field sorted in ascending order. Format the text box controls containing the letters. Arrange and adjust label and text box controls to display all data. Save as **Lastname Firstname 7K Special Programming Index** If you are instructed to submit this result, create a paper printout or PDF electronic image of the report.

(Project 7K Special Programming continues on the next page)

CONTENT-BASED ASSESSMENTS (CRITICAL THINKING)

GO! Solve It Project 7K Special Programming (continued)

Performance Level

Performance Criteria	Exemplary: You consistently applied the relevant skills	Proficient: You sometimes, but not always, applied the relevant skills	Developing: You rarely or never applied the relevant skills
Create 7K TV Shows Form	Form created with the correct controls and formatted as directed	Form created with no more than two missing elements	Form created with more than two missing elements
Modify 7K Special Programs Report	Report modified and formatted correctly	Report modified with no more than two missing elements	Report modified with more than two missing elements
Modify 7K Special Programming Index	Index created to include the correct controls, grouping, sorting, and formatting	Index created with no more than two missing elements	Index created with more than two missing elements

END | You have completed Project 7K

OUTCOME-BASED ASSESSMENTS (CRITICAL THINKING)

RUBRIC

The following outcomes-based assessments are open-ended assessments. That is, there is no specific correct result; your result will depend on your approach to the information provided. Make Professional Quality your goal. Use the following scoring rubric to guide you in how to approach the problem and then to evaluate how well your approach solves the problem.

The *criteria*—Software Mastery, Content, Format and Layout, and Process—represent the knowledge and skills you have gained that you can apply to solving the problem. The *levels of performance*—Professional Quality, Approaching Professional Quality, or Needs Quality Improvements—help you and your instructor evaluate your result.

	Your completed project is of Professional Quality if you:	Your completed project is Approaching Professional Quality if you:	Your completed project Needs Quality Improvements if you:
1-Software Mastery	Choose and apply the most appropriate skills, tools, and features and identify efficient methods to solve the problem.	Choose and apply some appropriate skills, tools, and features, but not in the most efficient manner.	Choose inappropriate skills, tools, or features, or are inefficient in solving the problem.
2-Content	Construct a solution that is clear and well organized, contains content that is accurate, appropriate to the audience and purpose, and is complete. Provide a solution that contains no errors in spelling, grammar, or style.	Construct a solution in which some components are unclear, poorly organized, inconsistent, or incomplete. Misjudge the needs of the audience. Have some errors in spelling, grammar, or style, but the errors do not detract from comprehension.	Construct a solution that is unclear, incomplete, or poorly organized; contains some inaccurate or inappropriate content; and contains many errors in spelling, grammar, or style. Do not solve the problem.
3-Format & Layout	Format and arrange all elements to communicate information and ideas, clarify function, illustrate relationships, and indicate relative importance.	Apply appropriate format and layout features to some elements, but not others. Overuse features, causing minor distraction.	Apply format and layout that does not communicate information or ideas clearly. Do not use format and layout features to clarify function, illustrate relationships, or indicate relative importance. Use available features excessively, causing distraction.
4-Process	Use an organized approach that integrates planning, development, self-assessment, revision, and reflection.	Demonstrate an organized approach in some areas, but not others; or, use an insufficient process of organization throughout.	Do not use an organized approach to solve the problem.

Employee Records

PROJECT ACTIVITIES

In Activities 8.01 through 8.07, you will help Jordan Jones, human resources director for Providence & Warwick Hospital, customize the employee records database to make it easier for his staff to use. You will create macros to automatically display a form and message box when an individual opens the database. The form will be ready for the staff to edit and update employment data for the hospital. Mr. Jones also wants you to add a button with an embedded macro to a form and embed a macro within a report. Finally, you will display and print a report that documents the details of the macros you created. When completed, your results will look similar to Figure 8.1.

PROJECT FILES

If your instructor wants you to submit Project 8A in the MyITLab grader system, log in to MyITLab, locate Grader Project 8A, and then download the files for this project.

For Project 8A, you will need the following file:
a08A_Employee_Records

You will save your database as:
Lastname_Firstname_8A_Employee_Records

PROJECT RESULTS

GO!
Walk Thru
Project 8A

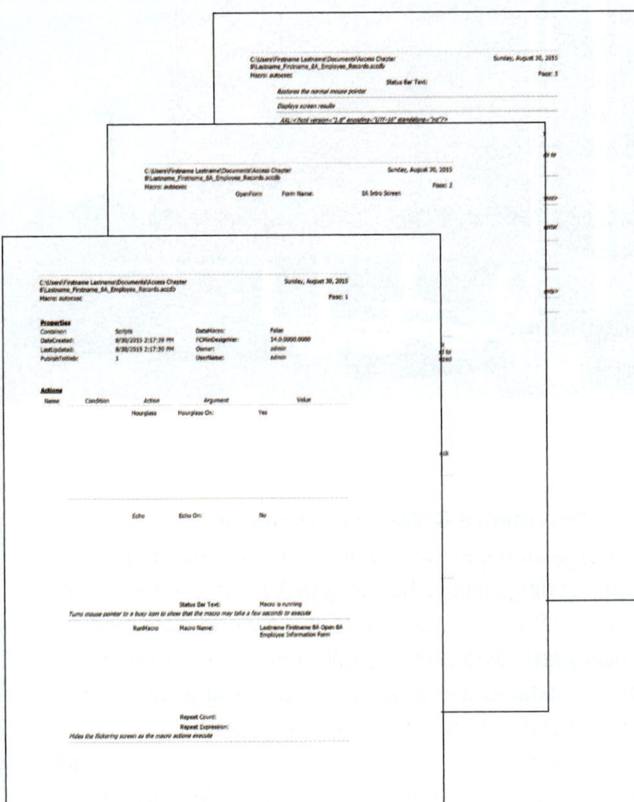

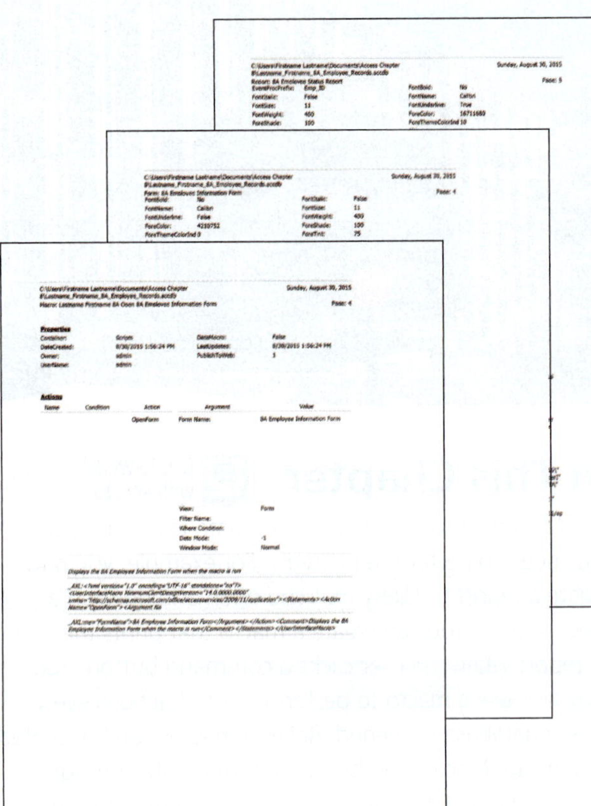

FIGURE 8.1 Project 8A Employee Records

PROJECT RESULTS

In this project, using your own name, you will create the following database and objects. Your instructor may ask for printouts or PDF electronic images:

Lastname_Firstname_Project8A_Employee_Records	Database file
Lastname_Firstname_Project8A_Activity8.07_Step4	Database Documenter report
Lastname_Firstname_Project8A_Activity8.07_Step8	Database Documenter report
Lastname_Firstname_Project8A_Activity8.07_Step12	Database Documenter report

Objective 1 Create a Standalone Macro with One Action

GO! Learn How Video A8-1

A ***macro*** is a series of actions grouped as a single command to accomplish a task or multiple tasks automatically adding functionality to your object or control. A ***standalone macro*** is an object displayed under Macros in the Navigation Pane. Some of the more commonly used actions are to open a report, find a record, or apply a filter to an object. An ***action*** is a self-contained instruction that can be combined with other actions to automate tasks.

Before creating a macro, you should list the actions you want to occur and in what order. You should determine if an argument applies to the action. An ***argument*** is a value that provides information to the action, such as the words to display in a message box. You should also determine if any conditions should be specified. A ***condition*** specifies that certain criteria must be met before the macro executes. A ***comment*** is used to provide explanatory information about the macro or the action.

Activity 8.01 | Creating a Standalone Macro

In this Activity, you will create a standalone macro that will display the *8A Employee Information Form* when the macro is run.

ALERT!

To submit this as an autograded project, log into MyITLab and download the files for this project, and begin with those files instead of a08A_Employee_Records. Begin working with the database in Step 2. For Grader to award points accurately, when saving an object or a macro, do not include your Lastname Firstname at the beginning of the name.

1. Start Access. Navigate to the location where the student data files for this textbook are saved. Locate and open the **a08A_Employee_Records** file. Create a new folder named **Access Chapter 8** and save the database as **Lastname_Firstname_8A_Employee_Records** in the folder. If necessary, add the Access Chapter 8 folder to the Trust Center.

   For this chapter, you must add the Access Chapter 8 folder to the Trust Center—you cannot just enable the content, because some of the macros will not execute properly if the database is not trusted.

2. In the **Navigation Pane**, under **Forms**, click **8A Employee Information Form** to select the form.

3. **Close** [«] the **Navigation Pane**.

8 In the **View** box, click the **arrow**. Notice that you can open the form in Form view, Design view, Print Preview, Datasheet view, PivotTable view, PivotChart view, or Layout view. Be sure that **Form** is selected.

The OpenForm action opens a form in Form view by default.

9 Point to the **Filter Name** box until the ScreenTip appears; read the description. Read the descriptions in the **Where Condition** box and the **Data Mode** box. Be sure that these arguments are left blank.

The Data Mode argument is used for forms that open in either Form view or Datasheet view. If left blank, Access opens the form in the data entry mode set in the form's Allow Edits, Allow Deletions, Allow Additions, and Data Entry property settings.

10 Point to the **Window Mode** box, and then read the description. Click the arrow, and notice the options for displaying the form. Be sure that the Window Mode setting is **Normal**.

11 In the **Action Catalog pane**, under **Program Flow**, double-click **Comment**. In the **Comment** text box that displays below the **OpenForm** action block, type **Displays the 8A Employee Information Form when the macro is run** Compare your screen with Figure 8.5.

You should always enter a description of a macro so that you and others can easily determine the actions that will occur when the macro runs. A green arrow displays to the right of the Comments dialog box; clicking it will move the comment above the action arguments.

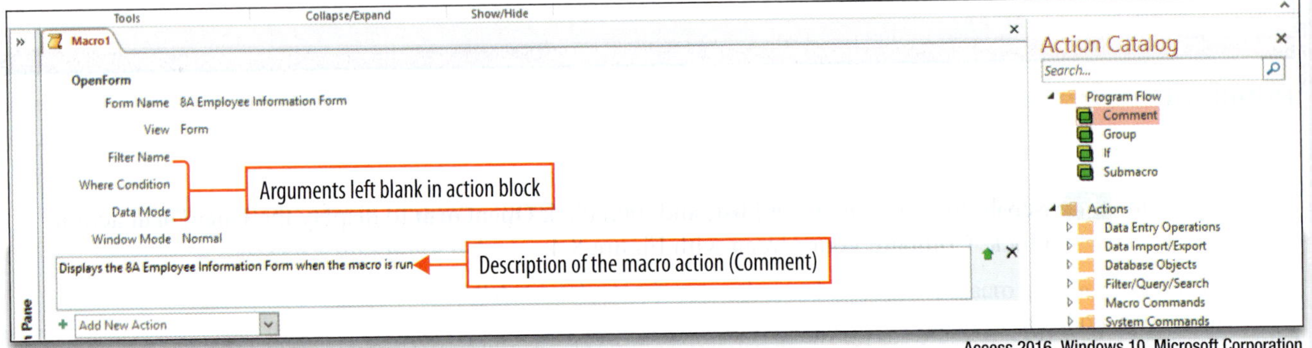

FIGURE 8.5

12 Under **Macro Tools**, on the **Design tab**, in the **Tools** group, click **Run**.

A message displays stating that you must save the macro before you run it.

13 In the displayed message box, click **Yes** to save the macro. In the **Save As** dialog box, type **Lastname Firstname 8A Open 8A Employee Information Form** and then click **OK**.

The macro is saved and runs. When the macro runs, it displays the 8A Employee Information Form.

14 **Close** [X] the **8A Employee Information Form**, and then **Close** [X] the Macro Designer. **Open** [»] the **Navigation Pane**, and then compare your screen with Figure 8.6.

In the Navigation Pane, a new group—Macros—displays, and the newly created macro object displays under the group name.

FIGURE 8.6

Access 2016, Windows 10, Microsoft Corporation

15 In the **Navigation Pane**, under **Macros**, double-click **8A Open 8A Employee Information Form**.

Double-clicking a macro object causes the macro to run.

16 **Close** ☒ the form.

Activity 8.02 | Opening a Form in Its Own Window

1.3.5, 4.2.5

In this Activity, you will modify the properties of a form to create a pop-up, modal window. A ***pop-up window*** displays (pops up), usually contains a menu of commands, and stays on the screen until the user selects one of the commands. A ***modal window*** is a child (secondary window) to a parent window—the original window that opened the modal window—that takes over control of the parent window. A user cannot press any controls or enter any information in the parent window until the modal window is closed. Both pop-up and modal windows are commonly used when the database designer wants to direct a user's focus to the information in the window.

1 In the **Navigation Pane**, under **Forms**, double-click **8A Intro Screen** to open the form in **Form** view.

Like most of the objects you have opened, the form displays with its own tab.

2 Switch to **Design** view. Under **Form Design Tools**, on the **Design tab**, in the **Tools group**, click **Property Sheet**, if necessary. If the Property Sheet does not display *Selection type: Form*, click the **Selection type** arrow, and then click **Form**.

3 On the **Property Sheet**, click the **Other tab**. Click the **Pop Up property setting arrow**, and then click **Yes**. Click in the **Modal property setting box**, click the **arrow**, and then click **Yes**. Compare your screen with Figure 8.7.

The Pop Up property setting of Yes displays the object in its own window on top of all other opened objects. A setting of No displays the object as a tabbed object. Changing the Pop Up setting to Yes is most common for objects that you want to get the attention of the individual using the database. The Modal property setting is used to keep the focus on the opened form, because you cannot change the focus to another database object until the form is closed.

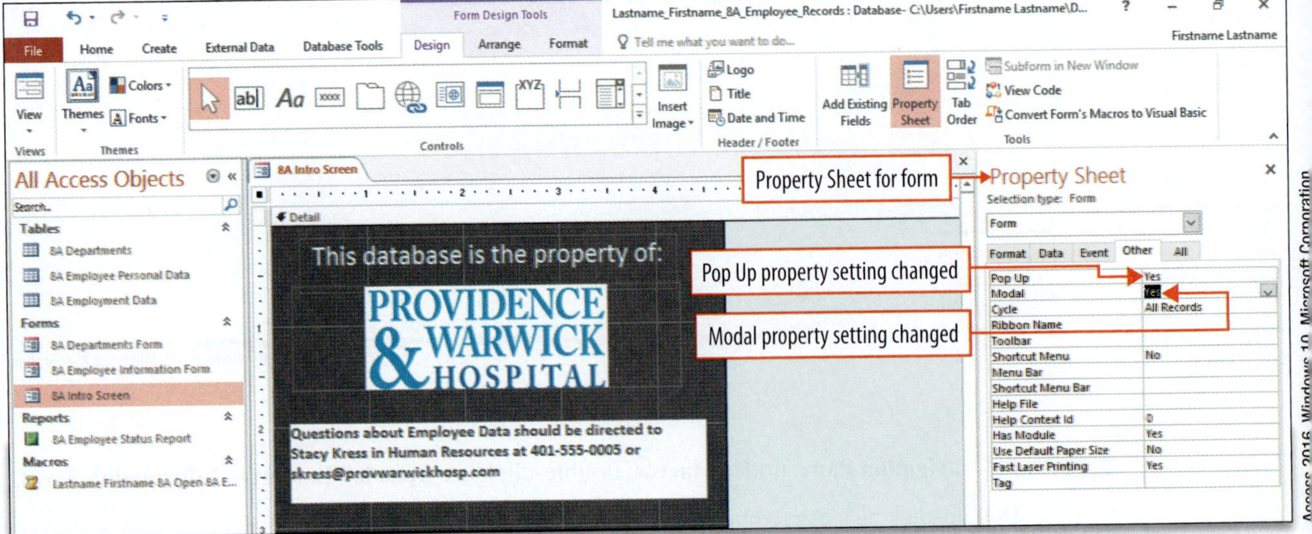

FIGURE 8.7

4 **Close** [X] the **Property Sheet**, and then **Close** [X] the form, saving changes when prompted. In the **Navigation Pane**, under **Macros**, double-click **Open 8A Employee Information Form**, and then under **Forms**, double-click **8A Intro Screen** to open both forms in Form view. Notice the text in the title bar of the pop-up window. In the **Navigation Pane**, under **Forms**, double-click **8A Departments Form**, and notice that the form does not open. Compare your screen with Figure 8.8.

8A Employee Information opens as a tabbed object, and *8A Intro Screen* opens in its own pop-up window. The pop-up window can be moved or closed. Until it is closed, the focus cannot be changed to another database object; that is why you cannot open the *8A Departments Form*. The *8A Intro Screen* form displays a Close button, but no Minimize or Maximize buttons, because the Modal property setting is Yes. A Modal property setting of No means the screen can display the Minimize and Maximize buttons.

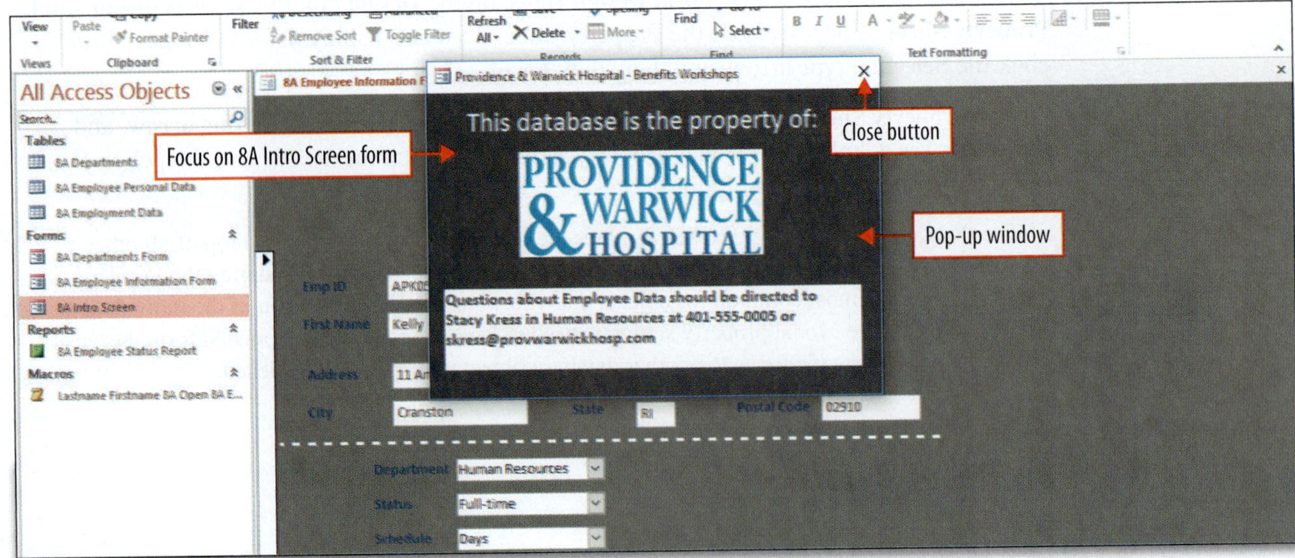

FIGURE 8.8

5 **Close** ☒ the **8A Intro Screen** form, and then **Close** ☒ the **8A Employee Information Form**. In the **Navigation Pane**, open the **8A Intro Screen** form in **Design** view.

6 Under **Form Design Tools**, on the **Design tab**, in the **Tools group**, click **Property Sheet**. Verify that the **Selection type** box displays **Form**. On the **Property Sheet**, click the **Format tab**, and then take a moment to review some of the property settings for this form while comparing your screen with Figure 8.9.

The text entered in the Caption property displays on the title bar of the form when in Form view. The Allow Form View property setting is Yes, while all of the other views are disabled. The Border Style property setting is Dialog, which is a thick border that can include a title bar with a Close button. The form cannot be resized, maximized, or minimized with this border style. Because this is a custom form that does not display any records from an underlying table or query, the Record Selectors, Navigation Buttons, and Scroll Bars property settings have been set to No or Neither.

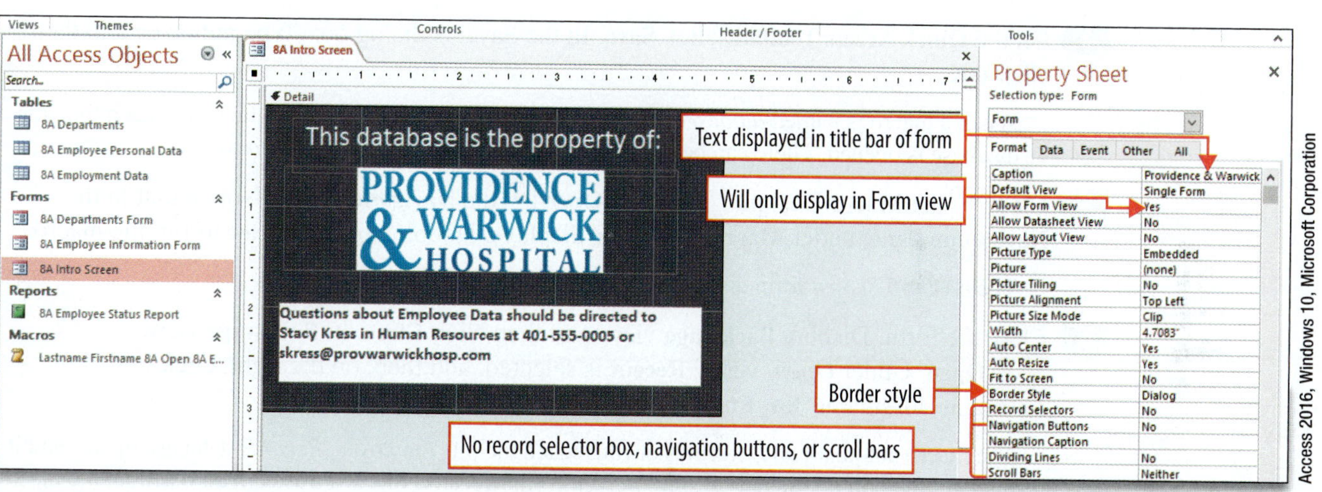

FIGURE 8.9

7 **Close** ☒ the **Property Sheet**, **Close** ☒ the form, and then **Close** « the **Navigation Pane**.

Activity 8.03 | Creating a Standalone Macro That Executes Automatically

In this Activity, you will create another standalone macro that will open the *8A Intro Screen* form when the database is opened.

1 On the **Create tab**, in the **Macros & Code group**, click **Macro** to display the **Macro Designer**.

2 In the **Macro Designer**, in the **Add New Action bar**, click the **arrow**, scroll down, and then click **OpenForm**. In the **OpenForm** action block, click the **Form Name arrow**, and then click **8A Intro Screen**.

3 If necessary, under **Macro Tools**, on the **Design tab**, in the **Show/Hide group**, click **Action Catalog** to display the **Action Catalog pane**. In the **Action Catalog pane**, point to **Comment**, and, holding down the left mouse button, drag it below the **OpenForm** action. Release the mouse button. In the **Comment** box, type **Opens the 8A Intro Screen form** Compare your screen with Figure 8.10.

In addition to double-clicking an action in the Action Catalog, an action can also be added by dragging it to the correct position. Comments are also used to identify or explain a macro action.

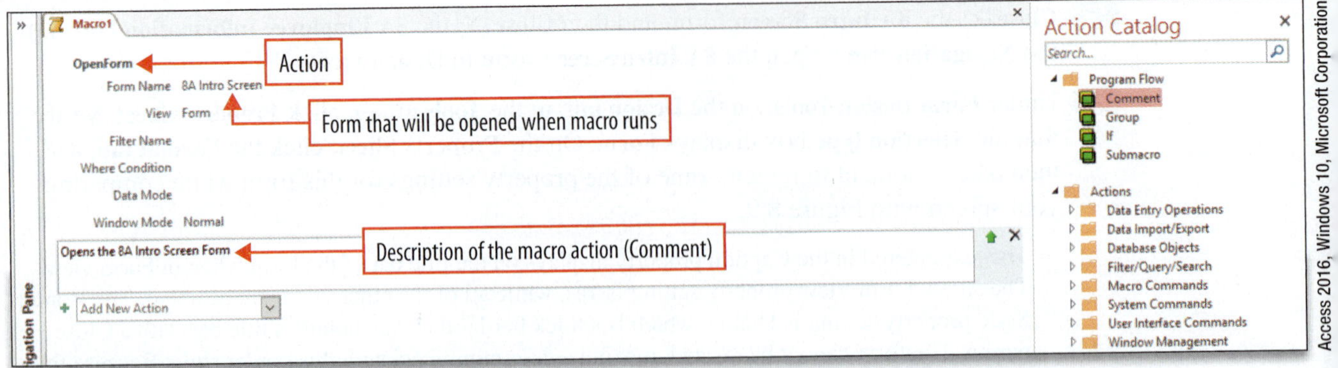

FIGURE 8.10

4 On the **Quick Access Toolbar**, click **Save**. In the **Save As** dialog box, type **autoexec** and then click **OK**.

When a macro is named *autoexec*, Access automatically runs or executes the macro each time the database is opened. There can be only one macro in a database named *autoexec*.

5 **Close** [X] the Macro Designer, and then **Open** [»] the **Navigation Pane**. Notice that in the **Navigation Pane**, under **Macros**, **autoexec** displays. Double-click **autoexec** to run the macro.

The *8A Intro Screen* form displays in its own pop-up, modal window.

6 **Close** the form. Display **Backstage** view, and then click **Close**. In **Backstage** view, click **Open**. Under *Open*, verify **Recent** is selected, and then, on the right, click **Lastname_Firstname_8A_Employee_Records**.

The macro automatically executes or runs when the *8A_Employee_Records* database opens, and it displays the pop-up, modal *8A Intro Screen* form. Because this is a trusted macro action, the macro will execute even if the database has not been trusted or the content enabled.

ANOTHER WAY The preferred method to open an object when the database is opened is the following. Display Backstage view, and then click Options. In the Access Options window, on the left side, click Current Database. Under Application Options, click the Display Form arrow, and then click the form that should be displayed when the database is opened. Because you will add more actions to the standalone macro, it is appropriate to open the 8A Intro Screen form as an auto executable action.

7 **Close** [X] the form.

Objective 2 Add Multiple Actions to a Standalone Macro

GO! Learn How Video A8-2

In the previous activities, you created macros that each contained only one action—opening a form. A macro can contain multiple actions that are executed in a specified order. For example, you can display a busy icon as the macro executes, which is especially useful for macros with multiple actions, to let the user know that Access is working on a process. This can be followed by an action that runs another standalone macro—for example, opening a form. You can then select the title bar on the form, maximize the form, and then turn off the busy icon.

Activity 8.04 | Adding Multiple Actions to an Existing Standalone Macro

In this Activity, you will modify the autoexec macro and add more actions to the macro.

1. In the **Navigation Pane**, under **Macros**, right-click **autoexec**, and then click **Design View**. **Close** « the **Navigation Pane**.

2. In the **Action Catalog pane**, click in the **Search** box, and then type **dis** Under **System Commands**, click **DisplayHourglassPointer** to display a description in the lower section of the Action Catalog.

   When you search for an action using the Action Catalog pane, a description of the macro you selected appears at the bottom of the pane. The Hourglass action changes the normal pointer to a busy icon to inform the user that some action is taking place. On a slower computer, the icon will keep the user from thinking that something is wrong with the database. If the computer is fast, the busy icon may not display. When the macro finishes running, the normal mouse pointer displays.

3. In the **Action Catalog pane**, double-click **DisplayHourglassPointer** to display the **DisplayHourglassPointer** action block. Notice that the default argument is *Yes*. Compare your screen with Figure 8.11.

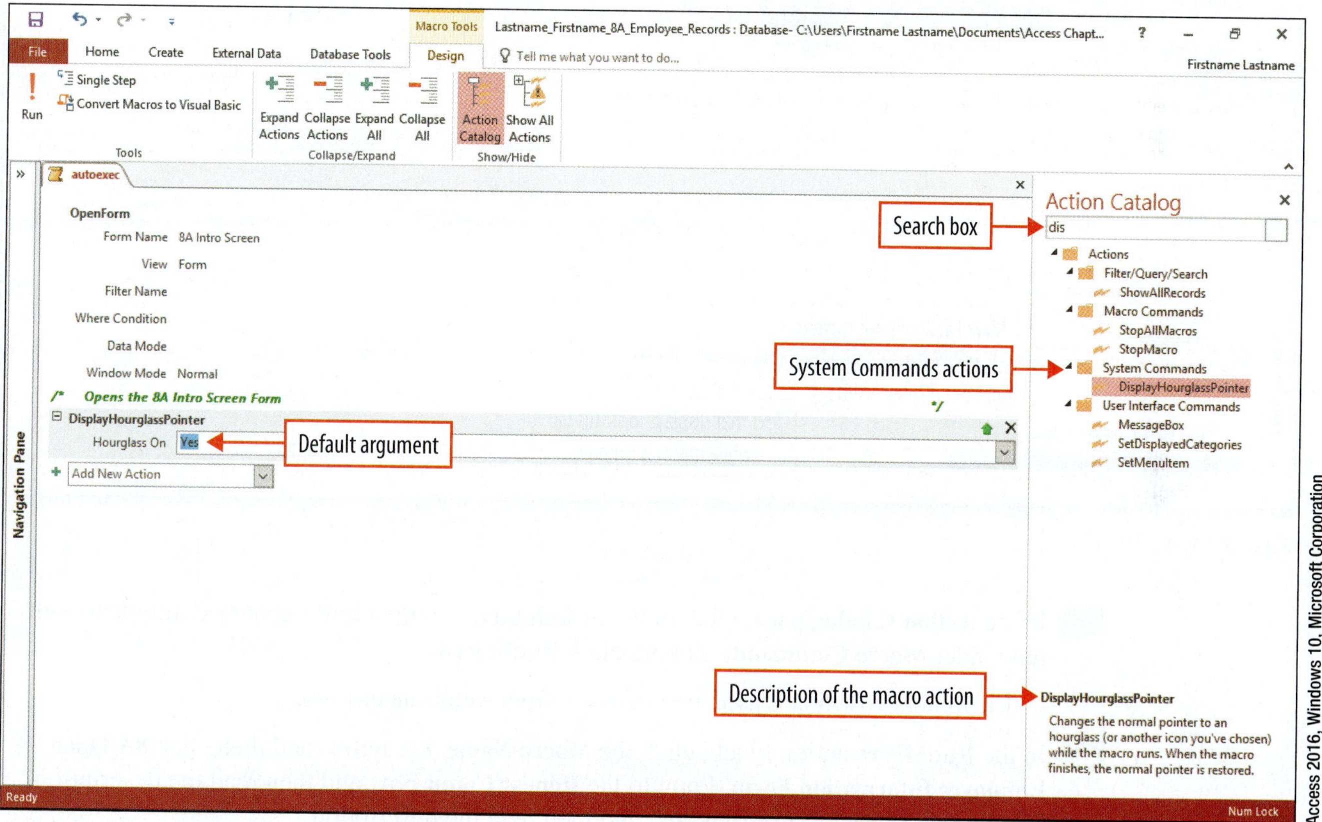

FIGURE 8.11

4. Click inside the **Add New Action bar**, and type **'Turns mouse pointer to a busy icon to show that the macro may take a few seconds to execute** and then press Enter.

   Typing a single quote before the comment identifies the text that follows as a comment. The Comment block displays after you press Enter.

5. Under **Macro Tools**, on the **Design tab**, in the **Show/Hide** group, click **Show All Actions**.

   Recall that the default list of macros displays only trusted macro actions. The next macro action that you will add to the macro is not a trusted macro action. For the macro to execute properly, you must add the location of the database to Trusted Locations or enable the content. Because this macro is used to open a pop-up, modal window, the database location must be trusted. The modal form will open automatically when the database is opened, and you cannot enable the content until the form is closed.

6 In the **Action Catalog pane**, click in the **Search** box, and then replace any existing text with **ech** Under **Macro Commands**, double-click **Echo**. In the **Echo** action block, in the **Echo On** box, click the **arrow**, and then click **No**. Click in the **Status Bar Text** box, and type **Macro is running** Click inside the **Add New Action bar** and type **'Hides the flickering screen as the macro actions execute** and then press Enter. Compare your screen with Figure 8.12.

The Echo macro action hides or displays the results of the macro while it runs; however, it will not hide error messages or property sheets. Changing the Echo On argument to No hides the results. The Status Bar Text argument displays text on the status bar while the macro is running with Echo On set to No. The icon that displays in the Action Argument box indicates that the macro action is not safe.

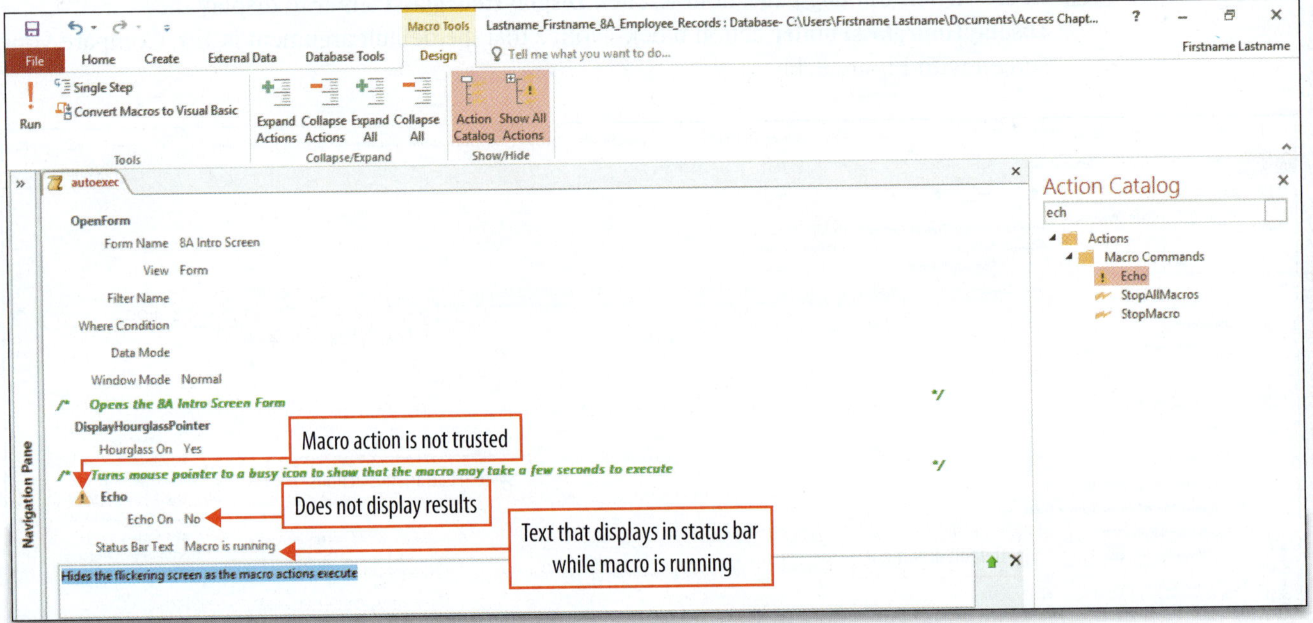

FIGURE 8.12

7 In the **Action Catalog pane**, click in the **Search** box, and then replace any existing text with **run** Under **Macro Commands**, double-click **RunMacro**.

The RunMacro action is used to run a macro from within another macro.

8 In the **RunMacro** action block, click the **Macro Name box arrow**, and then click **8A Open 8A Employee Information Form**. Point to the **Repeat Count** box, and then read the description. Point to the **Repeat Expression** box, and then read the description.

The Repeat Count and Repeat Expression action arguments are used when the macro should be run more than one time. Left blank, the macro will run only one time.

9 Click inside the **Add New Action bar**, type **'Opens the 8A Employee Information Form** and then press Enter.

10 In the **Action Catalog pane**, click in the **Search** box, and then replace any existing text with **mes** Under **User Interface Commands**, double-click **MessageBox**.

The MessageBox macro action is a trusted action that displays a message box that contains a warning or informational message. The MessageBox macro action can contain up to four arguments.

11 In the argument block, click in the **Message** box, and then type **Only employees of Providence & Warwick Hospital are authorized to access this database. Unauthorized use will result in legal action.**

12 Point to the **Beep** box, and read the description of the **Beep** argument. Verify that the **Beep** argument is **Yes**. Click the **Type arrow**, and then compare your screen with Figure 8.13.

There are five different message types listed. Each has a different icon that is displayed in the message box. None is the default message type because no icon displays in the message box.

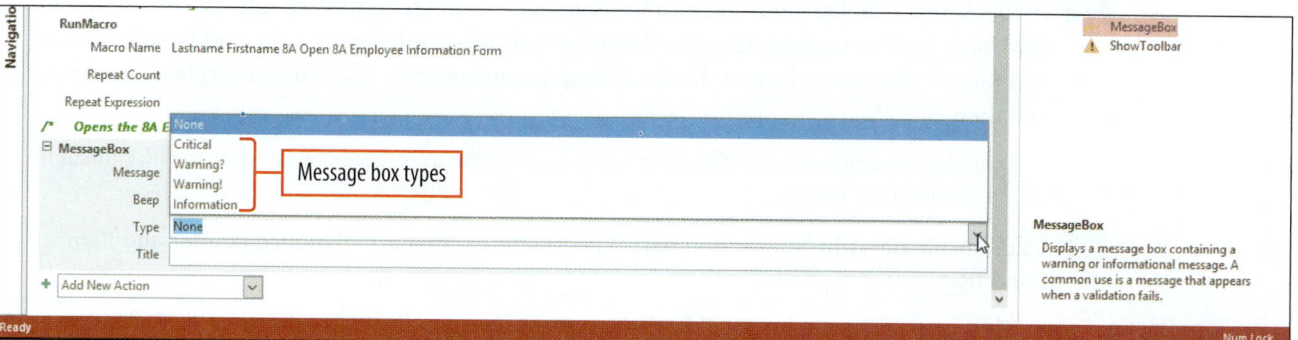

FIGURE 8.13

Access 2016, Windows 10, Microsoft Corporation

13 In the displayed list, click **Warning!** Point to the **Title** box, and read the description of the argument. Click in the **Title** box, and type **For Use by Providence & Warwick Hospital Employees Only!**

14 Click inside the **Add New Action bar**, type **'Displays a warning message box** and press Enter.

15 Scroll to the top of the **Macro Designer** window. Click the **OpenForm** action to make it active. At the right edge of the title, click the green **Move down arrow** two times to move the action below the **DisplayHourglassPointer** action. (Be sure to click twice, not double-click.) Click the green **Move down arrow** in the **OpenForm** action box five more times or until it appears below the comment *Opens the 8A Employee Information Form*. Compare your screen with Figure 8.14.

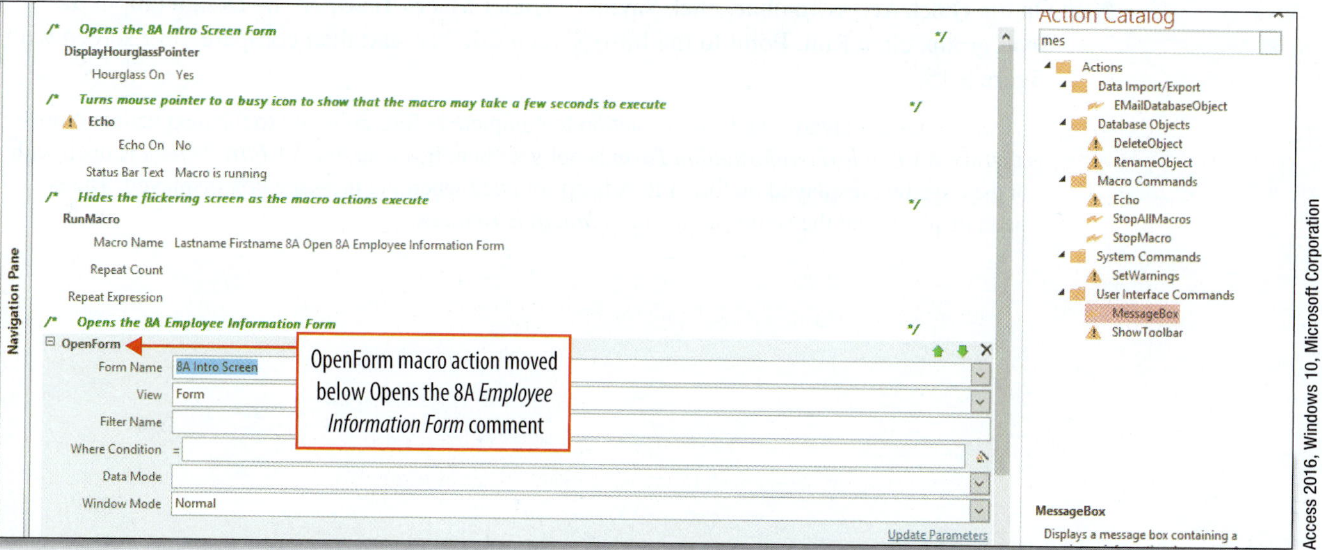

Access 2016, Windows 10, Microsoft Corporation

FIGURE 8.14

ANOTHER WAY Alternatively, you can point to the right edge of the Action or Comment block and drag it to a new position. When you point to the top edge of an Action or Comment block to move it, the mouse pointer does not change in appearance. As you drag the box, an orange line will appear at positions where the box can be dropped.

16 Click the green **Move down arrow** to the right of the **OpenForm macro comment** until you move it below the **OpenForm macro action**. In the **Designer** window, scroll down until the **Add New Action bar** is displayed.

17 In the **Action Catalog pane**, click in the **Search** box, and then replace any existing text with **dis** Under **System Commands**, drag **DisplayHourglassPointer** above the **Add New Action bar**, and release the mouse button. In the **Action Arguments** box, click the **Hourglass On arrow**, and then click **No**.

Dragging an action into the Designer window gives the user more control over the placement of the action in the macro.

18 Click inside the **Add New Action bar**, type **'Restores the normal mouse pointer** and then press Enter.

The normal mouse pointer will be displayed to let the user know that the macro is finished executing.

19 In the **Action Catalog pane**, click in the **Search** box, and then replace any existing text with **ech** Under **Macro Commands**, double-click **Echo**. Notice that in the action block, in the **Echo On** box, the setting is **Yes**. Click inside the **Add New Action bar,** type **'Displays screen results** and then press Enter.

Screen actions will no longer be hidden from the individual using the database. Status Bar Text is not displayed because the Echo On argument is set to Yes.

NOTE Turning Off Macro Actions

Access automatically restores Hourglass and Echo to the default settings after a macro has finished running to protect inexperienced macro programmers from causing the system to continue displaying the hourglass icon, which might lead the user to think that the database is operating incorrectly or is frozen. Even though Access restores these settings, it is good practice to always restore what you turn off. This will lead to better coding if you write Visual Basic code to execute commands.

20 On the **Quick Access Toolbar**, click **Save**. Under **Macro Tools**, on the **Design tab**, in the **Tools group**, click **Run**. Point to the Intro Screen title bar, and then compare your screen with Figure 8.15.

Access does not always wait for one action to complete before going on to the next action. Notice that the *8A Employee Information Form* is not yet open; however, the *8A Intro Screen* is open with a message box displayed on top of it. A beep sounded when the message box displayed. The busy icon displays, and the status bar displays *Macro is running*.

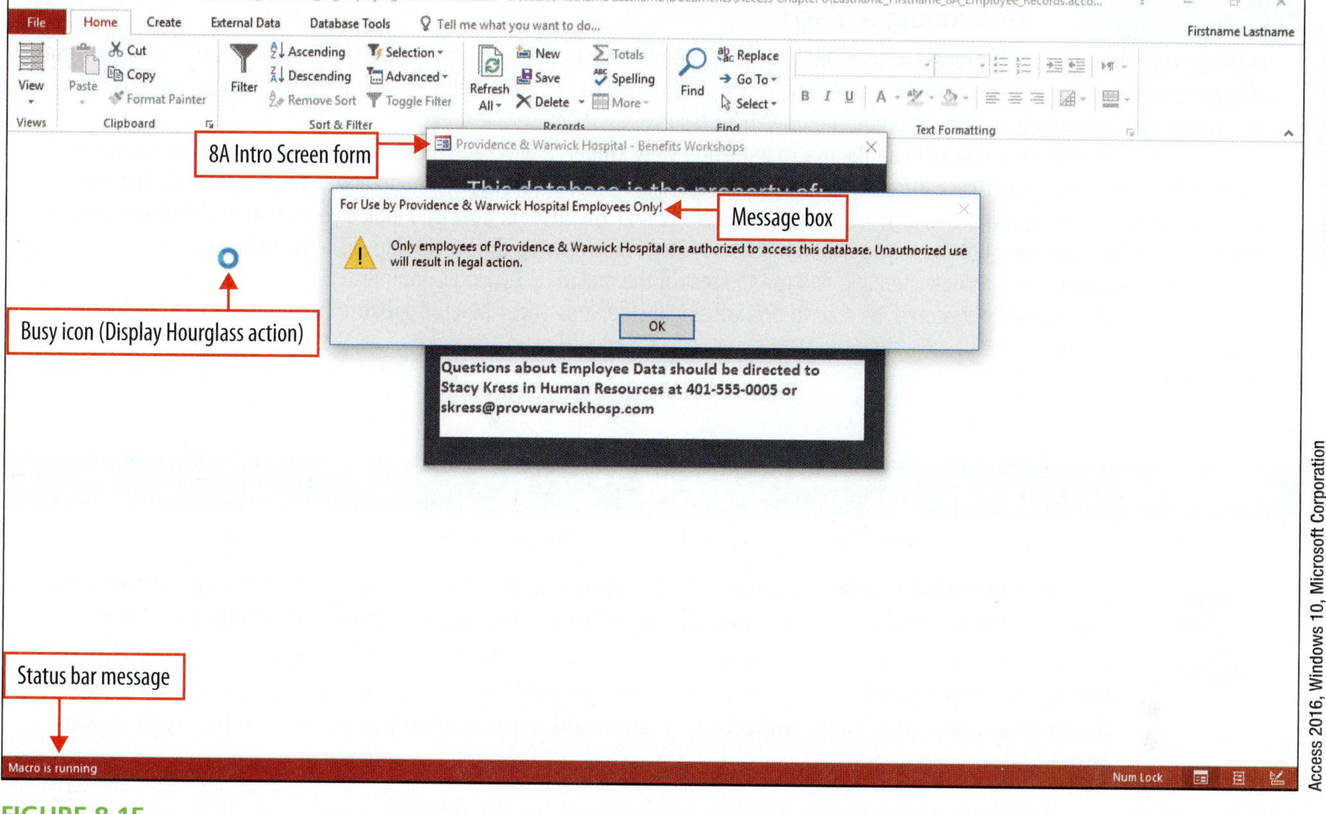

FIGURE 8.15

ALERT! Did a message box display?

If a message box displays stating that the Echo macro action cannot be run in disabled mode, you did not add the Access Chapter 8 folder to Trust Center. The Echo macro action is not trusted by default. To correct this, click OK, click Stop All Macros, and then add the Access Chapter 8 folder to the Trust Center.

21 In the displayed message box, click **OK**. The **8A Employee Information Form** displays underneath the **8A Intro Screen** form. **Close** ☒ the **8A Intro Screen** form. On the **tab row**, right-click any tab, and then click **Close All**.

22 Display **Backstage** view, and then click **Close**. Display **Backstage** view, click **Open** and then, under **Recent**, click **8A_Employee_Records**.

The Autoexec macro automatically executes or runs when the *8A_Employee_Records* database opens, and it displays the pop-up, modal *8A Intro Screen* form with the message box on top of it.

23 In the displayed message box, click **OK**. **Close** ☒ the **8A Intro Screen** form. Leave the **8A Employee Information Form** open for the next Activity.

More Knowledge **Debugging a Macro**

Debugging is using a logical process to find and reduce the number of errors in a program. To debug a macro, you can use ***single stepping***, which executes one action at a time. Single stepping allows you to observe the results of each macro action to isolate an action that may be causing an error or producing unwanted results.

To single step through a macro, open the macro in Design view. Under Macro Tools, on the Design tab, in the Tools group, click Single Step. In the Tools group, click Run. The Macro Single Step dialog box displays information about the macro, including the macro name, condition, action name, arguments, and an error number. An error number of 0 indicates that no error has occurred. In this dialog box, you can carry out the macro action by clicking Step. You can stop the macro and close the dialog box by clicking Stop All Macros, or you can turn off single stepping and run the rest of the macro by clicking Continue.

When the macro has fully executed, be sure to turn off single stepping. Under Macro Tools, on the Design tab, in the Tools group, click Single Step.

Objective 3 Create an Embedded Macro

GO! Learn How
Video A8-3

An ***embedded macro*** is a macro that is stored in the Event properties of forms, reports, or controls. Embedded macros are not displayed in the Navigation Pane under Macros. They are easier to manage because you do not have to keep track of the separate macro objects. Unlike standalone macros, when objects containing embedded macros are copied, imported, or exported, the macros are also copied, imported, or exported. Any standalone macro can be created as an embedded macro.

Activity 8.05 | Creating an Embedded Macro on a Form

1.3.5, 4.2.2, 4.2.5

In this Activity, you will create an embedded macro that will execute when the *Dept Info* button is clicked on the *8A Employee Information Form*.

1 Switch the **8A Employee Information Form** to **Design** view. Under **Form Design Tools**, on the **Design tab**, in the **Controls group**, click **Button** [xxxx]. In the **Detail** section, align the plus sign (+) of the pointer at **4.5 inches on the horizontal ruler** and **2.5 inches on the vertical ruler**, and then click. Compare your screen with Figure 8.16.

The button displays at the set position, and the Command Button Wizard dialog box displays.

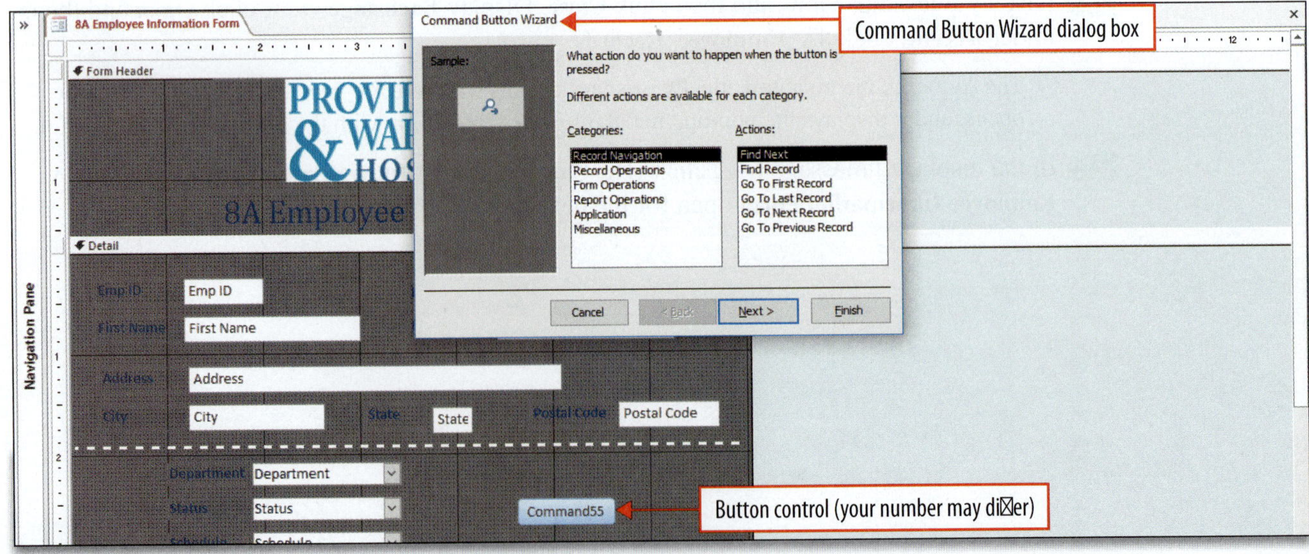

FIGURE 8.16

2 In the **Command Button Wizard** dialog box, click **Cancel**.

Recall that the Command Button Wizard can be used to associate a button with a preset action. Cancel the wizard to embed or assign a macro to the button. Because no name or picture has been associated with the button, it displays Command55. The number following the word Command may differ.

3 Right-click the button, and then click **Properties**. Verify that the **Property Sheet** displays *Selection type: Command Button* and the **Selection type** box displays *Command55*, identifying your command button. On the **Property Sheet Other tab**, in the **Name** property box, select the existing text and type **btnDeptInfo** and press Enter.

The button name has been updated to *btnDeptInfo*. The button name will now display in the Selection type box for easy identification.

4 On the **Property Sheet Format tab**, in the **Caption** property box, select the existing text and type **Dept Info** and press Enter. Compare your screen with Figure 8.17.

The button label has been updated to *Dept Info*, reflecting the caption property. However, no actions have been associated with the button.

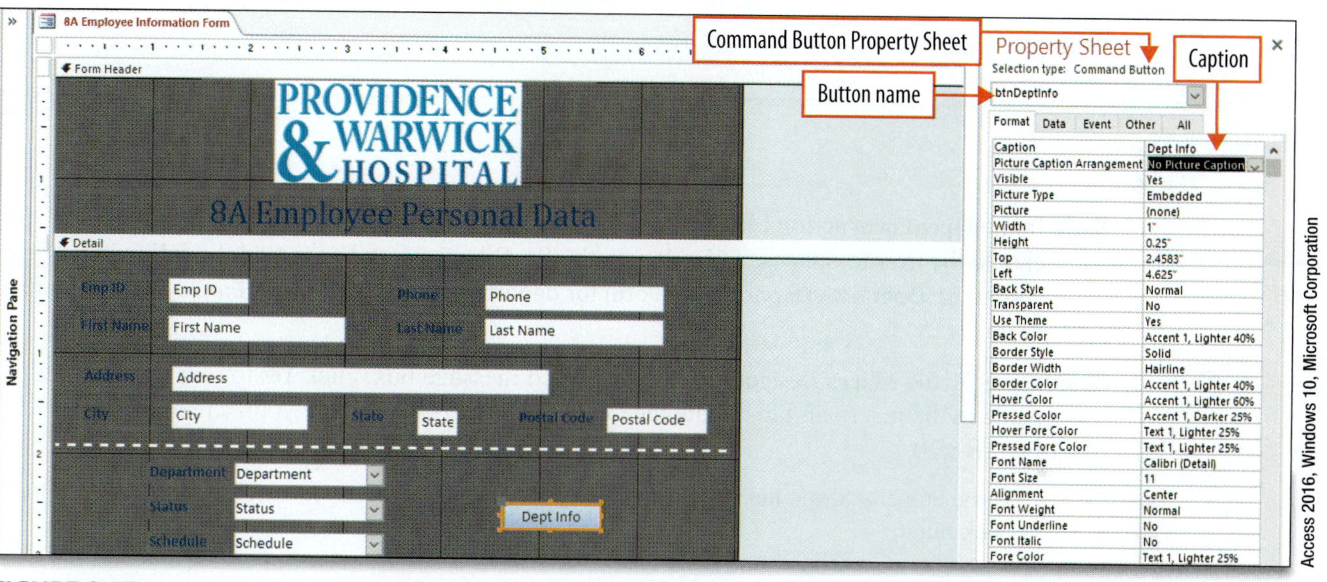

Access 2016, Windows 10, Microsoft Corporation

FIGURE 8.17

5 On the **Property Sheet**, click the **Event tab**. In the **On Click** property setting box, click **Build** [...], and then compare your screen with Figure 8.18.

The Choose Builder dialog box displays for you to select the Macro Builder, the Expression Builder, or the Code Builder. You have previously used the Macro Builder and the Expression Builder. The ***Code Builder*** is used for programming in Microsoft Visual Basic.

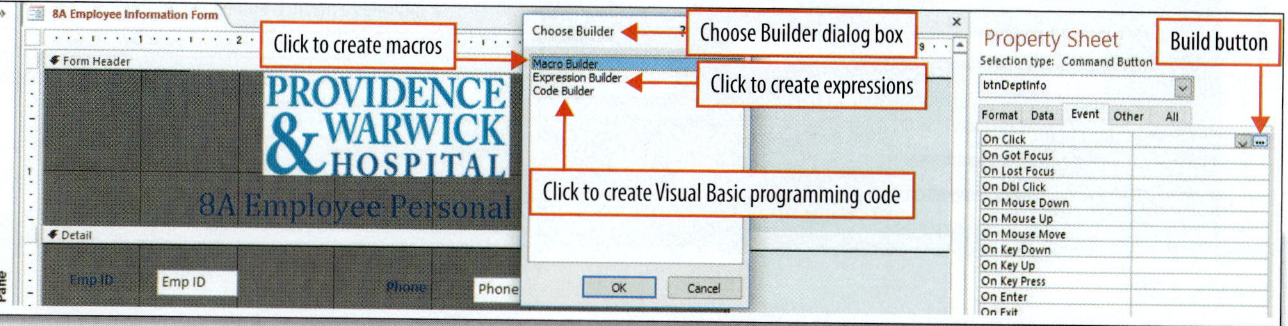

Access 2016, Windows 10, Microsoft Corporation

FIGURE 8.18

6 In the **Choose Builder** dialog box, if necessary, click **Macro Builder**, and then click **OK** to display the Macro Designer.

7 In the **Macro Designer**, add the **OpenForm** action using one of the techniques you have learned. In the **OpenForm** action block, click the **Form Name arrow**, and then click **8A Departments Form**. Click in the **Where Condition** box, type **[Dept ID]=[Forms]![8A Employee Information Form]![Department]** selecting items as they appear in the list to reduce errors, and then compare your screen with Figure 8.19.

The Where Condition property selects the records from the *8A Departments Form* for the Department displayed on the *8A Employee Information Form*.

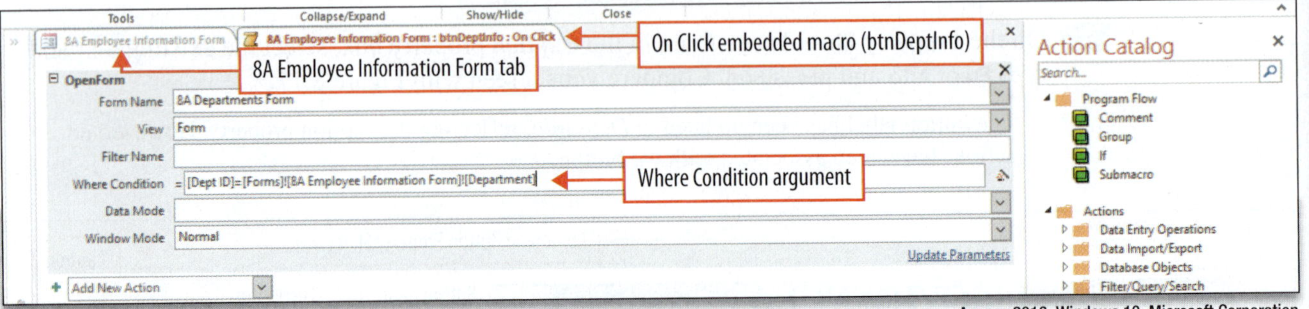

Access 2016, Windows 10, Microsoft Corporation

FIGURE 8.19

8 In the **OpenForm** action block, click the **Data Mode arrow**, and then click **Read Only** to enable the user to only view the data in the *8A Departments Form*. Add the following comment: **Opens 8A Departments Form for department indicated on 8A Employee Information Form**

9 **Close** [X] the **Macro Designer**. In the displayed message box, click **Yes** to save the changes made to the macro and to update the On Click property. Compare your screen with Figure 8.20.

In the Property Sheet, the On Click property displays *[Embedded Macro]*. To display the macro, click Build.

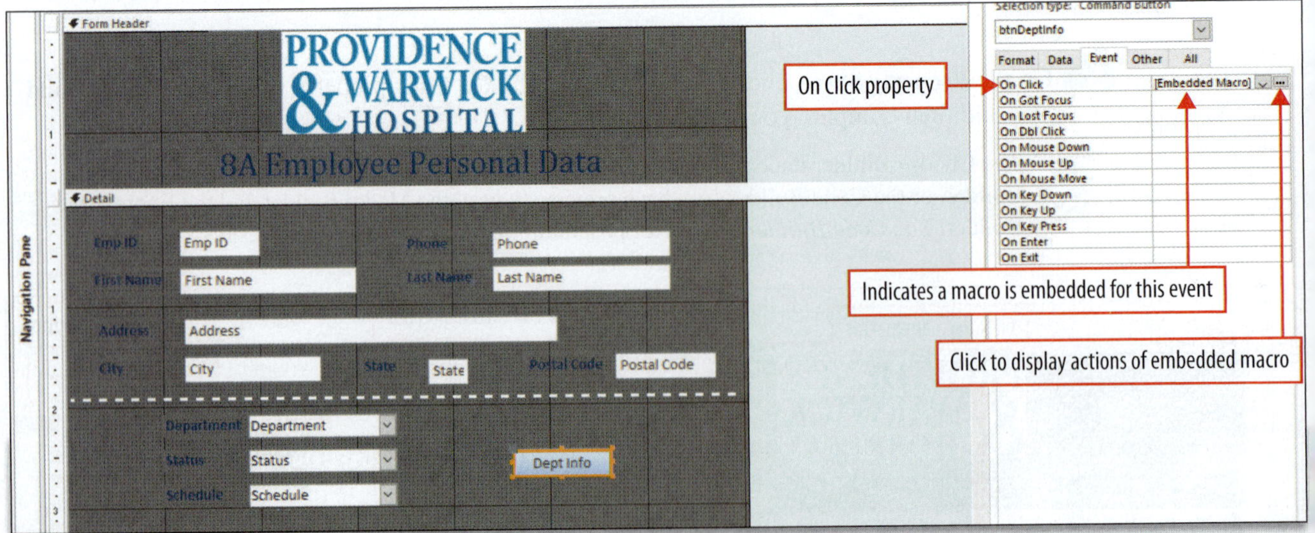

FIGURE 8.20

10 On the **Property Sheet**, click the **Format tab**. In the **Caption** box, click to the left of **Dept Info**, and then type **&** to create a shortcut key using the letter *D*. **Close** [X] the **Property Sheet**, **Save** [Save] the form, and then switch the *8A Employee Information Form* to **Form** view.

The ampersand (&) causes the letter that follows it to be underlined on the button, which will enable the user to use a shortcut key combination to access the button instead of clicking on the button. The user presses [Alt] + the letter to activate the button. For this button, the shortcut is [Alt] + [D].

11 On the **8A Employee Information Form**, click the **Dept Info** button or press [Alt] + [D].

The *8A Departments Form* displays as a pop-up window and provides directory information about the Human Resources department, the Department listed on the *8A Employee Information Form*.

12 **Close** [X] the **8A Departments Form**. In the **8A Employee Information Form**, in the record navigator, click **Last record** [Last record]. In the **8A Employee Information Form**, click the **Dept Info** button, and then compare your screen with Figure 8.21.

The pop-up window displays directory information for the Facilities department, the same department displayed on the *8A Employee Information Form*, as indicated by the Filtered button to the right of the record navigator in the *8A Departments Form*.

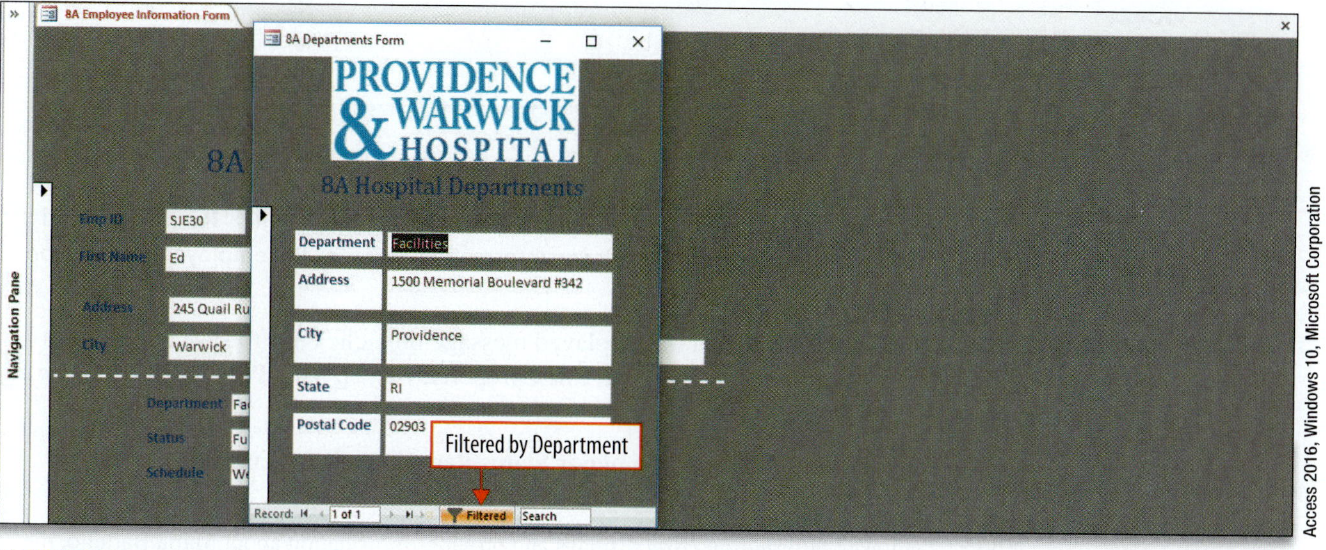

FIGURE 8.21

13 **Close** [X] the **8A Departments Form**, and then **Close** [X] the **8A Employee Information Form**, saving changes, if necessary. **Open** [»] the **Navigation Pane**. Notice that under **Macros**, the macro you created to display the *8A Departments Form* does not display—embedded macros do not display in the Navigation Pane.

Activity 8.06 | Creating an Embedded Macro on a Report

MOS 1.3.5, 4.2.2, 4.2.5

In this Activity, you will create an embedded macro that will execute when the *Emp ID* text box is clicked on the *8A Employee Status Report*.

1 Open the **8A Employee Status Report** in **Design** view. **Close** [«] the **Navigation Pane**. In the **Detail** section, right-click the **Emp ID** text box, and then click **Properties**. Verify that the **Property Sheet** displays *Selection type: Text Box* and the **Selection type** box displays *Emp ID*.

2 On the **Property Sheet Event tab**, in the **On Click** property setting box, click **Build** [...]. In the **Choose Builder** dialog box, verify that **Macro Builder** is selected, and then click **OK** to display the Macro Designer.

3 In the **Macro Designer**, add the **OpenForm** action using one of the techniques you have learned. In the **OpenForm** action block, click the **Form Name arrow**, and then click **8A Employee Information Form**. Click in the **Where Condition** box, type **[Emp ID]=[Reports]![8A Employee Status Report]![Emp ID]** selecting items as they appear in the list to reduce errors, and then compare your screen with Figure 8.22.

The Where Condition property selects the records from the *8A Employee Information Form* for the Employee selected on the *8A Employee Status Report*.

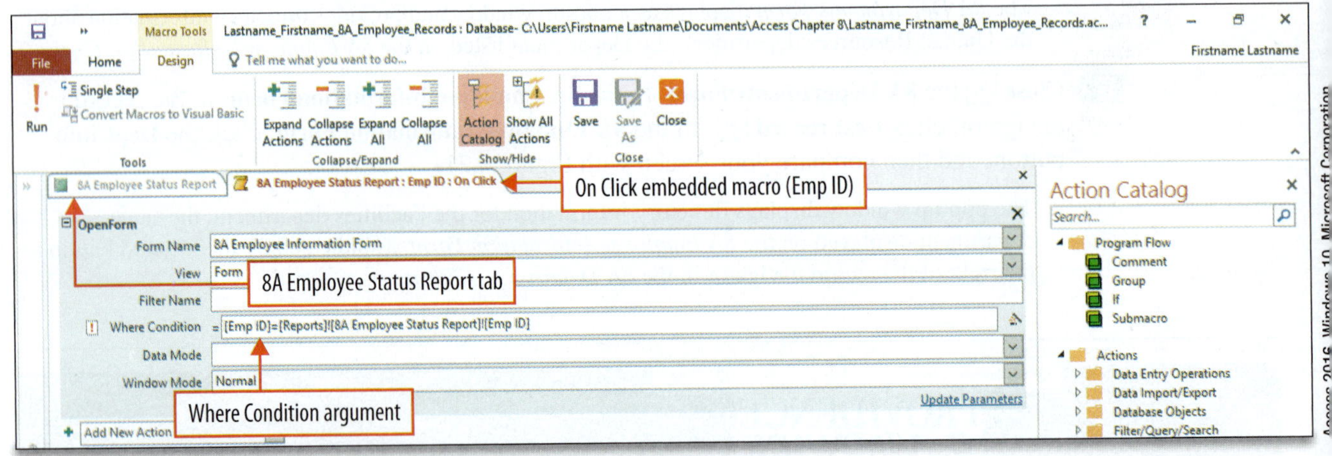

FIGURE 8.22

4 In the **OpenForm** action block, click the **Data Mode arrow**, and then click **Read Only**. Add the following comment: **Opens 8A Employee Information Form for the employee selected on 8A Employee Status Report**

5 **Close** the **Macro Designer**. In the displayed message box, click **Yes** to save the changes made to the macro and to update the On Click property. **Close** the **Property Sheet**. **Save** the report.

6 Switch to **Report** view. On the **8A Employee Status Report**, click the **Empl ID** text box for *BOM22* to run the macro.

The *8A Employee Information Form* displays and provides information about Maria Bartello, the employee whose Emp ID was selected on the *8A Employee Status Report*.

7 **Close** the **8A Employee Information Form**. **Close** the **8A Employee Status Report**, saving changes if necessary. **Open** the **Navigation Pane**. Notice that under **Macros**, the macro you created to display the *8A Employee Information Form* does not display because embedded macros do not display in the Navigation Pane.

Objective 4 Print Macro Details

GO! Learn How
Video A8-4

Use the ***Database Documenter*** to create a report that contains detailed information about the objects in a database, including macros, and to create a paper record.

Activity 8.07 | Printing Macro Details

In this Activity, you will use the Database Documenter to print out the details of the macros that you have created in this project.

1 **Close** « the **Navigation Pane**. On the **Database Tools tab**, in the **Analyze group**, click **Database Documenter**. In the displayed **Documenter** dialog box, click the **Macros tab**, and then compare your screen with Figure 8.23.

The Documenter dialog box displays tabs for each object type and a tab for the current database. Only standalone macros display on the Macros tab. Macros that are embedded with an object will display as a property of the object.

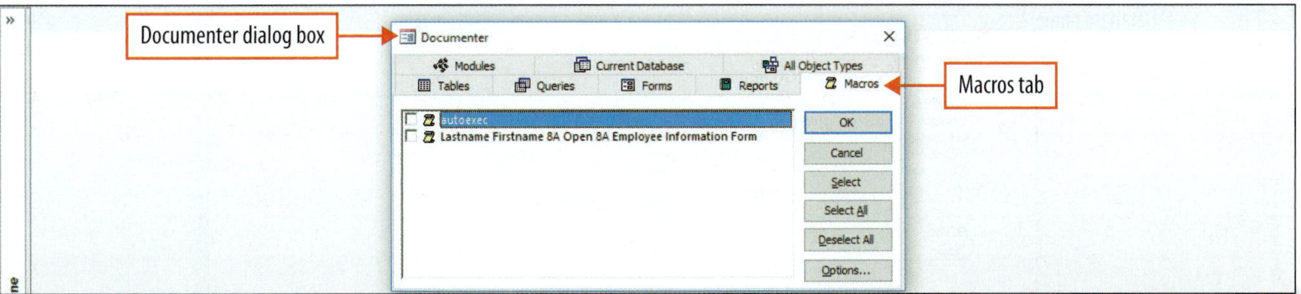

Access 2016, Windows 10, Microsoft Corporation

FIGURE 8.23

2 In the **Documenter** dialog box, click **Options**, and then compare your screen with Figure 8.24.

The Print Macro Definition dialog box displays. Properties, actions, arguments, and permissions by user and group can be displayed in the printed report.

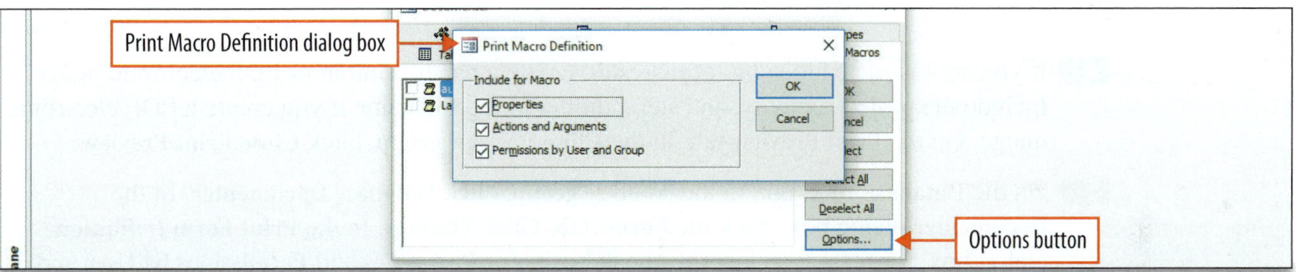

Access 2016, Windows 10, Microsoft Corporation

FIGURE 8.24

3 If necessary, click the **Permissions by User and Group** check box to clear it, and then click **OK**. In the **Documenter** dialog box, click **Select All**, and then click **OK**. Click in the middle of the document to zoom in, scroll up to display the top of the report, and then compare your screen with Figure 8.25.

The Object Definition opens in Print Preview and displays the first page of information about the macro named *autoexec*, including actions, arguments, conditions, and comments.

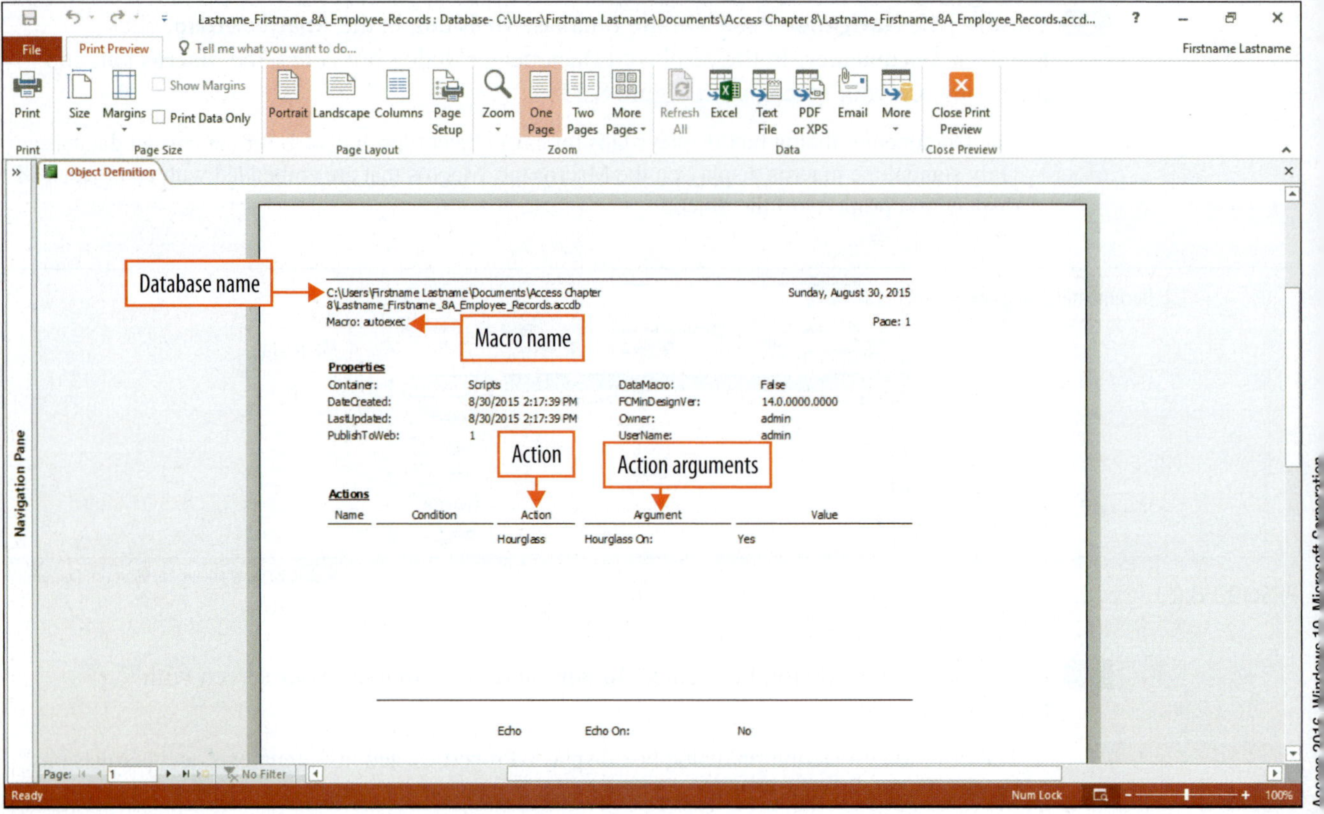

FIGURE 8.25

4 If you are instructed to submit this result, create a paper printout or PDF electronic image. Include the project, activity, and step number in the file name if you create a PDF electronic image. On the **Print Preview tab**, in the **Close Preview group**, click **Close Print Preview**.

5 On the **Database Tools tab**, in the **Analyze group**, click **Database Documenter**. In the **Documenter** dialog box, click the **Forms tab**. Click **Options**. In the **Print Form Definition** dialog box, if necessary, clear the check boxes for **Properties** and **Permissions by User and Group**, and then click **OK**.

6 In the **Documenter** dialog box, click the **8A Employee Information Form** check box.

This form has an embedded macro.

7 In the **Documenter** dialog box, click **OK**. In the **Object Definition** print preview, zoom in, and then scroll up to display the top of the first page, noticing that the report displays properties of the **8A Employee Information Form**. Click **Next Page three** times. Scroll down to display the bottom half of the page. Compare your screen with Figure 8.26.

The properties of the Dept Info button—Command Button: btnDeptInfo—display.

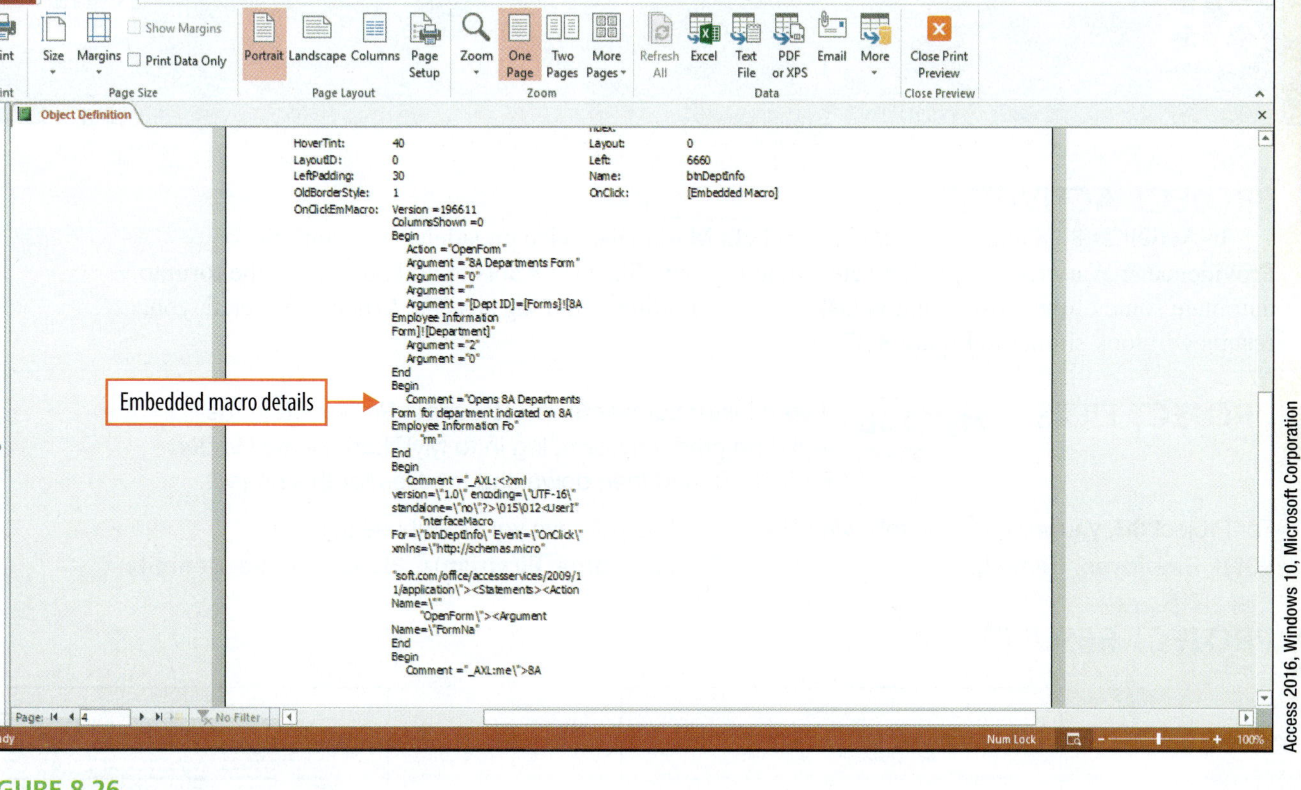

Access 2016, Windows 10, Microsoft Corporation

FIGURE 8.26

8. If you are instructed to submit this result, create a paper printout or PDF electronic image of page 4 only. Include the project, activity, and step number in the file name if you create a PDF electronic image. On the **Print Preview tab**, in the **Close Preview group**, click the **Close Print Preview** button.

9. On the **Database Tools tab**, in the **Analyze group**, click **Database Documenter**. In the **Documenter** dialog box, if necessary, click the **Reports tab**. Click **Options**. In the **Print Report Definition** dialog box, if necessary, clear the check boxes for **Properties** and **Permissions by User and Group**, and then click **OK**.

10. In the **Documenter** dialog box, click the **8A Employee Status Report** check box, and then click **OK**.

11. In the **Object Definition** print preview, zoom in, and click **Next Page four** times. Scroll down to display the bottom of the page.

    The OnClick property displays the embedded macro.

12. If you are instructed to submit this result, create a paper printout or PDF electronic image of page 5 only. Include the project, activity, and step number in the file name if you create a PDF electronic image. On the **Print Preview tab**, in the **Close Preview group**, click **Close Print Preview**.

13. Open [»] the **Navigation Pane**. Resize the **Navigation Pane** so all object names display fully. **Close** the database, and then **Close** Access.

14. As directed by your instructor, submit your database and the paper printout or PDF electronic image of the three Database Documenter reports that are the results of this project.

END | You have completed Project 8A

Employee Benefits

PROJECT ACTIVITIES

In Activities 8.08 through 8.12, you will help Maria Diaz, vice president of operations for Providence & Warwick Hospital, create a macro group. She also wants to add buttons on the form to automate some of the most common tasks, such as finding a training session. When completed, your results will look similar to Figure 8.27.

PROJECT FILES

If your instructor wants you to submit Project 8B in the MyITLab grader system, log in to MyITLab, locate Grader Project 8B, and then download the files for this project.

For Project 8B, you will need the following file:
a08B_Employee_Benefits

You will save your database as:
Lastname_Firstname_8B_Employee_Benefits

PROJECT RESULTS

GO! Walk Thru Project 8B

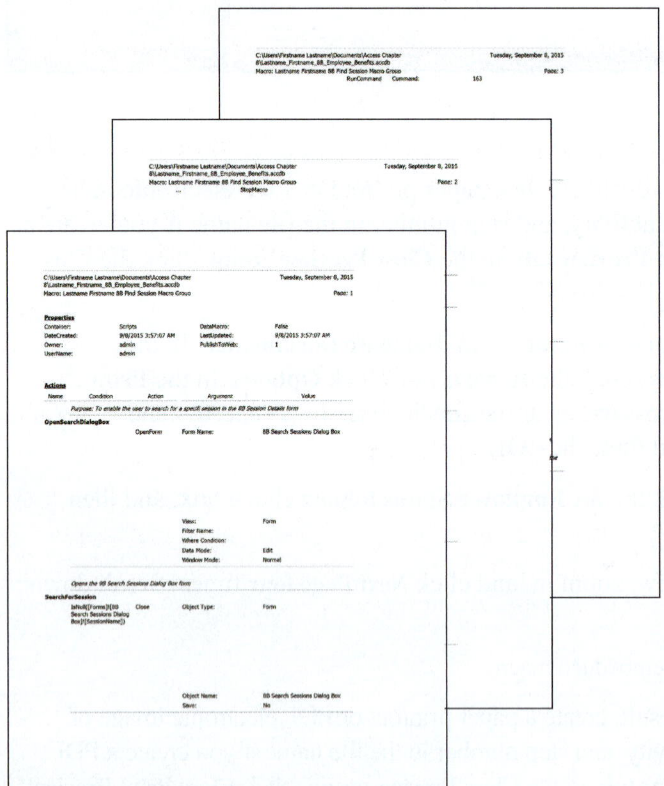

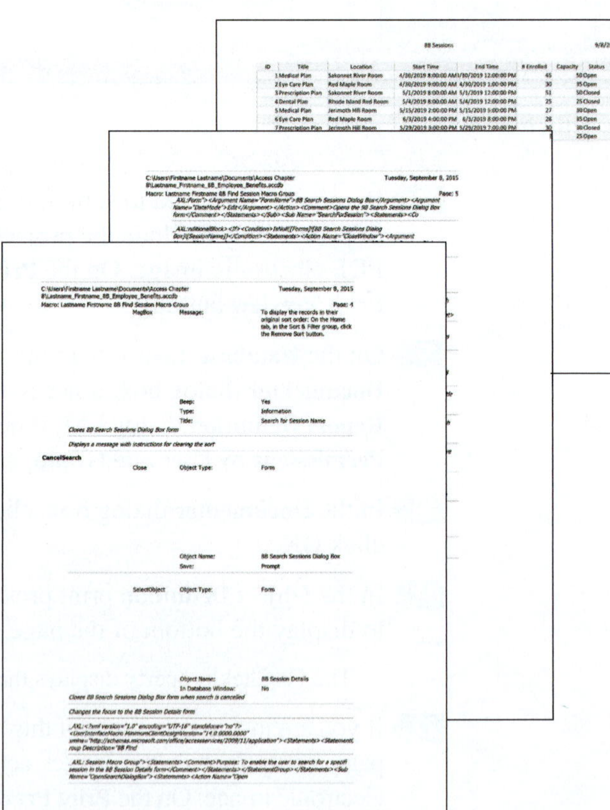

FIGURE 8.27 Project 8B Employee Benefits

PROJECT RESULTS

In this project, using your own name, you will create the following database and objects. Your instructor may ask for printouts or PDF electronic images:

Lastname_Firstname_Project8B_Employee_Benefits	Database file
Lastname_Firstname_Project8B_Activity8.11_Step21	Database Documenter report
8B Sessions	Table

Objective 5 Create a Macro Group

GO! Learn How
Video A8-5

In the previous Activities, you created a standalone macro with one action and another standalone macro with multiple actions. As you continue to create more macros, you may want to group related macros by creating a ***macro group***. A macro group is a set of submacros grouped by a common name that displays as one macro object in the Navigation Pane. For example, you might want to create a macro group that opens several forms or reports in a database.

Activity 8.08 | Creating the First Macro in a Macro Group

In this Activity, you will create the first macro in the macro group that will open the *8B Search Sessions Dialog Box* form.

ALERT!

To submit this as an autograded project, log into MyITLab and download the files for this project, and begin with those files instead of a08B_Employee_Benefits. Begin working with the database in Step 2. For Grader to award points accurately, when saving an object or a macro, do not include your Lastname Firstname at the beginning of the name.

1. Start Access. Navigate to the location where the student data files for this textbook are saved. Locate and open the **a08B_Employee_Benefits** file. **Save** the database in your **Access Chapter 8** folder as **Lastname_Firstname_8B_Employee_Benefits**

2. In the **Navigation Pane**, under **Forms**, double-click **8B Session Details**, and then double-click **8B Search Sessions Dialog Box** to open the forms in **Form** view. Point to the title bar of the **Search Sessions Dialog Box**, and then drag the pop-up form downward and to the right until, on the **8B Session Details** form, the Find Session button under the title displays. Compare your screen with Figure 8.28.

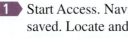

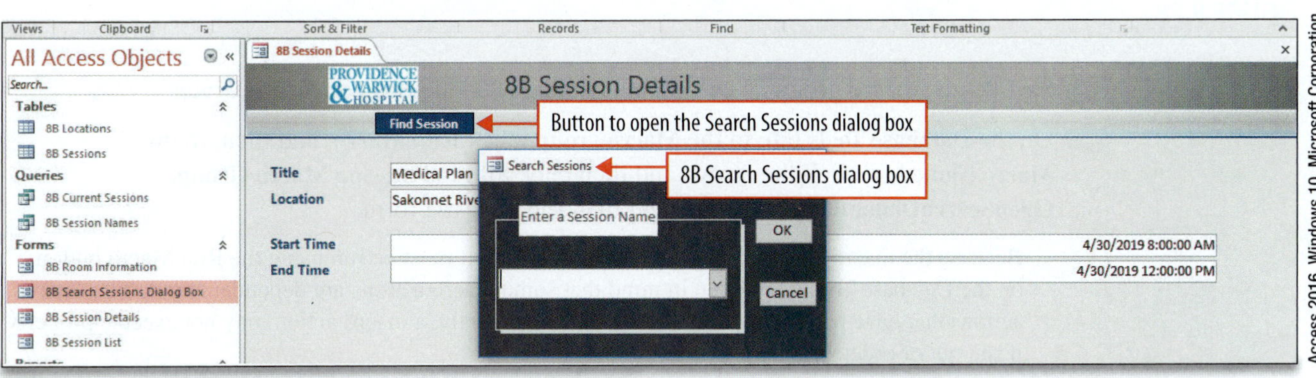

FIGURE 8.28

3 **Close** [X] the **Search Sessions Dialog Box** form, and then **Close** [X] the **8B Session Details** form. **Close** [«] the **Navigation Pane**.

4 On the **Create tab**, in the **Macros & Code group**, click **Macro**. Under **Macro Tools**, on the **Design tab**, in the **Show/Hide group**, click **Show All Actions**.

Recall that the Show All Actions button displays trusted and untrusted macro actions.

5 In the **Action Catalog pane**, double-click **Group**. In the **Macro Designer**, in the **Group** box, type **8B Find Session Macro Group** to identify the group. Add the following comment: **Purpose: To enable the user to search for a specific session in the 8B Session Details form**

It is a good practice to start a macro group with a name and the purpose of the macro group.

6 In the **Action Catalog pane**, double-click **Submacro** and then in the **Submacro** box, delete any text that is there and type **OpenSearchDialogBox**

In macro groups, submacro names are needed to distinguish the individual macros from one another. Within a macro group, the submacro name is entered before the macro actions in each submacro. The macro ends when *End Submacro* is encountered. Macro names are limited to 64 characters. Because macros perform an action or actions, it is good practice to start the name of the macro with a verb—in this case, *Open*.

7 In the **Submacro**, using one of the techniques you have learned, add an **OpenForm** action. In the **OpenForm** action block, click the **Form Name arrow**, and then click **8B Search Sessions Dialog Box**. Click the **Data Mode arrow**, and then click **Edit**. Add the following comment: **Opens the 8B Search Sessions Dialog Box form** Compare your screen with Figure 8.29.

Editing is enabled so that the user can enter a Session name in the combo box on the *8B Search Sessions Dialog Box* form. Because the form property has been set to open as a pop-up window, the Window Mode setting of Normal is appropriate.

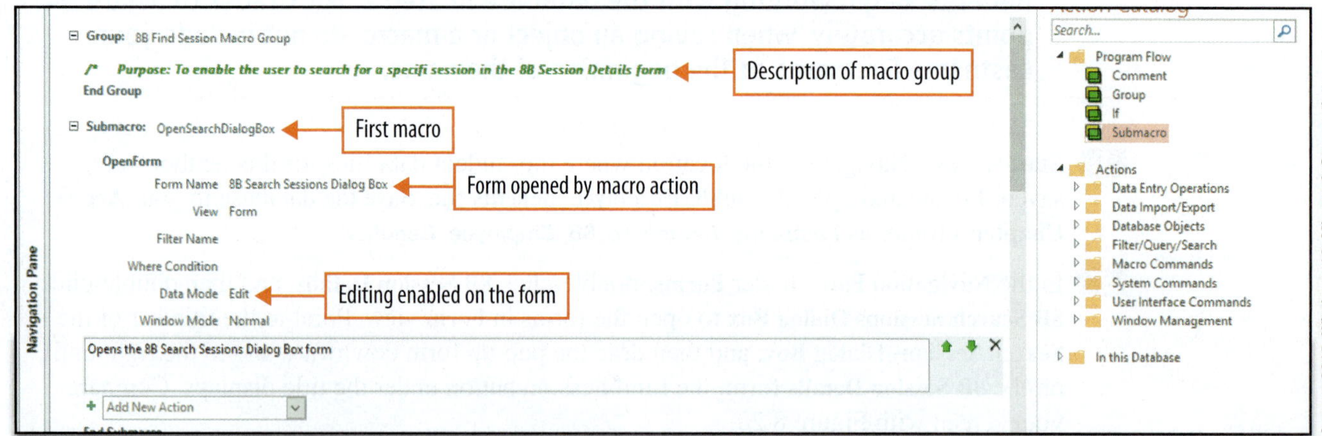

FIGURE 8.29

8 **Save** [save icon] the macro group as **Lastname Firstname 8B Find Session Macro Group**

9 On the **Database Tools tab**, in the **Macro group**, click **Run Macro**, and then, in the **Macro Name** list, click the arrow, and then click **8B Find Session Macro Group. OpenSearchDialogBox**. Click **OK**, and then **Close** [X] the form.

Because the macro is associated with a macro group, it must be run using the Run Macro button on the Database Tools tab. Keep in mind that some macro actions are dependent upon other macro actions that have previously executed, and independently, a macro action may not execute properly if run out of order.

Activity 8.09 | Creating a Second Macro in a Macro Group

In this Activity, you will create a second macro in the macro group that will check to see if a value is entered for the Session name in the *8B Search Sessions Dialog Box* form, hide the *8B Search Sessions Dialog Box* form, change the focus to the *8B Session Details* form, select the title of the Session on the *8B Session Details* form, sort the records by the Session name, find the requested Session, close the *8B Search Sessions Dialog Box* form, and display a message to the user with a reminder to display all of the records.

1 In the **Macro Designer**, in the **Action Catalog pane**, double-click **Submacro**, and in the **Submacro** box type **SearchForSession** In the **Action Catalog pane**, double-click **If**.

The If action block displays in the SearchForSession submacro to control the program flow. In some macros, an action should execute only if a condition is true. For example, if the user does not select a value in the combo box on the *8B Search Sessions Dialog Box* form, the macro should not execute.

2 In the **Submacro**, to the right of the **If** textbox, click **Builder**. In the **Expression Builder** dialog box, type **IsNull([Forms]![8B Search Sessions Dialog Box]![SessionName])** selecting items as they appear in the list to reduce errors. Compare your screen with Figure 8.30.

The expression used for the condition checks the SessionName combo box in the *8B Search Sessions Dialog Box* form to determine if the combo box is blank—IsNull. Recall that the exclamation mark (!) is the bang operator that separates the object type from the object name.

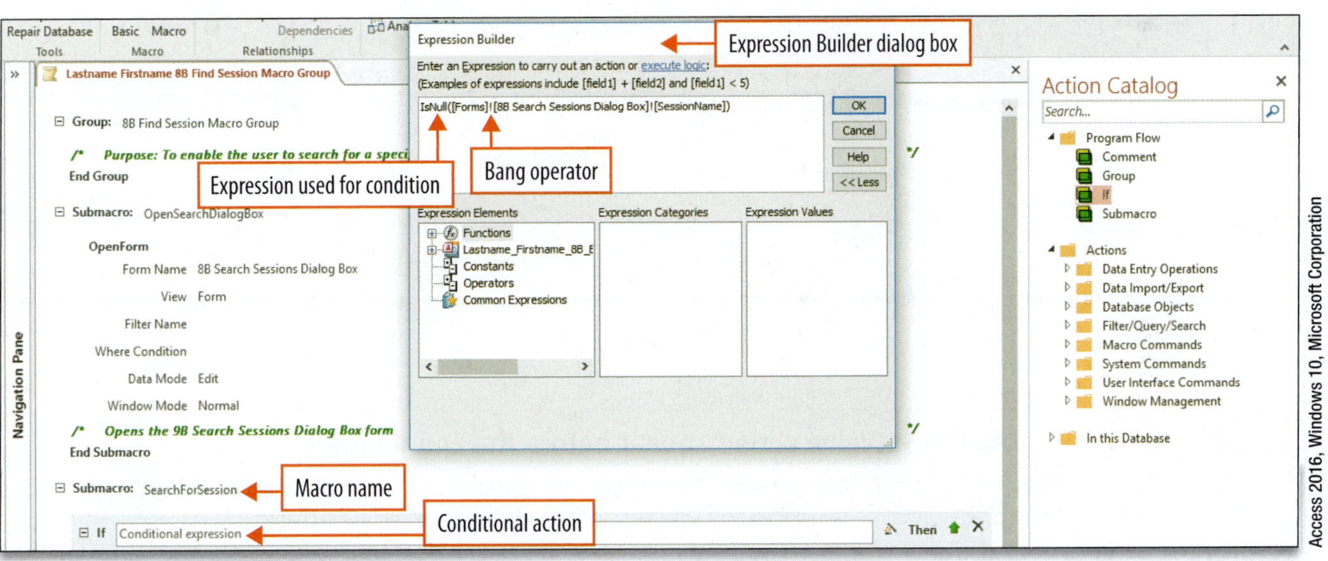

FIGURE 8.30

3 In the **Expression Builder** dialog box, click **OK**. In the **If** action block, add the **CloseWindow** action using one of the techniques you have learned. In the **CloseWindow** action block, click the **Object Type arrow**, and then click **Form**. Click the **Object Name arrow**, and then click **8B Search Sessions Dialog Box**. Click the **Save arrow**, and then click **No**. Add the following comment: **If a session is not selected, then close the 8B Search Sessions Dialog Box form**

If Access finds that the Sessions combo box is blank, it will close the *8B Search Sessions Dialog Box* form without saving changes made to the form. Recall that the warning symbol in the row selector box indicates that this macro action is not trusted.

4 In the **If Arguments Block**, add the **StopMacro** action. Notice that there are no action arguments for the StopMacro action. Add the following comment: **Exits the macro**

If the Sessions combo box is blank, and the form closes, the macro stops executing.

5 In the **Macro Designer**, click the **Submacro:SearchForSession** text box to activate the **Add New Action bar** below the **End If** label. Add the **SetValue** action. In the **SetValue** action block, to the right of the **Item** text box, click **Builder** to open the **Expression Builder**. Compare your screen with Figure 8.31.

The SetValue macro action is an untrusted action used to set the value of a field, control, or property on a form, a form datasheet, or a report. The item is the name of the field, control, or property whose value you want to set. You must use the full syntax to refer to the item—do not just type the field, control, or property name. ***Syntax*** refers to the spelling, grammar, and sequence of characters of a programming language.

The operator buttons and list boxes in the Expression Builder can help you build the expression using correct syntax. As you select an object in the first list box, the second and third list boxes will be populated. In the first list box, the plus sign (+) next to an object indicates that more items display under the object; click the plus sign (+) or double-click the object name to expand the list. The minus sign (–) indicates that the list under the object is fully expanded. Click the minus sign (–) or double-click the object name to collapse the list.

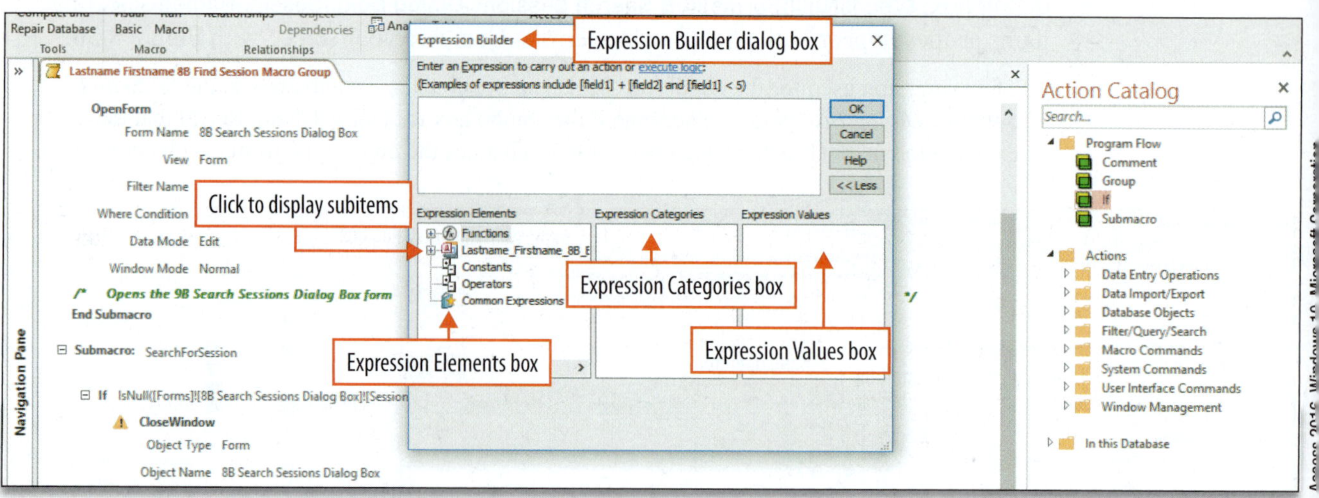

FIGURE 8.31

ALERT!

Did the SetValue action appear before the End If label?

If the SetValue action appears before the End If label, you didn't click the Submacro SearchForSession Action Block before adding the new action. To correct this, move the SetValue action below the End If label using either technique practiced in the chapter.

6 In the **Expression Builder** dialog box, in the **Expression Elements** list box, click the plus sign to the left of **Lastname_Firstname_8B_Employee_Benefits.accdb** to display the list of objects in the database—use the horizontal scroll bar to display the entire name of the database. Double-click **Forms** to expand the list, and double-click **All Forms**. Scroll down, and then click **8B Search Sessions Dialog Box**—use the horizontal scroll bar to display the entire name of the form.

The Expression Categories list box displays controls on the form. The Expression Values list box displays property settings and events that can be associated with the form or the controls on the form. An ***event*** is any action that can be detected by a program or computer system, such as clicking a button or closing an object. Selecting an object in the Expression Categories list box causes the values or events in the Expression Values list box to change, because different objects have different property settings or events associated with them.

7 In the **Expression Categories** list box, verify that <Form> is selected. In the **Expression Values** list box, scroll down, double-click **Visible**, and then compare your screen with Figure 8.32.

The Expression Builder displays the correct syntax for the Visible property of the *8B Search Sessions Dialog Box*, which is a form. Instead of using the Expression Builder, you can type the expression in the Item box in the action block. An advantage of using the Expression Builder is that Access will insert square brackets and parentheses where they are required.

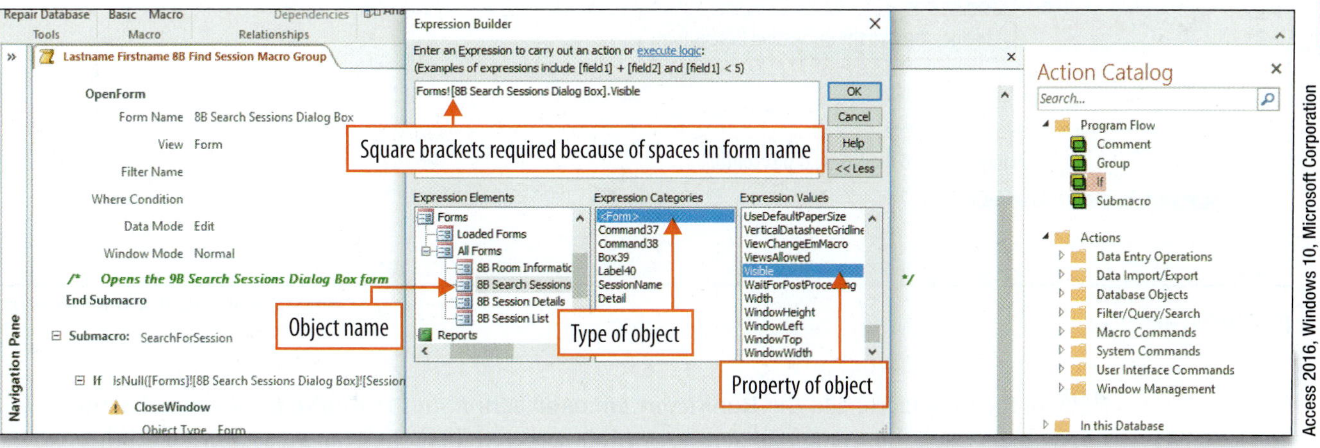

Access 2016, Windows 10, Microsoft Corporation

FIGURE 8.32

8 In the **Expression Builder**, click **OK**. In the **SetValue** action block, click in the **Expression** box, and then type **False**

This macro action sets the Visible property setting of the *8B Search Sessions Dialog Box* form to False; in other words, it will hide the *8B Search Sessions Dialog Box* form.

9 Add the following comment: **Hides the 8B Search Sessions Dialog Box form** Compare your screen with Figure 8.33.

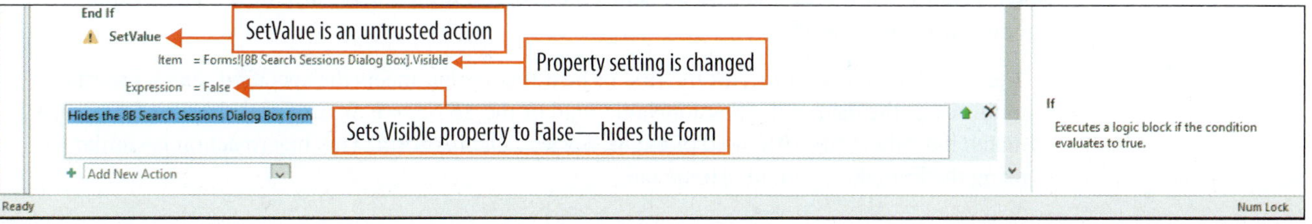

FIGURE 8.33

Access 2016, Windows 10, Microsoft Corporation

10 In the **Submacro**, add the **SelectObject** action. In the **SelectObject** action block, click the **Object Type arrow**, and then click **Form**. Click the **Object Name arrow**, and then click **8B Session Details**. Verify that the **In Database Window** box displays **No**. Add the following comment: **Changes the focus to the 8B Session Details form**

The SelectObject action is used to put the focus on a specified database object so that an action can be applied to that object. Recall that the *8B Session Details* form is automatically opened when the database is opened. Therefore, the In Database Window setting should be set to No. If the form is not open, Access needs to open it from the Navigation Pane, and the In Database Window setting should be set to Yes.

So far, the macro group will open the *8B Search Sessions Dialog Box* form and then check to see if the Sessions field displays data. If not, the macro stops executing. If data is displayed in the Sessions field, the *8B Search Sessions Dialog Box* form will be hidden, and the focus will shift to the *8B Session Details* form.

11 In the **Submacro**, add the **GoToControl** action. In the **GoToControl** action block, in the **Control Name** box, type **Title** Add the following comment: **Places focus on Title field on 8B Session Details form** Compare your screen with Figure 8.34.

In the previous action, the focus was changed to the *8B Session Details* form. With this action, the focus is placed on a specific text box control named *Title* on that form.

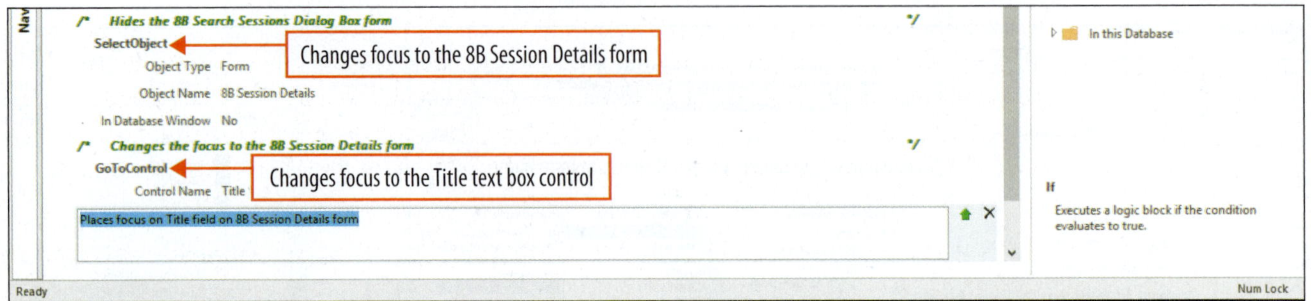

Access 2016, Windows 10, Microsoft Corporation

FIGURE 8.34

12 In the **Submacro**, add the **RunMenuCommand** action. In the **RunMenuCommand** action block, click the **Command arrow**, scroll down, and then click **SortAscending**. Add the following comment: **Sorts the session name (Title) in ascending order**

The RunMenuCommand action is used to execute an Access command, such as Sort Ascending or Save a Record.

13 In the **Submacro**, add the **FindRecord** action. In the **FindWhat** box, type **=[Forms]![8B Search Sessions Dialog Box]![SessionName]** selecting items as they appear in the list to reduce errors. Verify that you have entered the expression correctly. Click the **Match arrow**, and then click **Start of Field**. Point to each of the other argument boxes, reading the description of each argument and being sure not to change any of the settings. Add the following comment: **Finds the Title on the 8B Session Details form that matches the entry in the SessionName combo box on the 8B Search Sessions Dialog Box form** and then compare your screen with Figure 8.35.

The FindRecord action locates the first or next record that meets the specified search criteria; in this case, the data in the SessionName field of the *8B Search Sessions Dialog Box* form must match the data in the Title field of the *8B Session Details* form. This macro action is similar to using the Find button on the Home tab.

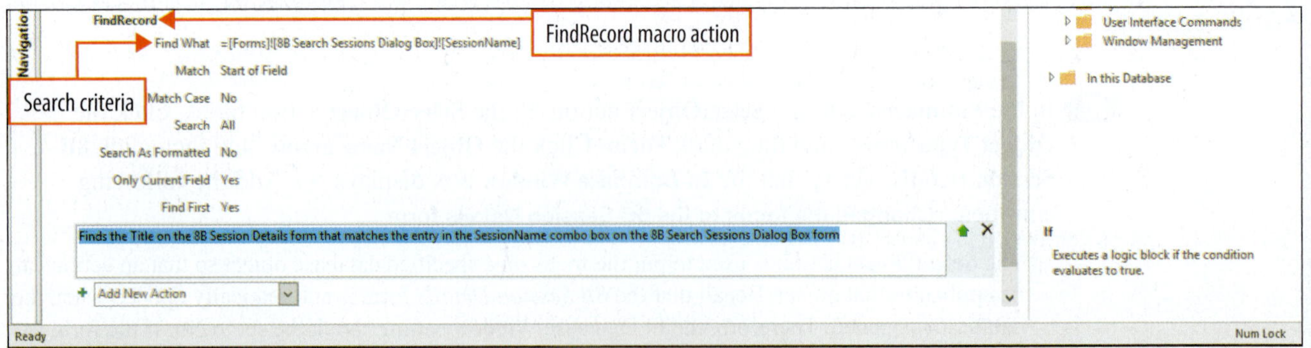

Access 2016, Windows 10, Microsoft Corporation

FIGURE 8.35

14 In the **Submacro**, add the **CloseWindow** action. In the **CloseWindow** action block, click the **Object Type arrow**, and then click **Form**. Click the **Object Name arrow**, and then click **8B Search Sessions Dialog Box**. Verify that **Prompt** appears in the **Save** box. Add the following comment: **Closes 8B Search Sessions Dialog Box form**

The Close action closes a specified object. If no object is specified in the Object Name box, the active object is closed.

15 In the **Submacro**, add the **MessageBox** action. In the **MessageBox** action block, click in the **Message** box, and then type **To display the records in their original sort order: On the Home tab, in the Sort & Filter group, click the Remove Sort button.** Click the **Type box arrow**, and then click **Information**. Click in the **Title** box, and then type **Search for Session Name** Add the following comment: **Displays a message with instructions for clearing the sort** Compare your screen with Figure 8.36.

Recall that if an individual filters or sorts records and closes the database, when the database is reopened, the filter or sort is still applied to the object.

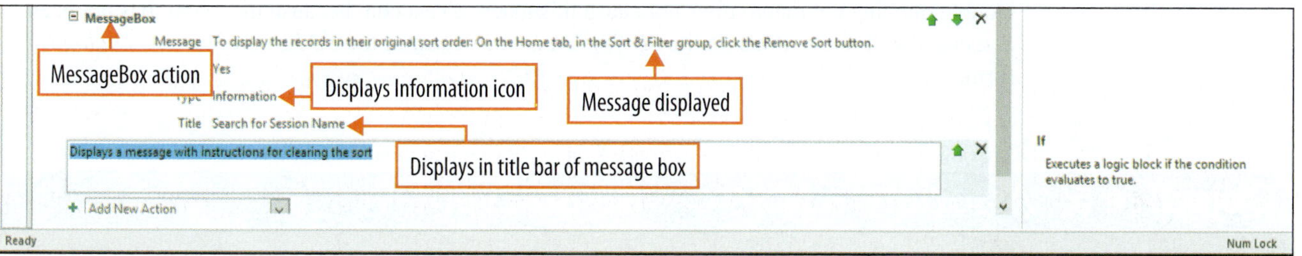

FIGURE 8.36

Access 2016, Windows 10, Microsoft Corporation

16 **Save** the macro group.

Activity 8.10 | Creating a Third Macro in a Macro Group

In this Activity, you will create a third and final macro in the macro group that will close the *8B Session Name Search* form.

1 In the **Macro Designer**, in the **Action Catalog pane**, double-click **Submacro**, and type **CancelSearch** to name the macro. Add the **CloseWindow** action. In the **CloseWindow** action block, click the **Object Type arrow**, and then click **Form**. Click the **Object Name arrow**, and then click **8B Search Sessions Dialog Box**. Verify that **Prompt** appears in the **Save** box. Add the following comment: **Closes 8B Search Sessions Dialog Box form when search is cancelled**

This macro will be used to close the *8B Search Sessions Dialog Box* form when the Cancel button on the form is clicked.

2 In the **Submacro**, add the **SelectObject** action. In the **SelectObject** action block, click the **Object Type arrow**, and then click **Form**. Click the **Object Name arrow**, and then click **8B Session Details**. Verify that the **In Database Window** box displays **No**. Add the following comment: **Changes the focus to 8B Session Details form** Compare your screen with Figure 8.37.

After the *8B Search Sessions Dialog Box* form is closed, the focus is placed on the *8B Session Details* form.

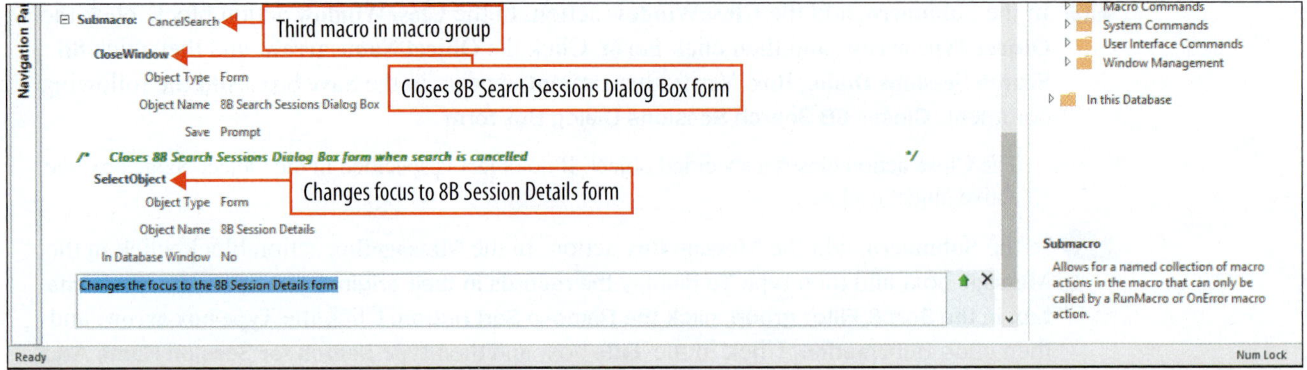

Access 2016, Windows 10, Microsoft Corporation

FIGURE 8.37

3 **Save** the macro group. **Close** the Macro Designer, **Open** the **Navigation Pane**, and notice that under **Macros**, the macro group displays as one macro object.

Double-clicking the macro does not cause this macro to execute because the macro has not been associated with the buttons on the *8B Session Details* form or the *8B Search Sessions Dialog Box* form.

Objective 6 Associate a Macro with an Event

GO! Learn How Video A8-6

Recall that an event is any action that can be detected by a program or computer system, such as clicking a button or closing an object. For example, clicking the Find Session button on the 8B Session Details form causes a system event, upon which Access can execute a macro.

Activity 8.11 | Associating a Command Button with a Macro

1.3.5, 4.2.5

In this Activity, you will associate clicking the Find Session button on the *8B Session Details* form with a macro—the *8B Find Session Macro Group* macro. Clicking the Find Session button will cause the macro to execute.

1 In the **Navigation Pane**, under **Forms**, double-click **8B Session Details** to display the form in **Form** view. On the form, click the **Find Session** button, and notice that nothing happens because the button is not associated with any event.

2 **Close** the **Navigation Pane**, and then switch the form to **Design** view. In the **Form Header section**, right-click the **Find Session** button, and then click **Properties**. Verify that the **Property Sheet** displays *Selection type: Command Button* and that the **Selection type** box displays *cmdFindSession*.

3 On the **Property Sheet**, click the **Event tab**, if necessary. Click the **On Click property setting arrow**. Notice that the complete names of some of the macros do not display. Point to the **left edge** of the **Property Sheet** until the pointer displays. Drag to the left to the **6.5-inch mark on the horizontal ruler** or until the complete names display. Click the **On Click property setting arrow**, and then compare your screen with Figure 8.38.

All of the macros that have been created display in the list.

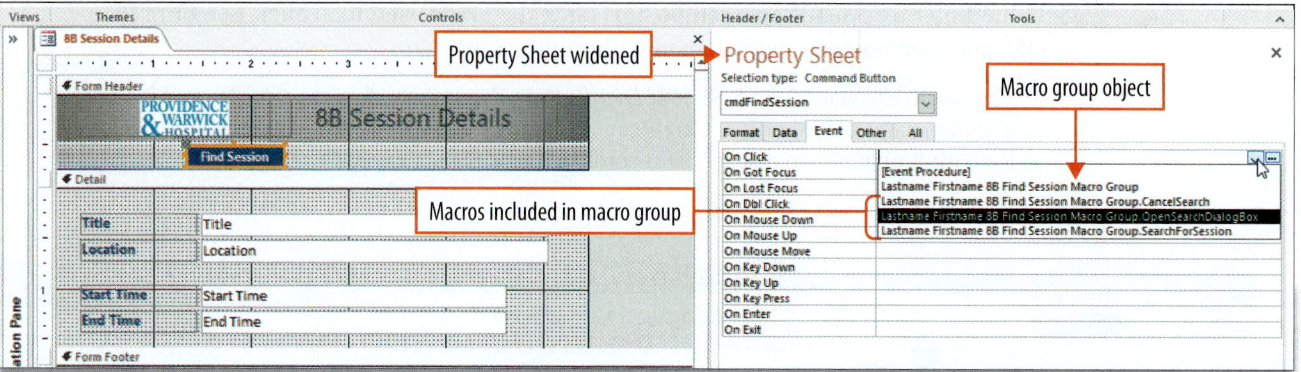

FIGURE 8.38 Access 2016, Windows 10, Microsoft Corporation

4 In the displayed list, click **8B Find Session Macro Group.OpenSearchDialogBox.**

When you click on the Find Session button in the *8B Session Details* form, the OpenSearchDialogBox macro in the *8B Find Session Macro Group* will execute.

5 On the **Property Sheet**, click the **Format tab**. In the **Caption** property setting box, click to the left of **Find Session**, and then type **&**

Recall that the ampersand (&) causes the letter that follows it to be underlined on the button, which will enable the user to use a shortcut key combination (Alt + the letter) to access the button instead of clicking on the button.

6 **Close** the **Property Sheet**, **Save** the form, and then switch to **Form** view. Notice that on the **Find Session** button, the letter **F** is underscored, which indicates that pressing Alt + F is the same action as clicking on the button.

7 Click the **Find Session** button, and then compare your screen with Figure 8.39.

The Search Sessions dialog box displays, which is the *8B Search Sessions Dialog Box* form.

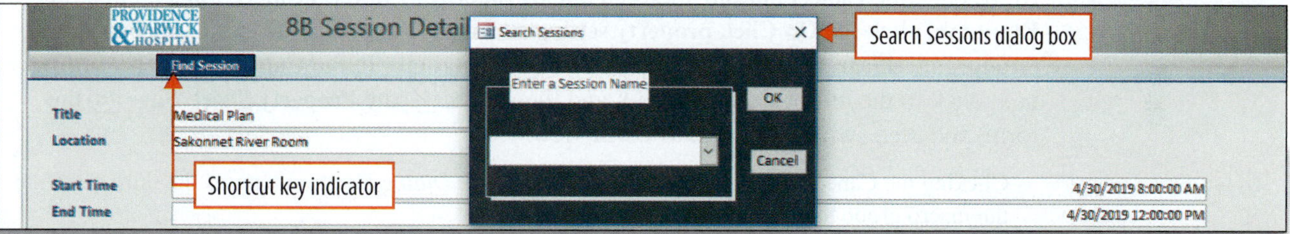

FIGURE 8.39 Access 2016, Windows 10, Microsoft Corporation

8 **Close** the **Search Sessions** dialog box.

> **ALERT!** **Did the Find and Replace dialog box display?**
>
> If you use the shortcut key and the Find and Replace dialog box displays instead of the Search Sessions dialog box, you held down Ctrl instead of Alt.

9 Do not close the **8B Session Details** form. **Open** the **Navigation Pane**. Under **Forms**, right-click **8B Search Sessions Dialog Box** and then click **Design View**. **Close** the **Navigation Pane**.

10 Right-click the **OK** button, and then click **Properties**. On the **Property Sheet**, click the **Event tab**. Click the **On Click property setting arrow**, and then click **8B Find Session Macro Group. SearchForSession**. On the **Property Sheet**, click the **Format tab**. In the **Caption** box, click to the left of **OK**, and then type **&** **Close** the **Property Sheet**. **Save** the form, and then switch the form to **Form** view.

When the OK button is clicked or the user presses Alt + O, the second macro in the *8B Find Session Macro Group* executes.

11 In the **Enter a Session Name combo box**, click the **arrow**, and then click **Eye Care Plan**. Click **OK**, and then compare your screen with Figure 8.40.

The macro executes, the *8B Session Details* form displays the first record—Record 3—with a session name (Title) of Eye Care Plan, and a message box displays, telling you to click the Remove Sort button to display the records in the original sort order.

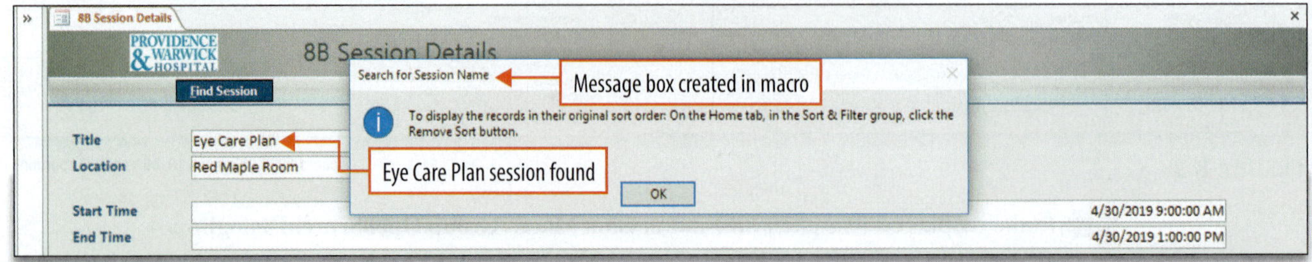

Access 2016, Windows 10, Microsoft Corporation

FIGURE 8.40

12 In the displayed message box, click **OK**. Press Alt + F to display the **Search Sessions** dialog box. In the **Search Sessions** dialog box, in the **Enter a Session Name** combo box, type **pr** and notice that Access displays Prescription Plan. Press Alt + O. In the displayed message box, click **OK**.

Instead of selecting an item from the list, you can type the first few letters of the Session name. If Access finds the Session name in the list, it displays in the combo box. Record 7 is displayed.

13 On the **Home tab**, in the **Sort & Filter** group, click **Remove Sort**.

14 **Open** » the **Navigation Pane**. Under **Forms**, open the **8B Search Sessions Dialog Box** form in **Design** view, and then **Close** « the **Navigation Pane**.

15 Right-click the **Cancel** button, and then click **Properties**. On the **Property Sheet**, click the **Event tab**, click the **On Click property setting arrow**, and then click **8B Find Session Macro Group.CancelSearch**. Click the **Property Sheet Format tab**. In the **Caption** property setting box, click to the left of **Cancel**, type **&** and then **Close** the **Property Sheet**. **Save** the form, and then switch the form to **Form** view.

Clicking the Cancel button on the *8B Search Sessions Dialog Box* form causes the third macro in the macro group to execute.

16 In the **Search Sessions** dialog box, click the **Cancel** button or press Alt + C.

The form closes, and the focus is placed on the *8B Session Details* form.

17 **Close** the **8B Session Details** form.

18 On the **Database Tools tab**, in the **Analyze group**, click **Database Documenter**.

The Documenter dialog box displays tabs for each object type and a tab for the current database. Only standalone macros display on the Macros tab. Macros that are run are embedded with an object and will display as a property of the object.

19 In the **Documenter** dialog box, if necessary, click the **Macros tab**. Click **Options**. If necessary, click the **Permissions by User and Group** check box to clear it, and then click **OK**. In the **Documenter** dialog box, click **Select All**. Click **OK**.

20 Click in the middle of the document to zoom in to display the details of the **8B Find Session Macro Group** macro.

21 If you are instructed to submit this result, create a paper printout or PDF electronic image. Include the project, activity, and step number in the file name if you create a PDF electronic image. On the **Print Preview tab**, in the **Close Preview group**, click **Close Print Preview**. **Open** » the **Navigation Pane**.

Objective 7 Create a Data Macro

GO! Learn How
Video A8-7

You have created macros using the Macro Designer and Macro Builder. Data macros are created and managed while you are viewing a table in Datasheet view. A ***data macro*** is a macro that is triggered by events, such as adding, updating, or deleting data within a table, form, or query. The macro is used to validate the accuracy of data in a table. It is also known as an event-driven macro.

Activity 8.12 | Creating an Event-Driven Macro

2.3.1

In this Activity, you will create an event-driven macro to determine the status of each session based on the # Enrolled.

1 In the **Navigation Pane**, under **Tables**, double-click **8B Sessions** to display the table in **Datasheet** view. Review the data displayed in the table. **Close** « the **Navigation Pane**.

The # Enrolled field displays how many employees have signed up for the session, and the Capacity field displays the maximum capacity in that room. The Status field will be used to display whether the session is still open for enrollment.

2 Under **Table Tools**, on the **Table tab**, in the **Before Events** group, click **Before Change** to display the **Macro Designer**.

3 In the **Macro Designer**, add the **If** action using one of the techniques you have learned. In the **If** action block, click in the **If** box, and type **[# Enrolled]>=[Capacity]** selecting items as they appear in the list to reduce errors.

The conditional expression comparison is used to determine the action that will occur.

4 In the **If** action block, add the **SetField** action using one of the techniques you have learned. In the **SetField** action block, click in the **Name** box, and type **Status** Click in the **Value** box, type **"Closed"** and then compare your screen with Figure 8.41.

The SetField action will update the *Status* field if the condition is true.

Access 2016, Windows 10, Microsoft Corporation

FIGURE 8.41

5 In the **If Arguments Block**, click **Add Else** on the right of the screen to add an additional condition to the If Arguments block. In the **Else Arguments Block**, add the **SetField** action using one of the techniques you have learned. In the **SetField** action block, click in the **Name** box, and type **Status** Click in the **Value** box, and type **"Open"**

The SetField action will update the *Status* field if the original conditional expression is false.

6 **Close** [X] the **Macro Designer**. In the displayed message box, click **Yes** to save the changes made to the macro and to update the property. **Save** [Save] the table.

7 In Record 7, click in the **# Enrolled** field, and type **30**. Press [↓] to move to the next record, type **22** and then click in the first **ID** field. Notice the updates to the **Status** field. Compare your screen with Figure 8.42.

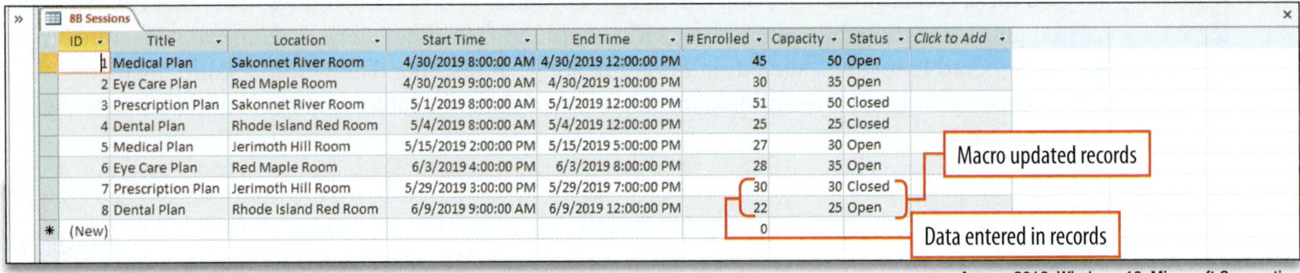
8B Sessions

ID	Title	Location	Start Time	End Time	# Enrolled	Capacity	Status	Click to Add
1	Medical Plan	Sakonnet River Room	4/30/2019 8:00:00 AM	4/30/2019 12:00:00 PM	45	50	Open	
2	Eye Care Plan	Red Maple Room	4/30/2019 9:00:00 AM	4/30/2019 1:00:00 PM	30	35	Open	
3	Prescription Plan	Sakonnet River Room	5/1/2019 8:00:00 AM	5/1/2019 12:00:00 PM	51	50	Closed	
4	Dental Plan	Rhode Island Red Room	5/4/2019 8:00:00 AM	5/4/2019 12:00:00 PM	25	25	Closed	
5	Medical Plan	Jerimoth Hill Room	5/15/2019 2:00:00 PM	5/15/2019 5:00:00 PM	27	30	Open	
6	Eye Care Plan	Red Maple Room	6/3/2019 4:00:00 PM	6/3/2019 8:00:00 PM	28	35	Open	
7	Prescription Plan	Jerimoth Hill Room	5/29/2019 3:00:00 PM	5/29/2019 7:00:00 PM	30	30	Closed	
8	Dental Plan	Rhode Island Red Room	6/9/2019 9:00:00 AM	6/9/2019 12:00:00 PM	22	25	Open	
(New)					0			

Access 2016, Windows 10, Microsoft Corporation

FIGURE 8.42

8 View the table in **Print Preview**. On the **Print Preview tab**, in the **Page Layout group**, click **Landscape**. If you are instructed to submit this result, create a paper printout or PDF electronic image. On the **Print Preview tab**, in the **Close Preview group,** click **Close Print Preview**.

9 **Close** the database, and then **Close** Access.

10 As directed by your instructor, submit your database and the paper printout or PDF electronic images of the two objects—one Database Documenter report and one table—that are the results of this project.

END | You have completed Project 8B

GO! To Work

Andres Rodriguez/Fotolia; FotolEdhar/Fotolia; Andrey Popov/Fotolia; Shutterstock

MICROSOFT OFFICE SPECIALIST (MOS) SKILLS IN THIS CHAPTER	
PROJECT 8A	**PROJECT 8B**
1.3.5 Change views of objects	**1.3.5** Change views of objects
4.2.2 Add form controls	**2.3.1** Update records
4.2.5 Set form control properties	**4.2.5** Set form control properties

BUILD YOUR E-PORTFOLIO

An E-Portfolio is a collection of evidence, stored electronically, that showcases what you have accomplished while completing your education. Collecting and then sharing your work products with potential employees reflects your academic and career goals. Your completed documents from the following projects are good examples to show what you have learned: 8G, 8K, and 8L.

GO! FOR JOB SUCCESS

Discussion: Career Satisfaction

Your instructor may assign these questions to your class, and then ask you to think about them or discuss them with your classmates:

When students talk about career plans, they inevitably hear advice like, "Follow your passion!" or "Do what you love and you'll be successful." But is that really true? Should everyone expect that following their dreams will lead to a successful career? Are you a failure if you don't follow your passion?

With millions of people unemployed but millions of jobs going unfilled, many career experts believe a new way of thinking about "passion" is needed. More realistic advice might be to find a passion for the job you have rather than struggling to find a job that fits your passion. A particular skill or area of knowledge will result in a successful career only if there is a need for it in the market—employers and customers must be willing to pay you to do it.

FotolEdhar/Fotolia

Do you think it's possible to be happy in a job or career that you are not passionate about, but that you like or are good at?

Do you think doing what you love is a requirement for a rewarding and successful career?

If you have a passion for an activity or cause, do you think it's realistic that you could make a living devoted to it, and do you think you would continue to be passionate about it if you had to do it for a living every day?

END OF CHAPTER

SUMMARY

Macros are created to automate database tasks. A database must be trusted in order for all macro actions to be enabled. The Database Documenter is used to print details of objects, including macros.

Standalone macros can run from the Navigation Pane. An autoexec macro runs automatically when the database is opened. Macros can also be embedded within buttons; embedded macros do not display in the Navigation Pane.

A macro group is a set of submacros grouped together and displayed as a single macro in the Navigation Pane. Submacros can then be associated with the clicking of a button on a form or report.

Data macros are associated with a table and triggered by events, such as adding, updating, or deleting data in a table, form, or query. Data macros are used to validate the accuracy of data in a table.

GO! LEARN IT ONLINE

Review the concepts, key terms, and MOS skills in this chapter by completing these online challenges, which you can find at **MyITLab**.

Matching and Multiple Choice: Answer matching and multiple-choice questions to test what you learned in this chapter.

Lessons on the GO!: Learn how to use all the new apps and features as they are introduced by Microsoft.

MOS Prep Quiz: Answer questions to review the MOS skills that you have practiced in this chapter.

PROJECT GUIDE FOR ACCESS CHAPTER 8

Your instructor will assign Projects from this list to ensure your learning and assess your knowledge.

PROJECT GUIDE FOR ACCESS CHAPTER 8			
Project	**Apply Skills from These Chapter Objectives**	**Project Type**	**Project Location**
8A **MyITLab**	Objectives 1–4 from Project 8A	**8A Instructional Project (Grader Project)** Guided instruction to learn the skills in Project 8A.	In MyITLab and in text
8B **MyITLab**	Objectives 5–7 from Project 8B	**8B Instructional Project (Grader Project)** Guided instruction to learn the skills in Project 8B.	In MyITLab and in text
8C	Objectives 1–4 from Project 8A	**8C Chapter Review (Scorecard Grading)** A guided review of the skills from Project 8A.	In text
8D	Objectives 5–7 from Project 8B	**8D Chapter Review (Scorecard Grading)** A guided review of the skills from Project 8B.	In text
8E	Objectives 1–4 from Project 8A	**8E Mastery (Scorecard Grading)** **Mastery and Transfer of Learning** A demonstration of your mastery of the skills in Project 8A with extensive decision making.	In text
8F	Objectives 5–7 from Project 8B	**8F Mastery (Scorecard Grading)** **Mastery and Transfer of Learning** A demonstration of your mastery of the skills in Project 8B with extensive decision making.	In text
8G **MyITLab**	Objectives 1–7 from Projects 8A and 8B	**8G Mastery (Grader Project)** **Mastery and Transfer of Learning** A demonstration of your mastery of the skills in Projects 8A and 8B with extensive decision making.	In MyITLab and in text
8H	Combination of Objectives from Projects 8A and 8B	**8H GO! Fix It (Scorecard Grading)** **Critical Thinking** A demonstration of your mastery of the skills in Projects 8A and 8B by creating a correct result from a document that contains errors you must find.	Instructor Resource Center (IRC) and MyITLab
8I	Combination of Objectives from Projects 8A and 8B	**8I GO! Make It (Scorecard Grading)** **Critical Thinking** A demonstration of your mastery of the skills in Projects 8A and 8B by creating a result from a supplied picture.	IRC and MyITLab
8J	Combination of Objectives from Projects 8A and 8B	**8J GO! Solve It (Rubric Grading)** **Critical Thinking** A demonstration of your mastery of the skills in Projects 8A and 8B, your decision-making skills, and your critical thinking skills. A task-specific rubric helps you self-assess your result.	IRC and MyITLab
8K	Combination of Objectives from Projects 8A and 8B	**8K GO! Solve It (Rubric Grading)** **Critical Thinking** A demonstration of your mastery of the skills in Projects 8A and 8B, your decision-making skills, and your critical thinking skills. A task-specific rubric helps you self-assess your result.	In text
8L	Combination of Objectives from Projects 8A and 8B	**8L GO! Think (Rubric Grading)** **Critical Thinking** A demonstration of your understanding of the chapter concepts applied in a manner that you would use outside of college. An analytic rubric helps you and your instructor grade the quality of your work by comparing it to the work an expert in the discipline would create.	In text
8M	Combination of Objectives from Projects 8A and 8B	**8M GO! Think (Rubric Grading)** **Critical Thinking** A demonstration of your understanding of the chapter concepts applied in a manner that you would use outside of college. An analytic rubric helps you and your instructor grade the quality of your work by comparing it to the work an expert in the discipline would create.	IRC and MyITLab
8N	Combination of Objectives from Projects 8A and 8B	**8N You and GO! (Rubric Grading)** **Critical Thinking** A demonstration of your understanding of the chapter concepts applied in a manner that you would use in a personal situation. An analytic rubric helps you and your instructor grade the quality of your work.	IRC and MyITLab

GLOSSARY

GLOSSARY OF CHAPTER KEY TERMS

Action A self-contained instruction that can be combined with other actions to automate tasks.

Argument A value that provides information to the macro action, such as the words to display in a message box or the control upon which to operate.

Code Builder A window used to type programming code in Microsoft Visual Basic.

Comment Explanatory information provided about the macro or the action.

Condition A statement that specifies that certain criteria must be met before the macro action executes.

Data macro A macro that is triggered by events, such as adding, updating, or deleting data within a table, form, or query. It is used to validate the accuracy of data in a table; also known as an event-driven macro.

Database Documenter An option used to create a report that contains detailed information about the objects in a database, including macros, and to create a paper record.

Debugging A logical process to find and reduce the number of errors in a program.

Embedded macro A macro that is stored in the properties of forms, reports, or controls.

Event Any action that can be detected by a program or computer system, such as clicking a button or closing an object.

Macro A series of actions grouped as a single command to accomplish a task or multiple tasks automatically to add functionality to your object or control.

Macro Designer Window that allows you to build the list of actions to be carried out when the macro runs.

Macro group A set of macros grouped by a common name that displays as one macro object on the Navigation Pane.

Modal window A child (secondary) window to a parent window—the original window that opened the modal window—that takes over control of the parent window.

Pop-up window A window that suddenly displays (pops up), usually contains a menu of commands, and stays on the screen only until the user selects one of the commands.

Single stepping Debugging a macro using a process that executes one action at a time.

Standalone macro A macro object that displays under Macros on the Navigation Pane.

Syntax The spelling, grammar, and sequence of characters of a programming language.

CHAPTER REVIEW

Apply 8A skills from these Objectives:

1. Create a Standalone Macro with One Action
2. Add Multiple Actions to a Standalone Macro
3. Create an Embedded Macro
4. Print Macro Details

Skills Review Project 8C Supervisory Staff

Maria Diaz, vice president of operations for Providence & Warwick Hospital, wants to customize her database of supervisory staff. In this project, you will create macros to automatically display a form and message box when the database is opened and embed macros within a form. Finally, you will display and print a report that documents the details of the macros you created. Your completed work will look similar to Figure 8.43.

PROJECT FILES

For Project 8C, you will need the following file:

a08C_Supervisory_Staff

You will save your database as:

Lastname_Firstname_8C_Supervisory_Staff

PROJECT RESULTS

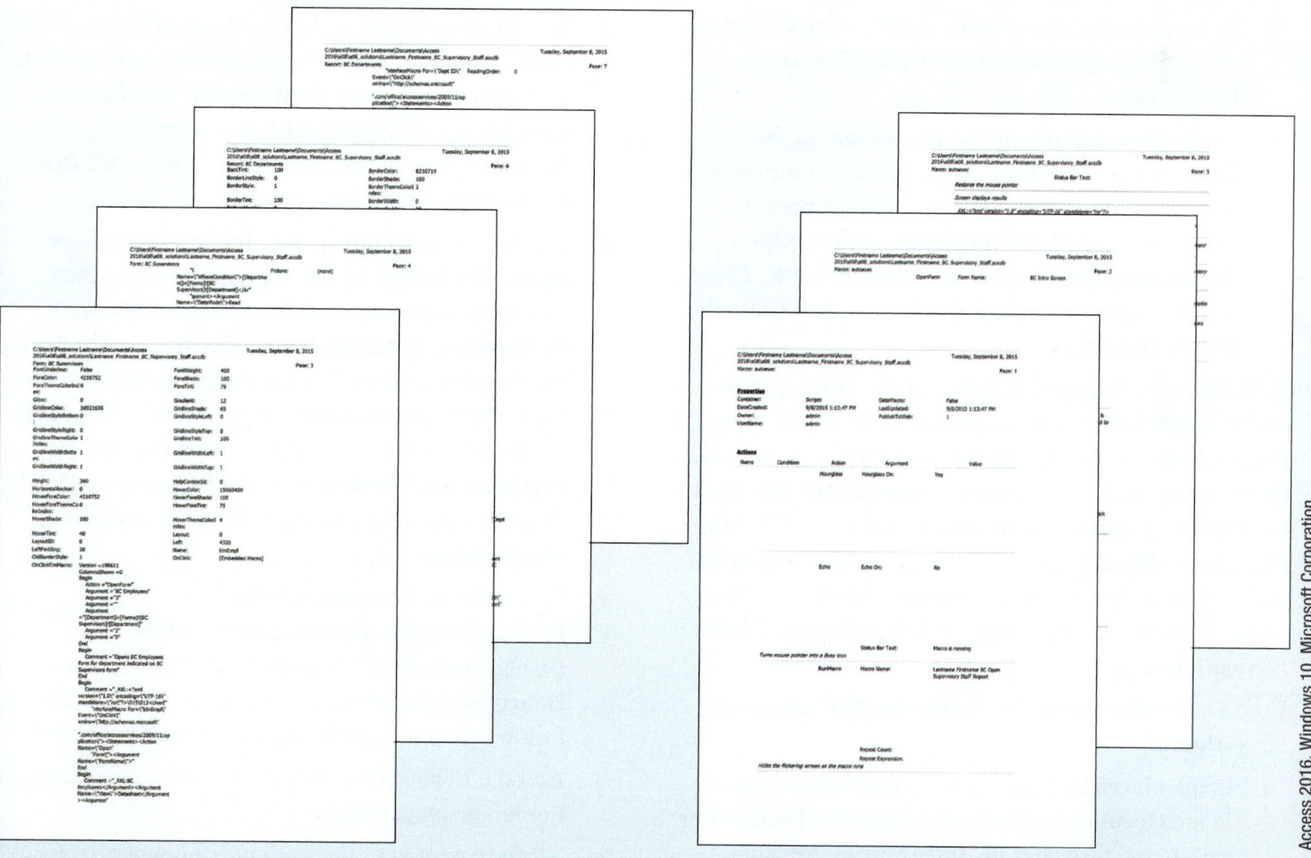

FIGURE 8.43

(Project 8C Supervisory Staff continues on the next page)

Skills Review Project 8C Supervisory Staff (continued)

1 Start Access. Locate and open the **a08C_Supervisory_Staff** file. Save the database in your **Access Chapter 8** folder as **Lastname_Firstname_8C_Supervisory_Staff** and then **Close** the **Navigation Pane**.

2 On the **Create tab**, in the **Macros & Code group**, click **Macro**.

a. In the **Macro Designer**, in the **Add New Action bar,** click the **arrow**, and then click **OpenReport**. In the **OpenReport** action block, in the **Report Name** box, click the **arrow**, and then click **8C Supervisory Staff**. In the **View** box, verify that **Report** is selected. The **Filter Name** and **Where Condition** boxes should be blank. In the **Window Mode** box, verify that the setting is **Normal**.

b. In the **Action Catalog pane**, double-click **Comment**, and type **Opens 8C Supervisory Staff report in Report view**

c. Under **Macro Tools**, on the **Design tab**, in the **Tools group**, click **Run**. In the displayed message box, click **Yes** to save the macro. In the **Save As** dialog box, type **Lastname Firstname 8C Open Supervisory Staff Report** and then click **OK**. **Close** the **8C Supervisory Staff** report, and then **Close** the Macro Designer.

3 **Open** the **Navigation Pane**. Under **Forms**, open the **8C Intro Screen** form in **Design** view. Under **Form Design Tools**, on the **Design tab**, in the **Tools group**, click **Property Sheet**. On the **Property Sheet Other tab**, click the **Pop Up property setting arrow**, and then click **Yes**. Click in the **Modal** property setting box, click the **arrow**, and then click **Yes**. Close the **Property Sheet**, and then **Close** the form, saving changes when prompted. **Close** the **Navigation Pane**.

4 On the **Create tab**, in the **Macros & Code group**, click **Macro**.

a. In the **Macro Designer**, add the **OpenForm** action. In the **OpenForm** action block, click the **Form Name arrow**, and then click **8C Intro Screen**. Add the following comment: **Opens 8C Intro Screen form**

b. On the **Quick Access Toolbar**, click **Save**. In the **Save As** dialog box, type **autoexec** and then click **OK**. **Close** the Macro Designer, and then **Open** the **Navigation Pane**. In the **Navigation Pane**, under **Macros**, double-click **autoexec** to run the macro. **Close** the form.

5 In the **Navigation Pane**, under **Macros**, right-click **Autoexec**, and then click **Design View**. **Close** the **Navigation Pane**.

a. Add the **DisplayHourglassPointer** action. Notice that the default argument is *Yes*. Add the following comment: **Turns mouse pointer into a Busy icon**

b. Under **Macro Tools**, on the **Design tab**, in the **Show/Hide group**, click **Show All Actions**. In the **Macro Designer**, add the **Echo** action. In the **Echo** action block, click the **Echo On arrow**, and then click **No**. Click in the **Status Bar Text** box, and type **Macro is running** Add the following comment: **Hides the flickering screen as the macro runs**

c. Add the **RunMacro** action. In the **RunMacro** action block, click the **Macro Name arrow**, and then click **8C Open Supervisory Staff Report**. The **Repeat Count** box and the **Repeat Expression** box should be blank. Add the following comment: **Runs 8C Open Supervisory Staff Report macro**

d. Add the **MessageBox** action. In the **MessageBox** action block, click in the **Message** box, and then type **Only supervisors at Providence & Warwick Hospital are authorized to access this database.** In the **Beep** box, verify that the Beep argument is **Yes**. Click the **Type box arrow**, and then click **Warning!** Click in the **Title** box, and then type **For Use by Providence & Warwick Hospital Supervisors Only!** Add the following comment: **Displays a warning message box**

e. In the **Macro Designer**, add the **DisplayHourglassPointer** action. In the **DisplayHourglassPointer** action block, click the **Hourglass On arrow**, and then click **No**. Add the following comment: **Restores the mouse pointer**

f. Add the **Echo** action. Add the following comment: **Screen displays results**

g. Scroll to the top of the **Action Argument** box. Click the **OpenForm** action to make it active, and then move the action below the comment **Runs 8C Open Supervisory Staff Report macro**.

h. Move the **OpenForm macro comment** below the **OpenForm action**.

(Project 8C Supervisory Staff continues on the next page)

Skills Review Project 8C Supervisory Staff (continued)

i. **Save** the macro. Under **Macro Tools**, on the **Design tab**, in the **Tools group**, click **Run**. In the displayed message box, click **OK**. **Close** the **8C Intro Screen** form. On the **tab row**, right-click any tab, and then click **Close All**. **Open** the **Navigation Pane**.

6 Open the **8C Supervisors** form in **Design** view. **Close** the **Navigation Pane**. Under **Form Design Tools**, on the **Design tab**, in the **Controls group**, click **Button**. In the **Details** section, align the plus sign (+) of the pointer at **3 inches on the horizontal ruler** and **2 inches on the vertical ruler**, and then click.

a. In the **Command Button Wizard** dialog box, click **Cancel**.

b. Right-click the button, and then click **Properties**. Verify that the **Property Sheet** displays *Selection type: Command Button* and the **Selection type** box displays *Command0* (your number may differ), identifying your command button. On the **Property Sheet Other tab**, in the **Name** property box, select the existing text and type **btnEmpl**

c. On the **Property Sheet Format tab**, in the **Caption** property box, select the existing text, type **Employee List** and then press Enter.

d. On the **Property Sheet Event tab**, in the **On Click** property setting box, click **Build**.

e. In the **Choose Builder** dialog box, click **Macro Builder**, if necessary, and then click **OK** to display the Macro Designer.

f. In the **Macro Designer**, add the **OpenForm** action using one of the techniques you have learned. In the **OpenForm** action block, click the **Form Name arrow**, and then click **8C Employees**. Click in the **Where Condition** box, and type **[Department]=[Forms]![8C Supervisors]![Department]** selecting items as they appear in the list to reduce errors.

g. In the **OpenForm** action block, click the **View arrow**, and then click **Datasheet**. Click the **Data Mode arrow**, and then click **Read Only**. Add the following comment: **Opens 8C Employees form for department indicated on 8C Supervisors form**

h. **Close** the **Macro Designer**. In the displayed message box, click **Yes** to save the changes made to the macro and to update the **On Click** property.

7 On the **Property Sheet**, click the **Format tab**. In the **Caption** box, click to the left of **Employee List**, and then type **&** to create a shortcut key using the letter *E*. **Close** the **Property Sheet**, **Save** the form, and then switch the **8C Supervisors** form to **Form** view.

a. On the **8C Supervisors** form, click the **Employee List** button or press Alt + E.

b. **Close** the **8C Employees** form, and then **Close** the **8C Supervisors** form, saving changes, if necessary. **Open** the **Navigation Pane**.

8 Open the **8C Departments** report in **Design** view. **Close** the **Navigation Pane**. In the **Detail** section, right-click the **Dept ID** text box, and then click **Properties**. Verify that the **Property Sheet** displays *Selection type: Text Box* and the **Selection type** box displays *Dept ID*.

a. On the **Property Sheet Event tab**, in the **On Click** property setting box, click the **Build** button. In the **Choose Builder** dialog box, verify that **Macro Builder** is selected, and then click **OK** to display the Macro Designer.

b. In the **Macro Designer**, add the **OpenForm** action using one of the techniques you have learned. In the **OpenForm** action block, click the **Form Name arrow**, and then click **8C Supervisors** form. Click in the **Where Condition** box, type **[Dept ID]=[Reports]![8C Departments]![Dept ID]** selecting items as they appear in the list to reduce errors.

c. In the **OpenForm** action block, click the **Data Mode arrow**, and then click **Read Only**. Add the following comment: **Opens 8C Supervisors form for the Dept ID selected on 8C Departments report**

d. **Close** the **Macro Designer**. In the displayed message box, click **Yes** to save the changes made to the macro and to update the **On Click** property. **Close** the **Property Sheet**. **Save** the report.

e. Switch to **Report** view. On the **8C Departments** report, click the **Dept ID** text box for *1233-D* to run the macro.

f. **Close** the **8C Supervisors** form. **Close** the **8C Departments** report, saving changes.

(Project 8C Supervisory Staff continues on the next page)

Skills Review Project 8C Supervisory Staff (continued)

9 On the **Database Tools tab**, in the **Analyze group**, click **Database Documenter**.

a. In the **Documenter** dialog box, click the **Macros tab**, and then click **Options**. If necessary, click the check box to deselect **Permissions by User and Group**, and then click **OK**. In the **Documenter** dialog box, click **Select All**.

b. In the **Documenter** dialog box, click the **Forms tab**, and then click **Options**. If necessary, click the check box to deselect **Properties** and **Permissions by User and Group**, and then click **OK**. In the **Documenter** dialog box, click the **8C Supervisors** form check box.

c. In the **Documenter** dialog box, click the **Reports tab**, and then click **Options**. If necessary, click the check box to deselect **Properties** and **Permissions by User and Group**, and then click **OK**. In the **Documenter** dialog box, click the **8C Departments** report check box, and then click **OK**.

d. If you are instructed to submit this result, create a paper printout or PDF electronic image of the pages that contain the embedded macros on the form, the embedded macros on the report, and the autoexec macro. Include the project number, 8C, in the file name if you create a PDF electronic image. On the **Print Preview tab**, in the **Close Preview group**, click **Close Print Preview**.

10 **Open** the **Navigation Pane**. **Close** the database, and then **Close** Access.

11 As directed by your instructor, submit your database and the paper printout or PDF electronic image of the three Database Documenter reports that are the result of this project. Specifically, in this project, using your own name you created the following database and printout or PDF electronic image:

1. Lastname_Firstname_8C_Supervisory_Staff	Database file
2. Lastname_Firstname_Project8C_Database_Documenter_Embedded_Form	Database Documenter report
3. Lastname_Firstname_Project8C_Database_Documenter_Embedded_Report	Database Documenter report
4. Lastname_Firstname_Project8C_Database_Documenter	Database Documenter report

END | You have completed Project 8C

Apply 8B skills from these Objectives:

5 Create a Macro Group

6 Associate a Macro with an Event

7 Create a Data Macro

Skills Review Project 8D Hospital Departments

Maria Diaz, vice president of operations for Providence & Warwick Hospital, wants to customize her database of department information, including automating the process to add new departments. You will associate command buttons with a macro group's submacros and create a data macro. Your completed work will look similar to Figure 8.44.

PROJECT FILES

For Project 8D, you will need the following file:

a08D_Hospital_Departments

You will save your database as:

Lastname_Firstname_8D_Hospital_Departments

PROJECT RESULTS

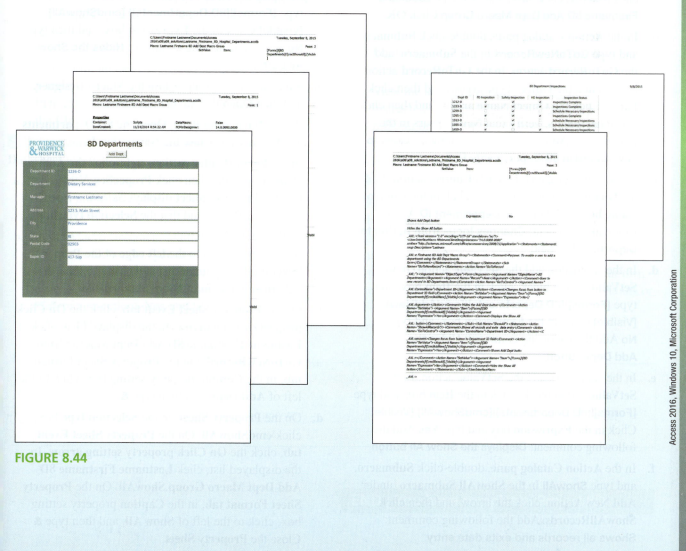

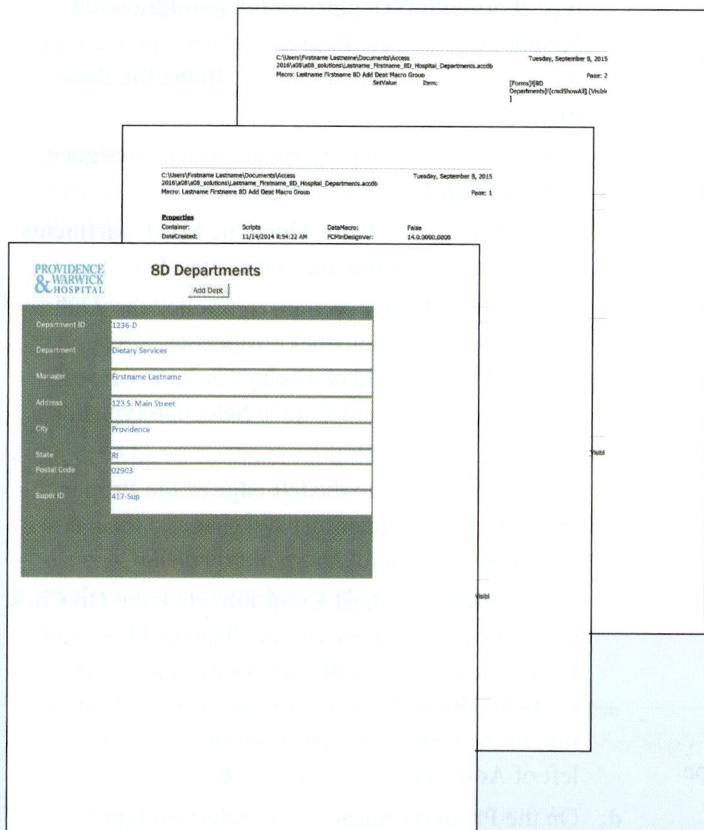

FIGURE 8.44

(Project 8D Hospital Departments continues on the next page)

Apply 8A skills from these Objectives:

1. Create a Standalone Macro with One Action
2. Add Multiple Actions to a Standalone Macro
3. Create an Embedded Macro
4. Print Macro Details

Mastering Access Project 8E Gift Shop

Maria Diaz, vice president of operations for Providence & Warwick Hospital, wants to customize the gift shop database and automate common tasks. In this project, you will create a macro to automatically display a form and message box when the user opens the database. In addition, you will embed macros within a form and report. Your completed work will look similar to Figure 8.45.

PROJECT FILES

For Project 8E, you will need the following file:

a08E_Gift_Shop

You will save your database as:

Lastname_Firstname_8E_Gift_Shop

PROJECT RESULTS

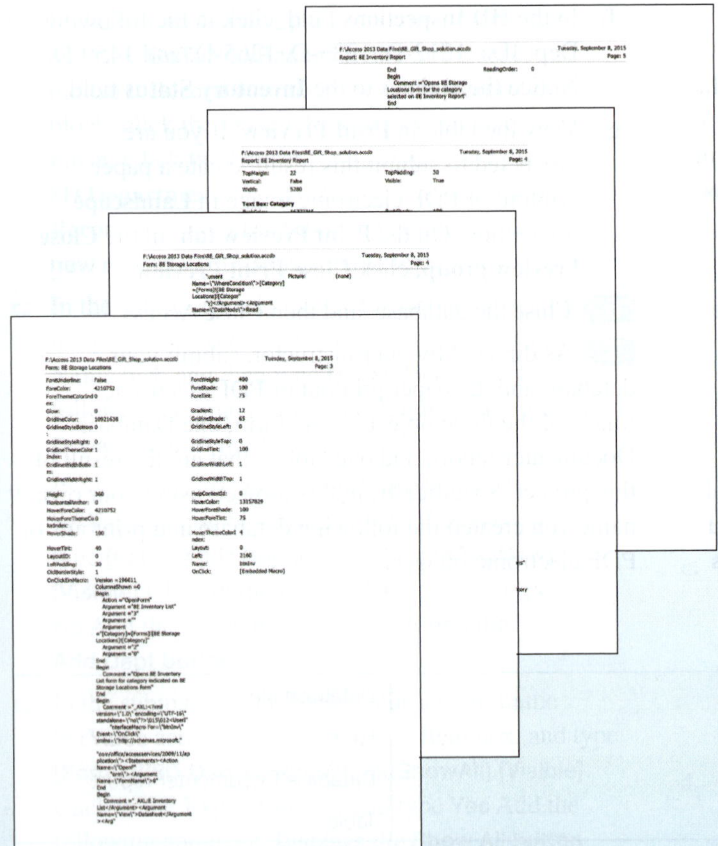

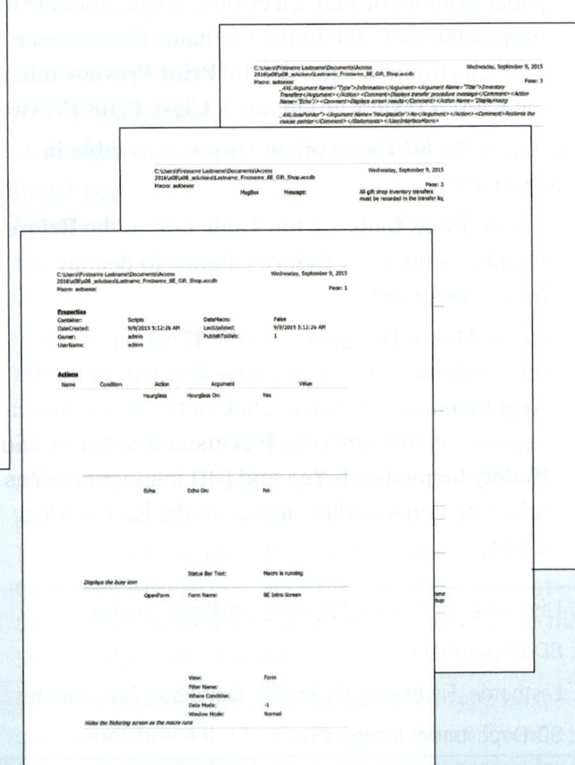

FIGURE 8.45

(Project 8E Gift Shop continues on the next page)

Mastering Access Project 8E Gift Shop (continued)

1 Start Access. Locate and open the **a08E_Gift_Shop** file. Save the database in your **Access Chapter 8** folder as **Lastname_Firstname_8E_Gift_Shop** **Close** the **Navigation Pane**.

2 Create a macro to open the **8E Intro Screen** form with a comment: **Opens 8E Intro Screen form** On the **Design tab**, in the **Show/Hide group**, verify that the **Show All Actions** button is active. **Save** the macro as **autoexec**

3 Modify the **Autoexec** macro. Add the action **DisplayHourglassPointer** with the **Comment Displays the busy icon** Add the **Echo** action with the **Comment Hides the flickering screen as the macro runs** In the **Echo** action block, change the **Echo On** box to **No**. In the **Status Bar Text** box, type **Macro is running** Move the **OpenForm** action and comment below the **Echo** macro comment.

4 In the **Macro Designer**, at the bottom of the current list of actions, add a **MessageBox** action. Type a **Message** that displays **All gift shop inventory transfers must be recorded in the transfer log.** Add a **Beep**, and change the **Type** box to **Information**. Title the **Message** box **Inventory Transfers** Add a **Comment** that reads **Displays transfer procedure message**

5 In the **Macro Designer**, add an **Echo** action. In the **Echo** action block, verify the **Echo On** box is set to **Yes**. Add a **Comment** that says **Displays screen results**

6 In the **Macro Designer**, add a **DisplayHourglassPointer** action. In the **DisplayHourglassPointer** action block, change the **Hourglass On** box to **No**. Add a **Comment** that says **Restores the mouse pointer**

7 **Close** the Macro Designer, and **Save** the macro. **Open** the **Navigation Pane**.

8 Open the **8E Storage Locations** form in **Design** view. **Close** the **Navigation Pane**. In the **Detail** section, add a **Button** control at **1.5 inches on the horizontal ruler** and **0.25 inches on the vertical ruler**. In the **Command Button Wizard** dialog box, click **Cancel**. Right-click the button, and then click **Properties**. On the **Property Sheet Other tab**, change the **Name** to **btnInv** On the **Property Sheet Format tab**, change the **Caption** to **Inventory List** On the **Property Sheet Event tab**, in the **On Click** property setting box, click the **Build** button. In the **Choose Builder** dialog box, verify that **Macro Builder** is selected, and then click **OK** to display the Macro Designer.

9 In the **Macro Designer**, add the **OpenForm** action to open the **8E Inventory List** form. In the **Where Condition** box, type **[Category]=[Forms]![8E Storage Locations]![Category]** For **View**, select **Datasheet**. For **Data Mode**, select **Read Only**. Add the comment: **Opens 8E Inventory List form for category indicated on 8E Storage Locations form** **Close** the **Macro Designer**, saving changes and updating the **On Click** property.

10 On the **Property Sheet Format tab**, in the **Caption** box, insert an **&** to the left of **Inventory List**. **Close** the **Property Sheet**, **Save** the form, and then switch **8E Storage Locations** to **Form** view. Click the **Inventory List** button. **Close** the **8E Inventory List** form. **Close** the **8E Storage Locations** form. **Open** the **Navigation Pane**.

11 Open the **8E Inventory Report** in **Design** view. **Close** the **Navigation Pane**. In the **Detail** section, display the **Property Sheet** for the **Category** text box. Verify that the **Property Sheet** displays *Selection type: Text Box* and the **Selection type** box displays *Category*. On the **Property Sheet Event tab**, in the **On Click** property setting box, click **Build**, and display the Macro Designer.

12 In the **Macro Designer**, add the **OpenForm** action to open the **8E Storage Locations** form. Add the **Where Condition [Category]=[Reports]![8E Inventory Report]![Category]** Change the **Data Mode** to **Read Only**. Add the comment: **Opens 8E Storage Locations form for the category selected on 8E Inventory Report** **Close** the **Macro Designer,** saving changes and updating the **On Click** property. **Close** the **Property Sheet**. **Save** the report.

13 Switch to **Report** view. On the **8E Inventory Report**, click the **Category** text box for *Food* to run the macro. **Close** the **8E Storage Locations** form. **Close** the **8E Inventory Report**, saving changes.

14 Open the **Database Documenter**. In the **Documenter** dialog box, click the **Macros tab**, and click **autoexec**. If necessary, in the **Options** dialog box, deselect **Permissions by User and Group.** In the **Documenter** dialog box, on the **Forms tab**, select the **8E Storage Locations** form. If necessary, in the **Options** dialog box, clear the **Properties** and **Permissions by User**

(Project 8E Gift Shop continues on the next page)

Mastering Access Project 8E Gift Shop (continued)

and Group check boxes. In the **Documenter** dialog box, on the **Reports tab**, select the **8E Inventory Report** and then click **OK**. If you are instructed to submit this result, create a paper printout or PDF electronic image of the pages for the embedded form, embedded report, and autoexec macros. Include the project number, 8E, in the file name if you create a PDF electronic image. **Close Print Preview**.

15 **Close** the database, and then **Close** Access.

16 As directed by your instructor, submit your database and the paper printout or PDF electronic image of the three Database Documenter reports that are the result of this project. Specifically, in this project, using your own name you created the following database and printouts or PDF electronic images:

1. Lastname_Firstname_8E_Gift_Shop	Database file
2. Lastname_Firstname_Project8E_Database_Documenter_Embedded_Form	Database Documenter report
3. Lastname_Firstname_Project8E_Database_Documenter_Embedded_Report	Database Documenter report
4. Lastname_Firstname_8E_Database_Documenter	Database Documenter report

END | You have completed Project 8E

Apply 8B skills from these Objectives:

5 Create a Macro Group
6 Associate a Macro with an Event
7 Create a Data Macro

Mastering Access Project 8F Orthopedic Supplies

Maria Diaz, vice president of operations for Providence & Warwick Hospital, wants to customize the orthopedic supplies database using macros. In this project, you will create a macro group, associate command buttons with a macro, and create a data macro. Your completed work will look similar to Figure 8.46.

PROJECT FILES

For Project 8F, you will need the following file:

a08F_Orthopedic_Supplies

You will save your database as:

Lastname_Firstname_8F_Orthopedic_Supplies

PROJECT RESULTS

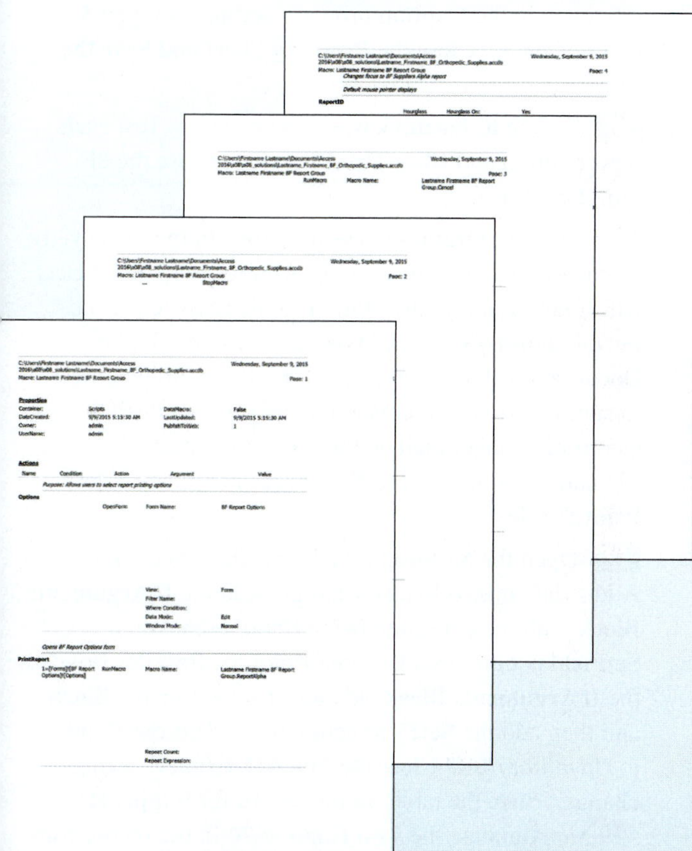

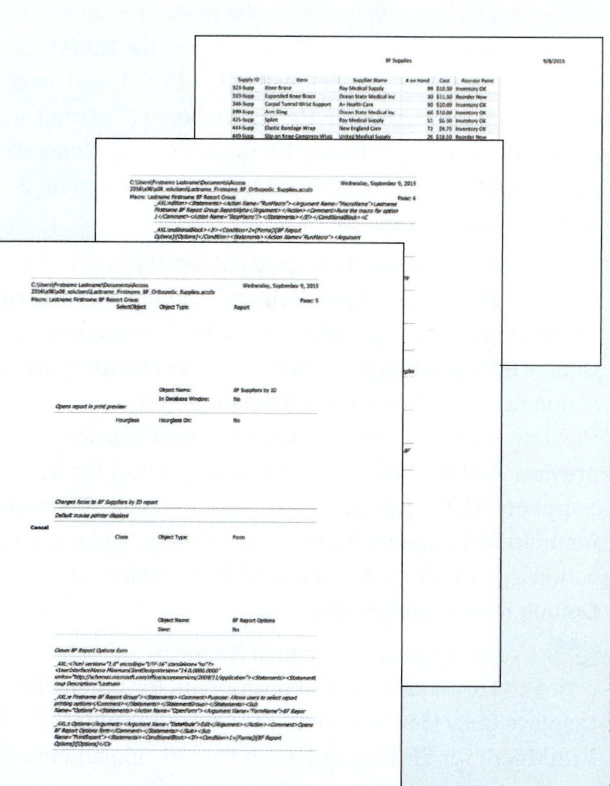

GURE 8.46

(Project 8F Orthopedic Supplies continues on the next page)

CONTENT-BASED ASSESSMENTS (MASTERY AND TRANSFER OF LEARNING)

Mastering Access Project 8F Orthopedic Supplies (continued)

1 Start Access. Locate and open the **a08F_Orthopedic_Supplies** file. Save the database in your **Access Chapter 8** folder as **Lastname_Firstname_8F_Orthopedic_Supplies** **Close** the **Navigation Pane**.

2 Create a **Macro Group** to print the reports. Name this macro group **Lastname Firstname 8F Report Group** with a comment: **Purpose: Allows users to select report printing options**

3 Create a **Submacro** named **Options** with the action **OpenForm** opening the **8F Report Options** form in Form view and Edit mode. Add the comment: **Opens 8F Report Options form**

4 Create a **Submacro** named **PrintReport** Add an **If** argument **1=[Forms]![8F Report Options]![Options]** and the **RunMacro** action for the **8F Report Group.ReportAlpha** macro. Add the comment: **Runs the macro for option 1** and then add the **StopMacro** action below the RunMacro action. In the submacro, below the first End If, add another **If** argument **2=[Forms]![8F Report Options]![Options]** and the **RunMacro** action for the **8F Report Group.ReportID** macro. Add the comment: **Runs the macro for option 2** and then add the **StopMacro** action.

5 Create a **Submacro** named **ReportAlpha** Add an action to **DisplayHourglassPointer**. Add the **RunMacro** for **8F Report Group.Cancel**, and add the comment: **Closes 8F Report Options form** Add the **OpenReport** action to open **8F Suppliers Alpha** report in Print Preview. Add the comment: **Opens report in print preview** Add the **SelectObject** action to select the **8F Suppliers Alpha** report, and add the comment: **Changes focus to 8F Suppliers Alpha report** Finally, add a macro action to turn off the hourglass with the comment: **Default mouse pointer displays**

6 Create a **Submacro** named **ReportID** Add an action to **DisplayHourglassPointer** with the comment: **Displays busy icon while macro is running** Add the **RunMacro** for **8F Report Group.Cancel**, and add the comment: **Closes 8F Report Options form** Next, add the **OpenReport** action to open the **8F Suppliers by ID** report in Print Preview. Add the comment: **Opens report in print preview** Add the **SelectObject** action to select the **8F Suppliers by ID** report, and add the comment: **Changes focus to 8F Suppliers by ID report** Finally, add a macro action to turn off the hourglass with the comment: **Default mouse pointer displays**

7 Create a **Submacro** named **Cancel** Add the **CloseWindow** action to close the **8F Report Options** form. Add the comment: **Closes 8F Report Options form**

8 **Close** the **Macro Designer**, saving the group as **Lastname Firstname 8F Report Group**

9 Open the **8F Report Options** form in **Design** view. Open the **Property Sheet** for the **Print Report** button. On the **Property Sheet Event tab**, click the **On Click property setting box arrow**, and click **8F Report Group. PrintReport**. On the **Property Sheet Format tab**, click in the **Caption** property setting and type **&** before *Print Report*. On the Design grid, click the **Cancel** button. On the **Event tab**, in the **On Click** property setting, select **8F Report Group.Cancel**. On the **Property Sheet Format tab**, click in the **Caption** property setting and type **&** before *Cancel*. **Close** the **Property Sheet** and **Save** the form.

10 Switch to **Form** view, saving changes**.** Test each report option and **Close Print Preview**. **Close** the **8F Suppliers** form.

11 Open the **Database Documenter**. In the displayed **Documenter** dialog box, on the **Macros tab**, click **Select All**. If necessary, in the **Options** dialog box, clear the **Permissions by User and Group** check box. In the **Documenter** dialog box, click **OK**. If you are instructed to submit this result, create a paper printout or PDF electronic image. Include the project number, 8F, in the file name if you create a PDF electronic image. **Close Print Preview**.

12 Open the **8F Supplies** table in **Datasheet** view. Add a data macro **Before Change**. Add the **If Arguments Block** with the condition **[# On Hand]<=36** Add the **SetField** action to set **Reorder Point** to **"Reorder Now"** In the **If Arguments Block**, add an **Else Arguments Block**, and then add the **SetField** action to set **Reorder Point** to **"Inventory OK"** **Close** the **Macro Designer**, saving changes. **Save** the table. In the record for **Supply ID** *519-Supp*, update the **# on Hand** to **70** In the record for *525-Supp*, update the **# on Hand** to **32** Click in the first field in the first record, and notice the updates to the **Reorder Point** field. View the table in **Print Preview**. If you are instructed to submit this result, create a paper printout or PDF electronic image in **Landscape** orientation. On the **Print Preview tab**, in the **Close Preview group**, click **Close Print Preview**.

(Project 8F Orthopedic Supplies continues on the next page)

Mastering Access Project 8F Orthopedic Supplies (continued)

13 **Close** the database, and then **Close** Access.

14 As directed by your instructor, submit your database and the paper printout or PDF electronic image of the two objects—one Database Documenter report and one table—that are the result of this project. Specifically, in this project, using your own name you created the following database and printouts or PDF electronic images:

1. Lastname_Firstname_8F_Orthopedic_Supplies	Database file
2. Lastname_Firstname_Project_8F_Database_Documenter	Database Documenter report
3. 8F Supplies	Table

END | You have completed Project 8F

CONTENT-BASED ASSESSMENTS (MASTERY AND TRANSFER OF LEARNING)

MyITLab grader

Apply 8A and 8B skills from these Objectives:

1 Create a Standalone Macro with One Action
2 Add Multiple Actions to a Standalone Macro
3 Create an Embedded Macro
4 Print Macro Details
5 Create a Macro Group
6 Associate a Macro with an Event
7 Create a Data Macro

Mastering Access Project 8G Hospital Expansion

Mara Bartello, facilities director of the Providence & Warwick Hospital in Providence, Rhode Island, is analyzing proposed expansion projects. In this project, you will create macros to automate the process. Your completed work will look similar to Figure 8.47.

PROJECT FILES

For Project 8G, you will need the following file:

a08G_Hospital_Expansion

You will save your database as:

Lastname_Firstname_8G_Hospital_Expansion

PROJECT RESULTS

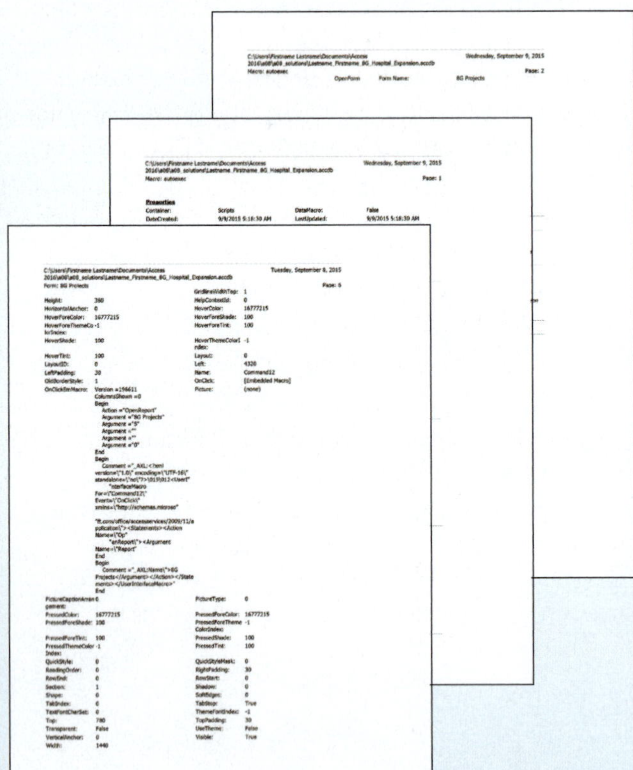

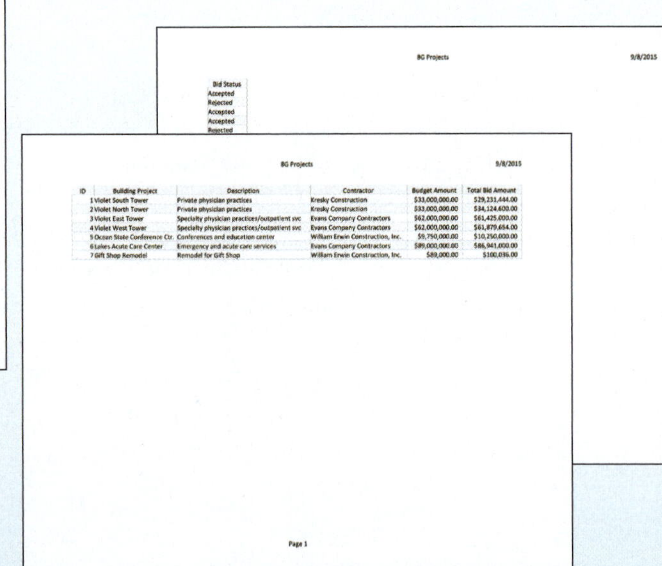

FIGURE 8.47

(Project 8G Hospital Expansion continues on the next page)

Mastering Access Project 8G Hospital Expansion (continued)

1 Start Access. Locate and open the **a08G_Hospital_Expansion** file. Save the database in your **Access Chapter 8** folder as **Lastname_Firstname_8G_Hospital_Expansion**

2 **Open** the **8G Intro Screen** form in **Design** view. Change the **Pop Up** and **Modal** properties to **Yes**. **Save** and **Close** the form.

3 Create a macro to open the **8G Intro Screen** form with an appropriate comment. In the **Show/Hide group**, be sure the **Show All Actions** button is active. **Save** the macro as **autoexec**

4 Modify the **autoexec** macro. Add the action **OpenForm** to open the **8G Projects** form with an appropriate comment. Add the action **DisplayHourglassPointer** with the **Comment Displays the busy icon** Add the **Echo** action. In the **Echo** action block, change the **Echo On** box to **No**. Click in the **Status Bar Text** box, and then type **Macro is running** Add the **Comment Hides the flickering screen as the macro runs** Move the first **OpenForm** action and comment below the **Echo** macro comment. **Save** and **Close** the macro. **Close** the database, and then reopen it.

5 **Close** the **8G Intro Screen**. Switch the **8G Projects** form to **Design** view. In the **Form Header**, add a **Button** control at the **3-inch mark on the horizontal ruler** and **0.5-inch mark on the vertical ruler** with the caption **&Summary** Embed a macro to **Open** the **8G Projects** report in **Report** view. **Save** and **Close** the macro. **Save** the form. Switch to **Form** view, and test the macro. **Close** the report and the form.

6 Run the **Database Documenter**. Select the **Forms tab**, if necessary, and select **8G Projects**. Click **Options** and under **Include for Form**, select the **Code** check box only, if necessary. Click **OK** two times. If you are instructed to submit this result, create a paper printout or PDF electronic image of the embedded macro page in the report. Include the project number, 8G, in the file name if you create a PDF electronic image. **Close Print Preview**.

7 Run the **Database Documenter**. Click the **Macros** tab, and click **Select All**. Click **OK**. If you are instructed to submit this result, create a paper printout or PDF electronic image of the report. Include the project number, 8G, in the file name if you create a PDF electronic image. **Close Print Preview**.

8 Open the **8G Projects** table in **Datasheet** view. Add a data macro **Before Change**. Add the **If Arguments Block** with the condition **[Total Bid Amount]<=[Budget Amount]** Add the **SetField** action to set **Bid Status** to **"Accepted"** In the **If Arguments Block**, add an **Else Arguments Block**, and then add the **SetField** action to set **Bid Status** to **"Rejected"** **Close** the **Macro Designer**, saving changes. **Save** the table. In Record 6, update the **Total Bid Amount** to **86941000** In Record 7 update the **Total Bid Amount** to **100036** Click in the first field in the first record, and notice the updates to the **Bid Status** field. View the table in **Print Preview**. If you are instructed to submit this result, create a paper printout or PDF electronic image in **Landscape** orientation. **Close Print Preview**.

9 **Open** the **Navigation Pane**. **Close** the database, and then **Close** Access.

10 As directed by your instructor, submit your database and the paper printout or PDF electronic image of the two objects—two Database Documenter reports and one table—that are the result of this project. Specifically, in this project, using your own name you created the following database and printouts or PDF electronic images:

1. Lastname_Firstname_8G_Hospital_Expansion	Database file
2. Project_8G_Database_Documenter_Embedded_Form	Database Documenter report
3. Project_8G_Database_ Documenter_Autoexec	Database Documenter report
4. 8G Projects	Table

END | You have completed Project 8G

Apply a combination of the 8A and 8B skills.

CONTENT-BASED ASSESSMENTS (CRITICAL THINKING)

GO! Fix It Project 8H Medical Transcription MyITLab

GO! Make It Project 8I Recruiting Events MyITLab

GO! Solve It Project 8J Dictation Department MyITLab

GO! Solve It Project 8K Stay Length

PROJECT FILES

For Project 8K, you will need the following file:

a08K_Stay_Length

You will save your database as:

Lastname_Firstname_8K_Stay_Length

The vice president of operations at the Providence & Warwick Hospital, Maria Diaz, is preparing for the upcoming recruiting season. Open the **a08K_Stay_Length** database and save it as **Lastname_Firstname_8K_Stay_Length** Create an autoexec standalone macro to display the *8K Intro Screen* form. On the *8K Facilities* form, embed a macro in the Patients button to display the *8K Patients* form for the facility selected in Datasheet view. In the *8K Facility* table, create a Before Change data macro to display **Outpatient** in the Facility type field if the Beds = 0; otherwise, it should display **Inpatient** Test the macro by entering **65** for the SMC facility and **0** for the WAC facility.

If you are instructed to submit this result, create a paper printout or PDF electronic image of the table in Landscape orientation. If you are instructed to submit the macro details, create a paper printout or PDF electronic image.

Performance Level

Performance Element	Exemplary: You consistently applied the relevant skills	Proficient: You sometimes, but not always, applied the relevant skills	Developing: You rarely or never applied the relevant skills
Create autoexec macro	Autoexec created with the correct actions, arguments, and comments	Autoexec created with no more than two missing actions, arguments, or comments	Autoexec created with more than two missing actions, arguments, or comments
Create embedded macro in Patients button on 8K Facilities form	Embedded macro created with the correct actions, arguments, and comments	Embedded macro created with no more than two missing actions, arguments, or comments	Embedded macro created with more than two missing actions, arguments, or comments
Create Before Change data macro in 8K Facility table	Data macro created with the correct actions, arguments, and comments	Data macro created with no more than two missing actions, arguments, or comments	Data macro created with more than two missing actions, arguments, or comments

END | You have completed Project 8K

OUTCOMES-BASED ASSESSMENTS (CRITICAL THINKING)

RUBRIC

The following outcomes-based assessments are open-ended assessments. That is, there is no specific correct result; your result will depend on your approach to the information provided. Make Professional Quality your goal. Use the following scoring rubric to guide you in how to approach the problem and then to evaluate how well your approach solves the problem.

The *criteria*—Software Mastery, Content, Format and Layout, and Process—represent the knowledge and skills you have gained that you can apply to solving the problem. The *levels of performance*—Professional Quality, Approaching Professional Quality, or Needs Quality Improvements—help you and your instructor evaluate your result.

	Your completed project is of Professional Quality if you:	Your completed project is Approaching Professional Quality if you:	Your completed project Needs Quality Improvements if you:
1-Software Mastery	Choose and apply the most appropriate skills, tools, and features and identify efficient methods to solve the problem.	Choose and apply some appropriate skills, tools, and features, but not in the most efficient manner.	Choose inappropriate skills, tools, or features, or are inefficient in solving the problem.
2-Content	Construct a solution that is clear and well organized, contains content that is accurate, appropriate to the audience and purpose, and is complete. Provide a solution that contains no errors of spelling, grammar, or style.	Construct a solution in which some components are unclear, poorly organized, inconsistent, or incomplete. Misjudge the needs of the audience. Have some errors in spelling, grammar, or style, but the errors do not detract from comprehension.	Construct a solution that is unclear, incomplete, or poorly organized, contains some inaccurate or inappropriate content, and contains many errors of spelling, grammar, or style. Do not solve the problem.
3-Format and Layout	Format and arrange all elements to communicate information and ideas, clarify function, illustrate relationships, and indicate relative importance.	Apply appropriate format and layout features to some elements, but not others. Overuse features, causing minor distraction.	Apply format and layout that does not communicate information or ideas clearly. Do not use format and layout features to clarify function, illustrate relationships, or indicate relative importance. Use available features excessively, causing distraction.
4-Process	Use an organized approach that integrates planning, development, self-assessment, revision, and reflection.	Demonstrate an organized approach in some areas, but not others; or, use an insufficient process of organization throughout.	Do not use an organized approach to solve the problem.

Apply a combination of the 8A and 8B skills.

OUTCOMES-BASED ASSESSMENTS (CRITICAL THINKING)

GO! Think Project 8L Patient Charges

PROJECT FILES

For Project 8L, you will need the following file:

a08L_Patient_Charges

You will save your database as:

Lastname_Firstname_8L_Patient_Charges

Paul Chin, CEO for Providence & Warwick Hospital, wants to study the patient charges accrued over the past few months at each of the facilities. Open the **a08L_Patient_Charges** database, close the Intro Screen, and save the database as **Lastname_Firstname_8L_Patient_Charges** Create a standalone macro that opens the *8L Patient Charges* report in Report view for the user to enter a facility name and then closes the *8L Display Charges* form. Save this macro as **Lastname Firstname 8L Charge Report** and associate the macro with the button on the *8L Display Charges* form. Using the form, generate the report for the P&W Rehab Center. Open the *8L Patient Charges* report in Design view and embed macros in both buttons in the Report Header. In the Display another facility button, embed a macro to close the current report without saving it and open the *8L Display Charges* form to allow selection of a different facility. In the Close Database button, embed a macro to close the report without saving it and close the database.

If you are instructed to submit this result, create a paper printout or PDF electronic image of the report and macro details.

END | You have completed Project 8L

GO! Think Project 8M Clinical Trials MyITLab

Build From Scratch

You and GO! Project 8N Club Directory MyITLab

Integrating Access with Other Applications

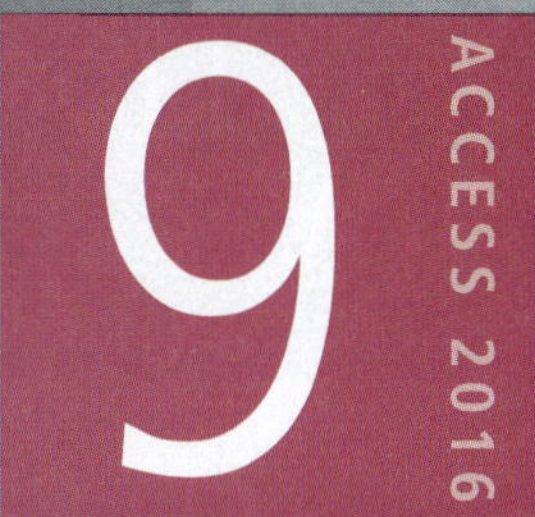

PROJECT 9A

OUTCOMES
Import data from and link to data in other Office applications.

OBJECTIVES

1. Import Data from a Word Table
2. Import Data from an Excel Workbook
3. Insert an Excel Chart into a Report
4. Import from and Link to Another Access Database

PROJECT 9B

OUTCOMES
Export data to Office applications, to HTML, and to XML files; create memos using mail merge.

OBJECTIVES

5. Export Data to Word
6. Use Mail Merge to Integrate Access and Word
7. Export Data to Excel
8. Export Data to an HTML File and an XML File

BestGreenScreen/Shutterstock

In This Chapter

Using Access with other applications maximizes the efficiency of managing information. Data can be imported from another source or linked to data in an external source, such as a Word table, an Excel worksheet, or another Access database. Data can also be exported from an Access database into other applications and platforms. For example, Access data can be used to create individualized letters in Word or analyze data in Excel. In addition, tables, forms, queries, or reports can be exported using HTML, the markup language used to create webpages, or XML, a markup language similar to HTML.

Liberty Motors has one of eastern Missouri's largest preowned inventories of popular car brands, sport utility vehicles, hybrid cars, sports cars, and motorcycles. Liberty also offers extensive customization options for all types of vehicles through its accessories division. Its sales, service, and finance staff are all highly trained and knowledgeable about their products, and the company takes pride in its consistently high customer satisfaction ratings in both sales and service. Liberty Motors and its employees are active members of their local community, where they sponsor and participate in activities and events.

PROJECT 9A

Liberty Motors

MyITLab
Project 9A Training
Project 9A Grader

PROJECT ACTIVITIES

In Activities 9.01 through 9.08, you will assist Phillip Garrett, president of Liberty Motors, and Jeanine Thomas, finance manager, in bringing data from Word, Excel, and other Access databases into a new Access database to create queries and reports. They need to import data from Microsoft Word and Excel as well as link information from another Access database. Your completed document will look similar to Figure 9.1.

PROJECT FILES

If your instructor wants you to submit Project 9A in the MyITLab Grader system, log in to MyITLab, locate Grader Project 9A, and then download the files for this project.

For Project 9A, you will need the following files:

New blank Access database
a09A_Employees.docx
a09A_Used_Auto_Inventory.xlsx
a09A_Logo.jpg
a09A_Used_Auto_Chart.xlsx
a09A_SUVs_and_Motorcycles.accdb

You will save your files as:

Lastname_Firstname_9A_Liberty_Motors.accdb
Lastname_Firstname_9A_Employees_Table.txt

PROJECT RESULTS

GO! Walk Thru Project 9A

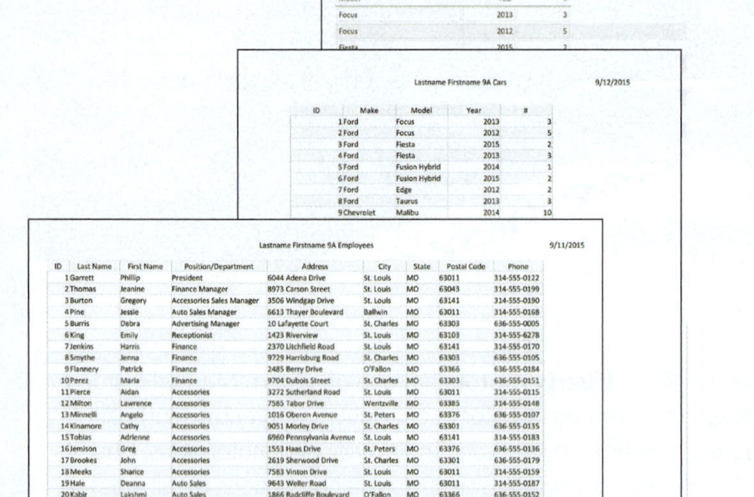

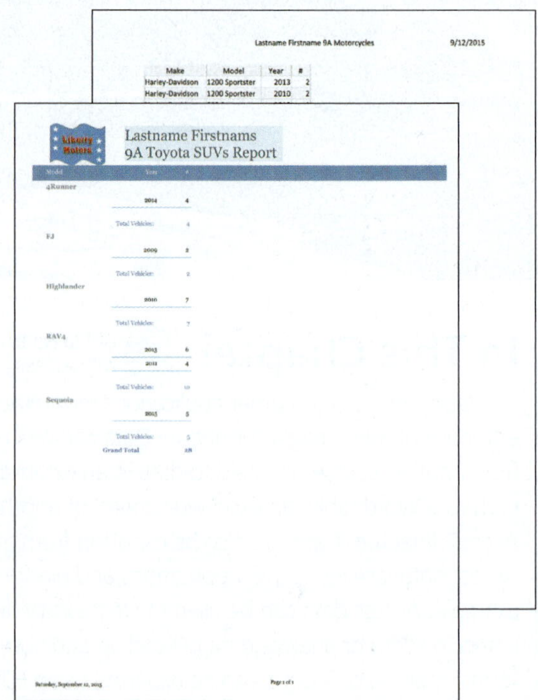

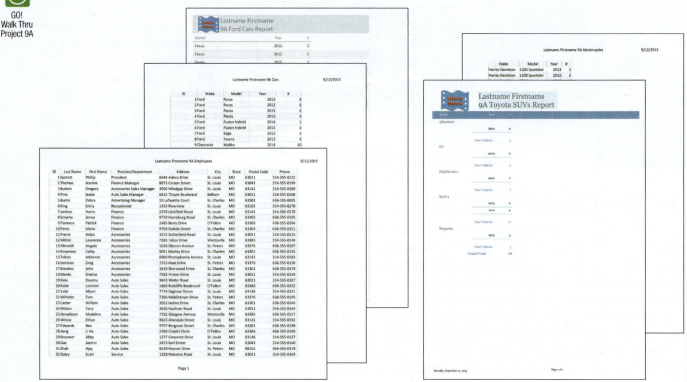

FIGURE 9.1 Project 9A Liberty Motors

9 ACCESS

PROJECT RESULTS

In this project, using your own name, you will create the following database and objects. Your instructor may ask for printouts or PDF electronic images:

Lastname_Firstname_9A_Liberty_Motors	Database file
Lastname Firstname 9A Employees	Table
Lastname Firstname 9A Ford Cars Report	Report
Lastname Firstname 9A Toyota SUVs Report	Report
Lastname Firstname 9A Motorcycles	Table

Objective 1 Import Data from a Word Table

GO! Learn How
Video A9-1

When you create a database, you can type the records directly into a table. You can also ***import*** data from a variety of sources. Importing is the process used to bring in a copy of data from one source or application to another application. For example, you can import data from a Word table or Excel spreadsheet into an Access database.

Data can be imported in various ways. An imported table can overwrite an existing table or append data to an object with the same name in the existing database. Linked data can change the data in the database, and the change will be updated in the source document and vice versa; imported data will not be synchronized between the imported object and the source object.

Activity 9.01 | Preparing a Word Table for Importing

ALERT!

To submit as an autograded project, log into MyITLab and download the files for this project and begin with those files instead of a new blank database and the accompanying files. For Project 9A, begin working with Step 3. For Grader to award points accurately, when saving an object, do not include your Lastname Firstname at the beginning of the object name.

In this Activity, you will create an empty database to store an imported Word table and then prepare the Word table for the import process.

1. **Start** Access. In the Access startup window, click **Blank desktop database**. In the **Blank desktop database** dialog box, to the right of the **File Name** box, click **Browse**. In the **File New Database** dialog box, navigate to the location where you are saving your databases for this chapter, create a **New folder** named **Access Chapter 9** and then press Enter. In the **File name** box, using your own name, replace the existing text with **Lastname_Firstname_9A_Liberty_Motors** and then click **OK** or press Enter. In the **Blank desktop database** dialog box, click **Create**, and then **Close** the displayed table.

   You have created an empty database to store the table that you will import from Word.

2. **Close** the database, and then **Close** Access.

3. **Start** Word, and then, on the bottom left, click **Open Other Documents**. Navigate to the location where the student data files for this textbook are saved. Locate and open the **a09A_Employees** file. Notice that employee data is saved in a table in this Word document.

4 Under **Table Tools**, click the **Layout tab**. In the **Data group**, click **Convert to Text**, and then compare your screen with Figure 9.2.

To import data from a Word table into an Access table, the data must be ***converted*** or changed to a ***delimited file***—a file where each record displays on a separate line and the fields within the record are separated by a single character called a ***delimiter***. A delimiter can be a paragraph mark, a tab, a comma, or another character.

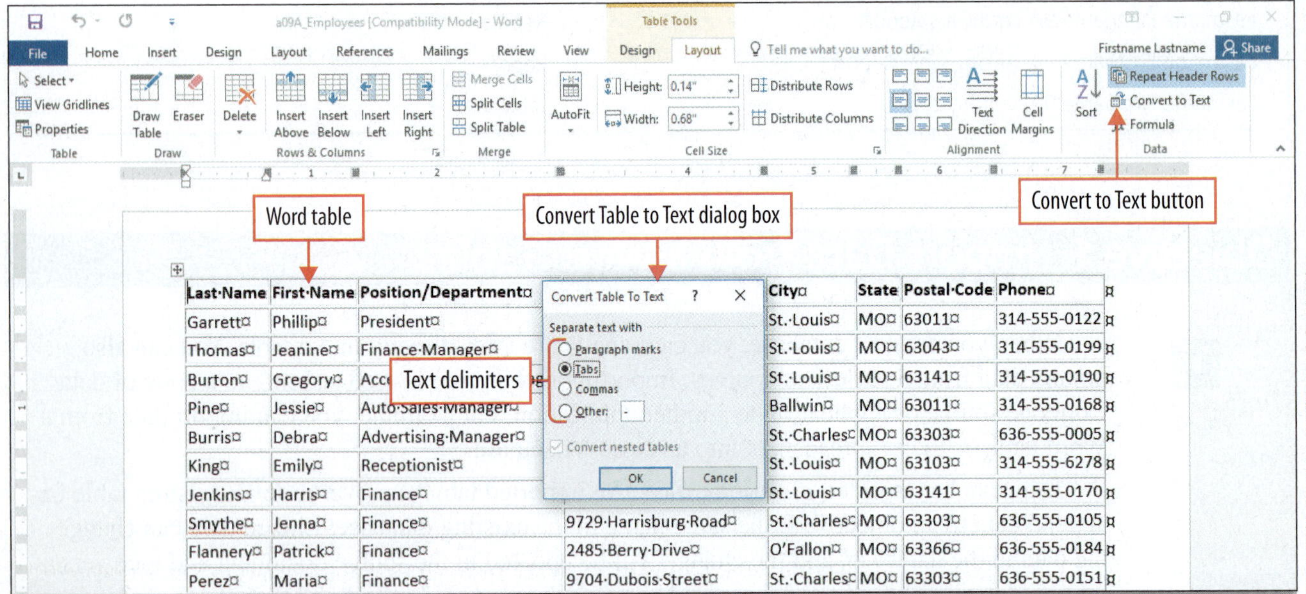

FIGURE 9.2

5 In the displayed **Convert Table to Text** dialog box, verify that the **Tabs** option button is selected—this is the delimiter character you will use to separate the data into fields—and then click **OK**.

6 On the **Home tab**, in the **Paragraph group**, click **Show/Hide** ¶ to display formatting marks if they are not already displayed. Click anywhere in the document to deselect the text, and then compare your screen with Figure 9.3.

Clicking Show/Hide enables you to see the tabs between the fields and the paragraph marks at the end of each line. Word also flags some proper names as spelling errors because they are not listed in the Word dictionary.

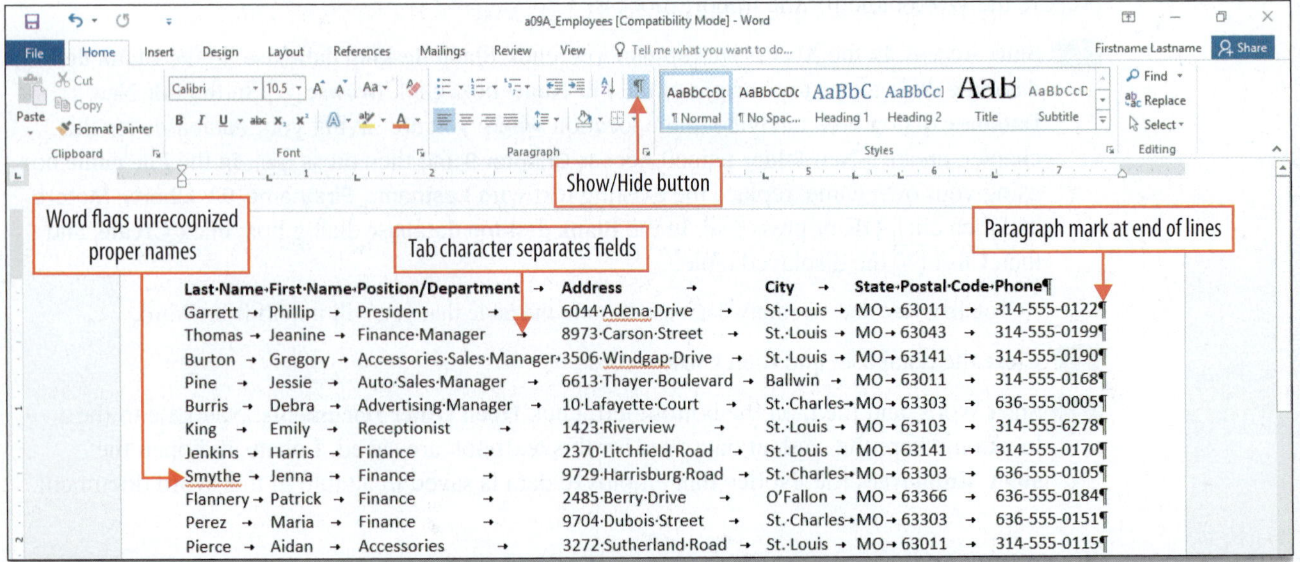

FIGURE 9.3

7 Display **Backstage** view, click **Save As**, and then, under *Save As*, click **Browse**. In the **Save As** dialog box, navigate to the **Access Chapter 9** folder, and then, in the **File name** box, select the existing text, and then type **Lastname_Firstname_9A_Employees_Table** Click the **Save as type arrow**, and from the displayed list, scroll down, and then click **Plain Text**. In the **Save As** dialog box, click **Save**, and then compare your screen with Figure 9.4.

A Word table must be converted to a delimited text file and then saved as either ***Plain Text*** or Rich Text. Data stored in Plain Text format contains no formatting, such as bold or italics. Plain Text stores the data using the ***ASCII***—American Standard Code for Information Interchange—character set. The File Conversion dialog box displays for you to confirm the conversion to a text file.

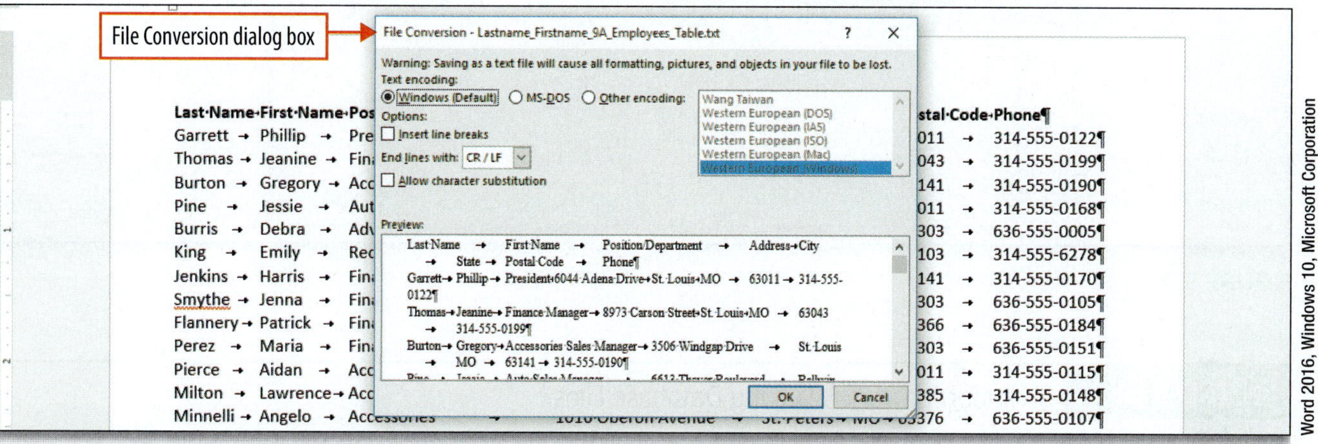

Word 2016, Windows 10, Microsoft Corporation

FIGURE 9.4

8 In the displayed **File Conversion** dialog box, accept the default settings by clicking **OK**. **Close** the document, and **Close** Word.

Activity 9.02 | Importing Data from a Word Table

2.1.2, 1.2.2, 2.4.5, 1.5.2

In this Activity, you will import the Word table data that is stored in a delimited text file into your 9A_Liberty_Motors database.

1 **Start** Access. On the left side of the opening screen, under **Recent**, click **9A_Liberty_Motors** to open the empty database. Enable the content or add the Access Chapter 9 folder to the Trust Center. Notice that in the Navigation Pane, there are no tables in the database.

2 On the **External Data tab**, in the **Import & Link group**, click **Text File**. In the displayed **Get External Data – Text File** dialog box, to the right of the **File name** box, click **Browse**. Navigate to the **Access Chapter 9** folder. In the **File Open** dialog box, double-click **9A_Employees_Table**, and then compare your screen with Figure 9.5.

The source file—the one being imported—is listed in the File name box. When importing, if a table with the same name as the imported table does not exist, Access creates the object. If a table with the same name exists in the database, Access may overwrite its contents with the imported data. If you modify data in the original text file, the data will not be updated in the Access database.

A ***link*** is a connection to data in another file. When linking, Access creates a table that maintains a link to the source data. You cannot change or delete data in a linked Access table; however, you can add new records.

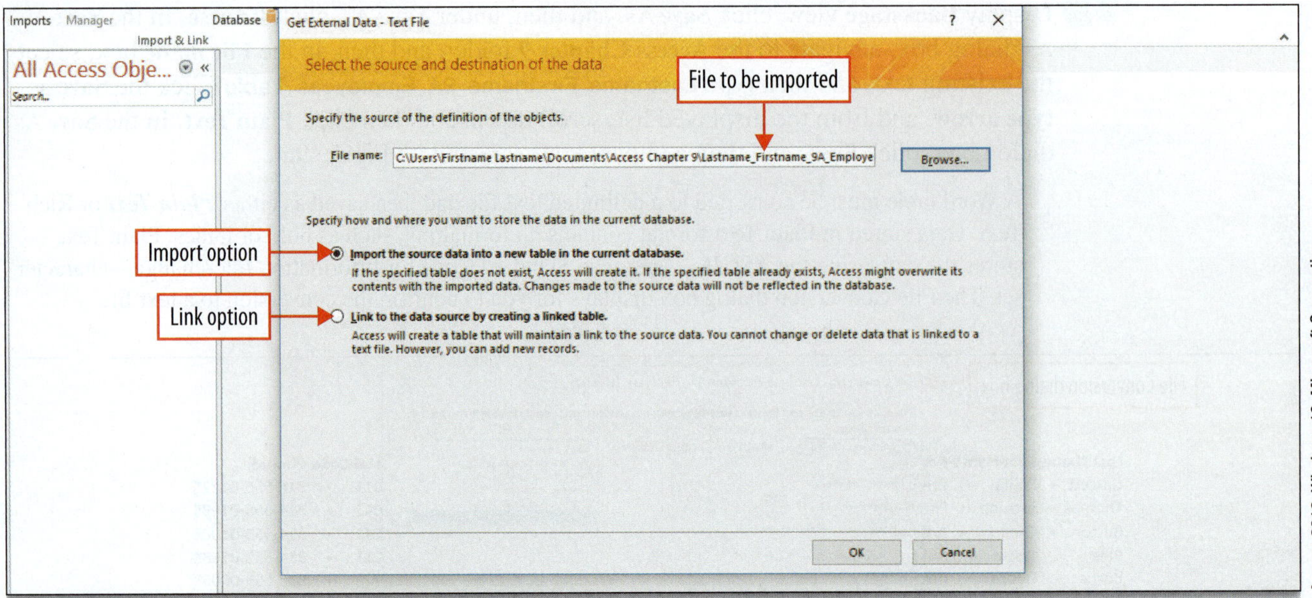

FIGURE 9.5

NOTE Importing versus Linking Database Files

Import when any of the following is true:

- The source file size is small and is changed infrequently.
- Data does not need to be shared with individuals using other database applications.
- You are replacing an old database application, and the data is no longer needed in the older format.
- You need to load data from another source to begin populating tables.
- You need the performance of Access 2016 while working with data from other database formats.

Link to a source when any of the following is true:

- The file is larger than the maximum capacity of a local Access database (2 gigabytes).
- The file is changed frequently, and the change needs to be reflected in the database.
- Data must be shared on a network with individuals using other database applications.
- The application is distributed to several individuals, and you need to make changes to the queries, forms, reports, and modules without changing the data already entered into the underlying tables.

3 In the **Get External Data – Text File** dialog box, verify that the **Import the source data into a new table in the current database** option button is selected, and then click **OK**. If a security message displays, click Open. Compare your screen with Figure 9.6.

The Import Text Wizard dialog box displays, indicating that the data seems to be in a delimited format, using a comma or tab to separate each field.

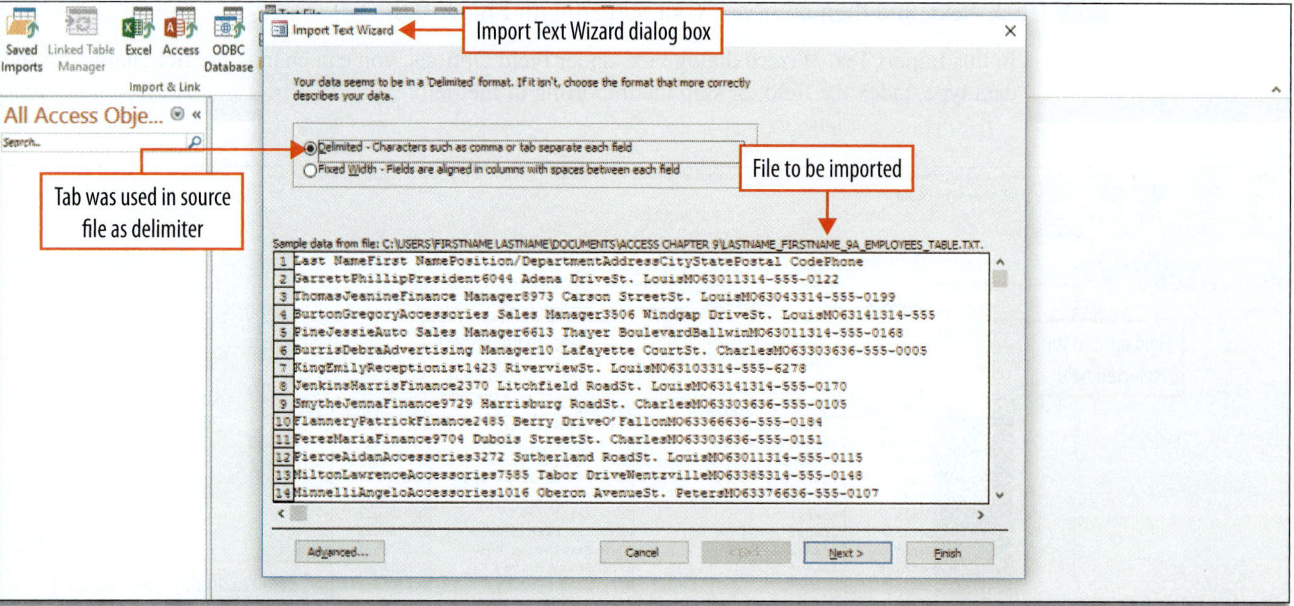

Access 2016, Windows 10, Microsoft Corporation

FIGURE 9.6

4 In the **Import Text Wizard** dialog box, verify that the **Delimited** option button is selected, and then click **Next**.

In this Import Text Wizard dialog box, you select the delimiter that you used when you created the text file.

5 Click each delimiter option button, and notice how the text is affected in the preview window. When you are finished, verify that the **Tab** option button is selected. Click the **First Row Contains Field Names** check box to convert the field names to column headings instead of first record data. Click the **Text Qualifier arrow**, and notice that a single quotation mark and a double quotation mark display. If you are working with a file that includes text in quotation marks, you would indicate this by selecting either the single quotation mark or the double quotation mark. Verify that **{none}** is selected, and then compare your screen with Figure 9.7.

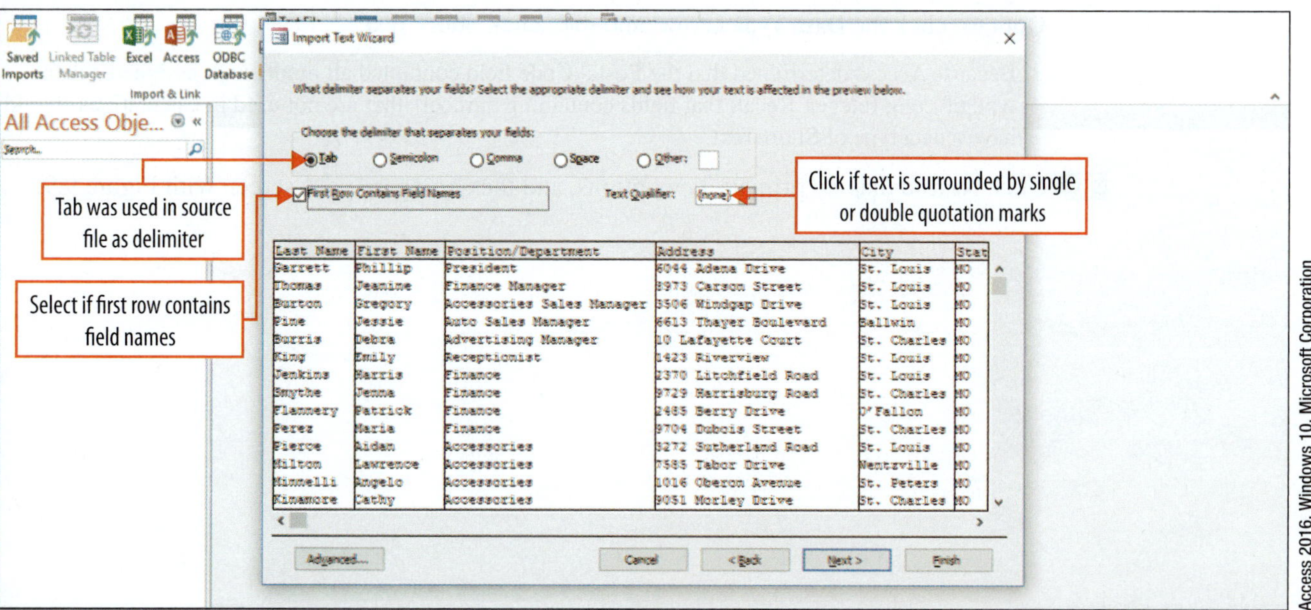

Access 2016, Windows 10, Microsoft Corporation

FIGURE 9.7

6 Click **Next**, and then compare your screen with Figure 9.8.

In this Import Text Wizard dialog box, under Field Options, you can change the field name, set the data type, index the field, or skip the importing of the field.

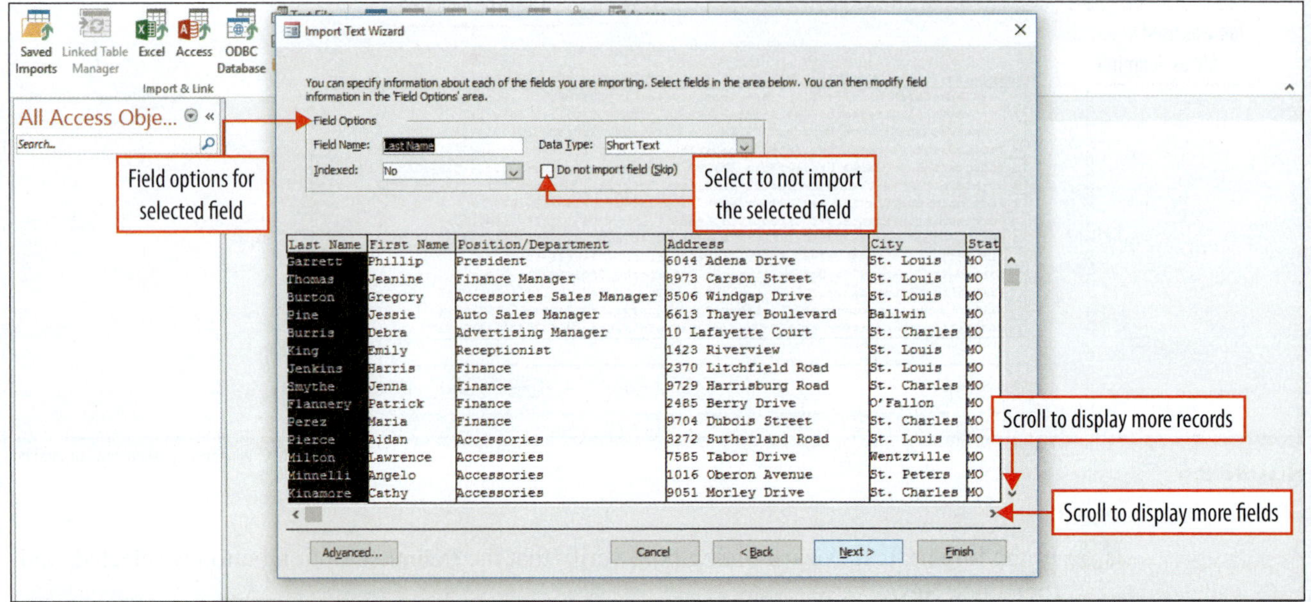

FIGURE 9.8

NOTE Saving Data as a New Table or Appending Data

If there is an existing table in the database, another Import Text Wizard dialog box displays before the one enabling you to change field options. This dialog box enables you to save the imported table as a new table or in an existing table. If you select the existing table, the data will be ***appended***—added—to the end of the existing table.

7 The Field Options for the **Last Name** field are correct. Use the horizontal scroll bar to display the fields on the right. Click in the **Postal Code** field to select the field. Under **Field Options**, click the **Data Type arrow**, and then click **Short Text**.

Because Access determined that the Postal Code field contained all numbers, it assigned a data type of Long Integer. Recall that fields containing numbers that are not used in calculations should have a data type of Short Text.

8 Click **Next** to display primary key options, and then compare your screen with Figure 9.9.

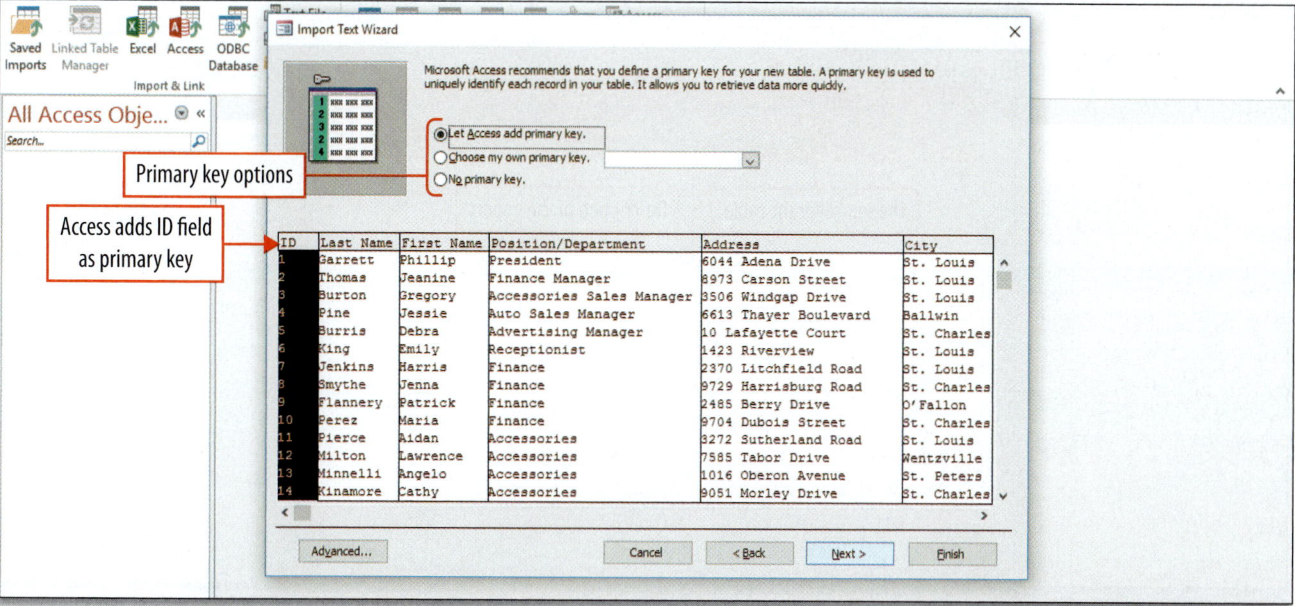

FIGURE 9.9

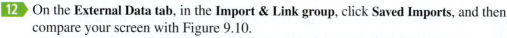

Access 2016, Windows 10, Microsoft Corporation

9 Verify that the **Let Access add primary key** option button is selected, and then click **Next**. In the **Import to Table** box, type **Lastname Firstname 9A Employees** and then click **Finish**.

In this dialog box, you can accept the default name of the table or type a new name.

10 Because there are no errors in the imported file, the **Get External Data – Text File** dialog box displays, which enables you to save the import steps for future use.

When you import or export data in Access, you can save the settings you used so that you can repeat the process at any time without using the wizard. The name of the source file, the name of the destination database, primary key fields, field names, and all the other specifications you set are saved. Even though all of the specifications are saved, you can still change the name of the source file or destination file before running the import or export specification again. You cannot save the specifications for linking or exporting only a portion of a table.

ALERT!

Did an error message box display after clicking finish?

If a message box displays, there may be extra blank lines at the end of the text file, which cause blank records to be inserted into the database. If this occurs, click OK two times. Open the new table, delete any empty records, display the table in Design view, and then set the appropriate field as the primary key.

11 Select the **Save import steps** check box to display additional options. Click in the **Description** box, and then type **Imports a tab-delimited file that was a Word table** Notice that if you are using Outlook, you can create an Outlook Task to remind you when to repeat the import operation. Click **Save Import**, and notice that in the **Navigation Pane**, the **9A Employees** table displays.

Access creates and saves the import specification in the current database. You cannot move or copy the specification to another database.

12 On the **External Data tab**, in the **Import & Link group**, click **Saved Imports**, and then compare your screen with Figure 9.10.

The Manage Data Tasks dialog box displays with two tabs—one for Saved Imports, and one for Saved Exports. Clicking Run performs the operation using the selected specification. You can schedule execution by clicking Create Outlook Task or delete a specification by clicking Delete. You can change the name or description of a specification, change the source file in an import operation, or change the destination file in an export operation by clicking the appropriate section in the specification.

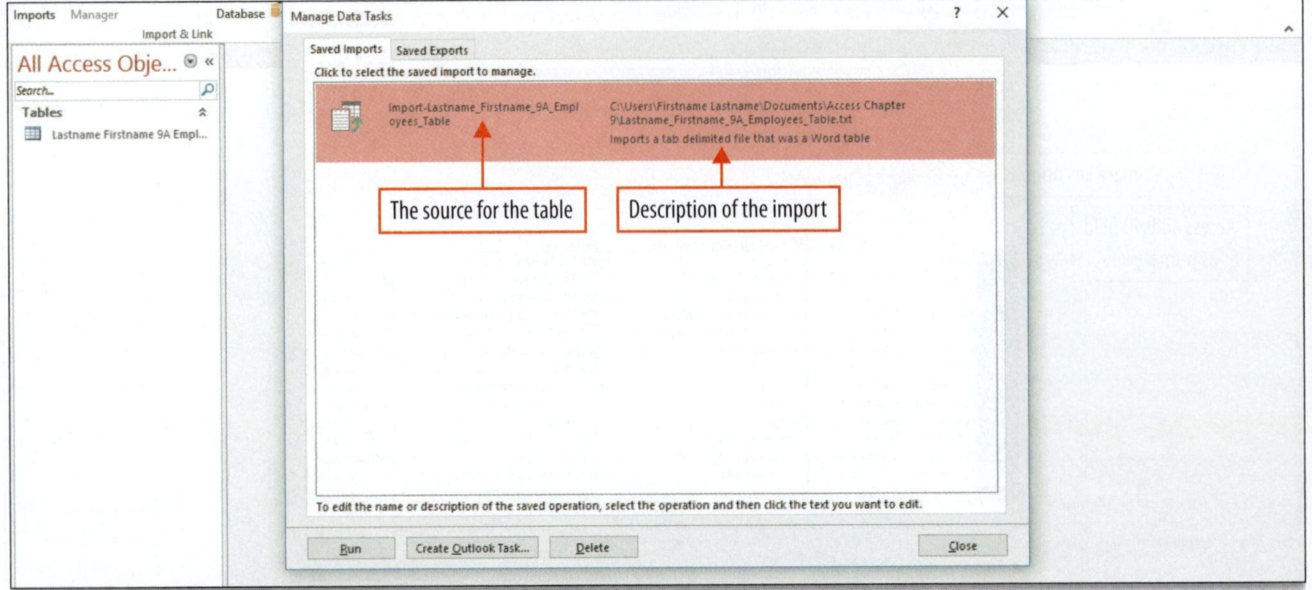

FIGURE 9.10

13 In the **Manage Data Tasks** dialog box, click **Close**.

14 Double-click **9A Employees** to open the table in **Datasheet** view, and then **Close** « the **Navigation Pane**. Apply **Best Fit** to adjust the widths of all of the fields to display all of the data and the entire field name for each field.

All of the data from the Word table, which was converted to a delimited file, has been imported successfully into a table within the database, saving you from typing the data.

More Knowledge **Importing from Other Applications**

If you have data in other applications that you would like to import or link to your Access database, explore the options on the External Data tab, in the Import & Link group, by clicking More. A ***SharePoint List*** is a list of documents maintained on a server running Microsoft Office SharePoint Server. A ***SharePoint Server*** enables you to share documents with others in your organization. You also can import data from other database applications, such as dBASE and ODBC databases. ***ODBC*** stands for ***Open Database Connectivity***, a standard that enables databases using SQL statements to interface with one another. You can also import or link to an Outlook folder. Data can also be imported from or linked to an HTML—HyperText Markup Language—document or Web document. HTML is a language used to display webpages.

15 If you are instructed to submit this result, create a paper printout or PDF electronic image of the **first page** of the table in **Landscape** orientation with **Normal** margins. **Save** the table, and then **Close** ☒ the table.

Objective 2 Import Data from an Excel Workbook

GO! Learn How Video A9-2

Jessie Pine, the auto sales manager, keeps an inventory of used cars, SUVs, and motorcycles in an Excel workbook. A ***workbook*** is an Excel file that contains one or more worksheets. A ***worksheet*** is the primary document used in Excel to save and work with data that is arranged in columns and rows. You can import the data from an Excel workbook into Access by copying the data from an open worksheet and pasting it into an Access datasheet, by importing a worksheet into a new or existing Access table, or by creating a link to a worksheet from an Access database.

There is no way to save the workbook as an Access database within Excel; the individual worksheets within a workbook must be imported into an Access database.

9 ACCESS

Activity 9.03 | Importing Data from an Excel Worksheet

2.1.2, 1.2.2

In this Activity, you will import an Excel worksheet containing the used car inventory, creating a new table in your database.

1 If necessary, click the **External Data tab**. In the **Import & Link group**, click **Excel**.

The Get External Data – Excel Spreadsheet dialog box displays, indicating that you can import the source data into a new table, append a copy of the records to an existing table, or link to the Excel worksheet.

2 In the **Get External Data – Excel Spreadsheet** dialog box, to the right of the **File name** box, click **Browse**. Navigate to the location where the student data files for this textbook are saved. Locate the **a09A_Used_Auto_Inventory** file, and then notice the icon to the left of the file name; it indicates the file is an Excel Worksheet file. Click **Open**.

3 In the **Get External Data – Excel Spreadsheet** dialog box, click **OK**, and then compare your screen with Figure 9.11.

The first Import Spreadsheet Wizard dialog box displays. A ***spreadsheet*** is another name for a worksheet. On this page you can select one worksheet—you can import only one worksheet at a time during an import operation. If you want to import several worksheets, save the import specification, and then change the source data. The first row displays column headings.

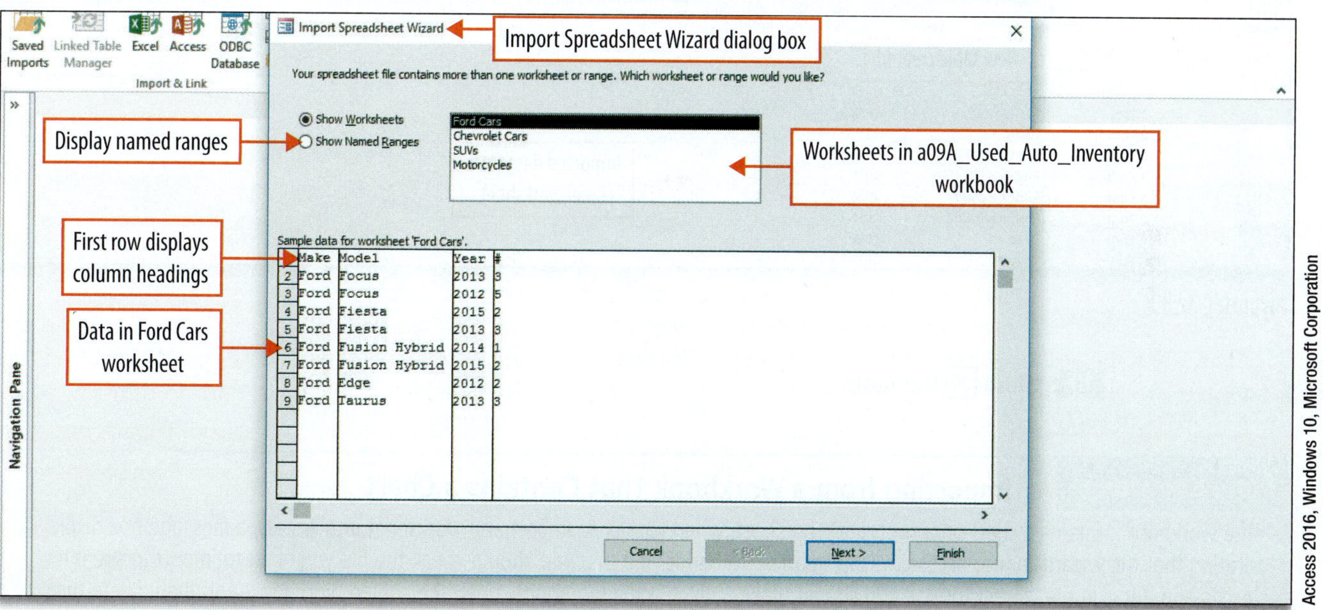

FIGURE 9.11

4 In the **Import Spreadsheet Wizard** dialog box, click the **Show Named Ranges** option button, and then in the box, click **Ford**.

This is the same data that displays in the *Ford Cars* worksheet, but without the column headings. If the Excel worksheet contains named ranges, you can select the Show Named Ranges option button. A ***range*** includes two or more selected cells on a worksheet that can be treated as a single unit. A ***named range*** is a range that has been given a name, making it easier to use the cells in calculations or modifications. A ***cell*** is the small box formed by the intersection of a column and a row.

5 Click the **Show Worksheets** option button, and verify that **Ford Cars** is selected. Click **Next** to display the second **Import Spreadsheet Wizard** dialog box. Notice that the wizard assumes that the first row contains column headings and that Access uses the column headings as field names.

6 Click **Next** to display the third **Import Spreadsheet Wizard** dialog box.

Just as you did when importing a text file, you can change the field name, index the field, set the data type, or remove the field from the import operation.

7 Click **Next**. In the fourth **Import Spreadsheet Wizard** dialog box, verify that **Let Access add primary key** is selected, and then click **Next**.

8 In the final **Import Spreadsheet Wizard** dialog box, in the **Import to Table** box, type **Lastname Firstname 9A Cars** and then click **Finish**. Because you do not want to save the import steps, in the **Get External Data – Excel Spreadsheet** dialog box, click **Close**. **Open** [»] the **Navigation Pane**. Resize the Navigation Pane so all object names display fully, and then notice that the table displays under *Tables*.

9 In the **Navigation Pane**, double-click **9A Cars** to open the table in **Datasheet** view. **Close** [«] the **Navigation Pane**, and then compare your screen with Figure 9.12.

The data from the *Ford Cars* worksheet in the *a09A_Used_Auto_Inventory* Excel workbook has been imported into this new table.

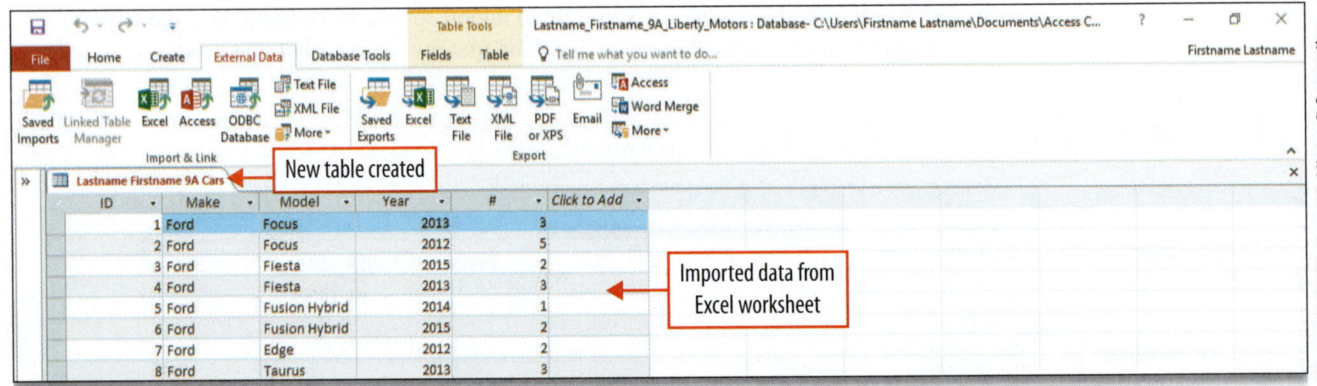

FIGURE 9.12

10 **Close** [X] the table.

> **More Knowledge** **Importing from a Workbook That Contains a Chart**
>
> If a workbook contains a chart on a separate worksheet, when you try to import any worksheet into Access, a message box displays stating that the wizard cannot access the information in the file and that you should check the file you want to import to see if it exists and if it is in the correct format. You should make a copy of the workbook, open the copied workbook, and then delete the worksheet containing the chart or move the chart to the sheet with the related data. Save the workbook, close it, and then import the data from any of the worksheets.

Activity 9.04 | Appending Data from Excel to an Access Table

2.3.4, 1.5.2

In this Activity, you will append data from an Excel worksheet to the 9A Cars table. To append data, the table must already be created.

1 If necessary, click the **External Data tab**. In the **Import & Link group**, click **Excel**. In the **Get External Data – Excel Spreadsheet** dialog box, click **Browse**. If necessary, navigate to the location where the student data files for this textbook are saved. Locate and **Open** the **a09A_Used_Auto_Inventory** file.

2 Under **Specify how and where you want to store the data in the current database**, click **Append a copy of the records to the table**. Click the **table name arrow** to display the names of the two tables that are saved in the database. Verify that **9A Cars** is selected, and then click **OK**.

3 In the first **Import Spreadsheet Wizard** dialog box, click the **Chevrolet Cars** worksheet, and then click **Next**. In the second **Import Spreadsheet Wizard** dialog box, notice that Access has determined that the first row matches the field names contained in the existing table and that you cannot clear the check box. Click **Next**.

4 In the **Import Spreadsheet Wizard** dialog box, click **Finish** to import the data into the **9A Cars** table in the current database.

5 In the **Get External Data – Excel Spreadsheet** dialog box, click **Close**, and then **Open** [»] the **Navigation Pane**. Double-click **9A Cars** to display the table in **Datasheet** view. **Close** [«] the **Navigation Pane**, and then compare your screen with Figure 9.13.

The data from the *Chevrolet Cars* worksheet in the *a09A_Used_Auto_Inventory* workbook is appended to the *9A Cars* table in your database.

Import & Link | Export

Lastname Firstname 9A Cars

ID	Make	Model	Year	#	Click to Add
1	Ford	Focus	2013	3	
2	Ford	Focus	2012	5	
3	Ford	Fiesta	2015	2	
4	Ford	Fiesta	2013	3	
5	Ford	Fusion Hybrid	2014	1	
6	Ford	Fusion Hybrid	2015	2	
7	Ford	Edge	2012	2	
8	Ford	Taurus	2013	3	
9	Chevrolet	Malibu	2014	10	
10	Chevrolet	Malibu	2015	7	
11	Chevrolet	Impala	2012	3	
12	Chevrolet	Impala	2014	6	
13	Chevrolet	Impala	2015	4	
14	Chevrolet	Impala	2012	8	
15	Chevrolet	Corvette	2006	3	
16	Chevrolet	Corvette	2012	8	
17	Chevrolet	Corvette	2014	10	
18	Chevrolet	Monte Carlo	2010	1	
19	Chevrolet	Monte Carlo	2012	4	
20	Chevrolet	Monte Carlo	2013	3	
(New)					

Navigation Pane

Data imported and appended

FIGURE 9.13

6 If you are instructed to submit this result, create a paper printout or PDF electronic image of the table. **Close** [X] the table.

Objective 3 Insert an Excel Chart into a Report

GO! Learn How Video A9-3

A ***chart*** is a graphic representation of data. Data presented in a chart is easier to understand than a table of numbers. ***Column charts*** display comparisons among related numbers, ***pie charts*** display the contributions of parts to a whole amount, and ***line charts*** display trends over time. Excel is the best tool for creating a chart because there are a wide variety of chart types and formatting options.

Activity 9.05 | Creating a Query and a Report

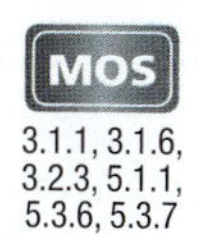

3.1.1, 3.1.6, 3.2.3, 5.1.1, 5.3.6, 5.3.7

In this Activity, you will create a query. Using the query, you will create a report that will be used in the next Activity.

1 On the **Create tab**, in the **Queries group**, click **Query Design**. In the **Show Table** dialog box, double-click **9A Cars** to add the table to the Query Design workspace, and then **Close** the **Show Table** dialog box.

2 If necessary, expand the field list to display the entire table name. In the field list, click **Make**. Hold down Shift, and then click **#** to select four fields. Drag the selected fields down into the first column of the design grid, and then compare your screen with Figure 9.14.

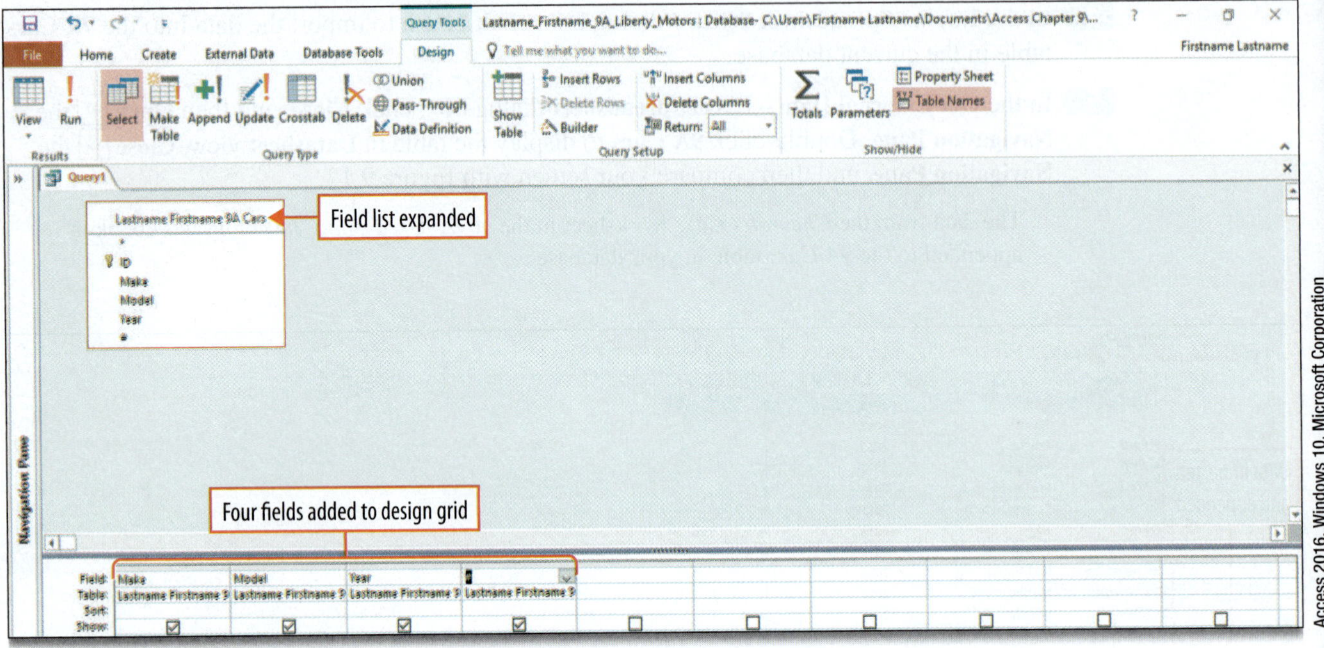

FIGURE 9.14

3 In the design grid, under **Make**, click in the **Criteria** box, type **Ford** and then press Enter.

4 Under **Query Tools**, on the **Design tab**, in the **Results group**, click **Run** to display only the Ford cars.

5 Switch the query to **Design** view. In the design grid, under **Make**, on the **Show** row, clear the check box, and then **Run** the query.

Recall that clearing the Show check box hides the field from the query. Because this query only displays Ford cars, hiding this field is appropriate.

6 **Save** the query as **Lastname Firstname 9A Ford Cars Query** and then **Close** the query. **Open** the **Navigation Pane**, and then notice that the query displays in the Navigation Pane.

7 In the **Navigation Pane**, under **Queries**, click **9A Ford Cars Query** to select the query, and then **Close** the **Navigation Pane**.

8 On the **Create tab**, in the **Reports group**, click **Report**. Switch to **Design** view.

9 In the **Report Header** section, in the **title**, delete the space before **9A**, and then press Shift + Enter. Double-click **Query** to select the word, and then type **Report** Press Enter.

10 Click the image to the left of the title to select it. Under **Report Design Tools**, on the **Design tab**, in the **Header/Footer group**, click **Logo**. If necessary, navigate to the location where the data files for this chapter are saved, and then double-click **a09A_Logo** to insert the logo. In the **Tools group**, click **Property Sheet**, and then click the **Format tab**. Click in the **Size Mode** property box, and select **Zoom**. Resize the image so the right edge aligns with the **1-inch mark on the horizontal ruler**. In the **Report Footer**, click the Totals control. On the **Property Sheet Format tab**, click in the **Height** property box, and type **0.2** and then press Enter. **Close** the **Property Sheet**.

11 In the **Report Header** section, delete the **Date** and **Time text box controls** and placeholders, if necessary. In the **Page Footer** section, delete the **Page number text box control**. Resize the report to 6.5 inches wide. Compare your screen with Figure 9.15.

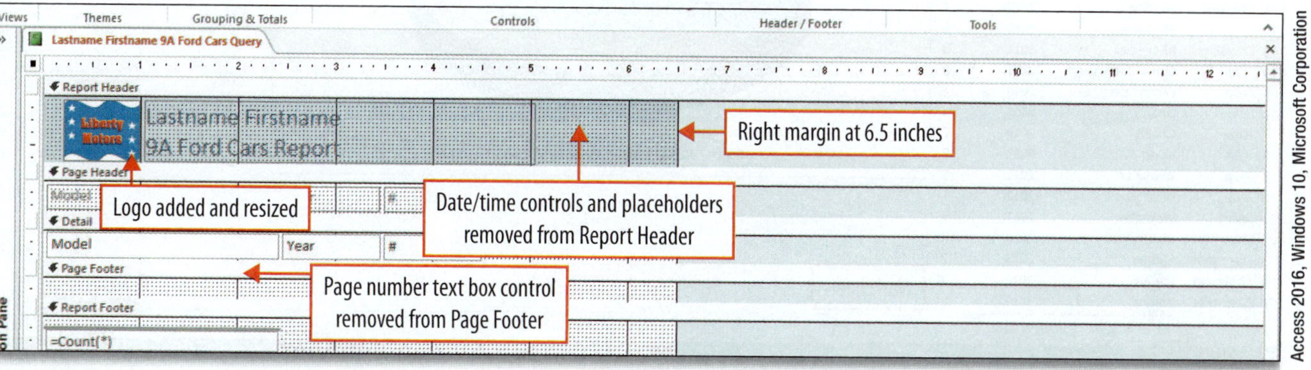

FIGURE 9.15

12 **Save** the report as **Lastname Firstname 9A Ford Cars Report**

5.3.6, 1.5.1

Activity 9.06 | Inserting an Excel Chart into a Report

In this Activity, you will insert an Excel chart into the 9A Ford Cars Report.

1 In the report, in **Design** view, point to the top of the **Report Footer section bar** until the pointer displays. Drag the section down to the **3-inch mark on the vertical ruler** to increase the size of the Page Footer section.

2 **Start** Excel. From **Backstage** view, click **Open Other Workbooks**. Navigate to the location where the data files for this chapter are saved, and then double-click **a09A_Used_Auto_Chart** to open the workbook. Compare your screen with Figure 9.16.

The workbook opens with the *Cars* worksheet displaying. A pie chart has been saved in the worksheet and displays the percentage of cars for each model of Ford vehicles.

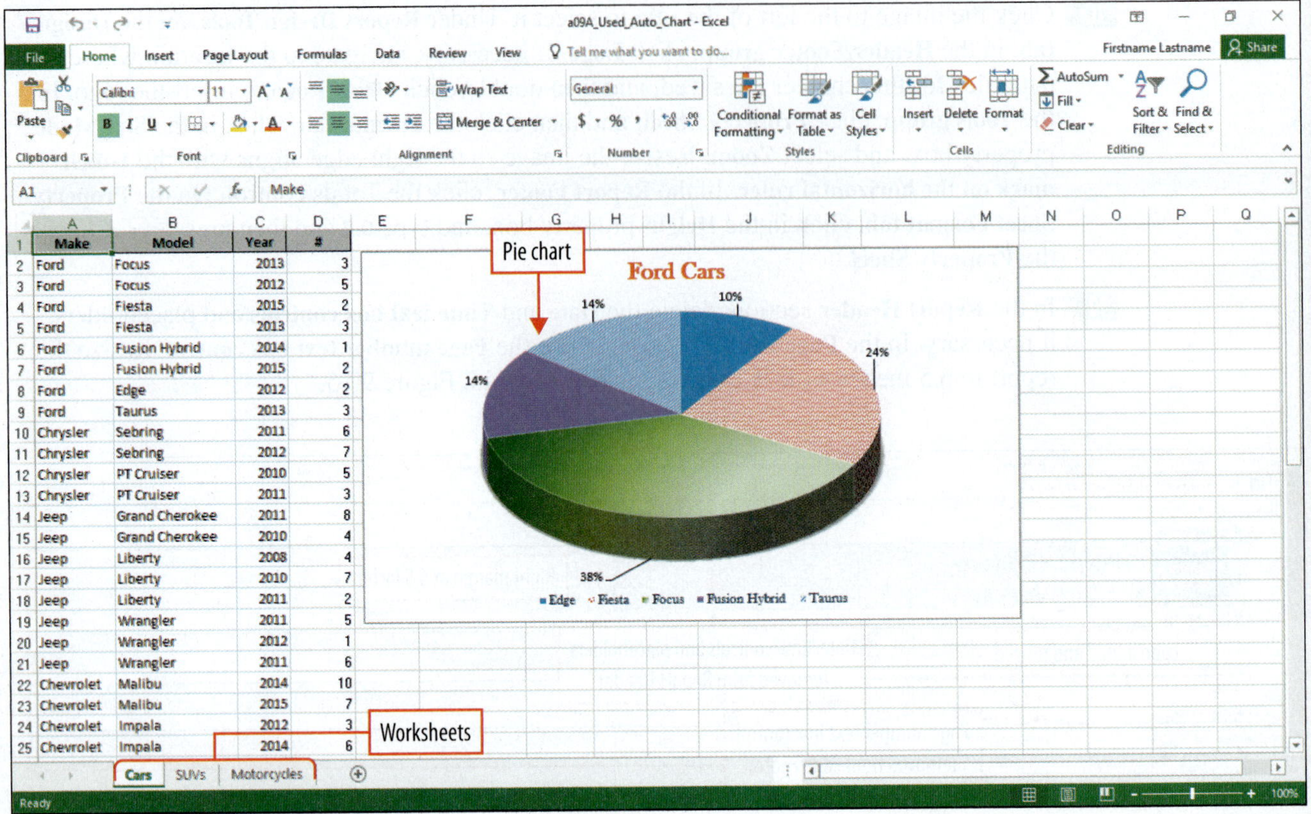

FIGURE 9.16

3 Click the outside edge of the **pie chart** to select the entire chart. On the **Home tab**, in the **Clipboard group**, click **Copy** to place a copy of the pie chart in the Office Clipboard. **Close** Excel.

4 Click the **Access** icon on the taskbar to activate the 9A Ford Cars Report in the database. In the **9A Ford Cars Report**, right-click the **Page Footer section bar**, and then click **Paste**. Compare your screen with Figure 9.17.

The pie chart is pasted into the Page Footer section of the report.

Excel chart copied into Access report

FIGURE 9.17

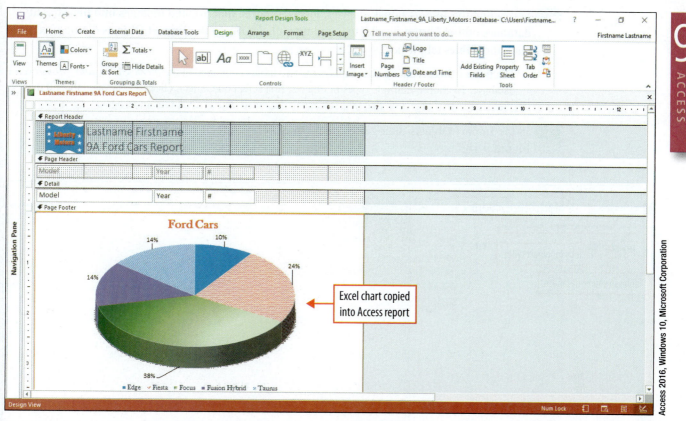

5 **Save** the report, and then switch to **Report** view. If you are instructed to submit this result, create a paper printout or PDF electronic image. **Close** the report.

Objective 4 Import from and Link to Another Access Database

GO! Learn How
Video A9-4

When you import data from another Access database, Access creates a copy of the source data without altering the source data. All of the objects in a database can be imported or copied to another Access database in a single operation. Import data from another Access database when you need to create similar tables or when you want to use the structure of the source database tables. Link to data in another Access database when the data is shared among multiple databases or if someone else needs to have the ability to add records and use the data, but not change the structure of the table.

Activity 9.07 | Importing Data from Another Access Database

1.1.3, 2.1.4, 5.3.4, 1.4.6

In this Activity, you will import the data contained in another Access database.

1 On the **External Data tab**, in the **Import & Link group**, click **Access**. In the **Get External Data – Access Database** dialog box, click **Browse**. If necessary, navigate to the location where the data files for this chapter are saved, and then double-click **a09A_SUVs_and_Motorcycles**.

The source database must be closed before you can import data from it. The destination database must be open. To import the data into a new database, you must create a blank database before starting the import operation.

2 Verify that the **Import tables, queries, forms, reports, macros, and modules into the current database** option button is selected, and then click **OK**. In the **Import Objects** dialog box, click the **Tables** tab, if necessary.

The Import Objects dialog box displays the two tables contained in the *a09A_SUVs_and_Motorcycles* database. To choose multiple types of objects, first select one object, click the relevant tab, and then click the desired object on that tab. To cancel a selected object, click the object again.

3 In the **Import Objects** dialog box, click **9A SUVs**, and then compare your screen with Figure 9.18.

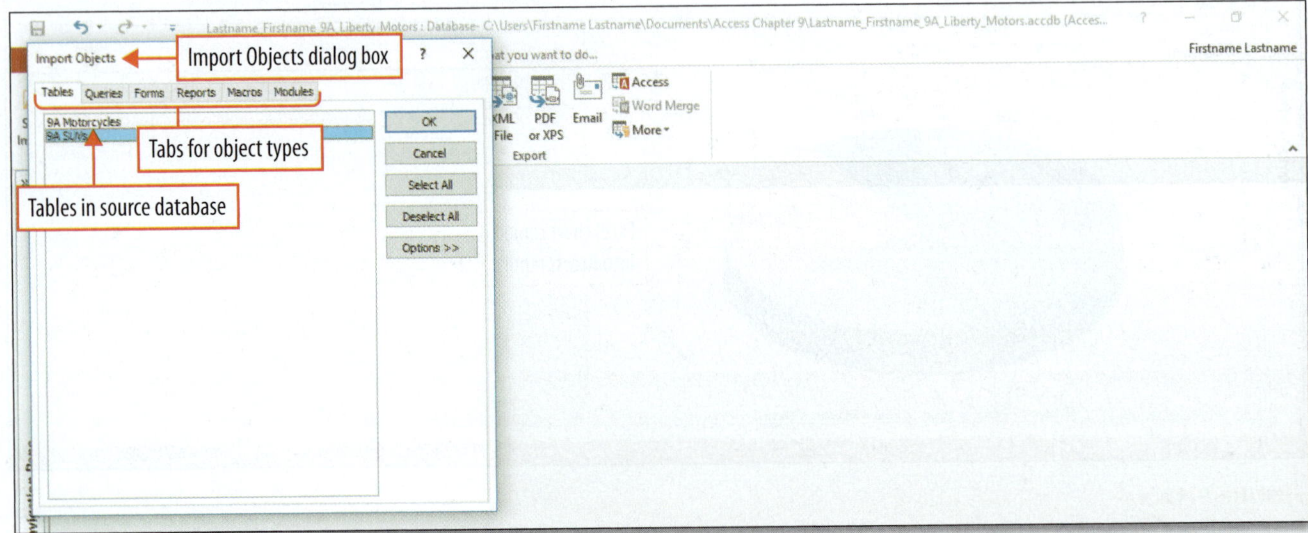

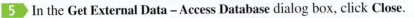

FIGURE 9.18

> **NOTE** Importing Queries, Forms, and Reports
>
> You can import table relationships, custom menus and toolbars, saved import/export specifications, and custom Navigation Pane groups. For tables, you can import the table definition and data or only the table definition. The ***definition*** is the structure of the database—the field names, data types, and field properties. You can import queries as queries or as tables. If you import a query as a query, you must also import the underlying table or tables used to create the query.
>
> Importing a query, form, report, subform, or subreport does not automatically import the underlying record sources. If you create one of these objects using the data in two related tables, you must also import those two tables; otherwise, these objects will not open properly.

4 In the **Import Objects** dialog box, click the **Queries tab**, and then click **9A Toyota SUVs Query**. Click the **Forms tab**, and then click **9A SUVs Form**. Click the **Reports tab**, click **9A Toyota SUVs Report**, and then click **OK**.

The Get External Data – Access Database dialog box displays, enabling you to save the import steps. If Access encounters any errors in the import operation, messages will display. To cancel the import operation during the importing process, press Ctrl + Break.

5 In the **Get External Data – Access Database** dialog box, click **Close**.

6 **Open** » the **Navigation Pane**, resize the pane so all object names display fully, and then compare your screen with Figure 9.19.

A table, query, form, and report have been imported to the open database.

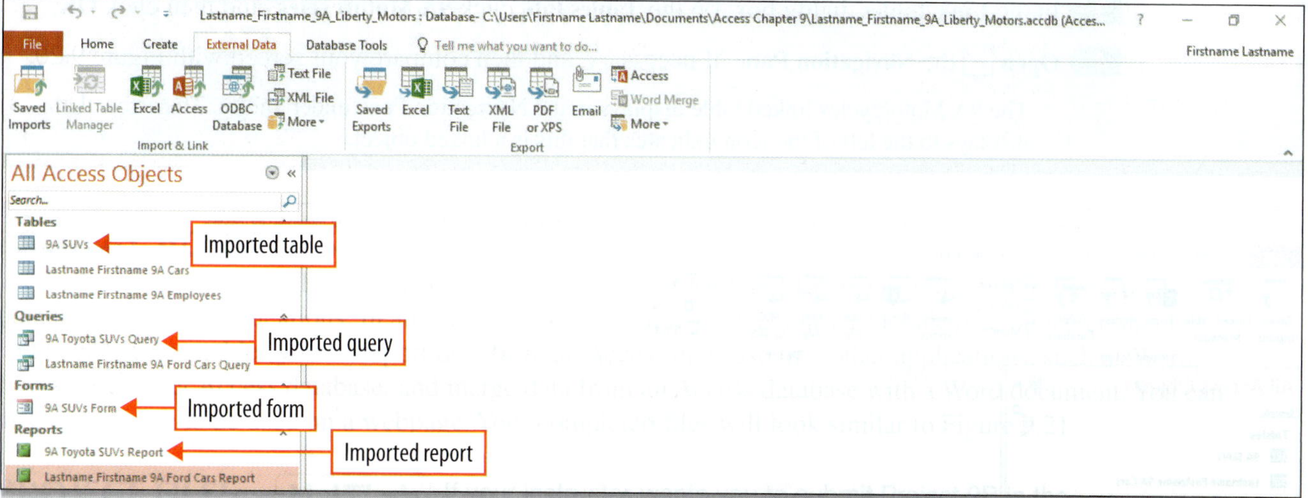

FIGURE 9.19

Access 2016, Windows 10, Microsoft Corporation

ALERT! **Were all four objects not imported?**

If all four objects were not imported, you may not have clicked the object in the Import Objects dialog box. To correct this, run the import operation again, and select the missing object or objects. Do not select objects that were imported correctly. For example, if you correctly imported the *9A SUVs* table, and then you import it again, a second *9A SUVs* table will be imported and will be named *9A SUVs1*.

7. In the **Navigation Pane**, under **Reports**, right-click **9A Toyota SUVs Report**, and then click **Layout View**. Click the title one time to select it. Click to the left of **9A** to enter into editing mode, type your **Lastname Firstname** and then press Shift + Enter. Press Enter. Under **Report Layout Tools**, on the **Format tab**, in the **Font group**, click the **Background Color arrow**, and then, under **Theme Colors**, in the second row, select the fifth color—**Blue, Accent 1, Lighter 80%**.

8. Switch to **Report** view. **Save** the report. If you are instructed to submit this result, create a paper printout or PDF electronic image.

9. **Close** the report, and then **Close** « the **Navigation Pane**.

More Knowledge **Recover Data from a Backup File**

If you are missing objects or they have become corrupt, import the clean objects from the most recent backup file using the technique you practiced in this Activity.

Activity 9.08 | Linking to a Table in Another Access Database

2.1.3

In this Activity, you will link to the data in the 9A Motorcycles table in the *a09A_SUVs_and_Motorcycles* database. You can link only to tables in another Access database; you cannot link to queries, forms, reports, macros, or modules.

1. On the **External Data tab**, in the **Import & Link group**, click **Access**. In the **Get External Data – Access Database** dialog box, **Browse** to the location where the data files for this chapter are saved, and then double-click **a09A_SUVs_and_Motorcycles**.

2. In the **Get External Data – Access Database** dialog box, click the **Link to the data source by creating a linked table** option button, and then click **OK**.

   Changes made to the data in Access will be propagated to the source data and vice versa. If the source database requires a password, that password is saved with the linked table. You cannot make changes to the structure of the table in the linked table.

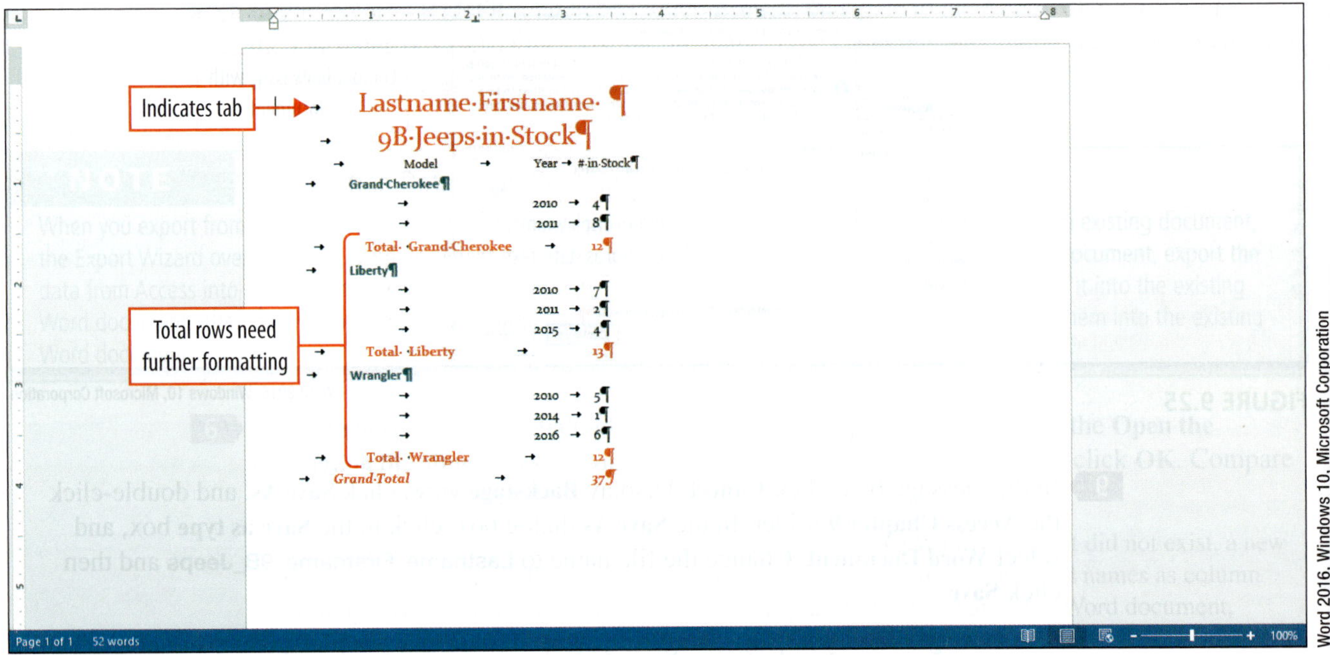

FIGURE 9.26

3 If you are instructed to submit this result, create a paper printout or PDF electronic image. **Close** [X] Word. In the **Export – RTF File** dialog box, click **Close**.

Objective 6 Use Mail Merge to Integrate Access and Word

GO! Learn How Video A9-6

Using Word's ***mail merge*** feature, letters or memos are created by combining, or ***merging***, two documents—a ***main document*** and a ***data source***. The main document contains the text of a letter or memo. The data source—an Access table or query—contains the names and addresses of the individuals to whom the letter, memo, or other document is being sent. Use the Mail Merge Wizard within Access to create a direct link between the table or query and the Word document.

Activity 9.11 | Merging an Access Table with a Word Document

1.5.4

In this Activity, you will create individual memos to the employees of Liberty Motors to inform them of an upcoming staff meeting. You will create the memos by merging the individual names and position or department in the 9B Employees Table with a memo created in Microsoft Word.

1 In the **Navigation Pane**, click the **9B Employees** table to select the table. On the **External Data tab**, in the **Export group**, click **Word Merge**. If a security message displays, click Open.

The Microsoft Word Mail Merge Wizard starts. In this first dialog box, you can link the data in the table to an existing Word document or create a new Word document and then link the data in the table to the new document.

2 Verify that **Link your data to an existing Microsoft Word document** is selected, and then click **OK**. In the **Select Microsoft Word Document** dialog box, navigate to the location where the student data files for this textbook are saved. Locate and open the **a09B_Memo** file; click the **Microsoft Word** icon on the taskbar to view the memo, and then compare your screen with Figure 9.27.

Microsoft Word opens with the memo on the left and the Mail Merge task pane on the right.

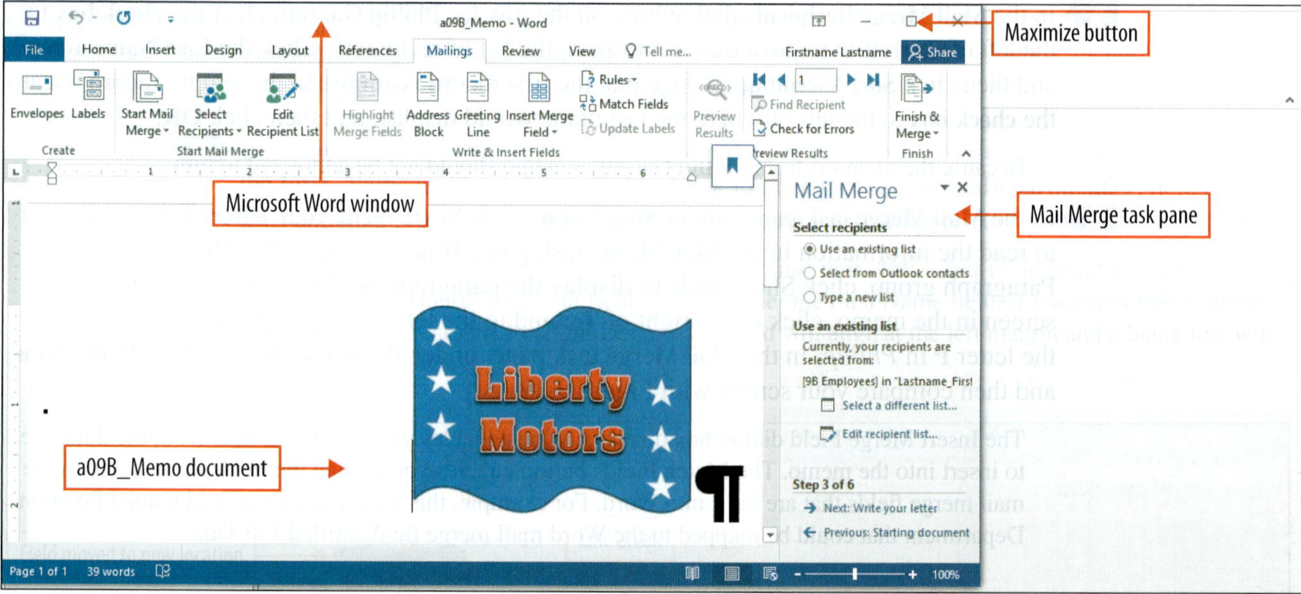

FIGURE 9.27

3 On the **Microsoft Word** title bar, click **Maximize** ☐. At the bottom of the **Mail Merge** task pane, notice that the wizard is on **Step 3 of 6**.

Because you are using an existing Word document, the first two steps are already defined.

4 In the **Mail Merge** task pane, under **Select recipients**, verify that the **Use an existing list** option button is selected. Under **Use an existing list**, click **Edit recipient list**, and then compare your screen with Figure 9.28.

The Mail Merge Recipients dialog box displays, enabling you to sort the list, filter the list, find duplicate entries, find a particular recipient or group of recipients, validate addresses, add recipients to the list, or remove recipients from the list.

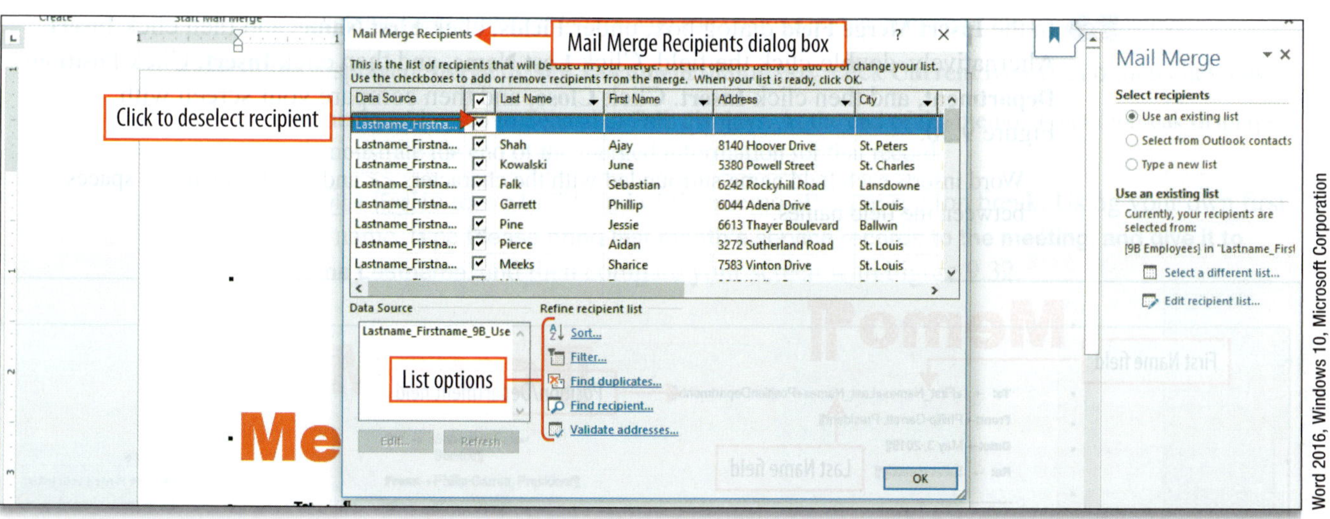

FIGURE 9.28

GLOSSARY

GLOSSARY OF CHAPTER KEY TERMS

Appended When data is added to the end of an existing table.

ASCII An acronym for American Standard Code for Information Interchange, a character set.

Cell The small box formed by the intersection of a column and a row in a worksheet.

Chart A graphic representation of data.

Column chart A chart used to display comparisons among related numbers.

Converted Changed from one format to another.

Data source An Access table or query that contains the names and addresses of the individuals to whom the letter, memo, or other document is being sent in a mail merge.

Definition The structure of the table—the field names, data types, and field properties.

Delimited file A file in which each record displays on a separate line, and the fields within the record are separated by a single character.

Delimiter A single character, which can be a paragraph mark, a tab, a comma, or another character, used to separate fields within a record.

Export The process used to send out a copy of data from one source or application to another application.

Extensible Markup Language The standard language for defining and storing data on the web.

HTML An acronym for HyperText Markup Language.

HyperText Markup Language The language used to display webpages.

Import The process used to bring in a copy of data from one source or application to another application.

Line chart A chart used to display trends over time.

Link A connection to data in another file.

Mail merge A Word feature used to create letters or memos that are created by combining a document and a record source.

Main document The document that contains the text of a letter or memo for a mail merge.

Merging Combining two documents to create one.

Named range A Excel range that has been given a name, making it easier to use the cells in calculations or modifications.

Notepad A simple text editor that comes with the Windows operating systems.

ODBC An acronym for Open Database Connectivity.

Open Database Connectivity A standard that enables databases using SQL statements to interface with one another.

Pie chart A chart used to display the contributions of parts to a whole amount.

Plain Text A document format that contains no formatting, such as bold or italic.

Range An area that includes two or more selected cells on an Excel worksheet that can be treated as a single unit.

SharePoint List A list of documents maintained on a server running Microsoft Office SharePoint Server.

SharePoint Server A server that enables you to share documents with others in your organization.

Spreadsheet Another name for a worksheet.

Tags HTML codes that the web browser interprets as the page is loaded; they begin with the < character and end with the > character.

Workbook An Excel file that contains one or more worksheets.

Worksheet The primary document used in Excel to save and work with data that is arranged in columns and rows.

XML An acronym for Extensible Markup Language.

XML presentation files Files that can be created so that the data can be viewed in a web browser.

XML schema A document with an .xsd extension that defines the elements, entities, and content allowed in the document.

CHAPTER REVIEW

Apply 9A skills from these Objectives:

1. Import Data from a Word Table
2. Import Data from an Excel Workbook
3. Insert an Excel Chart into a Report
4. Import from and Link to Another Access Database

Skills Review Project 9C Cars and Motorcycles

Liberty Motors maintains many of its records in Word, Excel, and Access files. Phillip Garrett, president, and Jeanine Thomas, finance manager, want to bring the data from these files into an Access database to create queries and reports. In this project, you will import data from Word, Excel, and another Access database and create a link to data in another application. Your completed files will look similar to Figure 9.41.

PROJECT FILES

For Project 9C, you will need the following files:

New blank Access database
a09C_Used_Cars_Inventory.accdb
a09C_Motorcycles.accdb
a09C_Logo.jpg
a09C_Domestic_Chart.xlsx
a09C_Customers.docx
a09C_Sports_Car_Sales.xlsx

You will save your files as:

Lastname_Firstname_9C_Cars_and_Motorcycles.accdb
Lastname_Firstname_9C_Customers_Table.txt

PROJECT RESULTS

Build from Scratch

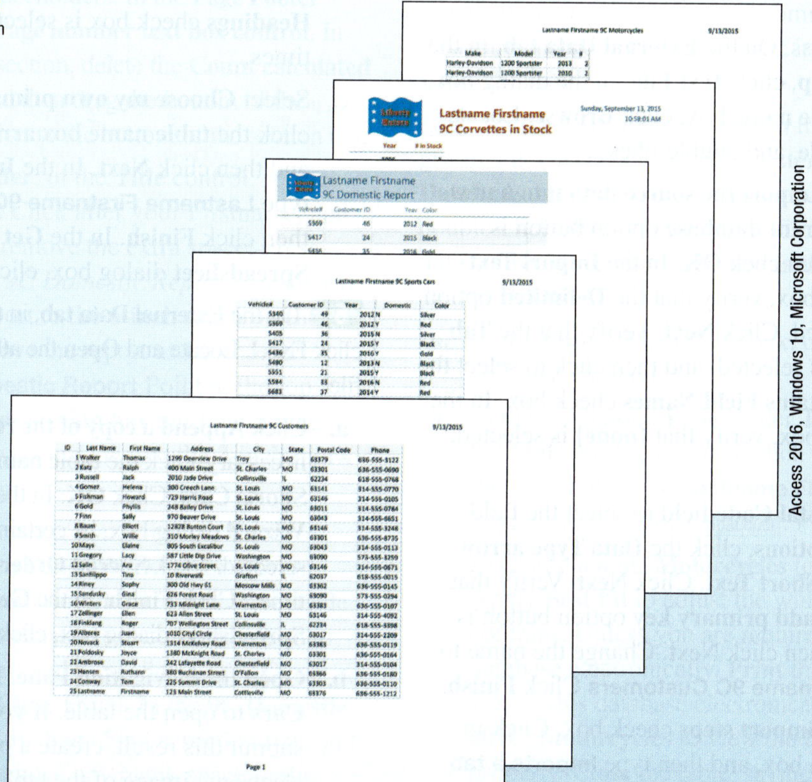

FIGURE 9.41

(Project 9C Cars and Motorcycles continues on the next page)

Mastering Access Project 9G Monthly Promotions (continued)

1 **Start** Access. **Create** a new blank database and save it in the **Access Chapter 9** folder as **Lastname_Firstname_9G_Monthly_Promotions** **Close** the table.

2 Import **External Data** from the **a09G_Customers** Excel file into a new table in the **9G_Monthly_Promotions** database. The **first row contains column headings**. Change the data type for the **Postal Code** field to **Short Text**. **Let Access add primary key**. Import to table **Lastname Firstname 9G Customers**

3 Open the **9G Customers** table, and **Best Fit** all columns. **Save** and **Close** the table. Merge it with the existing Microsoft Word document **a09G_Promotions_Letter**. The recipients will be selected from the existing list in the **9G Customers** table. Verify that **Show/Hide** is active. Place your insertion point at the beginning of the fifth blank line after the current date. Add the **Address Block**, and click **OK**. Insert the **First Name** and **Last Name** fields between the space and the colon in the salutation line. Place a space between these fields.

4 In the closing of the letter, replace **Firstname Lastname** with your first and last names. **Save** the document in your **Access Chapter 9** folder as **Lastname_Firstname_9G_Letter_Main**

5 **Preview your letters** and **Complete the merge** for only the eighth record. **Save** the Word document in your **Access Chapter 9** folder as **Lastname_Firstname_9G_Promotions_Letter** Unless you are required to submit your files electronically, **Print** the letter. **Close** the Word window, and then **Close** Word, saving changes if necessary.

6 Import **External Data** from the text file **a09G_Monthly_Promotions**. Import the source data into a new table in the current database. Use the **tab delimiter**. The **first row contains field names**. The data types are correct. **Let Access add primary key**. Import this text to **Lastname Firstname 9G Monthly Promotions** Do not save the import steps.

7 From the **9G Monthly Promotions** table, **Create** a report. In the **Title** of the report, move **9G Monthly Promotions** to a second line. Add the **a09G_Logo** to the report header. With the **Size Mode** property set to **Zoom**, resize the **logo control** until it reaches the **1.5-inch mark on the horizontal ruler**. Delete the **Date** and **Time** controls and placeholder. Resize the report to **6.5 inches** wide. **Save** the report as **Lastname Firstname 9G Monthly Promotions** and then **Close** the report.

8 Export the **9G Monthly Promotions** report as an **HTM Document**. **Save** the document in your **Access Chapter 9** folder as **Lastname_Firstname_9G_Monthly_Promotions_HTML** Open the destination file after the export operation is complete. In the **HTML Output Options** dialog box, click **OK**.

9 If you are instructed to submit this result, create a paper printout or PDF electronic image of the webpage. **Close** the web browser window. In the **Export – HTML Document** dialog box, click **Close**.

10 Resize the **Navigation Pane** so all object names are fully visible. **Close** Access.

11 As directed by your instructor, submit your database and the paper or PDF electronic images of the three objects that are the result of this project—two Word documents and one HTML file. Specifically, in this project, using your own name you created the following database and printouts or PDF electronic images:

1. Lastname_Firstname_9G_Monthly_Promotions	Database file
2. Lastname_Firstname_9G_Letter_Main	Word document
3. Lastname_Firstname_9G_Promotions_Letter	Word document
4. Lastname_Firstname_9G_Monthly_Promotions_HTML	HTML file

END | You have completed Project 9G

Apply a combination of the 9A and 9B skills

CONTENT-BASED ASSESSMENTS (CRITICAL THINKING)

GO! Fix It Project 9H Customer Service **MyITLab**

GO! Make It Project 9I Sponsored Events **MyITLab**

GO! Solve It Project 9J Sales Data **MyITLab**

GO! Solve It Project 9K Advertisements

PROJECT FILES

For Project 9K, you will need the following files:

a09K_Advertisements.accdb
a09K_Ad_Staff.txt

You will save your files as:

Lastname_Firstname_9K_Advertisements.accdb
Lastname_Firstname_9K_Ads_Workbook.xlsx

Jessie Pine, auto sales manager of Liberty Motors, explores many different venues to advertise the business. Most of the data for the advertisements is kept in a database. Some of the employees would like to see the data arranged in a worksheet to create a what-if analysis. Open the **a09K_Advertisements** database, and then save it as **Lastname_Firstname_9K_Advertisements** Import the **a09K_Ad_Staff.txt** file as a table, using the first row as field names, assigning a Short Text data type to the Postal Code field, and letting Access assign the primary key. Save the table as **Lastname Firstname 9K Ad Staff** and then Best Fit all columns in the table. Export the *9K Advertisements* table to an Excel workbook with formatting and layout. Save the workbook as **Lastname_Firstname_9K_Ads_Workbook** Rename the sheet tab **9K Data** If necessary, AutoFit the columns. Copy all of the data from the *9K Cost Analysis Summary* query to a second sheet in the same workbook. Rename this sheet **9K Analysis** AutoFit the columns. Type **Lastname Firstname 9K Advertisements** as a header for each of the sheets. Unless you are required to submit your files electronically, print the *9K Ad Staff* table and both worksheets in landscape orientation.

Performance Level

Performance Criteria	Exemplary: You consistently applied the relevant skills	Proficient: You sometimes, but not always, applied the relevant skills	Developing: You rarely or never applied the relevant skills
Import the a09K_Ad_Staff.txt file as a table	Table created with correct fields and settings as directed.	Table created with no more than two missing fields or settings.	Table created with more than two missing fields or settings.
Export the 9K Advertisements table to Excel	Worksheet created with correct fields and settings as directed.	Worksheet created with no more than two missing fields or settings.	Worksheet created with more than two missing fields or settings.
Export the 9K Cost Analysis Summary query to Excel	Worksheet created with correct fields and settings as directed.	Worksheet created with no more than two missing fields or settings.	Worksheet created with more than two missing fields or settings.

END | You have completed Project 9K

OUTCOMES-BASED ASSESSMENTS (CRITICAL THINKING)

Apply a combination of the 9A and 9B skills.

GO! Think Project 9L Employee Recognition

PROJECT FILES

For Project 9L, you will need the following files:

a09L_Employee_Recognition.accdb
a09L_Birthday_List.docx
a09L_Birthday_Card.docx

You will save your files as:

Lastname_Firstname_9L_Employee_Recognition.accdb
Lastname_Firstname_9L_Birthday_List.txt
Lastname_Firstname_9L_Birthday_Card.docx
Lastname_Firstname_9L_Card_Main.docx
Lastname_Firstname_9L_HTML_List.html

You have been asked to help with an employee recognition project at Liberty Motors. You will import the data from a Word table into a database table and then merge this table with cards created in Word. The birthday list will be uploaded to the company intranet, so it will need to be exported to HTML.

Open **a09L_Employee_Recognition** and save it as **Lastname_Firstname_9L_Employee_Recognition** Rename both objects to begin with your Lastname Firstname. Open **a09L_Birthday_List** and then convert the table to text. Save as a text file named **Lastname_Firstname_9L_Birthday_List** and then import it into your database as a table named **Lastname Firstname 9L Birthday List** with the first row as field names and no primary key. Best fit all columns, and add your name and birthday to the table. Merge it with **a09L_Birthday_Card** so the person's full name appears on the line after *Happy Birthday* and their favorite cake appears before the word *Cake*. Adjust the spacing as necessary. Merge your card only (Record 13), and save it as **Lastname_Firstname_9L_Card** Save the main document as **Lastname_Firstname_9L_Card_Main** If you are instructed to submit this result, create a paper printout or PDF electronic image of your birthday card.

Export the *9L Birthday List* table to HTML. Save the file as **Lastname_Firstname_9L_HTML_List.html** Unless you are required to submit your files electronically, print the webpage.

END | You have completed Project 9L

GO! Think Project 9M Service Records MyITLab

You and GO! Project 9N Club Directory MyITLab

Build from Scratch

Administering Databases and Writing SQL Statements

PROJECT 10A

OUTCOMES
Manage Access files.

OBJECTIVES

1. Create a Navigation Form
2. Use Microsoft Access Analysis Tools
3. Modify Access Views and Behaviors
4. Use the Database Splitter
5. Encrypt and Decrypt Databases
6. Create a Locked Database (ACCDE File)

PROJECT 10B

OUTCOMES
Write SQL statements.

OBJECTIVES

7. Modify a Query in SQL View
8. Create a Query in SQL View
9. Create a Union Query Using SQL
10. Create Calculated Fields and SQL Aggregate Functions

www.BillionPhotos.com/Shutterstock

In This Chapter

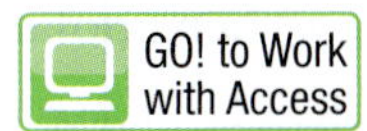

Throughout the life of a database, tables are added; design changes are made to queries, forms, and reports; and data is constantly updated and added. Understanding how to maintain a database is critical to the success of the individuals who rely on its data. Analysis tools enable users to identify potential problems and then fix them. Access also provides a set of security settings including password protection and a means to ensure the security of a database that you plan on sharing. Finally, Access provides a view for creating and modifying the SQL, or Structured Query Language, that makes all of its queries work.

Attorneys at **Loren-Renner Law Partners** counsel clients on a wide variety of issues including contracts, licensing, intellectual property, taxation, and the unique needs of the sports and entertainment industries. Entertainment clients include production companies, publishers, talent agencies, actors, writers, artists—anyone doing business in the entertainment industry. Sports clients include colleges and universities, professional sports teams, athletes, and venue operators. Increasingly, amateur and community sports coaches and organizations with concerns about liability are seeking the firm's specialized counsel.

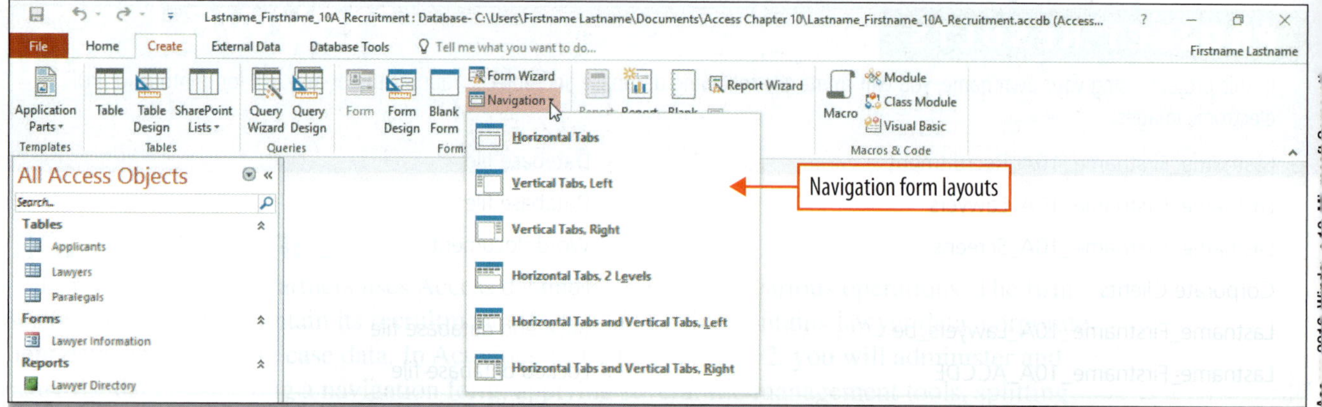

FIGURE 10.2

3 In the list, click **Vertical Tabs, Left**. If the Field List displays, close it. Compare your screen with Figure 10.3.

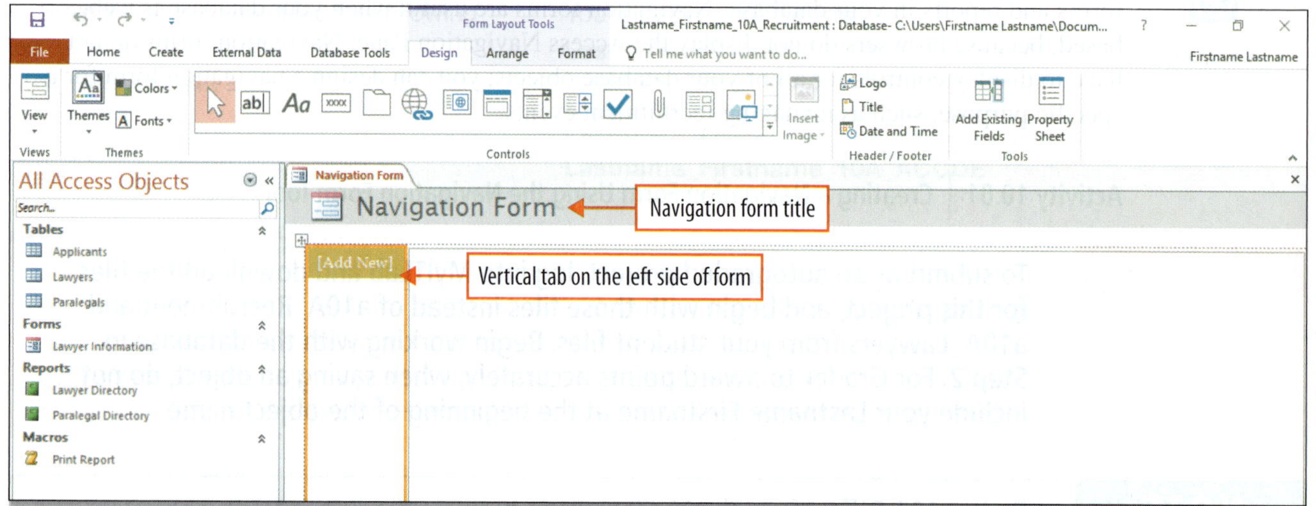

FIGURE 10.3

4 In the **Navigation Pane**, under **Forms**, point to **Lawyer Information**. Hold down the left mouse button, drag up and to the right to **[Add New]**, and then release the mouse button.

The Lawyer Information form is added to the navigation form as the first tab in the form.

5 Using the technique you just practiced, add the **Lawyer Directory** and the **Paralegal Directory** reports as the second and third tabs in the navigation form.

If you add an object as a tab in the navigation form by mistake, right-click the tab, and then click Delete.

6 At the top of the form, click the **Navigation Form** title to select it, and then click to the left of the *N* in *Navigation*. Type your **Lastname Firstname** press Spacebar, and then press Enter. Compare your screen with Figure 10.4.

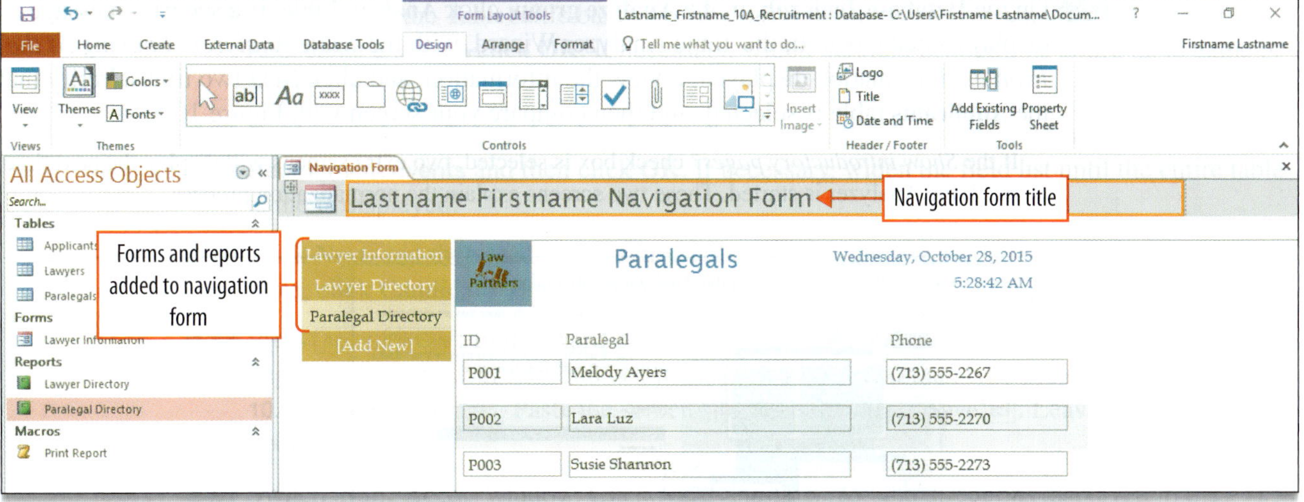

Access 2016, Windows 10, Microsoft Corporation

FIGURE 10.4

7 **Save** [Save] the navigation form as **Lastname Firstname Navigation Form Close** [«] the **Navigation Pane**. Switch to **Form** view.

8 Press Alt + PrintScrn. Create a new, blank Word document. In the **Word** document, type your first and last names, press Enter, and then type **Project 10A Activity 10.01 Step 8** Press Enter, and then **Paste** the screen shot. **Save** [Save] the document in your **Access Chapter 10** folder with the name **Lastname_Firstname_10A_Screens** Leave the Word document open.

9 Return to **Access**. **Close** [X] the navigation form, and **Open** [»] the **Navigation Pane**.

Objective 2 Use Microsoft Access Analysis Tools

GO! Learn How
Video A10-2

Microsoft Access contains several analysis tools that provide useful information to the database administrator. One tool scans tables for redundant data and then provides a mechanism to split them into smaller, related tables. Another tool analyzes all database objects and lists possible design flaws that decrease performance. Another analysis tool creates a highly detailed report listing the attributes for the entire database. These analysis tools are used to improve database performance and increase data reliability.

Activity 10.02 | Using the Table Analyzer

2.3.6, 1.2.2

Employees at Loren-Renner Law Partners notice that when they enter invoices into the database, they spend a significant amount of time typing the same recruitment information into multiple records. In this Activity, you will use the Table Analyzer to see if the table needs to be split. The ***Table Analyzer*** searches for repeated data in a table and then splits the table into two or more related tables to avoid data redundancy.

1 Open the **Applicants** table in **Datasheet** view. Click the **EventID column arrow**, and then click **Sort A to Z**. Scroll through the table, observe the duplicate entries in the EventID, Law School, and Event Date columns, and then **Close** [X] the table, saving changes. **Close** [«] the **Navigation Pane**.

The data in the Applicants table repeats information numerous times within the table, making it redundant.

8 In the left pane, click **Object Designers**. Under **Table design view**, in the **Default text field size**, replace the existing value with **50**

The default field size for new text fields will be 50 instead of 255.

9 Click **OK**. **Open** [»] the **Navigation Pane**. Open the **Paralegals** table in **Datasheet** view, and compare your screen with Figure 10.12.

The horizontal gridlines no longer display between the records. The font size is smaller for the entire table, allowing the columns to be smaller and still display all of the data.

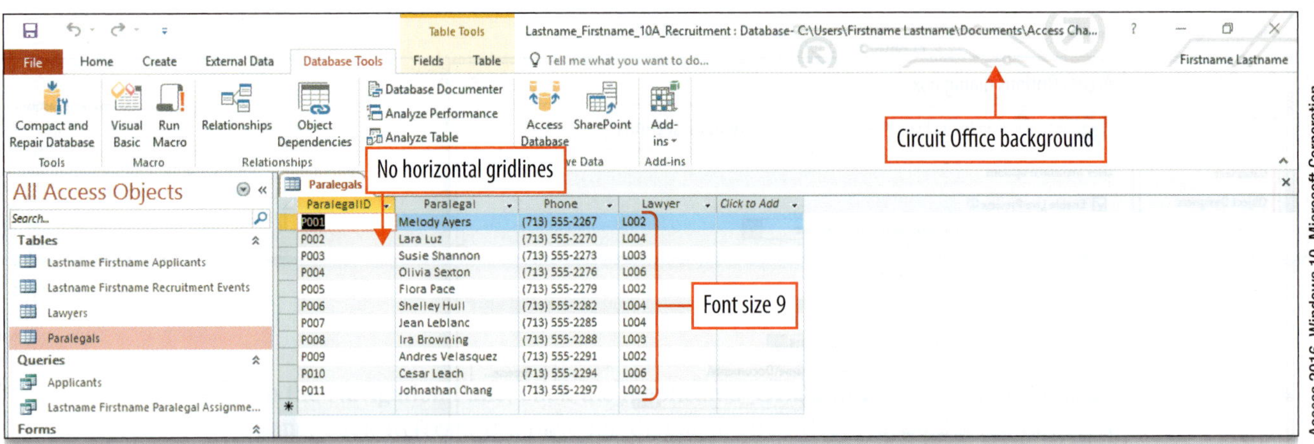

FIGURE 10.12

10 **Close** [X] the **Paralegals** table. **Close** [«] the **Navigation Pane**.

Activity 10.06 | Customizing the Quick Access Toolbar

Any Access command, including those not available on the ribbon, can be added to the Quick Access Toolbar. Loren-Renner Law Partners would like to add its commonly used commands to the Quick Access Toolbar. In this Activity, you will use two different methods to customize the Quick Access Toolbar.

1 Display **Backstage** view, and then click **Options**. In the left pane, click **Quick Access Toolbar**. Compare your screen with Figure 10.13.

Under *Choose commands from*, the commands from the Popular Commands group display. Under *Customize Quick Access Toolbar*, the commands on the current Quick Access Toolbar are listed. The *Customize Quick Access Toolbar* menu provides two options—the Quick Access Toolbar can be modified for all databases or just the current database.

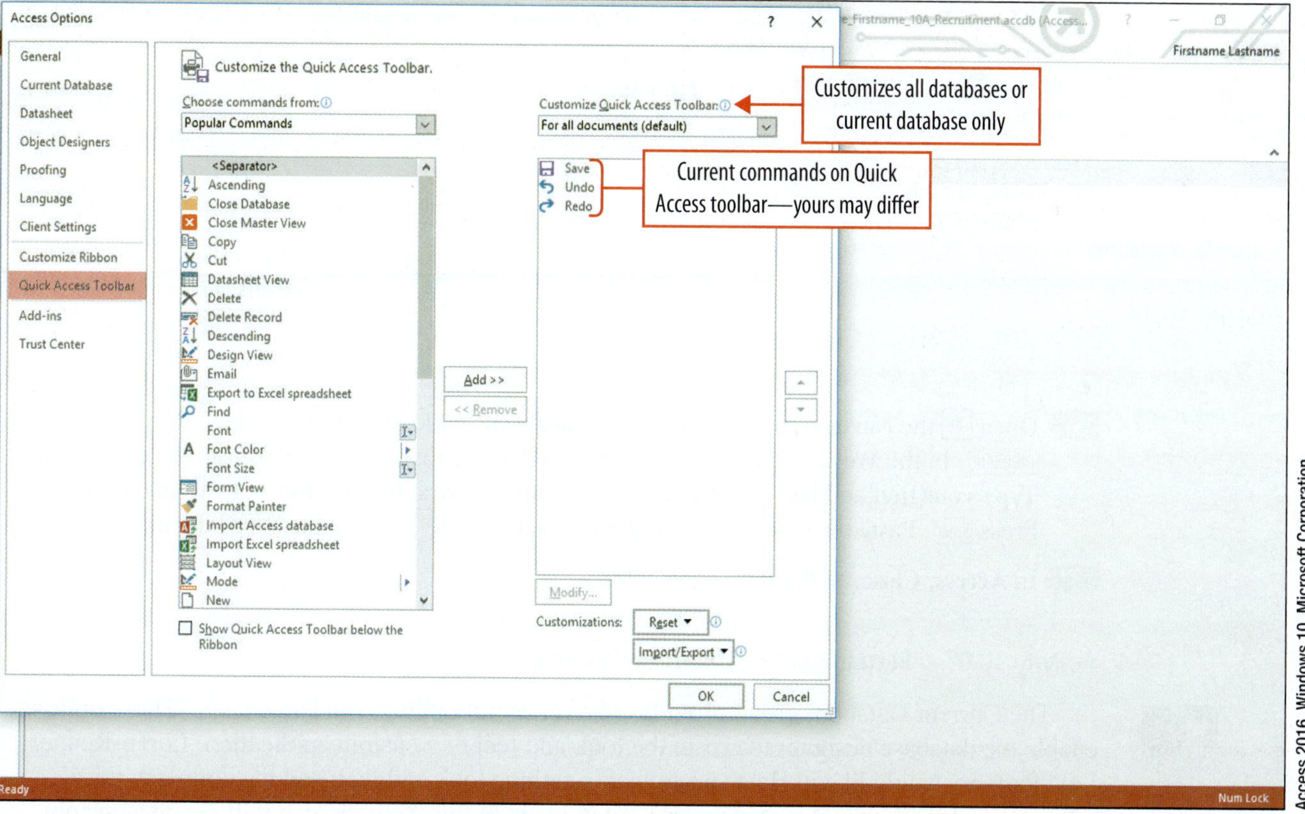

Access 2016, Windows 10, Microsoft Corporation

FIGURE 10.13

ANOTHER WAY On the Quick Access Toolbar, click the Customize Quick Access Toolbar arrow, and then click More Commands.

2 In the list below **Popular Commands**, click **Close Database,** and then click **Add**.

Loren-Renner Law Partners would like this button added for all databases opened on this computer.

3 In the upper-right corner, click the **Customize Quick Access Toolbar arrow**, and then click the path to the currently open database. In the list below **Popular Commands**, scroll down. Click **Quick Print**, and then click **Add**.

The firm would like this change for the currently opened database only.

4 Click **OK**, and then compare your screen with Figure 10.14.

The Close Database and Quick Print icons have been added to the Quick Access Toolbar. Icons added to just one database are placed to the right of the other icons.

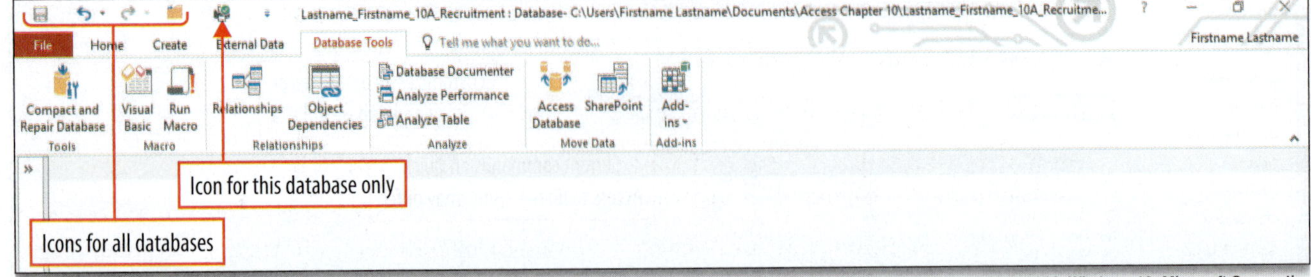

Access 2016, Windows 10, Microsoft Corporation

FIGURE 10.14

5 **Open** [»] the **Navigation Pane**. Open the **Paralegals** table in **Datasheet** view. Press Alt + PrintScrn. In the **Word** document, press Enter, and then press Ctrl + Enter to insert a page break. Type your first and last names, press Enter, and then type **Project 10A Activity 10.06 Step 5** Press Enter, **Paste** the screen shot, and then click **Save**. Leave the Word document open.

6 In **Access**, **Close** [X] the **Paralegals** table.

Activity 10.07 | Setting Current Database Options

1.3.3, 1.4.1, 1.4.2

The Current Database group provides several useful options you can change. These options enable the database designer to create the look and feel of a custom application. Loren-Renner Law Partners would like its database to have a unique look and feel, and the company does not want end users to make changes in Layout view. In this Activity, you will create a custom application title and application icon for the database, and then disable Layout view.

1 Display **Backstage** view, click **Options**, and then in the left pane, click **Current Database**.

2 Under **Application Options**, in the **Application Title** box, type **L-R Law Partners**

The ***application title*** is the text that displays in the Access title bar when that database is open. If the Application Title box is left blank, the file path, name, file, and application name display instead.

3 To the right of **Application Icon** box, click **Browse**. In the displayed **Icon Browser** dialog box, change the file type to **Bitmaps**.

4 In the **Icon Browser** dialog box, navigate to where the student files for this project are stored. Locate and click **a10A_Icon**, and then click **OK**. Click to select the check box next to *Use as Form and Report Icon*.

5 To the right of the **Display Form** box, click the down-pointing arrow, and then click **Navigation Form** to display this form when the database is opened.

Because the Navigation Pane does not display in web-based databases, the navigation form should be set to display as the default form when the database is opened.

6 Under **Application Options**, select the **Compact on Close** check box.

With this option selected, the database will be compacted and repaired each time it is closed. As a database is used, it creates temporary files and doesn't automatically recapture space from deleted objects. These situations can make the database run slowly or experience problems. ***Compact & Repair*** is a process in which an Access file is rewritten to store the objects and data more efficiently.

Display Backstage view, and under Info, click Compact & Repair if you experience file problems while working with a database.

7 Clear the **Enable Layout View** check box to remove the check mark.

With the check mark removed, Layout view is disabled.

8 Click **OK**, read the displayed message, and then click **OK** again.

9 Display **Backstage** view, click **Close**, and then, under *Recent*, click **Lastname_Firstname_10A_Recruitment**.

10 **Close** [X] the **Navigation Form**. **Open** the **Lawyer Directory** report in **Report** view, and then compare your screen with Figure 10.15.

The application title displays in the title bar. The application icon displays in the report's tab. If the database file or icon image file is renamed or moved to another location, the icon will no longer display.

FIGURE 10.15

11 **Close** [X] the report.

Activity 10.08 | Set Navigation Options

1.3.4, 1.5.3

The database designer can choose to customize the Navigation Pane to create a custom interface for the end user. Loren-Renner Law Partners would like its users to see objects in specialized groups in the Navigation Pane. In this Activity, you will customize the Navigation Pane by adding a custom category and two groups. You will then add the form and report to their respective groups.

1 Display **Backstage** view, click **Options**, and then in the left pane, if necessary, click Current Database.

2 Under **Navigation**, click the **Navigation Options** button, and then compare your screen with Figure 10.16.

The existing categories for the Navigation Pane display on the left and the groups for each existing category display on the right. Categories and Groups are edited using the buttons below the two columns.

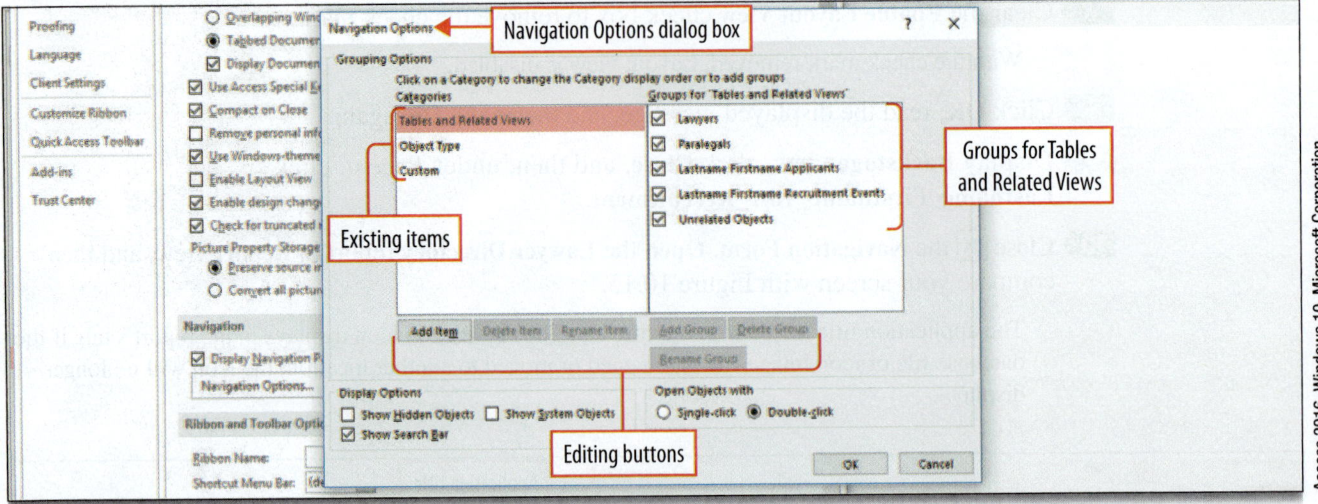

FIGURE 10.16

3 Click **Add Item**, type **L-R Law Partners** and then press Enter.

L-R Law Partners displays as a category. A ***Navigation Pane category*** is a top-level listing that displays when the Navigation Pane arrow is clicked.

4 With the **L-R Law Partners** category selected, click **Add Group**. Type **Lawyers** and then press Enter.

Lawyers displays as group. A ***Navigation Pane group*** is a second-level listing that displays when a Navigation Pane category is selected.

5 Click **Add Group**. Type **Paralegals** and then press Enter. Click **OK** twice to close the dialog boxes. Click **OK** to close the message box, if necessary.

6 **Close** the database. Display **Backstage** view, and under *Recent*, click **Lastname_Firstname_10A_Recruitment**. **Close** the **Navigation Form**.

7 Click the **Navigation Pane arrow**, and then click **L-R Law Partners**. In the **Navigation Pane**, under **Unassigned Objects**, drag the **Lawyers** table and drop it over the **Lawyers** group. Drag the **Lawyer Information** form and drop it over the **Lawyers** group. Drag the **Lawyer Directory** report and drop it over the **Lawyers** group.

8 Drag the **Paralegals** table and drop it over the **Paralegals** group. Drag the **Paralegal Directory** report and drop it over the **Paralegals** group. Compare your screen with Figure 10.17.

The objects display as shortcuts within their respective Navigation Pane groups, and they are no longer listed under Unassigned Objects.

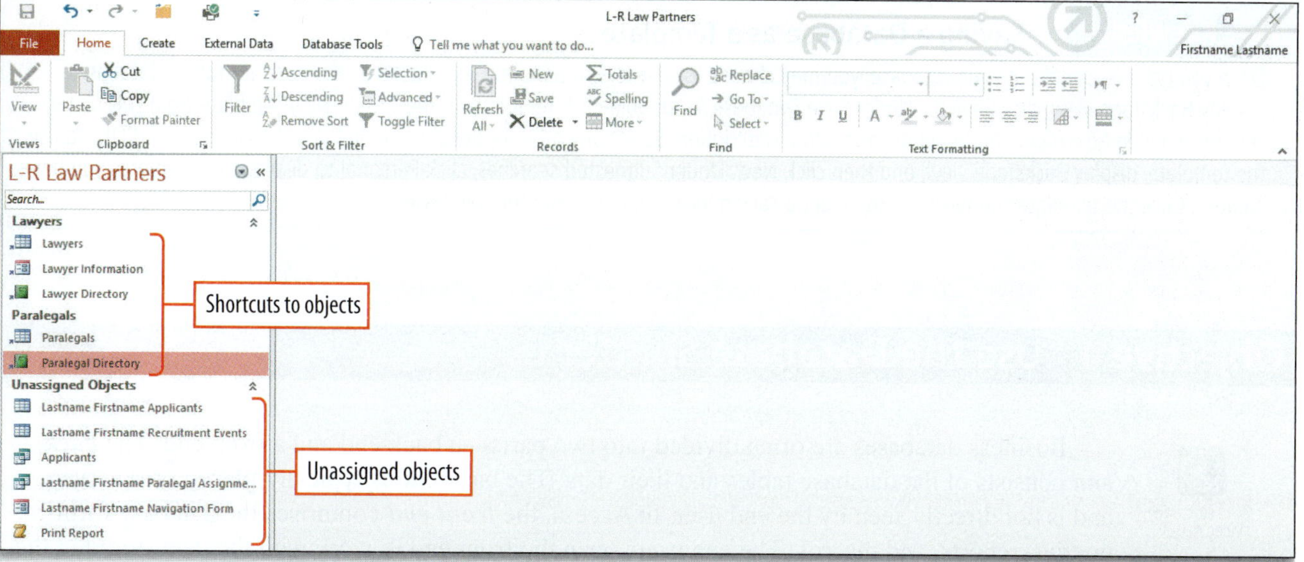

Access 2016, Windows 10, Microsoft Corporation

FIGURE 10.17

9 Display **Backstage** view, click **Options**, and then under **Navigation**, click the **Navigation Options** button. In the **Categories** column, click **L-R Law Partners**. In the **Groups** column, clear the **Unassigned Objects** check box, and then click **OK** two times to close the dialog boxes. Click **OK** to close the message box.

The two objects that you assigned earlier display in the Navigation Pane. You will need to close and reopen the database for the options to take effect.

10 **Close** the database. From the **Backstage** view, under *Recent*, click **Lastname_Firstname_10A_Recruitment**.

11 Right-click the **Lawyers** table, and in the displayed shortcut menu, click **Rename Shortcut**. Add your **Lastname Firstname** at the beginning of the object name. Use this same technique to add your last and first names to the other objects displayed in the Navigation Pane.

12 Press Alt + PrintScrn. In the **Word** document, press Enter, and then press Ctrl + Enter to insert a page break. Type your first and last names, press Enter, and then type **Project 10A Activity 10.08 Step 12** Press Enter, **Paste** the screen shot, and then click **Save**. Leave the Word document open.

13 Return to **Access**. On the **Quick Access Toolbar**, right-click the **Close Database button**, and then click **Remove from Quick Access Toolbar**. Use this same technique to remove the **Quick Print button** from the Quick Access Toolbar.

14 Display **Backstage** view, click **Options**, and then click **General**. Click the **Office Background arrow**, and then click **No Background**.

15 Click **Datasheet**. Click the **Default font size arrow**, and then click **11**. Under **Default gridlines showing**, select the **Horizontal** check box.

16 Click **Object Designers**, and then set the **Default text field size** back to **255**

17 Click **OK** to close the **Access Options** dialog box, and then click **OK** to close the message box. Close the **10A_Recruitment** database.

More Knowledge **Saving a Database as a Template**

Once you have personalized your database, you may choose to save it as a template to be used as the basis for future databases. Display Backstage view, click Save As. Under Save Database As, double-click Template. In the Create New Template from This Database dialog box, name the template, and add a description. Select any other options in the dialog box before clicking OK. To use the template, display Backstage view, and then click New. Under Suggested searches, click Personal to display the templates you have created. Click the template you wish to use, select a saving location, and name the database.

Objective 4 Use the Database Splitter

GO! Learn How
Video A10-4

Business databases are often divided into two parts—a back end and a front end. The ***back end*** consists of the database tables and their data. The back end is typically placed on a server and is not directly seen by the end user. In Access, the ***front end*** comprises the database forms, queries, reports, and macros. The end users open the front end to work with the data stored in the back-end tables. Dividing the database enables the database administrator to maintain a single source of data while designing multiple front ends to meet the needs of various departments in the company.

Activity 10.09 | Splitting a Database

1.4.4

A ***split database*** is an Access database that is split into two files—one containing the back end and one containing the front end. Several departments at Loren-Renner Law Partners need their own forms, reports, and queries. Instead of trying to coordinate separate databases, the company would like to place all of the database tables on a network server. Each department will then have its own custom front end that links to the tables in the back-end file. In this Activity, you will use the Split Database tool to create two separate files—one for the back end and one for the front end.

1. Navigate to the location where the student data files for this chapter are saved and open the **a10A_Lawyers** database. Save the database in your **Access Chapter 10** folder as **Lastname_Firstname_10A_Lawyers** If necessary, enable the content.

2. On the **Database Tools tab**, in the **Move Data group**, click **Access Database**. Compare your screen with Figure 10.18.

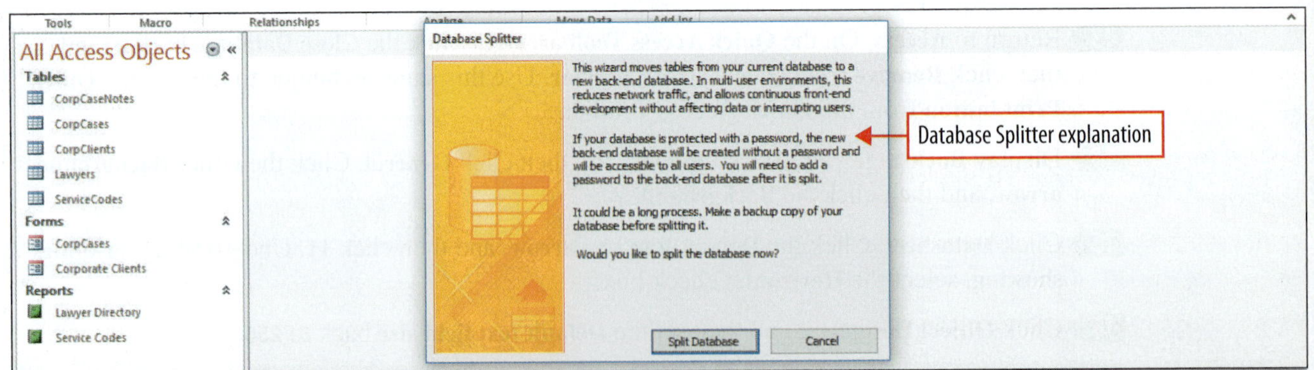

Access 2016, Windows 10, Microsoft Corporation

FIGURE 10.18

3 In the displayed **Database Splitter** dialog box, read the message, and then click **Split Database**. Compare your screen with Figure 10.19.

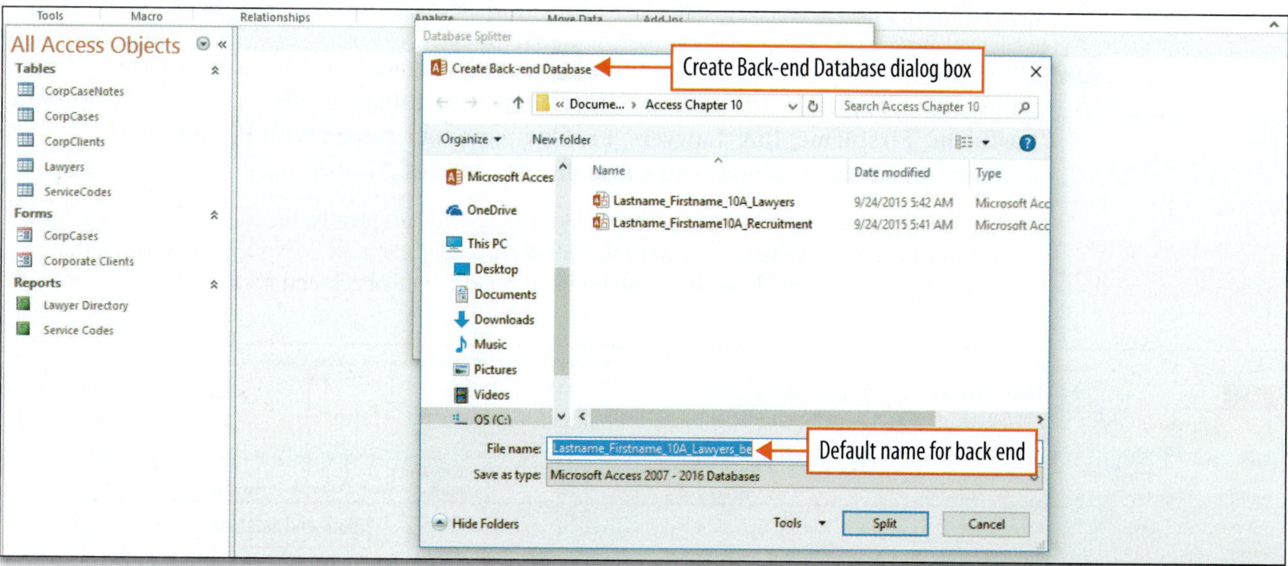

FIGURE 10.19

Access 2016, Windows 10, Microsoft Corporation

4 In the **Create Back-end Database** dialog box, if necessary, navigate to your **Access Chapter 10** folder. Notice the suggested file name, and then click **Split**. Read the displayed message, click **OK**, and then compare your screen with Figure 10.20.

In the Navigation Pane, the tables display the linked table icon and the other objects display as before. Recall that a linked table is a table that resides in a separate database file.

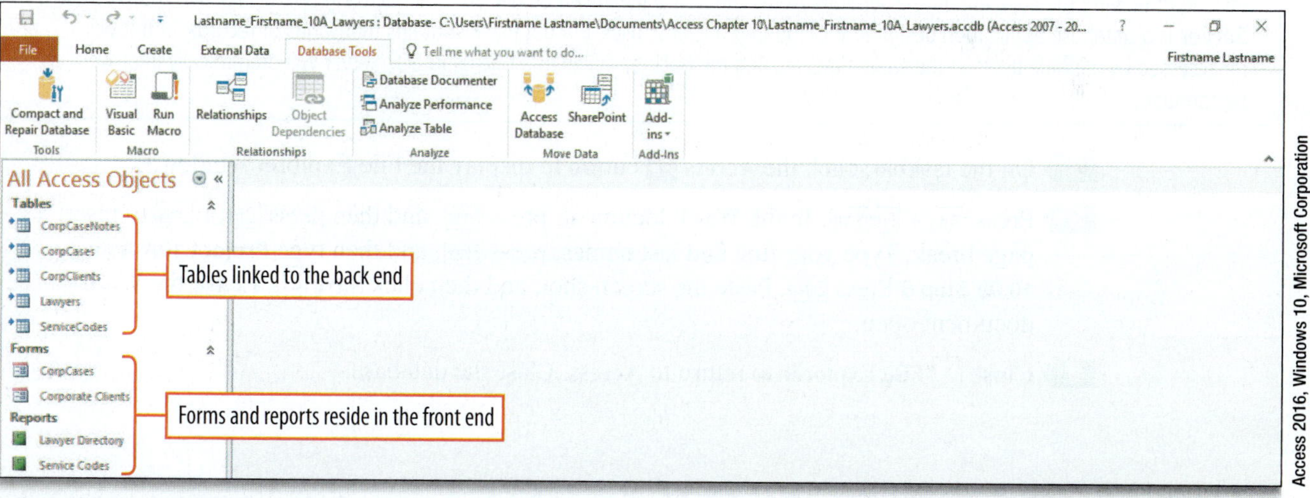

FIGURE 10.20

Access 2016, Windows 10, Microsoft Corporation

5 Press Alt + PrintScrn. In the **Word** document, press Enter, and then press Ctrl + Enter to insert a page break. Type your first and last names, press Enter, and then type **Project 10A Activity 10.09 Step 5** Press Enter, **Paste** the screen shot, and then click **Save**. Leave the Word document open.

6 On the taskbar, click the File Explorer icon. Navigate to the location where the Access Chapter 10 folder is saved, and open the folder. Double-click **Lastname_Firstname_10A_Lawyers_be**. Compare your screen with Figure 10.21, and then **Close** the database, and **Close** this instance of Access.

The five linked tables reside in this back-end database file. Typically, the file containing the back end would reside on a network server that all departments can access. Notice that none of the front-end objects in the Lawyers database were copied to this back-end file.

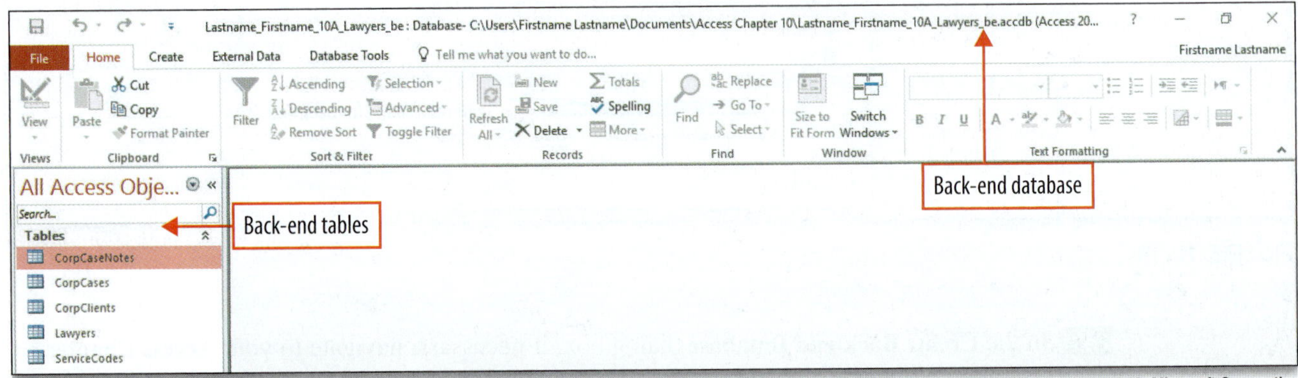

Access 2016, Windows 10, Microsoft Corporation

FIGURE 10.21

> **More Knowledge** **Moving the Back End to a Microsoft SQL Server**
>
> Instead of moving the back end into a separate Access database file, it can be placed on a Microsoft SQL Server. ***Microsoft SQL Server*** is a database application designed for high-end business uses. If a database contains thousands of records, or if it will be accessed by multiple users at the same time, moving the back-end files to a Microsoft SQL Server will dramatically improve performance.

7 On the taskbar, click the **Access** button to display the File Explorer window.

8 Press Alt + PrintScrn. In the **Word** document, press Enter, and then press Ctrl + Enter to insert a page break. Type your first and last names, press Enter, and then type **Project 10A Activity 10.09 Step 8** Press Enter, **Paste** the screen shot, and then click **Save**. Leave the Word document open.

9 Close **File Explorer** to return to **Access**. **Close** the database.

Objective 5 Encrypt and Decrypt Databases

GO! Learn How
Video A10-5

The data stored in any company's database is one of that company's most valuable assets. If proprietary knowledge is made public, the company could lose its competitive advantage. Further, personal information stored in the database needs to be protected from unauthorized access. For these reasons, the data needs to be hidden until the correct password is entered. Only authorized users should know what that password is.

Activity 10.10 | Encrypting a Database with a Password

Loren-Renner Law Partners has a moral and legal responsibility to keep the data it collects hidden from unauthorized individuals. If one of the company computers or laptops is ever lost or stolen, the data should be unreadable to anyone outside of the company. In this Activity, you will make an Access 2016 database unreadable until a password is entered.

1 Display **Backstage** view, and then click **Open**. Under Open, click **Browse**, and then navigate to the **Access Chapter 10** folder, if necessary. Click **Lastname_Firstname_10A_Lawyers** one time. In the lower-right corner of the **Open** dialog box, click the **Open arrow**, and compare your screen with Figure 10.22.

Three additional open modes display. ***Open Read-Only*** opens the database so that all objects can be opened and viewed, but data and design changes cannot be made. ***Open Exclusive*** opens the database so that changes can be made, but no one else may open the database at the same time. ***Open Exclusive Read-Only*** opens the database in both Exclusive and Read-Only modes.

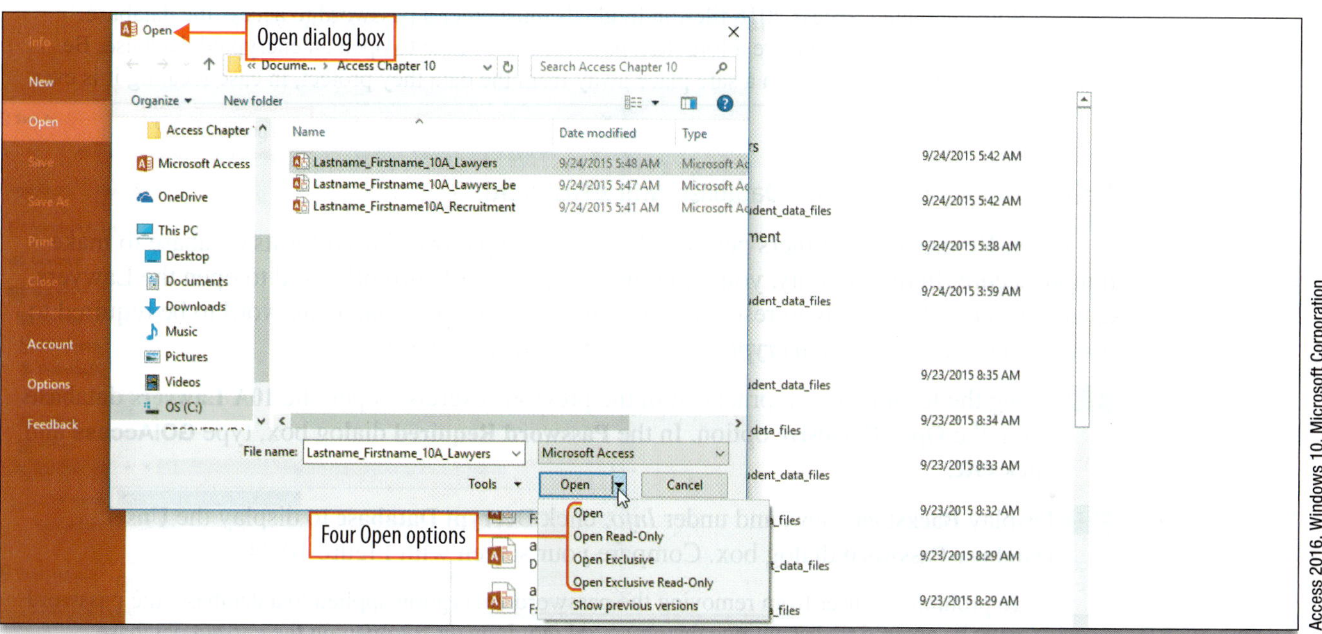

Access 2016, Windows 10, Microsoft Corporation

FIGURE 10.22

2 Click **Open Exclusive**.

The database must be opened in exclusive mode before it can be encrypted. To ***encrypt*** means to hide data by making the file unreadable until the correct password is entered.

3 Display **Backstage** view, and under *Info*, click **Encrypt with Password**. Compare your screen with Figure 10.23.

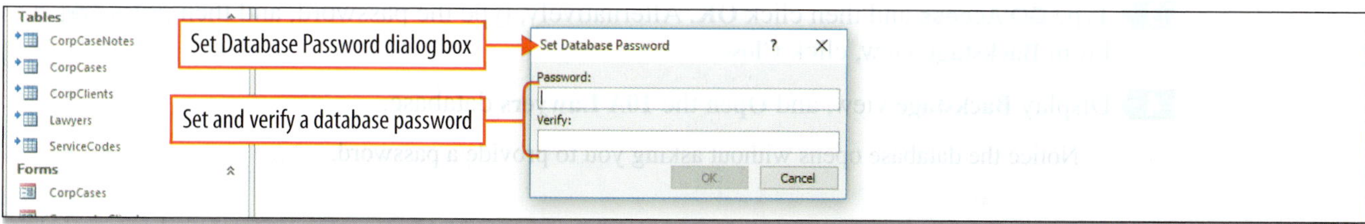

Access 2016, Windows 10, Microsoft Corporation

FIGURE 10.23

4 From the **FMLPersonalClients** table, add the following fields to the design grid: **PersonalID**, **FName**, **LName**, and **Phone**. From the **FMLFlatFeeBilling** table, add the **Paid** field to the design grid. In the **Criteria** box for the **Paid** column, type **No**

When you type *No*, do not accept an autocomplete entry of *Now*. You may need to press the space bar after typing *No*.

5 Click **Save**, type **FMLFlatFeesDue** using your own initials, and then click **OK**.

6 Locate the status bar in the lower-right corner of the database window, and then click **SQL View**. Click any blank area in the SQL workspace, and then compare your screen with Figure 10.29.

When you work in Query Design view, Access builds the equivalent SQL statement. An ***SQL statement*** is an expression that defines the SQL commands that should be performed when the query is run. SQL statements typically contain several SQL clauses that begin with keywords. ***Keywords*** are commands built into the SQL programming language. Keywords are typically written using uppercase letters. In SQL view, statements are edited in the design grid.

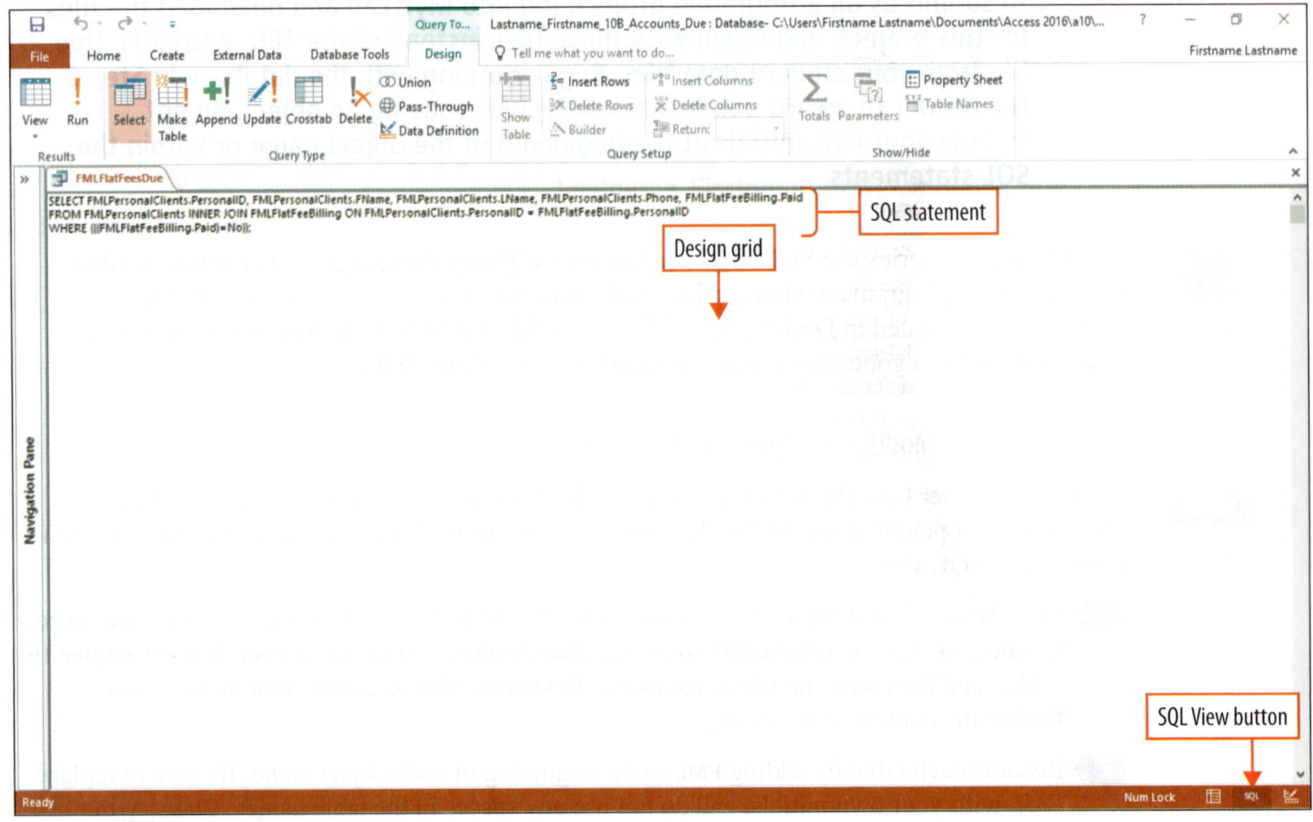

FIGURE 10.29

7 In the SQL statement, click to the left of the keyword *FROM*, and then press Enter.

This SQL statement starts with a SELECT clause. A ***SELECT clause*** lists which fields the query should display. The second clause in this SQL statement is a FROM clause. A ***FROM clause*** lists which tables hold the fields used in the SELECT clause.

8 Click to the left of the keyword *INNER*, and then press Enter two times.

A ***JOIN clause*** defines the join type for a query. Recall that an inner join displays only those records that have a corresponding record in both of the related tables. A ***WHERE clause*** defines the criteria that should be applied when a query is run.

Click to the left of the keyword *WHERE*, and then press Enter. In the **WHERE** clause, remove all six parentheses.

These parentheses would be needed only if a more complex WHERE clause were written. Often, the SQL generated while in Design view will not be as efficient as the SQL written by a database designer in SQL view.

10 Click **Save**. In the **Results group**, click **Run**. Click the **LName column arrow**, and then click **Sort A to Z**. Compare your screen with Figure 10.30.

Brandi Dorsey and Faye Wiley are each listed two times. This type of duplication may lead to duplicate phone calls being made to the client.

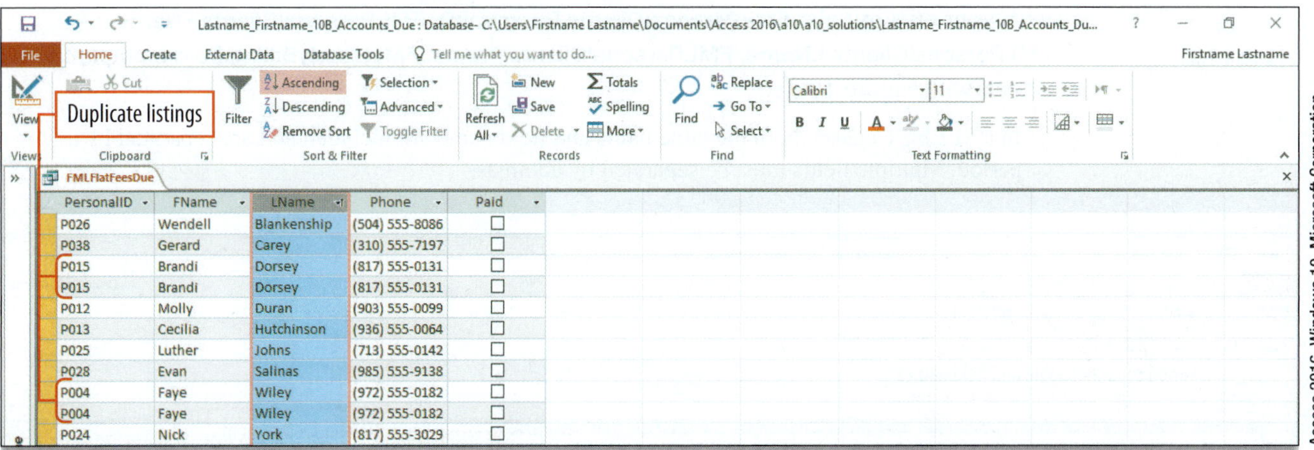

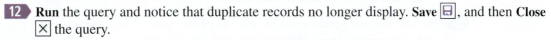

FIGURE 10.30

ALERT! **Does your SQL code disappear?**

Your SQL code may disappear when you click Save. The query will run, and the code will display after you run the query and click the SQL View button.

11 In the status bar, click the **SQL View** button. Click to the right of the keyword SELECT, press Spacebar, and then type **DISTINCT**

The ***DISTINCT*** keyword returns only a single instance of any duplicate values in query results. It always follows the SELECT keyword, and is added only in SQL View.

12 **Run** the query and notice that duplicate records no longer display. **Save**, and then **Close** the query.

Objective 8 Create a Query in SQL View

GO! Learn How Video A10-8

Many database designers find it easier to design their queries in SQL view. The typical SQL query uses the same three-step sequence. Understanding this sequence removes much of the complexity of the typical SQL statement. Working in SQL view enables the designer to write more efficient SQL and also provides more control than Design view. Several types of queries can be created only when working in SQL view.

Activity 10.14 | Creating an SQL Statement

3.1.1, 3.3.2, 3.1.6

Loren-Renner Law Partners needs a query that lists each client who was charged an hourly rate and has not yet paid the fee. Due to the nature of this query, you will need to work in SQL view to write a query not available in Design view. In this Activity, you will create that query in SQL view.

1 On the **Create tab**, in the **Queries group**, click **Query Design**. **Close** the **Show Table** dialog box, and then in the status bar, click the **SQL View** button.

Because you started with a select query, the SELECT keyword displays followed by a semicolon. Semicolons are used to mark the end of SQL statements.

2 Click before the semicolon, press Spacebar, and then type the following, substituting FML with your own initials: **FMLPersonalClients.PersonalID, FMLPersonalClients.FName, FMLPersonalClients.LName, FMLPersonalClients.Phone, FMLHourlyBilling.Paid** Compare your screen with Figure 10.31.

In a SELECT clause, both the table name and field name are included and are separated by a period. Multiple fields must be separated by commas.

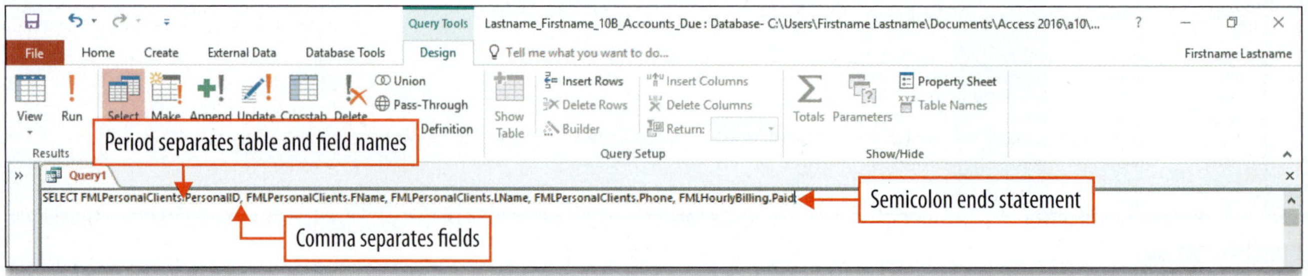

Access 2016, Windows 10, Microsoft Corporation

FIGURE 10.31

3 Press Enter, and then type the following FROM clause, substituting your own initials: **FROM FMLPersonalClients, FMLHourlyBilling**

All tables used in the SELECT clause must be listed in the FROM clause and are separated by commas.

4 Press Enter, and then type the following WHERE clause, substituting your own initials: **WHERE FMLHourlyBilling.Paid=No**

Recall that in the WHERE statement, the criteria for the query is defined.

5 Be sure that the semicolon is at the end of the query. Click **Save**, and then, substituting your own initials, type **FMLHourlyFeesDue** Click **OK**.

6 Click **Run**, and then compare your screen with Figure 10.32. If you receive a message that the query has errors or the Enter Parameter Value dialog box displays, go back and check your typing very carefully.

The result of this query is a cross join query. Recall that in a cross join query, every possible combination of records between two related tables will be returned. If no join type is defined or if there is a mistake in the WHERE clause, SQL returns a cross join query. When tables contain a large number of records, cross join queries will take a very long time to run. In this query, the join type needs to be defined.

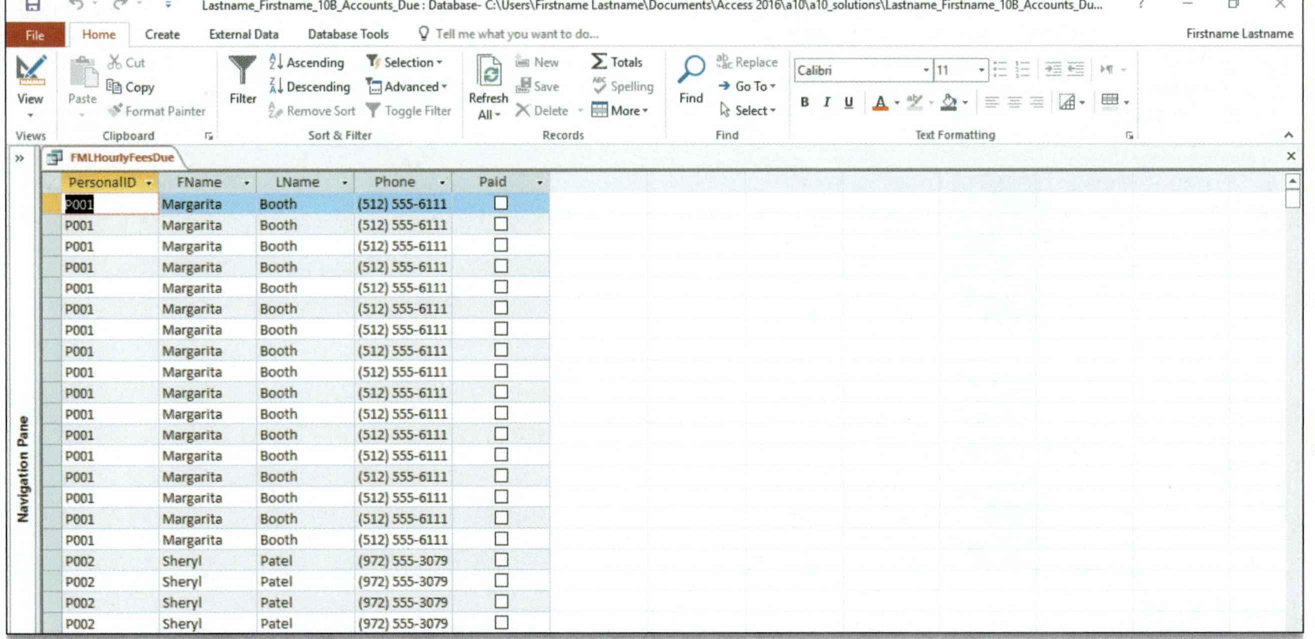

Access 2016, Windows 10, Microsoft Corporation

FIGURE 10.32

7 **Save** your query, and then return to **SQL** view.

Activity 10.15 | Specifying the Join Type in SQL

The Hourly Billing Due query currently returns a cross join. Once a join type is specified in the query, it will display one record per customer. In this Activity, you will add an SQL clause so that the two tables used in the query use an inner join.

1 In **SQL** view, in the **FROM** clause, click between *FMLPersonalClients* and the comma, and then press Enter.

2 Press Delete to remove the comma.

3 Type the following JOIN clause, **INNER JOIN**

The INNER JOIN keyword instructs the query to use an inner join between two tables.

4 Click to the right of *FMLHourlyBilling*, press Spacebar, and type the following ON clause: **ON FMLPersonalClients.PersonalID = FMLHourlyBilling.PersonalID**

The ***ON*** keyword is used to specify which field is common to two tables. The combination of the INNER JOIN and ON keywords creates a relationship between the two tables. In this query the PersonalID field is used to join the tables.

5 **Save**, and then **Run** the query. Sort the **LName** column in alphabetical order, and then compare your screen with Figure 10.33.

The tables are joined correctly, but customers with more than one outstanding bill are listed two or more times.

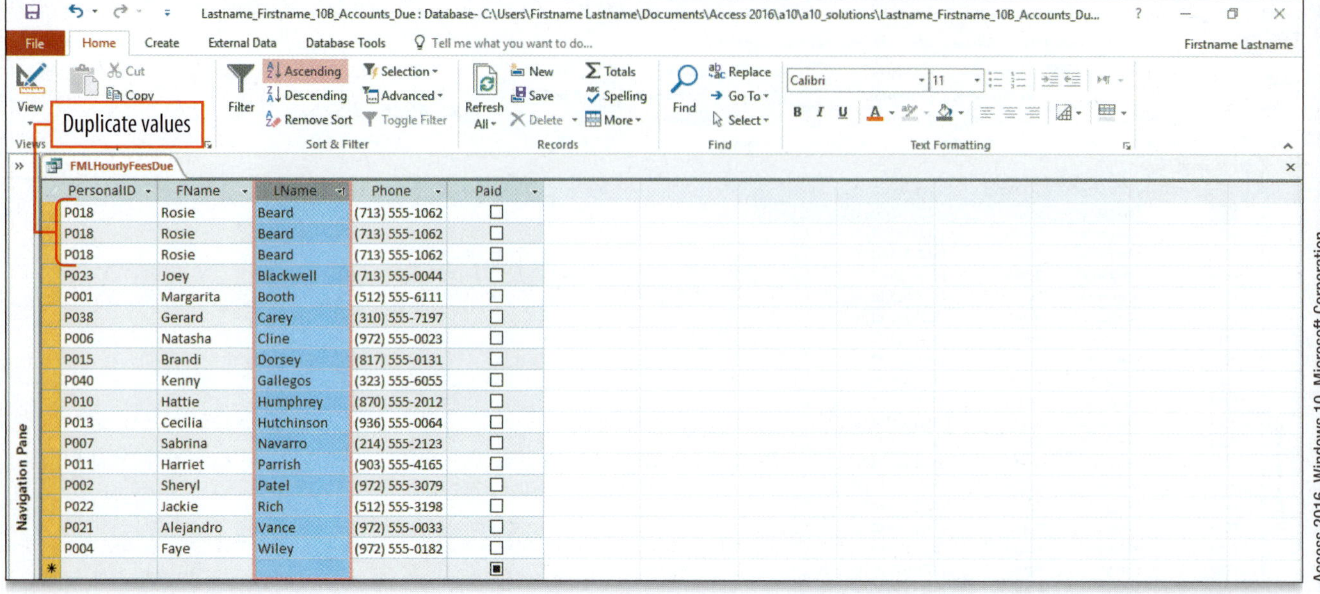

FIGURE 10.33

6 Return to **SQL** view. After the **SELECT** keyword, press Spacebar, and then type **DISTINCT**

7 **Run** the query. Check that no customer is listed more than once. **Save**, and then **Close** the query.

Objective 9 Create a Union Query Using SQL

GO! Learn How Video A10-9

Using SQL, the results of two or more queries can be displayed in one query. A ***union query*** combines the results of two or more similar select queries. The combined queries must have the same number of columns and the same data types in each corresponding column. Union queries are created only in SQL view.

Activity 10.16 | Creating a Union Query in SQL View

Recall that Loren-Renner Law Partners needs a list of all personal clients with amounts owed. In earlier projects, you built two separate queries, one for flat fees and the other for hourly fees. In this Activity, you will use SQL to combine the results of both queries into a single query.

1 On the **Create tab**, in the **Queries group**, click **Query Design**. **Close** the **Show Table** dialog box.

2 In the **Query Type group**, click **Union**. Notice that the query switches to SQL view.

3 **Open** the **Navigation Pane**. Open the **FMLFlatFeesDue** query, and then in the status bar, click the **SQL View** button. With the entire SQL statement selected, right-click anywhere in the design grid, and then click **Copy**.

4 **Close** the **FMLFlatFeesDue** query. In the union query, right-click anywhere in the design grid, and then click **Paste**.

5 At the end of the SQL statement, delete the semicolon, and then press Enter **two** times.

6 Type **UNION** and then press Enter **two** times. Compare your screen with Figure 10.34.

The ***UNION*** keyword is used to combine one or more queries in a union query.

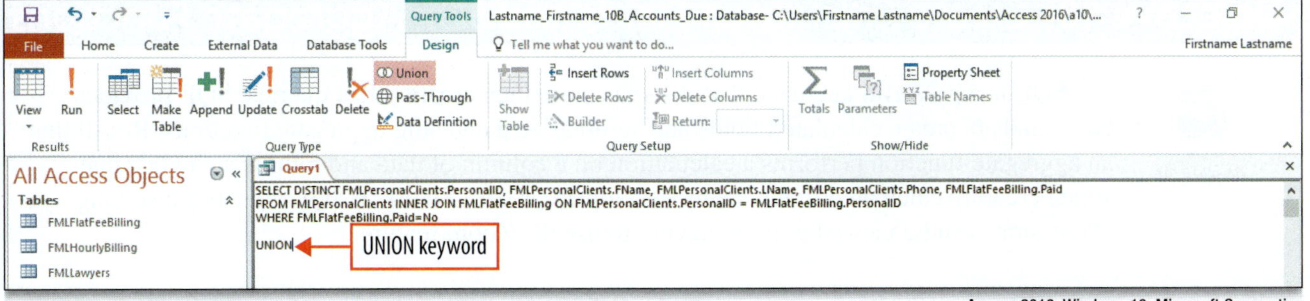

Access 2016, Windows 10, Microsoft Corporation

FIGURE 10.34

7 Open the **FMLHourlyFeesDue** query, and then in the status bar, click the **SQL View** button. With the entire SQL statement selected, right-click anywhere in the design grid, and then click **Copy**.

8 **Close** the **FMLHourlyFeesDue** query. In the union query that you are building, right-click next to the insertion point, and then click **Paste**.

9 Click **Save**, type **FMLAllFeesDue** using your own initials, and then click **OK**.

10 In the **Navigation Pane**, notice the union query icon to the left of the query's name. In the **Results group**, click the **View arrow**, and notice that Design view is not available for this query.

11 **Run** the query, and then compare your results with Figure 10.35.

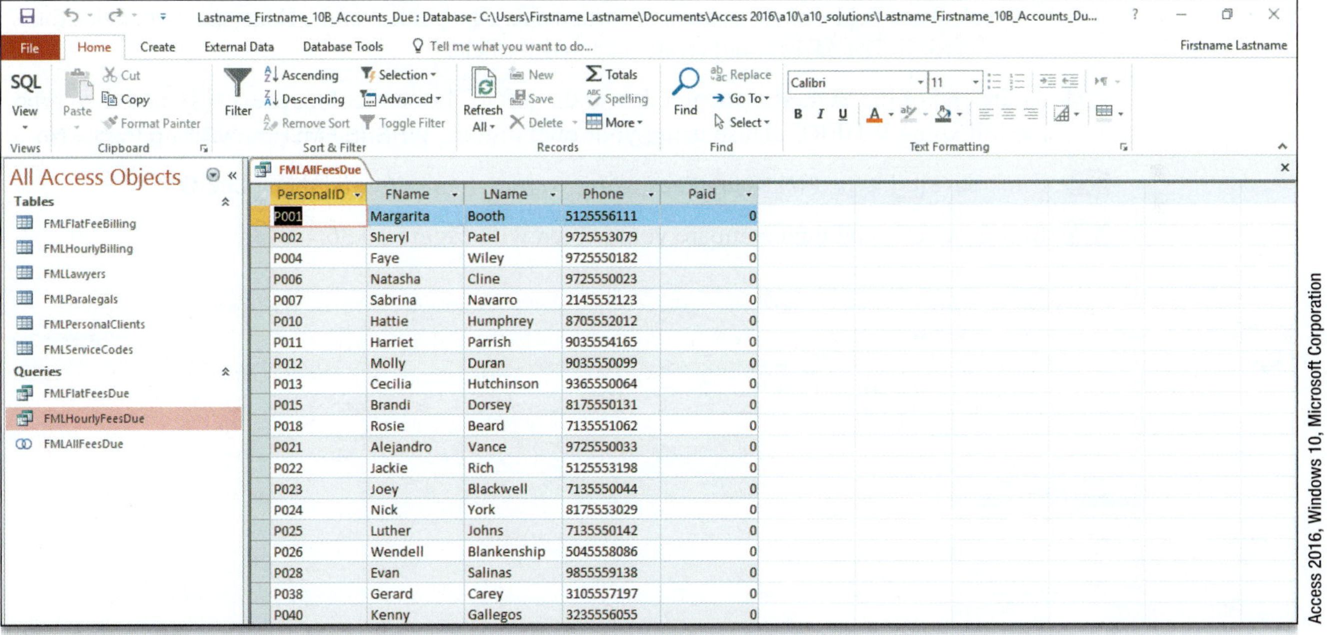

PersonalID	FName	LName	Phone	Paid
P001	Margarita	Booth	5125556111	0
P002	Sheryl	Patel	9725553079	0
P004	Faye	Wiley	9725550182	0
P006	Natasha	Cline	9725550023	0
P007	Sabrina	Navarro	2145552123	0
P010	Hattie	Humphrey	8705552012	0
P011	Harriet	Parrish	9035554165	0
P012	Molly	Duran	9035550099	0
P013	Cecilia	Hutchinson	9365550064	0
P015	Brandi	Dorsey	8175550131	0
P018	Rosie	Beard	7135551062	0
P021	Alejandro	Vance	9725550033	0
P022	Jackie	Rich	5125553198	0
P023	Joey	Blackwell	7135550044	0
P024	Nick	York	8175553029	0
P025	Luther	Johns	7135550142	0
P026	Wendell	Blankenship	5045558086	0
P028	Evan	Salinas	9855559138	0
P038	Gerard	Carey	3105557197	0
P040	Kenny	Gallegos	3235556055	0

Access 2016, Windows 10, Microsoft Corporation

FIGURE 10.35

12 If you are instructed to submit this result, create a paper printout or PDF electronic image of the query. Click **Save**, and then **Close** the query. **Close** the **Navigation Pane**.

Objective 10 Create Calculated Fields and SQL Aggregate Functions

SQL is a powerful language that does far more than create select queries. SQL provides commands to create calculated fields and summarize data using aggregate functions. Recall that an aggregate function performs a calculation on a column of data and returns a single value. When creating calculated fields, many developers prefer to work in SQL view because long expressions can be viewed without having to use the Zoom feature.

Activity 10.17 | Creating Calculated Fields in SQL

Loren-Renner Law Partners needs a list of total amounts due for the clients who were billed at an hourly rate. In this Activity, you will write an SQL statement with a field that calculates fees by multiplying the number of hours by the hourly rate.

1. On the **Create tab**, in the **Queries group**, click **Query Design**.

2. Use the displayed **Show Table** dialog box to add the **FMLPersonalClients** and **FMLHourlyBilling** tables, and then **Close** [×] the Show Table dialog box. Expand the field lists so all field names are displayed.

3. From the **FMLPersonalClients** table, add the **FName** field, and then add the **LName** field.

4. In the status bar, click the **SQL View** button [SQL].

   Starting this query in Design view saves you from having to type the SELECT, FROM, and INNER JOIN clauses.

5. To the right of the entire SELECT clause, type a comma, press Spacebar, and then type the following using your own initials: **FMLHourlyBilling.Hours * FMLHourlyBilling.Rate AS Fee**

   A calculated field with the caption *Fee* will display the product of the Hours and Rate fields for each record. The ***AS*** keyword creates captions for fields.

6. At the end of the SQL statement, click to the left of the semicolon, press Enter, and then type the following WHERE clause using your own initials: **WHERE FMLHourlyBilling.Paid = No**

7. Click **Save** [save icon], type **FMLHourlyFees** using your own initials, and then click **OK**.

8. **Run** the query, and then compare your screen with Figure 10.36.

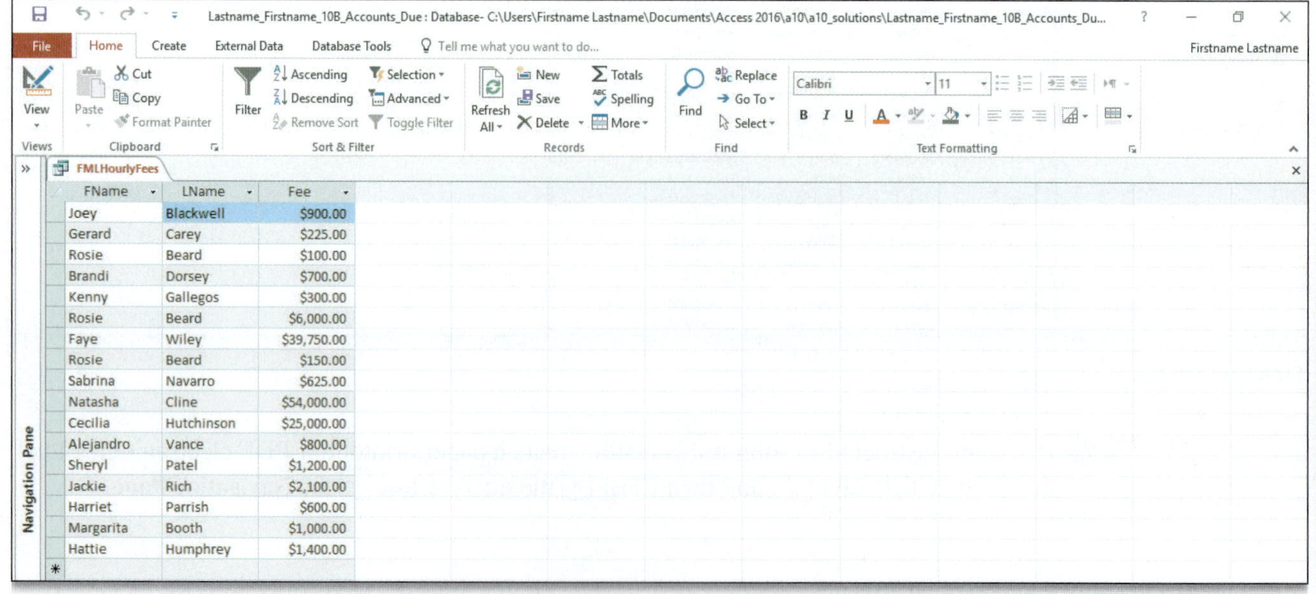

FIGURE 10.36

9 If you are instructed to submit this result, create a paper printout or PDF electronic image of the query. **Close** ☒ the query.

Activity 10.18 | Writing SQL Aggregate Functions

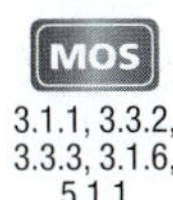

3.1.1, 3.3.2, 3.3.3, 3.1.6, 5.1.1

Loren-Renner Law Partners needs a report showing summary statistics for the amounts due from clients paying flat fees. In this Activity, you will use SQL aggregate functions to calculate summary statistics and then create a report based on the query.

1 On the **Create tab**, in the **Queries group**, click **Query Design**. **Close** ☒ the displayed **Show Table** dialog box. In the status bar, click the **SQL View** button SQL.

2 In the design grid, delete the semicolon, press Spacebar, and then, substituting *FML* with your own initials, type the following: **Count(FMLFlatFeeBilling.Fee) AS Count**

Count is an SQL aggregate function.

3 Press Enter, and then type the following FROM clause: **FROM FMLFlatFeeBilling**

4 Press Enter, and then type the following WHERE clause: **WHERE FMLFlatFeeBilling.Paid = No;**

5 Click **Save** 🖫, type **FMLFlatFeesStats** using your own initials, and then click **OK**.

6 Click **Run**, and then compare your screen with Figure 10.37.

The number of records in the query displays in a column that has *Count* as its caption.

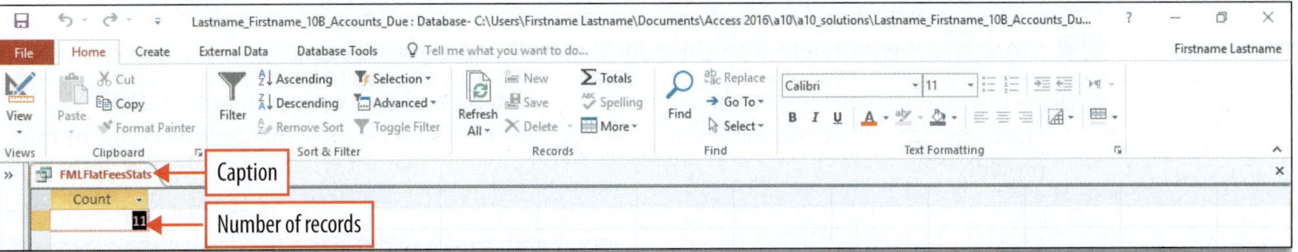

Access 2016, Windows 10, Microsoft Corporation

FIGURE 10.37

7 Return to **SQL View**. Click to the right of the entire **SELECT** clause, and then type a comma. Press Enter, and then type the following using your own initials: **Avg(FMLFlatFeeBilling.Fee) AS Average,** and then press Enter.

8 Continue adding to the SELECT clause by typing **Min(FMLFlatFeeBilling.Fee) AS Minimum,** and then press Enter. Type **Max(FMLFlatFeeBilling.Fee) AS Maximum,** and press Enter. Type **Sum(FMLFlatFeeBilling.Fee) AS [Total Flat Fees]**

Because Total Flat Fees contains spaces, it must be enclosed in square brackets. In Access SQL statements, any table name or field name that has spaces must be enclosed in square brackets. If there are no spaces, then the square brackets are optional. After [Total Flat Fees], no comma is needed because it is the end of the SELECT clause.

9 Compare your screen with Figure 10.38. **Save** 🖫 and then **Run** the query. Apply **Best Fit** so all data is visible.

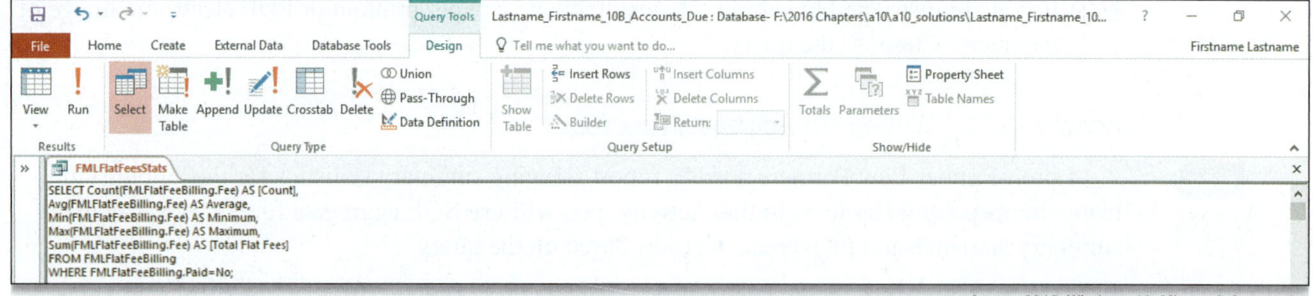

Access 2016, Windows 10, Microsoft Corporation

FIGURE 10.38

10 **Close** [X] the query, saving changes. **Open** [»] the **Navigation Pane**, and then click to select the **FMLFlatFeesStats** query. On the **Create tab**, in the **Reports group**, click **Report**.

11 Click anywhere in the **Total Flat Fees** column to select the column. Under **Report Layout Tools**, on the **Design tab**, in the **Grouping & Totals group**, click **Totals**, and then click **Sum** to remove the second displayed total for that column. Click the **Total** line, and then press Delete.

12 Delete the **Date** and **Time** boxes in the **Report Header**, and then delete the placeholders. Change the report's title to **Lastname Firstname Flat Fees Statistics** If necessary, resize the textbox so the title fits on one line. If you are instructed to submit this result, create a paper printout or PDF electronic image.

13 Click **Save** [save icon], and then accept the Report Name by clicking **OK**.

14 **Close** [X] the report, and then **Close** the database and **Close** Access.

15 As directed by your instructor, submit your database and the paper printouts or PDF electronic images of the three objects—two queries and a report—that are the result of this project.

END | You have completed Project 10B

GO! To Work

Andres Rodriguez/Fotolia; FotolEdhar/Fotolia; Andrey Popov/Fotolia; Shutterstock

10 ACCESS

MICROSOFT OFFICE SPECIALIST (MOS) SKILLS IN THIS CHAPTER	
PROJECT 10A	**PROJECT 10B**
1.1.4 Delete database objects	**2.2.4** Rename tables
1.2.2 Set the primary key	**3.1.1** Run a query
1.3.2 Create and modify a navigation form	**3.1.6** Save a query
1.3.3 Set a form as a startup option	**3.2.5** Sort data within queries
1.3.4 Display objects in the Navigation Pane	**3.3.1** Add calculated fields
1.4.1 Compact a database	**3.3.2** Set filtering criteria
1.4.2 Repair a database	**3.3.3** Group and summarize data
1.4.4 Split a database	**5.1.1** Create a report based on the query or table
1.4.5 Encrypt a database with a password	
1.5.3 Save a database as a template	
2.3.6 Sort records	
3.1.1 Run a query	
3.1.6 Save a query	

BUILD YOUR E-PORTFOLIO

An E-Portfolio is a collection of evidence, stored electronically, that showcases what you have accomplished while completing your education. Collecting and then sharing your work products with potential employees reflects your academic and career goals. Your completed documents from the following projects are good examples to show what you have learned: 10G, 10K, and 10L.

GO! FOR JOB SUCCESS

Discussion: Introverts

Your instructor may assign these questions to your class, and then ask you to think about them, or discuss them with your classmates:

Human beings generally lean one way or the other on the extroversion/introversion continuum. Extroverts are energized by groups, teams, and interaction; introverts are energized by quiet introspection, time to think, and deep focus on work.

The typical business culture is geared toward extroverts. Introverts may feel they have to hide their personalities to be successful, but this can inhibit the contributions they make. Some businesses have meetings with time for attendees to read materials, focusing everyone on the subject and giving everyone time to collect their thoughts.

FotolEdhar/Fotolia

What changes could be made to meetings to make introverts feel more comfortable sharing ideas?

Do you think you are an extrovert or an introvert, and how has this affected your participation in class assignments?

Do you notice the difference between introverts and extroverts? If so, what changes could you make so everyone feels comfortable?

END OF CHAPTER

SUMMARY

A navigation form is a form that displays navigational controls to display forms and reports in your database; it is useful for a web-based database where the Navigation Pane is not displayed.

Analysis tools improve performance. The Table Analyzer and Performance Analyzer analyze objects and offer improvement ideas. Viewing object dependencies protects the database before deleting objects.

Access Options customize database views, including the Navigation Pane. Using a locked-down ACCDE file format, a split database with the back end stored on a server, or a password provides security.

SQL provides more control and flexibility than Design view when designing queries, and more options. SQL can be used to join two queries in a union query, create calculated fields, and create statistics.

GO! LEARN IT ONLINE

Review the concepts, key terms, and MOS Skills in this chapter by completing these online challenges, which you can find at **MyITLab**.

Matching and Multiple Choice: Answer matching and multiple choice questions to test what you learned in this chapter.

Lessons on the GO!: Learn how to use all the new apps and features as they are introduced by Microsoft.

MOS Prep Quiz: Answer questions to review the MOS skills you have practiced in this chapter.

PROJECT GUIDE FOR ACCESS CHAPTER 10

Your instructor will assign Projects from this list to ensure your learning and assess your knowledge.

PROJECT GUIDE FOR ACCESS CHAPTER 10			
Project	**Apply Skills from These Chapter Objectives**	**Project Type**	**Project Location**
10A **MyITLab**	Objectives 1–6 from Project 10A	**10A Instructional Project (Grader Project)** Guided instruction to learn the skills in Project 10A.	In MyITLab and in text
10B **MyITLab**	Objectives 7–10 from Project 10B	**10B Instructional Project (Grader Project)** Guided instruction to learn the skills in Project 10B.	In MyITLab and in text
10C	Objectives 1–6 from Project 10A	**10C Skills Review (Scorecard Grading)** A guided review of the skills from Project 10A.	In text
10D	Objectives 7–10 from Project 10B	**10D Skills Review (Scorecard Grading)** A guided review of the skills from Project 10B.	In text
10E	Objectives 1–6 from Project 10A	**10E Mastery (Scorecard Grading) Mastery and Transfer of Learning** A demonstration of your mastery of the skills in Project 10A with extensive decision making.	In text
10F	Objectives 7–10 from Project 10B	**10F Mastery (Scorecard Grading) Mastery and Transfer of Learning** A demonstration of your mastery of the skills in Project 10B with extensive decision making.	In text
10G **MyITLab**	Combination of Objectives from Projects 10A and 10B	**10G Mastery (Grader Project) Mastery and Transfer of Learning** A demonstration of your mastery of the skills in Projects 10A and 10B with extensive decision making.	In MyITLab and in text
10H	Combination of Objectives from Projects 10A and 10B	**10H GO! Fix It (Scorecard Grading) Critical Thinking** A demonstration of your mastery of the skills in Projects 10A and 10B by creating a correct result from a document that contains errors you must find.	Instructor Resource Center (IRC) and MyITLab
10I	Combination of Objectives from Projects 10A and 10B	**10I GO! Make It (Scorecard Grading) Critical Thinking** A demonstration of your mastery of the skills in Projects 10A and 10B by creating a result from a supplied picture.	IRC and MyITLab
10J	Combination of Objectives from Projects 10A and 10B	**10J GO! Solve It (Rubric Grading) Critical Thinking** A demonstration of your mastery of the skills in Projects 10A and 10B, your decision-making skills, and your critical thinking skills. A task-specific rubric helps you self-assess your result.	IRC and MyITLab
10K	Combination of Objectives from Projects 10A and 10B	**10K GO! Solve It (Rubric Grading) Critical Thinking** A demonstration of your mastery of the skills in Projects 10A and 10B, your decision-making skills, and your critical thinking skills. A task-specific rubric helps you self-assess your result.	In text
10L	Combination of Objectives from Projects 10A and 10B	**10L GO! Think (Rubric Grading) Critical Thinking** A demonstration of your understanding of the chapter concepts applied in a manner that you would apply outside of college. An analytic rubric helps you and your instructor grade the quality of your work by comparing it to the work an expert in the discipline would create.	In text
10M	Combination of Objectives from Projects 10A and 10B	**10M GO! Think (Rubric Grading) Critical Thinking** A demonstration of your understanding of the chapter concepts applied in a manner that you would apply outside of college. An analytic rubric helps you and your instructor grade the quality of your work by comparing it to the work an expert in the discipline would create.	IRC and MyITLab
10N	Combination of Objectives from Projects 10A and 10B	**10N You and GO! (Rubric Grading) Critical Thinking** A demonstration of your understanding of the chapter concepts applied in a manner that you would apply in a personal situation. An analytic rubric helps you and your instructor grade the quality of your work.	IRC and MyITLab
Capstone Project for Access Chapters 7–10	Combination of Objectives from Projects 7A, 7B, 8A, 8B, 9A, 9B, 10A, and 10B	A demonstration of your mastery of the skills in Chapters 7–10 with extensive decision making. **(Grader Project)**	In IRC and MyITLab

GLOSSARY

GLOSSARY OF CHAPTER KEY TERMS

ACCDE file An Access file format that prevents individuals from creating or making design changes to forms, reports, and macros.

Application title The text that displays in the Access title bar when that database is open.

AS An SQL keyword that creates captions for fields.

Back end An Access database that consists of the database tables and their data. The back end is typically placed on a server and is not directly seen by the end user.

Compact & Repair A process where an Access file is rewritten to store the objects and data more efficiently.

Decrypt An action that removes a file's encryption or unsets a password.

Dependency An object that requires, or is dependent on, another database object.

DISTINCT An SQL keyword that returns only a single instance of any duplicate values in query results.

Encrypt A process to hide data by making the file unreadable until the correct password is entered.

FROM clause An SQL statement that lists which tables hold the fields used in the SELECT clause.

Front end An Access database that includes the database forms, queries, reports, and macros. The end users open the front end to work with the data stored in the back-end tables.

Indeterminate relationship A relationship that does not enforce referential integrity.

JOIN clause An SQL statement that defines the join type for a query.

Keywords Commands built into the SQL programming language.

Microsoft SQL Server A database application designed for high-end business uses.

Navigation form A form that displays navigational controls that enable you to display forms and reports in your database.

Navigation Pane category A top-level listing that displays when the Navigation Pane arrow is clicked.

Navigation Pane group A second-level listing that displays when a Navigation Pane category is selected.

Office background A small graphic in the upper-right corner of the Access application window used to personalize Office 2016.

ON An SQL keyword that is used to specify which field is common to two tables.

Open Exclusive An option that opens the database so that changes can be made, but no one else may open the database at the same time.

Open Exclusive Read-Only An option that opens the database in both Exclusive and Read-Only modes.

Open Read-Only An option that opens the database so that all objects can be opened and viewed, but data and design changes cannot be made.

Performance Analyzer A wizard that analyzes database objects, and then offers suggestions for improving them.

SELECT clause An SQL statement that lists which fields the query should display.

Split database An Access database that is split into two files—one containing the back end and one containing the front end.

SQL (Structured Query Language) A language used by many database programs to view, update, and query data in relational databases.

SQL statement An expression that defines the SQL commands that should be performed when the query is run.

Strong password A password that is very difficult to guess that may include upper-and lowercase letters, numbers, and special characters.

Table Analyzer A wizard that searches for repeated data in a table, and then splits the table into two or more related tables.

UNION An SQL keyword that is used to combine one or more queries in a union query.

Union query A query type that combines the results of two or more similar select queries.

Weak password A password that is easy to guess.

WHERE clause An SQL statement that defines the criteria that should be applied when a query is run.

Skills Review Project 10C Paralegals

Apply 10A skills from these Objectives:

1. Create a Navigation Form
2. Use Microsoft Access Analysis Tools
3. Modify Access Views and Behaviors
4. Use the Database Splitter
5. Encrypt and Decrypt Databases
6. Create a Locked Database (ACCDE File)

Loren-Renner Law Partners wants to secure the database tables used by its paralegals. You will encrypt the database using a secure password, create a locked ACCDE file, and split the database to allow Human Resources to design separate front-end databases to be used by various departments. Your completed documents will look like those shown in Figure 10.39.

PROJECT FILES

For Project 10C, you will need the following files:

a10C_Paralegals
a10C_Icon

You will save your files as:

Lastname_Firstname_10C_Paralegals
Lastname_Firstname_10C_Screens
Lastname_Firstname_10C_Paralegals_ACCDE
Lastname_Firstname_10C_Paralegals_be

PROJECT RESULTS

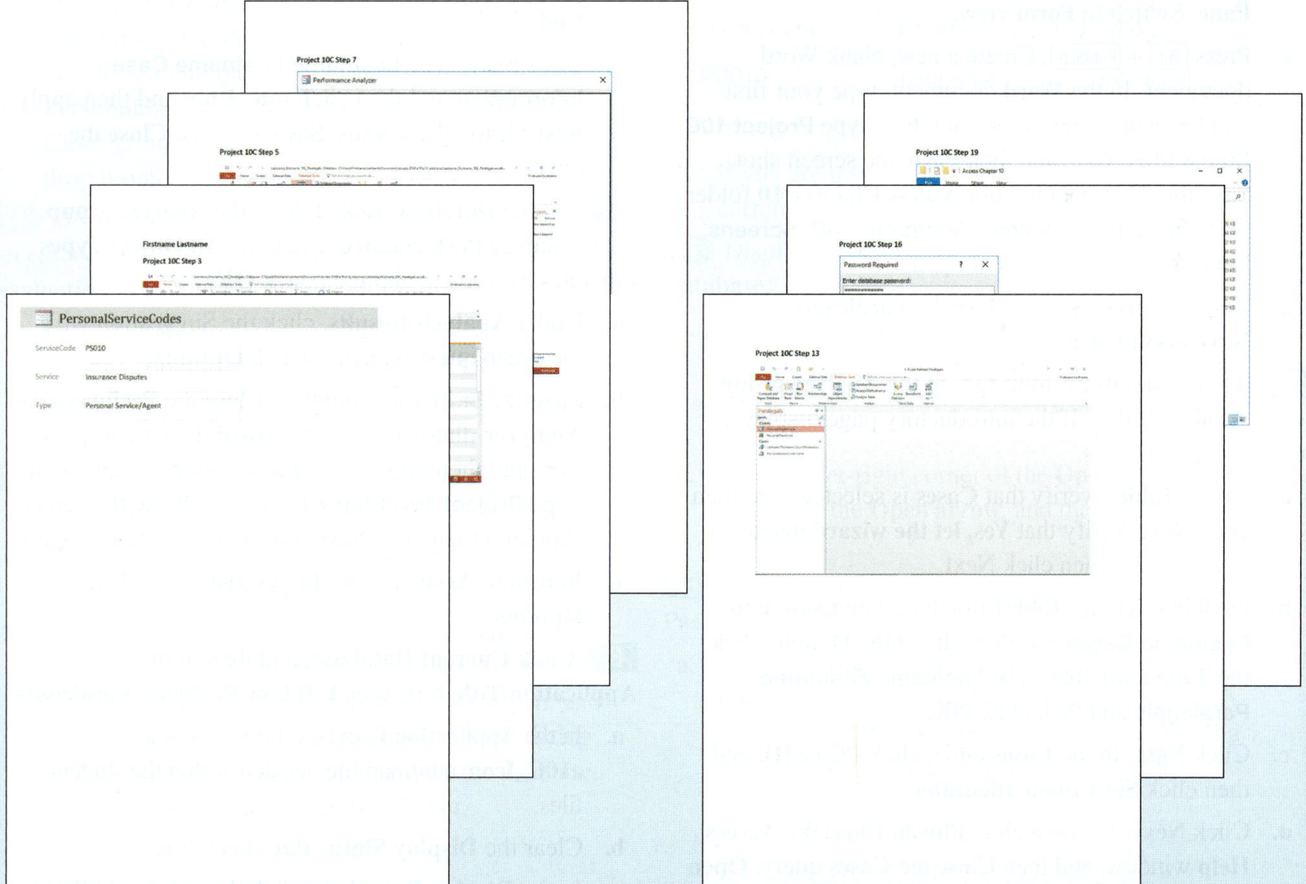

FIGURE 10.39

(Project 10C Paralegals continues on the next page)

CONTENT-BASED ASSESSMENTS (MASTERY AND TRANSFER OF LEARNING)

Apply 10A skills from these Objectives:

1. Create a Navigation Form
2. Use Microsoft Access Analysis Tools
3. Modify Access Views and Behaviors
4. Use the Database Splitter
5. Encrypt and Decrypt Databases
6. Create a Locked Database (ACCDE File)

Mastering Access Project 10E Accountants

Loren-Renner Law Partners wants to secure the databases used by its accounting and marketing departments. You will also create a new workgroup information file for the database used by the marketing department. Your results will look similar to that shown in Figure 10.41.

PROJECT FILES

For Project 10E, you will need the following files:

a10E_Accountants
a10E_Icon

You will save your files as:

Lastname_Firstname_10E_Accountants
Lastname_Firstname_10E_Screens
Lastname_Firstname_10E_Accountants_be
Lastname_Firstname_10E_ACCDE

PROJECT RESULTS

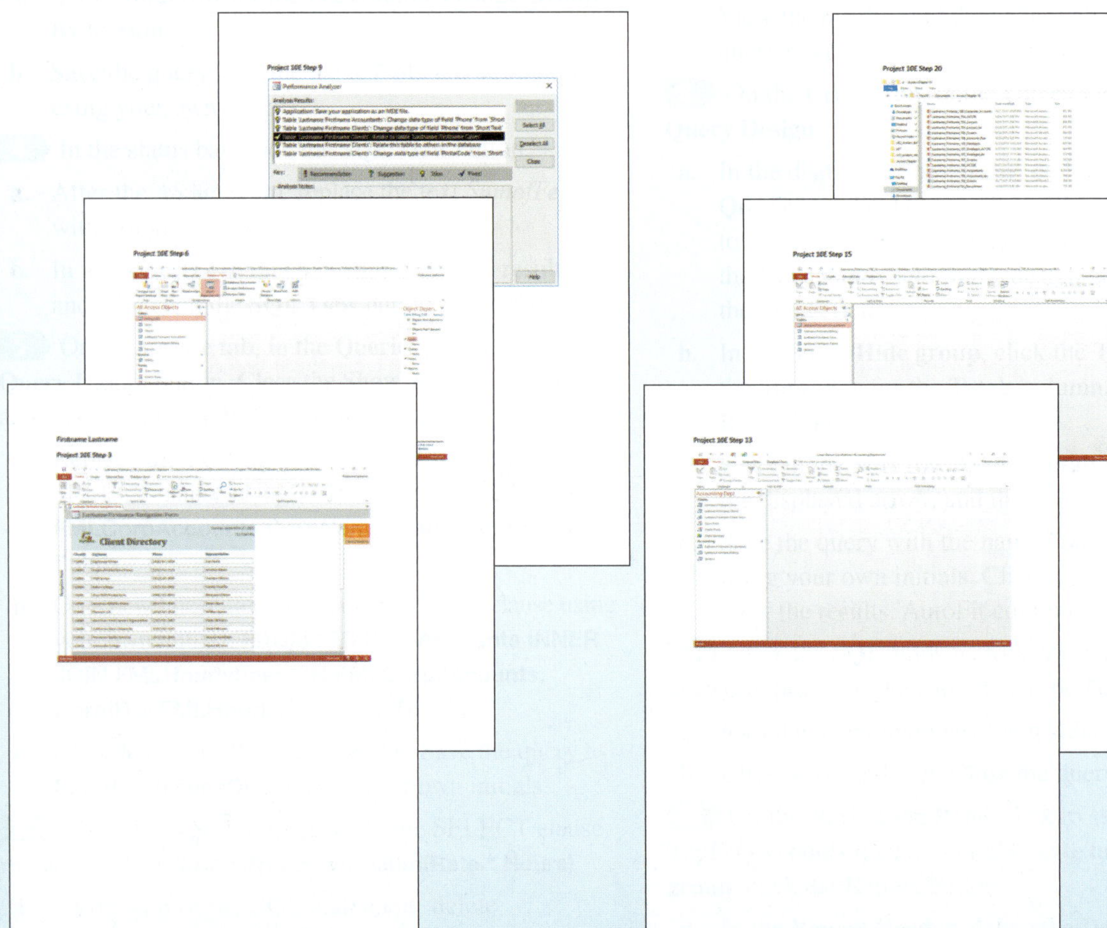

FIGURE 10.41

Access 2016, Windows 10, Microsoft Corporation

(Project 10E Accountants continues on the next page)

Mastering Access Project 10E Accountants (continued)

1 Start Access. Locate and open the **a10E_Accountants** file. **Save** the database in the **Access Chapter 10** folder as **Lastname_Firstname_10E_Accountants** If necessary, enable content.

2 Create a navigation form, **Vertical Tabs, Right**. If the Field List displays, close it. Add the **Cases Form**, **Clients Form**, and **Client Directory** to the navigation form. Edit the title to read **Lastname Firstname Navigation Form Save** the navigation form as **Lastname Firstname Navigation Form**

3 **Close** the **Navigation Pane**. Switch to **Form** view. Press Alt + PrintScrn. **Close** the **Navigation Form**. Create a new, blank Word document. In the **Word** document, type your first and last names, press Enter, and then type **Project 10E Step 3** Press Enter, and then **Paste** the screen shot. **Save** the document in your **Access Chapter 10** folder with the name **Lastname_Firstname_10E_Screens** Leave the Word document open.

4 Use the **Table Analyzer wizard** to analyze the **Billing** table. Have the wizard decide how to split the table, and then rename the suggested tables as follows:

Suggested Table	New Name
Table1	**Lastname Firstname Billing**
Table2	**Lastname Firstname Accountants**

5 In the **Billing** table, set **InvoiceID** as the **unique identifier**. Choose the option to create the query, and then **Finish** the wizard. **Close** the **Help** window, and **Close** the query.

6 Display all database objects that depend on the **Billing_OLD** table. Press Alt + PrintScrn, and then **Close** the **Object Dependencies** pane. In the **Word** document, press Enter, and then press Ctrl + Enter to insert a page break. Type **Project 10E Step 6** Press Enter, and then **Paste** the screen shot. **Save** the document.

7 Delete the **Billing_OLD** table. Rename the **Clients** table as **Lastname Firstname Clients** Rename the **Cases** table as **Lastname Firstname Cases**

8 Start a new query in **Query Design** view, and then add the **Clients** and **Cases** tables to the query. Resize the field lists so all fields and table names are visible. From the **Clients** table, add the **OrgName** field. From the **Cases** table, add the **CaseID** and **Closed?** fields. Create an indeterminate relationship between the **ClientID** field in the **Clients** table and the **Client** field in the **Cases** table, if necessary. Save the query as **Lastname Firstname Client-Cases Run** and then **Close** the query.

9 Run the **Performance Analyzer** wizard for **All Object Types**. Optimize the item with the **Suggestion** icon. Press Alt + PrintScrn, and then **Close** the dialog box. In the **Word** document, press Enter, and then press Ctrl + Enter to insert a page break. Type **Project 10E Step 9** Press Enter, **Paste** the screen shot, and then click **Save**.

10 Display **Backstage** view, display the **Access Options** dialog box. Under **Current Database**, change the **Application Title** to **Loren-Renner Law Partners Accounting Department** For the **Application Icon**, assign the bitmap **a10E_Icon**. Display the **Navigation Form**, and disable **Layout** view.

11 Edit the following **Navigation Pane** options: add a new item named **Accounting Dept** and then add two new groups: one named **Clients** and one named **Accounting** **Close** and then **Open** the database. In the **Navigation Pane**, display the **Accounting Dept** category. Drag the **Cases** and **Clients** tables into the **Clients** category. Drag the **Client-Cases** query into the **Clients** category. Drag the **Cases Form** and **Clients Form** into the **Clients** category. Drag the **Client Directory** report into the **Clients** category. Drag the **Accountants**, **Billing**, and **Services** tables into the **Accounting** category. Using the **Navigation** options, do not display Unassigned Objects in the Navigation Pane when the Accounting Dept category is selected. **Close** and then **Open** the database.

12 For the current database only, add the following commands to the Quick Access Toolbar: **Import Access database**, **Import Excel spreadsheet**, and **Open**.

13 Close all open dialog boxes and database objects. Press Alt + PrintScrn. In the **Word** document, press Enter, and then insert a page break. Type **Project 10E Step 13** Press Enter, **Paste** the screen shot, and then click **Save**.

14 Split the database into a back-end and front-end file. Save the back-end file in your **Access Chapter 10** folder with the name suggested by Access. **Close** the database.

15 Open **10E_Accountants_be**. Adjust the width of the **Navigation Pane** so all object names display fully. Press Alt + PrintScrn, and then **Close** the database. In the **Word** document, press Enter, and then insert a page break. Type **Project 10E Step 15** Press Enter, and then **Paste** the screen shot. **Save** the document.

(Project 10E Accountants continues on the next page)

CONTENT-BASED ASSESSMENTS (MASTERY AND TRANSFER OF LEARNING)

Mastering Access Project 10E Accountants (continued)

16 Open **10E_Accountants** using the **Open Exclusive** command. Encrypt the database using the password **GO!10EAccess** Click **OK**, and then **Close** the database.

17 Open **10E_Accountants** using the password. Create a secure ACCDE version of the database file. Save the ACCDE file in your **Access Chapter 10** folder as **Lastname_Firstname_10E_ACCDE**

18 **Close** the database, and **Close** Access.

19 Open **File Explorer**, and then open your **Access Chapter 10** folder. If necessary, maximize the File Explorer window and switch to Details view. Verify that all the files created in this project display and that the columns are wide enough to display all of the Name and Type descriptions. Press Alt + PrintScrn, and then **Close** File Explorer.

20 In the **Word** document, press Enter, and then press Ctrl + Enter to insert a page break. Type **Project 10E Step 20** Press Enter, **Paste** the screen shot, and then click **Save**. If you are instructed to submit this result, create a paper printout or PDF electronic image of the Word document.

21 As directed by your instructor, submit your databases and the printout or PDF electronic image of the Word document that is the result of this project. Specifically, in this project, using your own name you created the following databases and printout or PDF electronic image:

1. Lastname_Firstname_10E_Accountants	Database file
2. Lastname_Firstname_10E_Screens	Word document
3. Lastname_Firstname_10E_Accountants_be	Back-end database file
4. Lastname_Firstname_10E_ACCDE	Locked database file

END | You have completed Project 10E

Apply 10B skills from these Objectives:

7 Modify a Query in SQL View

8 Create a Query in SQL View

9 Create a Union Query Using SQL

10 Create Calculated Fields and SQL Aggregate Functions

Mastering Access Project 10F Legal Services

Loren-Renner Law Partners wants a report that describes the various services that it provides to corporations and organizations. To build the report, you will create two queries using SQL view. You will join the two queries into a single query. You will then create a query that summarizes the data in the union query and build the report from this query. Your completed report will look similar to the report shown in Figure 10.42.

PROJECT FILES

For Project 10F, you will need the following file:

a10F_Legal_Services

You will save your database as:

Lastname_Firstname_10F_Legal_Services

PROJECT RESULTS

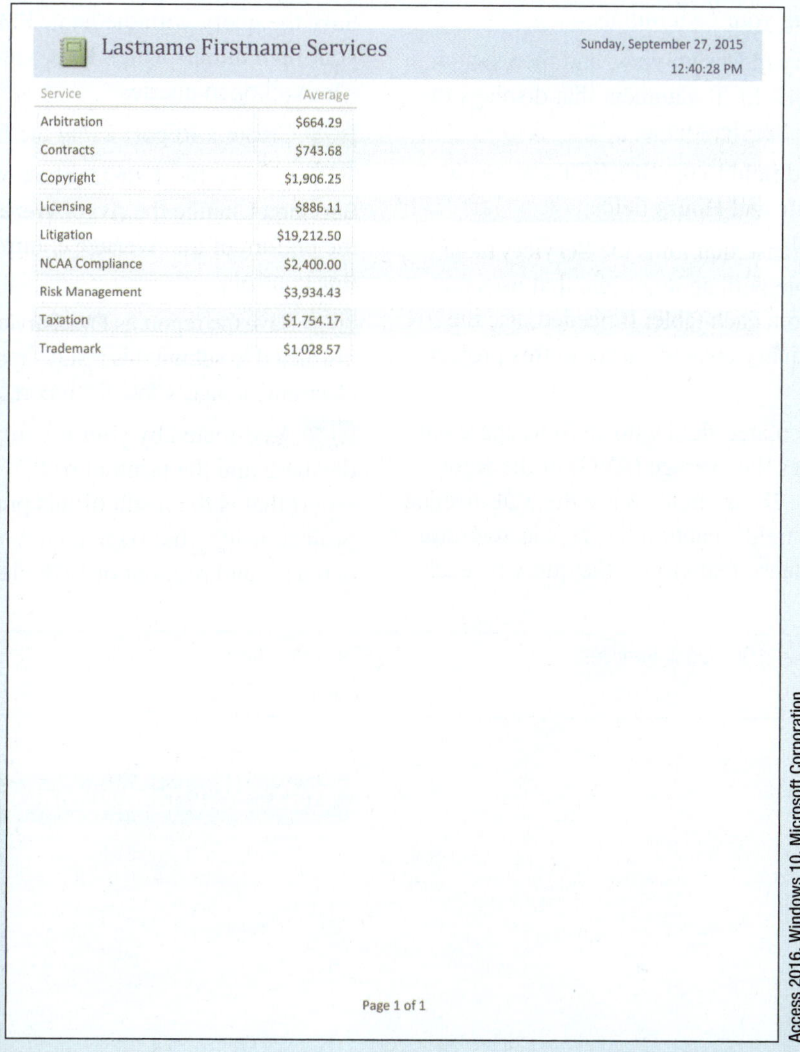

Lastname Firstname Services

Sunday, September 27, 2015
12:40:28 PM

Service	Average
Arbitration	$664.29
Contracts	$743.68
Copyright	$1,906.25
Licensing	$886.11
Litigation	$19,212.50
NCAA Compliance	$2,400.00
Risk Management	$3,934.43
Taxation	$1,754.17
Trademark	$1,028.57

Page 1 of 1

FIGURE 10.42

(Project 10F Legal Services continues on the next page)

Mastering Access | Project 10F Legal Services (continued)

1 Start Access. Locate and open the **a10F_Legal_Services** file. **Save** the database in the **Access Chapter 10** folder as **Lastname_Firstname_10F_Legal_Services** Enable content, if necessary. At the beginning of each table name, add **FML** using your own initials and no space.

2 Start a new query in **Design** view. Add the **Services** and **FlatFees** tables to the query. If necessary, expand the field lists to display all field names. From the **Services** table, add the **Service** field to the design grid. From the **FlatFees** table, add the **Fee** field.

3 In the **Show/Hide group**, click **Totals**. In the **Total** row for the **Fee** column, change **Group By** to **Avg**.

4 In **SQL** view, adapt the SELECT statement so that the calculated field's caption will display as **Average** **Run** the query and view the results. **Save** the query as **FMLFlatServices** using your own initials.

5 Start a new query in **Design** view, and then switch to **SQL** view. Add a SELECT statement that displays the *Service* field from the **Services** table.

6 Add a calculated field to the SELECT statement that multiplies the **Rate** and **Hours** fields.

7 Add a **FROM** clause that joins the **Services** table to the **HourlyFees** table with an inner join that uses the **ServiceCode** fields from each table. If needed, use the FROM clause in the query created earlier in this project as your reference.

8 Replace the calculated field with an SQL aggregate function that calculates the average (AVG) of the **Rate** field multiplied by the **Hours** field. Write the SQL needed so that the calculated field's caption displays as **Average** Add a GROUP BY clause that groups the query by each **Service**. If needed, use the query created earlier in this project as your reference.

9 **Run** the query and view the results. **Save** the query as **FMLHourlyServices** using your own initials.

10 Create a new **Union** query. **Copy** and **Paste** the SQL from the two queries created earlier and join them using the UNION keyword. **Run** the query, view the results, and then **Save** the query as **FMLServicesUnion** using your own initials.

11 Create a new query in **Design** view. In the displayed **Show Table** dialog box, click the **Queries tab**, add the **ServicesUnion** query, and then **Close** the dialog box. Add the **Service** field to the design grid, and then add the **Average** field.

12 In the **Show/Hide group**, click **Totals**. In the **Total** row for the **Average** column, change **Group By** to **Avg**. **Save** the query with the name **FMLServicesQuery** using your own initials. Click **Run**, view the results, and then **Close** all open queries.

13 Create a **Report** using the **ServicesQuery** query.

14 Change the **Title** text box to **Lastname Firstname Services** Change the **AvgofAverage** label to **Average** At the bottom of the **Average** column, delete the **total** and **line** controls.

15 **Save** the report as **FMLServicesReport**. If you are instructed to submit this result, create a paper printout or PDF electronic image. **Close** the report, and then **Exit** Access.

16 As directed by your instructor, submit your database and the printout or PDF electronic image of the report that is the result of this project. Specifically, in this project, using your own name you created the following database and printout or PDF electronic image:

1. Lastname_Firstname_10F_Legal_Services	Database file
2. FMLServicesReport	Report

END | You have completed Project 10F

Apply 10A and 10B skills from these Objectives:

1 Create a Navigation Form
2 Use Microsoft Access Analysis Tools
3 Modify Access Views and Behaviors
4 Use the Database Splitter
5 Encrypt and Decrypt Databases
6 Create a Locked Database (ACCDE File)
7 Modify a Query in SQL View
8 Create a Query in SQL View
9 Create a Union Query Using SQL
10 Create Calculated Fields and SQL Aggregate Functions

Mastering Access Project 10G Bonuses

The two lead partners, Alex Loren and David Renner, need to secure the front end of the database with a password before creating a confidential query that lists the lawyers who have generated the most business. You will create two queries using SQL view, join them in a union query, and then build another query summarizing the union query. Your completed report will look similar to Figure 10.43.

NOTE Project 10G Differs from the MyITLab Project

If you are completing this project in the MyITLab Grader system, your results will differ from the following project. In Grader the steps are all completed with one solution file instead of two in the project below.

PROJECT FILES

For Project 10G, you will need the following file:

a10G_Bonuses

You will save your files as:

Lastname_Firstname_10G_Bonuses
Lastname_Firstname_10G_Bonuses_be

PROJECT RESULTS

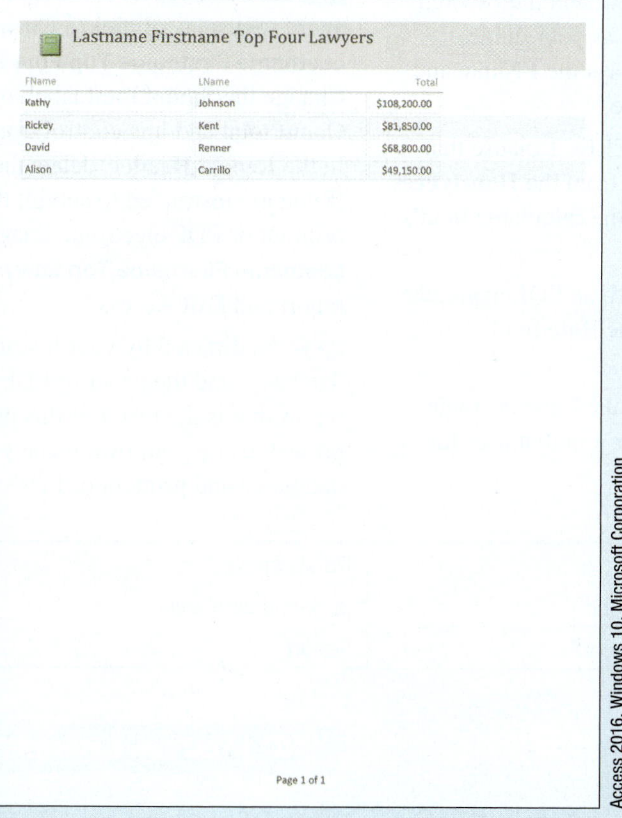

Lastname Firstname Top Four Lawyers

FName	LName	Total
Kathy	Johnson	$108,200.00
Rickey	Kent	$81,850.00
David	Renner	$68,800.00
Alison	Carrillo	$49,150.00

Page 1 of 1

Access 2016, Windows 10, Microsoft Corporation

FIGURE 10.43

(Project 10G Bonuses continues on the next page)

Mastering Access Project 10G Bonuses (continued)

1 Start Access. Locate and then open the **a10G_Bonuses** database. **Save** the database in your **Access Chapter 10** folder as **Lastname_Firstname_10G_Bonuses** At the beginning of each table name, add **FML** using your own initials and no space.

2 **Split** the database using the name Access suggests for the back end to save it in your **Access Chapter 10** folder.

3 **Close** the database. **Open** it again in **Exclusive mode**, and then encrypt it using the password **10GBonusGO!** If a message box displays, click **OK**.

4 Start a new query in **Design** view. Add the **Lawyers** and **FlatFees** tables to the query, expanding the field lists as necessary. From the **Lawyers** table, add the **FName** and **LName** fields to the design grid. From the **FlatFees** table, add the **Fee** field.

5 In the **Show/Hide group**, click **Totals**. In the **Total** row for the **Fee** column, change **Group By** to **Sum**.

6 In **SQL** view, change the caption for the calculated field to **Total Run** the query and view the results. **Save** the query as **FMLFlatFeesQuery** using your own initials.

7 Start a new query in **Design** view, and then switch to **SQL** view. Using the earlier query as your guide, write a SELECT statement that displays the **FName** and **LName** fields from the **Lawyers** table.

8 Add a calculated field to the SELECT clause that multiplies the **Rate** and **Hours** fields from the **HourlyFees** table. Write the SQL needed so that the calculated field's caption displays as **Total**

9 Replace the calculated field with an SQL aggregate function that calculates the sum of the **Rate** field multiplied by the **Hours** field.

10 Add a FROM clause that joins the **Lawyers** table to the **HourlyFees** table with an inner join that uses the **LawyerID** fields from each table.

11 Copy the GROUP BY clause from **FlatFeesQuery** and **Paste** it into the current query. **Run** the query and view the results. **Save** the query as **FMLHourlyFeesQuery** using your own initials.

12 Create a new **Union** query. **Copy** and **Paste** the SQL statements from the two queries created earlier and join them using the UNION keyword. **Run** the query, view the results, and then **Save** the query as **FMLUnion** using your own initials. **Close** all open queries.

13 Create a new query in **Design** view, add the **Union** query, and then add the **FName**, **LName**, and **Total** fields to the design grid. Add the **Total** row to the design grid, and then in the **Total** row for the **Total** column, change **Group By** to **Sum**.

14 In the **Total** column, change the **Sort** row value to **Descending**. Display the **Property Sheet**, and then, on the **General** tab, change the **Format** to **Currency**.

15 In **SQL** view, after SELECT, add the **TOP 4** keyword. **Save** the query as **FMLTopLawyers** using your own initials. **Run** the query, and then **Close** the query.

16 Create a report based on the **FMLTopLawyers** query to display all fields. Change the report title to read **Lastname Firstname Top Four Lawyers** on one line. Change the **SumofTotal** label to read **Total** Remove the **Count** total and line control from under the **FName** field. In the **Report Header**, delete the **date** and **time** controls. If you are instructed to submit this result, create a paper printout or PDF electronic image. **Save** the report as **Lastname Firstname Top Lawyers Report** **Close** the report and **Exit** Access.

17 As directed by your instructor, submit your databases and the paper or PDF electronic image of the report that is the result of this project. Specifically, in this project, using your own name you created the following databases and printout or PDF electronic image:

1. Lastname_Firstname_10G_Bonuses	Database file
2. Lastname_Firstname_10G_Bonuses_be	Back-end database
3. Lastname Firstname Top Lawyers Report	Report

END | You have completed Project 10G

Apply a combination of the 10A and 10B skills.

CONTENT-BASED ASSESSMENTS (CRITICAL THINKING)

GO! Fix It — Project 10H Annual Dinner — MyITLab

GO! Make It — Project 10I Professional Seminars — MyITLab

GO! Solve It — Project 10J Law Library — MyITLab

GO! Solve It — Project 10K Contracts

PROJECT FILES

For Project 10K, you will need the following file:

a10K_Contracts

You will save your files as:

Lastname_Firstname_10K_Contracts
Lastname_Firstname_10K_Screen

Open **a10K_Contracts**, and save it as **Lastname_Firstname_10K_Contracts** At the beginning of each table name, add **FML** using your own initials.

Create a Navigation Form using a Horizontal tab style. Add the form and both reports to the Navigation Form. Edit the title to read **Lastname Firstname Navigation Form** Save the form using the same name. Close the Navigation Pane, switch to Form view, and capture the screen. Paste it into a Word document saved as **Lastname_Firstname_10K_Screen** If you are instructed to submit this result, create a paper printout or PDF electronic image of the Word document.

Using SQL, create a query that lists personal clients who have cases listed in the *Cases* table. List only the clients where the *ServiceCode* is equal to SC08. Include the *Name*, *Street*, *City*, *State*, and *PostalCode* fields. Add the necessary SQL command so that clients are not listed more than one time in the query's results. Save the query as **FMLPersonalQuery** using your own initials.

Using SQL, create a query that lists corporate clients who have cases listed in the *Cases* table. List only the clients where the *ServiceCode* is equal to SC08. Include the *CompanyName*, *Street*, *City*, *State*, and *PostalCode* fields. Add the necessary SQL command so that clients are not listed more than one time in the query's results. Save the query as **FMLCorporateQuery** using your own initials.

Create a union query that combines the two queries. Save the query as **FMLAllClients** using your own initials. If you are instructed to submit this result, create a paper printout or PDF electronic image of the query.

Submit the database and the paper or PDF electronic images of the report that result of this project as directed by your instructor.

(Project 10K Contracts continues on the next page)

CONTENT-BASED ASSESSMENTS (CRITICAL THINKING)

GO! Solve It Project 10K Contracts (continued)

Performance Level

Performance Criteria	Exemplary: You consistently applied the relevant skills	Proficient: You sometimes, but not always, applied the relevant skills	Developing: You rarely or never applied the relevant skills
Create Contracts Navigation Form	Form created with correct tabs and title.	Form created with no more than two missing elements.	Form created with more than two missing elements.
Create PersonalQuery using SQL	Query created with correct syntax and format.	Query created with no more than two missing elements.	Query created with more than two missing elements.
Create CorporateQuery using SQL	Query created with correct syntax and format.	Query created with no more than two missing elements.	Query created with more than two missing elements.
Create AllClients union query using SQL	Query created with correct syntax and format.	Query created with no more than two missing elements.	Query created with more than two missing elements.

END | You have completed Project 10K

OUTCOMES-BASED ASSESSMENTS (CRITICAL THINKING)

RUBRIC

The following outcomes-based assessments are open-ended assessments. That is, there is no specific correct result; your result will depend on your approach to the information provided. Make Professional Quality your goal. Use the following scoring rubric to guide you in how to approach the problem and then to evaluate how well your approach solves the problem.

The *criteria*—Software Mastery, Content, Format and Layout, and Process—represent the knowledge and skills you have gained that you can apply to solving the problem. The *levels of performance*—Professional Quality, Approaching Professional Quality, or Needs Quality Improvements—help you and your instructor evaluate your result.

	Your completed project is of Professional Quality if you:	Your completed project is Approaching Professional Quality if you:	Your completed project Needs Quality Improvements if you:
1-Software Mastery	Choose and apply the most appropriate skills, tools, and features and identify efficient methods to solve the problem.	Choose and apply some appropriate skills, tools, and features, but not in the most efficient manner.	Choose inappropriate skills, tools, or features, or are inefficient in solving the problem.
2-Content	Construct a solution that is clear and well organized, contains content that is accurate, appropriate to the audience and purpose, and is complete. Provide a solution that contains no errors of spelling, grammar, or style.	Construct a solution in which some components are unclear, poorly organized, inconsistent, or incomplete. Misjudge the needs of the audience. Have some errors in spelling, grammar, or style, but the errors do not detract from comprehension.	Construct a solution that is unclear, incomplete, or poorly organized, contains some inaccurate or inappropriate content, and contains many errors of spelling, grammar, or style. Do not solve the problem.
3-Format and Layout	Format and arrange all elements to communicate information and ideas, clarify function, illustrate relationships, and indicate relative importance.	Apply appropriate format and layout features to some elements, but not others. Overuse features, causing minor distraction.	Apply format and layout that does not communicate information or ideas clearly. Do not use format and layout features to clarify function, illustrate relationships, or indicate relative importance. Use available features excessively, causing distraction.
4-Process	Use an organized approach that integrates planning, development, self-assessment, revision, and reflection.	Demonstrate an organized approach in some areas, but not others; or, use an insufficient process of organization throughout.	Do not use an organized approach to solve the problem.

Apply a combination of the 10A and 10B skills.

OUTCOMES-BASED ASSESSMENTS (CRITICAL THINKING)

GO! Think Project 10L Case History

PROJECT FILES

For Project 10L, you will need the following files:

a10L_Case_History
a10L_Icon

You will save your files as:

Lastname_Firstname_10L_Case_History
Lastname_Firstname_10L_ACCDE
Lastname_Firstname_10L_Screen

Loren-Renner Law Partners needs to secure the database containing a list of past cases. Open **a10L_Case_History** and save it as **Lastname_Firstname_10L_Case_History** Create an ACCDE file named **Lastname_Firstname_10L_ACCDE** At the beginning of each table name, add **FML** using your own initials. Customize the Access Options so the Application Title **L-R Case History** displays along with the **a10L_Icon**. Add the Open and Close Database icons to the Quick Access Toolbar for this database only. Capture the screen and paste it into a Word document named **Lastname_Firstname_10L_Screen** If you are instructed to submit this result, create a paper printout or PDF electronic image of the Word document.

Using SQL, create a query that lists corporate clients who have past cases listed in the *Cases* table. List only the client name and how many cases they have had. Group the data by *CompanyName*, and then display the count as **PastCases** Save the query as **FMLHistory** using your own initials. If you are instructed to submit this result, create a paper printout or PDF electronic image of the query.

Submit the project as directed by your instructor.

END | You have completed Project 10L

GO! Think Project 10M Phone List MyITLab

Build from Scratch

You and GO! Project 10N Club Directory MyITLab

Appendix

MICROSOFT OFFICE SPECIALIST ACCESS 2016			
Obj Number	**Objective Text**	**GO! Activity**	**Page Number**
1.0 Create and Manage a Database			
1.1	**Create and Modify Databases**		
1.1.1	create a blank desktop database	1.02	61
1.1.2	create a database from a template	1.18	97
1.1.3	create a database by using import objects or data from other sources	2.18, 9.07	167, 635
1.1.4	delete database objects	10.04	689
1.2	**Manage Relationships and Keys**		
1.2.1	create and modify relationships	2.03, 2.19	141, 169
1.2.2	set the primary key	2.18, 4.03, 9.02, 9.03, 10.02	167, 302, 623, 629, 685
1.2.3	enforce referential integrity	2.04, 2.19	144, 169
1.2.4	set foreign keys	2.03, 2.19	141, 169
1.2.5	view relationships	3.01, 3.16, 5.15, 5.16, 5.18, 7.04, 7.09	223, 251, 395, 398, 401, 503, 520
1.3	**Navigate through a Database**		
1.3.1	navigate specific records	4.07, 4.08	308, 310
1.3.2	create and modify a navigation form	10.01	683
1.3.3	set a form as the startup option	10.07	694
1.3.4	display objects in the Navigation Pane	1.21, 5.13, 10.08	103, 390, 695
1.3.5	change views of objects	1.08, 1.10, 2.13, 2.18, 2.21, 2.22, 2.23, 2.24, 2.26, 2.28, 2.29, 2.30, 2.31, 4.03, 4.09, 4.11, 5.01, 5.02, 5.03, 5.04, 5.12, 5.13, 5.15, 5.16, 5.17, 5.18, 5.19, 6.02, 6.03, 6.04, 6.05, 6.06, 6.07, 6.08, 6.09, 6.10, 6.12, 6.15, 6.16, 6.17, 6.18, 7.06, 7.07, 7.08, 7.10, 7.11, 7.12, 7.13, 7.15, 8.02, 8.05, 8.06, 8.11	72, 75, 155, 167, 171, 172, 174, 175, 178, 181, 182, 183, 185, 302, 312, 315, 365, 369, 371, 374, 389, 390, 395, 398, 399, 401, 403, 433, 435, 436, 440, 441, 443, 444, 446, 447, 454, 458, 460, 462, 464, 508, 512, 515, 522, 524, 526, 530, 532, 567, 576, 579, 592
1.4	**Protect and Maintain Databases**		
1.4.1	compact a database	10.07	694
1.4.2	repair a database	10.07	694
1.4.3	back up a database	4.01	299
1.4.4	split a database	10.09	698
1.4.5	encrypt a database with a password	10.10	701
1.4.6	recover data from backup	4.01, 9.07	299, 635

1.5	**Print and Export Data**		
1.5.1	print reports	1.16, 1.24, 2.05, 3.19, 3.24, 4.23, 6.12, 6.18, 7.12, 7.14, 715, 9.06	90, 107, 146, 256, 265, 338, 454, 464, 526, 531, 532, 633
1.5.2	print records	1.13, 1.25, 2.09, 3.06, 4.09, 4.11, 4.12, 6.10, 7.03, 7.04, 7.06, 7.07, 9.02, 9.04	80, 107, 150, 229, 312, 315, 316, 447, 501, 503, 508, 512, 623, 630
1.5.3	save a database as a template	10.08	695
1.5.4	export objects to alternative formats	9.09, 9.10, 9.11, 9.12, 9.14, 9.15	640, 643, 644, 648, 652, 653
2.0 Build Tables			
2.1	**Create Tables**		
2.1.1	create a table	1.03, 1.22, 4.13	63, 104, 319
2.1.2	import data into tables	1.11 , 5.14. 9.02, 9.03	76, 392, 623, 629
2.1.3	create linked tables from external sources	9.08	637
2.1.4	import tables from other databases	9.07	635
2.1.5	create a table from a template with application parts	1.22	104
2.2	**Manage Tables**		
2.2.1	hide fields in tables	4.09	312
2.2.2	add total rows	5.03	371
2.2.3	add table descriptions	1.09, 4.04	74, 303
2.2.4	rename tables	1.05, 2.02, 2.18, 3.01, 3.16, 4.13, 5.01, 5.11, 5.13, 5.14, 10.13	67, 140, 167, 223, 251, 319, 365, 387, 390, 392, 707
2.3	**Manage Records in Tables**		
2.3.1	update records	1.19, 4.08, 4.18, 4.23, 8.12	99, 310, 330, 338, 595
2.3.2	add records	1.05, 1.06, 1.23, 3.04	67, 68, 105, 227
2.3.3	delete records	2.07, 3.05, 4.07	147, 228, 308
2.3.4	append records from external data	1.07, 1.20, 4.04, 4.05, 4.06, 9.04	69, 102, 303, 305, 307, 630
2.3.5	find and replace data	3.05	228
2.3.6	sort records	2.08, 2.09, 4.03, 4.08, 5.15, 5.17, 10.02	149, 150, 302, 310, 395, 399, 685
2.3.7	filter records	3.07, 3.08, 3.09	231, 233, 235
2.4	**Create and Modify Fields**		
2.4.1	add fields to tables	1.03, 4.09, 4.12, 4.13, 4.14	63, 312, 316, 319, 323
2.4.2	add validation rules to fields	4.22	336
2.4.3	change field captions	1.04, 4.13, 5.04	66, 319, 374
2.4.4	change field sizes	1.09, 4.13, 4.14	74, 319, 323
2.4.5	change field data types	2.18, 4.11, 4.12, 4.14, 4.15, 4.16, 9.02	167, 315, 316, 323, 324, 326, 623

2.4.6	configure fields to auto-increment	1.04, 4.03	66, 302
2.4.7	set default values	4.20	334
2.4.8	use input masks	4.17, 4.18	327, 330
2.4.9	delete fields	1.08, 4.03, 4.05	72, 302, 305
3.0 Create Queries			
3.1	**Create a Query**		
3.1.1	run a query	1.14, 2.11, 2.13, 2.15, 2.16, 2.17, 2.20, 2.23, 2.24, 2.25, 2.26, 2.27, 2.28, 2.29, 2.30, 2.33, 5.01, 5.02, 5.03, 5.05, 5.07, 5.08, 5.09, 5.10, 5.11, 5.13, 5.14, 5.15, 5.16, 5.18, 9.05, 9.12, 10.03, 10.13, 10.14, 10.17, 10.18	85, 154, 155, 159, 161, 162, 171, 174, 175, 176, 178, 180, 181, 182, 183, 188, 365, 369, 371, 376, 380, 381, 383, 384, 387, 390, 392, 395, 398, 401, 631, 648, 688, 707, 710, 714, 715
3.1.2	create a crosstab query	2.32, 5.06	186, 378
3.1.3	create a parameter query	2.33, 5.09, 5.10	188, 383, 384
3.1.4	create an action query	5.12, 5.13, 5.14, 5.15, 5.16	389, 390, 392, 395, 398
3.1.5	create a multi-table query	2.25, 5.04, 5.05, 5.09, 5.10, 5.11, 5.13, 5.17, 5.18	176, 374, 376, 383, 384, 387, 390, 399, 401
3.1.6	save a query	2.11, 2.12, 2.13, 2.14, 2.15, 2.16, 2.17, 2.21, 2.22, 2.23, 2.24, 2.25, 2.26, 2.29, 2.31, 2.33, 5.01, 5.02, 5.03, 5.04, 5.05, 5.07, 5.08, 5.09, 5.10, 5.12, 5.13, 5.14, 5.15, 5.16, 5.19, 9.05, 10.03, 10.13, 10.14, 10.17, 10.18	154, 155, 157, 159, 161, 162, 171, 172, 174, 175, 176, 178, 182, 185, 188, 365, 369, 371, 374, 376, 380, 381, 383, 384, 389, 390, 392, 395, 398, 403, 631, 688, 707, 710, 714, 715
3.2	**Modify a Query**		
3.2.1	rename a query	2.12	155
3.2.2	add fields	2.10, 2.13, 2.15, 2.16, 2.17, 2.20, 2.22, 2.23, 2.24, 2.25, 2.26, 2.27, 2.30, 2.33, 5.01, 5.02, 5.03, 5.04, 5.05, 5.07, 5.08, 5.09, 5.10, 5.11, 5.14, 5.15, 5.16, 5.17, 5.18	152, 155, 159, 161, 162, 171, 172, 174, 175, 176, 178, 180, 183, 188, 365, 369, 371, 374, 376, 380, 381, 383, 384, 387, 392, 395, 398, 399, 401
3.2.3	remove fields	2.13, 9.05	155, 631
3.2.4	hide fields	2.16, 2.20, 2.26	161, 171, 178
3.2.5	sort data within queries	2.14, 2.16, 2.17, 2.25, 2.27, 2.33, 5.05, 5.18, 10.13	157, 161, 162, 176, 180, 188, 376, 401, 707
3.2.6	format fields within queries	2.29, 2.31, 2.32, 5.02	182, 185, 186, 369

3.3	Create Calculated Fields and Grouping within Queries		
3.3.1	add calculated fields	2.27, 2.28, 5.01, 5.02, 5.03, 517, 10.17	180, 181, 365, 369, 371, 399, 714
3.3.2	set filtering criteria	2.15, 2.16, 2.17, 2.20, 2.22, 2.23, 2.24, 5.02, 5.10, 5.13, 5.15, 5.16, 5.17, 10.13, 10.14, 10.17, 10.18	159, 161, 162, 171, 369, 383, 384, 390, 395, 398, 399, 707, 710, 714, 715
3.3.3	group and summarize data	2.30, 2.31, 5.04. 5.05, 10.18	183, 185, 374, 376, 715
3.3.4	group data by using comparison operators	2.21, 2.22, 2.23, 2.24	171, 172, 174, 175
3.3.5	group data by using arithmetic and logical operators	2.23, 2.24, 2.25. 2.26	174, 175, 176, 178
4.0 Create Forms			
4.1	**Create a Form**		
4.1.1	create a form	1.15, 3.02, 3.10, 3.03, 6.01, 7.01, 7.04, 7.05, 7.08	87, 225, 226, 237, 431, 495, 503, 507, 515
4.1.2	create a form from a template with application parts	7.05	503
4.1.3	save a form	1.15, 3.02, 3.03, 3.10, 6.01, 7.01, 7.04, 7.05, 7.08	87, 225, 226, 237, 431, 495, 503, 507, 515
4.2	**Configure Form Controls**		
4.2.1	move form controls	3.13, 6.03, 6.04. 7.06	240, 435, 436, 508
4.2.2	add form controls	3.13, 3.15, 6.01, 6.04, 7.02, 7.05, 7.08	240, 244, 431, 436, 497, 507, 515, 576, 579
4.2.3	modify data sources	3.13, 6.01, 7.08	240, 431, 515
4.2.4	remove form controls	7.02, 7.06, 7.07	497, 508, 512
4.2.5	set form control properties	3.11, 3.13, 3.14, 3.15, 6.04, 6.06, 6.08, 6.09, 6.10, 7.02, 7.03, 7.06, 7.08	238, 240, 243, 244, 436, 441, 444, 446, 447, 497, 501, 508, 515, 567, 576, 579, 592
4.2.6	manage labels	3.12, 3.13, 3.14, 3.15, 6.07, 7.03, 7.06, 7.07	240, 243, 244, 443, 501, 508, 512
4.2.7	add sub-forms	7.04, 7.05, 7.07	503, 507, 512
4.3	**Format a Form**		
4.3.1	modify tab order	6.10	447
4.3.2	configure print settings	3.06, 6.10, 7.02, 7.03	229, 447, 497, 501
4.3.3	sort records by form field	6.10, 7.04	447, 503
4.3.4	apply a theme	3.12, 6.05	240, 440
4.3.5	control form positioning	6.10, 7.04	447, 503
4.3.6	insert backgrounds	6.05, 6.06	440, 441
4.3.7	insert headers and footers	3.15, 6.02, 7.04	244, 433, 503
4.3.8	insert images	6.02, 6.04, 6.06, 7.02. 7.06	433, 436, 441, 497, 508

5.0 Create Reports			
5.1	**Create a Report**		
5.1.1	create a report based on the query or table	1.16, 3.17, 6.11, 6.13, 9.05, 10.18	90, 253, 452, 455, 631, 715
5.1.2	create a report in Design view	6.13	455
5.1.3	create a report by using a wizard	3.20, 6.11, 7.13, 7.15	256, 452, 530, 532
5.2	**Configure Report Controls**		
5.2.1	group and sort fields	3.18, 3.20, 3.21, 6.11, 6.17, 7.15	253, 256, 259, 452, 462, 532
5.2.2	modify data sources	6.13, 7.09, 7.11	455, 520, 524
5.2.3	add report controls	6.13, 6.15, 6.16, 6.18, 7.09, 7.10	455, 458, 460, 520, 522
5.2.4	add and modify labels	3.18, 3.23, 3.21, 6.14, 6.15, 6.18, 7.09, 7.12, 7.13, 7.14, 7.15	253, 259, 263, 456, 458, 464, 520, 526, 530, 531, 532
5.3	**Format a Report**		
5.3.1	format a report into multiple columns	3.20, 6.11, 6.13	256, 452, 455
5.3.2	add calculated fields	3.18, 6.18, 7.12	253, 464, 526
5.3.3	control report positioning	6.17, 7.12, 7.13	462, 526, 530
5.3.4	format report elements	3.18, 3.21, 3.22, 3.24, 6.12, 6.16, 7.10, 7.11, 7.12, 9.07	253, 259, 260, 265, 454, 460, 522, 524, 526, 635
5.3.5	change report orientation	6.11	452
5.3.6	insert header and footer information	3.23, 6.14, 6.15, 7.12, 7.14, 9.05, 9.06	263, 456, 458, 526, 531, 631, 633
5.3.7	insert images	6.14, 6.16, 9.05	456, 460, 631
5.3.8	apply a theme	3.17, 3.21, 6.12, 6.13	253, 259, 454, 455

Glossary

ACCDE file An Access file format that prevents individuals from creating or making design changes to forms, reports, and macros.

Action A self-contained instruction that can be combined with other actions to automate tasks.

Action query A query that creates a new table or changes data in an existing table.

Aggregate function A function that groups and performs calculations on multiple values and returns a single value.

Alignment The placement of text or objects relative to the left and right margins.

Alignment guides Green lines that display when you move an object to assist in alignment.

Alphabetic index Grouping of items by a common first character.

Alt text Another name for alternative text.

Alternative text Text added to a picture or object that helps people using a screen reader understand what the object is.

AND condition A condition in which records display only when all of the specified criteria are present in the selected fields.

App A self-contained program usually designed for a single purpose and that runs on smartphones and other mobile devices.

Append To add on to the end of an object; for example, to add records to the end of an existing table.

Append query An action query that adds new records to an existing table by adding data from another Access database or from a table in the same database.

Appended When data is added to the end of an existing table.

Application title The text that displays in the Access title bar when that database is open.

Apps for Office A collection of downloadable apps that enable you to create and view information within Office programs, and that combine cloud services and web technologies within the user interface of Office.

Argument A value that provides information to the macro action, such as the words to display in a message box or the control upon which to operate.

Arithmetic operators Mathematical symbols used in building expressions.

AS An SQL keyword that creates captions for fields.

Ascending order A sorting order that arranges text alphabetically (A to Z) and numbers from the lowest number to the highest number.

ASCII An acronym for American Standard Code for Information Interchange, a character set.

AutoNumber data type A data type that describes a unique sequential or random number assigned by Access as each record is entered and that is useful for data that has no distinct field that can be considered unique.

Back end An Access database that consists of the database tables and their data. The back end is typically placed on a server and is not directly seen by the end user.

Backstage tabs The area along the left side of Backstage view with tabs to display screens with related groups of commands.

Backstage view A centralized space for file management tasks; for example, opening, saving, printing, publishing, or sharing a file. A navigation pane displays along the left side with tabs that group file-related tasks together.

Backup A feature that creates a copy of the original database to protect against lost data.

Bang operator The exclamation (!) mark that tells Access that what follows is an object that belongs to the object that precedes it in the expression.

Best Fit An Access command that adjusts the width of a column to accommodate the column's longest entry.

Between ... And operator A comparison operator that looks for values within a range.

Blank desktop database A database that has no data and has no database tools—you must create the data and tools as you need them; the database is stored on your computer or other storage device.

Bookmark A command that identifies a word, section, or place in a document so that you can find it quickly without scrolling.

Bound A term used to describe objects and controls that are based on data that is stored in tables.

Bound control A control that retrieves its data from an underlying table or query; a text box control is an example of a bound control.

Bound report A report that displays data from an underlying table, query, or SQL statement as specified in the report's Record Source property.

Button control A control that enables individuals to add a command button to a form or report that will perform an action when the button is clicked.

Calculated control A control that contains an expression, often a formula or function, that most often summarizes a field that contains numerical data.

Calculated field A field that obtains its data by using a formula to perform a calculation or computation.

Caption A property setting that displays a name for a field in a table, query, form, or report different from the one listed as the field name.

Cascade Delete Related Records A cascade option that enables you to delete a record in a table and also delete all of the related records in related tables.

Cascade options Relationship options that enable you to update records in related tables when referential integrity is enforced.

Cascade Update Related Fields A cascade option that enables you to change the data in the primary key field in the table on the one side of the relationship and update that change to any fields storing that same data in related tables.

Cell The small box formed by the intersection of a column and a row in a worksheet.

Center alignment The alignment of text or objects that is centered horizontally between the left and right margin.

Chart A graphic representation of data.

Check Accessibility A command that checks the document for content that people with disabilities might find difficult to read.

Check Compatibility A command that searches your document for features that may not be supported by older versions of Office.

Clipboard A temporary storage area in Windows that can hold up to 24 items that you select and then cut or copy.

Cloud computing Applications and services that are accessed over the Internet, rather than accessing applications that are installed on your local computer.

Cloud storage Online storage of data so that you can access your data from different places and devices.

Code Builder A window used to type programming code in Microsoft Visual Basic.

Collaborate To work with others as a team in an intellectual endeavor to complete a shared task or to achieve a shared goal.

Column chart A chart used to display comparisons among related numbers.

Combo box A control that enables individuals to select from a list or to type a value.

Commands Instructions to a computer program that cause an action to be carried out.

Comment Explanatory information provided about the macro or the action.

Common field A field included in two or more tables that stores the same data.

Compact & Repair A process where an Access file is rewritten to store the objects and data more efficiently.

Comparison operators Symbols that are used to evaluate data in the field to determine if it is the same (=), greater than (>), less than (<), or in between a range of values as specified by the criteria.

Compound criteria Multiple conditions in a query or filter.

Compressed file A file that has been reduced in size and thus takes up less storage space and can be transferred to other computers quickly.

Concatenation Linking or joining strings.

Condition A statement that specifies that certain criteria must be met before the macro action executes.

Conditional formatting A way to apply formatting to specific controls based on a comparison to a rule set.

Content app An app for Office that integrates web-based features as content within the body of a document.

Context-sensitive commands Commands that display on a shortcut menu that relate to the object or text that you right-clicked.

Context menus Menus that display commands and options relevant to the selected text or object; also called *shortcut menus*.

Contextual tabs Tabs that are added to the ribbon automatically when a specific object, such as a picture, is selected, and that contain commands relevant to the selected object.

Control An object, such as a label or text box, in a form or report that displays data or text, performs actions, and lets you view and work with information.

Control layout The grouped arrangement of controls on a form or report; for example, the Stacked layout.

ControlTip A message that displays descriptive text when the mouse pointer is paused over the control.

Converted Changed from one format to another.

Copy A command that duplicates a selection and places it on the Clipboard.

Creative Commons A nonprofit organization that enables sharing and use of images and knowledge through free legal tools.

Criteria Conditions in a query that identify the specific records you are looking for.

Cross join A join that displays when each row from one table is combined with each row in a related table, usually created unintentionally when you do not create a join line between related tables.

Crosstab query A query that uses an aggregate function for data that is grouped by two types of information and displays the data in a compact, spreadsheet-like format. A crosstab query always has at least one row heading, one column heading, and one summary field.

Currency data type An Access data type that describes monetary values and numeric data that can be used in mathematical calculations involving values with one to four decimal places.

Custom web app A database that you can publish and share with others over the Internet.

Cut A command that removes a selection and places it on the Clipboard.

Data Facts about people, events, things, or ideas.

Database An organized collection of facts about people, events, things, or ideas related to a specific topic or purpose.

Database Documenter An option used to create a report that contains detailed information about the objects in a database, including macros, and to create a paper record.

Database management system (DBMS) Database software that controls how related collections of data are stored, organized, retrieved, and secured; also known as a *DBMS*.

Database template A preformatted database that contains prebuilt tables, queries, forms, and reports that perform a specific task, such as tracking events.

Data entry The action of entering the data into a record in a database table or form.

Data macro A macro that is triggered by events, such as adding, updating, or deleting data within a table, form, or query. It is used to validate the accuracy of data in a table; also known as an *event-driven macro*.

Datasheet view The Access view that displays data organized in columns and rows similar to an Excel worksheet.

Data source The table or tables from which a form, query, or report retrieves its data.

Data type Classification identifying the kind of data that can be stored in a field, such as numbers, text, or dates.

Data validation Rules that help prevent invalid data entries and ensure data is entered consistently.

Date control A control on a form or report that inserts the current date each time the form or report is opened.

DBMS An acronym for database management system.

Debugging A logical process to find and reduce the number of errors in a program.

Decrypt An action that removes a file's encryption or unsets a password.

Default The term that refers to the current selection or setting that is automatically used by a computer program unless you specify otherwise.

Default value A specified value to be automatically entered in a field in new records.

Definition The structure of the table—the field names, data types, and field properties.

Delete query An action query that removes records from an existing table in the same database.

Delimited file A file in which each record displays on a separate line, and the fields within the record are separated by a single character.

Delimiter A single character, which can be a paragraph mark, a tab, a comma, or another character, used to separate fields within a record.

Dependency An object that requires, or is dependent on, another database object.

Descending order A sorting order that arranges text in reverse alphabetical order (Z to A) and numbers from the highest number to the lowest number.

Deselect The action of canceling the selection of an object or block of text by clicking outside of the selection.

Design view An Access view that displays the detailed structure of a table, query, form, or report. For forms and reports, some tasks must be performed in this view; only the controls, not the data, display in this view.

Desktop app A computer program that is installed on your PC and requires a computer operating system such as Microsoft Windows; also known as a *desktop application*.

Desktop application A computer program that is installed on your PC and requires a computer operating system such as Microsoft Windows; also known as a *desktop app*.

Destination table In an append query, the table to which you are appending records, attempting to match the fields.

Detail section The section of a form or report that displays the records from the underlying table or query.

Dialog Box Launcher A small icon that displays to the right of some group names on the ribbon and that opens a related dialog box or pane providing additional options and commands related to that group.

DISTINCT An SQL keyword that returns only a single instance of any duplicate values in query results.

Document properties Details about a file that describe or identify it, including the title, author name, subject, and keywords that identify the document's topic or contents; also known as *metadata*.

Drag The action of holding down the left mouse button while moving your mouse.

Dynamic An attribute applied to data in a database that changes.

Edit The process of making changes to text or graphics in an Office file.

Ellipsis A set of three dots indicating incompleteness; an ellipsis following a command name indicates that a dialog box will display if you click the command.

Embedded macro A macro that is stored in the properties of forms, reports, or controls.

Encrypt A process to hide data by making the file unreadable until the correct password is entered.

Enhanced ScreenTip A ScreenTip that displays more descriptive text than a normal ScreenTip.

Event Any action that can be detected by a program or computer system, such as clicking a button or closing an object.

Export The process of copying data from one file into another file, such as an Access table into an Excel spreadsheet.

Expression A combination of functions, field values, constants, and operators that produces a result.

Expression Builder A feature used to create formulas (expressions) in calculated fields, query criteria, form and report controls, and table validation rules.

Extensible Markup Language The standard language for defining and storing data on the web.

Field A single piece of information that is stored in every record; represented by a column in a database table.

Field list A list of field names in a table.

Field properties Characteristics of a field that control how the field displays and how data can be entered in the field; they vary for different data types.

Fill The inside color of an object.

Filter by Form An Access command that filters the records in a form based on one or more fields, or based on more than one value in the field.

Filter by Selection An Access command that displays only the records that contain the value in the selected field and hides the records that do not contain the value.

Filtering The process of displaying only a portion of the total records (a subset) based on matching specific values to provide a quick answer to a question.

Find Duplicates Query A query used to locate duplicate records in a table.

Find Unmatched Query A query used to locate unmatched records so they can be deleted from the table.

First principle of good database design A principle of good database design stating that data is organized in tables so that there is no redundant data.

Flagged Action of highlighting a word that Spell Check does not recognize from the Office dictionary.

Flat database A simple database file that is not related or linked to any other collection of data.

Focus A control that is selected and currently being acted upon.

Font A set of characters with the same design and shape.

Font styles Formatting emphasis such as bold, italic, and underline.

Footer A reserved area for text or graphics that displays at the bottom of each page in a document.

Foreign key The field that is included in the related table so the field can be joined with the primary key in another table for the purpose of creating a relationship.

Form An Access object you can use to enter new records into a table, edit or delete existing records in a table, or display existing records.

Formatting The process of establishing the overall appearance of text, graphics, and pages in an Office file—for example, in a Word document.

Formatting marks Characters that display on the screen, but do not print, indicating where the Enter key, the Spacebar, and the Tab key were pressed; also called *nonprinting characters*.

Form Footer Information displayed at the bottom of the screen in Form view or Layout view that is printed after the last detail section on the last page of a printout.

Form Header Information such as a form's title that displays at the top of the screen in Form view or Layout view and is printed at the top of the first page when records are printed as forms.

Form selector The box in the upper-left corner of a form in Design view where the rulers meet; used to select the entire form.

Form tool An Access tool that creates a form with a single mouse click, which includes all of the fields from the underlying data source (table or query).

Form view The Access view in which you can view, modify, delete, or add records in a table but you cannot change the layout or design of the form.

Form Wizard An Access tool that walks you step by step through the creation of a form and that gives you more flexibility in the design, layout, and number of fields in a form.

FROM clause An SQL statement that lists which tables hold the fields used in the SELECT clause.

Front end An Access database that includes the database forms, queries, reports, and macros. The end users open the front end to work with the data stored in the back-end tables.

Gallery An Office feature that displays a list of potential results instead of just the command name.

Gradient fill A fill effect in which one color fades into another.

Group Footer Information printed at the end of each group of records to display summary information for the group.

Group Header Information printed at the beginning of each new group of records; for example, the group name.

Group, Sort, and Total pane A pane that displays at the bottom of the window in Design view in which you can control how information is sorted and grouped in a report; provides the most flexibility for adding or modifying groups, sort orders, or totals options on a report.

Groups On the Office ribbon, the sets of related commands that you might need for a specific type of task.

Header A reserved area for text or graphics that displays at the top of each page in a document.

HTML An acronym for HyperText Markup Language.

HyperText Markup Language The language used to display webpages.

Image control A control that enables individuals to insert an image into any section of a form or report.

Import The process of copying data from another file, such as a Word table or an Excel workbook, into a separate file, such as an Access database.

Indeterminate relationship A relationship that does not enforce referential integrity.

Index A special list created in Access to speed up searches and sorting.

Information Data that is accurate, timely, and organized in a useful manner.

Info tab The tab in Backstage view that displays information about the current file.

Inner join A join that allows only the records where the common field exists in both related tables to be displayed in query results.

Innermost sort field When sorting on multiple fields in Datasheet view, the field that will be used for the second level of sorting.

Insertion point A blinking vertical line that indicates where text or graphics will be inserted.

Inspect Document A command that searches your document for hidden data or personal information that you might not want to share publicly.

Is Not Null A criteria that searches for fields that are not empty.

Is Null A criteria that searches for fields that are empty.

Join A relationship that helps a query return only the records from each table you want to see, based on how those tables are related to other tables in the query.

JOIN clause An SQL statement that defines the join type for a query.

Join line In the Relationships window, the line joining two tables that visually indicates the common fields and the type of relationship.

Junction table A table that breaks down the many-to-many relationship into two one-to-many relationships.

Keyboard shortcut A combination of two or more keyboard keys, used to perform a task that would otherwise require a mouse.

KeyTip The letter that displays on a command in the ribbon and that indicates the key you can press to activate the command when keyboard control of the Ribbon is activated.

Keywords Commands built into the SQL programming language. Also, custom file properties in the form of words that you associate with a document to give an indication of the document's content; used to help find and organize files. Also called *tags*.

Label control A control on a form or report that contains descriptive information, usually a field name or title.

Landscape orientation A page orientation in which the paper is wider than it is tall.

Layout Options A button that displays when an object is selected and that has commands to choose how the object interacts with surrounding text.

Layout selector A small symbol that displays in the upper left corner of a selected control layout in a form or report that is displayed in Layout view or Design view and is used to move or format an entire group of controls.

Layout view The Access view in which you can make changes to a form or report while the data from the underlying data source displays.

Left outer join A join used when you want to display all of the records on the one side of a one-to-many relationship, whether or not there are matching records in the table on the many side of the relationship.

Line chart A chart used to display trends over time.

Line control A control that enables an individual to insert a line into a form or report.

Link A connection to data in another file.

Linked form A form related to the main form that is not stored within the main form.

List box A control that enables individuals to select from a list but does not enable individuals to type anything that is not in the list.

Live Preview A technology that shows the result of applying an editing or formatting change as you point to possible results—*before* you actually apply it.

Location Any disk drive, folder, or other place in which you can store files and folders.

Logical operators Operators that combine criteria using AND and OR. With two criteria, AND requires that both conditions be met and OR requires that either condition be met for the record to display in the query results.

Macro A series of actions grouped as a single command to accomplish a task or multiple tasks automatically to add functionality to your object or control.

Macro Designer Window that allows you to build the list of actions to be carried out when the macro runs.

Macro group A set of macros grouped by a common name that displays as one macro object on the Navigation Pane.

Mail app An app for Office that displays next to an Outlook item.

Mail merge A Word feature used to create letters or memos that are created by combining a document and a record source.

Main document The document that contains the text of a letter or memo for a mail merge.

Main form A form that contains a subform.

Main report A report that contains a subreport.

Make table query An action query that creates a new table by extracting data from one or more tables.

Many-to-many relationship A relationship between tables where one record in one table has many matching records in a second table, and a single record in the related table has many matching records in the first table.

Merging Combining two documents to create one.

Message Bar The area directly below the ribbon that displays information such as security alerts when there is potentially unsafe, active content in an Office document that you open.

Metadata Details about a file that describe or identify it, including the title, author name, subject, and keywords that identify the document's topic or contents; also known as *document properties*.

Microsoft SQL Server A database application designed for high-end business uses.

Mini toolbar A small, semitransparent toolbar containing frequently used formatting commands that displays as a result of selecting text or objects.

Modal window A child (secondary) window to a parent window—the original window that opened the modal window—that takes over control of the parent window.

MRU Acronym for most recently used, which refers to the state of some commands that retain the characteristic most recently applied; for example, the Font Color button retains the most recently used color until a new color is chosen.

Multi-page form A form that displays the data from the underlying table or query on more than one page.

Multiple-items form A form that enables you to display or enter multiple records in a table.

Multivalued field A field that holds multiple values.

Named range A Excel range that has been given a name, making it easier to use the cells in calculations or modifications.

Navigation area An area at the bottom of the Access window that indicates the number of records in the table and contains controls in the form of arrows that you click to move among the records.

Navigation form A form that displays navigational controls that enable you to display forms and reports in your database.

Navigation Pane An area of the Access window that displays and organizes the names of the objects in a database; from here, you open objects for use.

Navigation Pane category A top-level listing that displays when the Navigation Pane arrow is clicked.

Navigation Pane group A second-level listing that displays when a Navigation Pane category is selected.

Nested subform A subform that is embedded within another subform.

Nonprinting characters Characters that display on the screen, but do not print, indicating where the Enter key, the Spacebar, and the Tab key were pressed; also called *formatting marks*.

Normalization The process of applying design rules and principles to ensure that your database performs as expected.

Notepad A simple text editor that comes with the Windows operating systems.

Number data type An Access data type that represents a quantity, how much or how many, and may be used in calculations.

Objects Text boxes, pictures, tables, or shapes that you can select and then move and resize. Also, the basic parts of a database that you create to store your data and to work with your data, such as tables, queries, forms, and reports.

Object tab In the object window, a tab that identifies the object and which enables you to make an open object active.

Object window An area of the Access window that displays open objects, such as tables, queries, forms, or reports; by default, each object displays on its own tab.

ODBC An acronym for Open Database Connectivity.

Office 365 A version of Microsoft Office to which you subscribe for an annual fee.

Office background A small graphic in the upper-right corner of the Access application window used to personalize Office 2016.

Office Store A public marketplace that Microsoft hosts and regulates on Office.com.

ON An SQL keyword that is used to specify which field is common to two tables.

OneDrive Microsoft's free cloud storage for anyone with a free Microsoft account.

One-to-many relationship A relationship between two tables where one record in the first table corresponds to many records in the second table—the most common type of relationship in Access.

Open Database Connectivity A standard that enables databases using SQL statements to interface with one another.

Open dialog box A dialog box from which you can navigate to, and then open on your screen, an existing file that was created in that same program.

Open Exclusive An option that opens the database so that changes can be made, but no one else may open the database at the same time.

Open Exclusive Read-Only An option that opens the database in both Exclusive and Read-Only modes.

Open Read-Only An option that opens the database so that all objects can be opened and viewed, but data and design changes cannot be made.

Option button In a dialog box, a round button that enables you to make one choice among two or more options.

Options dialog box A dialog box within each Office application where you can select program settings and other options and preferences.

OR condition A compound criteria used to display records that match at least one of the specified criteria.

Outer join A join that is typically used to display records from both tables, regardless of whether there are matching records.

Outermost sort field When sorting on multiple fields in Datasheet view, the field that will be used for the first level of sorting.

Page Footer Information printed at the bottom of every page in a report and most often includes the page number.

Page Header Information printed at the top of every page in a report.

Page number control A control on a form or report that inserts the page number when displayed in Print Preview or when printed.

Page Width A view that zooms the document so that the width of the page matches the width of the window. Find this command on the View tab, in the Zoom group.

Paragraph symbol The symbol ¶ that represents the end of a paragraph.

Parameter A value that can be changed.

Parameter query A query that prompts the user for one or more criteria before running.

Paste The action of placing text or other objects that have been copied or cut from one location to a new location.

Paste Options gallery A gallery of buttons that provides a Live Preview of all the Paste options available in the current context.

Path The location of a folder or file on your computer or storage device.

PDF The acronym for *Portable Document Format*, which is a file format that creates an image that preserves the look of your file, but that cannot be easily changed; a popular format for sending documents electronically, because the document will display on most computers.

Performance Analyzer A wizard that analyzes database objects, and then offers suggestions for improving them.

Picture Alignment property A property that determines where the background picture for a form displays on the form.

Picture Size Mode property A property that determines the proportions of a picture in a form.

Pie chart A chart used to display the contributions of parts to a whole amount.

Plain Text A document format that contains no formatting, such as bold or italic.

Point A unit of measure that is 1/72 of an inch.

Pointer Any symbol that displays on your screen in response to moving your mouse.

Pop-up window A window that suddenly displays (pops up), usually contains a menu of commands, and stays on the screen only until the user selects one of the commands.

Populate The action of filling a database table with records.

Portable Document Format A file format that creates an image that preserves the look of your file, but that cannot be easily changed; a popular format for sending documents electronically, because the document will display on most computers; also called a *PDF*.

Portrait orientation A page orientation in which the paper is taller than it is wide.

Primary key A required field that uniquely identifies a record in a table; for example, a Student ID number at a college.

Print Preview A view of a document as it will appear when you print it.

Propagate To disseminate or apply changes to an object.

Properties The characteristics that determine the appearance, structure, and behavior of an object.

Property Sheet A list of characteristics—properties—for fields or controls on a form or report in which you can make precise changes to each property associated with the field or control.

Property Update Options button An option button that displays when you make changes to the design of a table; it enables individuals to update the Property Sheet for a field in all objects that use a table as the record source.

Protected View A security feature in Office 2016 that protects your computer from malicious files by opening them in a restricted environment until you enable them; you might encounter this feature if you open a file from an e-mail or download files from the Internet.

pt The abbreviation for point; for example, when referring to a font size.

Query A database object that retrieves specific data from one or more database objects—either tables or other queries—and then, in a single datasheet, displays only the data you specify.

Query design grid The lower area of the query window that displays the design of the query.

Quick Access Toolbar In an Office program window, the small row of buttons in the upper left corner of the screen from which you can perform frequently used commands.

Range An area that includes two or more selected cells on an Excel worksheet that can be treated as a single unit.

Read-only A property assigned to a file that prevents the file from being modified or deleted; it indicates that you cannot save any changes to the displayed document unless you first save it with a new name.

Record All of the categories of data pertaining to one person, place, event, thing, or idea; represented by a row in a database table.

Record selector bar The vertical bar at the left edge of a record when it is displayed in a form, and which is used to select an entire record in Form view.

Record selector box The small box at the left of a record in Datasheet view that, when clicked, selects the entire record.

Record source The tables or queries that provide the underlying data for a form or report.

Record Source property A property that enables you to specify the source of the data for a form or a report; the property setting can be a table name, a query name, or an SQL statement.

Redundant In a database, information that is duplicated in a manner that indicates poor database design.

Referential integrity A set of rules that Access uses to ensure that the data between related tables is valid.

Relational database A sophisticated type of database that has multiple collections of data within the file that are related to one another.

Relationship An association that you establish between two tables based on common fields.

Report A database object that summarizes the fields and records from a query or table in an easy-to-read format suitable for printing.

Report Footer Information printed at the bottom of the last page of a report.

Report Header Information printed on the first page of a report that is used for logos, titles, and dates.

Report tool An Access tool that creates a report with one mouse click and displays all of the fields and records from the record source that you select.

Report Wizard An Access tool that walks you step by step through the creation of a report and that gives you more flexibility in the design, layout, and number of fields in a report.

Required A field property that ensures a field cannot be left empty.

Rich Text Format (RTF) A standard file format that contains some formatting such as underline, bold, font sizes, and colors. RTF documents can be opened in many applications.

Right-click The action of clicking the right mouse button one time.

Right outer join A join used when you want to display all of the records on the many side of a one-to-many relationship, whether or not there are matching records in the table on the one side of the relationship.

Run The process in which Access searches the records in the table(s) included in the query design, finds the records that match the specified criteria, and then displays the records in a datasheet; only the fields that have been included in the query design display.

Sans serif font A font design with no lines or extensions on the ends of characters.

Screen reader Software that enables visually impaired users to read text on a computer screen to understand the content of pictures.

ScreenTip A small box that that displays useful information when you perform various mouse actions such as pointing to screen elements or dragging.

Second principle of good database design A principle stating that appropriate database techniques are used to ensure the accuracy and consistency of data as it is entered into the table.

Section bar In Design view, a gray bar in a form or report that identifies and separates one section from another; used to select the section and to change the size of the section.

SELECT clause An SQL statement that lists which fields the query should display.

Selecting Highlighting, by dragging with your mouse, areas of text or data or graphics, so that the selection can be edited, formatted, copied, or moved.

Select query A type of Access query that retrieves (selects) data from one or more tables or queries, displaying the selected data in a datasheet; also known as a *simple select query*.

Serif font A font design that includes small line extensions on the ends of the letters to guide the eye in reading from left to right.

Share button Opens the Share pane from which you can save your file to the cloud—your OneDrive—and then share it with others so you can collaborate.

SharePoint Microsoft collaboration software with which people in an organization can set up team sites to share information, manage documents, and publish reports for others to see.

SharePoint List A list of documents maintained on a server running Microsoft Office SharePoint Server.

SharePoint Server A server that enables you to share documents with others in your organization.

Shortcut menu A menu that displays commands and options relevant to the selected text or object; also called a *context menu*.

Short Text data type An Access data type that describes text, a combination of text and numbers, or numbers that are not used in calculations, such as the Postal Code.

Simple select query Another name for a select query.

Single-record form A form that enables you to display or enter one record at a time from a table.

Single stepping Debugging a macro using a process that executes one action at a time.

Sizing handles Small squares or circles that indicate a picture or object is selected.

Sorting The process of arranging data in a specific order based on the value in a field.

Source file When importing a file, refers to the file being imported.

Source table In a make table or append query, the table from which records are being extracted or copied.

Split button A button divided into two parts and in which clicking the main part of the button performs a command and clicking the arrow opens a menu with choices.

Split database An Access database that is split into two files—one containing the back end and one containing the front end.

Split form An object that displays data in two views—Form view and Datasheet view—on a single form.

Spreadsheet Another name for a worksheet.

SQL (Structured Query Language) A language used by many database programs to view, update, and query data in relational databases.

SQL statement An instruction using Structured Query Language.

Stacked layout A control layout format that is similar to a paper form, with label controls placed to the left of each text box control; the controls are grouped together for easy editing.

Standalone macro A macro object that displays under Macros on the Navigation Pane.

Static data Data that does not change.

Status bar The area along the lower edge of an Office program window that displays file information on the left and buttons to control how the window looks on the right.

Status Bar Text property A form property that enables individuals to enter text that will display in the status bar for a selected control.

String A series of characters.

Strong password A password that is very difficult to guess that may include upper-and lowercase letters, numbers, and special characters.

Structure In Access, the underlying design of a table, including field names, data types, descriptions, and field properties.

Style A group of formatting commands, such as font, font size, font color, paragraph alignment, and line spacing that can be applied to a paragraph with one command.

Subdatasheet A format for displaying related records when you click the plus sign (+) next to a record in a table on the one side of the relationship.

Subform A form that is embedded within another form.

Subreport A report that is embedded within another report.

Subset A portion of the total records available.

Synchronization The process of updating computer files that are in two or more locations according to specific rules—also called *syncing*.

Syncing The process of updating computer files that are in two or more locations according to specific rules—also called *synchronization*.

Syntax The set of rules by which words and symbols in an expression are combined; the spelling, grammar, and sequence of characters of a programming language.

System tables Tables used to keep track of multiple entries in an attachment field that you cannot work with or view.

Tab control A control that is used to display data on the main form on different tabs, similar to the way database objects, such as forms and tables, display on different tabs.

Table A format for information that organizes and presents text and data in columns and rows; the foundation of a database.

Table Analyzer A wizard that searches for repeated data in a table, and then splits the table into two or more related tables.

Table area The upper area of the query window that displays field lists for the tables that are used in a query.

Tables and Related Views An arrangement in the Navigation Pane that groups objects by the table to which they are related.

Tab order The order in which the insertion point moves from one field to another in a form when you press the Tab key.

Tabs (ribbon) On the Office ribbon, the name of each task-oriented activity area.

Tags Custom file properties in the form of words that you associate with a document to give an indication of the document's content; used to help find and organize files. Also called *keywords*. Also, HTML codes that the web browser interprets as the page is loaded; they begin with the < character and end with the > character.

Task pane app An app for Office that works side-by-side with an Office document by displaying a separate pane on the right side of the window.

Tell Me A search feature for Microsoft Office commands that you activate by typing what you are looking for in the Tell Me box.

Tell me more A prompt within a ScreenTip that opens the Office online Help system with explanations about how to perform the command referenced in the ScreenTip.

Template A preformatted document that you can use as a starting point and then change to suit your needs.

Text box control A bound control on a form or report that displays the data from the underlying table or query.

Text string A sequence of characters.

Theme A design tool that simplifies the process of creating professional-looking objects within one program or across multiple programs; includes theme colors and theme fonts that can be applied consistently throughout the objects in a database or to individual objects in the database.

Title bar The bar at the top edge of the program window that indicates the name of the current file and the program name.

Toggle button A button that can be turned on by clicking it once, and then turned off by clicking it again.

Toolbar In a folder window, a row of buttons with which you can perform common tasks, such as changing the view of your files and folders.

Totals query A query that calculates subtotals across groups of records.

Triple-click The action of clicking the left mouse button three times in rapid succession.

Truncated Data that is cut off or shortened because the field or column is not wide enough to display all of the data or the field size is too small to contain all of the data.

Trust Center A security feature that checks documents for macros and digital signatures.

Trusted Documents A security feature in Office that remembers which files you have already enabled; you might encounter this feature if you open a file from an e-mail or download files from the Internet.

Trusted source A person or organization that you know will not send you databases with malicious content.

Unbound control A control that does not have a source of data, such as the title in a form or report.

Unbound report A report that does not display data from an underlying table, query, or SQL statement and has an empty Record Source property setting.

Unequal join A join used to combine rows from two data sources based on field values that are not equal; can be created only in SQL view.

UNION An SQL keyword that is used to combine one or more queries in a union query.

Union query A query type that combines the results of two or more similar select queries.

Unmatched records Records in one table that have no matching records in a related table.

Update query An action query used to add, change, or delete data in fields of one or more existing records.

Validation rule An expression that precisely defines the range of data that will be accepted in a field.

Validation text The error message that displays when an individual enters a value prohibited by the validation rule.

Weak password A password that is easy to guess.

WHERE clause An SQL statement that defines the criteria that should be applie when a query is run.

Wildcard character In a query, a character that represents one or more unknown characters in criteria; an asterisk (*) represents one or more unknown characters, and a question mark (?) represents a single unknown character.

Windows apps An app that runs on all Windows device families—including PCs, Windows phones, Windows tablets, and the Xbox gaming system.

Wizard A feature in Microsoft Office that walks you step by step through a process.

WordArt An Office feature in Word, Excel, and PowerPoint that enables you to change normal text into decorative stylized text.

Workbook An Excel file that contains one or more worksheets.

Worksheet The primary document used in Excel to save and work with data that is arranged in columns and rows.

XML An acronym for Extensible Markup Language.

XML Paper Specification A Microsoft file format that creates an image of your document and that opens in the XPS viewer.

XML presentation files Files that can be created so that the data can be viewed in a web browser.

XML schema A document with an .xsd extension that defines the elements, entities, and content allowed in the document.

XPS The acronym for XML Paper Specification—a Microsoft file format that creates an image of your document and that opens in the XPS viewer.

Zero-length string An entry created by typing two quotation marks with no spaces between them ("") to indicate that no value exists for a required text or memo field.

Zoom The action of increasing or decreasing the size of the viewing area on the screen.

Index

D

E

F

N

O

P

Q

R

T

U

V

W

X

Z